# Handbook of School Neuropsychology

# Handbook of School Neuropsychology

Edited by
Rik Carl D'Amato, Elaine Fletcher-Janzen, and
Cecil R. Reynolds

**WILEY**

John Wiley & Sons, Inc.

Copyright © 2005 by John Wiley & Sons, Inc. All rights reserved.

Published by John Wiley & Sons, Inc., Hoboken, New Jersey.
Published simultaneously in Canada.

*Library of Congress Cataloging-in-Publication Data:*

Handbook of school neuropsychology / edited by Rik Carl D'Amato, Elaine
   Fletcher-Janzen, and Cecil R. Reynolds.
      p.      cm.
   Includes bibliographical references.
   ISBN-13 978-0-471-46550-8
   ISBN-10 0-471-46550-X (cloth : alk. paper)
   1. Pediatric neuropsychology.  2. School psychology.  3. School children—Mental health services   4. Behavioral assessment of children.  I. D'Amato, Rik Carl.  II. Fletcher-Janzen, Elaine.  III. Reynolds, Cecil R., 1952–
   [DNLM: 1. Learning Disorders—Adolescent.  2. Learning Disorders—Child.  3. Developmental Disabilities—Adolescent.  4. Developmental Disabilities—Child.  5. Mental Health Services—Adolescent  6. Mental Health Services—Child.  7. Neuropsychological Tests—Adolescent.  8. Neuropsychological Tests—Child.  9. Neuropsychology—methods—Adolescent.  10. Neuropsychology—methods—Child.  11. School Health Services. WS 110 H23692      2005]
   RJ486.5.H285      2005
   61892'8—dc22

                                                                              2004059093

Printed in the United States of America.

10   9   8   7   6   5   4   3   2   1

*To Marcia, Michael, and David,*
*my anchors in the sea of life. Your love and faith have provided me*
*unwavering support and direction in our dynamic yet demanding world.*

*Rik*


*To David, Emma, and Leif with thanks for all the fish.*

*Elaine*


*To Julia, as always.*
*Cecil*

# Foreword

WE ARE NOW in the midst of a full-fledged revolution in how reading is taught—a true paradigm shift from an era in which choice of methods and programs was based on philosophy and anecdotal information—to one based on rigorous science and evidence of effectiveness. The results indicate that using proven, evidence-based methods to teach reading is helping almost all readers become much better readers. This extremely promising and converging data demonstrates that virtually all children benefit from the application of scientifically based methods, which should inspire all practitioners to want to understand and to know how to apply the findings from this new science of reading. It is essential that pedagogical policy is intimately connected to, and reflects, our new understanding of reading, beginning at the level of the brain itself.

Modern brain-imaging technology now allows scientists to non-invasively peer into, and literally watch the brain at work—in children and in adults. Using this new technology, we and other laboratories around the world have now identified the specific neural systems used in reading, demonstrated how these systems differ in good and struggling readers, pinpointed the systems used in compensation, and identified the systems used in skilled or fluent reading. In addition, we have identified different types of reading disabilities and also demonstrated the malleability or plasticity of the neural circuitry for reading in response to an evidence-based reading intervention. These and other studies have provided a new and unprecedented level of insight and understanding about common neuropsychological disorders affecting children and adults, their mechanisms, their identification, and their effective treatment.

My dream has been to see this powerful and relevant knowledge from the laboratory integrated into educational practices in classrooms and universities across the United States. We must make education a priority and implement the kinds of evidence-based treatments that are advocated in this volume.

The complexity of the brain and its relation to learning is extraordinary. This book attempts to explain the neurobiological basis of learning, and tackles one of the most complicated of all subjects. It helps us understand the brain and the many disorders and disabilities that relate to glitches or disruptions in brain circuitry. Then, it masterfully links what we know empirically from current, rigorous research to how educators and psychologists may most effectively practice in the classroom.

Where should we start to help all students and adults learn? It will take all of us, dedicated to helping children learn, applying our newly developed knowledge, if we are to make a difference in the educational enterprise. The knowledge is there, we must ensure that it is embraced and applied. This text provides the information that you need to implement many of the recent interventions that our and other studies indicate that are highly effective. During my talks and in my practice, parents and educators alike often ask me if I can recommend books that apply this knowledge in an understandable format. This is why I wrote *Overcoming Dyslexia,* to bring this new scientific knowledge to those who need it most. And now, the *Handbook of School Neuropsychology* brings to the reader the promise of the newest scientific discoveries applied to interventions for a range of neuropsychological disorders affecting children and adults. It is a most welcome and valued addition to my library and I know it will be to the readers' as well.

SALLY E. SHAYWITZ, MD
Co-Director, Yale Center for the Study of Learning and Attention
Author, *Overcoming Dyslexia*

# Preface

FOR MORE THAN a hundred years, the brain has been the focus of passionate study. Experiments have been conducted, books have been written, courses have been taught, in-services have been offered, and university programs have offered training focused on the brain. Even training standards of the American Psychological Association and the National Association of School Psychologists (NASP) have integrated the study of the brain into their requirements. For many years, the largest interest group in NASP was the Neuropsychology in the Schools Interest Group. Nevertheless, it is important to remember that there was a time when scientists argued against the biological bases of our behavior—and many psychologists, especially school psychologists, did just that. *But that time has passed.*

The story is told of a major university, which sported a large and quite prominent psychology department, where all professors' offices were located down a long, straight, sterile, colorless corridor. At first, all of the offices were filled with psychoanalytic psychologists. Some years later with much apprehension, a single behaviorist joined the faculty. Some years later, all of the offices were filled with behavioral psychologists and a single psychoanalytic psychologist. When the psychoanalytic psychologist retired, he was replaced by a psychologist who had been trained as a clinical neuropsychologist. The neuropsychologist had a great deal of apprehension but joined the faculty nonetheless. And as behavioral psychologists retired, they were replaced with more neuropsychologists, experimental psychologists, or neuroscientists. In fact, the department now offers a specialization in the brain and behavior. Is neuropsychology a novel and contemporary trend or a fundamental building block on which the science of psychology rests?

The generation, dissemination, and preservation of new neuropsychological knowledge continues at a rapid and untamed pace. While some of the well-seasoned scientists and practitioners tell of a time when neuropsychology was not accepted in psychology or in education, it currently has become one of the most popular areas of study. A. R. Luria, the most famous of all neuropsychologists, is argued by some to be the most referenced psychologist in the world.

The educational enterprise is in dire need of capable and lucid leadership. Many have reported how public schools flip and flop in the winds of political pressure. While all join in the quest searching for successful educational progress for all, a panacea has been slow to emerge. Although some in school psychology still cling to their long-held belief that neuropsychology does not represent the future of our field, if we are to truly take a scientific or evidence-based view of the origin of our behavior, we are forced to recognize the behavioral orchestration that our brain directs. While many of the difficulties with our "No Child Left Behind" law have been widely debated, data supports the view that educational practices should be improved, and neuropsychological principles are available to help us meet the challenge. That is one reason for the creation of this *Handbook.*

We can choose to use neuropsychological knowledge as an accent to our current psychological practice or we may choose to pursue additional study. Our psychologists-in-training have completed day or weekend in-services, doctoral programs with neuropsychological specialization, and even postdoctoral study in the field. No longer must we advocate for a neuropsychological view when seeking to understand behavior. Our scanning techniques now allow us to evaluate brain functioning more rapidly and more accurately. The biological basis of our behavior can now be demonstrated before completion of an autopsy. The value of such data is inestimable.

Another purpose of this book is to bridge the gap between the scientific/medical research in neuropsychology and the practice of public education, including how students learn *best*. Remarkable advances in sophisticated brain scanning have led to important clues about how the brain works. Concomitantly, school districts clamor for training that helps teachers understand how children (and thus the brain) learn. We advocate moving from the medical center into the public classrooms. School psychologists are already the largest providers of rehabilitation services in the United States and school *neuropsychologists* can do much more.

It is a daunting task to serve as editors of a broadly based but scientifically focused book. Add to the mix the many rapid changes in the field—which can be conceptualized as a veritable explosion of new knowledge and skills each day. This was our motivation for seeking a great variety of talented authors. It is our belief that no single individual or small group of individuals could possess the degree of advanced knowledge that is expressed in nearly a thousand pages of text.

The *Handbook* focuses on interventions and is organized into five sections—it begins with an exploration of the foundations of school neuropsychological practice; investigates the development, structure, and functioning of the brain; considers neuropsychological assessment for intervention; focuses on understanding and serving learners with diseases, disorders, and from special populations; and finally, examines neuropsychological intervention in the schools.

This *Handbook* is exceptionally comprehensive. The contributors comprise a diversity of individuals from a range of specialties. We searched and found contributors who could take their scientific understanding of the brain and make it understandable for initiated and uninitiated professors, practitioners, students, and teachers. You will not find such comprehensive coverage anywhere. While the three of us certainly share the credit of having the idea for the book, our many contributors, our book publisher, and our editors brought our dream to fruition and, for that, we are especially thankful. Their dedication and hard work cannot be overlooked. We also have been surrounded by supportive and talented deans, graduate assistants, and office staff.

We hope to offer information in a format that is so useful, informative, and scientifically challenging that traditional practice in our field will be changed. We feel that is the *promise of school neuropsychology.* While we realize this is a lofty goal, we believe these changes are needed if we are to meet the many challenges present within the ever-demanding, and not always child or family friendly, educational enterprise. For the sake of all children, we hope you will join us in striving to reach these essential goals.

RIK CARL D'AMATO
ELAINE FLETCHER-JANZEN
CECIL R. REYNOLDS

# Contributors

**Tim R. Allen Jr.**
School of Professional Psychology
College of Education and
    Behavioral Sciences
University of Northern Colorado
Greeley, Colorado

**Andrea Beebe**
Department of Educational
    Foundations and Special Services
College of Education
Kent State University
Kent, Ohio

**Erin D. Bigler**
Department of Psychology and
    Neuroscience
College of Family, Home, and
    Social Sciences
Brigham Young University
Provo, Utah

**Kendra J. Bjoraker**
Department of Pediatric
    Neuropsychology
University of Minnesota
    Medical School
Minneapolis, Minnesota

**John J. Brinkman Jr.**
Neuropsychology Laboratory
Department of Educational Psychology
Teachers College
Ball State University
Muncie, Indiana

**Ronald T. Brown**
Department of Public Health
Temple University
Philadelphia, Pennsylvania

**Laura Arnstein Carpenter**
Department of Health Professions
College of Medicine
Medical University of South Carolina
Charleston, South Carolina

**Mary M. Chittooran**
Department of Educational Studies
College of Public Service
Saint Louis University
St. Louis, Missouri

**Hee-sook Choi**
Division of Counseling and
    Psychology in Education
School of Education
University of South Dakota
Vermillion, South Dakota

**Elizabeth Christiansen**
Department of Educational Psychology
College of Education
University of Utah
Salt Lake City, Utah

**Elaine Clark**
Department of Educational Psychology
College of Education
University of Utah
Salt Lake City, Utah

**Jane Close Conoley**
Office of the Dean
College of Education
Texas A&M University
College Station, Texas

**Rik Carl D'Amato**
School of Professional Psychology
    and Office of the Dean
College of Education and
    Behavioral Sciences
University of Northern Colorado
Greeley, Colorado

**Andrew S. Davis**
Neuropsychology Laboratory
Teachers College
Ball State University
Muncie, Indiana

**Raymond S. Dean**
Neuropsychology Laboratory
Teachers College
Ball State University
Muncie, Indiana

**Scott L. Decker**
Department of Counseling and
    Psychological Services
College of Education
Georgia State University
Atlanta, Georgia

**James P. Donnelly**
Department of Counseling, School and
    Educational Psychology
Graduate School of Education
University at Buffalo, State University
    of New York
Buffalo, New York

**Thomas M. Dunn**
School of Psychological Sciences
College of Education and
    Behavioral Sciences
University of Northern Colorado
Greeley, Colorado

**Phyllis Anne Teeter Ellison**
Department of Educational Psychology
School of Education
University of Wisconsin–Milwaukee
Milwaukee, Wisconsin

**Jodene Goldenring Fine**
Department of Educational Psychology
College of Education
University of Texas
Austin, Texas

**Elaine Fletcher-Janzen**
Department of Psychology
University of Colorado–
    Colorado Springs
Colorado Springs, Colorado

**Christine L. French**
Department of Educational Psychology
College of Education
Texas A&M University
College Station, Texas

**Aimee Gerrard-Morris**
Department of Educational Psychology
College of Education
University of Texas
Austin, Texas

**Lana Harder**
Department of Educational Psychology
College of Education
University of Texas
Austin, Texas

**Lora Tuesday Heathfield**
Department of Educational Psychology
College of Education
University of Utah
Salt Lake City, Utah

**Robyn S. Hess**
School of Professional Psychology
College of Education and
    Behavioral Sciences
University of Northern Colorado
Greeley, Colorado

**Arthur MacNeill Horton Jr.**
Psych Associates
Towson, Maryland

**Arthur MacNeill Horton III**
Saint Luke's Treatment Center
Bethesda, Maryland

**Leesa V. Huang**
Department of Psychology
College of Behavioral and
    Social Sciences
California State University at Chico
Chico, California

**David Hulac**
School of Professional Psychology
College of Education and
    Behavioral Sciences
University of Northern Colorado
Greeley, Colorado

**George W. Hynd**
Office of the Dean
College of Education
Purdue University
West Lafayette, Indiana

**Judy A. Johnson**
New Caney Independent
    School District
New Caney, Texas

**Laurice M. Joseph**
School Psychology Program
School of Physical Activity and
    Educational Services
College of Education
The Ohio State University
Columbus, Ohio

**Alexandra Kutz**
Department of Educational Psychology
College of Education
University of Texas
Austin, Texas

**Donghyung Lee**
Department of Educational Psychology
College of Education
Texas A&M University
College Station, Texas

**Cherise D. Lerew**
University of Northern Colorado
    & Adams County
    School District # 14
Greeley, Colorado

**Lawrence Lewandowski**
Department of Psychology
College of Arts and Sciences
Syracuse University
Syracuse, New York

**Dalene M. McCloskey**
School of Professional Psychology
College of Education and
    Behavioral Sciences
University of Northern Colorado
Greeley, Colorado

**Elizabeth A. McGrain**
School of Professional Psychology
College of Education and
    Behavioral Sciences
University of Northern Colorado
Greeley, Colorado

**David E. McIntosh**
Department of Educational Psychology
Teachers College
Ball State University
Muncie, Indiana

**LeAdelle Phelps**
Department of Counseling, School,
    and Educational Psychology
Graduate School of Education
University at Buffalo, State University
    of New York
Buffalo, New York

**Kelly Pizzitola-Jarratt**
Department of Educational Psychology
College of Education
Texas A & M University
College Station, Texas

**Janiece L. Pompa**
Department of Educational Psychology
College of Education
University of Utah
Salt Lake City, Utah

**Elizabeth Portman**
Department of Educational Psychology
College of Education
University of Texas
Austin, Texas

**Sherri L. Provencal**
Department of Psychology
College of Family, Home, and
    Social Sciences
Brigham Young University
Provo, Utah

**Paul D. Retzlaff**
School of Psychological Sciences
College of Education and
    Behavioral Sciences
University of Northern Colorado
Greeley, Colorado

**Cecil R. Reynolds**
Department of Educational Psychology
College of Education
Texas A&M University
College Station, Texas

**Robert L. Rhodes**
Department of Special Education/
    Communication Disorders
College of Education
New Mexico State University
Las Cruces, New Mexico

**Cynthia A. Riccio**
Department of Educational Psychology
College of Education
Texas A&M University
College Station, Texas

**Kimberly A. Root**
School of Professional Psychology
College of Education and
    Behavioral Sciences
University of Northern Colorado
Greeley, Colorado

**Margaret Semrud-Clikeman**
Department of Educational Psychology
College of Education
University of Texas
Austin, Texas

**Susan M. Sheridan**
Department of Educational Psychology
College of Education and Human
    Sciences
University of Nebraska-Lincoln
Lincoln, Nebraska

**Emily Strassner**
Department of Educational Psychology
College of Education
University of Texas
Austin, Texas

**Raymond C. Tait**
Department of Psychiatry
School of Medicine
Saint Louis University
St. Louis, Missouri

**Cathy F. Telzrow**
Department of Educational
    Foundations and Special Services
College of Education
Kent State University
Kent, Ohio

**Michael J. Tincup**
Capistrano Unified School District
Capistrano, California

**Jonathan E. Titley**
School of Professional Psychology
College of Education and Behavioral
    Sciences
University of Northern Colorado
Greeley, Colorado

**Matthew C. Traughber**
School of Professional Psychology
College of Education and Behavioral
  Sciences
University of Northern Colorado
Greeley, Colorado

**Tasha McMahon Wellington**
Department of Educational Psychology
College of Education
University of Texas
Austin, Texas

**Alison Wilkinson**
Department of Educational Psychology
College of Education
University of Texas
Austin, Texas

**W. Grant Willis**
Department of Psychology
College of Arts and Sciences
University of Rhode Island
Kingston, Rhode Island

**Julie Wojcik**
Department of Educational
  Foundations and Special Services
College of Education
Kent State University
Kent, Ohio

**Patricia H. L. Work**
Douglas County Education
  Service District
Roseburg, Oregon

# Contents

SECTION IV   UNDERSTANDING AND SERVING LEARNERS WITH
DISEASES AND DISORDERS OR FROM SPECIAL POPULATIONS

# SECTION I

# FOUNDATIONS OF SCHOOL NEUROPSYCHOLOGICAL PRACTICE

CHAPTER 1

# School Neuropsychology: The Evolution of a Specialty in School Psychology

GEORGE W. HYND and CECIL R. REYNOLDS

R EFERENCE TO SCHOOL neuropsychology as a specialty area in school psychology first appeared in an article by the senior author of this chapter
published in the *Journal of School Psychology* in 1981 (Hynd & Obrzut, 1981).
By a coincidence of history, the second author of this chapter was acknowledged
in a footnote to that article for his helpful comments on an earlier draft. So once
again we are united in articulating why specialization in school neuropsychology
is relevant to the practice of psychology with school-age children. At the time our
paths first crossed, both of the authors of the present chapter had graduated from
doctoral training programs in school psychology and had completed either internships or postdoctoral fellowships in clinical neuropsychology.

Now, more than a quarter of a century later, several hundred school psychologists have received doctorates in school psychology with specialization in neuropsychology, and tens of thousands of practicing school psychologists have
attended workshops or continuing education experiences on the neuropsychological basis of childhood learning and behavioral disorders. Yearly convention programs for the National Association of School Psychologists (NASP) regularly have
speakers on neuropsychological assessment- and intervention-related issues, one

Preparation of this chapter was supported in part by a grant to the first author (GWH) from the
National Institute of Child Health and Human Development (NICHD), National Institutes of
Health (NIH; RO1 HD26890-08).

Preparation of sections of this chapter reflect in part an address the first author (GWH) gave in
his "Legends of School Psychology" address at the annual meeting of the National Association of
School Psychologists in Dallas, April 2004. Certain other sections are based in part on the Division
of School Psychology presidential address of the second author (CRR), "Differentiating Doctoral
School Psychology: Doing What Works," at the annual convention of the American Psychological
Association, Honolulu, July 2004.

entire NASP convention (called Mind Matters) was dedicated to the brain, and books such as this one meet the escalating demand for information about the practice of neuropsychology in the educational environment. Moreover, formation of a Neuropsychology in the Schools Interest Group in the late 1980s, one of several interest groups sponsored by NASP, revealed both the vision and needs of current NASP members. The second author has conducted special training workshops at NASP and on multiple occasions at the National Academy of Neuropsychology annual convention on Neuropsychology for School Psychologists. How has all this come about in such a short period of time?

## GENESIS OF SCHOOL NEUROPSYCHOLOGY AS A SPECIALTY AREA

As odd as it seems today, there was a time remembered by some still in the profession when there was no universal law that addressed the constitutional rights of those in need of special education services. The passage of PL 94-142 (the Education for All Handicapped Children Act of 1975) changed that, and with the more recent reauthorization of the Individuals with Disabilities Education Act (IDEA), children with special education needs are guaranteed a free and appropriate education aimed at meeting their individual needs. Much has been and will be written about the impact of these public laws; the important point is that for the first time, the educational needs of learners with dyslexia or developmental aphasia were referenced (U.S. Office of Education, 1976) as being a priority for services in the educational environment. Advocates at that time for the use of criterion-referenced or behaviorally based identification procedures argued that these and other learners with neurodevelopmental disorders (e.g., Autism) provided a compelling rationale for the use of improved clinical assessment procedures by school psychologists and an improved knowledge of the biological bases of their difficulties (e.g., Gaddes, 1968, 1969; Rourke, 1976). Essentially, the passage of PL 94-142 in 1975 legitimized viewing learning disabilities and their various forms as neurologically based disorders of developmental origin. Gone was the older perspective that children with learning disabilities suffered from minimal brain damage (MBD) of some sort. From a more conceptual perspective, Gaddes (1969) argued that educators and school psychologists typically viewed actions by children at strictly a behavioral level, often failing to consider the obvious mediation of the central nervous system. He attributed this historically evident perspective (Skinner, 1938) to an aversion by many to consider the fields of neurology and psychology as interrelated. How this aversion was constructed is a complex matter but was likely influenced by the failure of earlier, simplistic models of brain functioning to help children with learning problems, particularly those of Doman and Delacato, the failure of perceptual-motor training to remediate learning deficits, and the use of such amorphous, and inadequate, terminology as MBD to describe many of these children, all of which coincided with the rise of behaviorism as the dominant philosophy of psychology.

How did this historical aversion to appreciate the interactions between the external environment and the central nervous system manifest itself in the training of school psychologists at the time? A survey of the 200 school psychology training programs in the country in 1980 revealed that only 18% of 6th-year certification programs in school psychology required a course in the physiological basis of behavior (Hynd, Quackenbush, & Obrzut, 1980). At the doctoral level, 41% of the training programs required such a course of their students. However, with the passage of PL 94-142 and with the increased interest in better understanding brain-behavior relationships, the directors of school psychology training programs desired more required coursework in the biological basis of behavior and in neuropsychological assessment for their students. Some 74% of the directors of 6th-year specialist programs and 93% of the doctoral training programs indicated their desire in this regard (Hynd et al., 1980).

While there was clearly a renaissance of appreciation for the importance of understanding the neurobiological basis of learning and behavioral disorders (chiefly in the early 1980s), there was also a concurrent recognition that practicing school psychologists would need to become better informed so they could communicate effectively with parents and health care professionals about increasingly complex, medically involved cases in the schools. It was recognized at the time that the professional preparation of clinical neuropsychologists was wholly inadequate (Craig, 1979), thus underscoring the importance of the role of the school psychologist as the informed consultant in neuropsychology.

Some 25 years ago, the stage was set for school psychologists to develop a better appreciation of how brain-behavior interactions manifest in typical and atypical developmental contexts. Two separate but clearly important endeavors supported this rapidly developing appreciation of a neuropsychological perspective in the schools.

## NEUROBIOLOGICAL BASIS OF CHILDHOOD LEARNING DISABILITIES AND ATTENTION-DEFICIT/HYPERACTIVITY DISORDER

First and foremost, research began to address the notion of what was the neurobiological basis of learning disabilities. This was an important development because, until the passage of PL 94-142, some well-respected scholars had argued that the neurological correlates of severe learning disabilities would never be understood despite the fact that much of the available evidence supported the view that some disturbance of the central nervous system existed in most children with this diagnosis. The available evidence at that time relied heavily on what might be considered "soft" neurological signs, which are defined as behaviors that exist only under certain circumstances but are thought to reflect neurological dysfunction of some sort. Examples include weak manual preference, reversals of figures on drawing tasks, motor clumsiness, and subtle errors of speech or language.

As it is beyond the scope of this chapter to review the explosion of research that has provided compelling evidence of the neurobiological basis of learning and behavioral disorders, let it be noted that in the past 25 years, multidisciplinary research has supported the following conclusions.

First, evidence supports the view that there are disturbances in the migration of neurons during fetal development in the brains of learners with severe reading disabilities (Galaburda, Sherman, Rosen, Aboitiz, & Geschwind, 1985). These migration errors seem to be associated with the atypical development of the language areas of the brain (Hynd & Semrud-Clikeman, 1989; Hynd, Semrud-Clikeman, Lorys, Novey, & Eliopulos, 1990). Furthermore these deviations in the normal trajectory of brain development seem to be associated with the memory and neurolinguistic deficits seen in children with severe reading disabilities (Kibby et al., 2004; Semrud-Clikeman, Hynd, Novey, & Eliopulos, 1991) and with the deficits observed on tasks assessing perceptual asymmetries (Foster, Hynd, Morgan, & Hugdahl, 2002). Brain imaging research has also supported the view that the brains of children diagnosed with Attention-Deficit/Hyperactivity Disorder (ADHD) are characterized by disturbances in the development of typical patterns of brain development in regions subserving behavioral regulation, attention, and impulse control (Hynd et al., 1993). Thus, as advocacy for a neuropsychological perspective in the schools continued over the years, research increasingly provided a rationale for school psychologists to become more informed about the neurological and developmental aspects of severe learning disabilities.

Second, more recent research began investigating how the behaviors associated with severe learning disabilities might be transmitted over generations. If the neurolinguistic deficits commonly seen in reading disabilities, for example, were related to deviations during fetal brain development, it was a reasonable question to ask if there was some genetic influence in this regard.

It had long been observed that severe learning disabilities seemed to run in families (Hinshelwood, 1900; Morgan, 1896). However, it was not until the late 1990s that molecular geneticists turned their attention to the potential heritability of learning disabilities. Research in the past 15 years has revealed that at least two chromosomes (6 and 15) seem linked to severe reading disabilities (Pennington, 1999), with linkage to chromosome 6 being associated with the deficits in phonological decoding, phoneme awareness, and orthographic coding (Olson, Datta, Gayan, & DeFries, 1999). Other recent linkage studies investigating the genetic basis of dyslexia suggest that a specific region on chromosome 15 is important in brain development and maturation and may be related to the functional cellular anomalies observed in this form of severe learning disability (Taipale et al., 2003).

Although there seems to be a strong case for neurobiological differences between typically achieving children and those with severe learning disabilities, possibly of genetic origin, there is also the view that our genetic makeup accounts for only approximately 50% of the variability in human cognitive abilities. The rest of the variance must be accounted for by the environment. This, of course, makes sense, otherwise we could not learn and adapt to our environment and we would rapidly become an extinct species. And, not surprisingly, there is good evidence that functional brain differences in persons with severe reading disabilities vary with the impact of culture and native language (Siok, Perfetti, Jin, & Tan, 2004). Learning from and adapting to environmental demands is an essential attribute, and evidence suggests that the brains of persons with severe learning disabilities can adapt and profit from their remedial experience.

Third, and in this context, neuroimaging procedures have shown quite dramatically that the brains of learners with severe reading disabilities actually change metabolically in response to intervention and that this change is seen both behaviorally and during functional imaging procedures (S. E. Shaywitz et al., 1998). The conclusion is that carefully targeted intervention, based on a sound theoretical and applied rationale, can impact dramatically how the brains of children process aspects of the language code typically impacted in severe learning disabilities (B. A. Shaywitz et al., 2004).

These and other research findings have continued to argue in support of neurobiological research informing educational practice, that there was indeed a neurobiological basis to learning and behavioral disabilities, that genetics were relevant in our understanding about the transmission of learning disabilities but that sound and carefully constructed interventions could indeed offer promise of educational progress.

From the perspective of many school psychologists, the research was impacting our understanding so quickly that opportunities for advanced study in clinical neuropsychology, either through continuing educational experiences or through the pursuit of an advanced degree, was inviting. Concurrently, other health care professionals, including those in the medical profession, began turning to school psychologists to provide more relevant clinical assessments. Advances in neuropsychological assessment of children made this possible. It was in this context that many in the field found arguments in favor of preparing school psychologists in neuropsychology inviting.

## TRAINING SCHOOL PSYCHOLOGISTS IN CLINICAL NEUROPSYCHOLOGY

Recognizing that there was interest among school psychology training directors for the preparation of school psychologists in neuropsychology, Hynd (1981) proposed a curriculum aimed at providing appropriate graduate courses and supervised clinical experiences in clinical neuropsychology for subdoctoral and doctoral students in school psychology. Texas A&M University began offering a specialization strand in neuropsychology in its PhD program in school psychology in 1981 as well.

What was envisioned was not to prepare school psychologists in how to diagnose brain impairment, but rather to prepare school psychologists in clinical neuropsychology to a sufficient degree that they could bring a *neuropsychological perspective* to the increasingly complex medical challenges found in some school-age children. At the time, Hynd (1981) proposed an appropriate sequence of graduate coursework and applied supervised clinical experiences for the preparation of the 6th-year/certification-level school psychologist. This proposal was based on recognition at that time that there was a role and function for subdoctoral professionals. However, reality dictated that there was not enough curricular flexibility in the traditional 6th-year school psychology training program to accommodate all of the necessary coursework and supervised clinical experience. Thus, the more realistic approach was to prepare doctoral-level school psychologists who met standards for professional preparation in both school psychology and clinical neuropsychology. Although this added 1 to 2 extra years to the typical PhD program in school psychology, the approach proved to be both feasible and appropriate considering professional standards at the time (Hynd, 1981).

Still relevant today, projected roles for the doctoral-level school psychologist trained in clinical neuropsychology include the following:

1. Interprets the results of neuropsychological assessment and develops strategies of intervention.
2. Presents recommendations for remediation based on knowledge of scientifically validated interventions.

3. Consults with curriculum specialists in designing approaches to instruction that more adequately reflect what is known about neuropsychological development.
4. Acts as an organizational liaison with the medical community, coordinating and evaluating medically based interventions.
5. Conducts in-service workshops for educational personnel, parents, and others on the neuropsychological basis of development and learning.
6. Conducts both basic and applied educational research investigating the efficacy of neuropsychologically based interventions and consultation in the schools.

So that the doctoral-level school psychologist would meet appropriate training standards, the curriculum and supervised clinical experiences had to reflect recommended training guidelines in school psychology and in clinical neuropsychology. In school psychology, this meant that the curriculum of the training program needed to represent the standards set by both the National Association of School Psychology/National Council for the Accreditation of Teacher Education and the American Psychological Association (APA). Reflecting the work of a task force of the International Neuropsychological Society (INS) and Division 40 (Clinical Neuropsychology) of the APA, training guidelines had been developed in clinical neuropsychology (Bieliauskas & Boll, 1984). Essentially, to add the proficiencies and expertise expected of the clinical neuropsychologist to the preparation of the doctoral-level school psychologist required considerably more coursework in the generic psychology core, including such courses as biological foundations of behavior, neuroanatomy, clinical neuropsychological assessment, psychopathology, developmental neuropsychology, neuropsychological rehabilitation, and an appropriate clinical internship where at least 50% of the time was spent engaged in the supervised duties of a clinical neuropsychologist. Because of required internship experiences in school psychology, students typically had to complete a half to a full year of internship in the school setting and another year in a clinical setting appropriate for training in clinical neuropsychology. Because of the blended nature of the educational and clinical experiences at the time, many of the graduates of programs reflecting this perspective were in many regards better prepared with more relevant coursework in assessment and supervised clinical experience than those trained solely as clinical neuropsychologists. This was to prove the deciding factor in the success of these training programs in the recruitment of students and in the successful placement of students in highly competitive clinical internship sites and professional positions upon graduation.

## Case Study of a Successful Training Program

While the senior author to this chapter was at the University of Georgia, a successful model was set in place aimed at preparing doctoral-level school psychologists with expertise in clinical neuropsychology. Part of the challenge in building such a program was that, in addition to appropriate professional standards, the program had to meet departmental requirements, college and university requirements, and state certification and applied licensure requirements for the practice of psychology.

The curriculum was built on an APA-approved PhD program in school psychology, incorporated the INS recommended training standards in clinical neuropsychology, required collaboration with other neuropsychologists on campus, had available practica/internship experiences in child neuropsychology under a licensed neuropsychologist at Medical College of Georgia, and typically required an additional year or two of coursework. Many of the students successfully pursued Association of Psychology Postdoctoral Internship Centers internship sites with a clinical neuropsychology emphasis.

Since 1982, when the program was initiated, over 62 PhDs in school psychology have been granted from the University of Georgia's school psychology program with appropriate specialization in child neuropsychology. The typical PhD program with specialization in child neuropsychology took 5 years to complete (4 years plus the internship, often after entering the program with a master's degree), was a year-round program, and included four to six supervised practica in the School Psychology Clinic and two other supervised practica at the Child Neuropsychology Service Center at the Medical College of Georgia or at the Center for Clinical and Developmental Neuropsychology at the University of Georgia. Most of the students pursued APPIC internship sites, including those at Harvard University, the Kennedy Krieger Institute at Johns Hopkins University, Massachusetts General Hospital, Oklahoma Health Science Center, University of Arkansas Children's Hospital, University of Chicago School of Medicine, University of North Carolina School of Medicine, University of South Carolina School of Medicine, and Vanderbilt University School of Medicine. These internship sites were often embedded in departments of psychiatry, neurology, or pediatrics and were pursued after internship requirements were met in school psychology.

It is a reasonable question to ask: Where have these students gone and what have they accomplished? Nineteen have pursued careers in academia (e.g., University of Texas, University of Rhode Island, University of North Carolina School of Medicine, Texas A&M University, Medical College of Georgia, University of Chicago School of Medicine, Medical College of South Carolina), 18 are in private practice, 15 are in traditional school psychology positions, and 10 are in other allied health settings (e.g., mental health clinics). Such specific data are not available on graduates of the Texas A&M University program, but we know that many are now employed in hospitals and related health care settings and at least one is chief of pediatric neuropsychology at a major pediatric specialty hospital in the southern United States.

The achievements of these individuals are notable and include authoring clinical assessment instruments used by school psychologists and clinical neuropsychologists (e.g., Children's Memory Scale; Cohen, 1998); receiving nationally significant awards, including the Orton Dyslexia Society Dissertation of the Year Award (Margaret Semrud-Clikeman) and the APA Division 16 Lightner Witmer Award (Cynthia Riccio); and receiving Fulbright Fellowships (e.g., Alison Lorys, Finland; Amy Clinton, Colombia; Jason Craggs, Norway).

Other successful training programs have offered similar or alternative approaches to preparing doctoral-level school psychologists in clinical neuropsychology. Included among these are the aforementioned program at Texas A&M University and those at the University of Texas, Ball State University, University of Northern Colorado, University of Utah, and University of Washington. It is clear that the graduates of these and other programs have contributed significantly to the practice of school psychology and to clinical neuropsychology as well.

## THE CHANGING TIMES

However, national initiatives and training standards for school psychologists and clinical neuropsychologists have evolved significantly in the past quarter-century, and market forces may require a reexamination of how school psychologists may be appropriately prepared in both disciplines. Consider, for example, the many different boards and associations that have input into the professional preparation, licensure, specialty board status, and practice of clinical neuropsychologists. These include (in addition to state-level licensing boards) the INS, National Academy of Neuropsychology, Association for Internship Training in Clinical Neuropsychology, Association for Doctoral Education in Clinical Neuropsychology, Association of Postdoctoral Programs in Clinical Neuropsychology, American Board of Professional Psychology, American Board of Professional Neuropsychology, the Clinical Neuropsychology Synarche, and the newly formed Coalition of Clinical Practitioners in Neuropsychology. Also, in contrast to what Craig found in 1979, there are now over 40 recognized graduate programs that offer appropriate PhD-level training in clinical neuropsychology. Much has happened in regard to both the number of training programs available in clinical neuropsychology and the depth of the training offered at the doctoral and postdoctoral levels. Can the same be said for the profession of school psychology?

Other than a few doctoral-level training programs in school psychology that continue to prepare school psychologists in clinical neuropsychology, it is unfortunate that not as much has changed in the context of the curriculum for preparing school psychologists. Many different employment opportunities continue to exist for the doctoral-level school psychologist prepared in clinical neuropsychology in academia or in medical settings in departments of psychiatry, neurology, and pediatrics, but the need for more in-depth training in neuropsychology among nondoctoral-level school psychologists remains as present as it was when Hynd et al. (1980) surveyed school psychology program directors.

We anticipate that dynamics in the larger profession of applied psychology may have some impact in encouraging 6th-year certification or continuing education programs in school psychology to begin incorporating more specific coursework in the neurobiological basis of behavior. Considering the fact that some states are now licensing rigorously prepared applied doctoral-level psychologists to prescribe medications appropriate to their practice (e.g., New Mexico, Georgia, Louisiana) and the noted success of the Department of Defense Prescribing Psychologist Program, it might be said that the main thrust of most applied psychology programs is increasingly more biomedically oriented. Will school psychologists continue to be prepared in a narrowly defined, behaviorally focused discipline that increasingly separates them from their doctoral-trained colleagues? Considering the demands of currently legislated mandates, this may indeed be the case for many, though not all, practicing school psychologists.

Professions, especially those engaged in clinical activities and those in education, are notoriously slow to embrace change, but they must change if they are to survive. Professions typically have had a considered, meticulous response to proposals for change. This is in part related to the many layers of regulation of such professions. At least six layers of regulation exist for the profession of school psychology that include regulation through state (and sometimes federal) laws, case law, personal injury and related malpractice litigation, tradition, codes of ethics and professional conduct, and professional standards and administrative rules of practice. Significant changes in a profession must coordinate at all layers of regulation. At present, there is no legal or professional recognition of subspecialties in school psychology. For school neuropsychology to exist, programs must offer training in biologically based systems of diagnosis and intervention coupled with training in schools as systems and the other traditional aspects of school psychology to be conjointly available to those who desire to specialize. Thus, recognition of the need to specialize in school must occur at many levels (and more areas than school neuropsychology will need to be made available), denoting the need for a fundamental change in how we view professional development and education in school psychology broadly.

Professions have a systematic response to change and an inherent need for innovation, slow as it may seem to develop. This response to efforts at fundamental change is a careful and considered response that must be steeped in research. One of the defining principles of the concept of a profession states that there is a body of knowledge that underlies the activities of those engaged in it. In health care and related psychological professions, this body of knowledge is drawn from the sciences that support and accumulate knowledge in the discipline. Thus, change must have a basis in need but also a basis in science: Is there a scientific body (or bodies) of knowledge that support the results of the call for change? Change is the lifeblood of a profession as its science changes, but it is simultaneously a slow, active, and adversarial process. Change cannot be allowed to occur on the basis of faddism, research without replication, or personal persuasion. Rather, change is governed by professional standards and law. Practice, and thus changes in practice, must be based ultimately on strong science.

We view the science of the past 25 years as having demonstrated overwhelmingly the relationship of the brain and neurodevelopment broadly to behavioral development and learning (e.g., samples of this research noted earlier and also reviewed in Reynolds & Fletcher-Janzen, 1997). The science supports the need for having individuals in the schools who understand clinical neuropsychology (neuropsychology being defined as the study of brain-behavior relationships and clinical neuropsychology as the application of the findings of this field of study to individual outcomes). School psychologists, who already receive some training in the biological bases of behavior and who are particularly well trained in psychological testing and assessment, are the natural professionals to take on this role. However, to ensure what amounts to proper patient care, considerable additional doctoral-level training is required, and we have outlined some of the methods for obtaining such a knowledge base in this chapter.

School psychologists are being asked to deal with a broader and broader array of problems in the schools with each redesign of IDEA and with the growing demands for successful schooling for all learners. The knowledge explosion has been tremendous in many areas relevant to school psychology, and not just neuropsychology (e.g., learning systems and environments, public health and the prevention sciences, neurodevelopmental disorders and pediatric psychology, alcohol and drug abuse or the addiction sciences, and pediatric psychopharmacology). We believe it is no longer possible for the school psychologist to master all of the areas of knowledge needed to function ethically and effectively in so many domains. *The time for the development of specializations in school psychology has come.*

This will require recognition of this need from NASP, from various levels within APA, and, ultimately, from state-level licensing and certification agencies and individual school districts. Some doctoral-level training programs in school psychology have been developing and producing students with de facto specialization for many years, and in some cases, for many decades. When university programs are looking to hire faculty with particular expertise in such areas as consultation, behavioral psychology, or neuropsychology, it is not at all clandestine knowledge that particular programs are contacted and asked about their graduates. We have known for a long time that we cannot train our graduates to equal and effective levels of knowledge and skill in all areas demanded in practice, and we have not done so.

It is time to recognize this process formally and to begin the process of setting professional standards for subspecialty designation in school psychology (and perhaps other areas of professional psychology as well, but that is not our concern here). School neuropsychology exists and school neuropsychologists have been trained for more than 2 decades. It is no fluke that the *Handbook of Clinical Child Neuropsychology* (its third edition now in preparation) is edited by two school psychologists, that the widely adopted text *Pediatric Neuropsychology* (Hynd & Willis, 1988) was coauthored by school psychologists with expertise in clinical child neuropsychology, or that more than one school psychologist has served as president of the National Academy of Neuropsychology and that several school psychologists have held various offices and committee chairships for the Division of Clinical Neuropsychology of the APA (including the office of president). Several school psychologists have served as president and in other capacities on the executive boards of diplomate-granting boards in the field of neuropsychology as well.

## CONCLUSION

There is a long and distinguished history of school psychologists actively being engaged in leadership roles in the profession of clinical neuropsychology. These school psychologists have also been actively engaged in changing the professional landscape of school psychology itself through their leadership in various specialty interest groups such as the NASP Neuropsychology Interest Group, one of the largest such groups in NASP. In this sense, much has changed in the past 25 years, and each profession has profited from the involvement of school psychologists appropriately trained according to standards established by each profession. As has been argued, however, it is time now for the development of appropriate training standards for a new doctoral-level specialty that incorporates the best practices from each profession. In this way, practice will represent the best each profession offers in our effort to understand and help children in need of services.

As a metaphor for the relationship between school psychology, traditionally a behaviorally oriented field, and clinical neuropsychology, the following quote seems appropriate:

> The boundary between behavior and biology is arbitrary and changing. It has been imposed not by the natural contours of the disciplines, but by lack of knowledge. As our knowledge expands, the biological and behavioral disciplines will

merge at certain points, and it is at these points of merger that our understanding of mentation will rest on particularly secure ground. . . . Ultimately, the joining of these two disciplines represents the emerging conviction that a coherent and biologically unified description of mentation is possible. (Kandel, 1985, p. 832)

## REFERENCES

Bieliauskas, L., & Boll, T. (1984). Division 40/INS task force on education, accreditation, and credentialing. *APA Newsletter, 40,* 1–5.

Cohen, M. (1998). *Children's memory scale.* San Antonio: The Psychological Corporation.

Craig, D. L. (1979). Neuropsychological assessment in public psychiatric hospitals: The current state of the practice. *Clinical Neuropsychology, 1,* 1–7.

Gaddes, W. H. (1968). A neuropsychological approach to learning disorders. *Journal of Learning Disabilities, 1,* 523–534.

Gaddes, W. H. (1969). Can educational psychology be neurologized. *Canadian Journal of School Psychology, 1,* 38–49.

Galaburda, A. M., Sherman, G. F., Rosen, G. D., Aboitiz, F., & Geschwind, N. (1985). Developmental dyslexia: Four consecutive patients with cortical anomalies. *Annals of Neurology, 18,* 222–233.

Hinshelwood, J. (1900). Congenital word-blindness. *Lancet, 1,* 1506–1508.

Hynd, G. W. (1981). Training the school psychologist in neuropsychology: Perspectives, issues, and models. In G. W. Hynd & J. E. Obrzut (Eds.), *Neuropsychological assessment of the school-age child* (pp. 379–404). New York: Allyn & Bacon.

Hynd, G. W., Hern, K. L., Novey, E. S., Eliopulos, D., Marshall, R., Gonzalez, J., et al. (1993). Attention deficit hyperactivity disorder (ADHD) and asymmetry of the caudate nucleus. *Journal of Child Neurology, 8,* 339–347.

Hynd, G. W., & Obrzut, J. E. (1981). School neuropsychology. *Journal of School Psychology, 19,* 45–50.

Hynd, G. W., Quackenbush, R., & Obrzut, J. E. (1980). Training school psychologists in neuropsychological assessment: Current practices and trends. *Journal of School Psychology, 18,* 148–153.

Hynd, G. W., & Semrud-Clikeman, M. (1989). Dyslexia and brain morphology. *Psychological Bulletin, 106,* 447–482.

Hynd, G. W., Semrud-Clikeman, M., Lorys, A. R., Novey, E. S., & Eliopulos, D. E. (1990). Brain morphology in developmental dyslexia and attention deficit disorder and hyperactivity. *Annals of Neurology, 47,* 919–926.

Hynd, G. W., & Willis, W. G. (1988). *Pediatric neuropsychology.* New York: Grune & Stratton.

Kandel, E. R. (1985). Nerve cells and behavior. In E. R. Kandel & J. H. Schwartz (Eds.), *Principles of neural science* (2nd ed., pp. 316–330). New York: Elsevier.

Kibby, M. Y., Kroese, J. M., Morgan, A. E., Hiemenz, J. R., Cohen, M. J., & Hynd, G. W. (2004). The relationship between perisylvian morphology and verbal short-term memory functioning in children with neurodevelopmental disorders. *Brain and Language, 89,* 122–135.

Morgan, W. P. (1896). A case of congenital word-blindness. *British Medical Journal, 2,* 1378.

Olson, R. K., Datta, H., Gayan, J., & DeFries, J. C. (1999). A behavioral-genetic analysis of reading disabilities and component processes. In R. N. Klein & P. McMullen (Eds.), *Converging methods for understanding reading and dyslexia* (pp. 133–151). Cambridge, MA: MIT Press.

Pennington, B. F. (1999). Toward an integrated understanding of dyslexia: Genetic, neurological, and cognitive mechanisms. *Development and Psychology, 11*, 629–654.

Reynolds, C. R., & Fletcher-Janzen, E. (Eds.). (1997). *The handbook of clinical child neuropsychology.* New York: Plenum Press.

Rourke, B. P. (1976). Issues in the assessment of children with learning disabilities. *Canadian Psychological Review, 17*, 89–102.

Semrud-Clikeman, M., Hynd, G. W., Novey, E., & Eliopulos, D. (1991). Dyslexia and brain morphology: Relationships between neuroanatomical variation and neurolinguistic tasks. *Learning and Individual Differences, 3*, 225–242.

Shaywitz, B. A., Shaywitz, S. E., Blachman, B. A., Pugh, K. R., Fulbright, R. K., Skudlarski, P., et al. (2004). Development of left occipitotemporal systems for skilled reading in children after a phonologically-based intervention. *Biological Psychiatry, 55*, 926–933.

Shaywitz, S. E., Shaywitz, B. A., Pugh, K., Fulbright, R. K., Constable, R., Fletcher, J., et al. (1998). Functional disruption of the organization of the brain for reading in dyslexia. *Proceedings of the National Academy of Sciences USA, 95*, 2636–2641.

Siok, W. T., Perfetti, C. A., Jin, Z., & Tan, L. H. (2004). Biological abnormality of impaired reading is constrained by culture. *Nature, 431*, 71–76.

Skinner, B. F. (1938). *The behavior of organisms.* New York: Appleton-Century.

Taipale, M., Kaminen, N., Nopola-Hemmi, J., Haltia, T., Myllyluoma, B., Lyytinen, H., et al. (2003). A candidate gene for developmental dyslexia encodes a nuclear tetratricopeptide repeat domain protein dynamically regulated in brain. *Proceedings of the National Academy of Sciences USA, 105*, 1–6.

U.S. Office of Education, Department of Health, Education and Welfare. (1976). Education of handicapped children and incentive grants program. *Federal Register, 41*, 46977.

CHAPTER 2

# Providing Neurodevelopmental, Collaborative, Consultative, and Crisis Intervention School Neuropsychology Services

KIMBERLY A. ROOT, RIK CARL D'AMATO, and CECIL R. REYNOLDS

SCHOOL NEUROPSYCHOLOGY EXAMINES the functioning of the brain and its relation to the behavior of learners in the schools (Obrzut & Hynd, 1986). Initially, the field of clinical neuropsychology focused on the detection of brain lesions and brain pathology. Such a focus is no longer the case. Although the field of clinical neuropsychology is relatively new, the advancement of medical technology such as magnetic resonance imaging (MRI), positron emission tomography (PET), computerized axial tomography (CAT) scans, regional cerebral blood flow (rCBF) scans, and functional magnetic resonance imaging (fMRI) techniques has documented our biological basis of behavior. This has forced clinical child neuropsychologists to develop advanced skills in neuropsychological assessment, behavioral diagnosis, treatment planning, and intervention facilitation (Kalat & Wurm, 1999; Teeter & Semrud-Clikeman, 1997). Further, disorders that were once thought to be clearly behavioral or functional (nonorganic) have now been found to be neurobiological or neurochemical in nature (Obrzut & Hynd, 1986). Thus, the line between psychology and biogenetics is not definitive (Hynd & Willis, 1988).

Clinical child neuropsychology has developed as an important discipline for understanding a variety of disorders in youth and adolescents and in their treatment (Reynolds & Fletcher-Janzen, 1997). Taking a neuropsychological perspective allows one to understand developmental, psychiatric, psychosocial, and learning disorders in greater depth than is afforded by traditional behavioral or psychoeducational or even medical models (D'Amato & Rothlisberg, 1992). The utility of neuropsychological models in the schools is not a new discovery, but widespread application of neuropsychological principles is relatively recent and

15

even extends to the development of specific psychological tests for school psychologists to apply in assessment and diagnosis (e.g., Kaufman & Kaufman, 1983; Reynolds, 2003). Moreover, federal and state laws now require public schools to be responsible for a variety of services traditionally provided by rehabilitation specialists or clinical/medical professionals (Clark & Hostetter, 1995; Sattler & D'Amato, 2002), including the provision of services to children with traumatic brain injuries. The National Association of School Psychologists (NASP) and the American Psychological Association (APA) have long required formal training in the biological basis of behavior to be included in training programs seeking accreditation by either organization (Kalat & Wurm, 1999). With this as a backdrop, some school psychologists have felt obligated to develop expertise in the area of clinical child neuropsychology because of the growing number of children with severe needs in the schools. Some of these doctoral-level psychologists now call themselves school neuropsychologists. These individuals practice at the doctoral level and have typically received comprehensive training (see Chapter 1).

## WHAT IS SCHOOL NEUROPSYCHOLOGY
## AND WHY IS IT IMPORTANT?

School neuropsychology has developed as an area of training and practice in clinical, counseling, and school psychology programs and is concerned with treating the neuropsychological and neuropsychiatric needs of learners of all ages both in and out of public schools. This is not surprising, as survey data (e.g., D'Amato, Hammons, Terminie, & Dean, 1992) indicated that neuropsychology is a frequently requested topic in training programs and at professional conventions. Some of the interest comes from the relative lack of neuropsychology training in many school psychology programs. Survey data indicated that the majority of programs do *not* offer training in this area; of these, 86% reported no plans to add training in neuropsychology in the future (Walker, Boling, & Cobb, 1999). Walker, Boling, and Cobb found that only 27% of the programs reporting had full-time school psychology faculty members with neuropsychological expertise, most being trained at the doctoral level and focusing on adult neuropsychology. Of those faculty members with expertise, most received their training through postdoctoral training and applied experience. Very few were board certified. Twenty-three percent of programs surveyed required a course in neuropsychology. In most cases, this course was a general neuropsychology overview. Very few required a child or pediatric neuropsychology course. Usually, course content concentrated on the characteristics and effects of brain injury rather than intervention and placement considerations. A need to train school psychologists in neuropsychological principles relevant to school practice is evident (D'Amato, Rothlisberg, & Leu Work, 1999). It appears that neuropsychology is an area of training that is growing dramatically. In fact, the theme of the 2004 NASP conference was "Mind Matters." Clinical neuropsychology has also been recognized formally by the APA as a distinct area of professional practice in psychology.

School neuropsychologists provide an array of neuropsychological assessment, intervention, prevention, health promotion, and evaluation services. Kalat and Wurm (1999) have suggested that school psychologists are in a position to be critical contacts for children with biologically related disorders (e.g., Fragile X Syndrome, Infantile Autism, Rett's Syndrome, Attention-Deficit/Hyperactivity

Disorder, lead exposure, Dyslexia, Tourette's Syndrome) who receive services from neurologists, endocrinologists, and other medically related specialists. Infant, childhood, and adolescent disorders are now being considered from a neuropsychological perspective as well as in more traditional ways (e.g., behavioral, ecological, psychosocial).

Teeter and Semrud-Clikeman (1997) have suggested that by examining brain functioning and environmental influences in human behaviors, one can begin to meet the needs of children and adolescents with severe disorders more comprehensively than has been the common case in the schools. Some have argued that a neurodevelopmental perspective is needed to understand childhood disorders because:

- The influence of developing brain structures on mental development is sequential and predictable.
- Numerous studies have documented the effects of brain injury on children's ability to learn.
- The nature and persistence of learning problems is dependent on an interaction between dysfunctional and intact neurological systems.
- The developing brain is highly vulnerable to numerous genetic and environmental conditions that can result in severe childhood disorders.
- Children are increasingly being exposed to drugs and a variety of neurotoxins in the environment.
- Malnutrition is prevalent in the United States and has significant neuropsychological consequences to which the developing brain is also highly vulnerable.
- Neuropsychology is a well-established science with knowledge relevant to childhood disorders.
- There is a growing body of evidence suggesting that "behavior and neurology are inseparable" (Hynd & Willis, 1988, p. 5).
- Neuropsychology provides a means for studying the long-term sequelae of head injury in children.
- Neuropsychology provides a means for investigating abnormalities in brain function that increase the risk for psychiatric disorders in children.
- Neuropsychology provides a means for early prediction and treatment of reading disabilities.
- Neuropsychology provides a more comprehensive understanding of human behavior (D'Amato, Chittooran, & Whitten, 1992; Felton & Brown, 1991; Gaddes & Edgell, 1994; Goldstein & Levin, 1990; Hynd & Willis, 1988; Teeter & Semrud-Clikeman, 1997; Tramontana & Hooper, 1989; Whitten, D'Amato, & Chittooran, 1992).

The neuropsychological approach fits well with the current suggestion that clinicians develop practical problem-solving skills because it considers the full gamut of possible interventions. Some have argued that lack of a neuropsychological approach leads to gaps in the data and thus decreased intervention options and related success (D'Amato et al., 1999; Reynolds, 1986; Telzrow, 1985).

Nevertheless, although neuropsychology is important, one should not exclude other paradigms, such as behavioral, humanistic, and cognitive, when seeking to understand human behavior (Gaddes & Edgell, 1994). Information should be collected from all psychological fields of inquiry. School neuropsychologists should use interventions that take into consideration psychosocial, ecological, neurocognitive, biogenetic, and neurochemical elements of behavior (D'Amato et al., 1999). The collection and analysis of such information helps school professionals to understand children more fully—how they learn, interactions between their brain-based systems (e.g., sensory/perception)—and to develop and implement evidence-based interventions.

## COMPARING SCHOOL NEUROPSYCHOLOGY TO ADULT NEUROPSYCHOLOGY

Over the past several decades, research related to neuropsychology with adults has begun to be applied to children (Teeter & Semrud-Clikeman, 1997). Unfortunately, knowledge about adult brain functioning may not directly relate to the functioning of children's brains. The neuropsychology of adults and children *are* different. Specifically, although there are consistent relationships between specific brain diseases and behaviors in adults, that same association may not apply to children. In fact, the tests used to determine adult abilities and brain functioning may *not* relate to the same functioning in children and youth. Each child's brain undergoes dramatic developmental changes, both physiologically and neurodevelopmentally, from birth through late adolescence (Dise-Lewis, Calvery, & Lewis, 2002). These changes include refinements of various centers of the brain and the connections among parts of the brain. Typical brain development leads to growth in cognitive abilities, behavior, emotional regulation, and social capabilities (Reynolds & Fletcher-Janzen, 1997). When a neuropsychological trauma occurs with a child, the area of the brain currently developing is most vulnerable to being impacted (Dise-Lewis et al., 2002). These same areas are likely to be of concern for the child throughout his or her development. Because the brain also possesses greater plasticity during the developmental period, brain insult during this time will impact other developing areas of the brain as they attempt to coordinate and replace damaged functions (and, at times, in unpredictable ways). Damaged or dysfunctional areas of the brain may also have an adverse impact on other brain structures, to which they regularly communicate faulty impulses, producing dysfunction in seemingly disparate anatomical regions of the developing brain, but regions that are part of a set of common functional systems.

### STAGES OF NEURODEVELOPMENT

There are some common misconceptions by parents and professionals regarding neuropsychological difficulties in children (Dise-Lewis et al., 2002). Many individuals believe that children recover from a neuropsychological impairment more easily than adults do because the child's brain is more malleable and the parts of the brain not affected will take over for the parts that were injured. In some cases, this may be true, but the question has roused great controversy (Dise-Lewis et al., 2002). In fact, as previously mentioned, the opposite can be true. When a child's brain is developing, it can be injured easily, providing the child less time to acquire knowledge, skills, and competencies (Dise-Lewis et al.). An injury in one area may affect functioning in many other areas and throughout life (Reynolds & French, 2003). Some believe that a child's recovery is easy to predict, but brain development (like normal development) does not follow a consistent time line, and thus it is easier to predict recovery in adults (Dise-Lewis et al.). Because adults also have a history of relationships and employment and an ability to perform certain activities, a comparison can be made between previous and current functioning. In the case of children, although some information, such as grades and discipline reports, is usually available, children's brains change throughout development, making it difficult to determine which skills have not yet emerged or may be affected by learning or emotional problems. Neurodevelopmental areas that may be affected include sensory development, motor skills, speech and language abilities, memory, new learning, organization of thinking and behavior, mental processing efficiency, mental fatigue, executive processes, personal development, and social relationships—that is, any function that requires cognitive processing (Dise-Lewis et al.). Also, children's personality develops as they grow, making it difficult for parents and professionals to differentiate what is due to normal development and what is due to the cerebral injury. Finally, whereas some have argued that a child's brain heals faster than an adult's, others argue that more recent data indicate that a child's brain requires a longer recovery period (Dise-Lewis et al.).

Traumatic brain injuries are sometimes not reported to the school if they occur when school is not in session, such as during vacations and before entry into school. Parents and children may not report injuries resulting from embarrassing circumstances or because they believe mild brain injuries have no lasting consequences. Common neuropsychologically related trauma may result from sports injuries, vehicle accidents, family violence, assault, chemical toxins, alcohol or drug use, school violence, or malnutrition (Benedict & Horton, 1992; D'Amato, Chittooran, & Whitten, 1992 ; Drew & Templer, 1992; Geffner & Rosenbaum, 1992; Hartlage & Rattan, 1992; Lilliquist & Bigler, 1992; Lundberg-Love, 1992; Miller & Miller, 1992; Singer, 1992; Templer, 1992; Templer & Drew, 1992). Current learning is often affected by previous neuropsychological impairments, which may lead to academic and behavior problems (D'Amato et al., 1999). Often, schools will not become aware of the problem until later years, when the educational demands get tougher and the child's functioning decreases. It is therefore necessary for school personnel to look for past traumatic brain injury and be aware that a child's current neurological difficulties may be due to circumstances that have not been reported. School personnel should also encourage parents to be forthcoming with this information.

FETAL PERIOD

Birth defects can lead to long-term deficits and dysfunction in children (Keelean, Pierpont, Wiley, & McGinty, 2004; Yoon et al., 2002). Alcohol consumption and cigarette use during pregnancy are two preventable leading contributors to birth defects and health complications such as placenta previa, placental abruption, low birthweight, premature rupture of membranes, preterm delivery, miscarriage, stillbirth, and Sudden Infant Death Syndrome (SIDS; Keelean, Pierpont, Wiley, & McGinty, 2004). Each year, more than 50,000 babies are born with alcohol-related birth defects, and 12,000 may be born with Fetal Alcohol Syndrome (FAS). Children with FAS are at risk for mental retardation, growth retardation, congenital heart defects, short attention span, aggressiveness, destructiveness, and nervousness. Alcohol-Related Neurodevelopmental Disorder (ARND) and Alcohol-Related Birth Defects (ARBD) can also occur. ARND refers to functional impairments and "cognitive abnormalities including learning difficulties, poor school performance, poor impulse control, and mathematical, memory, attention, and judgment difficulties" (Centers for Disease Control and Prevention [CDC], 2002, p. 8). ARBD refers to "malformations of the skeletal system and major organ systems, such as defects to the heart, kidneys, bones, and/or auditory system" (p. 17). School neuropsychologists can be instrumental in providing interventions for children with birth deficits acquired during the fetal period. It is important that practitioners consider the possibility of brain injury in their clients because primary deficits are often responsible for frustrating behaviors displayed by children in the school and home environments (Gray & Dean, 1991). Early intervention is important, as are individualizing interventions, because typical interventions may not be successful. Practitioners must balance helping the child reach his or her potential and keeping appropriate expectations in mind. Effective partnerships between the school, family, and all service providers are also critical (Christenson, 2003).

### INFANCY (BIRTH THROUGH 3)

Unfortunately, trauma during birth is not an uncommon phenomenon. Perinatal complications include hypoxic states of varying degrees of severity (a deprivation of oxygen to the brain, and the most common form of perinatal central nervous system injury), seizures (Aylward & Pfeiffer, 1991), and structural damage related to stroke, infarct, and other forms of internal bleeding, as well as the use of forceps in some cases. Of the numerous perinatal complications that can occur, low birthweight and prematurity have the most reliable detrimental effects on a child's future education (Telzrow, 1991) because lung development in these infants is inadequate to support all of the body systems and a prolonged state of hypoxia may exist. Difficulties resulting from low birthweight may include lower cognitive scores, physical deficits (e.g., central nervous system disorders, mental retardation, and sensory problems), behavioral difficulties (e.g., social skill deficits, insecurity, immaturity), academic and learning problems (e.g., language, school readiness, and academic difficulties), seizures, and hydrocephalies (Aylward & Pfeiffer, 1991; Telzrow, 1991). There is also a higher incidence of mild handicaps in infants who experience perinatal complications than in the general population. These may include lower cognitive abilities, hyperactivity, associated behavior deficits, and significant learning problems. For such children, difficulties may *not* be present in preschool but may become apparent when they reach school age, when other learning difficulties are usually identified. It is important for school neuropsychologists to keep in mind that IQ is *not* a good predictor of the educational outcome of children with perinatal complications (Telzrow, 1991). Many children do not score significantly lower than their peers on formal intelligence tests, but they do display significant learning and/or behavioral problems (Aylward & Pfeiffer, 1991; Telzrow, 1991). Further, these difficulties generally persist for at least 8 to 10 years, disputing the claim that the gap between low birthweight children and their peers dissipates over time. In the case of frontal lobe involvement, the behavioral complications of any perinatal injury may be exacerbated in adolescence. Telzrow reported that socioeconomic status, parental education level, and early intervention are mitigating factors for perinatal complication effects on children's education. This makes clear that all psychologists in the schools should advocate for free or reduced-cost breakfast and lunch programs and parent education.

As children pass out of the perinatal stage of development, accidental droppings, falls, vehicle accidents, and physical abuse (including shaken baby syndrome) become the most common causes of brain injury for infants and preschoolers (Rapp, 1999). Prenatal and postnatal malnutrition are other factors that can lead to educational difficulties in children, especially when the malnutrition occurs during critical points in a child's brain development (D'Amato, Chittooran, & Whitten, 1992). Children's brains are growing rapidly at this age, resulting in significant cognitive difficulties if a child sustains a cerebral impairment. Skills developed during this period include refinements of and interconnections between the sensory and motor systems, regulation of sleep cycles, language acquisition, basic understanding of cause-and-effect relationships, beginning self-awareness, and responsiveness to others (Dise-Lewis et al., 2002). Disease, disabilities, or impairment at this age can lead to difficulties in self-regulation, sleep-wake cycles, toilet training, language development, understanding of cause-and-effect relationships, emotional regulation, impulsivity, self-awareness, externalizing behaviors (e.g., hitting), transitions, and social and academic skills (Dise-Lewis et al., 2002). As noted earlier, parents may not report early injuries when the child reaches school age. It is therefore necessary that school personnel collect complete information from the family; in some cases, they may need to seek out the family physician and obtain the related medical records. A measure such as the Bayley Infant Neurodevelopmental Screener (Aylward, 1995) may be used to assess infants at this age. Preventive measures can be put in place to avoid further injuries that can produce more difficulties for the child. School practitioners can help by establishing routines for these children to develop understanding of cause-effect relationships, maintaining predictable environments, teaching relaxation techniques, and teaching functional behavior routines (Dise-Lewis et al., 2002).

## PRESCHOOL (AGES 3 THROUGH 6)

Injuries during the preschool years usually include serious falls, vehicle accidents, and physical abuse (Clark & Hostetter, 1995). During this stage, children are developing self-control over physical abilities, a greater understanding of cause-and-effect relationships, the ability to experience multiple emotions at the same time, perspective-taking skills, behavioral control (e.g., inhibiting aggressive behaviors, thinking before they act), friendship skills, social skills, the ability to accept changes in their routine, and the ability to judge right from wrong (Dise-Lewis et al., 2002). Injury during this stage usually leads to difficulties with toilet training, understanding cause-effect situations, learning from consequences, emotional regulation, impulsivity, organization, rigid thinking, changes in routines, externalizing behaviors, self-preservation skills, obedience, and acquiring preschool concepts. School neuropsychologists can help these students by teaching emotional regulation (both individually and in groups), creating structure and a network of adult support for the child, maintaining routines to increase predictability for the child, and providing assistance during especially difficult times such as transitions.

## ELEMENTARY SCHOOL (AGES 6 THROUGH 12)

Preadolescents most commonly incur brain injuries due to vehicle accidents, falls, recreation or sports injuries, or assault (Clark & Hostetter, 1995; Dise-Lewis et al., 2002). At this age, a child's brain is still growing, though not as rapidly as in the earlier years. Elementary students may go through a period of rapid brain development, followed by a slower period when cognition is developing. If a child sustains a disease, disability, or impairment during this period, it interrupts the developmental process and could have long-term consequences. For example, the child may have difficulty sustaining attention or acquiring new information during a time when he or she is supposed to be gaining new skills and academic information. This is particularly important if the child has not already mastered the skill.

Children at this stage are developing multiple cause-effect relationships, academic skills, strategies for new learning and memory, appropriate behaviors, the ability to distinguish intention from outcome, a positive self-image, social skills, and collaboration skills (Dise-Lewis et al., 2002). A cerebral impairment during this stage can lead to difficulties with academics, organization, mental flexibility, impulsivity, frustration tolerance, understanding others' behaviors, and social skills and behavior. Children's peer relationships may be affected, as these children may have difficulty reading social cues, make poor social judgments, and may overreact in play, to the point where peers may find their behaviors threatening or inappropriate. All psychologists are in a position to prevent many of these injuries and problems by providing workshops to educate teachers, school personnel, and students as to vehicle and bike safety (Rapp, 1999). A common problem is that teachers and parents do not realize that difficulties are not related to the child's motivation, effort, or desire to change (D'Amato et al., 1999), but to the child's neuropsychological state. Even problems that appear to be due to lack of motivation can easily be related to less than optimal development of frontal lobe functions. School neuropsychologists can also help individuals in the child's life to reduce stress and the demands placed on the child; create functional, context-based, multisensory learning experiences; reduce coursework and homework; and provide opportunities for activities such as scouting, clubs, or individual sports.

During this stage, higher-order problem-solving skills, reasoning, abstraction, planning, organization, and the ability to complete complex projects, learn new information independently, become autonomous, assume limited responsibility for self, and form friendships based on mutual interests take center stage. School neuropsychologists can provide these students with opportunities to talk to non-family members about concerns regarding their difficulties. School neuropsychologists must conduct a comprehensive evaluation to gain information on cognitive strengths and weaknesses to understand more thoroughly the source of the emotional or learning difficulties. Following a neuropsychological framework, school neuropsychologists can create accommodations to ensure academic and social success, provide as much structure as possible in the child's environment, increase collaboration between the home and the school regarding assignments, encourage teachers to use multimodal teaching strategies (such as videos, movies, picture books, and field trips) to create a context and familiarity with new topics, and at the same time encourage parents to identify clear roles and responsibilities at home, with monitoring done by the school neuropsychologist.

### ADOLESCENCE (AGES 13 THROUGH 19)

Adolescents and young adults are the age group at the highest risk for traumatic brain injuries, with the exception of the elderly. These individuals commonly sustain their injuries in motor vehicle or sports accidents (Dise-Lewis et al., 2002). During this period, the adolescent is *refining* brain development in a number of areas, especially the frontal lobe, as well as social development, *although full development will not occur until the late 20s*. The frontal lobe system controls executive functioning, including independent judgment and problem solving, abstraction and generalization, and inhibitory controls of thought, emotions, and behavior (Dise-Lewis et al.; Lezak, 1995). In fact, Luria, the most referenced neuropsychologist, who played an influential role in the development of the field of neuropsychology, reported that the frontal lobe system plays a major role in intellectual functioning (Reynolds & French, 2003). Adolescents are also going through transitions in education and in life. A disruption of functioning at this age can affect graduation and further education (e.g., vocational training, university study). Also, adolescents may deny an injury or be resistant to accommodations for other categorical areas like learning disabilities and significant identifiable emotional disorders in areas where they previously had no problems. This adds an additional challenge to programming and intervening for these young adults. School neuropsychologists can help adolescents by trying to combat the general feeling among adolescents, "This won't happen to me" (sometimes referred to in the developmental literature as optimistic bias or adolescent invulnerability).

Adolescents with neuropsychological difficulties may have problems with rigid thinking, mental processing, attending to complex situations, identifying the most important part of a problem, decision making and judgment, spontaneous behavior, organization, desire for independence, self-image, social image and social skills, defensiveness regarding emotional and cognitive difficulties, significant academic problems, and depression. Peer support groups or individual peer mentors can be arranged for students with neuropsychological difficulties to help with the social aspect of reentry into school as well as to provide peer tutoring in needed areas (Dise-Lewis et al., 2002). School neuropsychologists should be aware of the effect injuries at this stage of development have on an adolescent's personal, social, and emotional life. They should also be aware of the impact such an impairment can have on a parent's life and the functioning of the family. The family is a crucial part of a child's life, and family members' support and cooperation are important factors in a child's success in school when dealing with a neuropsychological or neurological impairment or injury (Havey, 2002). Family members may feel confused, guilty, sorrowful, or angry or may be experiencing a mixture of emotions. (Family considerations are discussed further later in this chapter.) When working with adolescents with neurological deficits, coursework can be reduced and assignments should be tailored to the student's strengths. Psychologists can advocate waiving grade point average requirements for students to participate in sports. They can also provide therapy, serve as a point of contact where the adolescent can check in on a daily basis to relay progress, and serve as coordinators bridging the gap between medicine and education.

The effects of a neurological or neuropsychological impairment over the course of development can have profound repercussions for an infant's, toddler's, child's, or adolescent's academic, social, emotional, and personal growth. Families, parents, siblings, and peers also may be impacted.

## THE MANDATE FOR EDUCATION OF STUDENTS WITH NEUROPSYCHOLOGICAL DIFFICULTIES

Historically, students with neurological or neuropsychological impairments were often excluded from school, as were most children with handicapping conditions, mental or physical. School district policies often required students to meet specific criteria to be admitted into the public education setting, criteria that many students with disabilities could not meet (Jacob & Hartshorne, 2003). One of the school psychologist's primary functions was to assess students for eligibility purposes and to excuse those students from school who did not meet the requirements, had behavioral difficulties, or were simply thought to be too challenging to teach. Prior to the 1960s, these children were often institutionalized, sent to private schools if parents could afford it, or kept at home (Jacob & Hartshorne, 2003).

In the late 1960s, parents began to sue schools on their children's behalf, leading to the development of federal legislation to provide a free and appropriate public education to all children, regardless of disability status (Jacob & Hartshorne, 2003). The most important legislation to arise was the Education of All Handicapped Children Act of 1972, which later became the Individuals with Disabilities Education Act (IDEA; 1997). Because schools were now required to provide a free and appropriate education to all learners, regardless of the severity of disability, learners with neurological or neuropsychological impairments began to be offered services.

Limited funds are provided for special education and related services under IDEA-Part B for children with certain disabilities. These include mental retardation, hearing impairments, speech or language impairments, visual impairments, serious emotional disturbance, orthopedic impairments, Autism, traumatic brain injury, other health impairments, and specific learning disabilities. Also included are students "who, by reason thereof, need special education and related services" (PL No. 105-17, § 602, 111 Stat. 43, 1997). Thus, it is mandated that students with neurological or neuropsychological impairments receive services. However, volumes of research suggest that schools often do not follow through appropriately with these mandates (e.g., Hynd & Hooper, 1992; Prentiss, 1997; Reynolds & Gutkin, 1999).

D'Amato and Rothlisberg (1996) emphasized the importance of a comprehensive approach to intervention for learners with neurological or neuropsychological disabilities. They have argued for an SOS model that encompasses three broad categories of intervention: structure, organization, and strategies. Structural intervention includes creating home-school partnerships, developing work-release programs, increasing teacher consistency, augmenting child behavioral consistency, controlling environmental stimulation, considering endurance and stamina, and supporting and validating emotions. Organizational interventions include developing instructional tactics, organizing assignments, adopting life skills curricula, and offering career education. The development of learning strategies is also important. This can be accomplished by developing student profiles that highlight strengths and needs, using compensatory strategies to work around skill deficits, offering remediation when appropriate, providing role models, and teaching social skills.

## THE CURRENT CRISIS IN EDUCATION

There is a growing list of issues and concerns that children, youth, and families face when interacting in the educational setting, including violence, suicide, homicide, bullying, abuse and neglect, and poverty (Sheridan & Gutkin, 2000). Garbarino (1995) explained that "the mere act of living in our society today is dangerous to the health and well-being of children and adolescents. . . . The social world of children, the social context in which they grow up, has become poisonous to their development" (p. ix, 4). Clearly, the methods used in the past few decades are not working or are working in limited areas.

Since the Spring Hill and Olympia conferences in the 1980s, which brought together practitioners and educators in the field of school psychology with the purpose of identifying the needs, worries, and future of school psychology (Spring Hill conference) and creating strategies to resolve those issues (Olympia conference), school psychology as a field has been pushing for a paradigm shift away from assessment (for the purposes of special education eligibility) and toward evidenced-based interventions, with a focus on evaluation of the effectiveness of interventions that have been implemented (Reschly, 1988; Reschly & Yesseldyke, 2002). Sheridan and Gutkin (2000) have argued that psychologists must collaborate with other professionals if they are to bring about the necessary changes. School neuropsychology training, practice, and research must take into account multiple settings, systems, and populations, being reflective of the changes within the systems in which we operate (Sheridan & D'Amato, 2004; Reynolds & Fletcher-Janzen, 1989). This shift, based on ecological theory, conceptualizes human behavior as a function of individuals interacting with their multiple environments. In an ecological paradigm, school psychologists should be less concerned with determining what is *wrong* with a child and more concerned with *prevention* and promoting what is going well with the child, thereby focusing on students' successes instead of their failures. School neuropsychologists must work with educators, parents, and other professionals in the community functioning within all systems (D'Amato et al., 1999). In schools, psychologists must collaborate with teachers, counselors, administrators, social workers, special educators, teachers, other support staff, and parents. Unfortunately, very few training programs provide opportunities where this type of educational collaboration is comprehensively taught.

## COLLABORATION BETWEEN THE MEDICAL FACILITY AND THE SCHOOL

Due to advances in medical research and technology, children who have neurological disorders are now living longer and returning to school earlier (Rapp, 1999;

Havey, 2002). Given these changes, school psychological service providers now offer more rehabilitation services than any other service providers (Reynolds & Fletcher-Janzen, 1997; Teeter & Semrud-Clikeman, 1997). Further, the emphasis in education on inclusion of all children leads to more of these children being in the regular education classrooms. The reauthorization of Public Law 94-142, requiring children with a variety of exceptionalities, including traumatic brain injuries and Autism, to receive special services in the school adds to the responsibilities of the educational system to be able to accommodate these populations of children (D'Amato & Rothlisberg, 1996).

Due to the nature of neurological disorders and injuries, children often receive services from a variety of professionals (e.g., psychiatrists, physicians, speech pathologists, occupational therapists), and these professionals may employ numerous psychosocial, behavioral, and medical treatments and interventions (Teeter & Semrud-Clikeman, 1997). Although the professionals may all have the same goals for the child, the techniques they call on are very different. For example, the physical therapist may be helping the child to learn to walk again, while the special education teacher may be helping to control the child's behavioral problems. Consequently, it is important that professionals communicate so that one intervention is not interfering with another and so that parents and school personnel are not given two different and contradictory interventions, leaving them to decide what to do for the child. A second concern is the high cost of neuropsychological assessments and interventions. Case collaboration is important so that duplication of assessments is avoided as much as possible. It becomes redundant, invalid, and costly for parents and teachers to fill out the same questionnaires or rating scales given by a variety of professionals in a short period of time. Another issue concerns the use of medication. Many children who suffer from neuropsychological disorders are prescribed medications that need to be monitored by all professionals who interact with these children. Concerns should be relayed to the primary care physician, psychiatrist, or neurologist so that adjustments can be made in a timely fashion. Many medications have side effects that teachers and parents need to know about so that interventions or accommodations can be planned when a medication has an adverse effect.

Similarly, when children with a neurologically related disease or disorder reenter the school system, teachers and other staff need to be knowledgeable about their needs (and the needs of the family) so as to best serve them. These needs may be medical, psychosocial, academic, and behavioral. School professionals should be in regular contact with physicians. The school neuropsychologist can educate the staff about each child's needs and act as a liaison between the school, the medical facility, the physician, and the parents. If the learner makes rapid improvements or rapid declines, school personnel are most likely to see these changes; they will then be able to relay these concerns to others (e.g., occupational therapist, physical therapist) so that interventions and medications can be modified appropriately.

Communication with parents is also of critical importance. It is stressful and confusing for parents to have a child with neuropsychological or neurological needs. Parents may be put in the unwanted position of being the liaison among a horde of professionals. Further, parents may have questions or needs of their own, and professionals must be available to answer these concerns in an effort to provide for their child in the best manner possible. Parents themselves may have been injured and have their own problems, making it difficult for them to concentrate on their child's circumstances. Just as each professional may have unique information that is useful to the others to best intervene for the child, parents are also useful as a resource. They have the most substantial impact on a child's life and course of recovery. In fact, schools that work in collaboration with parents often receive better results for the children to whom they are providing services (Christenson, 2003).

Confidentiality is an important consideration when communicating between and across systems. Parental permission must be obtained to share information, and sensitive information should be shared only on a need-to-know basis. Also of importance is that a regular plan or schedule be set up so that everyone is on the same page and each professional knows who is responsible. A schedule helps facilitate regular communication among parties. Professionals may need to communicate quite often in the beginning; this may taper off as the child begins to progress and meet therapeutic and intervention goals (Teeter & Semrud-Clikeman, 1997). Teeter and Semrud-Clikeman have advocated for follow-up at 6-, 12-, 18-, and 24-month intervals.

## CONSULTING AS A CRITICAL ASPECT OF SCHOOL NEUROPSYCHOLOGY

The importance of consultation in school psychology has been recognized for years (Gutkin & Curtis, 1999). To serve children appropriately in schools, school neuropsychologists need to work with all of the adults in the children's system, with a strong focus on the individuals who are going to be implementing the interventions developed. Numerous individuals are going to be working with a learner with neuropsychological difficulties; this creates a variety of different options and methods of intervention for each child. School neuropsychologists are in an ideal position and have the appropriate knowledge to collect all the needed information from the professionals (e.g., personal care physicians, neurologists, psychiatrists) and disseminate it back to parents and teachers as needed. They can be available to answer questions and concerns as they arise and to coordinate care for nonmedical interventions. A teacher is not going to implement a strategy that he or she does not understand or consider appropriate; it is the school neuropsychologist's responsibility to consult with teachers so that concerns are addressed and fitting interventions are put into place.

One of the first steps when providing educational services to children with neurological or neuropsychological impairments is preparing for the transition from the medical center to the school. This transition can be a difficult one if the medical facility and the educational system have different philosophies, structures, or goals, leading to problems in communication and ultimately to inadequate or poorly coordinated services for learners (Havey, 2002). Often, children arrive at school having been released from a primary care hospital, specialty care facility, or rehabilitation facility with no advance or coordinated planning with the school. Further complications can arise from transitions occurring over several weeks. This necessitates frequent communication between the school, the medical facility, and the family to ensure that services are provided in a cohesive manner that is best for the child's educational, social, and emotional growth. School neuropsychologists can facilitate this process by urging that school-based special education teams become involved at the hospital or rehabilitation facility, providing in-service training to all staff who will be in contact with the student, developing short- and long-term planning for support services for the child, and continuing to follow up with the professionals in the medical facility who are or were working with the child (Havey, 2002; Savage & Carter, 1988).

Clinical neuropsychologists have traditionally displayed difficulties with the consultation role. They are often trained in a medical center using the "expert" medical model. If they follow this model, they dispatch orders to school personnel in place of consulting or collaborating. Some school neuropsychologists may also be trained in this paradigm. The old adage "If they do not know you care, they do not care you know" is sage advice for any school neuropsychologist. Further, interventions for neuropsychological difficulties may look very different from what a teacher typically uses in his or her classroom. In this case, it is important for the school neuropsychologist to consult with the teacher so that the teacher knows what, when, and how he or she should be implementing interventions. Moreover, the teacher is going to be the individual seeing the results of the interventions on a day-to-day basis; thus, consultation is important so that data can be collected and aggregated and necessary modifications can be made. Teachers may also need help and support to continue to maintain suitable interventions.

Dealing with neuropsychological interventions may pose a unique challenge to teachers who are not trained to deal with learners with neuropsychological impairments. This is particularly important as children begin to make progress or if a child is on a new medication. Interventions or medication dosages may need to be modified rapidly, and teachers are in the best position to collect such information and relay it back to the school neuropsychologist or family physician. Some of these difficulties may be eased by fostering increased communication between teachers and between teachers and parents as children move from grade to grade. To ease the transition, Savage, Pearson, McDonald, Potoczny-Gray, and Marchese (2001) have recommended that the following information be passed along when a student enters a new grade: (1) school work (i.e., sample work, lists of books and materials used, effective and ineffective compensatory strategies, behavior management techniques, adaptive/assistive equipment or interventions, learning style/general strengths and needs); (2) a current medical summary (i.e., brief history of the injury/illness and medical interventions, current medications, including purpose and possible side effects, medical issues that may occur at school and the appropriate response if they do); (3) a special service summary (i.e., neuropsychological, psychological, physical therapy, occupational therapy, speech/language therapy, adapted physical education); and (4) a list of important participants and/or contacts (i.e., family members, educational advocates, therapists, physicians). What may be new and confusing to the educator is not new to the student or parent. By passing along information, transitions can be eased and the child can continue to progress instead of starting over each year (Savage et al., 2001). One of the authors (CRR) made it a practice to conduct (with appropriate parental consent) a one-hour in-service with the teachers of each of his traumatic brain injury clients at the beginning of each school year, detailing the specific nature and general characteristics of the child's difficulties and what might be expected with regard to learning and behavioral challenges.

Consultation with family and friends of the student is important for additional reasons. These individuals are in a position to see the improvements (or lack thereof) that infants, children, or adolescents may display outside the classroom and in areas other than academics (social, emotional, behavioral, personality) that may have been affected by the neuropsychological deficit. School neuropsychologists need this information to better serve the child. Further, it is difficult to have a child, sibling, or friend with a neurological deficit (Gaddes & Edgell, 1994; Savage & Wolcott, 1994). Friends and siblings may have a difficult time adjusting to changes in the way the child interacts with them or personality changes that may occur. Activities that these children could once engage in easily (e.g., sports) may be more difficult after the injury. Significant individuals in the child's life may need support to understand and cope with all the changes that have occurred in their relationship with the child. Providing information and training for the family is necessary. Even from the beginning stages, family members can learn about their child's difficulties, how to advocate for their child, what resources are available, where to refer their child for special services, and how to ensure that their child is receiving the best services (Savage et al., 2001). School neuropsychologists can provide this education by connecting with the medical facility early on and then continuing when the child reenters school.

As mentioned previously, family members may feel confusion, grief, guilt, sadness, or anger regarding their loved one's impairments. Children with traumatic brain injury may also experience guilt over surviving an accident when other family or friends died. Denial is a part of the recovery process for families and may last months or even years. Family dynamics may change in the way members interact and communicate, along with changing responsibilities and demands. Adjusting to and coping with these changes can be scary and exhausting for a family. Finances may be stretched thin due to medical bills. Parents may have to consider changing careers, or at least their daily routine, to care for the child. Siblings may receive less attention from parents. The child's changes in behavior at school may be embarrassing or cause social isolation for siblings. Family members' lives, including activities and social outlets, may be put on hold indefinitely while the needs of their loved one are taken care of, which may lead to stress, anger, or resentment. It is necessary that school neuropsychologists include families in decisions and address all their concerns and stressors to ensure the wellbeing of all involved.

Similarly, classmates are often affected by a learner's neurological deficits or neuropsychological injuries (D'Amato et al., 1999). As with siblings, peers may be embarrassed or confused by changes in their classmate's behaviors and capabilities. Further, just as in families, more attention may be given to the child with the impairment, leading to disorder in the classroom. School neuropsychologists can help maintain order in the class by educating peers (with the family's permission) as to the nature of their classmate's difficulties, changes they may see, and ways that they can help the child, thereby dispelling rumors. Transition back into the classroom can be eased by creating teams of peers and school personnel who can help the child integrate socially back into the school environment.

## CRISIS INTERVENTION SERVICES IN SCHOOL NEUROPSYCHOLOGY

Children today are facing numerous obstacles to healthy lifestyles, including difficulties with peers, parents, teachers, learning, and development. In the context of schools, the majority of these obstacles are not new, which leads one to believe that we live in a child-toxic society (Sheridan & D'Amato, 2004). Crockett (2003) outlined some of the issues facing children in the twenty-first century during the Future of School Psychology Conference. Thirty-seven percent of children in the United States live in poverty, 80% of whom live in working-poor households. Poverty rates are highest for African Americans (30%) and Latinos (28%). It is important to note that poverty and its correlates are the factors that most strongly negatively impact educational achievement (e.g., Carlson, Paavola, & Talley, 1995) and are related to cerebral development and neuropsychological functioning (D'Amato, 1990; D'Amato, Rothlisberg, & Rhodes, 1997).

Homicide is the second leading cause of death for all 15- to 24-year-olds, the leading cause of death for African Americans in this age group, and the second leading cause of death for Hispanic youths (Crockett, 2003). More than 800,000 children are victims of physical abuse (this reflects only those incidents of abuse reported). Crockett has indicated that one in seven children reports being bullied at school. One out of three students who were bullied had plans of retaliating against their aggressor. Moreover, 30% of girls and 18% of boys in grades 8 to 11 reported harassment that occurs almost on a daily basis. While births to girls age 15 and under have steadily declined for the African American and Latino population, this is not true for Caucasians (and teens are at high risk for having low birthweight babies and account for a disproportionate number of cases of intrauterine growth retardation). Further, sexually transmitted diseases are increasing for children age 15 to 19 (including pediatric HIV, which leads to cognitive impairment in about 50% of cases). Fifty percent of motor vehicle accidents and 30% of suicides involving adolescents are related to alcohol or other drugs. Suicide is the third leading cause of death for 15- to 24-year-olds. For Native Americans, 64% of suicides are in the 15- to 24-year-old age range. Although suicide for young children is rare, the CDC reported dramatic (109 percent) increases in suicide rates for children age 10 to 14 from 1980 to 1997. Surprisingly, only 36% of youths at risk for suicide during 2003 received mental health services. In addition, while the United States has become more diverse, hate crimes based on sexual orientation have increased and hate crimes based on race and religion continue to be a problem (Crockett, 2003). Moreover, children are exposed to violent images more than ever before (Balcerzak & D'Amato, 2000). Media depict violence as a way to solve conflict and to vent frustration and anger. Children may learn that violence has no consequence and is often rewarded. As a result, school violence is of great concern.

Schools currently are unable to handle many of the problems children are faced with due to structural and financial constraints (Carlson et al., 1995). A high student-to-school psychologist ratio is one factor contributing to schools' inability to be content about student mental health needs. Another is the fact that the IDEA covers only students suffering from behavioral and emotional disorders. While there are estimates of up to 15% of children having behavioral or emotional difficulties, fewer than 1% are identified under IDEA (Carlson et al., 1995). Schools rely on community professionals to provide services to these children, yet only 3% of school-age children and youth receive community mental health services, leaving a 12% gap between those needing and those obtaining services.

## INTERVENTIONS

In response to these dilemmas, Carlson et al. (1995) have advocated for school-based/school-linked comprehensive services for children and families. Schools would become seamless health service settings to meet the all-inclusive needs of children. The role of the school neuropsychologist fits well into this model as he or she would be bringing some of those services into the schools and collaborating among other professionals (hospitals, clinics, neuropsychologists, etc.). A move toward full-services schools, which would meet many of the needs of children outlined previously, has been discussed (Adelman & Taylor, 1998; Carlson et al., 1995). Recommendations include promoting a national agenda for screening and establishing national standards for personnel working with children, utilizing No Child Left Behind to provide prevention and early intervention services and training, and collaborating with community agencies. It will also be critical to develop multidisciplinary teams at the local level that include juvenile justice personnel, mental health professionals, school personnel, medical personnel, parents, and others (Harrison et al., 2004).

*Violence Interventions*   As children are increasingly faced with myriad problems within the school, the diverse needs of children are becoming more difficult for school neuropsychologists to handle (Reynolds & Gutkin, 1999). Referrals, consultation, and collaboration are necessary, as one person cannot meet all the needs of all the children. School psychologists and school neuropsychologists are in a unique position to provide training in appropriate and safe behavior, as well as to teach social and emotional skill development and conflict resolution. Balcerzak and D'Amato (2000) have called for these skills be taught through the development of each school as a "caring community," which involves a variety of initiatives such as youth development (character education) and peer mediation for an entire school. Family involvement in upholding values such as pride, respect, responsibility, caring, and honesty is also a primary focus of the program.

School neuropsychologists are also in a position to use their training in collaboration and organization to focus efforts during school emergencies. Larson, Smith, and Furlong (2002) have suggested a three-tier process including the *community,* the *district,* and the *school building* to deal with school violence. Tier 1 involves organizing a task force. At the community level, a task force may consist of the school district superintendent, a school board representative, educational support staff, law enforcement, businesses, clergy, the medical and mental health community, municipal government, juvenile justice, media, parents, and students. At the district level, the superintendent, grade-level administrators, support services representatives, school security, classified staff, parents, and students can be included in a task force. Building-level school safety planning teams may include the principal, grade-level/disability teacher representatives, support services representatives, students (keeping in mind age-appropriate considerations), parents, and qualified staff. This team is responsible for moving beyond crisis readiness and response to plan for a wide range of psychological and physical safety concerns. Tier 2 calls on the team to analyze the problem and to make sure all team members fully understand the problem. Tier 3 involves developing response proposals. In all tiers, collaboration is necessary.

Poland, Pitcher, and Lazarus (2002) have emphasized the importance of a comprehensive, multifaceted approach to dealing with school emergencies, including media, families, and community members. They recommended exposing all learners to conflict resolution, social problem-solving methods, and anger management. Interventions they support include mentoring programs, teaching better social/life skills, improving environmental factors (e.g., lowering violence, controlling crowds, creating a positive school atmosphere), intervening with at-risk students, and involving parents, students, and staff.

*Chronic Illness or Injury Interventions*   Medical crises are another area requiring attention by the schools. These may involve children who have been diagnosed with chronic and life-threatening diseases, children who are prone to acute injury, and children who live with chronic, life-threatening disease in their family. The need for intervention becomes particularly evident when children are not only faced with a medical emergency, but also are living with families with limited social, economic, and personal resources to cope, often leading to multiple stressors (Steward, 2002). Steward outlined a number of interventions for working with children dealing with chronic illness or injury.

Methods recommended for high-risk children include active listening, helping children reclaim control of their body by focusing on areas of physical competence, utilizing technology and the Internet for resources and support, and encouraging and nurturing friendships (Steward, 2002). Children with illness often have difficulties with social relationship skills and peer acceptance. Teachers, parents, peers, and school neuropsychologists can all work together to foster supportive friendships between children with illness or injury and their classmates. Group interventions are also effective for children with illness or injury. Summer camps, social skills training, and focus groups are all possibilities for working with these children (Steward, 2002). Preparing children for the death of a chronically ill classmate is also important for their mental health. Seat belt and helmet safety education is paramount. Education in this area should include monitoring, feedback, and reinforcement to be effective. School neuropsychologists can work in concert with the school, hospitals, and the community to provide comprehensive education in this area. Steward also emphasized the importance of three-way communication among the school, parents, and teachers, and in-service training, both of which school neuropsychologists can provide.

*Unresolved Grief and Death Interventions*   A large number of youth are exposed to momentous loss each year (Hilarski, 2004). Children who are not provided the opportunity to talk about loss and change may be at risk for unresolved grief, a chronic state that requires intervention and is linked with health consequences. Such loss could involve parents or siblings (typically, from an automobile accident) and peers or peers' parents or family members. Suicide can also be an important part of the clinical picture and must be dealt with seriously, judiciously, and empathetically (Rapp-Paglicci, Dulmus, & Wodarski, 2004). There are no formal prevention or intervention programs to deal with unresolved grief, but age-appropriate death education and group sharing are thought to be important elements of the school curriculum beginning as early as kindergarten (Hilarski, 2004). Children with unresolved grief are likely to be experiencing trauma reactions and therefore need to be assessed for trauma; intervention efforts should include trauma and bereavement components. It is a myth that "time heals"; therefore, early intervention is paramount (Hilarski, 2004).

*Additional Interventions*   Although it is not possible to recount intervention strategies for every area affecting children's mental and neurodevelopmental health or families' needs, there are some areas that warrant consideration, such as child maltreatment, dropping out of school, and substance abuse. There are numerous evidence-based intervention programs to deal with child maltreatment. Among them, a common theme is that they are family-centered, contain multiple components, and are implemented during early childhood (Thomlison, 2004). Interventions implemented at the earliest signs of risk factors and that incorporate parenting education have been shown to be most effective (Thomlison, 2004).

Adolescent school dropout is another area of great concern. Doll and Hess (2004) have advocated convincingly for universal prevention programs that include academic support and remediation and alternatives to retention, create a supportive school community, involve parents, attend to early warning signs, and encourage school reform. Selective preventive interventions involve increasing school engagement, easing school transitions, and providing community service opportunities; effective indicated prevention interventions involve high-intensity programming in school, alternative schools, and dropout retrieval programs.

Substance abuse is a growing area of concern with neuropsychologically impacted children in the schools. Effective interventions incorporate personal, life, social skills, and parent training, social influence, changing the school climate, mentoring, parent and family involvement, legal and policy changes, coalitions, youth clubs, and multicomponent interventions (LeCroy & Mann, 2004).

## CONCLUSION

By using their understanding of brain-behavior relationships, school neuropsychologists can provide effective intervention for learners with neurological or neuropsychological difficulties to supplement traditional interventions. Collaboration and consultation with parents, teachers, and professionals in the community enable school neuropsychologists to gain a comprehensive view of children and provide children, families, and teachers with the support they may need. By collaborating with community practitioners, school neuropsychologists will know what services are available and what can be offered to the learner. As always, it is necessary for school psychologists to refer children with neuropsychological difficulties or who are faced with a crisis requiring emergency school services to the appropriate professional. Some school psychologists may use neuropsychological skills to enhance their practice; others will complete the required classes and pre- and postdoctoral internships to provide appropriate services, including neuropsychological services.

The need for school neuropsychology services is evident. These professionals have a distinctive body of knowledge and can provide unique and comprehensive services to children with neurological or neuropsychological trauma across the entire developmental spectrum. School neuropsychologists can be the focal point of services provided to children, as demonstrated in Figure 2.1. The need for services for children with neuropsychological difficulties, as mandated by federal law, has inspired recent legislation, such as No Child Left Behind, and the current drive in school psychology for a paradigm shift and evidence-based interventions. Moreover, there is an increasing need for mental health services for children given the rise in societal violence and the educational problems children are faced with daily. The school neuropsychologist must be an essential and erudite partner in meeting

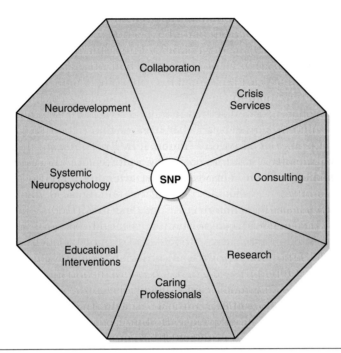

**Figure 2.1**  Graphic Display of the Various Components of School Neuropsychological Practice

the varied needs of children, families, peers, school professionals, and community partners.

## REFERENCES

Adelman, H. S., & Taylor, L. (1998). Mental health in schools: Moving forward. *School Psychology Review, 27*(2), 175–190.

Aylward, G. P. (1995). *The Bayley infant neurodevelopment screener.* San Antonio, TX: Psychological Corporation.

Aylward, G. P., & Pfeiffer, S. I. (1991). Perinatal complications and cognitive/neuropsychological outcome. In J. W. Gray & R. S. Dean (Eds.), *Neuropsychology of perinatal complications* (pp. 128–160). New York: Springer.

Balcerzak, A., & D'Amato, R. C. (2000). Changing society one classroom at a time: A school-wide approach to the development of social and emotional skills. *Communique, 29*(1), 6–9.

Benedict, R. H. B., & Horton, A. M. (1992). The neuropsychology of alcohol induced brain damage: Current perspectives on diagnosis, recovery, and prevention. In D. I. Templer, L. C. Hartlage, & W. G. Cannon (Eds.), *Preventable brain damage: Brain vulnerability and brain health* (pp. 146–160). New York: Springer.

Carlson, C., Paavola, J., & Talley, R. (1995). Historical, current, and future models of schools as health care delivery settings. *School Psychology Quarterly, 10*(3), 184–202.

Centers for Disease Control and Prevention. (2002). *Fetal alcohol syndrome prevention: Increasing public awareness of the risks of alcohol use during pregnancy through targeted media campaigns.* Retrieved May 12, 2004, from http://www.cdc.gov/ncbddd/fas.

Christenson, S. L. (2003). The family-school partnership: An opportunity to promote the learning competence of all students. *School Psychology Quarterly, 18*(4), 454–482.

Clark, E., & Hostetter, C. (1995). *Traumatic brain injury: Training manual for school personnel.* Longmont, CO: Sopris West.

Crockett, D. (2003). Critical issues children face in the 2000s. *School Psychology Quarterly, 18*(4), 446–453.

D'Amato, R. C. (1990). A neuropsychological approach to school psychology. *School Psychology Quarterly, 2,* 93–101.

D'Amato, R. C., Chittooran, M. M., & Whitten, J. D. (1992). Neuropsychological consequences of malnutrition. In D. I. Templer, L. C. Hartlage, & W. G. Cannon (Eds.), *Preventable brain damage: Brain vulnerability and brain health* (pp. 193–213). New York: Springer.

D'Amato, R. C., Hammons, P. F., Terminie, T. J., & Dean, R. S. (1992). Neuropsychological training in American Psychological Association-accredited and nonaccredited school psychology programs. *Journal of School Psychology, 30,* 175–183.

D'Amato, R. C., & Rothlisberg, B. A. (1992). *Psychological perspectives on intervention: A case study approach to prescriptions for change.* White Plains, NY: Longman. (Reissued by Waveland, Prospect Heights, IL, 1997).

D'Amato, R. C., & Rothlisberg, B. A. (1996). How education should respond to students with traumatic brain injuries. *Journal of Learning Disabilities, 29,* 670–683.

D'Amato, R. C., Rothlisberg, B. A., & Leu Work, P. (1999). Neuropsychological assessment for intervention. In C. R. Reynolds & T. B. Gutkin (Eds.), *Handbook of school psychology* (3rd ed., pp. 452–475). New York: Plenum Press.

D'Amato, R. C., Rothlisberg, B. A., & Rhodes, R. I. (1997). Utilizing a neuropsychological paradigm for understanding common educational and psychological tests. In C. R. Reynolds & E. Fletcher-Janzen (Eds.), *Handbook of clinical child neuropsychology* (2nd ed., pp. 270–295). New York: Plenum Press.

Dise-Lewis, J. E., Calvery, M. L., & Lewis, H. C. (2002). *Brainstars: Brain injury: Strategies for teams and re-education for students.* Denver, CO: Brainstars.

Doll, B., & Hess, R. (2004). School dropout. In L. A. Rapp-Paglicci, C. N. Dulmus, & J. S. Wodarski (Eds.), *Handbook of preventative interventions for children and adolescents* (pp. 359–380). Hoboken, NJ: Wiley.

Drew, R. H., & Templer, D. I. (1992). Contact sports. In D. I. Templer, L. C. Hartlage, & W. G. Cannon (Eds.), *Preventable brain damage: Brain vulnerability and brain health* (pp. 15–29). New York: Springer.

Felton, R. H., & Brown, I. S. (1991). Neuropsychological prediction of reading disabilities. In J. E. Obrzut & G. W. Hynd (Eds.), *Neuropsychological foundations of learning disabilities: A handbook of issues, methods, and practice* (pp. 387–410). San Diego, CA: Harcourt Brace Jovanich.

Gaddes, W. H., & Edgell, D. (1994). *Learning disabilities and brain function: A neuropsychological approach* (2nd ed.). New York: Springer-Verlag.

Garbarino, J. (1995). *Raising children in a socially toxic environment.* San Francisco: Jossey-Bass.

Geffner, G. M., & Rosenbaum, A. (1992). Brain impairment and family violence. In D. I. Templer, L. C. Hartlage, & W. G. Cannon (Eds.), *Preventable brain damage: Brain vulnerability and brain health* (pp. 58–71). New York: Springer.

Goldstein, F. C., & Levin, H. S. (1990). Epidemiology of traumatic brain injury: Incidence, clinical characteristics and risk factors. In E. Bigler (Ed.), *Traumatic brain injury.* Austin, TX: ProEd.

Gray, J. W., & Dean, R. S. (Eds.). (1991). *Neuropsychology of perinatal complications.* New York: Springer.

Gutkin, T. B., & Curtis, M. J. (1999). School-based consultation theory and practice: The art and science of indirect service delivery. In C. R. Reynolds & T. B. Gutkin (Eds.), *Handbook of school psychology* (3rd ed., pp. 598–637). New York: Wiley.

Harrison, P. L., Cummings, J. A., Dawson, M., Short, R. J., Gorin, S., & Palomares, R. (2004). Responding to the needs of children, families, and schools: The 2002 multisite conference on the future of school psychology. *School Psychology Review, 33*(1), 12–33.

Hartlage, L. C., & Rattan, G. (1992). Brain injury from motor vehicle accidents. In D. I. Templer, L. C. Hartlage, & W. G. Cannon (Eds.), *Preventable damage: Brain vulnerability and brain health* (pp. 3–14). New York: Springer.

Havey, J. M. (2002). Best practices in working with students with traumatic brain injury. In A. Thomas & J. Grimes (Eds.), *Best practices in school psychology IV* (Vol. 2, pp. 1433–1446). Bethesda, MD: National Association of School Psychologists.

Hilarski, C. (2004). Unresolved grief. In L. A. Rapp-Paglicci, C. N. Dulmus, & J. S. Wodarski (Eds.), *Handbook of preventative interventions for children and adolescents* (pp. 49–66). Hoboken, NJ: Wiley.

Hynd, G. W., & Hooper, S. R. (1992). *Neurological basis of childhood psychopathology.* Newbury Park, CA: Sage.

Hynd, G. W., & Willis, W. G. (1988). *Pediatric neuropsychology.* Orlando, FL: Grune & Stratton.

Individuals with Disabilities Education Act (PL No. 101-476), 20 U.S.C. Chapter 33. Amended by PL No. 105-17 in June, 1997. Regulations appear at 34 C.F.R. Part 300.

Jacob, S., & Hartshorne, T. S. (2003). *Ethics and law for school psychologists* (4th ed.). New York: Wiley.

Kalat, J. W., & Wurm, T. (1999). Implications of recent research in biological psychology for school psychology. In C. R. Reynolds & T. B. Gutkin (Eds.), *The handbook of school psychology* (3rd ed., pp. 271–290). New York: Wiley.

Kaufman, A. S., & Kaufman, N. L. (1983). *Kaufman assessment battery for children.* Circle Pines, MN: AGS.

Keelean, D., Pierpont, J. H., Wiley, J., & McGinty, K. (2004). Birth defects. In L. A. Rapp-Paglicci, C. N. Dulmus, & J. S. Wodarski (Eds.), *Handbook of preventative interventions for children and adolescents* (pp. 133–148). Hoboken, NJ: Wiley.

Larson, J., Smith, D. C., & Furlong, M. J. (2002). Best practices in school violence prevention. In A. Thomas (Ed.), *Best practices in school psychology IV* (Vol. 2, pp. 1081–1098). Bethesda, MD: National Association of School Psychologists.

LeCroy, C. W., & Mann, J. E. (2004). Substance abuse. In L. A. Rapp-Paglicci, C. N. Dulmus, & J. S. Wodarski (Eds.), *Handbook of preventative interventions for children and adolescents.* Hoboken, NJ: Wiley.

Lezak, M. D. (1995). *Neuropsychological assessment* (3rd ed.). New York: Oxford University Press.

Lilliquist, M. W., & Bigler, E. D. (1992). Neurological and neuropsychological consequences of drug abuse. In D. Templer, L. Hartlage, & W. G. Cannon (Eds.), *Preventable brain damage: Brain vulnerability and brain health* (pp. 161–192). New York: Springer.

Lundberg-Love, P. K. (1992). Industrial toxins. In D. Templer, L. Hartlage, & W. G. Cannon (Eds.), *Preventable brain damage: Brain vulnerability and brain health* (pp. 111–131). New York: Springer.

Miller, W. G., & Miller, F. (1992). Accidental injuries of children. In D. Templer, L. Hartlage, & W. G. Cannon (Eds.), *Preventable brain damage: Brain vulnerability and brain health* (pp. 41–57). New York: Springer.

Obrzut, J. E., & Hynd, G. W. (1986). *Child neuropsychology: Theory and research volume 1.* Orlando, FL: Academic Press.

Poland, S., Pitcher, G., & Lazarus, P. M. (2002). Best practices in crisis prevention and management. In A. Thomas & J. Grimes (Eds.), *Best practices in school psychology IV* (Vol. 2, pp. 1057–1080). Bethesda, MD: National Association of School Psychologists.

Prentiss, D. (1997). Pediatric brain injury and families: The parental experience. *Dissertation Abstracts International, 60*(02), 840. (UMI No. 9827968)

Rapp, D. L. (1999). Interventions for integrating children with traumatic brain injury into their schools. In C. R. Reynolds & T. B. Gutkin (Eds.), *The handbook of school psychology* (3rd ed., pp. 863–884). New York: Wiley.

Rapp-Paglicci, L. A., Dulmus, C. N., & Wodarski, J. S. (Eds.). (2004). *Handbook of preventative interventions for children and adolescents.* Hoboken, NJ: Wiley.

Reschly, D. J. (1988). Special education reform: School psychology revolution. *School Psychology Review, 17,* 459–475.

Reschly, D. J., & Yesseldyke, J. E. (2002). Paradigm shift: The past is not the future. In A. Thomas & J. Grimes (Eds.), *Best practices in school psychology.* National Association of School Psychologists.

Reynolds, C. R. (1986). Transactional models of intellectual development, yes. Deficit models of process remediation, no. *School Psychology Review, 15,* 256–260.

Reynolds, C. R. (2003). *Comprehensive trailmaking test.* Austin, TX: ProEd.

Reynolds, C. R., & Fletcher-Janzen, E. (1989). *Handbook of clinical child neuropsychology.* New York: Plenum Press.

Reynolds, C. R., & Fletcher-Janzen, E. (1997). *Handbook of clinical child neuropsychology: Critical issues in neuropsychology* (2nd ed.). New York: Plenum Press.

Reynolds, C. R., & French, C. L. (2003). The neuropsychological basis of intelligence revised: Some false starts and a clinical model. In A. M. Horton Jr. & L. C. Hartlage (Eds.), *Handbook of forensic neuropsychology* (pp. 35–92). New York: Springer.

Reynolds, C. R., & Gutkin, T. B. (1999). *The handbook of school psychology* (3rd ed.). New York: Wiley.

Sattler, J. M., & D'Amato, R. (2002). Brain injuries: Theory and rehabilitation programs. In J. M. Sattler (Ed.), *Assessment of children: Behavioral and clinical applications* (4th ed.). San Diego, CA: Jerome M. Sattler.

Savage, R. C., & Carter, R. R. (1988). Transitioning pediatric patients into educational systems: Guidelines for rehabilitation professionals. *Cognitive Rehabilitation, 6,* 4.

Savage, R. C., Pearson, S., McDonald, H., Potoczny-Gray, A., & Marchese, N. (2001). After hospital: Working with schools and families to support the long term needs of children with brain injuries. *Neurorehabilitation, 16*(1), 49–58.

Savage, R. C., & Wolcott, G. F. (1994). *Educational dimensions of acquired brain injury.* Austin, TX: ProEd.

Sheridan, S. M., & D'Amato, R. C. (2004). Partnering to chart our futures: *School Psychology Review* and *School Psychology Quarterly* combined issue on the multisite conference on the future of school psychology. *School Psychology Quarterly, 19,* 7–11.

Sheridan, S., & Gutkin, T. (2000). The ecology of school psychology: Examining and changing our paradigm for the 21st century. *School Psychology Review, 29,* 485–502.

Singer, R. (1992). Agricultural and domestic neurotoxic substances. In W. G. Cannon, L. Hartlage, & D. L. Templer (Eds.), *Preventable brain damage: Brain vulnerability and brain health* (pp. 132–145). New York: Springer.

Steward, M. S. (2002). Illness: A crisis for children. In J. Sandoval (Ed.), *Handbook of crisis counseling, intervention, and prevention in the schools* (2nd ed.). Hillsdale, NJ: Erlbaum.

Teeter, P. A., & Semrud-Clikeman, M. (1997). *Child neuropsychology: Assessment and interventions for neurodevelopment disorders.* Needham Heights, MA: Allyn & Bacon.

Telzrow, C. F. (1985). The science and speculation of rehabilitation in developmental neuropsychological disorders. In L. C. Hartlage & C. F. Telzrow (Eds.), *The neuropsychology of individual differences: A developmental perspective* (pp. 271–307). New York: Plenum Press.

Telzrow, C. F. (1991). The school psychologist's perspective on testing students with traumatic brain injury. *Journal of Head Trauma Rehabilitation, 6,* 23–34.

Templer, D. I. (1992). Assault. In W. G. Cannon, L. Hartlage, & D. L. Templer (Eds.), *Preventable brain damage: Brain vulnerability and brain health* (pp. 72–79). New York: Springer.

Templer, D. I., & Drew, R. H. (1992). Noncontact sports. In W. G. Cannon, L. Hartlage, & D. L. Templer (Eds.), *Preventable brain damage: Brain vulnerability and brain health* (pp. 30–40). New York: Springer.

Thomlison, B. (2004). Child maltreatment. In L. A. Rapp-Paglicci, C. N. Dulmus, & J. S. Wodarski (Eds.), *Handbook of preventative interventions for children and adolescents.* Hoboken, NJ: Wiley.

Tramontana, M. G., & Hooper, S. R. (1989). Neuropsychology of child psychopathology. In C. R. Reynolds & E. Fletcher-Janzen (Eds.), *Handbook of clinical child neuropsychology* (2nd ed., pp. 120–139). New York: Plenum Press.

Walker, W. N., Boling, M. S., & Cobb, H. (1999). Training of school psychologists in neuropsychology and brain injury: Results of a national survey of training programs. *Child Neuropsychology, 5*(2), 137–142.

Whitten, J. C., D'Amato, R. C., & Chittooran, M. M. (1992). A neuropsychological approach to intervention. In R. C. D'Amato & B. A. Rothlisberg (Eds.), *Psychological perspectives on intervention: A case study approach to prescriptions for change* (pp. 112–136). White Plains, NY: Longman. (Reissued by Waveland, Prospect Heights, IL, 1997)

Yoon, P. W., Rasmussen, S. A., Lynberg, M. C., Moore, C. A., Anderka, M., Carmichael, S. L., et al. (2002). National birth defects prevention study. *Public Health Reports, 116*(Suppl.1), 32–40.

# SECTION II

## DEVELOPMENT, STRUCTURE, AND FUNCTIONING OF THE BRAIN

# CHAPTER 3

# Foundations of Developmental Neuroanatomy

W. GRANT WILLIS

T HE NERVOUS SYSTEM comprises a highly organized set of subsystems, structures, and processes, and it is useful to consider the gestalt before addressing more specific levels of analysis. Table 3.1 provides an organizational scheme of the nervous system in the form of an outline. Although those of us interested in the field of school neuropsychology often are drawn to cerebral, and especially cortical, explanations for behavior and cognitive processes, it is important to remember that the central nervous system is only one component of the nervous system, that the brain is only one component of the central nervous system, and that the cortex is only one component of the brain. Nearly all aspects of human functioning depend on the effective integration of functional systems that are comprised by the entire nervous system. This is a primary reason why a basic understanding of the foundations of developmental neuroanatomy can be so useful to research and clinical practice in school psychology.

## NERVOUS SYSTEM CELLS

Regardless of the particular level of the nervous system (i.e., level of *neuraxis*) on which we focus, two basic kinds of cells are apparent: nerve cells (i.e., *neurons*) and glial cells (i.e., *glia*). The human brain comprises an estimated 100 billion neurons, which can be classified into as many as 1,000 different subtypes (Kandel, 2000). Even so, nearly all of these cells include four primary features: (1) a cell body (i.e., soma or perikaryon), (2) an axon, (3) presynaptic terminals, and (4) dendrites. The *cell body* contains the nucleus of the cell, within which are the cell's genes, and is responsible for the metabolic and protein-synthesis functions of the neuron. Extending from the cell body are the *axon,* which is a tubular process that transmits electrical signals (i.e., *action potentials*) across distances as short as 0.1 mm to as long as 3 m, and usually several short, branching *dendrites,* which receive incoming action potentials. At the end of the axon are

**Table 3.1**
Organization of the Nervous System

I. Central nervous system
   A. Brain
      1. Hindbrain (rhombencephalon)
         a. Medulla (myelencephalon)
         b. Metencephalon
            i. Pons
            ii. Cerebellum
      2. Midbrain (mesencephalon)
      3. Forebrain (prosencephalon)
         a. Diencephalon
            i. Thalamus
            ii. Hypothalamus
            iii. Epithalamus
            iv. Subthalamus
         b. Telencephalon
            i. Cerebral cortex
            ii. Basal ganglia
            iii. Forebrain limbic structures
   B. Spinal cord
II. Peripheral nervous system
   A. Autonomic system
      1. Parasympathetic division
      2. Sympathetic division
   B. Somatic system

fine branches, the specialized endings of which are called *presynaptic terminals.* When the action potential reaches these terminals, a chemical neurotransmitter is released that allows the electrical signal to be propagated to the dendrite of a receiving neuron (or sometimes to the receptive surface of another neuron) or to an effector cell such as those in muscles and glands. The region where two neurons communicate is called the *synapse,* and therefore the transmitting neuron is often referred to as the *presynaptic* cell and the receiving neuron as the *postsynaptic* cell. With some specific variations, action potentials propagated in this fashion form the basic informational units of the motor, sensory, perceptual, emotional, and cognitive aspects of human experience.

The other kind of nervous system cells, the glial cells, which are much more numerous than neurons in humans, are probably not involved in information processing, but instead play a number of other important roles. For example, they establish a structure, or kind of scaffolding, within which the neurons can function, as well as a variety of regulation, nourishment, and support functions. Some glial cells help to form the *blood-brain barrier,* which is a protective mechanism that helps to prevent toxins in the bloodstream from entering the brain. Still others (i.e., *oligodendrocytes* in the central nervous system and *Schwann cells* in the peripheral nervous system) wrap concentric layers of a substance called *myelin* around the axons of neurons, which serve to insulate them and to improve the speed and efficiency of neural conduction.

NEURAL INDUCTION

Nervous system cells develop through an orderly epigenetic process that includes (1) the initial proliferation and early differentiation of cells into glia and immature neurons; (2) the migration of neurons from germinal regions to final positions; (3) the further differentiation of neurons, including growth of axons and formation of synaptic connections; and (4) the modification of those synaptic connections, including programmed neuronal death (see Jessell, 1995). As Jessell emphasized, this epigenetic process is influenced by intracellular factors within the developing organism itself as well as factors from the external environment (e.g., nutrition, sensory function). Thus, genetic-environmental interactions extend even from these very early stages of development. The interconnections between specialized classes of neurons form the basis for our behavior, and the sensitivity of these connections to cellular and environmental influences may lead to a variety of individual differences associated with human functioning that are of special interest to professionals such as school neuropsychologists.

## NEURULATION

*Neurulation* describes the early differentiation of embryonic cells toward the formation of a closed cylinder called the *neural tube*, the presumptive beginning of the brain and spinal cord. Prior to a discussion of the process of neurulation, it may be useful to review a number of directional terms frequently used to describe locations of neuroanatomical regions.

ORIENTATION AND PLANES OF REFERENCE

*Dorsal* (or *superior*) refers to the back surface. *Ventral* (or *inferior*) is the side opposite the dorsal and refers to the front. Other directions are *anterior* (or *rostral,* meaning "head") and *posterior* (or *caudal,* meaning "tail"), which are oriented along the longitudinal head-to-tail axis (or neuraxis). These terms sometimes cause confusion because, in the mature human brain (as opposed to lower vertebrates'), there is a *flexure* (or curvature) of the longitudinal axis at about the upper-middle level of the brain, so that the dorsal or back side of the body extends to the top side of the head (i.e., the scalp), whereas the ventral side of the body (e.g., chest region) extends to the bottom side of the head, under the chin. Thus, in the spinal cord and at lower levels of the human brain, rostral means toward the head and caudal means toward the tail bone; ventral means toward the front of the body and dorsal means toward the back. At higher levels of the human brain, however, rostral refers to the facial side of the head and caudal to the back side of the head; dorsal to the top side of the head and ventral to the chin side of the head.

When imaging studies of the brain are conducted, for example, with computerized tomography or magnetic resonance imaging procedures, three common planes of reference are the *coronal* (also called transverse or frontal), *axial* (also called horizontal), and *saggital* planes. In humans, the coronal plane is parallel to the face, the axial plane is parallel to the top of the head, and the saggital plane is parallel to the side of the head. Coronal images typically are oriented as if the viewer were standing and facing a standing patient, whereas axial images typically are oriented as if the viewer were standing at the patient's feet looking toward the patient's head while the patient is in a prone position laying on the back. Thus, for both coronal and axial images, the patient's right side typically is on the left side of the image.

## Germinal and Early Embryonic Stages of Development

Human conception occurs when an egg cell (i.e., ovum) is fertilized by a sperm cell in the fallopian tube. The cells of the resulting zygote begin to subdivide as they travel through the fallopian tube to become implanted in the wall of the uterus. At this early stage of development, which occurs around 1 week after conception (i.e., approximately 3 menstrual weeks as counted from the mother's last menstrual period), the embryo comprises two layers of tissue: the dorsal, overlying *ectoderm,* and the *endoderm.* At about 9 days after conception, a presumptive third layer of tissue, the *mesoderm,* migrates into a medial position between these two layers. This process, called *gastrulation,* is essential to neurulation because it initiates neural induction (see Saxen, 1980).

About 2 weeks after conception, the *notochord* develops along the longitudinal axis of the mesoderm. The notocord directs a portion of the overlying ectoderm to begin to thicken to form the *neural plate.* Around the 18th day, a longitudinal fissure appears in the neural plate, and its edges (called *neural folds*) continue to become thicker and to buckle. The neural groove becomes deeper and the neural folds become thicker; by about the 21st day, the folds eventually meet and fuse together, forming the cylindrically shaped neural tube. This fusion begins in what will later become the cervical (or neck) region of the cranio-caudal axis and proceeds in both rostral and caudal directions. The neural tube becomes divided into two longitudinal halves by a pair of grooves known as the *sulcus limitans.* Along the dorsal half of the neural tube, the *floor plate* joins a pair of longitudinal cell columns called the *basal plates.* In caudal regions of the neural tube, the basal plates develop into the ventral gray columns (or horns) of the mature spinal cord, which subserve primarily motoric functions. Similarly, along the ventral half of the neural tube, the *roof plate* joins the *alar plates.* Again, in caudal regions of the neural tube, the alar plates develop into the *gracile* and *cuneate nuclei* of the mature spinal cord, which subserve primarily sensory functions. The rostral opening of the neural tube (i.e., the *anterior neuropore*) closes around 24 days after conception, and the caudal opening (i.e., the *posterior neuropore*) closes shortly thereafter, forming the beginning of the structure of the central nervous system.

Other cells of the neural plate that are not incorporated into the neural tube form the *neural crest,* the presumptive beginning of the peripheral nervous system. As the neural folds fuse to form the neural tube, the overlying ectoderm is drawn medially over the dorsal side of the rostral-caudal axis. The ectoderm separates from the neural tube, and the resulting layer of cells comprises the neural crest. This layer of tissue then divides longitudinally along the rostral-caudal axis, and the two resulting columns migrate laterally. The columns then become segmented to form beadlike aggregations of cells called *spinal ganglia.* Fibers originate from the spinal ganglia and grow toward the neural tube. In what will become the *cervical* (or neck), *thoracic* (chest), *lumbar* (lower back), and *sacral* (tailbone) regions of the spinal cord, these fibers form the dorsal roots of the spinal nerves, which are specialized for sensory functions. In more rostral regions of the neural tube (in what will later become the brain), neural crest cells develop into cranial nerve ganglia for the trigeminal (V), facial (VII), glossopharyngeal (IX), and vagus (X) nerves (Carpenter & Sutin, 1983). The functions associated with these cranial nerve nuclei hold high survival value for the neonate because they mediate important primitive reflexes stimulated by gustatory, vestibular, and cutaneous sensations.

As the neural tube develops, particular regions grow at different rates. This causes the longitudinal rostral-caudal axis to bend, forming flexures, so that as the process of neurulation nears completion, the cephalic end of the neural tube has become bent in an anterior direction (with the convex side of the curve on the dorsal side of the neural tube) forming a nearly right angle with the more posterior region of the neural tube. During embryonic development, three of these flexures occur: the *cephalic,* as described, the *cervical,* and the *pontine.* The latter two flexures relax, however, and only the cephalic flexure persists, accounting for the curved neuraxis of the mature human brain as opposed to the straight neuraxis of lower vertebrates.

A number of neurodevelopmental errors can occur during these early and critically important stages of embryonic development. Such neurodevelopmental errors are referred to as *dysraphic* or neural tube defects and include disorders such as anencephaly, which results from a failure of the anterior neuropore to fuse properly, and spina bifida, which results from a failure of more posterior regions of the neural tube to fuse properly. A number of studies have shown that supplements of folic acid, a vitamin found in green, leafy vegetables, can be remarkably effective in preventing these and other dysraphic defects from occurring (Scott et al., 1994). Because the process of neurulation occurs so early in gestation, however, an expectant mother may not have been able to confirm a pregnancy until after the neural tube already has been formed.

## DIFFERENTIATION OF THE BRAIN VESICLES

As the process of neurulation nears completion between the 3rd and 4th weeks of gestation, three dilations or *primary brain vesicles,* demarcated by the more caudal cervical flexure and the more rostral cephalic flexure, appear at the rostral end of the neural tube. These major subdivisions of the human embryonic brain comprise the rostral forebrain (or prosencephalon), the intermediate midbrain (or mesencephalon), and the caudal hindbrain (or rhombencephalon). There is a narrowed region demarcating the juncture of the midbrain and hindbrain that is called the *isthmus.*

During the 5th week of gestation, another flexure (i.e., the cephalic flexure) develops that subdivides the forebrain into two secondary brain vesicles: the more rostral telencephalon and the more caudal diencephalon. Subsequently, yet another flexure (i.e., the pontine flexure) develops that subdivides the hindbrain into its relatively more rostral metencephalon and its relatively more caudal myelencephalon. The pontine flexure diminishes with further development, and its only residual evidence in the mature human brain is a dorsal fissure called the *transverse rhombencephalic sulcus.* The midbrain does not further subdivide; therefore, the embryonic brain comprises five secondary brain vesicles at this stage of development. These vesicles become the presumptive sites of the major neuroanatomical structures of the mature human brain.

Ventricular System

Cerebrospinal fluid (CSF) eventually flows through a ventricular system of *lumina* (or cavities) throughout the five secondary brain vesicles that is continuous with the spinal canal in the more caudal neural tube. The telencephalon comprises the two lateral ventricles, the diencephalon comprises most of the third ventricle (which is connected with the lateral ventricles via the *intraventicular foramina*), the mesencephalon comprises the *cerebral aqueduct* (which interconnects the third and fourth ventricles), the rhombencephalic derivatives comprise the fourth ventricle, and the spinal cord comprises the central canal. The *choroid plexus* develops in the lateral, third, and fourth ventricles and begins to secrete the CSF. Initially, this system of lumina is closed, but during the 3rd and 4th months of gestation, openings (the *foramen of Magendie* and the *foramina of Luschka*) appear in the fourth ventricle that allow the CSF to flow into the subarachnoid space, which surrounds the brain and spinal cord (Corbett, Haines, & Ard, 2002).

The *subarachnoid space* is a region between meninge layers, which surround the central nervous system. The human *meninges* comprise the *pia mater,* the *arachnoid mater,* and the *dura mater,* which develop from neural crest and mesoderm cells that migrate into position between 20 and 35 days of gestation and attain their basic form as observed in the mature brain by about the end of the first trimester of pregnancy (Haines, 2002). The dura mater, which adheres to the inner surface of the skull, overlies and adheres to the arachnoid mater, which overlies the subarachnoid space, which in turn overlies the pia mater, which adheres to the surface of the brain and spinal cord. Within the subarachnoid space, strands of cells called *arachnoid trabeclae* bridge the gap between the pia mater and the overlying arachnoid mater. It is within this space that the CSF flows; therefore, the brain is essentially suspended in the CSF of the subarachnoid space. As Haines noted, because these arachnoid trabeclae are not rigid, the brain can move within the fluid of the subarachnoid space; therefore, closed head injuries may result in brain damage either at the site of trauma (i.e., *coup* injury) or at the site opposite trauma (i.e., *contrecoup* injury).

Beyond traumatic injuries, a number of events, including neurodevelopmental errors, infections, and glial-cell neoplasms (i.e., tumors), may occur that are associated with the ventricular system of the central nervous system (Corbett et al., 2002). For example, as cells in the midbrain proliferate through normal developmental processes, the cerebral aqueduct becomes narrower and provides a potential site of blocking the CSF between the third and fourth ventricles. Such blockage may result in hydrocephalus associated with the enlargement of the lateral and third ventricles and consequent compression of surrounding brain tissue.

## MAJOR NEUROANATOMICAL STRUCTURES

With continued prenatal development, the five secondary brain vesicles form the major neuroanatomical structures of the mature human brain. Proceeding in a caudal to rostral direction, the following discussion addresses the myelencephalon, which differentiates into the *medulla* (sometimes called the medulla oblongata); the metencephalon, which differentiates into the *pons* and the *cerebellum;* the mesencephalon, which becomes the *midbrain;* the diencephalon, which differentiates into the *thalamus, hypothalamus, epithalamus,* and *subthalamus;* and the telencephalon, which differentiates into the *cerebral cortex, basal ganglia,* and forebrain *limbic* structures.

MYELENCEPHALON

The most rostral structure of the mature human brain is the medulla. It is demarcated caudally by the first pair of spinal nerves in the cervical region and rostrally by the beginning of the pontine flexure. At its caudal region, the medulla is structurally similar to the spinal cord and, therefore, has been considered a transitional region serving to link the spinal cord with the brain in an integrated functional system (Arey, 1974). The spinal central canal continues into the medulla, and the sulcus limitans, which demarcates dorsal sensory regions from ventral motor regions, also is clearly present. More rostrally, however, those structures common to the medulla and spinal cord become more differentiated and displaced to different locations. Here, the central canal widens to become the fourth ventricle, and this widening displaces the alar plates to a location lateral to the basal plates. Around 6 weeks after conception, the basal plates differentiate into pairs of cell columns that retain their motor function specialization. In a similar fashion, the alar plates subsequently differentiate into cell columns that retain their sensory function specialization.

The cell columns arising from the alar plates are commonly referred to as general somatic afferent (GSA), general and special visceral afferent (G/SVA), and special somatic afferent (SSA), with reference to their functions. Those columns arising from the basal plates are commonly referred to as general somatic efferent (GSE), general visceral efferent (GVE), and special visceral efferent (SVE), again in reference to their functions (there is no SSE column). These columns become segmented to form the nuclei of the *cranial nerves,* which are an important group of sensory and motor fibers in the peripheral nervous system that have direct connections with these particular regions of the brain. There are 12 pairs of cranial nerves, numbered I through XII, and their nuclei range from the most rostral region of the brain (the olfactory cranial nerve, I) through the most caudal regions of the brain in the medulla (the hypoglossal cranial nerve, XII). The names of the cranial nerves, their associated nuclei, and major functions are listed in Table 3.2.

At the level of the medulla, the GSE column includes the *hypoglossal nucleus* (for cranial nerve XII); the SVE column includes the *nucleus ambiguous* (for cranial nerves IX and X); the GVE column includes the *inferior salivatory nucleus* (for cranial nerve IX) and the *dorsal motor nucleus of vagus* (for cranial nerve X); the G/SVA column includes the *solitary nucleus* (for cranial nerves VII, IX, and X); the GSA column includes the *spinal trigeminal nucleus* (for cranial nerves V, VII, IX, and X); and the SSA column includes the *vestibular nucleus* (for cranial nerve VIII). The glossopharyngeal (IX), vagus (X), and hypoglossal (XII) cranial nerves connect with their respective nuclei at the level of the medulla. (The spinal accessory nerve, XI, connects with the upper cervical level of the spinal cord.) Table 3.3 (p. 49) lists the cranial nerve nuclei that are associated with the cell columns deriving from the basal and alar plates at the level of neuraxis at which they occur.

**Table 3.2**
Cranial Nerves, Nuclei, and Functions

| Cranial Nerve | Nuclei | Functions |
| --- | --- | --- |
| I Olfactory | Neuroepithelial cells in nasal cavity | *Sensory:* Smell |
| II Optic | Ganglion cells in retina | *Sensory:* Vision |
| III Oculomotor | Edinger-Westphal nucleus (midbrain) | *Motor:* Eye movement, pupillary constriction, and lens accommodation |
| IV Trochlear | Trochlear nucleus (midbrain) | *Motor:* Eye movement |
| V Trigeminal | Trigeminal motor and principal sensory trigeminal nuclei (pons); spinal trigeminal nucleus (spinal cord, medulla, pons) | *Sensory:* Cutaneous and proprioceptive sensations from face and mouth <br> *Motor:* Innervates muscles of mastication |
| VI Abducens | Abducens nucleus (pons) | *Motor:* Eye movement |
| VII Facial | Facial motor and superior salivatory nuclei (pons); solitary nucleus (medulla); spinal trigeminal nucleus (spinal cord, medulla, pons) | *Sensory:* Taste and sensation from external ear canal <br> *Motor:* Innervates muscles of facial expression and salivary glands |
| VIII Vestibulocochlear | Cochlear nucleus (pons); vestibular nuclei (medulla, pons) | *Sensory:* Hearing and motion sense |
| IX Glossopharyngeal | Inferior salivatory and solitary nuclei and nucleus ambiguous (medulla); spinal trigeminal nucleus (spinal cord, medulla, pons) | *Sensory:* Taste <br> *Motor:* Swallowing |
| X Vagus | Dorsal motor nucleus of vagus, nucleus ambiguous, and solitary nucleus (medulla) | *Sensory:* Taste, sensation from pharynx, larynx, and thoracic and abdominal organs <br> *Motor:* Innervates smooth muscle and glands of cardiovascular, pulmonary, and gastrointestinal systems |
| XI Spinal accessory | Accessory nucleus (spinal cord) | *Motor:* Innervates neck and shoulder muscles |
| XII Hypoglossal | Hypoglossal nucleus (medulla) | *Motor:* Innervates tongue muscles |

**Table 3.3**
Cranial Nerve Nuclei Arising from Cell Columns of the Basal and Alar Plates

| Level of Neuraxis | GSE | SVE | GVE | G/SVA | GSA | SSA |
|---|---|---|---|---|---|---|
| | Cell Column | | | | | |
| Prosenephalon | | | | I | | II |
| Mesencephalon (midbrain) | III IV | | III | | V | |
| Metencephalon (pons) | VI | V VII | VII | VII | V VII IX X | VIII |
| Myelencephalon (medulla) | XII | IX X | IX X | VII IX X | V VII IX X | VIII |
| Spinal cord | | XI | | | V VII IX X | |

Other structures in the medulla, known collectively as the relatively diffuse *reticular nuclei* and the more concentrated *raphe nuclei,* are part of the *reticular formation* (or *reticular activating system*) and extend throughout the medulla and pons into the midbrain. These nuclei serve various functions in the control of heart rate and respiration; in the modulation of pain, postural reflexes, and muscle tone; and in the regulation of arousal and consciousness (see Delcomyn, 1998; Haines & Mihailoff, 2002a). In medial regions of the medulla, the reticular nuclei include the *central nucleus* and the *gigantocellular reticular nucleus* and, in more lateral regions, the *lateral reticular nucleus,* the *parvocellular nucleus,* and the *ventrolateral reticular area.* The raphe nuclei form bilateral columns adjacent to the midline and include the *nucleus raphes pallidus,* the *nucleus raphes obscurus,* and the *nucleus raphes magnus.*

Another set of structures in the medulla comprises ascending and descending pathways that innervate the somatosensory and motor systems. Fibers in the ascending (sensory) pathways originate in the spinal cord; some terminate in the medulla and others continue toward more rostral regions of the brain. One of these sets of pathways, the *medial lemniscal system,* which includes the gracile and cuneate nuclei, is specialized for discriminative touch (i.e., tactile discrimination) and position sense. Another set of pathways, the *anterolateral system,* which includes tracts that terminate in the thalamus and midbrain, is specialized for nondiscriminative touch (i.e., crude or poorly localized touch) and sensations of pain and temperature. Other ascending pathways continue on to the cerebellum. Descending (motor) pathways originate in the cerebral cortex (e.g., the *corticospinal* or *pyramidal* tract), midbrain (e.g., the *rubrospinal* tract), pons (e.g., the *reticulospinal* tract), and cerebellum (e.g., *fastigiospinal* tract). Most fibers in the descending pathways and in the ascending medial lemniscal system cross over the midline (i.e., *decussate*) at the level of the medulla, the latter slightly rostral to the former, but the fibers of the anterolateral system decussate at the level of the spinal cord.

## Metencephalon

The metencephalon is the more rostral secondary brain vesicle of the rhomben-cephalon and is demarcated by the caudal pontine flexure and the rostral isthmus. The metencephalon differentiates into two major neuroanatomic structures: the pons on the ventral side and the cerebellum on the dorsal side. The fourth ventricle is situated between the pons and cerebellum. The roof of this lumen ruptures between 3 and 4 months after conception to form the previously noted foramen of Magendie (medially positioned) and the two foramina of Luschka (laterally positioned) and thereby permits the CSF to flow into the subarachnoid space.

*Pons*  The cell columns arising from the basal and alar plates continue into the pons, and, like the medulla, nuclei for particular cranial nerves derive from these cell columns. At the level of the pons, the GSE column includes the *abducens nucleus* (for cranial nerve VI). The SVE column includes the *facial motor nucleus* (for cranial nerve VII) and the *trigeminal motor nucleus* (for cranial nerve V). The GVE column includes the *superior salivatory nucleus* (for cranial nerve VII). The solitary nucleus, which is present throughout most of the medulla, continues the G/SVA column into the medulla/pons junction. The rostral spinal trigeminal nucleus (for cranial nerves V, VII, IX, and X) in the GSA column of the medulla continues into the pons; at this level of neuraxis, this column also includes the *principal sensory trigeminal nucleus* (for cranial nerve V) as well as the beginning of the *mesencephalic trigeminal nucleus* (for cranial nerve V). The vestibular nucleus (for cranial nerve VIII) of the SSA column in the medulla continues into the pons and also includes the *cochlear nucleus* (for cranial nerve VIII). The trigeminal (V), abducens (VI), facial (VII), and vestibulocochlear (VIII) cranial nerves connect with their respective nuclei at the level of the pons.

The dorsal region of the pons that contains these cranial nerve nuclei is called the pontine *tegmentum,* which forms the floor of the fourth ventricle (between the pons and cerebellum). The pontine tegmentum also contains the reticular and raphe nuclei of the reticular formation, which originate at the level of the medulla. At the level of the pons, the more diffuse reticular nuclei include the relatively medially located *magnocellular* (i.e., large cell) and laterally located *parvocellular* (i.e., small cell) reticular areas, each of which comprises a number of specific nuclei, such as the gigantocellular reticular nucleus, *caudal* and *pontine reticular nuclei, lateral reticular formation,* and *medial* and *lateral parabrachial nuclei.* The bilateral columns of raphe nuclei adjacent to the midline of the pons include the *nucleus raphes magnus, nucleus raphes pontis, superior central nucleus,* and *posterior (dorsal) raphe nucleus* (Mihailoff & Haines, 2002b).

An important group of cells in the reticular formation of the pons, especially from the perspective of school neuropsychologists, is the *locus ceruleus.* This group of cells is the largest source of *noradrenergic* neurons in the central nervous system (Mihailoff & Haines, 2002b). Noradrenergic neurons, which constitute one of the major modulatory systems of the brain, use the neurotransmitter norepinephrine at their synaptic junctions. The locus ceruleus is thought to be associated with attention and therefore is especially relevant to cognitive functions (Kandel, Schwartz, & Jessell, 2000). Saper (2000) described this group of neurons as functioning to maintain vigilance and responsiveness to novel stimuli. Given the far-reaching projections of their axons caudally as well as rostrally, these neurons influence sensory perception and motor tone at the level of the pons, medulla, and spinal cord as well as modulate arousal at the level of the forebrain (Saper, 2000).

The ascending somatosensory pathways of the medial lemniscal and anterolateral systems present in the medulla continue into the pons, and some specific tracts of the anterolateral system (e.g., the *spinoreticular* tract) terminate in the reticular nuclei of the pons. The descending motor pathways of the corticospinal-pyramidal system originating in the cerebral cortex and midbrain course through the pons toward the medulla, and other specific tracts in this system originate in the pons (e.g., the reticulospinal and *vestibulospinal* tracts).

*Cerebellum*   The dorsolateral regions of the pontine alar plates migrate in posterior and medial directions to form structures called the *rhombic lips.* The rhombic lips meet and fuse together to form the transverse cerebellar plate. By about 3 months after conception, the lateral aspects of the transverse cerebellar plate swell into bulges. These bulges later become the cerebellar hemispheres, whereas the more medial aspects of the cerebellar plate become the region known as the *vermis.*

In its mature configuration, the cerebellum is subdivided parallel to its rostral-caudal axis into the medially located *vermis,* the intermediate areas or *paravermis,* and the laterally located hemispheres of the surface (or *cortex*) of the cerebellum. In the horizontal plane, the cerebellum comprises three rostral-caudal lobes: the *anterior,* the *posterior,* and the *flocculonodular,* which are demarcated by the *primary fissure* (between the anterior and posterior lobes) and the *posterolateral fissure* (between the posterior and flocculonodular lobes). These fissures begin to appear between 3 and 5 months after conception. With further development, additional lobules and smaller folds of cortex become separated from each other by other fissures, and the cerebellum attains its mature configuration by about the 7th month of gestation (Arey, 1974). The cerebellum is attached to the dorsal side of the pons by three thick pairs of fibers called the *cerebellar peduncles* (i.e., *superior, middle,* and *inferior*), which comprise axons of neurons traveling between these structures.

The cortex of the lobes and lobules of the cerebellum is composed of three distinct layers of cells. The outermost layer is called the *molecular* layer, the intermediate layer is called the *Perkinje cell* layer, and the innermost layer is called the *granular* layer of cerebellar cortex. There also is a subcortical layer of white matter under the granular layer that contains afferent fibers from the cerebellar cortex and various brain nuclei, such as the inferior olivary nucleus in the medulla and efferent fibers from the four cerebellar nuclei to other regions of the brain. The most lateral of the cerebellar nuclei, the *dentate nucleus,* receives information primarily from the lateral areas of the cerebellar cortex. The more intermediate nuclei, the *emboliform* and *globose nuclei,* receive information primarily from the intermediate areas of the cerebellar cortex; the most medial of the cerebellar nuclei, the *fastigial nucleus,* receives information primarily from the vermis.

MESENCEPHALON

Directly rostral to the pons is an in-folded or narrowed region called the isthmus, which demarcates the caudal region of the mesencephalon. As one of the primary brain vesicles, the mesencephalon (or midbrain) arises early in prenatal development. At this level of neuraxis, the growth and differentiation of the alar and basal plates compresses the ventricular cavity into a narrow canal called the *cerebral aqueduct,* with the alar plates dorsal to this lumen and the basal plates ventral to it. The caudal regions of the midbrain are contiguous with the pons, and the rostral regions border the caudal diencephalon.

The midbrain often is conceptualized as comprising three primary regions that are evident when viewed in horizontal section: the dorsally positioned *tectum* (or roof), the medially positioned *tegmentum,* and the ventrally positioned *basis pedunculi.* The tectum of the midbrain contains two major pairs of structures important for sensorimotor functioning known as the *superior* and *inferior colliculi,* which are components of the visual and auditory systems, respectively. The cerebral aqueduct lies in the ventromedial region of the tectum and is surrounded by a group of cells called the *periaqueductal gray.* These cells are associated with the suppression and modulation of pain (Mihailoff, Haines, & May, 2002). The basis pedunculi comprise two major regions, the more dorsomedially placed cells of the *substantial nigra* and the more ventrolaterally placed *crus cerebri.* Cells of the substantial nigra are involved in the motor system, and the crus cerebri primarily contain descending motor fibers.

At the level of the midbrain tegmentum, the GSE column includes the oculomotor and trochlear nuclei for cranial nerves III and IV, respectively. The *Edinger-Westphal nucleus,* which also is associated with cranial nerve III, is present in the GVE column at this level of neuraxis, and the mesencephalic trigeminal nucleus (for cranial nerve V), which begins in the GVE column of the pons, also continues into the midbrain. There are no cranial nerve nuclei in the SVE, G/SVA, or SSA columns at this level of neuraxis. The oculomotor (III) and trochlear (IV) cranial nerves connect with their respective nuclei at the level of the midbrain. Other structures contained in the tegmentum of the midbrain include the prominent *red* (i.e., *rubro*) nuclei and the decussation of the superior cerebellar peduncles. The red nuclei develop during the 3rd month of gestation and are involved in motor functioning. They receive input from the *ipsilateral* (i.e., same-sided) cerebral cortices and the *contralateral* (i.e., opposite-sided) cerebellar nuclei, and they project to the olivary nuclei in the medulla and the spinal cord. The superior cerebellar peduncles cross over at the level of the midbrain; most of these fibers continue on rostrally to other regions in the midbrain and the thalamus, but some proceed caudally to regions in the pons and medulla.

Also within the midbrain tegmentum are the reticular cells of the reticular formation, which extend from more caudal levels of neuraxis. At the level of the midbrain, these include the *cuneiform* and *subcuneiform nuclei* that are involved with the regulation of consciousness. More medially, the posterior (dorsal) raphe nucleus extends from the pons into the periaqueductal gray of the midbrain. These cells project to regions of the cerebral cortex and are believed to modulate neuronal activity characteristic of sleep and dream cycles (Mihailoff et al., 2002).

The ascending somatosensory pathways of the medial lemniscal and anterolateral systems of the medulla and pons continue into the midbrain. The descending motor pathways of the corticospinal-pyramidal system (originating in the cerebral cortex) pass through the crus cerebri of the midbrain toward the pons and medulla. Still other descending tracts in this system, such as the rubrospinal tract from the red nucleus, originate in the midbrain.

## DIENCEPHALON

The forebrain differentiates into the more caudal diencephalon and the more rostral telencephalon during the 5th week of gestation. The diencephalon is situated between the brainstem regions of the central nervous system and the telencephalon, demarcated caudally by the anterior limits of the midbrain and rostrally by the interventricular foramina (which interconnect the lateral and third ventricles). In its mature configuration, the diencephalon comprises four basic neuroanatomic regions: (1) the thalamus, (2) the hypothalamus, (3) the epithalamus, and (4) the subthalamus. The basal and floor plates of brainstem regions do not proceed rostrally into the diencephalon; thus, the structures comprised by the diencephalon develop from the roof and alar plates. The most caudal portion of the roof plate develops into the epithalamus. The alar plates become subdivided into dorsal and ventral regions by a groove called the *hypothalamic sulcus.* The dorsal region becomes the thalamus, which is principally involved in sensory and coordinating functions, and the ventral region becomes the hypothalamus, which is principally involved in motor functions. Thus, despite the absence of preeminent basal and floor plates at this level of neuraxis, the dorsal sensory and ventral motor specializations present at brainstem levels of neuraxis persist into the diencephalon.

*Thalamus*   The largest structure of the diencephalon is the thalamus. This structure is sometimes referred to as the *dorsal thalamus* to differentiate it from the subthalamus, also known as the *ventral thalamus* (see Mihailoff & Haines, 2002a). The dorsal thalamus comprises two nearly symmetrical, egg-shaped structures on each side of the third ventricle. There are three major groups of nuclei comprised by the dorsal thalamus: (1) *relay* nuclei, from which fibers are projected to regions of the cerebral cortex that are modality-specific (e.g., visual or auditory or somatosensory); (2) *association* nuclei, from which fibers are projected to the cerebral cortex that are specialized for multimodal integrative functions; and (3) *diffuse projecting* or *nonspecific* nuclei, from which fibers are projected to the cerebral cortex broadly rather than to particular cortical regions. Thus, nearly all input to the cerebral hemispheres is first processed by the thalamus, leading many to refer to this structure as a sensory "relay station" (Delcomyn, 1998, p. 74) or as a "gateway" (Mihailoff & Haines, 2002a, p. 223) to the cerebral cortex. These projections, which form a fan-like structure called the *internal capsule,* however, are also reciprocal, and nearly all regions of the cerebral cortex project back to the thalamus. Thus, fibers do not simply pass through the thalamus on their way to the cerebral cortex; rather, a substantial amount of information processing occurs at this level of neuraxis.

The relay nuclei of the thalamus include the *medial* and *lateral geniculate* nuclei, which are involved in the auditory and visual functional systems, respectively; the *ventral posterolateral* (VPL) and *posteromedial* (VPM) nuclei; the *ventral anterior* (VA) and *lateral* (VL) nuclei; and the *anterior (A)* nucleus. Association nuclei include the *dorsomedial* (DM) nucleus, the *lateral dorsal* (LD) and *posterior* (LP) nuclei, and cells in the *pulvinar.* Diffuse projecting nuclei include the *centromedian* (CM) and *parafascicular* (PF) nuclei, the *paratenial nucleus,* and some cells within the VA nucleus. In contrast to this functional grouping, thalamic nuclei also are sometimes grouped by their relative locations as comprising anterior (i.e., A), medial (i.e., DM), lateral (i.e., LD, LP, pulvinar, VA, VL, VPL, and VPM), intralaminar (i.e., CM and PF), and midline (i.e., paratenial) nuclei (Mihailoff & Haines, 2002a). One additional group of thalamic nuclei are the *thalamic reticular nuclei.* Rather than interconnecting the thalamus and cerebral cortex, these nuclei project back to other thalamic nuclei and are thought to modulate the effect of those other nuclei on afferent cortical input.

*Hypothalamus*   Ventral and anterior to the thalamus is the hypothalamus. The most ventral aspect of the hypothalamus is called the *infidibulum,* and it is to this structure that the *pituitary gland* is attached. This region of the hypothalamus undergoes structural differentiation during the 3rd through the 6th weeks of gestation (Reinis & Goldman, 1980). As noted, whereas the thalamus is principally sensory in function, the hypothalamus is principally motoric in function. Like the thalamus, however, the hypothalamus comprises a number of nuclei. These nuclei are located in three major areas: the *lateral* area, the *medial* area, and the *periventricular* area. The medial area comprises several clusters of nuclei in each of three regions that include the anteriorly placed *chiasmatic* region, which overlies the optic chiasm (i.e., the location where optic fibers from cranial nerve II cross; e.g., *preoptic, supraoptic, paraventricular, anterior,* and *suprachiasmatic nuclei*); the intermediately placed *tuberal* region, which overlies the stalk of the pituitary gland (e.g., *dorsomedial, ventromedial,* and *arcuate nuclei*); and the posteriorly placed *mammillary* region (e.g., *posterior nucleus* and *mammillary nuclei*). The third area, the periventricular region of the hypothalamus, includes those nuclei that surround the third ventricle. Each of these specific nuclei has been studied, and most of their connections and functions are well understood (see Iversen, Iversen, & Saper, 2000; Mihailoff & Haines, 2002a). In general, the hypothalamus serves to coordinate autonomic, endocrine, and behavioral functioning and to maintain homeostasis. More specifically, particular hypothalamic nuclei are involved in regulating hormone release and inhibition, some with cardiovascular function and circadian rhythms, and others with pupillary dilation, body temperature, growth, maturation, food intake, and reproduction.

*Epithalamus and Subthalamus*   The epithalamus is positioned at the most dorsal region of the thalamus, whereas the subthalamus is positioned at its most ventral region. The epithalamus comprises the *pineal gland,* the *habenular nuclei,* and the *stria medullaris thalami.* The pineal gland plays a role in circadian rhythms. The functional significance of the habenular nuclei and the stria medullaris thalami may relate to interconnections between the brainstem and telencephalic structures or a possible "limbic system-midbrain circuit" (Brodal, 1981, p. 673). The subthalamus comprises the *subthalamic nuclei,* which are rostral to the substantia nigra of the midbrain; the *prerubral area* (or *field H of Forel*), which is rostral to the red nucleus of the midbrain; and the *zona incerta.* These structures interconnect with basal ganglia structures (discussed subsequently) and motor areas of the cerebral cortex and seem to be associated with motor planning and execution.

TELENCEPHALON

The telencephalon is the most anterior of the secondary brain vesicles, becomes a highly specialized region in the human central nervous system, and is of special interest to school neuropsychologists because of its cognitive information-processing functions. The telencephalon comprises the cerebral hemispheres, which appear during the 6th week of gestation (Arey, 1974). The lumina of the telencephalon are the lateral ventricles, one of which is in each cerebral hemisphere.

Three major groups of gray matter structures comprised by the telencephalon are the cerebral cortex, the basal ganglia, and the forebrain limbic structures. There also is an extensive system of subcortical white matter that includes interhemispheric (i.e., *commissural*) fibers, which interconnect corresponding regions of opposite hemispheres; intrahemispheric (i.e., *association*) fibers, which interconnect regions within a given hemisphere; and *projection* fibers, which subserve rostral-caudal connections.

*Cerebral Cortex*    The cerebral cortex is a six-layered structure that covers the surfaces of the two cerebral hemispheres (collectively known as the *cerebrum*). In early stages of prenatal development, the cortex appears smooth (i.e., *lissencephalic*), but soon, *gyri*, which are convolutions separated by fissures of various depths (called *sulci*), develop, and by birth, full-term human neonates show a gyral pattern similar to that of adults. This pattern develops in an orderly and bilaterally symmetrical progression, with a marked increase in the number of gyri appearing between 26 and 28 weeks of gestation (Dooling, Chi, & Gilles, 1983). The gyri and sulci subdivide the cortex into four major lobes. In lateral saggital view, the most anterior lobe is the *frontal* lobe and the most posterior is the *occipital* lobe. In the intermediate region are the dorsal *parietal* lobe and the ventral *temporal* lobe. Haines and Mihailoff (2002b) classify two other lobes, but others (e.g., Amaral, 2000, p. 325) simply refer to these areas as "additional regions of the cerebral cortex." One is the *insular* area, which is a region of cortex deep inside the lateral fissure. The insular cortex cannot be seen in lateral view because it is obscured by the overlying regions of the temporal, parietal, and frontal lobes, called the *operculum*, but is clearly seen in coronal section. The other region is the *cingulate gyrus*, which is a band of cortex that surrounds the dorsal side of the *corpus callosum* (a group of interhemispheric fibers connecting the two cerebral hemispheres) on the medial surface of each hemisphere.

The first sulcus to develop is the *longitudinal fissure* at 10 weeks of gestation. The longitudinal fissure divides the cerebrum into the left and right hemispheres. About 4 weeks later, the *lateral sulcus* (sometimes called the *Sylvian fissure*) appears; it defines the boundary between the frontal/parietal lobes and the anterior temporal lobe on the lateral surface of the hemispheres. The *parietooccipital sulcus* appears at around 16 weeks of gestation; this sulcus defines the boundary between the parietal lobe and the occipital lobe on the medial surface of the cerebral hemispheres. The *central sulcus* (or *Rolandic fissure*) appears at around 20 weeks of gestation and defines the boundary between the frontal lobe and the parietal lobe on the lateral surface of the cerebral hemispheres.

For each of the lobes, cortical cells within gyri form particular zones. *Primary projection zones* to the temporal, parietal, and occipital lobes are specialized for auditory, somatosensory, and visual stimuli, respectively. For example, the *transverse temporal gyrus* (or *Heschl's gyrus*), which lies at the upper edge of the temporal lobe and extends into the lateral fissure, is the location of the primary auditory cortex. The laterally positioned *postcentral gyrus* follows directly posterior along the central sulcus and extends medially as the *posterior paracentral gyrus*; together, these regions form the primary somatosensory cortex. The parts of the *cuneus* and the *lingual gyrus* that border the *calcarine sulcus* of the occipital lobe, which extends medially toward the caudal extreme of this lobe (i.e., *the occipital pole*), form the primary visual cortex. The cortex in the primary zones of these three posterior lobes is distinguished by its particularly numerous neurons of cortical layers II and IV. This kind of cortex (which is known as the granular cortex of the temporal, parietal, and occipital lobes) characterizes regions that receive primary afferent sensory information.

Information from the projection zones in the temporal, parietal, and occipital lobes then extends via association fibers to *secondary* or *association zones* that surround these primary cortical regions. Cytoarchitectonically, these regions are distinguished by the especially numerous neurons in cortical layers II and III. Higher levels of perceptual processing occur in these secondary zones, and other association fibers then transmit information on to *tertiary* or *multimodal integrative zones* such as the angular gyrus, which is located in the overlapping region of the parietal, occipital, and temporal lobes. This tertiary region is characterized by the cellular differentiation of the middle and upper sublayers of cortical layers II and III.

The lateral surface of the frontal lobe comprises five major gyri: the *precentral* gyrus; the *superior, middle,* and *inferior frontal* gyri; and the *orbital* gyrus. All of these gyri are visible by 28 weeks of gestation (Miller, 1999). The precentral gyrus follows directly anterior along the central sulcus and extends medially as the *anterior paracentral gyrus.* Together, these regions form the primary motor cortex, which, in contrast to primary sensory regions, is characterized by especially well-developed cortical layers III and V (or *agranular* cortex). There also is a more anterior premotor area, which extends into the dorsal regions of the superior and middle frontal gyri. This region forms a secondary or association zone for the frontal lobe that is characterized by a more marked development of the deep sublayers of cortical layer III than in the primary motor cortex.

The inferior frontal gyrus and the ventral regions of the superior and middle frontal gyri together constitute the prefrontal tertiary region, which forms a highly developed and differentiated region of the brain in humans. This region has been referred to as the "granular frontal cortex" (Luria, 1973) because of the dearth of the large neurons found in layer V of the motor and premotor cortices. This region also is distinguished by its especially highly differentiated system of bilateral interconnections with subcortical regions in the brain. The middle frontal gyrus is anterior to the precentral gyrus, and the superior frontal gyrus, which lies anterior and dorsal to the middle frontal gyrus, extends to the medial surface of the cerebral hemispheres. The more ventrally positioned inferior frontal gyrus includes three smaller areas called *pars triangularis, pars opercularis,* and *pars orbitalis.* The region of pars triangularis and pars orbitalis in the left cerebral hemisphere (for most people) is the location of the well-known *Broca's area,* which is functionally specialized for the expression of language. The orbital gyrus lies at the most ventral region of the lateral surface of the frontal lobe and extends medially as the *gyrus rectus.* This is the location of the *olfactory bulb* and *tract,* where input from the olfactory cranial nerve (I) is processed.

The development of the primary, secondary, and tertiary cortical zones follows a distinct course. Relying on morphological evidence, Luria (1980) noted that although the primary cortical zones appear mature by birth in human neonates, the maturation of secondary and tertiary zones occurs during the first few postnatal months and years, respectively. Moreover, it is likely that the structural-functional interrelationships among these zones covary with age. For example, during neonatal and early infancy periods of development, relatively direct and associative sensory processes are dominant. In contrast, by early childhood, more complex integration related to language and higher-order cognitive processes has become pronounced. From this perspective, it is reasonable to speculate that early trauma to relatively basic sensory processes can produce deleterious effects on higher-order cognitive processes due to a disturbance in the foundation for those processes. Similar trauma occurring at later developmental stages might be expected to have a much more limited effect, however, owing to the fact that the structural-functional systems providing the substrate for higher-order cognitive functions already have been developed (see Hynd & Willis, 1988). The often cited "Kennard principle," which essentially states the opposite, that is, that early brain damage is less devastating than later brain damage perhaps owing to plasticity, is unfortunately widely believed but empirically unfounded (Hart & Faust, 1988).

*Basal Ganglia*   The basal ganglia are a group of nuclear masses deep in the cerebral hemispheres that are interconnected with the thalamus and cerebral cortex. In its contemporary use, the term *ganglia* typically refers to groups of neurons in the peripheral nervous system, whereas the term *nuclei* typically refers to groups of neurons in the central nervous system. Thus, some sources (e.g., Ma, 2002, p. 406) refer to these structures as "basal nuclei," although most retain the now outdated but more traditional designation "ganglia" (e.g., Delcomyn, 1998, pp. 76–77).

These structures are grouped in a variety of ways, and this can sometimes lead to confusion. For example, the basal ganglia typically are considered to comprise five major groups of nuclei: the *globus pallidus, caudate nucleus,* and *putamen* of the telencephalon; the subthalamic nuclei of the ventral thalamus; and the substantia nigra of the midbrain (however, cf. Ma, 2002, pp. 245–246). The globus pallidus and the putamen together often are referred to as the *lentiform* nucleus (given its lens-shaped appearance); the globus pallidus by itself as the *paleostriatum;* the putamen and caudate nucleus together as the *neostriatum* (or *striatum*); and the globus pallidus (i.e., paleostriatum) and the putamen and caudate nucleus (i.e., neostriatum) together as the *corpus striatum* (Delcomyn, 1998).

The lentiform nucleus (i.e., putamen and globus pallidus) is separated from the caudate nucleus in intermediate and posterior regions of the telencephalon by the fibers of the internal capsule (which interconnects thalamic and cortical structures), but these nuclei are adjacent to each other at anterior regions of the telencephalon. The caudate nucleus forms a curved structure around the lateral ventricle when viewed in midsaggital section. It is subdivided into three major regions: the head at its anterior bulging, the body, and the tail at its posteroventral narrowing. The more medial region of the lentiform nucleus is the globus pallidus, which itself is subdivided into a more medial and a more lateral part. The more lateral region of the lentiform nucleus is the putamen.

Although considered to have a major motor influence on behavior, the basal ganglia do not have any direct connections with the spinal cord, but instead mediate motor behavior via influence on the prefrontal and premotor cortices. In early prenatal development, the basal ganglia are separated from the diencephalon by a deep fissure, but this fissure disappears in the 3rd month of gestation owing to an enlargement of midbrain and thalamic nuclei (Arey, 1974). The caudate nucleus and the putamen (i.e., the neostriatum) have the same embryological origins and have similar connections (Ma, 2002).

Nevertheless, there seems to be some specialization of function of these structures into motor and nonmotor or cognitive functions. For example, motor functions may be mediated primarily by the putamen, the output of which may be directed to the premotor cortex and supplementary motor area, whereas cognitive functions may be mediated primarily by the caudate nucleus, the output of which may be directed to the prefrontal cortex (see Brodal, 1981; Kandel & Schwartz, 1985). Of particular interest to school neuropsychologists, the corpus striatum has been implicated in Attention-Deficit/Hyperactivity Disorder, but more neuroimaging research is needed before the specificity and clinical importance of potential neuroanatomic differences can be evaluated (see Willis & Weiler, 2005).

*Limbic Structures*   Forebrain structures of the limbic system include the cingulate gyrus, the *hippocampal formation,* the *amygdaloid complex,* and the *septal area.* The limbic system also contains thalamic, hypothalamic, and midbrain nuclei. This system has extensive interconnections with structures at many different levels of neuraxis and functionally is involved in emotion and a number of higher-order cognitive processes such as memory and learning.

As already noted, the cingulate gyrus forms a band of cortex surrounding the dorsal side of the corpus callosum on the medial surface of each hemisphere. The cingulate gyrus is often considered to be a major feature of the *circuit of Papez,* a limbic pathway involved in the modulation of emotion, but it also receives significant input from the prefrontal cortices. The hippocampal formation lies deep within the subcortical region of the temporal lobe and includes the dorsally located *dentate nucleus,* the intermediate *hippocampus,* and the ventrally located *subiculum.* The hippocampus projects fibers through a tract called the *fornix,* which bends in a ventral-anterior location dorsal to the corpus callosum and proceeds toward the septal area. Functions of the hippocampal formation are believed to be related to consolidating immediate and short-term memory into long-term memory stores. The subiculum of the hippocampal formation, for example, is among the first to be affected by the neuronal changes associated with Alzheimer's disease, a primary symptom of which is memory loss (Chronister & Hardy, 2002). The amygdaloid complex, also located in the subcortical regions of the temporal lobe, lies anterior to the hippocampal formation. It includes several nuclei, some of which are related to the olfactory bulb and the sense of smell, and others that interconnect with cortical structures. The septal region is dorsal and anterior to the amygdaloid complex and includes a number of small nuclei that receive input from the hippocampal formation and amygdaloid complex and project to hippocampal, thalamic, and hypothalamic nuclei. Specific functions of the septal area are not well established, but behavioral overreaction to environmental events has been observed following lesions of septal nuclei (Brodal, 1981).

## CONCLUSION

A fundamental understanding of developmental neuroanatomy is essential for professionals in the field of school neuropsychology. Many neurodevelopmental disorders can be understood fully only in the context of deviations from normal developmental sequences. Just as important, however, our understanding of the basic sensory, motor, perceptual, and higher-order cognitive and social-emotional processes that characterize all human functioning requires a foundation in the biological underpinnings of those processes, and, of course, this requires an appreciation of neurologic structure.

Approximately 20 years ago, Kandel (1985, p. 832) stated, "The boundary between behavior and biology is arbitrary and changing. . . . As our knowledge expands, the biological and behavioral disciplines will merge, and it is at these points of merger that our understanding of mentation will rest on particularly secure ground." It is clear that we have now progressed well beyond the time when neuropsychological and behavioral approaches to school psychology can be contrasted against one another. Effective research and clinical practice require that school psychologists integrate these approaches in ways that improve understanding of psychoeducational processes and that can effect change in individuals and systems.

In this chapter, foundations of developmental neuroanatomy have been presented to facilitate these goals in the field of school neuropsychology. This requires a consideration of the role of nervous system cells, the embryonic development of the neural tube, the early development of the brain into primary brain vesicles, and a perspective on mature neuroanatomical structures as derivatives of secondary brain vesicles. Of course, this perspective forms but one aspect of a comprehensive understanding of children. Behavior is modulated by neurological characteristics, but also by a variety of other intraindividual characteristics as well. Moreover, functional analyses have taught us that behavior is a function of (1) antecedent stimuli that occur in specific environments, (2) the consequences of that behavior, and (3) the way those consequences are linked to the behavior. Importantly, this entire antecedent stimulus–intraindividual variables–behavior–contingency–consequence chain of events occurs in an environmental context of families, schools, communities, and cultures. All are of equal importance to the field of school neuropsychology, which strives for a comprehensive understanding of individuals in contexts.

## REFERENCES

Amaral, D. G. (2000). The anatomical organization of the central nervous system. In E. R. Kandel, J. H. Schwartz, & T. M. Jessell (Eds.), *Principles of neural science* (4th ed., pp. 317–336). New York: McGraw-Hill.

Arey, L. B. (1974). Developmental anatomy: A textbook and laboratory manual of embryology (7th ed., rev.). Philadelphia: Saunders.

Brodal, A. (1981). *Neurological anatomy in relation to clinical medicine* (3rd ed.). New York: Oxford University.

Carpenter, M. B., & Sutin, J. (1983). *Human neuroanatomy* (8th ed.). Baltimore: Williams & Wilkins.

Chronister, R. B., & Hardy, S. G. P. (2002). The limbic system. In D. E. Haines (Ed.), *Fundamental neuroscience* (2nd ed., pp. 493–504). New York: Churchill Livingstone.

Corbett, J. J., Haines, D. E., & Ard, M. D. (2002). The ventricles, choriod plexus, and cerebrospinal fluid. In D. E. Haines (Ed.), *Fundamental neuroscience* (2nd ed., pp. 93–106). New York: Churchill Livingstone.

Delcomyn, F. (1998). *Foundations of neurobiology.* New York: Freeman.

Dooling, E. C., Chi, J. G., & Gilles, F. H. (1983). Telencephalic development: Changing gyral patterns. In F. H. Gilles, A. Leviton, & E. C. Dooling (Eds.), *The developing human brain: Growth and epidemiologic neuropathology* (pp. 94–104). Boston: John Wright.

Haines, D. E. (2002). The meninges. In D. E. Haines (Ed.), *Fundamental neuroscience* (2nd ed., pp. 107–120). New York: Churchill Livingstone.

Haines, D. E., & Mihailoff, G. A. (2002a). The medulla oblongata. In D. E. Haines (Ed.), *Fundamental neuroscience* (2nd ed., pp. 159–171). New York: Churchill Livingstone.

Haines, D. E., & Mihailoff, G. A. (2002b). The telencephalon. In D. E. Haines (Ed.), *Fundamental neuroscience* (2nd ed., pp. 235–251). New York: Churchill Livingstone.

Hart, K., & Faust, D. (1988). Prediction of the effects of mild head injury: A message about the Kennard principle. *Journal of Clinical Psychology, 44,* 780–782.

Hynd, G. W., & Willis, W. G. (1988). *Pediatric neuropsychology.* Orlando, FL: Grune & Stratton.

Iversen, S., Iversen, L., & Saper, C. B. (2000). The autonomic nervous system and the hypothalamus. In E. R. Kandel, J. H. Schwartz, & T. M. Jessell (Eds.), *Principles of neural science* (4th ed., pp. 960–981). New York: McGraw-Hill.

Jessell, T. M. (1995). Development of the nervous system. In E. R. Kandel, J. H. Schwartz, & T. M. Jessell (Eds.), *Essentials of neural science and behavior* (pp. 89–110). Norealk, CT: Appleton & Lange.

Kandel, E. R. (1985). Cellular mechanisms of learning and the biological basis of individuality. In E. R. Kandel & J. H. Schwartz (Eds.), *Principles of neural science* (2nd ed., pp. 816–833). New York: McGraw-Hill.

Kandel, E. R. (2000). Nerve cells and behavior. In E. R. Kandel, J. H. Schwartz, & T. M. Jessell (Eds.), *Principles of neural science* (4th ed., pp. 19–35). New York: McGraw-Hill.

Kandel, E. R., & Schwartz, J. H. (Eds.). (1985). *Principles of neural science* (2nd ed.). New York: Elsevier.

Kandel, E. R., Schwartz, J. H., & Jessell, T. M. (Eds.). (2000). *Principles of neural science* (4th ed.). New York: McGraw-Hill.

Luria, A. R. (1973). *The working brain: An introduction to neuropsychology.* New York: Basic Books.

Luria, A. R. (1980). *Higher cortical function in man.* New York: Basic Books.

Ma, T. P. (2002). The basal nuclei. In D. E. Haines (Ed.), *Fundamental neuroscience* (2nd ed., pp. 405–422). New York: Churchill Livingstone.

Mihailoff, G. A., & Haines, D. E. (2002a). The diencephalon. In D. E. Haines (Ed.), *Fundamental neuroscience* (2nd ed., pp. 219–234). New York: Churchill Livingstone.

Mihailoff, G. A., & Haines, D. E. (2002b). The pons and cerebellum. In D. E. Haines (Ed.), *Fundamental neuroscience* (2nd ed., pp. 173–185). New York: Churchill Livingstone.

Mihailoff, G. A., Haines, D. E., & May, P. J. (2002). The midbrain. In D. E. Haines (Ed.), *Fundamental neuroscience* (2nd ed., pp. 187–198). New York: Churchill Livingstone.

Miller, C. A. (1999). Neuroanatomy of the frontal lobes. In B. L. Miller & J. L. Cummings (Eds.), *The human frontal lobes: Functions and disorders* (pp. 71–82). New York: Guilford Press.

Reinis, S., & Goldman, J. M. (1980). *The development of the brain: Biological and functional perspectives.* Springfield, IL: Charles C. Thomas.

Saper, C. B. (2000). Brain stem modulation of sensation, movement, and consciousness. In E. R. Kandel, J. H. Schwartz, & T. M. Jessell (Eds.), *Principles of neural science* (4th ed., pp. 889–909). New York: McGraw-Hill.

Saxen, L. (1980). Neural induction: Past, present, and future. In R. K. Hunt (Ed.), *Current topics in developmental biology: Vol. 15. Neural development* [Part 1: Emergence of specificity in neural histogenesis] (pp. 409–418). Orlando, FL: Academic Press.

Scott, J. M., Weir, D. G., Molly, A., McPartlin, J., Daly, L., & Kirke, P. (1994). Folic acid metabolism and mechanisms of neural tube defects. *Ciba Foundation Symposium, 181,* 180–191.

Willis, W. G., & Weiler, M. D. (2005). Neural substrates of childhood Attention-Deficit/Hyperactivity Disorder: Electroencephalographic and magnetic resonance imaging evidence. *Developmental Neuropsychology, 27,* 135–182.

# CHAPTER 4

# Abnormalities of
# Neurological Development

CYNTHIA A. RICCIO and KELLY PIZZITOLA-JARRATT

THE TRAJECTORY OF neurological development begins at conception and is believed to continue through adolescence (Kolb & Fantie, 1997; White, Andreasen, Nopoulos, & Magnotta, 2003). There is an ontogenetic (from origin to development) process from cellular development to the formation of structures and eventual functional expression. Functional development follows the cephalocaudal principle and occurs from anterior to posterior in an orderly fashion. At the same time, development follows the proximodistal principle, such that development occurs from medial to lateral and the cortex matures from inner to outer surfaces. Because the development of the brain is an orderly process, each point in the developmental process is vulnerable to interference (Andersen, 2003). Further, abnormal development at one point in time, even if only affecting one area, leads to associated abnormalities at all levels and probably impacts multiple functional systems. Although specific types of abnormalities occurring during neurological development rarely happen, when taken together, low-incidence occurrences account for the underlying problems experienced by large numbers of individuals (Paciorkowski, Lerer, & Brunquell, 2002). For more commonly occurring developmental disorders (e.g., learning disability, Attention-Deficit/Hyperactivity Disorder, Autism), there is a *presumption* that the underlying cause of the disorder is due to abnormal development of the neural system. For this reason, it is important to be aware of the multiple factors that can interfere with normal brain development. Abnormalities in brain development that may contribute to learning and behavioral problems are listed in Table 4.1.

Although the foundation of the neural system predominantly occurs prior to birth, it is important to keep in mind that development of the central nervous system begins at conception (Kolb & Fantie, 1997). Genetic predisposition as well as external factors (e.g., virus, infection) can affect neural development at any time in the developmental process. These effects on neuroanatomy may occur in terms

**Table 4.1**

Abnormalities in Brain Development

| Abnormality | Description | Possible Causes | Other Associated Features |
|---|---|---|---|
| Agenesis of corpus callosum | Complete or partial absence of the corpus callosum. | Genetically transmitted in some cases; metabolic disorders; other teratogens. | Anterior commissure may become hyperatrophied to compensate, mental retardation, seizure disorder, language disorders. |
| Agyria (lissencephaly) | Brain development does not proceed normally and remains smooth; decreased white matter. | Genetically transmitted in some cases; deletions of chromosome 17, possibly due to arrest in cell proliferation and neuronal migration in first trimester. | Associated with microencephaly, severe or profound mental retardation, seizure disorder, hypotonia, death. |
| Anencephaly | Failure of neural tube to close at rostral end; absence of differentiated cerebral hemispheres, diencephalon, and midbrain. | Maternal diabetes, radiation, neurotoxins, excess vitamin A. | Possibly no development of spinal cord, distorted facial features. |
| Angelman syndrome | Rare congenital genetic disorder involving chromosome 15. | Loss of maternally imprinted contributions in the 15q11-q13 region by genetic mechanisms. | Developmental delays, mental retardation, severe speech impairment or absence of speech, gait ataxia or tremulousness of the limbs, mild cortical atrophy or dysmyelination, microcephaly, seizure disorders, episodic laughter, hand flapping, short attention span, excitability, hypopigmentation of skin and eyes, sucking and swallowing disorders, hyperactive tendon reflexes. |
| Cerebral asymmetry | Hemispheres are of significantly unequal size. | Variable. | Reading disorders. |

| | | | |
|---|---|---|---|
| | Viral infection caused by a communicable DNA virus found in the herpes family. | Virus transmitted congenitally or postnatally. | Microcephaly, small body size, petechiae, hepatomegaly, splenomegaly, jaundice, low blood count, abnormal muscle tone, progressive hearing loss, blindness, mental retardation, seizures, cerebral palsy, calcium deposits in the brain, developmental and learning delays; some may be asymptomatic. |
| Double cortex syndrome | Characterized by subcortical bands of heterotopic gray matter beneath the cortex bilaterally; may be anterior-biased, posterior-biased, global, or a combination. | Genetically transmitted, X-linked. | Epilepsy, mental retardation, and other seizure disorders. |
| Down syndrome (trisomy 21) | Genetic disorder involving chromosome 21. | Genetically transmitted, autosomal disorder. | Mental retardation, dysmorphic facial features, brachycephaly, Brushfield spots, short/broad neck, broad/stubby hands and feet, seizure disorders, other medical difficulties, dementia, Alzheimer's disease, death. |
| Dysplasia (heterotopia) | Development of abnormal cell clusters when migration is interrupted or stops prematurely; the clusters are in the wrong location for their genetically coded function. | Presence of teratogens; mechanisms that interfere or disrupt process are usually unknown. | Developmental disorders, learning disabilities, Attention-Deficit/ Hyperactivity Disorder; some may be asymptomatic. |

*(continued)*

**Table 4.1** (Continued)

| Abnormality | Description | Possible Causes | Other Associated Features |
|---|---|---|---|
| Encephalocele | Lesions that contain cerebral tissue; usually found in occipital region, but may occur in frontal region; affected cerebral hemisphere is somewhat smaller with some distortion in shape; subset of myelomeningeoceles associated with spina bifida. | Associated with disruption in formation and closure of neural tube. | May affect other brain structures, cranial nerves, and circulatory system of brain; may have other congenital abnormalities (e.g., agenesis of corpus callosum). |
| Fetal Alcohol Syndrome | Syndrome caused by maternal consumption of alcohol or ethanol; associated with malformations of neural tube development, including holoprosencephaly, myelomeningocele, and spina bifida. | Maternal consumption of alcohol or ethanol. | Dysmorphic facial features, microcephaly, cortical thinning, prenatal and/or postnatal growth deficiency, learning disorders, Attention-Deficit/Hyperactivity Disorder, memory loss, perceptual problems, delayed adaptive behavior, mild mental retardation. |
| Holoprosencephaly | Cortex develops as one undifferentiated hemisphere. | Maternal diabetes, retinoic acid exposure, cytomegalovirus, rubella, other teratogens. | Possible absence of olfactory nerve, some vesicles may fail to develop, seizure disorder, mental retardation, abnormalities in facial features. |
| Hydranencephaly | Replacement of cerebral hemispheres with cysts containing cerebral spinal fluid; may be some development of subcortical structures or of temporal and occipital lobes. | Massive necrosis possibly due to blockage in the vascular system, umbilical cord strangulation, blunt trauma to mother's abdomen during pregnancy. | Abnormal acceleration of head growth after birth. |

| | | | |
|---|---|---|---|
| Macrogyria (pachygyria) | Relatively smooth brain; gyri are usually wide and few in number. | Ischemia, viral infection. | Mental retardation, seizure disorders; tuberous sclerosis. |
| Megalencephaly | Abnormally large brain, excess number of neurons and glia cells, larger cell size, increased frontal and parietal white matter, large corpus callosum. | Genetically transmitted; abnormal production of cells, abnormal pruning, or combination of two. | Large head, decreased cognitive ability, seizure disorder, possible high nonverbal abilities. |
| Microencephaly | Subnormal brain size, small frontal and occipital lobes, small cerebellum, reduced white matter, normal-size basal ganglia. | Genetically transmitted, due to deletions or other transformations, malnutrition, metabolic disorders, inflammatory disease, radiation during first trimester, other teratogens. | Small head, thickened scalp, absent forehead, disproportionate facial features, possible decreased cognitive ability and learning disabilities. |
| Microgyria (micropolygyria, polymicrogyria) | Gyri are numerous, smaller, and poorly developed; no new gyri develop after 26 weeks, but existing gyri deepen; smooth appearance. | Carbon monoxide poisoning, intrauterine infections, maternal asphyxia, other trauma; due to focal necrosis during neuronal migration; associated with genetic disorders such as Zellweger syndrome and neonatal adrenal leukodystrophy; autosomal recessive genetic transmission. | Developmental delays, hypertonia; associated with other abnormalities such as agenesis of corpus callosum and vascular abnormalities; focal locations of micropolygyria may be associated with specific disorders. |
| Pediatric Human Immuno-deficiency Virus | Viral infection that attacks the immune system, often infecting the macrophages and microglia of the brain by releasing toxic substances; damaging white matter, causing demyelination of nerve tracks; altering blood-brain barrier. | Viral infection transmitted congenitally or postnatally. | Many infections, central nervous system difficulties, wasting syndromes, malignant disease, encephalopathy; decline in cognition, expressive motor and language functioning, and adaptive functioning; death. |

*(continued)*

**Table 4.1** (Continued)

| Abnormality | Description | Possible Causes | Other Associated Features |
|---|---|---|---|
| Porencephaly | Symmetrical cavities or cysts where white matter and cortex should have developed; usually occur in insular region and are bilateral. | Associated with disruption of neuronal migration and necrosis, possibly due to fetal stroke or ischemia. | Possible decreased thalamic size; polymicrogyria may be evident; gyral pattern may be atypical; mental retardation, paralysis, speech disorders, epilepsy; some are asymptomatic. |
| Schizencephaly | Cleft in cortex (usually in ventricle and extend to pia); present in one or both hemispheres. | Associated with disruption in neural tube closure. | Seizure disorder. |
| Spina bifida | Failure of neural tube to close at caudal end; malformation of spinal cord, vertebral column, and individual vertebrae. | Maternal fevers, intrauterine viral infections, hormonal effects, vitamin deficiencies, excess of vitamin A, maternal diabetes, maternal alcohol use, other teratogens. | Visible lesion on back, lipomas, decreased sensitivity to pain, paralysis, weakness of lower extremities, incontinence, hydrocephalus, meningitis, pneumonia. |

of overall brain mass or hemispheric differences, as well as at a cortical or subcortical level. The effects also may occur at the cell level, specifically related to proliferation, migration, and cell death (necrosis). These effects may result in changes to cortical organization that lead to variations in function (Janszky et al., 2003). Differential effects also may impact neurochemistry and metabolism. The extent to which cortical development is altered correlates significantly with clinical disability (Paciorkowski et al., 2002).

The impact of any interference or complication is determined in part by the stage in the developmental process in which the interference or complication occurs. For example, Janszky et al. (2003) found differences in activation for malformations associated with earlier interference as compared to later interference. It was initially believed that better recovery and prognosis was associated with brain injury the earlier the age at the time of the injury (Kennard, 1940); this is called the Kennard principle. Later research suggested that although there is sparing of function with early damage (less focal deficit), there is an overall effect of the injury on total functioning (diffuse deficits). Presently, it is believed that, in general, the earlier in the development the interference occurs, the more the neural developmental sequence and the trajectory can be disturbed; thus, complications that occur earlier (e.g., in the first trimester through birth) are likely to have more profound and more diffuse effects than complications that occur later in life (e.g., adulthood). Further, interventions and rehabilitation can affect brain function; plasticity is no longer believed to be limited to the expansion of intercortical connections (Rosenzweig, 2003).

## GROSS BRAIN SIZE

There is expected variation in the bulk or total mass of the brain; however, the typical brain-to-body proportion is approximately 1:30 (Hynd, Morgan, & Vaughn, 1997). As with any distribution, there are few abnormalities associated with gross brain mass within 1 to 2 standard deviations. As the difference from the typical proportion increases in either direction, the likelihood of relations between functional level and brain size increases (Hynd et al., 1997).

### MICROENCEPHALY

One of the most obvious differences across individuals is the gross weight of the brain and the circumference of the head. In microencephaly, there is an interruption in brain growth such that subnormal brain size is the dominant feature. Microencephaly is associated with a small head (microcephaly) as defined by a head circumference 2 to 3 standard deviations below the mean for the child's age and sex. Other features often associated with microencephaly include a thickened scalp, an absent forehead, and disproportionate facial features such as hypertellerism (i.e., disproportionate distance between eyes; Dobyns, 1992).

Neuroimaging of microencephalic individuals has revealed small frontal and occipital lobes, as well as a small cerebellum. Further examination indicates that the basal ganglia tend to be normal in size. This suggests that interference with neuronal development leading to microencephaly most likely occurs at about the 5th to 6th month of gestation. Overall, white matter may be reduced and the cortex may have a thick appearance (Dobyns, 1992).

There is evidence that microencephaly can be transmitted genetically as an autosomal dominant trait, an autosomal recessive trait, or an X-linked trait (Optiz & Holt, 1990); it may be due to deletions or other genetic transformations (Hynd & Willis, 1988). Microencephaly also may be associated with malnutrition (Winick & Russo, 1969), phenylketonuria (PKU) or other metabolic disorders, inflammatory disease, or radiation during the first trimester (Yamazaki & Schull, 1990). Other teratogens that are associated with microencephaly include alcohol and cocaine.

It is not uncommon for children with microencephaly to experience epilepsy, mental retardation, and delayed speech and motor function (Friede, 1989). Microencephaly has been found to be associated with prematurity, perinatal asphyxia, and respiratory distress syndrome as well as other disorders (Watemberg, Silver, Harel, & Lerman-Sagie, 2002). At the same time, in their sample of children ($N$=1,393), Watemberg and colleagues found that mental retardation was strongly correlated with microencephaly only when it co-occurred with cerebral palsy. In other studies, there is a high incidence of learning disability and decreased cognitive ability in conjunction with seizure disorder (Abdel-Salam, Halász, & Czeizel, 2000).

## MEGALENCEPHALY

In contrast to the underdevelopment of the brain in microencephaly, megalencephaly is the overdevelopment (hyperplasia) of brain tissue (Renowden & Squier, 1994). This condition may be due to abnormal production of cells, abnormal pruning, or a combination of the two (Friede, 1989). Research suggests that there is an increase in the actual number of both neurons and glia cells as well as larger cell size (Renowden & Squier, 1994). The overabundance of brain tissue may occur in one (referred to as hemimegalencephaly) or both hemispheres. Megalencephaly is manifested as a somewhat large head (e.g., twice the expected size for age and sex) such that the increased size is due to overproduction of cerebral tissue and not some other disorder (Hynd & Willis, 1988).

Other than a large head, usually associated with increased head growth in the first 4 months of life (Lorber & Priestly, 1981), there may be no specific manifestations (Friede, 1989). At the same time, there is some evidence that an extreme, rapid rate of brain growth (as evidenced by increased head circumference) in the first 6 months of life may be associated with Autism (Courchesne, Carper, & Akshoomoff, 2003; Deutsch & Joseph, 2003; Ghaziuddin, Zaccagnini, Tsai, & Elardo, 1999; Lainhart, 2003).

There may or may not be related medical or educational problems in conjunction with megalencephaly. Megalencephaly can be associated with low intelligence (Lorber & Priestly, 1981; Petersson, Pedersen, Schalling, & Lavebratt, 1999), seizures, and other problems (Aicardi, 1992); however, it also has been associated with high nonverbal abilities (Deutsch & Joseph, 2003). Megalencephaly is known to be genetically transmitted via both autosomal recessive and dominant paths (Friede, 1989; Lorber & Priestley, 1981; Petersson et al., 1999). Megalencephaly frequently occurs with neurofibromatosis type 1, with particular increases noted in frontal and parietal white matter (Cutting et al., 2002) and a larger corpus callosum (Moore, Slopis, Jackson, DeWinter, & Leeds, 2000). Differences in the ratio of gray to white matter were more pronounced in younger than in older children (Moore et al., 2000). In their comparison of the brain structures of children with Autism Spectrum Disorder, children with developmental delay, and normally developing children, Sparks et al. (2002) found that the brains of both boys and girls with Autism were significantly larger than the brains of children in either of the two control groups. Enlargement was noted for specific structures; however, once overall brain size was considered, these differences disappeared.

## NEURAL TUBE ABNORMALITIES

From about 2 to 4 weeks gestation, the neural tube is developing. The rostral (anterior) end of the neural tube becomes the brain, and the caudal (posterior) end becomes the spinal cord. At about 4 weeks, there is closure of the neural tube, and cell differentiation and proliferation occur. When partial or incomplete closure of the neural tube occurs, various abnormalities may result that affect neural development.

### ANENCEPHALY

If the neural tube fails to close at the rostral end, the result is anencephaly. With anencephaly, there is an absence of differentiated cerebral hemispheres, diencephalon, and midbrain (Kolb & Fantie, 1997); without closure of the neural tube at the anterior end, there is no further cell proliferation at this end. There may or may not be development of the spinal cord, and cranial nerves can be identified only from the trigeminal nerve down (Friede, 1989).

Although anencephaly is the most common cause of stillbirths, some infants with anencephaly may live hours, days, or weeks (Hynd & Willis, 1988). The abnormality is estimated to occur at approximately the 18th day of gestation, when facial features are forming in normal development. With anencephaly, the facial features of the infant are usually distorted. Anencephaly is associated with diabetes of the mother, radiation, neurotoxins, and excess vitamin A.

### SPINA BIFIDA

In contrast to anencephaly, failure to close at the caudal end of the neural tube, or spina bifida, is not usually fatal. The effects may be profound and obvious at birth, as in spina bifida cystica, or the effects may be benign, and the abnormality may not be discovered until later in life, when it is associated with back pain, as in spina bifida occulta. The defect involves malformation of the spinal cord, vertebral column, and individual vertebrae (Evans, 1987). Maternal fevers, intrauterine virus infections, hormonal effects, vitamin deficiencies, excess of vitamin A, maternal diabetes, maternal alcohol use, and other teratogens have been associated with the occurrence of spina bifida (Friede, 1989; Hynd & Willis, 1988). In terms of prevalence, there is a significantly lower incidence of spina bifida in African Americans than in Caucasians.

Spina bifida cystica involves a visible lesion on the back, primarily in the lumbosacral region. In myelomeningeocele, part of the spinal cord is enclosed in the cyst and protrudes (Friede, 1989). In contrast, the lesion may be flatter and is then referred to as myeloschisis (Aicardi, 1992). In either case, associated problems include decreased sensitivity to pain, paralysis, weakness of the lower extremities, and incontinence (Friede, 1989). Approximately 80% to 90% of children with spina bifida develop hydrocephalus (i.e., excess of cerebrospinal fluid in the ventricles that damages the cortex) and other complications, including meningitis and pneumonia (Friede, 1989). Thirty years ago, the prognosis for children with spina bifida cystica was fairly bleak; however, with medical advances, the prognosis has improved dramatically, both in terms of life expectancy and functional ability (Hynd et al., 1997).

## Schizencephaly

Schizencephaly is so named as a result of the appearance of a cleft(s) in the cortex. The cleft may be present in one or both hemispheres; however, effects are more pronounced in bilateral presentation and depending on the size of the cleft (Barkovich & Kjos, 1992). The cleft usually forms in the area of the ventricle and extends to the pia. Cerebrospinal fluid may or may not separate the sides of the cleft. In almost all cases of schizencephaly, there is some form of seizure disorder. In milder cases, where seizure disorder is the only manifestation, the occurrence of schizencephaly may not be detected unless neuroimaging is conducted. With larger clefts (involving greater areas of the cortex) and bilateral presentation, mental retardation and cerebral palsy are common (Clark, 2002).

## Encephalocele

Encephaloceles are lesions that contain cerebral tissue (Friede, 1989) and are a subset of the myelomeningeoceles associated with spina bifida. Encephaloceles tend to be found in the occipital region but may occur in the frontal area of the brain. The cerebral tissue within the encephalocele may be connected to the cerebral hemisphere via glial tissue. The affected cerebral hemisphere is somewhat smaller than the contralateral hemisphere, with some distortion of the shape of the brain (Friede, 1989). The presence of the encephalocele may affect other structures of the brain, the cranial nerves, and the circulatory system of the brain. Encephaloceles also may be associated with other congenital abnormalities, including agenesis of the corpus callosum. There is some evidence that encephaloceles are more frequent in females than males (Friede, 1989).

# CEREBRAL HEMISPHERE AND CORPUS CALLOSUM

## Holoprosencephaly

Holoprosencephaly occurs when the cortex develops as a single, undifferentiated hemisphere instead of cleaving into two hemispheres (Clark, 2002). In some cases, the olfactory nerve does not develop, a condition called olfactory aplasia; however, it is possible for olfactory aplasia and holoprosencephaly to occur separately (Friede, 1989). In effect, the vesicles fail to develop into hemispheres, suggesting that development was interrupted at about the 3rd to 6th week of gestation, when cleavage between hemispheres should develop (Friede, 1989).

Holoprosencephaly is generally incompatible with life and may be associated with seizure disorder and severe mental retardation (Aicardi, 1992; Plawner et al., 2002). Due to the interruption in development, there are frequent abnormalities of facial features (Aicardi, 1992; Friede, 1989) that can be detected by ultrasonography as early as the 9th week of gestation in severe cases and by the 16th week in most cases (Aicardi, 1992). These include cyclopia (formation of one eye and no nose), formation of a nose with a single nostril or flat nose, and midline cleft lip (Souza, Siebert, & Beckwith, 1990). The extent of functional deficits depends on the level of separation (or nonseparation) of the caudate, lentiform, and thalamic nuclei as well as the degree (or level) of holoprosencephaly (Plawner et al., 2002).

The occurrence of holoprosencephaly has been associated with maternal diabetes (Kobori, Herrick, & Urich, 1987), retinoic acid exposure, cytomegalovirus, and rubella (Cohen & Lemire, 1983), as well as exposure to neurotoxins (e.g., alcohol, drugs; Hynd & Willis, 1988). There also is evidence of possible familial transmission involving the 13–15 trisomy (Friede, 1989; Verloes et al., 1991).

## PORENCEPHALY

In porencephaly, there are symmetrical cavities where white matter and cortex should have developed (Kolb & Fantie, 1997); cysts may be evident in the place of the cortex. These cysts or cavities most likely occur in the insular region and are usually bilateral (Aicardi, 1992; Friede, 1989). Although evidence of decreased thalamic size may occur, other structures (e.g., basal ganglia, cerebellum) may not be affected. In some cases, polymicrogyria may be evident; however, when polymicrogyria are not evident, the gyral pattern may be atypical (Friede, 1989). It has been suggested that the interruption in normal development that results in porencephaly occurs during the 5th month of gestation. Porencephaly may be associated with disruption of neuronal migration but is not caused by disrupted migration. In fact, porencephaly is believed to result from necrosis, possibly due to fetal stroke or ischemia (Aicardi, 1992; Friede, 1989). Behavioral correlates vary in direct relation to the size of the cysts or lesions, the location of the lesion, and the extent to which the presence of the lesion has affected cortical development in that area (Aicardi, 1992). Some individuals may be asymptomatic, whereas others may evidence mental retardation, paralysis, speech disorders, or epilepsy (Aicardi, 1992).

## HYDRANENCEPHALY

The replacement of cerebral hemispheres by cysts containing cerebral spinal fluid (CSF) is called hydranencephaly (Friede, 1989). Caused by massive necrosis, there may be some evidence of development of subcortical structures such as the thalamus, basal ganglia, and brain stem; less frequently, there may be evidence of temporal or occipital lobes (Friede, 1989). Although the head may be of normal size at birth, there is an abnormal acceleration of head growth within the first weeks of life. The necrosis that leads to hydranencephaly is believed to be related to blockage in the vascular system, either in conjunction with umbilical cord strangulation or due to blunt trauma to the mother's abdomen during pregnancy (Friede, 1989).

Agenesis of the Corpus Callosum

The intercerebral commissures (i.e., anterior commissure, hippocampal commissure, corpus callosum) begin to develop at 7 weeks gestation; however, in some cases, these commissures do not develop. Agenesis of the corpus callosum refers to the complete or partial absence of the corpus callosum (Hynd et al., 1997; Kolb & Fantie, 1997) and is believed to be a result of interruption of normal development at about 12 to 22 weeks gestation (Hynd & Willis, 1988). Agenesis can be diagnosed at about 20 weeks gestation (Aicardi, 1992).

The effects of agenesis of the corpus callosum are not as severe as surgical "split brain" patients. This is due to increased development of other commissures and reorganization of the functional systems involved in interhemispheric communication. For example, there is some evidence that the anterior commissure may become hyperatrophied to compensate for the absent corpus callosum (Fischer, Ryan, & Dobyns, 1992). In those cases when it is symptomatic, mental retardation and seizure disorder are common (Jeret, Serur, Wisniewski, & Fisch, 1987). The manifestation generally involves a language disorder and linguistic-semantic deficits (e.g., Chiarello, 1980).

Familial transmission, specifically X-linked (from father to son) transmission, have been indicated with regard to agenesis of the corpus callosum (Aicardi, 1992; Jeret et al., 1987). Agenesis also may be associated with metabolic disorders or neurotoxin exposure (Jeret et al., 1987).

Cerebral Asymmetry

Variations in cerebral asymmetry have been reported for adults with dyslexia (e.g., Galaburda & Kemper, 1979; Galaburda, Sherman, Rosen, Aboitiz, & Geschwind, 1985). Both CT and postmortem studies document that about 66% of normal brains are asymmetric (L > R), favoring the left planum temporale in the posterior region; the reverse is true in the anterior portion (R > L) for about 75% of individuals (Duara et al., 1991). In contrast, for persons with a reading disability, the posterior asymmetry is reversed (R > L) or absent (R=L). Only about 10% of adults with dyslexia evidence the L > R posterior asymmetry. Normally, the planum temporale (area behind and above the ear) also is L > R, but in individuals with dyslexia, it tends to be R > L. This is due to greater right planum as opposed to smaller left planum when the surface areas are compared (normal–dyslexia; Galaburda et al., 1985; Leonard et al., 1993). Similarly, in the angular gyrus (association area that provides cross-modal integration such as writing and reading), Duara et al. found that normal controls tend to be symmetrical, whereas persons with dyslexia evidenced R > L asymmetry.

## INTERFERENCE WITH CELL MIGRATION

Cell differentiation and proliferation are based on function; cells multiply and differentiate from the time of conception (Kolb & Fantie, 1997). With increased development of the fetus, cell migration occurs in conjunction with the increased specificity to structures in the central nervous system (CNS). The function and area of the brain dictate when cell migration occurs. In normal development, continued cell proliferation results in the formation of the sulci or folds of the brain between 10 and 20 weeks gestation. Continued cell proliferation results in formation of gyri up until 26 weeks gestation (Kolb & Fantie, 1997). White et al. (2003) asserted that "gyrification is an important index of brain development" (p. 418).

In the past few years, methods for measuring cortical depth and curvature of the sulci and gyri have been developed (White et al., 2003). Using these methods, White and colleagues found that adults with schizophrenia, as a group, tended to have sharper or steeper gyral patterns but flattened sulcal patterns, depending on the region of the brain. They suggested that these differences reflected corresponding differences in the gyrification process during neurodevelopment, possibly related to problems with pruning or cell proliferation. In effect, at about 12 weeks gestation, the brain is lissencephalic (relatively smooth); by 24 weeks gestation, cell proliferation and migration have begun to establish gyral patterns. Gyrification continues through the gestational period and actually through the first years of life. With these new methods, further advances in identifying the timing and causes of specific anomalies in gyral patterns may emerge in the future (White et al., 2003). Some of the more clearly defined anomalies associated with gyrification are described briefly.

## Agyria

Agyria or lissencephaly is said to occur when brain development does not proceed with normal development of gyri (i.e., it remains smooth). It is believed to be the result of arrest in neuronal migration in the first trimester (Brodsky & Lombroso, 1998). In about 25% of cases, agyria is genetic and usually autosomal recessive. Specific genetic syndromes (e.g., Miller-Dieken phenotype) include lissencephaly associated with deletions to chromosome 17 that can be detected through amniocentesis (Brodsky & Lombroso, 1998; Ledbetter, Kirwano, Dobyns, & Ledbetter, 1992).

With the interruption in cell proliferation and neuronal migration, agyria is often associated with microencephaly (Pavone, Rizzo, & Dobyns, 1993) and reduced white matter (Kuchelmeister, Bergmann, & Gullotta, 1993). With decreased white matter, agyria often is accompanied by severe/profound retardation, seizure disorder, and hypotonia (Aicardi, 1992; Pavone et al., 1993).

## Macrogyria or Pachygyria

Although some gyri are present, macrogyria (also called pachygyria) is similar to agyria in that the brain is smoother than with normal cell proliferation. These gyri are generally wide and few in number (Kolb & Fantie, 1997). Some researchers have suggested that the difference between agyria and macrogyria is the level of severity (McLone, 1982). It has been suggested that whereas the interference that results in agyria occurs at about 11 weeks gestation, the interruption with macrogyria occurs at about 13 weeks gestation (Jellinger & Rett, 1976). Generally, the outcomes for children with macrogyria are somewhat more positive than for agyria, but there is still an increased likelihood of mental retardation and seizures (Hynd & Willis, 1988). Macrogyria also has been associated with tuberous sclerosis (Sener, 1993). The problems with cell proliferation and migration that result in macrogyria may be due to ischemia or viral infection (Pavone et al., 1993).

## MICROPOLYGYRIA, MICROGYRIA, OR POLYMICROGYRIA

After 26 weeks gestation, no new gyri develop; however, existing gyri deepen due to increased cell proliferation. With microgyria (also called micropolygyria or polymicrogyria), the gyri are numerous, smaller, and poorly developed. The shallow quality of the gyri and sulci may be perceived as increased cortical thickness as well as resulting in a smoother appearance (Clark, 2002). Microgyria is associated with genetic disorders such as Zellweger syndrome as well as neonatal adrenal leukodystrophy; the occurrence of microgyria also can be autosomal recessive. Prognosis depends on the extensiveness and diffuseness of the microgyria. When it is more diffuse (more of the brain is involved), there may be severe developmental delays and hypertonia (Clark, 2002).

Micropolygyria is often associated with other abnormalities, including agenesis of the corpus callosum and vascular abnormalities (Aicardi, 1992; Friede, 1989). Other precipitating events may include trauma, carbon monoxide poisoning, intrauterine infections, and maternal asphyxia (Aicardi, 1992). There also is tentative evidence of possible genetic transmission (Andermann, Palmini, Andermann, Tampieri, & Leonard, 1992). Micropolygyria is possibly due to focal necrosis during neuronal migration at about the 5th to 6th week of gestation.

It is believed that any complication or abnormality in the development of structures of the brain has a synergistic impact. That is, whenever a structure in the brain is missing, this impacts the orientation of the surrounding tissues and the organization of subcortical structures. In the presence of lesions (damage) in the developmental process or the failure to develop a structure, the gyral pattern changes such that the gyri point to the location of the lesion or absent structure. As such, with micropolygyria, the pattern is atypical as well as being characterized by small gyri (Aicardi, 1992). The clinical manifestation of microgyria depends on the extent of abnormality in development (Guerreiro et al., 2002). At the same time, focal locations of micropolygyria may be associated with specific disorders. For example, micropolygyria in Wernicke's area tends to be associated with learning disabilities and in the posterior parietal area tends to be associated with perisylvian syndrome and developmental language disorders (Guerreiro et al., 2002).

## DYSPLASIAS AND HETEROTOPIA

If migration is interrupted or stopped prematurely, groups of cells may be scattered among inner layers of cells or on the external surface, but may not form connections to brain structures. Dysplasias are believed to arise from deviations in the migration process that lead to the development of abnormal cell clusters (Kolb & Fantie, 1997). More specifically, the cells that make up the dysplasia, often called heterotopia, are normal neurons, but the clusters are in the wrong location for their genetically coded function (Clark, 2002). Mechanisms that interfere with or disrupt the migration process are usually unknown but may relate to the radial glial cells involved in the migration process (Clark, 2002).

Heterotopias are made of cortical material (gray matter) that is found deep in subcortical structures due to problems with migration. The presence of gray matter heterotopias also may suggest the presence of a disorder long before the disorder has manifested. Multiple studies suggest that heterotopias may be one indicator of predisposition to schizophrenia, with location of the heterotopias or dysplasias determining the disorder (White et al., 2003). Among potential causes for disrupted migration is the presence of teratogens (e.g., maternal drug use); less frequently, heterotopias follow a familial pattern (Moro et al., 2002).

Many developmental disorders (e.g., learning disabilities) are characterized by dysplasias or cells that are believed to have migrated incorrectly (Hynd & Willis, 1988). Autopsy studies identified the presence of disproportionate clustering of cellular abnormalities (focal dysplasias) in the left planum of individuals with learning disabilities (Galaburda et al., 1985). Cortical anomalies also have been found in the left inferior frontal and right frontal regions (Galaburda et al., 1985). In some cases, disorganization of subcortical pathways specific to the lateral geniculate nucleus of the thalamus have been found (Livingstone, Rosen, Drislane, & Galaburda, 1991). In general, for individuals with a learning disability, there is a higher incidence of cerebral anomalies (i.e., missing or duplicated gyri bilaterally in the planum and parietal operculum) relative to nondisabled individuals (Leonard et al., 1993). It is hypothesized that these focal, cellular differences may be the result of differences in cell migration during the 5th to 7th months of gestation and that the location and distribution of clusters may result in variation in learning disability subtypes. Heterotopias also are found more frequently in children with Attention-Deficit/Hyperactivity Disorder as compared to control children (Nopoulos et al., 2000).

At the same time, the presence of dysplasia or heterotopia, depending on the number and location, may be asymptomatic. The extent to which migrational abnormalities occur is associated with the clinical manifestation, but not necessarily the severity or type (Palmini et al., 1993). This is because, although migration of some neurons may be disrupted, the migration of other cells may not be affected at all. Further, there is less impact generally than with agyria or other gyral anomalies, as the disruption is believed to occur later in the process (Palmini et al., 1993).

## DOUBLE CORTEX SYNDROME

Double cortex (DC) syndrome or subcortical band heterotopia is a specific neuronal migration disorder that is associated with epilepsy and mental retardation (Gleeson et al., 2000). It consists of bands of heterotopic gray matter beneath the cortex bilaterally. DC syndrome can be anterior-biased, posterior-biased, global, or some combination of bias and global. In many cases of anterior-biased and anterior-biased/global, DC occurs in the presence of mutations in the X-linked doublecortin gene (Xq22.3); this was not found to be as common with posterior-biased DC (Gleeson et al., 2000). Some have suggested that this is the X-linked variant of lissencephaly (Dobyns et al., 1996). The presence of the double cortex of subcortical laminar band is usually associated with seizures; however, there is evidence that this band is involved in normal functional activity of the brain as well (Pinard et al., 2000).

Interference to cortical development is not limited to migration disorders. Following cell migration, there is axonal and dendritic elaboration of various cells that allow for connections between neurons. Selective cell death (pruning or apoptosis) occurs at approximately 8 to 9 months gestation (Andersen, 2003), and myelination of axons begins at approximately 8 months gestation, continuing through adolescence and into adulthood (Kolb & Fantie, 1997).

## COMPLICATIONS TO NEURAL DEVELOPMENT

Many environmental agents, including viral infections and other teratogenic (toxic) sources, can negatively influence neural development. Environmental agents may trigger a genetic susceptibility causing abnormal brain development or create structural lesions in the brain (Joseph, 1996). These toxic agents are known to cause congenital abnormalities such as microencephaly, hydrocephaly, encephalopathy, necrosis, demyelization, and other impairments. Drug and alcohol abuse and viral infections such as cytomegalovirus and human immunodeficiency virus (HIV) infection are a few examples of detrimental environmental agents.

### Cytomegalovirus

Cytomegalovirus (CMV) is a viral infection that may negatively impact a child's developmental course; it is described as a communicable DNA virus found in the herpes family (Sessoms, 2003). CMV infections occur in approximately 1% of all live births (Conboy et al., 1986) and are the most common viral disease transmitted in utero (Aylward, 2003; Williamson et al., 1982). The CMV infection can be transmitted congenitally to an unborn infant when the mother has a primary infection (CMV causes an infection for the first time) or a recurrent CMV infection (a suppressed infection reactivates and acts like a new infection) at the time of birth (National Congenital CMV Disease Registry, 1998). Congenital CMV is more likely to be transmitted when a woman contracts the virus for the first time during pregnancy and is concurrently symptomatic (Sessoms, 2003). CMV also is commonly transmitted postnatally to newborn babies through the mother's breast milk or by cervico-vaginal secretions at the time of birth (National Congenital CMV Disease Registry, 1998).

Although the virus is silent in most people (i.e., no signs or symptoms of the infection may be evident), unborn babies and people with weakened immune system are at great risk for significant health problems (National Congenital CMV Disease Registry, 1998). Approximately 10% of children with congenital CMV will manifest one or more symptoms and/or varying degrees of abnormalities at birth, such as microcephaly, small body size, petechiae (little red spots under the skin), hepatomegaly (enlarged liver), splenomegaly (enlarged spleen), jaundice, low blood count, pneumonia, and abnormal muscle tone (National Congenital CMV Disease Registry, 1998; National Congenital CMV Disease Registry, 1995b). CMV also is associated with macrogyria (Hayward, Titelbaum, Clancy, & Zimmerman, 1991). Chronic conditions involving the CNS that also may occur include deafness, blindness, mental retardation, seizures, cerebral palsy, calcium deposits in the brain, and developmental and learning delays (Aylward, 2003; National Congenital CMV Disease Registry, 1995b).

The most common disability associated with CMV infections is progressive hearing loss, with symptomatic infants being at higher risk. In addition, roughly 5% to 15% of asymptomatic infants also will develop some degree of hearing loss in their lifetime due to the infection (Sessoms, 2003). With regard to infectious diseases, CMV is considered the leading cause of nonhereditary sensorineural hearing loss and mental retardation (National Congenital CMV Disease Registry, 1995a). It has been reported that approximately 75% of CMV survivors will have some degree of mental retardation (Williamson et al., 1982). Children with CNS insults such as CMV are at risk for developmental and learning disabilities as well as social, emotional, and behavioral problems (Reiter-Purtill & Noll, 2003; Schuman & La Greca, 1999; Tramontana & Hooper, 1997).

## PEDIATRIC HUMAN IMMUNODEFICIENCY VIRUS INFECTION AND ACQUIRED IMMUNODEFICIENCY DISEASE

Another viral infection that significantly impacts a child's rapidly developing CNS is the HIV infection and acquired immunodeficiency disease (AIDS). HIV "is a single-stranded RNA retrovirus that is attracted to the CD4 surface molecule of T-cells, part of the human immune system. The HIV becomes incorporated into the DNA of the T-cell, replicates HIV-specific RNA proteins, kills the T-cell, and releases new HIV to continue the infection process"; in turn, immune function is impaired (Armstrong, Willen, & Sorgen, 2003, p. 359). The HIV infection can have profound effects on cognitive, social, and emotional development and can be detected as early as infancy. Children with HIV are specifically at risk for infections, direct effects on the CNS, wasting syndromes, lung disease, malignant disease (i.e., lymphoma), and even death (Armstrong et al., 2003). Older children and adolescents also are at risk for repeated infections of the brain such as toxoplasmosis, herpes simplex, and CMV (Armstrong et al., 2003).

HIV and AIDS have a serious impact on neurological development in children, and rapid or significant declines in neurocognitive functioning may be an indicator of the progression of the disease (Armstrong et al., 2003). HIV often infects the macrophages and microglia of the brain by releasing toxic substances (Armstrong et al., 2003), subsequently damaging white matter, causing demyelination of nerve tracks, and altering the blood-brain barrier (Mintz, 1999). This process also may cause cerebral atrophy, ventricular enlargements, and calcifications in the basal ganglia, cerebellum, and subcortical frontal white matter (Llorente, LoPresti, & Satz, 1997; Mintz, 1999). CNS encephalopathy is one of the most significant symptoms found in children with HIV; it can cause serious deviations in normal development and even death (Armstrong et al., 2003; Llorente et al., 1997). Specifically, encephalopathy causes the slowing and plateauing of brain development and, in severe cases, progressive deterioration of brain structures (Mintz, 1999). Llorente et al. noted that progressive encephalopathy is marked by a gradual and progressive decline in neurological functioning, affecting cognition, expressive motor and language functioning, and adaptive functioning, as well as loss of attained developmental milestones and death, in some cases.

## FETAL ALCOHOL SYNDROME

Not all complicating agents are viral or hormonal in nature. In the past two decades, there has been increased evidence of the effects of maternal alcohol consumption on fetal development. Specific effects of consumption depend on timing, pattern, duration, polydrug usage, and the amount of alcohol consumption (Aylward, 2003). Moderate to high maternal consumption during pregnancy is primarily associated with Fetal Alcohol Syndrome (FAS); however, when a clear diagnosis cannot be made due to a vague phenotype of FAS or an incomplete history regarding alcohol consumption, the term fetal alcohol effects (FAE) often is used (Carey & McMahon, 1999). Features of FAS include dysmorphic facial features, microcephaly, and cortical thinning, as well as prenatal growth deficiency (i.e., low birthweight) and postnatal growth deficiency (i.e., short stature, failure to thrive; Streissguth, Clarren, & Jones, 1985). A majority of children with FAS also evidence neurodevelopmental problems such as learning difficulties, attention deficit and hyperactivity problems, memory loss, perceptual problems, delayed adaptive behavior, and mild mental retardation (Aylward, 2003; Carey & McMahon, 1999). Specifically, many infants with FAS are often small for gestational age and demonstrate irritability, tremulousness, difficulties with sucking, and hypotonia (Aylward, 2003). High levels of alcohol consumption or ethanol exposure "may affect all organ systems and induce fetal hypoxia" (Aylward, 2003, pp. 260–261), and is associated with malformations in neural tube development, including holoprosencephaly, myelomeningocele, and spina bifida.

### GROWTH FACTORS AND RELATION TO NEURAL DEVELOPMENT

Various neurotrophics are implicated in neural development. These include brain-derived neurotrophic factor (BDNF), nerve growth factor (NGF), glia-derived growth factor (GDNF), CNTF, and IGF-1 (Andersen, 2003). Growth factors are involved early on in the developmental process and have a role in innervation, migration and retraction of neurons, and dendritic branching. Based on animal studies, the growth factors are believed to exert their strongest influence during gestation but continue to affect the individual across the life span.

## ASSOCIATION WITH OTHER DISORDERS

In addition to environmental and health factors that may affect brain development, there are specific disorders that directly impact brain function. As already noted, many abnormalities of neural development are genetically determined. Genes are intrinsically involved in brain development, regulating anatomical and functional aspects of development as well as the processes involved in cell proliferation and migration (Clark, 2002). Of genetic disorders, the most commonly studied are autosomal disorders. Autosomal (i.e., non-sex linked) disorders affect the CNS and typically result in multiple physical abnormalities (Hynd & Willis, 1988). The three most common of the autosomal abnormalities include Down syndrome (trisomy 21), Edwards' syndrome (trisomy 18), and Patau syndrome (trisomy 13). Most infants with Edwards' or Patau die before reaching 1 year of age.

### DOWN SYNDROME

Historically, there have been numerous studies on Down syndrome regarding its phenotype and sequelae. Down syndrome is one of the chief causes of mental retardation and includes many other distinctive physical characteristics. Persons with this syndrome may present with brachycephaly (broad head), hypoplasia of the midfacial bones, epicanthal folds, a delay of closure of the fontanels, obliquely placed palpebral fissures, depressed nasal bridge, Brushfield spots (white spots on the periphery of the iris), hyper- or hypoterlorism, overlapping or folding of the helix of the ear, tongue protrusion, fissured tongue, thickened lips, short and broad neck, broad and stubby hands and feet, umbilical hernias, a single palmar transverse crease, partial or complete syndactyly, and a wide space between the first and second toes (Pueschel, 1992). Some features associated with Down syndrome will remain consistent over time, whereas others may become increasingly more or less noticeable. Mental retardation may range from mild to profound in these individuals (Pueschel, 1992).

There are many medical implications associated with Down syndrome, including ophthalmological concerns, oral problems, cardiac problems, respiratory concerns, gastrointestinal anomalies, and dermatological conditions (Cody & Kamphaus, 1999). Down syndrome interferes with fetal development, resulting in various brain abnormalities, including seizure disorders, and reduced volume and weight of various cortical and subcortical structures due to a reduction in the neuronal density and decreased dendritic arborization (Florez, 1992; Jernigan, Bellugi, Sowell, Doherty, & Hesselink, 1993). In addition to a reduction in neurons, Down syndrome also causes abnormalities within the neurons and problems in the neurons' ability to communicate with each other (Florez, 1992). Additionally, features associated with dementia and Alzheimer's disease have been found to be evident in persons with Down syndrome, such as cortical atrophy, neurofibrillary tangles, and neuritic plaques (Lai, 1992). Other problems related to this syndrome include mild immune deficiency, hematological abnormalities such as transient myelodysplasia in infancy, red cell macrocytosis, and increased susceptibility to leukemia (Lubin, Cahn, & Scott, 1992), as well as possible endocrine dysfunction (i.e., thyroid problems; Pueschel & Bier, 1992). Due to the many medical complications associated with Down syndrome, premature death often occurs (Cody & Kamphaus, 1999).

## ANGELMAN SYNDROME

In the past few years, Angelman syndrome has become a specific genetic disorder of interest. Angelman syndrome is a rare congenital neurodevelopmental disorder with a number of etiologies and is estimated to occur in approximately 1 in 10,000 to 1 in 20,000 persons (Steinman, 2003). Angelman syndrome is caused by the loss of maternally imprinted contribution(s) in the 15q11-q13 region and is known to occur by five different genetic mechanisms; 3 to 5 Mb deletion (70%), uniparental disomy (maternal, 7%), imprinting defect (3%), UBE3A mutation (11%), cytogenetic rearrangement (1%), and unknown etiology (11%; Williams, Lossie, & Driscoll, 2000). The microdeletion is detected on the same chromosome indicated in Prader-Willi syndrome; however, with Prader-Willi syndrome, the paternal chromosome is affected.

Angelman syndrome is often difficult to diagnose in infancy due to a typically normal phenotype and birth history; however, developmental delays may occur as early as 6 months of age and unique clinical features often are noted after 1 year of age (Steinman, 2003; Williams et al., 2000). When Angelman syndrome is suspected, it can be detected using a variety of techniques, including fluorescent in situ hybridization (approximately 70% of cases), cytogenetic analysis, DNA methylation analysis, and UBE3A mutation analysis (Williams et al., 2000). Angelman syndrome primarily is characterized by severe developmental delays or mental retardation, severe speech impairment or absence of speech, gait ataxia or tremulousness of the limbs, and mild cortical atrophy or dysmyelination. These children also have a distinctive behavior pattern manifested by a happy demeanor with frequent smiling, episodic laughter, hand flapping, short attention span, and excitability (Summers & Feldman, 1999; Williams et al., 2000). Angelman syndrome often is referred to as the "happy puppet syndrome" due to the incessant happy demeanor and marionette-like movements (Steinman, 2003).

Approximately 80% of children with Angelman syndrome also will manifest delayed or slowed growth in head circumference resulting in microcephaly, seizures after 3 years of age, and an abnormal EEG pattern (Clayton-Smith & Laan, 2003; Williams et al., 2000). Other features that may occur in relation to the disorder include flat back of the head, strabismus, hypopigmentation of the skin and eyes, tongue thrusting, frequent drooling, sucking and swallowing disorders, wide mouth, wide-spaced teeth, uplifted arms while walking, hyperactive tendon reflexes, increased sensitivity to heat, and an attraction or fascination with water (Clayton-Smith & Laan, 2003; Williams et al., 2000).

## CONCLUSION

With increased advances in scientific inquiry and medicine, what is known about neurodevelopmental disorders and anomalies changes rapidly. Some understanding of the potential problems and disruptions that can occur is helpful in our appreciation of normal development and in our understanding and treatment of children and families who experience firsthand some of these problems. At the same time, Hynd et al. (1997) cautioned that there is still no direct connection between abnormality of neural development and outcome. Further, Whelan and Walker (1997) discussed the potential trap of losing sight of the individual child and the totality of the child's experiences, including the systems in which he or she functions. For each of the conditions described herein, there are exceptions, and the majority of these anomalies occur on a continuum. More important, appropriate medical, psychological, and educational intervention can affect the prognosis and life course for some of these children and their families.

Regardless of the type of abnormality, the etiology, or the severity, it is important for school psychologists and others who work with children to integrate what they know about abnormalities of neurological development with what they know about an individual child. The range of individual differences and the extent to which environment, stimulation, and support can affect prognosis demand individualized programming and frequent monitoring of progress toward short- and long-term goals. The more extensive the interference with normal development, the more diffuse the impact on brain function and the more domains of functioning that will likely be affected. The ability and willingness to approach assessment and intervention from varying perspectives will increase the usefulness of the information gleaned.

## REFERENCES

Abdel-Salam, G. M. H., Halász, A. A., & Czeizel, A. E. (2000). Association of epilepsy with different groups of microcephaly. *Developmental medicine and child neurology, 42,* 760–767.

Aircardi, J. (1992). *Diseases of the nervous system in childhood.* New York: MacKeith Press.

Andermann, E., Palmini, A., Andermann, D., Tampieri, D., & Leonard, G. (1992). Familial bilateral congenital perisylvan syndrome: Genetic determination of a localized neuronal disorder. *Neurology, 42*(Suppl. 3), 354.

Andersen, S. L. (2003). Trajectories of brain development: Point of vulnerability or window of opportunity? *Neuroscience and Biobehavioral Reviews, 27,* 3–18.

Armstrong, F. D., Willen, E. J., & Sorgen, K. (2003). HIV and AIDS in children and adolescents. In M. C. Roberts (Ed.), *Handbook of pediatric psychology* (3rd ed., pp. 358–374). New York: Guilford Press.

Aylward, G. P. (2003). Neonatology, prematurity, NICU, and developmental issues. In M. C. Roberts (Ed.), *Handbook of pediatric psychology* (3rd ed., pp. 253–268). New York: Guilford Press.

Barkovich, A. J., & Kjos, B. (1992). Schizencephaly: Correlation of clinical findings with MR characteristics. *American Journal of Neuroradiology, 13,* 85–94.

Brodsky, M., & Lombroso, P. J. (1998). Molecular mechanisms of developmental disorders. *Development and Psychopathology, 10,* 1–20.

Carey, J. C., & McMahon, W. M. (1999). Neurobehavioral disorders and medical genetics. In S. Goldstein & C. R. Reynolds (Eds.), *Handbook of neurodevelopmental and genetic disorders in children* (pp. 38–60). New York: Guilford Press.

Chiarello, C. (1980). A house divided? Cognitive functioning with callosal agenesis. *Brain and Language, 11,* 128–158.

Clark, G. D. (2002). Brain development and the genetics of brain development. *Neurologic Clinics, 20,* 917–939.

Clayton-Smith, J., & Laan, L. (2003). Angelman syndrome: A review of the clinical and genetic aspects. *Journal of Medical Genetics, 40,* 87–95.

Cody, H., & Kamphaus, R. W. (1999). Down syndrome. In S. Goldstein & C. R. Reynolds (Eds.), *Handbook of neurodevelopmental and genetic disorders in children* (pp. 385–405). New York: Guilford Press.

Cohen, M. M. J., & Lemire, R. J. (1983). Syndromes with cephaloceles. *Teratology, 25,* 161–172.

Conboy, T. J., Pass, R. F., Stagno, S., Britt, W. J., Alford, C. A., McFarland, C. E., et al. (1986). Intellectual development in school-aged children with asymptomatic congenital cytomegalovirus infection. *Pediatrics, 77*(6), 801–806.

Courchesne, E., Carper, R., & Akshoomoff, N. (2003). Evidence of brain overgrowth in the first year of life in autism. *Journal of the American Medical Association, 290,* 337–344.

Cutting, L. E., Cooper, K. L., Koth, C. W., Mostofsky, S. H., Kates, W. R., Denckla, M. B., et al. (2002). Megalencephaly in NF1: Predominantly white matter contribution and mitigation by ADHD. *Neurology, 59,* 1388–1394.

Deutsch, C. K., & Joseph, R. M. (2003). Brief report: Cognitive correlates of enlarged head circumference in children with autism. *Journal of Autism and Developmental Disorders, 33,* 209–215.

Dobyns, W. B. (1992). Cerebral dysgenesis: Causes and consequences. In G. Miller & J. C. Ramer (Eds.), *Static encephalopathies of infancies and childhood* (pp. 235–248). New York: Raven.

Dobyns, W. B., Andermann, E., Andermann, F., Czapansky-Beilman, D., Dubeau, F., Dulac, O., et al. (1996). X-linked malformations of neuronal migration. *Neurology, 47,* 331–339.

Duara, R., Kushch, A., Gross-Glenn, K., Barker, W. W., Barker, W., Jallad, B., et al. (1991). Neuroanatomic differences between dyslexic and normal readers on magnetic resonance imaging scans. *Archives of Neurology, 48,* 410–416.

Evans, O. B. (1987). *Manual of child neurology.* Edinburgh: Churchill Livingstone.

Fischer, M., Ryan, S. B., & Dobyns, W. B. (1992). Mechanisms of interhemispheric transfer and patterns of cognitive function in acallosal patients of normal intelligence. *Archives of Neurology, 49,* 271–277.

Florez, J. (1992). Neurologic abnormalities. In S. M. Pueschel & J. K. Pueschel (Eds.), *Biomedical concerns in persons with Down syndrome.* Baltimore: Paul H. Brookes.

Friede, R. L. (1989). *Developmental neuropathology* (2nd ed.). Berlin, Germany: Springer-Verlag.

Galaburda, A. M., & Kemper, T. C. (1979). Cytoarchitectonic abnormalities in developmental dyslexia: A case study. *Annals of Neurology, 6,* 94–100.

Galaburda, A. M., Sherman, G. F., Rosen, G. D., Aboitiz, F., & Geschwind, N. (1985). Developmental dyslexia: Four consecutive patients with cortical anomalies. *Annals of Neurology, 18,* 222–233.

Ghaziuddin, M., Zaccagnini, J., Tsai, L., & Elardo, S. (1999). Is megalencephaly specific to autism? *Journal of Intellectual Disability Research, 43,* 279–282.

Gleeson, J. G., Luo, R. F., Grant, P. E., Guerrini, R., Huttenlocher, P. R., Berg, M. J., et al. (2000). Genetic and neuroradiological heterogeneity of double cortex syndrome. *Annals of Neurology, 47,* 265–269.

Guerreiro, M. M., Hage, S. R. V., Guimaràes, C. A., Abramides, D. V., Fernandes, W., Pacheco, P. S., et al. (2002). Developmental language disorder associated with polymicrogyria. *Neurology, 59,* 245–250.

Hayward, J. C., Titelbaum, D. S., Clancy, R. R., & Zimmerman, R. A. (1991). Lissencephaly-pachygyria associated with congenital cytomegalovirus infection. *Journal of Child Neurology, 6,* 109–114.

Hynd, G. W., Morgan, A. E., & Vaughn, M. (1997). Neurodevelopmental anomalies and malformations. In C. R. Reynolds & E. Fletcher-Jantzen (Eds.), *Handbook of clinical child neuropsychology* (2nd ed., pp. 42–62). New York: Plenum Press.

Hynd, G. W., & Willis, W. G. (1988). *Pediatric neuropsychology.* Boston: Allyn & Bacon.

Janszky, J., Ebner, A., Kruse, B., Mertens, M., Jokeit, H., Seitz, R. J., et al. (2003). Functional organization of the brain with malformations of cortical development. *Annals of Neurology, 53,* 759–767.

Jellinger, K., & Rett, A. (1976). Agryia-pachygyria (lissencephaly syndrome). *Neuropädiatrie, 7,* 66–91.

Jeret, J. S., Serur, D., Wisniewski, K., & Fisch, C. (1987). Frequency of agenesis of the corpus callosum in the developmentally disabled population as determined by computerized tomography. *Pediatric Neuroscience, 12,* 101–103.

Jernigan, T. L., Bellugi, U., Sowell, E., Doherty, S., & Hesselink, J. R. (1993). Cerebral morphologic distinctions between Williams and Down syndromes. *Archives of Neurology, 50,* 186–191.

Joseph, R. (1996). *Neuropsychiatry, neuropsychology, and clinical neuroscience: Emotion, evolution, cognition, language, memory, brain damage, and abnormal behavior* (2nd ed.). Baltimore: Williams & Wilkins.

Kennard, M. A. (1940). Relation of age to motor impairment in man and in subhuman primates. *Archives of Neurology and Psychiatry, 44,* 377–397.

Kobori, J. A., Herrick, M. K., & Urich, H. (1987). Arhinencephaly: The spectrum of associated malformations. *Brain, 110,* 237–260.

Kolb, B., & Fantie, B. (1997). Developmental of the child's brain and behavior. In C. R. Reynolds & E. Fletcher-Jantzen (Eds.), *Handbook of clinical child neuropsychology* (2nd ed., pp. 17–41). New York: Plenum Press.

Kuchelmeister, K., Bergmann, M., & Gullotta, F. (1993). Neuropathology of lissencephalies. *Childs Nervous System, 9,* 394–399.

Lai, F. (1992). Alzheimer disease. In S. M. Pueschel & J. K. Pueschel (Eds.), *Biomedical concerns in persons with Down syndrome*. Baltimore: Paul H. Brookes.

Lainhart, J. E. (2003). Increased rate of head growth during infancy in autism. *Journal of the American Medical Association, 290,* 393–394.

Ledbetter, S. A., Kirwano, A., Dobyns, W. B., & Ledbetter, D. H. (1992). Microdeletions of chromosome 17p13 as a cause of isolated lissencephaly. *American Journal of Human Genetics, 50,* 182–189.

Leonard, C. M., Voeller, K. K., Lombardino, L. J., Morris, M. K., Hynd, G. W., Alexander, A. W., et al. (1993). Anomalous cerebral structure in dyslexia revealed with magnetic resonance imaging. *Archives of Neurology, 50,* 461–469.

Livingstone, M. S., Rosen, G. D., Drislane, F. W., & Galaburda, A. M. (1991). Physiological and anatomical evidence for a magnocellular defect in developmental dyslexia. *Proceedings of the National Academy of Science, 88,* 7943–7947.

Llorente, A., LoPresti, C. M., & Satz, P. (1997). Neuropsychological and neurobehavioral sequelae associated with pediatric HIV infection. In C. R. Reynolds & E. Fletcher-Janzen (Eds.), *Handbook of clinical child neuropsychology* (2nd ed., pp. 634–650). New York: Plenum Press.

Lorber, J., & Priestly, B. L. (1981). Children with large heads: A practical approach to diagnosis in 557 children, with special references to 109 children with megalencephaly. *Developmental Medicine and Child Neurology, 23,* 494–504.

Lubin, B. H., Cahn, S., & Scott, M. (1992). Hematologic manifestations. In S. M. Pueschel & J. K. Pueschel (Eds.), *Biomedical concerns in persons with Down syndrome*. Baltimore: Paul H. Brookes.

McLone, D. G. (1982). Congenital malformations of the brain. In R. L. McLaurin (Ed.), *Pediatric neurosurgery: Surgery of the developing nervous systems* (pp. 95–110). Orlando, FL: Grune & Stratton.

Mintz, M. (1999). Clinical features and treatment interventions for human immunodeficiency virus-associated neurologic disease in children. *Seminars in Neurology, 19,* 165–176.

Moore, B. D., III, Slopis, J. M., Jackson, E. F., DeWinter, A. E., & Leeds, N. E. (2000). Brain volume in children with neurofibromatosis type 1: Relation to neuropsychological status. *Neurology, 54,* 914–920.

Moro, F., Carrozzo, R., Veggiotti, P., Tortorella, G., Toniolo, D., Volzone, A., et al. (2002). Familial periventricular heterotopia: Missense and distal truncating mutations of the FLN1 gene. *Neurology, 58,* 916–921.

National Congenital CMV Disease Registry (1995a). Advances in CMV vaccine research. *CMV Updates, 1*(2), 1.

National Congenital CMV Disease Registry (1995b). What is CMV? *CMV Updates, 1*(1), 1.

National Congenital CMV Disease Registry. (1998). *What everyone should know about CMV* [Brochure]. Houston, TX: Author.

Nopoulos, P., Berg, S., Castellenos, X., Delgado, A., Andreasen, N. C., & Rapoport, J. L. (2000). Developmental brain anomalies in children with attention-deficit hyperactivity disorder. *Journal of Child Neurology, 15,* 102–108.

Optiz, J. M., & Holt, M. C. (1990). Microcephaly: General considerations and aids to nosology. *Journal of Craniofacial, Genetic, and Developmental Biology, 10,* 175–204.

Paciorkowski, A. R., Lerer, T., & Brunquell, P. J. (2002). Structure-function correlations in patients with malformations of cortical development. *Epilepsy and Behavior, 3,* 266–274.

Palmini, A., Andermann, F., DeGrissac, H., Tampieri, D., Robitaille, Y., Langevin, P., et al. (1993). Stages and patterns of centrifugal arrest of diffuse neuronal migration disorders. *Developmental Medicine and Child Neurology, 35,* 331–339.

Pavone, L., Rizzo, R., & Dobyns, W. B. (1993). Clinical manifestions and evaluation of isolated lissencephaly. *Childs Nervous System, 9,* 387–390.

Petersson, S., Pedersen, N. L., Schalling, M., & Lavebratt, C. (1999). Primary megalencephaly at birth and low intelligence level. *Neurology, 53,* 1254–1259.

Pinard, J.-M., Feydy, A., Carlier, R., Perez, N., Pierot, L., & Burnod, Y. (2000). Functional MRI in double cortex: Functionality of heterotopia. *Neurology, 54,* 1531–1533.

Plawner, L. L., Delgado, M. R., Miller, V. S., Levey, E. B., Kinsman, S. L., Barkovich, A. J., et al. (2002). Neuroanatomy of holoprosencaphly as predictor of function: Beyond the face predicting the brain. *Neurology, 59,* 1058–1066.

Pueschel, S. M. (1992). Phenotypic characteristics. In S. M. Pueschel & J. K. Pueschel (Eds.), *Biomedical concerns in persons with Down syndrome.* Baltimore: Paul H. Brookes.

Pueschel, S. M., & Bier, J. B. (1992). Endrocrinologic aspects. In S. M. Pueschel & J. K. Pueschel (Eds.), *Biomedical concerns in persons with Down syndrome.* Baltimore: Paul H. Brookes.

Reiter-Purtill, J., & Noll, R. B. (2003). Peer relationships of children with chronic illness. In M. C. Roberts (Ed.), *Handbook of pediatric psychology* (3rd ed., pp. 176–197). New York: Guilford Press.

Renowden, S. A., & Squier, M. (1994). Unusual magnetic resonance and neuropathological findings in hemimegalencephaly: Report of a case following hemispherectomy. *Developmental Medicine and Child Neurology, 36,* 357–361.

Rosenzweig, M. R. (2003). Effects of differential experience on the brain and behavior. *Developmental Neuropsychology, 24,* 523–540.

Schuman, W. B., & La Greca, A. M. (1999). Social correlates of chronic illness. In R. T. Brown (Ed.), *Cognitive aspects of chronic illness in children* (pp. 289–311). New York: Guilford Press.

Sener, R. N. (1993). Tuberous sclerosis associated with pachygyria CT findings. *Pediatric Radiology, 23,* 489–490.

Sessoms, A. (2003). Cytomegalovirus, congenital. In E. Fletcher-Janzen & C. R. Reynolds (Eds.), *Childhood disorders diagnostic desk reference* (pp. 164–165). Hoboken, NJ: Wiley.

Souza, J. P., Siebert, J. R., & Beckwith, J. B. (1990). An anatomic comparison of cebocephaly and ethmocephaly. *Teratology, 42,* 347–357.

Sparks, B. F., Friedman, S. D., Shaw, D. W., Aylward, E. H., Echelard, D., Artur, A. A., et al. (2002). Brain structural abnormalities in young children with autism spectrum disorder. *Neurology, 59,* 184–192.

Steinman, D. R. (2003). Angelman syndrome. In E. Fletcher-Janzen & C. R. Reynolds (Eds.), *Childhood disorders diagnostic desk reference* (pp. 40–42). Hoboken, NJ: Wiley.

Streissguth, A. P., Clarren, S. K., & Jones, K. L. (1985). National history of the fetal alcohol syndrome: A 10-year follow-up of eleven patients. *Lancet, ii,* 85–91.

Summers, J. A., & Feldman, M. A. (1999). Distinctive pattern of behavioral functioning in Angelman syndrome. *American Journal on Mental Retardation, 104*(4), 376–384.

Tramontana, M. G., & Hooper, S. R. (1997). Neuropsychology of child psychopathology. In C. R. Reynolds & E. Fletcher-Janzen (Eds.), *Handbook of clinical child neuropsychology* (2nd ed., pp. 121–139). New York: Plenum Press.

Verloes, A., Aymé, S., Gambarelli, D., Gonzalez, M., Le Merrer, M., Mulliez, N., et al. (1991). Holoprosencephaly-polydactyly (pseudotrisomy 13) syndrome: A syndrome with features of hydrolethalus and Smith-Lemli-Opitz syndromes. A collaborative multicentre study. *Journal of Medical Genetics, 28,* 297–303.

Watemberg, N., Silver, S., Harel, S., & Lerman-Sagie, T. (2002). Significance of microcephaly among children with developmental disabilities. *Journal of Child Neurology, 17,* 117–122.

Whelan, T. B., & Walker, M. L. (1997). Coping and adjustment of children with neurological disorder. In C. R. Reynolds & E. Fletcher-Jantzen (Eds.), *Handbook of clinical child neuropsychology* (2nd ed., pp. 688–711). New York: Plenum Press.

White, T., Andreasen, N. C., Nopoulos, P., & Magnotta, V. (2003). Gyrification abnormalities in childhood- and adolescent-onset schizophrenia. *Biological Psychiatry, 54,* 418–426.

Williams, C. A., Lossie, A. C., & Driscoll, D. J. (2000). *Angelman syndrome.* Retrieved May 2, 2001, from http://www.geneclinics.org/profiles/angelman/details.html.

Williamson, W. D., Desmond, M. M., LaFevers, N., Taber, L. H., Catlin, F. I., & Weaver, T. G. (1982). Symptomatic congenital cytomegalovirus. *American Journal of Diseases of Children, 136,* 902–905.

Winick, M., & Russo, P. (1969). The effect of severe early malnutrition on cellular growth of human brain. *Pediatric Research, 3,* 181–184.

Yamazaki, J. N., & Schull, W. J. (1990). Perinatal loss and neurological abnormalities among children of the atomic bomb: Nagasaki and Hiroshima revisited, 1949 to 1989. *Journal of the American Medical Association, 264,* 605–609.

# CHAPTER 5

# The Brain as a Dynamic Organ of Information Processing and Learning

CECIL R. REYNOLDS and CHRISTINE L. FRENCH

INTELLIGENCE IS A neuropsychological phenomenon. By that, we mean it is steeped in brain function, is closely associated with our biology, but is measured through behavior, as it should be. Intelligence must be manifested through behavior to be seen, to be useful, and to be measured and studied. Behavioral manifestations of intelligence may be overt or covert, although to assess the latter, we must question, observe, and make inferences from the former. In this chapter, we provide a view of intelligence from a functional, clinical perspective that we believe will be of utility in clinical practice but less of a heuristic for current research. Our intent is to relate a model of the working brain that will aid clinicians in understanding the neuropsychological dynamics of a brain that has been compromised.

We begin by reviewing several false starts that were amazingly, and unduly, influential in educational and related settings. Ultimately, we adopt a current view of Luria's theory of the working brain, integrated with research on lateral cerebral specialization, as a strong, useful paradigm for clinicians.

## CEREBRAL DOMINANCE

Cerebral dominance, as first described informally by Dax in 1836 (see Harris, 1980; Joynt & Benton, 1964; Penfield & Roberts, 1959) and later in formal presentations by Broca (1861, 1863; Harris, 1980), meant the hemisphere of the brain responsible for language functions, which is the left hemisphere for the vast

This chapter is based in part on prior work of the authors, including "The Neuropsychological Basis of Intelligence," by C. R. Reynolds, in *Neuropsychological Assessment and the School-Aged Child*, G. Hynd and J. Obrzut (Eds.), 1981, New York: Grune & Stratton; and "The Neuropsychological Basis of Intelligence Revised: Some False Starts and a Clinical Model," by C. R. Reynolds and C. L. French, in *Handbook of Forensic Neuropsychology*, A. M. Horton Jr. and L. C. Hartlage (Eds.), 2003, New York: Springer.

majority of individuals. The right hemisphere traditionally was believed to house few, if any, important cognitive functions. Throughout the history of the field of neuropsychology, investigations have focused on cerebral dominance in hopes that it would lead to an understanding of the neuropsychological basis and processes underlying human mental abilities. Cerebral dominance also has been used in some instances to refer to the establishment of lateral preference with regard to handedness, footedness, eyedness, and even earedness. Research over the past several decades has presented serious challenges to this traditional approach to the neuropsychology of intelligence and the general organization of the brain as an information-processing model. Past concepts of the relationship between lateral preference and other indices of cerebral dominance have been discarded as more contemporary concepts are introduced.

## LATERAL PREFERENCE AND CEREBRAL DOMINANCE

Supporters of lateral preference theory assume that cerebral dominance can be determined by observing or measuring motoric and sensory preferences. Lateral preference is distinct from cerebral dominance in that it is voluntary and involves the peripheral nervous system, whereas individuals have no input regarding their cerebral dominance and central nervous system functioning (Beaton, 2003; Obrzut & Obrzut, 1982). Although some researchers would like to think otherwise, it must be noted that the relationship between handedness or other lateral preference and cerebral dominance can never be directly espied, but only inferred from performance on particular measures or as reported by the individual (Beaumont, 1997).

Lateral preference and its relationship to cerebral dominance and language functions has been a concern of researchers and theoreticians for some time. Handedness is indeed the most ubiquitously investigated area of lateral preference, with footedness, eyedness, and, more recently, earedness quickly gaining in popularity. In fact, some researchers have attempted to use facedness as a measure of lateral preference (Borod, Caron, & Koff, 1981). Neurologists, psychologists, and others interested in the field of neuropsychology, with particular emphasis on using lateral preference to predict cerebral dominance, are finding conflicting and often insignificant results based on their investigations (e.g., Beaumont, 1997; Brown & Taylor, 1988; Coren, 1993; Coren & Porac, 1982; DiNuovo & Buono, 1997; Eisenmann, 1993; Grouios, Sakadami, Poderi, & Alevriadou, 1999; Rider, Imwold, & Griffin, 1985; Strauss, 1986).

Handedness itself has been studied extensively since at least the sixteenth century, and theories of how handedness develops abound. Beaton (2003) provides an excellent review of the many different theories, ranging from very simple to far-fetched, supporting right-hand dominance and its relationship to cerebral lateralization. Some of the hypotheses that argue for right-hand dominance include the following: the right hand was used as the offensive hand in battle, while the left hand held the shield to protect the heart; there is better blood supply to the left hemisphere, thereby making the contralateral motor functions more adept than those on the ipsalateral side; right-hand dominance counterbalances the body's center of gravity in the left side of the body; as a result of developmental instability, even in symmetric organisms, one side of the body will be larger or stronger than the other side; and early cerebral insult causes the left hemisphere to be more dominant than the right (see Beaton, 2003; Eckhert & Leonard, 2003).

In an early review, Harris (1980) discussed five categories of theories of handedness that have been proffered since the 1400s, a number of which stretch the imagination rather vigorously. These categories included structural asymmetry (visceral imbalance, blood flow, weight and density of the cerebral hemispheres, arm length, etc.); positional asymmetry (orientation of infant at time of birth or while in the womb); heredity; cultural conditioning (arm used to carry infants, carrying of war shield in left hand to protect heart, etc.); and the ambidextral culture (a movement begun in the late 1800s that proposed humans were "either-handed" and, as such movements seem to do, actually started an educational craze of training pupils to be ambidextrous). Though it now appears that handedness is a preordained, genetic function for most individuals (Saudino & McManus, 1998), deviations from the predetermined state can occur under a variety of conditions and are likely the result of an individual's neurobiology as well as the environment (see Beaton, 2003; Hoosain, 1990; Porac, Rees, & Buller, 1990). The issue of precisely how and why handedness develops as it does and its subsequent effects on the study of brain-behavior relationships is far from being settled (Annett, 1972; Boklage, 1978; Fuller, 1978; Grouios et al., 1999; Hardyck & Petrinovich, 1977; Harris, 1990; Herron, 1980; Morgan & Corballis, 1978; Robison, Block, Boudreaux, & Flora, 1999; Schwartz, 1990; Yeo, Gangestad, & Daniel, 1993).

Eyedness and earedness are even more complex phenomena than handedness and are not as simple to measure or equate with other indices of lateral preference. During the past 2 decades, earedness and eyedness have become sensory indices by which investigators have attempted to measure lateral preference and, consequently, cerebral dominance. With regard to eyedness, rather than each eye being under the principal control of a single cerebral hemisphere, each hemisphere processes visual information from the contralateral visual hemifield of each eye. In view of the complexity of the eyedness phenomenon, it is not surprising to note the disappointing results of numerous studies that have attempted to relate consistency of eye-hand preference in individuals (Balow, 1963; Balow & Balow, 1964; Brown & Taylor, 1988; Coleman & Deutsch, 1964; Hillerich, 1964; Metalis & Niemiec, 1984; Polemikos & Papaeliou, 2000; Robison et al., 1999; Strauss, 1986). Similarly, the facility with which earedness is measured is troublesome because it is not something that people are as familiar with compared to their general knowledge of which hand they prefer. Reiß and Reiß (2000) discussed the various ways in which earedness has been measured, noting that some investigators have relied not on ear preference, but on relative proficiency of the ears to perform their designed tasks. Proficiency of the right ear does not necessarily mean that the right ear is the preferred ear, therefore contaminating the data and complicating interpretation. Furthermore, ear preference is often measured by means of a self-report inventory (see Coren, 1993; Mandal, Pandey, Singh, & Asthana, 1992; Polemikos & Papaeliou, 2000; Saudino & McManus, 1998; Strauss, 1986), therefore introducing additional elements of error.

Some may assume that as the majority of individuals are right-handed, those same individuals would therefore demonstrate left hemisphere dominance, which coincides with the contralateral hand preference theories (Dean & Reynolds, 1997). Notably, reviews of the literature have indicated that in almost all people, the left hemisphere is the dominant hemisphere for symbolic language and speech regardless of the handedness of the subject (Bauer & Wepman, 1955; Coren & Porac, 1982; Strauss, 1986; White, 1969). Some exceptions have been noted, however (Lewis & Harris, 1990; McKeever, 1990). Witelson (1980) and others (Beaton, 2003; Coren & Porac, 1982; Eckhert & Leonard, 2003; Hartlage & Gage, 1997) conclude that left-handedness may be associated with a lesser degree of cerebral specialization for speech and language. Dysphasia associated with right hemisphere lesions in both right- and left-handers has also been reported (e.g., Newcombe & Ratcliff, 1973). Geffen (1978) reports that as many as 6% of normal right-handers have other than left hemisphere specialization for speech. Beaton (2003) noted these incidences of "crossed aphasia," in which individuals with right-hand dominance do not demonstrate language lateralized in the left hemisphere. It is apparent that handedness is not always the best indicator of hemispheric specialization.

Problems with using motoric and sensory indices as measures of cerebral dominance stem from disagreements about how these indices should be measured. Research results often differ dramatically depending on how these indices are measured. With regard to handedness, some researchers approach it from a dichotomous perspective: Individuals are considered right-handed or non-right-handed. Other researchers define right, left, and either or no preference as categories for the study of handedness. Early dichotomous measures attempted to assess an individual's pencil grip and posture of the hand to determine lateral preference (Beaton, 2003).

More recently, handedness (and hence, lateral preference) has come to be considered a continuous variable (Annett, 1972; Beaton, 2003). Subsequently, a variety of efforts have been made to measure lateral preference as a continuous variable. These measures include the use of manual tapping-speed instruments (e.g., Peters & Durding, 1978), eye-dominance wands (e.g., Robison et al., 1999), hole-in-the-hand techniques (e.g., Robison et al., 1999), other demonstration techniques (e.g., Brown & Taylor, 1988; Osburn & Klingsporn, 1998), and self-report inventories, such as the Lateral Preference Inventory and other questionnaires questioning hand, eye, and foot preference for a series of activities (e.g., Coren, 1993; Dean & Kulhavy, 1977; Dean & Reynolds, 1997; Strauss, 1986). Even percentage of time each hand is used for a task has been used as a method for determining lateral preference (Hartlage & Gage, 1997). It appears that measures assessing individuals' hand or eye preference by having them perform tasks (e.g., throwing a ball or looking through a peephole) would result in a more valid and reliable assessment of lateral preference. Presumably, measures of lateral preference based on self-report leave room for error and inaccurate results (see Beaton, 2003; Eisenman, 1993). Truly, how many individuals know which eye they would use to look through the sight of a rifle or which ear they would use to eavesdrop through a closed door? Beaton (2003) indicates that self-report inventories of hand preference are likely less predictive of true hand dominance as measured by objective measures of handedness, especially in self-reported left-handed individuals. Beaton argues that left-hand-dominant individuals tend to use their right hand with more frequency in comparison to right-handed individuals' use of their left hand. If one is to assume that hand preference truly represents lateral preference and language localization, this observation lends support to the greater frequency of mixed-hemisphere language dominance in left-handed individuals.

A number of motor-based programs intended to affect brain-behavior relationships have been developed over the years. Most of these programs assume that the failure to establish hand (and thus cerebral) dominance or consistent lateral preference is an underlying cause of learning or intellectual deficits. The first such program we have located apparently was a physical exercise therapy program by

Buzzard (1882) for the treatment of aphasia based on the theory that the various exercises employed would cause the right hemisphere to develop a "convolution for speech." Probably the most influential programs of this nature in American education have been those of Orton and of Doman and Delacato. Though the Doman and Delacato methods have been principally designed from the maxim "Ontogeny recapitulates phylogeny," the notion of cerebral dominance remains central to their theory of brain function and intelligence. Other theories of brain-behavior relationships have affected professional practices in a number of fields (see Harris, 1980; Zarske, 1982).

## SAMUEL T. ORTON'S THEORY

Orton's theory and writings (1925, 1928, 1931, 1937) have had marked effects on remedial practices in education, many of which remain in use today. However, few employing Orton-based techniques can even begin to explain his theory. Orton's theory of cerebral dominance and reading disability was novel for his time (Obrzut & Obrzut, 1982). He based his theory of cerebral dominance and learning (particularly reading) on the structural symmetry of the brain (though it is now widely known that the human brain does not display perfect morphological or structural symmetry, and it shows sexual dimorphism as well), and he assumed that any event recorded in one hemisphere was recorded in its mirror image in the opposite hemisphere. The dominant, or major, hemisphere was thought to record perceptual events in their correct spatial orientation. The reversals exhibited by dyslexic children were therefore believed to result from competition with the mirror images available in the nondominant, or minor, hemisphere. Although these hypotheses are not nearly as common at present, others continue to support the theory of greater learning, especially reading, difficulties and lower verbal ability in individuals who are not right-hand-dominant (Eckhert & Leonard, 2003). With incomplete, unestablished, or mixed dominance (as determined by lateral prefer-ence), the frequency of reversals occurring would be substantially greater due to the intrusion of the minor hemisphere into the process than when a single hemi-sphere exhibits clear, dominant control over cognitive functions. Orton's (1931) as-sertions essentially represent a storage or retrieval problem and *not* a problem of initial perception, as many believe.

Although initially accepted, the theoretical basis of Orton's position has been seriously questioned by Corballis and Beale (1976). As part of their convincing ar-gument, Corballis and Beale put forth that Orton was wrong in his basic assump-tions that the brain could not possibly respond to stimuli in a mirror-opposite way. Further negating Orton's theoretical basis, evidence proliferated throughout the past century supporting the view that there is no clear relationship between lateral preference (handedness, footedness, eyedness, and earedness) and cere-bral dominance (Belmont & Birch, 1963; Benton, 1955, 1959; Brysbaert, 1994; Coren & Porac, 1982; DiNuovo & Buono, 1997; Eisenman, 1993; Hardyck & Petri-novich, 1977; Hardyck, Petrinovich, & Goldman, 1976; Levy & Nagylaki, 1972; Milner, Branch, & Rasmussen, 1964; Naylor, 1980; Penfield & Roberts, 1959; Polemikos & Papaeliou, 2000; Reynolds, Hartlage, & Haak, 1980).

It is tempting to hypothesize that the lesser degree of lateralization of cogni-tive processes found with left-handers is responsible for the Orton effect. How-ever, this is contradicted by evidence related to gender differences in the degree of lateral cerebral specialization of cognitive functioning (Beaton, 2003). With regard to lateralization of verbal functions to the left hemisphere and spatial-oriented functions to the right hemisphere, males show consistently greater lateralization of function than females. Females tend to have a less rigid scheme of specialization. If less lateralization of cognitive function is associated with left-handedness and the lack of established dominance, and these two conditions are subsequently related to intellectual or cognitive dysfunctions, why do males (the more highly lateralized sex) outnumber females 4 to 1 in classes for learning-disabled children?

Dean (1979), using a self-report measure of lateral preference, found that children with higher Wechsler Intelligence Scale for Children-Revised (WISC-R) verbal IQs (VIQ) than performance IQs (PIQ) were significantly more bilateral than children with VIQ equal to PIQ and VIQ less than PIQ. The latter children tended to be more right-dominant. Orton's theory states that bilaterality underlies cognitive dysfunction in reading disabilities. However, the right-dominant children in Dean's study display the pattern of VIQ-PIQ discrepancies (PIQ greater than VIQ) that are most frequently found with samples of learning-disabled children (Anderson, Kaufman, & Kaufman, 1976; Kaufman, 1979b; Sattler, 1981; Smith, Coleman, Dokecki, & Davis, 1977; Zingale & Smith, 1978), and the bilateral children show the intellectual pattern least often associated with reading deficits.

Reynolds et al. (1980) attempted to replicate and extend Dean's (1979) findings to determine the relationship between lateral preference and intelligence-achievement discrepancies. Instead of relying on self-report studies, however, Reynolds and colleagues determined lateral preference (hand, eye, and foot) by summing each child's score on 26 neuropsychological tests that contrasted the two sides of the body. Correlations were then determined between each child's lateral preference score, verbal-performance IQ difference (with and without the sign retained), and the difference between achievement test scores (reading, spelling, and arithmetic) and each of the three WISC-R IQ scores. Of the 12 correlations generated by this method, *none* revealed any significant relationship between lateral preference and the variables described earlier. Neither was lateral preference significantly related to any of the intellectual or achievement variables when taken in isolation. Although the two studies have contradictory results, both are inconsistent with the Orton hypothesis and other traditional theories of dominance and intellectual function.

A more recent study was completed by Mayringer and Wimmer (2002). They attempted to replicate a study (Crow, Crow, Done, & Leask, 1998) that found that hemispheric indecision, as demonstrated by equal hand skill, was associated with cognitive and academic difficulties. However, results of the study indicated that there were no significant difficulties in cognitive ability, reading achievement, or spelling achievement in the presence of hemispheric indecision. These findings directly contradict Orton's theory and further cast doubt on his hypothesis.

Many researchers have offered modifications of Orton's theory since the 1930s. One modification contends that mixed cerebral dominance creates an antagonistic state of affairs, resulting in the right hemisphere fighting for control of language functions to the neglect of its normal involvement in perceptual and spatial functions. The antagonism between the two hemispheres and the subsequent loss of efficiency in perceptual and spatial functions is believed to play a major role in the development of intellectual dysfunctions during childhood. Noble (1968) has offered another, attractive alternative to Orton's proposal, yet he still relies on mirror-image perceptual transfers between hemispheres. Orton's theory and its derivatives continue to rely on the traditional notion of cerebral dominance. It now seems unlikely that measurements based on hand, eye, foot, and possibly even ear preference can bear more than a peripheral relationship to a dynamic understanding of the cognitive aspects of hemispheric functioning. Based on the theory's presupposition, a major fault of motoric and sensory indices of cerebral dominance concerns attempts to relate dominance of the motor cortex for physical activities to cortical dominance for intellectual functioning and preference for a single mode of cognitive processing. To better understand the intellectual workings of the brain, traditional concepts of dominance must give way to more contemporary notions of hemisphericity and the view of the brain as a dynamic organ (Reynolds, 1978, 1980, 1981).

## DOMAN AND DELACATO'S THEORY

The therapeutic system for children with learning disabilities or problems with motor skills (i.e., children with cerebral palsy), known as the Doman and Delacato (D-D) method, has been described principally in the writings of Delacato (1959, 1963, 1966) and can be traced directly to Orton's (1928) early writings on dominance and structural symmetry. The controversial D-D theory relies on vertical and horizontal development and organization of function in the human brain. The neuropsychological theory of D-D is based on the biogenetic principle that "ontogeny recapitulates phylogeny" and contends that if one does not follow this sequential continuum of neurological development, problems of mobility and/or communication will develop. Thus, children with learning disabilities or cerebral palsy are viewed as having inadequate neurological organization, which the D-D method contends it can ameliorate. The therapeutic methods of D-D are designed to overcome early deficiencies in development so that the optimal level and pattern of neurological organization may be achieved. In short, the goal of the D-D method is to achieve cerebral dominance, which can be accomplished only by successfully completing all prior levels of development.

Doman and Delacato maintain that there are six major functional attainments of humans: motor skills, speech, writing, reading, understanding, and stereognosis. The attainment of these skills is dependent on the individual's uninterrupted and successful neuroanatomical progress toward neurological organization. According to Zarske (1982), the D-D method is founded on an upward developmental trend through primary centers of the central nervous system (i.e., the spinal cord and cerebellum), continuing sequentially through the midbrain and forebrain. Neurological organization is complete when developmental progression extends horizontally through the neocortex.

Each higher level of functioning is dependent on successful progression through the earlier levels. The D-D theory contends that if the highest level of functioning (cerebral dominance) is incomplete or nonfunctioning, then a lower level of neurological organization dominates the intellectual behavior. The highest level of neurological organization, complete lateral cerebral dominance, is, according to Delacato (1959), what gives humans their great capacity for communication and completely sets them apart from lower animals. Unfortunately for the D-D theory of brain function and intelligence, there is evidence for cerebral dominance in other primates (Dewson, 1977; Gazzaniga, 1971; Johnson

& Gazzaniga, 1971a, 1971b; LeMay, 1976; Warren & Nonneman, 1976). In addition, the highest level of neurological organization is deemed to exist only when an individual has achieved consistency of hand, eye, and foot preference. Accordingly, the D-D method utilizes observations of lateral preference to determine an individual's level of cerebral dominance and, therefore, complete neurological organization (Zarske, 1982). As noted earlier, mixed eye-hand dominance is a common finding in children at least through age 8½ years (and likely beyond). Orton and Delacato would perhaps have fared better using a closer review of available literature. Woo and Pearson (1927), after an exhaustive study of 7,000 men, concluded that there was "no evidence whatsoever of even a correlation between ocular and manual lateralities" (p. 181). It is not unreasonable to suspect that the lack of completely consistent hand, eye, and foot preference is the rule rather than the exception, further supported by the earlier discussion of the literature regarding lateral preference.

The inherent goal of the D-D therapeutic methods is to stimulate and treat the ineffectual areas of the brain (Zarske, 1982), and treatment techniques are designed to pinpoint the level of neurological development and concentrate the remediation in that area of the brain. If a child is unable to perform the required exercises on his or her own, the patterning exercises are imposed on the child, some even during sleep, even though a series of studies with both animals and humans (Held, 1965; Held & Bossom, 1961; Held & Freedman, 1963; Held & Hein, 1963) has demonstrated the ineffectual nature of passive participation. Unfortunately for D-D supporters, the practice of passive participation is absent from modern techniques of cognitive rehabilitation. The recent work of Prigatano (2000) enumerates 13 principles of neuropsychological rehabilitation, none of which includes anything remotely related to passive participation of the affected individual. In fact, Prigatano and many others (e.g., Ben-Yishay, 2000; Braga & Campos da Paz, 2000; Christensen, 2000; Daniels-Zide & Ben-Yishay, 2000; Trexler, 2000) advocate for a comprehensive and dynamic treatment program that consists of cognitive, psychological, and neuropsychological therapeutic interventions.

As mentioned earlier, neurological development is believed to progress upward from the spinal cord through the medulla, the pons, and the midbrain (the evolutionarily older portions of the cortex) to the neocortex, resulting in lateral hemispheric dominance. Although there are any number of cogent theoretical arguments against a theory of neurological organization such as that proposed by Doman and Delacato (e.g., Bever, 1975; Kinsbourne, 1975), perhaps the more grave damage to their theory is the lack of positive results and methodological difficulties of the D-D remedial methods (for a review of these studies, see Cornish, 1970; Glass & Robbins, 1967; O'Donnell & Eisenson, 1969; Robbins, 1966). Studies touting the effectiveness of the D-D method failed to control for regression effects, randomly assign individuals to groups or conditions, and maintain equivalent experimental conditions (i.e., control and experimental groups met at different times of day, in different classrooms, and with different teachers). Such confounding variables severely restrict any interpretation of mean group differences. In fact, the conclusions of the study believed to be the best designed of all indicated that all differences found in the study were due to a Hawthorne effect!

Traditional dominance-based theories of neurological organization and intelligence find little empirical support. The relationship of dominance to motor and sensory functions can be only peripherally related to a preference for intellectual or cognitive processing of information, the forte of intelligent behavior. To cast further doubt on the functional importance of general dominance by the major hemisphere as indicated by motor and sensory indices of dominance, researchers have reported that hemispheric dominance for many cognitive tasks is quite malleable and responds to training and to the principles of reinforcement (e.g., Bever, 1975; Bever & Chiarello, 1974; Bogen, 1969; Johnson & Gazzaniga, 1971a, 1971b).

Although traditional concepts of dominance will remain an interesting area of theoretical research, reconceptualization of dominance as related to intellectual functioning is clearly necessary. Several influential theorists have developed neuropsychological models of intellectual functioning with considerably less reliance on traditional notions of cerebral dominance. Luria's theory in particular appears to hold great promise for understanding the neuropsychological basis of intelligence and for developing remedial or compensatory techniques for use with cognitively dysfunctional individuals.

## HALSTEAD'S THEORY OF BIOLOGICAL INTELLIGENCE

The early work of Halstead and associates, principally described in Halstead (1947) and Shure and Halstead (1959), has tremendously affected the development of many of the techniques and methods of clinical neuropsychology. Halstead's major thesis regarding the relationship between the brain and intelligence was published in 1947. This volume essentially reported the research of Halstead and his colleagues that began in 1935 at the Otho S. S. Sprague Memorial Institute and the Division of Psychiatry of the Department of Medicine at the University of Chicago. Halstead focused principally on the study of the cortex in relation to intelligence and more specifically on the role of the frontal lobes. (The frontal lobes also play a major role in Luria's conceptualization of intelligence.)

Halstead differentiated between biological intelligence and psychometric intelligence. He considered the latter to be what is measured by intelligence tests, specifically, the measurement of verbal abilities, including vocabulary skills, and the prediction of academic achievement (Broshek & Barth, 2000; Reitan, 1994). Halstead considered the former to be the true, innate ability of the individual. He did not want to weigh down theorists or psychometricians of his time with trying to decipher the dichotomy between the two types of intelligence. In fact, Halstead indicated that the difference between psychometric and biological intelligence could be attributed more to methodology than to true differences between the two measures of intelligence (Pallier, Roberts, & Stankov, 2000). According to Reitan (1994), Halstead considered biological intelligence best viewed as "the adaptive abilities represented by a healthy brain and nervous system" (p. 55). Halstead did not believe that measures of psychometric intelligence had the capability to denote the true state of the nervous system (Reed, 1985). In fact, Reitan noted incidences of patients with tremendous loss of brain mass continuing to score relatively high on measures of psychometric intelligence. However, an examination of the biological intelligence of these individuals would result in a greater understanding of their true capabilities. In short, Halstead conjectured that his theory of biological intelligence represented "the normal outcome of the functioning of a healthy nervous system" (Reitan, 1994, p. 56).

Halstead unquestionably realized that psychometric and biological intelligence were not independent of one another. In recognition of this, Halstead, and subsequently Reitan, routinely included a standardized test of intelligence, such as the Henmon-Nelson Tests of Mental Ability or a member of the Wechsler series of intelligence scales, in their neuropsychological test battery. Nevertheless, Halstead's research focused on determining the nature and underlying factors of biological intelligence.

From an original battery of 27 behavioral indicators (i.e., psychological tests), Halstead selected 13 measures for his study of biological intelligence. These 13 tests were selected because they yielded objective scores and because they "seemed likely to reflect some component of biological intelligence" (Halstead, 1947, p. 39). Some of the tests dropped from the larger battery were essentially personality or affective measures (e.g., Minnesota Multiphasic Personality Inventory, a modified version of the Rorschach); were one-item, dichotomously scored tests (Halstead Closure Test); or were purely sensory measures (e.g., Halstead-Brill Audiometer). Based on independent factor analyses of the correlation matrix for this set of tests, determined from the responses of a sample of what he considered normal individuals (50 adults fully recovered from a "concussive type" head injury), Halstead extracted four basic factors of biological intelligence, which he labeled C, A, P, and D. He hoped that these factors would help others begin to fathom the intricacy of brain-behavior relationships (Reed, 1985). Factor analyses of the data were conducted separately by Karl Holzinger and L. L. Thurstone. Each analysis produced essentially the same results. Halstead defined these four factors as follows.

### C, THE INTEGRATIVE FIELD FACTOR

Halstead considered this factor to represent an individual's experiences (Reitan, 1994). Central to this factor is the ability to adapt to new situations and to integrate new information and stimuli that were not a part of one's previous experiences in order to form new symbols and frameworks or orientation when necessary. The C factor creates order from the chaos of new stimuli from the external world constantly bombarding one and gives these stimuli an internal referent. The C factor was characterized in Halstead's initial factor analysis by large loadings by the Halstead Category Test, the Henmon-Nelson Tests of Mental Ability, the Speech-Sounds Perception Test, the Halstead Finger Oscillation Test, and the Halstead Time-Sense Test.

### A, THE ABSTRACTION FACTOR

The A factor represents Halstead's conceptualization of a basic factor of intelligence and the aptitude for abstraction. Abstraction is the ability to draw meaning from a series of events, to hold ideas apart from their concrete referents, and to grasp essential similarities in the face of apparent differences and vice versa without the use or reliance on past experience. It also includes the ability to draw a principle or set of rules governing a series of seemingly unconnected stimuli. The A factor was characterized in Halstead's initial factor analysis by large loadings from the Carlo Hollow-Square Performance Test for Intelligence, the Halstead Category Test, the Halstead Tactual Performance Test (memory component), and the Halstead Tactual Performance Test (localization component).

### P, THE POWER FACTOR

Halstead believed P to represent the undistorted power factor of the functioning brain and related it analogously to the reserve power available to an amplifier not already functioning at peak wattage. Halstead's description of the P factor relies heavily on flicker-fusion research and indicates that the brain with more available power (P) has a higher critical fusion frequency. For Halstead, P was certainly related to the electrical facilitation of cognition (mentation) in the brain and was controlled principally through the frontal lobes. Halstead also proposed some relationships between affect and its effects on intelligence and the P factor. According to Reitan (1994), P was critical in individuals' expression of their biological intelligence. Banich (2003) further expands on the idea of the brain's capacity to efficiently and adequately process information. The P factor was characterized in Halstead's factor analytic study by large loadings by the Halstead Flicker-Fusion Test, the Halstead Tactual Performance Test (recall component), the Halstead Dynamic Visual Field Test (central form), and the Halstead Dynamic Visual Field Test (central color).

## D, THE DIRECTIONAL FACTOR

The D factor was, in Halstead's interpretation, the most difficult of his biological factors of intelligence to legitimize statistically through factor analysis. Nevertheless, Halstead seemed satisfied with its existence and determined that D was the "medium of exteriorization of intelligence, either from within or from without the individual" (1947, p. 84). Intelligence must be expressed, whether through reading, writing, listening, speaking, composing, or painting, and Halstead believed that D represented the modality of expression of intelligence. In one sense, it was also an attentional factor, for to utilize a modality, one must be able to focus or direct the energy and power of thought toward that modality. Banich (2003) supports this idea of attentional capacities and executive functioning as resulting directly from hemispheric interaction. Results of the factor analysis showed D to be characterized by large loadings by the Halstead Tactual Performance Test (speed component) and the Halstead Dynamic Visual Field Test (peripheral component). A potentially important secondary loading was apparent by the Halstead Tactual Performance Test (incidental localization component). In the normally functioning human brain, Halstead believed that D faded into the background of the other three factors except when a new medium of expression was encountered.

As should be clear by now, C, A, and P were considered the process factors of intelligence and D the factor through which externalization of these processes occurred. In his subsequent research with brain-injured individuals, Halstead observed these various factors in operation and believed that he had thereby demonstrated their biological validity. Unfortunately, no replications of Thurstone and Holzinger's factor analysis have been completed (Broshek & Barth, 2000; Reitan, 1994), therefore limiting the validity for the concept of biological intelligence. Once having delineated these factors, Halstead and his associates turned their attention to the localization of intelligence in the brain and to the role of these four factors in various types of psychopathology. It is from this latter work that much of current clinical neuropsychology has grown.

The next step in Halstead's validation of his factors of biological intelligence was the development of the now well-known Halstead Impairment Index, which was created by collecting the 10 best discriminating tests into a battery. Halstead reasoned that if C, A, P, and D were indeed biological factors of intelligence, then individuals with known neuropathology should suffer impairment in their ability to perform tasks representing these factors. Halstead set out to investigate the neuroanatomical localization of biological intelligence as indicated by the Impairment Index.

Based on a series of findings with neurosurgical patients for whom the exact site of brain lesion was known, Halstead concluded that the factors of biological intelligence were principally controlled through the frontal lobes. Only a very slight difference occurred between left and right frontal lesions; left-sided lesions caused only slightly greater impairment than did right-sided lesions. Frontal lesions (typically in the form of lobotomy) resulted in an impairment index 6 times that of normal controls and 3 times that of nonfrontal lesions. The least amount of impairment occurred with occipital lesions, followed by parietal and temporal lesions, though parietal and temporal lesions were very similar in the degree of impairment produced. Although partial replication of these results was achieved by Shure and Halstead (1959), the strong relationship between the frontal lobes and Halstead's Impairment Index has not been validated in subsequent research (Reitan, 1975, 1994). However, Halstead retained his interest in the localization of the factors of biological intelligence.

Shortly after the publication of Halstead's 1947 monograph, Reitan and others recognized the need for a more diverse array of neuropsychological tests to make more exact and stringent diagnoses of neuropathology. It is important to remember that although Halstead apparently engaged in diagnosing various neurological disorders on the basis of performance on his battery of tests (Reitan, 1975), he was trained as an experimental physiological psychologist and was principally interested in developing a broad theory of the biology of behavior and concomitant brain-behavior relationships, an obvious precursor to the present-day practice of neuropsychology.

Reitan subsequently turned to highly empirical methods in an almost atheoretical fashion in expanding Halstead's original battery of tests. Reitan never developed a comprehensive theory of the biological basis of intelligence, though his contributions to the applied field of clinical neuropsychological assessment have been many and of great significance. One of these contributions included laying a foundation for test validation studies. Reitan completed extensive blind studies using test results, which were later reviewed and corroborated by others in the field of neuropsychology (Broshek & Barth, 2000; Reitan, 1994). Reitan also modified and updated the test battery and made headway in research based on brain-behavior relationships (Reed, 1985).

In addition, Reitan (1964a) engaged in some evaluation of Halstead's theory. In evaluating the effects of cerebral lesions of various locations in the cortex, Reitan concluded that the consensus of data indicated that non-frontal lobe lesions are most frequently associated with specific types of disorders while frontal lobe lesions result in more general disturbances that are difficult to specify in detail. Reitan apparently felt that these findings disconfirmed Halstead's notion of the frontal lobes as the principal anatomical site of biological intelligence (Reitan, 1975), yet this is not necessarily the case. If one conceptualizes intelligence as the coordinating and planning activity of the brain (the executive branch) and as directing the processing activities of other areas, then damage to the frontal lobes should produce a more generalized, diverse set of disorders.

Reitan's work (1955, 1964a, 1964b, 1966, 1975; Reitan & Davison, 1974; Wheeler & Reitan, 1962) has caused researchers and clinicians to appreciate the complexities of elaborating a theory of brain function and intelligence from deficits in the higher cognitive processes following brain lesions. Considerable research has been done with the Halstead-Reitan Neuropsychological Test Battery (HRNTB) regarding brain-behavior relationships (Reitan & Wolfson, 1996). In reviewing this research as it applies to clinical assessment and the development of a comprehensive theory of the neuropsychological basis of intelligence, one must keep in mind the methodological difficulties inherent in this line of research. Many of the methodological problems discussed early by Shure and Halstead (1959) remain. Additionally, researchers have not been vigilant in their reporting of subject descriptions in research utilizing the HRNTB (Hevern, 1980; Parsons & Prigatano, 1978), which is unfortunate because a variety of demographic variables are known to affect the outcome of neuropsychological assessment (Golden, Espe-Pfeifer, & Wachsler-Felder, 2000; Hevern, 1980; Parsons & Prigatano, 1978; Reynolds & Gutkin, 1979). Nevertheless, the HRNTB continues to be a widely used neuropsychological assessment measure, and multiple interpretive models add power to its clinical use (Nussbaum & Bigler, 1997).

A thorough assessment of Halstead's theory of biological intelligence is not yet available. It appears to have fallen by the wayside at present in favor of number-crunching empiricism. A strong theory of the neuropsychological basis of intelligence is requisite to important advances in the field.

## THE LURIA MODEL: A KEY TO CLINICAL UNDERSTANDING

Alexander R. Luria was a Russian neuropsychologist who was a major force in the development of the scientific discipline of neuropsychology. Although his research spans some 4 decades, his influence on American neuropsychology was minimal until around the mid-1960s. Luria was a prolific researcher and published extensively throughout his career, which ended with his death in 1977. His later work continued to be published into 1979. In fact, according to Tupper (1999), Luria's works continue to be the most popular books in the field of neuropsychology. Luria's major theoretical contributions to understanding the neuropsychological basis of intelligence are well summarized in his publications of 1961, 1964, 1966, 1969, 1970, and 1973. One of the major contributions he made to the field of neuropsychology was the concept of the functional system (Golden et al., 1982). Like Halstead, Luria believed the frontal lobes of humans to play a major role in intelligence. Luria's position with respect to frontal lobes is well reflected in the title of his 1969 address to the 19th International Congress of Psychology, "Cerebral Organization of Conscious Acts: A Frontal Lobe Function." Much of the following presentation is taken from these references to Luria's work and represents a decades' old conceptualization that remains among the most, if not the most (in our view), clinically useful conceptualizations of brain function.

Luria was greatly influenced in his clinical and experimental research in neuropsychology by the well-known Soviet psychologist L. S. Vygotski. Throughout Luria's work, one finds that he relied extensively on a clinical research methodology not at all unlike the *methodé clinique* of Piaget, in addition to his more formalized experimental research. In developing his clinical research methods, Luria designed a rich battery of neuropsychological tests that he used to obtain an essentially qualitative evaluation of an individual's neurological status and integrity. Indeed, it has been the qualitative (often seen as descriptive or subjective; Golden, Purisch, & Hammeke, 1979; Spiers, 1982; Tupper, 1999) nature of Luria's neuropsychological examination that has fostered the reluctance to adopt his techniques in American neuropsychology. However, after Luria's death, a standardized version of the Luria battery was developed and made available for experimental and clinical use in the United States (Golden et al., 1979). A children's version of this battery, the Luria Nebraska Neuropsychological Battery-Children's Revision, also has been developed (Golden, 1987). However, the quantification and standardization of Luria's assessment techniques has been criticized as tending to remove much of the richness that was the essence of Luria's methods. A clear understanding of Luria's theory of the functioning organization of the brain and an appreciation for the brain as a dynamic organ should avert the loss of information through the standardization of his methods. Standardization of such methods has a number of advantages that should add to the richness of information about brain function that is available (Golden et al., 1982). However, there still remains in North American psychology a general compulsion toward psychometrically sound, data-driven, quantitative research and assessment procedures, whereas the procedures proffered by Luria were driven by theory and flexibility and were qualitative in nature (Tupper, 1999).

Luria conceptualized the working brain as organized into three major components, which he termed "blocks of the brain." The first block of the brain is composed of the brainstem, including the reticular formation, the midbrain, pons, and medulla. The second block of the brain is essentially composed of the parietal, occipital, and temporal lobes, the sections of the brain frequently referred to as the association areas of the cortex. The third block of the brain is essentially composed of the remaining area of the cortex anterior to the central sulcus and the sensorimotor strip, principally the frontal lobes. It is important to note that the three blocks of the brain do not operate independently of each other. In fact, there is a dynamic interaction between the areas, and any weakness in one area of the brain may interact with and affect the functioning of the other areas (Languis & Miller, 1992; Reynolds, 1981). Before turning to the localization of function within each of the three blocks of the brain, it is important to fully understand the concept of dynamic localization of function in the human brain.

The sensory and motor functions of the brain have highly specific functional localizations. The locations of these functions have been mapped in precise and meticulous detail by neurologists and psychologists over the past decade. Higher-order, complex mental processes require the coordination of many areas of the brain and are not conducive to such rigid or narrow localization of function. In essence, Luria's theory of functional localization may be summed up as structure following function (Languis & Miller, 1992). There is not a direct correspondence between an area of the brain and a specific behavior (Reynolds, 1981). It is well known, for example, that impairment and lesions of the right parietal lobe result in extreme difficulty with the Block Design subtest of the Wechsler series, yet it is incorrect to consider Block Design performance as being localized to the right parietal lobe. Extensive damage to portions of the frontal or occipital lobes may also produce impaired performance on this task. Yet, if the parietal lobe remained intact, the *nature* of the difficulty on this task would change as a function of the localization of any neuropathology. Cortical specialization for cognitive tasks is not task- or stimulus-specific; it is much more process-specific, though processing specialization is gross, and any specific type of information processing itself requires coordination of several anatomical sections of the cortex. Also, functional localization of cognitive processes (as opposed to purely sensorimotor processes) more closely resembles the integrative, synergistic, and dynamic activities of the brain than would be achieved by a one-to-one correspondence of behaviors to brain areas (Ashman & Das, 1980).

The notion of the brain as a dynamic functional system is by no means a new idea. Hughlings Jackson presented a similar premise in the nineteenth century, as did Monakow in the early twentieth century. The concept of dynamic localization of higher cognitive processes has perhaps been best explained by Luria (1964). According to Luria, the higher mental processes are formed as a function of people's activity in the process of communication with one another and represent "*complex functional systems* based on jointly working zones of the brain cortex" (p. 11). Once one conceptualizes the brain as an interdependent systemic network, "it becomes completely understandable that a higher (mental) function may suffer as a result of the destruction of *any link which is a part of the structure of a complex functional system* and . . . may be disturbed even when the centers differ greatly in localization" (pp. 11–12). Banich (2003) further supports this idea of the greater breadth of hemispheric interactions during complex cognitive tasks. Central to this approach is the contention that each link in the system has a particular function in the processing of the problem at hand. Hence,

> when one or another link has been lost, the whole functional system will be disturbed in a particular way, and symptoms of disturbance of one or another higher (mental) function will have a *completely different structure, depending on the location of the damage.* (Luria, 1964, p. 12)

By thoroughly analyzing the nature of the difficulty experienced in performing a task such as reading, writing, or counting, one may determine the localizing significance of the observed disturbance. It was for this purpose that Luria developed his qualitative neuropsychological assessment methods. Keeping the concept of dynamic functional localization in mind, it is appropriate to turn to a functional appraisal of Luria's three blocks of the brain.

## Block 1

The first block of the brain, often called the arousal and attention unit, is responsible for regulating the energy level and tone of all other portions of the cortex. In serving this regulatory function, the first block provides a stable basis for the conscious organism to organize the various other functions and processes of the brain. The regulatory functions are especially controlled by the reticular formation, the posterior hypothalamus, and the brainstem, portions of which control the waking center of the brain. The reticular formation is responsible for the relative levels of arousal or activation found at any given time in the cortex. The first block of the brain, then, regulates consciousness, and any interruption of impulses from the first block of the brain to the cortex can result in coma or a lowering of the level of consciousness in the cortex, giving rise to confused behavior characterized by potentially bizarre associations and great difficulty in stimulus distinction. The subjective experience is not unlike alcohol- or barbiturate-induced intoxication. Though involved in all processes of the brain, the first block seems especially important in the maintenance of Halstead's P factor.

## BLOCK 2

The second block is undoubtedly the most widely and frequently researched area of the brain. It is essentially the area posterior to the central sulcus and is composed principally of the parietal, occipital, and temporal lobes. It is sometimes called the sensory input and integration unit. Most of the (simultaneous or successive) cognitive information processing of the brain, including receiving, processing, and storing of information, occurs in the second block. According to Luria's conceptualization, the various areas of block 2 that are responsible for the analysis and encoding of specific types of stimuli (e.g., auditory in the temporal region, visual or optic in the occipital region, and kinesthetic or tactile in the parietal lobe) are each organized into three hierarchical zones. The *primary zone* of each area is responsible for sorting and recording incoming sensory organization. Lesions or dysfunction in this area may result in confabulation and gap filling (Joseph, 1996). The *secondary zone* organizes and codes information from the primary zone. Damage in the secondary zone may result in agnosias and aphasias (Joseph, 1996). The *tertiary zone* is where data are merged from multiple sources of input and collated as the basis for organizing complex behavioral responses. Damage to this area may result in apraxia, anomia, impairment in temporal-sequential motor control, and visual-spatial neglect (Joseph, 1996).

Damage to the second block of the brain produces the most specific of all behavior changes. For example, damage to the primary zone of the acoustic area of the second block may result in a loss of hearing but is highly unlikely to have any direct effect on the complex, higher mental processes of the brain. As one moves up the hierarchy of processing, however, alterations in behavior become more complex and less predictable. It is in the second block of the brain that the principal information-processing functions of the brain are carried out. The brain essentially uses two methods of processing information, one a sequential, successive method and the other a method of simultaneous synthesis of information. These two modes of cognitive processing are explored further when the work of Kaufman and Kaufman (1983) and Naglieri and Das (1996) is examined.

## BLOCK 3

"The third block of the brain, comprising the frontal lobes, is involved in the formation of intentions and programs for behavior" (Luria, 1970, p. 68). It is often called the executive planning and organizing unit and is dependent on the successful operation of the first and second blocks of the brain (Obrzut & Obrzut, 1982). The frontal lobes organize and implement conscious actions on the part of an individual. As Luria points out, the frontal lobes have no responsibility for simple sensory or motor functions. They are, however, intimately involved in every complex, higher-order behavior of humans.

The frontal lobes are also closely tied to the reticular formation and are involved in the activation and regulation of the remainder of the cortex. The frontal lobes serve an important function in regulating and focusing attention in the brain. It is well known that intense anxiety interferes with complex thought and behavior and can produce behavior that appears confused. As a subjective state, anxiety appears to be experienced in the frontal lobes, causing global disruptions of behavior. Violent or highly active victims of psychosis who experience hallucinations are, as a rule, intensely anxious. Treatment of such patients through the psychosurgical process of frontal lobotomy (the severing of nerve fibers between the frontal lobes and the first block of the brain, particularly the thalamus, resulting in considerable bilateral lesions to the frontal lobes) does not effectively stop hallucinations or many other psychotic symptoms, but does calm the patient, apparently through reducing the intense anxiety promulgated by the psychotic symptomatology. These patients frequently become listless, however, seeming to lose their will to behave. The frontal lobotomy causes the loss of ability to plan, organize, and execute complex behavior functions due to the tremendous loss of communication between the third block and the other blocks of the brain.

The role of the frontal lobes in directing the attentional focus of the association areas also is extremely important. Interaction between the two hemispheres of the frontal lobe helps to modulate general attentional capacities; they also aid in selective attention tasks (Banich, 2003). The direction of attention is closely related to the method by which information is processed in the brain (simultaneous or successive). Kinsbourne (1978a, 1978b, 1997) believes that an attentional bias between the hemispheres is one potential basis for hemispheric differences and specialization of processing. Attentional biases in the receipt of sensory information are well documented. These attentional biases are quite likely mediated by the frontal lobes through interaction with the first block of the brain, though the second block is where the principal processing takes place. The view of the frontal lobes as the executive branch of intelligence in the human brain is neither new nor unique to Luria's model. It will be recalled that Halstead (1947) considered the frontal lobes to be the central anatomical locus of intelligence. The frontal lobes play an important role in Pribam's (1971) theory of brain function (though this is not surprising, as Pribam spent 6 months in Luria's laboratory studying patients with frontal lobe damage). Intelligent behavior, in the Luria model, is the product of the dynamic interplay of the three blocks of the brain, with activation, regulation, and planning of conscious acts falling to the frontal lobes.

SIMULTANEOUS AND SUCCESSIVE COGNITIVE PROCESSES

As Naglieri, Kamphaus, and Kaufman (1983) and Gunnison, Kaufman, and Kaufman (1982) noted, the field of psychology has a history replete with dichotomies, with the simultaneous-successive dichotomy enduring into theoretical formulations and assessment practices today. Luria's theory of cognitive processing arose out of a need to interpret the results of studies that other theories of hierarchical cognitive processing could not explain (Klich, 1987). Luria's model of successive and simultaneous processing, as indicated, is not hierarchical. Rather, the two modes of cognitive processing are complementary, working together for the individual to most efficiently and effectively accomplish tasks throughout the day (Hunt, 1980). Simultaneous and successive (or sequential) cognitive processes are the two principle information-processing strategies of the second block of the brain and therefore are central to any neuropsychological theory of intelligence.

These two processes seem to be deployed primarily in the secondary and tertiary zones of block 2 of Luria's model. Simultaneous and successive processes are neither modality- nor stimulus-specific (Ashman & Das, 1980; McCallum & Merritt, 1983). Verbal and nonverbal information may be processed either simultaneously or successively (Watters & English, 1995). Any type of stimulus information can be processed through simultaneous or successive means; however, certain functions are processed much more efficiently through one process than the other (Banich, 2003). Particularly for young children whose preferential means of cognitive processing is not yet solidified, the means of cognitive processing an individual uses for a task may change depending on the task demands, genetic predisposition, cultural traditions, the individual's level of attention to the task, and the individual's preferred means of completing the task (Cumming & Rodda, 1985; Hall, Gregory, Billinger, & Fisher, 1988; McCallum & Merritt, 1983; Watters & English, 1995; Willis, 1985). Though there are always exceptions to any rule, language is processed at peak efficiency through successive methods, in other words, placing the elements of the composition into a linear sequence, each part of which is dependent on its preceding component. Figure copying and solving visual analogies are examples of problems most efficiently solved through simultaneous-processing strategies.

*Simultaneous Processing*   As described by Das, Kirby, and Jarman (1979), "Simultaneous integration refers to the synthesis of separate elements into groups, these groups often taking on spatial overtones. The essential nature of this sort of processing is that any portion of the result is at once surveyable without dependence upon its position in the whole" (p. 49). This type of processing is linked to the occipital and parietal lobes of the brain, usually in the right hemisphere (Naglieri et al., 1983; Willis, 1985). The creation of a mental image, conversations regarding relationships (i.e., sister's mother, greater than), inductive reasoning, Raven's Matrices, figure-copying tests, the Graham-Kendall Memory-for-Designs Test, and Backward Digit Span and Similarities subtests of the Wechsler scales are excellent examples of simultaneous integration of stimuli (Das et al., 1979; Kirby & Das, 1977; Watters & English, 1995).

*Successive Processing*   Das et al. (1979) describe successive (or sequential) information processing as the "processing of information in a serial order. The important distinction between this type of information processing and simultaneous processing is that in successive processing the system is not totally surveyable at any point in time. Rather, a system of cues consecutively activates the components" (p. 52). This type of processing is linked to the frontotemporal areas of the brain, usually in the left hemisphere (Naglieri et al., 1983; Willis, 1985). Successive information processing is linear and sequential, with information being dealt with in an interdependent serial order. The syntactical structure of language makes it a task most efficiently processed through successive methods (although the concept behind the words is of a simultaneous nature), as do tests requiring the maintenance of a temporal order of input of information for the generation of an appropriate response. Other tasks that are most efficiently completed by successive means include digit-span tests (forward only), sequential visual short-term memory tests, and serial recall tests. Although it is obvious that all of these tasks are memory tests, extensive research (Das et al., 1979) indicates that these tests do not simply define a memory factor. These memory tasks all require the maintenance of a temporal order. In other words, each idea is directly related to the preceding and the following ideas (Gunnison et al., 1982).

## MEASURES OF INTELLIGENCE AND THE LURIA MODEL

With the advent of the Kaufman Assessment Battery for Children (K-ABC; Kaufman & Kaufman, 1983) and the more recent Cognitive Assessment System (CAS; Naglieri & Das, 1996), the sequential and simultaneous cognitive processing model has earned a notable position in the assessment field. Both measures are grounded in a convergence of theory and research (Kamphaus, 1993; Kamphaus & Reynolds, 1984, 1987; Naglieri & Das, 1990) and were developed based on Luria's theoretical framework of cerebral specialization and functional localization (Daleo et al., 1999; Reynolds, Kamphaus, Rosenthal, & Hiemenz, 1997).

Kaufman and Kaufman were the first to present a practical assessment measure that utilized the simultaneous-successive theory proposed by Luria. Reynolds and colleagues (Reynolds et al., 1997) argued that a child must have the mental ability to synthesize information, regardless of the mode of presentation (spatial or analogic), to most efficiently perform the simultaneous processing tasks on the K-ABC. Likewise, a child must have the ability to arrange stimuli in a sequential order to complete tasks in the successive processing cluster. Although tasks may be completed by any means of information processing, they have been placed into their respective clusters (simultaneous or successive) based on the respective modality by which they can be solved in the most efficient manner. Now that nearly 2 decades have passed since its original publication, the K-ABC is in the process of being revised. As with the original version, the revised version of the K-ABC is sure to bring new understanding to the field of intellectual assessment.

Like the K-ABC, the CAS was designed to fit nicely with Luria's conceptualization of the three blocks of the brain (Tupper, 1999). The CAS attempts to ascertain an individual's abilities in the areas of planning, attention, and simultaneous and successive processes (Naglieri, 1997). Rather than relegating to a single score, $g$, to explain an individual's cognitive functioning, Naglieri and Das (1990) created a battery of tasks in an attempt to more adequately describe the process of intelligence. Furthermore, the authors of the test were concerned not only with the results of an individual's performance, but the process by which the task is completed (Meikamp, 2001).

## HEMISPHERICITY AND COGNITIVE PROCESSING

Hemisphericity, briefly defined, is the tendency of an individual to rely primarily on the problem-solving or information-processing style of one or the other hemisphere in the course of normal daily functions. In this theory, there is the presupposition that an individual has a preferred mode of cognitive processing and is possibly able to actively choose the mode of processing (Beaumont, Young, & McManus, 1984). It is vital to understand that hemisphericity is conceptualized as a type of dominance for an information-processing style and is independent of traditional notions of cerebral dominance and unrelated to the motorically determined lateral preference of the individual. It is a form of dominance for a style of mentation that, if the term had not already acquired an established meaning in psychology, could be described accurately as a true cognitive style. Hemisphericity, meaning the cognitive style of the two hemispheres, has also been described as modes of consciousness (Deikman, 1971; Galin, 1974). The theory of hemisphericity is utilized in a wide variety of settings beyond the field of neuropsychology (Beaumont et al., 1984).

Conflicting theories of hemisphericity abound. Allen (1983) described the theory of unilateral specialization, wherein each hemisphere performs its own unique operations, completely independent of and without integration or interference from the other hemisphere. This theory of hemispheric specialization was sparked by the research of Dax, Broca, and Hughlings Jackson (Allen, 1983; Finger & Roe, 1999). Some of the functions originally believed to occur in only one hemisphere include language, visuospatial abilities, and motor tasks. Another theory of hemisphericity is cooperative interaction, which was basically what Luria was advocating for in his theory of functional lateralization (Allen, 1983). Also known as bilateralization, cooperative interaction occurs when both hemispheres are equally capable of performing a task, although one hemisphere may be slightly better at it. Banich (2003) stated, "Dividing processing across the hemispheres can increase the overall processing capacity of the brain, suggesting that the dynamic coupling and decoupling of the hemispheres helps to modulate the allocation of attentional resources" (p. 284). The hemispheres work cooperatively, therefore integrating functions, especially on complex tasks. Whereas the unilateral specialization theory would not lend credit to the maxim "More than the sum of the parts," cooperative interaction theory does. Other models, including negative interaction (inhibition), parallel processing, and allocation, also have been touted as plausible explanations for the hemispheric processing of the brain. Indeed, some argue that parallel processing is the most efficient and plausible method of cognitive processing (Beaumont, 1997). However, it seems that Luria's model has once again proven itself as the foundation for current treatment and assessment processes. Recent reviews of cognitive processing and hemispheric specialization continue to support Luria's model (Banich, 2003; Dean & Reynolds, 1997).

The notion of a dominant or preferential mode of information processing is not new. Bogen, DeZure, TenHouten, and Marsh (1972) describe the concept of hemisphericity as defined earlier and measure relative hemispheric dependence as a ratio of performance on appositional and propositional tasks. Das et al. (1979) frequently refer to individuals who display a "habitual mode of information processing." The development of hemisphericity may occur prior to the age of 3 years, but seems well established in most children by $3\frac{1}{2}$ to 4 years of age. A variety of studies have indicated the presence of hemisphericity in adult subjects. Hemispheric specialization has begun to replace cerebral dominance as a major concept in our understanding of brain-behavior relationships. Hemisphericity (the dominant or preferential information-processing modality of an individual) holds great promise for helping to understand both normal and dysfunctional intelligence. Normally functioning individuals appear to be able to utilize the two modes of information processing separately or in conjunction with one another and possibly shift at will depending on the type of information to be processed (Gazzaniga, 1974, 1975), though such decisions are more likely to be made at an unconscious level in interaction between the stimuli to be processed and the direction of hemisphericity. At the highest level of function, the two modes of processing operate in a complementary manner, achieving maximal interhemispheric integration of processing or, in Bogen et al.'s (1972) terminology, "cerebral complementarity." For example, right-hemisphere function (simultaneous processing) is important in contributing to letter and word recognition during reading, a function handled primarily through successive processing, due to its linguistic nature, in the formative stages of learning to read (Gardiner, 1987; Gunnison et al., 1982; Kwantes & Mewhort, 1999). Highly skilled readers who have mastered the component skills of reading, making it an automatic function, demonstrate extensive use of both processes in reading (Cummins & Das, 1977).

When first learning to read, successive processing (left hemisphericity) is most important, and many children with difficulties in learning to read have problems with successive processing (Cummins & Das, 1977; Gardiner, 1987; Gunnison et al., 1982; Kwantes & Mewhort, 1999). This is also consistent with the findings of higher performance than verbal IQ in most groups of reading-disabled children discussed earlier. Performance IQ is almost certainly more closely related to the simultaneous processing of information than to successive processing, while the converse relationship holds for the verbal IQ (Bell, 1990; Bloom, 2000).

A variety of direct and indirect methods are available for measuring hemisphericity, including studies on lateral eye movements, self-report questionnaires, electrophysiological measures, dichotic listening tasks, and tests of cognitive ability, although there is much controversy regarding their validity. Nevertheless, some interesting relationships have been reported between measures of hemisphericity and cognitive outcome measures. In a blind evaluation of written scenarios of the future (using an objective scoring system developed by Torrance for use in the National Future Problem Solving Program), individuals previously classified as having right hemisphericity versus left hemisphericity on the basis of performance on "Your Style of Learning and Thinking" (Torrance, Reynolds, & Riegel, 1977) were compared on the eight scoring scales of the future scenarios (Torrance & Reynolds, 1978). The right-hemisphericity group significantly outperformed the left-hemisphericity group on seven of the eight scales. This had been anticipated because future scenario writing is a creative task, and creative functions seem better subserved by simultaneous-processing methods. This is probably related to the nature of simultaneous processing that makes that entire schema constantly surveyable, making the tryout of new innovations more readily surveyed for outcome and more easily and efficiently modified. Differences in hemisphericity also appear to be partially responsible for black-white IQ discrepancies observed on traditional left-hemisphere-oriented intelligence tests (Reynolds & Gutkin, 1980; Reynolds, McBride, & Gibson, 1981). Furthermore, differences in reading ability and gender seem to account for at least some of the variance with regard to hemisphericity (Newell & Rugel, 1981; Roubinek, Bell, & Cates, 1987).

Much research evidence seems to suggest that traditional concepts of dominance should give way to concepts that pertain more to the dynamics of hemispheric specialization and cerebral complementarity. This is especially true as lateralization of cortical functions may be predisposed genetically (Bradshaw-McAnulty, Hicks, & Kinsbourne, 1984; Gorynia & Egenter, 2000; Kinsbourne, 1975, 1997; Kolb & Fantie, 1997; McCallum & Merritt, 1983; Tous, Fusté, & Vidal, 1995) and, without specific intervention, continues essentially unaltered throughout the normal life span (Borod & Goodglass, 1980; Elias & Kinsbourne, 1974; Woodruff, 1978; Zelinski & Marsh, 1976). Hemisphericity should take its place in the research literature as a potentially powerful explanatory variable with many pragmatic implications. Although the mode of processing underlying hemisphericity is carried out in the second block of the brain, the first block is undoubtedly the decision-making center that directs and coordinates processing and is thus "in charge" of hemisphericity. Hemisphericity can be altered through trauma or training (Bever & Chiarello, 1974; Reynolds & Torrance, 1978; Satz, Strauss, & Whitaker, 1990) or by intense emotional responses, especially anxiety. When experiencing high levels of anxiety, individuals tend to lapse into a single, preferential mode of processing. Notably, with the advent of the learning styles movement in the school system, recent research also has focused on identifying students' preferred mode of processing (hemisphericity) to remediate problems and facilitate successful academic performance (Faust, Kravetz, & Babkoff, 1993; Gunnison et al., 1982; Paquette, Tosoni, Lassonde, & Peretz, 1996; Roubinek et al., 1987; Sonnier, 1992; Sonnier & Goldsmith, 1985).

## THE ROLE OF *G* IN NEUROPSYCHOLOGICAL MODELS OF INTELLIGENCE

If one were to apply the theory of parsimony, *g* would indeed be the most suitable and efficient means of describing the general cognitive abilities of an individual. Rather than attempt to delineate each function as a means of accounting for intelligence, it would be parsimonious to relegate all cognitive functioning to one variable. The idea of using a single variable to describe intellectual functioning is not new by any means, nor is it completely outdated (Aluja-Fabregat, Colom, Abad, & Juan-Espinosa, 2000; Brand, 1996; Head, 1926; Jensen, 1998; Kane, 2000). Aristotle was the first to conceive an individual's intellect based on a single variable, *nous* (Detterman, 1982). However, during the past few decades, especially as more is learned about the specialized functioning of the two human cerebral hemispheres, it has been in vogue to dismiss the notion of *g* as outmoded, archaic, and having little pragmatic or explanatory value. The dismissal of *g* has been especially prominent in processing (Das et al., 1979; Naglieri & Das, 1988) and componential (Sternberg, 1980) models of intelligence. Even one of the foremost authorities and proponents of intelligence testing has seen fit to relegate *g* to the past (Kaufman, 1979a). Similarly, others state that the model of a single variable to explain cognitive functioning is simply not satisfactory (Detterman, 1982).

Das et al. (1979) and many others have devoted much time to arguing against even the existence of *g*. Researchers have made considerable and important progress in documenting the presence of simultaneous and successive cognitive processes across a variety of ages, races, and cultures (Das et al., 1979; Detterman, 1982; Jensen, 1997; Vernon, 1983, 1998). Das and colleagues maintain that isolation of these factors indicates the nonavailability of *g* and further downplay the concept of ability as well, indicating that processing, and not ability, is the more correct variable for study. However, isolation of simultaneous and successive processes as separate factors does not mean that the performance of these processes is independent of some general ability.

There is excellent evidence at present that one cause of learning disorders is difficulty with specific types of information processing or an overreliance on a single mode of cognitive processing. Yet, the differences between normally functioning individuals with intact brains and cognitive-processing systems cannot be swept under the theoretical rug. Essentially, barring trauma or other insult, $g$ controls the level and efficiency of cognitive processing (though almost certainly in interaction with a number of other factors) that any individual is able to undertake. A careful review of the literature will find $g$ to have many pragmatic aspects as well. For example, Travers (1977), Luborsky, Auerbach, Chandler, Cohen, and Bachrach (1971), and Lezak (1995) point out that, in study after study of psychotherapy outcome research, the general intellectual level (tantamount to $g$) of the individual turns out to be the best or one of the best predictors of success. The premorbid level of general intellectual functioning also is the best predictor of rehabilitative success of patients with acute brain trauma and a number of neurological diseases (Golden, 1978).

What is the nature of $g$? Undoubtedly, $g$ is determined by the particular anatomy, physiology, and chemistry of the brain of the individual (Ardila, 1999; Brand, 1996; Evans, 1977; Harmony, 1997; Head, 1926; Jensen, 1978; Languis & Miller, 1992; Vernon, 1983, 1998). Any comprehensive theory of intelligence must not only take into account the method and components of information processing in the brain, but must also account for the ability to use the available information-processing strategies to their fullest potential. Ignoring $g$ and its basic properties can easily lead one into such simplistic statements as Bijou's (1966) claim that there is no mental retardation, only retarded behavior. This directly implies that $g$ can be "taught" through behavior-modification techniques. We have yet to see any individual functioning in the mild, moderate, or lower ranges of $g$ become a doctor, lawyer, or other successful professional even with the most rigorous behavior-modification program; $g$ cannot be dismissed with such simplistic statements.

## CONCLUSION

Are there separate, independent mechanisms of biological and psychological intelligence? Does $g$ represent a biological intelligence based in the physiology of the brain, while psychological intelligence is represented by the executive, coordinating, and planning functions of the frontal lobes in interaction with Luria's first two blocks of the brain? The former type of intelligence would necessarily seem to be much more genetically based, though certainly dependent to some extent on the nurturance of the environment pre- and postnatally, such as is height. Psychological intelligence would be under much greater environmental control, though undoubtedly some genetic template is present, giving guidance to the functional development of the various anatomical structures of the brain.

Biological intelligence, in referring to higher-order thought, represents the general physiological efficiency of the brain. Psychological intelligence is the mechanism, or processes, through which intelligence is manifested. Biological intelligence is the principal determinant of an individual's level of function, and psychological intelligence is the principal determinant of an individual's method of performing intelligent functions. The theories of Halstead, Luria, Das and colleagues, and others referred to in this chapter are all, in reality, theories of psychological intelligence. Their further elaboration will continue to enhance greatly our understanding of how the human brain carries out higher-order thinking. Discovering and elaborating the mechanisms of biological intelligence remains in a primitive state and will likely fall to the neuropsychologist and behavioral neurochemist for resolution.

The notion of biological and psychological intelligence briefly described here is now several decades old and still in need of further elaboration. New approaches to dominance such as hemisphericity and habitual modes of information processing are contributing to a rich investigation of early learning in school and of school-related subjects. The reconceptualization of dominance continues to explode into new areas of research in the quest for the aptitude-treatment interaction. Is right or left hemisphericity related to performance in particular subject areas? Can accurate measures of hemisphericity be used to predict response to particular curriculum methods? A number of logical connections exist that are amenable to direct experimental investigation. It is not unlikely that an overdependence on right-hemisphere processing will be found to be associated with difficulties in early reading acquisition.

It should be clear that level of function, as denoted by $g$, must be included in any comprehensive theory of human intellect. Psychological intelligence appears to be best described at present by Luria's model of the three blocks of the brain as elaborated on by Das et al. (1979) and modified here to account for lateralization of processing in the brain. As new, better, comprehensive measures of psychological intelligence are developed, as they have been in the past 2 decades (e.g., Kaufman & Kaufman, 1983; Naglieri & Das, 1996), our understanding of brain function will increase and our theories will need modification. However, it is through the use of new techniques of measurement based on current theories of intelligence that understanding will come most readily. Perhaps through such methods, the neuropsychologist, the developmentalist, and the psychometrician, all with interests in the origins and development of intelligence, will be able to coalesce their now divergent views of intelligence. Certainly, each has a unique, significant view to contribute to our ultimate understanding of how the human brain processes information.

## REFERENCES

Allen, M. (1983). Models of hemispheric specialization. *Psychological Bulletin, 93*, 73–104.

Aluja-Fabregat, A., Colom, R., Abad, F., & Juan-Espinosa, M. (2000). Sex differences in general intelligence defined as $g$ among young adolescents. *Personality and Individual Differences, 28*, 813–820.

Anderson, M., Kaufman, A. S., & Kaufman, N. L. (1976). Use of the WISC-R with a learning disabled population: Some diagnostic implications. *Psychology in the Schools, 13*, 381–386.

Annett, M. (1972). The distribution of manual asymmetry. *British Journal of Psychology, 63*, 343–358.

Ardila, A. (1999). A neuropsychological approach to intelligence. *Neuropsychology Review, 9*, 117–136.

Ashman, A. F., & Das, J. P. (1980). Relation between planning and simultaneous-successive processing. *Perceptual and Motor Skills, 51*, 371–382.

Balow, I. H. (1963). Lateral dominance characteristics and reading achievement in the first grade. *Journal of Psychology, 55,* 323–328.

Balow, I. H., & Balow, B. (1964). Lateral dominance and reading achievement in second grade. *American Educational Research Journal, 1,* 139–143.

Banich, M. T. (2003). Interaction between the hemispheres and its implications for the processing capacity of the brain. In K. Hugdahl & R. J. Davidson (Eds.), *The asymmetrical brain* (pp. 261–302). Cambridge, MA: MIT Press.

Bauer, R. W., & Wepman, J. M. (1955). Lateralization of cerebral function. *Journal of Speech and Hearing Disorders, 20,* 171–177.

Beaton, A. A. (2003). The nature and determinants of handedness. In K. Hugdahl & R. J. Davidson (Eds.), *The asymmetrical brain* (pp. 105–158). Cambridge, MA: MIT Press.

Beaumont, J. G. (1997). Future research directions in laterality. *Neuropsychology Review, 7,* 107–126.

Beaumont, J. G., Young, A. W., & McManus, I. C. (1984). Hemisphericity: A critical review. *Cognitive Neuropsychology, 1,* 191–212.

Bell, T. K. (1990). Rapid sequential processing in dyslexic and ordinary readers. *Perceptual and Motor Skills, 71,* 1155–1159.

Belmont, C., & Birch, H. (1963). Lateral dominance, lateral awareness, and reading disability. *Child Development, 34,* 257–270.

Benton, A. L. (1955). Right-left discrimination and finger localization in defective children. *Archives of Neurology and Psychiatry, 74,* 583–589.

Benton, A. L. (1959). *Right-left discrimination and finger localization development and pathology.* New York: Harper & Row.

Ben-Yishay, Y. (2000). Postacute neuropsychological rehabilitation: A holistic perspective. In A. C. Christensen & B. P. Uzzell (Eds.), *International handbook of neuropsychological rehabilitation* (pp. 127–136). New York: Kluwer Academic/Plenum Press.

Bever, T. G. (1975). Cerebral asymmetries in humans are due to the differentiation of two incompatible processes: Holistic and analytic. In D. Aaronson & R. Reiber (Eds.), *Developmental psycholinguistics and communication disorders* (pp. 251–262). New York: New York Academy of Sciences.

Bever, T. G., & Chiarello, R. S. (1974). Cerebral dominance in musicians and nonmusicians. *Science, 186,* 537–539.

Bijou, S. W. (1966). A functional analysis of retarded development. *International Review of Mental Retardation, 1,* 1–19.

Bloom, A. S. (2000). When academic performance is higher than WISC-III IQs, is the sequential-processing model of intelligence the preferred approach to assessment? *Perceptual and Motor Skills, 90,* 883–884.

Bogen, J. E. (1969). The other side of the brain: Parts, I, II, and III. *Bulletin of the Los Angeles Neurological Society, 34,* 73–105, 135–162, 191–203.

Bogen, J. E., DeZure, R., TenHouten, W., & Marsh, J. (1972). The other side of the brain IV: The A/P ratio. *Bulletin of the Los Angeles Neurological Society, 37,* 49–61.

Boklage, C. E. (1978). On cellular mechanisms for heritability transmitting structural information. *The Behavioral and Brain Sciences, 2,* 282–286.

Borod, J. C., Caron, H. S., & Koff, E. (1981). Asymmetry of facial expression related to handedness, footedness, and eyedness: A quantitative study. *Cortex, 17,* 381–390.

Borod, J. C., & Goodglass, H. (1980). Lateralization of linguistic and melodic processing with age. *Neuropsychologia, 18,* 79–83.

Bradshaw-McAnulty, G., Hicks, R. E., & Kinsbourne, M. (1984). Pathological left-handedness and familial sinistrality in relation to degree of mental retardation. *Brain and Cognition, 3,* 349–356.

Braga, L. W., & Campos da Paz, A., Jr. (2000). Neuropsychological pediatric rehabilitation. In A. C. Christensen & B. P. Uzzell (Eds.), *International handbook of neuropsychological rehabilitation* (pp. 283–295). New York: Kluwer Academic/Plenum Press.

Brand, C. (1996). Doing something about *g*. *Intelligence, 22*, 311–326.

Broca, P. (1861). Remarques sur le siége de la faculté du language articulé, suivies d'une observation d'aphémie (perte de la parole). *Bulletins do la Societé Anatomique, 6*, 330–357.

Broca, P. (1963). Localisation des functions cérébrales. Siége du language articulé. *Bulletins de la Societé d'Anthropologie de Paris, 4*, 200–203.

Broshek, D. K., & Barth, J. T. (2000). The Halstead-Reitan Neuropsychological Test Battery. In G. Groth-Marnat (Ed.), *Neuropsychological assessment in clinical practice: A guide to test interpretation and integration* (pp. 223–262). New York: Wiley.

Brown, E. R., & Taylor, P. (1988). Handedness, footedness, and eyedness. *Perceptual and Motor Skills, 66*, 183–186.

Brysbaert, M. (1994). Lateral preferences and visual field asymmetries: Appearances may have been overstated. *Cortex, 30*, 413–429.

Buzzard, T. (1882). *Clinical lectures on diseases of the nervous system.* London: Churchill.

Christensen, A. (2000). Neuropsychological postacute rehabilitation. In A. C. Christensen & B. P. Uzzell (Eds.), *International handbook of neuropsychological rehabilitation* (pp. 151–163). New York: Kluwer Academic/Plenum Press.

Coleman, R. I., & Deutsch, C. P. (1964). Lateral dominance and right-left discrimination: A comparison of normal and retarded readers. *Perceptual and Motor Skills, 19*, 43–50.

Corballis, M. C., & Beale, I. L. (1976). *The psychology of left and right.* Hillsdale, NJ: Erlbaum.

Coren, S. (1993). The lateral preference inventory for measurement of handedness, footedness, eyedness, and earedness: Norms for young adults. *Bulletin of the Psychonomic Society, 31*, 1–3.

Coren, S., & Porac, C. (1982). Lateral preference and cognitive skills: An indirect test. *Perceptual and Motor Skills, 54*, 787–792.

Cornish, R. D. (1970). Effects of neurological training on psychomotor abilities of kindergarten children. *Journal of Experimental Education, 39*, 15–19.

Crow, T., Crow, L., Done, D., & Leask, S. (1998). Relative hand skill predicts academic ability: Global deficits at the point of hemispheric indecision. *Neuropsychologia, 36*, 1275–1282.

Cumming, C. E., & Rodda, M. (1985). The effects of auditory deprivation on successive processing. *Canadian Journal of Behavioural Science, 17*, 232–245.

Cummins, J., & Das, J. P. (1977). Cognitive processing and reading difficulties: A framework for research. *Alberta Journal of Educational Research, 23*, 245–256.

Daleo, D. V., Lopez, B. R., Cole, J. C., Kaufman, A. S., Kaufman, N. L., Newcomer, B. L., et al. (1999). K-ABC simultaneous processing, Das nonverbal reasoning, and Horn's expanded fluid-crystallized theory. *Psychological Reports, 84*, 563–574.

Daniels-Zide, E., & Ben-Yishay, Y. (2000). Therapeutic milieu day program. In A. C. Christensen & B. P. Uzzell (Eds.), *International handbook of neuropsychological rehabilitation* (pp. 183–194). New York: Kluwer Academic/Plenum Press.

Das, J. P., Kirby, J. R., & Jarman, R. F. (1979). *Simultaneous and successive cognitive processes.* New York: Academic Press.

Dean, R. S. (1979). Cerebral laterality and verbal-performance discrepancies in intelligence. *Journal of School Psychology, 17*, 145–150.

Dean, R. S., & Kulhavy, R. W. (1977). *Dean-Kulhavy lateral preference schedule.* Tempe, AZ: Arizona State University.

Dean, R. S., & Reynolds, C. R. (1997). Cognitive processing and self-report of lateral preference. *Neuropsychology Review, 7*, 127–142.

Deikman, A. J. (1971). Bimodal consciousness. *Archives of General Psychiatry, 25,* 481–489.

Delacato, C. H. (1959). *The treatment and prevention of reading problems: The neuropsychological approach.* Springfield, IL: Charles C. Thomas.

Delacato, C. H. (1963). *The diagnosis and treatment of speech and reading problems.* Springfield, IL: Charles C Thomas.

Delacato, C. H. (1966). *Neurological organization and reading.* Springfield, IL: Charles C. Thomas.

Detterman, D. K. (1982). Does "g" exist? *Intelligence, 6,* 99–108.

Dewson, J. H. (1977). Preliminary evidence of hemispheric asymmetry of auditory function in monkeys. In S. Harnad, R. Doty, L. Goldstein, J. Jaynes, & G. Krauthamer (Eds.), *Lateralization in the nervous system.* New York: Academic Press.

DiNuovo, S. F., & Buono, S. (1997). Laterality and handedness in mentally retarded subjects. *Perceptual and Motor Skills, 85,* 1229–1230.

Eckhert, M. A., & Leonard, C. M. (2003). Developmental disorders: Dyslexia. In K. Hugdahl & R. J. Davidson (Eds.), *The asymmetrical brain* (pp. 651–679). Cambridge, MA: MIT Press.

Eisenmann, R. (1993). Some problems in the assessment of handedness: Comment on Coren. *Bulletin of the Psychonomic Society, 31,* 285–286.

Elias, M. F., & Kinsbourne, M. (1974). Age and sex differences in the processing of verbal and nonverbal stimuli. *Journal of Gerontology, 29,* 162–171.

Evans, J. R. (1977). Evoked potentials and learning disabilities. In L. Tarnopol & M. Tarnopol (Eds.), *Brain function and reading disabilities.* Baltimore: University Park Press.

Faust, M., Kravetz, S., & Babkoff, H. (1993). Hemisphericity and top-down processing of language. *Brain and Language, 44,* 1–18.

Finger, S., & Roe, D. (1999). Does Gustave Dax deserve to be forgotten? The temporal lobe theory and other contributions of an overlooked figure in the history of language and cerebral dominance. *Brain and Language, 69,* 16–30.

Fuller, J. L. (1978). If genes are not right handed, what is? *The Behavioral and Brain Sciences, 2,* 295.

Galin, D. (1974). Implications for psychiatry of left and right cerebral specialization. *Archives of General Psychiatry, 31,* 78–82.

Gardiner, M. F. (1987). General temporal-sequential processing capability required for reading: New evidence from adults with specific reading difficulties. *Annals of the New York Academy of Sciences, 504,* 283–285.

Gazzaniga, M. S. (1971). Changing hemisphere dominance by change reward probabilities in split-brain monkeys. *Experimental Neurology, 33,* 412–419.

Gazzaniga, M. S. (1974). Cerebral dominance viewed as a decision system. In S. Dimond & J. Beaumont (Eds.), *Hemisphere functions in the human brain.* London: Halstead Press.

Gazzaniga, M. S. (1975). Recent research on hemispheric lateralization of the human brain: Review of the split-brain. *UCLA Educator, May,* 9–12.

Geffen, G. (1978). Human laterality: Cerebral dominance and handedness. *The Behavioral and Brain Sciences, 2,* 295–296.

Glass, G. V., & Robbins, M. P. (1967). A critique of experiments on the role of neurological organization in reading performance. *Reading Research Quarterly, 3,* 5–52.

Golden, C. J. (1978). *Diagnosis and rehabilitation in clinical neuropsychology.* Springfield, IL: Charles C Thomas.

Golden, C. J. (1987). *Luria-Nebraska Neuropsychological Battery-Children's Revision.* Los Angeles: Western Psychological Services.

Golden, C. J., Ariel, R. N., McKay, S. E., Wilkening, G. N., Wolf, B. A., & MacInnes, W. D. (1982). The Luria-Nebraska Neuropsychological Battery: Theoretical orientation and comment. *Journal of Consulting and Clinical Psychology, 50,* 291–300.

Golden, C. J., Espe-Pfeifer, P., & Wachsler-Felder, J. (2000). *Neuropsychological interpretations of objective psychological tests.* New York: Kluwer Academic/Plenum Press.

Golden, C. J., Purisch, A. D., & Hammeke, T. A. (1979). *The Luria-Nebraska Neuropsychological Test Battery: A manual for clinical and experimental uses.* Lincoln, NE: The University of Nebraska Press.

Gorynia, I., & Egenter, D. (2000). Intermanual coordination in relation to handedness, familial sinistrality and lateral preferences. *Cortex, 36,* 1–18.

Grouios, G., Sakadami, N., Poderi, A., & Alevriadou, A. (1999). Excess of non-right handedness among individuals with intellectual disability: Experimental evidence and possible explanations. *Journal of Intellectual Disability Research, 43,* 306–313.

Gunnison, J., Kaufman, N. L., & Kaufman, A. S. (1982). Reading remediation based on sequential and simultaneous processing. *Academic Therapy, 17,* 297–306.

Hall, C. W., Gregory, G., Billinger, E., & Fisher, T. (1988). Field independence and simultaneous processing in preschool children. *Perceptual and Motor Skills, 66,* 891–897.

Halstead, W. C. (1947). *Brain and intelligence.* Chicago: University of Chicago Press.

Hardyck, C., & Petrinovich, L. F. (1977). Left-handedness. *Psychological Bulletin, 84,* 385–404.

Hardyck, C., Petrinovich, L. F., & Goldman, R. D. (1976). Left-handedness and cognitive deficit. *Cortex, 12,* 266–279.

Harmony, T. (1997). Psychophysiological evaluation of neuropsychological disorders in children. In C. R. Reynolds & E. Fletcher-Janzen (Eds.), *Handbook of clinical child neuropsychology* (2nd ed., pp. 356–370). New York: Plenum Press.

Harris, L. J. (1980). Left-handedness: Early theories, facts, and fancies. In J. Herron (Ed.), *Neuropsychology of left-handedness.* New York: Academic Press.

Harris, L. J. (1990). Cultural influences on handedness: Historical and contemporary theory and evidence. In S. Coren (Ed.), *Left-handedness: Behavioral implications and anomalies* (pp. 195–258). Amsterdam, The Netherlands: Elsevier Science Publishers, B. V.

Hartlage, L. C., & Gage, R. (1997). Unimanual performance as a measure of laterality. *Neuropsychology Review, 7,* 143–156.

Head, H. (1926). *Aphasia and kindred disorders of speech* (Vol. 1). New York: Macmillan.

Held, R. (1965). Plasticity in sensory-motor systems. *Scientific American, 213,* 84–94.

Held, R., & Bossom, J. (1961). Neonatal deprivation and adult rearrangement: Complementary techniques for analyzing plastic sensory-motor coordination. *Journal of Comparative and Physiological Psychology, 54,* 33–37.

Held, R., & Freedman, J. (1963). Plasticity in human sensory-motor control. *Science, 142,* 455–462.

Held, R., & Hein, A. (1963). Movement-produced stimulation in the development of visually guided behavior. *Journal of Comparative and Physiological Psychology, 56,* 872–876.

Herron, J. (Ed.). (1980). *Neuropsychology of left-handedness.* New York: Academic Press.

Hevern, V. W. (1980). Recent validity studies of the Halstead-Reitan approach to clinical neuropsychological assessment: A critical review. *Clinical Neuropsychology, 2,* 49–61.

Hillerich, R. L. (1964). Eye-hand dominance and reading achievement. *American Educational Research Journal, 1,* 121–126.

Hoosain, R. (1990). Left handedness and handedness switch amongst the Chinese. *Cortex, 26,* 451–454.

Hunt, D. (1980). Intentional-incidental learning and simultaneous-successive processing. *Canadian Journal of Behavioural Science, 12,* 373–383.

Jensen, A. R. (1978, September). "g": Outmoded concept or unconquered frontier? Invited address at the annual meeting of the American Psychological Association, New York.

Jensen, A. R. (1997). Adoption data and two g-related hypotheses. *Intelligence, 25*, 1–6.

Jensen, A. R. (1998). *The g factor: The science of mental ability.* Westport, CT: Praeger.

Johnson, J. D., & Gazzaniga, M. S. (1971a). Reversal behavior in split-brain monkeys. *Physiology and Behavior, 6*, 706–709.

Johnson, J. D., & Gazzaniga, M. S. (1971b). Some effects of non-reinforcement in split-brain monkeys. *Physiology and Behavior, 6*, 703–706.

Joseph, R. (1996). *Neuropsychiatry, neuropsychology, and clinical neuroscience: Emotion, evolution, cognition, language, memory, brain damage, and abnormal behavior* (2nd ed.). Baltimore: Williams & Wilkins.

Joynt, R. J., & Benton, A. L. (1964). The memoir of Marc Dax on aphasia. *Neurology, 14*, 851–854.

Kamphaus, R. W. (1993). *Clinical assessment of children's intelligence.* Boston: Allyn & Bacon.

Kamphaus, R. W., & Reynolds, C. R. (1984). Development and structure of the Kaufman Assessment Battery for Children. *Journal of Special Education, 18*, 213–228.

Kamphaus, R. W., & Reynolds, C. R. (1987). *Clinical and research applications of the K-ABC.* Circle Pines, MN: American Guidance Service.

Kane, H. D. (2000). A secular decline in Spearman's g: Evidence from the WAIS, WAIS-R and WAIS-III. *Personality and Individual Differences, 29*, 561–566.

Kaufman, A. S. (1979a). *Intelligent testing with the WISC-R.* New York: Wiley-Interscience.

Kaufman, A. S. (1979b). Cerebral specialization and intelligence testing. *Journal of Research and Development in Education, 12*, 96–107.

Kaufman, A. S., & Kaufman, N. L. (1983). *Administration and scoring manual for the Kaufman Assessment Battery for Children.* Circle Pines, MN: American Guidance Service.

Kinsbourne, M. (1975). The ontogeny of cerebral dominance. In A. Aaronson & R. Reiber (Eds.), *Developmental psycholinguistics and communication disorders.* New York: New York Academy of Sciences.

Kinsbourne, M. (1978a). Biological determinants of functional bisymmetry an asymmetry. In M. Kinsbourne (Ed.), *Asymmetrical function of the brain.* Oxford, England: Cambridge University Press.

Kinsbourne, M. (1978b). Evolution of language in relation to lateral action. In M. Kinsbourne (Ed.), *Asymmetrical function of the brain.* Oxford, England: Cambridge University Press.

Kinsbourne, M. (1997). Mechanisms and development of cerebral lateralization in children. In C. R. Reynolds & E. Fletcher-Janzen (Eds.), *Handbook of clinical child neuropsychology* (2nd ed., pp. 102–119). New York: Plenum Press.

Kirby, J. R., & Das, J. P. (1977). Reading achievement, I.Q., & simultaneous-successive processing. *Journal of Educational Psychology, 69*, 564–570.

Klich, L. Z. (1987). A focal review of research on the Luria-Das model of cognitive processing. In S. H. Irvine & S. E. Newstead (Eds.), *Intelligence and cognition: Contemporary frames of reference* (pp. 313–347). Dordrecth, The Netherlands: Martinus Nijhoff.

Kolb, B., & Fantie, B. (1997). Development of the child's brain and behavior. In C. R. Reynolds & E. Fletcher-Janzen (Eds.), *Handbook of clinical child neuropsychology* (2nd ed., pp. 17–41). New York: Plenum Press.

Kwantes, P. J., & Mewhort, D. J. K. (1999). Evidence for sequential processing in visual word recognition. *Journal of Experimental Psychology: Human Perception and Performance, 25*, 376–381.

Languis, M. L., & Miller, D. C. (1992). Luria's theory of brain functioning: A model for research in cognitive psychophysiology. *Educational Psychologist, 27,* 493–511.

LeMay, M. (1976). Morphological cerebral asymmetries of modern man, fossil man, and nonhuman primate. *Annals of the New York Academy of Sciences, 280,* 349–366.

Levy, J., & Nagylaki, T. (1972). A model for the genetics of handedness. *Genetics, 72,* 117–128.

Lewis, R. S., & Harris, L. J. (1990). Handedness, sex, and spatial ability. In S. Coren (Ed.), *Left handedness: Behavioral implications and anomalies* (pp. 319–341). Amsterdam, The Netherlands: Elsevier Science Publishers, B. V.

Lezak, M. D. (1995). *Neuropsychological assessment* (3rd ed.). New York: Oxford University Press.

Luborsky, L., Auerbach, A. H., Chandler, M., Cohen, J., & Bachrach, H. M. (1971). Factors influencing the outcome of psychotherapy: A review of quantitative research. *Psychological Bulletin, 75,* 145–185.uria, A. R. (1961). *The role of speech in the regulation of normal and abnormal behavior.* Oxford, England: Pergamon Press.

Luria, A. R. (1964). Neuropsychology in the local diagnosis of brain damage. *Cortex, 1,* 3–18.

Luria, A. R. (1966). *Higher cortical functions in man.* New York: Basic Books.

Luria, A. R. (1969). *Cerebral organization of conscious acts: A frontal lobe function.* Speech to the 19th International Congress of Psychology, London, England.

Luria, A. R. (1970). The functional organization of the brain. *Scientific American, 222,* 66–78.

Luria, A. R. (1973). *The working brain.* London: Penguin.

Mandal, M. S., Pandey, G., Singh, S. K., & Asthana, H. S. (1992). Degree of asymmetry in lateral preferences: Eye, foot, ear. *Journal of Psychology, 126,* 155–162.

Mayringer, H., & Wimmer, H. (2002). No deficits at the point of hemispheric indecision. *Neuropsychologia, 40,* 701–704.

McCallum, R. S., & Merritt, F. M. (1983). Simultaneous-successive processing among college students. *Journal of Psychoeducational Assessment, 1,* 85–93.

McKeever, W. F. (1990). Familial sinistrality and cerebral organization. In S. Coren (Ed.), *Left handedness: Behavioral implications and anomalies* (pp. 373–412). Amsterdam, The Netherlands: Elsevier Science Publishers, B. V.

Meikamp, J. (2001). Das Naglieri cognitive assessment system. In J. C. Impara & B. S. Plake (Eds.), *The fourteenth mental measurements yearbook.* Lincoln, NE: The Buros Institute of Mental Measurements.

Metalis, S. A., & Niemiec, A. J. (1984). Assessment of eye dominance through response time. *Perceptual and Motor Skills, 59,* 539–544.

Milner, B., Branch, C., & Rasmussen, T. (1964). Observations on cerebral dominance. In A. V. S. de Rueck & M. O'Conner (Eds.), *Ciba Foundation symposium on disorders of language.* London: Churchill.

Morgan, M. J., & Corballis, M. C. (1978). On the biological basis of human laterality: II. The mechanisms of inheritance. *The Behavioral and Brain Sciences, 2,* 270–277.

Naglieri, J. A. (1997). Planning, attention, simultaneous, and successive theory and the Cognitive Assessment System: A new theory-based measure of intelligence. In D. P. Flanagan, J. L. Genshaft, & P. L. Harrison (Eds.), *Contemporary intellectual assessment: Theories, tests, and issues* (pp. 247–267). New York: Guilford Press.

Naglieri, J. A., & Das, J. P. (1988). Planning-Arousal-Simultaneous-Successive (PASS): A model for assessment. *Journal of School Psychology, 26,* 35–48.

Naglieri, J. A., & Das, J. P. (1990). Planning, attention, simultaneous, and successive (PASS) cognitive processes as a model for intelligence. *Journal of Psychoeducational Assessment, 8,* 303–337.

Naglieri, J. A., & Das, J. P. (1996). *Das Naglieri Cognitive Assessment System*. Chicago: Riverside.

Naglieri, J. A., Kamphaus, R. W., & Kaufman, A. S. (1983). The Luria-Das simultaneous successive model applied to the WISC-R. *Journal of Psychoeducational Assessment, 1*, 25–34.

Naylor, H. (1980). Reading disability and lateral asymmetry: An information processing analysis. *Psychological Bulletin, 87*, 531–545.

Newcombe, F., & Ratcliff, G. (1973). Handedness, speech lateralization and ability. *Neuropsychologia, 11*, 399–407.

Newell, D., & Rugel, R. P. (1981). Hemispheric specialization in normal and disabled readers. *Journal of Learning Disabilities, 14*, 296–298.

Noble, J. (1968). Paradoxical interocular transfer of mirror-image discrimination in the optic chiasm sectioned monkey. *Brain Research, 10*, 127–151.

Nussbaum, N. L., & Bigler, E. D. (1997). Halstead-Reitan Neuropsychological Test Batteries for Children. In C. R. Reynolds & E. Fletcher-Janzen (Eds.), *Handbook of clinical child neuropsychology* (2nd ed., pp. 219–236). New York: Plenum Press.

Obrzut, J. E., & Obrzut, A. (1982). Neuropsychological perspectives in pupil services: Practical application of Luria's model. *Journal of Research and Development in Education, 15*, 38 47.

O'Donnell, D. A., & Eisenson, J. (1969). Delacato training for reading achievement and visual motor integration. *Journal of Learning Disabilities, 2*, 441–447.

Orton, S. T. (1925). "Word-blindedness" in school children. *Archives of Neurology and Psychiatry, 14*, 581.

Orton, S. T. (1928). A physiological theory of reading disability and stuttering in children. *New England Journal of Medicine, 199*, 1046–1052.

Orton, S. T. (1931). Special disability in reading. *Bulletin of the Neurological Institute of New York, 1*, 159–162.

Orton, S. T. (1937). *Reading, writing, and speech problems in children*. New York: Norton.

Osburn, D. M., & Klingsporn, M. J. (1998). Consistency of performance on eyedness tasks. *British Journal of Psychology, 89*, 27.

Pallier, G., Roberts, R. D., & Stankov, L. (2000). Biological versus psychometric intelligence: Halstead's (1947) distinction revisted. *Archives of Clinical Neuropsychology, 15*, 205–226.

Paquette, C., Tosoni, C., Lassonde, M., & Peretz, I. (1996). Atypical hemispheric specialization in intellectual deficiency. *Brain and Language, 52*, 474–483.

Parsons, O. A., & Prigatano, G. P. (1978). Methodological considerations in clinical neuropsychological research. *Journal of Consulting and Clinical Psychology, 46*, 608–619.

Penfield, W., & Roberts, L. (1959). *Speech and brain mechanisms*. Princeton, NJ: Princeton University Press.

Peters, M., & Durding, B. M. (1978). Handedness measured by finger tapping: A continuous variable. *Canadian Journal of Psychology, 32*, 257–261.

Polemikos, N., & Papaeliou, C. (2000). Sidedness preference as an index of organization of laterality. *Perceptual and Motor Skills, 91*, 1083–1090.

Porac, C., Rees, L., & Buller, T. (1990). Switching hands: A place for left hand use in a right hand world. In S. Coren (Ed.), *Left-handedness: Behavioral implications and anomalies* (pp. 259–290). Amsterdam, The Netherlands: Elsevier Science Publishers, B. V.

Pribam, K. H. (1971). *Languages of the brain*. Englewood Cliffs, NJ: Prentice-Hall.

Prigatano, G. P. (2000). A brief overview of four principles of neuropsychological rehabilitation. In A. C. Christensen & B. P. Uzzell (Eds.), *International handbook of neuropsychological rehabilitation* (pp. 115–125). New York: Kluwer Academic/Plenum Press.

Reed, J. (1985). The contributions of Ward Halstead, Ralph Reitan and their associates. *International Journal of Neuroscience, 25,* 289–293.

Reiß, M., & Reiß, G. (2000). The dominant ear. *Perceptual and Motor Skills, 91,* 53–54.

Reitan, R. M. (1955). Certain differential effects of left and right cerebral lesions in human adults. *Journal of Comparative and Physiological Psychology, 48,* 474–477.

Reitan, R. M. (1964a). Psychological deficits resulting from cerebral lesions in man. In J. M. Warren & K. Akert (Eds.), *The frontal granular cortex and behavior.* New York: McGraw-Hill.

Reitan, R. M. (1964b). Relationships between neurological and psychological variables and their implications for reading instruction. In K. A. Robinson (Ed.), *Meeting individual differences in reading.* Chicago: University of Chicago Press.

Reitan, R. M. (1966). A research program on the psychological effects of brain lesions in human beings. *International Review of Research in Mental Retardation, 1,* 153–218.

Reitan, R. M. (1975). Assessment of brain-behavior relationships. In P. McReynolds (Ed.), *Advances in psychological assessment* (Vol. 3). San Francisco: Jossey Bass.

Reitan, R. M. (1994). Ward Halstead's contributions to neuropsychology and the Halstead-Reitan Neuropsychological Test Battery. *Journal of Clinical Psychology, 50,* 47–69.

Reitan, R. M., & Davison, L. A. (1974). *Clinical neuropsychology: Current status and applications.* Washington, DC: V. H. Winston.

Reitan, R. M., & Wolfson, D. (1996). Theoretical, methodological, and validational bases of the Halstead-Reitan Neuropsychological Test Battery. In I. Grant & K. M. Adams (Eds.), *Neuropsychological assessment of neuropsychiatric disorders* (2nd ed., pp. 3–42). New York: Oxford University Press.

Reynolds, C. R. (1978, April). *Current conceptualizations of hemisphericity.* Colloquium presented to the Department of Educational Psychology, the University of Texas at Austin, TX.

Reynolds, C. R. (1980, August). *The neuropsychology of intelligence and a reconceptualization of dominance.* Invited address to the Utah State University conference on Brain Research and Teaching, Logan, UT.

Reynolds, C. R. (1981). The neuropsychological basis of intelligence. In G. Hynd & J. Obrzut (Eds.), *Neuropsychological assessment and the school-aged child.* New York: Grune & Stratton.

Reynolds, C. R., & Gutkin, T. B. (1979). Predicting the premorbid intellectual status of children using demographic data. *Clinical Neuropsychology, 1,* 36–38.

Reynolds, C. R., & Gutkin, T. B. (1980, September). *Intellectual performance of Blacks and Whites matched on four demographic variables: A multivariate analysis.* Paper presented at the annual meeting of the American Psychological Association, Montreal, Canada.

Reynolds, C. R., Hartlage, L. C., & Haak, R. (1980, September). *Lateral preference as determined by neuropsychological performance and aptitude/achievement discrepancies.* Paper presented at the annual meeting of the American Psychological Association, Montreal, Canada.

Reynolds, C. R., Kamphaus, R. W., Rosenthal, B. L., & Hiemenz, J. R. (1997). Applications of the Kaufman Assessment Battery for Children (K-ABC) in neuropsychological assessment. In C. R. Reynolds & E. Fletcher-Janzen (Eds.), *Handbook of clinical child neuropsychology* (2nd ed., pp. 252–269). New York: Plenum Press.

Reynolds, C. R., McBride, R. D., & Gibson, L. J. (1981). Black-white IQ discrepancies may be related to differences in hemisphericity. *Contemporary Educational Psychology, 6,* 180–184.

Reynolds, C. R., & Torrance, E. P. (1978). Perceived changes in styles of learning and thinking (hemisphericity) through direct and indirect training. *Journal of Creative Behavior, 12,* 247–252.

Rider, R. A., Imwold, C. H., & Griffin, M. (1985). Comparison of hand preference in trainable mentally handicapped and nonhandicapped children. *Perceptual and Motor Skills, 61*, 1280–1282.

Robbins, M. P. (1966). A study of the validity of Delacato's theory of neurological organization. *Exceptional Children, 32*, 517–523.

Robison, S. E., Block, S. S., Boudreaux, J. D., & Flora, R. J. (1999). Hand-eye dominance in a population with mental handicaps: Prevalence and a comparison of methods. *Journal of the American Optometric Association, 70*, 563–570.

Roubinek, D. L., Bell, M. L., & Cates, L. A. (1987). Brain hemispheric preference of intellectually gifted children. *Roeper Review, 10*, 120–122.

Sattler, J. M. (1981). *Assessment of children's intelligence and special abilities.* Boston: Allyn & Bacon.

Satz, P., Strauss, E., & Whitaker, H. (1990). The ontogeny of hemispheric specialization: Some old hypotheses revisited. *Brain and Language, 38*, 596–614.

Saudino, K., & McManus, I. C. (1998). Handedness, footedness, eyedness and earedness in the Colorado Adoption Project. *British Journal of Developmental Psychology, 16*, 167–174.

Schwartz, M. (1990). Left-handedness and prenatal complications. In S. Coren (Ed.), *Left handedness: Behavioral implications and anomalies* (pp. 75–97). Amsterdam, The Netherlands: Elsevier Science Publishers, B. V.

Shure, G. H., & Halstead, W. C. (1959). Cerebral lateralization of individual processes. *Psychological Monographs: General and Applied, 72*, 12.

Smith, M. D., Coleman, J. M., Dokecki, P. R., & Davis, E. E. (1977). Intellectual characteristics of school labeled learning disabled children. *Exceptional Children, 43*, 352–357.

Sonnier, I. L. (1992). Hemisphericity as a key to understanding individual differences. In I. L. Sonnier (Ed.), *Hemisphericity as a key to understanding individual differences* (pp. 6–8). Springfield, IL: Charles C. Thomas.

Sonnier, I. L., & Goldsmith, J. (1985). The nature of human brain hemispheres: The basis for some individual differences. In I. L. Sonnier (Ed.), *Methods and techniques of holistic education* (pp. 17–25). Springfield, IL: Charles C. Thomas.

Spiers, P. A. (1982). The Luria-Nebraska Neuropsychological Battery revisited: A theory in practice or just practicing? *Journal of Consulting and Clinical Psychology, 50*, 301–306.

Sternberg, R. J. (1980, April). *Factor theories of intelligence are all right almost.* Paper presented at the annual meeting of the American Educational Research Association, Boston, MA.

Strauss, E. (1986). Hand, foot, eye and ear preferences and performance on a dichotic listening test. *Cortex, 22*, 475–482.

Torrance, E. P., & Reynolds, C. R. (1978). Images of the future of gifted adolescents: Effects of alienation and specialized cerebral functioning. *Gifted Child Quarterly, 22*, 40–54.

Torrance, E. P., Reynolds, C. R., & Riegel, T. R. (1977). Your style of learning and thinking—Forms A & B: Preliminary norms, abbreviated technical notes, scoring keys, and selected references. *Gifted Child Quarterly, 21*, 563–573.

Tous, J. M., Fusté, A., & Vidal, J. (1995). Hemispheric specialization and individual differences in cognitive processing. *Personality and Individual Differences, 19*, 463–470.

Travers, R. M. W. (1977). *Essentials of learning* (4th ed.). New York: Macmillan.

Trexler, L. E. (2000). Empirical support for neuropsychological rehabilitation. In A. C. Christensen & B. P. Uzzell (Eds.), *International handbook of neuropsychological rehabilitation* (pp. 137–150). New York: Kluwer Academic/Plenum Press.

Tupper, D. E. (1999). Introduction: Alexander Luria's continuing influence on worldwide neuropsychology. *Neuropsychology Review, 9*, 1–5.

Vernon, P. A. (1983). Recent findings on the nature of *g. Journal of Special Education, 17*, 389–400.

Vernon, P. A. (1998). From the cognitive to the biological: A sketch of Arthur Jensen's contributions to the study of *g. Intelligence, 26,* 267–271.

Warren, J. M., & Nonneman, A. J. (1976). The search for cerebral dominance in monkeys. *Annals of the New York Academy of Sciences, 280,* 732–744.

Watters, J. J., & English, L. D. (1995). Children's application of simultaneous and successive processing in inductive and deductive reasoning problems: Implications for developing scientific reasoning skills. *Journal of Research in Science Teaching, 32,* 699–714.

Wheeler, L., & Reitan, R. M. (1962). The presence and laterality of brain damage predicted from responses to a short aphasia screening test. *Perceptual and Motor Skills, 15,* 783–799.

White, M. J. (1969). Laterality differences in perception: A review. *Psychological Bulletin, 72,* 387–405.

Willis, W. G. (1985). Successive and simultaneous processing: A note on interpretation. *Journal of Psychoeducational Assessment, 4,* 343–346.

Witelson, S. W. (1980). Neuroanatomical asymmetry in left-handers. In J. Herron (Ed.), *Neuropsychology of left-handedness.* New York: Academic Press.

Woo, T. L., & Pearson, K. (1927). Dextrality and sinistrality of hand and eye. *Biometrika, 19,* 165–169.

Woodruff, D. S. (1978). Brain activity and development. In P. B. Bates (Ed.), *Life-span development and behavior* (Vol. 1). New York: Academic Press.

Yeo, R. A., Gangestad, S. W., & Daniel, W. F. (1993). Hand preference and developmental instability. *Psychobiology, 21,* 161–168.

Zarske, J. A. (1982). Neuropsychological intervention approaches for handicapped children. *Journal of Research and Development in Education, 15,* 66–74.

Zelinski, E. M., & Marsh, G. R. (1976, September). *Age differences in hemispheric processing of verbal and spatial information.* Paper presented at the annual meeting of the American Psychological Association, Washington, DC.

Zingale, S. A., & Smith, M. D. (1978). WISC-R patterns for learning disabled children at three SES levels. *Psychology in the Schools, 15,* 199–204.

# CHAPTER 6

# Lateralization of Cerebral Functions and Hemispheric Specialization: Linking Behavior, Structure, and Neuroimaging

ANDREW S. DAVIS and RAYMOND S. DEAN

A CASUAL OBSERVATION of the human brain will reveal that it clearly consists of two seemingly identical hemispheres. Although similar in appearance, evidence suggests that each hemisphere typically serves different functions, processes information in a unique fashion, and, in some cases, is structurally asymmetrical (Watt, 1990). Recent research using functional magnetic resonance imaging (fMRI) and positron emission tomography (PET) scans confirms that each hemisphere may be specialized for discrete tasks and that structural asymmetries in the hemispheres may lead to functional differences (Robichon, Levrier, Farnarier, & Habib, 2000; Xu et al., 2001). These differences in cerebral lateralization are evident from the perinatal to the adult stage (Dean & Anderson, 1997) and are salient to research that examines gender differences (Shaywitz et al., 1995), differences in language (Posner & Raichle, 1994), and differences in emotional processing and personality (Atchley, Iiardi, & Enloe, 2003). This chapter discusses cerebral lateralization and hemispheric specialization as they relate to developmental and clinical neuropsychology, including the history of cerebral lateralization, differences in hemispheric structure and specialization, developmental language differences, and gender differences.

## HISTORY OF CEREBRAL LATERALIZATION AND HEMISPHERIC SPECIALIZATION

Although the history of cerebral lateralization and hemispheric dominance traces primarily back to the Zeitgeist of cortical localization in the second half of the nineteenth century, theories of cerebral specialization were brought forward as early as the middle of the eighteenth century. Swedenborg (1688–1772) was likely the first to generate a theory of cortical localization. He wrote that separate areas of the brain were necessary to prevent psychological chaos and charted his ideas of discrete areas for vision and hearing based on his studies of pathology and anatomy (Finger, 1994). Swedenborg wrote that discrete areas of processing are most likely separated by fissures and gyri. He was ahead of his time, and his ideas were not published until the end of the nineteenth century, when cortical localization theory was broadly accepted and researchers were interested in attributing learning and behavioral problems to structural abnormalities and aberrations within the brain (e.g., Broca, 1861/1997; Jackson, 1874/1932).

Paul Broca (1824–1880), a French surgeon-anthropologist, and Cark Wernicke (1848–1904) significantly contributed to the understanding of cortical localization. Broca is best remembered for identifying an area of the brain that is related to expressive speech. Damage to this area is called Broca's aphasia and usually results from a lesion to the left hemisphere of the brain in either the frontal operculum or the corticocortical association pathways in the white matter of the temporal, parietal, and frontal lobes, which relate to motor speech areas (Martin, 1989). After performing an autopsy on his famous patient, Leborgne (also called Tan), who had suffered from a degenerative ability to produce speech, Broca was able to identify the area of the cerebrum responsible for the damage. On autopsy, Broca identified several areas of the brain that were destroyed and noted that the brain weighed about 400 grams, or 1 pound less than a normal brain (Schiller, 1979). As the relationship between cortical localization and impairment of function was being debated at the time of Broca's discovery, he provided widely accepted evidence for cortical localization theory and an early theory of hemispheric specialization. Broca is primarily responsible for starting the trend in which the left hemisphere was regarded as the dominant hemisphere.

Carl Wernicke postulated that the ability to understand spoken language had a particular localized site in the brain, specifically in the posterior half of the left superior temporal gyrus. The disorder now known as Wernicke's aphasia is generally characterized by defective comprehension of spoken words and fluent, yet incoherent speech. Wernicke's findings added weight to the cortical localization and hemispheric specialization theories by demonstrating that language is located in at least two different cortical areas in the left hemisphere.

The history of cerebral lateralization and hemispheric dominance is also marked by theories that became widely accepted in the twentieth century, which denoted a departure from the strict idea of localization of functions. Hughlings Jackson (1835–1911), an English neurologist interested in epileptic seizures and the connection between body movements and associated areas of the brain, hypothesized that higher mental functions are not discrete actions unto themselves but are combinations of a series of simpler mental processes (Jackson, 1874/1932). He disagreed with localization theorists who proposed that the brain had a single speech center lateralized to the left hemisphere. He viewed speech as a chain reaction of simple mental abilities, such as hearing, fine motor movements, and kinesthetic control of the mouth involving both hemispheres. If an injury to the brain resulted in loss of speech, it did not necessarily occur in Broca's or Wernicke's area. Instead, the injury could disrupt any one of the many processes in either hemisphere that is necessary to create speech. Jackson also suggested that a lesion causing a loss of speech ability did not indicate localization of the brain area responsible for speech; localizing damage that destroys speech and localizing speech are two different tasks (Zillmer & Spiers, 2001).

In regard to hemispheric specialization, Jackson (1874/1932) has written that there are two different modes of cognitive processing divided along hemispheric lines. He reported that language and verbal skills were left-hemispheric-dominated, and visual and spatial processing were the domain of the right hemisphere. Although Jackson recognized the necessity of the complex interaction of brain areas, he also supported the localization viewpoint, believing that each part of the brain was responsible for a specific function.

The second half of the twentieth century marked the emergence and acceptance of the equipotentiality theory, and it is still the basis for theories of cortical processing that are accepted today. Basically, equipotentiality theory proposes that all parts of the cortex contribute to complex functions (Rains, 2002), which makes it difficult to identify an area of the brain that is primarily responsible for a specific task. Despite the influence of the equipotentiality theory, the discussion of cerebral lateralization and hemispheric specialization remains a relevant topic, because even Luria (1970, 1973) acknowledged that complex psychological activity exists through the coordination of discrete cortical zones. Hemispheric specialization and cerebral dominance remain a much researched issue, and the field is marked by conflict, uncertainty, and dissension regarding the structural and functional roles of the left and right hemispheres in higher cortical processing (Dronkers, 2001). However, the progressive advancement of medical technology has started to allow neurologists and neuropsychologists to confirm earlier findings regarding the right and left hemispheres as well as not supporting some earlier beliefs.

As is apparent from this historical review, the role of the clinical neuropsychologist and neuroanatomist until the middle of the twentieth century was to localize function. But the advent of technological advances (e.g., fMRI, PET scans) has largely alleviated that role. Instead, their primary task now is to draw conclusions about the structural functioning of the brain and how it relates to behavior. To help accomplish this task, neuropsychologists have relied on traditional IQ tests, yet these tests do a poor job of localizing functions and identifying hemispheric differences. There has long been an erroneous assumption that verbal IQ tasks rely exclusively on the left hemisphere, and nonverbal IQ tasks rely mostly on the right hemisphere. This approach has been used to incorrectly diagnose childhood disorders ranging from learning disabilities to traumatic brain injury. In general, traditional IQ tests like the Wechsler Intelligence Scale for Children, third edition (Wechsler, 1991), have failed to demonstrate a direct relationship between verbal impairment and left hemispheric damage, and nonverbal impairment and right hemispheric damage (Kaufman, 1994). Perhaps, as Springer and Deutsch (1998) have pointed out, it is more appropriate to assess the hemispheres in terms of an *information-processing model,* as opposed to a strict task approach. This theory has been confirmed with fMRI, which demonstrated that hemispheric specialization depends on the construct of the task, not the stimulus (Stephan et al., 2003). Furthermore, traditional IQ tests often have mixed verbal and nonverbal components in tasks that supposedly solely measure one or the other. Using a simultaneous and successive processing model may be a more apt way to study hemispheric specialization through tests of cognitive processing, such as the Cognitive Assessment System (Das & Naglieri, 1997), which is composed of tasks that measure planning, attention, and simultaneous and successive processing from a brain-based cognitive processing model.

Traditional neuropsychological batteries such as the Halstead-Reitan Neuropsychological Test Battery (HRNB; Reitan & Wolfson, 1993) and the newer Dean-Woodcock Neuropsychological Battery (DWNB; Dean & Woodcock, 2003) can greatly assist school neuropsychologists to identify functional differences between the hemispheres, as well as behavioral implications of lateralized impairment. These batteries and their role in aiding neuropsychologists in their evolving role are briefly discussed in this section; for a more in-depth discussion of these instruments, please see Chapters 10, 11, and 12 in this volume.

The DWNB is a new standardized neuropsychological test battery that can be administered along with the Woodcock-Johnson Tests of Cognitive Abilities (Woodcock, McGrew, & Mather, 2001a) and the Woodcock-Johnson Tests of Achievement (Woodcock, McGrew, & Mather, 2001b). The DWNB offers a sensorimotor battery of 18 subtests that measure auditory, visual, and tactile stimulation. Many of the tasks are performed with both hands, which offers insight into the localization of damage, as impairment in the hemisphere contralateral to the impaired hand typically indicates impairment in that hemisphere (Dean & Woodcock, 2003). For example, on one of the subtests, Tactile Examination–Palm Writing, the patient is required to identify letters and numbers written lightly on the palm of his or her hand. Asymmetric difficulty on this task with one of the patient's hands will indicate possible impairment in the patient's contralateral hemisphere.

The HRNB is the most widely used neuropsychological test battery in the United States and has a rich, well-established history of validation (Dean, 1985b; Guilmette & Faust, 1991). The HRNB consists of different versions for adults, children and adolescents, and younger children. The tests on the HRNB are considered classic neuropsychological tasks, some of which have been widely used since 1947 (Halstead, 1947). Several tests on the HRNB are used to determine laterality, including the Finger Tapping Test, Grip Strength, and Sensory-Perceptual Examination (Reitan & Wolfson, 2001). Although the HRNB is well validated, it lacks a comprehensive normative sample and can be difficult to interpret without extensive training in neuropsychological assessment (Dean, 1985b).

Until recently, the primary role of the neuropsychologist was to identify cerebral lateralization and hemispheric specialization using traditional assessment instruments. Although this approach was amazingly accurate during the past century, the best system for measuring the functioning of the brain is through direct observation. Directly observing the processing of living brains was not possible until the past few years. But this has changed with the increased sophistication of our observation systems, namely, fMRI, single photon emission computed tomography (SPECT) scans, and PET scans, which allow a noninvasive, in-depth examination of brain functioning. Until these innovations became more refined, neurologists could observe structural anomalies only by using techniques such as magnetic resonance imaging (MRI) or computerized tomography (CT) scans. The link between cerebral hemodynamics and neuronal activity was first suggested more than 100 years ago (Roy & Sherrington, 1890). PET scans work by introducing intravenous tracers that allow the observation of cerebral blood flow and volume by monitoring the abundance of the tracer (Joseph, Noble, & Eden, 2001). fMRI can be used as oxygenated blood flow increases during local blood flow; this results in more oxygenated blood than is needed during neuronal tasks, which leads to a relative decrease in deoxyhemoglobin. The contrast between deoxygenated and oxygenated hemoglobin affects the image intensity, which allows observers to note the locale of increased cerebral blood flow (Joseph et al., 2001).

In regard to the future role of the neuropsychologist in analyzing hemispheric specialization and neuropsychological assessment, it is likely that a combined approach of using traditional batteries and newer technology will be employed. Currently, traditional neuropsychological assessment batteries can guide neurologists to utilize medical technology to look for structural impairment that may have been previously unsuspected, and neuroimaging can lead neuropsychologists to assess for specific behavioral impairments as a result of brain lesions or abnormalities. As knowledge increases regarding how the brain processes information, it is likely that a parallel increase in the sophistication of assessment instruments will ensue.

## FUNCTIONAL DIFFERENCES IN CEREBRAL LATERALIZATION AND HEMISPHERIC SPECIALIZATION

Although many different areas of the brain are ultimately responsible for the production of behaviors, it is true that the left and right hemispheres are separately responsible for the generation and etiology of different neuropsychological functional systems. Table 6.1 displays complex cognitive functions that are typically attributed to either the right or left hemisphere. This specialization has been demonstrated in studies involving patients with surgical resections of the corpus callosum or with specific localized lesions lateralized to one hemisphere. Recent advances using fMRI and PET technology illuminated other aspects of hemispheric specialization.

A review of Table 6.1 and recent research suggests that left-right hemispheric differences are reflected in language production and comprehension, visual-spatial ability, volitional attention, inhibition, successive processing, the processing of emotions, and the style of information processing. This left-right lateralization of functions is presented with caution, for not only are many areas of the brain engaged in most behaviors, especially complex ones, but individual differences exist, and a strict verbal-nonverbal lateralization is an oversimplification.

Dean and Hua (1982) proposed that hemispheric specialization is a dynamic process that renders the type of encoding dependent on attention and other individual differences in the lateralization of functions. Dean and Hua's theory is supported by research showing that visual-spatial information can be encoded semantically (Conrad, 1964) and verbal material can be processed along a visual system (Paivio, 1971). From a practical standpoint, it seems that learners can generate verbal or visual strategies to encode and process information regardless of the nature of the original stimuli (Dean & Anderson, 1997). Additionally, some modern theories of cognitive processing have been built on the equipotentiality theories of Jackson and Luria to conceive a brain-based system of processing whereby harmonious, conjoint processing between the two hemispheres is

**Table 6.1**

Lateralized Complex Cognitive Functions of the Left and Right Hemispheres

| Function | Reference |
|---|---|
| **Right Hemisphere** | |
| Processing Modes | |
| Simultaneous | Sperry (1974) |
| Holistic | Sperry (1974), Dimond & Beaumont (1974) |
| Visual/nonverbal | Weisenberg & McBride (1935), Sperry (1974), Savage & Thomas (1993) |
| Imagery | Seamon & Gazzaniga (1973) |
| Spatial reasoning | Sperry (1974), Poizner, Bellugi, & Klima (1990) |
| Nonverbal Functions | |
| Depth perception | Carmon & Bechtold (1969) |
| Melodic perception | Shankweiler (1966) |
| Tactile perception | Boll (1974), Coghill, Gilron, & Iadarola (2001) |
| Haptic perception | Witelson (1974) |
| Nonverbal sound recognition | Milner (1962) |
| Motor integration | Kimura (1967) |
| Visual constructive performance | Parsons, Vega, & Burn (1969) |
| Pattern recognition | Eccles (1973) |
| Memory and Learning | |
| Nonverbal memory | Stark (1961) |
| Face recognition | Milner (1967), Hecaen & Angelergues (1962) |
| **Left Hemisphere** | |
| Processing Modes | |
| Sequential | Sperry, Gazzaniga, & Bogen (1969) |
| Temporal | Mills (1977), Efron (1963) |
| Analytic | Morgan, McDonald, & McDonald (1971), Eccles (1973) |
| Verbal Functions | |
| Speech | Blank, Scott, Murphy, Warburton, & Wise (2002), Wada (1949), Eccles (1973) |
| General language/verbal skills | Friedman et al. (1998), Gazzaniga (1970), Smith (1974) |
| Calculation/arithmetic | Reitan (1955), Eccles (1973), Gerstmann (1957) |
| Abstract verbal thought | Gazzaniga & Sperry (1962) |
| Writing (composition) | Sperry (1974), Hecaen & Marcie (1974) |
| Complex motor functions | Dimond & Beaumont (1974) |
| Body orientation | Gerstmann (1957) |
| Vigilance | Dimond & Beaumont (1974) |
| Learning and Memory | |
| Verbal paired associates | Dimond & Beaumont (1974) |
| Short-term verbal recall | Kimura (1961) |
| Abstract and concrete words | McFarland, McFarland, Bain, & Ashton (1978), Seamon & Gazzaniga (1973) |
| Verbal mediation/rehearsal | Dean (1983), Seamon & Gazzaniga (1973) |
| Learning complex motor function | Dimond & Beaumont (1974) |

Much of this table was reproduced from "Lateralization of Cerebral Functions," by R. S. Dean and J. L. Anderson, in *The Neuropsychology Handbook,* 2nd ed., A. M. Horton, D. Wedding, and J. Webster (Eds.), 1997, New York: Springer Publishing.

possible. For example, the planning, attention, simultaneous, and successive theory (Naglieri, 1999) postulates that although each area can be independently tested, complex behavioral functions may require a combination of different processing systems. With these cautions noted, the following discussion addresses research highlighting left and right hemispheric functional differences.

As Broca and Wernicke first indicated, expressive and receptive language are generally lateralized to the left hemisphere for about 95% of right-handed individuals and about 70% of left-handed individuals (Springer & Deutsch, 1998). Much of the research that has attempted to ascertain and separate right-left hemispheric differences has been conducted on patients with brain injuries, and patients with left hemispheric damage have tended to exhibit different behavioral qualities than do patients with right hemispheric damage. Although the predominance of the left hemisphere for receptive and expressive language processing was substantially revealed by Broca, it was not until several decades later that the importance of the right hemisphere became evident. Springer and Deutsch indicate that the reason it may have taken scientists 70 years after Broca's discoveries to note the importance of the right hemisphere is that the right hemisphere may be able to sustain more damage without producing salient impairments. Small amounts of damage to the left hemisphere can produce dramatic observable impairment in language functioning, but small amounts of damage to the right hemisphere may not produce visible problems. This may indicate that the processes controlled by the right hemisphere are dispersed over a wider area than is true of the left hemisphere (Springer & Deutsch, 1998).

An early study that examined individuals with brain damage indicated that whereas damage to the left hemisphere produced poor performance on tests of verbal ability, damage to the right hemisphere resulted in poor performance on tasks of visual-spatial ability, manipulation of figures and puzzles, and other nonverbal tasks (Weisenberg & McBride, 1935). Research has revealed that the right hemisphere seems to more efficiently conduct simultaneous cognitive processes that involve a gestalt-like integration of stimuli to solve problems with maximum efficiency, as well as transformations of complex visual patterns and information that are not easily processed by verbal mediation (e.g., Gray & Dean, 1990; Levy, Trevarthen, & Sperry, 1972; Milner, 1962). Table 6.1 reveals that individuals tend to employ the right hemisphere to process nonverbal spatial information, nonverbal memory, depth perception, and auditory information that does not have a strong language component (such as a melody). The right hemisphere has also been shown to process parallel spatial information (Bogen & Gazzaniga, 1965) and to be dominant in somatosensory processing (Coghill, Gilron, & Iadarola, 2001).

Some new research has started to implicate the right hemisphere as being a factor in Attention-Deficit/Hyperactivity Disorder (ADHD). For example, some studies have led investigators to conclude that ADHD is more of a right hemispheric problem, finding decreased volume of the right anterior frontal area (Castellanos et al., 1996). This is consistent with problems experienced by children with ADHD; indeed, sensory-attentional skills and motor-intentional skills are both right-hemispheric-dominant. Mostofsky, Cooper, Kates, Denckla, and Kaufman (2002) investigated cerebral volumes for a group of boys with ADHD using MRIs. They discovered that there was a global reduction in gray and white matter for both the left and right hemispheres. However, more reduction in frontal white matter was found in the left hemisphere, and there was a greater reduction in frontal gray matter volume in the right hemisphere. The authors suggested:

> The findings from our study appear to suggest a differential contribution of both the right and left hemisphere, with gray matter abnormalities (most likely reflecting anomalies in neuronal structure) being present bilaterally, although to a greater degree in the right hemisphere, and white matter abnormalities (possibly reflecting disrupted efferent or afferent connections of the frontal lobe, including those with the basal ganglia) being lateralized to the left hemisphere. (p. 791)

Indeed, the right hemisphere may be more likely to be involved with volitional attention skills and inhibition of response difficulties observed in children with ADHD.

Due to the findings of Broca and Wernicke, the left hemisphere has traditionally been known as the hemisphere where speech and language are localized. The left hemisphere is better equipped to engage in successive processing: the placement of stimuli into a discrete, serial order where the detection of one portion of the stimuli depends on its position relative to the other incoming stimuli (Naglieri, 1999). Additionally, the left hemisphere has demonstrated superiority in processing information in an analytical and logical manner, which facilitates the ease of processing language (Dean & Anderson, 1997; Kimura, 1967). The left hemisphere is more engaged in general language and verbal abilities, mathematical functions, body orientation, verbal learning, and short-term memory.

Functional neuroimaging has confirmed the early findings of Broca and Wernicke by looking at prepropositional and nonpropositional speech. Prepropositional speech is the formulation of a deliberate, volitional utterance in response to a question or as a result of independent thought. Nonpropositional speech is the act of repeating or uttering overlearned material, such as the alphabet and nursery rhymes. Blank, Scott, Murphy, Warburton, and Wise (2002) used PET scans to determine that phonological and phonetic coding during prepropositional and nonpropositional speech were attributed to the areas of the brain in the left hemisphere known as Broca's and Wernicke's areas. Additionally, the Blank et al. study was the first to demonstrate that the production of speech involves three distinct areas in the left perisylvian cortex.

Recent research has provided evidence that the processing of emotional material is affected by hemispheric specialization. The majority of research has indicated that the right hemisphere is dominant for the encoding and comprehension of emotions (Atchley, Iiardi, & Enloe, 2003; Borod, 1992; Borod et al., 2000). However, the valence model states that expressed affect, internal emotional experiences, and mood have a differential effect for each cerebral hemisphere (Lee, Meador, Loring, & Bradley, 2002). For example, the valence model indicates that left hemispheric functioning is responsible for more positive emotions, and the right hemisphere is better suited for dealing with negative emotions (Rodway, Wright, & Hardie, 2003). Rodway et al. investigated the valence model and discovered that a valence-specific lateralization exists in females but not in males. Specifically, women tended to discriminate negative emotional experiences more accurately with information presented on the left side and were able to discriminate positive emotions when stimuli was presented on the right side. Their findings supported the valence model for women, but not necessarily for men. However, it has been demonstrated that females tend to be more bilaterally organized in terms of some functions, such as language (Shaywitz et al., 1995). Thus, it is possible that females tend to have a more bilateral representation of emotion as well as language.

Another area of gender difference between the two hemispheres is the style or fashion in which the brain processed information. It has been mentioned that the left hemisphere is more specialized for verbal, linguistic, and successive or temporal processing, and the right hemisphere is more specialized for visual, nonverbal, and simultaneous processing. Springer and Deutsch (1998) proposed that there may be a different way to conceptualize hemispheric differences; instead of analyzing hemispheric specialization based on the type of *task* to be processed, it may be more accurate to examine the type of *information* that is to be processed. For example, they suggested that the left hemisphere's ability to process linguistic information is a result of the left hemisphere's superior analytic processing skills, whereas the right hemisphere's strengths in visual-spatial skills are a consequence of the right hemisphere's superior successive, gestalt-like processing skills. Indeed, Springer and Deutsch have cited research suggesting that the analytical and holistic fashion of processing information has been the most influential process in moving away from the traditional approach of assigning verbal tasks to the left hemisphere and nonverbal tasks to the right hemisphere. This approach seems to fit a more modern approach in the fields of school psychology and neuropsychology, as possible reauthorizations of federal laws may place more emphasis on processing differences and less emphasis on discrepancy models of aptitude and achievement.

Although it is clear that salient hemispheric differences exist, there is also considerable evidence of hemispheric symmetrical processing. For example, in regard to simple sensory stimuli, it appears that both hemispheres demonstrate equal proficiency in encoding and storage, and the amount of functional lateralization seems to increase in direct relation to the amount of conceptual reformulation (Dean & Anderson, 1997; Gordan, 1974; Milner, 1962). Additionally, individuals with unilateral lesions in either hemisphere often demonstrate greater difficulties with the interpretation of stimulus attributes such as brightness, color, pitch, or tone compared to individuals without brain impairment (Gordan, 1974; Milner, 1962). Thus, it seems that both hemispheres contribute at least some interpretive aspects of sensory stimuli. But "it would seem that as the degree of cognitive processing necessary for a task increases, so too does the extent to which the function is asymmetrically lateralized . . . or when information must be interpreted in light of prior knowledge" (Dean & Anderson, 1997, p. 145). An in-depth discussion of hemispheric specialization and language processing appears in the next section.

## CEREBRAL LATERALIZATION AND THE DEVELOPMENT OF LANGUAGE FUNCTIONS

Structural differences in the right and left hemispheres have been observed, with areas of the left hemisphere being significantly larger than in the right (Geschwind

& Levitsky, 1968) in individuals without language problems. Specifically, the left temporale planum, implicated in language and reading (Robichon et al., 2000), is larger than the right planum temporale for most right-handed individuals without language difficulties. A landmark paper by Geschwind and Levitsky found a marked difference between the left and right planum temporale in 65% of 100 brains examined postmortem. Of the 65%, the left hemispheric temporale was larger in 54% of the cases. Galaburda, Consigliore, Rosen, and Sherman (1987) followed up on these findings and concluded that the left planum temporale remains relatively constant in size in different brains, yet the right planum temporale demonstrates developmental differences in size for both asymmetrical and symmetrical brains. This suggests that the right planum temporale's growth is malleable compared to a consistently sized left planum temporale. Research conducted by Geschwind and Levitsky and Galaburda et al. has suggested that an asymmetrical relationship between the left and right hemispheres may contribute to developmental language difficulties.

In a more recent study, Dalby, Elbro, and Stodkilde-Jorgensen (1998) investigated left-right temporal lobe asymmetry and dyslexia using MRIs. The temporal lobes contribute significantly to production and comprehension of language (Duara et al., 1991; Leonard et al., 1993). Dalby et al. found that individuals with dyslexia had symmetry or reversed right asymmetry on measures of temporal lobe size compared to the control group. In fact, 72% of the control group had a larger temporal cortical/subcortical area on the left side, but only 17% of the individuals with dyslexia had a larger left temporal area. Other studies have confirmed findings that individuals with reading problems have atypical symmetry of the left and right hemispheres, including the neuronal size of the visual pathway (Jenner, Rosen, & Galaburda, 1999).

This structural difference between individuals with and without learning problems may indicate the evolutionary importance of the rapid development of language, as the brain may be "prewired" to process language at the time of birth. The theory of equipotentiality of language (Lenneberg, 1967) indicates that the two hemispheres have equal potential to develop specialization for language, yet this possibility is limited by structural differences in the planum temporale. However, even if the hemispheres lack equal potential for development of language and other functions, the possibility that functional lateralization is a developmental process should not be ruled out (Dean & Anderson, 1997).

Although the ideas of cerebral lateralization and language in children trace back to Broca's findings (1861/1997), a pragmatic focus on learning problems and cerebral dominance starts with Orton's (1937) hypothesis. Orton noted that children with dyslexia often reverse letters and numbers and demonstrate bilateral hand and eye preference. Incorporating the belief that language is lateralized to the left hemisphere, he hypothesized that the right hemisphere stores letters and numbers in a mirror image, and then the letters and numbers are transferred to the left hemisphere in their correct spatial orientation. However, he believed that children with dyslexia have a lag in left hemispheric development that prevents the correct translation from the right hemisphere. Thus, Orton hypothesized that children with dyslexia fail to develop proper left hemispheric dominance and that led to a reading problem. But if an individual has language lateralized to a dominant left hemisphere, it would be expected that the individual would demonstrate greater acuity in the right visual and auditory field. Thus, if Orton was correct, it would be hypothesized that individuals with dyslexia would demonstrate a less dominant right eye and right ear (Gray & Dean, 1990). However, most research has indicated that individuals with dyslexia have the same strength as normal subjects in right visual and auditory acuity (Sparrow & Satz, 1970; Witelson, 1977).

Overall, Orton's (1937) idea of asymmetrical bilateralization leading to learning disabilities in children has undergone decades of scrutiny, and it is still difficult to ascertain the validity of his claims (Dean, 1981). It may be safest to conclude that in the majority of individuals, language is served in the left hemisphere, although it is likely that both the right and left hemispheres contribute to language, the degree to which may be mediated by *gender* and *handedness.* Although some of the details of Orton's hypothesis have not been sustained, his view that anomalous cerebral lateralization may be at the root of language problems has continued to be accepted (Richardson, 1995).

Handedness and cerebral lateralization as they relate to the cerebral development of language functions have been extensively studied. Orton's (1937) observation that the failure to develop hemispheric dominance was responsible for reading problems was partially based on his studies of bilateral hand and eye preference. Because handedness and other peripheral activities are controlled by the contralateral hemisphere, Zangwill (1962) proposed that the lack of consistent dominance with behavioral tasks indicates confusion at the cortical level. He reached this hypothesis after finding that 88% of individuals with developmental dyslexia show some mixed-hand tendencies (Zangwill, 1960). Springer and Deutsch (1998) reported that left-handed individuals had a better prognosis for recovering from aphasic language symptoms following a stroke than did right-handed individuals. This may indicate that language is more bilaterally organized in left-handed individuals. Orton initially noted a large number of non-right-handed individuals who had language problems. Although handedness has been found to relate to structural brain asymmetries (Annett, 1992), research has consistently failed to establish that non-right-handedness is related to dyslexia, although many of the studies have been marked by inconsistencies and contradictions relating to the actual definition and measurement of handedness (Richardson, 1995). It is likely that hand preference falls along a continuum, and lateral preference should be measured in this fashion (Dean & Woodcock, 2003). Indeed, some research has indicated that this is the case, with approximately 25% of the population showing some mixed-hand preferences (Annett, 1970). The percentage breakdown of handedness, with about 65% of individuals expressing consistent right-hand preference, 10% of individuals expressing left-hand preference, and 25% expressing mixed preference, mirrors the distribution for planum temporale asymmetry (Richardson, 1995), which suggests that handedness may indeed be related to language-processing disorders.

Besides the theory of cerebral dominance, other theories exist that relate to developmental dyslexia, or congenital difficulties with language and reading. One of these theories is the magnocellular processing theory. The magnocellular pathway has been implicated in reading problems for individuals with dyslexia (Facoetti et al., 2003; Fawcett, 2003). The magnocellular pathway is a visual pathway that starts in the retina and sends information back to the occipital lobe for processing; individuals with reading problems may have significantly fewer neurons in the magnocellular pathway than do normal readers, which can result in slower or blurred reading (Feifer & DeFina, 2000). Recently, Stein (2003) noted that individuals with reading problems have difficulties with phonemic segmentation and in sequencing visual symbols, skills that involve the magnocellular visual-processing system. He also noted that individuals with reading problems have reduced flicker and motion sensitivity, which is linked to abnormal hemispheric lateralization. From these findings, Stein concluded that normal magnocellular system development is related to normal cerebral lateralization and that deficits in the magnocellular processing system may lead to abnormal cerebral lateralization, which can cause language problems.

Richardson (1995) conducted a study in which he observed visual motion sensitivity in a group of individuals with dyslexia compared to a group of controlled normals. In addition to finding poorer motion sensitivity (measuring the magnocellular visual-processing system) among individuals with dyslexia, a main effect indicated that non-right-handers also demonstrated poorer motion sensitivity. Richardson's findings strengthen the idea that abnormal cerebral lateralization and the magnocellular processing system are related to language problems and that deficits with the magnocellular processing system may actually lead to abnormal hemispheric specialization.

Similar to the arresting influence of an impaired magnocellular processing system and development of language, Dean (1978) hypothesized that a possible bilateralization of language functions can impede the development of the right hemisphere. The verbal functions that are subsumed by the right hemisphere may occupy the processing areas that would normally be used for the development of visual processing, regularly a right hemispheric function. Dean (1980) indicated that readers who possess good decoding skills but lack the syntax-processing abilities required to comprehend written sentences, termed *difference-poor readers* by Wiener and Cromer (1967), are suffering from their poor ability to organize visual information compared to the more traditionally assumed verbal deficit. The distinction is important from an evidence-based practice point of view, as difference-poor readers will likely require visual-spatial right hemispheric academic interventions, as opposed to verbal, left-hemispheric-dominated interventions.

It is not clear to what degree functional development is lateralized. Dean (1985a) proposed that the functional lateralization of the hemispheres develop in a progressive pattern parallel to the child's neurological development. However, there is a question of whether some hemispheric specialization is innate or develops when the corresponding skill is acquired. For example, left hemispheric asymmetries related to language are present at birth (Preis, Jancke, Schmitz-Hillebrecht, & Steinmetz, 1999). However, these findings contrast with research showing that language can develop normally in children who sustain unilateral lesions to the left hemisphere (Muter, Taylor, & Vargha-Khadem, 1997). Balsamo et al. (2002) have indicated that there are two possible answers to this conundrum: Either language is solely localized in the left hemisphere from birth, or language is equally localized in both hemispheres but becomes gradually subsumed by the left hemisphere as development progresses. Balsamo et al. performed fMRI on a group of children with a mean age of 8.5 years and determined that hemispheric lateralization of language was similar to that in adults, which indicates that by age 8, language is no longer bilaterally evident. Earlier studies (e.g., Booth et al., 2001) have found contrasting results. As time progresses, it is hoped that these questions will be answered, as the development of cerebral lateralization can guide the nature of interventions for children following a unilateral or bilateral lesion.

Although it is clear that for the vast majority of individuals language is lateralized in the left hemisphere, the right hemisphere also plays a role in how we communicate. One way to study the effect the right hemisphere has on language is to examine patients who have had either their left hemisphere removed or their corpus collosum severed through surgery, a procedure used primarily to control severe epilepsy. A review of this research reveals that in some patients who have undergone this surgery, their right hemispheres have subsumed many of the language functions previously controlled by the now defunct left hemisphere (Springer & Deutsch, 1998). This process occurs over time (Springer & Deutsch, 1998) and is more evident in children under age 5 than in adults (Zillmer & Spiers, 2001). In addition to the right hemisphere's ability to subsume language functions, it aids in the visual-spatial processing of words that is necessary for reading (Posner & Raichle, 1994).

The knowledge base regarding the neural circuitry of language has increased because of the use of fMRI and PET scans, and recent research further illuminates the role of both the left and right hemispheres in language. A seminal study on the topic of the neural circuitry of reading and hemispheric specialization was conducted by Posner and Raichle (1994) using PET scans. In this study, individuals were required to complete four different reading tasks during a PET scan. The first task involved reading images of nonletter symbols. On this task, the right hemisphere became activated when interpreting these symbols, and the left hemisphere remained dormant. The second task required the subjects to read real letters that formed nonwords. Once again, the right hemisphere was more active than the left. In both cases, the activation of the right hemisphere was triggered by the analysis of visual and spatial information that required little contribution from the left hemisphere. The third task, though, asked subjects to read pseudowords, or strings of letters that formed nonwords organized according to the rules of the English language. Here, PET scans indicated that both hemispheres were activated, indicating that the right hemisphere was analyzing the spatial components of the nonwords, while the left hemisphere was attempting to transfer the symbols into a meaningful linguistic code. The final task required subjects to read real words. This primarily activated the left hemisphere. This research added credence to the specialization of each hemisphere, highlighting the left hemisphere's role in language and the right hemisphere's role in visual-spatial processing.

Other studies using PET scans further implicated the dominance of the left hemisphere in language processing. For example, research on orthographical processing (analyzing the printed structures of letters that compose words) generally implicates Broca's, Wernicke's, and other left hemispheric areas (Benson et al., 1996; Friedman et al., 1998; & Paulesu et al., 1997). Phonological processing studies involving the interpretation of the sound-symbol association of words also confirms the left hemisphere's role in language processing. Although, from an equipotentiality perspective, phonological processing, like other processing skills, requires different areas of the brain, PET studies have generally indicated that phonological processing tasks require activation of the left insula (Paulesu et al., 1997), the left posterior superior temporal gyrus (Paulesu et al., 1997), and Broca's area (Paulesu et al., 1997; Rumsey et al., 1997).

## GENDER DIFFERENCES IN CEREBRAL LATERALIZATION AND HEMISPHERIC SPECIALIZATION

Clear structural neurological differences are known to exist between males and females, and the literature has indicated several neuropsychological gender differences that are attributable to lateralization differences (Lewald, 2004). Gender differences in hemispheric specialization and lateralization of functions should be expected, as females tend to mature at a quicker rate than males, and neurological development is no exception to this more rapid maturation (Shaywitz et al., 1995). For example, Shaywitz et al. indicated that males and females process reading tasks differently, and Lynn (1995) indicated that there are structural differences in the brain between males and females. Anatomical brain differences between males and females render cognitive differences self-evident. For example, the area of the corpus callosum that connects the functional asymmetric temporo-parietal regions is larger in women (Witelson, 1989). This supports the theory that females' brains are more bilaterally organized in their representation of cognitive functions (Jancke & Steinmetz, 1994).

Recent studies that indicate structural brain differences between males and females have helped lead to the conclusion of gender lateralization differences. Shaywitz et al. (1995) used echo-planar fMRI, an electronic brain imaging technique, to determine that when males are engaged in phonological tasks, the brain activation is lateralized to the left inferior frontal gyrus regions. For females, phonological tasks activated a more diffuse neural system that involved both the front left and right inferior frontal gyrus. These gender differences in neural construction led to a conclusion that gender differences also exist in how information is processed within and between hemispheres. For example, it has been suggested that phonological processing is more bilaterally organized in females than in males, and fMRI studies have indicated differential hemispheric specialization for phonological processing (Pugh et al., 1996).

Xu et al. (2001) investigated the relationship between language, gender, and lateralization by using high-resolution three-dimensional PET scans. They found that "there are highly lateralized epicenters engaged in the phonological processing of words and pseudowords. These epicenters appear to be in the left hemisphere for both males and females" (p. 272). Although the lateralization of language to the left hemisphere corresponds with previous research, these results are contrary to other findings (e.g., Shaywitz et al., 1995) that indicate language is more bilaterally organized in females.

One theory pertaining to gender differences regarding hemispheric specialization postulates that neuropsychological differences between males and females are more attributable to functional-organizational attributes than to salient structural dissimilarities (Dean, 1985a). For example, Naglieri and Rojahn (2001) found a gender discrepancy in planning processing abilities in children age 11 to 17 years. Because females generally reach puberty several years before males, gender cognitive processing differences may be related to their rate of development, not pervasive cognitive differences. Indeed, Davis (2003) discovered that adult males and females demonstrate equivalency on planning processing skills. Other studies indicate that males and females, especially younger children, may demonstrate differences in the functional allocation of resources, with females generally allocating more brain resources to skills such as planning, attention, and verbal skills, whereas males tend to have better visual-spatial skills (Macoby & Jacklin, 1974; Naglieri & Rojahn, 2001; Voyer, Voyer, & Bryden, 1995).

It has been hypothesized that the etiology of gender neurological differences is at least partially attributable to perinatal and postconception hormonal differences (Geary, 1989; Gur, Gunning-Dixon, Bilker, & Gur, 2002). Hormones can have a significant effect on the structure of the central nervous system because hormones permeate the blood-brain barrier and have a high level of access to the brain early in a fetus's life (Baum, 1979; Schmeck, 1980). Consequently, exposure to hormones may alter the development of hemispheric specialization. Nass, Baker, Sadler, and Sidtis (1990) discovered that an increase in the activity of the adrenal glands prior to puberty (adrenarche) may limit the development of the right hemisphere and produce a subsequent deficit in visual-spatial skills in females who reach this stage of development before males.

Voyer et al. (1995) were interested in investigating the hypothesis that males have better spatial abilities than females. They conducted a comprehensive meta-analysis of previous studies that examined gender differences in spatial abilities and concluded that there does appear to be superiority in spatial processing for males. They found that the spatial ability differences between males and females were greatest in the area of mental rotation, less consistent for spatial perception, and highly variable and often nonsignificant for spatial visualization. Spatial visualization ability is a clear right hemispheric function, and it has been suggested that testosterone may stimulate growth in the right hemisphere or delay development in the left hemisphere (de Lacoste, Horvath, & Woodward, 1991). This may help explain why females tend to have better-developed left hemispheric specialized language ability, especially earlier in life. Indeed, males are 10 times more likely than females to have severe dyslexia (Sutaria, 1985).

The research reviewed in this section attributes the gender differences in hemispheric specialization and lateralization of functions to myriad causes, including hormonal differences, structural differences, organizational differences, and developmental differences. Despite these findings, one must be careful not to attribute differences in neuropsychological functioning solely to organic causes and overlook behavioral and social influences (Dean & Anderson, 1997). Males and females are treated differently in our society; for example, demographic data indicate that a higher percentage of males are referred for assessment, receive special education services, and are identified with reading problems (D'Amato, Dean, Rattan, & Nickell, 1988; Share & Silva, 2003). It is important to consider whether gender differences in social expectations and treatment are causing observable behavioral differences, or may even be contributing to the development of structural or functional differences in the lateralization of functions and hemispheric specialization.

## CONCLUSION

The lateralization of cerebral functions has been a topic of research and interest for the past 150 years, yet hemispheric specialization is still poorly understood (Stephan et al., 2003). As medical technology has improved, the field of neuropsychology has learned more about the structure, function, and processing abilities of the left and right hemispheres. This chapter noted differences in cerebral hemispheric processing that have been found in the areas of language, nonverbal skills, visual-spatial skills, memory, and many other important behavioral functions. Additionally, each hemisphere processes information differently depending on the nature of the task. However, there is a tendency in the educational system to favor tasks that have a left hemispheric basis, and this can be seen from academic classroom tasks to traditional IQ tests (Springer & Deutsch, 1998).

The finding that the two hemispheres differ in structure and functioning led to the conclusion that children with left or right hemispheric impairments may struggle with certain types of information processing. For example, if the right hemisphere is superior at processing simultaneous information, and the left hemisphere is better at successive processing, then a child with reading difficulties who has impairment in the left hemisphere may struggle with a successive phonemic approach but succeed with a holistic whole-word approach. Traditionally, schools have not taken children's hemispheric differences into account when planning instruction and education. Hartlage and Golden (1990) write:

> The focus of educators on exposing all children of a given age to a common set of achievement expectancies tends to neglect all that is known about individual differences in human cerebral hemisphere specialization, and contributes in a major way to maximizing the likelihood that at any given age a number of children in a given classroom will be unable to process information at a rate sufficient for academic success. (p. 433)

However, it is important to note that there is a lack of evidence to support the use of tasks such as simple visual exercises or laterality training to improve linguistic performance (Michaels, 1974). This suggests the lack of effectiveness of remediation for children with deviations in functional symmetry and the need for compensatory strategies. Indeed, cerebral lateralization and hemispheric specialization have direct applicability to school psychologists when taking neuropsychological strengths and weaknesses into account to plan compensatory interventions.

## REFERENCES

Annett, M. (1970). A classification of hand preference by association analysis. *British Journal of Psychology, 67,* 587–592.

Annett, M. (1992). Parallels between asymmetries of planum temporale and of hand skill. *Neuropsychologia, 30,* 951–962.

Atchley, R. A., Iiaridi, S. S., & Enloe, A. (2003). Hemispheric asymmetry in the processing of emotional content in word meanings: The effect of current and past depression. *Brain and Language, 84,* 105–119.

Balsamo, L. M., Xu, B., Grandin, C. B., Petrella, J. R., Braniecki, S. H., Elliot, T. K., et al. (2002). A functional magnetic resonance imaging study of left hemisphere language dominance in children. *Archives of Neurology, 59,* 1168–1174.

Baum, M. J. (1979). Difference of coital behavior in mammals: A comparative analysis. *Neuroscience and Biobehavioral Reviews, 3,* 268–284.

Benson, R. R., Logan, W. J., Cosgrove, G. R., Cole, A. J., Jiang, H., LeSueurr, L. L., et al. (1996). Functional MRI localization of language in a 9 year old child. *The Canadian Journal of Neurological Sciences, 23,* 213–219.

Blank, S. C., Scott, S. K., Murphy, K., Warburton, W., & Wise, R. J. S. (2002). Speech production: Wernicke, Broca and beyond. *Brain, 125,* 1829–1838.

Bogen, J. E., & Gazzaniga, M. S. (1965). Cerebral commissurotoma in man: Minor hemispheric dominance for certain visuo-spatial functions. *Journal of Neurosurgery, 23,* 394–399.

Boll, T. J. (1974). Behavioral correlates of cerebral damage in children age 9–14. In R. M. Reitan & L. A. Davison (Eds.), *Clinical neuropsychology: Current status and application.* Washington, DC: Hemisphere Press.

Booth, J. R., MacWhinney, B., Thulborn, K. R., Sacco, K., Voyvodic, J. T., & Feldman, H. M. (2001). Developmental and lesion effects in brain activation during sentence comprehension and mental rotation. *Developmental Neuropsychology, 18,* 139–169.

Borod, J. C. (1992). Interhemispheric and intrahemispheric control of emotion: A focus on unilateral brain damage. *Journal of Consulting and Clinical Psychology, 60,* 339–348.

Borod, J. C., Rorie, K. D., Pick, L. H., Bloom, R. L., Andelman, F., Campbell, A. L., et al. (2000). Verbal pragmatics following unilateral stroke: Emotional content and valence. *Neuropsychology, 14,* 112–124.

Broca, P. (1997). Bulletin de la Societe anatomiaque de Paris, 6. In L. Benjamin, *A History of psychology: Original sources and contemporary research.* McGraw-Hill: United States. (Original work published 1861)

Carmon, A., & Bechtoldt, H. (1969). Dominance of the right cerebral hemisphere for stereopsis. *Neuropsychologia, 7,* 29–39.

Castellanos, F. X., Giedd, J. N., Marsh, W. L., Hamburger, S. D., Vaituzis, A. C., & Dickstein, D. P. (1996). Quantitative brain magnetic resonance imaging in attention-deficit-hyperactivity disorder. *Archives of General Psychiatry, 53,* 607–616.

Coghill, R. C., Gilron, I., & Iadarola, J. (2001). Hemispheric lateralization of somatosensory processing. *Journal of Neurophysiology, 85,* 2602–2612.

Conrad, R. (1964). Acoustic confusions in immediate memory. *British Journal of Psychology, 55,* 75–83.

Dalby, M. A., Elbro, C., & Stodkilde-Jorgensen, H. (1998). Temporal lobe asymmetry and dyslexia: An in vivo study using MRI. *Brain and Language, 62,* 51–69.

D'Amato, R. C., Dean, R. S., Rattan, G., & Nickell, K. (1988). A study of psychological referrals for learning disabled children. *Journal of Pyschoeducational Assessment, 6,* 118–124.

Das, J. P., & Naglieri, J. A. (1997). *Cognitive Assessment System.* Itasca, IL: Riverside.

Davis, A. S. (2003). *Evaluating gender differences in experimental planning, attention, simultaneous and successive neuropsychological tasks in participants with and without learning disabilities.* Unpublished doctoral dissertation, University of Northern Colorado, Greeley, CO.

Dean, R. S. (1978). Cerebral laterality and reading comprehension. *Neuropsychologia, 16,* 633–636.

Dean, R. S. (1980). Cerebral lateralization and reading dysfunction. *Journal of School Psychology, 18,* 324–332.

Dean, R. S. (1981). Cerebral dominance and childhood learning disorders: Theoretical perspectives. *School Psychology Review, 10,* 373–380.

Dean, R. S. (1983, February). *Dual processing of prose and cerebral laterality.* Paper presented at the annual meeting of the International Neuropsychological Society, Mexico City.

Dean, R. S. (1985a). Foundation and rationale for neuropsychological bases of individual differences. In L. C. Hartlage & C. F. Telzrow (Eds.), *The neuropsychology of individual differences: A developmental perspective* (pp. 8–39). New York: Plenum Press.

Dean, R. S. (1985b). Review of Halstead-Reitan Neuropsychological Test Battery. In J. V. Mitchell (Ed.), *The ninth mental measurements yearbook* (pp. 642–646). Highland Park, NJ: The Gryphon Press.

Dean, R. S., & Anderson, J. L. (1997). Lateralization of cerebral functions. In A. M. Horton, D. Wedding, & J. Webster (Eds.), *The neuropsychology handbook* (2nd ed.). New York: Spring Publishing.

Dean, R. S., & Hua, M. (1982). Laterality effects in cued auditory asymmetries. *Neuropsychologia, 20,* 685–690.

Dean, R. S., & Woodcock, R. W. (2003). Examiners manual. *Dean-Woodcock Neuropsychological Battery.* Itasca, IL: Riverside.

de Lacoste, M. C., Horvath, D. S., & Woodward, D. J. (1991). Possible sex differences in the developing human fetal brain. *Journal of Clinical and Experimental Neuropsychology, 13,* 831–846.

Dimond, S., & Beaumont, J. (1974). *Hemispheric function in the human brain.* New York: Wiley.

Dronkers, N. F. (2001). The pursuit of brain-language relationships. *Brain and Language, 71,* 59–61.

Duara, R., Kushch, A., Gross-Glenn, K., Barker, W. W., Jallad, B., Pascal, S., et al. (1991). Neuroanatomic differences between dyslexic and normal readers on magnetic resonance imaging scans. *Archives of Neurology, 48,* 410–416.

Eccles, J. C. (1973). *The understanding of the brain.* New York: McGraw-Hill.

Effron, R. (1963). The effect of handedness on the perception of simultaneity and temporal order. *Brain, 86,* 261–284.

Facoetti, A., Lorusso, M. L., Paganoni, P., Cattaneo, C., Galli, R., & Mascetti, G. G. (2003). The time course of attentional focusing in dyslexic and normally reading children. *Brain and Cognition, 53,* 181–184.

Fawcett, A. (2003). Dyslexia and literacy: Theory and practice. *British Journal of Developmental Psychology, 21,* 619–620.

Feifer, S. G., & DeFina, P. A. (2000). *The neuropsychology of reading disorders: Diagnosis and intervention workbook.* Middletown, MD: School Neuropsych Press.

Finger, S. (1994). History of neuropsychology. In D. Zaidel (Ed.), *Neuropsychology.* San Diego: Academic Press.

Friedman, L., Kenny, J. T., Wise, A. A. L., Wu, D., Stuve, T. A., Miller, D. A., et al. (1998). Brain activation during silent word generation evaluated with functional MRI. *Brain and Language, 38,* 278–287.

Galaburda, A. M., Corsiglia, J., Rosen, G. D., & Sherman, G. F. (1987). Planum temporale asymmetry reappraisal since Geschwind and Levitsky. *Neuropsychologia, 25,* 853–868.

Gazzaniga, M. S. (1970). *The bisected brain.* New York: Appleton-Century-Crofts.

Gazzaniga, M. S., & Sperry, R. W. (1962). Language after section of the cerebral commissures. *Brain, 90,* 131–148.

Geary, D. (1989, August). A model for representing gender differences in the pattern of cognitive abilities. *American Psychologist,* 1155–1156.

Gerstmann, J. (1957). Some notes on the Gerstmann syndrome. *Neurology, 7,* 866–869.

Geschwind, N., & Levitsky, W. (1968). Human brain: Left-right asymmetries in temporal speech region. *Science, 161,* 186–187.

Gordan, H. W. (1974). Auditory specialization of the right and left hemispheres. In M. Kinsborne & W. L. Smith (Eds.), *Hemispheric disconnection and cerebral function.* Springfield, IL: Charles C. Thomas.

Gray, J. W., & Dean, R. S. (1990). Implications of neuropsychological research for school psychology. In T. B. Gutkin & C. R. Reynolds (Eds.), *The handbook of school psychology* (2nd ed., pp. 431–457). Oxford, England: Wiley.

Guilmette, T. J., & Faust, D. (1991). Characteristics of neuropsychologists who prefer the Halstead-Reitan or the Luria-Nebraska Neuropsychology Battery. *Professional Psychology: Research and Practice, 22,* 80–83.

Gur, R., Gunning-Dixon, F., Bilker, W., & Gur, R. (2002). Sex differences in temporo-limbic and frontal brain volumes of healthy adults. *Cerebral Cortex, 12,* 998–1003.

Halstead, W. C. (1947). *Brain and intelligence: A quantitative study of the frontal lobes.* Chicago: University of Chicago Press.

Hartlage, L. C., & Golden, C. J. (1990). Neuropsychological assessment techniques. In T. B. Gutkin & C. R. Reynolds (Eds.), *The handbook of school psychology* (2nd ed., pp. 431–457). Oxford, England: Wiley.

Hecaen, H., & Angelergues, R. (1962). Agnosia for faces (prosopagnosia). *Archives of Neurology, 7,* 24–32.

Hecaen, H., & Marcie, P. (1974). Disorders of written language following right hemisphere lesions: Spatial dysgraphia. In S. J. Dimond & J. G. Beaumont (Eds.), *Hemisphere function in the human brain* (pp. 345–366). New York: Wiley.

Jackson, J. H. (1932). On the duality of the brain. In J. Taylor (Ed.), *Selected writings of John Hughlings Jackson* (Vol. 2). London: Hodder and Stoughton. (Original work published 1874)

Jancke, L., & Steinmetz, H. (1994). Interhemispheric-transfer time and corpus collosum size. *NeuroReport, 5,* 2385–2388.

Jenner, A. R., Rosen, G. D., & Galaburda, A. M. (1999). Neuronal asymmetries in primary visual cortex of dyslexic and nondyslexic brains. *Annals of Neurology, 46,* 189–196.

Joseph, J., Noble, K., & Eden, G. (2001). The neurobiological basis of reading. *Journal of Learning Disabilities, 34,* 566–579.

Kaufman, A. S. (1994). *Intelligent testing with the WISC-III.* New York: Wiley.

Kimura, D. (1961). Cerebral dominance and the perception of visual stimuli. *Canadian Journal of Psychology, 15,* 166–171.

Kimura, D. (1967). Functional asymmetry of the brain in dichotic listening. *Cortex, 3,* 163–178.

Lee, G. P., Meador, K. J., Loring, D. W., & Bradley, K. P. (2002). Lateralized changes in autonomic arousal during emotional processing in patients with unilateral temporal lobe seizure onset. *International Journal of Neuroscience, 112,* 743–757.

Lenneberg, E. H. (1967). *Biological foundations of language.* New York: Wiley.

Leonard, C. M., Voeller, K. K. S., Lombardino, L. J., Morris, M. K., Hynd, G. W., Alexander, A. W., et al. (1993). Anomalus cerebral structure in dyslexia revealed with magnetic resonance imaging. *Archives of Neurology, 50,* 461–469.

Levy, J., Trevarthen, C., & Sperry, R. W. (1972). Perceptions of bilateral chimeric figures following hemispheric disconnection. *Brain, 95,* 61–78.

Lewald, J. (2004). Gender-specific hemispheric asymmetry in auditory space perception. *Cognitive-Brain Research, 19,* 92–99.

Luria, A. R. (1970). *Traumatic aphasia, its syndromes, psychology and treatment.* Oxford, England: Mouton.

Luria, A. R. (1973). *The working brain.* Harmondsworth, UK: Basic Books.

Lynn, R. (1995). Sex differences in intelligence and brain size: A paradox resolved. *Personality and Individual Differences, 17,* 257–271.

Macoby, E. E., & Jacklin, C. N. (1974). *The psychology of sex differences.* Stanford, CA: Stanford University Press.

Martin, J. H. (1989). *Neuroanatomy: Text and atlas.* Norwalk, CT: Appleton and Lange.

McFarland, K., McFarland, M. L., Bain, J. D., & Ashton, R. (1978). Ear differences of abstract and concrete word recognition. *Neuropsychologia, 16,* 555–561.

Michaels, D. D. (1974). Ocular dominance. *Surgery of Ophthalmology, 17,* 151–163.

Milner, B. (1962). Laterality effects in audition. In V. B. Mountcastle (Ed.), *Interhemispheric relations and cerebral dominance.* Baltimore: Johns Hopkins University Press.

Milner, B. (1967). Brain mechanisms suggested by studies of the temporal lobes. In C. H. Millian & F. L. Darley (Eds.), *Brain mechanisms underlying speech and language* (pp. 381–414). New York: Grune and Stratton.

Mills, L. (1977). *Left hemispheric specialization in normal subjects for judgments of successive order and duration of nonverbal stimuli.* Unpublished doctoral dissertation, University of Western Ontario, London, Ontario, Canada.

Morgan, A., McDonald, P. J., & McDonald, H. (1971). Differences in bilateral alpha activity as a function of experimental tasks, with a note on lateral eye movements and hypnotizability. *Neuropsychologia, 9,* 459–469.

Mostofsky, S. H., Cooper, K. L., Kates, W. R., Denckla, M. B., & Kaufman, W. E. (2002). Smaller prefrontal and premotor volumes in boys with attention-deficit/hyperactivity disorder. *Biological Psychiatry, 52,* 785–794.

Muter, V., Taylor, S., & Vargha-Khadem, F. (1997). A longitudinal study of early intellectual development in hemiplegic children. *Neuropsychologia, 35,* 289–298.

Naglieri, J. A. (1999). *Essentials of CAS assessment.* New York: Wiley.

Naglieri, J. A., & Rojahn, J. (2001). Gender differences in planning, attention, simultaneous and successive (PASS) cognitive processes and achievement. *Journal of Educational Psychology, 93,* 430–437.

Nass, R., Baker, S., Sadler, A. E., & Sidtis, J. J. (1990). The effects of precocious adrenarche on cognition and hemispheric specialization. *Brain and Cognition, 14,* 59–69.

Orton, S. T. (1937). *Reading, writing, and speech problems in children.* New York: Norton.

Paivio, A. (1971). *Imagery and verbal processes.* New York: Holt, Rinehart and Winston.

Parsons, O. A., Vega, A., & Burn, J. (1969). Different psychological effects of lateralized brain damage. *Journal of Consulting and Clinical Psychology, 33,* 551–557.

Paulesu, E., Goldacre, B., Scifo, P., Cappa, S. F., Gilardi, M. C., Castiglioni, D. P., et al. (1997). Functional heterogeneity of left inferior frontal cortex as revealed by fMRI. *NeuroReport, 8,* 2011–2016.

Poizner, H., Bellugi, U., & Klima, E. S. (1990). Biological foundations of language: Clues from sign language. *Annual Review of Neuroscience, 13,* 283–307.

Posner, M. I., & Raichle, M. E. (1994). *Images of the mind.* New York: Freeman Company.

Preis, S., Jancke, L., Schmitz-Hillbrecht, J., & Steinmetz, H. (1999). Child age and planum temporale asymmetry. *Brain and Cognition, 40,* 1038–1043.

Pugh, K. R., Shaywitz, B. A., Constable, R. T., Shaywitz, S. A., Skudlarski, P., Fulbright, R. K., et al. (1996). Cerebral organization of component processes in reading. *Brain, 119,* 1221–1238.

Rains, G. D. (2002). *Principles of human neuropsychology.* Boston: McGraw-Hill.

Reitan, R. M. (1955). An investigation of the validity of Halstead's measure of biological intelligence. *Archives of Neurology and Psychiatry, 73,* 28–35.

Reitan, R. M., & Wolfson, D. (1993). *The Halstead-Reitan Neuropsychological Test Battery.* Tucson, AZ: Neuropsychology Press.

Reitan, R. M., & Wolfson, D. (2001). Halstead-Reitan Neuropsychological Test Battery: Research findings and clinical application. In A. S. Kaufman & N. L. Kaufman (Eds.), *Specific learning disabilities and difficulties in children and adolescents: Psychological assessment and evaluation* (pp. 309–346). New York: Cambridge University Press.

Richardson, A. J. (1995). Handedness and visual motion sensitivity in adult dyslexics. *The Irish Journal of Psychology, 16,* 229–247.

Robichon, F., Levrier, O., Farnarier, P., & Habib, M. (2000). Developmental dyslexia: Atypical cortical asymmetries and functional significance. *European Journal of Neurology, 7,* 35–46.

Rodway, P., Wright, L., & Hardie, S. (2003). The valence-specific laterality effect in free viewing conditions: The influence of sex, handedness and response bias. *Brain and Cognition, 53,* 452–463.

Roy, C. S., & Sherrington, C. S. (1890). On the regulation of the blood supply of the brain. *Journal of Physiology, 11,* 85–105.

Rumsey, J. M., Horwitz, B., Donohue, B. C., Nace, K., Maisog, J. M., & Andreason, P. (1997). Phonologic and orthographic components of word recognition. A PET rCBF study. *Brain, 120,* 739–759.

Savage, C. R., & Thomas, D. G. (1993). Information processing and interhemispheric transfer in left- and right-handed adults. *International Journal of Neuroscience, 71,* 201–219.

Seamon, J. G., & Gazzaniga, M. D. (1973). Coding strategies and cerebral laterality effects. *Cognitive Psychology, 5,* 249–256.

Schiller, F. (1979). *Paul Broca: Founder of French anthropology, explorer of the brain.* Berkeley: University of California Press.

Schmeck, H. H. (1980). His brain, her brain. *Science and Living Tomorrow, 15,* 23–24.

Shankweiler, D. (1996). Effects of temporal-lobe damage on perception of dichototically presented melodies. *Journal of Comparative Psychology, 62,* 115–119.

Share, D., & Silva, P. (2003). Gender bias in IQ-discrepancy and post-discrepancy definitions of reading disability. *Journal of Learning Disabilities, 36,* 4–14.

Shaywitz, B. A., Shaywitz, S. E., Pugh, K. R., Constable, R. T., Skullarski, P., Fulbright, R. K., et al. (1995). Sex difference in the functional organization of the brain for language. *Nature, 373,* 607–609.

Smith, A. (1974). Dominant and nondominant hemispherectomy. In M. Kinsborne & W. L. Smith (Eds.), *Hemispheric deconnection and cerebral function.* Springfield, IL: Charles C Thomas.

Sparrow, S., & Satz, P. (1970). Dyslexia, laterality, and neuropsychological development. In D. J. Bakker & P. Satz (Eds.), *Specific reading disability: Advances in theory and method.* Rotterdam: Rotterdam University Press.

Sperry, R. W. (1974). Lateral specialization in the surgically separated hemispheres. In F. O. Schmitt & F. G. Worden (Eds.), *The neurosciences: Third study program.* New York: Wiley.

Sperry, R. W., Gazzaniga, M. S., & Bogen, J. H. (1969). Interhemispheric relationships: The neocortical commissures: Syndromes of hemispheric disconnection. In P. Vinken & G. W. Bruyn (Eds.), *Handbook of clinical neurology* (Vol. 4). New York: Wiley.

Springer, S. P., & Deutsch, G. (1998). *Left brain, right brain: Perspectives from cognitive neuroscience.* New York: Freeman.

Stark, R. (1961). An investigation of unilateral cerebral pathology with equated verbal and visual-spatial tasks. *Journal of Abnormal and Social Psychology, 62*, 282–287.

Stein, J. (2003). Visual motion sensitivity and reading. *Neuropsychologia, 41*, 1785–1793.

Stephan, K. C., Marshall, J. C., Friston, K. J., Rowe, J. B., Ritzl, A., Zilles, K., et al. (2003). Lateralized cognitive processes and lateralized task control in the human brain. *Science, 301*, 384–386.

Sutaria, S. D. (1985). *Specific learning disabilities: Nature and needs.* Springfield, IL: Charles C. Thomas.

Voyer, D., Voyer, S., & Bryden, P. M. (1995). Magnitude of sex differences in spatial abilities: A meta-analysis and consideration of critical variables. *Psychological-Bulletin, 117*, 250–270.

Wada, J. (1949). A new method for the determination of the side of cerebral speech dominance: A preliminary report on the intra-carotid injection of sodium amytal in man. *Medical Biology, 14*, 221.

Watt, D. F. (1990). Higher cortical functions and the ego: Explorations of the boundary between behavioral neurology, neuropsychology and psychoanalysis. *Psychoanalytic Psychology, 7*, 487–527.

Wechsler, D. (1991). *Wechsler Intelligence Scale for Children* (3rd ed.). San Antonio, TX: Psychological Corporation.

Weisenberg, T., & McBride, K. E. (1935). *Aphasia: A clinical and psychological study.* New York: Commonwealth.

Wiener, M., & Cromer, W. (1967). Reading and reading difficulty: A conceptual analysis. *Harvard Educational Review, 37*, 620–642.

Witelson, S. F. (1974). Hemispheric specialization for linguistic and nonlinguistic tactual perception using a dichotomous stimulation technique. *Cortex, 10*, 1–17.

Witelson, S. F. (1977). Developmental dyslexia: Two right hemispheres and none left. *Science, 195*, 309–311.

Witelson, S. F. (1989). Hand and sex differences in the isthmus and genu of the human corpus collosum. *Brain, 112*, 799–835.

Woodcock, R. S., McGrew, K. S., & Mather, N. (2001a). *Woodcock-Johnson III Tests of Cognitive Ability.* Itasca, IL: Riverside.

Woodcock, R. S., McGrew, K. S., & Mather, N. (2001b). *Woodcock-Johnson III Tests of Achievement.* Itasca, IL: Riverside.

Xu, B., Grafman, J., Gaillard, W. D., Ishii, K., Vega-Bermudez, F., Pietrini, P., et al. (2001). Conjoint and extended neural networks for the computation of speech codes: The neural basis of selective impairment in reading words and pseudowords. *Cerebral Cortex, 11*, 267–277.

Zangwill, O. L. (1960). *Cerebral dominance and its relationship to psychological function.* London: Oliver & Boyd.

Zangwill, O. L. (1962). Dyslexia in relation to cerebral dominance. In J. Money (Ed.), *Reading disability.* Baltimore: Johns Hopkins.

Zillmer, E., & Spiers, M. (2001). *Principles of neuropsychology.* Belmont, CA: Wadsworth.

# SECTION III

# NEUROPSYCHOLOGICAL ASSESSMENT FOR INTERVENTION

CHAPTER 7

# The Pediatric Neurological Examination and School Neuropsychology

TIM R. ALLEN JR., DAVID HULAC, and RIK CARL D'AMATO

I N A PRESIDENTIAL proclamation in 1990, President George H. W. Bush officially named the 1990s the "Decade of the Brain." During that decade, a vast amount of research helped to both answer and create numerous questions for brain-related medical practitioners such as pediatric neurologists, neurosurgeons, and neuropsychologists, as well as individuals suffering from neurological or nervous system problems or diseases (Reynolds & Fletcher-Janzen, 1997; Sattler & D'Amato, 2002a). While knowledge about neurology has increased exponentially and changed practice accordingly, the basis of understanding pediatric neurological functioning has long been the neurological examination. This chapter discusses the pediatric neurological examination in light of its history, components, and applications to the education enterprise.

## THE PEDIATRIC NEUROLOGICAL EXAMINATION

The pediatric neurological examination is a procedure that describes the general assessment of an individual's nervous system. The goal of the neurological examination is to locate a lesion or impairment within the nervous system. A lesion is generically defined as a dysfunction or an area of damage within the nervous system (Lundy-Ekman, 2002). Typically, neurologists or other physicians conducting this examination are most interested in the physical and motor functioning of the *central nervous system* (CNS), which consists of the brain and the spinal cord. The *peripheral nervous system* (PNS) is composed of the network of nerves that connect the CNS to the rest of the body (Curtis, 1990).

The pediatric neurological examination provides information regarding structural brain integrity after evaluating and observing behavior, development, and the standard neurological abilities of an individual (Bigler, Nilsson, Burr, &

Boyer, 1997). Through this series of observations, interview questions, and brief exams, the medical practitioner attempts to understand if a patient is experiencing neurological impairment. If such an impairment is found, the practitioner will investigate the nervous system further to better understand the patient's neurological problems, offer a diagnosis, and present treatment options, which could include a referral to another medical specialist.

## Why Is a Neurological Examination Administered?

Neurological examinations may be administered for a wide variety of reasons. Most individuals who have visited a physician for an annual physical have received a brief neurological examination. In this case, the physician is investigating a likely healthy body to screen for possible symptoms of disease. However, there are more in-depth examinations that may be conducted with patients who are at risk for neurological problems or display various medical or psychological symptoms (Haerer, 1992). Such patients include those involved in problematic births or car or bicycle accidents and who suffer from various diseases. So too, patients with attentional and educational problems, as well as those with multiple sclerosis, brain tumors, drug overdoses, and other disorders of the CNS may need to be evaluated. It may also be important to examine a patient to determine psychopharmacological side effects or to monitor the course of a disease. In an educational setting, a neurological examination may be warranted for learners who have displayed a sudden change in behavior, problematic academic performance, or a variety of medical problems (e.g., headaches or seizures) or have suffered a recent injury (Hynd & Willis, 1988). An evaluation may also be helpful to determine whether or not a learner has suffered from a previously undiagnosed injury or problem. Primary care physicians usually will make the referral to a neurologist if they believe it is warranted.

## How Does a Neurological Examination Differ from a Neuropsychological Examination?

Because they are commonly confused, it is important to distinguish the neurological examination from the neuropsychological examination. Both seek to examine the behavioral correlates of brain functions and neurodevelopmental problems (Hebben & Milberg, 2002). However, the approaches of the two examinations are quite different. A neurological examination considers the physical functioning of the nervous system, and it generally determines if and where there is damage. It also focuses on issues such as etiology and the biochemical issues associated with nervous system dysfunction (Hohol, Stewart, & Jenkinson, 2001; Meador & Nichols, 1987). A common complaint from individuals who have suffered from neurological damage is that the initial neurological examination revealed little if any damage to the nervous system (D'Amato & Dean, 1988). Although examinations may be able to pinpoint neurological abnormalities as never before, it is rarely possible to predict specifically how these abnormalities will be expressed behaviorally (D'Amato & Dean, 1988). For example, it may be months after a neurological examination that an individual with a traumatic brain injury begins experiencing neurological deficits.

A neuropsychological examination focuses, however, on biogenetic causes of cognitive, behavioral, learning, and emotional strengths and needs through a study of the functional brain-behavior systems (D'Amato, Rothlisberg, & Leu Work, 1999). The neuropsychological examination describes changes in these abilities in terms of the presence and severity of higher cognitive impairments (e.g., executive abilities, intelligence) and emotional-behavioral difficulties (Hebben & Milberg, 2002). It can serve to determine how a lesion or deficit found in the neurological examination affects the patient's ability to interact with his or her world (Meador & Nichols, 1987). Further, the neuropsychological examination provides quantitative data to complement the more qualitative findings of the neurological examination (Kirshner, 2002).

## How Does the Neurological Examination Differ from Neuroimaging?

One way technology has dramatically increased the ability of physicians to locate specific problems within the brain is through the use of neuroimaging techniques. Neuroimaging is a series of techniques used to create visual images of the brain. The regions of the brain that are showing the most activity can be highlighted (Atkinson, Atkinson, Smith, Bem, & Nolen-Hoeksema, 2003). These techniques can aid in identifying specific structural and physiological brain abnormalities. Neuroimaging techniques include magnetic resonance imaging (MRI), positron emission tomography (PET), single photon emission computed tomography (SPECT), functional magnetic resonance imaging (fMRI), computerized electroencephalography (EEG), and nuclear magnetic resonance spectroscopy (NMR; Johnstone & Stonnington, 2001; Wedding & Reeves, 1997). Chapter 14 of this volume provides a more detailed discussion regarding neuroimaging techniques.

It is important to note the distinction between a neurological examination and these popular neuroimaging techniques. Whereas neuroimaging may be able to suggest a problem, or the possibility of a problem, and provide information on the physical structure of the nervous system, the neurological examination is designed to look at the functioning of the nervous system and to determine whether or not functional weaknesses or strengths exist. In essence, the neurological examination may look for symptoms, whereas neuroimaging may be used to look for the physical causes of the symptoms, such as a brain tumor.

Regardless of when a lesion occurs, other developmental consequences may not become apparent until later stages in a person's life. Early damage in some individuals may not result in deficits relating to behavioral outcomes because of the plasticity of nondamaged regions of the brain, where they may adapt to become responsible for the function of the damaged areas (Kirshner, 2002). Thus, a particular lesion may be extremely invasive in its size and location by neuroimaging standards, but the immature brain could develop around the lesion, such that the lesion is no longer predictive of current behavioral outcomes (Bigler et al., 1997). Of course, the inverse can also occur, where a small lesion can be responsible for extensive behavioral impairments. Normally, neuroimaging techniques will not always be employed, but instead will be used when the neurological examination is inconclusive or does not reveal specific neuropathology or when neurological concerns persist (Lewis & Dorbad, 2000). Neuroimaging techniques have not replaced the need for the pediatric neurological examination.

A neurological examination is typically administered by a primary care physician, neurologist, or psychiatrist. However, as nurses and nurse practitioners become more highly trained, they may also conduct many of the components of the neurological examination (Murray, Kelly, & Jenkins, 2002). Primary care physicians usually screen a patient's general neurological functioning as part of an annual physical examination. A psychiatrist may conduct a neurological examination as part of a neuropsychiatric assessment to assess behavior in the context of emotional and biochemical interactions within the brain. By the time a patient has been referred to a pediatric neurologist, neurological damage is usually evident. A neurologist often conducts the most comprehensive neurological examination to determine the location of neurological damage, a diagnosis, possible course of the damage, and appropriate treatment.

## HISTORY OF THE PEDIATRIC NEUROLOGICAL EXAMINATION

The neurological examination is one element of one of the most dynamic and cutting-edge fields of science, the neurosciences, yet many of its components date back nearly 5,000 years. Certainly, the history and evolution of the neurological exam is closely tied to advances in neurology and other related fields, such as anatomy, medicine, and physiology, to the development of technology, and to the observations of physicians over time.

As far as the history of the neurological evaluation itself, Egypt is often attributed with the first record of neurological evaluations, around the thirteenth century B.C. (Patten, 1992). The patients in these exams were apparently asked to contract facial muscles and body movements, including moving the head up, down, left, and right. Galen of Pergamon was also credited with neurological work, including the labeling of cranial nerves, in the late second century (Patten, 1992). Descartes is attributed with the first book on physiology, in 1662, in which the nervous system was attributed to animal sprits working their way through hollow nerve tubes. Galvani strayed from animal spirits when he explained nerve action as a process of electricity in 1794 (Patten, 1992). As human cadaver dissection increased, so did theories of anatomy and, later, neuroanatomy. A common trend in these emerging theories was the increasing importance of the role of the brain. The brain became linked not only to cognition, but also to other aspects of bodily functioning, such as motor and sensory functions. As these theories developed, so did the physician's knowledge of the brain and its relationship to the rest of the body.

Before technology allowed practitioners to actually see the minute aspects of neuroanatomy, much of the information the physician considered was based on his or her observations. These observations included assessing gross physical symptoms but also observations of general and specific functioning of certain abilities, such as motor functions. Broca was led to his theory on the localization of the brain in part by observing patients with specific deficits in functioning, such as speech, and then integrating the patients' behavior with information gained from their autopsy (Lezak, Howieson, & Loring, 2004). Indeed, even today much of the neurological examination is based on the physician's observations of the patient. These observations allow the physician to determine if brain functions are impaired and to offer a diagnosis and treatment options.

Today, neuroimaging and neuropsychological methods are often employed as part of a team approach to assessing the neurological functioning of patients. Neuroimaging may be employed in an attempt to locate the abnormality in the brain, and neuropsychological methods may be used to determine affected psychological and biological functioning and to assess prognosis and intervention options (Hebben & Milberg, 2002). In its beginnings, neuropsychology had a rehabilitation context, when professionals developed strategies to improve cognitive functioning of soldiers returning from battle with brain injuries (Johnstone & Stonnington, 2001). Even today, educationally related rehabilitation continues to remain one of the field's leading contributions (Rothlisberg, D'Amato, & Palencia, 2003).

## COMPONENTS OF THE PEDIATRIC NEUROLOGICAL EXAMINATION

Many of the components of the neurological examination have remained the same for years. When conducting a neurological examination, there are four essential questions to be answered:

1. Does an injury or lesion to the nervous system exist?
2. Where in the nervous system does the lesion lie?
3. What conditions or diseases are known to cause such a lesion?
4. In a patient whose behavior or development appears irregular or pathological, what previous events or diseases may be consistent with the patient's profile? (Bickerstaff & Spillane, 1989; Hynd & Willis, 1988)

The neurological examination is comprehensive in that it evaluates all of the major structures of both the CNS and the PNS. Although the examination is often described in discrete steps, it is important to understand that the neurological systems of the human body are interconnected (Lundy-Ekman, 2002). As a result, a problem that may manifest itself through an evaluation of a cranial nerve may also impact motor functioning, mood, and sensory capabilities. Typically, six components are considered by the examiner during the pediatric neurological examination: (1) results of the mental status exam, (2) cranial nerves, (3) motor functioning, (4) coordination and balance, (5) reflexes, and (6) sensory functioning. By assessing these components, it is possible for the examiner to make inferences about the brain and nervous system functioning, and their subsequent impact on the body.

When completing a neurological exam, the examiner must keep in mind several different issues. The first is whether the patient is experiencing a significant discrepancy between the left and right sides of his or her body, which may indicate which part of the brain is affected. The physician then tries to establish whether or not there is a significant difference between functions that are considered to be part of the central or the peripheral nervous system. The examiner may also try to determine if a patient's difficulties are associated with the upper half or the lower portions of the body, which may indicate if the problem is at the CNS or PNS level. Finally, the physician will try to determine if a weakness (e.g., articulation) can be localized to a specific neurological lesion or if the weakness is suggestive of a comprehensive neurological problem (Bickerstaff & Spillane 1989). Each component of the neurological examination is briefly reviewed.

### The Mental Status Examination

The mental status examination (MSE) is a measure of a person's awareness of his or her environment. Most practitioners use a standardized form, such as the Mini Mental Status Exam, in combination with their own individualized procedures (Sattler & D'Amato, 2002a, 2002b). As a result, literally dozens of versions of the MSE are available and range from 5 minutes to 2 hours to complete (Kirshner, 2002). Although many neurological examinations measure mental status formally, it is not uncommon for many components of the MSE to be covered while the practitioner is asking the patient about his or her history (Maher, 1999). Moreover, a modified format of this examination is sometimes used with young children and a more standard format with children who are age 8 or older (Sattler & D'Amato, 2002a). The examiner will often observe the level of functioning in a number of areas.

*Alertness, Attention, and Cooperation*   This information is gathered through observation. To measure attention, the examiner may ask a patient to perform a relatively simple task that requires sustained concentration, such as reciting the alphabet backward or the serial 7s task, which asks the individual to start from 100 and subtract by 7 until reaching 70. Attention span and distractibility are also noted during this portion of the exam (Kirshner, 2002). Level of alertness, or sensorium, may be graded as normal, lethargic, or obtunded (requires external stimuli to be aroused). When considered together, these tasks also can indicate average, below average, or above average levels of cognitive functions in the patient (Greenberg, Aminoff, & Simon, 2002).

*Orientation*   Individuals who are functioning optimally are oriented to time, place, person, and situation. They will know who they are, who the other people in the room are, where they are, including the state, town, and building they are in, the time of day and approximate date, and the events that are occurring around them. Not only does this assess long-term and short-term memory, but it is another indication of alertness and attention. Disoriented patients are often unsure about time and place, but sometimes know the people around them (Andrefsky & Frank, 2002).

*Memory*   Memory can be assessed by showing patients several pictures or telling them words, and then asking them to remember the pictures or words. At some point later in the exam, the patient is again asked to restate those words or to describe the pictures. Inability to remember may indicate a short-term memory loss. A common assessment of short-term memory is to ask patients what they ate for a recent meal. Short-term memory loss suggests problems with the limbic memory structures (Blumenfield, 2001). The patient may be asked to perform other simple tasks such as recalling the days of the week or the months of the year (Bickerstaff & Spillane 1989). Patients may also be asked to recall certain events that have occurred in their life, including events before and after any possible head trauma. This could include asking about past vacations, previous jobs, or names of people with whom the patient has had contact. When assessing memory tasks that are unique to a patient (e.g., remembering previous friends or educational settings), it is essential to have access to a family member or colleague with whom life facts can be corroborated; this will assess remote memory (Greenberg et al., 2002).

*Language*   Language may be assessed by attending to the speech fluency and thought expression of the patient (Strub & Black, 1997). Additional assessments include asking the individual to name common items, to solve simple logic problems, to repeat a sentence, and to read a short passage. Language problems may suggest problems with the left frontal lobe, such as Broca's area, as well as the left temporal and parietal lobes, such as Warneke's area (Blumenfield, 2001). Typically, dysphasias are a result of small or medium-size lesions located in different parts of the dominant lobe (Curtis, 1990). Dysphasias include expressive and receptive problems that may impair individuals' ability to understand the words they hear or to express their thoughts (Tallal, 1987).

*Object Recognition*   Gnosis is the ability to recognize and discern objects. Agnosia is the inability of a particular body part to perform an object discernment task (Kirshner, 2002). For example, finger agnosia is the inability to name and identify each finger (Kirshner, 2002). Patients who are unable to visually identify an object but can use their fingers to feel it may have visual agnosia. To assess agnosias, a neurologist may have a series of objects, such as pens, paper clips, toy cars, and objects that make sounds, such as whistles and bells. Difficulty recognizing any of these is used to rule out Gerstmann's Syndrome or lesions in the left (or dominant) parietal lobe. Gerstmann's Syndrome is described as an inability to write, accompanied by right-left disorientation and finger agnosia (Damasio, 1987; Loring, 1999).

*Calculations*   Calculation ability is assessed by addition, subtraction, and multiplication tasks. The serial 7s task, which assesses a patient's concentration ability, can also be used to measure calculation skills. If patients are able to do the serial 7s task, it can be assumed that they have reasonably intact calculation skills. A right hemisphere lesion, which may impact visual-spatial skills, could be responsible for an inability to perform basic mathematical skills (Kirshner, 2002).

*Neglect and Self-Care*   The neurological exam should also evaluate the learner's level of hygiene. Individuals with brain injury may be unable to care for one side of their body. For example, they may have combed one side of their hair and washed only one half of their body. Another sign of neglect that is unintentional is anosognosia. Anosognosic patients are unaware that they have a disorder of any kind (Blumenfield, 2001). Problems of neglect may indicate possible lesions. For example, individuals who neglect the entire left side of their body are likely to have an impairment of their right parietal lobe (Greenberg et al., 2002).

*Delusions and Hallucinations*   Delusions and hallucinations are observed informally during the examination to see if a patient is experiencing any unusual thought patterns. The examiner may also ask patients if they see things that others do not see, if there are people who speak to them that others do not hear, and if there are people who are out to hurt them. Hallucinations can be the result of many different brain dysfunctions, including seizures in any of the four lobes of the brain (Joseph, 1996).

*Logic, Sequencing, and Abstraction*   Assessing individuals' ability to use logic includes asking them to complete a simple logical syllogism, such as "If Mary is taller than Jane and Jane is taller than Michelle, who is the tallest?" Patients may also be asked to explain proverbs or complete a common phrase, such as "A stitch in time . . ." (saves nine). Although difficulty on these tasks may not be localized to a single part of the brain, such tasks are useful for understanding patient difficulties and planning interventions (Blumenfield, 2001). If an individual has difficulty shifting cognitive strategies and a tendency to perseverate, the task will be difficult. Perseveration may be problematic among those who have lesions in their frontal lobes (Joseph, 1996).

*Affect and Mood*   Assessing mood includes observing if the patient is feeling depressed, anxious, apathetic, or inappropriately elated (Bickerstaff & Spillane 1989). The frontal lobes of the brain are not only responsible for sequencing tasks, but they also play an important role in an individual's mood and behavioral regulation (Joseph, 1996). Sudden changes in mood may indicate damage to the frontal lobe or biochemical brain imbalances.

### Evaluating Infants, Toddlers, and Young Children

Seeking to understand the neurodevelopment of young children is often more difficult than similar assessments with older children or adults. Due to their lack of academic, cognitive, and other emotional abilities, performing an MSE requires more thought and creativity on the part of the examiner. An infant or young child is often unable to follow complicated directions, and so the practitioner must rely more heavily on observations and environmental reports from others (Sattler & D'Amato, 2002a). Further challenges in assessing young children may result from the high degree of developmental variability that is common in children (Hynd & Willis, 1988). In assessing infants, a neurologist or other physician will look for such features as a baby's level of arousal, ability to be soothed, and response to painful or other stimulations (Diadori & Carmant, 2002). For younger children, academic and intellectual abilities can be evaluated by observing a child's nonverbal responses to questions, asking the child to draw and name pictures, and seeking answers to simple questions. Other techniques to assess a child's functional language abilities include asking the child who, what, where, and when questions. The examiner should also note the presence of drooling, nasal speech, and stuttering. The child's behavior should also be assessed for signs of impulsivity, short attention span, hyperactivity, and distractibility. The nature of the parent-child relationship and interactions and degree of eye contact with the examiner and caregivers can be clues to the child's emotional or psychological state (Diadori & Carmant, 2002).

A further accommodation made for younger children receiving a neurological examination is the addition of a parallel assessment format. In these settings, an educator with experience in neurobiological functioning of children works in accordance with a neurologist and will engage a child in many of the different activities of the MSE. Throughout the process, the neurologist will observe the child's interactions with the examiner and take necessary notes (Denckla, 1997).

Clearly, the developmental expectations for infants, toddlers, and young children are much different neurodevelopmentally from those of adults. For example, many reflexes are present after an infant is born but are suppressed later in the child's development (Hynd & Willis, 1988). In fact, some of the newer neuropsychological batteries focus on these differences (e.g., Dean-Woodcock Neuropsychological Battery; Dean & Woodcock, 2003). Other reflexes are also emerging or developing during this time. The same is true for motor skills, such as walking, and sensory skills, such as recognition of objects, vision, touch, and hearing.

All newborns receive a gross neurological examination known as the Apgar test. The Apgar measures heart rate, respiration, reflex irritability, muscle tone, and color when the infant is 1 minute, 5 minutes, and 10 minutes old. Each of the five categories is scored on a scale of 0 (absent), 1 (present), or 2 (optimal), with a total of 10 being optimal and 0 being problematic. Many have questioned this evaluation system and advocated for a more contemporary version of the Apgar (Gray & Dean, 1989).

The neurological examination for infants and toddlers is developmental in nature. After all, the expectations of the sensing, motor, and reflexive skills are much different for a 12-month-old than for a newborn. For example, an infant does not typically gain head control until he or she is 6 to 8 weeks old, is unable to crawl and pull into a standing position until 10 months, and usually is able to walk at 14 months (Hynd & Willis, 1988). One reason pediatric neurology is a difficult area of study is because the neurologist is attempting to predict what may develop in the future. For instance, over the first 8 weeks of life, the results of a neurological examination for an infant with anencephaly or hydranencephaly are similar to those of a normal infant (Ashwal et al., 1990). Indeed, understanding neurological developmental milestones is the key to diagnosing possible neurological dysfunction in children (Sattler & D'Amato, 2002a).

A number of neurologically based standardized instruments have been created to assess a child's neurological functioning. The Bayley Infant Neurodevelopmental Screener (BINS) is an instrument that measures posture, tone, movement, developmental status, and basic neurological capacity of infants and toddlers from the ages of 3 to 24 months (Aylward, 1995; Bayley, 1993). The BINS assesses how optimal a particular function is and places children in three categories: high risk, moderate risk, and low risk. Other standardized instruments include the Milani-Comparetti Examination, which measures spontaneous behavior, such as posture control and evoked responses, such as reflexes (Aylward, 1995). The Neonatal Neurodevelopment Examination, the Brief Infant Neurobehavioral Optimality Scale, and the Neurobehavioral Assessment of the Preterm Infant are additional measures that can be used to assess the neurological functioning of children under the age of 24 months (Aylward, 1995). However, a direct neurological examination is more common than the use of any standardized instrument (Gray & Dean, 1989).

*Infant Reflexes*   In newborns, reflexes predominate to aid the infant in developing head control, trunk control, limb extension, hand-eye coordination, and coordination of movements (Willis & Widerstrom, 1986). These reflexes are mediated by

**Table 7.1**
Infant Reflexes

| Reflex Name | What It Does | When it Develops | When It Disappears |
|---|---|---|---|
| Rooting and sucking | Sucking begins when hungry or when mouth is stimulated. | Prenatally | 3 to 4 months |
| Grasp reflex | Pressure to palm when stimulated. | Prenatally | 3 to 4 months |
| Withdrawal and extension reflexes | Legs and feet move in and out through the first or second month. | Prenatally | 1 to 2 months |
| Crossed extension reflex | When sole of foot is stimulated, that foot extends while the other foot flexes. | Prenatally | 3 to 4 months |
| Moro | Head lowers into supine position when arms and arms are thrown to the sides, then return to a flexed position. Aids in the development of muscles. | At its maximum at 2 months | 4 months |
| Galant response | Stroking part of the infant's back results in the infant flexing their trunk in order to avoid the stimulation. | Prenatally | 6 months |
| Positive support reflex | By touching to soles of the feet on a hard surface, there is a tendency to stand on the toes. | Prenatally | 10 months |
| Landau reflex | When in the prone position, the infant extends arm and legs when the head is raised and flexes these limbs when head is lowered. | 3 months | 2nd year of life |

Adapted from "Neuropsychological Development" (pp. 13-53), by G. W. Willis and A. H. Widerstrom, in *Child Neuropsychology: Theory and Research* (Volume 1), J. E. Obrzut and G. W. Hynd (Eds.), 1986, Orlando, FL: Academic Press.

lower brain centers compared to the automatic reflexes that develop later in a child's life. One of the important tasks of neurodevelopment is to suppress these infant reflexes (Willis & Widerstrom, 1986). Table 7.1 lists some of the reflexes that should predominate in early development but normally are extinguished.

Developmental Evaluation of Neurological Domains

A pediatric neurologist who is evaluating a child's nervous system will assess if the following reflexes are displayed or inhibited at an appropriate age.

*Automatic Reflexes*   The automatic reflexes support normal development and should continue as a healthy child develops into adulthood (Willis & Widerstrom, 1986). These reflexes include righting reactions, which allow the child's body to move in tandem, and parachute reactions, which allow a child to break his or her fall. As children become more ambulatory, their arms will go toward the ground if they begin to fall. If these automatic reflexes fail to form, it may suggest a serious CNS problem.

*Movements*  As neurology has become more sophisticated, some neurologists have begun to rate children's movements as they relate to neurological functioning. This may include assessment of the child's gait, unusual or abnormal eye movements, excessive or few body movements, or tremors (Blumenfield, 2001). Developmentally normal motor activities in children include being able to support their own neck at 6 to 8 weeks, being able to hold their face and head off the ground at approximately 12 weeks, being able to bear their weight on one hand and sit while leaning forward at 28 weeks, and at 36 weeks being able to pull themselves into a standing position (Diadori & Carmant, 2002). Walking with support should occur by the child's first birthday, and walking without support should occur by the time the child is 14 months (Hynd & Willis, 1988). Significant delays in these activities may be suggestive of further neurological problems.

*Muscle Tone*  Children with neurological difficulties often display unusual muscle tone. If they are hypertonic, they will have an usually high concentration of muscle in one area that will result in rigidity. Children who are too resistive to pressure may be diagnosed with hypertonia. Children with hypotonia have an unusually low concentration of muscles in a particular area, resulting in a flaccid presentation so that the child is unable to resist any pressure that the examiner places on different joints or extremities.

When performing the neurological examination on children, it is important for the examiner to understand the relationship between neural and developmental functioning. A child may have a neurological deficit (such as decreased muscle tone in the lower extremities) but may still be able to meet normal developmental functions (Blumenfield, 2001; Hynd & Willis, 1988). Thus, a neurological deficit may not indicate a functional deficit; by the same token, a functional deficit may not indicate a neurological deficit. It is the experienced pediatric neurologist who is able to work through many of these confusing signs.

## THE CRANIAL NERVES

The primary care physician, neurologist, or other medical specialist will move on to a more deliberate evaluation of the nervous system with a focus on individual nerves. This evaluation usually begins with the cranial nerves. The cranial nerves comprise 12 pairs of nerves that travel between the head, face, and neck regions. Each set of cranial nerves is responsible for functioning on either side of the face. As a result, one side's nerves may function normally while the other side displays abnormal functioning. These nerves are responsible for both movements and sensations in the face, as well as some of the body's critical functions, including hearing, seeing, smelling, and tasting (Lundky-Ekman, 2002). Given the importance of these nerves, testing is undertaken systematically but individually, while at the same time the examiner conducts a series of critical observations.

*Olfactory Nerve (I)*  The olfactory nerve controls an individual's sense of smell. The nerve connects the nose to an area directly underneath the frontal lobes. The most common reason for failure to smell is nasal decongestion. An inability to smell may also indicate problematic frontal lobe functioning or possible impairment. These are commonly tested using a series of vials composed of different scents: a subtle smell, such as mint, or a stronger smell, such as coffee or oranges. Initially, however, it is important to determine if the individual can detect any odor at all, rather than name the source of a particular odor (Greenberg et al., 2002).

*Optic Nerve (II)*   The optic nerve controls vision. There are several steps involved in testing this second nerve. To begin, a patient's visual acuity is tested using the Snellen eye chart or a handheld Jaeger print card (Corbett, 2002). The examiner will then stand directly in front of a patient with extended hands to test the patient's periphery vision. The examiner wiggles his or her fingers on either side and asks patients to indicate on which side they see the fingers moving. If these test results appear unusual, additional evaluations will be undertaken. The examiner will likely observe the patient's eyes in response to direct light. Here, an examiner is testing the reflexes of the patient's eyes, looking at the pupils dilating and contracting, and is observing any differences between the responses of each eye. Problems with eye reflexes may indicate damage to the ganglion cells (cells outside the CNS) or the optic disk (the area of the retina where the optic fibers converge to leave the back of the eye), as well as to the optic nerve (Loring, 1999; Reitan & Wolfson, 1993). Finally, the examiner may ask the patient to look at the examiner's finger placed 10 centimeters from the middle of the patient's line of sight. While having the patient look at the finger with either eye, the clinician watches the pupil's reaction to the stimulus (Corbett, 2002; Rathe, 2000). Problems with the functioning of the optic nerve may be due to a variety of reasons. The practitioner may evaluate for papilledema, a blurring of the margins of the optic disk that results from increased intracranial pressure (Loring, 1999). This is important because some practitioners use this as a sign of possible brain damage. Concerns may range from problems with the occipital lobe to tumors or damage within the optic nerve itself (Corbett). Another example of impairment is optic neuritis, a painful swelling of the optic nerve itself that is often found in women younger than 45 (Solomon, 1998).

*Oculomotor (III), Trochlear (IV), and Abducens Nerves (VI)*   While the optic nerve deals with the eye's function, the oculomotor nerve helps an individual's eye move into the correct position to allow for the detection of visual stimulus. There are six possible eye movements, and the oculomotor nerve assists with four of them. The medial rectus moves the muscles toward the nose, as when patients cross their eyes. The superior rectus allows the eye to move up and away from the nose. The inferior oblique muscle allows the eye to move up and toward the nose. The inferior rectus controls the eye's movements down and away from the nose.

The fourth cranial nerve is the trochlear nerve, which controls downward eye movement toward the nose. The abducens nerve controls the lateral rectus nerve, which controls eye movement away from the nose. Lateral eye movement may be restricted if this nerve is damaged (Lundy-Ekman, 2002).

*Trigeminal Nerve (V)*   The fifth nerve is responsible for sensation within the face and the oral and nasal cavities. An examiner may test this nerve by applying both tactile pressure and a mildly painful stimulus to the nose and mouth. This nerve is also evaluated in conjunction with the optic and oculomotor nerves to judge sensations within the cornea. Any jaw movement will also be controlled via the fifth nerve, which is assessed by asking patients to open and close their jaw against pressure (Wiederholt, 1982).

*Facial Nerve (VII)* All facial muscles are controlled by this seventh facial nerve, which is assessed by a series of exercises whereby patients wrinkle their forehead, close their eyes, and attempt to blow out of their cheeks while feeling pressure from the examiner (Wiederholt, 1982). The facial nerve is also responsible for the sensation of taste in the tongue.

*Auditory/Acoustic Nerve (VIII)* As its name suggests, the auditory nerve, also called the acoustic nerve, controls the ability to hear. A complete hearing test serves as the bulk of the assessment for the auditory nerve. This usually occurs through a referral to an audiologist. Both the pitch and volume of a sound are tested. Another important function of this nerve is its responsibility for vestibular functions, which help individuals maintain their balance (Curtis, 1990).

*Glossopharyngeal (IX) and Vagus Nerves (X)* The glossopharyngeal nerve is responsible for the gag reflex and is assessed in conjunction with the tenth cranial nerve, the vagus nerve. These nerves are tested by listening to the words an individual says while swallowing a sip of water. Patients suffering from damage to this tenth cranial nerve may have difficulty swallowing and using their tongue to generate language. An examiner will likely listen for hoarseness and will evaluate vocal cord movement in determining the possible problem (Curtis, 1990). There have also been some experimental treatments for depression that have involved electrical stimulation of the vagus nerve, indicating that this nerve may play an important part in emotional regulation (Rush et al., 2000).

*Spinal Accessory (XI) and Hypoglossal Nerves (XII)* The spinal accessory nerve is evaluated by having the individual rotate his or her head to one side and resist movement in the opposite direction. This nerve controls the muscles in the head and the shoulders, so the individuals may also be asked to shrug their shoulders (Curtis, 1990). The hypoglossal nerve controls movement and provides strength to the tongue. The tongue's strength can be tested by asking the patient to stick it out and move it around, or by asking the patient to extend it into the cheek while the examiner is trying to push it back (Wiederholt, 1982).

## MOTOR SYSTEM

Besides assessing for cranial nerve function, it is often necessary to assess how well an individual's nervous system allows him or her to control motion in the rest of the body. The motor system is evaluated throughout the course of the neurological examination. Normal motor functioning depends on intact upper and lower motor neurons, sensory pathways, and input from a number of other neurological systems. Throughout the process of assessing motor functioning, an examiner will look for signs of muscle atrophy or weakness. The motor examination will rely on observations and inspections of individual muscle areas, muscle tone, and the functionality of individual muscles and muscle groups. Informally, the patient may be assessed by watching him or her walk into the examination room or move about during the normal course of conversation. The more formal measures of strength and motor functioning require the patient to move a limb or part of a limb while the examiner adds resistance (Wiederholt, 1982). The motor functioning of the upper extremities of the body involve assessment of grip, wrist rotation, and wrist strength. The lower extremities of the body can be assessed by watching the patient stand, walk, and hop. If these evaluations support the existence of a problem, the neurologist may evaluate the patient's ability to lift one leg, move both knees one at a time, and attempt to rotate both legs while the examiner provides resistance. Although there will certainly be some difference between the amount of strength in the left and right sides of the body, one side may appear significantly stronger than the other. This is a critical characteristic of the evaluation and will help the examiner to locate nervous system weaknesses. Diseases that affect the motor neurons include amyotropic lateral scleroris (ALS), which is more commonly known as Lou Gehrig's disease; spastic paraplegia, a slowly progressive paralysis whereby the muscles contract but do not relax; and syringomyelia, or cavities in the spinal column (Solomon, 1998).

## Coordination and Balance

Assessment of a patient's coordination may help determine if there are nervous system problems that affect the outer extremities of the body, such as the hands and feet. The physician evaluates the patient's ability to move his or her body in the environment; accordingly, this assessment is closely related to the motor functioning component of the examination. This component of the neurological examination is commonly broken down into three areas: (1) appendicular coordination, (2) the Romberg test, and (3) gait.

Appendicular coordination is the term used to describe the fine motor movements of the toes and hands. Tests of upper body coordination may include rapid alternating movements of the fingers, assessing how quickly and smoothly the thumb and forefinger are able to move together, and using the finger-to-nose assessment, which is commonly used by police officers to screen drivers they suspect of driving under the influence of alcohol. Coordination of the lower extremities can be assessed using a heel-to-shin test. Problems with fine motor control may be due to problems in the basal ganglia or cerebellum (Hynd & Willis, 1988). When conducting the Romberg test, an examiner will ask patients to stand up and then close their eyes. Typically, there are three nervous subsystems that help prevent a patient from falling over while standing: the visual, vestibular, and proprioception systems. The proprioception subsystem is a communication system whereby individual parts of the body are able to know and react to changes in other parts of the body. Typically, when there are problems with the latter two systems, the visual system is able to compensate. However, when the visual system is compromised, a vestibular or proprioception problem could become rapidly apparent, causing a loss of balance (Blumenfield, 2001).

## Reflexes

Reflexes are "stereotyped motor responses to well defined stimuli" (Curtis, 1990, p. 45). Essentially, reflexes are automatic movements that do not require conscious thought to be expressed. The reflexes may follow neural pathways that travel through the brain or may travel only through the spinal cord or other, less centralized areas. There are several different assessments that look specifically at the reflexes: the deep tendon, clonus, and Babinski tests. The deep tendon reflexes are tested using the common reflex hammer. An examiner will test the reflexes inside the biceps, triceps, ankle, abdomen, knee, and wrist. The physician reports normal reflex functioning, an absence of reflex functioning, a weakened response, or a hyperactive response (Rathe, 2000). A hyperactive response may be accompanied by a clonus test, which is when a muscle vibrates or contracts repeatedly (Blumenfield, 2001). It is normal for newborns to experience some repeated muscular contractions, but in older children and adults it is suggestive of a problem in the CNS (Rathe, 2000). The Babinski reflex occurs at birth, when the infant, feeling the underside of his or her foot stroked from the ankle to the bottom of the toes, splays or spreads the toes. In adults, this response should be absent, and if present may indicate significant corticospinal disease (Voeller, 1981).

There are several other reflexes that usually wane shortly after infancy: the sucking reflex; the palmar reflex, whereby an individual automatically grasps the fingers that are stroking the palm of the hand; and the rooting reflex, whereby "stimulation of the lips causes them to deviate toward the stimulus" (Greenberg et al., 2002, p. 10). The existence of these reflexes in older children and adults may suggest brain impairment, but they do not guarantee the existence of a lesion (Greenberg et al., 2002).

SENSORY EXAMINATION

An important component of the neurological examination is an assessment of how well the patient's sense of touch functions. There are several major components of the sensory examination, but overall, the neurologist will assess the ability of an individual to recognize the sensations of touch, pain, temperature, and vibrations. Light touch is often examined using a cotton swab. Throughout this portion of the assessment, the examiner will ask patients if they feel a sensation on different parts of their body. Pain may be assessed using a safety pin while asking patients to determine whether the sharp or dull portion of the pin is making contact with different parts of their skin. An individual's ability to sense temperature can be assessed by asking patients whether they feel the touch of a cold tuning fork. A tuning fork placed on different points of the body is used to assess the sense of vibration. The physician also assesses extinction, which is diagnosed if the body is unable to feel two sensations at once. Extinction is tested by determining if a patient is able to hear sounds coming from opposite sides of the body, see visual stimuli on either side of the body, or feel different sensations on either side of the body. If a patient is experiencing localized problems with touch or vibrations (e.g., the patient recognizes touches to the arms but not to the fingers), it is suggestive of a possible PNS problem (Meador & Nichols, 1987).

Judging which parts of the body are able to feel different external stimuli is an important assessment of nerve endings on the skin, as well as possible spinal cord injuries. Injuries to one area of the spinal cord will typically obstruct the nerve functioning of the parts of the body that are controlled by the rest of the column below the injury. As a result, patients who have injuries along their spinal column may be able to feel sensations only in the parts of their body that are connected to the nervous system by the area of the spinal cord that is above the injured portion (Maynard et al., 1996). The sensory examination also helps the physician diagnose a potential injury on one side of the body or the other, and likely then the brain. Lesions that occur on only the left or the right side of the body may also be due to a conversion disorder, which could be a manifestation of nervous system damage that appears to be psychosomatic in nature, or could be due to subcortical lesions (Meador & Nichols, 1987).

## ADDITIONAL RELATED SCALES

Two scales, the Glasgow Coma Scale and the Rancho Los Amigos Level of Cognitive Functioning Scale (RLCF), can be used to assess fundamental neurological functioning (Hagen, 2004; Hynd & Willis, 1988). The Glasgow Coma Scale takes into account the depth and duration of a coma. This scale has been modified for use with children (e.g., Simpson & Reilly, 1982) by adding child norms that score a child's best response in motor, verbal, and eyes-open modalities. These scores are then compared to an aggregate score of children with comparable ages. Originally developed by Hagen, Malkmus, and Durham (1972), the RLCF is a comprehensive and systematic measure that allows for the evaluation of an individual's level of current cognitive functioning. For example, it places the individual in 1of 10 categories, from Level I, No Response: Total Assistance (e.g., complete absence of observable change in behavior when presented visual, auditory, tactile, proprioceptive, vestibular, or painful stimuli) to Level X, Purposeful, Appropriate: Modified Independent (e.g., able to handle multiple tasks simultaneously in all environments but may require periodic breaks; social interaction behavior is consistently appropriate). These scales are often used with the most severe cases to derive a score that indicates the abilities of an individual who has suffered a severe trauma.

## SOFT AND HARD NEUROLOGICAL SIGNS

Some evidence indicates the presence of CNS damage, such as an abnormal Babinski reflex or markedly asymmetric motor or sensory patterns (Tupper, 1986). Other evidence may be seen as less reliable or as suggesting only minor impairment. These signs are often referred to as soft signs and are looked at as just that: signs, as opposed to symptoms, of neurological problems (Tupper, 1987). Examples of soft signs are motor coordination problems and right-left confusion, which may indicate difficulties or developmental delays. Based on such observations, Tupper (1986) categorized soft signs into two categories: developmental soft signs and soft signs of abnormality. Developmental soft signs referred to those signs that may be considered abnormal only when they persist in an individual beyond the age that they are traditionally observed, such as in a delayed appearance of a developmental milestone (i.e., walking, handedness). Soft signs of abnormality refer to those signs whose appearance at any age would be considered abnormal, such as tremors (Tupper, 1986). Determining the type, location, and severity of damage is vital to understanding a patient's clinical profile (D'Amato et al., 1999; Katz, 1997).

## SUMMARY OF THE PEDIATRIC NEUROLOGICAL EXAMINATION

The intention of this section was to define and describe the components of the neurological examination and to connect each of these components to the area of the nervous system with which it is linked. Understanding the results of the examination will help the school psychologist or school neuropsychologist make appropriate school modifications or referrals to additional medical personnel. A school neuropsychologist who has an in-depth understanding of neurology may also help explain the results of the examination to parents and school personnel who are working with a student with a neurological impairment. A thorough understanding of such results will likely provide the information needed to implement evidence-based interventions to help the student succeed in a school setting.

## SCHOOL-BASED IMPLICATIONS OF THE NEUROLOGICAL EXAMINATION

Neurological problems can express themselves in a number of ways in the life of a child. Some of the more overt manifestations can become evident when observed during the school day. Because most school psychologists have developed skills in the observation of children in a school setting, they are in an ideal position to notice signs early so as to refer the child to a medical doctor for treatment or to establish an intervention. School psychologists may have opportunities to observe a number of signs of neurological impairment that may have been missed or misinterpreted because they are able to monitor behavior across a variety of settings as well as with a mix of individuals. Such neurological signs include gross motor, fine motor, and speech and language problems.

Gross motor impairment can be observed throughout the school day of a child, such as on the playground at recess, in the hallways, and in the physical education setting. A child with a neurological impairment may exhibit difficulties running after peers, kicking, throwing, and catching balls, and maintaining balance, such as falling down more often than his or her peers. A child who has trouble walking in a straight line may actually be experiencing a neurological difficulty rather than expressing defiant or disrespectful behavior. A child may choose not to engage in such activities because he or she may find them difficult or awkward or may feel embarrassed in front of the other children at school. Observation of such behaviors may then be more difficult and may go unnoticed for a longer period of time.

Signs of fine motor difficulty often first present themselves in the classroom. Examples are poor handwriting skills and problems with art skills that require manipulation of small materials. A student exhibiting these kinds of difficulties should be observed for possible tremors, seizures, or involuntary movements when initiating or completing a task or for the amount of effort it takes the child to complete the task. Some children may tire easily when writing because of the amount of effort it takes them to write legibly.

Speech and language problems may present themselves in a number of ways. Articulation problems, gross syntax errors, and poor word choice or elaboration of ideas in a given context may all be signs of neurological impairment. Some speech problems could also be the result of motor difficulty in controlling the tongue, which could in turn be the result of damage to the associated cranial nerves. A professional in the school who interacts closely with the child can observe additional signs that are often assessed in a complete neurological examination. Unusual or abnormal facial responses can be an example of cranial nerve dysfunction. These responses can include asymmetry of facial responses, such as one side of the child's face not responding when the child smiles, drooping eyelids, involuntary movements, and difficulty controlling movement (Yule & Taylor, 1987).

The child's medical history often provides important information regarding possible neurological damage and may suggest the need to refer the child for a neurological examination. Prenatal and birth history are obviously vital factors in the health of a child, including possible drug use by the mother during her pregnancy and periods of oxygen deprivation of the child during birth. Incidence of hospitalizations should be followed up by the school professional; thyroid disorders, for example, can sometimes affect reflexes (Goldberg, 2003a). Problems with headaches, depending on the cause and type, as well as frequent dizziness, can also be indicative of neurological problems (Wiederholt, 1982). A family medical history is important in the case of biogenetically based disorders.

Problems in the reflexes of a child can reflect impairment of sensory or motor functions. Decreased or absent reflexes can suggest an impairment of lower motor neuron activity. Conversely, hyperactive reflexes can suggest an impairment of upper motor neuron activity, such as in the brain (Goldberg, 2003b). Problems in balance and coordination can suggest impairment in the cerebellum; other possible causes of problems with coordination, including walking, could lie in visual, motor, and sensory deficits, all of which may be affected by neurological impairment, such as with the cranial nerves associated with each function.

Some assessment tools used by a school psychologist may give clues about sensory problems. For example, some tests have a multisensory component (Berninger, 2001). One such example is where the child is asked to tell which finger is touched with a stylus when his or her hand is shielded from view (Hebben & Milberg, 2002). The child is also asked what letter or number is drawn on his or her hand. Such tasks can give insight into the sensory discrimination abilities of the child. A quick way to get an idea of children's sensory discrimination skills is to place common objects in their hand when their eyes are closed and ask them to name the object. Another clue of possible sensory deficits is if a child is frequently involved in accidents, especially involving a slow reaction, or none at all, to painful stimuli, such as a hot stove (Reynolds & Fletcher-Janzen, 1997).

Often, educators and other professionals have assessed a learner in certain areas that can give important insight into their neurological functioning. Becoming familiar with such assessments given by other professionals can often help practitioners recognize problems in the academic, developmental, and neuropsychological areas in the life of a learner. One such measure is the Brigance Diagnostic Inventory of Early Development (Brigance, 1991), which measures academic and preacademic skills as well as motor skills. Some items on the Brigance assess gross motor abilities, such as how well a child can skip, hop, and walk on heels or toes. Other items look at fine motor abilities, such as how well a child can copy certain shapes. These observations may give important information about possible visual-motor integration difficulties. Teacher reports involving abrupt changes in behavior or skills can sometimes be clues to possible neurological trauma. Impairment in the attainment of developmental milestones can also indicate possible neurological problems. However, because some of these tests are used with young children, simple developmental delay may be eventually attributed as the cause and not neurological impairment (see Chapter 23).

## INTERVENTIONS IN THE SCHOOLS

The most common interventions used for neurological problems are medical, including pharmacological and surgical methods. Often, the purpose of these interventions is to alleviate the problem directly, as in the case of surgery, or to compensate for any loss of normal functioning that the neurological problem may cause, as with physical assistance devices. Although many of these procedures seem efficacious, or even are so, from a neurological point of view, the child patient may still be left with *life-altering* neuropsychological injuries that impact school and life skills. Thus, many neuropsychological interventions are needed after neurological procedures. Professionals in the school setting have the same goals in mind when implementing neuropsychological interventions (D'Amato & Rothlisberg, 1996). Teaching is often a part of a neurological intervention (e.g., teaching a patient how to walk in school). For instance, in school, teaching is often the main component of any intervention aimed at rehabilitation. This can involve the teaching of skills lost or the teaching of new skills never acquired. Compensatory interventions often involve modifying the delivery of information to the student, such as altering teaching methods and putting books on tape (Reynolds & Fletcher-Janzen, 1997). Another example is modifying the way students are allowed to convey knowledge, such through the use of voice dictation software or oral formats for tests, as opposed to using written measures (D'Amato & Rothlisberg, 1996).

Some common medications, including some sold over the counter, can potentially have adverse effects on a patient's CNS, possibly leading to regression of cognitive functioning (Cassidy, 1997). This possibility necessitates that those involved with a child be alert to any unexpected loss in cognitive functioning.

### IMPLICATIONS OF NEUROLOGICAL INTERVENTIONS

There is a wide range of specific areas of functioning that can be affected by neurological impairments that can negatively impact an individual's performance in the school setting. Five areas are briefly described here, followed by implications for interventions. For more strategies, refer to Section V of this *Handbook*. The five areas discussed in this chapter are (1) sensorimotor/visual-perceptual, (2) language/communication, (3) learning/memory, (4) executive functions, and (5) social-emotional/behavioral.

*Sensorimotor* problems include difficulties with vision, reading, headaches, and balance and coordination. Interventions include scheduling breaks for the student to avoid burnout, preferential seating, and occupational therapy and physical therapy consultations (Dise-Lewis, Calvery, & Lewis, 2002). *Visual-perceptual* problems may be in the area of visual discrimination, depth perception, spatial perception, or spatial orientation, as well as the cognitive processing of information gained through these abilities (Shaw, 2001). Impairment in any of these abilities can lead to inefficient learning or no learning at all. Interventions include presenting information via a variety of modalities, for example, both visually and verbally, and including other senses as much as possible, such as tactile activities and enlarging the size of written material (Dise-Lewis et al., 2002).

*Language and communication* abilities include both expressive and receptive language abilities, nonverbal and verbal, and written abilities. Such skills include the articulation of speech, the coherence of thoughts conveyed to others, and how well the individual understands information. Interventions include supplementing verbal directions with nonverbal gestures, checking for understanding of material covered as well as instructions given, using visual cues in the form of pictures and symbols, modifying assignments and tests, and providing assistive communicative devices, such as speech synthesizers (D'Amato & Rothlisberg, 1996; Dise-Lewis et al., 2002).

*Learning and memory* skills include the ability to understand and recall information, synthesize information from multiple sources, generalize skills to other environments, and make inferences using the material being presented or read. Reading and reading comprehension are common problems in the learning and memory domain. Interventions include teaching strategies such as breaking down tasks into steps, pulling out main ideas by using highlighting methods, outlining chapters, rehearsing information, having the teacher use multiple modalities in presenting information, tape recording lectures, and having someone take notes covering the material presented in class so that copies can be given to the individual for study.

*Attention* is an area in this domain that is often affected by neurological problems. The concept of attention includes the skills needed to attend to a stimulus, focus on that stimulus while filtering out competing information, focus on more than one stimuli at a time, and maintaining attention over an extended period of time (Levitt & Johnstone, 2001). Interventions include placing the learner in an environment with fewer distractions, employing developmentally appropriate self-monitoring systems, giving the child frequent breaks, varying the type of educational tasks, and praising on-task behavior.

*Executive functions*, for psychoeducational purposes, include abilities to quickly process and work with information, organize, plan, problem-solve, and self-monitor and regulate one's behavior (Dise-Lewis et al., 2002). Interventions include increasing time limits for projects and tests, providing outlines for material being covered, teaching organization and planning skills (such as using planners for assignments and schedules), and teaching self-monitoring techniques.

*Social-emotional and behavioral* concerns involve both internalizing issues, such as withdrawal, anxiety, and depression, and externalizing issues, such as challenging behaviors and conduct. Interventions include teaching social skills, social skills groups, role-playing relevant social situations, providing a mentor, behavior management that is constant among settings and incorporates positive attention, and counseling and therapy services (D'Amato & Rothlisberg, 1996).

## DIAGNOSIS LINKED TO INTERVENTION

There are a number of causes that need to be ruled out when considering possible neurological impairments. Tools available to the physician include a general physical examination, a review of the patient's medical records, a biographical history, ordering laboratory tests, conducting further medical procedures that may measure brain structure or activity, and making referrals to other professionals. Many of these activities are undertaken before a medical diagnosis is offered. A difficulty with some traditional medical diagnoses is that they sometimes search for simple lines of causation, as with a biologically based disturbance of the brain. Mental health problems, however, often have multiple etiologies that involve interactions of environmental and biological elements (Emde & Robinson,

2000). Preexisting and comorbid conditions are important to recognize in order to distinguish between which problems are directly attributable to a neurological cause and which are not (Katz, Mills, & Cassidy, 1997). A child with a traumatic brain injury, for example, needs to be differentiated from a child with a congenital or degenerative brain injury or birth trauma (D'Amato et al., 1999). Acquired brain injuries can exaggerate preexisting learning, behavioral, and psychological problems, as well as precipitate previously dormant physical or emotional disorders (Dise-Lewis et al., 2002).

As previously discussed, it is important to include in the history a description of the current severity, pervasiveness, and duration of symptoms, as well as the time of onset and progression of each individual's neuropsychological sequelae. Past treatment success, current medications, and prior evaluations are all important information to gather as well (Cassidy, 1997; Hebben & Milberg, 2002). In regard to the severity of the injury, such as with a traumatic brain injury, impairment can be viewed along a continuum, taking into account such indicators as depth and duration of coma and posttraumatic amnesia (D'Amato et al., 1999). In one case, an individual recovering from an accident may be struggling to recover the ability to walk or use his or her arms, whereas in another case, an individual may be working to regain social skills or reading abilities.

Many neurologists often focus on motor and sensory (i.e., neurological) processes and are pleased to report that patients will most probably recover all neurological functions. This means they will have the skills to see, hear, taste, smell, walk, and talk, for example; it does not mean they will recover all *neuropsychological* abilities. The family may think the patient was not affected by the accident, but this often is not the case. Similar injuries can produce radically diverse results in different individuals, and for this reason it is not enough to just label a learner as having a traumatic brain injury (Katz et al., 1997).

The pace at which a particular disorder develops also offers clues to the origin of the problem. A stroke, for example, results in an abrupt loss of function, whereas toxin-induced damage results in a more gradual onset of symptoms (Goldberg, 2003b). Patients with acute neurological symptoms often have impaired cognitive or language functions, and so attaining the necessary information and history may prove difficult. These individuals may have a prolonged period of examination before a diagnosis is offered (Murray et al., 2002). Information gathered from the neurological examination can also help decide what level of injury has taken place. For example, in the case of a spinal cord injury, an acute injury may result in the inability to sense a pin prick below the injury and an inability to move the lower extremities. A partial injury may result in the inability to sense the pin prick on one side of the body below the injury or an inability to move one leg, depending on the location of the injury (Goldberg, 2003b).

Applied Differential Diagnosis in Schools

A specific differential diagnosis needs to be made when diagnosing neurological problems. When abnormal reflexes are found, possible causes include impaired sensory input and abnormal motor nerve function. It will take compiling all available data to make an educated diagnosis as to what system(s) is/are impaired, such as the sensory limb or lower or upper motor neuron problems. Diseases such as diabetes and thyroid disorders can also affect reflexes, as can a stroke (Goldberg, 2003b). Trouble with coordination, as in touching one's nose with one's finger, may be a result of a problem with the cerebellum, but may also be attributed to vision or muscle problems (Goldberg, 2003b). The ability to stand, for instance, is dependent on a number of systems as well, including visual, cerebellar, motor, and sensory systems; a problem with any of these systems can produce difficulty with walking (Goldberg, 2003b).

In the area of vision, an individual with loss of half or more of his or her field of vision may actually have a pituitary tumor (Murray et al., 2002). The size and reaction of the pupils can indicate neuropathology, but medications, narcotics, and intracranial pressure can also affect the pupils (Goldberg, 2003a). In a patient presenting with a hearing difficulty, certain tests may differentiate between a conductive and a sensorineural hearing loss. A conductive hearing loss is where the passage of sound from the outside to the nerve is affected, such as with wax buildup in the external canal. A sensorineural hearing loss is where the transmission of sound from the nerve to the brain is affected, as in a tumor on the nerve. The Webber test can be used to differentiate between these two types of hearing loss (Goldberg, 2003a). In this test, the physician uses a tuning fork to send vibrations to the nerve via touch, on the skull, and via air, with the tuning fork next to the ear. An individual with a conductive hearing loss will be able to hear the tone better when the fork is placed on the skull rather than next to the ear, whereas an individual with a sensorineural hearing loss will still not be able to hear the tone as well in the ear with the affected nerve.

When dealing with individuals with possible learning disabilities, other information other than difficulties in school may be needed to rule out such possible contributing factors as emotional problems, environmental factors, and undiagnosed neurological problems. An example is the case of a learner who does not appear to be paying attention when he or she may actually be experiencing seizures, which can cause the student to appear to be daydreaming (Reynolds & Fletcher-Janzen, 1997; Wiederholt, 1982). Language problems also need to be ruled out, both expressive and receptive, because they will impact an individual's ability to learn and to express what has been learned (Murray et al., 2002; Wiederholt, 1982).

Damage to certain parts of the brain can differentially affect the patient's outcome. Neurologists work with radiologists and neurosurgeons to diagnose and treat brain abnormalities (D'Amato & Dean, 1988). Procedures typically include the neurological examination, laboratory tests, and a neuroimaging study, as well as other related medical procedures as needed (e.g., spinal tap). Damage to the temporal lobe, for example, could result in damage to sound discrimination and recognition, as well as to visual memory storage. Lesions in areas of the brain that serve more discrete functions often have more predictable neurological outcomes. An example is when a lesion in the right, primary visual cortex produces left visual field deficits (Katz, 1997). Brain tumors can result in symptoms that mimic dementia, but again, such symptoms usually arise more gradually (Wedding & Reeves, 1997). Approximately half of all patients with brain tumors present with psychiatric symptoms, and over 90% of patients with temporal lobe tumors display a similar presentation. Frontal lobe tumors may also produce symptoms such as depression, apathy, and irritability; temporal lobe tumors may produce depression and anxiety as well. Tumors in the hypothalamus are associated with higher incidences of amnesia, personality disturbances, Anorexia Nervosa, and disturbances in sexual functioning. Tumors affecting the pituitary region can result in sleep disturbances (Wedding & Reeves, 1997). All of these medical conditions could be misdiagnosed by a school psychologist without considering all information and making appropriate referrals.

When dealing with a motor dysfunction, a physician may look for patterns in the target muscle that may suggest a problem with either upper motor neuron processes, which lie in the spinal cord and brain, or lower motor neuron processes, which lie in the target muscle. An example of an upper motor neuron process is weakness and spasticity in the target muscle, of which either a cord lesion or brain impairment could be the cause. A cord lesion affects both sides of the body, whereas problems in the brain tend to affect one hemisphere and thus present with contralateral symptoms. A problem in a lower motor neuron process often presents as weakness and flaccidity in the target muscle (Goldberg, 2003b).

## CONCLUSION

Learning is driven by how the brain processes information. Significant damage to the brain can lead to death, and mild damage can lead to impaired life abilities (e.g., loss of speech) or neuropsychological impairment (e.g., poor planning abilities). Neuropsychological damage to the brain often leads to impairment in cognitive, memory, academic, emotional, social, and personal domains of behavior. When pediatric neurologists work regularly as part of a school team, their recommendations can lead to essential psychoeducational programming. Collaboration among professionals is important in addressing the needs of the learner, often by drawing on physical, occupational, and speech and language services, in addition to medical and psychological services. Because the neurological examination may *not* assess higher-level, integrative functioning, this area may need to be evaluated by a school neuropsychologist. Such an evaluation often includes assessing the learner's ability to integrate visual, auditory, and tactile systems in new learning, executive functioning, memory, and educational areas and emotional and behavioral issues. It is often up to the professional working in the school setting to understand how the students' learning is impacted by their strengths and needs and how best to accommodate those issues in an effort to assist students in achieving success.

## REFERENCES

Andrefsky, J. C., & Frank, J. I. (2002). Approach to the patient with acute confusional state (delirium/encephalopathy). In J. Biller (Ed.), *Practical neurology* (2nd ed., pp. 3–18). Philadelphia: Lippincott, Williams, & Wilkins.

Ashwal, S., Peabody, J. L., Schneider, S., Tomasi, L., Emery, J. R., & Peckham, N. (1990). Anencephaly: Clinical determination of brain death and neuropathological studies. *Pediatric Neurology, 6*(4), 233–239.

Atkinson, R. L., Atkinson, R. C., Smith, E. E., Bem, D. J., & Nolen-Hoeksema, S. (2003). *Hilgard's introduction to psychology: Glossary* (12th ed.). Retrieved April 13, 2004, from http://lms.thomsonelearning.com/hbcp/glossary/glossary.taf?gid=3.

Aylward, G. P. (1995). *Bayley infant neurodevelopmental screener.* San Antonio, TX: Psychological Corporation.

Aylward, G. P., Lazzara, A., & Meyer, J. (1978). Behavioral and neurological characteristics of a hydranencephalic infant. *Developmental Medicine and Child Neurology, 20*(2), 211–217.

Bayley, N. (1993). *Bayley scales of infant development* (2nd ed.). San Antonio, TX: Psychological Corporation.

Berninger, V. W. (2001). *Process assessment of the learner: Test battery for reading and writing.* San Antonio, TX: Psychological Corporation.

Bickerstaff, E. R., & Spillane, J. A. (1989). *Neurological examination in clinical practice* (5th ed.). Oxford, England: Blackwell Scientific.

Bigler, E. D., Nilsson, D. E., Burr, R. B., & Boyer, R. S. (1997). Neuroimaging in pediatric neuropsychology. In C. R. Reynolds & E. Fletcher-Janzen (Eds.), *Handbook of clinical child neuropsychology* (2nd ed., pp. 342–355). New York: Plenum Press.

Blumenfield, H. (2001). *An interactive online guide to the neurological examination: Neuroanatomy through clinical cases.* Retrieved February 4, 2004, from http://www.neuroexam.com.

Brigance, A. H. (1991). *Brigance diagnostic inventory for early development: Revised.* North Billerica, MA: Curriculum Associate.

Bush, G. H. W. (1990, July 17). *Presidential Proclamation 6158.* Retrieved April 14, 2004, from http://lcweb.loc.gov/loc/brain/proclaim.html.

Cassidy, J. W. (1997). Problem patients: Outliers in rehabilitation. In V. M. Mills, J. W. Cassidy, & D. I. Katz (Eds.), *Neurologic rehabilitation: A guide to diagnosis, prognosis, and treatment planning* (pp. 307–338). Malden, MA: Blackwell Science.

Corbett, J. J. (2002). Approach to the patient with visual loss. In J. Biller (Ed.), *Practical neurology* (2nd ed., pp. 119–134). Philadelphia: Lippincott, Williams, & Wilkins.

Curtis, B. A. (1990). *Neurosciences: The basics.* Philadelphia: Lea & Febiger.

D'Amato, R. C., & Dean, R. S. (1988). School psychology practice in a department of neurology. *School Psychology Review, 17*(3), 416–420.

D'Amato, R. C., & Rothlisberg, B. A. (1996). How education should respond to students with traumatic brain injury. *Journal of Learning Disabilities, 29,* 670–683.

D'Amato, R. C., Rothlisberg, B. A., & Leu Work, P. H. (1999). Neuropsychological assessment for intervention. In T. B. Gutkin & C. R. Reynolds (Eds.), *Handbook of school psychology* (3rd ed., pp. 452–475). New York: Wiley.

Damasio, A. R. (1987). Agraphia. In G. Adelman (Ed.), *Encyclopedia of neuroscience* (p. 24). Boston: Birkhäuser.

Dean, R. S., & Woodcock, R. W. (2003). *Dean-Woodcock Neuropsychological Battery.* Itasca, IL: Riverside.

Denckla, M. B. (1997). The neurobehavioral examination in children. In T. E. Feinberg & M. J. Farah (Eds.), *Behavioral neurology and neuropsychology* (pp. 721–728). New York: McGraw-Hill.

Diadori, P., & Carmant, L. (2001). The neurological examination. In B. L. Maria (Ed.), *Current management in child neurology* (2nd ed., pp. 28–34). Hamilton, Ontario: B.C. Decker.

Dise-Lewis, J. E., Calvery, M. L., & Lewis, H. C. (2002). *Brainstars. Brain injury: Strategies for teams and re-education of students.* (Available from the BrainSTARS program, 1056 East 19th Avenue, B285, Denver, CO 80218)

Emde, R. N., & Robinson, J. (2000). Guiding principles for a theory of early intervention: A developmental-psychoanalytic perspective. In J. P. Shonkoff & S. J. Meisels (Eds.), *Handbook of early childhood intervention* (pp. 160–178). Cambridge, United Kingdom: Cambridge University Press.

Goldberg, C. (2003a). *The neurological examination: Introduction.* Retrieved November 14, 2003, from the University of California, San Diego, School of Medicine and VA Medical Center Web site: http://medicine.ucsd.edu/clinicalmed/neuro2.htm.

Goldberg, C. (2003b). *The neurological examination: Reflex testing.* Retrieved November 14, 2003, from the University of California, San Diego, School of Medicine and VA Medical Center Web site: http://medicine.ucsd.edu/clinicalmed/neuro3.htm.

Gray, J. W., & Dean, R. S. (Eds.). (1989). *Neuropsychology of perinatal complications.* New York: Springer.

Greenberg, D. A., Aminoff, M. J., & Simon, R. P. (2002). *Clinical neurology* (5th ed.). New York: McGraw-Hill.

Haerer, A. F. (1992). *The neurological exam.* Philadelphia: J. B. Lippincott.

Hagen, C. (2004). *Rancho Los Amigos Scale.* Retrieved October 8, 2004, from http://www.neuroskills.com/tbi/rancho.html.

Hagen, C., Malkmus, D., & Durham, P. (1972). *Rancho Los Amigos Scale.* Retrieved on October 8, 2004, from http://www.neuroskills.com/tbi/rancho.html.

Hebben, N., & Milberg, W. (2002). Essentials of neuropsychological assessment. In A. S. Kaufman & N. L. Kaufman (Series Eds.), *Essentials of psychological assessment.* New York: Wiley.

Hohol, M., Stewart, P. A., & Jenkinson, J. (2001). *The neurological examination.* Retrieved February 2, 2004, from the University of Toronto School of Medicine Web site: http://icarus.med.utoronto.ca/NeuroExam.

Hynd, G. W., & Willis, W. G. (1988). *Pediatric neuropsychology.* Orlando: Grune & Stratton.

Johnstone, B., & Stonnington, H. H. (2001). Introduction. In B. Johnstone & H. H. Stonnington (Eds.), *Rehabilitation of neuropsychological disorders* (pp. 1–25). Philadelphia: Psychology Press.

Joseph, R. (1996). *Neuropsychiatry, neuropsychology, and clinical neuroscience* (2nd ed.). Baltimore: Williams & Wilkins.

Katz, D. I. (1997). Traumatic brain injury. In V. M. Mills, J. W. Cassidy, & D. I. Katz (Eds.), *Neurologic rehabilitation: A guide to diagnosis, prognosis, and treatment planning* (pp. 105–143). Malden, MA: Blackwell Science.

Katz, D. I., Mills, V. M., & Cassidy, J. W. (1997). The neurologic rehabilitation model in clinical practice. In V. M. Mills, J. W. Cassidy, & D. I. Katz (Eds.), *Neurologic rehabilitation: A guide to diagnosis, prognosis, and treatment planning* (pp. 1–27). Malden, MA: Blackwell Science.

Kirshner, H. S. (2002). *Behavioral neurology: Practical science of mind and brain* (2nd ed.). Boston: Butterworth-Heinemann.

Lezak, M. D., Howieson, D. B., & Loring, D. W. (2004). *Neuropsychological assessment* (4th ed.). New York: Oxford University Press.

Levitt, T., & Johnstone, B. (2001). The assessment and rehabilitation of attention disorders. In B. Johnstone & H. H. Stonnington (Eds.), *Rehabilitation of neuropsychological disorders* (pp. 27–52). Philadelphia: Psychology Press.

Lewis, D. W., & Dorbad, D. D. (2000). The utility of neuroimaging in the evaluation of children with migraine or chronic daily headaches who have normal neurological examinations. *Journal of Head and Face Pain, 8,* 629–632.

Loring, D. W. (Ed.). (1999). *INS Dictionary of neuropsychology.* New York: Oxford University Press.

Lundy-Ekman, L. (2002). *Neuroscience: Fundamentals of rehabilitation* (2nd ed.). Philadelphia: Saunders.

Maher, L. (1999). A quick neurologic examination. *Patient Care, 33*(2), 19.

Maynard, F. M., Bracken, M. B., Creasey, G., Ditunno, J. F., Donovan, W. H., & Ducker, T. B., et al. (1996). *International standards for neurological and functional classification of spinal cord injury.* Chicago: American Spinal Injury Association.

Meador, K. J., & Nichols, F. T. (1987). The neurological examination as it relates to neuropsychological issues. In L. C. Hartlage (Ed.), *Essentials of neuropsychological assessment* (pp. 30–45). New York: Springer.

Murray, T. A., Kelly, N. R., & Jenkins, S. (2002). The complete neurological examination: What every nurse practitioner should know. *Advance for Nurse Practitioners, 10*(7), 25–30.

Patten, B. M. (1992). The history of the neurological examination: Part 1. Ancient and premodern history—3000 BC to AD 1850. *Journal of the History of the Neurosciences, 1,* 3–14.

Rathe, R. (2000). *Basic clinical skills: The neurological examination.* Retrieved February 2, 2004, from http://medinfo.ufl.edu/year1/bcs/clist/neuro.html.

Reitan, R. M., & Wolfson, D. (1993). *The Halstead-Reitan Neuropsychological Test Battery: Theory and clinical interpretation* (2nd ed.). South Tucson, AZ: Neuropsychology Press.

Reynolds, C. R., & Fletcher-Janzen, E. (Eds.). (1997). *Handbook of clinical child neuropsychology* (2nd ed.). New York: Plenum Press.

Rothlisberg, B. A., D'Amato, R. C., & Palencia, B. N. (2003). Assessment of children for intervention planning following traumatic brain injury. In C. R. Reynolds & R. W. Kamphaus (Eds.), *Handbook of psychological and educational assessment of children: Personality, behavior, and context* (2nd ed., pp. 685–706). New York: Guilford Press.

Rush, A. J., George, M. S., Sackeim, H. A., Marangell, L. B., Husain, M. M., Giller, C., et al. (2000). Vagus nerve stimulation (VNS) for treatment-resistant depression: A multicenter study. *Biological Psychiatry, 47,* 276–286.

Sattler, J. M., & D'Amato, R. C. (2002a). Brain injuries: Formal batteries and informal measures. In J. M. Sattler (Ed.), *Assessment of children: Behavioral and clinical applications* (4th ed., pp. 440–469). San Diego, CA: Jerome M. Sattler.

Sattler, J. M., & D'Amato, R. C. (2002b). Brain injuries: Theory and rehabilitation programs. In J. M. Sattler (Ed.), *Assessment of children: Behavioral and clinical applications* (4th ed., pp. 401–439). San Diego, CA: Jerome M. Sattler.

Shaw, J. (2001). The assessment and rehabilitation of visual-spatial disorders. In B. Johnstone & H. H. Stonnington (Eds.), *Rehabilitation of neuropsychological disorders* (pp. 125–160). Philadelphia: Psychology Press.

Simpson, D., & Reilly, P. (1982). Pediatric coma scale. *Lancet, 2,* 450.

Solomon, D. (1998). Diseases of the cranial nerves and brainstem. In R. N. Rosenberg & D. E. Pleasure (Eds.), *Comprehensive neurology* (2nd ed., pp. 625–658). New York: Wiley.

Strub, R. L., & Black, F. W. (1997). The mental status exam. In T. E. Feinberg & M. J. Farah (Eds.), *Behavioral neurology and neuropsychology* (pp. 25–42). New York: McGraw-Hill.

Tallal, P. (1987). Dysphasia, developmental. In G. Adelman (Ed.), *Encyclopedia of neuroscience* (pp. 351–353). Boston: Birkhäuser.

Tupper, D. E. (1986). Neuropsychological screening and soft signs. In J. E. Obrzut & G. W. Hynd (Eds.), *Child neuropsychology: Vol. 2. Clinical practice* (pp. 139–186). Orlando, FL: Academic Press.

Tupper, D. E. (1987). The issues with "soft signs." In D. E. Tupper (Ed.), *Soft neurological signs* (pp. 1–16). Orlando, FL: Grune & Stratton.

Voeller, K. (1981). A proposed extended behavioral, cognitive and sensorimotor pediatric neurological examination. In R. Ochroch (Ed.), *The diagnosis and treatment of minimal brain dysfunction in children* (pp. 65–90). New York: Human Sciences Press.

Wedding, D., & Reeves, D. (1997). Neurological disorders. In A. M. Horton Jr., D. Wedding, & J. Webster (Eds.), *The neuropsychology handbook: Vol. 1. Foundations and assessment* (2nd ed., pp. 91–138). New York: Springer.

Wiederholt, W. C. (1982). *Neurology for non-neurologists*. New York: Academic Press.

Willis, W. G., & Widerstrom, A. H. (1986). Neuropsychological screening and soft signs. In J. E. Obrzut & G. W. Hynd (Eds.), *Child neuropsychology: Vol. 1. Theory and research* (pp. 13–53). Orlando, FL: Academic Press.

Yule, W., & Taylor, E. (1987). Classification of soft signs. In D. E. Tupper (Ed.), *Soft neurological signs* (pp. 19–43). Orlando, FL: Grune & Stratton.

# CHAPTER 8

# The School
# Neuropsychological Examination

ELAINE FLETCHER-JANZEN

THE ADAPTATION OF child neuropsychological assessment principles to the school setting is not a new endeavor. Eminent pediatric neuropsychologists, clinical psychologists, and school psychologists with training in neuropsychology have long understood the importance of attempting to answer referral questions about children in a competent manner that results in positive outcomes in the classroom (Bigler, Nussbaum, & Foley, 1997; Haak & Livingston, 1997; Hale & Fiorello, 2004; Lyon, Fletcher, & Barnes, 2003; Reynolds & Fletcher-Janzen, 1997; Sattler & D'Amato, 2002; Spreen, 2001; Teeter & Semrud-Clikeman, 1997).

The school psychologist with appropriate training in neuropsychology knows that a standard psychoeducational battery commonly used in the public schools will assist most children referred for evaluation. However, he or she also knows that there are many children who need much more. The regular battery used for activities such as discrepancy analysis simply do not address the breadth and depth of information necessary to help children with birth defects, brain injuries, chronic illnesses, and a myriad of disorders and diseases that affect brain-behavior relationships. Indeed, the discrepancy formula for learning disability determination under federal guidelines is being replaced with a consensus of opinion that a problem-solving model using information from multiple sources should guide special education assessments (National Dissemination Center for Children with Disabilities, 2004).

In addition, the reduction in funding from the private and public sectors for inpatient and outpatient services for children has also placed an onus on school psychologists to work with children who ordinarily would be served by professionals in clinical settings. In the years to come, school psychologists will need as much training as they can obtain on the finer points of assessment of children with neuropsychological needs.

This chapter focuses on neuropsychological assessments that can take place in the school setting. The training needed to be able to conduct a neuropsychological assessment in the schools is discussed at length elsewhere in this book and will not be reiterated here. Let it suffice to say that conducting assessments of this nature without proper training and periods of supervision is not appropriate and may well do more harm than good.

The school neuropsychological assessment is a process, not a product. The child study is not simply a set of neuropsychological tests, and the assessment does not end with a diagnosis and recommendations for intervention written in a report. Every part of the assessment is as important as any other. Small nuances of the child-teacher relationship are just as important as the results of formal neuropsychological tests. One is no less neuropsychological than the other. Indeed, Luria conducted most of his bedside assessments with objects that just happened to be in his pocket that day (Christensen, 2000), and he believed that "the fundamental purpose of neuropsychological assessment is to describe the functional nature of neuropsychological symptoms, rather than their presence or absence in a given case" (p. 273).

In this sense, the school neuropsychological assessment is a living and breathing process written into a functional treatment plan that can evolve over a period of years. The written document is not the end of the assessment because it may well be just the beginning of a series of trials. The school neuropsychological assessment process changes from moment to moment because a team has to carry it out, it is under constant review, it has an ecological focus, and services may be ongoing as long as the child is present in that school. The assessment is fluid, dynamic, and constantly evolving.

Historically, texts about child clinical neuropsychology have focused on neuropsychological test batteries with implied or cursory acknowledgment about the importance of detailed history taking and responsibility for ongoing case management or ecological validity of assessment results and treatment interaction. Currently, texts reflect the ecological validity of neuropsychological assessment but still omit much of the nuts and bolts of practice in the school setting (Bigler & Clement, 1997; Bigler, Nussbaum, & Foley, 1997; Teeter & Semrud-Clikeman, 1997). The assessment information in this chapter is not confined to a list of instruments that the clinician can simply add to his or her battery when brain-behavior referral questions are raised. The school neuropsychological assessment is broadly defined in this chapter and is geared to creating positive outcomes in an educational setting on an ongoing basis. Other chapters in this book speak to the concrete description and value of quantitative neuropsychological measures published in test batteries. This chapter attempts to describe the overall assessment process in the school setting and how it differs from the traditional clinical setting.

The referral question that initiates an assessment in the public schools often differs from that in clinical settings because it always loops back to how the child can be helped in the classroom. The school clinician basically has a different referral focus and a different outcome agenda than the outpatient or inpatient clinician. The reality of clinical practice is that it must have a source of funding whether services are inpatient or outpatient. The financial support of clinical neuropsychology is time-limited and setting-specific because of the financial constraints determined by managed care and insurance parameters. On the contrary, school neuropsychologist services are funded by the public sector and can be ongoing while the child is enrolled in the school district. Clinical and school neuropsychological practices are essentially opposite ends of a continuum. On one end is the private and individually funded patient in an inpatient hospital, and on the other is a child in a publicly funded school setting. Each has a specific source of funding and the constraints of practice and services determined by that source.

School neuropsychological services differ from state to state and school district to school district. An important reason school psychologists have found the need for further training in neuropsychology is because the current private and public systems of funding have substantially reduced lengths of stay and limits of assessment in inpatient and outpatient settings (Haak & Livingston, 1997). Hence, children with severe brain injuries and the like are discharged to the schools much earlier than ever before, and the school district becomes responsible for a much more intense level of care than has been previously required in that setting. The new demands on school psychologists are partly due to the decline of funds for treatment for children with neuropsychological needs. When there are no private funds, someone has to positively intervene in the lives of these many children, and school psychologists are natural delegates.

## DIFFERENCES BETWEEN CLINICAL AND SCHOOL NEUROPSYCHOLOGY PRACTICE

How does the practice of a school neuropsychologist differ from that of a child clinical neuropsychologist? Just as clinical and school psychology differ in populations served, treatment goals, and place of practice, so do their neuropsychology counterparts. Table 8.1 describes some of the ways the practice of neuropsychology differs in the clinical and school settings.

In general, the school neuropsychologist always has an educational goal in mind. The entire assessment process focuses on helping the child meet the demands of everyday living in the classroom and school environment. This approach keeps in mind that a child's quality of life is greatly influenced by academic and social success in school. Therefore, an accurate statement of the child's neuropsychological status and how that translates into learning becomes the basis for the assessment. Interventions based on the neuropsychological assessment are designed, carried out, supervised, and evaluated by the school neuropsychologist working in tandem with an educational team. In addition, the relationship with the child and the team may go on for the child's entire school career. The school neuropsychologist, therefore, has the potential to have a long-term relationship with every child with whom he or she works.

Long-term professional relationships allow the school neuropsychologist to have a unique clinical perspective. School neuropsychologists have opportunities to follow children to determine whether diagnostic formulations are correct, especially when the course of a disorder is expected to resolve, stabilize, or worsen (McCaffrey, Palav, O'Bryant, & Labarge, 2003). They witness the children growing up and meeting developmental milestones, sometimes watching them grow into disabilities, sometimes watching them overcome and outgrow disabilities, and, more important, helping children and their teachers and families prevent negative outcomes that so often occur with children who have neuropsychological deficits. In comparison, clinical neuropsychologists have much shorter and clinically intense opportunities with their clients that often end with a diagnosis and written recommendations (McCaffrey et al., 2003).

**Table 8.1**
Differences between Practice Parameters of School and Clinical Child
Neuropsychological Assessment

| Area of Specialty | School | Clinical |
|---|---|---|
| Outcome agenda | Ecological validity of school neuropsychological assessment. | Diagnosis, recommendations, and possible short-term management/intermittent consultation. |
| Neuropsychological assessment | Educationally focused. Inclusion of academic and achievement measures. Primarily academic/educational interventions. Evaluated by sustained and evidence-based gains in classroom. | *Outpatient:* Clinically focused, diagnosis/report, and sometimes short-term follow-up. *Inpatient:* Clinically focused, initial diagnosis, short-term treatment goals, master treatment plan evaluation, discharge preparation. |
| Informants for the assessment | Parents, teachers, school personnel, physicians, community members, siblings, school nurse, school counselor, social worker, office staff, librarian, support staff. | Parents, school reports, consulting physicians. |
| Prior personal knowledge of child | Can be up to years. | Usually none. |
| Clinician's relationship with parents | Ongoing and indefinite. | For the period of assessment and possible follow-up. |
| Clinician's relationships with consulting physicians | Ongoing. | Ongoing. |
| Clinician's relationship with child | Ongoing or as needed. | Time-limited for assessment and focused treatment. |
| Clinician's relationship with teacher | Consultative and ongoing. | Little or no contact. |
| Clinician's relationship with treatment team | Can be supervisory, consultative, or direct care provider. Long-term. | *Outpatient clinician:* None/limited. *Inpatient:* Clinician time-limited treatment team member. |
| Clinician's responsibility for ongoing medication monitoring | Frequent and long-term. | Infrequent and short-term. |

The school neuropsychologist also has to rely on consultation skills to create change through other school personnel and parents. For the most part, school psychologists spend the bulk of their professional time assessing children. Therefore, individuals who do not have training in neuropsychology have to deliver the services that will create good outcomes. Clinical psychologists in inpatient settings share direct care therapeutic duties with other qualified personnel who generally have smaller caseloads than staff in the public schools. In outpatient settings, clinical psychologists are often restricted to working with just the family, as school consultations usually are not funded by insurance and sheer distance limits how much supervision of treatment can occur by a nonemployee of the school district.

School neuropsychologists are much more likely to have extended personal contact with informants (D'Amato, Rothlisberg, & Leu Work, 1999). Over the years, the school psychologist forms close professional relationships with teachers and other personnel. The school psychologist knows the classroom climate from experience and knows the structure and expectations in a given classroom. Indeed, the school psychologist may know a child very well before he or she is even referred. Clinical psychologists, on the other hand, are much less likely to have these kinds of relationships with school personnel, and their fund of knowledge about the child, the personnel who work with the child on a daily basis, and the setting will be limited. Having a deep understanding and familiarity of the child's daily living and the personnel who will be recruited to help the child simply creates better chances for treatment success and accountability (D'Amato et al., 1999). Objective verification of the latter statement, however, needs to be evaluated as the practice of school neuropsychology grows.

Why is a discussion of the differences between the practice of child neuropsychology in the schools and in clinical settings related to the topic of neuropsychological assessment? The goals of school neuropsychological assessment and the competencies that a school neuropsychologist must have are related by the shift in perspective demanded by the setting of service delivery. To achieve positive outcomes, the school neuropsychologist has to handle assessment and group process in a real-world setting. It is clinical child neuropsychology "without walls."

The educational team brings the referral; the team has vital information that provides a large portion of the assessment information; the team has to formulate and buy into the intervention/treatment plan; the team has to carry out the plan; and the team has to evaluate the plan. The school neuropsychologist is the only team member who has the training and expertise to lead the team in directions that are specific to the neuropsychological needs of the individual child. Therefore, the diagnosis must be accurate, but the assessment is ongoing. The process of neuropsychological assessment in the schools does not end when a diagnosis is made, as it often does in clinical settings. It ends when a positive, evidence-based outcome is documented for some time in the classroom.

## ASSESSMENT APPROACHES

At this point, the research literature has not delineated an assessment approach that has been demonstrated to work effectively for school neuropsychological applications. Recently, Hale and Fiorello (2004) have proposed a promising approach designed specifically for school psychologists, though its effectiveness remains to be seen. Historically, assessment approach issues in child neuropsychology have centered on the battery and process approaches (Batchelor & Dean, 1996; Fennell, 1994) that reflect the early medical model settings. In recent years, there has been a tendency for these models to be expanded into less medically oriented settings, and ecological aspects have been included (e.g., Bigler et al., 1997; Fennell, 1994, 2002; Hartlage & Williams, 1990; Rourke, Van Der Vlugt, &

Rourke, 2002; Teeter & Semrud-Clikeman, 1997). For example, Teeter and Semrud-Clikeman use a transactional model whose basic premise is that because "the child's biobehavioral status acts and is acted on by the environment, it is important that this assessment evaluate home, school, and community functioning as well as neuropsychological performance" (p. 103).

## FIXED AND FLEXIBLE BATTERIES

Some neuropsychologists prefer the fixed battery approach, whereby the decision of which tests to administer is determined a priori. Standardized batteries such as the Luria-Nebraska Children's Battery (Golden, 1986) and the Halstead-Reitan Neuropsychological Test Batteries for Children (Reitan & Wolfson, 1985) fit well into this approach. These batteries have been shown to be quite effective in detecting the presence, lateralization, and localization of brain dysfunction (Bauer, 1994).

Others prefer a flexible approach to assessment, whereby instruments are chosen depending on the presenting issues or suspected pathologies and are sometimes based on a short screening battery. The flexible battery approach is an "experiment-in-evolution," and the course of the battery changes as the "early data returns" are obtained (Bauer, 1994, p. 263). Both approaches have advantages and disadvantages (Bauer, 1994; Kamphaus, 2001; Rourke, Van Der Vulgt, & Rourke, 2002; Russell, 1994; Teeter & Semrud-Clikeman, 1997), and the clinician has to determine which approach is best for the setting and the populations involved.

In the end, the job of the clinician is to answer the referral question. Sometimes the question can be answered in the context of a fixed approach to the assessment, and sometimes hypotheses need to be tested by bringing in other tests to satisfy lingering questions. Indeed, it has been argued that there is really no substantial difference between the fixed and flexible approaches (Bauer, 1994), and there are essentially no data suggesting superiority of one over the other (Kamphaus, 2001).

One bright point in the use of any battery is that the field of psychometrics is advancing, and more reliable and valid instruments geared toward neuropsychological constructs with children are available and affordable. These tests will hopefully increase predictive validity and provide compensation for tests that historically have been downward extensions of adult tests and batteries that had little or no reliability data (Batchelor & Dean, 1996; Hartlage & Williams, 1990; Marlowe, 2000).

## PROCESS APPROACH

Very much a qualitative approach to assessment, the process approach uses an initial set of tests to sample different domains of functioning. The child's performance on these tests is then analyzed from both a quantitative and a qualitative perspective to aid in the formation of hypotheses that will be tested further (Lezak, 1995). Based in the Lurian tradition (Bauer, 1994; Kamphaus, 2001; Kolb & Whishaw, 1990), observations about how a test is solved is considered to be more important than reporting success or failure of the task (Bauer, 1994). The limits of performance are tested in the process approach, and then the treatment plan is informed (Teeter & Semrud-Clikeman, 1997). This approach melds quantitative and qualitative data, and individual cases wander or vary on a continuum between the two methods of data collection (Batchelor, 1996; Kaplan, 1998).

A process-oriented approach may be suited for the school setting because it relies on clinical observations in standardized and experimental situations. The school neuropsychologist has the luxury of forming hypotheses of pathology and compensatory skills and seeing how they relate to everyday functioning in the real world. The school neuropsychologist has, if you will, a working laboratory in the classroom within which to test hypotheses that emerge from the assessment.

## ECOLOGICAL/TREATMENT MODELS

There have been many models for neuropsychological assessment in the past that have had a clinical or medical focus. Today, assessment models take on much more of a developmental, adaptive, and child-oriented treatment focus (Yeates & Taylor, 1998). For example, Rourke, Bakker, Fisk, and Strang (1983) created the "preliminary developmental neuropsychological remediation/ habilitation model," which was later revised and is now called the treatment-oriented model. This model accommodates the continuing relationship between neuropsychological assessment and intervention during the course of treatment (Rourke, Van Der Vlugt, & Rourke, 2002).

Teeter and Semrud-Clikeman (1997) have a similar model emphasizing a more ecological and transactional focus; it includes:

> (1) a description of the neuropsychological correlates of the disorder; (2) identification of behavioral characteristics of various childhood disorders; (3) takes into consideration moderator variables such as family, school, and community interactions; and (4) determines how the existing neuropsychological constraints interact with the child's coping ability and developmental changes that occur at various ages. (p. 104)

Fennell (1994) has used a more patient-centered approach, with emphasis on the isolation of the specific neuropsychological mechanism that underlies a particular behavior disorder. Taylor and Fletcher (1990) propose the biobehavioral approach that recognizes four types of variables present in the assessment: (1) presenting complaint; (2) cognitive and psychosocial characteristics; (3) environmental, sociocultlural, and historical variables; and (4) biological and genetic variables.

Recently, an ecological model has been proposed that builds on many of these approaches and responds much better to the school neuropsychologist's needs. Hale and Fiorello (2004) have developed the cognitive hypothesis-testing (CHT) model. This model emphasizes developmental criteria shaping "the nature of the assessment, interpretation of results, and recommendations for intervention" (p. 85). The model also calls for a screening battery whereby testable hypotheses are formed. Hale and Fiorello admit that the CHT model is not unlike others proposed by D'Amato, Rothlisberg, and Rhodes (1997) and Fennell and Bauer (1997). However, they suggest that the CHT model differs because it calls for the examination of input, processing, and output demands of the tests administered and relating the data to all other information in the assessment. Hale and Fiorello also emphasize the link between diagnosis and evidence-based interventions for academic deficits.

The efficacy of the CHT model has not been tested at this point, and because it supports some features of the process approach, it is unlikely that attempts to verify its effectiveness over other models could be methodologically realistic. This limitation is not specific to the CHT approach but will compromise any school model applications because developmental, environmental, and quality of life issues interact forcefully with individual school neuropsychological assessments. However, their emphasis on interpretation of the individual subtest-level performance on batteries such as the Wechsler scales is contrary to current evidence.

Regardless of the assessment approach taken by the school neuropsychologist, several components of a neuropsychological assessment are agreed on by most practitioners and are summarized here (and described in detail in Reynolds & Mayfield, 1999):

1. All (or at least a significant majority) of a child's educationally relevant cognitive skills or higher-order information-processing skills should be assessed.
2. Testing should sample the relative efficiency of the right and left hemispheres of the brain.
3. Testing should sample both anterior and posterior regions of cortical function.
4. Testing should determine the presence of specific deficits.
5. Testing should determine the acuteness versus the chronicity of any problems or weaknesses found.
6. Testing should locate intact complex functional systems.
7. Testing should assess affect, personality, and behavior.
8. Test results should be presented in ways that are useful in school settings, not just in acute care or intensive rehabilitation facilities or to physicians.
9. If consulting directly with a school system, an evaluator must be certain that the testing and examination procedure are efficient (p. 13, 14).

Several points come to mind when creating an appropriate neuropsychological assessment approach in the public schools. School neuropsychologists, as with neuropsychologists in any other setting, will need to identify a theoretical perspective that accommodates the setting and populations served. The theoretical perspective will need to take into account the developmental context of child neuropsychology, the ecological validity of measures used, and the practical application of neuropsychological principles in the classroom.

## OUTLINE OF THE SCHOOL NEUROPSYCHOLOGICAL ASSESSMENT

Adding another model of assessment to the array that is already available appears to be redundant. School neuropsychologists should already have extensive training in the different models of assessment, and it is up to the individual clinician to choose which methods are appropriate for each school setting. It is difficult to describe a one-size-fits-all process of assessment for a school neuropsychological examination because the clinician will most likely be faced with a wide variety of ages, disorders, and referral questions.

It is unlikely that a school psychologist would be used only for neuropsychological assessment in the public schools. It is much more likely that the school psychologist will have to wear different hats depending on the individual school needs and the demands of the referral questions. Cases in the school differ from day to day, and the assessment demands may progress from informal consultation with a teacher, to psychoeducational assessment, to a comprehensive psychological assessment, and on to a wideband neuropsychological assessment. The full spectrum of problems in the public schools is far wider than problems that come to a specific inpatient setting, and the treatment goals have a much less restrictive application. Therefore, above all, the school neuropsychologist has to be flexible and has to be able to adapt service delivery at a moment's notice and for a wide variety of brain-behavior problems that range from very mild to severe.

The information in this chapter about the assessment process progresses in a linear fashion through a school neuropsychological assessment. The investigative process is divided into sections that slowly build a picture of why the child has come to be referred for assessment; an in-depth medical, developmental, social, emotional, and academic history; the child's current neuropsychological functioning; and efficacy of current treatment and medications. This picture is then applied to possible evidence-based interventions that are a direct result of the diagnosis, and a follow-up plan and timetable for evaluating the efficacy of the interventions is clearly set forth.

Table 8.2 describes a school neuropsychological assessment outline. The steps that are depicted are customary and inclusive and reflect the use of quantitative and qualitative data. The steps are subject to the demands of the referral question, the parameters of practice set by the school district, the clinician's theoretical orientation, and the needs of the individual child. The reader is invited to change, delete, or adapt the sections as needed.

## EXAMINATION OF REFERRAL QUESTION

*Problem Definition*    It is important for the clinician to fully understand the reason the child is being referred for evaluation. Sometimes that determination is easy. For example, a third-grade boy was involved in an automobile accident, sustained a brain injury, was treated in an inpatient facility, and is now returning to school.

**Table 8.2**
Outline of a School Neuropsychological Assessment

---

1. Examination of referral question
2. File review
3. Developmental and medical history
4. Current medical management regimen
5. Observations
6. Social, emotional, psychological assessment data
7. Achievement data
8. Neuropsychological battery
9. Qualitative data
10. Report
11. Intervention/Evaluation/Reintervention

---

He is referred by his parents and teacher for a comprehensive assessment to determine current functioning and appropriate school placement.

Sometimes the reason for referral is hard to discern. For example, a kindergartener is referred in late spring because she does not recognize most of the letters of the alphabet, and the teacher is concerned about promoting her to first grade. There is a concrete reason (not recognizing letters), but there may also be other reasons prompting the concern (e.g., parent's refusal to hold the child back in kindergarten next year, suspicion of neglect, or the child has staring spells that last for a few seconds). It is important to understand exactly what the concerns of the referring party are and if different people around the child see the presenting problem differently.

Many times, referral questions will be addressed in global or vague terms, such as "Julie just can't pay attention" or "Miguel can't keep up with his classmates." It is important to help the referring party define exactly what the problem is and is not. The more information gained at this point, the more the clinician will be able to frame exactly what is problematic and not waste time and energy on incidental issues.

Another reason for spending time framing the referral question is for the clinician to gain information about the child's strengths. The child's ability to adapt and cope with everyday activities in the classroom tells us just as much about brain-behavior relationships as the examination of pathology. Too often, the referral question leads the clinician into fixing what is wrong and emphasizing pathology, deficits, or weaknesses. From a functional point of view, how the child accommodates and functions, notwithstanding his or her weaknesses, may well lead the clinician to intervention strategies that are more neuropsychologically and ecologically sound.

*Referral Source*   It is important to know who is referring the child. Is this a parent request without teacher support, or the opposite? Valuable information is gained from knowing if the problem behaviors are observed across settings. If all interested parties are observing the same issues and say that the problem is outside the normal range, then the informal raters seem to be in agreement. However, it is all too common that one party will see a problem and the home or school denies any problems at all. This divergence of opinion may simply reflect settings where behaviors are or are not a problem. It may also give clues as to who is a stakeholder in helping this child and who is not.

Answering referral questions is not easy at the best of times. It is important to deliver assessment results that respond directly to the referral question so as to satisfy the parties as much as possible. Defining and answering the referral question in appropriate and realistic terms is important not only for the case at hand but also for future credibility and buy-in for treatment recommendations.

### FILE REVIEW

Children's referrals come with varying amounts of history. A file review looks for patterns in information, omissions of information, conflicting information, previous test results, clues to premorbid functioning (Vanderploeg, 1994), and clues as to when and how the child's problems began and took hold. Following is a list of items that are of particular interest to a school neuropsychologist.

*Absences from School*   Lack of exposure to the school curriculum may be responsible for some low scores on achievement tests and social or adaptive tests. Many children with chronic illness or severe injuries from accidents may miss a great deal of the school year and therefore not evidence age-appropriate academic skills. This factor may not influence neuropsychological tests results per se, but it will affect how those results are interpreted. The interventions for children with lack of exposure to the curriculum are different from interventions for those who have neuropsychological deficits who do not miss school. Simply put, the school neuropsychologist seeks to find out why low achievement scores are present, and exposure to the curriculum is a very good place to start.

*History of Chronic Illness*   A large part of differential diagnosis for children with chronic illness is weighing the neuropsychological effects of the disorder, the effects of medications for the disorder (positive and negative), the existence of secondary or comorbid effects of the disorder (e.g., depression), expectations of family and teachers regarding stereotypes associated with the disorder, quality and duration of medical attention, and exposure to the curriculum. Even with a detailed file, this assessment is difficult at best. The interventions for each of these effects by themselves or together are different and therefore they need to be identified as specifically as possible. The clinician needs to mark questions about the disorder for future use during the history taking with the family.

*Evidence of Events That Could Have Induced Psychological Trauma*   The neuropsychological detective waits for diagnostic cues. Often, the file review will note an event with no mention of its severity or the reaction to the event. For example, the file may note that the child was in an automobile accident in which a family member died, but there will be no mention of any injuries sustained, psychological trauma incurred, or follow-up treatment. At other times, the file review will note multiple moves, major life changes, and other stressors known to evoke adjustment problems. Again, the clinician needs to make notes for further questioning about these events during history taking with the family.

*Evidence of Events That Could Be Reflective of Neurotoxin Exposure*   An unfortunate characteristic of neurotoxin exposure in children is that it is often unidentified, especially if the exposure did not cause an emergency room visit, as with an accidental overdose of medicine, for example. Therefore, the clinician needs to be alert for negative symptoms that happen suddenly, or if a sibling exhibits the same symptoms, or symptoms occur after a move to a new home. Notes in the file that suggest normal early development and then a change in behavior and skill levels should be investigated for many obvious reasons, including neurotoxin exposure.

*Prior Assessments*   The file review often provides previous assessment results. More often than not, the previous school assessments will deal with the psychoeducational aspects of special education eligibility rather than neuropsychological assessments. The former assessments are helpful indicators of how the child has functioned in the past, how the child responded to individual testing, and what recommendations were offered and implemented. The clinician should note if the prior referral question was the same as the present question and how previous school systems coped with the child's deficits and strengths.

## Developmental/Medical History Taken with Caregivers

It is imperative that the school neuropsychologist conduct a thorough history of the child with the primary caregivers. Standard psychological texts mention the importance of background data in the process of assessment (e.g., Sattler, 2001). However, the history-taking process in neuropsychological assessment is often much more diagnostic, prescriptive, and influenced by medical references. In addition, young children have smaller "repertoires of objectively measurable behaviors" (Hartlage & Williams, 1990, p. 47). Therefore, developmental indices that can be documented by other means are crucial for creating a comprehensive diagnostic picture. Berg, Franzen, and Wedding (1987) suggest:

> A careful history is the most powerful weapon in the arsenal of every clinician, whether generalist or specialist. Brain-behavior relations are extremely complex and involve many different moderator variables, such as age, level of premorbid functioning, and amount of education. Without knowledge of values for these moderator variables, it is virtually impossible to interpret even specialized, sophisticated test results. (p. 47)

This statement takes on more emphasis when working with children and adolescents because estimates of premorbid functioning often rely on subjective accounts from caregivers about dynamic developmental processes (Baron & Gioia, 1998), despite the availability and increased accuracy of empirical methods.

Teeter and Semrud-Clikeman (1997) have suggested that the history is important for several reasons: identifying risk factors during pregnancy and delivery that have been associated with neurodevelopmental disorders; uncovering previous head trauma or other health factors; determining the presence of similar or related disorders in other family members or hereditary linkages that might be helpful for understanding the etiology of a particular disorder; determining the nature and extent of the developmental correlates of the child's problem; and determining the presence of coexisting disorders that affect long-term outcomes.

During the history-taking session, it is possible to forge a relationship with the family that will maximize cooperation and provide them a stake in the assessment process. It is a good opportunity to show the family that the clinician cares about the child and that their input is important. It is an opportunity to form a trusting relationship so that information that ordinarily may remain hidden comes to light. The treatment process really begins with the initial contact with the family. There may be opportunities to correct misconceptions about the child's condition and even mismanagement of illnesses and other conditions that might be exacerbating the issues at hand.

It is important for the clinician to determine if there are any socioeconomic issues facing the family that have affected the child or may get in the way of appropriate treatment in the future. Families from lower socioeconomic groups may not have access to health care and may have difficulty prioritizing the needs of the child with the needs of the family. If there are socioeconomic obstacles to treatment, the clinician needs to include these variables in the treatment plans.

All in all, the history taking provides a wealth of information that puts the referral question in perspective and colors the choice of further assessment strategies. For the most part, the school neuropsychologist has to struggle with differential diagnosis and determine if the manifested problems are a result of neurodevelopmental issues or reflective of poor living conditions, poor schooling, or inadequate environmental modeling or support (Teeter & Semrud-Clikeman, 1997). In the end, the amount of effort put into gathering information in the file review and history taking is never wasted and may well prevent inaccurate diagnoses and the frustration of failed interventions.

There are many fine examples of background interviews and structured histories available on the market (e.g., Reynolds & Kamphaus, 1992, 2004; Swaiman, 1999). It is appropriate to use and adapt these instruments but also important to make sure that detailed questions that might illuminate disorders or conditions that may have a significant effect on brain-behavior functioning are included. For example, there should be adequate space on forms for descriptions about possible brain injury, chronic illness, repeated ear infections, and vision and hearing examination results, just to name a few. Table 8.3 shows some of the elements that neurologists use in history taking. Most of the time, clinicians use the form with which they are most comfortable. Some use established forms like those of Reynolds and Kamphaus (2004), and others feel more comfortable creating their own. Clinician-designed forms have the advantage of reflecting the information needed for special settings and populations.

Long before any objective neuropsychological tests enter the assessment process, the clinician investigates any data related to central nervous system (CNS) functioning. Most of the time, the history will be negative for telling CNS events. When the conversation proceeds from one developmental period to another, or from one story to another, the clinician has to be aware of when to probe and when to move on to other topics. All of this information claims the clinician's attention and becomes magnified or recedes depending on how it fits into the diagnostic picture. The history-taking session should not be viewed as a "netting operation with data to be subsequently sorted" (Swaiman, 1999, p. 10); it should be a system in which data are synthesized as they are collected and then used to change the direction, breadth, and depth of questions. Differential diagnosis hypotheses should be pretty well formed by the time the clinician starts to use the objective test portion of the assessment. The information from the referral question, file review, and developmental history creates hypotheses and questions that objective testing can help to answer.

Neurologists follow a similar history-taking sequence as they organize incoming information to help with differential diagnosis. Of course, neurologists work from the medical model, but it is not uncommon for neuropsychologists and neurologists to work together, and it is important to know how neurologists regard history taking. Swaiman (1999) explains:

> The chief complaint should trigger the process of differential diagnosis in the examiner's thinking, which begins as a listing of the disease conditions that could cause the chief complaint at the child's age. The following three specific questions should be answered, if possible, in the history of the present illness: (1) Is the process acute or insidious? (2) Is it focal or generalized? And (3) Is it progressive or static? The order in which disease findings develop and the precise time of onset of symptoms and signs may be critical factors in the process of accurate diagnosis. The presence of repeated episodes or associated phenomena should be determined. Detailed questions should be asked of the caregivers and child to elucidate the facts. (p. 1)

**Table 8.3**

Family history of illness
Family history of perception about illness
Family current health
    –Siblings
    –Extended family
Genetic illnesses in family
Prenatal
    –Medications taken by mother
    –Substances taken by mother (alcohol, tobacco, other)
    –Illnesses during pregnancy
    –Stressors during pregnancy
    –Prenatal care
Labor and delivery
    –Breech or unusual position
    –Forceps used
    –Delay in respiration or cry
    –Apgar score
    –Oxygen administered
    –Type of anesthesia employed for mother
Newborn period
    –Jaundice
    –Cyanosis
    –Infections
    –Seizures
    –Anemia
    –Medications administered
    –Home from hospital in _____ days
Development
    –Smiled
    –First words
    –Put words together (e.g., "bye-bye")
    –Complete sentences
    –Rolled over
    –Sat without support
    –Pulled to standing
    –Walked around furniture
    –Walked unassisted
Illnesses
    –Hospitalizations
    –Operations
    –Injuries
    –Accidental poisonings
    –History of being knocked out, unconscious
    –History of convulsions/seizures
    –History of ear infections
    –History of sleep disturbances
    –History of somatic complaints
Other
    –Eating habits
    –Sudden changes in development
    –Early traumatic events
    –Hearing screening results
    –Vision screening results

*Source:* Adapted from "Neurologic Examination of the Older Child," by K. E. Swaiman, 1999, in K. E. Swaiman and S. Ashwal (Eds.), *Pediatric Neurology* (pp. 676–691). St. Louis, MO: Mosby.

The neurologist wants to know if the chief complaint is acute or insidious because the way a condition manifests in time can help determine which systems are involved. For example, degenerative disease symptoms progress over weeks or months, whereas infectious diseases may reach highest levels within a day to several days. The neurologist also wants to know if the condition symptoms manifest in a focal, multifocal, or generalized indicators. This knowledge helps determine where a problem might be located in the brain. In addition, knowing if the condition is progressive or static is gained from the history taking and usually takes the form of finding out that the child can no longer perform some developmental milestones that were previously marked. Conditions that are static or that improve spontaneously are sometimes the result of traumatic or anoxic episodes, acute toxicity, or resolving infection (Hartlage & Williams, 1990; Swaiman, 1999).

The school neuropsychologist has to go outside of the familiar research disciplines to be aware of the breadth and depth of possible factors that can affect a child's neuropsychological functioning. It is not possible, in the context of this chapter, to describe each element of the history taking in detail. However, descriptions of certain areas of history taking may provide some insight into why we ask the questions and what we can do with the answers.

*Family History of Illness*   Finding a family history of a particular disorder or disease sets the diagnostic journey for the clinician. It is important to couch questions in terms that are easily understood by the family. At the same time, the clinician needs to be alert to language used by the family and help them define conditions. For example, symptoms may be described by the family in vague terms, such as "fainting spells" or "nervous breakdown"; these terms need to be clarified and documented (Swaiman, 1999). The clinician may also have to avoid using medical terms to help the family understand what types of illnesses are being investigated. In general, the most important fact is to determine if the child in question suffers from any problems that are shared with other family members and if the information suggests alternative neuropsychological interpretations (Hartlage & Williams, 1990).

*Family History of Perception about Illness*   Not all families have the same perceptions about illness. Cultural practices and beliefs vary, and the clinician needs to be aware of how the family perceives illness and the clinician. For example, some Native American tribes prefer to focus on positive aspects of life, and pathology needs to be reframed to the positive aspects of getting well or maintaining harmony (King & Fletcher-Janzen, 2000). Members of some cultures may have difficulty trusting or working with a clinician from another culture (Marlow, 2000; Sue & Sue, 1990). Cultural competence in the practice of neuropsychology is just as demanding (if not more) as in other areas of psychology (Wong, Strickland, Fletcher-Janzen, Ardila, & Reynolds, 2000). History taking is often a social process and an opportunity to bond with the family; therefore, cultural factors and awareness play an important part in rapport building.

*When History Is Positive for Problems with Attention*   Attention is not a pure brain function. It is really a group of processes dependent on many other brain functions, and it is very difficult to define (Light et al., 1996). Light et al. define attention as "a flexible state of cognitive alertness directed toward stimuli over time and in the face of competing stimuli associated with a task-appropriate response" (p. 273).

The diagnosis of attentional problems is established on the positive history for inattention, impulsivity, and hyperactivity (Barkley, 2003; Shaywitz, Fletcher, & Shaywitz, 1999). There are several interrelated components of attention: arousal, sustained attention/vigilance, selective/divided attention, and shifting/alternating attention (Barkley, 2003; Light et al., 1996). It might be possible when taking a history to help the family delineate different aspects of attention by asking questions about functional behaviors associated with attention. For example, instead of asking if the child exhibits sustained attention or vigilance, it might be more appropriate to ask, "Does he start his homework and then stay with it until it is finished?" or "Does she concentrate on her homework even if her favorite song comes on the radio?"

During history taking, it is important to note if the family has a realistic expectation of attentional capacity in the child. Many behaviors that are considered to be inattentive at one age may be perfectly normal for a young child (Shaywitz et al., 1999). Inattention is also highly comorbid with brain injury, neurotoxic effects, learning disabilities, and psychiatric disorders; therefore, the clinician needs to make sure that previous diagnoses of Attention-Deficit/Hyperactivity Disorder (ADHD) or a lay diagnosis of ADHD does not color the interview process by preconceived notions of what ADHD is or is not.

*When History Is Positive for Ear Infections/Hearing Problems*   There are many genetic, congenital, and acquired reasons for hearing loss in children, and the single most important variable related to education is age of onset (Rapin, 1999). The ramifications of language and cultural development differ greatly for children who experience hearing loss prelingually because they are not able to experience the usual course of language development.

One diagnostic area for the school neuropsychologist is the investigation of intermittent hearing loss in children who have experienced repeated otitus media. Otitus media is responsible for more reading problems than any other physical illness. For many years, the research literature has suggested that chronic conditions, regardless of onset, can also significantly interfere with language/speech acquisition (Cowley, 1996; Johnson, 1997; Rapin, 1999).

A detailed history should be taken for those children positive for repeated ear infections. The clinician should take note of the frequency, intensity, and duration of infections and the treatment history. In addition, the clinician should ask about concomitant behaviors that might signal hearing loss, for example, the child's not responding when his or her name is called, ignoring verbal/social cues, or having trouble with beginning phonological awareness skills.

Rapin (1999) suggests that "the mere suspicion of hearing loss in such children requires prompt, definitive assessment of hearing and middle ear function with physiologic testing, without wasting time on repeated and unreliable behavioral tests" (p. 87). This is good advice because there are so many varying degrees of hearing loss that have different consequences, and the technology to definitively evaluate hearing loss is readily available in most school districts.

Clinicians should note that some children are able to pass hearing screenings in the school because they may have sloping hearing losses; these are common and affect hearing of higher tones to a much greater degree than lower frequencies.

Activities and tests that measure lower frequencies will not catch the subtle high-frequency losses, and the child might appear quite normal. Screening may also miss fluctuating hearing loss resulting from chronic middle ear effusion that can last for weeks after an ear infection (Rapin, 1999).

*When History Is Positive for Vision Problems*   Vision disorders are the fourth most common disability among children in the United States. As many as 2% to 5% of preschool children are estimated to have impaired vision. Despite the prevalence of vision disorders, however, there is not a set of universally accepted standardized guidelines for vision screening in the public schools. In addition, vision screening conducted in the United States varies by state and geographic region. Although as many as 94% of children from birth to 17 years old in the United States have access to an ongoing source of health care, studies estimate that only 21% of all preschool children are screened for vision problems and only 14% receive a comprehensive vision exam (American Academy of Pediatrics, 2003).

Multiple studies suggest that children from ethnic minorities and low socioeconomic status have a much higher incidence of vision disorders (e.g., Johnson, Blair, & Zaba, 2003; Maples, 2001; Mozlin, 2001) and that the majority of children identified with vision screenings fail to obtain treatment with an eye care professional who can correct the vision problem (Zaba, Mozlin, & Reynolds, 2003). Indeed, visual factors are more robust predictors of scores on the Illinois Test of Basic Skills (ITBS) than factors of race or socioeconomics. Although race and socioeconomic status are significant factors in academic performance on the ITBS, visual skills appear to play a larger role (Maples, 2001).

Many school vision screenings are limited to visual acuity measures and are inadequate because they do not address visual efficiency problems such as near focus, near point convergence, tracking saccades and pursuits, and other diseases of the eye (Swaiman, 1999). These fine eye movements make up a large portion of the visual sensory motor components needed for reading. In terms of reading (and written language), research is rapidly expanding, and the study of eye movements has played a pivotal role (Radach & Kennedy, 2004), especially in European research circles (Rayner, 2004).

Experimental reading researchers view reading as a task that includes visual processing, linguistic processing, and oculomotor control. Some researchers are interested in studying eye movements such as saccades, where the eyes move in a sequence of very fast, relatively well-coordinated movements (Radach, 2004). Usually, the eyes land or fixate on different places depending on word length and orthographic cues in surrounding text (White & Liversedge, 2004). Other researchers are more interested in using eye movements to study the more cognitive aspects of comprehension (Radach, Inhoff, & Heller, 2004; Rayner & Juhasz, 2004). Whatever the area of study, there is consensus that text is read in a sequential, word-by-word manner; that the eyes are moved to attentional units; and that saccades are triggered, normally, by a cognitive event (Yang & McConkie, 2004).

Any child that is referred with reading problems should be evaluated regarding the oculomotor movements that he or she makes when reading (American Academy of Pediatrics, 2003). There are some behavioral indicators associated with visual efficiency problems; sample behaviors suggested by the Oregon Optometric Physician's Association Children's Vision Committee (2000) are depicted in Table 8.4. Children with near point convergence problems, for example,

**Table 8.4**
Sample Behavioral Indicators of Visual Efficiency Problems

General Visual Problem Sample Behaviors
Reduced reading comprehension
    –Holding materials very close to face
    –Rapidly tires when reading
    –Poor attention span
Tracking Problem Sample Behaviors
    –Moving head back and forth while reading
    –Rereading or skipping lines while reading
    –Losing place when copying from board
    –Must use a marker to keep place
Near-Point Convergence Problem Sample Behaviors
    –Complaining of double vision
    –Covering one eye during near work
Focusing Problem Sample Behaviors
    –Transient blur at near or distance
    –Headaches
    –Burning and/or itchy eyes

*Source: The Effects of Vision on Learning and School Performance*, by Oregon Optometric Physician's Association, 2000, Milwaukee, OR: Author.

have trouble getting both eyes to focus on the same point, especially in close-up activities. Behaviors that are common to this problem are covering one eye during visually taxing activities, complaining of double vision, complaining of headaches, and other behaviors that reflect severe eyestrain. On the other hand, children with tracking problems tend to lose their place when they are reading, skip lines, and have problems with reading comprehension because of the missed or mixed-up text.

School psychologists and neuropsychologists can obtain training from eye care professionals to perform basic screenings for visual efficiency disorders. The results should be carefully evaluated against behavioral indicators and reading test results. Currently, there are no data to suggest that visual efficiency disorders are revealed by visual processing or visual-motor subtests commonly found on ability batteries or any other standardized measures of visual processing. However, behavioral optometrists and pediatric ophthalmologists are well aware of visual efficiency problems and have accurate instruments that can define and remediate small oculomotor problems (American Academy of Pediatrics, 2003).

In summary, passing a general vision screening does not necessarily mean that a child does not have visual/oculomotor problems that are interfering in academic near work. The school neuropsychologist needs to tease out the behavioral and neurological indicators from the information given by the vision screening, teacher, and parents. Any question of ability to near focus, track saccades, or track pursuits, near point convergence, or eye disease warrants referral to an eye professional.

As with any other salient information in the school neuropsychological history taking, a small piece of accurate information can inform the differential diagnosis and change the whole course of the assessment and intervention. There is growing evidence that visual efficiency problems are currently going undetected, are not causes for referrals when they are detected, are not included in school vision screenings, are not mentioned in school psychology training programs, and can be major sources of reading problems in children. School neuropsychologists, therefore, need to seek training in the field of vision disorders to enhance their diagnostic abilities with children referred for academic problems.

*When History Is Positive for Febrile Seizures*    A febrile seizure is defined as "a seizure in association with a febrile illness in the absence of a CNS infection or acute electrolyte imbalance in children older than 1 month of age without prior afebrile seizures" (International League Against Epilepsy, 1993, p. 592). Physicians can make the diagnosis of a febrile seizure only if other causes have been ruled out. Because meningitis, encephalitis, serious electrolyte imbalance, and other acute neurologic illnesses may be involved, a detailed history of the presenting illness may help with differential diagnosis (Shinnar, 1999). On the whole, febrile seizures are benign; very few signal the beginning of epilepsy or other neurologic disorder.

Febrile seizures occur in the United States in 2% to 4% of the population, with the peak incidence at 18 months of age (American Academy of Pediatrics, 1996). The risk factors for recurrent febrile seizures are a family history of febrile seizures, being younger than 18 months, height of temperature, and duration of fever. Between 2% and 10% of children who have febrile seizures will go on to develop epilepsy. The risk factors for this relationship are neurodevelopmental abnormality, complex febrile seizure, family history of epilepsy, and duration of fever (Shinnar, 1999).

In general, if the developmental history of the child is positive for febrile seizures, it may be appropriate for the clinician to dig a little deeper into the details of the frequency, duration, and medical management of the seizures. The risk of febrile seizures developing into epilepsy or being indicative of neurologic disease is small, but neuropsychologists often deal with small brain factors that can have large behavioral effects.

*When History Is Positive for Afebrile Seizures or Epilepsy*    School neuropsychologists will rarely be involved in helping diagnose epilepsy. Involvement is usually for purposes of establishing a baseline or for evaluation of neurocognitive and neurobehavioral status (Hartlage & Williams, 1990). Epilepsy is diagnosed after a child has had two or more seizures that are not related to a concurrent illness such as brain injury, fever, or drug intoxications. Hauser and Hesdorffer (1990) estimate that 1% of children will have a seizure by age 14, and 0.4% to 0.8% will have epilepsy by age 11. The definition of epilepsy encompasses a large variety of disorders because the age of onset, etiology, severity, comorbid diagnoses, medication management, and prognosis vary widely (Camfield & Camfield, 1999). Issues associated with the negative cognitive, social, and emotional sequelae of antiepileptic medications are also added to the management of epilepsy, yielding a general call for neuropsychologists to be involved in cases of epilepsy right from the beginning of treatment (Dodrill & Warner 1996; Dreifuss, 1999; Hartlage & Williams, 1990).

Differential diagnosis of seizure disorders is difficult and in many cases cannot stand on the results of an EEG or imaging results alone (Camfield & Camfield, 1999). Reflexive seizures resulting from vasodepressor syncope or cyanotic breath holding are easily misinterpreted as epilepsy; disorders such as tic disorder, migraines, vertigo, night terrors, sleep walking, self-stimulatory behaviors, cardiac dysrhythmias, startle disease, and temper tantrums with amnesia for the rage event are commonly mistaken for seizure activity (Camfield & Camfield, 1999).

School neuropsychologists cannot diagnose epilepsy, but they can be of considerable help to physicians who are in the process of making a diagnosis. A detailed history of seizure-like behaviors and a thorough knowledge of the child's medical history with current observations can help with differential diagnosis. For those children who are referred with a known seizure disorder, the school neuropsychologist can help with the treatment goal of minimal medication side effects with little or no seizure activity. This goal is difficult to reach and is made much easier by the services of a professional who is trained to document brain-behavior activities.

*When History Is Positive for Sleep Disorders*   Sleep disorders in childhood are often age-dependent and related to the child's physical, emotional, and neurological development. The medical field acknowledges that sleep disorders require a multidisciplinary approach to diagnosis and treatment (Kohrman, 1999). An in-depth investigation is therefore supported by the school neuropsychologist, but children should be referred if pathological indicators are present.

Questions about sleep history should include information about bedtime, sleep onset, during nighttime sleep, morning awakening, daytime behavior/naps, and general concerns. This may help the clinician decide if the sleep problem fits into the differential diagnosis of dyssomnia, those disorders associated with initiating and/or maintaining sleep or producing excessive daytime sleepiness. The parasomnias are phenomena associated with arousal, partial arousal, and sleep state transition. The third group includes sleep problems associated with medical or psychiatric disorders (American Sleep Disorders Association, 1990).

The relationship between sleep interruption and deprivation and its negative effects on social, emotional, and academic functioning has long been established (Kohrman, 1999), and the examination of the sleep habits of any child or adolescent is well worth the time and effort.

*When History Is Positive for Headaches*   Serious neurological disorders are uncommon causes of headaches. Various conditions such as tumors, brain abscesses, hypertension, vasculitis, subdural hematoma, and hemorrhage do, however, create headaches (Rothner, 1999). Common headache types that are the primary disorder are migraine, tension, or cluster headaches and are classified using the temporal pattern of the headache plotted against its severity. There are five patterns that can be identified: acute, acute recurrent, chronic progressive, chronic nonprogressive, and mixed (Rothner, 1999).

During the history taking, the clinician should attempt to denote if the headaches are acute or chronic, static or progressive, or run in the family; this will help the clinician to get a general idea of the scope and severity of the headache episodes. Of course, the proper diagnosis of a significant history of headaches needs to be confirmed by a medical professional.

*When History Is Positive for Traumatic Brain Injury*   An in-depth discussion of pediatric brain injury is present elsewhere in this book and will not be reiterated here. The incidence of different types of pediatric brain injury is high, and all episodes of loss of consciousness, brain injury, concussions, contusions, lacerations, and hematomas concerning the brain should be investigated in detail by the school neuropsychologist.

Approximately 200,000 children are hospitalized each year in the United States with head trauma, and approximately 5,000 of those children die (Rosman, 1999). Almost 30,000 persons under the age of 19 suffer permanent disabilities from a brain injury; these include epilepsy, severe motor disturbances, cognitive impairment, learning difficulties, and behavioral and emotional problems (Rosman, 1999).

The incidence of mild brain injury is much harder to quantify but is considered to be extremely common (Ryan, Lamarche, Barth, & Boll, 1996). Repeated concussions, from playing sports, for example, cause cumulative neuropsychological and neuroanatomical damage, even when the incidents are months or years apart. Interestingly, the incidence of a football player sustaining a concussion is 4 to 6 times higher for the football player who has sustained a previous concussion than for players with no history of concussion (Taylor & Ashwal, 1999).

Linking neurological sequelae to sports injuries or other incidents common to active children and adolescents (falls, bicycle accidents) is difficult. Symptoms of mild brain injury or concussion vary widely and may include dizziness, headaches, irritability, memory problems, and impaired concentration lasting from days to months (Taylor & Ashwal, 1999; Teeter & Semrud-Clikeman, 1997). These types of symptoms may have serious behavioral consequences for social relationships and academic performance but are simply not recognized by many professionals in the public schools.

Any intimation that the child in question has sustained a concussion, mild brain injury, or moderate to severe brain injury should be investigated at length by the school neuropsychologist. The exact circumstances and date of the injury should be ascertained. The course of immediate and then ongoing treatment should be documented. In addition, determination of postinjury symptoms is essential.

There is always the question of nonaccidental brain injuries, especially in young children. Gilles (1999) suggests that those evaluating a child with suspected abuse should ask certain questions: What is the distribution of the injuries? Are there any pattern injuries (e.g., bruising)? What forces were needed to produce the injuries? Is the history congruent with the injuries? Is there an accidental mechanism that would explain the injuries? Has the child been reported to the authorities on previous occasions? If the school neuropsychologist suspects child abuse or neglect during the history taking, the questions pertaining to the nature of sustained brain injuries may become very sensitive, and he or she must proceed carefully and follow ethical guidelines.

*When History Is Positive for Hypoxic-Ischemic Injury of the Brain*   Children with a positive history for near drowning, electric shock, severe acute asthma, airway obstruction, aspiration, or cardiac arrest may have sequelae of oxygen deprivation. All incidents should be investigated. Incidents creating hypoxic-ischemic encephalopathy can be quite common. For example, submersion or near-drowning episodes are frequently reported for young children. In the United States, there are 4,000 deaths, 8,000 hospitalizations, and 31,000 emergency room visits a year for childhood immersion (Perkin & Ashwal, 1999). The brain damage resulting from hypoxic-ischemic episodes is represented by cell necrosis and programmed cell death, especially in the hippocampus and cortical layers III and V. Five minutes of oxygen deprivation will create cell death within 48 to 72 hours (Perkin & Ashwal, 1999). Neuropsychological deficits after oxygen deprivation of this nature vary widely and are related to the length of deprivation and type of treatment received during the emergency.

Special attention should be paid to learners with asthma, which is a condition that is on the increase. Hypoxic episodes for young children with asthma are not uncommon. They create loss of consciousness and cyanosis related to mild brain damage (Berg & Linton, 1997). Indeed, severe asthma attacks are the leading cause of pediatric hospitalizations and school absenteeism. The morbidity and mortality rates for asthma are climbing. Mortality is associated with lack of proper diagnosis of asthma severity and lack of adequate treatment due to limited funds for access (Perkin & Ashwal, 1999). Therefore, careful attention should be paid to the family's history of access to health care during the history taking. The clinician should also pay attention to how the disease has been medically treated and screen for side effects of medications, such as growth delay, cognitive deficits, nervousness, nausea, hyperactivity, drowsiness, and problems with visual and tactile motor tasks.

Diseases like asthma frequently have comorbid conditions of trauma (Panic Disorder, Posttraumatic Stress Disorder) associated with the hypoxic incidents and depression that can cloud a diagnostic picture (Taylor & Ashwal, 1999). In addition, from the school neuropsychological point of view, there is always the impact of lack of exposure to the curriculum (because of excessive medical absences), further compounding differential diagnosis.

*When History Is Positive for Neurologic Complications of Immunizations*   Most of the time, neurological disorders attributed to immunizations do not differ from those that are not attributed to immunizations. Therefore, establishing a causal link between immunization and subsequent adverse events is difficult. The link is further confounded by the fact that most immunizations are administered with several vaccines at once (Fenichel, 1999). Further complications arise as adverse events are usually specific to a vaccine and each version of the vaccine (Fenichel, 1999).

Any adverse events related to immunizations should be carefully examined and documented by the clinician. Determining who made the causal connection, what symptoms accompanied the adverse events, and what treatment was obtained is useful and may add not only to differential diagnostic information but also to information that can be given to referral sources.

*When History Is Positive for Poisoning/Neurotoxin Exposure*   Children are more likely at risk than adults for neurotoxic exposure to many substances (Hartman, 1995). Most reports of poisonings are for persons under 20 years of age and are accidental (Walsh & Garg, 1999). Human neurotoxic damage can occur directly, from toxic injury to the neuron, or indirectly, insofar as injury to other body systems (e.g., pulmonary, renal) produces secondary neuronal damage with consequent neuropsychological dysfunction (Tarter, Edwards, & Van Thiel as cited in Hartman, 1995).

There are many different sources of toxins. Industrial toxins range from localized sources such as industrial factory emissions near to a child's home to household items such as pesticides, solvents, and cleaning items. Biological agents can range from tobacco products to flowers, plants, and venom from snakes. Medications, of course, are a common source of neurotoxins affecting children (Walsh & Garg, 1999). Younger children may copy adults taking medications and ingest inappropriate substances, may ingest accidental overdoses from caregivers, may simply like the taste of some medications and drink or eat them without the parent's knowledge, or have access to medications that do not have child-protective locks. Teenagers are much more likely to ingest toxic substances in suicide attempts or through substance abuse. Common suicide methods include exhaust inhalation, overdose on medications, and ingesting substances together with alcohol (Walsh & Garg, 1999).

Emergency room diagnosis of toxic substance ingestion is difficult but often is made easier by a presenting set of symptoms clustering around specific types of poisonings. These clusters of symptoms are called "toxidromes" and aid differential diagnosis greatly (Walsh & Garg, 1999). Then again, chronic or intermittent poisoning, such as in pesticide applications in the home or ingestion of lead products, may take on individual and dose-related symptomatology that renders the symptoms more subclinical and chronic and medical attention more variable (Hartman, 1995).

Any history that is positive for toxin exposure presents a unique problem for the school neuropsychologist because it will require finding out exactly what the substance was, age at exposure, short-term reaction to exposure, long-term reaction to exposure, and establishment of level of monitoring required. This profile is highly individualized and substance-specific. The clinician may be required to research information about the toxin and consult with medical personnel for clarification.

The history surrounding a neurotoxic event (and other acquired brain injuries) also has to focus on premorbid functioning, which, in the case of children, is compounded by natural physical, cognitive, social, emotional, and academic development. Children are moving targets of assessment, and the school neuropsychologist has to weigh natural development, subclinical symptoms becoming visible, a child's growing into disabilities caused by toxic substances, and possible medical treatment effects.

Behavioral toxicology batteries for children have received comparatively little attention in the research literature (Hartman, 1995). General core batteries that cover all areas of neuropsychological functioning should be administered so that important areas of functioning are not unwittingly left out. The clinician should also keep in mind that nonverbal abilities tend to be differentially more affected by common neurotoxins, and therefore, the choice of neuropsychological tests (either from a fixed or flexible battery) should load heavily on nonverbal ability assessment (Hartman, 1995).

*Summary*   The developmental and medical history of the child is important for many reasons. The history can lead the clinician to areas of diagnostic curiosity, where a vein of investigation is opened up in the hope that it points the way to a competent diagnosis. The history can direct the entire case, from an established diagnosis to case management, prevention, and quality of life issues. The clinician should ask the right questions, know why he or she is asking the questions, and know what to do with the answers. This level of knowledge takes many years to obtain, but is an extremely productive endeavor that will inform the entire assessment over and over again.

## CURRENT MEDICAL MANAGEMENT REGIMEN

For those children with a history of ongoing or chronic illness, it is vital to include a detailed medical management history. At this point, the clinician will have to make a determination of whether the medical management is appropriate and if there are possible secondary issues that need to be investigated.

*Medication History*   Almost any medication has the potential to affect a child's neuropsychological functioning, including his or her performance on tests of cognitive skills (Yeates & Taylor, 1998). The clinician needs to be familiar with the negative side effects, adverse reactions, and drug interactions of any medication (prescribed or over-the-counter) that the child is currently taking or has taken in the past. Reference materials that evaluate research results other than from the drug company should be kept handy for this purpose (Green, 2001; Konopasek, 2004).

If the child is taking medications that may interfere with cognitive processes or physical performance, such as reaction time, then the clinician will need to determine if there is a possibility of the medications confounding test results. The clinician has options at this point to go ahead and conduct tests knowing that there are predictable effects from the medications, wait for a change in medications and hope for a window of opportunity in between prescriptions, or request a drug holiday and work with the attending physician. Remaining vigilant for opportunities to test children when they are off medication is important.

In cases where several team members note medication side effects detrimental to learning, the school neuropsychologist may need to speak with the family and/or physician to mark concerns and take problem-solving action (Teeter & Semrud-Clikeman, 1997). Medications such as anticonvulsants, antipsychotics, antioxiolytics, stimulants, steroids, and other potent medications do have side effects that can confound test results (Cepeda, 1997; Hartlage & Hartlage, 1997; Teeter & Semrud-Clikeman, 1997). The clinician needs to keep a careful record of behavioral responses in the classroom to different medications and needs to document and work around the impact of medications on test results.

Also of note, it is important to check with the caregivers as to the need for medication-level checks and routine checks for toxicity. Sometimes the correct dosage is prescribed, but backup checks for liver toxicity, for example, are not done on a regular basis. In addition, just because a medication is prescribed correctly, this does not mean that it is administered correctly. Therefore, the clinician needs to check that it is being administered correctly and that the family has the means to provide the medication.

*Consultation with Medical Personnel*   Over years of practice, school psychologists become familiar with local physicians who take care of students in the school. Depending on the practice philosophy of the physician, it is quite possible for the school psychologist to join in and help with the study of medication effects, medication dosage, and medical management of children with ongoing issues. School neuropsychologists, on the other hand, do not necessarily have a choice as to whether they have relationships with physicians treating the children in the school. Often, the school neuropsychologist will be working with medically complicated cases and issues with chronic illness and quality of life (Teeter & Semrud-Clikeman, 1997). This is very difficult to do without a partnership with the attending physician.

In some cases, it may be possible to administer double-blind trials of medications, whereby the school neuropsychologist manages behavioral documentation of different medications or dosage. Sometimes response to medication is the only way to determine a correct diagnosis, and the determination should be based on data that reflect as many objective facts as possible. The clinician can be of great assistance to the attending physician in these cases.

*Chronic Illness*   Good quality treatment of chronic illness by a school neuropsychologist can save lives and significantly improve quality of life. Fourteen people with asthma die every day in the United States (Asthma & Allergy Foundation of America [AAFA], 2004). Nearly all of the cases could be prevented with appropriate medical management.

The best way to manage asthma is through prevention of exposure to allergens. The learner with asthma has to have a supportive and knowledgeable family, expert physician care, and the support of school personnel. Asthma is the leading cause of child hospitalizations and school absences because management depends on the child's not engaging with allergic triggers and expert medical attention when negative effects take hold (AAFA, 2004). Asthmatic reactions to stress, posttraumatic triggers, and environmental allergens trigger inflammation, constriction, and the production of mucus in the lungs. These factors make it very difficult to breathe, and so the asthma attack comes full force and often results in hypoxia and emergency room visits (Berg & Linton, 1997).

The more episodes of hypoxia or cyanosis the child experiences, the more the likelihood of mild or subtle brain damage. The behavioral effects of multiple episodes of lack of oxygen show up on neuropsychological tests as deficits in memory, concentration, executive functions, visual-spatial ability, and problem solving (Berg & Linton, 1997). This, coupled with possible effects of prolonged use of steroid medications, posttraumatic stress from near-death experiences, and excessive absences from school, can significantly affect academic quality of life for the asthmatic child.

The school neuropsychologist can provide multiple services to help the child with asthma prevent negative outcomes:

- Especially for the child that has severe hypoxic episodes, the school neuropsychologist can administer a battery of tests that will establish a baseline of current cognitive and psychological functioning. These tests may also indicate areas of concern, depending on how long the child has had asthma.
- The clinician can determine if there are any posttraumatic/anxiety-related symptoms that may be inducing or helping induce attacks. If there are, then stress reduction/relaxation training therapy with the child and family may be appropriate.
- An evaluation of the quality of health care is important. Many families from low socioeconomic circumstances may not have regular health care and rely

more on emergency room medicine. The latter does not focus on prevention or maintenance. Therefore, the child receiving attention only during emergencies is receiving poor medical management that may make the condition worsen over time (Fletcher-Janzen, 2000).

- Allergic triggers should be identified and reduced or removed from the classroom, if possible. Teachers should be alerted to possible allergens and antecedent behaviors or conditions (e.g., physical education on hot days) that might trigger an attack.
- The clinician should be aware of age-appropriate management skills for asthma and help the child achieve maximum self-management skills.
- School personnel (teachers, nurse, staff, principals) should be aware of the special circumstances, have a medical management plan that is designed to reduce emergency room visits, and have homework contingencies for days when the child cannot come to school.
- The school neuropsychologist should follow the case and measure quality of life at appropriate intervals. In many circumstances, the school neuropsychologist is the only professional who understands the brain-behavior consequences of poor control of asthma and the long-term quality of life issues that face the child.

Other chronic illnesses such as diabetes and seizure disorders have similar patterns and require specialized knowledge on the part of the school neuropsychologist (Berg & Linton, 1997; Fletcher-Janzen, 2000). Other school personnel, such as school nurses, may assist children with chronic illness, but the school neuropsychologist has the specialized knowledge of the social, affective, psychological, and medical aspects that affect brain-behavior relationships and performance in the classroom.

OBSERVATIONS

It is very important that formal and informal observations of the learner are conducted in more than one setting (Yeates & Taylor, 1998). The classroom usually has a predictable schedule and set of expectations regarding structure. Although the child does spend most of his or her time in the classroom, it is also important to see how the child responds when the structure changes. The expectations on the playground, in the gym, and in the cafeteria are much less formal, staff-pupil ratios are larger, and the learner must orient his or her sociability, attention, impulse control, and judgment in more independent ways. These are rich settings for observations that inform the hypotheses about how brain processes translate into everyday behaviors.

In clinical settings, it is often the case that the child is seen only in one setting, and the clinician has to rely on anecdotal information from the family or information from behavior questionnaires (Hartlage & Williams, 1990). However, in schools, the clinician can follow the child and see how the child negotiates the environment as it shifts and readjusts as the day goes along. For example, a child with suspected Autism may do quite well with the schedule in the classroom but may be unable to make the environmental shift to the gym for physical education. The noises in the gym may echo, the ceilings are high, and physical education activities may seem random and frightening to this child. Observation of this problem with sensory exposure confirms some symptoms associated with the diagnosis. In addition, observing the child with suspected Autism in the gym will also allow the clinician to determine what adaptive and compensatory skills the child already possesses. Does the child run to the teacher and express being overwhelmed? Or does the child stand and cover his ears and scream? Good observation will uncover diagnostic information as well as compensatory strategies and possible interventions. Again, the school neuropsychologist has the luxury of observing the child in many different activities that vary in expectations and structure. This allows for naturalistic and functional information to flow into the assessment and interventions.

## QUANTITATIVE AND QUALITATIVE MEASURES OF SOCIAL/EMOTIONAL/ADAPTIVE FUNCTIONING

Observations and experiences of school personnel who have worked with the child over the long term contain invaluable information. These professionals have taken the child through different cognitive, academic, social, and emotional experiences and basically know the child very well. Anecdotal information allows the clinician to get a real-world understanding of how others perceive the child and clues about how and where interventions should be placed.

Peers are also an invaluable source of information about how the child manages everyday demands in the classroom. Direct observations of the child interacting with other children is possible but also are situation-specific. Sociograms are a helpful way to informally measure how the child is perceived by his or her peers. Sociograms are easy to administer and score, and they help determine the sociohistorical context of the child's condition.

In addition, having an ecological understanding of how the child has functioned for years in this setting will help inform the school neuropsychological assessment as to adaptive functioning, areas of functional strength and weakness, areas of interest, and the situations that elicit the best and worst of behaviors. Diagnosis must have a sharp and clear direct line to the intervention. However, diagnosis must be informed by a competent and careful analysis of what brought the problem about in the first place and if social issues are helping or hurting the situation. All of this information relates to treatment success.

Objective measures of social, emotional, and behavioral functioning are plentiful. Several well-designed batteries are available (e.g., Achenbach & McConaughy, 2004; Conners, 1997; Reynolds & Kamphaus, 1992). The results of both the qualitative and quantitative measures should be integrated because together the information creates a holistic picture of how the child is functioning in the target intervention setting.

## QUANTITATIVE AND QUALITATIVE MEASURES OF SCHOOL ACHIEVEMENT

The academic history of the child tells us how the child has been meeting the performance demands of everyday living in the classroom so far (Yeates & Taylor, 1998). In the past, teachers and parents have provided grades, work samples, and anecdotal information to help give us a picture of the child's actual everyday academic performance. This qualitative information provides a rich picture of the child's performance on a daily basis and of the context in which the interventions are going to take place.

In terms of quantitative data, the reauthorization of the Individuals with Disabilities Education Act has not been finalized at this writing, but it is most likely that school psychologists in the future will also have "response to intervention" data. The data that are presented will probably include a basic assessment of phonological and reading skills, levels of academic achievement, and progress over time. This information needs to be compared with standardized achievement measures given by the examiner.

The school neuropsychologist has the opportunity to examine group achievement scores and administer individual achievement tests as well. Comparing the child to same-age peers across the country provides an objective base for examination of academic skills, and comparing the norm-referenced scores to daily performance grades in the class helps the examiner determine differences between levels of skills and the production of academic work.

Problems with reading are exceedingly common in children referred for assessment, and so basic reading skill tests should be included in any set of achievement tests. Fluent reading, of course, is central to success in academics; the elements of fluent reading can be assessed with phonological awareness and rapid automatic naming tests.

Phonological awareness is described as the ability to understand and use the sound components of language. Phonological awareness is closely related to problems in speech perception, naming and vocabulary ability, and auditory short-term memory with sounds. When phonological awareness deficits are present, reading comprehension suffers because the cognitive processes that are required for comprehension are slowed and engaged primarily in decoding and word recognition (Stanovich, 1994). This leaves the child with a word-level focus on the elements of the text and few resources for fluid reading and comprehension. There is evidence to support interventions in phonemic awareness with young elementary school-age children not only from an academic outcome perspective but also from a neuropsychological growth perspective in that neural networks that support reading can be enhanced with the appropriate instruction (Lyon et al., 2003).

Rapid automatic naming (RAN) is defined as the automaticity with which a learner can retrieve the names of things (e.g., objects, colors, letters) from his or her lexical store. It has been found to be related to reading ability among early readers (Lyon et al., 2003). Naming facility and phonological awareness are the components of the "double-deficit hypothesis" that proposes that a deficit in either of these areas interferes with learning to read, and deficits in both produce an additive effect (Wolf, 1997, p. 47).

Phonological and RAN skills should be evaluated with other basic reading skills such as simple decoding, reading of nonsense words, measures of reading fluency, and reading comprehension. In addition, tests that measure auditory processing such as auditory discrimination, auditory perception, auditory memory, and visual processing skills all help to complete an in-depth picture of the skills and abilities needed for successful reading.

In summary, achievement information from multiple sources is an important part of the school neuropsychological assessment. For those children referred with reading problems, an analysis of phonological awareness, RAN, and other reading skills tests meld with neuropsychological and cognitive test results to build a picture about reading ability. Results of this comprehensive assessment of reading skills should directly prescribe interventions, especially for young readers.

### NEUROPSYCHOLOGICAL ASSESSMENT BATTERY

It is wise to begin a section on the objective measurement of brain-behavior relationships with a caveat from Berg et al. (1987):

> Because test scores are the most easily quantifiable components of test performance, they are the most often used variables in the evaluation of the validity of tests. But the classification of individuals as brain impaired simply on the basis of test scores is a simplistic and dangerous practice. The data from tests should always be integrated with information obtained through a clinical interview, information regarding the appearance of the person, and information regarding the qualitative aspects of performance. (p. 48)

With this advice in mind, the clinician needs to design a battery of objective tests that reflect the referral question, clinical hypotheses brought about by file review and history taking, other pertinent information, the practical resources of time, and the fatigue level of the child.

*Domains*    The neuropsychological domains covered by a school neuropsychological assessment should be comprehensive for all aspects of brain-behavior relationships (Batchelor, 1996; Haak & Livingston, 1997; Reitan & Wolfson, 1985). Rourke, Van Der Vlugt, and Rourke (2002) suggest:

> The gold standard in neuropsychological assessment with respect to content validity is clear and straightforward: Unless all relevant dimensions are measured, none should be. The probability of false positives, false negatives, and other grossly erroneous conclusions increases as a function of the narrowness and brevity of the assessment. . . . For example, arriving at conclusions about "memory" (on the basis of tests for various dimensions of "memory") without knowing (i.e., measuring) and taking into consideration concept-formation, problem-solving, word-finding, attentional capacities, and so on, is patently absurd. (p. 43)

The domains that are commonly accepted in the research literature center around problem solving, memory, attention, executive functions, language, visual-spatial processing, auditory processing, and sensorimotor functions (Haak & Livingston, 1997). The domains represented in a neuropsychological assessment vary from clinician to clinician and many times depend on the theoretical orientation of the examiner. Table 8.5 shows domains measured by a sample of researchers and practitioners in the field of child neuropsychology.

*Clinician Competencies*    The interpretation of neuropsychological data depends on the clinician's conceptual model of brain-behavior relationships and the desired outcome of the assessment. Cimino (1994) describes Lezak's conceptual model of four domains of knowledge essential for the clinician in neuropsychological assessment: (1) knowledge of functional neuroanatomy, (2) knowledge of neuropathological conditions and their sequelae, (3) knowledge of clinical psychology and psychopathology, and (4) knowledge of psychometric properties and

**Table 8.5**
Samples of Neuropsychological Domain Lists

Bigler, Nussbaum, & Foley (1997)
 –Motor (fine and gross)
 –Visual-spatial processing
 –Body awareness
 –Auditory verbal processing
 –Sequential processing
 –Memory
 –Cognitive development (knowledge, reasoning)
 –Attention
 –Language
 –Academic skills
 –Personality/behavioral
 –Psychosocial factors
D'Amato, Rothlisberg, & Leu Work (1999)
 –Sensory and perceptual
 –Motor functions
 –Intelligence/cognitive abilities
 –Memory/learning/processing
 –Communication/language skills
 –Personality/behavior/family
 –Environment fit
Fennell (1994)
 –Intelligence
 –Memory
 –Learning
 –Language
 –Motor
 –Visual-spatial functions
 –Frontal executive
 –Achievement
 –Social-emotional functioning
Korkman, Kirk, & Kemp (1998)
 –Attention/executive functions
 –Language
 –Sensorimotor functions
 –Visual-spatial processing
 –Memory and learning
Rourke, Van Der Vlugt, & Rourke (2002)
 –Sensation/perception
 –Motor/psychomotor skills
 –Language
 –Problem solving
 –Concept formation
 –Attention
 –Memory
 –Psychosocial
Sattler & D'Amato (2002)
 –Intellectual functioning
 –Educational achievement
 –Motor functioning

*(continued)*

**Table 8.5** *(Continued)*

---

Sattler & D'Amato (2002) *(continued)*
   –Auditory perceptual functioning
   –Tactile perceptual functioning
   –Visual-spatial perceptual functioning
   –Oral language ability
   –Memory processes and attentional processes
   –Behavior
Teeter & Semrud-Clikeman (1997)
   –Gross motor
   –Fine motor
   –Visual-perceptual
   –Sensorimotor
   –Verbal fluency
   –Expressive language
   –Receptive language
   –Memory
   –Abstraction/reasoning
   –Learning
   –Executive functions
   –Attention

---

principles. For the school neuropsychologist, these four domains need to be expanded to include knowledge of development processes (Fennell, 1994, 2002), knowledge of brain-behavior relationships with dynamic learning activities, and knowledge of evidence-based interventions associated with academic deficits.

*Systems for Interpretation*   A common system for interpretation of neuropsychological test results was developed in the 1960s and 1970s and remains popular today (Sattler & D'Amato, 2002; Teeter & Semrud-Clikeman, 1997). It is a medically oriented system with four levels of inference for neuropsychological assessment: pathognomonic signs, patterns of performance, level of performance, and right-left differences.

The pathognomonic signs approach was developed because certain responses to items on some neuropsychological tests occurred exclusively in brain-damaged individuals (Teeter & Semrud-Clikeman, 1997). Pathognomonic signs are indicators of specific deficits that are commonly not seen in normal individuals (Nussbaum & Bigler, 1997) and are skills that were present prior to an injury or insult. Determining premorbid skills can be problematic in children because of the interaction among the course of development, the level of skill acquisition (emerging, mastery, generalization), and the wide variety of skill acquisition in normal children. Used alone, the pathognomonic approach tends to generate false negatives because the absence of signs is not necessarily an indication of health (Sattler & D'Amato, 2002).

The patterns of performance approach interprets strengths and weaknesses from disparate subtest results. The neuropsychologist looks at performance on different tests and within tests and obtains information of patterns of processing on which to build inferences about specific and global brain functioning (Teeter & Semrud-Clikeman, 1997). This approach has been used extensively in the subgrouping of learning disabilities but is very difficult to perform with young children with severe deficits (Nussbaum & Bigler, 1997; Rourke, Van Der Vlugt, & Rourke, 2002).

Pattern analysis with intelligence tests has been described as unreliable (Reynolds & Kamphaus, 2003), yet it is necessary, when scores are significantly different within a scale, to examine possible reasons for differences and to test out hypotheses with other information (Kaufman & Kaufman, 2001). However, the drawbacks to pattern analysis are not so evident on tests that are poor measures of intelligence. Tests that measure simple perceptual skills, for example, are low in $g$ and tend to represent the perceptual skill with less confounding from problem solving and reasoning (Reynolds & Kamphaus, 2003). Hence, analysis of strengths and weaknesses from these types of tests, many of which are neuropsychological in nature, do not tend to run into reliability and base rate problems (Reynolds & Kamphaus, 2003).

The levels of performance approach makes comparisons between the child's scores and those of a normative group. Scores that are significantly below the mean for the child's age group on neuropsychological measures may be considered to identify neuropsychological deficits (Nussbaum & Bigler, 1997). This approach also uses cutoff points based on the normative sample (Sattler & D'Amato, 2002). As with other approaches, there are drawbacks to using this approach in isolation. First, the performances of normal children on neuropsychological measures vary greatly and therefore render the interpretation of significant scores difficult (Nussbaum & Bigler, 1997). Second, deficient scores can be due to other factors during testing, such as motivation or attention. This approach is associated with high false positive rates (Sattler & D'Amato, 2002).

The right-left differences approach attempts to determine lateralization of lower brain functions for motor and sensory-perceptual tasks (Nussbaum & Bigler, 1997). This approach can differentiate brain-damaged from normal children, but unilateral injury may not always produce lateralized motor or sensory difficulties (Sattler & D'Amato, 2002); therefore, it is not recommended in isolation or as a substitute for a full neuropsychological assessment (Teeter & Semrud-Clikeman, 1997). The examination of right-left differences, however, is particularly helpful with younger children, especially with tests of reaction time and measurement time (Hartlage & Williams, 1990).

All four of the inferential approaches have advantages and disadvantages, and combining the approaches appears to be the best way to minimize the overall disadvantages (Nussbaum & Bigler, 1997; Sattler & D'Amato, 2002). Clinicians have to make decisions about how to use the various tests in the school neuropsychological battery based on appropriateness, reliability, validity, specificity, interpretability, and practicality. In the end, the battery of tests has to be chosen for its ability to support the resolution of the referral question.

For school neuropsychologists, the addition of multiple and comprehensive achievement tests to the battery is essential for relating assessment results to the classroom. They provide much of the description of how the brain responds to academic tasks and therefore much of the evidence on which to base interventions. The interpretation of the brain processes and functions from neuropsychological tests have to be extended one step further and related to academic performance in the classroom. After all, academic performance in the assessment is usually reflective of optimal performance conditions, whereas academics in the classroom may well introduce environmental variables that detract from performance in unintended ways (Crosson, 1994). Understanding the relationship between brain and academic behavior is a difficult and long process that often requires the clinician's going back to the drawing board as hypotheses about brain-behavior functioning may pan out or diffuse in the classroom. The task is to revisit school neuropsychological test results as many times as necessary to answer the referral question, prescribe interventions, and follow up. This is the nature of the relationship between the school neuropsychologist and the educational objectives of the children they serve.

### QUALITATIVE INFORMATION

Batchelor (1996) suggests that there is an "illusive dichotomy that has historically evolved between advocates of quantitative and qualitative approaches to neuropsychological assessment" p. 12. Hartman (1995) states, "Variables including the patient's approach to testing, motivation, medical history and other ipsative information are as important in their own ways as the statistical properties of the exam" (p. 10). The dichotomy between the two kinds of information is probably on a continuum, as Batchelor suggests, rather than being discrete areas of practice. In the end, scores on objective tests and neuroimaging are useless unless there is someone there to interpret the scores in light of subjective data such as history, present living conditions, test behaviors, and medication changes.

Young children present their own test of the clinician's ability to switch from quantitative to qualitative evaluation of assessment results on a moment's notice. Many times, the very young child will simply refuse to perform an item, completely lose attention in the testing process, or indicate fatigue (Hartlage & Williams, 1990). At this point, the clinician has to determine if there is enough of a partially administered test to interpret, readminister at a later stage, or simply abandon! Therefore, the clinician has to make decisions about the reliability and validity of each piece of information that is pertinent to the assessment regardless of its level of intended objectivity.

Another way of looking at qualitative information gained during the assessment is the examination of test-taking behavior. There have been several attempts to codify test-taking behaviors (Aylward & MacGruder, 1996; Sattler, 1988, 2001; Watson, 1951). All of these instruments contained 30 or fewer items, usually measured on a Likert scale to be filled out immediately after administering a test or battery of tests. Most of the items centered on motivation, attitudes toward testing, attitudes toward examiners, and the like. However, a specific theoretical model for constructs included in these instruments was lacking. Glutting and Oakland (1993) developed the first standardized instrument that measured test session behaviors, the Guide to Assessment of Test Session Behavior (GATSB). The GATSB was conormed with the Wechsler Intelligence Scale for Children III (Wechsler, 1991). Glutting and Oakland included types of behavior "that reflect a child's temperament and personality, including attention, interest, cooperation, avoidance, motivation, effort, persistence, and the ability to shift perceptual sets or to shift task focus and remain flexible" (p. 25).

Recently, McConaughy and Achenbach (2004) have published the Test Observation Form (TOF). The TOF "is a standardized form for rating observations of behavior, affect, and test-taking style during testing sessions for children aged 2 to 18" (p. 1). The TOF was standardized on the same norm sample as the Stanford-Binet Intelligence Scales, fifth edition (Roid, 2003), and yields scores on five syndrome scales, internalizing and externalizing scales, and a *DSM*-oriented Attention-Deficit/Hyperactivity Scale. The TOF can also be a part of the Achenbach System of Empirically Based Assessment (Achenbach & McConaughy, 2004) system that measures parent and teacher observations of child behavior. The 5 syndrome scales of the TOF are factor analytically based and are labeled Withdrawn/Depressed, Language/Thought Problems, Anxious, Oppositional, and Attention Problems. The authors state that the TOF can be used with any individual cognitive ability test or achievement test. It will be interesting to see the role of the TOF unfold in the years to come and also see if it has utility in the school neuropsychological assessment.

In summary, there are many different sources of qualitative information in the assessment process, even if the process approach is not used. The reader is referred to the chapter in this book by Semrud-Clikeman, Wilkinson, and McMahon entitled "Qualitative Approaches to Neuropsychological Assessment" for more information on this subject.

REPORT

The school neuropsychological report must conform to report-writing guidelines appropriate for the setting. Different states and school districts have specific guidelines to which the school neuropsychologist has to adhere. In addition, the use of neuropsychological jargon may be out of place on an individual education plan, not only in terms of understanding by laypersons, but also as a potential indicator of liability for the school district. Therefore, report-writing style and content need to be approved by district administration before being adopted.

Reynolds and Mayfield (1999) cite several important points regarding report writing. First, the reports should "go beyond a simple descriptive presentation of test data and findings"(p. 33) in that the clinician should integrate information across sources and history and the information should be interpreted for the reader. Second, reports should be provided in a professional manner, with correct grammar and formal language structure. Third, Reynolds and Mayfield stress the importance of using language that is easily understood. Fourth, the report should be written about the child and not about the tests used in the assessment. Too often, reports contain test data with little or no integration. The fifth point made by Reynolds and Mayfield suggests that clinicians should draw diagnostic conclusions or summaries for the reader because diagnoses are "treatment relevant and should be noted" (p. 34). The sixth and final point is that the report should describe treatment implications of the neuropsychological findings. Chapter 9 of this text, "Clinical Interviewing and Report Writing in School Neuropsychology," written by Pompa, Tuesday-Heathfield, and Clark, addresses the more in-depth parameters of report writing in the public school setting.

The ecological validity of a school neuropsychological assessment is the degree to which it provides information about the child that will be useful in his or her classroom (Bigler & Clement, 1997). The clinician has to establish a direct line from the referral question to the choice of assessment, creation of a diagnosis/

hypotheses, and execution of the intervention/evaluation. All the points on the line have to relate to one another and sometimes coexist (as opposed to being present in a discrete and linear, step-by-step, fashion). No one point in the assessment process is more important than another because the end result must be synergistic and ecologically balanced.

Many suggest that interventions are best created with the team or major members of the team such as the teacher or parents. Due to the fact that these team members will most likely be the individuals who will carry out the interventions, this seems reasonable. Of course, the school neuropsychologist will need to quietly guide the intervention design and execution with neuropsychological principles in mind. Sometimes this will demand that the clinician give a detailed explanation of the diagnosis and how it relates to the intervention, and sometimes it may just require the dictation of good ideas. At the end of the day, the person implementing the intervention has to have a stake in its success. How buy-in is achieved in consultative relationships differs from one situation to another, and the complexity of a neuropsychological case does not necessarily make it any easier. Fortunately, school psychologists have extensive training and experience in consultation and are not new to the intricacies of consultative relationships.

There are several chapters in this book that focus on neuropsychological interventions for individuals, classrooms, and schools linked to such areas as reading, mathematics, and written expression. The reader is advised to study the different kinds of evidence-based interventions presented in these chapters in depth. Probably the most difficult task during the school neuropsychological assessment is matching the processing strengths and weaknesses of the child to interventions that are known to be valid. The ecological validity of school neuropsychological assessment is still relatively new in the research literature, as discussed in the final chapter of this volume. It is hoped that the uncovering of evidence-based interventions for children with neuropsychological deficits will continue rapidly in the years to come.

## CONCLUSION

School neuropsychology is a fledgling area of expertise for many school psychologists. Economic changes in health care have created a situation in which school psychologists have to be aware and competent caregivers to many children who, years ago, would have been treated in inpatient settings for extended periods of time before being discharged back to the public schools. In addition, there has been a welcome trend in the field of neuropsychology to examine the ecological validity of neuropsychological assessments. This, coupled with scientific exploration and the understanding of child neuropsychology, has created readily available information and training to school psychologists.

School neuropsychology has some specific characteristics not found in other settings. School neuropsychologists focus on ecological validity of treatment in the classroom; often, they are very familiar with the child before the assessment; they have a wealth of contact with the child, caregivers, and interventionists; they have the time to see through the recommendations that are proposed in the assessment report; they have the opportunity to create preventive care plans; and they are often the only professional in the system who fully understands the child's brain-behavior functioning. Now is the time when it is possible to have a fully credentialed professional with neuropsychological expertise administer child neuropsychological services that range from prevention to follow-up and redesign of interventions. What an opportunity! Let us hope that the field of school psychology, at all levels, supports and leads this venture.

## REFERENCES

Achenbach, T. M., & McConaughy, S. H. (2004). *School-based practitioners' guide for the Achenbach system of empirically based assessment (ASEBA).* (4th ed.). Burlington, VT: University of Vermont, Research Center for Children, Youth, and Families.

Alyward, G. P., & MacGruder, R. W. (1986). *Test behavior checklist.* Brandon, VT: Clinical Psychology.

American Academy of Pediatrics. (1996). Practice parameter: The neurodiagnostic evaluation of the child with a first simple febrile seizure. [Provisional Committee on Quality Improvement, Subcommittee on Febrile Seizures] *Pediatrics, 97,* 769.

American Academy of Pediatrics. (2003). Policy statement: Eye examination in infants, children, and young adults by pediatricians. *Pediatrics, 111,* 902–907.

American Sleep Disorders Association. (1990). *The international classification of sleep disorders.* Lawrence, KS: Allen Press.

Asthma & Allergy Foundation of America. (2004). *A closer look at asthma.* Retrieved May 24, 2004, from http://www.aafa.org.

Barkley, R. A. (2003). Attention-deficit/hyperactivity disorder. In E. J. Mash & R. A. Barkley (Eds.), *Child psychopathology* (pp. 75–145). New York: Guilford Press.

Baron, I. S., & Gioia, G. A. (1998). Neuropsychology of infants and young children. In G. Goldstein, P. D. Nussbaum, & S. R. Beers (Eds.), *Neuropsychology* (pp. 9–29). New York: Plenum Press.

Batchelor, E. S. (1996). Neuropsychological assessment of children. In E. S. Batchelor & R. S. Dean (Eds.), *Pediatric neuropsychology* (pp. 9–26). Needham Heights, MS: Allyn & Bacon.

Batchelor, E. S., & Dean, R. S. (1996). *Pediatric neuropsychology.* Needham Heights, MS: Allyn & Bacon.

Bauer, R. M. (1994). The flexible battery approach to neuropsychological assessment. In R. D. Vanderploeg (Ed.), *Clinician's guide to neuropsychological assessment* (pp. 259–290). Hillsdale, NJ: Erlbaum.

Berg, R., Franzen, M., & Wedding, D. (1987). *Screening for brain impairment: A manual for mental health practice.* New York: Springer.

Berg, R. A., & Linton, J. C. (1997). Neuropsychological sequelae of chronic medical disorders in children and youth. In C. R. Reynolds & E. Fletcher-Janzen (Eds.), *The handbook of clinical child neuropsychology* (2nd ed., pp. 663–687). New York: Kluwer/Plenum Press.

Bigler, E. D., & Clement, P. F. (1997). *Diagnostic clinical neuropsychology* (3rd ed.). Austin, TX: University of Texas Press.

Bigler, E. D., Nussbaum, N., & Foley, H. (1997). Child neuropsychology in the private medical practice. In C. R. Reynolds & E. Fletcher-Janzen (Eds.), *The handbook of clinical child neuropsychology* (2nd ed., pp. 725–742). New York: Kluwer/Plenum Press.

Camfield, P. R., & Camfield, C. S. (1999). Pediatric epilepsy: An overview. In K. E. Swaiman & S. Ashwal (Eds.), *Pediatric neurology* (pp. 629–646). St. Louis, MO: Mosby.

Cepeda, M. L. (1997). Nonstimulant psychotropic medication: Desired effects and cognitive/behavioral adverse effects. In C. R. Reynolds & E. Fletcher-Janzen (Eds.), *The handbook of clinical child neuropsychology* (2nd ed., pp. 573–586). New York: Kluwer/Plenum Press.

Christensen, A. (2000). Neuropscholgical postacute rehabilitation. In A. Christensen & B. Uzzell (Eds.), *International handbook of neuropsychological rehabilitation* (pp. 151–166). New York: Kluwer/Plenum Press.

Cimino, C. (1994). Principles of neuropsychological interpretation. In R. D. Vanderploeg (Ed.), *Clinician's guide to neuropsychological assessment* (pp. 69–112). Hillsdale, NJ: Erlbaum.

Conners, C. K. (1997). *Conners' Rating Scales-Revised.* North Tonawanda, NY: Multi-Health Systems.

Cowley, J. (1996). Longitudinal studies-are they worth it? *Australian Research in Early Childhood Education, 1,* 225–226.

Crosson, B. (1994). Application of neuropsychological assessment results. In R. D. Vanderploeg (Ed.), *Clinician's guide to neuropsychological assessment* (pp. 113–163). Hillsdale, NJ: Erlbaum.

D'Amato, R. C., Rothlisberg, B. A., & Rhodes, R. L. (1997). Utilizing a neuropsychological paradigm for understanding common educational and psychological tests. In C. R. Reynolds & E. Fletcher-Janzen (Eds.), *The handbook of clinical child neuropsychology* (2nd ed., pp. 270–295). New York: Kluwer/Plenum Press.

D'Amato, R. C., Rothlisberg, B. A., & Leu Work, P. H. (1999). Neuropsychological assessment for intervention. In T. B. Gutkin & C. R. Reynolds (Eds.), *Handbook of school psychology* (3rd ed., pp. 452–475). New York: Wiley.

Dodrill, C. B., & Warner, M. H. (1996). Seizure disorders. In E. S. Batchelor & R. S. Dean (Eds.), *Pediatric neuropsychology* (pp. 303–324). Needham Heights, MA: Allyn & Bacon.

Dreifuss, F. E. (1999). Partial seizures (focal and multifocal). In K. E. Swaiman & S. Ashwal (Eds.), *Pediatric neurology* (pp. 646–666). St. Louis, MO: Mosby.

Fenichel, G. M. (1999). Neurologic complications of immunization. In K. E. Swaiman & S. Ashwal (Eds.), *Pediatric neurology* (pp. 1470–1473). St. Louis, MO: Mosby.

Fennell, E. B. (1994). Issues in child neuropsychological assessment. In R. D. Vanderploeg (Ed.), *Clinician's guide to neuropsychological assessment* (pp. 113–163). Hillsdale, NJ: Erlbaum.

Fennell, E. B. (2002). Ethical issues in pediatric neuropsychology. In S. S. Bush & M. L. Drexler (Eds.), *Ethical issues in clinical neuropsychology* (pp. 75–86). Lisse, The Netherlands: Swets & Zeitlinger.

Fennell, E. B., & Bauer, R. M. (1997). Models of inference in evaluating brain-behavior relationships in children. In C. R. Reynolds & E. Fletcher-Janzen (Eds.), *Handbook of clinical child neuropsychology* (pp. 204–218). New York: Kluwer/Plenum Press.

Fletcher-Janzen, E. (2000). Multicultural perspectives on the neuropsychological assessment and treatment of epilepsy. In E. Fletcher-Janzen, T. L. Strickland, & C. R. Reynolds (Eds.), *Handbook of cross-cultural neuropsychology* (pp. 185–203). New York: Kluwer/Plenum Press.

Gilles, E. E. (1999). Nonaccidental head injury. In K. E. Swaiman & S. Ashwal (Eds.), *Pediatric neurology* (pp. 898–914). St. Louis, MO: Mosby.

Glutting, J. J., & Oakland, T. (1993). *The guide to the assessment of test session behavior.* San Antonio, TX: Psychological Corporation.

Golden, C. J. (1986). *The Luria-Nebraska Neuropsychological Battery: Children's Revision.* Los Angeles: Western Psychological Services.

Green, W. H. (2001). *Child and adolescent clinical psychopharmacology* (3rd ed.). Philadelphia: Lippincot Williams and Wilkins.

Haak, R. A., & Livingston, R. B. (1997). Treating traumatic brain injury in the school. In C. R. Reynolds & E. Fletcher-Janzen (Eds.), *Handbook of clinical child neuropsychology* (pp. 482–516). New York: Kluwer/Plenum Press.

Hale, J. B., & Fiorello, C. A. (2004). *School neuropsychology.* New York: Guilford Press.

Hartlage, P. L., & Hartlage, L. C. (1997). The neuropsychology of epilepsy: Overview and psychosocial aspects. In C. R. Reynolds & E. Fletcher-Janzen (Eds.), *Handbook of clinical child neuropsychology* (pp. 506–516). New York: Kluwer/Plenum Press.

Hartlage, L. C., & Williams, B. L. (1990). Neuropsychological assessment in the childhood and adolescent years. In A. MacNeill Horton (Ed.), *Neuropsychology across the life-span: Assessment and treatment* (pp. 44–63). New York: Springer.

Hartman, D. E. (1995). *Neuropsychological toxicology* (2nd ed.). New York: Plenum Press.

Hauser, W. A., & Hersdorffer, D. C. (1990). *Epilepsy: Frequency, causes and consequences.* New York: Demos.

International League Against Epilepsy. (1993). Guidelines for epidemiologic studies on epilepsy. *Epilepsia, 34,* 592.

Johnson, D. L. (1997, April). *The effects of early otitis media with effusion on child cognitive and language development at ages three and five.* Paper presented at the Biennial Meeting of the Society for Research in Child Development, Washington, DC.

Johnson, R. A., Blair, R. J., & Zaba, J. (1997). The visual screening of Title I reading students. *Journal of Behavioral Optometry, 20,* 14.

Kamphaus, R. W. (2001). *Clinical assessment of child and adolescent intelligence.* Needham Heights, MA: Allyn & Bacon.

Kaplan, E. (1998). A process approach to neuropsychological assessment. In T. Boll & B. K. Bryant (Eds.), *Clinical neuropsychology and brain function: Research, measurement, and practice* (pp. 125–167). Washington, DC: American Psychological Association.

Kaufman, A. S., & Kaufman, N. L. (Eds.). (2001). *Specific learning disabilities and difficulties in children and adolescents* (pp. 283–306). New York: Cambridge University Press.

Kaufman, A. S., & Kaufman, N. L. (2004). *The Kaufman Assessment Battery for Children* (2nd ed.). Circle Pines, MN: AGS.

King, J., & Fletcher-Janzen, E. (2000). Neuropsychological assessment and intervention with Native Americans. In E. Fletcher-Janzen, T. L. Strickland, & C. R. Reynolds (Eds.), *Handbook of cross-cultural neuropsychology* (pp. 105–122). New York: Kluwer/Plenum Press.

Kohrman, M. H. (1999). Pediatric sleep disorders. In K. E. Swaiman & S. Ashwal (Eds.), *Pediatric neurology* (pp. 773–785). St. Louis, MO: Mosby.

Kolb, B., & Whishaw, I. Q. (1990). *Fundamentals of human neuropsychology* (3rd ed.). New York: Freeman.

Konopasek, D. E. (2004). *Medication fact sheets.* Longmont, CO: Sopris-West.

Korkman, M., Kirk, U., & Kemp, S. (1998). *NEPSY: A developmental neuropsychological assessment manual.* San Antonio, TX: Psychological Corporation.

Lezak, M. D. (1995). *Neuropsychological assessment* (3rd ed.). New York: Oxford University Press.

Light, R., Satz, P., Asarnow, R. F., Lewis, R., Ribbler, A., & Neumann, E. (1996). Disorders of attention. In E. S. Batchelor & R. S. Dean (Eds.), *Pediatric neuropsychology* (pp. 269–302). Needham Heights, MA: Allyn & Bacon.

Lyon, G., Fletcher, J., & Barnes, T. (2003). Learning disabilities. In E. J. Mash & R. A. Barkley (Eds.), *Child psychopathology* (pp. 390–345). New York: Guilford Press.

Maples, W. C. (2001). A comparison of visual abilities, race and socio-economic factors as predictors of academic achievement. *Journal of Behavioral Optometry, 12,* 60–65.

Marlowe, W. B. (2000). Multicultural perspectives on the neuropsychological assessment of children and adolescents. In E. Fletcher-Janzen, T. L. Strickland, & C. R. Reynolds. *Handbook of cross-cultural neuropsychology* (pp. 145–168). New York: Kluwer/Plenum Press.

McCaffrey, R. J., Palav, A. A., O'Bryant, S. E., & Labarge, A. S. (2003). *Practitioner's guide to symptom base rates in clinical neuropsychology.* New York: Kluwer/Plenum Press.

McConallghy, S., & Achenbach, T. (2004). *Manual for the Test Observation Checklist Form for Ages 2–18.* Burlington, VT: University of Vermont.

Mozlin R. (2001). Poverty neurodevelopment and vision a demonstration project with an adolescent population. *Journal of Behavioral Optometry, 12,* 71–74.

National Dissemination Center for Children with Disabilities. (2004). *The National Dissemination Center for Children with Disabilities: The latest scoop!* Retrieved May 25, 2004, at http://www.nichcy.org/reauth.

Nussbaum, N. L., & Bigler, E. D. (1997). Halstead-Reitan Neuropsychological Test Batteries for Children. In C. R. Reynolds & E. Fletcher-Janzen (Eds.), *Handbook of clinical child neuropsychology* (pp. 219–326). New York: Kluwer/Plenum Press.

Oregon Optometric Physician's Association. (2000). *The effects of vision on learning and school performance.* Milwaukee, OR: Author.

Perkin, R. M., & Ashwall, S. (1999). Hypoxic-ischemic encephalopathy in infants and older children. In K. E. Swaiman & S. Ashwal (Eds.), *Pediatric neurology* (pp. 915–944). St. Louis, MO: Mosby.

Radach, R., Inhoff, A., & Heller, D. (2004). Orthographic regularity gradually modulates saccade amplitudes in reading. *European Journal of Cognitive Psychology, 16,* 27–51.

Radach, R., & Kennedy, A. (2004). Theoretical perspectives on eye movements in reading: Past controversies, current issues, and an agenda for future research. *European Journal of Cognitive Psychology, 16,* 3–26.

Rapin, I. (1999). Hearing impairment. In K. E. Swaiman & S. Ashwal (Eds.), *Pediatric neurology* (pp. 77–94). St. Louis, MO: Mosby.

Rayner, K., & Juhasz, B. J. (2004). Eye movements in reading: Old questions and new directions. *European Journal of Cognitive Psychology, 16,* 340–352.

Reitan, R. M., & Wolfson, D. (1985). *The Halstead-Reitan Neuropsychological Battery: Theory and clinical interpretation.* Tucson, AZ: Neuropsychological Press.

Reynolds, C. R., & Fletcher-Janzen, E. (1997). *The handbook of clinical child neuropsychology* (2nd ed.). New York: Kluwer/Plenum Press.

Reynolds, C. R., & Kamphaus, R. W. (1992). *The Behavior Assessment System for Children.* Circle Pines, MN: AGS.

Reynolds, C. R., & Kamphaus, R. W. (2003). *Reynolds Intellectual Assessment Scales.* Lutz, FL: Psychological Assessment Resources, Inc.

Reynolds, C. R., & Kamphaus, R. W. (2004). *The Behavior Assessment System for Children* (2nd ed.). Circle Pines, MN: AGS.

Reynolds, C. R., & Mayfield, J. W. (1999). Neuropsychological assessment in genetically linked neurodevelopmental disorders. In S. Goldstein & C. R. Reynolds (Eds.), *Handbook of neurodevelopmental and genetic disorders in children* (pp. 9–38), New York: Guilford Press.

Roid, G. H. (2003). *Standford-Binet Intelligence Scales* (5th ed.). Itasca, IL: Riverside.

Rosman, N. P. (1999). Traumatic brain injury in children. In K. E. Swaiman & S. Ashwal (Eds.), *Pediatric neurology* (pp. 57–58). St. Louis, MO: Mosby.

Rothner, A. D. (1999). Headaches. In K. E. Swaiman & S. Ashwal (Eds.), *Pediatric neurology* (pp. 747–758). St. Louis, MO: Mosby.

Rourke, B. P., Bakker, D. J., Fisk, J. L., & Strang, J. D. (1983). *Child neuropsychology.* New York: Guilford Press.

Rourke, B. P., Van Der Vlugt, H., & Rourke, S. B. (2002). *Practice of child-clinical neuropsychology: an introduction.* Exton, PA: Swets & Zeitlinger.

Russell, E. W. (1994). The cognitive-metric fixed battery approach to neuropsychological assessment. In R. D. Vanderploeg (Ed.), *Clinician's guide to neuropsychological assessment* (pp. 259–290). Hillsdale, NJ: Erlbaum.

Ryan, T. V., Lamarche, J. A., Barth, J. T., & Boll, T. J. (1996). Neuropsychological consequences and treatment of pediatric head trauma. In E. S. Batchelor & R. S. Dean (Eds.), *Pediatric neuropsychology* (pp. 117–138). Boston: Allyn & Bacon.

Sattler, J. (1988). *Assessment of children: Cognitive applications* (2nd ed.). San Diego, CA: Author.

Sattler, J. (2001). *Assessment of children: Cognitive applications* (4th ed.). San Diego, CA: Author.

Sattler, J., & D'Amato, R. C. (2002). Brain injuries: Theory and rehabilitation programs. In J. Sattler (Ed.), *Assessment of children: Behavioral and clinical applications* (4th ed.). San Diego, CA: Author.

Shaywitz, B. A., Fletcher, J. M., & Shaywitz, S. E. (1999). Attention-deficit hyperactivity disorder. In K. E. Swaiman & S. Ashwal (Eds.), *Pediatric neurology* (pp. 585–597). St. Louis, MO: Mosby.

Shinnar, S. (1999). Febrile seizures. In K. E. Swaiman & S. Ashwal (Eds.), *Pediatric neurology* (pp. 676–691). St. Louis, MO: Mosby.

Spreen, O. (2001). Learning disabilities and their neurological foundations, theories, and subtypes. In A. S. Kaufman & R. N. L. Kaufman (Eds.) *Specific learning disabilities in children and adolescents* (pp. 281–282). New York: Cambridge Press.

Stanovich, K. E. (1994). Developmental reading disorder. In S. R. Hooper, G. W. Hynd, & R. E. Mattison (Eds.), *Developmental disorders: Diagnostic criteria and clinical assessment* (pp. 173–208). Hillsdale, NJ: Erlbaum.

Sue, D. W., & Sue, D. S. (1990). *Counseling the culturally different* (2nd ed.). New York: Wiley.

Swaiman, K. E. (1999). Neurologic examination of the older child. In K. E. Swaiman & S. Ashwal (Eds.), *Pediatric neurology* (pp. 676–691). St. Louis, MO: Mosby.

Taylor, D. A., & Ashwal, S. (1999). Impairment of consciousness and coma. In K. E. Swaiman & S. Ashwal (Eds.), *Pediatric neurology* (pp. 861–872). St. Louis, MO: Mosby.

Taylor, H. G., & Fletcher, J. M. (1990). Neuropsychological assessment of children. In G. Goldstein & M. Hersen (Eds.), *Handbook of psychological assessment* (pp. 239–401). New York: Pergamon Press.

Teeter, P. A., & Semrud-Clikeman, M. (1997). *Child neuropsychology.* Needham Heights, MA: Allyn & Bacon.

Vanderploeg, R. D. (1994). Estimating premorbid level of functioning. In R. D. Vanderploeg (Ed.), *Clinician's guide to neuropsychological assessment* (pp. 43–68). Hillsdale, NJ: Erlbaum.

Walsh, L. E., & Garg, B. P. (1999). Poisoning and drug-induced neurologic disease. In K. E. Swaiman & S. Ashwal (Eds.), *Pediatric neurology* (pp. 1363–1384). St. Louis, MO: Mosby.

Watson, R. (1951). Test behavior observation guide. In R. Watson (Ed.), *The clinical method in psychology* (pp. 231–254). New York: Harper.

Wechsler, D. (1991). *The Wechsler Intelligence Scale for Children* (3rd ed.). San Antonio, TX: Psychological Corporation.

White, S. J., & Liversedge, S. P. (2004). Orthographic familiarity influences initial eye fixation positions in reading. *European Journal of Cognitive Psychology, 16,* 52–78.

Wolf, M. (1997). A provisional, integrative account of phonological and naming-speed deficits in dyslexia: Implications for diagnosis and intervention. In B. Blachman (Ed.), *Cognitive and linguistic foundations of reading acquisition: Implications for intervention research* (pp. 123–146). Hillsdale, NJ: Erlbaum.

Wong, T. M., Strickland, T. L., Fletcher-Janzen, E., Ardila, A., & Reynolds, C. R. (2000). Theoretical and practical issues in the neuropsychological assessment and treatment of culturally dissimilar patients. In E. Fletcher-Janzen, T. L. Strickland, & C. R. Reynolds (Eds.), *Handbook of cross-cultural neuropsychology* (pp. 3–18). New York: Kluwer/Plenum Press.

Yang, S. N., & McConkie, G. W. (2004). Saccade generation during reading: Are words necessary? *European Journal of Cognitive Psychology, 16,* 226–261.

Yeates, K. O., & Taylor, G. (1998). Neuropsychological assessment of older children. In G. Goldstein, P. D. Nussbaum, & S. Beers (Eds.), *Neuropsychology* (pp. 35–61). New York: Plenum Press.

Zaba, M. A., Mozlin, R., & Reynolds, W. T. (2003). Insights on the efficacy of vision examinations and vision screenings for children first entering school. *Journal of Behavioral Optometry, 14,* 5.

# CHAPTER 9

# Clinical Interviewing and Report Writing in School Neuropsychology

JANIECE L. POMPA, LORA TUESDAY HEATHFIELD, and ELAINE CLARK

T HE SCHOOL IS the most natural, yet often most neglected, setting for the practice of child neuropsychology. Children spend a majority of their weekday in school, engaged in academic tasks, interacting with peers and adults; as a result, the school is both the arena for children's cognitive and emotional development, as well as a rich source of data regarding their cognitive, emotional, and behavioral characteristics. The school psychologist with expertise in neuropsychology is in a unique position to evaluate the learner's functioning and develop meaningful interventions to promote the child's success in mastering the academic and developmental challenges inherent in the school experience. Guare and Dawson (2001) note that the practice of neuropsychology in the schools differs from practice in other settings, as the primary purpose of neuropsychological evaluation in the school is to generate meaningful academic and/or behavioral interventions rather than differential diagnosis or description of brain-behavior relationships or localization of function.

The information provided by a thorough child neuropsychological evaluation can be crucial to accurately describing a struggling student's cognitive strengths and weaknesses. As a result of a thorough assessment, interventions specifically tailored to maximize the child's ability to benefit from instruction can be prescribed. This can potentially minimize the frustration and academic regression that can occur when a child's academic difficulties are not properly understood or are misattributed to other factors such as lack of motivation or acting-out behavior. In addition, neuropsychological data can be critical in understanding the cognitive and psychological sequelae of acquired brain disorders, genetic syndromes, and medical illnesses that affect brain functioning. School psychologists can help identify cognitive problems secondary to traumatic brain injuries, Tourette's syndrome, alcohol-related syndromes, seizure disorder, Down syndrome, cerebral palsy, and diabetes, to name just a few. The neuropsychological evaluation—including thorough interviews; review of medical, psychological, and educational records; behavioral observations; test administration; and report writing—can reveal important aspects of the child's cognitive and psychological approach to academic tasks that are key to devising successful interventions for the child who is struggling in the classroom.

In the schools, students may be appropriately referred for neuropsychological evaluation if they have experienced a neurological event that has impacted their academic or emotional functioning to a degree that they are unable to benefit from classroom instruction. Teeter and Semrud-Clikeman (1997) recommend referral for neuropsychological evaluation not only if a child suffers from conditions affecting the central nervous system, but also for "chronic and severe" learning disabilities that do not respond to special education interventions; severe emotional or behavioral disturbances that result in significant learning, intellectual, or developmental delays "that are particularly resistant to traditional psychopharmacological, psychological, or behavioral interventions"; or sudden onset of deficits in intellectual functioning, language, visuospatial abilities, memory, motor skills, reasoning, academics, or behavior that are not adequately explained by previous psychological evaluations. For example, it is often the case that a teacher identifies a student with learning problems and implements preferral interventions that prove unsuccessful, following which the student is referred for evaluation. Then, following in-depth neuropsychological assessment, it is discovered that the student suffers from a previously unrecognized cognitive deficit that has doomed the intervention to failure. On one occasion, one of the authors evaluated a very quiet and shy adolescent whose writing was so slow that it was recommended that he be allowed to give his answers to exam questions orally rather than in written form, so that he would not be handicapped by the time requirements of the test. After this modification proved unsuccessful, neuropsychological testing revealed that the student had pronounced difficulty in both mentally organizing his thoughts and expressing them in a coherent verbal form. Teaching the student keyboarding skills and having him type his answers to test questions proved much more effective.

The current trend in special education mandating the identification of a processing disorder for special education classification of a student will call on the school psychologist to be trained in the use and interpretation of test instruments that provide specific information regarding cognitive processing difficulties. The neuropsychological assessment taps a broader range of cognitive abilities than does the traditional psychological assessment, thus improving the ability of the school psychologist to identify processing deficits in children referred for special education evaluation. At present, the Individuals with Disabilities Education Act (IDEA) defines a specific learning disability as a deficit in "one or more of the basic psychological processes" that form the building blocks of academic achievement. Accordingly, Springfield, Illinois, School District 186 requires that:

> the student demonstrates a processing deficit(s) that is chronic and intrinsic in nature and exists across settings as determined by multiple measures and manifested in classroom behavior. Such deficits can be documented through cognitive assessment, observation, error analysis, curriculum-based measurement, record review, test scores, interviews, etc. (District 186 eligibility requirements, n.d.; processing deficit criterion section, paragraph 1)

The fear has been expressed that the possible de-emphasis on the intellectual-academic discrepancy as the main criterion for eligibility due to severe learning disability following IDEA reauthorization in 2004 will result in reduced need for the services of the school psychologist. However, the authors believe that IDEA reauthorization will provide an even greater role for the school psychologist skilled in neuropsychological evaluation and the analysis of a child's cognitive strengths and weaknesses as they affect his or her academic achievement.

## THE CLINICAL INTERVIEW

The clinical interview is a critical component of the assessment process. The interview itself is typically structured by an agenda or purpose, namely, to elicit relevant information that will be helpful in designing effective interventions that will improve the academic success of the referred student. What follows is an overview of the interview process.

### INITIAL CONTACT

Once a child has been screened by the school's multidisciplinary student support team and deemed appropriate for special education evaluation, parental permission to evaluate the child must be obtained. Contact to obtain consent to evaluate may represent the initial opportunity for the school psychologist to discuss the assessment process with the parents, describe the reasons for referral and the referral questions and procedures involved, address parental concerns regarding the child, and answer any questions the parents might have regarding the evaluation process. The school psychologist may also need to explain how a neuropsychological evaluation differs from a traditional psychological evaluation and how the information gained from the evaluation will benefit the child in school. It is often helpful to discuss with the parents what the child will be told about the evaluation, so that the child knows who the examiner is, the purpose of the evaluation, and what kinds of activities the child and the examiner will be doing together. The child who knows what to expect is less likely to be frightened or intimidated by the evaluation process, and the psychologist may be able to achieve rapport more readily with a student who is well-informed and comfortable in the test setting.

### BACKGROUND INFORMATION

The process of gathering background information on the referral question includes a review of the child's cumulative file to obtain basic demographic information, school grades, school attendance records, standardized test scores, and results of hearing and vision screenings. Review of the child's special education file, if one exists, will yield results of previous psychoeducational evaluations, classification and placement information, and medical records. In neuropsychological record review, there is frequently a need for the school psychologist to review the part of the child's medical records that pertains to his or her cognitive functioning or the neurologic injury or illness that may be affecting brain functioning. If the child suffers from a medical condition that may be interfering with his or her ability to benefit from classroom instruction and no medical information is available in the school files, the school psychologist should always request the relevant medical records. If the child has been treated as an outpatient by a physician, the history and physical examination of the child, progress notes, and results of any diagnostic procedures relevant to the medical condition under consideration (CT, MRI scans of the brain, EEG, etc.) should be requested. If the child has been treated as an inpatient, the preceding records should also be requested, together with the hospital discharge summary and any relevant consultations performed while the child was an inpatient (such as neurologic consultation). If the child was treated on a rehabilitation unit, records of the child's progress and school recommendations should be obtained to facilitate the child's transfer from the hospital to the community school.

When reviewing medical records, the psychologist should know the meaning and implications of common abbreviations, medical terminology, and values (such as an abnormal Glasgow Coma Scale score). If questions arise, the psychologist should consult a reputable medical dictionary such as *Stedman's Medical Dictionary* (Stedman, 2000). On one occasion, one of the authors consulted with a student services team with regard to premature, low-birthweight twins, one of whom was functioning much more poorly than the other. School officials were mystified until the psychologist reviewed the medical record, which revealed that the lower-functioning twin suffered from SDH at birth; no one had known that the abbreviation stood for "subdural hemorrhage [of the brain]," which almost certainly explained the poorer functioning of the affected twin. Record reviews, as well as interviews with parents and school personnel, are the backbone of the information-gathering process that enables the psychologist to provide a context for the evaluation of the child, clarify the specific referral questions that will be addressed during the evaluation, allow the formulation of initial hypotheses regarding the child's functioning that will be tested during the assessment process, and determine the most appropriate instruments and procedures to test these hypotheses, answer the referral questions, and generate meaningful recommendations that can be implemented to benefit the child.

PARENT INTERVIEW

The purpose of the interview with the parent(s) or guardian is to obtain a history of the child's difficulties and information regarding factors that may be affecting the child's school performance. It is preferable to conduct the interview in person, although a telephone interview can substitute, if necessary. Parent interviews should be conducted with sensitivity to familial cultural and/or linguistic differences. Puente, Sol Mora, & Munoz-Cespedes (1997) discuss caveats with regard to the assessment of Hispanic children, suggesting that family involvement is essential, rationale and procedures of the evaluation should be discussed with the family in a courteous and respectful manner, the parents should be reassured regarding the evaluator's care and concern for their child, and the importance of the results to the child's future welfare should be emphasized. Parental expectations for child learning and behavior differ from one culture to another, and this may make it difficult for the family and the school to agree on the need for, or goals of, an evaluation. One of the authors once conducted an interview with the parents of a child from an Eastern European country. The parents were in violent disagreement with the teacher about the need for evaluation of their kinder-gartener's extreme impulsivity, inability to sit, listen, and follow directions, and frequent hitting of other children; in their home country, kindergarten children were there "to play, not sit still and learn." Obviously, such value conflicts must be thoroughly discussed, with respect for parental values and viewpoints, before a meaningful interview and evaluation can take place.

When working with a child of another culture, ideally the neuropsychologist should conduct the interview in the parents' dominant language. However, it is apparent that this guideline is often not followed. Echemendia, Congett, Harris, DIaz, & Puente (1998) report that, of neuropsychologists performing neuropsychological evaluations with Hispanic clients, only a small percentage reported being fluent in Spanish. If it is not possible to interview in the parents' dominant language, a translator trained in the parents' language and culture and the accurate translation of psychological and neuropsychological concepts should be utilized. Echemendia et al. suggest that the use of family members as translators creates difficulties due to the risk of inaccurate translation and possible disruption of family dynamics.

During the face-to-face interview, the interviewer may want to use a written guide or outline of questions to be asked to ensure that all relevant areas are covered. To save time during the interview process, a questionnaire may be sent home and completed by the parents prior to the interview. Sample child neuropsychological questionnaires and directed interview forms can be found in Baron (2004) and Franzen and Berg (1998). In addition, there are several neuropsychological symptom checklists and developmental history forms that provide neuropsychological information appropriate for children that can be completed by the parents prior to interview (Barkley, 1998; Greenberg, 1990; Levine, 1996; Melendez, 1978). Maloney and Ward (1976) recommend beginning the interview with an open-ended question (such as "What are your concerns about your child?"); this allows parents to select the information they believe to be important, which may reveal their attitude toward the child, the school, and the evaluation itself. According to the parents' responses, the interview then becomes progressively more structured to clarify details and inconsistencies. The case history obtained during the child neuropsychological interview generally reveals numerous variables that can influence the results and interpretation of neuropsychological data. These may include the following, depending on the child's age, developmental level, and reason for referral:

- *Demographic information:* Child's full name, date of birth, age, grade, handedness, country of origin, socioeconomic status, home culture, ethnicity, and primary language spoken.
- *Current complaints:* Who made the referral; parents' perspective on the reason for referral; when the problem started; precipitating event, if any; developmental course of the problem; whether the problem seems to occur in certain circumstances, settings, or in the presence of certain people; what the responses of others are to the child when the problem occurs.
- *Family situation and history:* Who the child lives with; whether the child is adopted or biological; age, gender, and number of siblings; academic achievement and learning problems of siblings; level of education of parents; academic achievement and learning problems of parents; family history of

genetic disorder or psychiatric or medical illness; stress and/or recent changes in home or family.

- *Pre- and perinatal history:* Maternal substance use, exposure to toxins, illness, injury during pregnancy; gestational age and birthweight; complications during delivery (fetal distress, use of forceps), Apgar score.
- *Early developmental history:* Achievement of developmental milestones in language (speaking single words and sentences, speech quality, ability to follow sequential commands) and fine and gross motor skills (sitting up, crawling, walking, riding a bike, drawing, tying shoes); siblings with whom to compare developmental rates.
- *School history:* Age at school entrance; school grades; academic and behavioral difficulties, including special education referral and placement; problems with attention, memory, expressive or receptive language, spatial ability, reasoning, or other cognitive problems; standardized test scores; attitude and motivation toward school; response to authority figures; peer relationships.
- *Psychiatric history:* Symptoms of depression, anxiety, psychosis, aggression, or other psychiatric illness; trauma or abuse; psychotherapy or psychiatric hospitalization; premorbid and current personality characteristics; quality of interpersonal relationships.
- *Physical status and medical history:* Eating and sleeping habits; injuries and significant illnesses and sequelae; current treatment regimen and medications; visual and hearing acuity.
- *Legal history:* History of serious violations of rules; legal offenses; court involvement; child's current legal status.
- *Occupational training and history:* Type of vocational training, if any; number and type of jobs; work habits and work ethic; length of jobs held; reason for leaving or dismissal.
- *Strengths:* Child's talents, hobbies, and interests.

The information obtained from the parent interview is generally broad in scope and will enable the school psychologist to identify and focus on cognitive, emotional, and behavioral areas of concern; develop hypotheses with regard to the origin and etiology of the child's problems; help identify specific tests and assessment techniques to clarify the referral questions; and begin formulating ideas for appropriate interventions to improve the child's school performance. For example, a child who is the only left-hander in the family and had a difficult birth raises the possibility of pathological left-handedness, which describes an individual who may have been genetically predisposed to right-handedness but whose handedness switched as a result of pre- or perinatal trauma to the left hemisphere of the brain. It would be helpful to know that the father of a child who demonstrates a math disability suffered from similar learning problems and was helped by a particular technique or curriculum, as genetic factors might suggest that his child would be helped by a similar intervention. The school psychologist might hypothesize that a child recently transferred to a new elementary school, who was referred for severe reading and writing problems and oppositional behavior, may have a verbal learning disability; however, the knowledge that the child's dominant language is Bosnian, that he moved to the United States 1 year ago after witnessing atrocities in his homeland, following which he was traumatized, and that his low-income parents speak only Bosnian at home introduces a host of other, nonneurologic factors that are certain to impact this child's learning abilities and emotional development. Such information can be gained only from a thorough, careful interview of the parents of a child referred for neuropsychological evaluation.

## INTERVIEW WITH TEACHERS AND SCHOOL PERSONNEL

Another source of interview data often overlooked by neuropsychologists practicing in nonschool settings is the interview with teachers and other school personnel. The teacher's perspective on a child's classroom functioning may be similar to or different from the parent's perspective and serves to round out the evolving picture of the child's functioning. The psychologist should regard the teacher with respect and realize that rapport with the teacher is the key to successful consultation and implementation of interventions in the classroom. Franzen and Berg (1998) note that teachers can provide useful information regarding the child's attention span, impulsivity, frustration tolerance, peer relationships, cognitive strengths and weaknesses in approach to academic material, and emotional adjustment. An interview with the teacher can also provide information on what motivates the child, as well as contingencies that are likely to improve or reduce the child's chances for academic success (providing frequent reinforcement, peer tutoring, use of the computer instead of writing, etc.). Sattler (1988) provides an example of a semistructured interview with the teacher, including specific questions regarding the teacher's perception of the child's problem behavior, the teacher's reaction to the child's behaviors, the academic performance of the child, the child's strengths, the teacher's view of the child's family, and the teacher's expectations of the child's behavior and suggestions for intervention. The teacher's responses to these questions will also provide insight regarding the teacher's ability and willingness to implement interventions in the classroom.

Interviews with other school personnel who have had contact with the child can also provide information about the child's characteristics and functioning in different settings. The school guidance counselor may have insight into the child's emotional issues, psychological characteristics, and peer relationships, while related servers such as the speech pathologist or occupational or physical therapist can add information with regard to the child's language and fine and gross motor abilities. The school secretary and office staff can provide information on the child's behavior with parents and other children "when no one is looking." Office staff may observe how the child separates and reunites with parents, how the parents speak to the child, and what the parents and child spontaneously discuss while waiting in the informal office setting, which may not be manifest in the formal interview setting.

## INTERVIEW OF THE CHILD

Much has been written regarding the clinical interview of the child (Brems, 2002; Franzen & Berg, 1998; Sattler, 1988; Semrud-Clikeman, 1995), and a full description of child interviewing techniques may be obtained from those sources. Semrud-Clikeman notes that the interview of the child is usually shorter than the adult interview and that children should be allowed more control and freedom of activity in the interview setting to promote increased involvement in the session.

Playing, drawing, acting with puppets, and sitting on the floor are often appropriate to help the child feel at ease and to elicit information. Although the psychologist may want to conduct a traditional interview with the child to obtain the child's perspective on his or her difficulties (see Sattler, 1988), the interview also provides a setting in which the clinician can conduct an unstructured behavioral observation of the child. In fact, this type of behavioral observation may be one of the most informational aspects of the child interview itself.

BEHAVIORAL OBSERVATIONS

Behavioral observations of the child are not only helpful when assessing the child's cognitive and psychological status, but are mandated by some states as part of the special education evaluation process for some diagnostic categories. In addition, it is important to observe child behaviors that may affect the reliability or validity of test performance (poor attention or motivation), indicate sensory or motor handicaps that will influence the choice of tests to be used with the child (poor visual acuity, severe motor incoordination), aid in interpretation of test results (memory problems, disorganization), or be diagnostic of neurological problems (tremor, nystagmus). Observation of the child during the individual interview and testing, as well as in the classroom and/or the playground, provides several venues for the assessment of consistency of child behavior in structured, unstructured, academic, and social settings. Child characteristics and behaviors of interest to the school psychologist include physical appearance, level of activity, gait, eye contact, attention span, expressive and receptive language, logic and reasoning process, and nonverbal behavior, including motor activity.

Careful observation of the child's physical appearance may reveal dysmorphic characteristics suggestive of genetic disorder, such as wide-set eyes, abnormally large or small head circumference, flat nasal bridge, unusual height or weight, or abnormal mouth, ear, or chin shape. Observation of the child's gait may be indicative of various neurologic conditions, such as cerebral palsy or traumatic brain injury. Bitten nails, scars or scratches on the body, physical or vocal tics raise the possibility of psychiatric disorders such as anxiety, depression, or Tourette's syndrome, respectively. Is the child able to sit quietly in a chair during the session, or is he frequently out of his seat, tapping his pencil, playing with test materials or other objects, or under the table? Conversely, is he sleepy, lethargic, slow-moving, and sluggish? Does he demonstrate an age-appropriate attention span; does he frequently have to be redirected to tasks; or does he obsess and perseverate over topics and tasks and have difficulty transitioning to new activities? Difficulties in regulation of attention may suggest Attention-Deficit/Hyperactivity Disorder (ADHD), anxiety, depression, sleep problems, medication side effects, Obsessive-Compulsive Disorder, or problems with executive functioning (see Table 9.1).

Observation of the child's spontaneous conversation provides an opportunity to assess expressive and receptive language. What is the child's vocal quality, rate and volume of speech, verbal fluency, and the quality of her articulation? Does she have difficulty with word retrieval, as indicated by hesitations in speech, word substitutions, or use of incorrect words? Does she talk "around" the topic (circumlocution) rather than getting to the point, or speak in short, choppy sentences? Is her use of vocabulary and grammar age-appropriate? Do questions have

**Table 9.1**

Sampling of Neurologic Conditions of Childhood with Possible Cognitive Effects

Prenatal/Perinatal Onset
    Cerebral palsy
    Chromosomal abnormalities (e.g., fragile X, Down's syndrome)
    Fetal alcohol syndrome/effects
    Hydrocephalus
    Muscular dystrophy
    Metabolic disorder
    Spina bifida
Infections/Postinfectious Disorders
    Meningitis (viral or bacterial)
    Encephalitis
    Guillain-Barre syndrome
    Reye syndrome
Head Trauma
    Intracranial hematoma
    Cerebral contusion
    Mild head injury
Vascular Disease
    Heart disease
    Intraventricular hemorrhage
    Sickle cell anemia
Other
    Chronic fatigue syndrome
    Fibromyalgia
    Leukemia
    Seizure disorder
    Tourette's syndrome
    Brain tumor

to be repeated or rephrased for her to understand what is being asked? Does she mishear words? Can she follow a three-step command? Problems in these areas suggest a need for auditory acuity and formal language testing and can help distinguish whether the child is suffering from ADHD, auditory processing problems, developmental language disorder, or acquired aphasia, depending on her history. Poor logic during conversation, flight of ideas, and jumping from topic to topic can be symptoms of mental disorganization characteristic of disorders such as ADHD, Schizophrenia, and Bipolar Disorder.

In addition, the psychologist may want to take this opportunity to observe the child performing informal or formal tasks, and then teach the child how to do the task, observing the child's rate and efficiency of learning, compensatory techniques the child may be using, and cognitive process used to perform the task. This could constitute a dynamic assessment of the child's abilities from which conclusions may be drawn and compared with the results of standardized testing, both of which should be included in the evaluation report.

Abnormal nonverbal and motor behaviors can represent neurological symptomatology and/or symptoms of psychiatric illness. How long and under what circumstances does the child maintain eye contact? Does his posture reflect excessive or poor muscle tone? Does he demonstrate motor tics, overflow or mirror movements, tremors, clumsiness, self-stimulatory behavior, stereotyped movements, facial grimacing, or odd mannerisms? Does he have an abnormal gait or problems with motor coordination? What are his facial expressions, and are they appropriate to the situation or topic being discussed? Does he accurately comprehend nonverbal cues and gestures from others? Such neurologic "soft signs" may represent immature development of the central nervous system (CNS), may be symptomatic of CNS injury, or may be part of the symptom picture of nonverbal learning disability, Autistic Spectrum Disorder, or Tourette's syndrome. In addition, eye contact, facial expressions, and body language enable the clinician to make inferences with regard to the child's mood and affect in the interview situation.

Other observed behaviors displayed by the child may add a dimension of ecological validity to interview impressions and test findings. The clinician may observe a child who has attended the same school for several years, yet has difficulty finding his way back to the classroom, repeatedly leaves his personal possessions in the school psychologist's office, or forgets school supplies at home, who also scores poorly on memory tests. The hypothesis that the child has memory problems is borne out by the neuropsychological test data and vice versa. One of the authors observed a 5-year-old girl in a diagnostic kindergarten who, despite daily prompting for almost the entire school year, was not only the sole child in her class who could not remember her school lunch number, but she did not even understand that the number had to be entered so she could buy her lunch; the cashier had to grasp the child's forefinger and help her punch in the number manually. Of course, a discrepancy between test scores and a child's observed behavior, an occurrence that is not unusual in the school setting, is also worth mention and may have implications for intervention as well as prognostic significance. The 10-year-old boy who scores poorly on tests of memory and learning yet can accurately program the examiner's cell phone after one demonstration may be a child whose executive functioning abilities are relatively intact and who can learn better with hands-on instruction. The school psychologist's final report should combine such observations with history and test data to create a clear picture of the child's strengths and weaknesses in performing activities of daily living and other practical, as well as academic, tasks.

## REPORT WRITING

The neuropsychological report is the product of the neuropsychological evaluation and represents the analysis and synthesis of the information gained through record reviews, interviews, observations of the child, and history and test data. From this often complex database of information, the school psychologist applies training, experience, and judgment to generate conclusions regarding the cause of the child's difficulties and formulate recommendations for interventions that will improve the child's ability to benefit from instruction. The purpose of the report is to accurately describe the child; present the assessment results in a clear and organized fashion; offer conclusions that are supported by the data, setting forth the logic and data points that were used to derive these conclusions; and address the referral question, presenting practical strategies for intervention that are described in sufficient detail so that the individuals responsible for their implementation have a clear and comprehensible road map or way to proceed following the completion of the evaluation.

## GENERAL ISSUES

Tallent (1993) has observed that in the past, the psychological test report was a consultation between professionals, but now, the report may be read by nonprofessionals as well. Armengol, Kaplan, and Moes (2001) opined that making neuropsychological reports more "consumer-oriented" or "user-friendly" would promote the understanding and appreciation of the potential contributions of neuropsychology; they wrote *The Consumer-Oriented Neuropsychological Report* to fulfill that purpose. The authors describe many neuropsychological reports as overly technical, providing excessive or inadequate detail, lacking in information critical for treatment planning, and failing to describe how conclusions were reached. School personnel who may read the child's neuropsychological evaluation report, including the principal, teacher, guidance counselor, social worker, and related servers such as speech pathologists, will vary widely with regard to training, background, and familiarity with psychological, neurological, and neuropsychological concepts. Therefore, it is in the child's best interest if the report is written in plain language, with potentially unfamiliar concepts briefly described in a way that is understandable to the lay reader. A report that reads "This 7-year-old boy with prenatal IVH and periventricular encephalomalacia demonstrates deficits in executive functioning and bilateral hemispheric compromise, and requires accommodations in the classroom" may confound the average reader and adds little to the school's understanding of the child's needs. It is preferable for the examiner to provide a clear description of the child's condition and practical recommendations, such as:

> Johnny suffered bleeding in both sides of the brain prior to birth, resulting in softening of brain tissue. These changes in the brain have likely resulted in his struggle to keep information in immediate memory long enough to act on it, as well as problems in performing sequential steps to solve a math problem or complete an assignment. It is recommended that successive steps to solve a problem be presented to him in written form. As he is able to successfully master and remember the problem-solving process, the first step can be covered with a piece of paper. If he can remember it, successive steps can be covered up (or *faded*) until he can remember each step in order.

Bradley-Johnson and Johnson (1998) present other pitfalls of style in the report, such as:

> use of jargon, use of inconsistent verb tense, incorrect presentation of names and abbreviations of published tests, redundancy, wordiness, misuse of hyphens, use of contractions, overuse of *very* and *it is,* lack of subject-verb agreement, prepositions at the ends of sentences, misplaced modifiers, misuse of *that, which, since,* and *because,* and incorrect forms of commonly used terms.

Ownby's (1997) research indicated that reports written by psychologists in clinical settings are "sometimes considered useful" by other mental health professionals who receive them, frequently criticized by these professionals due to content and style, and may or may not make a meaningful contribution to client treatment plans. Several studies of teachers with regard to the reports of school psychologists (Hagborg & Aiello-Coultier, 1994; Salvagno & Teglasi, 1987) indicate that teachers find most helpful numerous specific, concrete recommendations for intervention. Rucker (1967) found that elementary school teachers were critical of school psychologists' reports that were too brief, were poorly organized, omitted or failed to explain results, failed to provide answers to referral questions, and provided vague, brief, or unrealistic suggestions for intervention. They positively rated reports that were understandable, were interesting to read, provided adequate interpretations and explanations to the reader, explained the etiology of the problem, answered specific referral questions, and provided a variety of specific recommendations that could be easily implemented in the classroom.

## Expository Process Model

Following their exhaustive review of the literature on psychological report writing, Ownby and Wallbrown (1986) developed the Expository Process Model (EPM) to reduce the use of jargon and relate data to theory in a way that would be understandable to the untrained reader. Ownby and Wallbrown assert that the use of jargon in reports occurs not only when the author uses obscure terminology, but when he or she invokes a theoretical construct to explain the child's behavior that is not clearly explained in the report. These theoretical concepts, which they term "middle level constructs" (MLC), are necessary to link assessment data to conclusions but often are not well understood by either the untrained reader or the professional colleague who may be reading the report. For example, the term "overflow movements" may not be understood by the average reader; the explanatory sentence "When the child tapped a key with one hand, the other hand involuntarily moved as well, a neurological 'soft sign' that may indicate developmental delay" is more easily understood. Following an initial explanation of a possibly ambiguous term, the term may subsequently be used in the report, with the assumption that the report writer and reader have a mutual understanding of the meaning of that term. Ownby and Wallbrown further state, "The possibility exists that what's wrong with the use of MLC's in reports is not their content—the terms themselves—but their relation to data (the degree to which they are clearly explained) and their relation to the child (the degree to which their importance to the child is explained)" (p. 26). The EPM proposes:

1. "Any MLC in a report must have a directly shared referent in data either implicitly or explicitly contained in the report" (Ownby, 1997, pp. 55–56). In other words, all MLCs used in a report must be terms clearly understood by the reader and the writer. If not, the writer must present a concrete description of the MLC in terms that a lay reader would understand.
2. "Conclusions are evaluative statements about the MLC [which was invoked to explain an aspect of the child's cognition or behavior] and must be supported by data" (pp. 55–56).
3. "Recommendations must be logically related to conclusions stated in the report" (pp. 55–56).

In this manner, the clinician's conclusions are supported by a particular theoretical construct, which in turn is validated by assessment data. Widespread implementation of this model would go a long way toward eliminating the problems of vagueness, ambiguity in the use of psychological and neuropsychological terms, presentation of conclusions that are not supported by data, and difficulty following the clinician's logic in formulating conclusions presented in the report. For example, non-EPM conclusions such as the following are all too common in neuropsychological reports: "This child appears to be suffering from a nonverbal learning disability and learning disability in mathematics. Presentation of stimuli in verbal form in the classroom, as well as referral to a study skills class, are recommended." In this case, the MLC *nonverbal learning disability* is presented without explanation of the meaning of this term as it relates to that particular child, as well as the specific test behaviors that led the clinician to invoke that particular MLC to explain the child's behavior. A revision of this conclusion according to the EPM model might read as follows:

> The child's deficits in performance of nonverbal tasks such as assembling blocks to match a model, drawing and remembering complex shapes, and assembling jigsaw puzzles, when compared to his superior performance on verbal tasks such as word retrieval, knowledge of vocabulary words, and fund of general information, suggests that he is suffering from a nonverbal learning disability that is affecting his ability to perform math calculations. He is likely to remember and understand material better if concepts are presented in lecture or written form; graphs, charts, and other visual methods of presentation should be avoided. His nonverbal learning disability is characterized by difficulty in visual organization when performing math problems, so the use of graph paper with horizontal and vertical lines to help him keep numbers in the proper relation to each other when adding and subtracting is recommended.

These EPM statements explain the ways the child displayed nonverbal difficulties during the assessment, thus connecting the data to the MLC. In addition, the recommendations link directly to both the MLC and the performance problems the child displayed during the assessment. Ownby and Wallbrown (1986) noted that EPM statements "may be seen to be more vivid and to communicate in a concrete and more easily understandable fashion the psychologist's message . . . statements using the EPM were rated significantly more credible and persuasive than non-EPM equivalents" (p. 28). The reader is referred to Ownby and Wallbrown (1986) for further details with regard to the EPM model.

## ORGANIZATION OF THE REPORT

The content, format, and organization of the neuropsychological report vary widely, according to the training of the clinician, the purpose of the evaluation, and the requirements of the practice setting. There are many templates of neuropsychological reports in the literature (Baron, 2004; Mendoza, 2001), most of which include the following elements.

*Identifying Information*   Agencies and school districts generally have their own formats for reporting the child's demographic information, but many include headings for the child's name, date of birth, age, school, grade, date of testing, and examiner's name. School districts that serve a significant number of English-language learners may also include headings for the languages spoken by the child and language(s) in which the interview and testing was conducted.

*Reason for Referral*   This section provides a brief statement of the reason the child was referred for evaluation, which structures the evaluation and the conclusions to follow. Referral questions from the school should be specific, answerable by the procedures and techniques available to the school psychologist, and pertinent to the child's school performance, academic curriculum, and/or class placement. A referral made to investigate a child's cognitive strengths and weaknesses because he is significantly below grade level in reading and can learn something one minute and forget it the next is a legitimate request; wanting to know why an adequately functioning child's verbal and performance IQ are so discrepant is not.

*History and Background Information*   This section presents the information gathered during record review and interviews to provide a context for and shape the interpretation of test results obtained. In some cases, organization of information under relevant subheadings may improve the readability of the report, for example, *Early history* (including significant prenatal and perinatal events in the child's life and achievement of developmental milestones); *School history* (grades, standardized testing, level of achievement in academic subjects, previous evaluations); *Cognitive symptoms* (problems with memory, attention, reasoning and executive functioning, visuospatial ability, sensorimotor problems); *Psychological and behavioral difficulties* (problems with mood or affect, fears, nightmares, hallucinations, emotional lability, aggression, obsessions or compulsions, poor social skills); *Medical history and physical symptoms* (visual and auditory acuity, past and present medical or neurologic illness, current medications); and *Family history* (genetic syndromes, learning problems, emotional problems, family living situation, family stresses). If the child is an English-language learner, and if the family is of a different ethnicity or culture, that information may also be included here.

Donders (2001), in his survey of a sample of practicing neuropsychologists, found that in their reports, the majority of respondents commented only occasionally on sensitive personal information such as physical or sexual abuse. The authors noted that this practice is consistent with the *Ethical principles of psychologists and code of conduct* (Standard 4.04 (a)), which suggests that only information that is relevant to the purpose of the professional communication should be reported (American Psychological Association, 2003). Drake and Bardon (1978) also suggest that information that may be harmful or prejudicial to the child be excluded from the report. The school psychologist should be mindful of the potential prejudicial effect of certain types of information regarding the child or family that can impact the child's education and should omit potentially sensitive information in reports unless it is germane to the purpose of the evaluation or conclusions derived from test data. For example, when evaluating a child for ADHD in the school, the fact that the parents were divorced due to one party's infidelity is not likely to be relevant and should not be included in the report.

*Behavioral Observations*   The psychologist's observations of the child's behavior during interview and testing may be included here. This section can be organized into two paragraphs, the first describing the notable aspects of the child's stature and physical appearance, behavior, mood and affect, attitude, and interaction with parents and the examiner, and the second describing the child's behavior during testing, including attention to task, activity level, motivation, factors potentially affecting the child's test performance (e.g., medication status, lack of sleep), and examiner's judgment of the reliability and validity of test results, with the reasons for that judgment.

*Tests Administered (or Assessment Procedures)*   Each test administered to the child is listed here, properly spelled and with its abbreviation if used later in the report. Other assessment procedures, such as child, parent, and collateral interviews and record review, are listed here. The information gained from record review is usually presented in the history and background information section, and test scores are usually presented in the test results section.

*Test Results*   This section is the heart of the report, presenting the child's scores on the tests administered as compared to a normative sample. Mendoza (2001) suggests that this section be structured either (1) in a test-by-test fashion, reporting the results of each test separately; (2) by grouping the results of various tests assessing similar types of cognitive functioning; (3) by theoretical models of brain organization and/or brain function; (4) by the client's strengths versus weaknesses; or (5) by a combination of these schemas. The author also notes that the multifactorial nature of most neuropsychological tests poses difficulties when attempting to organize test results by the putative cognitive ability assessed. Mendoza states, however, that organizing the report in a test-by-test manner may be problematic, as the failure to integrate test results places the burden on the reader to try to interpret results and interrelationships and frequently results in failure to resolve inconsistencies in the data set.

Psychologists also must choose between writing a *quantitative* (data-focused) report and writing a *qualitative* (descriptive) report. Some psychologists prefer to report scores for each test as compared to a normative group, usually in the form of standard scores, T-scores, Z-scores, percentile ranks, and/or age or grade equivalents. Because most psychologists are familiar with the meaning of the tests and these types of scores, other psychologists reviewing the report can easily see and understand the data generated by the client and can formulate their own opinions with regard to the implications of the scores and the child's functioning. However, it is still incumbent upon the writer of the report to explain, interpret, and derive conclusions from raw test data. As previously mentioned, readers of the report may vary widely in their training and understanding of test scores and may come to incorrect conclusions with regard to their meaning. For example, one of the authors once consulted with a professional group that had decided to deny testing accommodations to a student whose measured IQ fell within the superior range. They had interpreted the student's reported standard scores on academic tasks, which fell within the 70 to 80 range, as percentile ranks.

## CURRENT ISSUES

An issue that is specific to child neuropsychological assessment as a relatively new and developing discipline is the use of different sets of norms to interpret test scores, as well as the use of tests that are not well validated psychometrically. Traditionally, psychologists have used assessment instruments that have been normed on relatively large numbers of children, with manuals describing the psychometric properties of the normative group and, sometimes, special populations as well (developmentally disabled, learning-disabled, head-injured, etc.). However, many neuropsychological instruments used with both children and adults are normed on small numbers of subjects or have been normed on groups of subjects with different demographic characteristics, which are scattered throughout the literature. Several texts have been published in an attempt to gather this information in one source (Baron, 2004; Mitrushina, Boone, & D'Elia, 1999; Spreen & Strauss, 1998). Donders (2001) reports that 23% of pediatric neuropsychologists in his survey always included information regarding the source of the norms that were used, which is more than twice the rate for adult or geriatric neuropsychologists. He noted that, due to debate in the literature on the need for age-based norms for children's neurobehavioral abilities and "serious concerns" regarding the adequacy of present norms for child neuropsychological tests, "it is understandable that pediatric neuropsychologists may be especially inclined to clarify the nature of the norms that were used to interpret psychometric data" (p. 145). Given the large differences between normative samples on some neuropsychological tests and the widely different inferences that can be drawn from test scores as a result, it is preferable for report authors to specify the source of the norms used to derive their conclusions about a child's cognitive abilities.

It is also the psychologist's job to explain the child's test scores in the context of his or her history and the influence of other variables such as the child's attention, motivation, and language status, adequacy of past instruction, or other situational factors that may have affected the test results. Without the analysis and synthesis of all information about the child, the reader may arrive at inaccurate conclusions with regard to that child's functioning. A school principal who glances at a report and reads that a child who suffered a head injury 6 months ago in an automobile-bike accident has a current Full Scale IQ of 95 may quickly conclude that the child is capable of learning at a normal rate. However, a trained school psychologist who knows that this child displayed superior learning ability and academic skills prior to his injury and now scores very poorly on tests of verbal memory and learning can clarify that the child's inability to remember the steps in solving an algebra equation he had learned the day before, and his subsequent lack of attention and low frustration tolerance in the classroom, are sequelae of his head injury that should be accommodated in the classroom. The psychologist can also explain that the child's performance may drop dramatically over time if no effective interventions are implemented.

The *qualitative* report is a narrative report, employing qualitative descriptors to indicate the child's performance on assessment tasks compared to a normative group. Instead of "The child's Full Scale IQ was 72," the report will state, "The child's Full Scale IQ falls within the *borderline* range." Profile analysis is accomplished through indication of the severity level of a child's deficits (mild, moderate, or severe) on each test, or strengths and weaknesses compared to a normative group, as well as the child's own scores on and across tests. This style has been criticized because the description of the child's level of performance is dependent on the examiner's interpretation and judgment, descriptors are ambiguous and may have different meanings to different readers, and lack of scores can make test-retest comparisons more difficult (Mendoza, 2001). Mendoza has suggested that a compromise between the quantitative and qualitative styles could be struck by describing the behavior of the child during each test that pertains to the skills or abilities tested and by drawing inferences from those behaviors, which can in turn generalize to extratest behaviors. However, he acknowledges that, like the criticisms of the qualitative report, inferences and judgments regarding cognitive abilities from samples of behavior on standardized tests are highly subjective and require considerable examiner training and experience to be accurate. It is also more time-intensive to record, report, and make judgments on relevant behaviors.

The differences between report writing styles have led to a lively debate in the neuropsychological literature concerning reporting test scores within the body of the report or writing a narrative, more qualitative report and appending a list of test scores to the end of the report (Friedes, 1993, 1995; Matarazzo, 1995; Naugle & McSweeney, 1995). It has been argued that test data are sensitive information that should be protected and not included in the report and, conversely, that written interpretation of data is no less sensitive than the data itself. Traditionally, school psychological reports have included test scores in the body of the report, accompanied by interpretive statements regarding the child's level of functioning, according to the psychologist's judgment. This is undoubtedly the case because, in most states, test scores are critical in determining a child's eligibility for special education placement. Therefore, a narrative report containing descriptive statements and no test scores is unlikely to gain widespread acceptance among school psychologists, as it would be of limited utility in the school setting.

The school neuropsychological report may present the test results organized according to the following subheadings:

- *Intellectual functioning:* Results of intelligence testing and discrepancies between subtest scores or indexes are reported here.
- *Verbal abilities:* This section includes the results of tests of verbal ability administered by the school psychologist. In some cases, a brief summary of tests performed by the school's speech pathologist may be reported here, if relevant to the psychologist's conclusions and recommendations.
- *Visuospatial abilities:* The results of tests assessing visual-constructional and visuospatial abilities are reported here.
- *Memory and attention:* This section may include the results of tests of verbal and nonverbal immediate and long-term memory, working memory, visual and auditory attention, and concentration. Results of questionnaires completed by the parent and/or child that give information regarding the child's functioning in these areas may also be included (attentional subtests of the Conners' and Achenbach rating scales and Behavior Assessment System for Children [BASC]; Attention Deficit Disorders Evaluation Scale; etc.).
- *Executive functioning/abstract reasoning/mental tracking:* This section may include the results of interview data, questionnaires, and tests in either the verbal or visual modality that shed light on the child's executive functioning. Results of batteries specifically designed to evaluate different aspects of executive functioning (such as the Delis-Kaplan Executive Functioning System or NEPSY), including ability to formulate a mental plan of action, carry it out in proper sequence, evaluate the quality of performance, and make corrections if necessary, as well as questionnaires describing the

child's behavior in these areas (such as the Behavior Rating Inventory of Executive Function) may be reported here. In addition, it is important to comment on the way a child formulates and executes any activity or task, not just those labeled as "executive functioning" tasks, as executive function is involved in all complex human behaviors. The child who rushes through Block Design or arithmetic calculations, making careless errors because he did not check his work, demonstrates a problem in the self-monitoring aspect of executive functioning.

- *Sensorimotor abilities:* This section may include a report of the child's visual and auditory acuity, as well as results of testing that bear on the child's visual, motor, and tactile sensory abilities.

- *Academic abilities:* In this section are reported results of academic testing, such as the Woodcock-Johnson Tests of Achievement III and Wechsler Individual Achievement Test II. Typically, standard scores and percentile ranks are reported in a table. It is also important to specify the type of normative sample to which the child's score is being compared (age versus grade). Results of curriculum-based assessment or other forms of alternative academic assessment may also be reported here.

- *Personality and behavioral assessment:* This section usually includes the results of projective and objective tests and questionnaires regarding the child's psychological characteristics, personality, and behavior. Results of the personality and behavior scales of the BASC, Achenbach, and Conners, Minnesota Multiphasic Personality Inventory for Adolescents, Millon Adolescent Clinical Inventory, and other questionnaires are described here, usually in a table with standard scores. If adaptive behavior measures have been administered, results may be reported here or in a separate section devoted to adaptive behavior and/or functional living skills.

- *Summary and conclusions:* The summary generally reiterates the child's basic demographic information and reason for referral in one or two brief sentences. The bulk of this section is devoted to the clinician's proposed answer to the referral questions, conclusions with regard to the child's strengths and weaknesses, etiology of the child's problems, and the logic and data on which those conclusions were based. Clinical lore holds that many readers tend to flip to the summary, conclusions, and recommendations first, so this section should be able to stand alone, providing a concise summary of basic demographic information, the important data obtained through the course of the evaluation, and the reasons for the conclusions derived.

- *Recommendations:* Driven by the referral questions, the recommendations are analogous to a doctor's prescription in that they provide the referral source with definite steps to take to address the referral questions following the evaluation. Recommendations may include referral of the child to a physician for medication evaluation, referral for counseling or psychotherapy, suggested educational classification of the child for special education services, and specific techniques or curricular materials that match the child's cognitive strengths to enhance the child's learning capabilities. Braden and Kratochwill (1997) describe the process that drives school psychologists' recommendations, in which psychologists develop a profile of the child's strengths (or aptitudes) and weaknesses inferred from the pattern of test results. The psychologist then recommends interventions that are matched to the child's strengths, under the assumption that cognitive aptitudes interact with treatments to affect learning ability (aptitude-treatment interactions, or ATIs). This approach has been criticized on the grounds that there is little research to substantiate a connection between a child's scores on a test battery and learning efficacy. Braden and Kratochwill note that there is truth to the assertion that test publishers do not provide evidence directly linking test scores to educational interventions, although the connection is implied. Cronbach and Snow (1977) explain that aptitudes and instructional treatments interact in complex ways and are influenced by task and situation variables. Future studies on ATIs are eagerly awaited by school psychologists, as is research that describes empirically validated interventions for children with brain injuries and learning disorders (see Section V of this volume).

School neuropsychological recommendations may be grouped into separate categories for ease of understanding. Recommendations may involve changes at the level of (1) the environment, such as the teacher or the classroom; (2) the individual child; and (3) the parents. Environmental changes occur when aspects of the child's external environment, curriculum, or academic requirements are modified to facilitate the child's learning ability. Examples of different types of environmental modifications include the following:

- Preview and preteach material (*teacher* modification).
- Provide an outline of the textbook, allowing the student to take notes on the outline while peers are reading (*textbook* modification).
- Allow extended time to complete homework or in-class tests (*curricular* modification).

Individual child modifications occur when a change is desired in some aspect of the child's cognition, academic ability, or behavior, which is then addressed through the intervention. Examples include:

- Use of a personal digital assistant with keyboard or AlphaSmart (a device that allows the student to enter text from a keyboard, then send it to a computer or printer) to take notes (modification utilizing *assistive technology*, targeted to deficit in cognitive abilities such as visual-motor speed or problems with fine motor coordination or attentional ability).
- Having the child view a tape of himself or herself attending to the teacher and completing classwork (intervention using the self-as-a-model technique to improve the child's attention and task completion).
- Referral for medication evaluation by a physician (intervention targeted toward improving the child's cognition through biobehavioral means).

Intervention at the parental level requires collaboration with the parents, the most influential persons in the child's life, to change the parents' behavior to help the child improve his or her performance at school. This might involve:

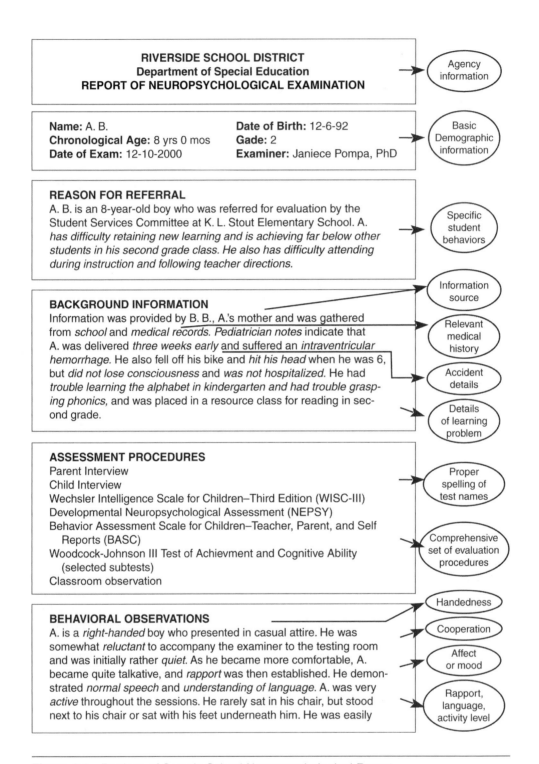

**Figure 9.1** Portions of Sample School Neuropsychological Report

- Recommending books for the parents to read regarding their child's cognitive, academic, or behavioral difficulties (intervention that may be directed toward modifying parental attitudes or behavior toward the child, communication styles, or discipline in the home).
- Suggesting that the parents read to the child for 20 minutes a day, periodically asking the child questions about the story (intervention aimed at improving the child's reading comprehension through auditory means).

An example of a school neuropsychological report that follows the format described is presented in Figure 9.1.

## CONCLUSION

The school is a gold mine of information on the functioning of the learner. The school psychologist is in a unique position to obtain that information, having ready access to teachers, school records, and the child himself or herself. The psychologist's interviews of parents, school personnel, and the child lay the groundwork for the neuropsychological evaluation, and the school neuropsychological report, like a road map, provides directions for educators, parents, and the child to help improve the child's school performance. Accordingly, the overall report, especially the summary, conclusions, and recommendations, should clearly describe interview, background information, and test results, the logic used to derive conclusions about the child, and the steps that should be taken following the evaluation to help improve the child's academic performance, emotional condition, and/or behavior. An example of the school neuropsychological report is presented, but clinicians need to determine the format that is most appropriate to use in their practice setting. Through the implementation of the neuropsychological evaluation process and the writing of a readable and practical report, the school psychologist can make a meaningful difference in a child's school performance, growth, and development to ensure that "no child [will be] left behind."

## REFERENCES

American Psychological Association. (2003). *Ethical principles of psychologists and code of conduct.* Retrieved December 13, 2003, from www.apa.org/ethics.

Armengol, C., Kaplan, E., & Moes, E. (Eds.). (2001). *The consumer-oriented neuropsychological report.* Lutz, FL: Psychological Assessment Resources.

Barkley, R. A. (1998). *Attention-deficit hyperactivity disorder: A handbook for diagnosis and treatment* (2nd ed.). New York: Guilford Press.

Baron, I. S. (2004). *Neuropsychological evaluation of the child.* New York: Oxford University Press.

Braden, J. P., & Kratochwill, T. R. (1997). Treatment utility of assessment: Myths and realities. *School Psychology Review, 26,* 475–485.

Bradley-Johnson, S., & Johnson, C. M. (1998). *A handbook for writing effective psychoeducational reports.* Austin, TX: ProEd.

Brems, C. (2002). *A comprehensive guide to child psychotherapy* (2nd ed.). Boston: Allyn & Bacon.

Cronbach, L., & Snow, R. (1977). *Aptitudes and instructional methods: A handbook of research on interactions.* New York: Irvington Press.

District #186 eligibility requirements; Springfield, Il. (n.d.). Retrieved January 14, 2003, from http://www.springfield.k12.il.us/schools/ses/ld.html.

Donders, J. (2001). A survey of report writing by neuropsychologists: General characteristics and content. *Clinical Neuropsychologist, 15*(2), 137–149.

Drake, E. A., & Bardon, J. I. (1978). Confidentiality and inter-agency communication: Effect of the Buckley Amendment. *Hospital and Community Psychiatry, 29*, 312–315.

Echemendia, R. J., Congett, S. M., Harris, J. G., Diaz, M. L., & Puente, A. D. (1998). Neuropsychology training and practices with Hispanics. *Clinical Neuropsychologist, 11*, 229–243.

Franzen, M. D., & Berg, R. A. (1998). *Screening children for brain impairment.* New York: Springer.

Friedes, D. (1993). Proposed standard of professional practice: Neuropsychological reports display all quantitative data. *Clinical Neuropsychologist, 7*, 234–235.

Friedes, D. (1995). Interpretations are more benign than data? *Clinical Neuropsychologist, 9*, 248.

Greenberg, G. D. (1990). *Child neuropsychological history.* Worthington, OH: International Diagnostic Systems.

Guare, R., & Dawson, M. (2001). Neuropsychological assessment in the schools. In C. Armengol, E. Kaplan, & E. Moes (Eds.), *The consumer-oriented neuropsychological report* (pp. 191–201). Lutz, FL: Psychological Assessment Resources.

Hagborg, W., & Aiello-Coultier, M. (1994). Teachers' perceptions of psychologists' reports of assessments. *Perceptual and Motor Skills, 78*, 171–176.

Levine, M. D. (1996). *Manual for the ANSER system.* Cambridge, MA: Educators Publishing Service.

Maloney, M. P., & Ward, M. P. (1976). *Psychological assessment: A conceptual approach.* New York: Oxford University Press.

Matarazzo, R. G. (1995). Psychological report standards in neuropsychology. *Clinical Neuropsychologist, 9*, 249–250.

Melendez, F. (1978). *Child Neuropsychological Questionnaire.* Odessa, FL: Psychological Assessment Resources.

Mendoza, J. (2001). Reporting the results of the neuropsychological evaluation. In C. Armengol, E. Kaplan, & E. Moes (Eds.), *The consumer-oriented neuropsychological report* (pp. 95–113). Lutz, FL: Psychological Assessment Resources.

Mitrushina, M. N., Boone, K. B., & D'Elia, L. F. (1999). *Handbook of normative data for neuropsychological assessment.* New York: Oxford University Press.

Naugle, R. I., & McSweeny, A. J. (1995). On the practice of routinely appending raw data to reports. *Clinical Neuropsychologist, 9*, 245–247.

Ownby, R. L. (1997). *Psychological reports: A guide to report writing in professional psychology* (3rd ed.). New York: Wiley.

Ownby, R. L., & Wallbrown, F. (1986). Improving report writing in school psychology. In T. Kratochwill (Ed.), *Advances in school psychology: Vol. V.* Hillsdale, NJ: Erlbaum.

Puente, A., Sol Mora, M., & Munoz-Cespedes, J. M. (1997). Neuropsychological assessment of Spanish-speaking children and youth. In C. Reynolds & E. Fletcher-Janzen (Eds.), *Handbook of clinical child neuropsychology: Critical issues in neuropsychology* (2nd ed., pp. 371–383). New York: Plenum Press.

Rucker, C. N. (1967). Report writing in school psychology: A critical investigation. *Journal of School Psychology, 5*, 101–108.

Salvagno, M., & Teglasi, H. (1987). Teacher perceptions of different types of information in psychological reports. *Journal of School Psychology, 25*, 415–424.

Sattler, J. (1988). *Assessment of children* (3rd ed.). San Diego, CA: Jerome M. Sattler.

Semrud-Clikeman, M. (1995). *Child and adolescent therapy.* Needham Heights, MA: Allyn & Bacon.

Spreen, O., & Strauss, E. (1998). *A compendium of neuropsychological tests: Administration, norms and commentary.* New York: Oxford Press.

Stedman, T. L. (2000). *Stedman's medical dictionary.* Baltimore: Lippincott, Williams, & Wilkins.

Tallent, N. (1993). *Psychological report writing* (4th ed.). Englewood Cliffs, NJ: Prentice-Hall.

Teeter, P. A., & Semrud-Clikeman, M. (1997). *Child neuropsychology: Assessment and interventions for neurodevelopmental disorders.* Needham Heights, MA: Allyn & Bacon.

CHAPTER 10

# Evaluating and Using Long-Standing School Neuropsychological Batteries: The Halstead-Reitan and the Luria-Nebraska Neuropsychological Batteries

ANDREW S. DAVIS, JUDY A. JOHNSON, and RIK CARL D'AMATO

A NEUROPSYCHOLOGICAL APPROACH TO assessment can be viewed as a comprehensive ecological approach to link a child's behavior with underlying brain processes. In fact, neuropsychology synthesizes all areas of a child's life, including biochemical factors, behavioral functioning, communication skills, educational styles, hemispheric processing, community resources, and family functioning (Batchelor, Gray, & Dean, 1990; Lezak, 1995; Sattler & D'Amato, 2002). If the origin of all observable behavior is an interconnected series of brain activity, then it is practical for researchers and practitioners alike to assess behavior by analyzing the integrity of brain functions and functional systems through the filter of the child's environment. A neuropsychological approach to assessment allows psychologists to reach beyond the traditional reductionist approach of narrowing cognitive functioning to a simple number that is not representative of the array of cognitive skills that are necessary for academic and social success (Rothlisberg, D'Amato, & Palencia, 2003). Neuropsychological assessments in the schools differ from psychoeducational assessments in that *all* functional domains are evaluated (D'Amato, Rothlisberg, & Leu Work, 1999). Domains are areas of functioning that can affect a child's life, including, but not limited to, social, emotional, and academic functioning as viewed from a brain-behavior perspective. Some of the domains that are assessed in a typical neuropsychological examination include fine and gross motor skills, memory, attention and concentration, personality, social-emotional functioning, visual-spatial skills, sensory skills, communication and language, academic achievement, and intelligence and cognition (Rothlisberg et al., 2003).

The use of *fixed* batteries (a set of consistent tests given to every child regardless of the referral question) in evaluating children is not the domain of neuropsychologists alone. It is common for school psychologists to employ a fixed battery approach to assessment in the schools. A typical assessment for a child who is being evaluated for problems in school may include a cognitive or intellectual assessment, a test of academic achievement, a behavioral rating scale for emotional and acting-out problems, an interview with the teacher, an interview with the parent and child, collection of work samples, and a test of visual-motor integration. The fixed battery approach consists of administering the same set of tests to every patient or examinee (D'Amato et al., 1999). An alternative method is the *flexible* battery approach, in which the psychologist administers a variety of tests based on the examinee's signs and symptoms. Typically, the flexible battery approach creates a constantly changing set of tests, which denotes that there is not a chance to evaluate or validate the group of tests holistically (Horton, 1997). A strength of the flexible battery approach is the opportunity to tailor the assessment more carefully to the referral question, allowing a more intense investigation of the examinee's difficulty within the allotted time period (Reynolds & Fletcher-Janzen, 1997; Reynolds & French, 2003). A drawback with using the flexible battery approach is the recursive, self-validating nature of the approach. Psychologists may choose to administer a series of instruments based on a description of the patient's difficulties. Therefore, using only instruments that are designed to elucidate the patient's complaints are *unlikely* to reveal unrelated areas of impairment, which may be the underlying cause of the referral question. The fixed battery approach, which historically has been employed by neuropsychologists in the Western hemisphere, theoretically allows each child to receive a comprehensive, thorough evaluation regardless of the referral question (Reitan & Wolfson, 1993). An area of impairment may be uncovered that is unrelated to the referral question, or an underlying processing problem may be disclosed that is at the root of the referral question. In addition, the fixed battery approach allows for research and validation of an established set of tests (Reitan & Wolfson, 1993). The obvious disadvantage of the fixed battery approach is that the examiner and examinee's time may be wasted when nonessential areas of the brain are assessed. Horton (1997) has cautioned that the neuropsychologist's imagination can be stifled, and the fixed battery approach may curtail investigation of some needed areas. Despite these difficulties, the fixed battery approach has been the traditional and most popular route that school psychologists and school neuropsychologists have employed since the second half of the twentieth century.

There have been a large number of tests that purport to test neuropsychological features; however, two tests emerged during the past 50 years as the popular choice of neuropsychologists. These are the Halstead-Reitan Neuropsychological Test Battery (HRNB; Reitan & Wolfson, 1993) and the Luria-Nebraska Neuropsychological Test Battery (LNNB; Golden, Purisch, & Hammeke, 1985). Both tests have seen several different versions, and various child and adolescent tests have been created from these batteries. The two measures differ widely in theory, structure, and content, yet historically they have been the two most widely used measures of neuropsychological functioning (Guilmette & Faust, 1991). A survey of neuropsychologists from across the United States reported that between the two measures, 51% preferred the HRNB, 23% preferred the LNNB, and 26% expressed little preference (Guilmette & Faust, 1991). Furthermore, the same survey indicated that the primary reasons practitioners preferred the HRNB were what they believed to be the superior *norms* and the more extensive *research* base. The LNNB was preferred mainly due to the *ease* of administration, including a shorter administration time and more *portability.* Guilmette and Faust matched other historical surveys, which revealed that the HRNB, or selected subtests from the battery, were among the most widely used neuropsychological test instruments (i.e., Camara, Nathan, & Puente, 2000; Retzlaff, Butler, & Vanderploeg, 1992; Seretny, Dean, Gray, & Hartlage, 1986). Indeed, in reviewing the HRNB in the *Ninth Mental Measurements Yearbook,* Dean (1985) wrote:

> Neuropsychological assessment in North America has focused on the development of test batteries that would predict the presence of brain damage while offering a comprehensive view of a patient's individual functions. Numerous batteries have been offered as wide-band measures of the integrity and functioning of the brain. However, the HRNB remains the most researched and widely used measure. (p. 644)

Although it is clear that the HRNB remains the more popular of the two standardized batteries, the LNNB remains widely used, and for that reason these two standardized batteries are reviewed in this chapter.

## THE HALSTEAD-REITAN NEUROPSYCHOLOGICAL TEST BATTERY

This section describes the history of the Halsead-Reitan Neuropsychological Test Battery.

### HISTORY OF THE HALSTEAD-REITAN NEUROPSYCHOLOGICAL TEST BATTERY

Halstead (1947) laid the foundation for the Halstead-Reitan Neuropsychological Test Battery when he noted that current theories of intelligence failed to account for the organic basis of intelligence, and he wrote that there was a need to measure and identify intelligence in relation to brain functions. His clinical observations led him to develop a biologically based theory of intelligence that included four factors: (1) central integrative field, (2) abstraction, (3) power, and (4) direction. Although his four-factor model of intelligence has not been widely replicated, his theories and test instruments became the basis of the HRNB, as well as part of the model of brain-behavior relations that is most commonly used to implement and interpret the HRNB (Reitan & Wolfson, 1993). Halstead noted that individuals with cerebral lesions had myriad deficits, including motor problems, sensory perceptual problems on one or the other side of the body, and general or specific confusion about events and activities. He did not believe that a single test was capable of measuring and assessing this wide range of deficits (Halstead, 1947; Reitan & Wolfson, 1993). Halstead addressed this problem by creating a series of 10 tests that were based on his biological theory of intelligence. To do this, he experimented with psychological testing procedures that differed from traditional evaluations in that he required his participants not only to solve problems, but also to observe the nature of the problem, analyze the problem, and then define the problem (Reitan & Wolfson, 1993). His testing procedures and the tests themselves were offered to the psychological community in his 1947 text, *Brain and Intelligence: A Quantitative Study of the Frontal Lobes.* Seven of Halstead's tests have stood the test of time and now form the core of the HRNB.

Reitan, a doctoral student of Halstead's, started experimenting with Halstead's (1947) tests of neuropsychological functioning in the 1950s. Reitan (1955) was able to differentiate patients with and without brain injury at a then astonishing rate using only 7 of the 10 tests. Reitan and Wolfson (1992) have noted that Reitan's results were being produced at a time when studies had shown minimal differences between patients with and without brain injury, and Hebb (1939, 1941) had reported cases of people with IQs in the superior range despite having had as much as one-third of their cerebral hemisphere removed through surgery. The differences exhibited on Halstead's tests, in light of the inability of IQ tests to detect cerebral damage, indicated the clinical utility of a different and more comprehensive approach to assessment for detecting cerebral impairment. More recently, studies have indicated that traditional IQ tests are still not sufficient to encapsulate the wide range of cognitive functions exhibited by the brain, with only about a 10% overlap between traditional IQ measures and measures of neuropsychological functioning (D'Amato, Dean, & Rhodes, 1998; D'Amato, Gray, & Dean, 1988; Sattler & D'Amato, 2002). In the following years, Reitan removed the three Halstead tests that were not statistically differentiating between patients with and without brain injuries and added measures to the battery (i.e., Trail Making A, Trail Making B, Sensory Perceptual examination, and the Reitan-Indiana Aphasia Screening Test) that constitute the current battery and provide an in-depth assessment of a broad spectrum of neuropsychological functions. In addition to Halstead's tests and the other tests described in *The Halstead-Reitan Neuropsychological Test Battery: Theory and Clinical Interpretation,* second edition (Reitan & Wolfson, 1993), the current HRNB typically includes the age-appropriate Wechsler intelligence scale (i.e., Wechsler, 1997, 2003) and a comprehensive measure of personality (e.g., the Behavioral Assessment System 2 and/or the Minnesota Multiphasic Personality Inventory, second edition [MMPI-2]) with older examinees. These additional tests are not described in this chapter; for more information, the reader is directed to other texts (D'Amato et al., 1999; D'Amato, Rothlisberg, & Rhodes, 1997; Graham, 2000; Sattler, 2002). However, it is important to note that assessment of behavior, personality, and affect is a crucial component of any neuropsychological evaluation.

The HRNB has been adapted for use with *children* and *adolescents* into two different batteries, the Halstead-Reitan Neuropsychological Test Battery for Older Children (HRNB-C; Reitan & Davison, 1974) and the Reitan-Indiana Test Battery for Children (RITB-C; Reitan, 1969). The HRNB-C is designed for examinees age 9 to 14 years, and the RITB-C is designed for examinees age 5 to 8 years. Both children's versions are based on the subtests from the HRNB, but with different instructions, and in some cases, different subtests have been added or subtracted. This section of this chapter describes the two children's revisions of the HRNB as well as the subtests of the HRNB, which can be used for older adolescents. Table 10.1 presents the various subtests for each version of the HRNB.

**Table 10.1**

Subtests of the Three Versions of the Halstead-Reitan Neuropsychological Test Batteries

| HRNB | HRNB-C | RITB-C |
|---|---|---|
| Reitan-Indiana Aphasia Screening Test | Reitan-Indiana Aphasia Screening Test | Reitan-Indiana Aphasia Screening Test |
| Finger Tapping Test | Finger Tapping Test | Finger Tapping Test |
| Grip Strength | Grip Strength | Grip Strength |
| Sensory-Perceptual Examination | Sensory-Perceptual Examination | Sensory-Perceptual Examination |
| Tactile Form Recognition Test | Tactile Form Recognition Test | Marching Test |
| Rhythm Test | Rhythm Test | Color Form Test |
| Speech-Sounds Perception Test | Speech-Sounds Perception Test | Progressive Figure Test |
| Trail Making Test for Adults | Trail Making Test | Individual Performance Test |
| Tactual Performance Test | Tactual Performance Test | Tactual Performance Test |
| Category Test | Category Test | Category Test |
| | | Target Test |

USER QUALIFICATIONS FOR ADMINISTERING THE HALSTEAD-REITAN
NEUROPSYCHOLOGICAL TEST BATTERY FOR CHILDREN AND THE
REITAN-INDIANA TEST BATTERY FOR CHILDREN

Most test instruments that school psychologists are familiar with have a section in the test manual labeled "User Qualifications." For example, in the manual for the Wechsler Intelligence Scale for Children, third edition (WISC-III; Wechsler, 1991), there is a three-paragraph section on page 10 that clearly explains who should be using the test, what training is required prior to administration and interpretation, and steps for safeguarding the testing materials. The HRNB-C and RITB-C do not have a section that discusses this issue or the issue of a school psychologist's using neuropsychological tests. Two comprehensive books written by Reitan and Wolfson (1992, 1993) discuss the rationale and theory behind the tests, describe the tests, provide instructions for administration and scoring, give interpretive guidelines, provide general information on neuropsychological disorders, and report case studies. Because these texts take the place of test manuals, it is recommended that the reader purchase one of these if he or she plans to complete training using one of these tests. However, the issue of who should be using the HRNB-C was not addressed. Ethically, it should be clear that only psychologists trained in neuropsychological test administration and interpretation and child development and evaluation should purchase or use these instruments (see Chapter 1).

At minimum, the examiner should have graduate training in neuropsychological test administration, scoring, and interpretation. Some authors have suggested that the examiner have graduate training *and* postgraduate training in neuropsychology (Reitan & Wolfson, 1992). In some cases, it may be necessary for school psychologists to seek additional training at a local university. Cecil Reynolds, one of the most widely published authors in the fields of school psychology and special education and a prominent school neuropsychologist, explained: "The question should not be, is this a neuropsychological test, or a psychological test, but rather, am I qualified to make the interpretations that can be drawn from this test, and will my interpretations be supported by the scientific literature" (Davis, 2003, p. 27).

Caution should be used when interpreting *any* scores and generating recommendations or interventions. So, too, drawing neuropsychological conclusions about areas of brain impairment, difficulty with brain dysfunction, and functional cerebral systems should be limited to school neuropsychologists (i.e., those with specialized training and supervised experience in clinical applications of neuropsychology in the schools). If a school psychologist is uncomfortable or unfamiliar with typical neuropsychological procedures, knowledge about the batteries is still of great value. In many cases, school psychologists will be presented with neuropsychological assessments that were conducted outside of the schools, and the information contained in the neuropsychological evaluation must be implemented into an examinee's individualized education program (IEP). If the school psychologist is familiar with the more commonly used neuropsychological batteries, transferring recommendations drawn from these batteries into an IEP will be greatly facilitated (Davis & Warnygora, 2002).

Subtests from the Halstead-Reitan Neuropsychological Test Battery, the Reitan-Indiana Neuropsychological Test Battery for Children, and the Halstead-Reitan Neuropsychological Test Battery for Older Children

This section describes the subtests of the three Halstead-Reitan Neuropsychological Test Batteries.

*Reitan-Kløve Lateral Dominance Examination*    This examination can be given prior to the administration of the HRNB, RITB-C, or HRNB-C. The Reitan-Kløve Lateral Dominance Examination examines a child's preference for using his or her left or right hand. Determining a child's dominant hand is an important component of a neuropsychological battery, because many subtests require examinees to use their dominant hand first for a task (Dean & Woodcock, 2003). The child is asked to mime performing somewhat familiar tasks such as throwing a ball, hammering a nail, or using an eraser. Reitan and Wolfson (1992) have recommended that regardless of which hand the child uses to perform these tasks, the hand with which the child writes his or her name should be the hand regarded as the dominant hand for performance on the battery. Nevertheless, differences should be noted when interpreting the examinee's scores.

*Reitan-Indiana Aphasia Screening Test*    This subtest is a modification of the Halstead-Wepman Aphasia Screening Test (Halstead & Wepman, 1949). The examinee is required to name objects, understand spoken language, identify body parts, copy simple geometric shapes, identify numbers and letters, produce spoken language, use simple mathematical skills, and discriminate between left and right. As the name implies, these activities constitute a screening task and are used to elicit responses that are indicative of pathognomic signs of brain impairment or indications that can greatly facilitate a diagnosis. Failure or excessive difficulty on any of the tasks of the Reitan-Indiana Aphasia Screening Test is used to begin identification of dyscalculia, expressive aphasia, receptive aphasia, auditory dysgnosia, visual dysgnosia, dysnomia, and spelling and construction dyspraxia. With children, especially those suspected of academic impairment, special care must be taken to ensure that these examinees possess the preacademic and academic skills necessary to complete these tasks (Reitan & Wolfson, 1992, 2001).

Different approaches to scoring of the Reitan-Indiana Aphasia Screening Test have been offered. Some examiners prefer to score each item as either passed or failed, and then total the number of errors. Another approach is to look at each task independently and gauge failures as a suspected deficit in the domain being tested. For example, difficulty in copying geometric shapes may be indicative of constructional dyspraxia (Reitan & Wolfson, 1993). This approach can lead to a high number of false positives, which is why it is important to remember to use these tasks as a screening device that may suggest the existence of a possible problem. This subtest differs between the RITB-C and the HRNB-C in that there are fewer and less difficult items.

*Finger Tapping Test (Finger Oscillation Test)*    The Finger Tapping Test (FTT), one of Halstead's original tests, is a measure of fine motor speed and coordination as measured by the speed with which an examinee can depress a small lever. An electronic finger tapper is available for use with small children. Unlike some other measures of fine motor skills, this task does not involve pencil and paper or require any objects other than the tapping key to be manipulated. Sometimes this task is referred to as the Finger Oscillation Test (FOT). The FTT is often thought to be one of the tests on the battery that is most sensitive to determining fine motor problems, brain impairment, and laterality of brain lesions (Reitan & Wolfson, 1996; Russell, Neuringer, & Goldstein, 1970). Examinees are first required to use their dominant hand to tap the lever as rapidly as possible for five trials of 10 seconds each. This process is then repeated with the nondominant hand. Fatigue is avoided by giving rest periods between the trials as needed. The examinee's performance is based on the average score of the five trials for the dominant hand and the average score of the five trials for the nondominant hand. Decreased performance in one hand generally indicates a contralateral hemispheric weakness.

*Grip Strength Test*   The Grip Strength Test measures upper extremity gross motor skills. Examinees are required to stand and hold their arms at their sides while gripping a hand dynamometer. Examinees are then instructed to squeeze the dynamometer as hard as they can. The hand dynamometer can be adjusted to fit different hand sizes and thus can be used for children, adolescents, and adults. Alternating trials are used for the dominant and nondominant hand. Similar to the FTT, the Grip Strength Test is sensitive to lateralized impairment in the hemisphere contralateral to a weakness observed in either hand. Grip strength is thought to be sensitive to impairment or lesions in the motor strip and has been found to be sensitive to examinees with a traumatic brain injury (TBI) as well as sensorimotor difficulties and degenerative diseases with motor components (Haaland, Temkin, Randahl, & Dikmen, 1994).

*Sensory Perceptual Examination*   The Sensory Perceptual Examination (SPE) is composed of several different tasks that are used to assess the integrity of the examinee's auditory, tactile, and visual sensory abilities. The SPE consists of a tactile finger localization task, auditory perception task, visual perception task, and the identification of how accurately examinees can perceive unilateral and bilateral sensory stimulation. Examinees are required to identify shapes without visual stimuli, identify the location of unilateral and bilateral sensory stimulation, and demonstrate their visual and auditory acuity. The auditory, kinesthetic, and visual sensory modalities are tested independently of one another (Lezak, 1995). In fact, to evaluate an examinee's sensory abilities, this subtest is useful for contributing to a determination of laterality of impairment. Indeed, examinees with lateralized lesions, or traumatic disruptions of brain tissue, can often identify stimulation when it is limited to one side of the body but may fail to recognize stimulation that occurs simultaneously on both sides of the body (Reitan & Wolfson, 1992). The presentation of some tasks has been simplified for use on the RITB-C.

*Rhythm Test*   The Rhythm Test is used only on the HRNB and the HRNB-C. Most often referred to as the Seashore Rhythm Test, this task requires the child to listen to pairs of rhythmic beats and determine if the beats are the same or different. The child is presented with 30 trials. Many neuropsychologists initially assumed that this test served as a measure of right hemispheric functioning, as nonverbal rhythmic tasks are typically thought to be subsumed within the right hemisphere (Dean & Anderson, 1997). Yet research has demonstrated that groups with left or right hemispheric damage are equally impaired on this measure (Reitan & Wolfson, 1992). Certainly, this task serves as a measure of nonverbal auditory discrimination, auditory perception, and auditory attention (Lezak, 1995; Selz, 1981). The child's score is the number of correctly identified items.

*Speech-Sounds Perception Test* The Speech-Sounds Perception Test is used only on the HRNB and the HRNB-C. The child is required to listen to 60 spoken nonsense words, all of which have the "ee" sound. After hearing a nonsense word, the examinee is required to select one of three options, one of which was the spoken word, while the other two are distracters. Research has indicated that individuals with left hemispheric impairment tend to perform poorly on this task due to the verbal comprehension component (Reitan & Wolfson, 1990). This subtest assesses auditory-visual integration, auditory attention, and concentration (Lezak, 1995; D'Amato, 1990). It is useful to contrast this subtest with the Rhythm Test, which measures nonverbal perception. Both this subtest and the Rhythm Test are presented on an audiotape, which many psychologists may find to be low tech, based on the quality of the recording. However, given the normative procedures, these tapes are required. This test, considered in concert with the Rhythm Test, has proven to be extremely helpful in psychoeducational diagnosis.

*Trail Making Test* This subtest appears only on the HRNB and the HRNB-C. It is composed of two tasks, Trail Making A and Trail Making B. Trail Making A requires the child to use a pencil to connect 15 circles, each of which contains a number from 1 to 15, in a sequential manner. Trail Making B has the same number of circles, but 8 circles are numbered from 1 to 8 and the other 7 circles are filled with letters from A to G. The examinee must connect the circles by alternating from numbers to letters in a correct sequential fashion. The score is the number of seconds to complete each task. Although one of the simplest tasks to administer and complete, the Trail Making Test remains one of the best measures of global cerebral functioning due to the symbolic recognition, which is a left hemispheric task, while the visual scanning component is more of a right hemispheric function (Reitan & Wolfson, 1985, 1992). The Trail Making Test is considered a measure of mental flexibility, inhibition, processing speed, visual attention, and visual perception (D'Amato, 1990; Dean, 1985). Although not part of the HRNB, a more current version of Trailmaking normed for ages 8 to 74 years that includes 5 trails that emphasize frontal functions more heavily has recently been introduced (see Comprehensive Trailmaking Test, Reynolds, 2003).

*Marching Test* The Marching Test appears only on the RITB-C. It is a test of gross motor coordination as measured by the examinee's ability to use a crayon to connect a series of circles in a specified order as rapidly as possible (Sattler & D'Amato, 2002). Alternating trials are conducted with the dominant and nondominant hand. Ability is measured by the total time and number of errors for each hand. The examinee is also required to imitate finger and arm movements of the examiner, using fingers to link the circles. A score is obtained by the total number of circles that are connected before the task is complete. The Marching Test derives its name from the examiner's instructions that examinees should "march" up the page with their crayon and their hands.

*Color Form Test*   The Color Form Test is limited to use on the RITB-C. On this subtest, examinees are presented with a series of shapes of varying colors. To complete this task, examinees are required to draw imaginary lines to connect figures having the same shape, and then the same color, continuing on until the task is complete. This subtest is an indicator of an examinee's mental flexibility, abstraction, inhibition, and sustained attention (Sattler & D'Amato, 2002). The examinee's ability is measured by the time in seconds for completion and the number of errors.

*Progressive Figures Test*   This subtest appears only on the RITB-C. It is similar to the Color Form Test in that they are both measures of attention, inhibition, mental flexibility, and abstraction. However, the Progressive Figures Test requires the examinee to use a pencil to connect a series of shapes; hence, it can also be considered a measure of abstraction, fine motor control, and speed (Sattler & D'Amato, 2002). This task consists of a printed page with a series of large figures. Inside each figure is a smaller figure. The examinee must draw from one large figure to the next, using the small figure inside as a guide for where to draw the next line. The examinee's score is the time required for the completion of the task.

*Individual Performance Test*   The Individual Performance Test is a series of four subtests that broadly measure visual perception and visual-motor ability (Sattler & D'Amato, 2002). This test is used only on the RITB-C. The first task, the Matching Figures Test, requires the examinee to match blocks with complex figures on them to cards with the identical picture. The examiner notes the time required to complete the task and the number of errors. The second task is the Star Test, for which the examinee copies a star that consists of two overlapping triangles. The score is the time in seconds required to complete the drawing, as well as an accuracy score. The next task is the Matching V's Test, which requires the examinee to match blocks with angles of varying degrees printed on them to picture cards that have the same figures. The examiner scores the number of errors and the time the examinee takes to complete the task. The last task is the Concentric Squares Test, which involves the examinee copying a series of three squares. Like previous tests, the examinee's abilities are measured by the time taken to complete the drawing, as well as an accuracy score.

*Tactual Performance Test*   The Tactual Performance Test (TPT) is one of the more complex tasks on the HRNB. The examinee is blindfolded before the test begins and seated in a chair. On a table in front of the examinee is a formboard into which a series of geometric shapes (cross, circle, square, etc.) can be placed. Different layouts of the formboard are used for the HRNB, RITB-C, and HRNB-C. Participants are first required to place the blocks in the formboard using only their dominant hand. After that task has been completed, examinees then use their nondominant hand to complete the task. The next step is to have the examinee complete the task a third time, this time using both hands. After the examinee has completed these three tasks, the formboard is placed out of sight and the blindfold is removed. The examinee is then asked to draw the formboard from memory. The TPT allows the clinician to compare the left and right hemispheres and estimate the general efficiency of the brain (Reitan & Wolfson, 1992, 2001). This task measures tactual discrimination, nonvisual spatial awareness, tactile awareness, motor skills, nonvisual figural memory, ability to learn, and commitment (Charter, 2000; D'Amato, 1990; Dean, 1985; Jarvis & Barth, 1994; Selz, 1981). Three *groups* of scores are obtained from this subtest: (1a) time taken for performance on the dominant hand, (1b) time taken for performance on the nondominant hand, and (1c) the total performance time; (2) a memory score for the number of correct shapes reproduced by the examinee; and (3) a localization score that assesses the accuracy of the location of the reproduced shapes.

*Category Test*   The Category Test is perhaps the most unique measure in the entire battery. It requires a very large projection box that is not portable. A computerized version of the Category Test exists, as well as a book version, for those looking for more portability, although these versions are typically said to have less available validity and reliability information. In this chapter, only the original HRNB version of the Category Test is discussed. For this task, the examinee sits in front of a 10-by-8-inch screen on which a series of figures are projected. The RITB-C uses 80 figures, and the HRNB-C uses 168 figures. The examinee must press down on one of four levers that correspond to the correct answer. Correct answers are rewarded with a pleasant-sounding bell, and incorrect answers are punished with an unpleasant buzzer. The examinee is presented with five trials on the RITB-C and six trials on the HRNB-C. Correct answers are abstractions drawn from color, shape, size, figure, and memory clues. The score is the total number of errors for all five trials. The Category Test is considered a classic measure of executive functioning. It measures concept formation, abstractions, memory, reasoning, new learning, and hypothesis testing (Lezak, 1995; Gontkovsky & Shouheaver, 2002; Reitan & Wolfson, 1992, 2001; Selz, 1981). This test is one of the only measures in the field that provides clear, but sometimes distressing, feedback. The Category Test differs from most other measures of hypothesis testing in that it allows the examinee to formulate and test hypotheses, receive positive or negative feedback regarding those hypotheses, and modify the hypotheses based on the immediate feedback (Reitan & Wolfson, 1992).

*Target Test*   The Target Test is used only on the RITB-C. On this task, the examinee is presented with a stimulus card that contains nine dots, which are divided into three rows and three columns. The examiner points out a design by connecting dots with a pointer on the stimulus card, and the examinee is required to use a red pencil to draw the design on a piece of paper containing the same dots. The Target Test measures an examinee's visual-spatial memory for figures (Nussbaum & Bigler, 1989). The score for this subtest is the number of correctly drawn items.

VALIDATION OF THE HALSTEAD-REITAN NEUROPSYCHOLOGICAL TEST BATTERY, THE REITAN-INDIANA NEUROPSYCHOLOGICAL TEST BATTERY FOR CHILDREN, AND THE HALSTEAD-REITAN NEUROPSYCHOLOGICAL TEST BATTERY FOR OLDER CHILDREN

Although the original purpose of the HRNB was to differentiate between brain-injured and normal individuals, more recently the battery has been used to provide a rich array of behavioral information from which school, home, and community interventions can be developed (D'Amato et al., 1999; Rothlisberg et al., 2003). Indeed, the shift from primarily diagnosis to intervention development and evaluation is one that the neuropsychological field has been forced to pursue as medical technology has become more sophisticated (Walsh, 1987). The manual for the HRNB does not include in-depth reliability and validity information, but focuses on the reason subtests were included in the battery (Dean, 1985). Universal standard scores for the HRNB drawn from a large normative sample are still not available, although there are several groups of independent normative scores available for interpretation. It is difficult to compare the results between individual tests due to the lack of standard score transformation data (Dean, 1985). However, despite these limitations, the HRNB remains one of the most researched and validated neuropsychological tests in the world (Horton, 1997). Many existing studies used subtests from the HRNB or the entire battery to investigate the validity of the battery, but only a few seminal studies are covered in this review. For a more detailed description of related research, see Dean (1985), Golden and Golden (2003), Kennedy, Clement, and Curtiss (2003), Lezak (1995), and Reitan and Wolfson (2001).

The initial study (Reed, Reitan, & Kløve, 1965) that investigated the HRNB-C indicated that children with brain impairment performed poorly on nearly every measure at the .01 level of significance. Another seminal study, conducted by Boll (1974), indicated that the vast majority of measures on the HRNB-C were successful in differentiating between brain-impaired and normal examinees. Early studies of 5- to 8-year-olds found similar results using the subtests of the HRNB (Klonoff, Robinson, & Thompson, 1969; Reitan, 1974). It seems clear that the HRNB is effective in detecting cerebral impairment in children and differentiating between brain-injured and average examinees. This is an important function in any neuropsychological test, as these batteries are sometimes employed in instances in which an examinee has suffered an insult to the brain.

Validation questions regarding the use of the HRNB in clinical practice should focus on assessing the neuropsychological strengths and weaknesses of examinees and how these examinee profiles relate to successful rehabilitation (Rothlisberg et al., 2003). Some of these questions have started to be answered (see Reitan & Wolfson, 2001). Leckliter, Forster, Klonoff, and Knights (1992) have conducted an extensive review of reference group data for the HRNB-C and concluded that caution should be used when interpreting impaired results for some subtests. From this same perspective, Leckliter et al. (1992) indicated that current norms used for the HRNB-C lack sufficient demographic representation. It is the lack of a large representative (normative) sample that school neuropsychologists may find most troubling concerning these various batteries.

Early on, Reitan and Boll (1973) examined children with minimal brain dysfunction and concluded that these examinees exhibited few differences from normal examinees in regard to sensorimotor functioning. However, children with brain dysfunction were significantly more impaired in terms of abstraction, attention, nonverbal intelligence, and verbal abilities. The factor structure of the HRNB-C has been evaluated for children with learning disabilities (LD). With a large sample of 934 children with LD, Chittooran, D'Amato, Lassiter, and Dean (1993) investigated the factor structure of the HRNB-C along with measures of intelligence, achievement, and receptive language. These authors reported that seven factors emerged, which they labeled: (1) Verbal Reasoning, (2) Academic

Achievement, (3) Visual-Perceptual Organization, (4) Developmental, (5) Visual-Motor Speed, (6) Spatial Memory, and (7) Attention and Concentration. Chittooran et al. indicated that factors 4, 5, and 6 were *unique* to the HRNB and noted that developmental, visual-motor speed, and spatial memory are *not fully analyzed* on typical school-related measures of intelligence, achievement, and receptive language. A similar study (D'Amato, Dean, et al., 1998) determined the need to venture beyond traditional IQ measures to understand the neuropsychological constructs of children with learning and emotional difficulties. These findings, as well as previously discussed research, argue for the inclusion of neuropsychological measures when working with the most difficult cases of examinees who fail in a traditional school setting (D'Amato, 1990; D'Amato, Dean, et al., 1998; D'Amato et al., 1999).

## INTERPRETING THE HALSTEAD-REITAN NEUROPSYCHOLOGICAL TEST BATTERY

There are several approaches to interpreting the HRNB, including a cut-off approach (referred to more commonly as the level of performance method), review of right-left differences, consideration of pathonomic signs, and review of some recently expanded indexes (Reitan & Wolfson, 1993). Nonetheless, psychologists accustomed to interpreting other tests that produce standard scores from subtests, as well as composite index scores, may be troubled by some of the nebulous interpretation when using the HRNB. Dean (1985) reported, "The manual for the HRNB lacks the basic psychometric documentation needed in interpretation. Moreover, interpretations are more dependent on the psychologist's knowledge and clinical acumen than reported psychometric properties for the battery" (p. 645). This lack of psychometric sophistication, combined with the lack of an extensive normative sample, limits the utility of all of the Halstead batteries, especially as newer neuropsychological test batteries are emerging that are psychometrically superior. Currently, neuropsychologists are becoming accustomed to tests that provide index scores as well as scores that provide evidence of strengths and weaknesses. Some of the HRNB normative samples use a cut-off approach that determines whether an examinee is impaired in the absence of standard scores. Although the HRNB does not have an overall composite score that reflects an individual's overall performance, the Halstead Impairment Index, which contains the subtests most sensitive to cerebral impairment, provides the psychologist an indicator of overall impairment by looking at the proportion of tests in which the examinee performed in the impaired range. The scores on the Halstead Impairment Index range from 0.0 (no brain impairment) to 1.0 (severe brain impairment).

Reitan and Wolfson (1992) provided a guide for clinical interpretation of the HRNB that involves the use of the Neuropsychological Deficit Scale (NDS). The NDS can be considered an overall gauge of the examinee's neuropsychological functioning that uses cut-off scores as a guide to compare test scores to the scores of learners with brain damage. The NDS leads the psychologist to consider an examinee's performance on the HRNB from a level of performance approach, right-left comparisons, and the consideration of dysphasia and other deficits. Reitan and Wolfson have also recommended that the examinee's NDS scores be compared to scores of examinees with brain damage for the following domains: Motor Functions, Sensory-Perceptual Functions, Attention and Concentration, Immediate Memory and Recapitulation, Visual-Spatial Skills, Abstraction and

Reasoning, and Dysphasia. As a final step, Reitan and Wolfson also recommended that the data obtained from the NDS scores be used as a framework from which to view the results of the other tests used as part of the HRNB, namely, measures of cognitive ability, academic achievement, and personality. For a more in-depth discussion of HRNB interpretation, see Reitan and Wolfson (1993, 2001) or Sattler and D'Amato (2002). To be sure, the HRNB has provided a foundation for the formation and further development of the field of clinical neuropsychology.

## THE LURIA-NEBRASKA NEUROPSYCHOLOGICAL TEST BATTERY AND THE LURIA-NEBRASKA NEUROPSYCHOLOGICAL TEST BATTERY-CHILDREN'S REVISION

A major contributor to the development of neuropsychology was a Russian neuropsychologist named A. R. Luria, whose books continue to be some of the most popular in the field of psychology (Reynolds & French, 2003). Luria (1966, 1980) proposed that human cognitive processing involves three functional units that work together and are needed for any type of mental processing. The *first* unit maintains a state of arousal or focus of attention, which is needed for effective mental activity. The *second* functional unit receives, processes, and retains information that an individual gets from the world and is composed of simultaneous and successive processing. The *third* unit allows an individual to form plans, carry them out, and evaluate whether they were effective.

Luria "designed a rich battery of neuropsychological tests that he used to obtain an essentially qualitative evaluation of an individual's neurological status and integrity" (Reynolds & French, 2003, p. 54). In 1970, an attempt was made to summarize his techniques in *Luria's Neuropsychological Investigation* (Christenson, 1975). Luria's qualitative approach to assessing individual differences differed significantly from the psychometric measures traditionally used at the time (Hynd & Semrud-Clikeman, 1990). To review a listing of many of Luria's informal tasks, see Hynd and Semrud-Clikeman (1990), Gaddes and Edgell (1994), and Chapter 27 of this volume. Golden and his colleagues (1985), like many others, were drawn to Luria's theory (see Chapters 3 and 4), the uniqueness of Luria's assessments, and how these tasks *linked* to neuropsychological rehabilitation. With Luria in mind, Golden developed a test battery that many argue *is* based on Luria's work (Golden et al., 1985).

The Luria-Nebraska Neuropsychological Battery was first published in 1978, and since that time, has received mixed reviews (Golden & Freshwater, 2001). Many of the critics argued that the qualitative approach of Luria could not be fused with a quantitative approach (Chittooran & D'Amato, 1989; Lezak, 1995; Purisch, 2001). The LNNB's goal was to standardize the test procedures of Luria to provide an objective scoring system. The resulting measure, the LNNB, currently has two equivalent forms that are commercially available.

Some research studies have used the LNNB III (Bradley, Teichner, Crum, & Golden, 2000; Devaraju-Backhaus, Espe-Pfeifer, Mahrou, & Golden, 2001; Teichner, Golden, Bradley, & Crum, 1999), but this version is not currently available. Form I of the LNNB has 269 items, and Form II has 279 items; both forms yield similar information (Golden et al., 1985), but Form II can only be computer-scored. This instrument was designed for examinees 15 years old or older, but the instrument has also been used with 13- and 14-year-olds. Primarily, the LNNB is used to diagnose cognitive deficits and detect specific problems and mild impairment that other measures may overlook. The LNNB can usually be administered in between 1½ to 2½ hours.

Almost 10 years after the introduction of the adult version, in 1987, a children's version of the LNNB, the *Luria-Nebraska Neuropsychological Test Battery-Children's Revision* (LNNB-C; Golden, 1987) was published for use with examinees ranging from age 5 to 12 years. Surprisingly, the children's version was originally developed by administering the LNNB to children and deleting items that appeared to be too difficult (Berg, 1999); this has led many to question the developmental appropriateness of this version of the test. Further development of the LNNB-C included gathering data on several different versions of the test, including adaptations and additions to the test content (Berg, 1999). The LNNB-C has 149 items and uses stimulus materials from Form I of the LNNB, three extra cards, and an audiotape. A typical administration of the LNNB-C takes 2½ hours and can be hand- or computer-scored.

### Scales from the Luria-Nebraska Neuropsychological Test Battery

The LNNB's structure is different from that of many typical instruments. Golden and Freshwater (2001) stated, "The LNNB scales are nontraditional because the same procedure or question is not asked repeatedly at different levels of difficulty" (p. 61). Some could advocate that this is like a projective personality test, with the same problems and strengths (e.g., each examinee gets a different measure based on individual differences). Each scale is heterogeneous to provide an evaluation of functional systems rather than unitary skills (Purisch, 2001). The evaluator can then examine the *impaired* items to interpret the examinee's score on the scale. The LNNB yields 11 clinical scales on Form I, and Form II added an Intermediate Memory Scale. In addition, 8 Localization Scales can be derived: (1) Left Frontal, (2) Left Sensorimotor, (3) Left Parietal-Occipital, (4) Left Temporal, (5) Right Frontal, (6) Right Sensorimotor, (7) Right Parietal-Occipital, and (8) Right Temporal. Further, the LNNB yields 5 summary scales, (1) Pathognomonic, (2) Left Hemisphere, (3) Right Hemisphere, (4) Profile Elevation, and (5) Impairment Scales, as well as 28 factor scales, which reflect more specific sensory and cognitive functions.

Descriptions of the clinical scales follow and are depicted in Table 10.2 (Golden et al., 1985).

*Motor (C1)*   The Motor Scale includes items that measure the motor speed of both hands by having the examinee perform both simple tasks (clenching and then extending each hand) and motor-related complex tasks (touching each finger with the thumb of the same hand in sequence). Items also require the examinee to perform, when directed verbally by the examiner, complex motor movements such as using a pair of scissors or threading a needle. Additionally, the scale measures a variety of oral motor movements such as sticking the tongue out of the mouth and rolling the tongue. Further, several items have the examinee draw simple items quickly and accurately. Some of the items are similar to a neurological exam (see Chapter 21).

**Table 10.2**
Subtests of Luria-Nebraska Neuropsychological Test Battery
(LNNB) and the Luria-Nebraska Neuropsychological Test
Battery-Children's Revision (LNNB-C)

| LNNB | LNNB-C |
| --- | --- |
| Motor (C1) | Motor (C1) |
| Rhythm (C2) | Rhythm (C2) |
| Tactile (C3) | Tactile (C3) |
| Visual (C4) | Visual (C4) |
| Receptive Speech (C5) | Receptive Speech (C5) |
| Expressive Speech (C6) | Expressive Speech (C6) |
| Writing (C7) | Writing (C7) |
| Reading (C8) | Reading (C8) |
| Arithmetic (C9) | Arithmetic (C9) |
| Memory (C10) | Memory (C10) |
| Intellectual Processes (C11) | Intellectual Processes (C11) |
| Intermediate Memory (C12) | |

*Rhythm (C2)*   Most of the rhythm items are presented on an audiotape; they evaluate the examinee's ability to listen to rhythmic patterns and musical tones, evaluate the auditory stimuli, and reproduce tones, patterns, and musical sequences. Early items require examinees to determine if patterns are the same or different, and later items ask examinees to sing a song or tap a rhythm they have heard (Golden et al., 1985).

*Tactile (C3)*   This scale measures the examinee's tactile functions (on both the left and right sides of the body) while blindfolded. Items include identifying where the examinee was touched by the examiner, estimation of the intensity of that touch (hard, soft, sharp, dull), which numbers or letters were written on the examinee's wrist, and identification of an object that was placed in the examinee's hand. The examinee is also directed to copy an arm position when directed.

*Visual (C4)*   This scale measures visual and visual-spatial skills and does not require the use of motor skills. Items include identification of objects and pictures, identification of pictures with missing parts, and identification of pictures with overlapping parts. Tasks using spatial skills include identifying directions, completing visual patterns, and solving problems in three dimensions (Golden et al., 1985).

*Receptive Speech (C5)*   The Receptive Speech Scale measures the comprehension of speech, including phonemes, words, and basic and complex sentences. On some items, the examinee is asked to follow multistep directions and answer increasingly complex questions.

*Expressive Speech (C6)*   Repeating sounds, words, series of words, sentences, and retelling a story are included on the Expressive Speech Scale. Other tasks include identifying letter-sound relationships, reading words, describing pictures, orally responding to questions, and giving a short speech. The reading items on this scale measure expressive fluency (Golden et al., 1985).

*Writing (C7)*   The Writing Scale measures both spelling and motor writing (the forming of letters and words using motor skills). Tasks include counting the letters in words, identifying letters in words, copying letters, and writing letters. This scale measures writing words after viewing them for a short time, writing words and phrases from dictation, and writing sentences on a specific topic. The Writing Scale measures spelling and basic writing skills up to a 7th-grade level (Golden et al., 1985).

*Reading (C8)*   The ability to identify letter sounds and to read single letters, words, sentences, and a paragraph are measured by the items of this Reading Scale. The items, which range from basic reading skills up to a 7th-grade level, are scored for accuracy, not expressive fluency skills, which are measured by the Expressive Speech Scale.

*Arithmetic (C9)*   The Arithmetic Scale measures the reading and writing of numbers and simple calculation skills. Items include writing numbers from dictation, identifying numerals, identifying the larger of two numbers, and solving simple addition, subtraction, and multiplication problems. Examinees are also asked to count down by subtracting a specific number each time. As with the other academic scales, the Arithmetic Scale measures basic skills up to a 7th-grade level (Golden et al., 1985).

*Memory (C10)*   Verbal and nonverbal memory are assessed on the Memory Scale, which includes items with and without interference. Repeating words in a series, utilizing picture memory with and without delays, using rhythmic and tactile-visual memory and verbal-visual memory are assessed on this scale.

*Intellectual Processes (C11)*   The Intellectual Processes Scale includes several items similar to those included on traditional intelligence measures. The Intellectual Processes Scale includes the following tasks: describing pictures, sequencing pictures (similar to Picture Arrangement on the Wechsler scales), answering questions about a story, interpreting proverbs, describing how two objects are alike (similar to the Similarities subtest on the Wechsler scales), and solving arithmetic word problems (similar to the Arithmetic subtest on the Wechsler scales). The Intellectual Processes Scale includes items that tap problem-solving skills and complex reasoning and yields an estimate of intellectual functioning (Golden et al., 1985).

*Intermediate Memory (C12, Form II only)*   The Intermediate Memory Scale has been called a measure of "delayed, unwarned recall and incidental memory" (Franzen, 1999, p. 2) because not all of the items involve information that the examinee was asked to learn and later remember. Items are verbal and nonverbal and include retention and recognition of material in previous sections of the test battery (delays typically range from 30 minutes to 2 hours).

SCALES FROM THE LURIA-NEBRASKA NEUROPSYCHOLOGICAL TEST
BATTERY-CHILDREN'S REVISION

In contrast to the LNNB, which has over 250 items, the LNNB-C has only 149 items. On the other hand, Berg (1999) has noted that most of these items have numerous tasks and components; thus, the actual number of individual items is much higher on the LNNB-C than it appears. Similar to the LNNB, the scales of the LNNB-C measure a domain of skills in an area rather than a specific skill. Although this approach provides broader coverage of a domain, further testing may be needed to gain more detailed information of specific skill deficits. The LNNB-C yields 11 clinical scales: (1) Motor, (2) Rhythm, (3) Tactile, (4) Visual, (5) Receptive Speech, (6) Expressive Speech, (7) Reading, (8) Writing, (9) Arithmetic, (10) Memory, and (11) Intellectual Processes. The LNNB-C also yields three summary scales, (1) Pathognomonic, (2) Left Sensorimotor, and (3) Right Sensorimotor, and two optional scales, (1) Spelling and (2) Motor Writing.

Each item of the LNNB-C is given a score of 0 (indicating normal performance), 1 (indicating borderline performance), or 2 (indicating abnormal performance); scores are totaled and converted into T-scores for each scale. Such a scoring system has been discussed and questioned by a variety of authors (e.g., Chittooran & D'Amato, 1989; Reynolds & Fletcher-Janzen, 1997). The LNNB-C clinical scales (Berg, 1999) are briefly described next.

*Motor (C1)*   The Motor Scale measures a variety of motor skills, ranging from simple hand movements to drawing tasks. The items measure basic motor speech, coordination, and imitation and construction skills.

*Rhythm (C2)*   The Rhythm Scale involves reproduction and analysis of tones and rhythms. Items measure the examinee's ability to hear and repeat simple tonal discriminations, to sing a song from memory and from an example, and to repeat and count rhythmic patterns (Berg, 1999).

*Tactile (C3)*   The Tactile Scale requires examinees to identify how hard they are touched and where they are touched without using vision. The scale involves cutaneous sensation at several different levels. Items measure finger and arm localization, two-point discrimination, shape discrimination, strength discrimination, movement detection, and stereognostic skills in hands and arms.

*Visual (C4)*   The Visual Scale requires visual-spatial organization and analysis. The examinee is asked to identify and name common pictures and objects, identify and name visually distorted objects, identify overlapping figures, and utilize visual memory (Berg, 1999).

*Receptive Speech (C5)*   The Receptive Speech Scale evaluates the ability to understand speech. Items range from simple phonemic analysis to understanding complex sentences.

*Expressive Speech (C6)*   The Expressive Speech Scale measures a variety of abilities, including repeating simple phonemes, words, and sentences and generating more complex speech forms (Berg, 1999).

*Writing (C7)*   The ability to analyze words phonetically and the ability to spell and write from dictation is measured by the Writing Scale.

*Reading (C8)*   The Reading Scale begins with simple reading skills, such as naming letters, sound-symbol relationships, and reading simple words, and progresses to more complex reading skills involving sentences and paragraphs (Berg, 1999).

*Arithmetic (C9)*   The Arithmetic Scale evaluates number recognition, number comparison, number writing, and simple mathematical processes.

*Memory (C10)*   The Memory Scale assesses verbal and short-term visual memory, verbal memory under interference conditions, and verbal-visual association memory (Berg, 1999).

*Intellectual Processes (C11)*   The Intellectual Processes Scale, designed to discriminate between examinees with brain damage and examinees with normal functioning, includes visual analysis of pictures, simple concept formation and definitions, simple arithmetic, story interpretation, and comparisons between objects. Some items are similar in content to several subtests of the Wechsler scales.

## Reliability and Validity of the Luria-Nebraska Neuropsychological Test Battery and the Luria-Nebraska Neuropsychological Test Battery-Children's Revision

Numerous psychometric methods have been used to determine the reliability of the LNNB (Form I and II), including internal consistency, interrater reliability, test-retest reliability, and split-half reliability methods. However, the empirical base is more extensive for Form I of the LNNB (Franzen, 1999). As expected, many of the reliability and validity studies on the LNNB were undertaken in the 1980s because it was a new neuropsychological measure at that time. The current literature contains several studies on a new version of the test, the LNNB-III (Bradley et al., 2000; Devaraju-Backhaus et al., 2001; Teichner et al., 1999), but this version is not available commercially at this time.

Internal consistency studies, using coefficient alpha, were completed on the LNNB by several researchers (Maruish, Sawicki, Franzen, & Golden, 1985; Moses, 1985; Moses, Johnson, & Lewis, 1983). Moses and his colleagues reported values in the range of .78 to .89 for the clinical and summary scales; similar coefficient alpha values were reported by Moses and by Maruish et al.

Interrater reliability of the LNNB was generally good. Golden and his associates (Golden, Hammeke, & Purisch, 1978) have found high rates of agreement between the raters (95% overall between raters) on the LNNB clinical scales. Similar results were found when this study was replicated by Moses and Schefft (1985). Another study evaluated interrater reliability using both clear and ambiguous responses (Bach, Harowski, Kirby, Peterson, & Schulein, 1981) and found interrater agreement was .75 for the ambiguous responses and .90 for the clearly scorable responses.

Early on, Campbell (1983) and Golden, Berg, and Graber (1982) investigated test-retest reliability of the LNNB. Campbell found a test-retest coefficient of .92, while Golden and his colleagues found a test-retest reliability coefficient of .88. Several studies found adequate split-half reliability (Campbell, 1983; Golden, Fross, & Graber, 1981; Maruish et al., 1985).

These early validity studies evaluating the construct validity of the LNNB were plagued with statistical flaws, including inadequate subject-to-variable ratios and inattention to the increase in error when multiple comparisons were made (Moses & Maruish, 1988, pp. 5–11). As with the construct validity research of the LNNB, the research methodology of many of the more concurrent validity studies were also statistically inadequate (Moses & Maruish, 1988, pp. 12–19), including an insufficient ratio of participants to variables and inattention to increased error due to multiple statistical comparisons. Nonetheless, there are some studies that have demonstrated concurrent validity of the LNNB Memory Scale with other measures of memory, as well as the LNNB Intellectual Processes Scale with the Wechsler Adult Intelligence Scale (WAIS). Moreover, some see results of the LNNB as comparable to those of the HRNB (Moses & Maruish, 1988, pp. 12–19). Some have found the LNNB to be especially useful in evaluating children with LD (Lewis, Hutchens, & Garland, 1993). These authors reported that the LNNB was accurate in diagnosing this group of children, and they suggested that use of the LNNB may reduce the diagnostic error that is present in using only a discrepancy model for identifying students with LD.

Several researchers have found significant inverse relationships (a high score on the LNNB indicates more cognitive deficits in that area) between the LNNB Memory Scale and other measures of memory (McKay & Ramsey, 1983; Ryan & Prifitera, 1982). So, too, several early studies examined the relationships between the WAIS and the LNNB Intellectual Processes Scale (McKay, Golden, Moses, Fishburne, & Wisniewski, 1981; Picker & Schlottmann, 1982; Prifitera & Ryan, 1981). These studies showed high negative correlations between the LNNB Intellectual Processes Scale and the WAIS. But some of these studies again used small sample sizes, which made the reliable interpretation of the results difficult (Koffler & Zehler, 1986).

The relationship between the LNNB and the HRNB has also been examined. Comparable findings were found between raters evaluating data from the LNNB and HRNB to assess clinical status (Kane, Sweet, Golden, Parsons, & Moses, 1981). In a combined study using both the LNNB and the HRNB to predict group membership for examinees with brain impairment ($N = 48$) and without brain impairment ($N = 60$), classification rates exceeded 85% for both measures (Golden, Kane, et al., 1981). Another early study found the HRNB and the LNNB to be comparable measures for detecting brain dysfunction (each with a classification rate of over 90%; Kane, Parsons, & Goldstein, 1985). However, a later study (Bryson, Silverstein, Nathan, & Stephen, 1993) found a lower rate of agreement (below 70%) between the two batteries in classifying those with Schizophrenia ($N = 55$) and affective disorders ($N = 64$). Some early success has been reported when using the HRNB in isolation with a psychiatric population, predicting primary affective depression using neuropsychological data (Gray, Dean, D'Amato, & Rattan, 1986).

The validity of the LNNB-C has been explored by analyzing studies investigating the use of the LNNB-C with special populations, including those with brain damage, LD, and Attention-Deficit/Hyperactivity Disorder (ADHD). Pfeiffer, Naglieri, and Tingstrom (1987) found that 27 of 32 students with LD were correctly identified using a criterion of three or more elevated (1 standard deviation from the mean) LNNB-C scales. Similarly, using the criteria of two or more scales above the critical level on the LNNB-C, Teeter, Boliek, Obrzut, and Malsch (1986) accurately classified 96% of those with and without LD. In a seminal study, Snow,

Hynd, and Hartlage (1984) found significant differences on the LNNB-C scales in differentiating between children with mild and more severe LD. Yet, other researchers have found that the LNNB-C *failed* to differentiate between students with LD (Morgan & Brown, 1988; Snow & Hynd, 1985), students with ADHD (Schaughency et al., 1989), and average learners. The findings from these studies are surprisingly mixed and certainly bring into question the use of these batteries from a psychometric view.

### Interpreting the Results from the Luria-Nebraska Neuropsychological Test Battery and the Luria-Nebraska Neuropsychological Test Battery-Children's Revision

A variety of approaches to interpretation of the LNNB and LNNB-C have been presented in the literature (Berg, 1999; Franzen, 1999; Golden & Freshwater, 2001; Golden, Freshwater, & Vayalakkara, 2000). Although there are many similarities in these approaches, the recently offered clinical interpretive strategies of Golden and Freshwater is evaluated in this chapter. Interpretation of the LNNB and LNNB-C includes the following strategies (Golden & Freshwater, 2001): (1) Quantify the profile as normal or abnormal; (2) conduct a pattern analysis of test scores; (3) do an item analysis of the examinee's test performance (What could the examinee do? What was the examinee unable to do?); (4) analyze qualitative data and integrate the results with quantitative data; (5) analyze the impact of the examinee's history; and (6) integrate all data on the examinee to create a *definitive picture* of the examinee's strengths and weaknesses, role of medical and personal history, and the implications of these data for rehabilitation and future functioning.

Several indicators of possible brain impairment are offered on the LNNB. The battery allows psychologists to determine a critical level (CL) for an examinee. The CL is based on a formula that calculates one standard deviation greater than the typical score expected for the individual based on age and education. First, a comparison of scores on the clinical scales and the Pathognomonic Scale is made to the CL. Having more than three scores above the CL indicates the presence of a brain injury. Other profiles are considered normal (none or one scale above CL) or borderline (two scales above CL). Another method used on the LNNB to identify brain impairment is a comparison between the highest and lowest T-scores. Those with brain injury often show greater variability, and a difference of over 30 points is indicative of such a condition (Golden & Freshwater, 2001). Other differences are classified in the borderline range (21 to 30 points) and normal range (20 points and under).

The third strategy involves interpreting the scales of the LNNB using pattern analysis (similar to the interpretation of the Minnesota Multiphasic Personality Inventory II). Golden and Freshwater (2001) stated that a 2-point profile is one in which "both of the 2 highest scales are at least 10 points higher than the 3rd highest scale among the 12 basic scales plus the Pathognomonic, Right Hemisphere, and Left Hemisphere scales" (p. 66), or in which the two scales are the only ones elevated above the critical level. Similarly, a 3-point profile must have three scales at least 10 points higher than the fourth scale, or the three elevated scales are the only ones higher than the critical level. Golden and Freshwater also noted that a scale is usually not included in a *high-point profile* unless it exceeds the critical level. Interpretations of the specific high-point profiles are provided in the test manual as well as in the literature (Golden & Freshwater, 2001; Golden et al., 1985, 2000).

The next or fourth interpretive strategy is an analysis of the pattern of errors made by the examinee. Item analysis begins with the highest T-score and examines errors to identify specific item groupings that may have been difficult for the examinee. The goal of this strategy is to identify the fewest problem areas that explain the full range of errors made by the examinee (Golden & Freshwater, 2001). Next, qualitative data are examined to aid in the interpretation of the examinee's performance. Qualitative data are more descriptive and are based on the observations of the clinician. Any behavior that was unusual or impacted testing procedures should be noted by the examiner. Behaviors may include descriptions of the examinee's level of inattentiveness or difficulty on tasks requiring motor skills. A skilled psychologist or neuropsychologist will have an understanding of how behavior is impacted by brain injuries and will apply this knowledge when observing and interpreting the examinee's performance (Golden & Freshwater, 2001).

The fifth interpretive strategy is analyzing the examinee's history to determine key factors that impact his or her current level of functioning. The collection of background information should include a detailed medical history, mental health history, and previous test results. Finally, all the different sources of data described are integrated to consider the examinee's strengths and weaknesses and to develop and then evaluate suitable neuropsychological interventions.

The LNNB has sparked controversy since its publication over 20 years ago, and the debate over the validity and reliability of this instrument most certainly will continue. There is a body of research that does *not* support the use of the LNNB or the LNNB-C based on their poor psychometric properties and limited links to intervention. Even so, Hynd and Semrud-Clikeman (1990) have reported that, despite continued controversy, the LNNB is frequently used due to its clinical efficiency and ability to differentiate between those with and without brain impairment as well as much longer batteries (such as the HRNB). It would seem that with the recent development and improvement of neuropsychological batteries, it is likely that the popularity of these batteries will decline and they will be replaced with newer measures such as the NEPSY that purportedly are conceptually and psychometrically sound.

## CONCLUSION

Currently, the HRNB and the LNNB remain the two most widely used neuropsychological test batteries. Although these comprehensive batteries originally may have been designed primarily for differentiating between brain-injured and normal individuals, they continue to offer a rich array of clinical information regarding brain-behavior relations. This chapter reviewed the history and development of the HRNB and the LNNB. Moreover, the differences and unique qualities of flexible and standardized batteries were presented. Limited reliability and validity information exist for these measures, especially compared to more modern neuropsychological and psychological tests. School neuropsychologists most certainly will find some elements of these batteries cumbersome and frustrating, such as their limited portability and a lack of normative tables. Indeed, school psychologists who are used to the slick look of cover sheets and test manuals will be disappointed by these batteries. But they will find new information that will lead to the development of novel interventions. The HRNB and the LNNB may have reached their peak in terms of popularity and clinical and research utility. It is likely that different instruments meeting more contemporary standards will become popular in the future, although many of the tasks on the newer batteries were obviously adopted from the classic tasks of the HRNB. Because it is likely that at some point in their careers, all school psychologists will be involved with examinees who require neuropsychological services if they are to succeed, it is critical to familiarize oneself with the assessment instruments used in the field of school neuropsychology.

## REFERENCES

Bach, P. J., Harowski, K., Kirby, K., Peterson, P., & Schulein, M. (1981). The interrater reliability of the Luria-Nebraska Neuropsychological Battery. *Clinical Neuropsychology, 111,* 19–21.

Batchelor, E. S., Gray, J. W., & Dean, R. S. (1990). Neuropsychological aspects of arithmetic performance in learning disability. *International Journal of Clinical Neuropsychology, 12,* 90–94.

Berg, R. A. (1999). The Luria-Nebraska Neuropsychological Battery-Children's Revision (LNNB-C). In C. Golden, W. Warren, & P. Espe-Pfeiffer (Eds.), *LNNB Handbook: 20th Anniversary: Vol. 1. A guide to clinical interpretation and use in special settings* (pp. 213–225). Los Angeles: Western Psychological Services.

Boll, T. J. (1974). Behavioral correlates of cerebral damage in children age 9–14. In R. M. Reitan & L. A. Davison (Eds.), *Clinical neuropsychology: Current status and application.* Washington, DC: Hemisphere Press.

Bradley, J. D., Teichner, G., Crum, T. A., & Golden, G. J. (2000). Concurrent validity and analysis of learning curves on the memory scales of the Luria-Nebraska Neuropsychological Battery—Third Edition. *International Journal of Neuroscience, 103,* 115–126.

Bryson, G., Silverstein, M., Nathan, A., & Stephen, L. (1993). Differential rate of neuropsychological dysfunction in psychiatric disorders: Comparison between the Halstead-Reitan and Luria-Nebraska Batteries. *Perceptual and Motor Skills, 76*(1), 305–306.

Camara, W. J., Nathan, J. S., & Puente, A. E. (2000). Psychological test usage: Implications in professional psychology. *Professional Psychology: Research and Practice, 31,* 141–154.

Campbell, B. R. (1983). Reliability and practice effects on the Luria-Nebraska Neuropsychological Battery. *Clinical Neuropsychology, 3*(3), 19–21.

Charter, R. A. (2000). Internal consistency reliability of the Tactual Performance Test trials. *Perceptual and Motor Skills, 91,* 460–462.

Chittooran, M. M., & D'Amato, R. C. (1989). Review of the screening tests for the Luria-Nebraska Neuropsychological Battery: Adult and Children's Forms. *Communiqué, 18,* 30.

Chittooran, M. M., D'Amato, R. C., Lassiter, K. S., & Dean, R. S. (1993). Factor structure of psychoeducational and neuropsychological measures of learning disabled children. *Psychology in the Schools, 30,* 109–118.

Christensen, A. L. (1975). *Luria's neuropsychological investigation.* New York: Spectrum.

D'Amato, R. C. (1990). A neuropsychological approach to school psychology. *School Psychology Quarterly, 5,* 141–160.

D'Amato, R. C., Dean, R. S., & Rhodes, R. L. (1998). Subtyping children's learning disabilities with neuropsychological, intellectual, and achievement measures. *International Journal of Neuroscience, 96,* 107–125.

D'Amato, R. C., Gray, J. W., & Dean, R. S. (1988). A comparison between intelligence and neuropsychological functioning. *Journal of School Psychology, 26,* 283–292.

D'Amato, R. C., Rothlisberg, B. A., & Leu Work, P. H. (1999). Neuropsychological assessment for intervention. In C. R. Reynolds & T. B. Gutkin (Eds.), *The handbook of school psychology*. New York: Wiley.

D'Amato, R. C., Rothlisberg, B. A., & Rhodes, R. I. (1997). Utilizing a neuropsychological paradigm for understanding common educational and psychological tests. In C. R. Reynolds & E. Fletcher-Janzen (Eds.), *Handbook of clinical child neuropsychology* (2nd ed., pp. 270–295). New York: Plenum Press.

Davis, A. S. (2003). Dr. Cecil Reynolds receives the neuropsychology interest group lifetime achievement award for 2003. *Communiqué, 31,* 27.

Davis, A. S., & Warnygora, N. (2002). *Neuropsychological assessment in the schools: A four step approach.* Workshop presented at the 34th Annual Convention of the National Association of School Psychologists, Chicago.

Dean, R. S. (1985). Review of Halstead-Reitan Neuropsychological Test Battery. In J. V. Mitchell (Ed.), *The ninth mental measurements yearbook* (pp. 642–646). Highland Park, NJ: Gryphon Press.

Dean, R. S., & Anderson, J. L. (1997). Lateralization of cerebral functions. In A. M. Horton, D. Wedding, & J. Webster (Eds.), *The neuropsychology handbook* (2nd ed.). New York: Springer.

Dean, R. S., & Woodcock, R. W. (2003). *Dean-Woodcock Neuropsychological Battery.* [Examiners manual.] Itasca, IL: Riverside.

Devaraju-Backhaus, S., Espe-Pfeifer, P., Mahrou, M. L., & Golden, C. J. (2001). Correlation of the LNNB-III with the WAIS-III in a mixed psychiatric and brain-injured population. *International Journal of Neuroscience, 111,* 235–240.

Franzen, M. D. (1999). Clinical interpretation of the LNNB. In C. Golden, W. Warren, & P. Espe-Pfeiffer (Eds.), *LNNB Handbook: 20th Anniversary: Vol. 1. A guide to clinical interpretation and use in special population settings* (pp. 1–11). Los Angeles: Western Psychological Services.

Gaddes, W. H., & Edgell, D. (1994). *Learning disabilities and brain function: A neuropsychological approach* (2nd ed.). New York: Springer-Verlag.

Golden, C. J. (1987). *Luria-Nebraska Neuropsychological Battery-Children's Revision* [Manual]. Los Angeles: Western Psychological Services.

Golden, C. J., Berg, R. A., & Graber, B. (1982). Test-retest reliability of the Luria-Nebraska Neuropsychological Battery in stable, chronically impaired patients. *Journal of Consulting and Clinical Psychology, 50,* 452–454.

Golden, C. J., & Freshwater, S. M. (2001). Luria-Nebraska Neuropsychological Battery. In W. Dorfman & M. Hersen (Eds.), *Understanding psychological assessment: Perspectives on individual differences* (pp. 59–75). Dordrecht, Netherlands: Kluwer Academic.

Golden, C. J., Freshwater, S. M., & Vayalakkara, J. (2000). The Luria Nebraska Neuropsychological Battery. In G. Groth-Marnat (Ed.), *Neuropsychological assessment in clinical practice: A guide to test interpretation and integration* (pp. 263–289). New York: Wiley.

Golden, C. J., Fross, K. H., & Graber, B. (1981). Split-half reliability of the Luria-Nebraska Neuropsychological Battery. *Journal of Consulting and Clinical Psychology, 49,* 304–305.

Golden, C. J., Hammeke, T. A., & Purisch, A. D. (1978). Diagnostic validity of a standardized neuropsychological battery derived from Luria's neuropsychological tests. *Journal of Consulting and Clinical Psychology, 46,* 1258–1265.

Golden, C. J., Kane, R., Sweet, J., Moses, J. A., Cardellino, J., Templeton, R., et al. (1981). Relationship of the Halstead-Reitan Neuropsychological Battery to the Luria-Nebraska Neuropsychological Battery. *Journal of Consulting and Clinical Psychology, 49,* 410–417.

Golden, C. J., Purisch, A. D., & Hammeke, T. A. (1985). *Luria-Nebraska Neuropsychological Battery Forms I & II* [Manual]. Los Angeles: Western Psychological Services.

Golden, Z., & Golden, C. J. (2003). Impact of brain injury severity on personality dysfunction. *International Journal of Neuroscience, 113,* 733–745.

Gontkovsky, S. T., & Souheaver, G. T. (2002). T-score and raw-score comparisons in detecting brain dysfunction using the Booklet Category Test and the Short Category Test. *Perceptual-and-Motor-Skills, 94,* 319–322.

Graham, J. R. (2000). *MMPI-2: Assessing personality and psychopathology* (3rd ed.). New York: Oxford University Press.

Gray, J. W., Dean, R. S., D'Amato, R. C., & Rattan, G. (1986). Differential diagnosis of primary affective depression using the Halstead-Reitan Neuropsychological Test Battery. *International Journal of Neuroscience, 35,* 43–49.

Guilmette, T. J., & Faust, D. (1991). Characteristics of neuropsychologists who prefer the Halstead-Reitan or the Luria-Nebraska Neuropsychology Battery. *Professional Psychology: Research and Practice, 22,* 80–83.

Haaland, K. Y., Temkin, N., Randahl, G., & Dikmen, S. (1994). Recovery of simple motor skills after head injury. *Journal of Clinical and Experimental Neuropsychology, 16,* 448–456.

Halstead, W. C. (1947). *Brain and intelligence: A quantitative study of the frontal lobes.* Chicago: University of Chicago Press.

Halstead, W. C., & Wepman, J. M. (1949). The Halstead-Wepman Aphasia Screening Test. *Journal of Speech and Hearing Disorders, 14,* 9–13.

Hebb, D. O. (1939). Intelligence in man after large removals of cerebral tissue: Report of four frontal lobe cases. *Journal of General Psychology, 21,* 73–87.

Hebb, D. O. (1941). Human intelligence after removal of cerebral tissue from the right frontal lobe. *Journal of General Psychology, 25,* 257–265.

Horton, A. M. (1997). The Halstead-Reitan Neuropsychological Test Battery: Problems and prospects. In A. M. Horton, D. Wedding, & J. Webster (Eds.), *The neuropsychology handbook* (Vol. 1). New York: Springer.

Hynd, G. W., & Semrud-Clikeman, M. (1990). Neuropsychological assessment. In A. S. Kaufman (Ed.), *Assessing adolescent and adult intelligence.* Needham, MA: Simon & Schuster.

Jarvis, P. E., & Barth, J. B. (1994). *The Halstead-Reitan Neuropsychological Battery: A guide to interpretation and clinical applications.* Odessa, FL: Psychological Assessment Resources.

Kane, R. L., Parsons, O. A., & Goldstein, G. (1985). Statistical relationships and discriminative accuracy of the Halstead-Reitan, Luria-Nebraska, and Wechsler IQ scores in the identification of brain damage. *Journal of Clinical and Experimental Neuropsychology, 7,* 211–223.

Kane, R. L., Sweet, J. J., Golden, C. J., Parsons, O. A., & Moses, J. A. (1981). Comparative diagnostic accuracy of the Halstead-Reitan and standardized Luria-Nebraska Neuropsychological Batteries in a mixed psychiatric and brain-damaged population. *Journal of Consulting and Clinical Psychology, 49,* 484–485.

Kennedy, J. E., Clement, P. F., & Curtiss, G. (2003). WAIS-III Processing Speed Index Scores after TBI: The influence of working memory, psychomotor speed, and perceptual processing. *Clinical-Neuropsychologist, 17,* 303–307.

Klonoff, H., Robinson, G. C., & Thompson, G. (1969). Acute and chronic brain syndromes in children. *Developmental Medicine and Child Neurology, 11,* 198–213.

Koffler, S., & Zehler, D. (1986). Correlation of the Luria-Nebraska Neuropsychological Battery with the WAIS-R. *International Journal of Clinical Neuropsychology, 8,* 68–71.

Leckliter, I. N., Forster, A. A., Klonoff, H., & Knights, R. M. (1992). A review of reference group data from normal children for the Halstead-Reitan Neuropsychological Test Battery for Older Children. *The Clinical Neuropsychologist, 6,* 201–229.

Lewis, R. D., Hutchens, T. A., & Garland, B. L. (1993). Cross-validation of the discriminative effectiveness of the Luria-Nebraska Neuropsychological Battery for Learning Disabled Adolescents. *Archives of Clinical Neuropsychology, 8,* 437–447.

Lezak, M. D. (1995). *Neuropsychological assessment* (3rd ed.). New York: Oxford University.

Luria, A. R. (1966). *Human brain and psychological processes.* New York: Harper & Row.

Luria, A. R. (1980). *Higher cortical functions in man* (2nd ed.). New York: Basic Books.

Maruish, M. E., Sawicki, R. E., Franzen, M. D., & Golden, C. J. (1985). Alpha coefficient reliabilities for the Luria-Nebraska Neuropsychological Battery summary and localization scales by diagnostic category. *International Journal of Clinical Neuropsychology, 7,* 10–12.

McKay, S., Golden, C. J., Moses, J. A., Fishburne, F. J., & Wisniewski, A. (1981). Correlation of the Luria-Nebraska Neuropsychological Battery with the WAIS. *Journal of Consulting and Clinical Psychology, 49,* 940–946.

McKay, S., & Ramsey, R. (1983). Correlation of the Wechsler Memory Scale and the Luria-Nebraska Memory Scale. *Clinical Neuropsychology, 5,* 168–170.

Morgan, S. B., & Brown, T. L. (1988). Luria-Nebraska Neuropsychological Battery-Children's Revision: Concurrent validity with three learning disability subtypes. *Journal of Consulting and Clinical Psychology, 56*(3), 463–466.

Moses, J. A. (1985). Replication of internal consistency reliability values for Luria-Nebraska Neuropsychological Battery summary, localization, factor and compensation scales. *International Journal of Clinical Neuropsychology, 6,* 200–203.

Moses, J. A., Johnson, G. L., & Lewis, G. P. (1983). Reliability analyses of the Luria-Nebraska Neuropsychological Battery summary, localization, and factor scales. *International Journal of Neuroscience, 21,* 149–154.

Moses, J. A., & Maruish, M. E. (1988). A critical review of the Luria-Nebraska Neuropsychological Battery Literature: II. Construct validity. *International Journal of Clinical Neuropsychology, 10*(1), 5–19.

Moses, J. A., & Schefft, B. K. (1985). Interrater reliability analyses of the Luria-Nebraska Neuropsychological Battery. *International Journal of Clinical Neuropsychology, 6,* 31–38.

Nussbaum, N. L., & Bigler, E. D. (1989). Halstead-Reitan Neuropsychological Test Batteries for Children. In C. R. Reynolds & E. Fletcher-Janzen (Eds.), *Handbook of clinical child neuropsychology: Critical issues in neuropsychology* (pp. 181–191). New York: Plenum Press.

Pfeiffer, S. I., Naglieri, J. A., & Tingstrom, D. H. (1987). Comparison of the Luria-Nebraska Neuropsychological Battery-Children's Revision and the WISC-R with learning disabled children. *Perceptual and Motor Skills, 65,* 911–916.

Picker, W. R., & Schlottmann, R. S. (1982). An investigation of the Intellectual Processes scale of the Luria-Nebraska Neuropsychological Battery. *Clinical Neuropsychology, 4*(3), 120–124.

Prifitera, A., & Ryan, J. J. (1981). Validity of the Luria-Nebraska Intellectual Processes scale as a measure of adult intelligence. *Journal of Consulting and Clinical Psychology, 49,* 755–756.

Purisch, A. D. (2001). Misconceptions about the Luria-Nebraska Neuropsychological Battery. *NeuroRehabilitation, 16,* 275–280.

Reed, H. B. C., Reitan, R. M., & Kløve, H. (1965). The influence of cerebral lesions on psychological test performances of older children. *Journal of Consulting Psychology, 29,* 247–251.

Reitan, R. M. (1955). An investigation of the validity of Halstead's measure of biological intelligence. *Archives of Neurology and Psychiatry, 73,* 28–35.

Reitan, R. M. (1969). *Manual for the administration of neuropsychological test batteries for adults and children.* Indianapolis, IN: Author.

Reitan, R. M. (1974). Psychological effects of cerebral lesions in children of early school age. In R. M. Reitan & L. A. Davison (Eds.), *Clinical neuropsychology: Current status and applications* (pp. 53–90). Washington, DC: Hemisphere Publishing.

Reitan, R. M., & Boll, R. (1973). Neuropsychological correlates of minimal brain dysfunction. *Annals of the New York Academy of Sciences, 205,* 65–87.

Reitan, R. M., & Davison, L. A. (1974). *Clinical neuropsychology: Current status and applications.* Washington, DC: Hemisphere Publishing.

Reitan, R. M., & Wolfson, D. (1985). *The Halstead-Reitan Neuropsychological Test Battery: Theory and clinical interpretation.* Tucson, AZ: Neuropsychology Press.

Reitan, R. M., & Wolfson, D. (1990). The significance of the Speech-sounds Perception Test for cerebral functions. *Archives of Clinical Neuropsychology, 5,* 365–272.

Reitan, R. M., & Wolfson, D. (1992). *Neuropsychological evaluation of older children.* Tucson, Arizona: Neuropsychology Press.

Reitan, R. M., & Wolfson, D. (1993). *The Halstead-Reitan Neuropsychological Test Battery: Theory and clinical interpretation* (2nd ed.). Tucson, AZ: Neuropsychology Press.

Reitan, R. M., & Wolfson, D. (1996). Relationships between specific and general tests of cerebral functioning. *The Clinical Neuropsychologist, 10,* 37–42.

Reitan, R. M., & Wolfson, D. (2001). Halstead-Reitan Neuropsychological Test Battery: Research findings and clinical application. In A. S. Kaufman & N. L. Kaufman (Eds.), *Specific learning disabilities and difficulties in children and adolescents: Psychological assessment and evaluation* (pp. 309–346). New York: Cambridge University Press.

Retzlaff, P., Butler, M., & Vanderploeg, R. D. (1992). Neuropsychological battery choice and theoretical orientation: A multivariate analysis. *Journal of Clinical Psychology, 48,* 666–672.

Reynolds, C. R. (2003). *Comprehensive trailmaking test.* Austin, TX: ProEd.

Reynolds, C. R., & Fletcher-Janzen, E. (Eds.). (1997). *Handbook of clinical child neuropsychology* (2nd ed.). New York: Plenum Press.

Reynolds, C. R., & French, C. L. (2003). The neuropsychological basis of intelligence revised: Some false starts and a clinical model. In A. M. Horton, Jr. & L. C. Hartlage (Eds.), *Handbook of forensic neuropsychology* (pp. 35–92). New York: Springer.

Rothlisberg, B. A., D'Amato, R. C., & Palencia, B. (2003). Assessment of children for intervention planning following traumatic brain injury. In C. R. Reynolds & R. W. Kamphaus (Eds.), *Handbook of psychological and educational assessment of children* (pp. 685–706). New York: Guilford Press.

Russell, E. W., Neuringer, C., & Goldstein, G. (1970). *Assessment of brain damage: A neuropsychological key approach.* New York: Wiley.

Ryan, J. J., & Prifitera, A. (1982). Concurrent validity of the Luria-Nebraska Memory scale. *Journal of Clinical Psychology, 38,* 378–379.

Sattler, J. M. (2002). *Assessment of children: Behavioral and clinical application* (4th ed.). San Diego, CA: Jerome M. Sattler.

Sattler, J. M., & D'Amato, R. C. (2002). Brain injuries: Formal batteries and informal measures. In J. M. Sattler (Ed.), *Assessment of children: Behavioral and clinical application* (4th ed., pp. 440–469). San Diego, CA: Jerome M. Sattler.

Schaughency, E. A., Lahey, B. B., Hynd, G. W., Stone, P. A., Piacentini, J. C., & Frick, P. J. (1989). Neuropsychological test performance and the attention deficit disorders:

Clinical utility of the Luria-Nebraska Neuropsychological Battery-Children's Revision. *Journal of Consulting and Clinical Psychology, 51*(1), 112–116.

Selz, M. (1981). Halstead-Reitan Neuropsychological Test Batteries for Children. In G. W. Hynd & J. E. Obrzut (Eds.), *Neuropsychological assessment and the school-age child: Issues and procedures* (pp. 195–235). New York, NY: Grune & Stratton.

Seretny, M. L., Dean, R. S., Gray, J. W., & Hartlage, L. C. (1986). The practice of clinical neuropsychology in the United States. *Archives of Clinical Neuropsychology, 1*, 5–12.

Snow, J. H., & Hynd, G. W. (1985). A multivariate investigation of the Luria-Nebraska Neuropsychological Battery-Children's Revision with learning-disabled children. *Journal of Psychoeducational Assessment, 3*(2), 101–109.

Snow, J. H., Hynd, G. W., & Hartlage, L. (1984). Differences between mildly and more severely learning disabled children on the Luria-Nebraska Neuropsychological Battery-Children's Revision *Journal of Psychoeducational Assessment, 2*, 23–28.

Teeter, P. A., Boliek, C. A., Obrzut, J. E., & Malsch, K. (1986). Diagnostic utility of the critical level formula and clinical summary scales of the Luria-Nebraska Neuropsychological Battery-Children's Revision with learning disabled children. *Developmental Neuropsychology, 2*(2), 125–135.

Teichner, G., Golden, C. J., Bradley, J. D., & Crum, T. A. (1999). Internal consistency and discriminant validity of the Luria Nebraska Neuropsychological Battery-III. *International Journal of Neuroscience, 98*, 141–152.

Walsh, K. (1987). *Neuropsychology: A clinical approach.* New York: Churchill Livingstone.

Wechsler, D. (1991). *Wechsler Intelligence Test for Children* (3rd ed.). San Antonio, TX: Psychological Corporation.

Wechsler, D. (1997). *Wechsler Adult Intelligence Scale* (3rd ed.). San Antonio, TX: Psychological Corporation.

Wechsler, D. (2003). *Wechsler Intelligence Test for Children* (4th ed.). San Antonio, TX: Psychological Corporation.

# CHAPTER 11

# Evaluating and Using Contemporary Neuropsychological Batteries: The NEPSY and the Dean-Woodcock Neuropsychological Assessment System

ANDREW S. DAVIS and RIK CARL D'AMATO

THE HALLMARK OF applied neuropsychological practice is neuropsychological assessment. The roles and goals of neuropsychological assessment have changed since the middle of the twentieth century, when standardized neuropsychological instruments started gaining popularity (Walsh, 1987). Modern clinical neuropsychology originated in traditional neurology and neurosurgery settings, and early research was concerned with the identification of penetrating wounds to the brain and the diagnosis of brain tumors and strokes (Zillmer & Spiers, 2001). Modern medical technology has rendered the task of identifying lesions (and structural anomalies) as no longer critical for practice, and neuropsychologists now focus on the identification of unique strengths and weaknesses that allow for rehabilitation of individual skill deficits (D'Amato, Rothlisberg, & Leu Work, 1999). Moreover, the focus of clinical neuropsychology is moving from diagnosis to intervention as medical and statistical technology become more sophisticated (Walsh, 1987). Neuropsychological assessment offers the practitioner an expanded, comprehensive view of a child's unique profile, as compared to the traditional assessment battery administered in most public schools. The ability to understand, employ, and interpret neuropsychological instruments in the schools is becoming a necessity for many school psychologists (D'Amato et al., 1999). A neuropsychological approach to assessment allows neuropsychologists the opportunity to tie behavioral output demonstrated by learners in the classroom to functional systems within the brain. Another advantage of using a neuropsychological approach is that it allows for interventions to be constructed that are theoretically based.

As new neuropsychological test batteries have recently been published, test authors and related companies must have recognized the current paradigm shift from assessment and diagnosis to neuropsychological assessment *for evidence-based interventions.* Newer standardized neuropsychological assessment batteries such as the Dean-Woodcock Neuropsychological Battery (DWNB; Dean & Woodcock, 2003a, 2003c), and the NEPSY: A Developmental Neuropsychological Assessment (NEPSY; Korkman, Kirk, & Kemp, 1998) facilitate a practical approach to assessment for intervention. Psychologists who are accustomed to well-organized protocols, portable test kits, instruments with thorough standardized instructions, and a representative normative sample will find older neuropsychological instruments such as the Halstead-Reitan Neuropsychological Test Battery (HRNB; Reitan & Wolfson, 1993) to be lacking in these areas when compared to newer measures. The DWNB and the NEPSY have addressed these issues, and school neuropsychologists should view these instruments as promising, pending further psychometric information. These instruments seem ideal for use in the schools, as they take a process approach to identifying the underlying neuropsychological processes that constitute academic skills, such as reading, writing, and math; yet questions remain about the utility and the validity of some of these new measures (Sattler & D'Amato, 2002). Some doctoral-level school psychologists with training in neuropsychology will be able to administer these instruments, but interpretation of neuropsychological constructs should remain in the domain of those with advanced neuropsychological training. In fact, the NEPSY manual (Korkman et al., 1998) has stated that when the NEPSY is used as part of a neuropsychological assessment, the examiner should have appropriate training in this area. This chapter reviews the two newest standardized neuropsychological test batteries, the NEPSY and the DWNB.

## THE NEPSY: A DEVELOPMENTAL NEUROPSYCHOLOGICAL ASSESSMENT

The authors of the NEPSY were interested in creating a comprehensive neuropsychological assessment battery for children that was based on the work of the Russian neuropsychologist Luria (e.g., 1966, 1973). Some of Luria's theories are briefly reviewed in this chapter to emphasize the theoretical basis of this innovative standardized measure. Test batteries that are based on theory help guide the interpretation of the data and intervention development. Luria did not view intelligence, or cognitive processing, as a product of a particular tissue or organ, but as the coordination of several different cerebral areas (e.g., Luria, 1973). For example, with regard to speech, he postulated that Wernicke's area was best suited for auditory to verbal transformations, but the execution of a complex activity, such as repeating a spoken word, would involve an extensive system of coordinating lexical and basic motor program units (Gouvier et al., 1997). Luria (1973) combined elements of localization and equipotentiality theory to create a conceptualization of the normally functioning brain as three major units. He advocated that:

> human mental processes are complex functional systems and they are not localized in narrow, circumscribed areas of the brain, but take place through the participation

of groups of concertedly working brain structures, each of which makes its own particular contribution to the organization of the functional system. (p. 43)

Luria (1973) hypothesized that when a *functional system* is not operating at an optimal level, it is unclear which cerebral structure in the brain is impaired. For example, according to Luria, a person with a learning problem may have a brain dysfunction resulting from an impairment of a functional system composed of one of three major units. The individual may not be attending to stimuli (Unit 1), he or she may not be able to analyze relevant stimuli (Unit 2), or he or she may not be actively trying to use the information (Unit 3; Gouvier et al., 1997). Impairment at any one of these sites would affect the individual's entire ability to process information (see Chapter 5, this volume). To assess which system is impaired, Luria proposed testing a series of hypotheses that call on each unit to demonstrate its functional integrity. His methods have also been employed to diagnose cortical and subcortical lesions resulting from trauma, tumors, vascular accidents, or inflammation and the efficacy of surgical interventions (Belopol'skaia & Grebennikova, 1997).

Luria's practice of independently evaluating each area of cognitive functioning for primary and secondary deficits, an approach he called "syndrome analysis," can be seen in the construction of the NEPSY. This process of conducting a series of hypothesis tests based on a pass/fail method is thought to work well with adults, but Korkman (1999) listed three reasons why the identification of strengths and weaknesses is more useful and practical for children in an educational setting. First, children tend to have comorbid deficits, which are troublesome for psychologists, who are often called on to differentiate learning problems from attention problems, behavioral problems, or emotional problems. Second, primary deficits may have different consequences for children. For example, a lesion in an area of a child's brain that is still developing will have implications for more advanced neurocognitive processes, the emergence of which is contingent on adequate functioning of the impaired area (Luria, 1973). Third, there is a paucity of generally accepted syndrome descriptions in the child neuropsychology literature that can serve as a model for interpretation (Fletcher-Janzen & Reynolds, 2003; Korkman, 1999). Hence, some elements of Luria's theories were adapted for use in the NEPSY, with the description of a comprehensive pattern of neuropsychological strengths and weaknesses serving as the goal of the test. An instrument with this goal is especially useful for school neuropsychologists, who may use a child's strengths to compensate for weaknesses in areas of academic functioning.

Korkman et al. (1998) believe that the NEPSY is different from other child neuropsychological tests because the subtests were specifically designed for *children* between the ages of 3 and 12. Many of the subtests on the NEPSY were adopted from traditional, well-researched neuropsychological tasks, but all of the tasks have been made child-friendly and user-friendly for the examiners. Moreover, the battery was standardized on a single sample of children. Indeed, the normative data are a primary strength of this battery, with 1,000 children constituting the standardization sample that closely approximates the U.S. population. Prior to the NEPSY, neuropsychologists were limited in their selection of comprehensive, well-standardized, and well-normed batteries for children, often requiring practitioners to assemble items drawn from several different tests, each with its own standardized data and normative sample. The third reason the NEPSY differs from other child neuropsychological tests is its construct validity. Finally, the NEPSY "was designed to assess basic and complex aspects of cognitive capacities that are critical to children's ability to learn and to be productive both in and outside of school settings" (Korkman et al., 1998, p. 1). On careful examination, it is evident that the test authors chose neuropsychological domains that seem to underlie the processes responsible for academic tasks, including reading, writing, mathematics, and some social skills.

The NEPSY is a unique tool in that it combines into one test a screening device, a complete battery, and a system of examining in-depth, complex neuropsychological problems in children age 3 to 12. The authors accomplished this goal by including 27 subtests that can be used to explore neuropsychological functioning in five domains:

1. Attention/executive functions
2. Language
3. Visual-spatial processing
4. Sensorimotor
5. Memory and language

Luria (1973) believed that behaviors such as language, learning, movement, and memory were the result of an interaction of simple and complex brain systems, and this viewpoint is reflected in the construction of the NEPSY. Some of the subtests in the NEPSY assess basic subcomponents of the previously discussed neuropsychological domains; other subtests tap into neuropsychological functions that require contributions and interactions between the subtests (Korkman et al., 1998). The genesis of many learning difficulties is a neuropsychological processing problem in one of the five functional areas assessed by the NEPSY. For example, a reading problem may be due to a limitation in phonological processing, poor planning ability when an unfamiliar word is encountered, poor attention and inhibition skills, insufficient memory processes, visual-spatial limitations, or even poor oral motor skills. All of these processing abilities are assessed under the five functional domains in the NEPSY. A diagnosis of a specific learning disorder includes a deficit in a processing skill that is often unclear at best on traditional measures of cognitive assessment. The NEPSY can assist in the identification of such specific processing skills. Unfortunately, the NEPSY is available for use with children only through age 12, so children in secondary education will not be able to benefit from this instrument.

It is not necessary to administer all 27 subtests to obtain a comprehensive measure of a child's functioning. The components of a NEPSY administration are flexible and dependent on the needs of the examiner and examinee (Ahmad & Warriner, 2001). Indeed, the subtests are divided into a group of *core subtests* and a group of *expanded subtests*. The NEPSY developers intended that the core subtests would be administered first, and if a child demonstrated a weakness in one of the domains, the expanded subtests could be administered to further investigate the child's area of difficulty. There are two different administration protocols, one for ages 3 and 4, and one for children age 5 to 12. For school-age children (5 to 12), 14 subtests compose the core battery, which can be administered in 1 to 1½ hours to children without major neurological deficits (Korkman et al., 1998).

**Table 11.1**
Core Subtests from the NEPSY: A Developmental
Neuropsychological Assessment

| Age 3 to 4 | Age 5 to 12 |
|---|---|
| **Attention/Executive Functions** | |
| Visual Attention | Visual Attention |
| Statue | Auditory Attention and Response Set |
| | Tower |
| **Language** | |
| Comprehension of Instructions | Comprehension of Instructions |
| Phonological Processing | Phonological Processing |
| Body Part Naming | Speeded Naming |
| **Sensorimotor** | |
| Imitating Hand Positions | Imitating Hand Positions |
| Visuomotor Precision | Visuomotor Precision |
| | Fingertip Tapping |
| **Visuospatial** | |
| Design Copying | Design Copying |
| Block Construction | Arrows |
| **Memory** | |
| Narrative Memory | Narrative Memory |
| Sentence Repetition | Memory for Faces |
| | Memory for Names |

Only the core subtests are briefly reviewed in this chapter; for a more complete description of these subtests, as well as descriptions of the expanded subtests, see the NEPSY manual (Korkman et al., 1998) or related research or reviews (Korkman, Kettunen, & Autti-Raemoe, 2003; Sattler & D'Amato, 2002; Stinnett, Oehler-Stinnett, Fuqua, & Palmer, 2002). Some of the core subtests reviewed in this text may be administered to children of different ages as part of the extended battery. The core subtests from the NEPSY appear in Table 11.1.

ATTENTION/EXECUTIVE FUNCTION CORE SUBTESTS

This section describes the administration and interpretation of the Attention/Executive Function Core Subtests.

*Visual Attention*    This subtest appears on both the preschool battery and the school-age battery and is designed to assess a child's ability to maintain a selected focus on visual targets within a wide array of distracters. Children are asked to mark all of the objects that are the same as a target object. The Visual Attention subtest is thought to measure attention, impulsivity, and memory deficits (Korkman et al., 1998). The score is based on the number of correct targets marked, the number missed, and the time taken to complete the task. Examiners are able to qualitatively record off-task behaviors that could contribute to poor scores on this task due to inattention or impulsivity (Kemp, Kirk, & Korkman, 2001).

*Statue*   As a core subtest, this task is administered only to children age 3 to 4. Children are required to maintain a constant standing body position with their eyes closed while they attempt to resist the impulse to respond to auditory distracters provided by the examiner. Impaired performance on this subtest may indicate deficits in impulse control, inhibition, or motor persistence (Korkman et al., 1998). Children are rated on their ability to resist the distracters during a series of time intervals.

*Tower*   This version of a classic Tower Test (e.g., Culbertson, Moberg, Duda, Stern, & Weintraub, 2004) is administered only to children age 5 to 12. Children are required to move three balls on a series of three wooden pegs from a set starting position to a new position indicated by the stimulus manual. Children are allowed a specified number of moves to complete the task. Historically, tasks similar to the Tower Test have been used to measure executive functions, as the task requires extensive planning. Cicerone and Tupper (1986) have reported the main elements of planning as the ability to formulate and develop a plan to reach goals, the ability to execute the plan, and the ability to monitor and review the plan. A deficit in one of these areas could have profound academic implications. Korkman et al. (1998) have indicated that low scores on the Tower subtest could result from an inability to generate new solutions to problems. Scores are determined on a pass/fail basis for each item completed within a time limit. Qualitative scoring can indicate the number of rule violations that occur when the children incorrectly move the balls; motor difficulty should also be noted, as it could be related to impaired performance (Kemp et al., 2001).

*Auditory Attention and Response Set*   This subtest is designed to be administered to children age 5 to 12 and measures the child's ability to resist distracters, exercise inhibition, and shift cognitive sets. Children and examiners both may find this subtest to be the most difficult to take and administer. Children are required to listen to a tape-recorded voice that names colors and other words and place different-colored foam squares in a box according to the examiner's instructions. The tape-recorded voice proceeds at a rapid pace, and children are required to maintain a high level of attention and concentration to ensure that the correct colored squares are placed in the box while ignoring distracter words. There are two parts to this test: The first part assesses the ability to maintain vigilance and attention during an auditory task; the second part requires the child to adopt a new set of instructions for the same task, which helps assess perseveration, the more complex ability to shift and maintain set (Korkman et al., 1998). Children are scored based on the number of colored foam squares correctly placed in the box in a rapid fashion minus commission errors, or incorrect responses. Simultaneously, off-task behavior is tallied qualitatively.

LANGUAGE CORE SUBTESTS

This section describes the administration and interpretation of the Language Core Subtests.

*Body Part Naming*   Naming tasks are a common component of many child neuropsychological examinations and often include parts of the body or other common objects. This subtest is administered only to children age 3 to 4 and can be used to assess a child's naming ability, dysnomia (difficulty naming objects), and dysarthria (difficulties with articulation). Children are required to respond to the examiner's query to name parts of the body as pointed to in a stimulus booklet. The total score is based on the number of body parts that are named by the child, and the examiner also can qualitatively rate the child's articulation abilities.

*Speeded Naming*   This task is administered to children age 5 to 12 from the stimulus booklet and requires children to name the size, shape, and color of some simple geometric objects in a rapid and alternating manner. Scores on this subtest are based on the number of characteristics named correctly for each figure and the total time taken to complete the task. Difficulty on this task is usually related to a number of factors, including poor phonological processing skills, poor recall ability, impulsivity, and slow processing speed (Korkman et al., 1998). Speeded Naming may also be an indicator of reading difficulties, as phonological awareness and rapid naming ability are excellent predictors of reading ability (Crews, 2003; Feifer & DeFina, 2000).

*Phonological Processing*   As previously stated, phonological processing and awareness are excellent indicators of reading ability. If phonological awareness is not obtained by age 10, it is very difficult for a child to adequately learn the sound-symbol associations necessary for reading (Rourke & Del Dotto, 1994). This subtest is part of the battery for children age 3 to 4 and 5 to 12. Part A of this task asks the child to use words from phonemic segments to identify pictures. Part B is more complex, as the child is required to create a new word from an old word that has had a phoneme changed by the examiner. Similar to other subtests on the NEPSY that have two parts, interpretation is facilitated by drawing comparisons between performances on the two components. Poor performance on these tasks could indicate difficulty with phonological processing or phonemic awareness. This subtest is scored based on the number of correct items identified and the number of correctly created words.

*Comprehension of Instructions*   This subtest appears on the battery for children age 3 to 4 and 5 to 12. It assesses a child's ability to follow spoken directions and point to different-colored geometric shapes or rabbits in a stimulus booklet based on increasingly complex directions read by the examiner. Korkman et al. (1998) noted that difficulty on this task may indicate impaired ability in receptive language for semantically and syntactically complex directions. Scores are based on the number of correct responses. Although many of the subtests of the NEPSY have obvious face validity as they relate to classroom tasks, Comprehension of Instructions clearly relates to a child's difficulty in following directions from a teacher, especially multistep directions.

### Sensorimotor Core Subtests

This section describes the administration and interpretation of the Sensorimotor Core Subtests.

*Fingertip Tapping*   This subtest, administered to children 5 to 12, is a derivation of a classic finger tapping test that extends back to an early version of the HRNB.

This task is considered to be very sensitive to brain impairment and laterality of brain lesions (Reitan & Wolfson, 1993, 1996). However, unlike other batteries that use an electric or manual tapping device, this subtest asks the child to rapidly tap the tip of the index finger against the other fingers. Part 1 of this task has children tap their index finger against their thumb, first with their preferred hand, and then with their nondominant hand. The second component of this task asks the child to tap the four fingers of the dominant hand against the thumb in a sequential pattern, and then repeat with the nondominant hand. Qualitative observations include rate changes, incorrect positions, opposite-hand mirroring, and speech action during finger movement. Scores are based on the time taken to complete the requisite number of fingertip taps for each task.

*Imitating Hand Positions*   This subtest is administered to children of all ages. The examiner models a variety of hand positions that the children must imitate, first with the preferred hand and then with the nonpreferred hand. Korkman et al. (1998) indicated that difficulty with this task may be linked to kinesthetic praxis (the ability to perform skilled movement; Loring, 1999), processing of tactile information, and fine motor skills. Qualitative observation on this task includes using the other hand to help set the acting hand into position (not allowed) and the other hand mirroring the task. Scoring on this task is based on the number of hand positions that are imitated correctly.

*Visuomotor Precision*   This subtest, administered to all ages, is somewhat related to tasks found on other cognitive tests, such as the Mazes subtest on the Wechsler Intelligence Test for Children, third edition (Wechsler, 1991). Children are required to use a pencil to quickly draw a line inside a track that resembles a racing track or train tracks. This task assesses graphomotor skills, fine motor ability, and visual-spatial integration. Korkman et al. (1998) have also reported that poor performance could indicate impulsivity, poor visuomotor coordination, and poor planning. Children's performance on this subtest is scored by tallying the number of errors made. Qualitative observations are made regarding the child's pencil grip.

## Visuospatial Core Subtests

This section describes the administration and interpretation of the Visuospatial Core Subtests.

*Design Copying*   Tasks that require children to copy designs have a salient visuoperceptual component and are difficult for individuals with poor perceptual abilities (Lezak, 1995). Children of all ages complete this subtest. Children are required to copy a series of two-dimensional drawings from a stimulus booklet. Drawing tests appear as part of many standardized batteries due to their sensitivity for assessing visual-spatial integration and fine motor control. Difficulty copying simple geometric shapes may be indicative of constructional dyspraxia. Additionally, Korkman et al. (1998) suggested that difficulty on this task may be caused by poor motor coordination, inadequate visual-spatial abilities, and difficulty using a tool to implement visual-spatial motor-guided planning. The examiner makes qualitative observations regarding the child's pencil grip, and children's scores are based on criteria included in an appendix of the examiner's manual.

*Block Construction*   Block Construction is administered solely to children age 3 to 4. Tasks that require blocks to be constructed into three-dimensional formations based on a model serve as an excellent indicator of visual-spatial ability and are also used in other tests of cognitive functioning, notably the Wechsler Intelligence Test for Children, fourth edition (WISC-IV; Wechsler, 2003), in which the Block Design subtest has demonstrated excellent psychometric qualities. A child's score is based on the number of correct models, with bonuses awarded for speedy time. Rotations are recorded, although they do not affect the score.

*Arrows*   This subtest is administered only to children age 5 to 12. This visual-spatial task requires children to look at a stimulus booklet, which contains a series of drawings with a target in the center of a page and numbered arrows that point in the direction of the target. However, only two arrows are pointing at the direct center of the target, and the child must choose the correct arrows. This is an interesting visual-spatial task because it is free of motor components and allows the examiner to focus on the integration of visual and spatial abilities without the confounds of fine motor difficulty or visual-motor integration. Korkman et al. (1998) stated:

> Poor performance on the Arrows subtest could indicate difficulty in visualizing spatial relationships; in judging directions and estimating distance, orientation, and angularity of lines; and in understanding the relative position of objects in space. Lack of previewing or advance planning (impulsivity) may also affect a child's performance on this subtest. (p. 259)

Scoring for this subtest is based on the number of correct arrows chosen. Qualitative scoring notes the number of errors in each visual field.

## Memory Core Subtests

This section describes the administration and interpretation of the Memory Core Subtests.

*Narrative Memory*   The Narrative Memory subtest is administered to children age 3 to 4 and 5 to 12. Children are read a story by the examiner and then are asked to retell the story. Both age groups receive the same story. After children retell the story, they are prompted for content that they missed. The score on this subtest is based on the number of items recalled (under free recall and prompted conditions), with items recalled under the free recall task receiving more points. This subtest assesses a child's auditory memory, auditory encoding, and auditory comprehension. The test authors have pointed out that this subtest should be considered in light of other subtests on the NEPSY that assess attention, language, and executive functions.

*Sentence Repetition*   This subtest is administered only to children age 3 to 4. Children are asked to repeat verbatim sentences of increasing length. Tasks that assess auditory memory generally follow this form, in which the child is required to rapidly encode and recall verbal information. One of the advantages of this subtest over memory span auditory tests is that the task contains a naturalistic component that is related to everyday functioning (Lezak, 1995). The total score is the number of correct sentences plus the number of sentences with fewer than two errors. Qualitative notations can be made concerning performance on this repetition task (Kemp et al., 2001).

*Memory for Faces*   The Memory for Faces subtest is administered only to children age 5 to 12. Memory for Faces has two parts, an immediate recall phase and a delayed recognition phase, which occurs about 30 minutes after the initial presentation of the stimulus. Participants are presented with pictures of children's faces from a stimulus book at an exposure duration of 5 seconds. Immediately following the presentation, children are asked to look at a page containing pictures of 3 faces, one of which is the same as that viewed during the stimulus presentation. Thirty minutes later, children repeat the delayed recognition part of the task. The total score for this task is the combined number of faces identified on the immediate and delayed recall. This subtest not only assesses visual memory, but also can be used to compare immediate and delayed visual memory based on differential performance between the two components of this subtest. The test authors believe that poor performance could be due to inadequate visuospatial processing, poor attention, or a limited memory span (Korkman et al., 1998).

*Memory for Names*   The Memory for Names subtest is similar in administration to the Memory for Faces subtest and is also administered only to children age 5 to 12. Participants are presented with a series of cards that have children's faces on them, and the examiner pairs each face with a name. The examiner then shuffles the cards and asks the child to identify the names. This is repeated for 3 trials. After 30 minutes, the child is again presented with the cards and asked to identify the name of each child pictured. In addition to measuring immediate and delayed verbal memory, this subtest assesses the storage and retrieval of verbal labels, attention, planning, and language skills (Korkman et al., 1998). The total score for this subtest is the number of correct names recalled for the immediate and delayed aspects of this subtest.

### INTERPRETATION OF THE NEPSY

As with any neuropsychological test or battery, caution should be exercised in drawing brain-related conclusions about test results unless the examiner is trained in neuropsychological assessment, interpretation, and intervention development. The NEPSY is easy to administer and score, and any school psychologist with sufficient training in neuropsychology will be able to perform these tasks. A computer-scoring program is also available (Korkman et al., 1998). The NEPSY is also relatively easy to interpret, and psychologists will be able to draw a tremendous amount of behavioral information from the core or expanded versions of the battery. Practitioners familiar with the WISC-III or WISC-IV will recognize the user-friendly interface of the protocol cover sheet. Some subtests allow the calculation of supplemental scores when the subtest scaled scores represent different facets, such as breaking down the Memory for Faces subtests into immediate and delayed recall standard scores.

Interpretation of the NEPSY should be a multifaceted process, the depth of which will depend on the user's familiarity with neuropsychology and the underlying paradigm that flows from the theoretical construct on which the NEPSY was based (Korkman et al., 1998). Normative and ipsative analyses are facilitated by the format of the protocol, which allows the examiner to look at children's scores relative to the standardization sample, as well as to compare within and between a child's own domain scores. Intraindividual analysis is especially useful on the NEPSY, as psychologists will be able to use neuropsychological strengths uncovered on the NEPSY to compensate for neuropsychological weaknesses in the planning of interventions. Although subtests tend to have lower reliability than index scores or domain scores, interpretation at the subtest level will provide information about behavioral functioning that will also suggest strengths and weaknesses. Another useful interpretation strategy is to examine intraindividual domain scores to elucidate a child's unique profile; for example, a child may demonstrate strength in phonological processing ability but have a weakness in the rapid, automatic recognition of concepts, which may explain the etiology of a reading problem in the presence of an average language domain score. The NEPSY manual has provided a wealth of information about interpreting and analyzing subtest and domain scores, and interested readers are directed toward that source (Kemp et al., 2001).

## PSYCHOMETRIC VALIDATION OF THE NEPSY

Like any new neuropsychological test, judgment regarding the *reliability* and *validity* of the test will have to be at least partially withheld until a number of outside validation studies have been conducted. Although the NEPSY falls in the category of a relatively recent test, some validity information has been collected and published that has begun to illuminate the psychometric properties of the instrument (Bjoraker, 2001; Crews, 2003; McClosky, 2000; Stinnett et al., 2002). In its present form, the NEPSY is a restructuring of older tests originally used in Finland (Korkman, 1980, 1988). Hence, there is more information regarding the validity and reliability of the battery than would be expected on a test battery published in 1998. Additionally, many of the subtests are adopted from classic neuropsychological tests that have an extensive history of validation, such as the Finger Tapping subtest, which appeared as early as 1947 (Halstead, 1947). The NEPSY manual presents more studies on its psychometric qualities than can be covered in this brief review; however, some seminal studies are briefly discussed.

Reliability coefficients are provided for the subtests and domains, and reliability coefficients are reported by the test authors for each age (3 to 12). For children age 3 to 4, the average core domain reliability coefficients were generally moderate to high and ranged from .70 to .91, and the subtest average reliability coefficients ranged from .50 to .91. The .50 was obviously an area of concern. For children age 5 to 12, the average core domain reliability coefficients ranged from .79 to .87, and the subtest average reliability coefficients ranged from .58 to .91. In general, users should feel comfortable with the reliability of both the subtests and the domains; the reliability of .70 for Attention/Executive Functions for children age 3 and 4 is the only area of concern. However, the test authors aptly point out that developmental variability can be extreme in this area of the brain for very young children (Korkman et al., 1998).

Numerous validity studies are reported in the test manual that were conducted on earlier versions of the NEPSY, as well as on the current version. Content validity was reportedly established following reviews by panels of neuropsychologists, school psychologists, and other experts and were used to modify the NEPSY. Construct validity on the NEPSY has been established by a broad series of comparison studies with normal and clinical populations to other neuropsychological and psychological tests, including the WISC-III, the Bayley Scales of Infant Development, second edition (Bayley, 1993), the Wechsler Individual Achievement Test (Psychological Corporation, 1992), the Children's Memory Scale (Cohen, 1997), and the Benton Neuropsychological Tests (Benton, Hamsher, Varney, & Spreen, 1983). In general, these comparison studies have indicated mostly acceptable levels of convergent and discriminant validity. So, too, when appropriate, aspects of the NEPSY were related to intellectual functioning, school performance, and measures of neuropsychological processing. Korkman, Kirk, and Kemp (2001) have attempted to provide further evidence of validity in a study that examined a subset of the standardization sample; they argued that the NEPSY was sensitive to age effects. In addition to the comparison studies presented in the test manual, the test authors have provided a number of studies that examined the NEPSY with specific clinical populations, such as children with learning disabilities and Attention-Deficit/Hyperactivity Disorder, as well as children with Fetal Alcohol Syndrome and traumatic brain injuries.

Reitan and Wolfson (1993) list three components that a neuropsychological test battery that measures brain-behavior relationships should possess. First, the test must measure brain-based neuropsychological functions. Second, a good test contains methods that enable the test results to demonstrate the uniqueness of individuals. Finally, the psychometric properties of the test must be validated through formal research in regard to clinical evaluation and utility. Although the NEPSY admirably meets the first two criteria set by Reitan and Wolfson, the third area is in development. Although some studies provide evidence of average to excellent validity and reliability, others suggest that the psychometric qualities of the NEPSY should be evaluated *with caution*. For example, Stinnett et al. (2002) conducted an exploratory principal axis factor analysis of the core subtest scores of children in the NEPSY standardization sample age 5 to 12 as reported in the NEPSY manual. The authors concluded that a 1-factor solution best described the core subtests. This is quite different from the NEPSY's presentation as a battery that measures five succinct neuropsychological domains. Stinnett et al. (2002) also cautioned that many of the subtests lacked the specificity required for independent interpretation of the underlying abilities the subtests purport to measure. However, Stinnett et al. (2002) stated that, "because the language factor was sufficient in explaining the structure of the test, interpretation of a child's NEPSY performance as if Attention/Executive Functions, Sensorimotor Functions, Visuospatial Processing, and/or Memory and Learning are separate neuropsychological functions is not warranted" (p. 78). McClosky (2000) used the NEPSY to evaluate the neuropsychological functioning of Hispanic children. In brief, she found that although teachers reported concerns about the neuropsychological functioning of children in their classrooms, the NEPSY *did not* identify these children as impaired. In contrast, Bjoraker (2001) found the NEPSY to be *sensitive* to the language deficits of children who had been identified as having a significantly identifiable emotional disorder. A more recent study by Crews (2003) used the

NEPSY to subtype children's learning disabilities. Clearly, more information is needed about the utility and validity of this battery. However, ease of administration, portability, and the seemingly abundant availability of clinical information the NEPSY provides make it an attractive instrument (Sattler & D'Amato, 2002).

## THE DEAN-WOODCOCK
## NEUROPSYCHOLOGICAL BATTERY

A positive trend in test development is the linking, co-norming, and concurrent development of one measure with others, so that measures can be combined to form a more comprehensive battery. This approach allows psychologists to administer a series of individual tests when more information is needed regarding a certain brain-related domain. For example, an auditory memory deficit suspected as the result of the administration of the WISC-IV (Wechsler, 2003) can be followed by selected subtests or the entire battery of the Wechsler Memory Scale, third edition (WMS-III; Psychological Corporation, 1997). Similarly, the new DWNB (Dean & Woodcock, 2003a) was designed to be administered as a stand-alone battery or to be used in conjunction with the Woodcock-Johnson Tests of Cognitive Abilities (WJ-III-COG; Woodcock, McGrew, & Mather, 2001a) and the Woodcock-Johnson Tests of Achievement (WJ-III-ACH; Woodcock, McGrew, & Mather, 2001b). The DWNB with these two measures together compose the comprehensive battery known as the Dean-Woodcock Neuropsychological Assessment System (DWNAS). The WJ-COG and the WJ-ACH contribute greatly to the battery because they encompass theory-based measures of cognitive functioning and academic achievement. Combining these three measures allows for the evaluation of *all* of the important neuropsychological domains of relevance in the majority of cases. Indeed, the DWNB manual states, "The DWNAS covers most of the major domains assessed in a comprehensive neuropsychological, or psychoeducational evaluation and provides a profile of an individual's sensory, motor, emotional, cognitive, and academic functioning" (Dean & Woodcock, 2003a, p. 1). The DWNB consists of the Dean-Woodcock Sensory-Motor Battery (DWSMB), the Dean-Woodcock Emotional Status Examination (Dean & Woodcock, 2003b), and the Dean-Woodcock Structured Neuropsychological Interview (Dean & Woodcock, 2003d). For a thorough discussion of the Woodcock-Johnson Tests of Cognitive Abilities (Woodcock et al., 2001a) and the Woodcock-Johnson Tests of Achievement (Woodcock et al., 2001b), the reader is directed to Mather, Wendling, and Woodcock (2001) and Schrank, Flanagan, Woodcock, and Mascolo (2001).

A review of the literature of current sensory and motor tests reveals a serious lack of information on reliability and validity, including little, if any, standardization data (Woodward, Ridenour, Dean, & Woodcock, 2002). The DWNB is quite different from the older, cumbersome, lengthy batteries with outdated normative samples. Additionally, the comprehensive assessment of sensory and motor skills is a key component that is often neglected by those administering traditional psychoeducational batteries. The DWSMB appears easy to administer and score, and a computer scoring system will soon be available. The DWSMB can be administered in about 30 to 45 minutes. The Structured Neuropsychological Interview and the Emotional Status Examination each take approximately 30 minutes to administer. However, as with all neuropsychological measures, administration time may increase if the child demonstrates significant impairment. An advantage of the DWNB when compared to other traditional standardized batteries is that it was designed for a wide range of practitioners, including school psychologists. The DWNB can be administered and interpreted by doctoral-level school psychologists who are qualified to administer and interpret psychological tests. Caution should be exercised, however, when drawing neuropsychological conclusions if the administrator is not fully trained in neuropsychology. Indeed, the manual states, "The DWNB is a specialized diagnostic aid that was designed to be administered and scored easily by a wide range of examiners. However, the battery should be administered only by properly trained examiners" (Dean & Woodcock, 2003c, p. 5). The manual is comprehensive and provides a wealth of information, not only about the DWNB, but also about neuropsychological assessment, and could serve as an introduction to the field for classes in neuropsychology.

## THE DEAN-WOODCOCK SENSORY-MOTOR BATTERY

The DWSMB consists of 18 subtests, 8 of which measure *sensory* functions such as visual, auditory, and tactile perception, and 10 of which measure *motor* functioning. The subtests from the DWSMB are displayed in Table 11.2.

The scores obtained on subtests from the DWSMB were derived from a normative sample of more than 1,000 individuals ranging from 4 to over 90 years of age. Many of the subtests on the DWSMB will seem familiar to neuropsychologists, yet

> many of the tests in the DWSMB are adapted standardized versions of neurological or neuropsychological measures that historically have been used to assess cortical and subcortical functioning. However, unlike their historic predecessors, both the administration and scoring of the clinical measures in the DWSMB have been standardized. (Dean & Woodcock, 2003c, p. 2)

Additionally, the subtests go beyond the traditional cut-off approach, and this greater specificity allows consideration of a few errors that could be indicative of sensorimotor impairment. Instructions for each subtest are provided in the examiner's manual in both English and Spanish. Each subtest of the DWSMB is briefly described next in the order in which they are presented in the examiner's manual (Dean & Woodcock, 2003c).

**Table 11.2**
Subtests from the Dean-Woodcock Sensory-Motor Battery

| Sensory Subtests | Motor Subtests |
|---|---|
| Near-Point Visual Acuity | Lateral Preference Scale |
| Visual Confrontation | Gait and Station |
| Naming Pictures of Objects | Romberg |
| Auditory Acuity | Construction |
| Tactile Examination: Palm Writing | Mime Movements |
| Tactile Examination: Object Identification | Left-Right Movements |
| Tactile Examination: | Finger Tapping |
|    Simultaneous Localization | Expressive Speech |
| Tactile Examination: Finger Identification | Grip Strength |
| | Coordination |

*Sensory Tests*  This section describes the administration and interpretation of the Sensory Tests.

NEAR-POINT VISUAL ACUITY  Visual acuity is a function that is not normally assessed during a standard school psychologist's assessment, yet the ability to see clearly can have a profound impact on an individual's performance and the validity of the findings. A cardboard eye occluder keeps one eye covered while the other eye is used to read a series of numbers on an eye chart placed 14 inches away. The process is repeated for the other eye, and scoring is based on Snellen notations (i.e., 20/20 vision).

VISUAL CONFRONTATION  Visual attention tasks, sometimes referred to as visual neglect tasks, can be sensitive to abrupt onset conditions, such as stroke or trauma (Lezak, 1995). This subtest assesses the subject's field of vision for any defects or inattention. The examinee is required to stare at the center of the examiner's face while the examiner sits 3 feet away with his or her arms extended and wiggles either the left, right, or both fingers. This subtest is important to neuropsychological functioning due to the contralateral nature of the visual field, which can aid examiners in determining cerebral lateralization, as well as whether lesions are prechiasmal, chiasmal, or postchiasmal, all of which can affect academic, social, and vocational functioning (Dean & Woodcock, 2003c).

NAMING PICTURES OF OBJECTS  Confrontation naming, the ability to volitionally access the correct word, is a skill that can be lost due to a variety of neuropsychological conditions that affect children and adults, such as traumatic brain injury (Lezak, 1995). Designed as a screening test, this subtest requires the subject to name 21 objects. None of the objects is overly complex, so this subtest should not be mistaken for an ability test of vocabulary. Rather, this task serves to screen for dysnomia (difficulty naming objects) or visual agnosia (failure to visually recognize objects). Although dysnomia and visual agnosia may exist in isolation, it is more common that they accompany receptive language problems. Evidence of either disorder should lead the examiner to further examine potential deficits on tests from the full battery that assess expressive and receptive language (Dean & Woodcock, 2003b).

AUDITORY ACUITY  Similar to visual acuity, auditory acuity is an area in which the psychologist generally relies on the self-report of the participant to provide information regarding hearing. Although most participants are aware of a hearing loss, those who may have recently incurred a brain trauma may be unaware of the deficit, especially when the hearing loss is slight or when aphasic deficits are contributing to speech problems (Lezak, 1995). On this task, the examiner stands behind the subject and gently rubs his or her fingers together 3 inches away from the examinee's ears. The examinee is required to identify which ear or if both ears are receiving the sound. Auditory Acuity aids in determining laterality in impairment when there is a difference in performance between the left and right auditory channels (Dean & Woodcock, 2003c). Like the Visual Acuity subtest, this subtest is designed as a screener and should not replace a formal assessment by an audiologist or ophthalmologist.

*Tactile Examination*  The tactile examination subtests are classic tests of perceptual discrimination, similar to those found on the HRNB (Reitan & Wolfson, 1993).

PALM WRITING  The first task of Tactile Examination-Palm Writing requires subjects to identify whether an X or an O is written on their palm; the second task requires subjects to identify numbers. A different number of errors between hands may be evidence of a contralateral cerebral impairment (an impairment opposite the hemisphere of the impaired hand). Difficulty on this task can also indicate a tactile discrimination problem, which can present as clumsiness and difficulty with dexterity (Dean & Woodcock, 2003c). Skin-writing tasks are also sometimes part of a neurological examination and can be used for lateralization information when no clear hemiparesis or aphasia is present, as well as provide information regarding the severity of a tactile or perceptual deficit (Lezak, 1995).

OBJECT IDENTIFICATION    The inability to identify common objects by tactile stimulation in the absence of visual aid is generally indicative of astereognosis (loss of an ability to recognize objects by touch). Generally, normal individuals are able to easily complete this task, and even one error or indication of hesitation may indicate cerebral problems (Dean & Woodcock, 2003c). In this subtest, the examinee is blindfolded and seated in a chair. Individuals are required to identify familiar objects by holding and manipulating them in their hands. Testing for astereognosis with this type of task is well validated and has appeared in many different forms (e.g., Luria, 1966; Reitan & Wolfson, 1993).

FINGER IDENTIFICATION    Designed to assess finger agnosia (the inability to recognize tactile stimulation in one's own fingers), this subtest requires the examinee to identify without visual help which finger the examiner is touching. A version of this task appears on the HRNB, and most normal participants will have few nonconcentration-related errors. However, errors on this task are thought to be associated with contralateral parietal lobe lesions or concentration problems (Reitan & Wolfson, 1993).

SIMULTANEOUS LOCALIZATION    The fourth of the tactile examination subtests, all of which assess broad sensory and tactile reception, uses double sensory stimulation and unilateral stimulation to increase the likelihood of identifying a sensory deficit because unilateral stimulation alone may not detect subtle lesions in the sensory cortex (Dean & Woodcock, 2003c). The technique of using double sensory stimulation on the participants' hands and cheeks to investigate tactile perception is a well-validated method, and versions of this task have been used since at least 1960 (Kahn, Goldfarb, Pollack, & Peck, 1960). The child's hands and cheeks are touched lightly with a stylus in a predetermined combination of right only, left only, and right and left together, and the child is required to identify the location of the stimulation.

*Motor Tests*    This section describes the administration and interpretation of the Motor Tests.

LATERAL PREFERENCE SCALE    Based on a task first standardized by Dean (1988), this subtest is designed to determine the handedness of the individual. This is an important issue, as handedness can help determine laterality of cerebral dysfunction, as well as guide the examiner when tasks requiring the dominant hand are required (see Chapter 6). Handedness is very consistent; Reitan and Davison (1974) found that nearly 100% of normal participants maintained the same dominant hand after a 5-year span. Subjects are required to answer a series of questions from the stimulus book regarding which hand or leg they would use to complete 17 different fine motor movements. This subtest differs from traditional tests of lateral preference in its use of a 5-point Likert scale that ranges from "left always" to "right always."

GAIT AND STATION    Gait and Station is composed of three separate tasks that broadly assess gait problems, or the ability to coordinate smooth motor movement (Davis, 2003). Gait is an important concept, yet despite the wide assessment of this motor ability by physicians, psychologists, and neuropsychologists, the assessment of gait is not found in any other major neuropsychological standardized battery (Dean & Woodcock, 2003c; Sattler & D'Amato, 2002). This series of tasks is thought to assess lower extremity gross motor functioning, coordination, and speed and can be sensitive to the presence of subcortical lesions. The first task, Gait-Free Walking, requires the subject to walk forward 10 feet and turn around. The second task, Gait-Heel-to-Toe, requires the examinee to walk by placing one foot directly in front of the other. The third task, Gait-Hopping, asks the subject to hop in place on one foot and then the other. The examiner assesses the degree to which the child is able to complete the task correctly and smoothly. For the fourth part of this subtest, Station, the subject's steadiness is examined while standing erect with his or her feet together and eyes open.

ROMBERG    This classic neurological test requires that the child stand erect with his or her eyes closed while the examiner watches for swaying and other signs of impaired balance. Here the utility of the Romberg test is enhanced due to the large standardization sample and the requirement that the subject stand in three different positions to increase the chance of detection of cerebral impairment. The positions become increasingly difficult for the child, and hence more subcortically dependent (Dean & Woodcock, 2003c).

CONSTRUCTION    Drawing tests are designed to detect pathognomic signs of construction dyspraxia (difficulty in motor tasks involving the construction of figures), visual-motor integration, and visuospatial awareness and memory. Drawing tests are popular and appear in many neuropsychological batteries, including the Bender Visual-Motor Gestalt Test, second edition (Brannigan & Decker, 2003) and the Reitan-Indiana Aphasia Screening Test (Reitan & Wolfson, 1992). Indeed, drawing tasks play a central role in neuropsychological testing due to their sensitivity to different types of brain impairment (Lezak, 1995; Sattler & D'Amato, 2002). The Construction task requires the subject to copy a cross from a stimulus book and to draw a clock that displays a specific time. In addition to identifying dyspraxia, construction tasks have historically been used as effective screening tests to differentiate elderly patients without Alzheimer's disease from elderly patients with Alzheimer's disease (Dean & Woodcock, 2003c).

COORDINATION    This subtest assesses an individual's upper extremity motor functioning by using a version of the classic neurological test of moving one's finger to one's nose. However, like the other subtests on the DWSMB, this task is now normed, which is an advantage compared to administering sensorimotor tests by qualitative observation alone. Participants are required to first touch the tip of their nose with their index finger, and then touch the examiner's finger as the examiner moves his or her finger across the participant's field of vision. Participants must also tap their thigh, alternating between the front and the back of their hand. Both of these tasks are administered with both of the participant's hands. These tasks assess coordinated motor movement at the cerebral and cerebellar levels (Dean & Woodcock, 2003c).

MIME MOVEMENTS    Mime Movements assesses an individual's ability to follow directions and execute skilled motor movements. Individuals are required to perform simple acts that involve the hands, mouth, and head (e.g., pretending to brush one's hair). When individuals possess adequate receptive language ability and are unable to execute well-rehearsed movements, it may indicate the presence of ideomotor dyspraxia (an inability to perform simple motor tasks when requested to do so; Dean & Woodcock, 2003c). Indeed, when used in conjunction with tests of receptive language, this subtest is useful in discriminating between receptive language difficulties and motor movement difficulties.

LEFT-RIGHT MOVEMENTS  Although it is rare for children over 9 to demonstrate confusion between the left and right hand, such confusion can interfere with daily living skills and may be indicative of a variety of brain difficulties (Dean & Woodcock, 2003c). This subtest assesses left-right confusion by asking the subject to perform a number of very simple tasks with both hands.

FINGER TAPPING  Finger tapping tests are one of the most widely used measures of manual dexterity (Sattler & D'Amato, 2002), and a version of this task, called the Finger Tapping Test or Finger Oscillation Test, appears on the HRNB. This subtest on the DWSMB assesses fine motor speed and dexterity and provides an indicator of the overall functioning of the motor strip and precentral gyrus (Dean & Woodcock, 2003c). Participants are required to tap the + key on a hand calculator as rapidly as possible for five 10-second trials with each hand.

EXPRESSIVE SPEECH  Some individuals are able to accurately understand language, yet have difficulty producing it. This subtest assesses for the presence of dysarthria (problems with speech due to muscle control) by asking participants to repeat a series of simple words and phrases. Participants who struggle with this task may be exhibiting deficits in the peripheral speech mechanisms, and it allows the separation of dysarthria from more global language impairments (Dean & Woodcock, 2003c).

GRIP STRENGTH  This classic neuropsychological test has long been used to measure upper extremity motor strength (Dean & Woodcock, 2003c). On this subtest, a hand dynometer is squeezed for three trials with each hand. Impaired performance with either hand may indicate deficits in the contralateral motor strip and the overall integrity of the cerebral hemispheres (Dean & Woodcock, 2003c). This popular test has been used for decades (Reitan & Wolfson, 1993).

## THE DEAN-WOODCOCK STRUCTURED NEUROPSYCHOLOGICAL INTERVIEW

An individual's performance on a neuropsychological battery is not always a pure indication of the individual's neuropsychological skills and abilities. Often, factors such as motivation, attention, emotional problems, and medical disorders may cause individuals to either perform better or worse than their true neuropsychological abilities. The Structured Neuropsychological Interview provides practitioners with a systematic measure for obtaining information about the child's or adult's current level of functioning. The Structured Neuropsychological Interview can be administered to the child directly or to a respondent familiar with the child. This easy-to-administer measure collects information from seven areas. The first section, Identifying Information/ Biographic Information, provides demographic information. The test authors indicate that such information should not be overlooked, because demographic information such as occupation may be an important predictor of premorbid functioning (Dean, 1989). The Referral Information/Chief Complaint section elicits the primary reason the individual is being referred for assessment, as well as information about the child's perceived complaint and his or her level of functioning. The Medical History section offers a wealth of information regarding the child's past and current medical history and its relationship to current neuropsychological functioning. The History of Psychiatric/Psychological Evaluation and/or Treatment section allows the examiner to collect information regarding previous emotional problems. This section focuses on psychiatric and psychological problems, including past mental illness/disorder, substance abuse, head injuries, seizures, and sensory impairments. The Personal and Social History section allows the examiner to obtain information about risk factors and resiliency, including social support systems and poor social or adaptive skills. The Psychiatric and Neurologic Family History focuses on the child's history of neuropsychological and neurological functioning. Dean and Woodcock (2003c) have argued that the biographical history may be the most important part of the overall evaluation. The final section focuses on prenatal development, the mother's pregnancy, and the rate at which the client reached developmental milestones.

## THE DEAN-WOODCOCK EMOTIONAL STATUS EXAMINATION

The Emotional Status Examination helps the clinician collect information that could be modulating the results of an assessment or affecting a child's functioning. Similar to the Structured Neuropsychological Interview, information can be collected either from the child or an informant who knows the child well. The Emotional Status Examination consists of three sections. The first section provides the examiner space to enter the client's demographic information. The second section entails a series of questions designed to explore signs and symptoms of psychiatric disorders. The third section, Clinical Observations and Impressions, permits the examiner to note observations of the client's functioning, including orientation, physical appearance, behavioral observations, emotional status, and cognitive status. The Emotional Status Examination is a valuable component to the battery; standardized neuropsychological batteries have rarely solicited such detailed information regarding emotional status.

## INTERPRETATION OF THE DEAN-WOODCOCK NEUROPSYCHOLOGICAL BATTERY

The DWNB provides data indicative of neuropsychological functioning across sensory, motor, personality, and emotional domains. The DWNB appears more sensitive to subcortical functioning than other measures of sensory and motor functioning (Woodward et al., 2002). Although parts of the battery are designed to provide information regarding pathognomic signs of cerebral dysfunction, psychologists will be able to gather information regarding behavioral functioning that can help guide interventions and determine strengths and weaknesses. Age-equivalent and W-scores are available for interpretation for each subtest of the DWSMB. W-difference scores are available that can provide information regarding the learner's functioning in terms of level of impairment, ranging from "above," to "within normal limits," to "severely impaired." In addition, summary indexes are available for Total Sensory, Total Motor, and Total Impairment. The authors offer four different approaches to interpreting the DWSMB that are grounded in traditional neuropsychological assessment: Functional Level of Performance approach, Right-Left Differences approach, Pattern Analysis, and Pathognomic Sign approach. For a more complete discussion regarding interpretation of the DWSMB and other neuropsychological tests, see Dean and Woodcock (2003c), Hebben and Milberg (2002), Reitan and Wolfson (1993), and Sattler and D'Amato (2002).

## Validation of the Dean-Woodcock Neuropsychological Battery

The test authors drew from classic neuropsychological tests with a long history of research and validation in their development of the DWSMB (Dean & Woodcock, 2002b). Due to the recent release of the DWNB, few validation studies are available in the literature. Like any new test, independent studies of the validity and reliability of the DWNB are needed. However, a few studies are reported in the manual that attest to the validity and reliability of this measure. In one study, Woodward et al. (2002) administered the DWSMB to 95 participants and videotaped the assessment. Interrater reliability was generally regarded as adequate to excellent for the subtests of the DWSMB. A study is reported in the test manual that examined the underlying factor construct of the DWSMB (Hill, Lewis, Dean, & Woodcock, 2001). Exploratory factor analysis involving 617 participants between the ages of 2 and 88 revealed that a 3-factor solution best fit the data, with the following three factors emerging: Sensory Functions, Cortical Motor Functions, and Subcortical Motor Functions. Overall, sufficient validity and reliability information seems to exists, warranting confidence in the interpretation of the DWSMB. However, it is important to note that further validation is necessary.

## CONCLUSION

School neuropsychologists have much to gain from the use and understanding of neuropsychological information. Neuropsychological tests offer school psychologists a perspective from which to understand disorders of school-age children, in addition to being able to provide a theoretical perspective for the planning of interventions based on a child's unique strengths and weaknesses from a number of functional domains (D'Amato et al., 1999). Historically, school psychologists have not relied on neuropsychological information due to its complexity and the seemingly minimal utility provided by traditional neuropsychological batteries. However, more recent, user-friendly neuropsychological test batteries such as the DWNB and the NEPSY have improved the assessment of neuropsychological functioning in children. Both of these batteries have been standardized on a large sample of children, have adequate to excellent norms, and possess emerging evidence of adequate reliability and validity. Although these batteries have yet to be put through the rigors of extensive independent analysis, in both cases, the test authors drew on traditional, well-validated neuropsychological tasks that have proven to be good indicators of pathognomic signs and neuropsychological abilities. However, some questions remain about both batteries. For example, independent research (Stinnett et al., 2002) suggested that using the NEPSY to generate interventions should be done with caution given findings that did not support the proposed factorial structure. The DWNB is so new that independent validation studies of the instrument have yet to appear in the literature. Despite these limitations, the DWNB and the NEPSY should be considered leaders in the new generation of theoretically based, well-constructed, user-friendly, and psychometrically sound neuropsychological test batteries. Well-constructed assessment devices are essential to the pragmatic assessment of functional behavioral systems, which should lead to the generation of neuropsychological interventions for instruction using compensatory activities. As school neuropsychologists modify their roles to focus on prevention, interventions, and system change (Ysseldyke & Elliot, 1999), select children and youth with significant impairments will continue to require comprehensive neuropsychological services. To meet these needs, school districts will have to have access to school neuropsychological services.

## REFERENCES

Ahmad, S. A., & Warriner, E. M. (2001). Review of the NEPSY: A developmental neuropsychological assessment. *Clinical Neuropsychologist, 15,* 240–249.

Bayley, N. (1993). *Bayley scales of infant development* (2nd ed.). San Antonio, TX: Psychological Corporation.

Belopol'skaia, N., & Grebennikova, N. (1997). Neuropsychology and psychological dimensions of abnormal development. In E. Grigorenko, P. Ruzgis, & R. Sternberg (Eds.), *Psychology of Russia: Past, present, future* (pp. 155–179). Commack, NY: Nova Science.

Benton, A. L., Hamsher, K. S., Varney, N. R., & Spreen, O. (1983). *Contributions to neuropsychological assessment: A clinical manual.* New York: Oxford University Press.

Bjoraker, K. J. (2001). *An examination of the neuropsychological basis of emotional difficulties in children.* Unpublished doctoral dissertation, University of Northern Colorado, Greeley, CO.

Brannigan, G. G., & Decker, S. L. (2003). *Bender Visual-Motor Gestalt Test* (2nd ed.). Itasca, IL: Riverside.

Cicerone, K. D., & Tupper, D. E. (1986). Cognitive assessment in the neuropsychological rehabilitation of head-injured adults. In B. P. Uzzell & Y. Gross (Eds.), *Clinical neuropsychology of intervention.* Boston: Marinus Nijhoff.

Cohen, M. J. (1997). *Children's memory scale.* San Antonio, TX: Psychological Corporation.

Crews, K. (2003). *Subtyping reading disabilities in children with neuropsychological measures.* Unpublished doctoral dissertation, University of Northern Colorado, Greeley, CO.

Culbertson, W. C., Moberg, P. J., Duda, J. E., Stern, M. B., & Weintraub, D. (2004). Assessing the executive function deficits of patients with Parkinson's disease: Utility of the Tower of London-Drexel. *Assessment, 11,* 27–39.

D'Amato, R. C., Rothlisberg, B. A., & Leu Work, P. H. (1999). Neuropsychological assessment for intervention. In C. R. Reynolds & T. B. Gutkin (Eds.), *The handbook of school psychology* (3rd ed., pp. 452–475). New York: Wiley.

Davis, A. S. (2003). Gait disturbance. In E. Fletcher-Janzen & C. R. Reynolds (Eds.), *The diagnostic manual of childhood disorders: Clinical and special education applications* (pp. 251–252). Hoboken, NJ: Wiley.

Dean, R. S. (1988). *Lateral preference schedule: Professional manual.* Odessa, FL: Psychological Assessment Resources.

Dean, R. S. (1989). Foundations of rationale for neuropsychological bases of individual differences. In L. C. Hartlage & C. F. Telzrow (Eds.), *The neuropsychology of individual differences: A developmental perspective.* New York: Plenum Press.

Dean, R. S., & Woodcock, R. W. (2003a). *Dean-Woodcock Neuropsychological Battery.* Itasca, IL: Riverside.

Dean, R. S., & Woodcock, R. W. (2003b). Emotional Status Examination. *Dean-Woodcock Neuropsychological Battery.* Itasca, IL: Riverside.

Dean, R. S., & Woodcock, R. W. (2003c). *Dean-Woodcock Neuropsychological Battery.* [Examiners manual]. Itasca, IL: Riverside.

Dean, R. S., & Woodcock, R. W. (2003d). Structured Neuropsychological Interview. *Dean-Woodcock Neuropsychological Battery.* Itasca, IL: Riverside.

Feifer, S. G., & DeFina, P. A. (2000). *The neuropsychology of reading disorders: Diagnosis and intervention workbook.* Middletown, MD: School Neuropsych Press.

Fletcher-Janzen, E., & Reynolds, C. R. (2003). *Childhood disorders: Diagnostic desk reference.* New York: Wiley.

Gouvier, W., Ryan, L., O'Jile, J., Parks-Levy, J., Webster, J., & Blanton, P. (1997). Cognitive retraining with brain-damaged patients. In A. Horton, D. Wedding, & J. Webster (Eds.), *The neuropsychology handbook: Vol. 2.* New York: Springer.

Halstead, W. C. (1947). *Brain and intelligence: A quantitative study of the frontal lobes.* Chicago: University of Chicago Press.

Hebben, N., & Milberg, W. (2002). *Essentials of neuropsychological assessment.* Hoboken, NJ: Wiley.

Hill, S. K., Lewis, M. N., Dean, R. S., & Woodcock, R. S. (2001). Constructs underlying measures of sensory-motor functioning. *Archives of Clinical Neuropsychology, 15,* 631–641.

Kahn, R. L., Goldfarb, A. I., Pollack, M., & Peck, A. (1960). Brief objective measures for the determination of mental status in the aged. *American Journal of Psychiatry, 117,* 326–328.

Kemp, S. L., Kirk, U., & Korkman, M. (2001). *Essentials of NEPS assessment.* New York: Wiley.

Korkman, M. (1980). *NEPS. Lasten neuropsykologinen tutkimus* [NEPS. Neuropsychological assessment of children]. Helsinki, Finland: Psyklolgien Kustannus Oy.

Korkman, M. (1988). *NEPSU. Lasten neuropsykologinen tutkimus. Uudistettu versio* [NEPSY. Neuropsychological assessment of children-Revised edition]. Helsinki, Finland: Psyklolgien Kustannus Oy.

Korkman, M. (1999). Applying Luria's diagnostic principles in the neuropsychological assessment of children. *Neuropsychology Review, 9,* 89–105.

Korkman, M., Kettunen, S., & Autti-Raemoe, I. (2003). Neurocognitive impairment in early adolescence following prenatal alcohol exposure of varying duration. *Child Neuropsychology, 9,* 117–128.

Korkman, M., Kirk, U., & Kemp, S. (1998). *NEPSY: A developmental neuropsychological assessment manual.* San Antonio, TX: Psychological Corporation.

Korkman, M., Kirk, U., & Kemp, S. (2001). Effects of age on neurocognitive measures of children ages 5 to 12: A cross sectional study on 800 children from the United States. *Developmental Neuropsychology, 20,* 331–354.

Lezak, M. D. (1995). *Neuropsychological assessment* (3rd ed.). New York: Oxford University.

Loring, D. W. (Ed.). (1999). *INS dictionary of neuropsychology.* New York: Oxford Press.

Luria, A. R. (1966). *Higher cortical functions in man.* New York: Basic Books.

Luria, A. R. (1973). *The working brain.* Harmondsworth, UK: Basic Books.

Mather, N., Wendling, B. J., & Woodcock, R. W. (2001). *Essentials of WJ III Tests of Achievement assessment.* New York: Wiley.

McCloskey, D. M. (2000). *Evaluating the neuropsychological and behavioral abilities of migrant children and non-migrant children of Hispanic background.* Unpublished doctoral dissertation, University of Northern Colorado, Greeley, CO.

Psychological Corporation. (1992). *Wechsler Individual Achievement Test.* San Antonio, TX: Author.

Psychological Corporation. (1997). *Wechsler Memory Scale* (3rd ed.). San Antonio, TX: Author.

Reitan, R. M., & Davison, L. A. (1974). *Clinical neuropsychology: Current status and applications.* Washington, DC: Hemisphere Publishing.

Reitan, R. M., & Wolfson, D. (1992). *Neuropsychological evaluation of older children.* South Tucson, AZ: Neuropsychology Press.

Reitan, R. M., & Wolfson, D. (1993). *The Halstead-Reitan Neuropsychological Test Battery.* Tucson, AZ: Neuropsychology Press.

Reitan, R. M., & Wolfson, D. (1996). Relationships between specific and general tests of cerebral functioning. *The Clinical Neuropsychologist, 10,* 37–42.

Rourke, B. P., & Del Dotto, J. (1994). *Learning disabilities: A neuropsychological perspective.* New York: Sage.

Sattler, J. M., & D'Amato, R. C. (2002). Brain injuries: Formal batteries and informal measures. In J. M. Sattler (Ed.), *Assessment of children: Behavioral and clinical application* (4th ed., pp. 440–469). San Diego, CA: Jerome M. Sattler.

Schrank, F. A., Flanagan, D. P., Woodcock, R. W., & Mascolo, J. T. (2001). *The essentials of WJ III Cognitive Abilities Assessment.* New York: Wiley.

Stinnett, T. A., Oehler-Stinnett, J., Fuqua, D. R., & Palmer, L. S. (2002). Examination of the underlying structure of the NEPSY: A Developmental Neuropsychological Assessment. *Journal of Psychoeducational Assessment, 20,* 66–82.

Walsh, K. (1987). *Neuropsychology: A clinical approach.* New York: Churchill Livingstone.

Wechsler, D. (1991). *Wechsler Intelligence Test for Children* (3rd ed.). San Antonio, TX: Psychological Corporation.

Wechsler, D. (2003). *Wechsler Intelligence Test for Children* (4th ed.). San Antonio, TX: Psychological Corporation.

Woodcock, R. S., McGrew, K. S., & Mather, N. (2001a). *Woodcock-Johnson III Tests of Cognitive Ability.* Itasca, IL: Riverside.

Woodcock, R. S., McGrew, K. S., & Mather, N. (2001b). *Woodcock-Johnson III Tests of Achievement.* Itasca, IL: Riverside.

Woodward, H. R., Ridenour, T., Dean, R. S., & Woodcock, R. S. (2002). Generalizability of sensory and motor tests. *International Journal of Neuroscience, 112,* 1115–1137.

Ysseldyke, J., & Elliot, J. (1999). Effective instructional practices: Implications for assessing educational environments. In C. R. Reynolds & T. B. Gutkin (Eds.), *Handbook of school psychology* (pp. 497–518). New York: Wiley.

Zillmer, E., & Spiers, M. (2001). *Principles of neuropsychology.* United States: Wadsworth.

# CHAPTER 12

# Evaluating and Using Qualitative Approaches to Neuropsychological Assessment

MARGARET SEMRUD-CLIKEMAN, ALISON WILKINSON, and
TASHA McMAHON WELLINGTON

THERE ARE MANY approaches to the evaluation of a child in neuropsychological practice. Most neuropsychologists use standardized tests as a method for determining behavior and functioning that differ from typical development for the age of the child evaluated. These tests provide quantitative information as to how the child completes tasks that require memory, attention, learning, language, and reasoning. However, the test is only as good as the person who is providing the interpretation. Many neuropsychologists use trained technicians or graduate students to administer the tests, but the interpretation is done by the professional with advanced postgraduate training.

Benton (1975) suggested that the neurodiagnostic approach should include tests of ability, memory, reasoning, perception, psychomotor functioning, and attention. The tests may vary depending on the need of the client, and a standardized battery may not be best practice. Prior to that time, surveys of practitioners found two-thirds using one of the two main batteries and only one-third using a mixture of psychological measures (Hartlage, 1985). Bigler (2001) suggested that the integration of the results plus the use of current technology (i.e., MRI) are the most important parts of neuropsychological assessment.

Quantitative approaches provide only the beginning for understanding the neuropsychological functioning of the child. The tests provide a benchmark for understanding how the child compares to others his or her age, but in isolation they do not tell the whole story. Children with severe head injury suffered at a young age are not expected to be able to read or do high-level abstract reasoning. Tests of these skills at their age level may not reveal difficulties that are later present. Mateer, Kerns, and Eso (1996) suggested that a child may grow into the deficit; in other words, we don't expect a young child to be cognitively flexible, yet these problems may arise as the child grows and may cause significant problems with adjustment.

Children's behavior and adjustment can alter their performance on standard-ized measures. Children who are oppositional, have attentional problems, or are anxious may not complete the tasks in the same manner as those without such ad-justment problems. Similarly, many disorders can mimic each other, and without qualitative information, a child with a significant anxiety or mood disorder can appear to have an attention deficit disorder.

Qualitative evaluation measures the child's behavior in the testing session as well as in informal observations of the child and parent in the waiting room. An observation of the child in the school setting is most helpful but may be difficult for practitioners who are not school based. It is particularly important to be aware of the child's ability to adapt to transitions both during the evaluation and in life. Additional areas that need to be qualitatively observed include attention, level of frustration tolerance, fatigability, need for routine, difficulty understanding di-rections, time needed to process information, and how consistent the child is.

Qualitative approaches also stress the way a child completes a task and not just what he or she does. How children approach a task can provide insight into how they understand the world. A child who gingerly approaches a challenging task and is very concerned about performance will work differently from a child who is open to such experiences. Similarly, a child who uses a trial-and-error approach to problem solving may arrive at the same score as a child who takes a thoughtful approach; however, the underlying difficulties may be quite different.

In addition to evaluating how a child solves a problem, qualitative information on the child's educational background, socioeconomic status, and cultural back-ground can assist in interpretation of the results of the evaluation. For example, in many cases, a child can appear to have a learning disability based on the dis-crepancy model. However, further evaluation of the child's ability to phonologi-cally process information can assist in determining whether a learning disability is the result of a *teaching disability* or of a biologically based *learning disability.*

A thorough clinical interview is a key piece of a neuropsychological assess-ment conducted from a qualitative perspective. The clinician must carefully ex-plore developmental, medical, and educational histories as well as the family structure and background. Additionally, a complete time line of the referring dif-ficulty should be obtained, including previous interventions that may have been tried. Ideally, the child will be interviewed informally as well. A great deal of in-formation about the child's social skills, ability to handle novel situations, and general approach to the world can be gained. This time can also be used to de-velop rapport with the child. These interviews, as well as a review of appropriate records and behavioral observations, are not only crucial to the selection of proper measures for the child, but also provide information that will be just as important as the test results.

To fully appreciate the role played by qualitative analysis of neuropsychological data, one must understand the roots of this process. Aleksander Luria (1980) was a forerunner in the use of qualitative data for understanding a neuropsychological deficit. The following section describes his theory and contributions to the field.

## LURIAN THEORY

Aleksander Romanovich Luria (1902–1977) was arguably one of the greatest in-fluences on modern neuropsychology. A Russian psychologist, Luria published his first book at the age of 20. His subsequent body of work covered a variety of topics, including cognitive development, memory, language, and higher cortical functioning. Perhaps most important, Luria developed a theory of brain functioning that has had a far-reaching impact on neuropsychological assessment.

## THEORETICAL INFLUENCES

Luria sought to resolve opposition between two major approaches to psychology: holistic and reductionistic thinking (Good, 2000). His extensive reading of Freud and Jung developed a respect for the richness of detailed case histories. His experience treating brain injuries during World War II increased his understanding of the organization of complex psychological processes (Good, 2000). Luria collaborated a great deal with Lev Vygotsky, and the two of them helped to develop a new school of thought in psychology that investigated the relationship between the brain and the environment (Good, 2000). Luria's model of cognitive functioning and resulting implications for assessment is fundamentally based on the idea that human behavior is rich and complex and must be viewed in context.

## UNDERLYING ASSUMPTIONS

Luria's (1980) theory represented a middle ground between localization and equipotential theories. Localization theory posits that discrete brain regions control discrete brain functions (Kolb & Whishaw, 1990). Equipotential theory emphasizes the plasticity of the brain, that when one portion of the brain is damaged, another part can take over part of its function (Kolb & Whishaw, 1990). Luria's theory, influenced by both of these approaches, was based on four major assumptions:

1. The brain is highly differentiated, and specific parts are responsible for different behaviors.
2. At birth, brain tissue is already specialized for different functions, psychologically as well as physiologically.
3. Human behavior is the result of systems of brain areas working together.
4. Any specific behavior can be produced by more than one system; therefore, if one system is damaged, another system can perform the behavior.

Luria's (1980) model of the brain centers on the idea of a functional system. A functional system consists of specific brain regions, as well as the connections between them, that work in concert to produce complex behaviors (Bauer, 2000). Luria's functional systems are grouped into three units.

## FUNCTIONAL UNITS

*Unit I: Arousal System*    This unit comprises the reticular activating system (RAS), pons, medulla, thalamus, and hypothalamus. Working together, these structures are responsible for maintaining arousal, filtering out unimportant stimuli from awareness, and maintaining attention and concentration. Damage to or dysfunction of this system can result in such symptoms as loss of consciousness, disorganization of memory, distractibility, insomnia, and attention problems (Teeter &

Semrud-Clikeman, 1997). However, in later adolescence and adulthood, Units II and III can compensate for problems in Unit I, such as by monitoring hyperactivity or impulsivity (Teeter & Semrud-Clikeman, 1997).

*Unit II: Sensory System*    In Luria's (1980) theory, the second unit is responsible for sensory reception and integration. This unit consists of the parietal lobe, the temporal lobe, and the occipital lobe. Luria argued that this sensory unit is organized according to three laws:

1. The structures within each zone do not remain constant during development.
2. Zones become more specified as development progresses.
3. Lateralization of function within zones increases as development progresses.

Each lobe within the sensory unit is further divided into hierarchical zones: the primary, secondary, and tertiary zones.

In each lobe, the primary zones have a point-to-point correspondence with their corresponding sense organ. These zones sort and record incoming sensory information. The organization of the primary zones is largely determined by genetics (Teeter & Semrud-Clikeman, 1997). The primary auditory zone is located in the temporal lobe and handles auditory perception. In the parietal lobe, the primary tactile zone is the sensory strip that handles tactile perception. The primary visual zone is in the occipital lobe and involves visual perception.

The secondary zones in each lobe are responsible for organizing the sensory information and coding it for retrieval later. Information is processed sequentially (Luria, 1980). The secondary auditory zones, located in the temporal lobe, analyze and synthesize the discrete parts of sound, such as phonemes and tone. Just beyond the sensory strip in the parietal lobe, the secondary tactile zones perform functions such as two-point discrimination and identifying objects by touch. The secondary visual zones are located in the occipital lobe. These areas perform visual functions such as identifying letters and shapes (Teeter & Semrud-Clikeman, 1997). The functions of the secondary zones are specialized by hemispheres. The secondary zones of the left hemisphere process verbal information, and the secondary zones of the right hemisphere process nonverbal material. Secondary zones of both hemispheres are involved in reading. The right hemisphere recognizes unfamiliar shapes (important in the acquisition of reading) and is involved in the comprehension of the emotional tone of passages. The left hemisphere recognizes words and letters that have already been learned and analyzes content for syntax and semantic meanings. The secondary zones are also specialized for writing, as the right hemisphere is more involved with visual-motor integration when learning to write, and the left hemisphere is more involved once writing becomes a rote task (Teeter & Semrud-Clikeman, 1997).

Finally, the tertiary zones of the sensory system are located in the parietal/occipital/temporal region, the area of the brain where these three lobes intersect (Luria, 1980). This area of the brain is also known as the association cortex. The tertiary zones are responsible for cross-modal integration of sensory information. Complex and simultaneous processing, such as reading comprehension, occurs in this area, as visual and auditory information must be integrated. Mathematics skills also involve these zones, as visual and spatial material is synthesized with language-based concepts. The tertiary zones are the primary seat of intelligence, and therefore damage or dysfunction in this area of the brain can result in impaired performance on IQ tests as well as on achievement tests (Teeter & Semrud-Clikeman, 1997).

*Unit III: Output and Planning System*  According to Luria (1980), the third unit, located in the frontal lobes, is responsible for planning and output. As with Unit II, it is divided into primary, secondary, and tertiary zones. The primary zone consists of the motor strip and is involved in simple motor output. The premotor areas of the frontal lobe constitute the secondary zone; these areas of the brain are responsible for motor planning and speech production. The tertiary zone of Unit III is located in the prefrontal region of the brain. This zone handles the abilities that are also known as the executive functions; skills such as monitoring, planning, and evaluating behaviors are performed in this area. Unit III is heavily interconnected to other areas of the brain and can therefore activate and modulate processes in other regions. Damage to this area of the brain can resemble psychiatric or behavior problems and can result in difficulties focusing attention, learning from past behavior, and controlling impulses (Teeter & Semrud-Clikeman, 1997).

IMPLICATIONS FOR ASSESSMENT

Because Luria viewed behavior as a result of the interaction of these functional systems in the brain, he argued that a person's symptoms would vary based on the location of the injury or dysfunction as well as the ability of the other systems to compensate (Bauer, 2000). Luria felt that observation was the most important assessment tool (Good, 2000). Therefore, he did not support the use of a fixed assessment battery, but believed that test selection should be based on the clinician's initial evaluation of the presenting problem. Luria also believed that the way problems were solved during the assessment was just as important as the answers given (Bauer, 2000). Human behavior, according to Luria, is best viewed as a complex interaction between functional systems and the environment. A thorough assessment must therefore include qualitative data from interview and observation and quantitative data from assessment tools selected based on that information. This information should be overlaid on a clinician's prerequisite knowledge of brain anatomy and functional system organization (Bauer, 2000; Good, 2000).

Since Luria's death in 1977, many attempts have been made to extend and supplement his work. Many of these attempts have been controversial. Christensen (1974) was the first to attempt to standardize Luria's methods, developing Luria's Neuropsychological Investigation. Although this is the most faithful of all standardizations to Luria's methods and actually uses many of the tasks Luria used in his clinics, Luria himself did not approve of the measure (Tupper, 1999). Golden (1981) placed Luria's functional units into a developmental framework and subsequently developed the Luria-Nebraska Neuropsychological Battery for use on adults and children. Several other neo-Lurian measures have been developed, attempting to measure mental processes rather than pure output (Tupper,

1999). These include the Das-Naglieri Cognitive Assessment System (Naglieri & Das, 1997), the Kaufman Assessment Battery for Children (Kaufman & Kaufman, 1983), and the NEPSY: A Developmental Neuropsychological Assessment (Korkman, Kirk, & Kemp, 1998).

In addition to influencing the development of these measures, Luria's theory has continued to affect the field of neuropsychology in significant ways. The flexible, process-oriented approach to assessment that he developed continues to be practiced, in some form, by a large number of neuropsychologists around the world. Luria's idea of viewing brain functioning *in context* with the *environment* seems simple, but it was novel in his time. His approach has been adapted for use through the Boston process approach described in the next section.

## BOSTON PROCESS APPROACH

The Boston Process Approach (BPA) to neuropsychological assessment is as concerned with the process by which an individual completes the task as with the score achieved (Kaplan, 1988). This approach suggests that two individuals can achieve a similar score for different reasons, such that an impaired score could be the result of deficits in different factors. For example, this approach illuminates that a poor performance on the Block Design subtest from the Weschler Intelligence tests may be attributed to inattention to detail, visuospatial deficits, poor visuospatial integration, or psychomotor and cognitive slowing (Kaplan, 1988). By examining the process by which the tasks are completed, the BPA attempts to delineate which areas are deficient for the individual. The BPA is a flexible battery that uses a hypothesis-testing approach in which an initial sampling of specific behaviors is completed, and from those measures additional tasks are added to further investigate possible areas of deficit (Teeter & Semrud-Clikeman, 1997). The measures used in the BPA are borrowed from other batteries and assess memory, language, visual-motor skills, and attention (Milberg, Hebben, & Kaplan, 1996). Given the flexible nature of the BPA, it can also be called the Boston Hypothesis-Testing Approach; it relies on the assumption that both the qualitative observations of behaviors and the quantitative scores will yield more information about a client's cognitive style, deficits, and strengths than using the scores alone.

### HISTORY

By the early 1970s, standardized and quantitative batteries, such as the Halstead-Reitan Neuropsychological Battery (HRNB), were being established as the gold standard for assessing patients with brain damage in the United States. However, some suggested that the approaches that used the standardized testing procedures were inadequate for truly understanding the problem-solving deficits of brain-injured patients. In addition, a process approach was already commonly being used in Europe (Poreh, 2000).

Researchers in the Boston area began to investigate the relationships between the brain and behavior and were strongly influenced by the relatively new focus on cognitive neuropsychology (Hebban & Milberg, 2002). Boston-based investigators researched diverse topics, such as memory, language, and perception, with the common thread of elucidating the neural structures in which the basic components of cognition may be located. Researchers Harold Goodglass, a clinical psychologist, and Norman Geschwind, a behavioral neurologist, and many others revolutionized how the brain and brain damage, such as aphasias and amnesia, were being studied (Hebban & Milberg, 2002). Edith Kaplan, a graduate student of developmental psychologist Heinz Werner at Clark University, began to work as a research assistant for Dr. Goodglass at the Boston Veteran's Affairs Medical Center.

Goodglass and Geschwind investigated the brain using a process of analysis and reduction to basic elements, reminiscent of anatomical localization theories, which was an experimental approach different from that of the Halstead-Reitan tradition. Heinz Werner's theory was that different cognitive processes could be used by different individuals to solve the same problem. Werner taught that cognitive development was characterized by changes in the mechanisms or cognitive approaches by which children solved problems as they developed. Kaplan applied her observation skills and the concept that individuals could use different cognitive processes to solve the same problem to research basic cognitive functions that were impaired when brain-damaged patients completed standard neuropsychological tests (Hebben & Milberg, 2002).

Influenced by the research environment at the Boston VA hospital, Kaplan investigated patients after neurosurgery to cut the corpus callosum, a fiber tract connecting the right and left hemispheres, for epilepsy treatment. Kaplan observed differences in how patients solved the Block Design, a puzzle construction task from the Wechsler Adult Intelligence Scale (WAIS), depending on whether the examiner placed the task to the right or left of the patient.

Kaplan continued her research and published a complete modification of the Wechsler Adult Intelligence Scale-Revised (WAIS-R) in the Wechsler Adult Intelligence Scale-Revised Neuropsychological Instrument (WAIS-R NI; Kaplan, Fein, Morris, & Delis, 1991). This modification included verbal multiple choice versions of several subtests, as well as her adaptations to subtest administration and observational recommendations. Examples of adaptations to subtest scoring include recording the locations of blocks as they are placed during the Block Design subtest and tallying the number of blocks correctly situated as well as specific errors (Kaplan et al., 1991).

Another adaptation to the WAIS-R, which was included in the WAIS-III, lies in the Digit-Symbol subtest. Kaplan et al. (1991) attempted to assess whether poor performance is due to failure to learn or failure to remember the digit-symbol combinations by adding an optional Digit-Symbol–Incidental Learning subtest. A second optional procedure, the Digit-Symbol-Copy, requires the examinee to copy symbols without having to match them to numbers. These modifications allow the clinician the option to utilize adaptations on a subtest-by-subtest basis depending on an ongoing subjective assessment of the client's strengths and weaknesses (Spreen & Strauss, 1998). Kaplan also developed modifications of Weschler Memory Scores, such as adding delayed recall and recognition memory trials that have become standard components of the revised Weschler Memory Scale (WMS) and other memory batteries.

This approach was termed the Boston Process Approach in 1986 (Milberg, Hebben, & Kaplan, 1996), and it continues to be used in research and practice. Kaplan and her colleagues have developed psychometrically validated measures based on advancements in cognitive information-processing theories; such measures include the Boston Diagnostic Aphasia Examination, Boston Naming Test (Kaplan, Goodglass, & Wintraub, 1983), the California Verbal Learning Test (CVLT-9; Delis, Kramer, Kaplan, & Ober, 1987), and the Delis-Kaplan Executive Function System (Delis, Kaplan, & Kramer, 2000).

## THE BOSTON PROCESS BATTERY

The BPA is a flexible battery approach that borrows measures from a long list of tests from various domains in order to address referral questions. Both standardized and experimental measures are utilized to understand the current level of functioning of the client and to guide treatment planning. The Boston Process battery is unpublished and can vary depending on the clinician and the population being assessed. The clinical interview plays an important role, as the information gathered about the client guides the assessment and assists in understanding how the client's skills have been impacted or spared by brain damage or pathology (Teeter & Sermud-Clikeman, 1997). This approach suggests that basic areas of function should be screened; these basic areas include cognitive/intellectual functioning, neuropsychological functioning, reasoning abilities, verbal language, memory, and perception. Optional assessment can be completed related to self-regulation and motor and academic functions, if required by the referral question (Teeter & Semrud-Clikeman, 1997; Kolb & Whishaw, 2003).

Initial tests of reasoning suggested for the Boston battery include the Stroop Color Word Test and the Wisconsin Card Sort Test, which provide an assessment of frontal lobe function. A measure that provides a screen for memory abilities is also recommended (i.e., Test of Memory and Learning [TOMAL], Wide Range Assessment of Memory and Learning, California Verbal Language Test-Children's Version). The Rey-Osterreith Complex Figure Test (ROCF; standardized by Osterreith in 1944) provides both an assessment of conceptual functioning and a memory component with later recall of the figure. The initial screening measures of the language skills frequently used in the BPA are the Boson Naming Test, which requires the child to name increasingly more difficult black-and-white pictures, and the Controlled Oral Word Association Test, which requires the child to name as many words as possible in one minute that start with the letter, F, then A, then S. The tests of perception include the Hooper Visual Organization Test, Benton Visual Perceptual Tests, Judgment of Line Orientation, Test of Facial Recognition, and Cancellation Tasks. The Wide Range Achievement Tests 3 is frequently used as the measure of achievement.

## RESEARCH APPLICATIONS OF THE BPA

Research has supported the observation made by Kaplan and her colleagues that individuals can demonstrate similar scores on a task using different underlying mechanisms (Kaplan, 1988). There is also evidence that although the score alone may not differentiate between groups, the analysis of how the task was preformed can aid diagnostic discrimination.

A significant amount of research has addressed qualitative aspects of the WAIS-R. Qualitative research on the Block Design has demonstrated that examining the type of errors made during the task can discriminate between damage to the right or left hemisphere. Patients with damage to the right hemisphere will make gross design violations, whereas left hemisphere damage tends to result in simplification and detail errors (Kaplan, 1988). Additional research found that the Digit-Symbol-Copy subtest, which requires the examinee to copy symbols without having to match them to numbers, can elucidate whether a poor performance on the Digit-Symbol Coding task is the result of graphomotor deficits (Kelly & Britton, 1996). The Digit Span subtest is usually considered a measure of attention and working memory and has not been found to discriminate between brain-injured children and normal children (Brooks, 1975). A qualitative study found that although children with traumatic brain injury (TBI) did not look significantly different from the control group on standard scores, an error analysis showed that children with TBI made more preceiling sequencing and omission errors than the control group (Warschausky, Kewman, & Selim, 1996).

A recent study by Giovannetti et al. (2001) found that different mechanisms may underlie deficits in verbal concept formation among patients with Alzheimer's Disease (AD) and ischaemic vascular dementia (IVD). Although the AD and IVD groups demonstrated no differences in standardized scores on the WAIS-R Similarities subtest, the type of errors made during the test were significantly different. Qualitative approaches to studying dementia have proved beneficial in aiding diagnostic discrimination and elucidate underlying differential deficits among a wide range of dementia syndromes. Disturbances in memory have been observed in all dementia syndromes, but the number of correct responses on the serial list learning tasks, like the nine-word CVLT-9, have not shown to discriminate between the various dementia syndromes. However, an analysis of the errors made by patients with AD versus patients with IVD illuminates the differences between these dementias (Davis, Price, Kaplan, & Libon, 2002). Davis et al.'s (2002) findings suggest that the verbal memory deficits demonstrated by patients with AD may be related to deficits in semantic knowledge, and the verbal memory deficits exhibited by patients with IVD may be associated with deficits in executive functions.

The ROCF is frequently used in process-based neuropsychological assessment given that it measures perceptual, visuospatial, and organizational skills (Meyers & Meyers, 1995). Studies investigating how individuals complete this task have found performance differences in patients with left versus right hemispheric deficits (Poreh & Shye, 1998). In addition, a recent study found that IQ can affect how an individual solves the ROCF, such that individuals with higher IQs utilize visual-spatial abilities, whereas individuals with lower IQs rely on organizational skills (Fujii, Lloyd, & Miyamoto, 2000).

More recently, Eden and her colleagues (Eden, Wood, & Stein, 2003) found that the qualitative Clock Drawing Test was a useful screening test for detecting visuospatial impairments in children with dyslexia. The results from this study suggest that some children with dyslexia may exhibit deficits in the right posterior parietal hemisphere. The Clock Drawing Test is a very simple measure that requires a limited amount of time to administer.

Process-guided research elucidates neural mechanisms underlying various neuropsychological disorders. It can also help fine-tune assessment batteries and provide clinicians with useful tools for diagnostic discrimination.

## Advantages of the Boston Process Approach

One advantage of the BPA is that it can be tailored to the referral question to address specific areas of concern. This can reduce the time spent administering the battery and provide more information about specific areas of concern. In addition, this approach can provide greater descriptive power and further understanding of neurological disorders and underlying neural systems (Kaplan et al., 1991). This process approach is particularly useful for tasks that tap multiple cognitive skills, such as verbal declarative memory tasks, which involve attention, concentration, and semantic knowledge. The BPA can improve differential diagnosis for disorders and brain pathology that are otherwise indistinguishable on raw and scaled score measures (Poreh, 2000; Stuss & Levine, 2002).

## Limitations of the Boston Process Approach

A limitation to the approach is that it has produced a limited amount of normative data for qualitative findings. Although recent research has provided support for Kaplan and her colleagues' observations (Joy, Fein, Kaplan, & Morris Freedman, 2001; Slick et al., 1996; Wecker et al., 2000) the BPA continues to have relatively limited normative information. The WAIS-R NI (Kaplan et al., 1991) is one of the few examples of tests published with some standard information about reliability and standard errors of measurement, although it continues to lack reliability and validity information for observational data used for making clinical inferences (Hebben & Milberg, 2002).

An additional limitation is that the BPA depends on observation skills, which can be difficult to standardize across clinicians and requires more specific training (Hebben & Milberg, 2002). With the exception of the WAIS-R NI, this is an unpublished battery and it can vary across clinicians. The nature of this method requires that the clinician have extensive knowledge and experience with a wide variety of measures, brain-behavior relationships, and normative child performance across a wide age range. Although research has supported many of the observations made in the BPA in adults, this approach still needs further research with children (Teeter & Semrud-Clikeman, 1997).

## Summary of the Boston Process Approach

The BPA is a flexible battery that allows for integration of clinical observations and standardized testing. It takes an initial overview of cognitive and behavioral functioning and then focuses on potential areas of concern based on the initial findings. The BPA also allows for the investigation and differentiation of neural mechanisms that underlie disorders that is not possible with only a raw or scaled score. Although it has its limitations, the qualitative information it offers can enhance diagnostic skills (Teeter & Semrud-Clikeman, 1997) and warrants further research and empirical validation.

*Alternative Forms*   The BPA is used in various forms by practitioners. Baron (2004) uses a technique called convergent profile analysis, which includes profile analysis plus all relevant data about the child. Baron describes profile analysis as the interpretation of scores among tests that are similar. Improvement in interpretation of these data was found for neuropsychologists who were most versed in understanding normative data as well as integrating information into domains (Garb & Lutz, 2001). This technique is very similar to the working hypothesis model suggested by Teeter and Semrud-Clikeman (1997).

The convergence of qualitative data with quantitative results provides important information about the child's functioning. Baron (2004) reports that when a child does poorly on a test, interpretation of that result must be tempered by consistent problems on similar measures. A hypothesis based on one data point is less reliable and viable than one that is based on data taken together. Clinical impressions must be backed up by quantitative support to be fully valid (Nesbit-Greene & Donders, 2002).

Qualitative observations may include perseverating on an answer, an inability to maintain a response pattern, or failure to self-monitor. Positive observations may include how the child manages failure, how he or she plans, what compensations the child has developed, and what strategies he or she employs to solve a problem (Baron, 2004). These observations can enrich the interpretation of the data and make the recommendations more appropriate and more useful to parents and teachers.

There are attempts to provide guidance as to qualitative approaches on new tests, including achievement testing and learning tasks. The Wechsler Individual Achievement Test (WIAT) and Woodcock-Johnson have rating scales for how the child completes the task. The CVLT-C now provides information on the child's tendency to repeat mistakes and/or to add information that is not presented.

Unfortunately, most of the progress evaluating attention and motivation has been developed for adult tests (Stern et al., 1999). Child psychologists continue to rely on their training and experience for the development of such qualitative norms and for interpretations. Baron (2004) suggests comparing scores calculated with time constraints to those when longer time is allowed to determine whether the child failed on Block Design solely because of time. If, when provided with sufficient time, he or she is able to solve the design, the problem is not one of perception but may be one of speed of information processing or slower cognitive tempo. Interventions would differ for each of these hypotheses.

*Working Hypothesis Approach*    The working hypothesis approach evaluates how the child solves the problem. The use of recognition cues can assist in determining what type of learning difficulty may be present. For example, on the CVLT-C the child is asked to select the target words embedded within a list of words. This type of situation is also present on the Weschler Memory Scale-Revised and on the TOMAL. The ability to contrast the child's performance on these tests without recognition aides and then to evaluate how the child performs once such aids are present provides a window into how to work with this child most effectively.

The type of errors is also an area for evaluation. Children who do not use feedback on their performance to change their response have difficulty managing their behavior. This type of difficulty has been related to orbitofrontal functioning. Children with lesions in the inferior frontal lobe were found to have difficulty choosing appropriate behavior and evaluating the consequences for their behavior (Levin et al., 2001).

*Flexible Batteries*    The use of a flexible battery lends itself to evaluating a child's performance in many aspects. A set battery (i.e., HRNB) requires the same tests to be administered to all children. Both approaches allow for the evaluation of the child's ability and possible areas of concern. The difficulty with the fixed battery is that the child may be required to complete tasks that are superfluous, thus increasing time spent as well as money. The fixed battery may also not evaluate the referral question at hand most appropriately.

Baron (2004) found that the HRNB (the most common fixed battery) generally is weak in evaluating attention, learning, free recall, and recognition memory, and some aspects of executive functioning. Hynd and Semrud-Clikeman (1990) reviewed the literature and found that the WAIS was as sensitive to brain dysfunction as the HRNB, and both tests measure similar functions, with the WAIS requiring 90 minutes and the Halstead up to 6 hours.

The use of multiple tests to evaluate an area of difficulty can provide insight into how the child learns. For example, the WIAT requires the child to read a passage and then answer questions. The Woodcock-Johnson Passage Comprehension subtest requires the child to supply a word from the context of the sentence. Both tests are called reading comprehension. However, a child may have difficulty reading a passage and then answering questions but be able to complete a fill-in-the-blank questionnaire. Reading interventions that tailor instruction to match the child's needs can utilize this information. Visual-motor functioning can also be evaluated qualitatively. The Developmental Test of Visual-Motor Integration (VMI) requires the child to copy figures that are contained within a set portion of the page. The Bender-Gestalt requires the child to copy figures on a page without assistance with order or presentation. The VMI can provide a measure of how the child completes a perceptual-motor task within a limit and then can be contrasted with the Bender, which is more ambiguous and requires more planning and organization. By contrasting these different methods of problem solving and learning, the child's performance sheds a light on how he or she learns and approaches a task.

The difficulty with this approach is selecting the most appropriate tests and becoming familiar with them. The tests need to span the areas of development, provide an idea of how the child learns best and with what materials, and identify areas of weakness. There are more and more tests available, and it is difficult to keep up with their proliferation. It is even more difficult to be aware of the crucial validity and reliability of these measures. However, the clinician must select the tests that fit the needs of the child and the referral question and that are most appropriate. It may be easier to utilize a fixed battery approach in the initial stages of one's career; however, it is likely that this approach will become binding and restricting. This is one reason neuropsychological assessment is so challenging and why additional training is crucial for practice.

QUALITATIVE ASSESSMENT DURING FEEDBACK

The ability to understand how the child approaches a task is an important part of helping parents and teachers understand the child's functioning. The process approach allows one to highlight the child's strengths as well as weaknesses. Many times, parents and teachers will receive a report with many scores on it, and although it is interesting, they will then wonder, Now what? Detailing the child's strengths and how he or she learns best is helpful.

Particularly important is the ability to place the child's skills in context. Helping parents and teachers to understand what is behind the child's behavior can assist in changing their approach to the child. Baron (2004) calls this a dynamic process that also can be fluid and provide a therapeutic change. A young man, referred for evaluation for attentional problems, was told repeatedly by his father that he was "lazy." The client accepted this view of his difficulty, and it became even more difficult for him to stay on task and plan and organize. Although there was an attentional deficit at the root of the difficulty, the client's attentional problems became more pronounced, as he now had an emotional reaction to tasks that required sustained effort. Assisting the father to reframe his frustration with his son provided support for the client and improved their relationship.

Likewise, helping patients and parents understand the way the brain processes information and difficulties that problems with auditory processing and/or listening comprehension can produce can assist with treatment for the child. Young children with severe speech and language disorders frequently experience behavioral difficulty as they are unable to use language to gratify their needs. Parents may be cognizant of the child's behavioral problems but not of the root cause of the behavior, namely, problems with expression. A parent who understands this difficulty will take a different approach to working with the child, and his or her resulting frustration may be lower.

Adjusting the tests to fit the child and the referral question is a challenging task but one that is also rewarding. Conducting parent and teacher feedback that is dynamic and supportive is useful for all involved and makes it far more likely that the recommendations generated from the testing will be utilized.

## CONCLUSION

While the purpose of this chapter was to describe qualititative approaches to neuropsychological assessment, the use of both quantitative and qualitative data is important for a comprehensive evaluation. Quantitative data provide a normative estimate of the child's functioning relative to his or her peer group. Qualitative data provide the observations of the child and his or her test-taking behavior. Observations of the child's dress, manner, tone of voice, mood, affect, language, and attentional abilities are crucial to understanding how he or she functions (Lezak, 1995). Some believe that the use of quantitative data alone is sufficient (Dawes, Faust, & Meehl, 1989); others believe a combination is most appropriate (Heaton, 1981). Lezak suggests that only simple diagnostic questions, such as the sequelae of set lesions on behavior, are appropriate for quantitative data alone, whereas most other referral questions require a combination. The use of qualitative data alone may be problematic as it is quite difficult to remain objective and to select the most appropriate areas for evaluation without comparing the child's performance to his or her age group. Developmental information is crucial for children, though not as important for adults.

The approaches described in this chapter assume sufficient training in the neuropsychological measures. Interpretation of these measures and evaluating multiple data points is an art that develops only over time and with experience. Understanding the relationship between domains is crucial for appropriate interpretation. Children with difficulties with attention may well experience problems with memory that are due to attentional difficulties and not to memory problems. Selecting tests that provide a window into how the child remembers something, whether a visual or recognition cue can aid in memory, or whether attentional variables are paramount can assist teachers and parents in developing appropriate interventions.

Qualitative interpretation is an important aspect of any evaluation but most crucial in a neuropsychological evaluation. Helping the child adjust to his or her environment and providing appropriate recommendations often hinges on the ability to understand *how* the child solves problems and *what* he or she is able to accomplish (Semrud-Clikeman, 2003). Intangible aspects of functioning such as motivation, temperament, frustration tolerance, and emotional stability are important aspects that have no set test but are generally inferred from performance. These are also the aspects that are most predictive of the child's later adjustment and success in life.

## REFERENCES

Baron, I. S. (2004). *Neuropsychological evaluation of the child.* New York: Oxford Press.

Bauer, R. M. (2000). The flexible battery approach to neuropsychological assessment. In R. D. Vanderploeg (Ed.), *Clinician's guide to neuropsychological assessment* (pp. 419–448). Mahwah, NJ: Erlbaum.

Benton, A. R. (1975). Psychological tests for brain damage. In A. M. Freedman & H. I. Kaplan (Eds.), *Diagnosing mental illness: Evaluation in psychiatry and psychology* (pp. 2–15). New York: Atheneum.

Bigler, E. D. (2001). Neuropsychological testing defines the neurobehavioral significance of neuroimaging-identified abnormalities. *Archives of Clinical Neuropsychology, 16,* 227–236.

Brooks, D. N. (1975). Long and short term memory in head injured patients. *Cortex, 11,* 329–340.

Christensen, A. L. (1974). *Luria's neuropsychological investigation.* Copenhagen, Denmark: Munksgaard.

Davis, K. L., Price, C. C., Kaplan, E., & Libon, D. J. (2002). Error analysis of the Nine-Word California Verbal Learning Test (CVLT-9) among older adults with and without dementia. *Clinical Neuropsychologist, 16*(1), 81–89.

Dawes, R. M., Faust, D., & Meehl, P. E. (1989). Clinical versus actuarial judgment. *Science, 243,* 1668–1674.

Delis, D. C., Kaplan, E., & Kramer, J. H. (2000). *Delis-Kaplan Executive Function System manual.* San Antonio, TX: Psychological Corporation.

Delis, D. C., Kramer, J. H., Kaplan, E., & Ober, B. A. (1987). *California Verbal Learning Test: Adult version manual.* San Antonio, TX: Psychological Corporation.

Eden, G. F., Wood, F. B., & Stein, J. F. (2003). Clock drawing in developmental dyslexia. *Journal of Learning Disabilities, 36,* 216–228.

Erikson, R. C. (1995). A review and critique of the process approach in neuropsychological assessment. *Neuropsychology Review, 5,* 223–243.

Fujii, D. E., Lloyd, H. A., & Miyamoto, K. (2000). The salience of visuospatial and organizational skills in reproducing the Rey-Osterreith complex figure in subjects with high and low IQs. *Clinical Neuropsychologist, 14*(4), 551–554.

Garb, H., & Lutz, C. (2001). Cognitive complexity and the validity of clinician's judgments. *Assessment, 8,* 111–115.

Giovannetti, T., Lamar, M., Cloud, B. S., Swenson, R., Fein, D., Kaplan, E., et al. (2001). Different underlying mechanisms for deficits in concept formation in dementia. *Archives of Clinical Neuropsychology, 16,* 547–560.

Golden, C. J. (1981). The Luria-Nebraska Children's Battery: Theory and formulation. In G. W. Hynd & J. E. Obrzut (Eds.), *Neuropsychological assessment and the school-age child: Issues and procedures* (pp. 277–302). Orlando, FL: Grune & Stratton.

Good, S. R. (2000). A. R. Luria: A humanistic legacy. *Journal of Humanistic Psychology, 40*(1), 17–32.

Hartlage, L. C. (1985, August). *Past, present, and emerging trends in clinical neuropsychology.* Presidential address at the meeting of the American Psychological Association, Los Angeles, CA.

Heaton, R. K. (1981). *Wisconsin Card Sorting Test.* Odessa, FL: Psychological Assessment Resources.

Hebben, N., & Milberg, N. (2002). *Essentials of neuropsychological assessment.* New York: John Wiley & Sons.

Hynd, G. W., & Semrud-Clikeman, M. (1990). Neuropsychological assessment. In A. S. Kaufman (Ed.), *Assessing adolescent and adult intelligence* (pp. 638–670). Boston: Allyn & Bacon.

Joy, S., Fein, D., Kaplan, E., & Morris Freedman, M. (2001). Quantifying qualitative features of block design performance among healthy older adults. *Archives of Clinical Neuropsychology, 16,* 157–170.

Kaplan, E. (1988). A process approach to neuropsychological assessment. In E. Dennis, M. Posner, D. Stein, & K. Thompson (Eds.), *Clinical neuropsychology and brain functioning: Research, measurement, and practice* (pp. 129–166). Washington, DC: American Psychological Association.

Kaplan, E., Fein, D., Morris, R., & Delis, D. (1991). *WAIS-R as a neuropsychological instrument.* New York: Psychological Corporation.

Kaplan, E. F., Goodglass, H., & Weintraub, S. (1983). *The Boston Naming Test* (2nd ed.). Philadelphia: Lea & Febiger.

Kaufman, A. S., & Kaufman, N. L. (1983). *Kaufman Assessment Battery for Children.* Circle Pines, MN: American Guidance Service.

Kelly, T. P., & Britton, P. G. (1996). Sex differences on an adaptation of the digit symbol subtest of the Wechsler Intelligence Scale for Children-III. *Perceptual and Motor Skills, 83,* 843–847.

Kolb, B., & Whishaw, I. Q. (1990). *Fundamentals of human neuropsychology* (3rd ed.). San Francisco: Freeman.

Kolb, B., & Whishaw, I. Q. (2003). *Neuropsychological assessment.* (5th ed., pp. 751–763). New York: Worth Publishing.

Korkman, M., Kirk, U., & Kemp, S. (1998). *NEPSY: A developmental neuropsychological assessment.* San Antonio, TX: Psychological Corporation.

Levin, H. S., Leplow, B., Herzog, A., Benz, B., Ritz, A., Stolze, H., et al. (2001). Children's spatial behavior is differentially affected after traumatic brain injury. *Child Neuropsychology, 7,* 59–71.

Lezak, M. D. (1995). *Neuropsychological assessment* (3rd ed.). New York: Oxford Press.

Luria, A. R. (1980). *Higher cortical functions in man* (2nd ed.). New York: Basic Books.

Mateer, C. A., Kerns, K. A., & Eso, K. L. (1996). Management of attention and memory disorders following traumatic brain injury. *Journal of Learning Disabilities, 29,* 618–632.

Meyers, J., & Meyers, K. (1995). *The Meyers scoring system for the Rey complex figure and the recognition trial: Professional manual.* Odessa, FL: Psychological Assessment Resources.

Milberg, W. P., Hebben, N., & Kaplan, E. (1996). The Boston Process Approach to neuropsychological assessment. In I. Grant & K. M. Adams (Eds.), *Neuropsychological assessment of neuropsychiatric disorders* (pp. 58–80). New York: Oxford University Press.

Naglieri, J. A., & Das, J. P. (1997). *Das-Naglieri cognitive assessment system.* Itasca, IL: Riverside.

Nesbit-Greene, K., & Donders, J. (2002). Latent structure of the Children's Category Test after pediatric traumatic head injury. *Journal of Clinical and Experimental Neuropsychology, 24,* 194–199.

Osterrieth, P. A. (1944). Le test de copie d'une figure complexe. Contribution a l'etude de la perception et de la memoire. *Archives de Psychologie, 30,* 206–353.

Poreh, A. M. (2000). The quantified process approach: An emerging methodology to neuropsychological assessment. *Clinical Neuropsychologist, 14*(2), 212–222.

Poreh, A., & Shye, S. (1998). Examination of the global and local features of the Rey-Osterreith complex figure using faceted smallest space analysis. *Clinical Neuropsychologist, 12,* 453–467.

Semrud-Clikeman, M. (2003). Executive functions and social communication disorders. *Perspectives, 29,* 20–22.

Slick, D., Hopp, G., Strauss, E., Fox, D., Pinch, D., & Stickgold, K. (1996). Effects of prior testing with the WAIS-R NI on subsequent retest with the WAIS-R. *Archives of Neuropsychology, 11,* 123–130.

Spreen, O., & Strauss, E. (1998). *A compendium of neuropsychological tests: Administration, norms and commentary.* Oxford, England: Oxford University Press.

Stern, R., Javorsky, D. J., Singer, E. A., Singer Harris, N. G., Somerville, J. A., Duke, L. M., et al. (1999). *The Boston qualitative scoring system for the Rey-Osterrieth complex figure.* Odessa, FL: Psychological Assessment Resources.

Stuss, D. T., & Levine, B. (2002). Adult clinical neuropsychology: Lessons from studies of the frontal lobes. *Annual Review of Psychology.*

Teeter, P. A., & Semrud-Clikeman, M. (1997). *Child neuropsychology.* Boston: Allyn & Bacon.

Tupper, D. E. (1999). Introduction: Neuropsychological assessment après Luria. *Neuropsychology Review, 9*(2), 57–61.

Warschausky, S., Kewman, D. G., & Selim, A. (1996). Attentional performance of children with traumatic brain injury: A quantitative and qualitative analysis of digit span. *Archives of Clinical Neuropsychology, 11,* 147–153.

Wecker, N. S., Kramer, J. H., Wisniewski, A., Delis, D. C., & Kaplan, E. (2000). Age effects on executive ability. *Neuropsychology, 14,* 409–414.

# CHAPTER 13

# Assessing and Understanding Brain Function through Neuropsychologically Based Ability Tests

JOHN J. BRINKMAN JR., SCOTT L. DECKER, and RAYMOND S. DEAN

T HIS CHAPTER PROVIDES a history of our understanding of cognitive ability by tracing the conceptualization of intelligence with the incorporation of theory applied to intelligence and neuropsychological tests. There has been a corresponding change in how ability measures are used and interpreted based on changes in the conceptualization and theoretical models of ability. This chapter also reviews how Carroll's hierarchical model of broad- and narrow-based abilities fits well with the current conceptualization of abilities in neuropsychology. Next, we present an overview of the Dean-Woodcock Cognitive Neuropsychology Model, which synthesizes neuropsychological models with contemporary psychometric models. Finally, we offer an educationally relevant case study of how information obtained from a well-developed, broad-based theory of abilities can be used in assessment practice.

As Reynolds (1981) pointed out some time ago, the interpretation of cognitive ability remains an essential part of a comprehensive neuropsychological examination. Such an examination includes a cognitive measure, a test of academic achievement, a sensorimotor battery, and a measure of emotionality. D'Amato, Gray, and Dean (1988) called into question the difference between tests of achievement and tests of ability. Along with these tests, a complete neuropsychological examination includes obtaining measures or indicators of an individual's emotional status and relevant background information through a structured interview. Though the ability test score is important, it is the collection of subtests that constitutes the overall ability score that is most important. Woodcock (1997) states that the primary purpose for cognitive ability testing is to "find out more about the problem, not to obtain an IQ." Thus, an understanding of the diverse tasks that make up an ability score proves the most useful both for interpretation and to guide interventions.

## SCHOOL PSYCHOLOGISTS

The school psychologist is in a primary position to provide an interpretation of ability test scores from a neuropsychological perspective. The school psychologist has training in testing and assessment, the available population of students referred with neuropsychological disorders, and training in linking assessment with the appropriate interventions. Traditionally, school psychologists have been trained as generalist practitioners, testing students with psychoeducational assessments to provide appropriate placement and/or accommodations for students with disabilities. Though this may still be true for school psychologists trained at the master's and educational specialist levels, doctoral training has allowed many programs to provide advanced training in a variety of educational and psychological domains. Doctoral programs offer specializations in many areas, including counseling, family/systems therapy, consultation, learning assessment/intervention, gifted studies, organizational development, program evaluation, childhood psychopathology, and neuropsychology (Fagan & Wise, 2000). Though not all doctoral programs offer training in neuropsychology, many offer coursework in neuropsychology. A recent survey of school psychology training programs found that out of 86 programs, 43 (50%) of the programs accredited by the National Association of School Psychologists required some level of training in neuropsychology to include a course, a module in a course, or classes within a course (Walker, Boling, & Cobb, 1999). Further, Fagan and Wise (2000) identified 16 doctoral programs that have subspecialties in neuropsychology, which they point out is one of the more popular specializations. Thus, with appropriate education and practical experience, there are many school psychologists with training in neuropsychological testing and assessment who are able to provide neuropsychological services in the school setting. As previously detailed in this text, many of these individuals call themselves school neuropsychologists. The school neuropsychologist has access to a population of learners referred with disorders having neurogenic etiologies. Such disorders include, but are not limited to, learning disorders, head injury, seizure disorders, genetic disorders, neurodevelopmental disorders, and disorders of attention. All of these represent a patient population that is shared by both the neuropsychologist and the school psychologist. By providing neuropsychological services in the school setting, students referred for such services are able to take advantage of having the same professional who administers the neuropsychological assessment the one who follows up with implementation and/or consultation of psychological and educational interventions. Thus, school neuropsychologists as well as some school psychologists are able to link assessment with intervention and provide ecologically relevant neuropsychological interventions for students in a learning environment. Finally, it should be noted that it is the school neuropsychologist who is able to bridge the gap between traditional psychoeducational assessment and neuropsychological assessment and provide an integrated and comprehensive interpretation of ability.

## HISTORY OF COGNITIVE ABILITY

The history of cognitive ability can be traced by looking at the conceptualization of intelligence. Though early conceptualizations of intelligence, based on intelligence tests, were atheoretical, later concepts of intelligence have incorporated theoretical models as the basis for test construction. Neuropsychological assessment in North America also has a tradition of being atheoretical. However, with the incorporation of theoretical cognitive ability testing, neuropsychological test construction has begun to embrace a theoretical orientation.

### CONCEPTUALIZATION OF INTELLIGENCE

There has been a clear trend in the conceptualization of intelligence from the simple to the more complex, as evidenced by theoretical and interpretive models applied to tests of intelligence. The concept of a single, general intellectual ability dominated test development and interpretation for the first half of the twentieth century. By the end of the twentieth century, attempts were being made to develop tests based on broad cognitive abilities. More recently, at the beginning of the twenty-first century, test development has witnessed the identification of a sizable set of specific, or narrow, cognitive abilities. In tracing the history of intelligence and cognitive abilities theory, five broad levels of conceptualizations emerge:

1. Intelligence as a single general ability
2. Intelligence as a pair of abilities
3. Intelligence as a limited set of multiple abilities
4. Intelligence as a complete set of multiple abilities
5. Intelligence as a hierarchy of narrow abilities underlying multiple broad abilities

This conceptualization of intelligence is presented by illustrating the relationship between the level of conceptualization and the publication date of numerous major intelligence batteries available since 1916.

*Level 1: Intelligence as a Single General Ability*   The earliest conceptualization of intelligence among clinicians, and still popular among some, at least operationally, is the view of intelligence as a single general ability. The Stanford-Binet (SB) test of 1916 (Terman, 1916) articulated that view of intelligence in the United States. Twenty-one years later, a revised SB was published with two alternate forms (Terman & Merrill, 1937). The third edition was published in 1960 (Terman & Merrill, 1960) as a single form that included the better test items from the previous two 1937 forms. Two scores were provided by these early SB tests: a mental age (MA) and a ratio IQ. The ratio IQ was obtained by dividing the MA by the subject's chronological age. In the eyes of most clinicians using the early SB tests, that single IQ score represented all that was to be known about a person's intelligence. It should be noted, however, that the early SB tests included a rich variety of test items. Many examiners studied the pattern of correct and incorrect responses among the subject's responses to the various test items for clues about the nature of individual differences, or strengths and weaknesses, in cognitive performance.

*Level 2: Intelligence Partitioned as a Pair of Abilities*   At Level 2, intelligence is perceived and measured as a pair of abilities, somewhat the opposite of each other (e.g., verbal versus nonverbal). This shift in the conceptualization of intelligence among clinicians primarily occurred following the publication of the Wechsler-Bellevue (WB) in 1939 (Wechsler, 1939) and several subsequent versions of the

Wechsler scales. In the eyes of most users, the WB was perceived as a measure of general intelligence or full-scale IQ (FSIQ), undergirded by two narrower abilities, verbal IQ (VIQ) and performance IQ (PIQ).

The WB was a scale for adults. The first Wechsler Intelligence Scale for Children (WISC) was published in 1949 (Wechsler, 1949), and the Wechsler Adult Intelligence Scale (WAIS), replacing the WB, was published in 1955 (Wechsler, 1955). Clinicians now had a Wechsler available for use with children and another for use with adults. Both provided VIQ and PIQ scores, plus an FSIQ. These two batteries were revised and released in 1974 and 1981 as the WISC-R (Wechsler, 1974) and the WAIS-R (Wechsler, 1981) with relatively little change from their earlier editions, quite possibly because little attention was paid to cognitive ability theory, at least among clinicians and the developers of the Wechsler scales, during these decades.

Other well-known tests associated with a Level 2 conceptualization include the Kaufman Assessment Battery for Children (K-ABC; Kaufman & Kaufman, 1983) and the Kaufman Adolescent and Adult Intelligence Test (KAIT; Kaufman & Kaufman, 1993). Though based on different theoretical approaches, each intelligence test measures a distinct pair of abilities. The K-ABC provides scales of simultaneous processing and sequential processing. The KAIT provides scales of crystallized and fluid intelligence.

*Level 3: Intelligence as a Limited Set of Multiple Abilities*  The third level of conceptualization reflects the advent and subsequent use of intelligence batteries measuring more than two broad cognitive abilities. The first major battery to break with the pairing tradition established by the Wechsler scales was the Woodcock-Johnson Tests of Cognitive Abilities (WJ; Woodcock & Johnson, 1977). The WJ provided scores for four broad cognitive functions, identified as verbal ability, reasoning, perceptual speed, and memory.

The next Level 3 battery, published in 1986, was the Stanford-Binet Intelligence Scale, fourth edition (SB IV; Thorndike, Hagen, & Sattler, 1986). That battery also measured four broad categories of abilities: verbal reasoning, quantitative reasoning, abstract/visual reasoning, and short-term memory. Other Level 3 batteries published since 1986 include the Differential Abilities Scales (Elliot, 1990), measuring three broad categories (verbal, nonverbal reasoning, and spatial), and the WISC-III (Wechsler, 1991), measuring four broad categories (verbal comprehension, perceptual organization, freedom from distraction, and processing speed). The WISC-III was the first Wechsler battery to move beyond a Level 2 conceptualization of intelligence. The Cognitive Assessment System (Naglieri & Das, 1997) measures four separate functions (planning, attention, simultaneous processing, and successive processing). The WAIS-III (Wechsler, 1997) measures four abilities (verbal comprehension, perceptual organization, working memory, and processing speed).

*Level 4: Intelligence as a Complete Set of Broad Cognitive Abilities*  The next step advancing clinicians' conceptualizations of intelligence is associated with the availability of intelligence batteries intended to measure the complete set of broad abilities. Many contemporary scholars of intelligence would agree that the structure of cognitive ability is best portrayed by the Cattell-Horn-Carroll (CHC) theory of cognitive abilities. The CHC theory is an amalgamation of Cattell and

Horn's Gf-Gc theory (Cattell, 1941; Horn, 1965, 1991; Horn & Noll, 1997) and Carroll's (1993, 1998) three-strata theory of intelligence (Carroll & Horn, personal communication, July 1999).

The 1989 revision of the WJ (WJ-R; Woodcock & Johnson, 1989b) measures seven broad abilities identify by the CHC theory. Two other broad abilities, quantitative knowledge and reading-writing, are measured as part of the companion achievement battery (Woodcock & Johnson, 1989a). The WJ-R was based on the Gf-Gc theory, now subsumed in the CHC theory.

Table 13.1 on page 308 lists and describes nine well-defined CHC broad abilities. The acronyms presented for each broad ability are standard in the literature, though some writers may use variations. The table also includes examples of implications for deficits in each of the nine abilities.

*Level 5: Broad Cognitive Abilities Underlined by Numerous Narrow Abilities*   This level of conceptualization recognizes that 60 or more narrow abilities underlie the nine broad abilities described in Table 13.1. The narrow abilities represent qualitatively different specialized abilities that have been rather well defined in the literature. Horn (1991, pp. 207–223) relates the concept of narrow abilities to the primary mental abilities concept (Thurston, 1938) and to well-replicated cognitive factors' primary abilities (Ekstrom, French, & Harmon, 1979). This is followed by Horn's presentation of several kinds of measures that are associated with each of nine broad Gf-Gc abilities. Carroll (1993) places narrow abilities in the first stratum of his three-stratum theory. The WJ-III (Woodcock, McGrew, & Mather, 2001a, 2001b) is a Level 5 battery. Each of the broad CHC abilities is measured by at least two qualitatively different narrow ability tests. Some 21 narrow abilities are documented as measured in the WJ-III Tests of Cognitive Ability, and 19 other narrow abilities are measured in the WJ-III Tests of Achievement.

Table 13.1 provides several examples of narrow abilities associated with each of the broad CHC abilities. The acronyms listed for the narrow abilities in Table 13.1 are rather standard in the literature. Comprehension-knowledge (*Gc*) is an example of a broad ability with a list of underlying narrow abilities (e.g., language development, listening ability, and general information). Each narrow ability is a verifiably separate and measurable aspect of broad comprehension-knowledge and provides qualitatively different information. An examinee may demonstrate a significant strength or weakness on one of the measures but not on the others. A parallel can be drawn with the assessment of reading, a broad area of achievement. A variety of reading tests may be administered, each assessing a different narrow reading ability (e.g., word attack, word identification, or reading comprehension). To find out more about a reading problem, it may be necessary to measure several narrow aspects of reading so that the nature of the problem can be determined and appropriate instruction planned. The same strategy applies to the assessment of a problem in one of the broad abilities.

## INTERPRETATION OF INTELLIGENCE TESTS

The practical application of theories of abilities has resulted in numerous intelligence and ability tests. As the conceptualization of intelligence has changed,

**Table 13.1**

Examples of Cattell-Horn-Carroll (CHC) Narrow Abilities

| CHC Broad Ability | CHC Narrow Abilities | |
|---|---|---|
| **Acquired Knowledge** | | |
| Comprehension-knowledge (Gc) | Language development (LD) | Oral production and fluency (OP) |
| | Lexical knowledge (VL) | General information (K0) |
| | Listening ability (LS) | Information about culture (K2) |
| Quantitative knowledge (Gq) | Mathematical achievement (A3) | Mathematical knowledge (KM) |
| Reading-writing (Grw) | Reading decoding (RD) | Writing ability (WA) |
| | Reading comprehension (RC) | English-usage knowledge (EU) |
| | Spelling ability (SG) | |
| **Thinking Abilities** | | |
| Long-term retrieval (Glr) | Associative memory (MA) | Ideational fluency (IF) |
| | Meaningful memory (MM) | Naming facility (NA) |
| | Figural fluency (FF) | |
| Visual-spatial thinking (Gv) | Visualization (Vz) | Length estimation (LE) |
| | Spatial relations (SR) | Visual memory (MV) |
| | Flexibility of closure (CF) | Spatial scanning (SS) |
| Auditory processing (Ga) | Phonetic coding (PC) | Resistance to auditory stimulus distortion (UR) |
| | Speech-sound discrimination (US) | Memory for sound patterns (UM) |
| | General sound discrimination (UG) | |
| Fluid reasoning (Gf) | Induction (I) | Quantitative reasoning (RQ) |
| | General sequential reasoning (RG) | |
| **Cognitive Efficiency** | | |
| Processing speed (Gs) | Perceptual speed (P) | Rate of test taking (R9) |
| | Semantic processing speed (R4) | Number facility (N) |
| Short-term memory (Gsm) | Working memory (WM) | Memory span (MS) |

there has been a corresponding change in how scores from such tests are interpreted. As the conceptualization of intelligence has changed from a single global ability to a hierarchy of narrow abilities underlying multiple broad abilities, a parallel series of developments corresponding to the interpretation of intelligence tests has developed as well. According to Kamphaus, Petoskey, and Morgan (1997), there have been four major waves of intelligence test interpretations. The first wave was based on the quantification of general ability and sought to classify individuals into a single category. Interpretation was based on an overall single score based on an IQ or an overall standard score. The first classification schemes used terminology such as "Idiot," "Imbeciles," and "Morons" to describe individuals' overall intelligence grouping (Levine & Mark, 1928). Similar use but different terminology (e.g., Defective, Borderline) was used on the first Wechsler scale (Wechsler, 1958).

The second wave was clinical profile analysis, which included the shape of test score profiles in addition to overall ability level. It incorporated differences between verbal and performance tests, similar to the conceptualization of intelligence as a pair of abilities. This "clinical" method, however, lacked scientific rigor, which opened the door for the third wave of interpretation, guided by measurement science. Statistical techniques such as factor analysis provided support for multiple abilities. The psychometric approach tempered clinical interpretation techniques with an appreciation of error variance and reliability issues involved with test interpretation. As the psychometric approach began to demonstrate the lack of validity and reliability of many clinical procedures, a fourth wave that included a theoretical basis for measurement was viewed as the most valid interpretive method (Kamphaus, 1993). Correspondingly, "Knowledge of theory is important above and beyond research findings, as theory allows the clinician to do a better job of conceptualizing a child's score" (Kamphaus, Petoskey, & Morgan, 1999; p. 44). Additionally, the development of a priori hypotheses is viewed as important and corresponds to a similar statistical shift from factor analysis to confirmatory factor analysis.

An important aspect of the most recent developments in the interpretation of ability measures is the need for theory. Although Carroll's hierarchical model is often viewed as a theory of cognitive abilities, it may more aptly be thought of as a description. Carroll's model describes the structure and types of abilities identifiable by statistical procedures. However, such a model does not explain the causal aspects or origins of ability. Although various theoretical models (e.g., Vygotsky's developmental model, Sternberg's triarchic theory, Gardner's multiple intelligences) are available, each with different assumptions, neuropsychological models stand to make the greatest theoretical contribution to interpreting ability tests by an appreciation of brain-behavior relationships. Theoretical models generated from an understanding of how the brain processes information will provide both the basis for understanding hierarchical models of ability and also the interpretive basis to develop a priori hypotheses that are tested through the assessment process.

Conceptualization of Neuropsychological Assessment

The conceptualization of neurological assessment has focused on two approaches. The first approach is the quantitative (structural) approach predominant in North

America. This approach was based on the development of test batteries that allowed for the identification of aberrant neurological conditions from a structural point of view using standardized methods and comparisons with normative samples. This point of view is exemplified by Reitan (1955, 1966) and reflected in the construction of the Halstead-Reitan Neuropsychological Test Battery (Reitan & Wolfson, 1993). Because the methods of the quantitative orientation have been adopted on the basis of predictive efficiency, this approach, which provides continuous predictive validation, is most frequently faulted as being atheoretical and lacking data necessary for understanding and documenting the loss of individual functions (Luria & Majovski, 1977).

In contrast, Luria (1966) proposed a more qualitative approach focusing on "pathognomonic signs" useful in understanding a patient's functioning. Luria's theoretical view of cortical functioning rests on the development of specific assessment techniques that would lead to rehabilitation strategies. Similar to many of Luria's arguments, a number of neuropsychologists have stressed methods that view neuropsychological assessment as a dynamic, interactive process. From this point of view, the importance of diagnosis is subserved by the concern for providing a comprehensive view of a patient's total functioning.

As opposed to other theorists who have argued that functions are discretely localized in specific areas of the brain, Luria (1970) and proponents of the qualitative school maintain that higher forms of human cognitive activity (e.g., memory) are based on the participation of all levels of cerebral activity and are more heuristically organized into functional systems of the brain. The crux of Luria's observation-based approach has been a syndrome analysis or a "qualification of the symptom" in which behaviors are described and hypotheses formulated regarding the dysfunction of the brain. Based on such an evaluation of the patient's symptoms, specific assessment techniques were developed to test early hypotheses (Luria, 1973). Hence, data resulting from the assessments were not viewed in terms of quantitative norms but considered in terms of patterns of "functioning" (Luria, 1973). The techniques used in this approach change from patient to patient as well as for the cerebral function being considered. Such flexibility during evaluation seems more indicative of the behavioral neurologist than what we in the West would consider neuropsychological assessment (Dean, 1986). As such, Luria's strategy is often criticized as employing a far too subjective approach with few opportunities to validate procedures or establish other than clinical norms (Luria, 1973).

The standardized test batteries of North America were developed using both the quantitative and qualitative approaches to neuropsychological assessment. Such test batteries have been criticized as either being atheoretical and ignoring descriptive data (e.g., Halstead-Reitan Neuropsychology Test Battery) or relying on case study methods and failing to systematically evaluate methods of assessment (e.g., Luria-Nebraska Neuropsychological Test Battery). These standardized test batteries were originally developed to predict brain damage (i.e., "brain damage, no damage") before sophisticated imaging techniques were available. However, the new generation of computer tomography (CT) scanning equipment and magnetic resonance imaging (MRI) and recent advances in positron emission tomography and functional MRI hold clear implications for the diagnosis and localization of neurological dysfunction. In the past, the noninvasive nature of neuropsychological assessment and the lack of radiological techniques to portray soft tissue made obvious the utility of neuropsychological assessment as a diagnostic tool. However, continued refinement of radiological procedures has reduced the dependence on neuropsychological assessment in the diagnosis of brain damage. As a result, increasing importance has been placed on outlining a functional impairment as well as defining the adaptive behavior remaining following brain damage (Dean & Gray, 1990). Although definitive knowledge concerning the anatomical integrity of the brain may be available, rarely is the neurologist or neurosurgeon in a position to predict the behavioral expression of a given lesion in the patient's postmorbid environment (e.g., school). This prediction is even less accurate in childhood because brain development must also be taken into account (Dean, 1987).

Although the discovery of a broad array of abilities in Carroll's model is at the forefront of contemporary psychometric research, neuropsychologists recognized very early that most measures of intelligence and ability lacked the inclusion of important abilities central to the notion of intelligence. Frontal lobe lesions had little impact on traditional measures of intelligence. Similar results have been found in other studies and generalize to contemporary measures. Additionally, the concept of intelligence as an all-encompassing concept of cognitive ability lacks the specificity needed for clinical utility. As such, Carroll's model, which specifies a hierarchy of multiple abilities, would seem especially fitting for neuropsychological assessment.

Much of contemporary neuropsychological test development of ability has sought to integrate psychometric models of intelligence with contemporary neuropsychological models. For example, the KAIT (Kaufman & Kaufman, 1993) integrates the Horn-Cattell theory of intelligence with neuropsychological models from Luria and developmental models from Piaget. Another recent battery is the Reynolds Intellectual Assessment Scales (Reynolds & Kamphouse, 2004). Based in part on the Gf-Gc model, the battery offers a number of tests that allows one to go beyond the simple model and provides measures of broad cognitive abilities. Although fluid and crystallized IQs are provided in many tests, important abilities from Carroll's model, which extends the Horn-Cattell model, are not provided. Similarly, the Cognitive Assessment System (Naglieri & Das, 1997) incorporates neuropsychological models from Luria using psychometric techniques, but does not specifically incorporate any of the ability models (g, Gf-Gc, Carroll). Other attempts, such as the WISC-III PI, include applying neuropsychological approaches to existing instruments with slight modification (Kaplan, Fein, Kramer, Delis, & Morris, 1999).

To apply a neuropsychological model but move beyond the level of a simple "brain damage, no damage" decision and address the criticisms of available neuropsychological test batteries and to fully incorporate a hierarchical broad ability model, Dean and Woodcock (2003a) have developed the Dean-Woodcock Neuropsychological Assessment System (D-WNAS). The D-WNAS focuses on empirically derived single function measures, having a theoretical base in present cognitive neuropsychological/information-processing theory. This approach departs from the traditional atheoretical approach seen in many of our presently available tests and moves us to the next conceptual level of neuropsychological assessment.

## THE DEAN-WOODCOCK COGNITIVE NEUROPSYCHOLOGY MODEL

The assessment of cognitive abilities or intelligence is an integral part of the neuropsychological examination. As such, the Dean-Woodcock cognitive neuropsychology model integrates the assessment of cognitive abilities with assessment of sensorimotor functions. The system integrates CHC theory, reflected in the WJ-III's Level 5 conceptualization of cognitive abilities, within a broader interpretation of an individual's neuropsychological functioning.

Figure 13.1 presents the Dean-Woodcock cognitive neuropsychology model. This model has been adapted for neuropsychology for the Gf-Gc information-processing model (Woodcock, 1993, 1998). It illustrates the interaction of cognitive and noncognitive factors in the production of cognitive and motor performance. An understanding of the model will aid in the interpretation of the impact of functional deficits observed in the performance of a learner or patient.

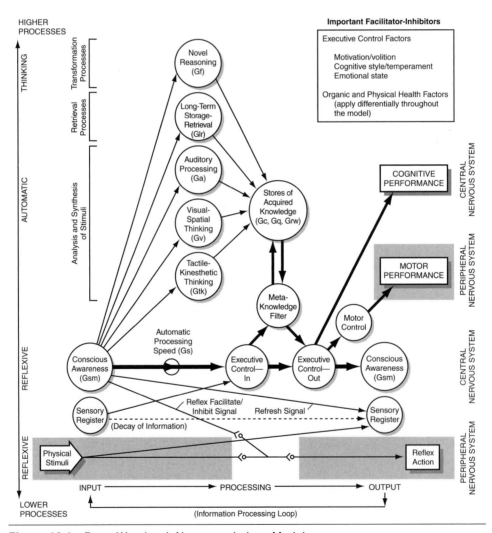

**Figure 13.1**  Dean-Woodcock Neuropsychology Model

DESCRIPTION OF THE COGNITIVE NEUROPSYCHOLOGICAL MODEL

Most models provide a simplified representation of the relationships among the components of a complex process. Though there may be some correlation, a model of cognition does not necessarily represent the underlying physical components and their connections. The Dean-Woodcock neuropsychology model (Figure 13.1) was derived from combining CHC theory with information-processing theory. The model is presented in a stepwise manner to aid the reader in its application. Before reading the explanation that follows, however, the reader should consider certain features of the model:

- The model in Figure 13.1 indicates whether a process or pathway involves the peripheral nervous system, the central nervous system, or both.
- The arrow in the lower left-hand corner of Figure 13.2 represents the input of physical stimuli from external or internal sources.
- The right-hand, or output, side of the model includes cognitive and motor outcomes.
- The horizontal dimension of Figure 13.1 represents a single cycle of cognitive processing, including input, processing, and output. The right-hand, or output, side of the model serves as the input for the next cycle. The model may be perceived as wrapped around a cylinder, with the output of one cycle becoming the input of the next cycle.
- The vertical dimension of the model represents the level of cognitive processing. Reflexive processes are represented in the lowest portion of the model. Above this level, automatic processes are represented. The upper region of the model includes the thinking and reasoning processes.
- The model recognizes that cognitive performance and motor performance are not determined by cognitive abilities alone, but also by the influence of noncognitive factors, called facilitator-inhibitors.

Although this model may appear complex at first, reading the following section will provide an appreciation of how cognitive and noncognitive influences interact to produce cognitive and motor performance. This, in turn, may contribute to a more insightful interpretation of neuropsychological information.

*Reflexive Level*   The lowest level in the cognitive neuropsychology model represents one of the most fundamental neurological functions: the reflex arc (Figure 13.2). For example, if you unexpectedly touch a very hot object (physical stimulus), your response will be a rapid retraction of your hand. This reflexive action is represented in Figure 13.2 by the line extending from physical stimuli to reflex action. Note that the reception of physical stimuli and motor response are located in the peripheral nervous system but that part of the reflex arc takes place in the spinal cord portion of the central nervous system. The protective reflex action occurs quickly, even before there is any conscious awareness of heat or pain.

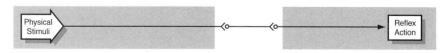

**Figure 13.2**   Reflexive Level of the Cognitive Neuropsychology System

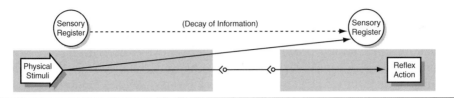

**Figure 13.3**   Input to Sensory Registers

While the reflex action is under way, a signal is traveling to the appropriate sensory register in the brain (Figure 13.2). Recall that because the horizontal dimension of the model represents only a single cycle of functioning, the contents of the sensory register of the right side of the model are simultaneously acting on the contents of the sensory register represented on the left side. The dotted line between the sensory register on the left and the sensory register on the right indicates that the sensory information will rapidly decay if there is no further input.

Figure 13.3 introduces the concept of conscious awareness onto Figure 13.4. The information that has reached the sensory register is routed through executive control into conscious awareness. You are now aware of having touched the hot object. Executive control operates as a traffic director in the cognitive system, allocating attention resources, directing automatic and nonautomatic activity, and monitoring operations. Though it is in the stream of conscious awareness, executive control usually performs its responsibilities automatically.

Conscious awareness, in concert with executive control, can exercise limited control over some reflex and sensory registers (Figure 13.5). At least four types of controlling actions may be initiated from conscious awareness. First, an inhibit signal can moderate the normal action of the reflex arc. For example, if one must pick up an object suspected of being hot, conscious awareness can suppress operation of the reflex arc and allow the object to be picked up even though it is painful. Second, a facilitate signal to the reflex arc can enhance its proclivity to initiate a reflex action even if the object is only slightly warm. The third controlling action can signal the sensory register to recycle its stored information through conscious awareness, a type of review process that is available only for a second or two. For example, if a sound is not immediately recognized, conscious

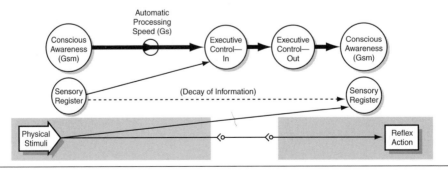

**Figure 13.4**   Automatic Level of the Cognitive Neuropsychology Model

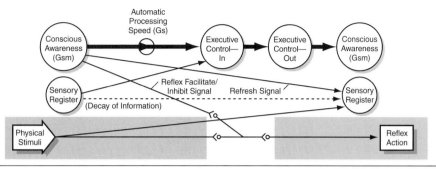

**Figure 13.5** Influence of Consciousness Awareness on Reflex Arcs and Sensory Registers

awareness may transmit a refresh signal to the sensory register so that its contents can be sent again into conscious awareness, thus providing a short-lived opportunity to "rehear" the sound. A similar function of the refresh signal facilitates the rehearsal of auditory stimuli. If the stimuli are a telephone number that you must remember long enough to dial, the refresh signal allows you to rehearse that number. Woodcock (1993) refers to this process as the "phonological loop." The fourth type of controlling action allows conscious awareness to attend to the contents of sensory registers that are being ignored, such as the pressure being exerted on your feet by the shoes you are wearing.

Note that the path from conscious awareness through executive control, and to certain other areas in the complete model, is represented by a broad line indicating that this is the "freeway" of cognitive functioning. Most of the activity at this level is automatic. Two Gf-Gc broad abilities, short-term memory (Gsm) and automatic processing speed (Gs), and certain facilitator-inhibitors play important roles along this freeway. These abilities reflect the individual's capacity to hold information in conscious awareness and to perform automatic tasks rapidly. If the individual has a processing speed limitation, this operates as if a partially closed valve is reducing the flow of information along the automatic pathway.

Figure 13.6 on page 316 adds a large circle to the model that represents the stores of declarative and procedural knowledge. In the pathway between executive control and these stores of knowledge lies the metaknowledge filter. This portion of the model decides, more or less imperfectly, whether the declarative and/or procedural knowledge is known and available. If not known, executive control may generate a strategy for attempting to solve the problem. The model now allows for the recognition of familiar stimuli, such as your name when you are called or the face of a friend.

Figure 13.7 on page 316 adds the components of cognitive performance (a central nervous system function) and motor performance (both a central and a peripheral nervous system function) to the model. Note that motor performance is moderated by motor control, which is part of the central nervous system. If you wish to write down a telephone number that is currently in conscious awareness, those pathways would be involved.

Now suppose the stimulus is the question "How do you spell your name?" We have already described the path that this stimulus (the question) would follow

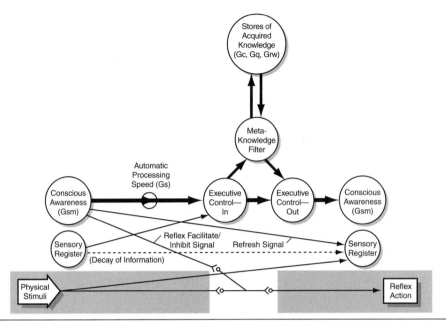

**Figure 13.6** The Metaknowledge Filter and Stores of Acquired Knowledge

from the arrow representing physical stimuli into conscious awareness, with executive control operating as a traffic director. The question "How do you spell your name?" is routed through the metaknowledge filter by executive control into the stores of knowledge. Assuming that you know how to spell your name, the retrieval of the spelling is automatic. Upon returning to executive control, the out-

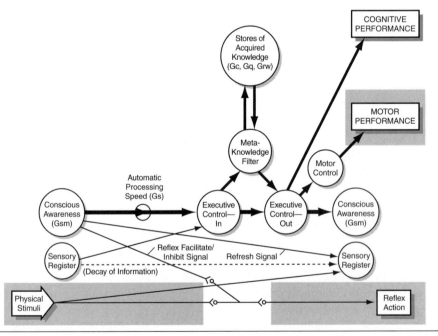

**Figure 13.7** Cognitive Performance and Motor Performance Components of the Cognitive Neuropsychology Model

put goes to cognitive performance and to a motor representation in either speech or writing. Of course, if you have not learned to spell your name, there is no store of that knowledge and you could not provide a correct response.

Note that the stores of acquired knowledge include three of the previously described Gf-Gc abilities: verbal comprehension-knowledge (Gc), quantitative knowledge (Gq), and reading-writing (Grw). In addition, though not normally included in discussions about Gf-Gc theory, various sensory and motor knowledge stores could be added to the model.

Now suppose that the stimulus (question) has changed and you are asked to spell your name backward. (As a personal experiment, try it!) The response no longer requires a simple automatic recall from stored knowledge; rather, you must think. Figure 13.8 adds the thinking abilities to the cognitive neuropsychology model. These include the traditional Gf-Gc abilities of visual-spatial thinking (Gv), auditory processing (Ga), long-term storage-retrieval (Glr), and novel reasoning

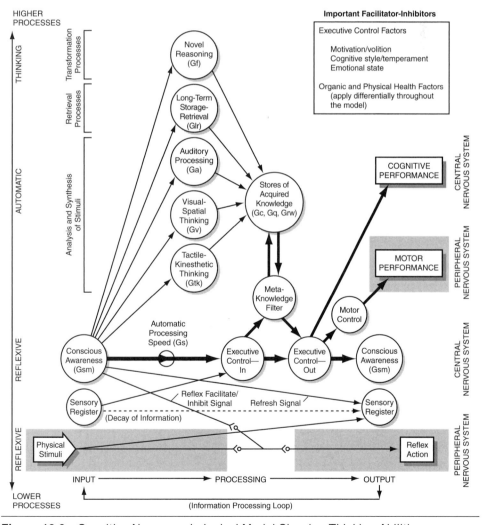

**Figure 13.8** Cognitive Neuropsychological Model Showing Thinking Abilities

(Gf). Neuropsychologists are also concerned with other types of processing, particularly motor, tactile, and kinesthetic (Gtk). Such processing represents a complex interaction of cortical and subcortical functions as well as pathways in the spinal cord and the peripheral nervous system.

As you have probably never attempted to spell you name backward, there is no chunk of stored knowledge from which to draw. As a result, your cognitive system must produce a strategy for attacking that problem. That strategy, along with the question, enters conscious awareness. Most people attack this problem by visualizing their name in the mind's eye and then spelling it backward. As this process is executed, the result flows through the stores of knowledge, through executive control, and on to cognitive and motor performance. The reversed spelling of your name, on its way through the stores of knowledge, leaves a trace in the memory systems. If this process is repeated enough times, that trace grows and becomes part of stored knowledge. Subsequently, at the request to spell your name backward, that information can be retrieved automatically and reported without invoking the previously required thinking process.

At this point, except for the facilitator-inhibitors, we are now back to the complete cognitive neuropsychology model as represented in Figure 13.1. Note the box in the upper right-hand corner of Figure 13.8. That box lists some of the facilitator-inhibitors that can exert a profound influence on cognitive and motor performance. Facilitator-inhibitors primarily operate on executive control in this model and include, for example, motivation/volition, cognitive style, temperament, and emotional state. In addition, various organic factors operate as facilitator-inhibitors and apply differentially throughout the model. The input of physical stimuli may be especially impacted by organic factors such as impaired vision or hearing.

This completes the description of the cognitive neuropsychology model, but two caveats are in order. First, as complex as this model may appear, it is an oversimplification of the neurological bases of cognitive processing. Most cognitive processing requires interaction of many components and, further, requires many cycles for completion. Second, the model represents functional relationships among the components, and there is not necessarily specific neuroanatomical correspondence that can be said to underlie a particular component or pathway.

## The Dean-Woodcock Neuropsychological Assessment System

To assess the sensorimotor functions presented in the Dean-Woodcock cognitive neuropsychology model, Dean and Woodcock (2003b) have developed the Dean-Woodcock Sensory-Motor Battery (D-WSMB). In conjunction with selected tests of the Woodcock-Johnson Tests of Cognitive Ability (WJ-III COG) and Achievement (WJ-III ACH), the D-WSMB provides a comprehensive neuropsychological evaluation system referred to as the Dean-Woodcock Neuropsychological Assessment System (D-WNAS).

*Educational Application of the Dean-Woodcock Neuropsychological Assessment System*
To provide a practical example of how the D-WNAS can be used in the school setting, an educationally relevant case study is presented. It should be noted that the scores for each subtest provided are given a qualitative label of functioning. As portrayed in Table 13.2, the scores for the WJ-III may be transformed in a number

**Table 13.2**
Good Measures of CHC Factors

| Factor | Battery | | | |
|---|---|---|---|---|
| | WJ III | Wechslers | SB-IV | K-ABC |
| Short-Term Memory (Gsm) | (Short-Term Memory) Numbers Reversed | Digit Span Letter-Number Sequencing (WAIS III)* | (Short-Term Memory) Memory for Digits Memory for Objects | (Sequential Processing) Number Recall Word Order |
| Comprehension Knowledge (Gc) | (Comprehension-Knowledge) Verbal Comprehension General Information | (Verbal Comprehension) Vocabulary Comprehension Information Similarities | (Verbal Reasoning) Vocabulary Verbal Relations Absurdities Comprehension | Riddles Faces and Places |
| Quantitative Knowledge (Gq) | (Quantitative Ability) Calculation Applied Problems Quantitative Concepts | Arithmetic | (Quantitative Reasoning) Equation Building Number Series Quantitative | Arithmetic |
| Visual-Spatial Thinking (Gv) | (Visual Processing) Picture Recognition Spatial Relations | (Perceptual Organization) Object Assembly Block Design Mazes Picture Completion | Pattern Analysis Copying Paper Folding and Cutting Memory for Objects* Bead Memory* | (Simultaneous Processing) Triangles Gestalt Closure Magic Window* |
| Auditory Processing (Ga) | (Auditory Processing) Auditory Attention Sound Blending Incomplete Words | | | |

*(Continued)*

**Table 13.2** *Continued*

| Factor | Battery | | | |
|---|---|---|---|---|
| | WJ III | Wechslers | SB-IV | K-ABC |
| Long-Term Retrieval (Glr) | (Long-Term Retrieval) Retrieval Fluency Visual-Auditory Learning | | | |
| Fluid Reasoning (Gf) | (Fluid Reasoning) Planning Concept Formation Analysis-Synthesis | Matrix Reasoning (WAIS-III)* | Matrices Equation Building* Number Series* | |
| Processing Speed (Gs) | (Processing Speed) Decision Speed Visual Matching | (Processing Speed) Coding (Digit Symbol) Symbol Search | | |

Adapted from Woodcock (1990, 1994); McGrew & Woodcock (2001), and Flanagan and Ortiz (2001).

of ways. One transformation that holds considerable interest in neuropsychology is termed "functional level." When Table 13.2 is consulted, scores from individual tests of the WJ-III may be transformed to functional levels ranging from within normal limits (WNL) to severely impaired. Because the scores for the D-WNAS are based on results of Rasch scaling, they have the same meaning at any age level and for any area measured (Woodcock, 1999, pp. 199–121).

### Case Study: John M.

John is a 7-year-old, left-handed, White male who just completed the first grade. He was accompanied by his mother, who reported a number of disruptive behaviors, including hypermotor behavior, distractibility, and problems with concentration. John stated that he "hears a little man's voice."

John lives with his mother, biological brother, and stepfather. He sees his biological father on alternate weekends. His peer relationships are reported to be good. His mother reports that John's teacher had some difficulty with him during the past year, identifying him as "the class clown." He completed the first grade, receiving no special education services. His grades were fair.

Medically, John experienced significant perinatal distress. He was the product of a premature delivery, weighing 5 lb. 20 oz. An emergency cesarean section delivery was required, and he had significant respiratory distress that required considerable intervention with steroids. He continues to take steroids as needed for asthma. He has allergies for a number of airborne particles. John has diminished appetite. Sleep patterns are reported to be normal.

His mother saw developmental milestones as being normal. He has never been seen by a mental health professional. Two years ago, the chief complaints noted earlier led his primary care physician to diagnose Attention-Deficit/Hyperactivity Disorder, Combined Type. Recently, the physician referred him for a neuropsychological evaluation.

John's Emotional Status Examination indicated moderate maladjustment with reported anxiety, depression, hypermotor behavior, and inattention. He was not taking psychoactive medication when seen.

John's overall intellectual ability is in the average range. Most of his cognitive functions (comprehension-knowledge, long-term retrieval, visual-spatial thinking, auditory processing, and fluid reasoning) are within normal limits, although he demonstrated mild impairment on measures of processing speed and short-term, or immediate, memory (less than 30 seconds), and his auditory working memory capacity, requiring the ability to manipulate and transform numbers and words, was mildly impaired. Although most measured areas of academic functioning are also within normal limits, he demonstrated mild impairment in the ability to comprehend written passages while reading.

The patient's sensory and motor assessment indicated that mild impairment was present for left-side tactile perception of upper extremities, left-hand finger agnosia, and balance/strength of the leg. An overview of his cognitive, sensory, motor, and emotional assessment is shown in Table 13.3 on page 322.

In summary, John M. is a young man of average cognitive ability with Attention-Deficit/Hyperactivity Disorder, Combined Type. In addition, as is often seen with ADHD, he has comorbid anxiety and depression. In general, his neuropsychological functioning ranged from mildly impaired to within normal limits.

**Table 13.3**

Overview of Patient's Cognitive, Sensory Motor, and Emotional Assessments

| | | | |
|---|---|---|---|
| **Name:** | John M. | **Handedness:** | Left |
| **Gender:** | Male | **Diagnosis:** | ADHD, Coordination |
| **Age:** | 7 years, 3 months | | |
| **Education:** | 2nd/Current/Reg. Ed. | **Time at Onset:** | Congenital |

| Function | Rating |
|---|---|
| **General Intellectual Ability** | |
| GIA (Standard) | 93 |
| **Comprehension-Knowledge** | |
| Verbal Comprehension | WNL |
| **Long-Term Retrieveal** | |
| Visual-Auditory Learning | WNL |
| Visual-Auditory Learning | |
| Delayed Recall | WNL |
| **Visual-Spatial Thinking** | |
| Spatial Relations | WNL |
| Picture Recognition | WNL |
| **Auditory Processing** | |
| Sound Blending | WNL |
| Incomplete Words | WNL |
| **Fluid Reasoning** | |
| Concept Formation | WNL |
| Analysis-Synthesis | WNL |
| Planning | WNL |
| **Processing Speed** | |
| Visual Matching | Mildly impaired |
| Decision Speed | Mildly impaired |
| **Short-Term and Working Memory** | |
| Memory for Words | Mildly impaired |
| Numbers Reversed | WNL |
| Auditory Working Memory | Mildly impaired |
| **Quantitative Ability** | |
| Calculation | WNL |
| Applied Problems | WNL |
| **Reading and Writing Ability** | |
| Letter-Word Identification | WNL |
| Passage Comprehension | Mildly impaired |
| Spelling | WNL |
| Writing Samples | WNL |
| **Sensory Assessment** | |
| Visual Acuity | WNL |
| Visual Confrontation | WNL |
| Naming Pictures of Objects | WNL |
| Auditory Acuity | WNL |
| Tactile Perception | Moderately impaired (left) |
| **Motor Assessment** | |
| Gait and Station | Mildly impaired (left leg) |
| Romberg (traditional, one foot, heel to toe) | WNL |
| Coordination/Gross Cerebellar Assessment | WNL |
| Construction | WNL |

**Table 13.3** *Continued*

| Function | Rating |
|---|---|
| Motor Assessment *continued* | |
|     Mime Movements | WNL |
|     Left-Right Movements | WNL |
|     Finger Tapping | Mildly impaired (left) |
|     Grip Strength | Mildly impaired (bilateral) |
|     Lateral Preference | Left |
|     Expressive Speech | WNL |
| History/Emotional Status | |
|     History: (medical, psychiatric, social, family) Premature; respiratory distress; emergency C-section; asthma; sees father every other week. | |
|     Emotional Status: Hypermotor behavior, depression, inattention, anxiety. | |

*Note:* WNL = Within normal limits.

Although most age-level cognitive and academic tasks should be manageable for John, tasks involving processing speed, auditory short-term memory, and reading comprehension will be very difficult for him. Mild impairments in these areas may be secondary effects of ADHD. Consequently, he should be considered for a trial on both an antidepressant and a stimulant medication. John also has a mild, left-side sensorimotor impairment; some motor tasks will be very difficult for him. Although the impairment is thought to be congenital in etiology, it should be reviewed by a neurologist to rule out any active neuropathology. Following a negative neurological examination, John should be considered for occupation and physical therapy. He should be reevaluated following stabilization on medication and a neurological examination.

This case study demonstrates how the WJ-III provides the foundation for assessing a broad range of behavioral functions not offered through any other single battery. With an examination of the Dean-Woodcock neuropsychological models shown in Figure 13.2, it becomes clear that Woodcock's (1993) extended Gf-Gc theory offers an information-processing model that combines theory with dimensions of input and output. The WJ-III, in conjunction with this model, gives neuropsychologists and school psychologists a way to assess cognitive strengths and weaknesses, a method of interpretation for intervention, and a means for follow-up planning.

## CONCLUSION

The neuropsychological interpretation of ability takes cognitive ability testing to the next level, providing a comprehensive evaluation of brain functioning. Moreover, this is keeping with the No Child Left Behind program, which reduces the use of ability testing that was stressed in the past The school neuropsychologist now has the means to assess neuropsychological ability using the D-WNAS or other measures. The D-WNAS not only provides a neuropsychological interpretation of ability, but it also provides a system describing functional levels (i.e., from within normal limits to severely impaired), which can be used to describe the ease or difficulty with which the student will find similar, real-world tasks. The school neuropsychologist is then able to link assessment with intervention, providing ecologically relevant neuropsychological interventions in a learning environment.

## REFERENCES

Carroll, J. B. (1993). *Human cognitive abilities: A survey of factor-analytic studies.* Cambridge, England: Cambridge University Press.

Carroll, J. B. (1998). Human cognitive abilities. A critique. In J. J. McArdle & R. W. Woodcock (Eds.), *Human cognitive abilities in theory and practice* (pp. 5–23). Mahwah, NJ: Erlbaum.

Cattell, R. B. (1941). Some theoretical issues in adult intelligence testing. *Psychological Bulletin, 38,* 592.

D'Amato, R. C., Gray, J. W., & Dean, R. S. (1988). Construct validity on the PPVT with neuropsychological, intellectual, and achievement measures. *Journal of Clinical Psychology, 44,* 934–939.

Dean, R. S. (1986). Perspectives on the future of neuropsychological assessment. In J. V. Mitchell (Series Ed.), B. S. Plake, & J. C. Witt (Vol. Eds.), *Buros-Nebraska symposium on measurement and testing: Vol. 2. The future of testing* (pp. 203–244). Hillsdale, NJ: Earlbaum.

Dean, R. S. (1987). Foundations of rationale for neuropsychological bases of individual differences. In L. C. Hartlage & C. F. Telzrow (Eds.), *The neuropsychology of individual differences: A developmental perspective.* New York: Plenum Press.

Dean, R. S., & Gray, J. W. (1990). Traditional approaches to neuropsychological assessment. In T. B. Gutkin & C. Reynolds (Eds.), *The handbook of school psychology* (pp. 269–288). New York: Wiley.

Dean, R. S., & Woodcock, R. W. (2003a). *Dean-Woodcock Neuropsychological Assessment System.* Itasca, IL: Riverside.

Dean, R. S., & Woodcock, R. W. (2003b). *Dean-Woodcock Sensory-Motor Battery.* Itasca, IL: Riverside.

Ekstrom, R. B., French, J. W., & Harmon, M. H. (1979). Cognitive factors: Their identification and replication. *Multivariate Behavioral Research Monographs, 79*(2).

Elliot, C. D. (1990). *Differential abilities scales.* San Antonio, TX: Psychological Corporation.

Fagan, T. K., & Wise, P. S. (2000). *School psychology: Past, present, and future.* Bethesda: NASP.

Golden, C. J., Purish, A. D., & Hammeke, T. A. (1985). *Luria-Nebraska Neuropsychological Battery.* Los Angeles: Western Psychological Services.

Horn, J. L. (1965). *Fluid and crystallized intelligence.* Unpublished doctoral dissertation, University of Illinois, Urbana-Champaign.

Horn, J. L. (1991). Measurement of intellectual capabilities: A review of theory. In K. S. McGrew, J. K. Werder, & R. W. Woodcock (Eds.), *WJ-R technical manual* (pp. 197–232). Chicago: Riverside.

Horn, J. L., & Noll, J. (1997). Human cognitive capabilities (*Gf-Gc*) theory. In D. P. Flanagan, J. L. Genshaft, & P. L. Harrison (Eds.), *Contemporary intellectual assessment: Theories, tests, and issues* (pp. 53–91). New York: Guilford Press.

Kaufman, A. S., & Kaufman, N. L. (1983). *Kaufman Assessment Battery for Children.* Circle Pines, MN: American Guidance Service.

Kaufman, A. S., & Kaufman, N. L. (1993). *The Kaufman Adolescent and Adult Intelligence Test.* Circle Pines, MN: American Guidance Service.

Levine, A. J., & Marks, L. (1928). *Testing intelligence and achievement.* New York: Macmillan.

Luria, A. R. (1966). *Higher cortical functions in man.* New York: Basic Books.

Luria, A. R. (1970). The functional organization of the brain. *Scientific American, 3,* 66–78.

Luria, A. R. (1973). *The working brain.* London: Penguin Press.

Luria, A. R., & Majovski, L. V. (1977). Basic approaches used in American and Soviet clinical neuropsychology. *American Psychologist, 32,* 959–968.

Naglieri, J. A., & Das, J. P. (1997). *Cognitive assessment system.* Itasca, IL: Riverside.

Reitan, R. M. (1955). An investigation of the validity of Halstead's measures of biological intelligence. *Archives of Neurology and Psychiatry, 73,* 28–35.

Reitan, R. M. (1966). Problems and prospects in studying the psychological correlates of brain lesions. *Cortex, 2,* 127–154.

Reitan, R. M., & Wolfson, D. (1993). *The Halstead-Reitan Neuropsychological Test Battery.* Tucson, AZ: Neuropsychology Press.

Reynolds, C. R. (1981). The neuropsychological basis of intelligence. In G. W. Hynd & J. E. Odrzut (Eds.), *Neuropsychological assessment and the school aged child: Issues and procedures* (pp. 87–124). New York: Grune & Stratton.

Reynolds, C. R., & Kamphaus, R. W. (2003). *Reynolds Intellectual Assessment Scales.* Lutz, FL: Psychological Assessment Resources.

Terman, L. M. (1916). *The measurement of intelligence.* Boston: Houghton Mifflin.

Terman, L. M., & Merrill, M. A. (1937). *Measuring intelligence: A guide to the administration of the new revised Stanford-Binet Tests of Intelligence.* Boston: Houghton Mifflin.

Terman, L. M., & Merrill, M. A. (1960). *Stanford-Binet Intelligence Scale: Manual for the third revision. Form L.-M.* Boston: Houghton Mifflin.

Thorndike, R. M., Hagen, E. P., & Sattler, J. M. (1986). *Stanford-Binet Intelligence Scale* (4th ed.). Itasca, IL: Riverside.

Thurstone, L. L. (1938). Primary mental abilities. *Psychometric Monographs, 1.*

Walker, N. W., Boling, M. S., & Cobb, H. (1999). Training of school psychologists in neuropsychology and brain injury: Results of a national survey of training programs. *Child Neuropsychology, 5*(2), 137–142.

Wechsler, D. (1939). *The measurement of adult intelligence.* Baltimore: Williams & Wilkins.

Wechsler, D. (1949). *Wechsler Intelligence Scale for Children.* San Antonio, TX: Psychological Corporation.

Wechsler, D. (1955). *Wechsler Adult Intelligence Scale.* San Antonio, TX: Psychological Corporation.

Wechsler, D. (1958). *The measurement and appraisal of adult intelligence* (4th ed.). Baltimore: Williams & Wilkins.

Wechsler, D. (1974). *Wechsler Intelligence Scale for Children-Revised.* San Antonio, TX: Psychological Corporation.

Wechsler, D. (1981). *Wechsler Adult Intelligence Scale-Revised.* San Antonio, TX: Psychological Corporation.

Wechsler, D. (1991). *Wechsler Intelligence Scale for Children* (3rd ed.). San Antonio, TX: Psychological Corporation.

Wechsler, D. (1997). *Wechsler Adult Intelligence Scale* (3rd ed.). San Antonio, TX: Psychological Corporation.

Woodcock, R. W. (1993). An information processing view of *Gf-Gc* theory. *Journal of Psychoeducational Assessment* [Monograph Series: WJ-R Monograph], 80–102.

Woodcock, R. W. (1997). New looks in the assessment of cognitive ability. *Peabody Journal of Education, 77*(2), 6–22.

Woodcock, R. W. (1998). *The WJ-R and Bateria-R in neuropsychological assessment: Research report number 1.* Itasca, IL: Riverside.

Woodcock, R. W., & Johnson, M. B. (1977). *Woodcock-Johnson Psycho-Educational Battery.* Itasca, IL: Riverside.

Woodcock, R. W., & Johnson, M. B. (1989a). *Woodcock-Johnson Tests of Achievement-Revised.* Itasca, IL: Riverside.

Woodcock, R. W., & Johnson, M. B. (1989b). *Woodcock-Johnson Tests of Cognitive Ability-Revised.* Itasca, IL: Riverside.

Woodcock, R. W., McGrew, K. S., & Mather, N. (2001a). *Woodcock-Johnson III Tests of Achievement.* Itasca, IL: Riverside.

Woodcock, R. W., McGrew, K. S., & Mather, N. (2001b). *Woodcock-Johnson III Tests of Cognitive Abilities.* Itasca, IL: Riverside.

# CHAPTER 14

# Behavioral Neuroimaging: What Is It and What Does It Tell Us?

SHERRI L. PROVENCAL and ERIN D. BIGLER

C HILDREN ARE UNIQUE persons with different rates of learning and individual differences in their cognition and behavior. Many teachers and school psychologists undoubtedly have worked with children who are different— different in their thoughts, actions, personalities, and learning styles. Behavioral neuroimaging provides neuropsychologists insight into the minds of children. Hopes for the future are better understanding of brain mechanisms underlying deviant development and the implementation of interventions aimed at preventing and/or ameliorating symptoms related to disorders of childhood.

Behavioral neuroimaging refers to a group of radiological techniques used to study brain structure and function. Some techniques provide pictures of brain anatomy, or structure; others provide information related to how the brain works, or function. Of most interest to the neuropsychologist is the complex interaction between brain anatomy, cognition, and behavior. Radiologic advances over the past several decades have been most useful for the study of childhood disorders and conditions. These techniques, while sometimes possessing challenges for the study of the brain in younger children, provide researchers the exciting opportunity to explore developmental changes in the brain and how it adapts to increased environmental demands in the typically developing child, as well as in the child with developmental inconsistencies and difficulties. This chapter introduces different types of behavioral neuroimaging techniques, presents case studies demonstrating the clinical application of neuroimaging, and provides insight into the utilization of neuroimaging to research the dynamic properties of the young brain.

## NEUROANATOMICAL OR STRUCTURAL IMAGING TECHNIQUES

The introduction of neuroanatomical imaging techniques in the 1970s provided in vivo assessment of brain structure and resulted in dramatic improvements in the evaluation of neurological disorders and brain abnormalities. For the study of neuropsychiatric disorders, a shift in research occurred whereby biological underpinnings of mental illness were sought. The ability to view the human brain as development unfolds undoubtedly impacts the field of neuropsychology and how we conceptualize brain-behavior relationships in children.

## Computerized Axial Tomography

As the first neuroimaging technique to make its way into clinical diagnostics, computerized tomography (CT) remains widely used in medical settings. CT is a form of x-ray examination in which a planar volume or slice of the body is imaged and the projections are reconstructed to form a picture of the area of interest. Throughout the past 3 decades, CT technique has significantly advanced, with better resolution images of the brain, quicker scan times, and safer levels of radiation exposure (Orrison & Sanders, 1995).

Modern-day CT scanners require the patient to lie still in a "gantry" or tube while an x-ray source and detection system assesses tissue density as the x-ray beam passes through the tissue. A mathematical algorithm is applied that allows the generation of a reconstructed computer image. In clinical settings in the past, the computer images were mostly transferred to traditional x-ray films for viewing, but now most imaging is reviewed in some digital format on an LCD or similar screen. Because CT images can be obtained quickly and can be done on patients requiring life support or other medical equipment, CT is the method of choice for the acute assessment of the head when intracranial abnormality is expected (Gean, 1994; Haydel et al., 2000). CT is an excellent tool for determining the presence of treatable brain lesions and providing baseline information concerning the location and nature of pathological conditions such as cortical contusion, intraparenchymal hemorrhage, petichial hemorrhage, and localized or generalized edema (Bigler, in press). CT is also excellent in detecting skull fracture and associated pneumocephalus, which may require surgical intervention. In children, CT imaging is used to diagnose suspected insult to the brain during the birth and delivery process, acquired injury to the head due to an accident, and other acquired benign insults such as tumors, brain infarction, and seizures. In traumatic brain injury (TBI), the most clinically important use of CT imaging is acute assessment of gross structural pathology of the brain for subsequent monitoring and surgical intervention for any treatable lesion (Bigler, in press). Often, however, morphological consequences from trauma take time to evolve; thus, multiple CT images are frequently obtained to monitor the extent of the injury. Figure 14.1 depicts CT scans of a 3-year-old restrained passenger involved in a high-speed motor vehicle accident and demonstrates the benefits of CT in the assessment and monitoring of pediatric head injury and the changes that occur over time.

In this child who sustained a severe TBI, the day of injury scan demonstrates a right intraparenchymal hemorrhage in the right internal capsule and putamen (see Figure 14.1). While the anterior horn is visible, the cortical sulci are less so, a sign of potential generalized edema. Two days postinjury, there is definite generalized edema, with the ventricular system barely noticeable—a clear sign of generalized edema. A scan obtained 1 year postinjury reveals a large cavitation in the right basal ganglia, which is a result of the focal hemorrhage in this region. Also note the enlarged ventricles, common sequelae of acquired head injury caused by the cell death and cerebral atrophy (Bigler, 1997). From a school psychology perspective, this type of imaging demonstrates extensive cerebral damage that

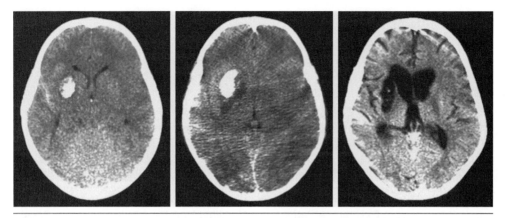

**Figure 14.1** Sequential CT Scans of a 3-Year-Old Closed Head Injury Patient. On the day of injury, an intraparenchymal hemorrhage is visible in the right internal capsule and putamen. There are also some early signs of generalized edema or swelling. Two days post-injury, the ventricular system is significantly reduced as a result of the generalized brain edema. At one-year post injury, lasting effects of the hemorrhage in the right basal ganglia are visible. Trauma-related global atrophy due to cell death is manifest by generalized ventricular dilation and prominent cortical sulci.

would be expected to markedly alter this child's cognitive and academic skills. Deficits were documented with neuropsychological assessment, and this child required a comprehensive special education program.

### MAGNETIC RESONANCE IMAGING

Despite the usefulness of CT as a clinical diagnostic tool, especially in acute trauma, magnetic resonance imaging (MRI) is preferred when a more detailed anatomical investigation is sought. MRI is similar to CT in that it provides a gross inspection of the macroscopically visible brain, although the acquisition of data is quite dissimilar (Orrison & Sanders, 1995). CT is a type of x-ray, whereas MRI is not. Instead, MRI is a noninvasive technique that takes advantage of anatomic properties of the human body and how anatomic nuclei (mostly hydrogen) react in the presence of an applied magnetic field generated briefly as presented in pulse sequences from a magnet inside the MRI scanner.

During MRI scans, patients lie still in a tube-like scanner while a magnetic field is applied. Because of the strong magnetic field used during MRI acquisition, there are safety concerns to consider. It is important, for example, for technicians to remove all free metal objects before entering the room and for patients to be free of metal. Usually this is not a problem with children, but in older patients, persons with pacemakers and other inserted metal material (e.g., aneurism clips) are usually restricted from undergoing MRI procedures. Metallic objects such as permanent or temporary dental fixtures, though not requiring exclusion from an MRI examination, cause signal artifact that distorts the image. Other artifacts also exist, most notably motion artifact that occurs when the patient moves during the scan acquisition. Movement artifact poses a particular challenge when scanning pediatric populations, who may require sedation to lie still for the 20- to 60-minute procedure (depending on the type and number of different pulse sequences used).

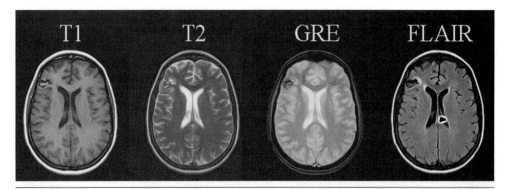

**Figure 14.2** This Illustration Demonstrates in the Same Patient How Four Different Image Sequences at Exactly the Same Level Highlight How Each Has a Different Sensitivity in Detecting Pathology. The patient sustained a severe traumatic brain injury three months prior to the imaging. Acutely, a right frontal contusion is clearly visible in each scan. Note the sensitivity of the GRE sequence in detecting blood byproducts that are not shown on the other sequences. The FLAIR sequence demonstrates not only the lesion but also white matter changes in areas adjacent to the lesion.

During the scan, different combinations of radiofrequency transmission, signal reception, pulse timing, and signal delay time are programmed through computer software programs called pulse sequences and applied during the scan to detect various types of tissue in the brain (Figure 14.2). Image slices are reconstructed off-line to form views of the brain in three planes or perspectives. T1- and T2-weighted sequences are most popularly used in clinical studies in which radiologic data are visually inspected and reviewed by a trained neuroradiologist for gross structural changes or abnormalities.

Because of the high spatial resolution and the ability to view slices of the brain from three perspectives, MRI is the preferred clinical tool for anatomic studies of the brain in which central diseases or injuries are suspected, including epilepsy, cerebrovascular insults, neoplasms, infections, and CNS degenerations (Symms, Jager, Schmierer, & Yousry, 2004). When a lesion or abnormality is seen on MRI, there are likely some behavioral deficits associated with the brain abnormality. Radiologic data, therefore, are an important part of a patient's medical history and add to the neuropsychologist's evaluation of current neurocognitive functioning of the patient.

### QUANTITATIVE MAGNETIC RESONANCE IMAGING

When clinicians or researchers are interested in a more refined analysis of the brain beyond visual inspection, a technique called quantitative magnetic resonance imaging (qMRI) may be applied. The brain is composed of two tissue types, gray matter (mostly cell bodies and dendritic trees) and white matter (mainly myelinated axons). These tissue types yield different signal characteristics on MRI. These dissimilar signal intensities permit their isolation, and therefore gray and white matter can be "segmented" from one another (Laidlaw, Fleischer, & Barr, 1998). Similarly, cerebral spinal fluid (CSF) spaces (i.e., ventricles) and bone also have different signal characteristics from the brain parenchyma. Once these different tissue-CSF compartments are segmented, accurate estimates of the volume of any region of interest can be made (Bigler & Tate, 2001). Because contemporary MRI has resolution of approximately 1 mm, fine structural analysis can be achieved of any region that can be visualized with gross inspection. Researchers may, for example, obtain MR images from a clinical population (e.g., children with Attention-Deficit/Hyperactivity Disorder) and compare variables of interest to those from a nonclinical population (e.g., typically developing children). Off-line quantitative analyses of the brain are performed to compare variables such as overall size of the brain, the amount of gray and white matter, and the size of certain brain regions/structures. This type of neuroimaging analysis is popular for investigating the etiology of pediatric disorders, and the number of published studies in this area is continually growing.

Conducting and interpreting qMRI research poses many challenges that frequently result in inconsistent findings across studies. When conducting volumetric analyses in pediatric clinical populations, particular attention must be paid to the sample size, patient and control group characteristics, scan acquisition methods, image analysis methods, and statistical control of variables potentially affecting results (i.e., age, gender, and intellectual ability; Giedd, 2001; Palmen & van Engeland, 2004). Nevertheless, image acquisition of every major brain structure is routinely achieved as part of the standard imaging when scans are performed.

## Diffusion Tensor Magnetic Resonance Imaging

A fairly recent advance in structural neuroimaging called diffusion tensor MRI (DT-MRI) allows for the visualization of brain fiber tracts and provides quantitative information on the connectivity of the brain. This noninvasive approach measures the random movement of hydrogen atoms in water of the brain. In white matter, the measured diffusion of water appears to be greatest along the fiber direction and more restricted in the perpendicular direction. White matter connectivity between different brain regions may be estimated from the long-range continuity in the diffusion tensor field, and it is believed to be correlated to the underlying white matter fiber system (Basser, Pajevic, Pierpaoli, Duda, & Aldroubi, 2000; Conturo et al., 1999; Poupon et al., 2000). Most MRI manufacturers now offer pulse sequences and semiautomated analysis software for DT-MRI. Several types of DT-MRI measurements, including the trace of the tensor, anisotropy, and tensor orientation, provide quantitative information regarding white matter structure in the brain. Advanced analysis methods like white matter tractography allow segmentation of white matter pathways in the brain as well as in certain white matter structures, such as the corpus callosum (Figure 14.3 on p. 332).

The application of DT-MRI to the investigation of pediatric disorders is promising, especially for neurological and neurodevelopmental disorders in which white matter disorganization or insult is suspected.

## Case Studies Demonstrating Structural Neuroimaging Techniques

Developing, implementing, and monitoring treatment plans for children in the school setting is challenging. Each child comes into the classroom with his or her own personal history, neurobehavioral strengths and weaknesses, and social context. Appropriate diagnostic, neuropsychological, and, in some cases, behavioral neuroimaging evaluation can greatly improve the efficacy of the individual's treatment and education plan.

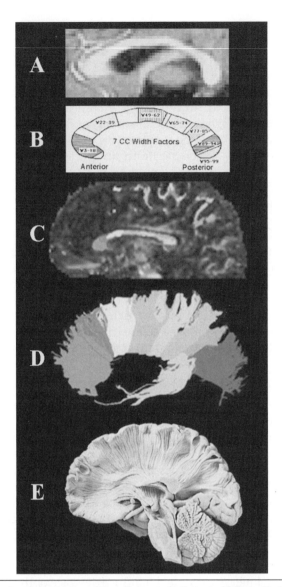

**Figure 14.3** Structural Analyses of the Corpus Callosum (CC) in Patients with Autism Using MRI and DT-MRI Methodologies. Clear boundaries between white and gray matter of the corpus callosum (CC) are clearly seen in this standard T1 weighted midsagittal view (A). The surface area of the CC can be obtained using a factor analytic approach outlined by Denenberg, Kertesz, and Cowell (1991) to section the CC into distinct regions for quantitative analysis (B). In the midsagittal diffusion tensor MRI (DT-MRI) scan, this post-processing image shows a color coded sectioning of the CC which is a reference where pixels were seeded to identify the inter-hemispheric tracts (C). Projections from the CC to different regions of the cortex are then identified to investigate the organization of white matter connectivity in the autistic brain. For example, all the red within the genu/rostrum of the CC projects to frontal areas (D). DT-MRI provides in vivo visualization and measurement of white matter tracts that closely resemble the white matter connections visible in a normal post-mortem brain and is useful in the investigation of brain organization in developmental disorders (E). Reproduced with permission from Andrew Alexander and Mariana Lazar from the University of Wisconsin, Madison.

**Case 1: Child with Hydrocephalus and Behavioral Problems**

This male was 13 years old when evaluated due to persisting emotional and behavioral problems. At 5 weeks of age, he underwent surgical intervention for removal of a right hemisphere cyst and received a shunt placement to reduce intracranial fluid. Routine follow-up neurologic and radiologic evaluations reported no difficulties with increased intracranial fluid, suggesting his shunt operated appropriately and his medical condition remained stable.

Several psychological evaluations were conducted throughout the years to address emotional and behavioral difficulties. As a young child, he was diagnosed with Oppositional Defiant Disorder. Intellectual functioning was estimated to be in the borderline to low average range. He was later hospitalized in a psychiatric institution and diagnosed with Depressive Disorder with Psychotic Features. More recently, behavioral problems, emotional lability, and poor social skills escalated and required placement in a residential facility for intensive treatment and educational intervention. He was diagnosed with Attention-Deficit/Hyperactivity Disorder (ADHD) and Bipolar Disorder. Medications at the time of evaluation included Adderall, Tegretol, and Seroquel.

A review of neuroimaging findings at age 13 years reflected significant enlargement of the lateral ventricles, probable congenital agenesis of the corpus callosum (i.e., callosal agenesis), and a right frontal shunt (Figure 14.4). No significant changes on ventricular size were noted on repeat exams and parents were informed that his shunt was operating properly and not contributing to his current behavioral and emotional functioning.

Table 14.1 displays neuropsychological findings for this teenager. Consistent with previous evaluations, intellectual abilities were in the low average range. Brief academic testing was average for his age and grade level. Performance on

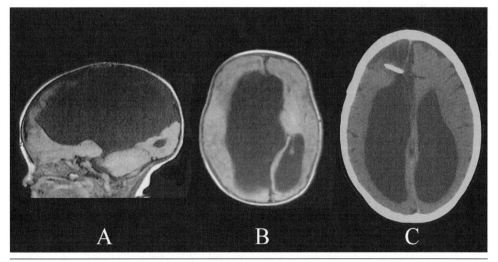

**Figure 14.4** Sagittal (A) and Axial (B) Views of CT Images from a 2-Month-Old with an Arachnoid Cyst in the Right Frontal Region and Shunted Hydrocephalus. At age 13 years, repeat CT imaging reveals no difficulties with increased intracranial fluid, suggesting proper functioning of the shunt. Because his medical condition was stable, poor behavioral and academic functioning were attributed to non-neurologic causes.

**Table 14.1**
Case Study 1: 13-Year-Old Male with Hydrocephalus

### Intellectual (WASI)

| | |
|---|---|
| FSIQ = 88 | |
| Vocabulary | 40 |
| Matrix Reasoning | 46 |

### Motor Examination

*Dominant Hand (right)*

| | |
|---|---|
| Finger Tap | z-score = −0.4 |
| Grip Strength | z-score = −1.8 |

*Nondominant Hand (left)*

| | |
|---|---|
| Finger Tap | z-score = −0.7 |
| Grip Strength | z-score = −1.5 |

### Language

| | |
|---|---|
| Verbal Fluency | z-score = −1.4 |

### Attention (TOMAL)

| | |
|---|---|
| Digits Forward | 8 |
| Digits Backward | 8 |
| Letters Forward | 10 |
| Letters Backward | 5 |

### Memory

| | |
|---|---|
| TOMAL Verbal Index = 83 | |
| Memory for Stories | 6 |
| Word Selective Remind | 7 |
| Object Recall | 7 |
| Paired Recall | 10 |
| RCFT Recall | z-score = −3.3 |

| | |
|---|---|
| TOMAL Nonverbal Index = 73 | |
| Facial Memory | 5 |
| Visual Selective Remind | 9 |
| Abstract Visual Memory | 5 |
| Memory for Location | 4 |
| Manual Imitation | 10 |

### Academic Achievement (WRAT-III)

| | |
|---|---|
| Read | 89 |
| Spell | 107 |
| Arithmetic | 94 |

### Visual Spatial/Motor

| | |
|---|---|
| TMT (Part A) | z-score = −2.3 |
| VMI, fourth edition | 91 |
| Hooper | T-score = 46 |
| RCFT Copy | z-score = 1.7 |

### Executive Functions

| | |
|---|---|
| TMT (Part B) | z-score = −0.7 |
| CCT Level 2 | T-score = 48 |

*Notes:* CCT = Children's Category Test; RCFT = Rey Complex Figure Test; TOMAL = Test of Memory and Learning; TMT = Trail Making Test; VMI = Beery Developmental Test of Visual-Motor Integration; WASI = Wechsler Abbreviated Scale of Intelligence; WRAT-III = Wide Range Achievement Test, third edition.

memory tests ranged from the borderline to low average range. Graphomotor and visual perception skills were slightly impaired. His approach to copying the Rey Complex Figure Test (RCFT) involved a piecemeal approach that focused on details of the design and failed to appreciate the overall gestalt of the design (see Figure 14.5 on p. 336). Verbal memory skills were better developed than nonverbal memory skills. On the RCFT, for example, he recalled only several details of the figure following a 15-minute delay (see Figure 14.5).

Although he endorsed few difficulties on self-report measures, his counselor and teacher reported symptoms of withdrawal, anxiety/depression, poor socialization, inattention, and aggression. Parental comments and ratings on the Neurobehavioral Signs and Symptoms Checklist were consistent with comments and ratings from personnel from the treatment facility. Given the medical history, imaging findings, and neuropsychological data, this child has made tremendous gains with regard to cognitive ability in spite of his significant neurological insult. Neurobehavioral weaknesses in the areas of visual-spatial abilities, motor coordination, attention/concentration, and socialization are typical of children with a history of hydrocephalus and are often conceptualized as a nonverbal learning disability type of syndrome.

What is most interesting about this case is how the neuroimaging findings were never appreciated by mental health clinicians and school personnel. Because the child, from the neurosurgical perspective, had been successfully treated with the shunting procedure, they assumed that the behavioral and learning deficits did not have a neurological basis and were merely related to "behavioral problems." Clearly, having the neuroimaging shows the extensive structural damage and the likelihood that the deficits in academic and behavioral performance are neurologically based. This is an excellent case illustrating the interface of neuropsychological test results and imaging to fully understand the sequelae of certain brain abnormalities.

### Case Study 2: Child with a Cerebral Artery Infarct Secondary to Traumatic Birth

At the time of assessment, this patient was a 7-year-old male with a history of a birth-related injury following persistence in an attempted pitocin-stimulated vaginal delivery. At 1 day of life, he had four tonic clonic seizures with oxygen desaturation below 80%. A CAT scan revealed the presence of a left middle cerebral artery (MCA) distribution stroke, resulting in a large left-posterior frontal-parietal porencephalic cyst. A follow-up MRI scan completed near the time of assessment is depicted in Figure 14.6 on page 337.

Despite the significance of the stroke and the presence of right-sided hemiparesis, the child met all developmental milestones in the broad context of average. Several neuropsychological evaluations were conducted when the child was school age to evaluate and monitor his developmental progress. Parental concerns included the presence of a lisp that has not developmentally corrected itself, residual right-side motor deficit, and the potential for learning and behavior problems. Table 14.2 on page 338 summarizes tests and standardized scores from his evaluation.

On the Edinburgh Handedness Inventory, he demonstrated a left hand dominance on tasks presented over three trials. Writing tasks were completed with his

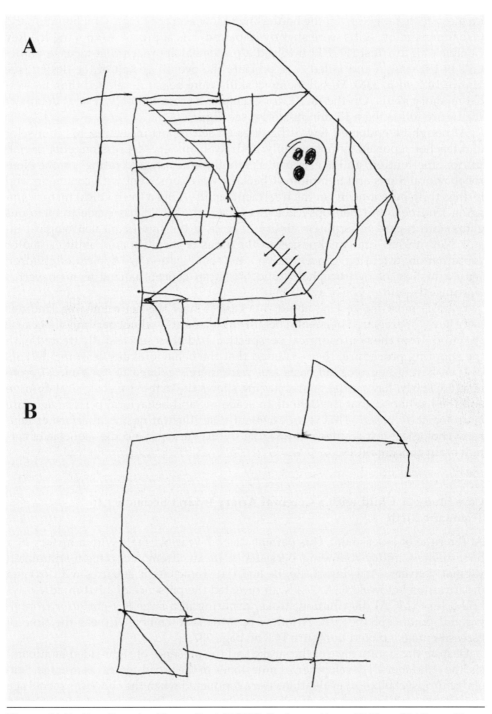

**Figure 14.5** Rey Complex Figure Test (RCFT) Performed by a 13-Year-Old Boy with Shunted Hydrocephalus. The patient's approach to copying the figure was poorly organized and involved a piece-meal approach commonly used by patients with right hemisphere dysfunction or damage (A). Recall of the figure following a 15-minute delay was below average for his age (B).

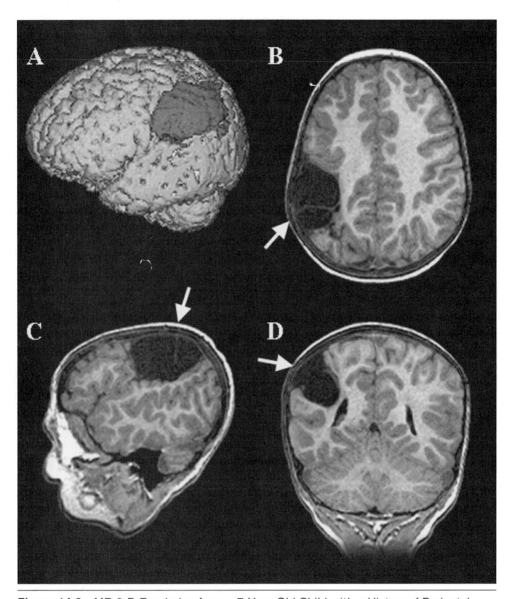

**Figure 14.6** MR 3-D Rendering from a 7-Year-Old Child with a History of Perinatal Stroke Demonstrating the Severity of the Damage (A). The axial (B), left hemisphere sagittal (C), and coronal (D) views show the large cavity containing cerebral spinal fluid in the left parietal and posterior frontal lobes consistent with a porencephalic cyst. Also note the loss of cortex and underlying white matter.

left hand. He preferred his left foot for kicking a ball and his right eye for visually focusing on objects. Motor skills were within normal limits for his left side, but mildly deficient for his right side. Performance on visuomotor integration tests were within normal limits for his age.

Based on performance on the Kaufman Assessment Battery for Children, general cognitive abilities were in the above-average range, with sequential processing

**Table 14.2**

Case Study 2: 7-Year-Old Male with Left Middle
Cerebral Artery Infarct at Birth

Neuropsychological findings are consistent with recovery of left hemisphere functions at the expense of:

### Intellectual (K-ABC)

| | |
|---|---|
| Sequential Processing =122 | |
| Hand Movements | 11 |
| Number Recall | 17 |
| Word Order | 12 |
| Simultaneous Processing = 111 | |
| Gestalt Closure | 14 |
| Triangles | 13 |
| Spatial Memory | 12 |
| Matrix Analogies | 10 |
| Photo Series | 9 |

### Academic Achievement (WRAT-III)

| | |
|---|---|
| Read | 105 |
| Spell | 117 |
| Arithmetic | 103 |

### Motor Examination

| | |
|---|---|
| *Dominant Hand (left)* | |
| Finger Tap | z-score = −1.0 |
| Grip Strength | z-score = −0.2 |
| *Nondominant Hand (right)* | |
| Finger Tap | z-score = −2.1 |
| Grip Strength | z-score = 1.0 |

### Language

| | |
|---|---|
| BNT | z-score = 0.2 |
| PPVT-III | 124 |

### Attention (TOMAL)

| | |
|---|---|
| Digits Forward | 15 |
| Digits Backward | 11 |
| Letters Forward | 14 |
| Letters Backward | 9 |

### Memory (TOMAL)

| | |
|---|---|
| Verbal Index = 103 | |
| Memory for Stories | 13 |
| Word Selective Remind | 8 |
| Object Recall | 8 |
| Paired Recall | 10 |
| Nonverbal Index = 112 | |
| Facial Memory | 11 |
| Visual Selective Remind | 10 |
| Abstract Visual Memory | 13 |
| Memory for Location | 13 |
| Manual Imitation | 7 |

**Table 14.2** *Continued*

**Visual Motor**

| | |
|---|---|
| TMT (Part A) | z-score = 0.7 |
| VMI, 4th edition | 109 |

**Executive Functions**

| | |
|---|---|
| TMT (Part B) | z-score = −1.1 |
| CCT Level 1 | T-score = 54 |

*Notes:* BNT = Boston Naming Test; CCT = Children's Category Test; K-ABC = Kaufman Assessment Battery for Children; PPVT-III = Peabody Picture Vocabulary Test, third edition; TMT = Trail Making Test; TOMAL = Test of Memory and Learning; VMI = Beery Developmental Test of Visual-Motor Integration; WRAT-III = Wide Range Achievement Test, third edition

skills better developed than simultaneous skills. Academic achievement scores were in the average range for his age and consistent with estimated cognitive abilities. Verbal and nonverbal memory abilities ranged from average to high-average. Executive functioning was in the average range. Parent report suggested symptoms of poor socialization, withdrawn behavior, anxiety/depression, inattention, and hyperactivity/impulsivity. His teacher reported no concerns regarding academic, social, or behavioral functioning.

Despite the size of his brain lesion, his neuropsychological findings were generally within the normal range. This case demonstrates the potential the brain has to reroute and develop around even a large lesion, a principle in neuropsychology known as the Kennard Principle (Finger & Wolf, 1988). Because the brain is in a very plastic and modifiable state early in its development, current theory proposes that the brain injury and tissue loss result in new neural connections that the brain was not predetermined to establish. Damage in infancy can show more rapid and more complete recovery of a particular function (e.g., language) compared to damage later in life. This forced reorganization and sparing of function, however, is not without its cost. In fact, more recent evidence suggests that injury in the first year of life results in more severe deficits than once thought (Duval, Dumont, Braun, & Montour-Proulx, 2002; Webb, Rose, Johnson, & Attree, 1996). Although good recovery of language and academics may occur, neuropsychological findings often reveal inconsistent performance across cognitive domains and deficits in higher-level functions, including reasoning, conceptualization, mental flexibility, and processing speed. Depending on the cognitive reserve or capacity that was given up or allocated during the adaptation, other cognitive deficits may also be noted as the child develops. In this case, early injury to the left hemisphere in a child likely to be right-hand dominant (and hence left-hemisphere dominant for language functions) likely resulted in recovery of language functions to the average range and deficits in speech production (i.e., articulation) and motor skills. The problem with brain injuries occurring in infants and children is that each brain is somewhat unique and later cognitive and behavioral functioning is difficult to predict. Children with early insults, as in this case, may later "grow into" their disabilities so that residual effects are not

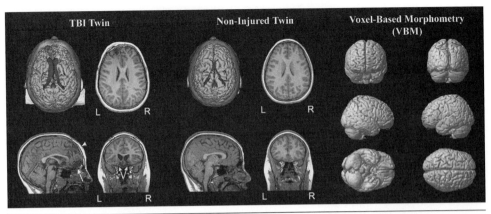

**Figure 14.7** MR Imaging and 3-D Rendering of the Brain of a 10-Year-Old Male Injured in a Motor Vehicle Accident. Note the residual bifrontal abnormalities and increased ventricular size for his age compared to MR imaging of his uninjured twin sister. Voxel-based morphometry (VBM), an advanced technique for comparing white and gray matter densities between two individuals or groups, highlights the region of the brain with the most significant tissue damage when compared to his twin sister.

apparent until adolescence, when environmental demands require efficient processing of higher-order cognitive functions.

### Case Study 3: Child with an Acquired Traumatic Brain Injury

This 10-year-old boy was referred for a neuropsychological evaluation following an automobile accident that occurred 3 years prior. At the accident scene and en route to the hospital, he exhibited a decreased level of consciousness, with a Glasgow Coma Scale of 8 to 9. He suffered multiple facial fractures, including a compound, comminuted fracture of the frontal bone, cerebral edema, and bifrontal intracerebral hemorrhages, left greater than right. He was unconscious for nearly 2 days following the accident. Figure 14.7 depicts three-dimensional MRI images of this patient compared to his twin sister 3 years postinjury. Although the frontal lobe hemorrhages and right frontal lobe hematoma resolved, follow-up scans demonstrate residual bifrontal encephalomalacia ("soft brain") and increased ventricular size for his age.

Preinjury, this child was described as an advanced reader who received straight As in school and participated in a program for the intellectually gifted. Postinjury, his mother reported significant cognitive and emotional changes in the patient, most notably difficulties with mathematics, problem solving, concentration, motivation, short-term memory, and judgment. The greatest reported change, however, was in his personality. Once calm and confident, he now required significant assistance and attention in performing everyday functions. Emotionally, his mother reported that the injury "set him back a couple of years." He also became more impulsive, easily frustrated, and emotional labile.

Table 14.3 displays neuropsychological tests administered and obtained standard scores. On the neuropsychological tests, this patient exhibited several areas of strength. For the most part, language, visual perceptual, verbal and nonverbal memory, simple attention, and reading skills were within normal limits. Areas of

**Table 14.3**
Case Study 3: 10-Year-Old Boy with Traumatic
Brain Injury

| Intellectual (WISC-III) | |
|---|---|
| VIQ = 106 | |
| Vocabulary | 12 |
| Information | 12 |
| Comprehension | 9 |
| Arithmetic | 8 |
| Digit Span | 9 |
| | |
| PIQ = 102 | |
| Picture Completion | 11 |
| Picture Arrangement | 11 |
| Block Design | 12 |
| Object Assembly | 11 |
| Symbol Search | 9 |
| Coding | 6 |
| Mazes | 17 |

| Academic Achievement (WRAT-III) | |
|---|---|
| Read | 124 |
| Spell | 103 |
| Arithmetic | 87 |

**Language Examination**

BNT 98th percentile
PPVT-III standard score = 124
DKEFS C-WIT Naming Speed scaled score = 8

**Memory (CVLT-C, CMS)**

*Verbal*

| | |
|---|---|
| List Trials 1–5 | T-score = 58 |
| List Delayed Recall | z = −0.5 to +1.0 |

List Recognition = 100%
Story Memory Immediate Recall = 14
Story Memory Delayed Recall = 17
Story Memory Delayed Recognition = 14

*Nonverbal*

Dot Location Immediate Recall = 12
Dot Location Delayed Recall = 13
RCFT Delay = 50th percentile

**Motor Examination**

| | | | |
|---|---|---|---|
| FOD | z-score = −1.4 | FOND | z-score = −0.4 |
| GPD | z-score = −0.9 | GPDND | z-score = −0.3 |

DKEFS TMT Motor Speed = 11

**Executive Function (D-KEFS)**

*Verbal Modality*

Word Context Test = 12
Color-Word Interference Test = 8
Letter Fluency = 9
Category Fluency = 6

*(continued)*

**Table 14.3** *Continued*

**Executive Function (D-KEFS)** *continued*

*Spatial Modality*
Tower Test = 10
Design Fluency = 13

*Concept Formation/Problem Solving*
Sorting Correct Sorts = 10
Sorting Spontaneous Description = 10
Sorting Structured Rule Description = 8
Twenty Questions Initial Abstraction = 19
Twenty Questions Total Questions = 12
Twenty Questions Achievement = 12

*Cognitive Shift*
TMT (Part 4) = 13
TMT Set Losses (4) 16th percentile
Verbal Fluency Shift = 13
Design Fluency Shift = 12
C-WIT Shift = 10

WCST Categorized Sorts 11th to 16th percentile
   (completed 2 out of 6 categorized sorts)
WCST Perseverative Responses 10th percentile
   (T-score = 37)
WCST Total Errors 5th percentile (T-score = 33)

**Attention**

| | |
|---|---:|
| CMS Picture Location | 6 |
| DKEFS TMT Visual Scan | 15 |
| DKEFS TMT Scan Omits | 7 errors |

**Spatial Cognition**
BVMIT standard score = 106
RCFT Copy 58th percentile

**Visual Motor Sequencing**
DKEFS TMT Number Sequence =13
DKEFS TMT Letter Sequence =14

*Note:* WICMS = Children's Memory Scale; CVLT-C = California Verbal Learning Test-Children's Version; C-WIT = Color-Word Interference Test; D-KEFS = Delis-Kaplan Executive Function System; FOD = Finger Oscillation Dominant; FOND = Finger Oscillation Non-Dominant; GPD = Grooved Pegboard Dominant; GPND = Grooved Pegboard Non-Dominant; RCFT = Rey Complex Figure Test; TMT = Trail Making Test; WCST = Wisconsin Card Sorting Test; WISC-III = Wechsler Intelligence Scale for Children, third edition; WRAT-III = Wide Range Achievement Test, third edition.

weakness, however, included mild deficits in complex auditory processing (i.e., digit span backward, spatial attention span, and generating words from semantic categories). He demonstrated omission errors due to impulsivity on a visual scanning task, set-loss errors on switching tasks, fluency, and a tendency to make perseverative errors on novel problem-solving tasks (i.e., Wisconsin Card Sorting Test and Delis-Kaplan Executive Function System). He exhibited a moderate deficit in his reading speed. In addition, his motor speed and fine-motor dexterity were significantly impaired in his right hand. Finally, he performed in the low end of the average range in terms of math skills, which represented an acquired impairment for him. Emotionally, behavioral concerns were noted, including impatience, some aggressiveness, and increased child-like behavior.

Overall conceptualization of this patient's reported history, medical records, and neuropsychological findings is consistent with a classic profile of frontal-lobe syndrome. That is, he tends to perform well on tasks requiring fundamental cognitive skills, but less well on tasks requiring higher-level cognitive skills. His personality and behavior changes are also typical of frontal-lobe damage (e.g., child-like behavior). He has a tendency to perform worse on verbal compared to spatial executive function tasks, and his motor dexterity is impaired in his right hand but not his left hand. This asymmetric pattern of scores is consistent with neuroimaging findings of bifrontal brain damage, with greater pathology in the left frontal regions relative to the right.

From an outsider's point of view, this young child may appear to be developing normally. He could easily be viewed as an average child with some very mild symptoms of inattention, impulsivity, and math difficulties compared to others his age. Yet, this child clearly suffered a significant brain injury resulting in lowered cognitive, emotional, and behavioral skills compared to preinjury functioning. As a result, he and his family require ongoing educational, psychological, and medical intervention and support to maximize his recovery and chances for a successful, independent life. The combination of behavioral and anatomical data can greatly assist in treatment planning for children with a history of traumatic brain injury.

## NEUROPHYSIOLOGICAL OR FUNCTIONAL IMAGINING TECHNIQUES

Because behavior and cognition are not necessarily localized to any one particular region of the brain, deficits can be the result of either focal or diffuse abnormalities that interrupt neural networks and information processing. Unlike CT and MRI, which depict the structure of the brain, several imaging techniques in use today directly measure brain activity or function. When combined with CT or MRI, neurophysiological or functional imaging techniques provide a valuable picture of what is happening in the brain and where it is happening. Neuroimaging tools, including positron emission tomography (PET), single photon emission computed tomography (SPECT), functional magnetic resonance imaging (fMRI), quantitative electroencephalography (qEEG), and magnetoencephalography (MEG), contribute to recent advances in the cognitive neurosciences (Orrison, Lewine, Sanders, & Hartshorne, 1995). Some play a role in clinical diagnosis of various neurological and medical disorders of childhood, although most are considered experimental by clinical standards and health insurance companies. Nonetheless, these behavioral neuroimaging techniques guide our understanding of how the brain works in both normally developing children and in those with neurodevelopmental disorders or neurological insults.

### Positron Emission Tomography

PET is a nuclear medicine neuroimaging approach sensitive to hemodynamic/metabolic changes in the brain. PET was one of the earliest techniques used to study localization of brain functions and paved the way for later behavioral neuroimaging techniques, including MEG, fMRI, and SPECT (Hartshorne, 1995a). During a PET scan, gamma-ray detectors placed around the head detect the radioactivity emitted from a radionucleotide that is intravenously injected during the scanning process. Computer reconstruction procedures are applied to produce tomographic images of the brain. The output images obtained from a PET study demonstrate the biochemical or physiologic processes involved in cerebral glucose metabolism and regional cerebral blood flow. The underlying assumption is that increased blood flow to a region indicates increased neuronal activity in that region. The spatial resolution of PET is approximately 4 to 6 mm and its temporal resolution is between 90 and 120 s (Calvert & Thesen, 2004).

Because PET detects metabolic changes in the body, disease processes may be diagnosed earlier than by neuroanatomical methods (CT and MRI), which require a substantial anatomical change (i.e., lesion or mass) noticeable on visual inspection of the scan. Clinically, a PET scan allows physicians to detect and monitor cancer, brain disorders (e.g., Alzheimer's, epilepsy), and heart disease. Figure 14.8 shows neuroimaging data obtained from a 17-year-old female with a history of anoxic brain injury secondary to complications following the delivery of her baby. Postinjury, patient complaints included migraine headaches, short-term memory problems, diminished mental acuity, anxiety, and depression. MR images were superimposed and compared with PET findings, which revealed decreased blood flow in the left temporal region (left right reversed) extending medially into the area of the left hippocampus and associated neocortex consistent with MRI findings of marked atrophy in this region. There was also evidence of decreased metabolic activity in focal regions throughout the brain, which correlated with abnormal signal intensity in the white matter noted on MR images.

PET studies investigating brain activation patterns associated with higher-order mental processes are also conducted, mostly for research purposes. For these investigations, a radionucleotide is injected while the participant performs

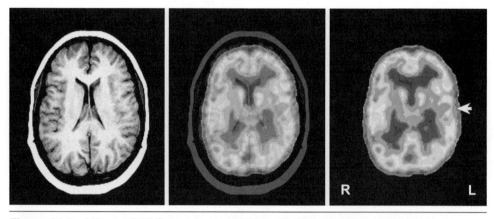

**Figure 14.8** MR and PET Scans from a 17-Year-Old Female with a Hypoxic Brain Injury. MR imaging (A) were superimposed onto PET data (B) for comparison of clinical findings regarding brain structure and function. Her PET scan (C) revealed decreased metabolic activity in the left temporal regions consistent with MR findings of atrophy in this region.

a series of cognitive tasks during a 45-minute examination. A common method for studying complex information-processing skills with PET is the subtraction method, which requires the researcher to break down the task into hierarchical components in order to eventually isolate the more advanced cognitive skill of interest (Bookheimer, 1996). Images of blood flow from the different conditions are compared to isolate cognitive components of the task. When the subtraction method is applied with proper experimental control, PET studies generate maps of brain regions activated during even complex cognitive functions.

### SINGLE PHOTON EMISSION COMPUTED TOMOGRAPHY

SPECT is another radioisotope nuclear medicine neuroimaging procedure that measures cerebral blood flow and metabolic activity patterns of the brain. SPECT is used for many of the same purposes as PET, although SPECT is less complex, less expensive, and more available compared to PET (Hartshorne, 1995b; Innis, 1992). Whereas PET requires precise timing of intravenous injection and scanning, SPECT radioisotopes are distributed in the brain within minutes and remain for up to 6 hours. For children who may have a difficult time remaining still during a functional brain scan, sedation may be used shortly after the injection of the radioisotope to minimize artifact from movement during the scan. SPECT output images depict underlying blood flow and brain activation that can be coregistered with anatomic data from CT or MRI to demonstrate brain function and structure. Clinical applications of SPECT include detection of abnormal physiology and monitoring of brain physiology following treatments for brain tumors (Kirton, Kloiber, Rigel, & Wolff, 2002; Paakko et al., 2003), epileptiform disorders (Buchhalter & So, 2004; Gupta et al., 2004; Kaminska et al., 2003; O'Brien et al., 2004), and traumatic brain injury (Bigler, 1999; Poussaint & Moeller, 2002).

Technological details regarding PET and SPECT instrumentation and data acquisition/analyses are complex. Initial installation and day-to-day operations of the systems are costly. From a research perspective, in vivo regional measurements of cerebral blood flow and metabolic rates of the developing brain contribute to our understanding of functional neuroanatomy. However, the injection of radiopharmaceuticals is considered invasive and the risk of radiation too high for typically developing children for whom there is no clinical benefit. Studies of abnormal brain development identified by PET/SPECT in pediatric populations, therefore, often lack experimental rigor due to the absence of a typically developing comparison group. Despite research design challenges, brain metabolism and activation patterns at rest and during cognitive tasks are ongoing research interests in studies investigating neurobiological correlates of developmental disorders such as Autism, dyslexia, and ADHD.

### FUNCTIONAL MAGNETIC RESONANCE IMAGING

The noninvasive imaging technique fMRI combines brain activation patterns with anatomical data from MRI. The technique does not require the injection of radionucleotides. Instead, fMRI uses high-speed imaging techniques to detect local blood volume, flow, and saturation associated with underlying changes in neuronal activity in response to a cognitive task (Sanders & Orrison, 1995). The fundamentals of fMRI methodology overlap with SPECT and PET in that neuronal activity is implied from hemodynamic changes in the brain. Functional MRI, however, offers better spatial and temporal resolution, does not require ionizing radiation, and costs less to operate (Sanders & Orrison, 1995). When combined with structural MR images, the spatial resolution of the computer-generated images localizes the neuronal activity within a few millimeters. The temporal resolution is more difficult to obtain due to the 6 to 8 s need for the ho-modynamic changes to happen poststimulus (Calvert & Thesen, 2004). As a re-sult, cognitive tasks are repeated a number of times during the recording session. For children, the task demands as well as the requirement to lie still for long pe-riods of time can prove difficult (Bookheimer, 2000). Nevertheless, this noninva-sive technique is a valuable research and clinical tool for understanding brain structure, function, and pathology in pediatric populations.

There is growing emergence of fMRI studies contributing to cognitive develop-ment and neurobiological correlates underlying behavioral deficits in neuro-developmental disorders. Deficits in social interactions, for example, are core characteristics of children with autism spectrum disorders. Using fMRI, re-searchers are investigating neurofunctional correlates of impoverished interper-sonal interactions in autism. A cognitive skill of particular interest is the recognition of human faces, an integral component of successful social interac-tions. There is converging evidence using fMRI that individuals with autism demonstrate atypical brain activation patterns during processing of human faces (Critchley et al., 2000; Hubl et al., 2003; Pierce, Muller, Ambrose, Allen, & Courchesne, 2001; Schultz et al., 2000). Figure 14.9 demonstrates the utility of fMRI for studying face processing in autism (Schultz et al., 2000). While in the scanner, participants performed simple discrimination tasks for both faces and objects (e.g., same or different). In healthy controls, the fusiform gyrus (FG) of the right hemisphere was most engaged by face stimuli. This lateral aspect of the FG is often called the "fusiform face area" (FFA) because of its specialty for pro-cessing human face recognition (Schultz et al., 2003). When presented with the object recognition task, greater ITG activation was found for healthy controls. Brain activation patterns for individuals with high-functioning autism, however, differed in that the right ITG region seemed more activated during face process-ing than the expected FG area. Cognitive resources used during the face discrim-ination task, therefore, were more similar to those used for object discrimination and less specialized than in typically developing individuals.

The application of fMRI to the field of developmental cognitive neuroscience is promising. Methodological and practical issues pose challenges to designing and implementing fMRI studies with pediatric populations, but future advances in technology and research designs likely will continue the popularity of fMRI as a research tool for studying the developing brain (Bookheimer, 2000).

## ELECTROENCEPHALOGRAM SOURCE IMAGING

EEG is not technically a neuroimaging tool, but a neuroelectric technique used to inspect temporal and spatial principles of brain activity. During the procedure, small metal discs or electrodes coated with a conductive gel are placed on standard locations of the scalp. Electrodes may be placed individually, which can be time-consuming, or, as is often the case with children, an electrode cap can be used. There are two types of recordings that can be obtained: spontaneous recordings of

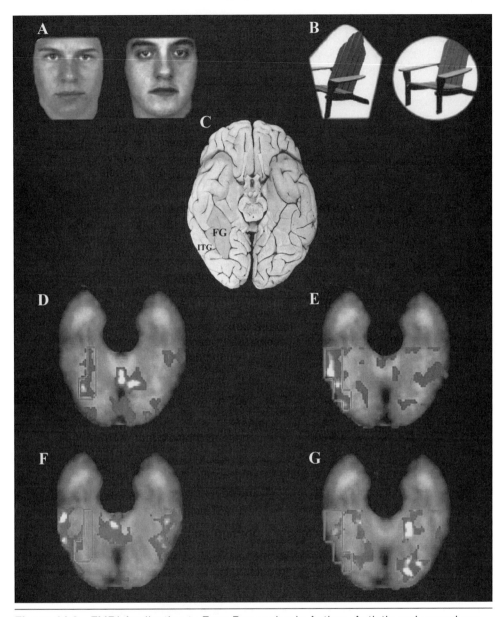

**Figure 14.9** FMRI Application to Face Processing in Autism. Autistic and normal controls performed a stimulus discrimination task (same versus different) for both human faces (A) and objects (B). Illustration of brain anatomy in a post-mortem brain showing the fusifom gyrus (FG) and inferior temporal gyrus (ITG) (C). In normal controls, the FG preferentially responds to face stimuli (D), whereas the ITG preferentially responds to object stimuli (E). The autism group used the ITG more than the controls for the face processing task (F) similar to the object processing task (G). Right and left are reversed by radiologic convention. Adapted from "Abnormal Ventral Temporal Cortical Activity during Face Discrimination among Individuals with Autism and Asperger Syndrome," by R. T. Schultz et al., 2000, *Archives of General Psychiatry, 57*(4), pp. 331–340.

neuroelectric activity and event-related and stimulus-evoked potentials. During spontaneous recordings, neuroelectric activity is compared to expected rhythms from the normal human brain. Event-related and stimulus-evoked potentials record repeated instances of brain activity following a time-locked event or stimulus presented during a mental task. When the recordings are averaged, the output is a waveform whose components can be analyzed for timing and amplitude. The excellent temporal resolution of EEG recording techniques allows for precise investigation of when distributed neural networks in the brain become active, as well as overall integrity of the human sensory processing systems (Halliday, 1993; Regan, 1989). The temporal resolution of EEG is in the order of milliseconds; the spatial resolution is less precise due to what is called the static electromagnetic inverse problem, or the difficulty assuming active neuronal generators are located under the peak activity measured on the scalp surface. Advanced signal processing and mathematical algorithms can be applied to improve solutions to the inverse problem (Babiloni et al., 1996; Fuchs, Wagner, Kohler, & Wischmann, 1999; Gevins, 1993; Gevins, Brickett, Costales, Le, & Reutter, 1990; He & Lian, 2002; Michel et al., 1999). EEG source imaging procedures add to traditional EEG by extracting information about brain activity beyond visual inspection of the recording and allowing for integration with other imaging techniques for improved localization of brain function (see Michel et al., 2004, for a review).

EEG source imaging is often used medically as an adjunct to traditional EEG for the diagnosis of neurological disorders, including epilepsy, dementia, and head injury. Underlying abnormalities in brain functioning are also studied using EEG source imaging in a number of psychiatric and neurodevelopmental populations, such as those with Schizophrenia, ADHD, and dyslexia. EEG biofeedback, neurofeedback, and neurotherapy are treatment approaches based on this technology. The data are used as a baseline measure of where in the brain and under what conditions brain activity is nonoptimal. EEG feedback-assisted cognitive-behavior modification therapy is then implemented to enhance brain activation and behavioral and cognitive functioning.

## MAGNETOENCEPHALOGRAPHY

MEG detects brain activity by measuring magnetic fields generated by electrical activity in the brain. The magnetic flux associated with electrical currents in activated sets of neurons is measured on the head surface by a byomagnetometer system containing detection coils and superconducting quantum interference devices. Like EEG recordings, MEG output signals can be either spontaneous or event-related waveforms. Using mathematical modeling, the activity source of the neurons contributing to a recorded signal at any instant in time can be estimated through the application of modeling techniques (Darvas, Pantazis, Kucukaltun-Yildirim, & Leahy, 2004; Lewine & Orrison, 1995; Pang, Gaetz, Otsubo, Chuang, & Cheyne, 2003; Tang, Pearlmutter, Malaszenko, Phung, & Reeb, 2002).

MEG signals recorded in response to repeated stimulus presentations allow researchers to study the timing and strength of brain activity associated with primary functions of the brain (i.e., somatosensory, auditory, visual, and motor) as well as more complicated functions (e.g., reading, working memory; Vellutino, Fletcher, Snowling, & Scanlon, 2004). MEG has excellent temporal resolution and adequate spatial resolution when mapping even higher-order cognitive tasks

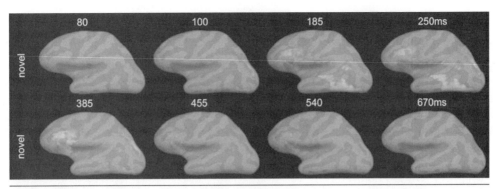

**Figure 14.10** Snapshots of Left Hemisphere MEG Shortly after Presentation of a Novel Word. fMEG is averaged across 4 healthy controls and painted onto the average left hemisphere. Activation is estimated to spread very rapidly from the occipital pole at 80ms, to the medioventral temporal lobe at 100ms, and then to lateral inferotemporal, intraparietal, prefrontal, anterior cingular cortices at 185ms. These areas remained active for about 400ms before weakening and eventually disappearing by 670ms. Adapted from "Dynamic Statistical Parametric Mapping: Combining Fmri and Meg for High-Resolution Imaging of Cortical Activity," by A. M. Dale et al., 2000, *Neuron, 26*(1), pp. 55–67.

(Dale et al., 2000). Given the high temporal resolution of MEG (i.e., the real-time, direct assessment of cognitive events), MEG complements other neuroimaging techniques characterized by high spatial resolution. In combination, MEG integrated with MRI (called magnetic source imaging or MSI) provides information about the timing of cognitive events and regions of the brain activated during the cognitive task. Both timing and localization are important in the study of complex cognitive processes.

Normal reading ability, for example, requires a complex interaction of both non-language-based (e.g., visual perception, memory) and language-based cognitive processes (e.g., phonological awareness, reading comprehension; Vellutino et al., 2004.) The spatiotemporal localization of complex tasks like reading are fairly new. Some advances in behavioral neuroimaging of complex cognitive tasks include the integration of the high spatial resolution of fMRI with the high temporal resolution of MEG. Using the fMRI findings to anatomically constrain the localization of the magnetic activity source from the same reading task, cognitive maps or "movies" depicting the sequence and localization of higher-order cognitive processes can be generated. Spatiotemporal maps of brain activity generated while reading words are shown in Figure 14.10 (Dale et al., 2000).

Disruption and/or abnormal development of any one of these processes theoretically leads to inefficient or poor reading in an individual. Neurobiological findings in dyslexia consistently implicate differences in the left temporo-parieto-occipital regions between impaired and nonimpaired readers (Eliez et al., 2000; Galaburda, Sherman, Rosen, Aboitiz, & Geschwind, 1985; Horwitz, Rumsey, & Donohue, 1998; Rumsey et al., 1992; B. A. Shaywitz et al., 2002; S. E. Shaywitz et al., 1998). In dyslexics, there seems to be a disruption of neural processing whereby different brain regions are activated during reading tasks. In neurologically typical individuals without a history of reading difficulty, MSI brain activation profiles

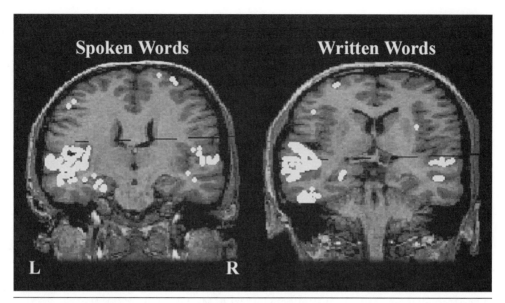

**Figure 14.11** MSI Activation During Language Tasks in Normal Readers. During aural and word recognition tasks with children without reading difficulties, there is a distinct pattern of brain activation, predominantly in the left hemisphere for both spoken (A) and printed (B) words. Adapted from "Brain Mechanisms for Reading in Children with and without Dyslexia: A Review of Studies of Normal Development and Plasticity," by A. C. Papanicolaou et al., 2003, *Developmental Neuropsychology, 24*(2/3), pp. 593–612.

are similarly predominant in the left hemisphere language areas whether subjects hear spoken words through earphones or view printed words on a screen (Figure 14.11; Papanicolaou et al., 2003).

In normal readers, therefore, there is overlap of brain mechanisms used for spoken comprehension and reading. When individuals with dyslexia perform the same two tasks, MSI brain activation patterns are similar to normal readers for spoken words, but different for printed words. In fact, brain activation profiles for the reading task shift to reflect brain activity predominantly in right hemisphere homologues of left hemisphere language areas (Figure 14.12).

Brain activity seen in regions not typically activated during phonological processing tasks is noteworthy. This shift in activation from one hemisphere to the other is commonly observed in recovery of function following left hemisphere damage (Cao, Vikingstad, George, Johnson, & Welch, 1999; Thulborn, Carpenter, & Just, 1999; Vikingstad et al., 2000) and likely represents efforts of compensation in the dyslexic brain. Interestingly, similar results are found for children who were identified at the end of kindergarten as being at risk for later reading problems based on their inability to master important concepts necessary to support early reading acquisition (e.g., knowledge of letter sounds; Papanicolaou et al., 2003). This implies that atypical brain organization is present early in development and results in poor phonetic awareness and reading.

Programs to improve reading skills in dyslexic children include direct remediation of the primary deficit in phonologic awareness and processing. Treatment outcome studies in pediatric populations are continuously plagued by a lack

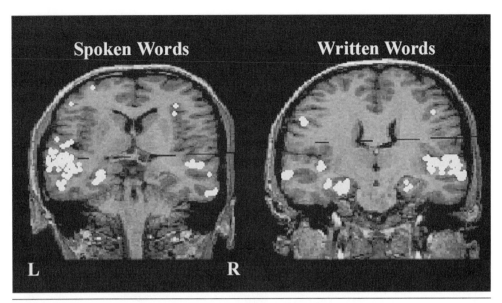

**Figure 14.12** MSI Activation During Language Tasks in Dyslexics. During the same aural and word recognition tasks with children with dyslexia, spoken words evoke similar left hemisphere brain regions as in typical readers. For printed words, however, there is a reversed functional asymmetry. Adapted from "Brain Mechanisms for Reading in Children with and without Dyslexia: A Review of Studies of Normal Development and Plasticity," by A. C. Papanicolaou et al., 2003, *Developmental Neuropsychology, 24*(2/3), pp. 593–612.

of appropriate outcome measures sensitive to detecting change as a result of the intervention. Investigators are exploring options in behavioral neuroimaging. Preliminary data for eight dyslexic children who participated in a reading intervention (Simos et al., 2002) demonstrate the usefulness of MSI in detecting neurofunctional changes following treatment (Figure 14.13).

Of particular interest is the increased activation in the left temporo-parieto-occipital region, the area involved in phonological processing and likely disrupted in poor readers. Improved activation in this area is cautiously interpreted as partial *normalization* of brain function attributed to the remediation. Although these findings are preliminary and in need of replication, findings from MSI data corroborate findings from other functional studies finding atypical increased right hemisphere brain activation during reading tasks in dyslexia followed by a shift to more typical patterns following remediation designed to improve auditory and language processing (Temple et al., 2003).

In summary, behavioral neuroimaging using various structural and functional methods offers promise of better clinical diagnostics and research understanding of pediatric neurologic and neurodevelopmental disorders. The developing brain undoubtedly is programmed for change as neural networks become established and modified by the environment. Perhaps the most impressive feature of the young brain is this amazing capability. Behavioral neuroimaging holds promise for investigating the cognitive neuroscience principle of brain plasticity both in typically developing children and in cases of abnormal development or insult, as presented in the following case study.

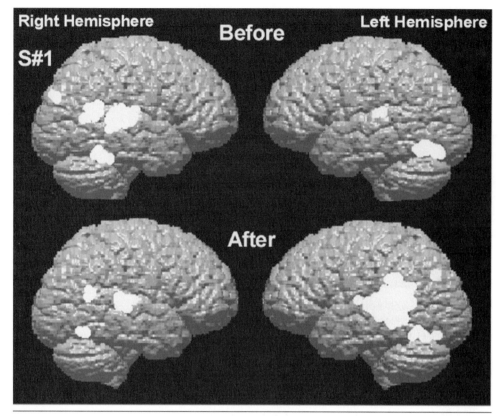

**Figure 14.13** MSI Activation Maps from a 9-Year-Old Dyslexic Child Before and After an Intensive Reading Remediation Program. MEG data was obtained during a pseudo-word rhyme-matching task. Note the shift in activation from the right temporoparietal regions to the left homologues (predominantly in the superior temporal gyrus) following treatment. Adapted from "Brain Mechanisms for Reading in Children with and without Dyslexia: A Review of Studies of Normal Development and Plasticity," by A. C. Papani-colaou et al., 2003, *Developmental Neuropsychology, 24*(2/3), pp. 593–612.

### Case Study 4: Normal Reading in the Absence of Visual Cortex

This 25-year-old patient was born with an occipital encephalocele, an external cranial sack at the base of her neck the same size as the head. The encephalocele was surgically removed at 4 days of age. No complications of the surgery were encountered, and surprisingly, the child progressed through developmental milestones on target, with the exception of some delays in perceptual-motor development. Pediatric neurological exams throughout her life revealed partial cortical blindness and visual acuity problems, as well as optic atrophy that remained stable throughout her life. Despite these obstacles, the child developed age-appropriate visually guided behavior sufficient for semi-independent ambulation, learned the alphabet, and ultimately to read.

At the time of neuropsychological testing and neuroimaging, she was successfully completing her 3rd year in a college program. Table 14.4 provides neuropsychological and academic data obtained at age 25 years.

**Table 14.4**

Case Study 4: 25-Year-Old Female with Average Reading
Despite Damaged Visual Cortex

| Intellectual (WAIS-R) | |
|---|---|
| VIQ = 108 | |
| Vocabulary | 12 |
| Information | 11 |
| Comprehension | 12 |
| Arithmetic | 14 |
| Digit Span | 13 |
| PIQ = 61 | |
| Picture Completion | 3 |
| Picture Arrangement | 4 |
| Block Design | 6 |
| Object Assembly | 1 |
| Digit Symbol | 2 |

| Academic Achievement (WRAT-III) | |
|---|---|
| Read | 108 (63%) |
| Spell | 89 (23%) |
| Arithmetic | 86 (18%) |

| Language Examination | |
|---|---|
| Boston Naming Test | 42/60 (< 1st%) |
| Verbal Fluency (FAS) | 42 (50th%) |

| Visual Spatial | |
|---|---|
| Ravens Coloured Progressive Matrices | 28/26 (10th–25th%) |
| Judgment of Line Orientation | 16/30 (1st%) |
| Benton Facial Recognition | 30/54 (<1st%) |
| Benton Visual Form Discrimination | 15/16 |
| Hooper Visual Organization Test | 8/30 (T = 87; impaired) |

| Memory | |
|---|---|
| WMS-R Verbal Memory Quotient | 105 |
| CVLT Trial 1–5 | T = 35 |
| Short Delay | z = –2.0 |
| Long Delay | z = –2.0 |
| Recognition | 16/16 |
| Benton Visual Retention Test-R | 11 errors (< 0.1%) |

| Attention/Auditory Discrimination | |
|---|---|
| Seashore Rhythm Test | 2 errors |

| Visual Motor | |
|---|---|
| VMI, 4th ed | 55 (0.2%) |

*Note:* CVLT = California Verbal Learning Test; PIQ = Performance Intelligence Quotient; VIQ = Verbal Intelligence Quotient; VMI = Beery Developmental Test of Visual-Motor Integration; WAIS-R = Wechsler Adult Intelligence Scale-Revised; WMS-R = Wechsler Memory Scale-Revised; WRAT-3 = Wide Range Achievement Test, third edition.

Neuropsychological findings revealed average or above average language abilities. Nonverbal intelligence was in the impaired range, which is not expected given her visual defect. Word reading was average for her age and commensurate with verbal abilities. Spelling and mathematics were in the low-average range. Verbal fluency skills were intact. She performed less well on a test of confrontation naming, although she was able to name some complex visual items. Likewise, she generated correct answers to several items on the Hooper Visual Organization Test and missed only one item on a visual discrimination task, a remarkable feat given her visual defects. Performance on other visual and visual-motor integration tests were impaired. Verbal memory was intact and consistent with intellectual ability. Visual limitations were too significant to perform visual memory tests.

Figure 14.14 depicts neuroimaging findings at the time of neuropsychological testing. Extensive bilateral structural (MR) and metabolic (SPECT) abnormalities are evident in the primary visual cortex. The MR study reveals enlarged ventricles and thinning of the cortex of the posterior parietal and occipital lobes. Sagittal view of the MR additionally demonstrates atrophic to absent corpus callosum from mid-body posteriorly. Thus, no interhemispheric integration of visual information could take place via traditional projections across the splenium. Most telling is the SPECT scan, which demonstrates an abnormal pattern of distribution of the radioactive tracer, most notably minimal to absent activity in the posterior parietal lobes and occipital lobes, consistent with structural findings. The perfusion pattern in the frontal, temporal, and anterior parietal lobes, however, appeared symmetric and unremarkable.

Remarkably, and as predicted if reading occurs outside the primary visual cortex, fMRI demonstrated activation of traditional temporofrontal regions, along with activation of a bilateral parietal area that appeared to be the primary site of visual activation (see Figure 14.14). Once visual information was processed as a word, the transfer of that information progressed normally to language-reading areas, where all functions then proceeded normally. On all other non-word-processing visual-perceptual tasks, as would be expected, the patient performed very poorly if at all (refer to Table 14.4). This case of normal reading in the context of significant visual dysgnosia is an excellent example of plasticity and reorganization of function in the developing brain.

## CHALLENGES RELATED TO BEHAVIORAL NEUROIMAGING IN PEDIATRIC POPULATIONS

Several challenges and ethical concerns exist regarding the neuropsychologist's role in the acquisition and interpretation of behavioral neuroimaging in pediatric patients. Whereas neuroanatomical imaging techniques are well established for clinical use in cases in which brain integrity is questioned, newer functional neuroimaging techniques are considered more investigational. Neuropsychologists adhere to guidelines for the ethical and competent practice of clinical neuropsychology, psychological assessment, and test use (American Psychological Association, 1992, 2002). With the advance of neuroimaging technology and the foreseeable increased application in pediatric neuropsychology, guidelines are needed that adequately cover the specific requirements and potential applications

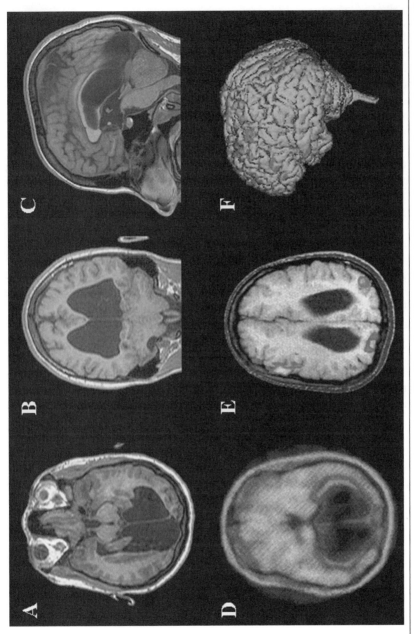

**Figure 14.14** MR Imaging in Three Planes of a 25-Year-Old Female with an Occipital Encephalocele Surgically Removed at Birth (A-C). MR study reveals enlarged ventricles, thinning of the cortex of the posterior parietal and occipital lobes, and thinning of the corpus callosum. The SPECT scan (D) demonstrates minimal to absent activity in the posterior parietal lobes and occipital lobes, consistent with structural findings. fMRI activation generated during a reading task depicts remarkable brain plasticity and reorganization of function following early insult. Data reflect the differential activity of novel words versus repeated words (E). Note the left frontal and bilateral parietal activation patterns as plotted on her 3-D rendered brain.

presented by neuroimaging. Several issues to be addressed are informed consent for the procedure, potential risks to the child, general competence in the development and refinement of neuroimaging measures, and an understanding of the clinical use and interpretation of neuroimaging techniques with children (Hinton, 2002; Rosen & Gur, 2002).

Neuroimaging offers insight into the developing brain that ultimately will better guide treatment for children with neurological and neurobehavioral disorders. Most techniques are considered noninvasive as long as the child is able to remain physically still throughout the examination to reduce motion artifact in the data. If unable to do so, sedation is an option. There is ongoing medical and ethical debate concerning the potential risk of sedation-related adverse effects compared to the benefits of neuroimaging (Freeman, 2001; Hoffman, Nowakowski, Troshynski, Berens, & Weisman, 2002; Olson, Sheehan, Thompson, Hall, & Hahn, 2001; Pilling, Abernethy, Wright, & Carty, 2001). When possible, behavioral desensitization procedures are recommended to reduce anxiety and discomfort to the child during the procedure, distress to family members, and the need for sedation (Rosenberg et al., 1997; Slifer, Cataldo, Cataldo, Llorente, & Gerson, 1993; Slifer, Koontz, & Cataldo, 2002).

## CONCLUSION

Until recently, understanding the developing brain has largely relied on inferences from behavioral testing paradigms and neuropathological studies of postmortem brains. Behavioral neuroimaging techniques now offer in vivo investigation of the anatomical, metabolic, and functional correlates of brain development from 24 weeks gestational age up through adulthood (Inder & Huppi, 2000). Potential application of pediatric neuroimaging is vast. The nature of the information obtained from each technique varies, as do the benefits and limitations. In the future, methodological advances in multimodal integration of imaging data are likely to be used to study complex interactions in the brain.

Learning disabilities, ADHD, and Autism spectrum disorders, for example, are the most common disorders of childhood facing teachers and school personnel. Disrupted development of the neural networks supporting cognition and behavior is thought to underlie neurodevelopmental disorders of childhood (Belmonte et al., 2004). Behavioral neuroimaging allows investigators to systematically study brain structure and function for abnormal trends contributing to poor developmental outcomes (Frank & Pavlakis, 2001). The field has not yet progressed to the point where behavioral imaging techniques can be used to clinically diagnose certain disorders of childhood. Future goals are to identify neuroanatomical and neurofunctional markers of common childhood disorders and provide biological markers to evaluate brain plasticity and treatment efficacy.

## REFERENCES

American Psychological Association. (1992). Ethical principles of psychologists and code of conduct. *American Psychologist, 47,* 1597–1611.

American Psychological Association. (2002). Ethical principles of psychologists and code of conduct. *American Psychologist, 57*(12), 1060–1073.

Babiloni, F., Babiloni, C., Carducci, F., Fattorini, L., Onorati, P., & Urbano, A. (1996). Spline Laplacian estimate of EEG potentials over a realistic magnetic resonance-constructed scalp surface model. *Electroencephalography and Clinical Neurophysiology, 98*(4), 363–373.

Basser, P. J., Pajevic, S., Pierpaoli, C., Duda, J., & Aldroubi, A. (2000). In vivo fiber tractography using DT-MRI data. *Magnetic Resonance in Medicine, 44*(4), 625–632.

Belmonte, M. K., Allen, G., Beckel-Mitchener, A., Boulanger, L. M., Carper, R. A., & Webb, S. J. (2004). Autism and abnormal development of brain connectivity. *Journal of Neuroscience, 24*(42), 9228–9231.

Bigler, E. D. (1997). Brain imaging and behavioral outcome in traumatic brain injury. In E. C. Erin, D. Bigler, & J. E. Farmer (Eds.), *Childhood traumatic brain injury* (pp. 7–29). Austin, TX: ProEd.

Bigler, E. D. (1999). Neuroimaging in pediatric traumatic head injury: Diagnostic considerations and relationships to neurobehavioral outcome. *Journal of Head Trauma Rehabilitation, 14*(4), 406–423.

Bigler, E. D. (in press). Structural imaging. In J. Silver, S. Yudofsky, & R. Hales (Eds.), *Neuropsychiatry of traumatic brain injury* (2nd ed., pp. 79–105). Washington, DC: American Psychiatric Association.

Bigler, E. D., & Tate, D. F. (2001). Brain volume, intracranial volume, and dementia. *Investigative Radiology, 36*(9), 539–546.

Bookheimer, S. Y. (1996). Positron emission tomography studies of cognition. In E. D. Bigler (Ed.), *Neuroimaging I: Basic science* (pp. 97–117). New York: Plenum Press.

Bookheimer, S. Y. (2000). Methodological issues in pediatric neuroimaging. *Mental Retardation and Developmental Disabilities Research Review, 6*(3), 161–165.

Buchhalter, J. R., & So, E. L. (2004). Advances in computer-assisted single-photon emission computed tomography (SPECT) for epilepsy surgery in children. *Acta Paediatrica, 93*(445), 32–35.

Calvert, G. A., & Thesen, T. (2004). Multisensory integration: Methodological approaches and emerging principles in the human brain. *Journal of Physiology, Paris, 98*(1/3), 191–205.

Cao, Y., Vikingstad, E. M., George, K. P., Johnson, A. F., & Welch, K. M. (1999). Cortical language activation in stroke patients recovering from aphasia with functional MRI. *Stroke, 30*(11), 2331–2340.

Conturo, T. E., Lori, N. F., Cull, T. S., Akbudak, E., Snyder, A. Z., Shimony, J. S., et al. (1999). Tracking neuronal fiber pathways in the living human brain. *Proceedings of the National Academy of Sciences of the United States of America, 96*(18), 10422–10427.

Critchley, H. D., Daly, E. M., Bullmore, E. T., Williams, S. C., Van Amelsvoort, T., Robertson, D. M., et al. (2000). The functional neuroanatomy of social behaviour: Changes in cerebral blood flow when people with autistic disorder process facial expressions. *Brain, 123*(Pt 11), 2203–2212.

Dale, A. M., Liu, A. K., Fischl, B. R., Buckner, R. L., Belliveau, J. W., Lewine, J. D., et al. (2000). Dynamic statistical parametric mapping: Combining fMRI and MEG for high-resolution imaging of cortical activity. *Neuron, 26*(1), 55–67.

Darvas, F., Pantazis, D., Kucukaltun-Yildirim, E., & Leahy, R. M. (2004). Mapping human brain function with, M. E. G., & EEG: Methods and validation. *Neuroimage, 23*(Suppl. 1), S289–S299.

Duval, J., Dumont, M., Braun, C. M., & Montour-Proulx, I. (2002). Recovery of intellectual function after a brain injury: A comparison of longitudinal and cross-sectional approaches. *Brain and Cognition, 48*(2/3), 337–342.

Eliez, S., Rumsey, J. M., Giedd, J. N., Schmitt, J. E., Patwardhan, A. J., & Reiss, A. L. (2000). Morphological alteration of temporal lobe gray matter in dyslexia: An MRI study. *Journal of Child Psychology and Psychiatry and Allied Disciplines, 41*(5), 637–644.

Finger, S., & Wolf, C. (1988). The "Kennard effect" before Kennard: The early history of age and brain lesions. *Archives of Neurology, 45*(10), 1136–1142.

Frank, Y., & Pavlakis, S. G. (2001). Brain imaging in neurobehavioral disorders. *Pediatric Neurology, 25*(4), 278–287.

Freeman, J. M. (2001). The risks of sedation for electroencephalograms: Data at last. *Pediatrics, 108*(1), 178.

Fuchs, M., Wagner, M., Kohler, T., & Wischmann, H. A. (1999). Linear and nonlinear current density reconstructions. *Journal of Clinical Neurophysiology, 16*(3), 267–295.

Galaburda, A. M., Sherman, G. F., Rosen, G. D., Aboitiz, F., & Geschwind, N. (1985). Developmental dyslexia: Four consecutive patients with cortical anomalies. *Annals of Neurology, 18*(2), 222–233.

Gean, A. (1994). *Imaging of head trauma.* New York: Raven Press.

Gevins, A. (1993). High-resolution EEG enters imaging arena. *Diagnostic Imaging, 15*(11), 77–78.

Gevins, A., Brickett, P., Costales, B., Le, J., & Reutter, B. (1990). Beyond topographic mapping: Towards functional-anatomical imaging with 124-channel EEGs and 3-D MRIs. *Brain Topography, 3*(1), 53–64.

Giedd, J. N. (2001, May). Neuroimaging of pediatric neuropsychiatric disorders. *Archives General Psychiatry, 58,* 443–444.

Gupta, A., Raja, S., Kotagal, P., Lachhwani, D., Wyllie, E., & Bingaman, W. B. (2004). Ictal SPECT in children with partial epilepsy due to focal cortical dysplasia. *Pediatric Neurology, 31*(2), 89–95.

Halliday, A. (1993). *Evoked potentials in clinical testing* (2nd ed.). Edinburg: Churchill Livingstone.

Hartshorne, M. F. (1995a). Positron emission tomography. In W. W. Orrison, J. D. Lewine, J. A. Sanders, & M. F. Hartshorne (Eds.), *Functional brain imaging* (pp. 187–212). St. Louis, MO: Mosby-Yearbook.

Hartshorne, M. F. (1995b). Single photon emission computed tomography. In W. W. Orrison, J. D. Lewine, J. A. Sanders, & M. F. Hartshorne (Eds.), *Functional brain imaging* (pp. 213–238). St. Louis, MO: Mosby-Yearbook.

Haydel, M. J., Preston, C. A., Mills, T. J., Luber, S., Blaudeau, E., & DeBlieux, P. M. (2000). Indications for computed tomography in patients with minor head injury. *New England Journal of Medicine, 343*(2), 100–105.

He, B., & Lian, J. (2002). High-resolution spatio-temporal functional neuroimaging of brain activity. *Critical Reviews in Biomedical Engineering, 30*(4/6), 283–306.

Hinton, V. J. (2002). Ethics of neuroimaging in pediatric development. *Brain and Cognition, 50*(3), 455–468.

Hoffman, G. M., Nowakowski, R., Troshynski, T. J., Berens, R. J., & Weisman, S. J. (2002). Risk reduction in pediatric procedural sedation by application of an American Academy of Pediatrics/American Society of Anesthesiologists process model. *Pediatrics, 109*(2), 236–243.

Horwitz, B., Rumsey, J. M., & Donohue, B. C. (1998). Functional connectivity of the angular gyrus in normal reading and dyslexia. *Proceedings of the National Academy of Sciences of the United States of America, 95*(15), 8939–8944.

Hubl, D., Bolte, S., Feineis-Matthews, S., Lanfermann, H., Federspiel, A., Strik, W., et al. (2003). Functional imbalance of visual pathways indicates alternative face processing strategies in autism. *Neurology, 61*(9), 1232–1237.

Inder, T. E., & Huppi, P. S. (2000). In vivo studies of brain development by magnetic resonance techniques. *Mental Retardation and Developmental Disabilities Research Review, 6*(1), 59–67.

Innis, R. B. (1992). Neuroreceptor imaging with SPECT. *Journal of Clinical Psychiatry, 53 Suppl,* 29–34.

Kaminska, A., Chiron, C., Ville, D., Dellatolas, G., Hollo, A., Cieuta, C., et al. (2003). Ictal SPECT in children with epilepsy: Comparison with intracranial, EEG, and relation to postsurgical outcome. *Brain, 126*(Pt 1), 248–260.

Kirton, A., Kloiber, R., Rigel, J., & Wolff, J. (2002). Evaluation of pediatric CNS malignancies with (99m)Tc-methoxyisobutylisonitrile SPECT. *Journal of Nuclear Medicine, 43*(11), 1438–1443.

Laidlaw, D. H., Fleischer, K. W., & Barr, A. H. (1998). Partial-volume Bayesian classification of material mixtures in MR volume data using voxel histograms. *IEEE Transactions on Medical Imaging, 17*(1), 74–86.

Lewine, J. D., & Orrison, W. W. (1995). Magnetoencephalography and magnetic source imaging. In W. W. Orrison, J. D. Lewine, J. A. Sanders, & M. F. Hartshorne (Eds.), *Functional brain imaging* (pp. 369–418). St Louis: Mosby-Yearbook.

Michel, C. M., Grave de Peralta, R., Lantz, G., Gonzalez Andino, S., Spinelli, L., Blanke, O., et al. (1999). Spatiotemporal EEG analysis and distributed source estimation in presurgical epilepsy evaluation. *Journal of Clinical Neurophysiology, 16*(3), 239–266.

Michel, C. M., Murray, M. M., Lantz, G., Gonzalez, S., Spinelli, L., & Grave de Peralta, R. (2004). EEG source imaging. *Clinical Neurophysiology, 115*(10), 2195–2222.

O'Brien, T. J., So, E. L., Cascino, G. D., Hauser, M. F., Marsh, W. R., Meyer, F. B., et al. (2004). Subtraction SPECT coregistered to MRI in focal malformations of cortical development: Localization of the epileptogenic zone in epilepsy surgery candidates. *Epilepsia, 45*(4), 367–376.

Olson, D. M., Sheehan, M. G., Thompson, W., Hall, P. T., & Hahn, J. (2001). Sedation of children for electroencephalograms. *Pediatrics, 108*(1), 163–165.

Orrison, W. W., Lewine, J. D., Sanders, J. A., & Hartshorne, M. F. (1995). *Functional brain imaging.* St. Louis: Mosbey-Yearbook.

Orrison, W. W., & Sanders, J. A. (1995). Clinical brain imaging: Computerized axial tomography and magnetic resonance imaging. In W. W. Orrison, J. D. Lewine, J. A. Sanders, & M. F. Hartshorne (Eds.), *Functional brain imaging* (pp. 97–143). St. Louis: Mosbey-Yearbook.

Paakko, E., Lehtinen, S., Harila-Saari, A., Ahonen, A., Jauhiainen, J., Torniainen, P., et al. (2003). Perfusion, M. R. I., & SPECT of brain after treatment for childhood acute lymphoblastic leukemia. *Medical and Pediatric Oncology, 40*(2), 88–92.

Palmen, S. J., & van Engeland, H. (2004). Review on structural neuroimaging findings in autism. *Journal of Neural Transmission, 111*(7), 903–929.

Pang, E. W., Gaetz, W., Otsubo, H., Chuang, S., & Cheyne, D. (2003). Localization of auditory N1 in children using MEG: Source modeling issues. *International Journal of Psychophysiology, 51*(1), 27–35.

Papanicolaou, A. C., Simos, P. G., Breier, J. I., Fletcher, J. M., Foorman, B. R., Francis, D., et al. (2003). Brain mechanisms for reading in children with and without dyslexia: A review of studies of normal development and plasticity. *Developmental Neuropsychology,* *24*(2/3), 593–612.

Pierce, K., Muller, R. A., Ambrose, J., Allen, G., & Courchesne, E. (2001). Face processing occurs outside the fusiform "face area" in autism: Evidence from functional MRI. *Brain, 124*(Pt 10), 2059–2073.

Pilling, D., Abernethy, L., Wright, N., & Carty, H. (2001). Sedation, safety and MRI. *British Journal of Radiology, 74*(885), 875–876.

Poupon, C., Clark, C. A., Frouin, V., Regis, J., Bloch, I., Le Bihan, D., et al. (2000). Regularization of diffusion-based direction maps for the tracking of brain white matter fascicles. *Neuroimage, 12*(2), 184–195.

Poussaint, T. Y., & Moeller, K. K. (2002). Imaging of pediatric head trauma. *Neuroimaging Clinics of North America, 12*(2), ix, 271–294.

Regan, D. (1989). *Human brain electrophysiology.* Amsterdam: Elsevier.

Rosen, A. C., & Gur, R. C. (2002). Ethical considerations for neuropsychologists as functional magnetic imagers. *Brain and Cognition, 50*(3), 469–481.

Rosenberg, D. R., Sweeney, J. A., Gillen, J. S., Kim, J., Varanelli, M. J., O'Hearn, K. M., et al. (1997). Magnetic resonance imaging of children without sedation: Preparation with simulation. *Journal of the American Academy of Child and Adolescent Psychiatry, 36*(6), 853–859.

Rumsey, J. M., Andreason, P., Zametkin, A. J., Aquino, T., King, A. C., Hamburger, S. D., et al. (1992). Failure to activate the left temporoparietal cortex in dyslexia. An oxygen 15 positron emission tomographic study. *Archives of Neurology, 49*(5), 527–534.

Sanders, J. A., & Orrison, W. W. (1995). Functional magnetic resonance imaging. In W. W. Orrison, J. D. Lewine, J. A. Sanders, & M. F. Hartshorne (Eds.), *Functional brain imaging* (pp. 239–326). St. Louis, MO: Mosby-Yearbook.

Schultz, R. T., Gauthier, I., Klin, A., Fulbright, R. K., Anderson, A. W., Volkmar, F., et al. (2000). Abnormal ventral temporal cortical activity during face discrimination among individuals with autism and Asperger syndrome. *Archives of General Psychiatry, 57*(4), 331–340.

Schultz, R. T., Grelotti, D. J., Klin, A., Kleinman, J., Van der Gaag, C., Marois, R., et al. (2003). The role of the fusiform face area in social cognition: Implications for the pathobiology of autism. *Proceedings of the Royal Society of London. Series B, Biological Sciences, 358*(1430), 415–427.

Shaywitz, B. A., Shaywitz, S. E., Pugh, K. R., Mencl, W. E., Fulbright, R. K., Skudlarski, P., et al. (2002). Disruption of posterior brain systems for reading in children with developmental dyslexia. *Biological Psychiatry, 52*(2), 101–110.

Shaywitz, S. E., Shaywitz, B. A., Pugh, K. R., Fulbright, R. K., Constable, R. T., Mencl, W. E., et al. (1998). Functional disruption in the organization of the brain for reading in dyslexia. *Proceedings of the National Academy of Sciences of the United States of America, 95*(5), 2636–2641.

Simos, P. G., Fletcher, J. M., Bergman, E., Breier, J. I., Foorman, B. R., Castillo, E. M., et al. (2002). Dyslexia-specific brain activation profile becomes normal following successful remedial training. *Neurology, 58*(8), 1203–1213.

Slifer, K. J., Cataldo, M. F., Cataldo, M. D., Llorente, A. M., & Gerson, A. C. (1993). Behavior analysis of motion control for pediatric neuroimaging. *Journal of Applied Behavior Analysis, 26*(4), 469–470.

Slifer, K. J., Koontz, K. L., & Cataldo, M. F. (2002). Operant-contingency-based preparation of children for functional magnetic resonance imaging. *Journal of Applied Behavior Analysis, 35*(2), 191–194.

Symms, M., Jager, H. R., Schmierer, K., & Yousry, T. A. (2004). A review of structural magnetic resonance neuroimaging. *Journal of Neurology, Neurosurgery, and Psychiatry, 75*(9), 1235–1244.

Tang, A. C., Pearlmutter, B. A., Malaszenko, N. A., Phung, D. B., & Reeb, B. C. (2002). Independent components of magnetoencephalography: Localization. *Neural Computation, 14*(8), 1827–1858.

Temple, E., Deutsch, G. K., Poldrack, R. A., Miller, S. L., Tallal, P., Merzenich, M. M., et al. (2003). Neural deficits in children with dyslexia ameliorated by behavioral remediation: Evidence from functional MRI. *Proceedings of the National Academy of Sciences of the United States of America, 100*(5), 2860–2865.

Thulborn, K. R., Carpenter, P. A., & Just, M. A. (1999). Plasticity of language-related brain function during recovery from stroke. *Stroke, 30*(4), 749–754.

Vellutino, F. R., Fletcher, J. M., Snowling, M. J., & Scanlon, D. M. (2004). Specific reading disability (dyslexia): What have we learned in the past four decades? *Journal of Child Psychology and Psychiatry and Allied Disciplines, 45*(1), 2–40.

Vikingstad, E. M., Cao, Y., Thomas, A. J., Johnson, A. F., Malik, G. M., & Welch, K. M. (2000). Language hemispheric dominance in patients with congenital lesions of eloquent brain. *Neurosurgery, 47*(3), 562–570.

Webb, C., Rose, F. D., Johnson, D. A., & Attree, E. A. (1996). Age and recovery from brain injury: Clinical opinions and experimental evidence. *Brain Injury, 10*(4), 303–310.

# UNDERSTANDING AND SERVING LEARNERS WITH DISEASES AND DISORDERS OR FROM SPECIAL POPULATIONS

# CHAPTER 15

# Understanding and Evaluating Special Education, IDEA, ADA, NCLB, and Section 504 in School Neuropsychology

DAVID E. McINTOSH and SCOTT L. DECKER

THIS CHAPTER BEGINS by providing a brief historical overview demonstrating the link between federal legislation and school neuropsychology. Although the application of neuropsychology in the schools has been well documented, the passage of special education and antidiscrimination legislation has had significant impact on how neuropsychological techniques are utilized and practiced in schools. In addition, medical and theoretical advancements in neuropsychology have also changed how neuropsychology is used in the schools. These issues are examined in light of laws and individual liberties.

A major portion of the chapter focuses on discussing the main education, special education, and antidiscrimination legislation of the past 40 years. The Individuals with Disabilities Education Act, No Child Left Behind Act, Section 504, and Americans with Disabilities Act are reviewed. A brief description is provided regarding each of these laws. The influence of legislation on school neuropsychology practice is discussed. Recommendations are provided on how neuropsychologists working in the schools can advocate for children given current federal regulations. The chapter concludes by discussing emerging neuropsychology theories and their application in education and the conceptual connection between emerging theory and federal legislation.

## THE HISTORICAL LINKS OF EDUCATION LEGISLATION, SECTION 504, AND SCHOOL NEUROPSYCHOLOGY

Although early and contemporary researchers consistently have made strong arguments for the inclusion of neuropsychological techniques when identifying children with learning disabilities (D'Amato, 1990; Hynd & Obrzut, 1981; Reitan,

1955), it was not until Public Law 94-142: Education for All Handicapped Children Act (1975) that school psychologists showed an increased interest in learning and applying these techniques in the school setting (D'Amato, 1990; Rothlisberg & D'Amato, 1988). Interestingly, long before Public Law 94-142 mandated the identification of students with disabilities, it was clear that neuropsychological assessment could assist in better understanding these children (Gaddes, 1981). Neuropsychology, as applied in the schools, also has expanded beyond the medical model; now, the focus is less on localizing specific brain lesions and more on gaining a better understanding of children's deficits with the goal of developing specific treatments (Hale & Fiorello, 2004). This change in perspective is primarily due to the increase in the use of brain imaging procedures (e.g., computerized tomography, magnetic resonance imaging), which localize brain lesions with a high degree of accuracy but provide little in terms of the resulting behavioral consequences (Dean & Woodcock, 2003; Dean, Woodcock, Decker, & Schrank, 2003; Hynd, 1981). Hynd suggests that school psychologists can apply their knowledge of neuropsychology when developing interventions or consulting with other school personnel when addressing children's learning problems. Hale and Fiorello have actually outlined a process for linking behavioral neuropsychology with the problem-solving consultation model. This consultation approach of combining neuropsychological assessment with behavioral methods fits well with service mandates prescribed in special education law, which, in turn, has facilitated the use of neuropsychological techniques in the schools.

## FEDERAL EDUCATION LEGISLATION

### INDIVIDUALS WITH DISABILITIES EDUCATION ACT

The Individuals with Disabilities Education Act (IDEA) amendments of 1997 (PL 105-117) are the latest of a series of federal statues mandating that all children, regardless of handicapping condition, are entitled to a free and appropriate public education in the least restrictive environment (Fagan & Sachs-Wise, 2000). Public Law 94-142 (1975) was the first in the series of federal statues to mandate that all children had a right to a free and appropriate education and required that each state must develop a plan to ensure that every child with disabilities receives special education services as outlined in an individualized education program (IEP; Jacob & Hartshorne, 2003). Public Laws 101-476 (1990) and 105-117 (1997) reauthorized and expanded on the statues outlined in Public Law 94-142. Specifically, services were extended to include infants and young children, provisions were made for assistive technology devices, and more emphasis was placed on family involvement when developing education programs for children with disabilities.

IDEA ensures that all children with handicaps are identified and classified. A multidisciplinary team determines eligibility for special education services. This team typically includes a school psychologist, a special education teacher with training in the area of the suspected disability, the regular education teacher, and the parents. In addition, the case conference committee, which may or may not be composed of the same members as the multidisciplinary team, determines eligibility for special education services. Hale and Fiorello (2004) outlined the criteria the case conference committee must address when determining eligibility for special education services:

- Does the child meet criteria for one or more of the existing disability categories?
- Does the child's disorder have an adverse impact on educational performance?
- Does the child need special instruction to ensure a free, appropriate public education? (p. 38)

For school neuropsychologists, IDEA poses certain challenges and considerations. While neuropsychological techniques can facilitate the diagnostic process and enhance our understanding of the underlying problems affecting learning, it is important to consider the consumers of neuropsychological information. Regular education teachers, special education teachers, administrators, and parents have a right to reports that are concise, clear, and jargon free. Therefore, neuropsychologists must be cognizant of the type of reports they generate and ensure that they are understandable. Case conference committees should be able to use the information in a neuropsychological report to facilitate discussion related to eligibility and develop specific objectives in the IEP.

Neuropsychologists working outside the school setting also should be sensitive when offering diagnostic recommendations. IDEA is clear that a multidisciplinary team must be involved in the assessment process. Therefore, in addition to the neuropsychological report, the multidisciplinary team may decide to conduct additional testing and classroom observations, review educational records, and gather any other information deemed necessary to make decisions regarding eligibility. It is important to note that schools do not have to consider an independent neuropsychological evaluation conducted outside the school setting when determining eligibility of special education services. In fact, the multidisciplinary team could decide to conduct additional neuropsychological testing and/or psychoeducational testing after considering the independent neuropsychological evaluation. However, most multidisciplinary teams work collaboratively with professionals outside the school setting and will consider independent neuropsychological evaluations when making eligibility decisions.

Although neuropsychologists make specific diagnoses, these diagnoses may or may not translate into a child's being eligible for special education services (Hale & Fiorello, 2004). IDEA mandates services for children who have been identified with specific disabilities (e.g., learning disability, speech and language impairment, mental retardation). Specifically, the diagnostic nomenclature used by neuropsychologists in private practice may or may not be consistent with the criteria needed for children to receive special education services in the school setting (Hale & Fiorello, 2004). This can be frustrating for neuropsychologists and confusing to parents. Therefore, neuropsychologists should be careful not to make assumptions regarding special education services and should educate parents regarding the process needed to pursue special education services in the schools. Neuropsychologists should at least help parents understand the difference between a clinical diagnosis and a special education classification and how the two may or may not overlap.

IDEA also mandates that children in need of special education services receive these services in the least restrictive environment. Therefore, the case conference committee must begin with the assumption that a child with a disability can be educated in the regular education classroom (Jacob & Hartshorne, 2003). In addition, the committee must consider whether or not a child with a disability can be educated in the regular classroom with the use of supplementary aids and services. Neuropsychologists can be immensely helpful to the committee if recommendations for interventions and accommodations are to be implemented in the regular classroom. For example, a child with a traumatic brain injury who is being considered for integration (i.e., inclusion) in a regular classroom could benefit from recommendations specifically stemming from a neuropsychological evaluation.

## No Child Left Behind Act

The No Child Left Behind Act of 2001 (PL 107-750) was the most recent amendment to the Elementary and Secondary Education Act of 1965 (PL 89-750). This latest amendment continues to focus on funding schools where a large majority of the children are from indigent families. The act also requires states to demonstrate the academic proficiency of all children in reading and math (Jacob & Hartshorne, 2003). Jacob and Hartshorne note that states now must implement statewide reading and mathematics testing for grades 3 to 8 by 2005 to 2006 and must offer supplemental tutoring for children who fail to demonstrate proficiency after 3 years.

How does the No Child Left Behind Act apply to school neuropsychology? Neuropsychologists can bring a unique perspective to working with children in regular education. Because neuropsychology has been shown to be helpful in understanding children's preferential processing styles and providing prognostic information related to daily living (D'Amato & DiUglio-Johnson, 1996), neuropsychologists working in the schools should become involved in the development and implementation of prevention programs. For example, neuropsychologists can become involved in prevention programs focused on educating parents, teachers, and students about environmental contagions commonly found in the homes of low-income families. Prevention programs focused on reducing health risks due to lead poisoning, exposed insulation, and insectides can be developed by neuropsychologists.

Due to their advanced training in the neurophysiology of behavior, neuropsychologists can bring a unique perspective to learning in the regular education classroom. Also, it is important to consider that in normal children and children with disabilities, neurological functions lie along a continuum and that the brain is directly related to learning and behavior (Hale & Fiorello, 2004). Therefore, neuropsychologists can assist in helping all children learn more effectively. Neuropsychologists and teachers can work together to develop curricula that will optimize learning, retention, and application of principles learned in the classroom. Thus, neuropsychologists working in the schools will need to keep pace with the momentum and educational reform spurred by the No Child Left Behind Act (Sheridan & D'Amato, 2003).

## Family Educational Rights and Privacy Act

The Family Education Rights and Privacy Act (FERPA; PL 93-380, 1974), also called the Buckley Amendment, assures parents the right to review, inspect, and request amendments to the educational records of their children. In addition, FERPA established rules for the copying and release of student records. The right to review and inspect records is accorded to parents, guardians, or surrogates (Warden, 1996a). Prasse (2002) indicated that FERPA was enacted in response to parent and student complaints related to lack of access to records and inaccuracy of records. Students 18 and over or students attending a postsecondary institution also are eligible to review and inspect their records. However, schools may also allow students under the age of 18 to review and inspect their records (Underwood & Mead, 1995).

There are several important considerations related to educational records, confidentiality, and amendment to records that school neuropsychologists should be familiar with when working in education:

- FERPA defines "educational records" as any records maintained by the schools or a party acting for the schools directly related to a student (Jacob & Hartshorne, 2003; Warden, 1996a). The personal records (i.e., notes) of the neuropsychologist are excluded if they have not been shared with anyone else. However, Jacob and Hartshorne note that a psychologist's personal notes can be subpoenaed.
- Schools that receive federal funds and do not restrict unauthorized access to educational records risk losing their funding (Sealander, 1999). Therefore, schools that receive federal funding must protect the privacy of students' educational records.
- The identifiable information of a student cannot be shared with anyone who does not have a legitimate educational interest related to the student. Typically, special education teachers, school counselors, psychologists, and other school service personnel have a legitimate need to have access to students' records.
- Schools cannot release information without the consent of parents, and parents must provide consent in writing to release records (Sealander, 1999). Sealander notes that parents have the right to modify information if they believe it is inaccurate or misleading.
- Test protocols should be considered part of a student's educational record. Because test protocols and raw psychological test data are used in forming a special education decision, it is difficult to argue that these records should be inaccessible to parents (Prasse, 2002). It also is important to note that test protocols are often copyrighted and copies cannot be made and given to parents; therefore, although parents have access to the records, they do not have the right to copy or make specific notes of information contained in protocols. One approach to addressing this problem is to allow parents to discuss and review protocols under the supervision of a psychologist (Jacob & Hartshorne, 2003). Prasse recommends that psychologists strive for balance when considering a parent's right to be informed and when complying with acceptable professional standards.
- Unless there is an outstanding request to inspect or review educational records, if they are no longer needed for educational purposes they may be destroyed after 5 years (Sealander, 1999). However, Jacob and Hartshorne (2003) recommend that psychologists working in the schools consult their state education laws and district policies prior to destroying educational records. Bernstein and Hartsell (1998) recommend that psychologists in independent private practice retain records for 5 to 10 years after a minor reaches the age that full civil rights are accorded.

School neuropsychologists and consulting neuropsychologists must be aware of parents' rights to review and inspect their children's educational records. Neuropsychologists must determine how and what information in a report should be shared with the school. There may be information in a report that they do not wish to become part of a student's educational record, yet they will want to include information that can assist in meeting the educational needs of the student (Jacob & Hartshorne, 2003).

School neuropsychologists will have to make similar decisions regarding information from professionals outside the school setting. Some information contained in a neurological report is irrelevant to meeting the educational needs of a student; in this case, it is recommended that neuropsychologists return the report to the neurologist and request that only information that would be helpful in meeting the educational needs of the student be retained in the report (Jacob & Hartshorne, 2003).

In summary, it is essential for neuropsychologists to become familiar with the federal, state, and local school district regulations related to the access, protection, confidentiality, and retention of educational records to ensure a high level of service to children and their families.

## FEDERAL ANTIDISCRIMINATION LEGISLATION

### SECTION 504 OF THE REHABILITATION ACT

Section 504 of the Rehabilitation Act of 1973 provides protection against discrimination for individuals with disabilities (Hicks, 1996). Although Section 504 was passed in the early 1970s, it was not until the late 1980s, when the Office of Civil Rights began enforcement efforts and the U.S. Department of Education clarified its regulations for Section 504, that its impact was felt by schools (Hicks, 1996; Jacob-Timm & Hartshorne, 1994). Compared to IDEA, Section 504 uses a broader definition of disability and focuses on determining whether an individual has a disability that substantially limits one or more major life activities. Section 504 uses the following definition:

> The term "physical or mental impairment" is defined as (a) any physiological condition, cosmetic disfigurement, or anatomical loss affecting one or more of the following body systems: neurological; musculoskeletal; special sense organs, respiratory, including speech organs; cardiovascular; reproductive; digestive; genito-urinary; hemic and lymphatic; skin; and endocrine; or (b) any mental or psychological disorder, such as mental retardation, organic brain syndrome, emotional or mental illness, and specific learning disabilities. (34 CFR § 104.3j; Rehabilitation Act, 1973)

It is important to note that children receiving special education services under IDEA also are protected under Section 504. In contrast, children afforded protection and services under Section 504 may not qualify for special education services under IDEA. Hicks (1996) suggested that children with "juvenile arthritis, acquired immunodeficiency syndrome (AIDS), or attention deficit disorder (ADD) who do not qualify as emotional disturbed, other health-impaired, or learning disability under IDEA" may be protected under Section 504. Students with mild traumatic brain injury also could be classified with a physical or mental impairment under Section 504 (Silver & Oakland, 1997).

Section 504 and IDEA both mandate a free and appropriate public education for children with handicaps. However, there are major differences between Section 504 and IDEA that neuropsychologists should be aware of when working in the schools. They are the following:

- There are no federal monies attached with Section 504, but federal funding is provided to schools under IDEA (Silver & Oakland, 1997). Schools must comply with antidiscrimination legislation if they receive any federal funds (Jacob-Timm & Harshorne, 1994).
- IDEA requires an IEP, and specific individuals are mandated to participate in the development of the IEP. Section 504 also requires that individuals knowledgeable about the student's particular condition or mental impairment must participate in the development of a 504 plan (Silver & Oakland, 1997).
- IDEA classifies children with one or more specific disabilities (e.g., reading disability or visual, hearing, or other health impairment). With Section 504, the more general definition cited earlier is used, but the handicap or condition must substantially limit a major life function.
- Children served under IDEA receive only special education services. Children served under Section 504 may receive regular or special educational services (Jacob-Timm & Harshorne, 1994). In both cases, services must be provided in the least restrictive environment.
- School districts are required to have a Section 504 coordinator and must annually publish public notices indicating the name of the coordinator (Perla, 1998).
- Procedural safeguards are required under IDEA and Section 504. Both require notice to the parent or guardian related to identification, evaluation, and/or placement of a student (Silver & Oakland, 1997). However, only IDEA requires written notice.

Section 504 appears to be a feasible alternative to providing much needed services to children with mild disabilities in the school setting. However, a common misunderstanding among professionals and parents is that Section 504 regulations are less stringent and its services are inferior compared to services provided under IDEA. It is important to remember that the primary objective is to meet the educational needs of learners regardless of whether learners are served under Section 504 or IDEA. School neuropsychologists must be aware of the various federal and state regulations if they are going to advocate for children classified with disabilities.

## AMERICANS WITH DISABILITIES ACT

The Americans with Disabilities Act of 1990 (ADA; PL 101-336, 1990) mandated the elimination of discrimination against individuals with disabilities. Warden (1996b) noted that ADA provided clear, consistent, and enforceable standards for addressing discrimination. Telecommunications companies, schools, and state and local government agencies also must meet the mandates specified in ADA. In addition, ADA applies to postsecondary institutions. In schools, ADA is often seen as less stringent compared to the criteria for special education services under IDEA. ADA provides a more general guideline, indicating that an individual with a "physical or mental impairment that substantially limits at least one major life activity" is eligible for services. Therefore, a child who qualifies for special education services under IDEA automatically is afforded ADA protections, but a child may qualify for services under ADA and not qualify for services under IDEA.

Because ADA does not specifically mention learning disabilities, there has been considerable confusion regarding whether children classified with a specific learning disability should be afforded ADA protections. Roberts and Mather (1995) have provided clarification by explaining how learning disabilities are consistent with the ADA definition of "substantially limiting a major life activity." They note that ADA and Section 504 consider "learning" a major life activity and that a learning disability affects the major life activity of learning. If the special education services provided under IDEA are discontinued for a child with a specific learning disability, the child may still be afforded the protections mandated under ADA. For children who are classified as having specific learning disabilities but who do not meet the criteria for services under IDEA, school neuropsychologists can recommend that school personnel and parents consider ADA and Section 504. Unfortunately, schools do not receive federal money for providing ADA and Section 504 services; as a result, schools may be less inclined to provide services under these federal mandates (Hale & Fiorello, 2004). Neuropsychologists must recognize when it is in the best interests of children to advocate for services and protections afforded under these federal mandates.

Along with being familiar with ADA and how to advocate for children with disabilities, school neuropsychologists also need to help students make the transition from school to postsecondary education and to work. The School-to-Work Opportunity Act (National Transition Network, 1994) established guidelines for supporting performance-based education and training programs for students. Specifically, the legislation helped established school-based counseling and career awareness and work-based experiences and mentoring for students with disabilities (Yesseldyke & Geenen, 1996). Yesseldyke and Geenen advocate for the participation of psychologists on case conference committees because their knowledge can be useful in establishing training programs and in the execution of transitional programs.

Many psychologists working in the schools are unaware of how essential a comprehensive psychological evaluation is in ensuring appropriate accommodations in work and postsecondary settings. A comprehensive psychological evaluation is recommended during a student's senior year because many postsecondary institutions request a current psychological evaluation and documentation of the specific learning disability or mental disorder. In addition, the evaluation should provide specific recommendations regarding accommodations the student may wish to request from the postsecondary institution he or she plans to attend. Because ADA requires trained admission officers who can interview prospective students with disabilities and who also are required to conduct seminars for faculty to increase their sensitivity to the needs of students with disabilities (Alston, Russo, & Miles, 1994), it can be very helpful if neuropsychologists are proactive in helping students identify needed accommodations prior to meeting with admission officers. Such accommodations include additional time when taking tests, taking tests in a quiet environment, the use of note takers, copies of instructors' overheads, books on tape, and preferential scheduling. Although these are some of the more common accommodations requested by college students with disabilities, it could save students time, unneeded testing, and frustration if these are specifically stated in the psychological report conducted during their senior year in high school. Neuropsychologists working with high school students with severe learning disabilities, traumatic brain injury, or other health impairments may recommend highly specific accommodations. Working with students and postsecondary institutions during the senior year, neuropsychologists can assist the institutions in developing appropriate accommodations and assist students in determining whether an institution can meet their educational needs.

For students classified with disabilities who are planning on entering the workforce directly after graduation, many states offer school-to-work transition services through vocational rehabilitation. Neuropsychologists can use their expertise to help students identify accommodations they will need in the work setting. Ideally, the school-to-work transition should begin prior to starting high school; for example, career exploration can begin during elementary school. Neuropsychologists can conduct situational assessments by visiting worksites with students and identifying the specific accommodations needed for students to be successful. Job shadowing also can assist students with disabilities identify jobs that they can be successful in after graduation. Neuropsychologists are encouraged to become actively involved when students participate in job shadowing; neuropsychologists and students can discuss with workers the specific demands and requirements needed to be successful, and neuropsychologists can assist students in making informed decisions regarding accommodations, vocational training, and career choice.

School neuropsychologists can advocate for students with disabilities and ensure that the protections afforded under ADA are implemented. Many students with disabilities graduating from high school often will need accommodations to succeed in their postgraduation endeavors and neuropsychologists can assist in this transition. Because the services and mandates provided under IDEA are specifically limited to the school setting, it is important to educate students and parents prior to graduation on the protections afforded individuals by ADA in work settings. Specifically, *all* public institutions that receive federal money and *all* private institutions with over 15 employees must provide accommodations for individuals with disabilities.

## SCHOOL NEUROPSYCHOLOGY AND APPLIED PRACTICE IN EDUCATIONAL SETTINGS

The interface between pediatric neuropsychologists and school systems has not always been straightforward. A neuropsychological evaluation in a school, like regular psychoeducational evaluations, may ultimately result in recommending educational accommodations for a learner. As such, the learner must be identified within a particular category designated by legal guidelines. Schools almost exclusively rely on diagnostic categories provided by the federal government, such as IDEA or Section 504, for determining eligibility for services. The diagnostic categories, rules for category inclusion, and measurement and assessment instruments used by neuropsychologists may not be the same as those used by the federal government or adopted by the state. Neuropsychologists not only must understand the legal guidelines that define and regulate special education but also must understand how neuropsychological categories and conditions relate to categories and conditions identified by federal or state law. Unless recommendations from a neuropsychological evaluation are specifically tailored to these unique aspects of the educational social system, it is *unlikely* that such recommendations will have any major impact for the child.

Because federal guidelines provide a specific category for brain injuries, school neuropsychologists have a primary role in evaluating children for special educational services. Assessment of brain injured children is typically outside the range of expertise of many school psychologists, which necessitates the role of the school neuropsychologist. The role of the neuropsychologist, however, is not limited to this subpopulation of learners. General categories exist in the federal guidelines for conditions that may presume some underlying neurological conditions but may not require evidence of neurological dysfunction for eligibility (e.g., individuals with learning disabilities). Other general categories provided by federal law may require neurological factors to be ruled out, which also may require the consultation of a school neuropsychologist. As such, services performed by neuropsychologists have direct reference to special education law, and the important role of the neuropsychologist in providing expertise in the area of brain-behavior relationships in both evaluations and consultation has been widely noted (D'Amato, Rothlisberg, & Rhodes, 1997).

The general categories and guidelines provided by the federal government are not sufficient to provide a detailed picture of the learner's problem (Kamphaus, Reynolds, & Imperato-McCammon, 1999). In contrast, terminology often used in neuropsychology is for the specific purpose of defining the underlying deficit. Whereas an individual may be classified as having a learning disability in the federal guidelines, neuropsychologists are apt to use different and more specific terminology, such as anomia, apraxia, and executive functions, in defining deficits. Although the use of such terms by school neuropsychologists is less likely, the conditions described by neuropsychologists generally have a reference to the underlying structure or functioning of the brain (Rothlisberg & D'Amato, 1988) based on brain-behavioral models derived through theory and research.

As the major importance of classification rests on a common nomenclature for the purpose of communicating with other professionals (Kamphaus, 1993), the discrepancy in terminology used by clinical neuropsychologists from the terminology that guides the legal definitions of diagnostic categories can provide a serious obstacle for interfacing neuropsychological techniques in schools for the purpose of obtaining accommodations for children. To decrease the number of such discrepancies, clinical neuropsychologists should obtain specialized training in the application of neuropsychology in school settings. Additionally, it is important for neuropsychologists to have open dialogues with school personnel and case conference members. It is often helpful for clinical neuropsychologists to review their recommendations with one or more of the case conference committee members in order to receive feedback on how the recommendations fit with the opinion of school personnel.

It is vital that clinical neuropsychologists are familiar with the federal guidelines, how the federal guidelines are implemented in particular states, and how the disorders specified in the federal guidelines relate to disorders specified through research in neuropsychology. Additionally, as radical improvement of current federal categories is unlikely, some have emphasized the responsibility to teach others to use such classification systems in an "enlightened fashion" (Kamphaus, Reynolds, & Imperato-McCammom, 1999). For clinical neuropsychologists, this may entail providing a more thorough explanation of the assessment results beyond that of a phone interview or short presentation at the case conference.

## APPLICATION OF NEUROPSYCHOLOGICAL PROCEDURES IN SCHOOLS

In addition to and in conjunction with the communication problems involved in translating clinical neuropsychological practices into legally defined diagnostic categories, the procedures, techniques, and rules that are used by neuropsychologists to determine category inclusion or diagnosis may be unfamiliar to nonneuropsychologists. A typical procedure used by school psychologists and special educators is to seek test results that fulfill the legal requirements. In the case of evaluating learning disabilities, this may include a few initial screening measures to determine if the difference between IQ and achievement nears the level of difference required by state guidelines. Such assessment approaches to determine eligibility for services resembles a "numbers game" rather than a clinical analysis of an individual's functional strengths and deficits. In contrast, such a restricted criterion is rarely of interest to clinical neuropsychologists, who place more emphasis on identifying the child's underlying problem. As such, test results are not the explanation of behavior but the behavior in need of an explanation. Using brain-behavioral models, neuropsychologists use the results of testing to make inferences related to deficits in psychological functions, and it is the inference to brain-behavior or cognitive neuropsychological models that help neuropsychologists understand the underlying problems in learning.

School personnel may conduct an assessment that meets all of the requirements set forth in the law but not gain any better understanding about the learner's specific problems. Then again, clinical neuropsychologists may conduct an assessment that helps identify the learner's specific problem but not meet the requirements set forth by law. This is a primary problem for neuropsychologists in schools and a paramount obstacle. A prime example of this conflict is the legal adoption of discrepancy guidelines to identify learning disabilities, for which some states have arbitrarily adopted a simple point-discrepancy model (see McGrew, 1994, for a comparison of models). The clinical approach to determining deficits by clinical neuropsychologists is in stark contrast to simple point-discrepancy methods, and how decisions are made when the two methodologies conflict has been an unaddressed problem. Technically, even if the methods used by neuropsychologists are more valid and have more research support, single-point discrepancy methods, or other less valid methodologies, would take priority over clinical neuropsychological methods due to their closer adherence to legal guidelines.

Many other procedural differences exist between clinical neuropsychologists and school psychologists. The inferential methods used in neuropsychology may be unfamiliar to those in a school-based environment, and the process of deriving sufficient evidence to warrant educational accommodations as defined by the law may be in dispute. A number of inferential techniques have been developed to interpret neuropsychological assessment results (Reitan, 1974) that continue to be generalized to contemporary tests (Dean & Woodcock, 2003; Dean et al., 2003). In more quantitative approaches, these methods, in terms of evaluating test data, include a review of the (1) level of performance, (2) pattern of performance, (3) lateralization of function, and (4) pathognomonic signs (Jarvis & Barth, 1994). These methods of inference, as well as qualitative methods in neuropsychology, are incorporated into a theoretical context in which hypotheses are derived concerning the individual's current level of functioning. Test results are used to evaluate a variety of hypotheses concerning an individual's cognitive functioning or neurological integrity.

Qualitative approaches to neuropsychology place more emphasis on idiographic approaches than nomothetic approaches. Such approaches rely on case studies to demonstrate the particular effects of brain lesions. Because more emphasis is placed on individual factors, less reliance is placed on normative testing. Such approaches rely more heavily on brain-behavior models. For example, Luria (1973, 1980) proposed three functional units of the brain, of which the second and third units were further defined by primary, secondary, and tertiary properties. He used this model, and some other theoretical postulates, to explain the functional deficits of case studies. Because of reliability issues, however, idiographic and qualitative approaches are best used to supplement or support normative approaches in test interpretation (Hale & Fiorello, 2004).

Regardless of perspective, clinical neuropsychologists often rely on brain-behavior models in test interpretation. In contrast, school psychologists and educational personnel rarely use theoretical models to guide test interpretation and primarily make decisions from a psychometric approach. Partially in reflection of test theory, the emphasis in educational assessment is almost completely in estimating the individual's overall ability level in a variety of domains. Trait or true score estimation is particularly focused on the overall magnitude of scores. Although an individual's overall score on a particular test has relevance for clinical neuropsychologists as well, other areas are of equal or greater importance, such as score profiles (comparison across different scores), processing characteristics, qualitative analysis, lateral differences, and pathognomic signs. Additionally, an individual's relative standing in a group, as conveyed by standard scores, is only one part of the information used to make decisions. School neuropsychologists may interpret differences between test scores as reflecting functional differences in cognitive processing and, in extreme cases, as double dissociations in cognition. Because score discrepancies are relative, to reflect processing differences similar patterns must be found among a variety of tests. In contrast to the neuropsychologist's profile approach, in educational evaluations score comparisons are made with rigidity and without a conceptual model to interpret the meaning of the discrepancy.

The behavioral domains observed or evaluated by neuropsychologists directly reflect the theoretical correspondence to areas of brain functioning (see D'Amato, Rothlisberg, & Leu Work, 1999, for a review). In contrast, educational testing typically involves two domains: intelligence and achievement. It has long been established that intelligence, or a global composite of multiple test results, has a substantial relationship to academic achievement. However, its usefulness in neuropsychology is outdated. Lezak's (1988) article "IQ: R.I.P." addressed many issues concerning the lack of specificity inherent in global test scores and composites and the misuses in interpreting IQ scores. This issue relates to the fact that neuropsychologists primarily evaluate learners to determine, diagnose, and understand the specific cognitive or neuropsychological strengths and difficulties that are manifested. As such, possessing a conceptual understanding of intelligence (i.e., intelligence versus cognitive abilities) is another noteworthy difference between neuropsychologists and school psychologists.

Given the complexity of terminology and procedures in neuropsychology, it is difficult for school personnel to judge how neuropsychological evidence coincides with existing legislative guidelines for determining eligibility for special education. Additionally, neuropsychological opinions may be less determined by federal guidelines than by theoretical perspectives on clinical disorders. School or clinical neuropsychologists may complete a lengthy evaluation that involves results from numerous brain-based systems/domains; such evidence may demonstrate a clear weakness in a particular psychological process. However, school personnel may look solely for particular data (e.g., a discrepancy between IQ and achievement) in the results. Sometimes these data sources are in conflict. For example, a neuropsychologist using his or her own methods of inference could determine a problem exists, whereas school personnel do not, or vice versa.

## SYNTHESIZING NEUROPSYCHOLOGICAL PROCEDURES WITH EDUCATIONAL LAW

Despite these procedural differences, there are many indicators of greater synthesis between school neuropsychological approaches and approaches used in education to determine eligibility for special education. Additionally, there are many alternative routes in which the neuropsychologists' opinion can be heard. Because, by law, the determination of a disability in schools is based on a case conference committee, the opinions and information provided by a neuropsychologist must be integrated in the existing framework of how schools work. At the point where school-based inferences and neuropsychological beliefs conflict, it is a matter of persuasion on the part of the neuropsychologist to help the case conference committee understand the collected data and how they relate to the child's functioning. This may be the reason many schools have hired their own school neuropsychologist rather than rely on consulting clinical neuropsychologists. A clear and methodical presentation of the facts and how the inferences were made based on evidence becomes a powerful tool. As brain-based teaching methods and other brain-related issues are being widely assimilated into educational contexts, such persuasion is becoming easier for both schools and clinical neuropsychologists.

As previously detailed, the school or clinical neuropsychologist must work within the existing guidelines of educational law. In some circumstances, in the best interests of the learner, this may include adapting and fitting the neuropsychological diagnosis into a category that fits federal guidelines. Indeed, this may indicate using all federal guidelines to this end. Children whose condition does not fit neatly into one of the 13 IDEA categories may still receive services under the other health impaired (e.g., learners with Attention-Deficit/Hyperactivity Disorder) category. Many contemporary evaluation techniques and tools used in education are become more like those used in neuropsychology; for example, various contemporary psychometric tests frequently used in educational settings advocate diagnostic approaches. Contemporary test developers whose tests have a long history in education advocate for the *diagnostic* use of testing. As stated by Woodcock (2002, p. 1), "The primary purpose of cognitive testing should be to find out more about the problem, not to obtain an IQ."

Constructs in many contemporary tests reflect neuropsychological approaches in that measurements are taken of neurocognitive functions (e.g., auditory processing, visual processing, language). Similarly, psychometric models of intelligence such as the Cattell-Horn-Carroll model (CHC; Carroll, 1993) have expanded psychometric models that include more functional areas and a cross-battery approach (Flanagan & Ortiz, 2001). School and clinical neuropsychologists rely on a broad range of tests to determine patterns across various areas of functioning (Lezak, 1995). The cross-battery approach resembles neuropsychological techniques, comparing results from numerous tests to look for patterns of strengths and weaknesses, as does the CHC psychometric framework.

Although the procedures and technology used in neuropsychological diagnosis are becoming more like those used by psychologists, and although federal law is changing to support such changes, the simplistic use of psychological tests in the past has undoubtedly impacted the perceived usefulness of testing in schools. Other professionals observing the one-dimensional criterion used to determine the existence of a complex clinical condition (e.g., simple-point discrepancy between IQ and achievement) no doubt perceive such technology as worthless and understandably have searched for better methods (e.g., curriculum-based assessment, consultation). Such resignation is only amplified by the underlying rationale provided by psychometric-based evaluations. What does a discrepancy signify about a child? Why 20 points, why not 19 or 18? So, too, the distinction between IQ and achievement is ill defined, and some tests even contain achievement-related content in the estimation of IQ. From a brain-based perspective, both IQ and achievement involve many of the same underlying neurocognitive processes that are based on the same underlying structure, the brain.

The use of diagnostic testing in schools has seen a decrease as alternative approaches deemed more useful have been on the rise. For example, curriculum-based assessment procedures have been advocated as the dominant assessment practice in school psychology (Fuchs, 2004). Likewise, functional behavioral assessment paradigms have been offered as an alternative to traditional psychometric models (Ervin & Ehrhardt, 2001). In contrast, surveys indicate that neuropsychologists increasingly spend a substantial amount of time administering and interpreting tests (Camara, Nathan, & Puente, 2000). Because school and clinical neuropsychologists place an emphasis on evaluation, there is a risk of neuropsychological services being viewed as "more of the same" and a lack of appreciation for the procedural differences between neuropsychologists and school psychologists. However, when the results and procedures of the neuropsychological evaluation are made clear, it is only in rare cases where educational personnel will not find value in the input of a neuropsychologist. Indeed, such input is usually of great value in developing accommodations and interventions, and when evaluations are thorough and professional, most school personnel come to view the input of the school or clinical neuropsychologist as critical.

Currently, IDEA is under reauthorization. A proposed aspect of the reauthorization is to lessen the emphasis on discrepancy models to diagnose children with learning disabilities. This could be good for school neuropsychologists, as it makes available alternative forms of evidence to inform diagnostic decision making in an effort to enhance instruction. However, there also is a proposed lessening of testing altogether in response to a more intervention-based model. These methods rely less on diagnostic testing to determine an individual's specific problem and tailoring the intervention to the problem, and more on curriculum-based measurement that simply monitors outcomes of general interventions. Identification of a disability is determined by how a child responds to an intervention. This proposed change is a direct challenge to the predominant evaluation-based methodology used to identify disabilities, as discrepancy models may misidentify children and take a "wait and fail" approach.

School psychologists must understand multiple approaches and be free to utilize all the tools at their disposal to help children. The growing antitesting movement in schools, as reflected in proposed changes in the law, is a result of frustration with the simplistic, outdated procedures used by many school psychologists. Although the degree of resistance legal changes will bring to neuropsychological evaluations in schools can only be approximated, it provides an additional opportunity and impetus for school neuropsychologists to share their techniques and procedures in the hope of improving educational instruction in the schools. Furthermore, changes in the law require school neuropsychologists to demonstrate the utility of their diagnostic procedures through a study of their ecological validity and their evidence basis (see Chapter 37 of this volume). In regard to neuropsychology as a whole, there has been a substantial lack of research on the ecological validity of neuropsychological testing, especially with children, and in the field of school neuropsychology it is nonexistent.

There are numerous obstacles to overcome when interfacing neuropsychological methods and procedures in the schools. As discussed in Chapter 1 of this volume, all of the obstacles point to the need for training that blends school psychology practice with neuropsychological rehabilitation. For neuropsychologists to function in the schools, they must understand both federal and state guidelines that regulate special services in schools, as well as how each state uniquely implements and follows the guidelines. Also, they must be aware that school-based psychologists and personnel typically have extremely different training from clinical neuropsychologists, who may have widely different beliefs about the causes of behavior.

For school psychologists to function as school neuropsychologists, it is important to obtain training in brain-behavioral models, clinical disorders, rehabilitation planning, and decision-making techniques. Proficiency in these areas is well beyond that of one or two university courses on the topic and should involve both practicum and internship experiences. Because school psychologists are traditionally trained in psychometric testing, which forms the foundation of neuropsychological assessment, the procedural and methodological aspects of neuropsychology should not be unfamiliar. In fact, contemporary approaches to psychometrics, such as problem-solving approaches to testing using the CHC model, are similar to neuropsychological techniques and make neuropsychological training less difficult.

As the field of school neuropsychology begins to flourish, it is important for the field to define itself and understand what part of it is neuropsychology and what part is school psychology. Systematic guidelines for such training must be developed. Finally, for school psychologists, complete reliance on pure psychometric approaches are of limited utility and will eventually go the way of IQ (R.I.P.).

Such approaches must be backed by clinical models of behavior as well as a better understanding of the cognitive processes involved in tests beyond that of factor descriptions. The emergence of these various areas will provide unprecedented aid when developing academic interventions.

## CONCLUSION

The acceptance and practice of neuropsychology in the schools is well documented. Over the past 30 years, the value of neuropsychological techniques in the diagnosis, evaluation, and treatment of children classified with disabilities in the schools has increased markedly. It is clear that school neuropsychology has become part of the educational landscape and will continue to play a significant role in meeting the educational needs of all learners.

This chapter focused on providing an overview of the major educational and antidiscrimination legislation passed in the past 30 years. The primary goal was to provide a summative overview of legislation, not an exhaustive discussion, with the objective of assisting neuropsychologists when providing psychological interventions in the school setting. The unique contributions made by school neuropsychologists when working with learners, parents, and school personnel were also discussed. This was accomplished by providing specific examples and recommendations that neuropsychologists may wish to consider when advocating for learners, given current federal, state, and district policies. The chapter also examined the theoretical orientation of neuropsychologists compared to other psychologists working in the schools. In summary, school neuropsychologists, like school psychologists, must become familiar with current legislative mandates and study legislative updates if they are to provide appropriate psychological services in the schools.

## REFERENCES

Alston, R. J., Russo, C. J., & Miles, A. S. (1994). Brown v. board of education and the American with disabilities act: Vistas of equal educational opportunities for African Americans. *Journal of Negro Education, 63*(3), 349–357.

American with Disabilities Act. (1990). 42 U.S.C.A. Sections 12101–12213.

Bernstein, B. E., & Hartsell, T. L. (1998). *The portable lawyer for mental health professionals.* New York: Wiley.

Camara, W. J., Nathan, J. S., & Puente, A. E. (2000). Psychological test usage: Implications in professional psychology. *Professional Psychology: Research and Practice, 31*(2), 141–154.

Carroll, J. B. (1993). *Human cognitive abilities: A survey of factor-analytical studies.* New York: Cambridge University Press.

D'Amato, R. C. (1990). A neuropsychological approach to school psychology. *School Psychology Quarterly, 5*(2), 141–160.

D'Amato, R. C., & DiUglio-Johnson, S. M. (1996). Neuropsychology laboratory. In T. K. Fagan & P. G. Warden (Eds.), *Historical encyclopia of school psychology* (pp. 234–235). Westport, CT: Greenwood.

D'Amato, R. C., Rothlisberg, B. A., & Leu Work, P. H. (1999). Neuropsychological assessment for intervention. In T. B. Gutkin & C. R. Reynolds (Eds.), *Handbook of school psychology* (3rd ed., pp. 452–475). New York: Wiley.

D'Amato, R. C., Rothlisberg, B. A., & Rhodes, R. L. (1997). Utilizing a neuropsychological paradigm for understanding common educational and psychological tests. In C. R.

Reynolds & E. Fletcher-Janzen (Eds.), *Handbook of clinical child neuropsychology* (2nd ed., pp. 270–295). New York: Plenum Press.

Dean, R. S., & Woodcock, R. W. (2003). *The Dean-Woodcock Neuropsychological Assessment System.* Itasca, IL: Riverside.

Dean, R. S., Woodcock, R. W., Decker, S. L., & Schrank, F. A. (2003). A cognitive neuropsychological assessment system. In F. L. Schrank & D. P. Flanagan (Eds.), *WJ III Clinical use and interpretation* (pp. 345-375). San Diego, CA: Elsevier Science.

Education for all Handicapped Children Act of 1975, PL No. 94-142, § 20 U.S.C., 34 C.F.R.

Elementary and Secondary Education Act of 1965 (20 U.S.C. § 631 *et seq.*).

Ervin, R. A., & Ehrhardt, K. E. (2001). Functional assessment: Old wine in new bottles. *School Psychology Review, 30*(2), 173–179.

Fagan, T. K., & Sachs-Wise, P. (2000). *School psychology: Past, present, and future* (2nd ed.). Bethesda, MD: National Association of School Psychologists.

Family Educational Rights and Privacy Act of 1974, PL No. 93-380, § 20 U.S.C., 34 C.F.R.

Flanagan, D. P., & McGrew, K. S. (1997). A cross-battery approach to assessing and interpreting cognitive abilities: Narrowing the gap between practice and cognitive science. In J. L. Genshaft and D. P. Flanagan (Eds.), *Contemporary intellectual assessment: Theories, tests, and issues* (pp. 314–325). New York: Guilford Press.

Flanagan, D. P., & Ortiz, S. (2001). *Essentials of cross-battery assessment.* New York: Wiley.

Fuchs, L. S. (2004). The past, present and future of curriculum-based measurement research. *School Psychology Review, 33*(2), 188–192.

Gaddes, W. H. (1981). An examination of the validity of neuropsychological knowledge of educational diagnosis and remediation. In G. Hynd & J. Obrzut (Eds.), *Neuropsychological assessment and the school-age child: Issues and procedures* (pp. 27–84). Boston: Allyn & Bacon.

Hale, J. B., & Fiorello, C. A. (2004). *School neuropsychology: A practitioner's handbook.* New York: Guilford Press.

Hicks, P. A. (1996). Section 504 of the rehabilitation act. In T. K. Fagan & P. G. Warden (Eds.), *Historical encyclopedia of school psychology* (pp. 353–354). Westport, CT: Greenwood Publishing Group.

Hynd, G. W. (1981). Training the school psychologist in neuropsychology: Perspectives, issues, and models. In G. Hynd & J. Obrzut (Eds.), *Neuropsychological assessment and the school-age child: Issues and procedures* (pp. 379–404). Boston: Allyn & Bacon.

Hynd, G. W., & Obrzut, J. E. (1981). School neuropsychology. *Journal of School Psychology, 19,* 45–50.

Individuals with Disabilities Education Act, 1990, PL No. 101-476, § 2, 104 Stat. 1103. (1991).

Individuals with Disabilities Act (Pub. L. No. 101-476), 20 U.S.C. chapter 33. Amended by Pub. L. No. 105-117 in June 1997. Regulations appear at 34 C.F.R. Part 30.

Jacob, S., & Hartshorne, T. S. (2003). *Ethics and law for school psychologists* (4th ed.). Hoboken, NJ: Wiley.

Jacob-Timm, S., & Hartshorne, T. S. (1994). Section 504 and school psychology. *Psychology in the Schools, 31,* 26–39.

Jarvis, P. E., & Barth, J. B. (1994). *The Halstead-Reitan Neuropsychological Battery: A guide to interpretation and clinical applications.* Odessa, FL: Psychological Assessment Resources.

Kamphaus, R. W. (1993). *Clinical assessment of children's intelligence.* Boston: Allyn & Bacon.

Kamphaus, R. W., Reynolds, C. R., & Imperato-McCammon, C. (1999). The roles of diagnosis and classification in school psychology. In C. R. Reynolds & T. B. Gutkin (Eds.), *The handbook of school psychology* (3rd ed., pp. 292–306). New York: Wiley.

Lezak, M. D. (1988). IQ: RIP. *Journal of Clinical and Experimental Neuropsychology, 10,* 351–361.

Lezak, M. D. (1995). *Neuropsychological assessment* (3rd ed.). New York: Oxford University Press.

Luria, A. R. (1973). *The working brain: An introduction to neuropsychology.* New York: Basic Books.

Luria, A. R. (1980). *Higher cortical functions in man.* New York: Basic Books.

McGrew, K. S. (1994). *Clinical interpretation of the Woodcock-Johnson Tests of Cognitive Abilities-Revised.* Needham Heights, MA: Allyn & Bacon.

National Transition Network. (1994, Summer). *Youth with disabilities and the School-to-Work Opportunities Act of 1994* [Policy update.] Minneapolis, MN: Author.

No Child Left Behind Act of 2001 (Pub. L. No. 107-110). Most recent set of amendments to the Elementary and Secondary Education Act of 1965. Available from www.ed.gov.

Perla, M. (1998). *Section 504: An introduction for parents.* Bethesda, MD: National Association of School Psychologists.

Prasse, D. P. (2002). Best practices in school psychology and the law. In A. Thomas & J. Grimes (Eds.), *Best practices in school psychology, IV* (pp. 57–75). Bethesda, MD: National Association of School Psychologists.

Rehabilitation Act of 1973, 29 U.S.C. § 794.

Reitan, R. M. (1955). Investigation of the validity of Halstead's measures of biological intelligence. *A. M. A. Archives of Neurology and Psychiatry, 73,* 28–35.

Reitan, R. M. (1974). Methodological problems in clinical neuropsychology. In R. M. Reitan & L. A. Davidson (Eds.), *Clinical neuropsychology: Current status and applications* (pp. 19–46). New York: Wiley.

Roberts, R., & Mather, N. (1995). Legal protections for individuals with learning disabilities: The IDEA, Section 504, and the ADA. *Learning Disabilities Research and Practice, 10*(3), 160–168.

Rothlisberg, B. A., & D'Amato, R. C. (1988). Increased neuropsychological understanding seen as important for school psychologists. *NASP Communiqué, 17,* 14.

Sealander, K. A. (1999). Confidentiality and the law. *Professional School Counseling, 3*(2), 6, 122.

Sheridan, S. M., & D'Amato, R. C. (2003). Partnering to chart our futures: *School Psychology Review* and *School Psychology Quarterly* combined issue on the multisite conference on the future of school psychology. *School Psychology Review, 33*(1), 7–11.

Silver, C. H., & Oakland, T. D. (1997). Helping students with mild traumatic brain injury: Collaborative roles within schools. In E. R. Bigler, E. Clark, & J. E. Farmer (Eds.), *Childhood traumatic brain injury: Diagnosis, assessment, and intervention* (pp. 239–258). Austin, TX: ProEd.

Underwood, J. K., & Mead, J. F. (1995). *Legal aspects of special education and pupil services.* Boston: Allyn & Bacon.

Warden, P. G. (1996a). Public Law 93-380: Family educational rights and privacy act. In T. K. Fagan & P. G. Warden (Eds.), *Historical encyclopedia of school psychology* (pp. 308–310). Westport, CT: Greenwood Publishing Group.

Warden, P. G. (1996b). Americans with disabilities act. In T. K. Fagan & P. G. Warden (Eds.), *Historical encyclopedia of school psychology* (pp. 22–23). Westport, CT: Greenwood Publishing Group.

Woodcock, R. W. (2002). New looks in cognitive assessment. *Peabody Journal of Education, 77*(2), 6–22.

Yesseldyke, J., & Geenen, K. (1996). Integrating the special education and compensatory education systems into the school reform process: A national perspective. *School Psychology Review, 25*(4), 418–430.

# CHAPTER 16

# Understanding the School Neuropsychology of Nosology, Pediatric Neuropsychiatry, and Developmental Disorders

MARGARET SEMRUD-CLIKEMAN, ELIZABETH PORTMAN, and
AIMEE GERRARD-MORRIS

DIAGNOSIS IN THE fields of psychology, psychiatry, and neurology share common ground in seeking to evaluate the child's functioning and determine the presence (or absence) of significant clinical difficulties. Psychiatry and neurology pursue diagnosis from a medical point of view, that is, looking for symptoms that fit a particular clinical picture. Although neurologists and psychiatrists may request laboratory tests, the history is the paramount part of data gathering for diagnosis.

Swaiman (1999) urges that the history-taking procedure be viewed as at least as important as the laboratory evaluations and describes it as a "dynamic diagnostic quest" that is crucial to the diagnostic purpose (p. 1). Psychologists and psychiatrists also use history taking as one of the most important parts of diagnosis, stressing the aspects of the child's development that are crucial for differential diagnosis. Neuropsychologists seek to understand the relationships between medical and psychological functioning in children. For all of these professionals, the history is paramount for diagnostic purposes. School psychologists also utilize the diagnostic process in evaluating children and determining appropriate educational placement. The emphasis for psychologists working in the schools is somewhat different, as it is important to determine the child's learning abilities and the effect that behavioral, academic, and emotional difficulties may have on the child's functioning. A medical point of view is not as useful for school psychologists, but it is important that they understand the diagnostic classifications frequently used in a medical setting.

## DIAGNOSTIC AND STATISTICAL MANUAL OF MENTAL DISORDERS

Psychiatrists and neurologists use diagnostic criteria that are generally discussed in one of two volumes: the *Diagnostic and Statistical Manual of Mental Disorders* (*DSM*; American Psychiatric Association, 2000) or the *International Classification of Diseases* (*ICD*). The *DSM* has been revised several times; the most recent version is the *DSM-IV-TR* (2002). The *ICD* has been revised to include clinical disorders as well as medical disorders; the current edition is *ICD-10* (WHO, 1992) with a clinical modification in the process of being finalized and implemented. The *DSM-TR* is generally considered more comprehensive and more frequently used by practitioners (American Psychiatric Association, 2000; Hynd, & Willis,1988).

The *DSM* editions are focused on clinical, research, and educational purposes and have sought to establish an *empirical basis* for the diagnostic criteria of mental disorders (American Psychiatric Association, 2000). The *DSM* is a product of 13 member work groups, each of which had responsibility for a designated section of the manual. Editions have been developed to assist in providing a common language for professionals as to the defining features of a disorder, which, of course, is critical to intervention planning. The *DSM* system utilizes field trials to study the various diagnoses and their response to treatment. These field trials also helped bridge the possible gulf between clinical and research practices.

The *DSM* revision conceptualized each disorder as a "clinically significant behavioral or psychological syndrome . . . that occurs in an individual and that is associated with present distress . . . or disability . . . or with significantly increased risk of suffering death, pain, disability, or an important loss of freedom" (American Psychiatric Association, 2002, p. xxxi). The *DSM* seeks to classify the disorder, not the person; as such, it does not refer to clients as schizophrenic but to persons with schizophrenia (American Psychiatric Association, 2000).

Although the classification system also seeks to divide mental disorders into defining features, few disorders are discrete, and individuals frequently show differing symptoms and degrees of symptoms. Thus, the categories should be considered a probabilistic method of diagnosis, with the recognition that clinical judgment, experience, and flexibility are of vital importance.

The *DSM-IV* provides a multiaxial approach that evaluates not only the diagnostic criteria but also medical and social/adaptive contributions. Each area is an axis with the following demarcations:

Axis I: Clinical disorders

Axis II: Personality disorders and mental retardation

Axis III: Medical disorders

Axis IV: Psychosocial and environmental problems

Axis V: Global assessment of functioning

The following sections discuss what each of these categories measure and how psychologists and psychiatrists use them to inform diagnosis.

### Axis I

This category consists of psychiatric disorders except for personality disorder and mental retardation, which are coded on Axis II. These disorders consist of the major categories of psychiatric diagnosis. Included in this category are depression, anxiety, posttraumatic stress disorder, bipolar disorder, psychotic disorders, dementia, and substance abuse. The categories most relevant to children are learning disorders and attention-deficit/hyperactivity disorders. In addition to the broad psychiatric diagnoses, this axis also includes the adjustment disorders. Adjustment disorders are of short duration and are seen as a reaction to environmental stressors. In addition, this axis contains eating disorders, sleep disorders, somatoform disorders, sexual and gender identity disorder, and dissociative disorders. In addition to these psychiatric conditions are V disorders that are also coded on Axis I. These include relational difficulties, problems related to abuse or neglect, and additional conditions that are a focus of clinical attention (not complying with treatment, malingering, and bereavement).

## Axis II

These disorders include the personality disorders as well as mental retardation. It is not clear why personality disorders and mental retardation are on the same axis, and this grouping is not explained in the *DSM* handbook. Axis II may also be used for delineating maladaptive personality features as well as behaviors. It is not uncommon to have an Axis I diagnosis and an Axis II diagnosis. The manual suggests that the primary diagnosis should be indicated in the list of diagnoses (American Psychiatric Association, 1987). Axis II is not considered a lesser diagnostic category compared to Axis I. These diagnoses were separated to provide emphasis on maladaptive personality features that interfere with adjustment. Included on this axis are borderline personality disorder, narcissistic personality disorder, antisocial personality disorder, dependent personality disorder, and histrionic personality disorder, to name a few.

## Axis III

Axis III includes general medical conditions that are relevant to the person's psychiatric diagnosis and treatment. These medical conditions are related to the mental disorders in that sometimes the medical diagnosis is directly related to the etiology of Axis I. In these cases, the disorder should be listed on both Axis I and III. For example, a common side effect of hypothyroidism is depression. Thus, hypothyroidism should be listed on Axis III and mood disorder due to hypothyroidism on Axis I (American Psychiatric Association, 1987). In other situations, the Axis I diagnosis may be an outgrowth of the Axis III diagnosis. For example, a person diagnosed with multiple sclerosis (Axis III) may also show an adjustment reaction (Axis I) or a depressive reaction (Axis I) to the diagnosis; both should be coded. Children with cystic fibrosis (Axis III) may show oppositional behavior, noncompliance to treatment, and other reactions that need to be classified on Axis I. All relevant medical disorders should be reported on Axis III. If no Axis III diagnosis is present, then a code of "none" should be applied; if clinicians are unsure about medical diagnoses that impinge on Axis I or II, this should be indicated by writing "deferred."

## Axis IV

Axis IV involves an estimation of the person's psychosocial functioning and any environmental problems that are present. These difficulties include negative life events (death, arrest, legal problems, problems in school), familial or interpersonal stress (divorce, breakup of a relationship), economic difficulties (loss of a job, bankruptcy), and lack of social support. These difficulties may go hand in hand with the person's Axis I or Axis II diagnosis, or they may be problems that need to be addressed in the treatment program. For multiple difficulties, the areas of concern that are relevant to the person's treatment should be listed. Problems are generally listed that have been present during the preceding year. Difficulties from the past that are continuing to influence the client's treatment should also be noted. This category is important for treatment planning as well as an estimation of how the client will respond to intervention.

## Axis V

Axis V is the global assessment of functioning (GAF). This category is the clinician's judgment of how the person is doing. Similar to Axis IV, it is a judgment of how the person is responding, or will respond, to treatment. The GAF is rated only in respect to "psychological, social and occupational functioning . . . and (does not) include impairment in functioning due to physical (or environmental) limitations" (American Psychiatric Association, 1987, p. 30). The rating is from 1 to 100, followed by the time period reflected in the rating. Some clinicians include two GAFs: one for the current level and one for the highest level in the past year. This is not an exact scale, and most clinicians use it broadly. Table 16.1 summarizes the broad categories.

## Summary

The *DSM* axial system is not meant to be an ironclad diagnosis but is a working system that communicates areas of concern to other professionals. In addition, it

**Table 16.1**

GAF Ratings

| | |
|---|---|
| 91–100 | Superior functioning |
| 81–90 | Minimal symptoms |
| 71–80 | Transient symptoms or expected reactions to environmental stressors |
| 61–70 | Some mild symptoms |
| 51–60 | Moderate symptoms |
| 41–50 | Serious symptoms |
| 31–40 | Impairment in reality testing or communication or impairment in several areas of life |
| 21–30 | Delusions/hallucinations present or serious impairment in communication or inability to function in all areas |
| 11–20 | Danger of hurting self or others, failure to maintain personal hygiene, or gross impairment in communication |
| 1–10 | Persistent danger of severely hurting self or others, inability to maintain minimal hygiene, or serious suicidal act with expectation of death |

Adapted with permission from *Diagnostic and Statistical Manual of Mental Disorders IV,* by American Psychiatric Association, 1994, Washington, DC: Author.

can assist in treatment planning as well as providing a gross yardstick of progress the person is making in treatment. The multiaxial approach uses diagnostic codes that are numbers assigned to each diagnosis by the *DSM.* An example of a multi-axial approach to a child with learning disabilities and anxiety disorder may look like the following:

| | | |
|---|---|---|
| Axis I: | 300.02 | Generalized anxiety disorder |
| | 315.0 | Reading disorder (primary) |
| Axis II: | None | |
| Axis III: | Otitis media, recurrent | |
| Axis IV: | Homeless, academic problems | |
| Axis V: | GAF = 53 (current) | |

The multiaxial system can be utilized in many different situations. For many clinicians, it is best used as a hypothesis to inform treatment. In other cases, it can be used to differentiate among various diagnoses. There is frequent comorbidity between diagnoses, and such overlap can assist in clearing up the diagnostic picture. For example, children who are anxious or sad can have difficulty with attention. Similarly, children with ADHD who are not succeeding in school or with friends may become sad. In such cases, it is possible to list what the clinician believes is the primary disorder and also place the secondary diagnosis in the system. In other cases, the diagnosis may not be clear and the clinician may specify "R/O" ("rule out") or "provisional," indicating that further evaluation and/or observation is necessary to obtain a diagnosis. The following section describes an approach to diagnosis that utilizes both the multiaxial system and testing to determine the most appropriate diagnostic category for the child/adolescent.

## HYPOTHESIS TESTING

An approach to evaluation that has been helpful and applicable to neuropsychology and school psychology is the use of hypothesis testing. This approach relies on the history taking as well as assessment of the child to determine possible alternative diagnoses. For example, a child may have difficulty with attention due to attention-deficit/hyperactivity disorder (ADHD), anxiety disorder, depression, or a metabolic disorder, to name a few. A comprehensive social history and the results of psychological tests can assist in determining the most appropriate diagnosis and, more important, the most effective intervention. The use of a hypothesis-testing approach requires familiarity with diagnostic nomenclature and disorders that are frequently comorbid or overlapping. This approach provides an opportunity to incorporate information from several sources, including medical personnel, school personnel, and family data. A well-trained clinical psychologist or school neuropsychologist or a school psychologist with some training in neuropsychology may be able to relate *medical, academic,* and *family* data to determine appropriate interventions. However, higher-level inferences needed to determine functional brain-behavior relationships are most appropriate for a trained clinical neuropsychologist (Hartlage & Long, 1997).

The following sections of this chapter are designed to provide the school psychologist with familiarity of the neuropsychology of internalizing and externalizing disorders. We do not mean to imply that after reading these sections, school psychologists will be prepared to conduct a working hypothesis diagnosis of the learners they evaluate (see Chapter 1).

## PSYCHOPATHOLOGY

Psychopathology has been related to brain dysfunction in several types of children, but the contribution of such brain dysfunction has not been fully examined empirically (Tramontana & Hooper, 1989). Direct effects are those related to specific behaviors of disinhibition, attention deficits, memory deficits, and the like. Indirect effects are those that produce an emotional or behavior disturbance as the learner attempts to deal with difficulties, such as frustration and failure. At times, the caretakers in the child's life may view him or her as unmotivated, difficult, or slow, thus serving to exacerbate the problems at home (Tramontana & Hooper, 1989). For example, a recently evaluated learner had an ateriovenous malformation that hemorrhaged and needed to be removed surgically. After 2 months in the hospital recuperating from this surgery, the child was mainstreamed back into school with little preparation or support provided. This learner was easily fatigued, did not complete his schoolwork, and appeared "depressed" and unmotivated. The teacher began enforcing consequences for these behaviors, and the child became more angry and sad and was referred for evaluation for "emotional disturbance." An evaluation found significant learning deficits, memory problems, and difficulty with attention, and recommendations were developed for an acquired brain injury support. In this case, the teacher's lack of understanding as well as the school's lack of preparation for this child's reentry by the medical personnel involved in the case set the child up for more difficulties than were originally present.

The relationship between brain dysfunction and psychopathology is likely nonspecific; children may simply show poor adaptability and problems in dealing with life's struggles (Boll & Barth, 1981). Support for this view comes from work that finds no identical psychiatric symptoms related to closed-head injury (Semrud-Clikeman, 2001), conduct disorders and depression (Tramontana & Hooper, 1989), and ADHD (Kusche, Cook, & Greenberg, 1993). In addition, a history of nonspecific neurological deficits or neuropsychological impairment appears to be more common in learners with internalizing behaviors such as depression, anxiety, and withdrawal (Rutter, Chadwick, & Schaffer, 1983; Shaffer et al., 1985).

## NEUROPSYCHOLOGY OF INTERNALIZING DISORDERS

Internalizing disorders are those that generally are not disruptive behaviors and that indicate the child is experiencing "internal" difficulties (Sattler, 2002). Such disorders are manifested in the form of depression, anxiety, withdrawal, and isolation. These disorders are generally covert and not readily observed—hence the difficulty in identification of depression and anxiety in children (Semrud-Clikeman, Bennett, & Guli, 2002). These disorders are more distressing to the child but less obvious to parents and teachers.

NEUROPSYCHOLOGY OF DEPRESSION IN CHILDREN

Depression is a heterogeneous construct that is primarily characterized by impaired mood or loss of pleasure; it can also include symptoms of irritability, insomnia, and fatigue (American Psychiatric Association, 2000). The disorder commonly co-occurs with anxiety or conduct problems as a result of complications of the depression (Kovacs, 1996). It is important to note that much of our current knowledge of childhood depression, its origins, and the neuropsychological implications come from research of depression in the adult population. Only a limited number of studies have investigated the neuropsychological features of childhood depression.

Several models have been developed to explain the neuroanatomical basis of depression in adults. Researchers have shown that there is an overall reduction of cerebral activity in depressed individuals (Kolb & Whishaw, 1990). The neuropsychological implications of this diffuse activity reduction are poor cognitive processing, reduced attention span, reduced memory, difficulty with new learning, difficulty with task completion, and impaired concentration (Teeter & Semrud-Clikeman, 1997).

Many researchers rely on the model that links the disorder to the right hemisphere. Generally speaking, the right cerebral hemisphere is thought to regulate emotion, arousal, and attention (Shenal, Harrison, & Demaree, 2003). Right frontal dysfunction has been found to impair nonverbal fluency and to promote perseverative responses to cognitive tasks. Empirical data involving children and adolescents support the right-hemispheric theory of depression. Researchers have demonstrated that children on antidepressants have improved performance on tasks sensitive to frontal and right-hemisphere functioning (Brumback, Staton, & Wilson, 1980; Staton, Wilson, & Brumback, 1981).

Children with depressive symptoms have demonstrated deficits in nonverbal reasoning on cognitive ability tests, specifically those that require attention to detail and memory (Blumberg & Izard, 1985; Kaslow, Rehm, & Siegel, 1984). For example, scores on the Children's Depression Inventory (CDI; Kovacs & Beck, 1977) have been shown to be negatively correlated with scores from the Block Design (Blumberg & Izard, 1985), Coding, and Digit Span subtests of the Wechsler Intelligence Scale for Children-Revised (Kaslow, Rehm, & Siegel, 1984; Wechsler, 1974). Thus, clinically significant ratings of depression are correlated with lowered performance on nonverbal reasoning tasks. In these studies, however, children's performance on verbal intelligence tasks were not related to CDI scores (Blumberg & Izard, 1985; Kaslow, Rehm, & Siegel, 1984). Tramontana and Hooper (1987) suggest that this pattern of performance on tasks that are less verbally mediated may be related to depressed concentration and motor speed rather than right hemisphere dysfunction.

NEUROPSYCHOLOGY OF BIPOLAR DISORDER

Bipolar disorder (BPD) is a chronic mental illness that typically is manifested in cycles of mania, depression, or mixed mood states. This mood disorder affects approximately 0.5% of all adults; its prevalence in children is less certain (American Psychiatric Association, 2000). The controversy about the presence of BPD in young learners warrants further attention. Due to the variance in manifestation of symptoms and the complexity in distinguishing it from other disorders (e.g., depression and ADHD), BPD in children is difficult to diagnose. Although manic symptoms resemble ADHD symptoms, making the ADHD diagnosis redundant, it is often the case that both disorders are present. Likewise, conduct and anxiety disorders are often comorbid disorders with BPD (Gellar & Luby, 1997). There is a need for expansion of knowledge about the cognitive functioning of children and adolescents with BPD (Shear, DelBello, Rosenberg, & Strakowski, 2002). Researchers' and practitioners' understanding of the cognitive and neuropsychological differences in this population of children is based partly on studies with bipolar adults and partly on studies involving children genetically at risk for BPD. Studies with children or adolescents who have a *DSM-IV* diagnosis of BPD are limited due to reasons previously cited.

Adult studies have shown that individuals with BPD experiencing abnormal moods are deficient in cognitive functioning, specifically in the areas of attention, memory, verbal fluency, and executive functioning (see Shear, DelBello, Rosenberg, & Strakowski, 2002, for a review). Some of these deficits have been shown in studies with children. For example, in groups of children genetically at risk for developing BPD based on having a parent with BPD, researchers demonstrated that significant discrepancies exist between Verbal and Performance IQ (VIQ > PIQ; Decina et al., 1983; McDonough-Ryan et al., 2002). Although PIQ scores remained in the average range, this discrepancy maintains practical significance as it implies relative right hemisphere deficits (Decina et al., 1983).

This discrepancy between cognitive abilities also has implications for the functioning of executive processes such as novel problem solving and fluid abilities (McDonough-Ryan et al., 2002; Shear, DelBello, Rosenberg, & Strakowski, 2002). Shear, DelBello, Rosenberg, and Strakowski investigated the executive functioning skills of 31 adolescents diagnosed with BPD or BPD and ADHD. The Behavior Rating Inventory of Executive Function (BRIEF; Gioia, Isquith, Guy, & Kenworthy, 2000) was administered to the caregivers of these participants. Compared to healthy controls, adolescents with BPD had significant impairments on tasks mediated by executive functions, including behavior regulation (e.g., inhibitory control and emotional control) and metacognitive functions (e.g., working memory, planning, organization, and self-monitoring). These results are consistent with other studies correlating BPD with frontal-subcortical brain circuitry dysfunction. As this region of the brain is thought to control executive functions, dysfunction in this skill is an "expected feature of the disorder" (Shear, DelBello, Rosenberg, & Strakowski, 2002, p. 292).

In addition to cognitive deficiencies, learners at risk for BPD and learners who have been diagnosed with BPD tend to have deficits in areas of academic achievement (McDonough-Ryan et al., 2002; Wozniak et al., 1995), language skills, social skills, and motor functioning (Sigurdsson, Fombonne, Sayal, & Checkley, 1999). Furthermore, children and adolescents diagnosed with BPD have been shown to have impairments on tasks requiring problem solving, short-term memory for faces and names, visual attention, and visual-motor speed and accuracy (Castillo, Kwock, Courvoisie, & Hooper, 2000).

## Neuropsychology of Anxiety Disorders

In general, anxiety disorders are characterized by excessive anxiety and worrying about specific stimuli (e.g., snakes, heights, socialization) or nonspecific stimuli. The disorder is commonly comorbid with other anxiety disorders, depression, and ADHD (see Bernstein & Shaw, 1997, for review). Evidence exists that anxiety disorders originate from an increased arousal in the limbic system (Kagan, Arcus, Snidman, & Feng-Wang-Yu, 1994). There is also evidence that early neurological soft signs, particularly in the area of coordination, are predictive of a psychiatric anxiety-withdrawal diagnosis (Shaffer et al., 1985). In their study, Shaffer et al. found a positive relationship between neurological abnormalities at age 7 and the presence of affective disorders in adolescence. The authors of this study speculate that the relationship between anxiety and neuromotor difficulties may be explained by organic factors directly leading to anxious behaviors (Shaffer et al., 1984).

Anxiety disorders in children may be overlooked by their parents and teachers due to the child's lack of overt displays of behavior problems and the presence of generally average intelligence (Kusché, Cook, & Greenberg, 1993; Toren et al., 2000). Specific cognitive processing deficits, however, are likely to be present, as shown in a study by Kusché, Cook, and Greenberg. These researchers compared three groups of children with psychopathology (i.e., anxiety/somatic-only, externalizing-only, and comorbid symptomatology) to normal controls. In general, all three psychopathology groups exhibited more cognitive and academic deficits compared to children without internalizing or externalizing symptoms. Specifically, weaknesses in executive functioning by all three symptomatic groups suggest that frontal lobe dysfunction may be related to psychopathology in general, rather than a specific type of psychopathology. Compared to controls, children in the anxiety/somatic-only group exhibited deficits in verbal tasks (i.e., Verbal Fluency and short-term verbal memory), some nonverbal tasks (i.e., Block Design and Nonverbal Analogies), and general intelligence. According to these authors, the comparable levels of these bilateral impairments suggest that "anxiety may be related to interference with specific aspects of tertiary processing in the temporal-parietal areas" (Kusché, Cook, & Greenberg, 1993, p. 189).

Other neuropsychological deficits have been shown in the executive function of cognitive flexibility (Toren et al., 2000). Deficits in nonverbal processes (Toren et al., 2000), visual-motor speed, right-left orientation, and perceptual motor ability (Kusché, Cook, & Greenberg, 1993) are not prevalent for children with anxiety disorders.

Linguistic deficits are a common feature reported in the body of research on child anxiety disorders. In a study of children with learning disabilities, Glooser and Koppell (1987) found that children with deficits on tasks associated with left hemisphere cognitive functions (e.g., word recognition) displayed depressive and anxious symptomatology at greater rates than those with right hemisphere cognitive impairments. Another study lending support to the link between anxiety and linguistic deficits demonstrated that children with anxiety disorders had significantly lower scores on a test that requires them to learn a list of words as compared to matched controls (Toren et al., 2000). This pattern of performance may be explained by the poor working memory or attention deficits that often characterize learners with anxiety (Tannock, Ickowicz, & Schachar, 1995). Livingston, Stark, Haak, and Jennings (1996) have contested that attention and concentration problems may result from the somatic symptoms or excessive worry that interfere with the learner's ability to focus on a task. In their study, these authors demonstrated that such attention problems are worse among learners with a comorbid anxiety/depressive disorder.

In summary, internalizing disorders are easily differentiated on paper, though slightly more challenging to differentiate in the clinical setting. The rates of comorbidity and the wide range of behavioral symptoms make distinguishing such internalizing disorders difficult. The behavioral manifestation of the internalized behavior problems also makes the child's neuropsychological profiles variant. It appears that children with depression have neuropsychological deficits indicative of right hemisphere dysfunction, including visuospatial processing and nonverbal reasoning. Children with BPD appear to have executive processing difficulties, perhaps due to the comorbid attention deficits that are common to this population. Memory deficits are also prevalent for children with BPD. Unlike children with depression or BPD, children with anxiety disorders have neuropsychological profiles dominated by verbal processing weaknesses. Children with comorbid anxiety and depression tend to have greater neuropsychological impairments, particularly attentional deficits, than children with a single diagnosis.

## ASSESSMENT WITH CHILDREN WITH INTERNALIZING DISORDERS

The evaluation of children with internalizing disorders can be difficult depending on how forthcoming the child is about his or her difficulties. As noted earlier, some disruption may be present on measures requiring attention and memory. Memory difficulties are often related to difficulties with attention, as if the input of information is faulty, and the child is unable to retrieve information that was not learned (Teeter & Semrud-Clikeman, 1997). In the assessment of internalizing disorders it is very important to use a multi-instrument, multi-informant method. Information needs to be obtained from parents, teachers, and the child and should include behavioral data as well as interviews and projective techniques as necessary. Most school psychologists are not trained in advanced projective measures and should refer the child to child psychologists or neuropsychologists for such assessments.

Given the strong comorbidity between internalizing disorders and neurological difficulties, it is very important to rule out medical and neurological causes prior to arriving at a diagnosis of depression, anxiety, or BPD. Moreover, it is very important to establish good rapport with the child, as research indicates that a good relationship increases the validity of the child's response, particularly for those with suspected depression (Birleson et al., 1987).

## NEUROPSYCHOLOGY OF EXTERNALIZING DISORDERS

Externalizing disorders are characterized by persistent behavioral deficits that clearly interfere with developmentally appropriate social, academic, or occupational functioning. Included in this category of impairment are children with ADHD and those with disruptive disorders such as conduct disorder (CD) and oppositional defiant disorder (ODD). Moreover, children with ADHD often have a comorbid diagnosis of CD or ODD (American Psychiatric Association, 2000). The behavioral problems that children with externalizing disorders exhibit can be linked to neurological impairments (Sattler, 1992; Teichner & Golden, 2000).

The following section provides a review of the neuropsychological underpinnings of children with ADHD and with disruptive behavior disorders.

### ATTENTION-DEFICIT/HYPERACTIVITY DISORDER

Inattention, hyperactivity, and impulsivity are the key problems related to ADHD. This disorder is appropriately diagnosed by indicating one of three subtypes that best fits the child's behavioral pattern: ADHD combined type, predominantly inattentive type, or predominantly hyperactive-impulsive type (American Psychiatric Association, 2000). Children with ADHD combined type exhibit significant behavioral difficulties associated with both inattention and hyperactivity-impulsivity. Children with the predominantly inattentive type demonstrate extreme symptoms associated with sustained attention (but not hyperactivity), whereas the predominantly hyperactive-impulsive type describes children who show severe problems primarily related to hyperactive and impulsive behaviors (but not inattention).

Disharmony can be common in families of children with ADHD and may be reflected through marital dissatisfaction between parents, high levels of parenting stress, and frequent discordant interactions between parents and children with ADHD (Hinshaw & Zalecki, 2001). In a study by Gerdes, Hoza, and Pelhaam (2003), the mothers and fathers of ADHD boys perceived their relationships with their children more negatively than did parents of the control sample. ADHD status of the boys in this sample significantly predicted mothers' and fathers' perceptions of their relationships with their children. Parents of ADHD children perceived themselves to display less warmth and more power assertion to their children. Peris and Hinshaw (2003) explored the relationship between parental expressed emotion and ADHD status of adolescent girls. Expressed emotion was examined as a two-dimensional construct assessed by levels of parental criticism and emotional overinvolvement. The researchers found that high parental expressed emotion is strongly positively associated with ADHD, and it is also linked with child aggression. These studies highlight the important link between family dynamics and ADHD-related behaviors.

Social difficulties are centrally associated with the performance deficits shown by ADHD children, and the social implications of this disability become especially salient during adolescence (Sattler, 1992). These individuals may be seen as socially immature because they lack the ability to regulate and plan their behavior, thereby making it difficult for them to appropriately reciprocate in social situations and inhibit inappropriate behaviors. Although these children have knowledge of social norms, they are unable to independently monitor their behavior in a way that allows them to carry out these socially appropriate behaviors (Clark, Prior, & Kinsella, 2002). For example, children with ADHD may find it challenging to focus on conversations with others. They may frequently interrupt conversations or be extremely fidgety in sedentary situations. During play, these children may have difficulty following rules and taking turns. They may make embarrassing or hurtful comments to peers, making friendships difficult to maintain.

Academic problems are common among the ADHD population, as reflected by lowered achievement test scores, special education placement, and high drop-out rates (Hinshaw & Zalecki, 2001). Symptoms of restlessness, inattention, and impulsivity make it difficult for these children to follow classroom rules, remain attentive during discussions, and focus on important details related to school-work. The problematic behaviors associated with ADHD may be especially obvious in the typical classroom setting, where children are often required to remain still, attentive, and engaged in repetitive tasks that lack novelty (American Psychiatric Association, 2000). The core symptoms of ADHD cause these children to miss out on important information taught in the regular classroom setting, which can potentially lead to academic struggles and eventual failure.

Barkley (1997) has proposed that ADHD is the manifestation of a core deficit in basic inhibitory functions that influence behavior. These children tend to perform poorly on tasks of sustained attention and on measures requiring a delay of impulse. Poor performance on such tasks likely reflects deficits of executive function (Sattler, 1992). Kalff et al. (2002) found that, in a sample of children ages 5 to 6, participants who had ADHD with and without comorbid CD/ODD were significantly impaired on measures of working memory and visual perceptual and motor integration ability when compared to control children and those with rated CD/ODD. The authors concluded that these impairments are associated with an ADHD diagnosis and imply deficient higher-order processes such as executive functioning. Clark, Prior, and Kinsella (2002) also found that, among a sample of adolescent participants, children with ADHD exhibited difficulties related to executive functioning when compared to children without an ADHD diagnosis. These impairments were reflected through participants' poor self-regulation and strategic planning skills that are related to social functioning and adaptive communication.

Language impairments have also been noted in children with ADHD. Hogg-Johnson and Tannock (2003) found that ADHD boys ages 9 to 12 had significantly more difficulty than normal children in higher-level comprehension skills such as making inferences and monitoring their comprehension of expository passages. The authors found that these comprehension difficulties were significantly related to impairments in working memory, which is suggested to be a key cognitive correlate of ADHD. Clark et al. (2002) found that deficient word reading abilities of adolescents was associated with an ADHD diagnosis. The authors suggested that these decoding weaknesses may be associated with poor strategic planning abilities.

Barkley (1997) conceptualizes ADHD as a disorder of *doing* rather than *knowing*, where impairments involve behavioral disinhibition instead of the acquisition of skills or knowledge. In a study conducted by Kalff et al. (2002), perceptual input processing skills in young ADHD children were intact, but their motor control output skills were deficient. Scheres, Oosterlaan, and Sergeant (2001) found that ADHD and ADHD+ODD children demonstrated slow response execution in the stop paradigm performance task compared to ODD-only and normal participants. These findings support the conceptualization of ADHD as a performance deficit, and they indicate that ADHD children have difficulties with the cross-modal transfer and planning of information to motor output. Furthermore, the difficulties in planning could be tied to impairments in executive functions.

## DISRUPTIVE BEHAVIOR DISORDERS

Delinquent children tend to more often have neuropsychological impairments than nondelinquent children (Sattler, 1992), and children with childhood-onset CD exhibit higher rates of neuropsychological dysfunction than the adolescent-onset group (Frick & McCoy, 2001). Luria (1980) theorized that behaviors such as aggression are the result of complex interactions between the brain and external environmental factors. For example, for the child who develops in an environment that does not encourage the use of inhibitory skills, the prefrontal areas of the brain will perhaps be dysfunctional, thereby resulting in an adolescent who exhibits no impulse control.

Like children with ADHD, those with CD and ODD are thought to have weaknesses in planning and carrying out proper behaviors, rather than in possessing the skills or knowledge to do so. Kalff et al. (2002) found that a sample of ODD/CD adolescents performed within the average range on a task of perceptual closure capacity, showing intact input processing abilities. Egan, Brown, Goonan, Goonan, and Celano (1998) found that the ability to emotionally decode video scenes across verbal, prosody, facial, and combined modalities was not impeded by a CD or ODD diagnosis among a sample of children. The authors of this study concluded that behavior disordered children have difficulty not with the decoding of emotions, but with the process of encoding emotion, which will influence the emission of social behaviors.

Disruptive behavior disorders are often associated with a lower IQ, particularly VIQ. The perceptual abilities of conduct disordered children tend to be better developed than their verbal abilities, although the presence of this discrepancy cannot be used as a diagnostic tool for the identification of CD (Sattler, 1992). Loney, Frick, Ellis, and McCoy (1998) found that verbal comprehension weaknesses were associated with an ODD or CD diagnosis among a sample of children without callous and unemotional traits. On the other hand, CD/ODD children with callous and unemotional traits did not show a verbal deficit; in fact, they showed a weak tendency toward nonverbal learning deficits. These results lead to the conclusion that behavior disordered children without callous and unemotional traits may more often display verbal difficulties, which can be an indicator of left-hemispheric brain dysfunction. These deficits can hamper abilities to engage in problem-solving activities, to engage in positive social exchanges, and to benefit from the academic learning environment.

Disruptive behavior disorders have also been linked to problems with executive functions, although research results related to this aspect of functioning vary. Executive functions are related to the prefrontal cortex, and they include ability to initiate goal-directed behavior and purposeful motor sequences, to sustain attention and concentration, and to inhibit impulsive behaviors. The research documenting a relationship between deficient executive functions and disruptive behaviors is equivocal. Moffit (1990) concluded in a literature review that delinquent children perform poorly on measures of executive functions, but Kalff et al. (2002) reported that children with ODD/CD did as well as control children on tasks of working memory and executive functions. Conduct disordered adolescents in Dery, Toupin, and Pauze's (1999) study did not differ from control children on measures of executive function.

Clark, Prior, and Kinsella (2002) found that although both CD/ODD adolescents and ADHD adolescents had underdeveloped social behavioral skills, the developmental pathways for these deficiencies differed for the two groups. Whereas executive function problems reflected the adaptive problems leading to social difficulties for ADHD children, hostile attributions more adequately explained the social deficiencies demonstrated by the delinquent child sample.

These results suggest that the behavioral difficulties related to problems of poor impulse control and attention may not be explained best by deficits in executive functions among this population of children. As suggested by Clark et al., negative behaviors among CD/ODD youth may be the result of faulty processing of social information.

In summary, children with externalizing disorders demonstrate difficulties in carrying out socially acceptable behaviors, although they do possess the skills for understanding social cues and norms. For children with ADHD, this performance deficit is linked to poor performance on tasks of executive functioning and language ability. In particular, these children tend to do poorly on tasks of sustained attention, visual-motor integration, and higher-level comprehension skills. Executive function impairments make it difficult for ADHD children to plan and carry out appropriate behaviors while inhibiting their impulses. Their struggles with language comprehension further block them from engaging in successful social interactions with others in their environment.

Children with disruptive behavior diagnoses of ODD or CD also exhibit verbal weaknesses that can hamper social problem-solving and classroom learning capabilities. Furthermore, the association between verbal difficulties and disruptive behavior problems may be less salient for children who demonstrate callous and unemotional traits. Although some research supports the presence of executive dysfunction among CD/ODD youth, several fairly recent studies (Dery et al., 1999; Kalff et al., 2000) have found that CD/ODD children perform as well as control children on tasks of executive functions. Researchers such as Clark et al. (2002) hypothesize that the negative behaviors of disruptive children may be the result of distorted social information processes such as negative attributional bias.

## ASSESSMENT WITH EXTERNALIZING DISORDERS

Similar to the assessment of children with internalizing disorders, psychologists evaluating those with acting-out disorders need to be cognizant of the behaviors that may occur. Children with ADHD may need more frequent breaks and support, and those with ODD or CD may require sufficient patience and behavioral control for them to complete the tasks appropriately. Children with developmental delays including retardation and/or autism are frequently challenging to evaluate and cause even the most experienced examiner difficulty. It is important that these difficulties be noted in the report because for many children, underestimates of ability may be due to challenging behaviors.

Many learners with neurological disorders may appear to have diagnoses of ADHD or ODD/CD but in fact be showing behaviors consistent with metabolic, head injury, or genetic disorders. Children with undiagnosed epilepsy may well appear to have attentional problems that are misdiagnosed as ADHD. The school psychologist may not be able to identify these disorders, so it is very important during the general assessment to take note of genetic risk factors as well as psychological test results that do not conform to an expected pattern.

The well-informed school psychologist will realize when a child should be referred for a neurological or psychiatric evaluation. A child who is experiencing difficulties that are unusual in nature or do not conform to expectations from testing needs to be further evaluated. For example, a child who shows difficulty with attention in the classroom, is not disruptive, appears to daydream, seems out of touch with reality, and has difficulty learning both academically and socially should be evaluated for possible seizure disorder, prepsychotic diagnoses, or genetic disorders.

An example may help to clarify this point. A high school student was referred for neuropsychological evaluation by her psychiatrist and school psychologist. She was experiencing significant difficulty with peer relationships, could become combative at home, frequently stared into space, and seemed to be out of touch with reality. A full neuropsychological assessment indicated no difficulties with attention, learning, or executive functions. Intellectual evaluation found above-average ability with no areas of weakness. Prior to this child's sophomore year, she had been an honor student. Her performance progressively became worse until she failed all of her junior-level courses. Medication for ADHD had not been helpful. An MRI and EEG were negative. Projective evaluation and diagnostic interviewing indicated the emergence of Paranoid Schizophrenia and the significant anxiety that frequently accompanies this disorder. Treatment plans were modified, as were medications for this young woman. Improvement was seen following intensive therapy and family support work. The initial diagnosis for this woman was ADHD based on behavioral rating scales completed by her teacher and parents. This unidimensional assessment neglected important aspects of the woman's functioning and did not utilize the differential diagnosis method suggested by the *DSM* (American Psychiatric Association, 1994). Tying together her emotional functioning with appropriate assessment techniques and consultation with medical personnel allowed for a more appropriate diagnosis.

## CONSULTATION WITH MEDICAL PROFESSIONALS

School psychologists are in the best position to translate information from medical personnel and records to school personnel. The neurological terms, aspects, and recommendations can at times be quite difficult to understand. It is, however, important that the school psychologist understand brain anatomy as well as functional relationships between brain and behavior.

One of the most important changes for children with neurological insults or psychiatric residential placements is reentry into the school setting. The ability of the school to program for these children has been found to be one of the main predictors for a good outcome (McKee & Witt, 1990; Ylvisaker et al., 1993). Variables such as teacher personality qualities, peer interactions, and school environment have been found to be the most predictive (Farmer & Peterson, 1995).

Many teachers are not prepared for the challenges provided by children with neurological and psychiatric difficulties. Some teachers may even be fearful of the child and feel intimidated by the diagnoses. For this reason, inservices for the reentry of these children and for those who are newly identified are crucial for success (Semrud-Clikeman, 2001). It has been suggested that these inservices are the responsibility of the individualized education plan (IEP) team. Required modifications to the curriculum and school day should be explained in detail, with opportunity for questions and concerns (Mira & Tyler, 1991).

The school psychologist is in a unique position to assist with this transition, not only in interpreting medical jargon to the teacher but also providing assistance in understanding the child's needs and requirements. The child mentioned earlier, who was recovering from neurosurgery, needed such interpretations for his teacher to understand his needs. Unfortunately, no adjustment was made and no transition between hospital and school was provided. Once the teacher became informed of this child's needs, he was very willing to assist and provided numerous accommodations that were beyond what was requested. It is enlightening that the teacher reported to the neuropsychologist, "I thought since he was released from the hospital, he was fine." This assumption is understandable but resulted in significant emotional distress.

It is therefore important that the school psychologist assist the teacher and the IEP team in developing a program for the child. Key behaviors can be readily misinterpreted by school personnel not familiar with neurological or psychiatric difficulties. Another example of misguided judgment involved a child who was experiencing florid hallucinations and was reported by his teacher to be very creative and in need of gifted and talented resources.

Learning environments are also important to consider when programming for these children. Most neurologists and psychiatrists are not familiar with academic requirements and are unable or unwilling to assist with academic intervention planning. This task is most appropriate for the school psychologist and IEP team. Determining the level of structure required by the child and then matching this level to the appropriate teacher can be of immeasurable help.

In addition to assisting with school transition, it is important to involve the parents in programming. Families report that the most helpful information about their child is the level of his or her health, the educational programs available to the child, and the agencies available for help (Miller, 1993). Many parents of children with significant neuropsychological disabilities will have worked with a number of professionals and may be disillusioned by numerous differences of opinions as to outcome and treatment. They may carry these feelings into the relationship with the school (Martin, 1988). It is very important that school personnel be aware of these stresses and provide as much support as possible for the parents.

Providing parents with practical information about the child's progress as well as educational needs is an important way school psychologists can translate neurological and psychiatric information into practical suggestions. Information may need to be frequently repeated, and patience is required. Parents may be struggling with many issues that are unknown to the school, including financial hardship, marital stress, and family discord that frequently accompany these disorders (Semrud-Clikeman, 2001).

Meetings that include large numbers of people are intimidating to most parents. Likewise, sending reports without explanation via the mail may result in parents not reading the report, being overwhelmed by the information, or feeling isolated and possibly angry at the school. It is important to assist parents in understanding the process as well as what the school expects of their child (Conoley & Sheridan, 1996). The school psychologist needs to remind the team that the parents' subjective burden (feelings about the child's disorder and the stress from the disorder) has been found to increase over time, and school meetings may exacerbate these feelings. Close follow-up between parents and teachers as well as school psychologists is very important.

## CONCLUSION

The diagnosis of a child's disorder, whether neurological, psychiatric, or educational, is just the beginning. A neurologist or psychiatrist will look at the needs of a learner quite differently from an educator. Many times, the needs of the parents or the child for learning are overlooked, as aspects of the disorder become of paramount importance. The medical model stresses the need to find areas of difficulty rather than areas of strength. In addition, this model stresses medical means of treatment, including psychopharmocology and hospitalization. This is in contrast to the educational model, which stresses the child's learning capabilities both academically and behaviorally and emotionally. Strengths as well as weaknesses are important aspects of the evaluation and provide a window into learning how to work with a child. An important difference in these models is that the neurologist or psychiatrist may see the patient only four times a year at most, whereas the teacher, school psychologist, and IEP team often interact with the learner on a daily basis. Developing the most appropriate program is not based solely on diagnosis but rather on *what* the child is able to do and *how* he or she is able to function.

Common developmental disorders discussed in this chapter indicate the need to understand how the child functions not only in a clinical setting but also in the real world. Many children are able to work fairly well in a structured setting but have great difficulty in situations such as recess and lunch, which are generally unstructured. One child deliberately misbehaved in order to miss recess and spend the lunch period with the teacher. When he had to earn this privilege, his behavior improved.

A school neuropsychologist can support the school system in understanding the information provided by medical personnel and in translating academic and educational needs for the medical profession. This bridging of information is very important for the success of the child. Consultation between professionals requires a common language, and a school psychologist with neuropsychological training can provide such assistance.

However, it is also important to recognize the boundaries of one's competence. It is the rare school psychologist who has sufficient training in neuropsychology to provide these services in the school system. It is even rarer for a doctoral-level school psychologist with postdoctoral training in neuropsychology to be employed by a school. It is important for most school psychologists to recognize their limitations in this regard and to know when to refer cases to appropriately trained school neuropsychologists. Working together can help the child develop to his or her full potential.

## REFERENCES

American Psychiatric Association. (1987). *Diagnostic and statistical manual of mental disorders-IIIR.* Washington, DC: Author.

American Psychiatric Association. (1994). *Diagnostic and statistical manual of mental disorders, IV.* Washington, DC: Author.

American Psychiatric Association. (2000). *Diagnostic and statistical manual of mental disorders* (4th ed., text rev.). Washington, DC: Author.

Barkely, R. A. (1997). *ADHD and the nature of self-control.* New York: Guilford Press.

Bernstein, G. A., Shaw, K., & the Work Group on Quality Issues. (1997). Practice parameters for the assessment and treatment of children and adolescents with anxiety disorders. *Journal of American Academy of Child and Adolescent Psychiatry, 36*(Suppl. 10), 69–84.

Blumberg, S. H., & Izard, C. E. (1985). Affective and cognitive characteristics of depression in 10- and 11-year-old children. *Journal of Personality and Social Psychology, 49*(1), 194–202.

Boll, T. J., & Barth, J. T. (1981). Neuropsychology of brain damage in children. In S. B. Fil-skov & T. J. Boll (Eds.), *Handbook of clinical neuropsychology* (pp. 418–452). New York: Wiley.

Brumback, R. A., Staton, R. D., & Wilson, H. (1980). Neuropsychological study of children during and after remission of endogenous depressive episodes. *Perceptual Motor Skills, 50,* 1163–1167.

Burns, G. L., & Walsh, J. A. (2002). The influence of ADHD-hyperactivity/impulsivity symptoms in a 2-year longitudinal study. *Journal of Abnormal Child Psychology, 30*(3), 245–256.

Castillo, M., Kwock, L., Courvoisie, N., & Hooper, S. R. (2000). Proton MR spectroscopy in children with bipolar affective disorder: Preliminary observation. *American Journal of Neuroradiology, 21,* 832–838.

Clark, C., Prior, M., & Kinsella, G. (2002). The relationship between executive function abilities, adaptive behavior, and academic achievement in children with externalizing behavior problems. *Journal of Child Psychology and Psychiatry, 43*(6), 785–796.

Conoley, J., & Sheridan, S. (1996). Pediatric traumatic brain injury: Challenges and inter-ventions for families. *Journal of Learning Disabilities, 29,* 662–669.

Decina, P., Kestenbaum, C. J., Farber, S., Kron, L., Gargan, M., Sackeim, H. A., et al. (1983). Clinical and psychological assessment of children of bipolar probands. *American Journal of Psychiatry, 140*(5), 548–553.

Dery, M., Toupin, J., & Pauze, R. (1999). Neuropsychological characteristics of adolescents with conduct disorder: Association with attention deficit-hyperactivity and aggres-sion. *Journal of Abnormal Child Psychology, 27*(3), 225–236.

Egan, G. J., Brown, R. T., Goonan, L., Goonan, B., & Celano, M. (1998). The development of decoding of emotions in children with externalizing behavioral disturbances and their normally developing peers. *Archives of Clinical Neuropsychology, 13*(4), 383–396.

Farmer, J., & Peterson, L. (1995). Pediatric traumatic brain injury: Promoting successful school entry. *School Psychology Review, 24,* 230–243.

Gerdes, A. C., Hoza, B., & Pelham, W. E. (2003). Attention-deficit/hyperactivity disor-dered boys' relationships with their mothers and fathers: Child, mother, and father perceptions. *Developmental and Psychopathology, 15,* 363–382.

Gioia, G. A., Isquith, P. K., Guy, S. C., & Kenworth, L. (2000). *Behavior rating inventory of ex-ecutive function.* Odessa, FL: Psychological Assessment Resources.

Glosser, G., & Koppell, S. (1987). Emotional-behavioral patterns in children with learn-ing disabilities: Lateralized hemispheric differences. *Journal of Learning Disabilities, 20*(6), 365–368.

Hartlage, L. C., & Long, C. J. (1997). Development of neuropsychology as a professional psychological specialty: History, training, and credentialing. In C. R. Reynolds & E. Fletcher-Janzen (Eds.), *Handbook of clinical child neuropsychology* (pp. 3–16). New York: Plenum Press.

Hinshaw, S. P., & Zalecki, C. (2001). Attention-deficit hyperactivity disorder. In H. Or-vaschel & M. Hersen (Eds.), *Handbook of conceptualization and treatment of child psycho-pathology* (pp. 77–104). New York: Pergamon Press.

Hynd, G. W., & Willis, G. W. (1988). *Pediatric neuropsychology.* Orlando, FL: Grune & Stratton.

Kalff, A. C., Hendricksen, J. M., Kroes, M., Vles, J., Steyaert, J., Feron, F., et al. (2002). Neurocognitive performance of 5- and 6- year-old children who met criteria for atten-tion deficit/hyperactivity disorder at 18 months and follow-up. *Journal of Abnormal Child Psychology, 30*(6), 589–599.

Kagan, J., Arcus, D., Snidman, N., & Feng-Wang, Yu. (1994). Reactivity in infants. *Develop-mental Psychology, 30,* 342–345.

Kaslow, N. J., Rehm, L. P., & Siegel, A. W. (1984). Social-cognitive and cognitive correlates of depression in children. *Journal of Abnormal Child Psychology, 12*(4), 605–620.

Kolb, B., & Whishaw, I. Q. (1990). *Fundamentals of human neuropsychology* (3rd ed.). San Francisco: Freeman.

Kovacs, M. (1996). Presentation and course of major depressive disorder during childhood and later years of the life span. *Journal of the American Academy of Child and Adolescent Psychiatry, 35,* 705–715.

Kovacs, M., & Beck, A. T. (1977). An empirical-clinical approach toward a definition of childhood depression. In J. G. Schulterbrandt & A. Raskin (Eds.), *Depression in childhood* (pp. 1–25). New York: Plenum Press.

Kusché, C. A., Cook, E. T., & Greenberg, M. T. (1993). Neuropsychological and cognitive functioning in children with anxiety, externalizing, and comorbid psychopathology. *Journal of Clinical Child Psychology, 22*(2), 172–195.

Lavigne, J. V., Cicchetti, C., Gibbons, R. D., Binns, H. J., Larsen, L., & Devito, C. (2001). Oppositional defiant disorder with onset in preschool years: Longitudinal stability and pathways to other disorders. *Journal of the American Academy of Child and Adolescent Psychiatry, 40*(12), 1393–1401.

Livingston, R. B., Stark, K. D., Haak, R. A., & Jennings, E. (1996). Neuropsychological profiles of children with depressive and anxiety disorders. *Child Neuropsychology, 2*(1), 48–62.

Looney, B. R., Frick, P. J., & McCoy, M. (1998). Intelligence, callous-unemotional traits, and antisocial behavior. *Journal of Psychopathology and Behavioral Assessment, 20*(3), 231–247.

Luria, A. R., 1980. *Higher cortical functions in man.* New York: Basic Books.

McKee, W. T., & Witt, J. C. (1990). Effective teaching: A review of instructional and environmental variables. In T. B. Gutkin & C. R. Reynolds (Eds.), *The handbook of school psychology* (pp. 821–846). New York: Wiley.

McDonough-Ryan, P., DelBello, M., Shear, P. K., Ris, M. D., Soutullo, C., & Strakowski, S. M. (2002). Academic and cognitive abilities in children of parents with bipolar disorder: A test of the nonverbal learning disability model. *Journal of Clinical and Experimental Neuropsychology, 24*(3), 280–285.

McInnes, A., Humphries, T., Hogg-Johnson, S., & Tannock, R. (2003). Listening comprehension and working memory are impaired in attention-deficit hyperactivity disorder irrespective of language impairment. *Journal of Abnormal Child Psychology, 31*(4), 427–444.

Martin, D. A. (1988). Children and adolescents with traumatic brain injury: Impact on the family. *Journal of Learning Disabilities, 21,* 464–470.

Miller, L. (1993). Family therapy of brain injury: Syndromes, strategies, and solutions. *American Journal of Family Therapy, 21,* 111–121.

Mira, M. P., & Tyler, J. S. (1991). Students with traumatic brain injury: Making the transition from hospital to school. *Focus on Exceptional Children, 23,* 1–12.

Peris, T. S., & Hinshaw, S. P. (2003). Family dynamics and preadolescent girls with ADHD: The relationship between expressed emotion, ADHD symptomatology, and comorbid disruptive behavior. *Journal of Child Psychology and Psychiatry, 44*(8), 1177–1190.

Rutter, M., Chadwick, O., & Shaffer, D. (1983). Head injury. In M. Rutter (Ed.), *Developmental neuropsychiatry* (pp. 83–111). New York: Guilford Press.

Sattler, J. M. (1992). *Assessment of children: Revised and updated* (3rd ed.). San Diego, CA: Jerome M. Sattler.

Sattler, J. M. (2002). *Assessment of children: Behavioral and clinical applications.* San Diego, CA: Jerome M. Sattler.

Semrud-Clikeman, M. (2001). *Traumatic brain injury in children and adolescents.* New York: Guilford Press.

Semrud-Clikeman, M., Bennett, L., & Guli, L. (2002). Assessment of childhood depression. In C. R. Reynolds & R. W. Kamphaus (Eds.), *Handbook of psychological and educational assessment of children* (2nd ed., pp. 259–290). New York: Guilford Press.

Scheres, A., Oosterlaan, J., & Sergeant, J. A. (2001). Response execution and inhibition in children with AD/HD and other disruptive disorders: The role of behavioural activation. *Journal of Child Psychology and Psychiatry, 42*(3), 347–357.

Shaffer, D., Schonfeld, I., O'Connor, P. A., Stokman, C., Trautman, P., Shafer, S., et al. (1985). Neurological soft signs: Their relationship to psychiatric disorder and intelligence in childhood and adolescence. *Archives of General Psychiatry, 42*(4), 342–351.

Shear, P. K., DelBello, M. P., Rosenberg, H. L., & Strakowski, S. M. (2002). Parental reports of executive dysfunction in adolescents with bipolar disorder. *Child Neuropsychology, 8*(4), 285–295.

Shenal, B. V., Harrison, D. W., & Demaree, H. A. (2003). The neuropsychology of depression: A literature review and preliminary model. *Neuropsychology Review, 13*(1), 33–42.

Sigurdsson, E., Fombonne, E., Sayal, K., & Checkley, S. (1999). Neurodevelopmental antecedents of early-onset bipolar affective disorder. *British Journal of Psychiatry, 174,* 121–127.

Staton, R. D., Wilson, H., & Brumback, R. A. (1981). Cognitive improvement associated with tricyclic antidepressant treatment of childhood major depressive illness. *Perceptual and Motor Skills, 53,* 219–234.

Swaiman, K. F. (1999). *Pediatric neurology: Principles and practice* (3rd ed.). St. Louis, MO: Mosby.

Tannock, R., Ickowicz, A., & Schachar, R. (1995). Differential effects of methylphenidate on working memory in ADHD children with and without comorbid anxiety. *Journal of the American Academy for Child and Adolescent Psychiatry, 34,* 886–896.

Teeter, P. A., & Semrud-Clikeman, M. (1997). *Child neuropsychology: Assessment and interventions for neurodevelopmental disorders.* Boston: Allyn & Bacon.

Teichner, G., & Golden, C. J. (2000). The relationship of neuropsychological impairment to conduct disorder in adolescence. *Aggression and Violent Behavior, 5*(6), 509–528.

Toren, P., Sadeh, M., Wolmer, L., Eldar, S., Koren, S., Weizman, R., et al. (2000). Neurocognitive correlates of anxiety disorders in children: A preliminary report. *Journal of Anxiety Disorders, 14*(3), 239–247.

Tramontana, M., & Hooper, S. (1989). Neuropsychology of child psychopathology. In C. R. Reynolds & E. Fletcher-Janzen (Eds.), *Handbook of clinical child neuropsychology* (pp. 87–106). New York: Plenum Press.

Weschler, D. (1974). *Wechsler Intelligence Scale for Children-Revised.* New York: Psychological Corporation.

Weinberg, W. A., & Emslie, G. J. (1988). Adolescents and school problems: Depression, suicide and learning disorders. In R. A. Feldman & A. R. Stiffman (Eds.), *Advances in adolescent mental health: Vol. 3. Depression and suicide* (pp. 181–205). Greenwich, CT: JAI Press.

World Health Organization. (1980). *International classification of diseases-9.* Brussels: Author.

Wozniak, J., Biederman, J., Kiely, K., Ablon, J. S., Faraone, S. V., Mundy, E., et al. (1995). Mania-like symptoms suggestive of childhood-onset bipolar disorder in clinically referred children. *Journal of the American Academy of Child and Adolescent Psychiatry, 34*(7), 867–876.

Ylvisaker, M., Feeney, T. J., & Urbanczyk, B. (1993). A social-environmental approach to communication and behavior after traumatic brain injury. *Seminars in Speech and Language, 14,* 74–87.

# CHAPTER 17

# Providing Neuropsychological Services to Students with Learning Disabilities

MARGARET SEMRUD-CLIKEMAN,
JODENE GOLDENRING FINE, and LANA HARDER

IT IS ESTIMATED that approximately 15% of children in the United States have a learning disability (LD), with the most common type being reading disorder (Sattler, 2001). Difficulties in mathematics and written language are also present but not at the same rate. There is controversy about the male-female ratio in learning disabilities, with some placing the incidence at 3 to 1 (DeFries & Gillis, 1991) and others at 1.5 to 1 (S. E. Shaywitz, 2003).

Part of the difficulty in determining incidence of learning problems is the varying definitions that are used. The current definition states that learning disabilities involve the central nervous system, with a significant discrepancy between ability and achievement. In addition, this difficulty is unexpected due to adequate cognitive abilities in other areas and adequate educational instruction (Lyon, Shaywitz, & Shaywitz, 2003). Difficulties may be found in listening comprehension, reasoning, reading, writing, spelling, and mathematics (Individual with Disabilities Education Act: Code of Federal Regulations, Title 34, Subtitle B, Chapter III, Section 200.7(b)(10)).

The definition requires that the learner has received adequate educational instruction. Children who are at risk for failing to learn may be from disadvantaged backgrounds and/or school systems. If the child's instruction is not adjusted for these early difficulties, reading failure that is not related to a *central nervous dysfunction* may occur due to instructional failure (Lyon, Shaywitz, et al., 2003). In this case, a LD does not exist, but an instructional disability does. Torgeson (2002) found that many children with reading failure identified in kindergarten and first grade who were then provided effective instruction went on to develop adequate skills. Lyon et al. (2003) suggests that children who do not profit from effective, empirically based instruction are those with a true LD, and those who receive inadequate instruction may not be truly learning disabled.

## DEFINITIONAL ISSUES

One controversy concerning the definition of a LD is the requirement of a severe or significant discrepancy between ability and achievement. In the past, the discrepancy has been defined as a difference between intelligence and a measure of academic achievement. Generally, tests such as the Wechsler Intelligence Scale for Children (WISC) and the Wechsler Individual Achievement Test (WIAT) or Woodcock-Johnson Achievement Battery (WJ) have been used to determine this discrepancy. States differ on the size of the discrepancy required for a child to qualify for services; some require 16 standard score points and others 27 to 30 standard score points. Lyon, Fletcher, and Barnes (2003) suggest that the use of a discrepancy formula eliminates children who truly require support and may overidentify those children who have reading problems due not to a biologically based LD but to poor teaching or lack of advantage.

This controversy has not been resolved and continues to be debated. The use of intelligence tests to identify children with learning disabilities may be based on faulty assumptions. IQ tests have been found to be good predictors of school success in children with no learning problems. However, Morrison and Siegel (1991) suggest that IQ tests are *not* good predictors of achievement in disabled learners. Performance on IQ tests is likely influenced by past learning, genetics, and situational factors (motivation, affect, temperament) and does not reflect aspects of behavioral and adaptive functioning that are crucial for success in school and in life (Fletcher et al., 1989; Siegel, 1989, 1992). It has been suggested that a variety of skills be evaluated, including but not limited to ability measures. Moreover, IQ and achievement have been found to be moderately correlated (Morrison & Siegel, 1991). With a moderate correlation present, approximately 50% of the variance is shared between the two measures.

These definitional problems have led many to suggest the use of empirically based learning tasks to differentiate between those children with and without biologically based learning problems. Children who respond to well-designed and well-implemented instruction are those who would not be identified as learning disabled. Those who continue to need additional support and whose response is not up to expectations are more likely to be children with a LD. Lyon, Fletcher, et al. (2003) suggest that identification must include an evaluation of skills related to the academic area being assessed, with underachievement determined by comparing the student to his or her peers. They further suggest that a team evaluate the child's needs and determine a diagnosis of LD.

Although the definition and method of evaluation continue to be controversial, the one common thread throughout the discussion has been the existence of academic underachievement. It is important to determine whether a child is continuing to experience problems in learning despite good teaching. If so, a neuropsychological evaluation can assist the team in determining whether the child needs specialized support.

Areas that have consistently been found to define learning problems in reading include word fluency, phonological processing, slow word processing, slow naming speed, and word accuracy (Chard, Vaughn, & Tyler, 2002). These areas need to be evaluated in children who are not responding to instruction. In mathematics, skills such as number facts, working memory, reasoning, and attention play a prominent role in learning (Jordan & Hanich, 2000; Shalev et al., 2001). These areas are more fully examined in the following section.

## COMORBIDITY

Children with learning disabilities have been found to show an increased incidence of attentional difficulties (Semrud-Clikeman, Hynd, Novey, & Eliopulos, 1991). However, the inattention and impulsivity characteristic of ADHD make it difficult to determine if academic difficulty is due to the presence of a LD or attentional deficits (Semrud-Clikeman et al., 1992). Language disorders, mood disorders, and social skill deficits are often experienced by those diagnosed with a LD (Kavale, Forness, & Lorsbach, 1991). Children with mathematics disabilities have been found to show more difficulty with adjustment, particularly with psychosocial functioning (Scarborough & Parker, in press). Almost three-fourths of a sample of second-grade children with mathematics disability showed significant behavioral difficulties, whereas those with sole reading disorder had behavioral scores similar to those of typically developing children. When these children were reevaluated 6 years later, the children with mathematics disorder continued to have more externalizing problems than did the other groups (Scarborough & Parker, in press).

Children with a sole diagnosis of reading disability may not show the same difficulties in adjustment as those with a dual diagnosis of reading and mathematics or those with a sole diagnosis of a mathematics-based LD. Many studies include children with reading and mathematics disabilities. The results of these studies have been equivocal, with some finding significant behavioral problems (Beitchman & Young, 1997; Cornwall & Bawden, 1992; Tsatsanis, Fuerst, & Rourke, 1997) and others finding behavioral problems only in those children with significant discrepancies between IQ and achievement or very low achievement (Hinshaw, 1992). Martinez and Semrud-Clikeman (2004) compared four groups—children with a reading disability, with a math disability, with a reading and comorbid math disability, and controls—on measures of adjustment. Findings indicated that the comorbid LD group evidenced greater maladjustment on measures of depression, adjustment, self-esteem, and feelings of adequacy relative to peers in the normally achieving group.

## BIOLOGICAL CONTRIBUTIONS TO LEARNING DISABILITIES

Emerging findings suggest that children with learning disabilities process information differently from those without learning problems. Differences in development have shown that fluent adult readers utilize the frontal regions more than children who are beginning to read (Schlaggar, 2003). The left frontal region becomes more active over development, with more fluent child readers activating this area more than children with difficulties (Schlaggar, Brown, & Lugar, 2002). Moreover, children with learning problems show a differential pattern from normal readers, activating the anterior word decoding system rather than the more fluent posterior whole-word recognition systems, as well as having more activation in the right hemisphere than do normally developing readers. The change from anterior (phonological decoding) to posterior (word-form) systems by more fluent readers suggests that fluency is built upon repeated decoding, and that disassociation of these systems in children with learning disabilities prevents fluency (B. A. Shaywitz, 2003). Moreover, children show a more diffuse activation when beginning to learn to read that gradually becomes more specialized as the reading process improves.

Similarly, when asked to read single words, normal readers showed left-hemispheric activation, whereas those with dyslexia showed more right-hemispheric activation (Breier, Fletcher, Foorman, Klaas, & Gray, 2003; Papanicolaou, 2003). Changes from right-hemispheric processing to left-hemispheric processing have been found to occur with improvement in reading skills. These changes are also found when improvement in language functioning occurs. Such changes are not found for children with dyslexia, as the reading process does not become automatic and effortless.

Gabrieli (2003) found that the region most responsible for auditory processing and language is more activated in good readers compared to those who had compensated for their dyslexia. The more activated the white matter tracts are that carry the signals throughout the brain, the better the scores on reading measures. These studies also found improvements in activation following remediation of auditory processing ability. Presently, it is not clear whether these changes continue over time, and further study is needed.

## VERBAL LEARNING DISABILITIES

Language-based learning disabilities are among the most recognizable and best researched of school-age problems. Although the various forms of language may be considered different systems (Berniger, Abbott, Abbott, Graham, & Richards, 2002), listening, speaking, reading, and writing share developmental reciprocity (Compton, 2002; Lerner, 1997; McCardle, Scarborough, & Catts, 2001). Each language mode facilitates the maturity of the other language skills from birth forward. It's not surprising, then, that verbal learning disabilities, or difficulty reading, spelling, and writing, that are unexpected in otherwise adequately developing children are often seen together in individually varying degrees rather than in isolation.

Evidence is mounting that both speech and reading disorders are familial and heritable (S. E. Shaywitz, 1998; Tunick & Pennington, 2002), making family history one of the most important risk factors. Genetic studies have begun to discern chromosomal loci that are implicated in reading disorders (Gayan & Olson, 2003; Grigorenko, 2001). Moreover, a review of brain imaging studies strongly indicates that there are structural differences between normal and clinically deficient readers (Grigorenko, 2001). Environmental influences, such as exposure to print, quality of instruction, and home environment, also interact reciprocally with developing language systems (Molfese & Molfese, 2002); thus, extrinsic variables should not be underestimated.

PREVALENCE

Reading difficulty is estimated to affect approximately 25% of schoolchildren in the regular classroom (Joshi, 2003), and estimates for the diagnosis of reading disability (RD) range from 5% to 10% (S. E. Shaywitz, 1998) to as high as 17.5% (Breier, Simos, et al., 2003) of the general population. School-based referrals for reading difficulties have been biased toward males, resulting in prevalence estimates two to four times higher for boys (Miles, Haslum, & Wheeler, 1999); however, research-based diagnosis of RD indicates that boys and girls are equally likely to have a reading disorder (S. E. Shaywitz, B. A. Shaywitz, Fletcher, & Escobar, 1990).

## PERSISTENCE ACROSS THE LIFE SPAN

Integrated and dependent on mutual development, deficits in language systems may be observed behaviorally in varying forms as children mature. Children with early articulation and speech delays at the age of 5 are likely to exhibit a reading disorder at 8 and a writing disorder at 14 (Lerner, 1997; Tunick & Pennington, 2002). The academic pressure to master reading in industrialized school systems (Grigorenko, 2001), coupled with the complexity of English and other irregular written languages (Goswami, 2003), has made reading disorders the most common of learning problems. Thus, LD researchers have focused on reading disorder, and it is from this body of literature that most of our information about verbal learning disabilities is derived.

Verbal learning disorders tend to be persistent across the life span. Children who have difficulty learning to read are likely to have reading deficits throughout adolescence (Grigorenko, 2001) and adulthood (Booth, Perfetti, MacWhinney, & Hunt, 2000; Felton, Naylor, & Wood, 1990; Ransby & Swanson, 2003), indicating that these deficits do not represent a transient developmental delay (B. A. Shaywitz et al., 1995; S. E. Shaywitz, 1998). Rather, early deficits in specific systems such as phonological processing may be remediated or compensated, but slow and effortful reading continues in adulthood in the form of short-term verbal memory (Snowling, 2000) and word-naming problems.

There is some disagreement as to whether reading disorders represent a graded continuum of normal processes on which children with deficits fall at the lower end of the curve (S. E. Shaywitz, Escobar, B. A. Shaywitz, & Fletcher, 1992) or are a discrete etiological condition (Grigorenko, 2001). As mentioned earlier, a child's response to remediation is one possible way of distinguishing garden-variety slow readers from the truly learning disabled. Although this question remains unanswered, investigation into the behavioral and neurological foundations of verbal learning disabilities consistently points to one of the basic language systems: phonological processing.

## PHONOLOGICAL PROCESSING

Phonological processing refers to the unconscious perception of the phonemic units of speech, though deficits in phonological processing are observed at the level of conscious processing, or "metaphonologic" ability (Brady, 2003). Phonological sensitivity develops in the early stages of preliteracy and refers to the awareness that words have phonological units such as beginning sounds and syllables. Over time, full phonemic awareness develops reciprocally with reading mastery as readers become able to recognize, segment, and manipulate the sound constituents of oral language (Habib, 2000). For example, normal readers can easily identify three sounds in the word *dog:* duh-aw-g. Furthermore, they can map the sounds to the alphabetic code. Language disorders related to phonological processing are conceived as a failure to perceive and extract phonemes from oral language, preventing efficient mapping of sound units to the appropriate symbols. Phonemic awareness has been proven to be a robust predictor of both reading (S. E. Shaywitz, 1998) and spelling disorders (Sawyer, Wade, & Kim, 1999).

## THE LEXICAL ROUTE

Early readers are thought to rely on conscious phonological decoding via print-to-sound conversion of letters to words. As readers mature, they develop a store of visual word forms that can be automatically recognized without phonological decoding. This process is sometimes referred to as the lexical, semantic, or orthographic route and is thought to be the foundation of reading fluency and comprehension. Researchers debate whether the lexical route is functionally and neurologically distinct from the phonological route (Berniger et al., 2002; Compton, 2002; Habib, 2000; Pugh et al., 2001; Wolf et al., 2002; Zeffiro & Eden, 2000). Snowling (2000) and others (Semrud-Clikeman, Guy, Griffin, & Hynd, 2000) suggest that the deficits seen in rapid automatic naming (RAN) of letters and numbers among persons with specific reading disability is a result of deficient phonological representations, not of poor word recognition. Others (Wolf et al., 2002) emphasize the modularity and independence of the two routes.

## MODELS OF READING DISORDER

All models of reading disorder assume a common core of phonological deficits, but there is much controversy over whether contributions from other cognitive domains are salient. At issue is whether there are identifiable subtypes within the broad definition of reading disability (RD). This discussion has given rise to several models of reading disorder.

Proponents of the dual-route model identify two RD subtypes based on a distinction between children with apparent phonological decoding versus word-reading deficits. Readers with phonological deficits (phonologic dyslexics) are poor decoders who read pseudo-words with great difficulty (e.g., *gluck, dring*) but may have relatively better irregular word identification skills (e.g., *weight, knight*). In contrast, "surface dyslexics" perform better at decoding than at recognizing irregular words (Stanovich, Siegel, & Gottardo, 1997). Although the existence of the two subtypes has been substantiated (Snowling, 2000), some research suggests that the surface dyslexic subtype is subsumed when reading-level rather than age-level matching to controls is used (Howes, Bigler, Burlingame, & Lawson, 2003).

Subtypes of reading disorder have also been identified on the basis of phonological and automatic word retrieval deficits. The speed and accuracy of lexical retrieval is observed when readers are asked to perform RAN of colors, objects, letters, or numbers. The underlying substrates of the task are controversial, as discussed earlier, but RAN tasks are known to be good predictors of RD (Grigorenko, 2001; Semrud-Clikeman et al., 2000). Wolf and colleagues (Wolf, 1986; Wolf & Bowers, 1999; Wolf et al., 2002) have proposed a three-subtype model for reading disorder: readers with a phonological deficit only, with a rapid naming deficit only, and those with a "double deficit" of both phonological and rapid naming deficits. Individuals with both deficits are expected to experience poorer outcomes.

Other theorists have emphasized temporal processing deficits affecting both the auditory and visuospatial modalities (Breier, Simos, et al., 2003; Tallal, Stark, & Mellits, 1985), memory (Howes et al., 2003), and visual timing in the magnosystem (for a review, see Habib, 2000). Alternatively, integrated "connectionist" models have been proposed emphasizing a single neural mechanism for verbal learning disabilities around which the developing brain reorganizes its functional systems in response to both genetic and environmental variables (Grigorenko, 2001).

## ASSESSMENT OF VERBAL LEARNING DISABILITIES

Traditional assessment for verbal learning disabilities has used the IQ-discrepancy model. The *Diagnostic and Statistical Manual of Mental Disorders* defines reading disability as underachievement based in part on "measured intelligence" (American Psychiatric Association, 1994, p. 50). However, as mentioned earlier, Stanovich (1993) and others (Joshi, 2003; Stage, Abbott, Jenkins, & Berniger, 2002) suggest that the IQ-discrepancy model has serious shortcomings. The relationship between IQ and reading changes over the life span (Stanovich, 1993), and the model tells us little about the specificity of the reading disorder, offers no guidance regarding remediation, and "undermines the very notion of Learning Disability and its usefulness as an educational concept" (Joshi, 2003, p. 13).

From the standpoint of program gatekeeping within the educational system, differentiating slow readers from those who are reading disabled is an economic reality. Stanovich (1993) suggested using cognitive measures other than IQ in learning disability assessment (cf. Teeter & Semrud-Clikeman, 1997). Joshi (2003) offers an assessment alternative to the IQ-discrepancy model, the componential model, which uses a discrepancy between listening and reading comprehension and emphasizes three independent components of reading: word recognition, comprehension, and speed of processing. It should be noted that sensory impairments, such as hearing and visual loss, should be ruled out first, especially in younger children.

*Word Recognition*   This first component of the componential diagnostic model includes assessment of phonological awareness, decoding skills, and spelling. There are several instruments available for testing phonological awareness, including the Comprehensive Test of Phonological Processing (CTOPP; Wagner, Torgesen, & Rashotte, 1999) and the Auditory Analysis Test (Rosner & Simon, 1971). Joshi (2003) emphasizes the importance of testing both speed and accuracy of pseudoword decoding, which can be accomplished with instruments such as the Test of Word Reading Efficiency (Torgesen, Wagner, & Rashotte, 1997). Poor spelling is more likely to be an indication of poor phonological skills than of visual memory deficits. Joshi suggests that spelling is a "more rigorous test of decoding than nonword reading" (p. 15), particularly when the spelling test includes only those words with which the child is familiar and has successfully read aloud. Careful analysis of spelling errors is encouraged to provide clues to the source of decoding errors indicated by the child's performance.

*Comprehension*   Joshi (2003), as has Stanovich (1993), suggests using the discrepancy between listening and reading comprehension as a method of parceling out reading disorder related to phonological deficits. Reading versus listening comprehension may also assist in determining whether a reading problem includes a comorbid ADHD contribution or may be in fact only a problem with attention regulation. Those with RD only can be expected to have a listening comprehension score higher than reading comprehension, whereas those with only an ADHD component are expected to have the opposite pattern: lower listening comprehension relative to reading comprehension (Aaron, 2003). The length of the reading comprehension stimulus can also be used to delineate ADHD/RD issues. Those with RD will perform equally poorly on both short (i.e., cloze-type) stimuli and paragraph-length stimuli, whereas those with ADHD and no RD will have paragraph-length scores lower than for the shorter, cloze-type stimuli. For a thorough assessment, tests of reading and listening vocabulary are encouraged, as vocabulary knowledge contributes to comprehension (Joshi, 2003).

*Processing Speed*   Speed and errors in RAN of letters or numbers reliably differentiate between poor and normal readers in childhood through adolescence, though color and object RAN are also predictive prior to the second grade (Semrud-Clikeman et al., 2000; Wolf, 1986). Rapid Alternating Stimulus (RAS: Wolf, 1986) tasks are also predictive and may additionally assist in disentangling ADHD comorbidity because it is a less boring task than RAN and children with ADHD are likely to perform within the average range on the RAS (Semrud-Clikeman et al., 2000).

### ADDITIONAL MEASURES: MEMORY, LEARNING, AND EXECUTIVE FUNCTIONS

Joshi's (2003) componential model is a good starting place, though several elements are noticeably lacking. The role of executive functions and, in particular, short-term working memory and learning strategies are relevant to the assessment of RD. The term "executive functions" has engendered many definitions, but most agree that executive functions refer to the higher-order cognitive processes that allow for the perception, integration, and response to environmental stimuli toward a purposeful goal (Baron, 2004). Attention, working memory, fluency, planning, and organization are all executive functions involved in reading and writing. Varying deficits in either or several of these areas may help explain the heterogeneity of children with LD (Lyon, 1998). It follows that assessment of executive functions can help us better to describe and to treat children with LD.

Working memory is susceptible to disruption due to neurological conditions such as LD (Baron, 2004). The Baddeley and Hitch (1974; Baddeley, 2000) model of working memory hypothesizes a phonological loop responsible for short-term storage involving phonemic processing and a visual "sketch pad" for visual and spatial information. The central executive system is responsible for attention and coordination, and the episodic buffer mnemonic storage system for scenes (cf. Baron, 2004). This system has limited capacity and can become overwhelmed when demands outstrip performance. If, for example, a child's processing speed is too slow for the decay rate in the phonological route, we could expect problems in fluency and comprehension.

Not surprisingly, poor short-term memory is a marker for LD. Sequential auditory memory should be evaluated for assessment of the ability to hold and retrieve context-reduced auditory stimuli. Many memory batteries include a sequential auditory memory task of repeating spoken numbers and/or letters, as does the CTOPP. Children with LD tend to employ anemic memory and learning strategies, so it is also important to investigate their compensatory skills. Word learning tasks such as the California Verbal Learning Test (Delis, Kramer, Kaplan, & Ober, 1994) and paired associate tasks available on many memory batteries help to assess whether a child is able effectively to employ weak clustering and schematic strategies.

## INTERVENTION BASED ON ASSESSMENT

The assessment model described earlier provides guidelines for intervention. Phonemic awareness training followed by multisensory instruction in decoding skills has been proven effective in the remediation of phonological skill deficits. Several studies suggest that phonological awareness training explicitly linked to reading activities is most successful (Snowling, 2000). Rapid naming speed appears to be a predictor of remediation success, with slow RAN readers experiencing poorer generalization and less reading progress in phoneme and whole-word training (Levy, Bourassa, & Horn, 1999). Many more repetitions will be needed for this group of readers to improve fluency.

Readers with deficits in comprehension can be taught to become more effective learners through metacognitive strategies. Swanson (1989) suggests that children with reading difficulties are "actively inefficient learners" (p. 10). Further, reading fluency has been linked to problems with reading comprehension, indicating that fluent reading is one of the most important skills for readers to develop (Chard et al., 2002).

Effective interventions appear to include the building of fluency, multiple opportunities to read familiar text with corrective feedback, and increasing text difficulty when the child meets criteria (Chard et al., 2002). Students who were provided with increasingly difficult text with the opportunity to read the text several times to different people have been found to show significant improvement (Weinstein & Cooke, 1992). When children were also taught strategies in reading with a coach in a small group, they showed gains in both fluency and comprehension (Vaughn et al., 2000). Chard, Simmons, and Kameenui (1998) found that repeated reading and daily instruction in fluency were the most important parts of a successful reading outcome.

## REMEDIATION

Research on effective remediation programs for disabled readers has, understandably, lagged behind research into the cognitive processes involved in reading disorders. However, findings from several studies suggest that with intense intervention, the brains of poorly developing readers reorganize as reading improves. Increases in activity in the left termporoparietal cortex associated with improved reading and more closely aligned with activity in that region for able readers have been reported. In addition, increased frontal lobe activity not normally seen in able readers that may be part of a compensatory workaround has also been reported (B. A. Shaywitz et al., 2004; Simos et al., 2002; Temple et al., 2003).

Remediation of less able readers in the schools usually takes the form of supplemental work in small groups. To be effective, programs of work with RD students need to be intense to close the gap between them and their normally developing peers. At a level of instruction similar to their more able reading peers, students with RD acquire reading skills more slowly; thus, to catch up, their pace of learning must be accelerated.

In contrast to comprehensive curricula designed with integrated word decoding, vocabulary building, comprehension, and writing, most RD remedial systems are aimed primarily at the phonological process but may include other reading components to a lesser degree. Most are multisensory, such as the Lindamood Phoneme Sequencing program (LiPS) and the various Orton-Gillingham-based programs. There are subtle differences in programs, however. For example, the LiPS program (www.lblp.com) focuses on teaching the oral-motor characteristics of speech sounds, a method that has been found to be effective with younger children.

There are several programs based on Orton-Gillingham methods, which are highly structured, sequenced, systematic, multisensory programs for teaching phonemic awareness, decoding, and spelling. Two Orton-Gillingham reading programs are GoPhonics (www.gophonics.com) for younger readers K through 2 and the Wilson Reading System (www.wilsonlanguage.com) for older elementary students. The PHAST Track Reading Program is a 70-lesson system that integrates phonological and metacognitive strategy training. This system currently is being evaluated by the National Institute of Child Health and Human Development and shows promise (Lovett, Barron, & Benson, 2003).

A computer-based program, Fast ForWard (www.scientificlearning.com), has recently been gaining attention, although little research by neutral parties has been conducted to verify the claims of the product developers. Fast ForWard presents acoustically modified speech, slowing and amplifying the frequency transitions. The system aims to improve phoneme recognition, memory, and attention. The protocol calls for 100-minute sessions 5 days per week for 4 to 8 weeks or a reduced session time over a longer number of weeks.

Which program is chosen, according to S. E. Shaywitz (1998), is less important than the adherence to an intense remediation program. As much as 150 to 300 hours of special instruction is needed for a reading disabled child to catch up to his or her peers. Further, outcomes have been reported to be variable depending on the quality of teaching; best results are yielded when highly qualified teachers are employed. Finally, once word decoding is adequately established, fluency and comprehension should be monitored and supported with further training.

S. E. Shaywitz (1998) notes that most children with a reading disorder will not be diagnosed until they are 9 years old, when they have already fallen behind. Reading progress typically slows by about the seventh grade (Francis, S. E. Shaywitz, Stuebing, Fletcher, & B. A. Shaywitz, 1996), creating a window of opportunity spanning only 3 to 4 years for optimal remediation. Remediation work with children who have already experienced several years of failure includes additional challenges. Clearly, earlier diagnosis and intervention is desirable. Single kindergarten screening measures are generally unreliable; evidence suggests that a well-designed battery of cognitive-linguistic and prereading skill measures may prove useful in predicting future poor readers (McCardle et al., 2001).

WRITTEN LANGUAGE DISORDER

The multivariate nature of writing suggests multiple pathways to a disorder in written language (WLD). Writing involves the formulation, organization, and sequencing of ideas, spelling, syntax, grammar, and graphomotor control. The very broad *DSM-IV* diagnostic criteria—that writing skills are below expected based on age, intelligence, and education not due entirely to sensory deficit (American Psychiatric Association, 1994)—allow for deficits in any combination of these areas.

The spelling dimension of writing can be directly tied to phonological skills discussed earlier, and as expected, many children with writing problems also have RD. However, some researchers have found that not all poor writers have co-occurring oral or reading disorders (Abbott & Berniger, 1993). Berniger and associates have performed a series of studies suggesting that automaticity of alphabet writing, rapid coding of orthographic information, and speed of sequential finger movements best predict writing disorder, and these variables may account for some types of written language disorders (see Lyon, 1998, for a review). Children with problems in attention and executive functions may also have writing problems, particularly with planning, organization, thematic development, and sequencing. Visuospatial skill deficits can affect letter and word spacing, which may be present in children with a Nonverbal Learning Disorder (NVLD) profile.

In contrast to reading disorders, research on writing is limited, and little is known about the etiology, characteristics, and treatment of WLD (Lyon, 1998). Epidemiological data on the incidence of WLD are also lacking. Clearly defined criteria for the assessment of WLD will be needed before these questions can be answered.

In recent years, it has been recognized that learning disabilities include deficits in the social realm, and that such deficits can profoundly affect learning. Such children do not have difficulty with word reading or fluency and so are not identified as early or as frequently as are those with verbal learning disabilities. The following section discusses the needs of these children from a neuropsychological viewpoint.

## NONVERBAL LEARNING DISABILITIES

Since the late 1960s, a distinct pattern of neuropsychological assets and deficits found in learning disabled children has been under investigation (Rourke, 1982; Rourke & Fisk, 1988). This pattern has been linked to systems in the right cerebral hemisphere and became known as "nonverbal" or "right hemisphere" learning disability (Denckla, 1983; Myklebust, 1975; Rourke, 1989; Rourke & Strang, 1978; Semrud-Clikeman & Hynd, 1990; Tranel, Hall, Olson, & Tranel, 1987; Wientraub & Mesulam, 1983). The prevalence of NVLD is estimated to be between 1% and 10% of the learning disabled population and between 0.1% and 1% of the general population, with a 1:1 sex ratio (Pennington, 1991; Rourke, 1989).

NVLD was first studied in the general context of learning disabilities; however, the functional impact of NVLD is unlike that of other learning disabilities because key features of the disorder include disturbances in the cognitive, social, and emotional domains. Individuals diagnosed with NVLD often possess age-appropriate rote verbal, simple motor, and psycholingustic skills, but their concept formation, abstract reasoning, cause-and-effect reasoning, psychomotor, tactile-perceptual, visual-spatial-organizational, and nonverbal problem-solving abilities lack in development (Harnadek & Rourke, 1994; Klin & Volkmar, 1995; Rourke & Fuerst, 1991; Rourke et al., 1990; Semrud-Clikeman & Hynd, 1990; Teeter & Semrud-Clikeman, 1997). Due to an inability to perceive, process, or enact nonverbal unrehearsed aspects of social situations, those with NVLD also experience significant social problems (Rourke & Fuerst, 1991; Rourke, Young, & Leenaars, 1989; Sisterhen & Gerber, 1989). An inability to cope with these deficits may lead to anxiety and depression (Rourke, Young, & Leenaars, 1989).

Rourke (1989) has proposed the most widely published NVLD model, which describes a unique combination of neuropsychological assets and deficits identified as primary, secondary, tertiary, and verbal. In this model, primary assets and deficits are thought to cause secondary assets and deficits and so forth. The interaction of these assets and deficits results in the patterns of academic and socioemotional deficits experienced by individuals with NVLD. Although Rourke has conceptualized a model for the disorder, specific clinical criteria have not yet been established (Harnadek & Rourke, 1994).

## MANIFESTATIONS OF NVLD THROUGHOUT DEVELOPMENT

NVLD is conceptualized as a developmental disorder, because it is evident when social skills become an important developmental task and persists into adulthood, presenting a unique set of challenges. Early childhood behavior is characterized by passivity, little exploration of the environment, and a lack of interaction with others (Johnson, 1987). Fine motor abilities necessary for dressing, such as buttoning clothes and tying shoes, are frequently impaired. As these children get older, they are often poorly coordinated and may appear clumsy.

In school, deficits associated with NVLD interfere with handwriting, arithmetic, higher-level comprehension, written expression, and novel reasoning (Gross-Tsur, Shalev, Manor, & Amir, 1995; Johnson, 1987; Pennington, 1991; Rourke & Tsatsanis, 1996; Strang & Rourke, 1985). Handwriting is often challenging for these students due to poor visual-motor integration (Pennington, 1991). For example, students may exhibit slow and labored handwriting as well as difficulty with the spatial organization of the letters such that letters are poorly spaced and vary in size and height.

Arithmetic errors are thought to be caused by difficulty in conceptually understanding (1) the problem that they are undertaking, (2) the subroutines needed to solve it, and (3) what a reasonable answer would be (Pennington, 1991; Strang & Rourke, 1985). As a result, these students frequently attempt problems that are too difficult and produce wildly incorrect answers. Moreover, poor visual-spatial organization abilities contribute to the misalignment of number columns.

Despite these relative weaknesses, basic reading is an area of strength for NVLD students. According to Johnson (1987), most NVLD students are excellent at decoding words due to strengths in phonological awareness and the acquisition of phonics; however, they often have difficulty with higher-level comprehension and novel reasoning. For example, in a literature course, they may be unable to perceive another person's point of view. As a result, NVLD students may appear narrow-minded and egocentric. Also, in terms of verbal abilities, individuals with NVLD demonstrate adequate skill in spelling and written syntax, but they may use a rather superficial high level of vocabulary.

One of the most debilitating features of the NVLD syndrome is the extent of social impairment (Roman, 1998). *Social competence* is defined as an individual's ability to adapt to his or her environment in an appropriate manner. It involves the ability to perceive facial expression, tone of voice, and body language, which subsequently affect the ability to learn, to understand another's point of view, and to work with adults and other children (Glass, Guli, & Semrud-Clikeman, 2000; Vaughn & Haager, 1994). Because much of social communication is nonverbal, impairments in visual processing and visual-spatial perception place individuals with NVLD at a significant social disadvantage (Johnson, 1987; Roman, 1998). Furthermore, the inability to understand tone of voice, emotional gesturing, and other social cues interferes with the development of interpersonal skills (Johnson, 1987). These problems are exacerbated by the failure to observe and benefit from the negative nonverbal feedback of others.

In early adulthood, a period typically associated with more independence, practical deficits begin to emerge. For example, NVLD sufferers often experience difficulty with math-based survival skills such as budgeting, balancing a checkbook, measuring, counting money, and shopping (Johnson, 1987). Moreover, a struggle to connect socially makes it difficult to create and maintain a support system. Nonetheless, stronger language-based abilities enable some higher-functioning individuals with NVLD to complete college.

The vast majority of the NVLD literature focuses on the K through 12 student population (Harder & Semrud-Clikeman, 2003). The transition to college, however, presents unique and challenging experiences for all students, particularly those with learning disabilities (Eaton & Coull, 1998). Four difficulties typically experienced by students with disabilities as they transition into college are a decrease in teacher-student contact, an increase in academic competition, a change in personal support networks, and a loss of the protective public school environment, which is largely determined by the legal mandates present in education (Rosenthal, 1989). Given the deficits associated with NVLD and the new educational and social-emotional demands of college, students with NVLD face a profound set of obstacles as they pursue a higher education degree (Harder, Semrud-Clikeman, & Dolit, 2003).

The Americans with Disabilities Act mandates academic support services to all college students with documented disabilities, including those with learning disabilities. College students with NVLD likely benefit from academic accommodations deemed appropriate in high school, which may have included extra time to complete work, use of a calculator and graph paper for math calculations, and assistance with taking notes. Because the functional impact of NVLD extends beyond the scope of academics, it is important to consider other sources of support found in higher education institutions. For example, to cope with social-emotional deficits, these students may benefit from university counseling center services, including individual and group therapy and, if available, social skills training.

Although college students with NVLD may succeed academically, cognitive and social deficits may lead to difficulty finding employment (Rourke & Fisk, 1981; Rourke, Young, & Leenaars, 1989; Weintraub & Mesulam, 1983). Ineffective strategies used to adapt to these challenges can lead to anxiety, depression, or even suicidal thoughts and behavior (Bender et al., 1999; Rourke, Young, & Leenaars, 1989; Rourke, Young, Strang, & Russell, 1986). Although difficulties related to internalizing emotional problems are evident in early childhood, problems with anxiety, social withdrawal, and depression are more common in adolescence and tend to increase with age (Roman, 1998; Rourke, 1987).

## Assessment of Nonverbal Learning Disability

To identify the NVLD syndrome, a thorough neuropsychological evaluation is warranted (Teeter & Semrud-Clikeman, 1997). Because consensus has not yet been reached regarding diagnostic criteria, good clinical judgment is essential. Assessment, however, typically reveals several distinct patterns.

First, strength in verbal, language-based cognitive abilities and relative weakness in nonverbal, visual-spatial cognitive abilities is commonly observed. A VIQ score that is higher than a PIQ score on formal measures of intelligence is often indicative of this pattern of abilities (Johnson, 1987; Weintraub & Mesulam, 1983). Second, math achievement is significantly below what would be expected based on measured cognitive abilities (Pennington, 1991). Third, individuals with NVLD exhibit deficits in tactile perception, tactile attention, and tactile memory. Bilateral tactile-perceptual and psychomotor coordination deficiencies are often present; these deficits are frequently more marked on the left side of the body (Harnadek & Rourke, 1994). Fourth, due to neuropsychological deficits in visual perception, visual attention, and visual memory, individuals with NVLD show significant deficiencies in tasks requiring visual-spatial organizational abilities (Rourke, 1989). Finally, social skills, including social perception and social judgment, must be impaired to a significant degree (Rourke, Young, & Leenaars, 1989).

## Interventions

There are no specific interventions that have been empirically validated for NVLD. Some recommendations have been made for therapy, social skills training, and social coaching. Social skills programs have operant conditioning (reinforcement, punishment, shaping), coaching (verbal instruction, guided rehearsal), social learning (modeling, role-playing, reinforcement), or cognitive-behavioral training (Matson, Sevin, & Box, 1995). Skill acquisition and performance have been emphasized through reducing interfering behaviors while generalizing skills across environments (Gresham, 1998). In general, programs teaching these skills rest on the assumption that problems with social interaction result from a lack of knowledge and can be taught. Unfortunately, these programs have been largely unsuccessful in effecting lasting change (McIntosh, Vaughn, & Zaragoza, 1991; Teeter and Semrud-Clikeman, 1997). Multimodal programs have been only slightly more successful, demonstrating a small long-term effect compared to programs that select one method of intervention (Beelman, Pfingsten, & Losel, 1994).

It has been hypothesized that the core deficits of poor visual-spatial perception leading to difficulty reading facial expression, and diminished perception of prosody (tone of voice) are most affected in children with NVLD (Rourke, 1995; Semrud-Clikeman & Hynd, 1990). Children with verbal learning disabilities and those with attentional problems may misperceive or misinterpret emotional cues due to processing difficulties but not perceptual problems (Greene et al., 1996; Kravetz, Faust, Lipshitz, & Shalhave, 1999).

Older learners tend to rely on situational cues more than facial expressions and to integrate all available information (Egan et al., 1998). Children with NVLD may be highly verbal but are generally less proficient at the pragmatic aspects of language. They tend to be more literal and do not understand the more subtle social context (Gross-Tsur et al., 1995; Rourke, 1995).

Development of a program based on creative drama that provides direct instruction in interpretation of environmental cues and facial expressions has been ongoing at the University of Texas. In SCIP (Social Competence Intervention Program), exercises were adapted from children's creative drama and theater classes to practice processes fundamental to social competence. The exercises were adapted from those originally used to assist actors in developing accurate perception and response to cues. Highly multimodal, the activities address various aspects of social perception. Theater games can be placed in the following categories: sensory games, space/movement games, mirroring activities, communication with sounds, and physical control (Spolin, 1986). These categories seem most appropriate for children with NVLD.

The exercises for SCIP are structured to move from perception of emotions (input) to interpretation (or integration) and then to response (or output; Glass, Guli, & Semrud-Clikeman, 2000). In each of these areas, the exercises begin with basic emotions and move to an understanding of subtler and less common emotions. Initial exercises involve facial expressions, followed by body movement and vocal cues such as intonation and speech rate. Integration of these various aspects of social interaction are then introduced in more advanced form and practice provided (Semrud-Clikeman & Schaefer, 2000). The increasingly complex novel experiences accumulated by the children are reviewed periodically during treatment, enhancing generalization.

Preliminary findings from SCIP indicate that children with NVLD and those with similar social difficulties (Asperger's Disorder, Pervasive Developmental Disorder, etc.) showed good growth in social understanding that generalized to the classroom (Guli, 2005). In contrast, children who did not show NVLD but who had social difficulties due to poor attention and impulse control did not improve significantly. Further evaluation of this program is being conducted, but it shows promise of working with children with NVLD.

## CONCLUSION

There are many unknowns that require further evaluation to promote our understanding of learning disabilities. Definitional issues, assessment practices, and identification are very important aspects of this field that continue to be debated and adjusted. In addition, the area of intervention requires much more attention and support than has been provided. Recent research indicating that interventions in kindergarten and first grade can be successful for children at risk for a learning problem is promising. However, intervention research on the performance of children and adolescents in higher grades is not as easy to achieve due to the requirements of various content areas and the complications of puberty and developmental concerns.

Reading assistance for children in middle school and high school is an area of continuing concern; few programs are currently provided that can assist in this area. Empirically validated research on programs that assist students in older grades is very important, particularly as these children may be at higher risk for emotional complications. Understandably, it is far more difficult to develop interventions for reading when one considers that a high school student may need assistance in reading his or her chemistry or physics textbook, completing essays for English, and navigating higher-order reasoning tasks for classes such as speech or debate.

It is important to understand the neuropsychology involved in learning problems and to more fully examine the relationship between the reading process and brain activity. The advent of MRI and fMRI has increased our understanding of brain mechanisms involved in reading. Emerging evidence that brain connections can and do change following intervention is promising. Continued support of such research is crucial for developing an understanding of how to assist children with learning differences.

## REFERENCES

Aaron, P. G. (2003, November). *Poor reading performance: Is it dyslexia or ADHD?* Paper presented at the 54th annual conference of the International Dyslexia Association, San Diego, CA.

Abbott, R. D., & Berniger, V. W. (1993). Structural equation modeling of relationships among developmental skills and writing skills in primary- and intermediate-grade writers. *Journal of Educational Psychology, 85,* 478–508.

American Psychiatric Association. (1994). *Diagnostic and statistical manual of mental disorders* (4th ed.). Washington, DC: Author.

Baddeley, A. D. (2000). The episodic buffer: A new component of working memory? *Trends in Cognitive Science, 4,* 417–423.

Baddeley, A. D., & Hitch, G. J. (1974). Working memory. In G. H. Bower (Ed.), *The psychology of learning and motivation* (Vol. 8, pp. 47–88). New York: Academic Press.

Baron, I. S. (2004). *Neuropsychological evaluation of the child.* New York: Oxford University Press.

Beelman, A., Pfingsten, V., & Losel, F. (1994). Effects of training social competence in children: A meta-analysis of recent evaluation studies. *Journal of Clinical Child Psychology, 23,* 260–271.

Beitchman, J. H., & Young, A. R. (1997). Learning disorders with a special emphasis on reading disorders: A review of the past 10 years. *Journal of the American Academy of Child and Adolescent Psychiatry, 36,* 1020–1032.

Bender, W. N., Rosenkrans, C. B., & Crane, M. K. (1999). Stress, depression, and suicide among students with learning disabilities: Assessing the risk. *Learning Disability Quarterly, 22*(2), 143–156.

Berniger, V. W., Abbott, R. D., Abbott, S. P., Graham, S., & Richards, T. (2002). Writing and reading: Connections between language by hand and language by eye. *Journal of Learning Disabilities, 35*(1), 39–56.

Booth, J. R., Perfetti, C. A., MacWhinney, B., & Hunt, S. B. (2000). The association of rapid temporal perception with orthographic and phonological processing in children and adults with reading impairment. *Scientific Studies of Reading, 4,* 101–132.

Brady, S. (2003, November). *Terminology matters: Sorting out the "phon" words.* Paper presented at the 54th annual conference of the International Dyslexia Association, San Diego, CA.

Breier, J. I., Fletcher, J. M., Foorman, B. R., Klaas, P., & Gray, L. C. (2003). Auditory temporal processing in children with specific reading disability with and without attention deficit/hyperactivity disorder. *Journal of Speech, Language, and Hearing Research, 46,* 31–42.

Breier, J. I., Simos, P. G., Fletcher, J. M., Castillo, E. M., Zhang, W., & Papanicolaou, A. C. (2003). Abnormal activation of temporoparietal language areas during phonetic analysis in children with dyslexia. *Neuropsychology, 17*(4), 1–12.

Chard, D. J., Simmons, D. C., & Kameenui, E. J. (1998). Word recognition: Instructional and curricular basics and implications. In D. C. Simmons & E. J. Kameenui (Eds.), *What reading research tells us about children with diverse learning needs: The bases and the basics* (pp. 169–182). Hillsdale, NJ: Elrbaum.

Chard, D. J., Vaughn, S., & Tyler, B. J. (2002). A synthesis of research on effective interventions for building reading fluency with elementary students with learning disabilities. *Journal of Learning Disabilities, 35,* 386–406.

Compton, D. L. (2002). The relationships among phonological processing, orthographic processing, and lexical development in children with reading disabilities. *Journal of Special Education, 35*(4), 201–210.

Cornwall, A., & Bawden, H. N. (1992). Reading disabilities and aggression: A critical review. *Journal of Learning Disabilities, 25,* 281–288.

DeFries, J. C., & Gillis, J. J. (1991). Etiology of reading deficits in learning disabilities: Quantitative genetic analysis. In J. Obrzut & G. W. Hynd (Eds.), *Neuropsychological foundations of learning disabilities* (pp. 29–48). San Diego, CA: Academic Press.

Delis, D., Kramer, J. H., Kaplan, E., & Ober, B. A. (1994). *California Verbal Learning Test-Children's Version.* San Antonio, TX: Psychological Corporation.

Denckla, M. B. (1983). The neuropsychology of social-emotional learning disabilities. *Archives of Neurology, 40,* 461–462.

Eaton, H., & Coull, L. (1998). *Transitions to post-secondary learning/student work guide.* Eaton Coull Learning Group Publishing.

Egan, S. K., Monson, T. C., & Perry, D. G. (1998). Social-cognitive influences on change in aggression over time. *Developmental Psychology, 34,* 996–1006.

Felton, R. H., Naylor, C. E., & Wood, F. B. (1990). Neuropsychological profile of adult dyslexics. *Brain and Language, 39*(4), 485–497.

Fletcher, F. J. M., Espy, K. A., Francis, D. J., Davidson, K. C., Rourke, B. P., & Shaywitz, S. A. (1989). Comparisons of cutoff and regression-based definitions of reading disabilities. *Journal of Learning Disabilities, 22,* 334–338.

Francis, D. J., Shaywitz, S. E., Stuebing, K. K., Fletcher, J. M., & Shaywitz, B. A. (1996). Developmental lag vs. deficit models of reading disability: A longitudinal individual growth curves analysis. *Journal of Educational Psychology, 86,* 13–17.

Gabrieli, J. (2003, November). *Neuroimaging evidence about the brain basis for dyslexia.* Paper presented at the annual conference of the International Dyslexia Association, San Diego, CA.

Gayan, J., & Olson, R. K. (2003). Genetic and environmental influences on individual differences in printed word recognition. *Journal of Experimental Child Psychology, 84,* 97–123.

Glass, K., Guli, L., & Semrud-Clikeman, M. (2000). Social competence intervention program: A pilot study program for the development of social competence. *Journal of Psychotherapy and Independent Practice, 1*(4), 21–33.

Goswami, U. (2003). Phonology, learning to read and dyslexia: A cross-linguistic analysis. In V. Csepe (Ed.), *Dyslexia: Different brain, different behavior* (Vol. 23, pp. 1–40). New York: Kluwer Academic/Plenum Press.

Greene, R. W., Biederman, J., & Faraone, S. V. (1996). Toward a new psychometric definition of social disability in children with attention-deficit hyperactivity disorder. *Journal of the American Academy of Child and Adolescent Psychiatry, 35*, 571–578.

Gresham, F. M. (1998). Social skills training with children: Social learning and applied
behavioral analytic approaches. In T. Watson & F. M. Gresham (Eds.), *Handbook of child
behavior therapy* (pp. 475–497). New York: Plenum Press.

Grigorenko, E. L. (2001). Developmental dyslexia: An update on genes, brains, and environments. *Journal of Child Psychology and Psychiatry, 42*(1), 91–125.

Gross-Tsur, V., Shalev, R. S., Manor, O., & Amir, N. (1995). Developmental right-
hemisphere syndrome: Clinical spectrum of the nonverbal learning disability. *Journal of
Learning Disabilities, 2*, 80–86.

Guli, L. (2005). *Nonverbal learning disabilities: A creative drama approach.* Unpublished dissertation, University of Texas at Austin.

Habib, M. (2000). The neurological basis of developmental dyslexia: An overview and
working hypothesis. *Brain, 123*, 2373–2399.

Harder, L., & Semrud-Clikeman, M. (2003, August). *Nonverbal learning disabilities in college
students: An integrative analysis.* Poster session presented at the annual meeting of the
American Psychological Association, Toronto, Ontario, Canada.

Harder, L., Semrud-Clikeman, M., & Dolit, C. (2003, July). *Nonverbal learning disabilities:
Potential implications for policy and practice in higher education.* Poster session presented at
the annual meeting of the Association on Higher Education and Disability (AHEAD),
Dallas, TX.

Harnadek, M. C., & Rourke, B. P. (1994). Principle identifying features of the syndrome of
nonverbal learning disabilities in children. *Journal of Learning Disabilities, 3*, 144–154.

Hinshaw, S. P. (1992). Externalizing behaviour problems and academic underachievement in childhood and adolescence: Causal relationships and underlying mechanisms.
*Psychological Bulletin, 111*, 127–155.

Howes, N.-L., Bigler, E. D., Burlingame, G. M., & Lawson, J. S. (2003). Memory performance of children with dyslexia: A comparative analysis of theoretical perspectives.
*Journal of Learning Disabilities, 36*(3), 230–246.

Johnson, D. J. (1987). Nonverbal learning disabilities. *Pediatric Annals, 16*(2), 133–141.

Jordan, N. C., & Hanich, L. B. (2000). Mathematical thinking in second-grade children
with different forms of LD. *Journal of Learning Disabilities, 567*–578.

Joshi, R. M. (2003, November). *Dyslexia: Myths, misconceptions, and some practical applications.* Paper presented at the 54th annual conference of the International Dyslexia Association, San Diego, CA.

Kavale, K. A., Forness, S. R., & Lorsbach, T. C. (1991). Definition for definitions of learning disabilities. *Learning Disability Quarterly, 14*, 257–266.

Klin, A., &, Volkmar, F. R. (1995). Autism and the pervasive developmental disorders.
*Child and Psychiatric Clinics of North America, 4*, 617–630.

Kravetz, S., Faust, M., Lipshitz, S., & Shalhav, S. (1999). LD, interpersonal understanding,
and social behavior in the classroom. *Journal of Learning Disabilities, 32*, 248–256.

Lerner, J. (1997). *Learning disabilities: Theories, diagnosis, and teaching strategies* (7th ed.).
Boston: Houghton Mifflin.

Levy, B. A., Bourassa, D. C., & Horn, C. (1999). Fast and slow namers: Benefits of segmentation and whole word training. *Journal of Experimental Child Psychology, 73*, 115–138.

Lovett, M., Barron, R. W., & Benson, N. J. (2003). Effective remediation of word identifi-
cation and decoding difficulties in school-age children with reading disabilities. In
H. L. Swanson, K. R. Harris, & S. Graham (Eds.), *Handbook of learning disabilities.* New
York: Guilford Press.

Lyon, G. R. (1998). Learning disabilities. In E. J. Mash & R. A. Barkley (Eds.), *Treatment of childhood disorders* (2nd ed., pp. 468–498). New York: Guilford Press.

Lyon, G. R., Fletcher, J. M., & Barnes, M. C. (2003). Learning disabilities. In E. J. Mash & R. A. Barkley (Eds.), *Child psychopathology* (2nd ed., pp. 520–586). New York: Guilford Press.

Lyon, G. R., Shaywitz, S. E., & Shaywitz, B. A. (2003). A definition of dyslexia. *Annals of Dyslexia, 53,* 1–14.

Martinez, R., & Semrud-Clikeman, M. (2004). Emotional adjustment of young adolescents with different learning disability subtypes. *Journal of Learning Disabilities, 37,* 411–420.

Matson, J. L., Sevin, J. A., & Box, M. L. (1995). Social skills in children. In E. W. O'Donohue & L. Krasner (Eds.), *Handbook of psychological skills training: Clinical techniques and applications* (pp. 36–53). New York: Allyn & Bacon.

McCardle, P., Scarborough, H. S., & Catts, H. W. (2001). Predicting, explaining, and preventing children's reading difficulties. *Learning Disabilities Research and Practice, 16*(4), 230–239.

McIntosh, R., Vaughn, S., & Zaragoza, N. (1991). A review of social interventions for students with learning disabilities. *Journal of Learning Disabilities, 24,* 451–458.

Miles, T. R., Haslum, M. N., & Wheeler, T. J. (1999). Gender ratio in dyslexia. *Annals of Dyslexia, 48,* 27–56.

Molfese, V. J., & Molfese, D. L. (2002). Environmental and social influences on reading skills as indexed by brain and behavioral responses. *Annals of Dyslexia, 52,* 121–137.

Morrison, S. R., & Siegel, L. S. (1991). Learning disabilities: A critical review of definitional and assessment issues. In J. E. Obrzut & G. W. Hynd (Eds.), *Neuropsychological foundations of learning disabilities: A handbook of issues, methods, and practice* (pp. 79–97). San Diego, CA: Academic Press.

Myklebust, H. R. (1975). Nonverbal learning disabilities: Assessment and intervention. In H. R. Myklebust (Ed.), *Progress in learning disabilities* (3rd ed., pp. 85–121). New York: Grune & Stratton.

Papanicolaou, A. C. (2003). *Brain imaging in normal and impaired reading: A developmental-educational perspective.* Paper presented at the annual conference of the International Dyslexia Association, San Diego, CA.

Pennington, B. F. (1991). Right hemisphere learning disorders. In B. F. Pennington (Ed.), *Diagnosing learning disabilities: A neuropsychological framework* (pp. 111–134). New York: Guilford Press.

Pugh, K. R., Mencl, W. E., Jenner, A. R., Katz, L., Frost, S. J., Lee, J. R., et al. (2001). Neurobiological studies of reading and reading disability. *Journal of Communication Disorders, 34,* 479–492.

Ransby, M. J., & Swanson, H. L. (2003). Reading comprehension skills of young adults with childhood diagnoses of dyslexia. *Journal of Learning Disabilities, 36*(6), 538–555.

Roman, M. A. (1998). The syndrome of nonverbal learning disabilities: Clinical description and applied aspects. *Current Issues in Education, 1*(1).

Rosenthal, I. (1989). Model transition programs for learning disabled high school and college students. *Rehabilitation Counseling Bulletin, 33*(1), 54–66.

Rosner, J., & Simon, D. P. (1971). The auditory analysis test: An initial report. *Journal of Learning Disabilities, 4,* 384–392.

Rourke, B. P. (1982). Central processing deficiencies in children: Toward a developmental neuropsychological model. *Journal of Clinical Neuropsychology, 4,* 1–18.

Rourke, B. P. (1987). Syndrome of nonverbal learning disabilities: The final common pathway of white-matter disease/dysfunction? *Clinical Neuropsychologist, 1,* 209–234.

Rourke, B. P. (1989). *Nonverbal learning disabilities: The syndrome and the model.* New York: Guilford Press.

Rourke, B. P. (1995). *Syndrome of nonverbal learning disabilities: Neurodevelopmental manifestations.* New York: Guilford Press.

Rourke, B. P., Del Dotto, J. E., Rourke, S. B., & Casey, J. E. (1990). Nonverbal learning disabilities: The syndrome and a case study. *Journal of School Psychology, 28*(4), 361–385.

Rourke, B. P., & Fisk, J. L. (1981). Socio-emotional disturbances of learning disabled children: The role of central processing deficits. *Bulletin of the Orton Society, 31,* 77–88.

Rourke, B. P., & Fisk, J. L. (1988). Subtypes of learning-disabled children: Implications for a neurodevelopmental model of differential hemisphere processing. In C. K. Molfese & S. J. Segalowitz (Eds.), *Brain lateralization in children: Developmental implications* (pp. 547–565). New York: Guilford Press.

Rourke, B. P., & Fuerst, D. R. (1991). *Cognitive processing, academic achievement, and psychosocial functioning: A neurodevelopmental perspective.* New York: Guilford Press.

Rourke, B. P., & Strang, J. D. (1978). Neuropsychological significance of variation in patterns of academic performance: Motor, psychomotor and tactile-perceptual abilities. *Journal of Pediatric Psychology, 3*(2), 62–66.

Rourke, B. P., & Tsatsanis, K. D. (1996). Syndrome of nonverbal learning disabilities: Psycholinguistic assets and deficits. *Topic in Language Disorders, 16*(2), 30–44.

Rourke, B. P., Young, G. C., & Leenaars, A. A. (1989). A childhood learning disability that predisposes those afflicted to adolescent and adult depression and suicide risk. *Journal of Learning Disabilities, 22*(3), 169–175.

Rourke, B. P., Young, G. C., Strang, J. D., & Russell, C. K. (1986). Adult outcomes of central processing deficiencies in childhood. In I. Grant & K. M. Adams (Eds.), *Neuropsychological assessment in neuropsychiatric disorders: Clinical methods and empirical findings* (pp. 244–267). New York: Oxford University Press.

Sattler, J. M. (2001). *Assessment of children: Cognitive approaches.* San Diego, CA: Author.

Sawyer, D. J., Wade, S., & Kim, J. K. (1999). Spelling errors as a window on variations in phonological deficits among students with dyslexia. *Annals of Dyslexia,* 137–159.

Scarborough, H. S., & Parker, J. D. (in press). Matthew effects in children with learning disabilities: Development of reading, IQ, & psycho-social problems from grade 2 to grade 8. *Annals of Dyslexia.*

Schlaggar, B. L. (2003, November). *FMRI and the development of single word reading.* Paper presented at the annual conference of the International Dyslexia Association, San Diego, CA.

Schlaggar, B. L., Brown, T. T., & Lugar, H. M. (2002). Functional neuroanatomical differences between adults and school-age children in the processing of single words. *Science, 296,* 1476–1479.

Semrud-Clikeman, M., Biederman, J., Sprich-Buckminster, S., Krifcher Lehman, B., Faraone, S. V., & Norman, D. (1992). The incidence of ADHD and concurrent learning disabilities. *Journal of the American Academy of Child and Adolescent Psychiatry, 31,* 439–448.

Semrud-Clikeman, M., Guy, K., Griffin, J. D., & Hynd, G. W. (2000). Rapid naming deficits in children and adolescents with reading disabilities and attention deficit hyperactivity disorder. *Brain and Language, 74,* 70–83.

Semrud-Clikeman, M., & Hynd, G. W. (1990). Right hemispheric dysfunction in nonverbal learning disabilities: Social, academic, and adaptive functioning in adults and children. *Psychological Bulletin, 107*(2), 196–209.

Semrud-Clikeman, M., Hynd, G. W., Novey, E. S., & Eliopulos, D. (1991). Relationships between neurolinguistic measures and brain morphometry in dyslexic, ADHD, and normal children. *Learning and Individual Differences, 3*, 225–242.

Semrud-Clikeman, M., & Shaefer, V. (2000). Social competence in developmental disorders. *Journal of Psychotherapy in Independent Practice, 4*, 3–20.

Shalev, R., Manor, O., Kerem, B., Ayali, M., Badichi, N., Friedlander, Y., et al. (2001). Developmental dyscalculia is a familial learning disability. *Journal of Learning Disabilities, 34*(1), 59–65.

Shaywitz, B. A. (2003, November). *Disruption of neural systems in dyslexia and their improvement with intervention.* Paper presented at the annual conference of the International Dyslexia Association, San Diego, CA.

Shaywitz, B. A., Holford, T. R., Holahan, J. M., Fletcher, J. M., Stuebing, K. K., Francis, D. J., et al. (1995). A Matthew effect for IQ but not for reading: Results from a longitudinal study. *Reading Research Quarterly, 30*(4), 894–906.

Shaywitz, B. A., Shaywitz, S. E., Blachman, B. A., Pugh, K. R., Fulbright, R. K., Skudlarski, P., et al. (2004). Development of left occipitotemporal systems for skilled reading in children after a phonologically-based intervention. *Biological Psychiatry, 55,* 926–933.

Shaywitz, S. E. (1998). Dyslexia. *New England Journal of Medicine, 338*(5), 307–312.

Shaywitz, S. E. (2003). *Overcoming dyslexia: A new and complete science-based program for reading problems at any level.* New York: Alfred A. Knopf.

Shaywitz, S. E., Escobar, M. D., Shaywitz, B. A., & Fletcher, J. M. (1992). Evidence that dyslexia may represent the lower tail of a normal distribution of reading ability. *New England Journal of Medicine, 326*(3), 145–150.

Shaywitz, S. E., Shaywitz, B. A., Fletcher, J. M., & Escobar, M. D. (1990). Prevalence of reading disability in boys and girls: Results of the Connecticut longitudinal study. *Journal of the American Medical Association, 264*(8), 998–1003.

Siegel, L. S. (1989). IQ is irrelevant to the definition of learning disabilities. *Journal of Learning Disabilities, 22,* 469–478.

Siegel, L. S. (1992). An evaluation of the discrepancy definition of dyslexia. *Journal of Learning Disabilities, 25,* 618–629.

Simos, P. G., Fletcher, J. M., Bergman, E., Breier, J. I., Foorman, B. R., Castillo, E. M., et al. (2002). Dyslexia-specific brain activation profile becomes normal following successful remedial training. *Neurology, 58,* 1203–1213.

Sisterhen, D. H., & Gerber, P. J. (1989). Auditory, visual, and multisensory non-verbal social perception in adolescents with and without learning disabilities. *Journal of Learning Disabilities, 22,* 245–249.

Snowling, M. J. (2000). *Dyslexia* (2nd ed.). Malden, MA: Blackwell.

Stage, S., Abbott, R. D., Jenkins, J. R., & Berninger, V. W. (2002). Predicting response to early reading intervention from verbal IQ, reading-related language abilities, attention ratings, and verbal-IQ word reading discrepancy: Failure to validate discrepancy model. *Journal of Learning Disabilities, 36*(1), 24–33.

Spolin, V. (1986). *Theater games for the classroom.* Evanston, IL: Northwestern University Press.

Stanovich, K. E. (1993). The construct validity of discrepancy definitions of reading disability. In C. R. Lyon, D. B. Gray, J. F. Kavanagh, & N. A. Krasnegor (Eds.), *Better understanding learning disabilities: New views from research and their implications for education and public policies* (pp. 273–308). Baltimore: Brookes.

Stanovich, K. E., Siegel, L. S., & Gottardo, A. (1997). Converging evidence for phonological and surface subtypes of reading disability. *Journal of Educational Psychology, 89,* 114–128.

Strang, J. D., & Rourke, B. P. (1985). Arithmetic disability subtypes: The neuropsychological significance of specific arithmetical impairment in childhood. In B. P. Rourke
(Ed.), *Neuropsychology of learning disabilities* (pp. 167–183). New York: Guilford Press.

Swanson, H. L. (1989). Strategy instruction: Overview of principles and procedures for
effective use. *Learning Disability Quarterly, 12,* 3–14.

Tallal, P., Stark, R. E., & Mellits, E. D. (1985). Identification of language-impaired children
on the basis of rapid perception and production skills. *Brain and Language, 25,* 314–322.

Teeter, P. A., & Semrud-Clikeman, M. (1997). *Child neuropsychology: Assessment and interventions for neurodevelopmental disorders.* Boston: Allyn & Bacon.

Temple, E., Deutsch, G. K., Poldrack, R. A., Miller, S. L., Tallal, P., & Merzenich, M. M.
(2003). Neural deficits in children with dyslexia ameliorated by behavioral remediation: Evidence from functional MRI. *Proceedings of the National Academy of Sciences,
100*(5), 2860–2865.

Torgeson, J. K. (2002). Empirical and theoretical support for direct diagnosis of learning
disabilities by assessment of intrinsic processing weaknesses. In R. Bradley & L.
Danielson (Eds.), *Identification of learning disabilities: Research to practice* (pp. 565–613).
Mahwah, NJ: Erlbaum.

Torgeson, J. K., Wagner, R. K., & Rashotte, C. A. (1997). *Test of word reading efficiency.*
Austin, TX: ProEd.

Tranel, D., Hall, L. E., Olson, S., & Tranel, N. N. (1987). Evidence for a right-hemisphere
developmental learning disability. *Developmental Neuropsychology, 3,* 113–117.

Tsatsanis, K. D., Fuerst, D. R., & Rourke, B. P. (1997). Psychosocial dimensions of learning
disabilities: External validation and relationship with age and academic functioning.
*Journal of Learning Disabilities, 30,* 490–502.

Tunick, R. A., & Pennington, B. F. (2002). The etiological relationship between reading
disability and phonological disorder. *Annals of Dyslexia, 52,* 75–95.

Vaughn, S., Chard, D. J., Bryant, D. P., Coleman, M., Tyler, B. J., Thompson, S., et al. (2000).
Fluency and comprehension interventions for third-grade students. *Remedial and Special Education, 21,* 325–335.

Vaughn, S. R., & Haager, D. (1994). Social competence as a multifaceted construct: How do
students with learning disabilities fare? *Learning Disability Quarterly, 17,* 253–266.

Wagner, R. K., Torgesen, J. K., & Rashotte, C. A. (1999). *Comprehensive test of phonological
processing.* Austin, TX: ProEd.

Weinstein, G., & Cooke, N. L. (1992). The effects of two repeated reading interventions on
generalization of fluency. *Learning Disability Quarterly, 15,* 21–28.

Weintraub, S., & Mesulam, M. (1983). Developmental learning disabilities of the right
hemisphere. *Archives of Neurology, 40,* 463–468.

Wolf, M. (1986). Rapid alternating stimulus naming in the developmental dyslexias. *Brain
and Language, 27,* 360–379.

Wolf, M., & Bowers, P. G. (1999). The double-deficit hypothesis for the developmental
dyslexias. *Journal of Educational Psychology, 91,* 415–438.

Wolf, M., Goldberg O'Rourke, A., Gidney, C., Lovett, M., Cirino, P., & Morris, R. (2002).
The second deficit: An investigation of the independence of phonological and naming-
speed deficits in developmental dyslexia. *Reading and Writing: An Interdisciplinary Journal, 15,* 43–72.

Zeffiro, T., & Eden, G. (2000). The neural basis of developmental dyslexia. *Annals of
Dyslexia, 50,* 3–30.

# CHAPTER 18

# Providing Neuropsychological Services to Learners with Traumatic Brain Injuries

MARGARET SEMRUD-CLIKEMAN,
ALEXANDRA KUTZ, and EMILY STRASSNER

TRAUMATIC BRAIN INJURY has been identified as a leading cause of death and acquired disabilities in children and adolescents (Anderson, Catroppa, Morse, Haritou, & Rosenfeld, 2001; Baron, Fennell, & Voeller, 1995). Many researchers have observed that it is difficult to obtain accurate statistics regarding the incidence of head trauma, especially for learners (Kraus, 1995; Yeates, 2000). This has been attributed to the dearth of head trauma registries in the United States on local, regional, and national levels. Existent registries often collect different types of data, which results in inconsistencies in definition, sources of data, and data collection methods. Additionally, most registries often only report head injuries that required medical treatment; thus, milder injuries tend to be underreported. Therefore, incidence rates can vary significantly among sources.

Generally, estimates vary from 193 per 100,000 to 367 per 100,000 (Baron et al., 1995). In a meta-analysis, Kraus (1995) reported an average annual incidence rate of 180 per 100,000 children per year in children younger than 15 years. Lowenthal (1998) reported a rate of 33 per 100,000 children per year for children under the age of 5 years. Researchers have suggested that these figures depend largely on the type and severity of the head injury.

Looking at the incidence of brain injury as a function of severity, a pattern emerges. Epidemiological research has shown that most head injuries are mild in nature, but the actual number of mild cases may be higher than reported as some mild head injuries are likely to be unreported or undetected. The U.S. National Coma Data Bank reported that approximately 85% of head injuries are considered to be mild, 8% moderate, and 6% severe in nature (Luerssen, Klauber, & Marshall, 1988). Similarly, the National Pediatric Trauma Registry reported that of

425

pediatric head injuries requiring medical attention, 76% are categorized as mild, 10% as moderate, and 13% as severe in nature (Lescohier & DiScala, 1993).

Research findings have also suggested that there seem to be critical developmental periods in which a learner is more vulnerable to incurring a head injury. Trends indicate that children are most likely to experience some type of head trauma during the first 5 years of life and again later, during mid- to late adolescence (Baron et al., 1995; Hooper & Baglio, 2001). Gender has also been connected to the incidence rate of head injury: Research has indicated that boys are more likely than girls to sustain a head injury, a discrepancy that becomes more pronounced as children grow older (Baron et al., 1995; Guthrie, Mast, Richards, McQuaid, & Pavlakis, 1999; Kraus, 1995). Specifically, Kraus (1995) reported that the ratio between boys and girls increases from 1.5:1 to 2:1 from preschool to school-age/adolescence. Also, ethnicity has been linked to incidence rates of head trauma: Research data suggest that ethnic minority groups have a higher rate of head injury compared to Caucasians (Baron et al., 1995; Kraus, 1987). Kraus (1987) suggests that this relationship may be conflated with socioeconomic status, as lower socioeconomic status has been correlated with higher rates of head injury as well. Finally, preexisting behaviors and disorders, for example, impulsivity, hyperactivity, depressive symptoms, antisocial behaviors, emotional disturbance, temperamental problems, and family dysfunction, have been linked to an increased risk for head injury (Guthrie et al., 1999; Hooper & Baglio, 2001).

## CAUSES

Epidemiological research has shown that the common causes for head injuries vary somewhat with the age of the child. Generally, the most common causes for head trauma fall into two broad categories: transportation-related injuries and falls. Kraus (1995) reported that approximately 75% to 80% of all brain injuries can be subsumed under one of these two categories. Data indicate that infants and young children are more likely to incur a brain injury due to a fall (Baron et al., 1995; Kraus, 1995). Infants and toddlers are also especially vulnerable to brain trauma as a result of caretaker abuse, such as in Shaken Baby Syndrome, in which the child is shaken so violently that neuronal shearing occurs (Lowenthal, 1998). Among school-age children, brain injuries are most likely to be linked to sports-related accidents and pedestrian/bicycle-motor vehicle collisions. Finally, motor vehicle accidents are the most cited reason for head trauma among adolescents (Baron et al., 1995; Kraus, 1995).

## TYPES OF BRAIN INJURIES

Traumatic brain injuries (TBI) are often classified into two categories: open-head (penetrating) and closed-head (nonpenetrating) injuries. Open-head injuries result when the force of a blow from an object fractures the skull and forces skull fragments to penetrate the dura and brain tissue or when a foreign body, for example, a bullet, penetrates the skull, the dura, and the brain tissue. Closed-head injuries occur when the mechanical forces associated with a blow to the head affect the brain within the skull without compromising the skull (Baron et al., 1995; Hooper & Baglio, 2001). According to research data, approximately 90% of brain injuries are a result of closed-head-type injuries (Hooper & Baglio, 2001). Although strokes, tumors, and infections can also cause brain damage, they are not included under TBI because the damage is not due to external forces.

During a TBI, mechanical forces injure the brain through compression, shearing, and/or tearing of neuronal tissues. The mechanical forces can be due to the acceleration or deceleration of the brain within the skull, and they can be translational, that is, moving along the same plane, and/or rotational, that is, angular, in nature (Hynd & Willis, 1988; Yeates, 2000). The severity of head injuries is directly related to these physical forces. Acceleration injuries occur when a moving object strikes the child's head, which is either stationary or moving at a slower rate than the object. Injuries due to violently shaking a child are also considered acceleration injuries because the brain is moving slower than the skull and repeatedly strikes the skull. Deceleration injuries occur when a child's moving head hits a relatively stationary object, such as in motor vehicle accidents and falls. The skull rapidly decelerates while the brain continues in motion until it strikes the skull. Injuries subsequent to either acceleration or deceleration forces usually result in an injury at the site of impact, that is, coup, and an injury at the site contralateral to the site of impact, that is, contra coup. Injuries tend to be more diffuse and severe at the contra coup site in acceleration injuries, whereas deceleration injuries have been linked to greater damage at the site of injury (Hynd & Willis, 1988).

Primary injuries are usually a direct result of the mechanical forces involved in head trauma resulting in neuronal tissues becoming compressed, strained/stretched, shearing across each other, and/or completely torn apart (Hooper & Baglio, 2001; Hynd & Willis, 1988; Yeates, 2000). It is possible for any combination of these to occur either successively or simultaneously. Commonly, there are both focal and diffuse effects of a TBI, though open-head injuries typically have more focal and localized damage compared to closed-head injuries, which tend to be more diffuse in nature. Shear-strain injuries, thought to be related to diffuse axonal injury, occur most often at white-gray matter junctures and tend to arise around the basal ganglia, near the hypothalamus, at the superior cerebellar peduncles, fornices, corpus callosum, and the fiber tracts of the brain stem (Guthrie et al., 1999; Yeates, 2000). Neuroimaging studies have indicated that focal lesions are larger and occur more frequently in the frontal and anterior temporal regions of the brain (Guthrie et al., 1999; Yeates, 2000). Yeates suggests that these areas are most vulnerable to becoming damaged by the bony protrusions in the anterior and middle fossa of the skull during head trauma. Finally, blood vessels in the dura and brain may become bruised, ruptured, or torn, which may give rise to focal contusions or subdural, subarachnoid, epidural, or intraventricular hemorrhaging (Guthrie et al., 1999; Hooper & Baglio, 2001; Yeates, 2000).

There are often secondary injuries present that arise as an indirect by-product of the initial head trauma. These injuries include brain swelling, edema, hypoxia, hypotension, increased intracranial pressure, contusions, hematomas, and seizures (Hooper & Baglio, 2001; Yeates, 2000). Young children appear to be more vulnerable to early posttraumatic seizures, but data do not indicate that these children are at a higher risk for later epilepsy. Recent research has also suggested that TBI may alter the brain's neurochemistry, which may lead to further damage, such as through the production of free radicals, excitatory amino acids, and the disruption of the normal calcium homeostasis (Novak, Dillon, & Jackson, 1996).

## GLASGOW COMA SCALE

The severity of TBI is usually classified into three categories: mild, moderate, or severe. Typically, classification is determined by considering three variables: (1) the duration of unconsciousness, (2) the extent of posttraumatic amnesia, and (3) the child's score on the Glasgow Coma Scale (GCS). The GCS was originally developed as a measure to assess impaired consciousness, to evaluate brain injury severity, and to provide a prognosis following brain injury (Lustig & Tompkins, 1998; Teasdale & Jennett, 1974).

The GCS can be used to measure the improvement or decline of a patient along three behavioral categories: motor, verbal, and eye movement. Motor responses, thought to reflect a gross central nervous system evaluation, are measured along a 6-point scale ranging from no response to a pinch (1) to being able to obey simple commands (6). Verbal responses, thought to reflect integration, are measured using a 5-point scale ranging from no verbal noise (1) to exhibiting orientation to person, time, and space (5). Finally, eye opening responses, thought to test brain stem arousal mechanisms, are measured along a 4-point scale ranging from no eye response to speech or pain (1) to spontaneously opening the eyes (4). Generally, scores ranging from 13 to 15 are believed to reflect a mild injury, 9 to 12 a moderate injury, and 8 or less are classified as a severe injury (Yeates, 2000). Table 18.1 provides the GCS measure.

**Table 18.1**
Glasgow Coma Scale

| Response | Score |
|---|---|
| **Eye Opening** | |
| Spontaneous (does not imply intact awareness) | 4 |
| To speech (nonspecific response to speech) | 3 |
| To pain | 2 |
| No response | 1 |
| **Motor Response** | |
| Follows simple commands | 6 |
| Localized movement to remove painful stimulus | 5 |
| Withdrawal from painful stimulus | 4 |
| Abnormal flexion (decorticate posturing) | 3 |
| Extension (decerebrate posturing) | 2 |
| No response | 1 |
| **Verbal Response** | |
| Oriented to time, person, and place | 5 |
| Confused (conversation reveals some disorientation) | 4 |
| No sustained or coherent conversation | 3 |
| Vocalizations but no recognizable words | 2 |
| No response | 1 |

Adapted with permission from "Assessment of Coma and Impaired Consciousness," by G. Teasdale and B. Jennett, 1974, *Lancet, 2,* pp. 81–84.

It is important to note that the GCS does not make any assumptions regarding the type or location of the head injury. Rather, it describes a patient's level of consciousness. Recent criticism against the GCS purports that the scale may not be adequately sensitive to distinguish mild from moderate head injuries and often underestimates functional impairment (Lustig & Tompkins, 1998; Winogren, Knights, & Bawden, 1984). Another criticism stems from the concern that the GCS requires certain premorbid language and communication skills that younger children may not have yet fully developed (Baron et al., 1995). In response, the Children's Coma Scale has been developed (Hahn et al., 1988). This scale includes the motor and eye opening modules from the GCS but offers a modified verbal component that includes behaviors that are not dependent on language skills; for example, oriented to sound, interaction, consolable crying, and inconsolable crying.

To understand the different types of injuries involved in pediatric TBI, it is important to review some basic neuroanatomy. The following section briefly reviews key structures that are frequently involved in TBI. The interested reader is referred to more in-depth reviews in Semrud-Clikeman (2001) or Carlson (2001).

## FUNCTIONAL NEUROANATOMY

Damage is generally either focal or diffuse. Focal damage involves a specified area of the brain as well as adjacent areas that may be affected by swelling or bruising. Diffuse damage is more debilitating and involves several areas of networks. The main region of the brain we are concerned with is the cortex, which accounts for approximately 80% of the human brain (Kolb & Whishaw, 1990). The cortex is composed of right and left hemispheres that have anatomical as well as functional differences (Semrud-Clikeman & Hynd, 1991). The left hemisphere contains more gray matter, and the right hemisphere contains more white matter. Gray matter is generally made up of the nuclei of neurons; white matter serves as the myelinated axonal tracts that move nerve impulses from one neuron to the next. The left hemisphere has short association fibers that allow for the processing of sequential information such as that involved in language (Semrud-Clikeman, 2001). The right hemisphere's longer white matter connections allow for the processing of materials that require holistic analysis, such as the processing of novel stimuli and social interactions (Goldberg & Costa, 1981). The hemispheres are able to act independently for some specific functions; integrative and higher-level functions are shared between the hemispheres, allowing for flexibility and adaptability (Zaidel, Clark, & Suyenobu, 1990).

Left hemisphere damage, particularly in the frontal and temporal lobes of the brain, results in difficulty with language and memory. Right hemisphere damage can result in problems with visual-spatial reasoning and nonverbal thinking. The cortex comprises four lobes in each hemisphere: the frontal, parietal, occipital, and temporal lobes. The frontal lobe includes the motor cortex. The parietal lobe encompasses the ability to sense heat and cold, a sense of touch, and kinesthetic sense. The temporal lobe is responsible for language, auditory processing, and short-term memory. Finally, the occipital lobe is involved with vision, depth perception, and visual perception. Regions of the posterior portion of the brain where the temporal, occipital, and temporal lobes merge are involved in long-term storage, association of learned material to new material, and the integration of learning.

## FRONTAL LOBES

Damage to frontal lobes often results in difficulty with attention, inhibition, and impulse control as well as difficulty with motor planning and motor control. The ability to use insight, to change one's behavior in accordance with environmental demands, and to compare and contrast previous experiences with current requirements are called executive functions and are generally thought to be frontal functions. Damage to the frontal lobe frequently impairs functioning in these areas. One can also see apathy, lowered activity level, and perseveration. Damage to the frontal lobes is seen in many head injuries and is the most difficult region to functionally evaluate. Frontal lobe difficulty is also one of the more debilitating injuries experienced by children, as difficulties with learning from mistakes, poor impulse control, and disinhibition frequently cause difficulty with learning and social relationships.

## TEMPORAL LOBES

The temporal lobe is important for the input of auditory stimuli, expressive language, and short-term memory. This lobe is also frequently involved in TBI as it lies next to the temporal bone in the skull and often makes contact with the skull in automobile and bicycle accidents. A pathway that connects the temporal and frontal lobes (arcuate fasciculus) is frequently involved in head injury. This pathway is important for the pairing of expressive and receptive language.

Areas of the temporal lobe (hippocampal formation) are important in the translating of information retained for a short period of time to longer-term storage in other areas of the brain. The difficulty many children with TBI experience in learning new materials is of particular concern when damage to this region occurs in the elementary years. Damage to this region results in the inability to learn new material as new memories are unable to be stored (Kupferman, 1991). Difficulties with reading comprehension, receptive language, and repetition of materials is seen with damage to this region.

The temporal lobe is also closely associated with the limbic system, which is intimately connected to the frontal lobe and involves the ability to control emotions, interpret emotional information, and relate these experiences to previous learning. Damage to this region can be related to problems with emotional control, inappropriate emotional responses, and impulse control.

## PARIETAL LOBES

The parietal lobe is involved in somatosensory functioning. Damage to this region generally is not readily apparent. Damage to the right parietal lobe can result in problems with identifying objects by touch. Problems may also be present with directionality and right-left confusion. Left hemispheric damage can result in problems following multiple-step directions, problems with speech and syntax, and difficulties with motor planning.

## OCCIPITAL LOBES

The occipital lobes are the most posterior region of the brain. Damage can result in problems with visual discrimination, visual integration, and identifying faces and objects (right hemisphere). In addition, problems can be present with left hemispheric damage in the ability to recognize a complex figure or draw the figure as a whole.

## NEUROPSYCHOLOGICAL DEFICITS IN PEDIATRIC TRAUMATIC BRAIN INJURY

Age is an important variable in the disruption of functioning. In addition, severity and location of the damage are also important prognostic aspects. For some functions, damage may not show up until the child is old enough to developmentally demonstrate the functions. Frontal and posterior brain region damage may not be evident until the child is older than 12 years (Kolb & Fantie, 1989). Younger children may show primary deficits in the areas of attention and emotional lability rather than in cognition; older children show more difficulties in intellectual and learning skills. Rourke, Bakker, Fisk, and Strang (1983) suggest that attentional problems mask later cognitive difficulties in young children. Damage acquired in late childhood or adolescence generally is consistent with damage seen in adults (Teeter & Semrud-Clikeman, 1997). In adults, maximum recovery is generally seen in the first 18 months, whereas in children, recovery can continue for more than 5 years after injury (Lezak, 1994).

Areas most commonly compromised in TBI include intelligence, perception, memory, attention, and social-emotional functioning (Ewing-Cobbs, Fletcher, & Levin, 1986). For some children, only one or two of these areas may be involved. For others with severe injury, many of the domains can be affected. The following sections briefly discuss these functional domains.

### INTELLIGENCE

Deficits in intelligence are more common in children with severe head injuries and who were in a coma for more than 24 hours (Fletcher, Ewing-Cobbs, Francis, & Levin, 1995). When injury is multifocal and diffuse, severe deficits are found in even young children with TBI. Those who experienced TBI prior to age 3 show lower ability scores than those with damage in late childhood and adolescence (Aram & Eisele, 1994). It may be that the difficulty in younger children lies in consolidating learned information into the developing networks that results in the lowered IQ (Dennis, Wilkinson, Koski, & Humphreys, 1995).

The Performance IQ has been found to be most susceptible to TBI and continues to be lower after recovery (Begali, 1992); Verbal IQ scores show improvement to the premorbid level. The area that appears to be most susceptible to damage is the ability to solve new problems (Bigler, Johnson, & Blatter, 1999). On the WISC-III, the factors that appears to be most vulnerable to TBI are processing speed and perceptual organization (Donders, 1996; Hoffman, Donders, & Thompson, 2000).

### ACADEMICS

Children with TBI often show difficulties with language, reading, arithmetic calculation, writing, and spelling (Levin, Ewing-Cobbs, & Eisenberg, 1995). Standardized testing often finds average performance coupled with poor performance in the classroom on day-to-day tasks. More than three-fourths of children with severe TBI have been found to be retained in a grade or receive special education services even though they scored in the average range on standardized tests (Ewing-Cobbs, Fletcher, Levin, Iovino, & Miner, 1998). Difficulties with memory, visual-spatial ability, and attention may be at the root of the problems with every-day functioning, for which standardized tests are insensitive measures.

## Attention and Executive Functions

The most frequent complaint among children with TBI is attentional deficits (Semrud-Clikeman, 2001). Attentional difficulties frequently interfere with measures of memory, and these two domains often coexist as areas of concern for children with TBI. Attentional deficits are generally seen immediately following injury, although for some children, these resolve within the first year of recovery (Van Zomeren & Brouwer, 1992). For children with severe head injuries, deficits in sustained and selective attention are most frequently present. Research has found that younger children show more attentional difficulties than those injured at an older age (Dennis et al., 1995). Continuing difficulty with attention appears to be more frequent with severe head injuries than in those with mild or moderate injuries (Asarnow et al., 1995).

Difficulties with executive functions are also frequently seen in children with TBI. Problems with planning and organization are most common, with particular difficulties noted in social functioning. Damage to the left hemisphere has been found to result in problems with verbal fluency, inhibition, and perseveration; right hemispheric damage is related to working memory and categorical reasoning (Levin, Culhane, Fletcher, & Mendelsohn, 1994).

## Memory

Difficulties are generally seen in the areas of verbal learning and verbal memory (Roman et al., 1998). These difficulties appear to persist and interfere with the child's ability to learn new information. Imaging studies have found lesions in the frontal and temporal lobes in children with memory deficits (Levin, Fletcher, Kusnerik, & Kufera, 1996).

Working memory deficits have also been found. Working memory is the ability to hold information in mind while solving a problem. Children with severe TBI have been found to show significant difficulties in the areas of working memory, with the deficit persisting following recovery (Dennis, Roncardin, Barnes, Guger, & Archibald, 2000).

## Psychosocial and Behavioral Functioning

Emotional difficulties are frequent in children with TBI and cause the most distress for teachers and parents (DiScala, Osberg, Gans, Chin, & Grant, 1991). Difficulties in the initial stages of recovery include agitation, poor receptive language, and regressive behaviors. Those that persist are generally more permanent and include difficulties with behavioral control, low self-esteem, emotional lability, and poor attention. Premorbid functioning is the single most predictive variable; those with difficulties prior to the injury show the more severe deficits following the injury (Jaffe, Brink, Hays, & Chorazy, 1990). Those children with

**Table 18.2**
A Checklist for School Psychologists for the Assessment of a
Child or Adolescent TBI

---

Intelligence
  –Performance IQ scores most susceptible and continues to be lower after TBI
  –Verbal IQ shows improvement to pre-morbid level
  –WISC-III factors most vulnerable: processing speed and perceptual organization
Academics
  –Language
  –Reading
  –Arithmetic calculation
  –Writing
  –Spelling
Attention and Executive Functions
  –Attention
  –Planning
  –Organization
Memory
  –Verbal learning and verbal memory
  –Working memory
Psychosocial and Behavioral Functioning
  –Emotional functioning
  –Social skills
  –Behavioral functioning

---

premorbid behavioral difficulties who have less social support and more chaotic family functioning show the poorest recovery from TBI (Semrud-Clikeman, 2001). Particular difficulty is seen in low frustration tolerance, problems with anger modulation, aggressive behavior, anxiety, and depression, as well as social isolation. These difficulties are of particular concern because they affect academic and cognitive progress and social competence (Rosenthal & Bond, 1990). Moreover, children with TBI often show a deterioration in social skills as they become aware of their disabilities and struggle to come to terms with their limitations (Fordyce, Roueche, & Prigatano, 1983).

Table 18.2 provides a list of commonly required measures for a comprehensive evaluation of a child with TBI.

Substance abuse is an area of particular concern for adolescents with TBI. One-third to one-half of head injury patients have been found to be intoxicated at the time of injury (Corrigan, 1995). Patients who were heavy drinkers prior to their injury show significant drinking in follow-up as well as an increase in drinking after release from the hospital (Kreutzer, Witol, & Marwitz, 1996). An imaging study found that patients with TBI who were also heavy drinkers showed more brain atrophy compared to those patients with TBI who did not drink (Barker et al., 1999). Thus, substance abuse at all times places the adolescent at higher risk for long-term damage and poor outcome and is an important variable that must be evaluated.

The support provided by the child's/adolescent's family and school is an important variable in recovery. The stresses experienced by the family are important to understand when planning reentry into school or developing an individual-ized education program (IEP).

## THE ROLE OF THE FAMILY

Families of children and adolescents with TBI progress through several general stages as they endeavor to adapt to the initial crisis and continuing care of their family member (Martin, 1988; Semrud-Clikeman, 2001). The initial stage that is most commonly reported is characterized by overwhelming shock. This shock oc-curs when families are informed that their child suffered a severe, and poten-tially lethal, head injury (Martin, 1988). In this initial stage, the family's first concern is the survival of the child. Once survival is assured, the focus changes to the eventual functioning of the child or adolescent (Conoley & Sheridan, 1996; Semrud-Clikeman, 2001). As the shock of the trauma diminishes, parents often shift into a phase of denial or disbelief regarding the child's injury. Initially, de-nial may be functional and serve as a protective mechanism for the family to gradually grasp the reality of the child's injury. On the other hand, persistent de-nial can prevent the family from accepting the child's actual losses and engaging in critical rehabilitation and educational programming (Martin, 1988).

The next stage the family may live through is characterized by an intense sense of sorrow and despondency. Parents begin to realize that their child is "forever changed." This sadness may remain latent for long periods and resurface when new difficulties confront the injured child or the family. Families may also expe-rience feelings of anger about their child's TBI. The anger may be directed toward the circumstances that led to the injury or stem from unresolved feelings that the injury was unjust. Over long periods this anger can be destructive and prevent the family from moving into the final stage of adaptation (Martin, 1988).

The last stage, adaptation, is reached when the family has arrived at an emo-tional equilibrium. Often, the family has undergone a process of reorganization and redefinition of roles that function to accommodate the needs of their injured child. Research has suggested that this stage is not static and should be envi-sioned as an extremely fluid process that may vary over time (Martin, 1988).

Recovery for the child or adolescent with TBI may occur rather quickly at first. Parents may experience feelings of euphoria in reaction to the noticeable im-provements in their children's language, attention, and motor skills (Conoley & Sheridan, 1996). Cognitive deficits or weaknesses may not be detectable in the acute phase following a TBI but may emerge later in development as more com-plex skills are needed. Parents and teachers may begin to notice a developmental lag between children who incurred a TBI and same-age peers (Gil, 2003). Thus, re-covery is often a very long process that can fluctuate over time.

Much of the research on family functioning following a child's or adolescent's TBI has been dedicated to measuring family stress and burden. Perrott, Taylor, and Montes (1991) found that parents reported a higher level of stress associated with parenting a child with TBI than with parenting a healthy sibling as mea-sured by the Parenting Stress Inventory. Researchers have also found severity of injury to be related to family functioning, such that families with children who sustained a severe TBI showed higher levels of family burden relative to families whose child incurred a mild or moderate TBI (Anderson, Catroppa, Haritou, et al., 2001; Rivara et al., 1992). Similar findings revealed that interviewer ratings of marital and peer relationships, as well as global family relationships and functioning, decreased more for families of children with a severe TBI than for families of children with mild or moderate TBI (Rivara et al., 1996).

Wade, Taylor, Drotar, Stanchin, and Yeates (1998) studied families with children with a TBI (moderate and severe) in comparison to families with children with orthopedic injuries that did not involve the central nervous system. To measure injury-related burden, the Family Burden of Injury Interview was administered to assess injury-related stress in three areas: concerns with the child's recovery and adjustment, the reactions of extended family and friends, and spouse's reactions. Additional self-report measures were included to assess global family functioning and caregiver psychological distress. Results from this research revealed that in the initial year postinjury, caregivers of children with severe TBI had significantly higher levels of burden, psychological distress, and injury-related stress than caregivers in the orthopedic group.

In a follow-up study on the same population of families, Wade and colleagues (2002) found that elevated injury-related stress and burden in the severe TBI group existed across multiple assessments. Even though the severe TBI group reported average levels of injury-related stress at extended follow-up, most continued to face at least one area of high injury-related stress many years after a severe TBI. Wade and colleagues found that caregivers of children with TBI did not report more psychological distress than caregivers of children with orthopedic injury at follow-up. Possible explanations offered by these researchers are that both injuries may be associated with longer-term caregiver distress or that families of children who sustain injury are often more distressed before the injury (Wade et al., 2002).

Wade and colleagues (2003) also studied the interactions between parents and adolescents after adolescent TBI. The results of their research showed that observations of criticism/coldness and self-rated conflict were more disruptive after TBI when compared to orthopedic injuries. Higher levels of criticism/coldness, greater parent-rated conflict, and poorer problem solving were related to poorer parent and family functioning. These associations were much stronger after severe TBI, suggesting that these factors may function differently in this population.

Siblings of children and adolescents with TBI are likely to exhibit distress and changes in their own functioning within the family. Wade and colleagues (Wade, Taylor, Drotar, Stanchin, & Yeates, 1996) found that severe TBI was likely to become a source of stress in interactions between siblings. Siblings may go through feelings of considerable conflict toward their injured sibling because they view their parents as focusing more of their attention on the injured sibling. This unbalanced attention toward the children from parents can trigger feelings of jealousy, anger, and anxiety and becomes especially pronounced in the case of a long-lasting recovery (Semrud-Clikeman, 2001). Siblings of children with TBI have been shown to display attitudes that are dysfunctional and often utilize inadequate problem-solving skills (Conoley & Sheridan, 1996). Sibling difficulties have been reported to be present for more than 5 years after the injury, and siblings have reported feeling that the injury is something they can "never live up to" (Orsillo, McCaffrey, & Fisher, 1993; Semrud-Clikeman, 2001). Swift and colleagues (2003) looked at sibling relationships 4 years postinjury for both TBI and orthopedic injuries. More negative sibling relationships in families of children with TBI than in families of children in the orthopedic injury group were discovered, but only for mixed-gender sibling pairings. Additionally, the results showed that behavior problems in children with TBI predicted both sibling relationships and sibling behavior problems.

Not all families report long-term negative effects after a child or adolescent experiences TBI. Wade et al. (1996) suggest that many families exhibit considerable resiliency when faced with trauma. Therefore, identifying factors that separate the families who cope well from those who experience ongoing difficulties is crucial to understanding predictors of long-term adjustment after a child or adolescent TBI. Wade and colleagues suggest that a comprehensive model of family adaptation to TBI would include stressors and resources, such as preinjury family functioning, persistent life stressors confronting the family, injury-related burden, community resources, and the availability of social supports and rehabilitative and therapeutic services. Taking all of these factors into consideration when working with a family that has experienced a prediatric TBI will assist in predicting family outcomes and adaptation.

## FAMILY INTERVENTIONS

Family interventions can be particularly helpful for family members coping with TBI. Some of the most commonly advocated interventions include family education, family counseling and therapy, family support groups, family networking, and family advocacy (Tyerman & Booth, 2001). Family counseling may be helpful if the family has not been able to assimilate the cognitive, behavioral, language, emotional, and other changes in the child or adolescent with TBI into the present family structure (Conoley & Sheridan, 1996). Tyerman and Booth advocate for an open-door approach with families; in their practice, they allow family members to recognize and adjust to the consequences of TBI at their own pace.

Conoley and Sheridan (1996) suggest that family counseling is both a preventive and a remedial strategy for families, and the therapist can teach the family strategies to effectively work with their injured child. Sibling adjustment and sibling relationships should also be monitored after TBI, and siblings should be included in family interventions (Swift et al., 2003). Conoley and Sheridan suggest that siblings of children with TBI would benefit from education about the possible negative effects of prolonged caretaking on both themselves and the rest of the family. In addition, learning effective support and problem-solving strategies would likely benefit siblings.

## COMMUNITY SUPPORT

Gathering information on available community resources is an important step in working with families of children with TBI. Legal and financial concerns become more pronounced as the recovery process begins. These additional stressors can impact both child and family functioning, and it is important for the school to be informed of these stressors (Semrud-Clikeman, 2001). Research has shown that successful coping during the early adjustment period has been related to obtaining adequate social support and information, attending support groups, involvement in religion, and becoming active in recreation. Strategies that families found useful in the later stages of adjustment to the TBI included maintaining a healthy outlook, participating in support groups, seeking respite, and acquiring additional information about the long-term effects of TBI, especially the impact on the emotional and behavioral capacities of the individual (Hibbard et al., 2002).

Case managers can assist the family in accessing all the community and educational services for which they qualify (Conoley & Sheridan, 1996; Semrud-Clikeman, 2001). Hibbard and colleagues (2002) explored the utility of a community-based peer support program for individuals and their families following a TBI. Although their study was based on an adult population, their findings revealed that participants reported positive impacts of peer support on enhancing their overall quality of life, increasing their knowledge about TBI, increasing their coping abilities, and improving their general outlook on life. In addition, connecting families with local or national organizations, such as the National Head Injury Foundation, can help the family acquire additional information and support (Conoley & Sheridan, 1996; Semrud-Clikeman, 2001).

## HOME-SCHOOL COLLABORATION

A fundamental component of family coping and involvement in the recovery of the learner with TBI is a solid connection between family and school. The first critical step is a meeting during which the goal is to develop an appropriate IEP. The school psychologist is a key member of the IEP team and can assist the team (including the parents) in preparing fitting educational goals by gathering the required information that will effectively address each learner's specific difficulties (Conoley & Sheridan, 1996).

Clark, Russman, and Orme (1999) suggest that the reintegration of learners with TBI into the school environment requires early identification of (1) the student's deficits and skills, (2) the teacher's management style and tolerance for inappropriate behavior, (3) the level of classroom structure, and (4) the degree of classroom control. Consultation between the school psychologist and the parents is important and provides a means for the school psychologist to collect information about the child's ability to function in the home and in the community. Additional important information that can be obtained through these collaborations includes the relationships the child has with siblings and peers and learning of any involvement the child has in social and recreational activities. Collaborations with parents also allow the school psychologist to grasp how the family is adjusting to the child's injury (Clark et al., 1999).

### SCHOOL REENTRY

It is estimated that approximately one-fifth of learners with TBI will require special education (Kraus, Rock, & Hemyarai, 1990), with many of them having been enrolled in special education services *prior* to the injury. A range of placements is possible, from residential treatment to homebound to special education classes, including self-contained and/or resource rooms. Many times, a child will begin with a half-day and progress to a full day of school. The timing of school reentry is important, with the child's ability to attend to simultaneous input and to work unassisted for 30 minutes being the most indicative for school readiness (Mira &

Tyler, 1991). Cohen (1996) suggests that to successfully reenter school, the child must be able to understand and attend to classroom instruction, retain new information, reason and express ideas, solve problems, and plan and monitor his or her behavior.

Planning is paramount for successful reentry, and the school psychologist is an important player in this planning. Interagency cooperation has been found to be imperative for the child's reentry, and the school personnel need to be competent in understanding medical terminology (DePompei & Bloser, 1993). The IEP needs to be developed in cooperation with the medical team and must include current levels of performance, goals and objectives, need for related services, and methods of evaluation of the child's needs. It is suggested that assessment be periodic; for a child with TBI, serial evaluation of progress is necessary. Interpretation of results differs from that for most children, as the results are not necessarily predictive of future performance but rather of current functioning (Semrud-Clikeman, 2001). To properly plan for the child's reentry into school, standardized tests may be used, although information as to the child's learning style and learning needs is most helpful for appropriate planning. A formal planning meeting is generally held at the end of the hospitalization, and though school personnel should attend, they are often not invited. It is imperative that the school psychologist remain in contact with the family to ensure that they are invited to the meeting and to prepare a smooth transition.

One of the key predictors for successful reentry is the teacher's acceptance and agreement to work with the child (Rosen & Gerring, 1986). Support from school psychologists and therapists has been found to improve communication and the delivery of services (Smith, 1991). In addition, because the program for a child with TBI must, by definition, change as he or she improves, the teacher needs to know that change is key and to be expected. Problems that are neuropsychologically based such as expressive language difficulties may present as difficulties in learning and at times with behavior as frustration mounts. A teacher who understands these key concepts can help the child to demonstrate learning through alternative methods besides paper-and-pencil tests. Teachers also need to understand that processing speed is lower for these children, and they may be hard-pressed to keep up with the classroom.

Learning environments have also been found to be important variables. Aspects of the classroom such as structured versus unstructured, independent versus teacher-led work, and classroom instructional methods can all have an effect on the child's learning ability. The use of actual classroom materials during speech/language, occupational, and physical therapy have been found to be most appropriate and helpful (Smith, 1991).

The most common deficits that interfere with school performance for children with TBI include the following (Ozer, 1988):

- Walking, writing, and self-help skills
- Ability to recall information and learn new material
- Language skills
- Attention
- Visual-spatial and motor deficits
- Planning and organization

Teachers who are informed of these difficulties have been found to be more successful with the children and have succeeded in building the child's self-esteem and willingness to try new tasks. Issues such as stamina, attention, and language disabilities continue after release from the hospital. Program goals need to emphasize the child's strengths as well as his or her weaknesses and account for subtle disabilities that can have major impacts on learning.

## CONCLUSION

Pediatric TBI is a fairly common occurrence with wide variation in any resulting deficits. It presents particular challenges to the school psychologist who has limited experience and training in neuropsychology. There are few training programs that include instruction in neuropsychology to assist in interpreting medical records. More children with severe head injuries are surviving their injuries and reentering the school environment. It becomes even more critical that school psychologists be able to converse with medical personnel as well as translate medical findings into educational terms. School psychologists with master's or specialist degrees are not trained in neuropsychological assessment and need to be aware of when children who are not learning and who may have a head injury need to be referred to a neuropsychologist for an evaluation. Doctoral-level school psychologists may have had a course or two in neuropsychology but are not generally trained sufficiently to conduct neuropsychological assessments. However, school psychologists are in an important position to provide support to teachers and families for children with TBI. In addition, providing a bridge between the medical community and the school is an invaluable contribution for the success of these children.

## REFERENCES

Anderson, V. A., Catroppa, C., Haritou, F., Morse, S., Pentland, L., Rosenfeld, J., et al. (2001). Predictors of acute child and family outcome following traumatic brain injury in children. *Pediatric Neuropsychology, 34,* 138–148.

Anderson, V. A., Catroppa, C., Morse, S., Haritou, F., & Rosenfeld, J. (2001). Outcome from mild head injury in young children: A prospective study. *Journal of Clinical and Experimental Neuropsychology, 23*(6), 705–717.

Aram, D. M., & Eisele, J. A. (1994). Intellectual stability in children with unilateral lesions. *Neuropsychologia, 32,* 85–96.

Asarnow, R. F., Satz, P., Light, R., Zaucha, K., Lewis, R., & McCleary, C. (1995). The UCLA study of mild closed head injury in children and adolescents. In S. Broman & M. E. Michel (Eds.), *Traumatic head injury in children and adolescents* (pp. 117–146). New York: Oxford University Press.

Barker, L. H., Bigler, E. D., Johnson, S. C., Anderson, C. V., Russo, A. A., Boineau, B., et al. (1999). Polysubstance abuse and traumatic brain injury: Quantitative magnetic resonance imaging and neuropsychological outcome in older adolescents and young adults. *Journal of the International Neuropsychological Society, 5,* 593–608.

Baron, I. S., Fennell, E. B., & Voeller, K. S. (1995). Head trauma. In *Pediatric neuropsychology in the medical setting* (pp. 292–315). New York: Oxford University Press.

Begali, V. (1992). *Head injury in children and adolescents* (2nd ed.). Brandon, VT: Clinical Psychology Publishing.

Bigler, E. D., Johnson, S. C., & Blatter, D. D. (1999). Head trauma and intellectual status: Relation to quantitative magnetic resonance imaging findings. *Applied Neuropsychology, 6,* 217–225.

Carlson, N. R. (2001). *Physiology of behavior* (7th ed.). Boston: Allyn & Bacon.

Clark, E., Russman, S., & Orme, S. (1999). Traumatic brain injury: Effects on school functioning and intervention strategies. *School Psychology Review, 28,* 242–251.

Cohen, S. B. (1996). Practical guidelines for teachers. In A. L. Goldberg (Ed.), *Acquired brain injury in childhood and adolescence: A team and family guide to educational program development and implementation* (pp. 126–170). Springfield, IL: Charles C. Thomas.

Conoley, J. C., & Sheridan, S. M. (1996). Pediatric traumatic brain injury: Challenges and interventions for families. *Journal of Learning Disabilities, 29,* 662–669.

Corrigan, J. (1995). Substance abuse as a mediating factor in outcome from traumatic brain injury. *Archives of Physical Medicine and Rehabilitation, 76,* 302–309.

Dennis, M., Roncardin, C., Barnes, M. A., Guger, S., & Archibald, J. (2000). Working memory after mild, moderate, or severe childhood head injury. *Journal of the International Neuropsychological Society, 6,* 132.

Dennis, M., Wilkinson, M., Koski, L., & Humphreys, R. P. (1995). Attention deficits in the long term after childhood head injury. In S. Broman & M. E. Michel (Eds.), *Traumatic head injury in children and adolescents* (pp. 165–187). New York: Oxford University Press.

DePompei, R., & Bloser, J. L. (1993). Professional training and development for pediatric rehabilitation. In C. J. Durgin, N. D. Schmidt, & L. J. Fryer (Eds.), *Staff development and clinical intervention in brain injury rehabilitation* (pp. 229–253). Gaithersburg, MD: Aspen Publications.

DiScala, C., Osberg, J. S., Gans, B. M., Chin, L. J., & Grant, C. C. (1991). Children with traumatic head injury: Morbidity and postacute treatment. *Archives of Physical Medicine and Rehabilitation, 72,* 662–666.

Donders, J. (1996). Cluster subtypes in the WISC-III standardization sample: Analysis of factor index scores. *Psychological Assessment, 8,* 312–318.

Ewing-Cobbs, L., Fletcher, J. M., & Levin, H. S. (1986). Neurobehavioral sequelae following head injury in children: Educational implications. *Journal of Head Trauma Rehabilitation, 1,* 57–65.

Ewing-Cobbs, L., Fletcher, J. M., Levin, H. S., Iovino, I., & Miner, M. E. (1998). Academic achievement and academic placement following traumatic brain injury in children and adolescents: A two-year longitudinal study. *Journal of Clinical and Experimental Neuropsychology, 20,* 769–781.

Fletcher, J. M., Ewing-Cobbs, L., Francis, D. J., & Levin, H. S. (1995). Variability in outcomes after traumatic brain injury in children: A developmental perspective. In S. H. Broman & M. D. Michel (Eds.), *Traumatic head injury in children* (pp. 3–21). New York: Oxford University Press.

Fordyce, D. J., Roueche, J. R., & Prigatano, G. P. (1983). Enhanced emotional reaction in chronic head trauma patients. *Journal of Neurology, Neurosurgery, and Psychiatry, 46,* 620–624.

Gil, A. M. (2003). Neurocognitive outcomes following pediatric brain injury: A developmental approach. *Journal of School Psychology, 41,* 337–354.

Goldberg, E., & Costa, L. D. (1981). Hemisphere differences in the acquisition and use of descriptive systems. *Brain and Language, 14,* 144–173.

Guthrie, E., Mast, J., Richards, P., McQuaid, M., & Pavlakis, S. (1999). Traumatic brain injury in children and adolescents. *Child and Adolescent Psychiatric Clinics of North America, 8*(4), 807–826.

Hahn, Y. S., Chyung, C., Barthel, M. J., Bailes, J., Flannery, A., & McLone, D. G. (1988). Head injuries in children under 36 months of age. *Child's Nervous System, 4*, 34–40.

Hibbard, M. R., Cantor, J., Charatz, H., Rosenthal, R., Ashman, T., Gundersen, N., et al. (2002). Peer support in the community: Initial findings of a mentoring program for individuals with traumatic brain injury and their families. *Journal of Head Trauma Rehabilitation, 17*, 112–131.

Hoffman, N., Donders, J., & Thompson, E. H. (2000). Novel learning abilities after traumatic head injury in children. *Archives of Clinical Neuropsychology, 15*, 47–58.

Hooper, S. R., & Baglio, C. (2001). Children and adolescents experiencing traumatic brain injury. In J. N. Hughes, A. M. LaGreca, & J. C. Conoley (Eds.), *Handbook of psychological services for children and adolescents* (pp. 267–283). New York: Oxford Press.

Hynd, G. W., & Willis, W. G. (1988). Intracranial injuries. In *Pediatric neuropsychology* (pp. 257–262). New York: Grune & Stratton.

Jaffe, K. M., Brink, J. D., Hays, R. M., & Chorazy, A. J. L. (1990). Specific problems associated with pediatric head injury. In M. Rosenthal, E. R. Griffith, M. R. Bond, & J. D. Miller (Eds.), *Rehabilitation of the adult and child with traumatic brain injury* (2nd ed., pp. 539–557). Philadelphia: Davis.

Kolb, B., & Fantie, B. (1989). Development of the child's brain and behavior. In C. R. Reynolds & E. F. Janzen (Eds.), *Handbook of clinical child neuropsychology* (pp. 17–40). New York: Plenum Press.

Kolb, B., & Whishaw, I. Q. (1990). *Fundamentals of human neuropsychology* (3rd ed.). San Francisco: Freeman.

Kraus, J. F. (1987). Epidemiology of head injury. In P. R. Cooper (Ed.), *Head injury* (pp. 1–19). Baltimore: Williams & Wilkins.

Kraus, J. F. (1995). Epidemiological features of brain injury in children: Occurrence, children at risk, causes and manner of injury, severity, and outcomes. In S. H. Broman & M. E. Michel (Eds.), *Traumatic head injury in children* (pp. 22–39). New York: Oxford Press.

Kraus, J. F., Rock, A., & Hemyarai, P. (1990). Brain injuries among infants, children, adolescents, and young adults. *American Journal of Diseases of Children, 144*, 684–691.

Kruetzer, J. S., Witol, A. D., & Marwitz, J. H. (1996). Alcohol and drug use among young persons with traumatic brain injury. *Journal of Learning Disabilities, 29*, 643–651.

Kupferman, I. (1991). Learning and memory. In E. R. Kandel, J. H. Schwartz, & T. M. Jessel (Eds.), *Principles of neural science* (3rd ed., pp. 997–1008). New York: Elsevier.

Lescohier, I., & DiScala, C. (1993). Blunt trauma in children: Causes and outcomes of head versus intracranial injury. *Pediatrics, 91*, 721–725.

Levin, H. S., Culhane, K. A., Fletcher, J. M., & Mendelsohn, D. B. (1994). Dissociation between delayed attention and memory after pediatric head injury: Relationship to MRI findings. *Journal of Child Neurology, 9*, 81–89.

Levin, H. S., Ewing-Cobbs, L., & Eisenberg, H. M. (1995). Neurobehavioral outcome of pediatric closed head injury. In S. Broman & M. E. Michel (Eds.), *Traumatic head injury in children* (pp. 70–94). New York: Oxford University Press.

Levin, H. S., Fletcher, J. M., Kusnerik, L., & Kufera, J. A. (1996). Semantic memory following pediatric head injury: Relationship to age, severity of injury, and MRI. *Cortex, 32*, 461–478.

Lezak, M. (1994). *Neuropsychological assessment* (4th ed.). New York: Oxford University Press.

Lowenthal, B. (1998). Early childhood traumatic brain injuries: Effects on development and interventions. *Early Child Development and Care, 146*, 21–32.

Luerssen, T. G., Klauber, M. R., & Marshall, L. F. (1988). Outcome from head injury related to patient's age: A longitudinal prospective study of adult and pediatric head injury. *Journal of Neurosurgery, 68,* 409–416.

Lustig, A. P., & Tompkins, C. A. (1998). An examination of severity classification measures and subject criteria used for studies on mild pediatric traumatic brain injury. *Journal of Medical Speech-Language Pathology, 6*(1), 13–25.

Martin, D. A. (1988). Children and adolescents with traumatic brain injury: Impact on the family. *Journal of Learning Disabilities, 21,* 464–470.

Mira, M. P., & Tyler, J. S. (1991). Students with traumatic brain injury: Making the transition from hospital to school. *Focus on Exceptional Children, 23,* 1–12.

Novak, T. A., Dillon, M. C., & Jackson, W. T. (1996). Neurochemical mechanisms in brain injury and treatment: A review. *Journal of Clinical and Experimental Neuropsychology, 18,* 685–706.

Orsillo, S. M., McCaffrey, R. J., & Fisher, J. M. (1993). Siblings of head-injured individuals: A population at risk. *Journal of Head Trauma Rehabilitation, 8,* 102–115.

Ozer, M. (1988). *The head injury survivor on campus: Issues and resources.* Washington, DC: Health Resource Center.

Perrott, S., Taylor, H. G., & Montes, J. (1991). Neuropsychological sequelae, family stress, and environmental adaptation following a pediatric head injury. *Developmental Neuropsychology, 7,* 69–86.

Rivara, J. B., Fay, G., Jaffe, K., Polissar, N., Shurtleff, H., & Martin, K. (1992). Predictors of family functioning one year following traumatic brain injury in children. *Archives of Physical Medicine and Rehabilitation, 73,* 899–910.

Rivara, J. B., Jaffe, K. M., Polissar, N. L., Fay, G. C., Liao, S., & Martin, K. M. (1996). Predictors of family functioning and change 3 years after traumatic brain injury in children. *Archives of Physical Medicine and Rehabilitation, 77,* 754–764.

Roman, M. J., Delis, D. C., Willerman, L., Magulac, M., Demadura, T. L., de la Pena, J. L., et al. (1998). Impact of pediatric traumatic brain injury on components of verbal memory. *Journal of Clinical and Experimental Neuropsychology, 20,* 245–258.

Rosen, C. D., & Gerring, J. P. (1986). *Head trauma educational reintegration.* San Diego, CA: College-Hill Press.

Rosenthal, M., & Bond, M. R. (1990). Behavioral and psychiatric sequelae. In M. Rosenthal, M. Bond, E. R. Griffith, & J. D. Miller (Eds.), *Rehabilitation of the adult and child with traumatic brain injury* (pp. 179–192). Philadelphia: Davis.

Rourke, B. P., Bakker, D. J., Fisk, J. L., & Strang, J. D. (1983). *Child neuropsychology: An introduction to theory, research, and clinical practice.* New York: Guilford Press.

Semrud-Clikeman, M. (2001). *Traumatic brain injury in children and adolescents: Assessment and intervention.* New York: Guilford Press.

Semrud-Clikeman, M., & Hynd, G. W. (1991). Specific nonverbal and social skills deficits in children with learning disabilities. In J. E. Obrzut & G. W. Hynd (Eds.), *Neuropsychological foundations of learning disabilities: A handbook of issues, methods, and practice* (pp. 603–630). San Diego, CA: Academic Press.

Smith, C. R. (1991). *Learning disabilities: The interaction of learner, task, and setting* (2nd ed.). Boston: Allyn & Bacon.

Swift, E. E., Taylor, H. G., Kaugars, A. S., Drotar, D., Yeates, K. O., Wade, S. L., et al. (2003). Sibling relationship and behavior after pediatric traumatic brain injury. *Journal of Developmental and Behavioral Pediatrics, 24,* 24–31.

Teasdale, G., & Jennett, B. (1974). Assessment of coma and impaired consciousness. *Lancet, 2,* 81–84.

Teeter, P. A., & Semrud-Clikeman, M. (1997). *Child neuropsychology: Assessment and interventions for neurodevelopmental disorders.* Boston: Allyn & Bacon.

Tyerman, A., & Booth, J. (2001). Family interventions after traumatic brain injury: A service example. *NeuroRehabilitation, 16,* 59–66.

Van Zomeren, A. H., & Brouwer, W. H. (1992). Assessment of attention. In J. R. Crawford, D. M. Parker, & W. W. McKinlay (Eds.), *A handbook of neuropsychological assessment* (pp. 241–266). Hillsdale, NJ: Erlbaum.

Wade, S. L., Taylor, H. G., Drotar, D., Stanchin, T., & Yeates, K. O. (1996). Childhood traumatic brain injury: Initial impact on the family. *Journal of Learning Disabilities, 29,* 652–661.

Wade, S. L., Taylor, H. G., Drotar, D., Stanchin, T., & Yeates, K. O. (1998). Family burden and adaptation during the initial year following traumatic brain injury in children. *Pediatrics, 102,* 110–116.

Wade, S. L., Taylor, H. G., Drotar, D., Stanchin, T., Yeates, K. O., & Minich, N. M. (2002). A prospective study of long-term caregiver and family adaptation following brain injury in children. *Journal of Head Trauma Rehabilitation, 17,* 96–111.

Wade, S. L., Taylor, H. G., Drotar, D., Stanchin, T., Yeates, K. O., & Minich, N. M. (2003). Parent-adolescent interactions after traumatic brain injury: Their relationship to family adaptation and adolescent adjustment. *Journal of Head Trauma Rehabilitation, 18,* 164–176.

Winogren, H. W., Knights, R. M., & Bawden, H. N. (1984). Neuropsychological deficits following head injury in children. *Journal of Clinical Neuropsychology, 6*(3), 269–286.

Yeates, K. O. (2000). Closed-head injury. In K. O. Yeates, M. D. Ris, & H. G. Taylor (Eds.), *Pediatric neuropsychology: Research, theory, and practice* (pp. 92–116). New York: Guilford Press.

Zaidel, E., Clark, M., & Suyenobu, B. (1990). Hemispheric independence: A paradigm case for cognitive neuroscience. In A. B. Scheibel & A. F. Wechsler (Eds.), *Neurobiology of higher cognitive function* (pp. 297–356). New York: Guilford Press.

# CHAPTER 19

# Neurological and Psychological Issues for Learners with Seizures

ELAINE CLARK and ELIZABETH CHRISTIANSEN

SEVENTY-FIVE PERCENT OF all individuals who have seizures will have a seizure episode before the age of 20 (Kim, 1991). According to the Epilepsy Foundation of America, approximately 120,000 children in the United States are diagnosed each year with seizures (www.efa.org), making this the most common neurologic condition of childhood. Children under the age of 5 are especially susceptible to seizures; in fact, nearly a third of all seizures occur in this young age group (Barrett, 1995). Although large numbers of young children have seizure episodes associated with high temperatures (estimated to be about 30 per 100,000), in approximately 70% of seizure cases the cause is unknown. When the etiology is identified, it is often due to such conditions as hypoxic brain damage, traumatic brain injuries, central nervous system (CNS) infections, cerebral vascular accident or stroke, or congenital (structural) brain abnormalities. Genetic and environmental factors have also been studied, and some researchers have found that males and children who are of African American decent, live in socially disadvantaged conditions, and have a mother or father with epilepsy are at increased risk for seizures.

Seizures are especially difficult to treat when they begin during childhood. According to Jarrar and Buchhalter (2003), approximately 25% of children diagnosed with epilepsy (i.e., have recurrent seizures) are nonresponsive to traditional antiepileptic drug (AED) therapy. Although alternative therapies are often tried, children who have a poor response to drug treatment are also difficult to treat with alternative therapies. The struggle to find effective treatments for seizures is not new, and neither are the treatment options. The ketogenic diet, still an alternative treatment, was first tried in the 1920s, long before the discovery of AEDs. Although the physiologic mechanism for seizures was documented for the first time in this century, the phenomenon has been recorded for centuries. The first account of seizures was in 2080 B.C. in the *Code of Hamurabi*. According to Barrett (1995), Mesopotamian and Babylonian writings were remarkably accurate in terms of the description of seizure behaviors. However, the mechanism of seizures was poorly understood. Although Hippocrates alluded to underlying physiological factors in his 357 book, *The Sacred Disease*, the condition was associated with spirituality not physiology. During the Roman Empire, seizures were thought to be caused by demonic possession, and even until the nineteenth century, seizures continued to have this negative association. Given the often phasic nature of the condition, seizures were also thought to be related to lunar cycles and psychiatric disturbance. It was not until the electroencephalogram (EEG) was developed in 1929 that seizures became more clearly understood as neurologic phenomena, that is, sudden involuntary, transient alterations in neurologic function caused by abnormal excessive electrical discharge in neurons (Thiele, Gonzalez-Heydrich, & Riviello, 1999).

## MEDICAL FACTS PERTINENT TO SCHOOL PSYCHOLOGISTS

Several groups have attempted to classify seizures. Some, like the International League Against Epilepsy, have attempted to use correlations of EEG data and seizure symptomatology. As a result of problems correlating EEG with behaviors, in particular, cases of very young children and infants, other systems have been used. This includes the International Classification of Epileptic Seizures (ICES), a widely known and accepted system of seizure classification. Because the ICES does not rely on correlation of seizure behaviors and EEG, terminology from this system will be used in the current chapter. For school psychologists to effectively communicate with parents and medical professionals who are treating children with seizures, it is important to have a reasonable lexicon. Although the following section does not substitute for a comprehensive medical dictionary, such as *Stedman's Medical Dictionary* (Stedman, 2000), it will provide readers with some basic terminology.

### Seizure Classification

In the ICES, seizures are classified as either partial or generalized. There are, further, two types of partial seizures, simple and complex, and two types of generalized seizures, tonic-clonic and absence. In addition to these seizures, a few of the more common seizure syndromes and types will be described.

*Partial Seizures*   Partial seizures are caused by activation of neurons in one part of the brain, specifically, one hemisphere. Partial seizures have a focal area of electrical malfunction and often present with sensory, motor, autonomic, and psychological symptoms. These seizures are often preceded by an aura that serves as a warning sign. The aura may include an odd odor or unusual taste, a feeling of déjà vu, fear, dizziness, and nausea, to name a few. The type of aura, like the clinical manifestation of the seizure itself, is associated with the location of the seizure; in other words, seizures that are caused by abnormal firing in the occipital cortex will have a visual manifestation (e.g., perceiving objects as smaller or larger than they are), whereas those in the parietal cortex will be somatosensory and those in the frontal area will be motor-related.

The chance of an individual with epilepsy having a partial seizure is about 40%. The etiology of partial seizures varies but includes both developmental and acquired phenomena (e.g., cerebral scarring, vascular lesions, porencephalic cysts, brain tumors, traumatic brain injury, and CNS infections such as encephalitis and meningitis). The severity of partial seizures ranges from mild (i.e., no loss of consciousness, no aura) to severe (i.e., impaired consciousness and awareness, complex sensory experiences).

Partial seizures can be categorized as simple partial and complex partial. With a simple partial seizure, there is no impairment of consciousness and no aura. Abnormal motor movements may involve one extremity or just part of that extremity and can include jerking, posturing, and hypertonia. Parasthesias, numbness, tingling, and auditory/visual sensations also occur, as do a combination of other sensory and motor responses. With complex partial seizures, the child's consciousness is impaired and there are often accompanying automatisms (e.g., facial grimaces, lip smacking, chewing, twisting clothing, fumbling with the hands) and postictal (postseizure) confusion and lethargy. It is also common to find these children staring into space and experiencing a change in postural tone. This type of seizure is also referred to as a psychomotor seizure.

*Generalized Seizures*    Generalized seizures are characterized by synchronous bilateral electrical epileptical discharges. Although primary generalized seizures typically begin at the same time in both hemispheres of the brain, in the case of a secondary generalized seizure, the abnormal electrical activity begins in one hemisphere (or a particular focal area), then spreads to other parts of the brain. When this occurs, the onset seizure is referred to as a partial seizure. These seizures are typically abrupt (no aura) and often result in a loss of consciousness. The most common type of generalized seizure is a tonic-clonic seizure, or what has been referred to as a grand mal seizure. This type of seizure typically occurs first during adolescence. The tonic phase of the seizure typically lasts several seconds to a minute and involves stiffening or contraction of the trunk and extremities. This is followed by rhythmical jerking, or what is called the clonic phase. These jerking movements can last up to 30 minutes but more often last just a few seconds. The child's eyes can also be observed to roll upward or deviate to one side, and the mouth is forcibly closed with increased salivation and sounds emitted from the contracted vocal chords and abdomen. Breathing often stops momentarily, and in some cases the child will appear cyanotic (bluish). After the seizure ends (the postictal phase), the child will often feel sleepy and will be difficult to arouse. After regaining consciousness, confusion and/or agitation frequently occur, and the child may also have slurred speech, visual problems, headache, and nausea/vomiting.

Absence seizures are the second most common form of generalized seizure, yet these account for less than 10% of all seizure types (Holmes, 1999). There is no evidence that a structural lesion causes the seizure; however, in 50% of the cases, children will have at least one generalized tonic-clonic seizure (Fenichel, 1997; Holmes, 1999). The typical absence seizure is associated with various etiologies, but the prognosis is typically good (e.g., 70% to 80% of children respond to AEDs and the seizure remits spontaneously; Holmes, 1999). Some learners with absence, however, will have neurocognitive sequelae, including slowed processing of information, problems completing academic tasks, and behavior problems (Menkes & Sankar, 2000). Although, in those with childhood onset, the impact does not seem as severe, this is not the case with juvenile onset, or what is referred to as juvenile absence epilepsy. This occurs in about 40% of children with absence (Berkovic, 1997) and often involves the development of generalized tonic-clonic seizures. According to Berkovic, individuals with juvenile absence epilepsy often experience persistent convulsive type seizures that continue into adulthood.

The absence seizure occurs more commonly in females and has a peak age of onset between 4 and 8 years (Fenichel, 1997). Most absence seizures remit during adolescence, but some will persist into adulthood (Menkes & Sankar, 2000). The absence seizure typically starts abruptly and without any warning (i.e., no aura). It is characterized by an abrupt cessation of activity with brief (5 to 30 seconds) but frequent (20 or more) episodes of staring. Sometimes children with absence will lose their posture, roll their eyes, and have rapid eyelid fluttering. In many cases, though, the seizure will be mistaken for daydreaming or inattentiveness suggestive of an attention deficit disorder. Following the ictus (actual seizure), these learners will immediately resume their normal activities without any postictal confusion or fatigue. Memory for the seizure itself, however, will be impaired, as will recall of events that took place during the seizure (e.g., they won't remember what the teacher said or what classmates were doing).

The simple absence seizure usually involves staring without prominent motor features, whereas complex absence involves prominent motor phenomena such as tonic and clonic movements and automatisms. The child with an atypical absence seizure can also have motor behaviors, including cloni and automatisms; however, these behaviors are not as frequent, and the seizure itself occurs more in cycles and lasts longer than typical absence. It also starts earlier in childhood and is more often associated with developmental delay, sometimes quite severe (Holmes, 1999; Holmes & Stafstrom, 1998; Menkes & Sankar, 2000). CNS insult is the most common cause of an atypical absence seizure.

Other generalized seizures include myoclonic and atonic. Myoclonic seizures are characterized as brief involuntary muscle contractions; atonic seizures involve an abrupt loss of muscle tone that causes a person to fall. The atonic seizure is often referred to as a drop attack. Myocloni can also cause falls due to bilateral or unilateral contractions, but more typically the person retains his or her posture. Myoclonic seizures often occur right after awakening but can be triggered by a number of conditions, including sleep deprivation, alcohol ingestion, and menstruation (hormonal change; Baram, 1999; Holmes & Stafstrom, 1998).

Infantile spasms and juvenile myoclonic epilepsy (sometimes confused with nervousness) are the most common types of myocloni. There are also two rare forms, benign myoclonic epilepsy and severe myoclonic epilepsy. Whereas the benign form can be controlled with medication (typically Depakote), the severe form is highly resistant to AEDs.

SYNDROMES

The following section discusses a number of syndromes and their associated causes.

*Febrile Seizures*   Febrile seizures are characterized as brief seizure episodes that accompany a high fever. The onset of febrile seizures typically occurs between the ages of 3 months and 5 years. These are one of the most common types of seizures in young children; in fact, they are estimated to occur in 2% to 5% of children 5 years and younger. Although the prognosis for a full recovery is typically good, in 3% to 6% of cases epilepsy later develops.

*Neonatal Seizures*   These seizures occur in very young infants but are often misdiagnosed given the typical infant's motor behavior (i.e., random motor movements). Although rare in full-term healthy infants (i.e., estimated to occur in only 0.5%), neonatal seizures occur at high rates in preterm infants. In fact, it is estimated that 20% of preterm infants will have this type of seizure. Besides immature brain development (e.g., cerebral dysgenesis), other causes for neonatal seizures include asphyxia, trauma, CNS infection, exposure to toxins, metabolic conditions, drug withdrawal of the mother, and accidental injection of anesthetics at the time of delivery (drugs intended for the mother). Although the prognosis can be related to the cause of the seizure, in general it is poor. Between 15% and 40% of infants with these seizures die, and 35% are diagnosed as having mental retardation and/or cerebral palsy.

Neonatal seizures are often difficult to distinguish from infantile spasms, or West Syndrome (WS). In WS, though, the infant has clusters of myoclonic seizures. Infantile spasms typically remit between 2 and 4 years of age; however, in 25% to 60% of cases, another seizure type develops. Infants with WS have a very poor prognosis: In 80% to 90% of cases, mental retardation is diagnosed. Death also occurs in a large number of children but mostly due to the underlying cause of the seizure (e.g., intrauterine asphyxia, CNS infection, traumatic brain injury, or neurodegenerative disease).

*Benign Rolandic Seizures*   Benign rolandic seizures are fairly common during childhood. These seizures, however, occur infrequently and typically at nighttime. In most cases, the seizures begin between the ages of 3 and 10 and remit by adolescence. The seizure involves rhythmical jerking of the face and upper extremities (one-sided). In rare cases, the focus of the seizure is the occipital lobe, causing visual symptoms such as illusions and hallucinations. AEDs are usually not necessary unless the seizures are frequent or occur in the daytime. These children are generally neurologically normal unless the benign rolandic seizure develops into a generalized tonic-clonic seizure. For the most part, though, developmental delays and neurocognitive impairments are not found and the prognosis is good.

*Lennox-Gastaut Syndrome*   Lennox-Gastaut Syndrome (LGS) accounts for at least 3% to 5% of all childhood epilepsies and is one of the most severe forms (Wheless & Constantinou, 1997). The syndrome consists of multiple types of seizures, including tonic, atonic, myoclonic, and atypical absence. Prognosis is very poor: More than 75% of children with LGS have mental retardation, many quite severe (Wheless & Constantinou, 1997). The earlier the age of onset, the more likely that mental retardation will occur (e.g., under the age of 2 years). Progressive loss of intellectual functioning is common during the course of the syndrome and is often attributed to hypoxia from intractable seizures and toxicity from continual AED use.

The age of onset for LGS is between 1 and 8 years (peak period between 3 and 5). LGS is slightly more common in males and in children with a prior history of infantile spasms. Possible etiologies include hypoxic ischemic encephalopathy due to a lack of oxygen at birth; intrauterine infection such as cytomegalovirus, rubella, and toxoplasmosis; traumatic brain injury; meningitis; tuberous sclerosis; brain tumors; and metabolic disorders. In one-third of cases, however, the seizure is considered idiopathic (unknown cause). Treatment is difficult secondary to the number and degree of functional impairments that these individuals have and the variety of seizures that are associated with the syndrome. Multiple AEDs are often necessary to control the seizures, but in 80% of cases the seizures will persist into adulthood. The National Institutes of Neurological Disease and Stroke (NINDS) estimate that 25% of individuals with LGS will have serious psychological and behavioral problems, including hyperactivity, aggressiveness, and poor social skills. NINDS data further indicate that only 20% of individuals with LGS will live independent lives.

*Landau-Kleffner Syndrome*   Landau-Kleffner Syndrome (LKS) is essentially an acquired aphasia with a convulsive disorder. LKS has an onset between the ages of 2 and 11 years and is characterized by deterioration in expressive language skills following a period of normal language development. Nonverbal cognitive abilities are not affected. The seizure is actually considered an epiphenomenon of the child's aphasia, not the cause. This condition is confused at times with Autism; however, with LKS the EEG is abnormal. The onset can be sudden, but it can also develop gradually.

*Pseudoseizures*   Pseudoseizures are episodes of altered movements that superficially resemble epileptic seizures but are not associated with abnormal neuronal firing. These seizure-like behaviors are found in 5% to 9% of patients referred to epilepsy centers but are more commonly found among adolescent females. According to Fenichel (1997), the ratio of adolescent females to males is 3:1.

Pseudoseizures lack the characteristic clinical features of a true seizure. For example, the seizure tends to begin suddenly without any aura or postictal (i.e., postseizure) confusion or fatigue. Further, children with these seizures rarely respond to AED therapy. More often than not, these seizures simulate generalized tonic-clonic seizures but have no identifiable physiologic etiology or associated EEG abnormality. The seizures, however, can also appear as complex partial seizures, generalized absence, or myoclonic or atonic episodes.

Many children who experience pseudoseizures have experienced a real seizure at some point, and a significant percentage also have true epilepsy, typically a complex partial or generalized motor seizure (Holmes & Stafstrom, 1998). Only through simultaneous EEG-video monitoring can pseudoseizures be conclusively diagnosed. There are some observable differences, however, between a pseudoseizure and a true seizure. Self-injury and urinary incontinence often occur in generalized tonic-clonic seizures but rarely occur with pseudoseizures. Further, in pseudoseizures combativeness and vulgar language often occur, whereas in tonic-clonic seizures both are rare. Epileptic seizures usually occur in single episodes, but pseudoseizures often occur in clusters. Although movements simulate true epileptic seizures, rather than tonic-clonic movements there is more thrashing and jerking (even flapping and pelvic thrusting).

Fenichel (1997) found that pseudoseizures often begin after a true (i.e., organic) seizure is under control. Controlling the true seizure is thought to remove potential for secondary gain from the child (e.g., attention from parents). This, however, is not the only precursor to the onset of a pseudoseizure. Emotional stress is also thought to bring on a pseudoseizure. There is evidence to suggest that children who have suffered from physical and sexual abuse and those who have posttraumatic stress are more prone to seizure episodes (Rosenberg, Rosenberg, Williamson, & Wolford, 2000). Although the prognosis for pseudoseizures is better for children than for adults (i.e., remits after 3 years in three-quarters of cases), research also shows that the younger the child, the worse the outcome given delays in appropriate treatment and longer reinforcement of maladaptive behaviors (Holmes & Stafstrom, 1998). It is, therefore, critical that children with seizures of any type, including those suspected to have a psychologically based seizure, be thoroughly evaluated by medical personnel.

## MEDICAL EVALUATION AND TREATMENT OPTIONS

The primary method used to diagnose a seizure is the EEG. The following section describes the EEG as well as other assessment measures.

### MEDICAL EVALUATION

Using electrodes placed on the scalp, the EEG records electrical activity from cells throughout the brain. The purpose is to locate an injured area or area of overactive brain cells by taking brain wave recordings. Although the EEG cannot be used alone to make a diagnosis (it is also critical that seizure behaviors be observed), the electrical pattern (i.e., the spike-wave pattern) can help distinguish different types of seizures and help rule out pseudoseizures. In about 60% to 70% of individuals with epilepsy, a single EEG taken during sleep and again during wakefulness will demonstrate the abnormal pattern. EEGs taken only during an awake state tend to be less reliable (Williams & Sharp, 2000). It is estimated that approximately 30% of seizures cannot be confirmed using EEG technology alone. Some individuals with seizure disorders have normal EEGs and some without seizure disorders have abnormal EEG patterns.

Because it is important that seizures be correctly identified so that physicians can begin treatment, adjunctive methods may be necessary to provide sufficient data to convince the physician (preferably a pediatric neurologist) that the child has a true seizure and what the likely type is. Often, neurologists request a telemetry video EEG. This method involves the video recording of children's behavior during a suspected seizure. This telemetry method has been used to distinguish true seizure activity from phenomena such as migraine, breath holding, hyperventilation, night terrors, and syncope (i.e., fainting). Because some children will not show abnormal EEG patterns even with this method, some neurologists may rely on behavioral reports from parents. When seizures are suspected at school and not observed at home, teachers can help by providing complete descriptions of behaviors and school psychologists can assist by helping them videotape the event so that physicians can later review the tape and give a diagnosis (videotaping may also need to be done at home to assist with diagnosis).

Children with a confirmed or even suspected seizure are also evaluated at times using x-ray, blood and urine studies, and neuroimaging (e.g., computerized tomography [CT] and magnetic resonance imaging [MRI]); however, these procedures are used to help identify the cause, not the seizure itself. The etiologies that these methods are seeking to identify include abnormal brain structure, CNS infection, and other diseases causing epileptiform activity in the brain.

## MEDICAL TREATMENT

*AED Therapy*   Because seizures occur when the basal level of neuronal excitability exceeds a critical level or threshold in individuals who are predisposed, the preferred treatment is AED therapy. AEDs keep the neuronal excitability level below the seizure threshold (Wong, 1999). In some cases, however, AEDs may not be used. For example, when children have only one unprovoked afebrile (non-fever) seizure and have up to a 70% chance of not having further seizures, AED therapy may not be indicated (Jarrar & Buchhalter, 2003). On the other hand, there are groups of children who need immediate aggressive drug therapy to get their seizures under control. This includes children who have seizures that have an identifiable etiology such as febrile seizures and infantile spasms.

Drug therapy has been shown to have a number of negative side effects, including sedation, sleeplessness, weight changes (gain or loss), dizziness, gastrointestinal distress, rash, and gait problems. Although these side effects are undisputed, there is considerable inconsistency in the research regarding the impact of seizures on cognitive and behavioral functioning. The drug that has been most associated with these problems is phenobarbital.

Phenobarbital is thought to cause problems with decreased psychomotor speed, impaired information processing and cognitive ability, diminished concentration and memory, impaired motor functions, increased irritability and hyperactivity, and depression (Williams, Bates, et al., 1998). Investigations of phenobarbital, however, have shown that when dosages are kept low but within a therapeutic range, side effects are rather minimal. The same has been found when using other drugs, including phenytoin (Dilantin). Studies with this drug have found progressive encephalopathy with personality and intellectual changes (Legarda, Booth, Fennell, & Maria, 1996). Although much of the problem with side effects appears to be related to high serum levels that cause drug toxicity, many of the children who require high dosages are those with complicated seizure disorders. These children are also the ones who often have coexisting cognitive and behavioral problems and are compromised by the etiology of their seizures, not necessarily the drugs to treat them. Williams and her colleagues, for example, failed to find adverse side effects on cognition (e.g., attention, immediate and delayed memory, complex motor speed) and behavior in children being treated during the first 6 months using a single AED (only one child in the study was taking phenobarbital; the majority were on valproic acid or Tegretol). Although valproic acid (Depakote) and carbamazepine (Tegretol) are considered to have some of the fewest side effects of all the AEDs, even these drugs in high dosages have been found to compromise cognitive functioning (e.g., Tegretol can negatively affect memory and learning efficiency).

Ideally, the preferred treatment is low-dose single-drug therapy (Legarda et al., 1996). Side effects are also more pronounced when several medications are combined. Although certain children seem to respond better in general to drug therapy (e.g., children with generalized tonic-clonic and absence seizures; Holmes, 1999), even these groups of children have been found to get a better response from certain select AEDs. For example, Jarrar and Buchhalter (2003) have found that children who have generalized tonic-clonic, myoclonic, and atonic seizures tend to do best on Depakote. Children with juvenile myoclonic epilepsy, in fact, have been found to have 85% to 90% seizure reduction on Depakote (Baram, 1999). When first-choice drugs are found to be ineffective, new drugs such as topiramate (Topomax), lamotrigine (Lamictal), and felbamate are often tried. Depakote has also been successfully used with typical absence seizures but is not the first-line drug. The preferred AED for absence is ethosuximide (Zarontin). Not all children respond to Zarontin, however, and are therefore placed on some of the other new line drugs (e.g., felbamate, gabapentin, lamotrigine, topiramate, tiagabine, leve-tiracetam, oxcarbazepine, and zonisamide).

Although a review of drugs is beyond the scope of this chapter, school psychologists need to be aware that a number of newer drugs are on the market for seizures, especially for children who have refractory seizures. This includes children with LGS. In this group, felbamate has been found to be effective. According to data from the Felbamate Study Group in LGS (1993), LGS seizures were reduced by 19%. Felbamate, like most newer drugs, has not been studied as extensively as others but has been found to have some serious side effects (e.g., aplastic anemia and hepatic failure). Many of the children who have serious complications with felbamate have also been shown to have problems with toxicity from other AEDs (Jarrar & Buchhalter, 2003). Serious side effects often lead to a discontinuation of drug therapy and use of alternative treatments, including diet changes.

*Ketogenic Diet*   The ketogenic diet requires about a 3 to 1 ratio of fat to carbohydrate/protein and is intended to induce the metabolic effects of starvation. Although the popularity of this method declined when AEDs were first developed, the diet became popular again when it was discovered that many individuals with seizures were nonresponsive to drug therapy or had problems with drug toxicity. Some researchers have found the diet to be effective in reducing refractory seizures by about 30% to 70% (Thiele et al., 1999). Seizures that have been shown to be most responsive to the diet include atonic, tonic, myoclonic, and atypical absence (Jarrar & Buchhalter, 2003).

The ketogenic diet has some negative side effects, including hypoglycemia, dehydration, and vomiting; however, these problems are suspected to be more a function of the way the diet is initiated rather than due to the diet itself (Jarrar & Buchhalter, 2003; Vining, 1999). Some children cannot tolerate the diet. In fact, in one study reported by the Epilepsy International group, 50% of children were forced to discontinue the diet (www.epilepsy-international.com). Although some of the side effects can be treated (e.g., dietary supplements for problems with vitamin and mineral deficiencies), others are more serious and require discontinuation of the diet. This includes significant increases in hepatic enzymes that cause hepatotoxicity. Researchers have found that many of the children who had this complication were also on Depakote, a drug that has also been associated with hepatotoxicity (Williams, Bates, et al., 1998).

*Surgery*   Surgery is another alternative treatment and consists of hemispherectomies (e.g., removing an entire hemisphere of the brain), temporal lobectomies (removing just the temporal lobe), and interhemispheric commissurotomy (disconnecting the commissural tissues that connect the right and left hemispheres).

Surgery is intended for a variety of purposes, including removal of damaged tissue that is contributing to ongoing epileptiform activity, eliminating the cause (e.g., resecting a brain tumor), and preventing the spread of epileptiform activity from one hemisphere to the other.

The rates of success from surgeries vary widely. In many cases, however, surgery improves the quality of children's lives; for example, research has demonstrated a reduction of seizures in 80% of children who have temporal lobectomies. Although delayed verbal memory is often impacted by this surgery, regardless of the hemisphere involved, typically the child's cognitive functioning is spared (Williams, Griebel, Sharp, & Boop, 1998). This is not always the case with surgeries that divide the hemispheres, such as a corpus callosotomy. Although this type of surgery has been found to improve seizure control in 25% to 75% of all cases of generalized tonic-clonic or partial seizures in children, these children are often compromised cognitively. Some argue, however, that the compromise predated the surgery; that is, the child is already intellectually compromised from intractable seizures or the etiology of these (Williams & Sharp, 2000). Even corpus callosotomies can improve the quality of a child's life by reducing the frequency of seizures and improving attention to tasks as well as task completion. Fortunately, unlike adults who have this type of surgery, children rarely have a disconnection syndrome. Another type of psychosurgery for epilepsy is a hemispherectomy. This operation is rarely performed due to high rates of complications (e.g., post-operative death in 6.6% of cases) and other serious complications in 17% to 35% of cases (e.g., hemorrhage and hydrocephalus; Fenichel, 1997).

## ANTICIPATED IMPACT ON LEARNING AND PSYCHOLOGICAL FUNCTIONING

### LEARNING OUTCOMES

Children with seizure disorders are clearly at risk for increased problems with learning. This is due in part to the disproportionately large number of school days and instructional opportunities that these children miss each year. Although some children with seizure disorders have below-average intelligence, researchers have found that even children with normal intelligence have greater problems learning than their nonepileptic peers. Bailet and Turk (2000), for example, found significant differences on reading and spelling measures for children with seizures who have normal-range IQ scores. Although children with significant cognitive impairments do even worse on academic measures, this group is not the largest. In fact, even in studies that have found IQ scores to be significantly below that of nonepileptic peers, the mean IQ was still average (e.g., FSIQ of 98 found for the Bailet and Turk subjects with seizures). What probably distinguished the children in the Bailet and Turk study were the abnormal EEG findings. Few studies have actually correlated EEG epileptiform activity with academic achievement, making this study unique and important in suggesting that such a relationship may exist. This may be a particularly important finding for school psychologists who conduct evaluations of children with seizures and want to develop an educational plan based on expectations for performance.

Other factors that have been found to correlate with learning outcomes include age at the time of seizure onset; foci of the seizure activity (e.g., temporal versus frontal); seizure type, duration, and frequency; and hand dominance. Strauss,

Hunter, and Wada (1995) found that the most potent predictors of learning were seizure location and handedness. Although age of seizure onset was also significant, a finding in many other studies as well, this was not as potent as seizure location and handedness. Strauss and her colleagues found that when children had temporal and extratemporal lobe seizures and left-hand dominance, they were significantly more likely to have cognitive and learning problems. Hershey, Craft, Glauser, and Hale (1998) similarly found that children who had temporal lobe epilepsy were at much greater risk for memory problems, especially memory for spatial material. Overall, research has suggested that handedness and seizure location account for 6% and 10% of the variance, respectively, in FSIQ scores. Although the correlation between lesion site and IQ may be apparent, handedness may not. Studies have found, however, that children who are left-handed have significantly lower IQs. In fact, some have found the IQ averages to be as low as 80, compared to 93 in right-handed peers with seizures. It is hypothesized that the left-handedness in these children is pathologic and signals neurodevelopmental abnormality. Although the effect is more subtle, cerebral speech dominance has also been found to correlate with intelligence, in particular, nonverbal reasoning, another indication of possible cerebral reorganization induced by early injury.

Age of seizure onset has also been found to correlate with FSIQ; that is, the earlier the onset, the lower the IQ. Although Strauss and her colleagues (1995) failed to show as dramatic a difference for children with earlier-onset seizures, other studies have found that this variable may account for as much as 8% of the variance in FSIQ. Dodrill (1992), in fact, found that mean FSIQ scores increase in a linear fashion from age of onset, with a mean IQ of 78.8 when seizures begin before the age of 1 year, a mean IQ of 96.6 with onset during childhood and adolescence, and a mean IQ of 96.5 with an adult onset. Similar to the finding of left-handedness, age of onset has been hypothesized to reflect a disruption of neuronal processes in early gestational and postnatal development. It is not clear, though, if the phenomenon in early onset is due to factors such as the etiology of the seizure and/or the use of medications that adversely impact cognitive functioning. For later-onset seizures, it is similarly unclear what role the frequency of seizures and years of education might play.

Another factor that seems to impact cognitive functioning is the type of seizure that a child has. This, however, appears to be related to both pathologic neurodevelopment and seizure. For example, children who have typical absence and benign rolandic seizures have been found to have normal ability levels, whereas children with atypical seizures (e.g., atypical absence), mixed seizures, infantile spasms, and syndromes such as LGS have unusually high rates of intellectual impairment. Children whose seizures are associated with chromosomal abnormalities, insults to the brain such as perinatal asphyxia, CNS infection, and neurodevelopmental conditions (e.g., tuberous sclerosis and Autism) are also at greater risk for lower than normal IQs, again assumed to be related to the underlying cause and not the seizure itself or its treatment. Children who have poorly controlled seizures are also at greater risk for intellectual deficits. This includes children with status epilepticus and seizures that are nonresponsive to first-line AED therapy, thus requiring unusually high dosages and alternative therapies. With the exception of phenobarbital and phenytoin, however, few AEDs have been associated with cognitive and learning problems (Williams & Sharp, 2000).

## PSYCHOLOGICAL AND BEHAVIORAL OUTCOMES

Children with seizures have been found to have disproportionately high rates of psychological disturbance. Although the cause of this has been debated, the existent of emotional and behavioral problems in many of these children seems clear. In one of the first community-based studies of children's psychological and behavioral status following seizure, Graham and Rutter (1968) found that 29% were diagnosed with psychiatric disorders, a rate much higher than either of their control groups (normals had a rate of 6.6%, and the children with chronic but nonneurologic illness had a rate of 12%). Dunn, Austin, and Huster (1999) also found that in their sample of children with seizures that 25% had identifiable behavior disorders. Other researchers have found even higher rates of psychopathology, some as high as 60% (e.g., Caplan, Arbelle, & Magharious, 1998). Although one might question the role of the neurologic condition versus that of the reaction to it, some research has clearly demonstrated that brain abnormality plays a major role. Studies found certain localized EEG findings being correlated with psychological disturbance (e.g., Kim's 1991 study showing left temporal spiking being associated); others have found psychological problems predating the seizure onset by several months (e.g., Austin, Harezlak, & Dunn's, 2001, research).

Although there has been a wide range of problems reported, including aggression and depression, many of the studies have found internalizing disorders to be occurring at a much higher rate. Ettinger, Wesbrot, and Nolan (1998) found that 26% of the children they studied who had seizures met criteria for depression, and 16% met criteria for anxiety. Austin and his colleagues (2002) demonstrated a direct positive relationship between recurrent seizures and degree of psychological disturbance.

Despite consistent findings in the literature that children with epilepsy are at increased risk for psychological problems, researchers have found that very few children are receiving any treatment for these. Ott and his colleagues (2003) found that fewer than 40% of the children they studied who were diagnosed with psychiatric disorders had received therapy. Although this is more encouraging than earlier studies that found no children with psychiatric conditions receiving treatment (i.e., Ettinger et al., 1998), the study by Ott et al. indicates that much still needs to be done to address the mental health needs of these children.

Some have hypothesized that one reason children with epilepsy fail to receive mental health services is that the psychological problems are misinterpreted as seizure manifestations. Others question the extent to which these children's problems are being overlooked because of their internalizing nature. In any case, there is a clear need to find and treat children with epilepsy who have emotional and behavioral difficulties. Data from studies on adults suggest that the problems are not likely to remit without intervention. In fact, some researchers have found high rates of psychiatric disorders in adults with epilepsy who had problems that began in childhood. Blumer, Montouris, and Hermann (1995) showed a rate as high as 80% for psychiatric disorders in adults with an epileptic disorder.

## CONCLUSION

There are a number of ways that school psychologists can help improve outcomes for children with seizures, including helping teachers and parents to better understand what to expect of children in terms of their emotional response to having seizures as well as their response to peers and the learning environment. As with any condition, seizures affect different children in different ways. It is therefore critical that every child be evaluated to determine treatment needs. Although research has been inconsistent, and sometimes contradictory in terms of how seizures are thought to impact a child's learning and behavior, data are fairly clear that children with seizures are at risk for poorer performance in school and greater social and emotional problems.

Factors that have been shown to predict the worst outcome are seizure onset after the age of 16, the onset of seizures following the initiation of AED treatment, polydrug therapy for seizure control, and history of generalized tonic-clonic or myoclonic seizures (Wong, 1999). Conversely, predicting the best outcome are first seizure before the age of 12 (but no history of a neonatal seizure), fewer than 21 seizures before the start of drug therapy, good response to a single AED, and normal premorbid intelligence. Although these factors are outside the control of professionals who are working with the child, understanding prognostic factors can help determine how high to set the bar when designing educational programs. Mcnelis (2001) found that children who do best academically are those whose teachers and parents set high expectations.

Often, though, children with seizures never come to the attention of the school psychologist. This seems to be due in part to the fact that these children are considered to have physical health impairments, not mental health problems. School psychologists can be valuable in assisting children with seizures by designing strategies to improve their academic performance and providing therapy to help them deal more effectively with their medical condition. Although these children may already be receiving classroom accommodations and/or special education services, professionals providing these services often are not familiar with the impact that seizures have on learning and behavior. This includes special education teachers assigned to work with these learners. Part of the problem is the trend toward noncategorical training in special education, but another problem is the diverse population of learners that special educators are required to work with. Although school psychologists also work with a wide range of problems and learners with disabilities and their training programs are often modeled after that of a general practitioner, many school psychologists receive preservice training in neuropsychology and medical conditions that may affect a child's education. School psychologists with a neuropsychological assessment background are at an advantage in being capable of providing comprehensive neuropsychological assessments in the schools at no cost to families, and they can provide practical treatment recommendations.

Working in the schools puts the school psychologist at a decided advantage in knowing what resources are available in the schools and how to obtain these. In addition, school psychologists have access to educational records and educational personnel who worked with the child and family (current and past), can observe the child in the classroom and interacting with peers, can monitor academic progress, and can design and evaluate educational strategies that are being used to improve a student's learning (e.g., reading instruction, study skills strategies, homework programs). Further, school psychologists can consult with parents about their child's progress and communicate parents' concerns to teachers and professionals who are involved with the child's treatment. School psychologists with knowledge about seizures can provide valuable information to physicians about a child's response to medical treatment (e.g., efficacy of AED therapy and problems with side effects) and inform them if the child demonstrates an inexplicable change in behavior that suggests deterioration or adverse response to therapy.

School psychologists can also help children to develop better social relationships and improve coping skills. Often, children with seizures are rejected by peers and experience social isolation. Providing peers with information about seizures may help, but research has focused more on psychological interventions to be used with children who have seizure disorders. Although each individual has different emotional issues, many children with seizures struggle to gain independence. It is not unusual, for example, for an adolescent looking forward to his 16th birthday to be refused a driver's license or for a graduating senior to be turned down for a job because of safety concerns or misinformation about seizures. Unemployment rates for individuals with epilepsy who are capable of working have been reported to be between 20% and 30%. School psychologists can help ensure that the young people they work with are not a part of this number by assisting these individuals to dispel myths about epilepsy and to communicate with potential employers about any problems they have that could interfere with work. Regardless of what the issue is, accurate information needs to be provided so that individuals with seizures have the opportunity to achieve their goals and live independent, self-determined lives.

In some cases, therapy will be needed to assist the child or adolescent with seizures to cope. Research has shown that children with seizures can benefit from stress management, relaxation therapy, and biofeedback (Holmes & Stafstrom, 1998; Mitchell, 1999). School psychologists may be in the best position to provide this type of treatment but may also know someone they would recommend to provide this. School psychologists can recommend child and adolescent psychiatrists to evaluate the child for the appropriateness of medication. Although psychotropic medications will not be necessary in all cases, children with seizures who have depression and other internalizing (or externalizing) disorders may benefit from medication and need to have this type of intervention considered. Finally, school psychologists can help parents by providing information about important resources, such as the Epilepsy Foundation of America (800-EFA-1000; www.epilepsyfoundation.org) as well as reading material that may be helpful for them (e.g., *Seizures and Epilepsy in Childhood: A Guide for Parents*, Freeman, Vining, & Pillas, 1997).

## REFERENCES

Austin, J., Dunn, D., Caffrey, H., Perkins, S., Harezlak, J., & Douglas, R. (2002). Recurrent seizures and behavior problems in children with first recognized seizures: A prospective study. *Epilepsia, 43,* 1564–1573.

Austin, J., Harezlak, J., & Dunn, D. (2001). Behaviour problems in children before first recognized seizure. *Pediatrics, 107,* 115–122.

Bailet, L., & Turk, W. R. (2000). The impact of childhood epilepsy on neurocognitive and behavioral performance: A prospective longitudinal study. *Epilepsia, 41*(4), 426–431.

Baram, T. Z. (1999). Myoclonus and myoclonic seizures. In K. Swaimann & S. Ashwall (Eds.), *Pediatric neurology: Principles and practice* (pp. 668–675). St. Louis, MO: Mosby.

Barrett, R. P. (1995). Seizure disorders: A review for school psychologists. *School Psychology Review, 24*(2), 131–146.

Berkovic, S. (1997). Childhood absence epilepsy and juvenile absence epilepsy. In E. Wyllie (Ed.), *The treatment of epilepsy: Principles and practice* (2nd ed., pp. 466). Baltimore: Williams & Wilkins.

Blumer, D., Montouris, G., & Hermann, B. (1995). Psychiatric morbidity in seizure patients on a neurodiagnostic monitoring unit. *Journal of Neuropsychiatry and Clinical Neuroscience, 7,* 445–456.

Caplan, R., Arbelle, S., & Magharious, W. (1998). Psychopathology in pediatric complex partial and generalized epilepsy. *Developmental Medicine and Child Neurology, 40,* 805–811.

Dodrill, C. (1992). Neuropsychological aspects of epilepsy. *Psychiatric Clinics of North America, 15,* 383–394.

Dunn, D., Austin, J., & Huster, G. (1999). Behavior problems in children with new onset epilepsy. *Journal of American Academy of Adolescent Psychiatry, 38,* 1132–1138.

Ettinger, A. B., Weisbrot, D. M., & Nolan, E. E. (1998). Symptoms of depression and anxiety in pediatric epilepsy patients. *Epilepsia, 39,* 595–599.

Felbamate Study Group in Lennox-Gastaut Syndrome. (1993). Efficacy of felbamate in childhood epileptic encephalopathy. *New England Journal of Medicine, 328,* 29–33.

Fenichel, G. M. (1997). *Clinical pediatric neurology: A signs and symptoms approach* (3rd ed.). Philadelphia: Saunders.

Freeman, J. M., Vining, E., & Pillas, D. (1997). *Seizures and epilepsy in childhood: A guide for parents.* Baltimore: Johns Hopkins University Press.

Graham, P., & Rutter, M. (1968). Organic brain dysfunction and child psychiatric disorder. *British Medical Journal, 3,* 695–700.

Hershey, T., Craft, S., Glauser, T. A., & Hale, S. (1998). Short-term and long-term memory in early temporal lobe dysfunction. *Neuropsychology, 12*(1), 52–64.

Holmes, G. L. (1999). Generalized seizures. In K. Swaimann & S. Ashwall (Eds.), *Pediatric neurology: Principles and practice* (pp. 634–645). St. Louis, MO: Mosby.

Holmes, G. L., & Stafstrom, C. E. (1998). The epilepsies. In R. B. David (Ed.), *Child and adolescent neurology* (pp. 183–234). St. Louis, MO: Mosby.

Jarrar, R. G., & Buchhalter, J. R. (2003). Therapeutics in pediatric epilepsy: The new antiepileptic drugs and the ketogenic diet. *Mayo Clinic Proceedings, 78,* 359–370.

Kim, W. J. (1991). Psychiatric aspects of epileptic children and adolescents. *Journal of the American Academy of Child and Adolescent Psychiatry, 30,* 874–886.

Legarda, S. B., Booth, M., Fennell, E. B., & Maria, B. (1996). Altered cognitive functioning in children with idiopathic epilepsy receiving valproate monotherapy. *Journal of Child Neurology, 11,* 321–330.

Mcnelis, A. M. (2001). Academic achievement in children with new onset seizures or asthma. *Dissertation Abstracts International, 61*(8-B), 4079.

Menkes, J. H., & Sankar, R. (2000). Paroxysmal disorders. In J. H. Menkes & H. B. Sarnat (Eds.), *Child neurology* (pp. 919–1026). Philadelphia: Lippincott, Williams, & Wilkins.

Mitchell, W. G. (1999). Behavioral, Cognitive, and Social Difficulties in childhood epilepsy. In K. Swaimann & S. Ashwall (Eds.), *Pediatric neurology: Principles and practice* (pp. 742–746). St. Louis, MO: Mosby.

Ott, D., Siddarth, P., Gurbani, S., Koh, S., Tournay, A., Shields, W., et al. (2003). Behavioral disorders in pediatric epilepsy: Unmet psychiatric need. *Epilepsia, 44,* 591–597.

Rosenberg, H. J., Rosenberg, S. D., Williamson, P. D., & Wolford, G. L. (2000). A comparative study of trauma and posttraumatic stress disorder prevalence in epilepsy patients and psychogenic nonepileptic seizure patients. *Epilepsia, 41,* 447–452.

Stedman's Medical Dictionary, 27th Edition. (2000). Baltimore: Williams & Wilkins.

Strauss, E., Hunter, M., & Wada, J. (1995). Risk factors for cognitive impairment in epilepsy. *Neuropsychology, 9*(4), 457–463.

Thiele, E. A., Gonzalez-Heydrich, & Riviello, J. J. (1999). Epilepsy in children and adolescents. *Child and Adolescent Psychiatric Clinics of North America, 8*(4), 671–694.

Vining, E. P. (1999). Clinical efficacy of the ketognic diet. *Epilepsy Research, 37,* 181–190.

Wheless, J. W., & Constantinou, J. (1997). Lennox-Gaustaut Syndrome. *Pediatric Neurology, 17,* 203–209.

Williams, J., Bates, S., Griebel, M. L., Lange, B., Mancias, P., Pihoker, C. M., et al. (1998). Does short-term antiepileptic drug treatment in children result in cognitive or behavioral change? *Epilepsia, 39*(10), 1064–1069.

Williams, J., Griebel, M. L., Sharp, G. B., & Boop, F. A. (1998). Cognition and behavior after temporal lobectomy in pediatric patients with intractable epilepsy. *Pediatric Neurology, 19,* 189–194.

Williams, J., & Sharp, G. B. (2000). Epilepsy. In K. O. Yeates, M. D. Ris, & H. G. Taylor (Eds.), *Pediatric neuropsychology: Research, theory, and practice.* (pp. 47–73). New York: Guilford Press.

Wong, D. (1999). *Whaley and Wong's nursing care of infants and children* (6th ed.). St Louis: Mosby.

# CHAPTER 20

# School Neuropsychology of Attention-Deficit/Hyperactivity Disorder

PHYLLIS ANNE TEETER ELLISON

THERE IS GROWING evidence that chronic, severe psychiatric disorders of childhood and adolescence have a neurobiological basis (Barkley, 1997, 1998; Teeter, 1998; Teeter & Semrud-Clikeman, 1997). As a result, school psychologists should be well versed in assessment and intervention paradigms that explore neurodevelopmental and neuropsychological correlates of disorders that are commonly assessed and treated in school settings. Attention-Deficit/Hyperactivity Disorder (ADHD) is one of the most common disorders of childhood, with recent studies showing that approximately 5% to 7% of school-age children (Bararesi et al., 2002; Leibson, Katusic, Barbaresi, Ransom, & O'Brien, 2001), between 2% and 6% of adolescents (Murphy & Barkley, 1996) have the disorder.

This chapter explores the neuropsychology of ADHD with a particular emphasis on practices suited for school settings. First, a rationale for a transactional paradigm for understanding ADHD is explored. Second, a review of brain functions and neurodevelopmental issues pertaining to ADHD is presented. Third, the concept of executive functions (i.e., self-modulation and self-regulation) is explored. Fourth, guidelines are presented for conducting school-based neuropsychological assessment and intervention plans for ADHD.

## NEED FOR TRANSACTIONAL PARADIGMS IN THE ASSESSMENT AND TREATMENT OF ADHD

It is critical to consider assessment-intervention paradigms that promote and recognize the need for an integrated orientation for understanding the complex relationships between brain functions and the psychosocial, emotional, behavioral, academic, and psychiatric consequences of ADHD. Although the literature is replete with examples of approaches that focus on single theoretical models—the most common being behavioral approaches—understanding the interaction of neurobiological and genetic factors underlying ADHD is essential. Although behavioral approaches and biological determinism have historical roots, integrative, transactional models are more defensible (see Barkley, 1998; Teeter, 1998; Teeter & Semrud-Clikeman, 1997). There is no doubt that a more definitive science of childhood psychiatric disorders requires a clearer understanding of abnormal behaviors, their neurobiological basis, and the context that affects their expression. Casey (2000) describes how disruption of inhibitory control systems—abnormal functions in the frontostriatal circuitry of the brain—forms the basis of a number of childhood disorders including ADHD, obsessive-compulsive disorders (OCD), Tourette Syndrome (TS), and schizophrenia. It is important to note that while a search for the neuropsychological basis of ADHD is important, it does not negate the need to fully explore the contextual, environmental variables associated with ADHD. It is the interaction of these factors that contribute to the associated problems that typically accompany the disorder. Hinshaw and Park (1999) make this argument cogently when addressing disruptive behavioral disorders (DBD) in general. "Whereas careful description and documentation of developmental patterns is indeed important, understanding of causal pathways will be facilitated by linking data with developmental, personality-related, psychobiological, and cultural theory. On the other hand, overarching 'theories of everything' that do not allow for the great individual and subgroup differences in causal pathways, underlying mechanisms, and response to intervention are doomed to failure. That is, theories must take into account the considerable individual, developmental and cultural differences that pertain to DBD" (Hinshaw & Park, 1999, p. 44). Furthermore integrated models are powerful because they begin to identify and link transactional pathways where neurobiological and genetic vulnerabilities (i.e., temperamental factors) interact with environmental factors such as parent-child fit; peer, school, family, and neighborhood influences; and socioeconomic status and cultural factors (Hinshaw & Park, 1999; Teeter, 1998; Teeter & Semrud-Clikeman, 1997). For these reasons, integrated transactional assessment and treatment models are most defensible.

The major rationales and tenets of an integrated model for assessing and treating ADHD in children and adolescents are as follows:

- Person-environment approaches are not dichotomous; and, dichotomous approaches are not empirically defensible. Although ADHD has a biogenetic basis, environmental factors interact with neuropsychological functions and contribute to a number of associated features of the disorder—impaired parent-child relations, poor social interactions, academic difficulties, and comorbid disorders (e.g., conduct disorders, depression, and anxiety). To investigate or emphasize one factor and ignore other variables is tantamount to poor science, and may lead to an incomplete and/or erroneous understanding and clinical treatment of ADHD. There is need for "person centered" models where neurobiological influences are investigated and where the child's individual experiential, environmental, and cultural context is better described.
- There is need to consider a full range of assessment and intervention strategies when treating children and adolescents with ADHD, particularly multimodal approaches that address child characteristics (i.e., symptom severity

including hyperactivity, inattention, and impulsivity), family distress and parenting styles, social relationships, and academic problems.

- There is a need for school psychologists to be knowledgeable about pharmacological treatments that modify biochemical activity and subsequent behavioral functioning of children receiving stimulant medications. Psychologists who can monitor medication efficacy and negative side effects can serve an important role in the management of children who are medicated in school settings.

- There is a need for a transactional, neurodevelopmental model of ADHD to better understand the developmental trajectory of the disorder, and to appreciate the need of interventions through the lifespan. Neurobiological risk factors early in life (e.g., temperamental variations, poor impulse control, and disinhibition) affect a child's overall social, psychological, emotional, and behavioral functioning into adolescence and adulthood. By approaching ADHD from a neurodevelopmental perspective, we can begin to better investigate how specific treatment approaches facilitate or interfere with normal development. We can begin to more clearly identify causal pathways of comorbid disorders with ADHD and to determine whether preventive measures alter these pathways.

- There is a need to develop a research base for understanding how gender and cultural differences influence the development, expression, and course of ADHD. It is surprising that at this stage, we know so little about how these factors are related to risk factors including temperamental dispositions, exposure to adverse environments, resiliency and coping mechanisms that ultimately affect child and adolescent adjustment and well-being. The extent to which of these factors interact with biological vulnerabilities should be explored.

- Finally, it is important that psychologists begin to identify competency and resiliency factors to reduce the negative impact of ADHD. Resiliency models should be incorporated into assessment and intervention processes within a transactional, neurodevelopmental context. We need to better identify factors that mediate competency and adaptability in young children with ADHD in order to reduce the development of other comorbid disorders, school and work failure, impaired relationships, and distress and unhappiness that often persists into later life.

In an effort to fully appreciate how brain functions affect the social, emotional, psychological, and behavioral functions of children and adolescents with ADHD, it is important to investigate basic brain regions involved with these complex functions. The following section briefly reviews these relationships.

## BRAIN FUNCTIONS AND NEURODEVELOPMENT: EFFECTS ON SOCIAL, EMOTIONAL, AND BEHAVIORAL FUNCTIONING

The direct role of brain function and development on psychological, social, and behavioral development is far from definitive in children (Kolb & Fantie, 1997). Empirical evidence of these relationships is generally correlational, and many studies have not addressed the impact of environmental and social-cultural factors on these relationships. However, there is emerging evidence to suggest that meaningful patterns can be discerned from the literature (Teeter & Semrud-Clikeman, 1997). A brief overview of the neuroanatomical mechanisms and functional systems of basic emotions is presented, followed by a summary of literature for these mechanisms for children with ADHD.

The basic organization of motivations and emotions are broad and encompass multisystemic relationships (Adrianov, 1996). Basic sensory, associative and activating-integrative (i.e., motoric) systems interact with neocortical and limbicoreticular formulations to directly impact aspects of personality function, and conscious and unconscious forms of activity (e.g., goal directed behavior, motivation). These systems are diverse and interrelated, such that neurochemical, neurohormonal and/or morphological variations produce a myriad of emotional and motivational states. Memory and other cognitive functions play a role in this dynamic and serve to anchor and interpret new experiences into existing memory traces. Furthermore many of these systems have built in feedback loops whereby subcortical and cortical regions constantly influence one another, and thus influence emotional, behavioral, and inhibitory reactions and processes.

While neuroscientists and clinicians are interested in how brain functions and neurodevelopment, affective and cognitive processes are also involved in these processes. The concept of affective styles has been explored in an effort to bring broad and at times divergent studies and theoretical orientations together for a more coherent model of emotional and motivational systems.

APPROACH AND WITHDRAWAL SYSTEMS

Researchers have explored the concept of "affective style," the neuroanatomical substrates of motivational/emotional systems, and the cognitive consequences of these relationships (Davidson, 1999). Davidson suggests that dispositional mood and emotional reactions are distinct in quality and intensity, and that individuals vary on these dimensions. Differences in affective states have been referred to as "affective style," and appear related to temperament, personality, and vulnerability to psychopathology (Davidson, 1999). Individual differences in "affective style" may provide insight into why some individuals have a tendency to be resilient in the face of adversity, while others tend to be overwhelmed by life events. It is likely that resiliency is a function of how quickly individuals recover from aversive experiences and the ability to regulate emotions under adverse situations.

"Emotion regulation refers to a broad constellation of processes that serve to amplify, attenuate, or maintain the strength of emotional reactions. Included among these processes are certain features of attention which regulate the extend to which an organism can be distracted from a potentially aversive stimulus (Derryberry & Reed, 1996) and the capacity for self-generated imagery to replace emotions that are unwanted with more desirable imagery scripts" (Davidson, 1999, p. 104). Furthermore, Davidson suggests that when emotions are generated, regulatory processes are also activated so that it is "difficult to distinguish sharply between when an emotion ends and regulation begins" (p. 104).

Approach-withdrawal systems have been the focus of much of the "affective style" research. The approach system is related to positive affective states such as pride, enthusiasm, and so on, and usually results in the individual moving toward a desired goal (DePue & Collins, 1999). The withdrawal system appears to facilitate the individual's withdrawal from aversive stimuli and negative reactions including fear and disgust (Davidson, 1999).

In functional magnetic resonance imaging (fMRI) studies, Irwin et al. (1996) showed that right hemisphere activation is prominent during aversive, withdrawal emotions and that the amygdala and the temporal pole regions are activated under these conditions. Studies employing positron emission tomography (PET) and electrophysiological activation patterns confirm these findings, and it is likely that prefrontal, basal ganglia and hypothalamic regions are also involved in the motoric and automatic components of withdrawal-related, negative affect. This system appears to facilitate withdrawal behaviors from aversive stimulation, and is activated during negative emotional states such as fear and disgust. On the other hand, the left prefrontal cortex and amygdala appear activated during positive affective states and may be related to approach, goal-directed behaviors. Davidson (1999) hypothesizes that left hemisphere activation may serve to inhibit negative emotions that interfere with the generation of positive affect and goal-directed, approach behaviors. Put another way "one function of positive affect is to inhibit concurrent negative affect" (Davidson, 1999, p. 109).

## Frontal Lobe Mechanisms, Executive Functions, and Emotional Regulation

Pribram (1992) describes the contributions of specific prefrontal regions on executive functions. The dorsal frontal region is involved with determining the importance of a situation. The lateral frontal region judges the effort needed to accomplish a goal and it determines whether the goal is worth the effort; while, the orbital frontal regions determine the appropriateness of actions taking into account the social and situational context of the behavior. It is the interplay of the frontal cortex with its influence on other cortical and subcortical regions that are thought to be involved with executive control functions (Thatcher, 1991).

The prefrontal lobes have rich connections to posterior brain regions for perceptual processing and to the limbic system for emotional processes. "By virtue of its unique anatomical connectivity, the prefrontal cortex is likely to play an important role in top-down influences on brain regions that are critical components of circuitry required for many complex emotional and cognitive functions" (Davidson, 1999, p. 115). In a series of studies, Davidson and colleagues (Davidson, 1995; Henriques & Davidson, 1990, 1991) investigated the relationship of frontal activation patterns and various psychological disturbances. They found that depressed individuals show a pattern of relative right prefrontal activation with accompanying decreased left hemisphere activation. This particular activation pattern was related to poor performance on tasks of visuospatial processing for individuals with depression compared to individuals without depression. It appeared that left prefrontal hypoactivation was related to relative hypoactivation of the right-sided posterior brain regions that were involved with the processing of visuospatial tasks.

Bell and Fox (1994) suggest that the frontal lobes are associated with three major facets of emotions, including "the motor component, the organization of the multisystemic response pattern that constitutes emotion, and the ability to inhibit or regulate emotions" (p. 335). In their studies, Bell and Fox found that frontal asymmetry of EEG recordings are related to affective behaviors in infants as early as 10 months of age. Specifically, infants with greater left frontal activation patterns showed a longer latency to cry when separated from their mothers while infants with greater right hemisphere activation showed a shorter latency period. Although all infants developed or learned to inhibit distress emotions when separated (typically by the end of the age of 2 into the 3rd year of life when language begins to develop), Bell and Fox (1994) hypothesize that shorter-latency-to-cry infants may have a lag in left hemisphere maturation. They suggest that this delay may represent an inability to inhibit or suppress negative right hemisphere emotions, and that there may be a small set of infants who continue to "display distinct patterns of distress to mild stressors . . . behaviors that may be related to underlying patterns of cerebral activation" and maturation (p. 338). The emergence of language may play a role in this process in that infants begin to develop internal speech that further serves to regulate and self-monitor responses that are associated with negative emotions. More research into the brain-emotion relationship will help clarify these important issues. It makes sense given what we know about temperament—that infants vary broadly on these dimensions.

Posner and Raichle (1994) identified various subcomponents of attention including four major areas: (1) Alerting refers to the ability to readily respond to stimuli involves a decrease in neural noise; (2) Orienting refers to preparedness to respond to a specific stimuli; and (3) Executing or executive control refers to the process of resolving conflict when two or more stimuli are present (see Swanson, 2003, for a discussion). Executive control involves the inhibition of over-learned responses and the use of new responses that are more appropriate or effective to the situation. Posner and Peterson (1990) suggest that the frontal lobes play a role in directing attention and vigilance. Sutton, Davidson, and Rogers (1996) investigated the role of prefrontal asymmetry on directing attention to positive or negative stimuli. Participants with greater left prefrontal activation selected more positive word-pairs than did individuals with more right hemisphere activation. "Selective attentional biases might act to maintain and preserve the dispositional affective characteristics of individuals who differ in their trait-levels of prefrontal activation asymmetry" (p. 117). A more detailed description of these relationships will be important in our understanding of how brain functions affect one's experiences as well as one's perceptions of those experiences.

The prefrontal lobes appear to regulate emotions that may be directly related to the inhibition of negative affect (Davidson, 1999). In unpublished reports Davidson suggests that individuals with relative left prefrontal activation show increased inhibition of negative emotions after exposure to negative stimuli. These individuals apparently are able to more rapidly terminate negative emotional responses once they are elicited and to recover more quickly, which is most likely due to modulating the activity of the amygdale. Davidson also indicates ". . . the prefrontal lobe is likely to play a role in the maintenance of reinforcement-related behavioral approach. Perhaps the dampening of negative affect and shortening of its time course facilitates the maintenance of approach-related positive affect" (1999, p. 118).

Disruption of Inhibitory Control: A Model of Frontostriatal Circuitry

Casey, Tottenham, and Fossella (2002) propose a model of inhibitory control, describe two major brain pathways, and discuss how these pathways are related to childhood disorders (e.g., ADHD, schizophrenia, obsessive compulsive disorder, and Tourette Syndrome). This model is based on data from neuroimaging (functional magnet resonance imaging fMRI), clinical, and animal research whereby inhibitory control is regulated by the basal ganglia and the thalamocortical circuits with five (5) major connections to other structures. First, the primary, supplementary, and premotor frontal cortex controls skeletal movements. Second, the oculomotor circuit in the supplementary eye fields controls eye movements. Third, the dorsolateral prefrontal lobes represent sensory information (e.g., object, spatial, and verbal stimuli). Fourth, the lateral orbital prefrontal cortex is involved with developing response information (e.g., different behavioral sets). Fifth, the limbic circuit with the medial prefrontal cortex (i.e., anterior cingulated and the medial orbitofrontal cortex) processes emotional information that helps determine when to approach and when to avoid an event—the approach-avoidance paradigm.

The thalamocortical projections are modulated by the basal ganglia through either direct (excitatory) or indirect (inhibitory) pathways. The direct pathway involves projections to the striatum (internal capsule of the globus pallidus and substantia nigra) that modulates inhibitory projections to the thalamus, and ultimately disinhibits the thalamus allowing for more cortically mediated behaviors as well as an increase in thalamic activity. The indirect pathway projects to the globus pallidus (external capsule) that modulates the subthalamic nuclei thereby leading to the excitation of the internal capsule globus pallidus and substantia nigra that inhibits the thalamus. The indirect pathway thus inhibits cortically mediated behaviors or behaviors that are conflicting (Casey et al., 2002).

The important question to address now is how do these circuits relate to inhibitory functions and specific childhood disorders especially ADHD. Casey et al. (2002) postulate that a disruption of the direct pathway, which facilitates cortically mediated behaviors, may explain the emergence of behaviors such as those observed in children with ADHD or interrupted thoughts such as those found in schizophrenia. Disruptions to the indirect pathway responsible for inhibiting cortically mediated behaviors may result in repetitive behaviors such as those observed in obsessive-compulsive disorder (OCD) and Tourette Syndrome or in obsessively depressive thoughts. Furthermore, Casey et al. (2002) postulate that "distinct symptomology across disorders is reflected in which of these circuits is disrupted since different types of information are represented in each. Accordingly, we propose that the inhibitory mechanism is the same across circuits (i.e., at the level of the indirect pathway of the basal ganglia) but the type of information represented by each within the frontal cortex is different. More generally, we propose that the basal ganglia thalamocortical circuits underlie inhibitory control and that inhibitory deficits observed in a range of developmental disorders reflect a disruption in the development of these circuits" (p. 7).

In summary, Casey et al. (2002) provide initial support for the hypothesis that the "basal ganglia are involved in suppression of actions while prefrontal cortex is involved in representing and maintaining information and conditions to which we respond or act. Developmentally we propose that the ability to support information from competing sources increase with age thereby facilitating inhibitory control. Relevant projections from the prefrontal lobe to the basal ganglia are enhanced while irrelevant projections are eliminated" (p. 17). Thus, the development of the frontal cortex is of interest when investigating the neuropsychological basis of ADHD.

## DEVELOPMENT OF THE FRONTAL LOBES: IMPACT ON EMOTIONAL AND BEHAVIORAL DEVELOPMENT

"The most important difference between development of the prefrontal cortex relative to other cortical regions (e.g., visual cortex) is in the gradual decrease in synapses in young childhood (Bourgeois, Goldman-Rakic, & Rakic, 1994). This decrease in synaptic density does not start until roughly puberty and coincides with the continued development of cognitive capacities. Accordingly, increasing cognitive capacity coincides with a gradual loss rather than formation of new synapses. These cognitive and biological processes may represent the behavioral and ultimate physiological suppression competing, irrelevant behaviors as appropriate behaviors are reinforced and enhanced (i.e., inhibitory control)" (Casey, 2002, p. 7). Eslinger, Biddle, Pennington, and Page (1999) suggest that it is important to identify the contributions of the prefrontal cortex to the neuropsychological development for determining "how cognitive systems become organized and regulate adaptive behavior in problem solving, social, and other complex domains" (p. 158). The development of the prefrontal cortex and executive functions which include "planning, working memory, inhibition, response shifting, and initiation" impact adaptation across academic, social, and emotional domains (Eslinger et al., 1999, p. 158).

The development of frontal lobe functions increases with age and is associated with behavioral, psychological, and social aspects of development for typical children and for those with ADHD. In a longitudinal study using MRI scans, Giedd et al. (1999) found predictable, linear changes in white matter across ages 4 to 22 (12.4% net increase) in 145 healthy subjects. This increase was less prominent for females than for males; and, white-matter changes were not significantly different for frontal, parietal, temporal, and occipital lobes. Conversely, nonlinear, regionally specific changes were reported in volume changes in cortical gray matter. "Gray matter in the frontal lobe increased during preadolescence with a maximum size occurring at 12.1 years for males and 11.0 years for females, followed by a decline during postadolescence that resulted in a net decrease in volume across this age span" (Giedd et al., 1999, p. 861). A similar growth curve was found in parietal regions but changes in gray matter were most distinct in the temporal regions (maximum size at 16.5 years for males and 16.7 years for females) with a slight decline after peak growth. The occipital regions increased linearly with age without a significant decline. Although the shape of the growth curves was similar, there were differences in the absolute size of gray matter for males (10% larger than females). Giedd et al. (1999) speculate "if increase is related to a second wave of overproduction of synapses, it may herald a critical stage of development when environment or activities of the teenager may guide selective elimination during adolescence" (p. 863). Giedd suggests that interests and experiences during the teenage years are critical in shaping lifelong synaptic processes in the frontal cortex. This research may have implications for interventions as well. The question as to whether the full effects of early damage to the frontal cortex can be discerned in early childhood needs further exploration. Given the maturational processes, it is reasonable to hypothesize that children may grow into deficits or they may manifest deficits at a later age than were presented at initial evaluation. A neurodevelopmental framework would account for these maturational anomalies.

## ADVANCES IN NEUROBIOLOGICAL BASIS OF ADHD

In recent years, neuroscientists have taken an interest in identifying the neurobiological basis of ADHD. In a summary of neuroimaging (magnetic resonance imaging, MRI) research, Castellanos (2000) indicates that a distributed circuit underlies some of the symptoms of ADHD. "At least in boys, this circuit appears to include right prefrontal regions, the caudate nucleus, globus pallidus, and subregion of the cerebellar vermis" (Castellanos, 2000, p. 5). In almost every instance, studies reported reduced brain volume suggesting hypofunctioning particularly in the cortico-striatal-thalamo-cortical (CSTC) circuits. The CSTC serve both excitatory and inhibitory functions whereby one response is selected while another is simultaneously inhibited. Indirect pathways in this circuit are implicated in ADHD. "The fundamental hypothesis motivating neuroimaging investigations of ADHD has been that this neuronal brake does not function optimally, and that such a functional deficit should be reflected in relevant anatomic abnormalities" (Castellanos, 2000, p. 3). Castellanos cautions that the methodologies for this research are evolving and sample sizes have been small. Furthermore these circuits may have other complex cognitive and motor functions in addition to inhibition. However, we do have provisional support from MRI studies that the CSTC circuits involved with executive functions are linked to ADHD.

In a review of research over the previous 25 years, Tannock (1998) reported the following: (1) differences between ADHD and normal controls were found in encephalography (EEG) studies, but there is little agreement over the precise nature of the abnormalities; (2) event related potentials (ERP) studies show altered characteristics of EEG wave patterns, specifically a reduced P3B amplitude, that appear related to difficulties in selecting and organizing responses; and (3) greater uptake asymmetry in the left frontal and parietal regions based on SPECT (measures of brain glucose metabolism). Further, there may be significant gender differences where females with ADHD show greater brain metabolic abnormalities compared to males. For example, Faraone et al. (1995) found that boys with ADHD may have diverse etiological risk factors while girls appear to have a stronger familial type with higher heritability. Tannock concludes "the most parsimonious interpretation of the findings is that fronto-striatal networks may be involved with ADHD. . . . Abnormalities can occur as a result of alterations in normal developmental processes (e.g., neuronal genesis, migration, synaptic pruning) that may be mediated by genetic, hormonal, or environmental effects or a combination of these" (1998, pp. 83–84). Although genetic heritability of ADHD is high, the high degree of comorbid conduct, mood, and anxiety disorders found in individuals with ADHD complicates how the disorder is manifested (Biederman, Faraone, Keenan, Steingard, & Tsuang, 1991).

### BIOGENETIC ABNORMALITIES IN ADHD

Controlled family studies have shown that ADHD is a familial disorder (Samuel et al., 1999). Family members of ADHD are likely to have ADHD, disruptive behavior disorders, substance abuse, and depression (see Barkley, 1998). Twin studies have shown that monozygotic twins have the highest rate of concordance for symptoms of ADHD (up to 81%), while the rates of ADHD for dizyogtic twins is somewhat lower (29%; Gilger, Pennington, & DeFries, 1992). Further, the trait of hyperactivity-impulsivity also seems to be more heritable (on average about 80%) across studies, and the genetic contribution is highest at the most extreme ends of the continuum of symptom severity. See Plomin, DeFries, McClearn, and Rutter (1997) for an extensive discussion of the genetic underpinnings of ADHD.

There is growing evidence that variants in dopamine-related genes have been implicated in children, adolescents, and adults with ADHD. Swanson et al. (1997, 2001) investigated the dopamine D4 receptor gene (DRD4), while others have investigated the dopamine transporter gene (DAT1; Cook, Stein, & Leventhal, 1997). Casey et al. (2002) found that variations in the dopamine-related genes were associated with variations in cognitive control measures for children with ADHD.

### SUMMARY

While brain imaging technology has been useful for investigating the neuro-anatomical basis of ADHD, we are not at a point where this technology can be used to diagnose the disorder. First, neuroimaging research has been used for detecting group, not individual, differences. Variations may occur across individuals so that MRI scans are not diagnostic. Giedd (2000) does indicate that MRI scans may be useful when children with ADHD also present with significant neurological abnormalities, comorbid psychotic features, have atypical symptoms that do not respond to conventional treatment, or when one identical twin has ADHD but the other does not. ADHD appears to be a familial disorder; with family members of children with ADHD are at risk for high rates of disruptive, mood, and substance abuse disorders. Variations in dopamine-related genes will play an important role in the search for genetic models of ADHD. Further "compromises within an individuals neural substrate is important and necessary but not sufficient to understand fully either the current or the future level of functioning of an individual. The emergence and manifestation of ADHD and its component symptoms are likely to arise from multiple interacting factors that cannot be understood in isolation. Since most forms of child psychopathology are likely to be attributable to multiple etiologies and their interactions, the incorporation of a developmental-systems perspective will be an important strategy for future research" (Tannock, 1998, p. 68).

## ASSESSMENT OF ADHD: CLINICAL PRACTICES IN SCHOOL CONTEXT

Despite the advances in understanding the neurobiological basis of ADHD, assessment and diagnosis of ADHD is primarily behavioral and psychological in nature. The next section provides an overview of the diagnosis of ADHD, and includes a review of measures of executive functions that can be incorporated into an assessment of ADHD in school-aged children.

## Diagnosis of ADHD

The question of who is responsible for diagnosing ADHD has become clarified by changes in federal guidelines for special education services. In the past pediatricians, psychiatrists, and clinical psychologists typically made the diagnosis of ADHD. However changes in federal law require that schools identify children with handicapping conditions, and in 1991, the U.S. Department of Education issued a memorandum indicating that children may be eligible for special education services on the basis of their ADHD under Section 504 of Public Law 93-112 or under the Individuals with Disabilities Education Act (IDEA). This regulation marked a change in responsibility whereby schools became legally responsible for assessing and diagnosing ADHD. See Barkley (1998), DuPaul and Stoner (2003), and Reynolds and Kamphaus (2002) for guidelines for making the diagnosis of ADHD.

Although children with ADHD often present with various neuropsychological, cognitive, and social interaction problems, the diagnosis of ADHD is typically made using behavioral criteria (Barkley, 1998; Platzman et al., 1992). Behavioral assessment paradigms provide methods for gathering information about the symptoms of ADHD, and can be useful for delineating the antecedent and consequential features of the disorder. Psychosocial and cognitive/academic measures are usually incorporated into the assessment to rule out other disorders of childhood (e.g., learning disabilities and cognitive delays), and to identify co-existing psychiatric disorders (e.g., conduct disorders and depression).

A review of background history, behavioral rating scales, parent and teacher interviews, and direct observation of the child in multiple settings form the basis of the evaluation process (American Academy of Pediatrics, 2000; Barkley, 1998; DuPaul & Stoner, 2003; Neul, Applegate, & Drabman, 2003; Platzman et al., 1992). Guidelines suggest that assessment be conducted from multiple sources, across multiple settings, and multiple methods. If differences arise across settings, informants, or observers then the assessment needs to take into consideration why such discrepancies occur. Although parent and teacher rating scales show low to moderate agreement, there is about a 77% probability that teacher ratings will result in a diagnosis of ADHD in children with positive parent ratings (Biederman, Faraone, Milberger, & Doyle, 1993). See Achenbach and McConaughy (2003), Barkley (2002), and Reynolds and Kamphaus (2002) for an in-depth discussion of how to interpret cross-informant comparisons (i.e., differences among parents, teachers, parents, and youth). For adolescents there is an added dimension—assessment can access the individual's self-perceptions using interviews and self-report forms. For example, the Youth Self-Report (YSF) of the Achenbach System of Empirically Based Assessment (ASEBA; Achenbach & Rescorla, 2001) and the Self-Report of Personality (SRP) of the Behavior Assessment Scale for Children (BASC; Reynolds & Kamphaus, 1992, 2002) measure how adolescents perceive their problem, identify their concerns, and the degree to which they endorse specific symptoms.

Barkley (1998, 2002) suggests that tests should possess strong psychometric properties in order to make a valid diagnosis of ADHD. Common multimethod, multidimensional rating scales for assessing behavior problems including symptoms of ADHD in children and youth include: (1) the Conners' Teacher Rating Scale-Revised (CTRS-R) and the Conners' Parent Rating Scale (CPRS; Conners, 1997); (2) the Child Behavior Checklist (CBCL) for parents, the Teacher's Report Form (TRF), and the Youth Self Report (YSR) from the ASEBA (Achenbach & McConaughy, 2003); and (3) the Teacher Rating Scale (TRS), the Parent Rating Scale (PRS), Self-Report of Personality (SRP), the Structured Developmental History (SDH), and the Student Observation System (SOS) from the BASC (Reynolds & Kamphaus, 2002). While research investigating the utility of the BASC, PRS, and the CBCL show equivalence for these scales for identifying ADHD-combined subtypes (Doyle et al., 1997), the BASC, PRS, and TRS scales are stronger than the CBCL and the TRF for identifying ADHD-predominantly inattentive type (Vaughn et al., 1997).

Other measures that are useful for evaluating ADHD symptoms in the home and school include the ADHD Rating Scale-IV (DuPaul, Erving, Hook, & McGoey, 1998), the School Situations Questionnaire-Revised (SSQ-R) and the Home-Situations Questionnaire-Revised (HSQ-R; DuPaul & Barkley, 1992). The School Archival Records Search (SARS; Walker, Block-Pedego, Todis, & Severson, 1998), a structured method for gathering crucial information on 11 variables (e.g., schools attended, days absent, grades, and discipline history), is also helpful for documenting the presence of school problems. See Reynolds and Kamphaus (2002) for guidelines for using objective data from the BASC to document emotional disturbance as defined by IDEA, and ADHD as defined by *DSM-IV*.

## Subtypes of ADHD

It is becoming increasingly more important that psychologists understand childhood disorders within a dimensional perspective that is complimentary to (not dichotomous with) categorical approaches (Hinshaw & Park, 1999). Dimensional approaches have empirical support (Mash & Barkley, 1996), and suggest that numerous behaviors and personality characteristics exist on a continuum. For example, all children may be impulsive or hyperactive to some degree, but it is only when impulsive/hyperactive behaviors are extreme and chronic, that these behaviors interfere with normal development. According to categorical approaches such as the Diagnostic Statistical Manual (*DSM-IV*; American Psychiatric Association, 1994), diagnosis of ADHD may be warranted when children display a specific set of symptoms.

*DSM-IV* criteria does differentiate ADHD with predominantly inattentive from ADHD with predominantly hyperactive-impulsive type, and a combined type.

Research investigating the relationships among psychological, behavioral, cognitive, and social interaction variables has explored the nature of ADHD, depending on the presence (ADD/H) or absence of hyperactivity (ADD/WO). Barkley, DuPaul, and McMurray (1990) report significant differences between the two groups related to attentional, memory, psychosocial, and familial correlates. Trommer, Hoeppner, Lorber, and Armstrong (1988) also found that the two groups differed in terms of impulse control on a choice task. Both groups showed initial difficulties with impulse control, but children with ADD/WO improved with training while children with and ADD/H did not improve. Children with ADD/WO were more likely to have a codiagnosis of tension-anxiety or anxiety/

depression than were hyperactive children. Children with ADD/H were more likely to have symptoms of aggression, antisocial activity, and impulsivity even though a codiagnosis of conduct disorder (CD) was not given. In addition, children with pervasive and severe hyperactivity appeared to be a more disordered group, showed problem behaviors at an earlier age, and had lower IQs, neurodevelopmental problems, and language delays compared to children with moderate levels of ADHD (Taylor, 1989).

In a series of carefully designed studies, Lahey and his associates systematically investigated differences between children identified as ADD/H or ADD/WO. Lahey, Schaughency, Hynd, Carlson, and Nieves (1987) reported that ADD/WO could be reliably differentiated from ADD/H in a clinic setting; although, both groups had a high frequency of codiagnoses with other childhood disorders (ADD/WO at 68% and ADD/H at 61%). The behavioral differences between the two groups were also important. The ADD/H group was found to have a higher incidence of and a more severe type of conduct disorder, and they were more impulsive. In contrast, "children with ADD/WO are more sluggish in their cognitive tempo and are more likely to display coexisting internalizing disorders" (Lahey et al., 1987, p. 721). These data were consistent with those reported earlier by Lahey, Schaughency, Strauss, and Frame (1984), where ADD/H children showed signs of externalizing disorders and ADD/WO children showed signs of internalizing disorders. Even when Lahey et al. (1987) eliminated all children with a codiagnosis of conduct disorder, the ADD/H and ADD/WO groups showed a different cognitive tempo and varying levels of anxiety.

Carlson, Lahey, Frame, Walker, and Hynd (1987) demonstrated that both groups of ADD/H and ADD/WO children were not popular with peers. Although these findings seem to contradict a distinction between these two groups, the authors did find that when children who had a codiagnosis were compared (i.e., ADD/H plus conduct disorders versus ADD/WO plus conduct disorders or plus major depression), the codiagnosed ADD/H group started more fights with peers than did the codiagnosed ADD/WO group.

A number of studies investigated the neurocognitive correlates of ADD/H and ADD/WO. Hynd et al. (1989) measured reaction time, speed, and accuracy on a classification task. In this study, children with ADD/H did not differ from ADD/WO, although they were slower than a clinic control group. The ADD/H group was much more inconsistent in terms of attention, leading these authors to conclude that the term "variable" (i.e., attentional variability) should be used to fully describe the attentional deficits present in this group. Barkley (1998) reports that children with ADD/H have persistence difficulties, working memory problems, and disinhibition. On the other hand, ADD/WO showed more deficiencies on focused or selective attention, information processing, and memory retrieval tasks (Barkley, 1998, 2002).

In summary, children with ADD/H and ADD/WO appear to differ in other domains, and the differentiation of children on the presence or absence of hyperactivity and impulsivity appears warranted. There are likely important differences between these groups on attention processing as well (Teeter & Semrud-Clikeman, 1997). Barkley (1998, 2002) suggests that ADD/WO may be a distinct disorder from ADD/H but there is not sufficient evidence to determine whether the two types have different disturbances in attention. Research to date has led to changes in the diagnostic criteria in *DSM-IV* and clearly differentiates predominantly inattentive type, predominantly hyperactive-impulsive type, and a combined type.

## ADHD WITH COMORBID DISORDERS

In their review of the ADHD literature, Biederman, Newcome, and Sprich (1991) found that ADHD is a heterogeneous disorder that occurs frequently with other disorders such that 30% to 50% of children with ADHD also meet criteria for conduct disorders (CD), 25% have comorbid anxiety disorders, and 20% to 30% have mood disorders. Moreover, Biederman and Steingard (1987) found that adolescents with ADHD plus major depression were at risk for suicide due partially to their poor impulse control. Others report that as many as 30% to 35% children with ADHD have comorbid learning disorders (LD; Semrud-Clikeman et al., 1992). Comorbid disorders appear to show patterns within families. Studies investigating the familial-genetic link suggest that ADHD and major depression share common familial vulnerabilities; while, ADHD and anxiety disorders appear to be separately transmitted (Biederman, Munir, & Knee, 1987). Seidman et al. (1995) also found that children with ADHD were impaired on measures of frontal lobe functioning (i.e., Wisconsin Card Sorting Test, the Stroop, and the Continuous Performance Test) compared to a control group, and those with a family history of ADHD were the most significantly impaired.

Academic underachievement also appears in children with ADHD+CD and the relationship appears to show developmental shifts. First, ADHD is related to underachievement in early to middle childhood. Second, antisocial, disruptive behaviors are associated with academic underachievement in some but not all teens.

While there is evidence that different brain systems are involved in ADHD (right frontal lobes) and learning disabilities (left perisylvian fissure; Hynd, Semrud-Clikeman, Lorys, Novey, & Eliopulus, 1990), some suggest that individuals with both ADHD+ learning disabilities may be a meaningful subgroup that warrants further study (Seidman et al., 1995). Klorman et al. (1999) found that only children with ADHD combined type showed executive functioning deficits (Tower of Hanoi and Wisconsin Card Sort Test) regardless of comorbid reading or oppositional disorder and displayed deficiencies in planning, working memory, and spatial skills.

These findings suggest that, at least for ADHD, a simplistic formulation using only one piece of an interwoven pattern allows for an incomplete understanding of the whole pattern particularly given the high rates of comorbid disorders that accompany ADHD. Goldstein and Goldstein (1998) describe useful methods for determining whether parental expectations, parenting style, and social interaction patterns significantly impact on the expression and maintenance of general behavioral problems in childhood or in more severe cases (e.g., ADHD). Direct observation and clinical interviews increase the ecological validity of the assessment process.

## MEASURES OF EXECUTIVE FUNCTIONS

Although neuropsychological tests do not form the basis for the assessment and diagnosis of ADHD, there is growing evidence that children and adults with

ADHD deficits in executive functions (EF). Executive functions are defined in various ways but it is generally agreed that they encompass skills necessary for "goal-directed activity" (Anderson, 1998). Lezak (1995) suggests that EFs are higher-order cognitive processes including initiation, planning, hypotheses generation, decision-making, self-regulation, and self-perception. Other conceptualizations include problem solving, abstract thinking, concept formation, perseveration, inability to correct errors and to profit from feedback, and rigid thought processes (see Anderson, 1998). Finally, Pennington (1997) outlined four major components of EFs: motor inhibition, planning, interference control, and shifting sets. Recently Barkley (1997, 1998) extended his model of ADHD to include deficits in self-regulation or behavioral disinhibition, involving: working memory (nonverbal, sense of time), internalization of speech (verbal working memory), self-regulation or affect/motivation/arousal, and reconstitution (analysis and synthesis of behavior). Table 20.1 presents a summary of select EF measures and includes a description of common rating scales measuring attention, hyperactivity, and impulsivity.

In his discussion of executive functions, Osmon (1999) includes the concept of mental set—which involves moving beyond the perceptual aspects of stimuli into the realm of abstract or internal representation. Internal representation of stimuli is referred to as working memory. Mental set includes both working memory and preparatory set or getting ready to respond. The concept of mental set includes the regulatory processes whereby ". . . top-down influences of the frontal lobe mediate or control posterior, perceptual processing. EF is the process of forming, maintaining, and switching mental set that regulates cognitive and socioemotional function to bring it under the control of both interoceptive processing (switching and maintaining set in the fronto-cortical limbic structures) and exteroreceptive processing for purposes of behaving in an adaptive fashion" (Osmon, 1999, p. 182).

Osmon (1999) also refers to interference as another aspect of executive functions including attention and response selection. Attentional tasks such as the Stroop and Go-No-Go tests appear to measure important aspects of frontal lobe activity, whereby "maintaining mental set is seen as a process where motor planning and motivated attention co-mingle in the medial frontal area in order to deal with interference between competing stimuli or responses. Inhibition . . . is a closely allied process. . . . Inhibition is seen as a process that compliments interference by stopping ongoing behavior or switching mental set" (Osmon, 1999, p. 183). Planning is also part of executive functions and involves the ability to envision a strategy, to generate the necessary steps for approach, and to execute the motor responses to achieve the strategy. Socioemotional aspects of EF are considered separate from the cognitive components.

Assessment of executive dysfunction should not be used instead of clinical interviews, review of medical and academic history, parent, teacher, and youth rating scales and general assessment of comorbid disorders. When evaluating ADHD, school psychologists should evaluate intellectual and academic functioning to identify or rule out comorbid disorders. Measures of sustained attention or Continuous Performance Tests (CPT), the ability to suppress responses or shift mental sets (e.g., Stroop), and measures of verbal learning and verbal fluency may also identify associated problems that can be targeted for intervention.

**Table 20.1**
Measures of Executive Control Functions

| Behavior Checklists | Purpose of Measure |
| --- | --- |
| Behavior Rating Inventory of Executive Functions (Gioi, Isquith, Guy, & Kenworthy, 2000) | Parent and teacher scales. Measures global executive functions, behavioral regulation (Inhibit, Shift, Emotional Control), and metacognition (Initiate, Working Memory, Plan/Organize, Organization of Materials, Monitor). Separate scales for inconsistency and negativity. Initiate: getting started; Working Memory: holding information in mind while thinking and planning; Plan/Organize: goal setting, following through, and estimating time; Organization of Materials: keeping room and so on in reasonable order; Monitor: evaluating effects of own behavior. |
| Behavior Assessment Scale for Children (Kamphaus & Reynolds, 1996; Reynolds & Kamphaus, 1992) | Comprehensive parent, teacher, and child scales. Broad measure for diagnosing maladaptive behaviors (externalizing and internalizing problems), including attention and hyperactivity. Eighteen items from the teacher and parent scales have been shown to measure frontal lobe/executive functions. The BASC Monitor for ADHD is a short form of the BASC used to measure treatment effectiveness. |
| Brown ADD Scales (Brown, 1996) | Measures six clusters: (1) Organizing, Prioritizing, and Activating to Work; (2) Focusing, Sustaining, and Shifting Attention to Tasks; (3) Regulating Alertness, Sustaining Effort, and Processing Speed; (4) Managing Frustration and Modulating Emotions; (5) Utilizing Working Memory and Accessing Recall; (6) Monitoring and Self-Regulating Action. |
| Child Behavior Checklist (Achenbach & Rescorla, 2001) | Comprehensive parent, teacher, and child scales. Broad measure of internalizing and externalizing disorders, including attention and hyperactivity. The Child Attention profile is taken from the teacher scales. |
| Conners Rating Scales–Revised (Conners, 1997) | Narrow-band measure of inattention, hyperactivity, and impulsivity. Includes parent, teacher, and adolescent forms. Includes screening tools: a 12-item ADHD Index and the 18-item *DSM-IV* Symptom Checklist. |

*(continued)*

**Table 20.1** *Continued*

| Neuropsychological Assessment Measures | Purpose of Measure |
| --- | --- |
| California Verbal Learning Test–Children (Delis et al., 2000) | Measures memory and learning in semantic categories (fruit, clothing, toys); clustered by semantic domains, perseverative responses, and intrusive responses. |
| Children's Category Test-Booklet Format (Boll, 1993) | Measures reasoning, ability to deduce classification principles, use of response-contingent feedback, and cognitive flexibility. |
| Cognitive Assessment System (Naglieri & Das, 1997) | Measures cognitive processing strategies, problem solving, planning and attention. |
| Colorado Neuropsychology Tests (Davis, Bajszar, & Squire, 1995); includes Tower of Hanoi and Tower of London | Measures memory and higher-order executive functions, problem solving, and monitoring. |
| NEPSY (Korkman, Kirk, & Kemp, 1998) | Measures planning, cognitive flexibility, impulsivity, vigilance, selective attention, monitoring, self-regulation, and problem solving. |
| Rey-Osterreith Complex Figure Drawing (see Waber & Holmes, 1985) | Measures planning, visual-spatial construction skills. |
| Stroop Color-Word Test (Stroop, 1935) | Measures selective attention, cognitive flexibility, ability to suppress responses. |
| Trail Making Test for Children (Halstead-Reitan Neuropsychological Battery; Reitan, 1979; Reitan & Wolfson, 1985) | Measures visual scanning, attention, motor speed, flexibility, and ability to establish and change mental set. |
| Wisconsin Card Sorting Test (Heaton, 1981) | Measures abstraction, conceptualization, ability to establish and change mental sets, attention, memory, and response to feedback. |

| Measures of Attention | Purpose of Measure |
| --- | --- |
| Conners Continuous Performance Test II (Conners, 2000) | Measures sustained attention and ability to inhibit. |
| d2 Test: Concentration Endurance Test (Brickenkamp, 1981) | Measures speed, accuracy, persistence, and learning. |
| Gordon Diagnostic System (Gordon, 1987). | Measures sustained attention and ability to inhibit. |
| Directed Attention (Mesulam, 1985) | Measures sustained attention, planning, search strategies, and self-monitoring abilities. |
| Test of Variable Attention (Greenberg & Kindschi, 1996) | Measures sustained attention and ability to inhibit. |

RESEARCH ON EXECUTIVE FUNCTIONS IN ADHD

Clinical measures of attention are often included in the assessment of ADHD, but there is a great deal of controversy over the utility of these measures. First, objective measures of attention and behavioral disinhibition are not demanding enough to have ecological validity (Teeter & Semrud-Clikeman, 1997). Tasks that are employed are initially interesting, short in duration, and generally administered in the presence of an adult. Despite their shortcomings, Barkley (1990) indicates that standardized laboratory tests of sustained attention (e.g., the Gordon Diagnostic System) may reduce the error inherent in rating scales and provide a method for valid and reliable assessment of vigilance. Barkley warns that scores on vigilance tasks should not be used as "the sole determinant of a diagnosis ADHD" (p. 329). See Riccio, Reynolds, and Lowe (2001) for a comprehensive review of continuous performance tests for measuring attention and impulsive responding in children and adults. Riccio et al. (2001) also provide guidelines for incorporating CPTs into a multimethod assessment of ADHD and describe methods for monitoring medication and treatment efficacy.

Goldstein and Goldstein (1998) discuss the use of other measures of attention, including: Coding and Digit Span (Wechsler Scales), Speech-Sounds Perception and Seashore Rhythm Tests (Halstead-Reitan Neuropsychological Battery), and the Digit Symbol Test. When employed in assessment, measures of inattention may support a diagnosis of ADHD but they also have inherent problems because they do not always capture the behavioral problems that are of greatest concern to parents and teachers (Barkley, 1990). While the Freedom from Distractibility Factor (FFD) on the Wechsler scales has been described as a measure of attention, Barkley et al. (1990) found that the FFD measure did not differentiate ADHD from normal or learning disabled children.

Seidman et al. (1995) found that a family history (FH) of ADHD was highly predictive of neuropsychological impairment on measures of flexibility and reasoning (Stroop and Wisconsin Card Sorting Test; WCST), and on measures of memory and learning. Children with ADHD+FH also had a different profile of neuropsychological deficits than children with ADHD+ learning disabilities (LD). Children with ADHD+LD were not specifically deficient on tasks of attention and executive controls but these individuals did show difficulties on motor speed. Possible reduction in cerebral dominance implicating the left hemisphere was hypothesized, and Seidman et al. (1995) suggest that ADHD+LD may be a meaningful clinical subgroup warranting further study. Riccio et al. (2001) found that the scores on the Attention Problem Scale of the BASC were highly related to perseverative errors on the WCST. Perseverative errors on the WCST have been shown to be a good measure of executive functions in children (Lezak, 1995). Barringer and Reynolds (1995) also identified 18 items of the BASC parent rating scales for children and adolescents that according to neuropsychology experts were judged to represent frontal lobe/executive functions. Scores on these items were significantly higher for children with ADHD when compared to the normative sample, and Reynolds and Kamphaus (2002) suggest that the items on the frontal lobe scale of the BASC are sensitive to organic impairment in ADHD, CD, and cognitive delays.

In a study of ADHD of subtypes Nigg, Blaskey, Huang-Pollock, and Rappley (2002) found that both ADHD-combined (ADHD-C) and ADHD-inattentive

(ADHD-I) had deficits on measures of behavioral inhibition, planning, interference control, shifting sets, and response speed. Both ADHD-C and ADHD-I groups performed poorly on the behavioral inhibition tests compared to controls; ADHD-I boys did not show deficits but ADHD-I girls were impaired; ADHD-C boys were slower than ADHD-I boys; and ADHD-C and ADHD-I girls did not differ. Compared to controls, ADHD-C groups had deficits in planning; the ADHD-I group was less impaired and did not differ from controls; and, the ADHD types did not differ. On interference control measures, the groups did not differ from each other but were impaired compared to controls. Finally, on shifting sets, the ADHD-I group showed significant deficits but the ADHD-C did not show significant deficits. In summary, this study found that ADHD-I groups had similar EF deficits as the ADHD-C groups in response speed, vigilance or effort and may differ on other EF measures by degree of severity. However only boys in the ADHD-C groups had deficits in response inhibition.

Barkley (1998, 2002) cautions that studies of EF deficits in children with ADHD have produced conflicting results. False-negatives can be high when using EF measures (e.g., Wisconsin Card Sort Test, WCST), overall accuracy rates can be poor, and prediction rates can be low. "Such findings do not encourage the diagnostic use of this test for ADHD" (1998, p. 301). Similar results were found for the Stoop test, the Rey-Ostrerrieth Complex Figure, and the Trail Making Test (Parts A and B). More recent attempts to refine measures of EF may be more useful and deserve further study. For example, the Comprehensive Trailmaking Test (CTMT) measures attention, concentration, resistance to distraction, and cognitive flexibility (Reynolds, 2003), and may be more sensitive than earlier versions of the Trail Making test. When used as part of a multimethod assessment protocol, measures of EF may be useful for designing interventions that target the cognitive features of ADHD.

## SUMMARY OF ASSESSMENT OF ADHD AND EF DEFICITS

The assessment and diagnosis of ADHD requires a comprehensive, multifaceted approach. Behavioral rating scales, and observational and interview techniques form the basis of the assessment. Other broad-based measures of psychological, cognitive, and academic functioning are incorporated to rule out competing diagnoses or to identify comorbid disorders. The literature shows that ADHD, CD, ODD, and LD co-occur at high rates. For children with ADHD+CD and/or ODD, parental psychopathology and family stress may be contributing factors to comorbidity. The prognosis for individuals with both ADHD+CD is guarded and treatment becomes more difficult because environmental stress and risk factors increase. In the case of comorbid LD, some researchers suggest that learning problems are secondary to primary process deficits (i.e., inattention) associated with ADHD. The fact that drug therapy often results in positive behavioral changes with no improvement in academics implies that there are different mechanisms underlying ADHD and LD.

Despite underlining EF deficits appear to be related to ADHD, measures of EF deficits should not be used to make diagnostic decisions regarding ADHD. However, several promising tests may be useful (e.g., the Cognitive Assessment System, the Comprehensive Trailmaking Test) and warrant further study. These neuropsychological measures may be used with rating scales, interviews, observations, and history to develop an in-depth understanding of the child's neurocognitive difficulties but should not substitute for a comprehensive behavioral assessment.

Treatment of ADHD is generally multimodal including stimulant medication, behavioral, and psychosocial approaches. Recent treatment plans include adding cognitive strategies for increasing attention, organization, and self-control. These are briefly reviewed next.

## MULTIMODAL TREATMENT OF ADHD: TREATING ADHD IN SCHOOL CONTEXT

Multimodal treatment generally includes parent and child education about ADHD, stimulant medication, classroom behavior management, and educational interventions for psychosocial and academic difficulties. The Multimodal Treatment Study of Children with ADHD (MTA Cooperative Group, 1999a, 1999b) ranked treatments in order of effectiveness were as follows: (1) combined medication and behavioral treatments (68% excellent responders), (2) medication management alone (56% excellent responders), (3) behavioral therapy alone (34% excellent responders), and (4) treatment received in the community (25% excellent responders). Stimulant medications produced clinical improvement in the core symptoms of ADHD—hyperactivity, inattention, and impulsivity. Combined treatment with medication and behavioral therapy was more effective than behavioral therapy alone and community care. The behavioral therapy was also found to be more effective than community care. These differences may have resulted from lower medication dose and frequency rather than the MTA management and the combined conditions. In general, stimulant medications produce improvement in compliance, impulsive aggression, social interactions, and academic performance (Wilens & Spencer, 2000).

Other studies have shown that the following behavioral treatments are highly effective for youth with ADHD.

- Contingency Management includes the application of positive (token or point systems) and negative consequences (time-out and response cost) in highly structured environments. Pelham and associates developed a summer treatment program that incorporates these principles with other psychosocial and academic interventions (Pelham, Greiner, & Gnagy, 1997). To be effective, behavioral strategies must be used consistently.
- Behavioral therapy has been shown to be effective both in home and in the school environment (Teeter, 1998). Parent training programs and teacher consultation for reducing disruptive behaviors generally include the use of token systems with rewards for targeted behaviors. When necessary punishment can be effective when it is nonphysical and consistently applied to a reward-rich environment. Home-school contingency plans also utilize these behavioral techniques with success.
- Social skills training has produced mixed results but when applied more systematically, positive results have been more robust (see Pfiffner & McBurnett, 1997).
- Peer tutoring of children with ADHD has been shown to be an effective intervention in the classroom (DuPaul et al., 1998).
- Self-management, self-instruction, and self-reinforcement techniques also show promise (DuPaul & Stoner, 2002).

While we do not have a research base to determine efficacy to date, there are some promising interventions that might be effective for promoting self-control and other executive skills in children. Strayhorn (2002) reviewed the empirical evidence of a number of systematic strategies for children with self-control difficulties. The methods generally incorporate goal setting, determining and arranging task difficulty, changing attributional style, modeling desired behaviors, practicing skills (rehearsal), reinforcing and punishment to foster delay gratification, and self-instruction.

Dawson and Guare (2004) have written a useful handbook that describes a number of promising interventions for increasing executive skills that focus on the environment and the individual. First, changes in the environment are made to adjust to the limitations of the child. These include: (1) changing the physical environment in the classroom may include changing the child's seating, matching the child with a highly structured teacher, and/or reduce the number of children in the classroom and increase the amount of supervision; (2) changing the nature of the task by making it shorter, making steps more explicit, making the task closed ended (e.g., fill-in-the-blank or true-false), building in choice, and providing scoring rubrics with each assignment; (3) changing the way in which cues are given by using verbal prompts and reminders, using visual cues, creating schedules, making lists, using audio taped cues for self-monitoring, and using pager systems for older youth; and (4) changing the way adults interact with child by anticipating problems and modifying the environment, by intervening early before the problem gets too big, by reminding and prompting the child, and by designing interventions that address the child's individual weaknesses.

Interventions that promote executive control skills that focus on the child teach planning, organization, and following specified directions (see Dawson & Guare, 2004). Initially these steps are followed under the direction of parents (or teachers) then supervision is faded. For example, specific steps include: describing the problem behavior; setting a goal; establishing steps to meet the goal; supervising the child to meet goals; evaluating the strategies and making changes if needed; and fading the supervision. These steps move the child to self-directed or self-monitored problem solving. An incentive system (i.e., behavioral contracts) is built into the steps to increase saliency of the strategies that are being taught. Other strategies include targeting skills for response inhibition, working memory, self-regulation of emotions, sustained attention, initiating tasks, planning goals, organization, time management, and goal-directed persistence. The techniques that are described utilize a number of behavioral and cognitive-behavioral strategies that may prove to be helpful in assisting children with ADHD. Other coaching techniques are suggested, including ways to integrate these into educational plans.

## CONCLUSION

Currently the science of ADHD suggests a biogenetic basis of ADHD, and variants in dopamine-related genes may underlie ADHD in children, adolescents, and adults with ADHD. Frontal-striatal circuits appear implicated in ADHD where projections from frontal regions into thalamic, limbic, and the basal ganglia regions are central to behavioral and affective inhibition, motivational, and attentional functions. Neurodevelopmental variations in these brain regions have been identified. Despite advances in the neurobiological basis of ADHD, assessment of the disorder remains primarily behavioral (i.e., rating scales, observations, clinical interviews). While measures of executive function deficits are the focus of current research they are not recommended for the diagnosis of ADHD. Measures of EF deficits may be helpful for exploring the neuropsychological basis of the disorder and may prove helpful for developing intervention plans for deficits in organization, planning, inhibition, and other executive control skills. Promising practices include systematic interventions that target self-control and executive deficits in children with ADHD.

## REFERENCES

Achenbach, T. M. (1991). *Manual for the child behavior checklist.* Burlington, VT: University of Vermont Department of Psychiatry.

Adrianov, O. S. (1996). Cerebral interrelationships of cognitive and emotional activity: Pathways and mechanisms. *Neuroscience and Behavioral Physiology, 26,* 329–339.

American Academy of Pediatrics. (2000). Clinical practice guidelines: Diagnosis and evaluation of the child with attention-deficit/hyperactivity disorder. *Pediatrics, 105,* 1158–1170.

American Psychiatric Association. (1994). *Diagnostic and statistical manual of mental disorders* (4th ed.). Washington, DC: Author.

Anderson, V. (1998). Assessing executive functions in children: Biological, psychological, and developmental considerations. *Neuropsychological Rehabilitation, 8,* 319–349.

Bararesi, W., Katisic, S., Colligan, R., Pankratz, S., Weaver, A., Weber, K., et al. (2002). *Archives of Pediatric and Adolescent Medicine,* 217–224.

Barkley, R. A. (1990). *Attention-deficit hyperactivity disorder: A handbook for diagnosis and treatment.* New York: Guilford Press.

Barkley, R. A. (1997). *ADHD and the nature of self-control.* New York: Guilford Press.

Barkley, R. A. (1998). *Attention-deficit hyperactivity disorder: A handbook for diagnosis and treatment* (2nd ed.). New York: Guilford Press.

Barkley, R. A., DuPaul, G., & McMurray, M. B. (1990). A comprehensive evaluation of attention deficit disorder with and without hyperactivity defined by research criteria. *Journal of Consulting and Clinical Psychology, 58,* 775–789.

Bararesi, W., Katisic, S., Colligan, R., Pankratz, S., Weaver, A., Weber, K., et al. (2002). *Archives of Pediatric and Adolescent Medicine,* 217–224.

Bell, M. A., & Fox, N. A. (1994). Brain development over the first year of life: Relations between EEG frequency and coherence and cognitive and affective behaviors. In G. Davidson & K. Fischer (Eds.), *Human behavior and the developing brain* (pp. 314–345). New York: Guilford Press.

Biederman, J., Faraone, S. V., Keenan, K., Steingard, R., & Tsuang, M. T. (1991). Family association between attention deficit disorder (ADD) and anxiety disorder. *American Journal of Psychiatry, 48,* 633–642.

Biederman, J., Faraone, S. V., Milberger, S., & Doyle, A. (1993). Diagnosis of attention-deficit hyperactivity disorder from parent reports predict diagnosis of teacher reports. *Journal of the American Academy of Child and Adolescent Psychiatry, 32,* 315–317.

Biederman, J., Munir, K., & Knee, D. (1987). Conduct and oppositional disorder in clinically referred children with attention deficit disorder: A controlled family study. *Journal of the American Academy of Child and Adolescent Psychiatry, 26,* 724–727.

Biederman, J., Newcome, J., & Sprich, S. (1991). Comorbidity of attention deficit hyperactivity disorder with conduct, depressive, anxiety, and other disorders. *American Journal of Psychiatry, 148,* 564–577.

Biederman, J., & Steingard, R. (1987). Attention-deficit hyperactivity disorder in adolescents. *Psychiatric Annals, 19,* 587–596.

Boll, T. (1993). *Children's Category Test.* San Antonio, TX: Psychological Corporation.

Bourgeois, J. P., Goldman-Rakic, P. S., & Rakic, P. (1994). Synaptogenesis in prefrontal cortex in rhesus monkeys. *Cerebral Cortex, 4,* 78–96.

Brickenkamp, R. (1981). *Test d2:/Aufmerksamkeits-Belastungs-test.* Handanweisung.

Brown, T. E. (1996). *Brown ADD scales.* San Antonio, TX: Psychological Corporation.

Carlson, C. L., Lahey, B. B., Frame, C. L., Walker, J., & Hynd, G. W. (1987). Socioeconomic status of clinically referred children with and without hyperactivity. *Journal of Abnormal Child Psychology, 15,* 537–547.

Casey, B. J. (2000). Disruption of inhibitory control in developmental disorders: A mechanistic model of implicated frontostriatal circuitary. In R. S. Siegler & J. L. McClelland (Eds.), *Mechanisms of cognitive development: The Carnegie Symposium on Cognition* (Vol. 28). Hillsdale, NJ: Erlbaum.

Casey, B. J., Tottenham, N., & Fossella, J. (2002). Clinical, imaging, lesion, and genetic approaches toward a model of cognitive control. *Developmental Psychobiology, 40,* 237–254.

Castellanos, F. X. (2000). Neuroimaging studies of attention-deficit/hyperactivity disorder. In M. Solanto, A. Arnsten, & F. X. Castellanos (Eds.), *Attention-deficit/hyperactivity disorder and stimulants: Basic and clinical neuroscience* (pp. 243–258). New York: Oxford University Press.

Conners, K. (1997). *Conners' Rating Scales–Revised.* North Tonawanda, NY: Multi-Health Systems.

Cook, E. H., Stein, M. A., & Leventhal, D. L. (1997). Family-based association of attention-deficit hyperactivity disorder and the dopamine transporter. In K. Blum (Ed.), *Handbook of psychiatric genetics* (pp. 297–310). New York: CRC Press.

Davidson, R. J. (1995). Cerebral asymmetry, emotion, and affective style. In R. J. Davidson & K. Hugdahl (Eds.), *Brain asymmetry* (pp. 361–387). Cambridge, MA: MIT Press.

Davidson, R. J. (1999). Neuropsychological perspectives on affective styles and their cognitive consequences. In T. Dalgleish & M. Power (Eds.), *Handbook of cognition and emotion* (pp. 103–123). New York: Wiley.

Davis, H. P., Bajszar, G. M., & Squire, L. R. (1995). *Colorado neuropsychology tests.* Colorado Springs, CO. Colorado Neuropsychology Company.

Dawson, P., & Guare, R. (2002). *Executive skills in children and adolescents.* New York: Guilford Press.

Delis, D., Kaplan, E., & Kramer, J. (2000). *Delis-Kaplan executive function scale.* San Antonio, TX: Psychological Corporation.

Delis, D., Kaplan, E., Kramer, J., & Ober, B. A. (2000). *The California verbal learning test* (2nd ed.). San Antonio, TX: Psychological Corporation.

Depue, R. A., & Collins, P. F. (1999). Neurobiology of the structure of personality: Dopamine, facilitation of incentive motivation, and extraversion. *Behavioral and Brain Sciences, 22,* 491–569.

Derryberry, D., & Reed, M. A. (1996). Regulatory processes and the development of cognitive representation. *Development and Psychopathology, 8,* 215–234.

DuPaul, G., Erving, R. A., Hook, C. L., & McGoey, K. (1998). Peer tutoring for children with attention-deficit hyperactivity disorder: Effects on classroom behavior and academic performance. *Journal of Applied Behavioral Analysis, 31,* 579–592.

DuPaul, G., & Stoner, G. (2002). *ADHD in the schools: Assessment and intervention strategies* (2nd ed.). New York: Guilford Press.

Eslinger, P. J., Biddle, K., Pennington, B., & Page, R. (1999). Cognitive and behavioral development up to 4 years after early right frontal lobe lesion. *Developmental Neuropsychology, 15,* 157–191.

Faraone, S. V., Biederman, J., Chen, W. J., Milberger, S., Warburton, R., & Tsuang, M. T. (1995). Genetic heterogeneity in attention-deficit hyperactivity disorder (ADHD): Gender, psychiatric comorbidity, and maternal ADHD. *Journal of Abnormal Psychology, 104,* 334–345.

Giedd, J. N., Blumenthal, J., Jeffries, N. O., Castellanos, F. X., Liu, H., Zijdenbos, A., et al. (1999). Cerebral cortical gray matter changes during childhood and adolescence: A longitudinal MRI study. *Nature Neuroscience, 2,* 861–863.

Gilger, J. W., Pennington, B. F., & DeFries, J. D. (1992). A twin study of the etiology comorbditiy: Attention-deficit hyperactivity disorder and dyslexia. *Journal of the American Academy of Child and Adolescent Psychiatry, 31,* 343–348.

Gioi, G. A., Isquith, P. K., Guy, S. C., & Kenworthy, L. (2000). *Behavior rating inventory of executive function.* Odessa, FL: Psychological Assessment Resources.

Goldstein, S., & Goldstein, M. (1998). *Managing attention deficit hyperactivity disorder: A guide for practitioners* (2nd ed.). New York: Wiley.

Gordon, M. (1987). *The Gordon diagnostic system.* DeWitt, NY: Gordon System.

Gray, J. A. (1994). Framework for taxonomy of psychiatric disorder. In S. H. M. vanGozzen & N. E. VandePoll (Eds.), *Emotions: Essays on emotion theory* (pp. 29–59). Hillsdale, NJ: Erlbaum.

Greenberg, L. M., & Kindschi, C. L. (1996). *TOVA Test of variables of attention: Clinical guide.* St. Paul, MN: TOVA Research Foundation.

Heaton, R. K. (1981). *Wisconsin Card Sorting Test (WCST).* Odessa, FL: Psychological Assessment Resources.

Henriques, J. B., & Davidson, R. J. (1990). Regional brain electrical asymmetries discriminate between previously depressed subjects and healthy controls. *Journal of Abnormal Psychology, 99,* 22–31.

Henriques, J. B., & Davidson, R. J. (1991). Left hypoactivation in depression. *Journal of Abnormal Psychology, 100,* 535–545.

Hinshaw, S., & Park, T. (1999). Research issues and problems: Toward a more definitive science of disruptive behavior disorders. In H. C. Quay & H. E. Hoza (Eds.), *Handbook of disruptive behavior disorders* (pp. 593–620). New York: Plenum Press.

Hynd, G. W., Nieves, N., Conner, R., Stone, P., Town, P., Becker, M. B., et al. (1989). Speed of neurocognitive processing in children with and without hyperactivity. *Journal of Learning Disorders, 22,* 573–580.

Hynd, G. W., Semrud-Clikeman, M., Lorys, A., Novey, E., & Eliopulus, D. (1990). Brain morphology in developmental dyslexia and attention-deficit disorder/hyperactivity. *Archives of Neurology, 47,* 919–926.

Irwin, W., Davidson, R. J., Lowe, M. J., Mock, B. J., Sorenson, J. A., & Turski, P. A. (1996). Human amygdala activation detected with echo-planar functional magnetic resonance imaging. *NeuroReport, 7,* 1765–1769.

Kamphaus, R., & Reynolds, C. R. (1996). *BASC Monitor for ADHD.* Circle Pines, MN: American Guidance Service.

Klorman, R., Hazel-Fernandez, L. A., Shaywitz, S. E., Fletcher, J. M., Marchione, K. E., Holahan, J. M., et al. (1999). Executive functioning deficits in attention-deficit hyperactivity disorder are independent of oppositional defiant disorder or reading disorder. *Journal of the American Academy of Child and Adolescent Psychiatry, 38,* 1148–1155.

Kolb, B., & Fantie, B. (1997). Development of the child's brain and behavior. In C. R. Reynolds & E. F. Janzen (Eds.), *Handbook of clinical child neuropsychology* (2nd ed., pp. 17–41). New York: Plenum Press.

Korkman, M., Kirk, U., & Kemp, S. (1998). *NEPSY.* San Antonio, TX: Psychological Corporation.

Lahey, B. B., Schaughency, E., Hynd, G., Carlson, C., & Nieves, N. (1987). Attention deficit disorder with and without hyperactivity: Comparison of behavioral characteristics of clinic-referred children. *Journal of the American Academy of Child Psychiatry, 28,* 718–723.

Lahey, B. B., Schaughency, E., Strauss, C., & Frame, C. (1984). Are attention deficit disorders with and without hyperactivity similar or dissimilar disorders? *Journal of the American Academy of Child Psychiatry, 23,* 302–309.

Leibson, C. L., Katusic, S. K., Barbaresi, W. J., Ransom, J., & O'Brien, P. C. (2001). Use and cost of medical care for children and adolescents with and without attention-deficit/hyperactivity disorder. *Journal of the American Medical Association, 285,* 60–66.

Lezak, M. D. (1995). *Neuropsychological assessment* (3rd ed.). New York: Oxford University Press.

Mash, E. J., & Barkley, R. A. (1996). *Child psychopathology.* New York: Guilford Press.

Mesulam, M. (1985). *Principles of behavioral neurology.* Philadelphia: Davis.

MTA Cooperative Group. (1999a). A 14-month randomized clinical trial of treatment strategies for attention-deficit/hyperactivity disorder. *Archives of General Psychiatry, 56,* 1073–1086.

MTA Cooperative Group. (1999b). Moderators and mediators of treatment response for attention-deficit/hyperactivity disorder. *Archives of General Psychiatry, 56,* 1088–1096.

Murphy, K., & Barkley, R. (1996). Attention deficit/hyperactivity disorder adults: Comorbidities and adaptive impairments. *Comprehensive Psychiatry, 37,* 393–401.

Naglieri, J., & Das, J. P. (1997). *Cognitive assessment system.* Itasca, IL: Riverside.

Nigg, J. T., Blaskey, L. G., Huang-Pollock, C., & Rappley, M. D. (2002). Neuropsychological executive functions and DSM-IV ADHD subtypes. *Journal of the American Academy of Child and Adolescent Psychiatry, 41,* 59–66.

Osmon, D. (1999). Complexities in the evaluation of executive functions. In J. J. Sweet (Ed.), *Forensic neuropsychology* (pp. 185–226). Lisse, The Netherlands: Swets & Zeitlinger.

Pelham, W. E., Greiner, A. R., & Gnagy, E. M. (1997). *Summer treatment program manual.* Buffalo, NY: Comprehensive Treatment for Attention Deficit Disorders.

Pennington, B. F. (1997). Dimensions of executive functions in normal and abnormal development. In N. A. Krasbegor, G. R. Lyon, & P. Goldman-Rakic (Eds.), *Development of the prefrontal cortex: Evolution, neurobiology, and behavior* (pp. 265–281). Baltimore: Brookes.

Pfiffner, L., & McBurnett, K. (1997). Social skills training with parent generalization: Treatment effects for children with attention deficit disorder. *Journal of Consulting and Clinical Psychology, 65,* 749–757.

Platzman, K. A., Stoy, M. R., Brown, R. T., Coles, C. D., Smith, I. E., & Falek, A. (1992). Review of observational methods in attention deficit hyperactivity disorder (ADHD): Implications for diagnosis. *School Psychology Quarterly, 7,* 155–177.

Plomin, R., DeFries, J. C., & McClearn, G. E. (1997). *Behavioral genetics: A primer* (3rd ed.). New York: Cambridge University Press.

Posner, M. I., & Peterson, S. E. (1990). The attention system of the human brain. *Annual Review of Neuroscience, 13,* 25–42.

Posner, M. I., & Raichle, M. E. (1994). Networks of attention. In M. I. Posner & M. E. Raichle (Eds.), *Images of mind* (pp. 153–179). New York: Scientific American Library.

Pribram, K. H. (1992). *Brain and perception: Holonomy and structure in figural processes.* Hillsdale, NJ: Erlbaum.

Reitan, R. (1979). *Manual for administration of neuropsychological test batteries for adults and children.* Tuscon, AZ: Neuropsychological Press.

Reitan, R., & Wolfson, D. (1985). *The Halstead-Reitan Neuropsychological Test Battery.* Tuscon, AZ: Neuropsychological Press.

Reynolds, C. R. (2003). *Comprehensive trailmaking test.* Austin, TX: ProEd.

Reynolds, C. R., & Kamphaus, R. (1992). *Behavior assessment system for children manual.* Circle Pines, MN: American Guidance Service.

Reynolds, C. R., & Kamphaus, R. (1996). *Behavior assessment system for children manual.* Circle Pines, MN: American Guidance Service.

Reynolds, C. R., & Kamphaus, R. (2000). *The clinician's guide to the Behavior Assessment System for Children.* New York: Guilford Press.

Reynolds, C. R., & Kamphaus, R. (2004). *Behavior assessment system for children* (2nd ed.). Circle Pines, MN: American Guidance Service.

Riccio, C. A., Reynolds, C. R., & Lowe, P. A. (2001). *Clinical applications of continuous performance tests: Measuring attention and impulsive responding in children and adults.* New York: Wiley.

Samuel, V. J., George, P., Thornell, A., Curtis, S., Taylor, A., Brome, D., et al. (1999). A pilot controlled family study of DSM-III-R and DSM-IV ADHD in African American children. *Journal of the American Academy of Child and Adolescent Psychiatry, 38,* 34–39.

Seidman, L. J., Biederman, J., Faraone, S. V., Milberger, S., Norman, D., Seiverd, K., et al. (1995). Effects of family history and comorbidity on the neuropsychological performance of children with ADHD: Preliminary findings. *Journal of the American Academy of Child and Adolescent Psychiatry, 34,* 1015–1024.

Semrud-Clikeman, M., Biederman, J., Sprich-Buckminister, S., Lehamn, B., Faraone, S., & Norman, D. (1992). Comorbidity between ADHD and learning disability: A review of and report in a clinically referred sample. *Journal of the American Academy of Child and Adolescent Psychiatry, 31,* 439–448.

Strayhorn, J. M. (2002). Self-control: Toward systematic training programs. *Journal of the American Academy of Child and Adolescent Psychiatry, 41,* 17–27.

Stroop, J. R. (1935). Studies of interference in serial verbal reactions. *Journal of Experimental Psychology, 18,* 643–662.

Sutton, S. K., Davidson, R. J., & Rogers, G. M. (1996). Resting anterior EEG asymmetry predicts affects-related information processing. *Psychophysiology, 33*(Suppl.), S81.

Swanson, J. (2003). Role of executive functions in ADHD. *Journal of Clinical Psychiatry, 64,* 35–39.

Swanson, J., Posner, M., Fusella, J., Wasdell, M., So, T., & Fan, J. (2001). Genes and attention deficit hyperactivity disorder. *Current Psychiatric Report, 3,* 100.

Swanson, J., Sunohara, G., Kennedy, J., Regino, R., Fineberg, E., & Wigal, E. (1997). *Association of the dopamine receptor D4 (DRD4) gene with a refined phenotype of attention deficit hyperactivity disorder (ADHD): A family-based approach.*

Tannock, R. (1998). Attention deficit hyperactivity disorder: Advances in cognitive, neurobiological, and genetic studies. *Journal of Child Psychology and Psychiatry, 39,* 65–100.

Taylor, E. A. (1989). On the epidemiology of hyperactivity. In T. Sagvolden & T. Archer (Eds.), *Attention deficit disorder: Clinical and basic research* (pp. 31–52). Hillsdale, NJ: Erlbaum.

Teeter, P. A. (1998). *Interventions for ADHD: Treatment in developmental context.* New York: Guilford Press.

Teeter, P. A., & Semrud-Clikeman, M. (1997). *Child neuropsychology: Assessment and interventions for neurodevelopmental disorders.* Boston: Allyn & Bacon.

Thatcher, R. W. (1991). Maturation of the frontal lobes: Physiological evidence for staging. *Developmental Neuropsychology, 7*, 397–419.

Trommer, B. L., Hoeppner, J. B., Lorber, R., & Armstrong, K. (1988). Pitfalls in the use of a continuous performance test as a diagnostic tool in attention deficit disorder. *Developmental and Behavioral Pediatrics, 9*, 339–346.

Waber, D., & Holmes, J. M. (1985). Assessing children's copy productions of the Rey Osterrieth complex figure. *Journal of Clinical and Experimental Neuropsychology, 7*, 264–280.

Walker, H. M., Block-Pedego, A., Todis, B., & Severson, H. H. (1998). *School archival records search.* Longmont, CA: Sopris West.

Wilens, T. E., & Spencer, T. J. (2000). The stimulants revisited. *Child and Adolescent Psychiatry Clinical North American, 9*, 573–603.

# CHAPTER 21

# Providing Neuropsychological Services to Learners with Otitis Media and Central Auditory Processing Disorders

DALENE M. McCLOSKEY

OTITIS MEDIA (OM) IS one of the most frequently diagnosed childhood illnesses and accounts for most cases of hearing impairment in learners (Arick, 1995; Hasentaub, 1987). The incidence rates vary, but studies have suggested that nearly all children between the ages of birth and 3 years sustain at least one episode of OM (Gravel, McCarton, & Ruben, 1988; Henderson & Roush, 1997; Owen, Baldwin, Luttman, & Howie, 1993). Minimally, between 3% and 17% of all children have three or more OM episodes during this same age period (Gottlieb, 1981; Rasmussen, 1994; Teele, Klein, & Rosner, 1980). Infants from birth to 6 months appear to be the most at risk of acquiring OM (Gravel & Wallace, 1995), followed by children between 6 and 18 months old (Bondy, Berman, Glazner, & Lezotte, 2000; Henderson & Roush, 1997). It is also during this time that children are learning language and are most at risk of missing critical auditory stimulation that will promote a mature auditory language system (Eimas & Clarkson, 1986; Hasentaub, 1987; Schwartz, Mody, & Petinou, 1997). Many authorities have suggested that children who have OM, and hearing impairment because of the OM, are at risk for developing language, learning, auditory processing, and behavioral disorders (Byrd & Weitzman, 1994; Gravel & Nozza, 1997; Kaplan, Gleshman, Bender, Baum, & Clark, 1973; Knishkowy, Palti, Adler, & Tepper, 1991; Roberts & Wallace, 1997; Silva, Chalmers, & Stewart, 1986; Wallace & Hooper, 1997). It is for this reason that school-based professionals must become acquainted with the factors associated with OM and potential disabilities that can result from it. By understanding the issues, psychologists can promote prevention and become better informed regarding diagnosis and treatment so that intervention can occur as quickly as possible.

It has been difficult to calculate the number of individuals who develop central auditory processing disorders (CAPD) because of a lack of consensus regarding the definition and terminology involved (Keith, 1988), but Chermak and Musiek (1997) have estimated the prevalence rate to be 2% to 3% of all Americans, including children and adults. There is evidence that 5% to 8% of American schoolchildren have learning disabilities, and many of these are *auditory* or *language-based processing problems* (Keith, 1988). Of the children who are diagnosed with auditory, language, or learning disorders, many have a history of chronic OM (Byrd & Weitzman, 1994; Lonigan, Fischel, Whitehurst, Arnold, & Valdez-Mechanca, 1992). However, *most* children who experience OM do not demonstrate functional CAPD or language or learning disorders (Gravel & Wallace, 1992; Teele, Klein, Rosner, & Greater Boston Otitis Media Study Group, 1984).

Recent U.S. estimates indicate that the direct cost of treating OM, such as physician visits and surgery to insert ventilating tubes, was approximately $5.3 billion in 1998, or an average of $239 per episode (Bondy et al., 2000). Indirect costs, such as parents taking time off from work for doctor appointments and supervision of sick children, were not calculated, but if included, costs would obviously be a great deal higher (Alsarraf & Gates, 1999; Bondy et al., 2000). The long-term effects of OM have not been studied despite nearly 50 years of research. Because there is no clear cause-and-effect connection between OM and subsequent deleterious effects, it is difficult to calculate the cost to society.

## DEFINING OTITIS MEDIA

Otitis media is the generic term used to identify middle ear disease (Daly, 1997). There are two major categories of OM. Acute otitis media (AOM) is characterized by a bacterial infection and is often preceded by an upper respiratory infection. With AOM, the child's tympanic membrane is inflamed and the child experiences fever and pain. With treatment, the child can recover from the infection, but fluid can remain for up to 8 weeks or even longer. A mild to moderate hearing loss occurs as long as the fluid remains (Pukander & Karma, 1988; Roberts & Medley, 1995). The second major category, otitis media with effusion (OME), is diagnosed when there is fluid in the middle ear but infection is absent. It often follows an episode of AOM (Alho, Oja, Koivu, & Sorri, 1995), and the child is often asymptomatic and does not complain of pain in the middle ear (Marchant et al., 1984). Most cases of OME are due to either unresolved or recurrent AOM or Eustachian tube dysfunction, such as blockage of the opening to the tubes because of allergy or edema or because the walls of the Eustachian tubes are floppy and have difficulty inflating (Arick, 1995).

### Diagnosis of Otitis Media

The diagnosis of OM is usually dependent on visual and tympanometric evaluation. Tympanometry involves the use of a tympanometer, a device used to measure pressure in the middle ear. When the normally translucent tympanic membrane (TM) is reddened, or a fluid level is visible, or when the malleus, a small bone in the middle ear, is not visible through the TM, there is evidence of fluid in the middle ear. If the TM is bulging outward, there is a likelihood of bacterial infection, and if left untreated, the TM can burst. OME can best be diagnosed with tympanometry because it provides evidence of positive or negative ear pressure.

## RISK FACTORS FOR OTITIS MEDIA

Children are more at risk for OM than adults because of structural and physiological differences. Children have shorter and more horizontal Eustachian tubes, making it easier for bacteria to migrate to the middle ear chamber (Lim, 1984). The Eustachian tube is also less functional, and greater effort is required to make it work, but this changes at about the age of 7, when the tube more closely resembles an adult-like structure (Bylander & Tjernstrom, 1983). Children also have smaller mastoid bones, compromising the middle ear's ability to absorb fluid and thus maintain normal middle ear pressure. Moreover, children tend to have more pathogenic bacteria in their nasopharynx and a reduced capacity to produce antibodies to fight infection (Prellner, Kalm, & Pedersen, 1984).

In addition to factors associated with childhood, there are certain characteristics that make specific children more susceptible to OM episodes. Prellner (1995) and Paden, Novak, and Beiter (1987) have pointed out that no single factor puts a child more at risk; rather, it is the unique combination of factors that contributes to possible OM. Despite this qualifier, there are certain factors that clearly appear in the research. The greatest risk for an episode of OM is the previous occurrence of OM within 3 months (Alho et al., 1995). Boys tend to have a greater incidence of OM than girls (Alho et al., 1995; Prellner, 1995). Children under the age of 12 months are more at risk (Alho et al., 1995; Bondy et al., 2000; Roberts, Burchinal, & Henderson, 1993), especially if they attend day care and if it is autumn or winter (Alho et al., 1995; Prellner, 1995). Being breastfed and living with caregivers who smoke also seem to be factors contributing to increased OM (Alho et al., 1995; Teele et al., 1980). Native American and Eskimo children have a higher rate of occurrence than Caucasian children, and African American children seem to have the lowest incidence (Alho et al., 1995; Teele et al., 1980). The effect of socioeconomic status on OM is ambiguous (Alho et al., 1995).

## PERIPHERAL AUDITORY PATHWAYS AND FUNCTIONS

To understand the neuropsychological implications and problems inherent in OM and central auditory processing, it is important to clarify the nature of audition, or the hearing process. Hearing is a complex activity that involves mechanical, hydraulic, and electrophysiological processing of the acoustic signal.

### MECHANICAL PROCESSES IN THE OUTER AND MIDDLE EAR

The mechanical portion of sound transmission begins when the pinna, or the outer ear, gathers sound waves and directs them toward the ear canal, which ends at the tympanic membrane. Sound waves enter the ear canal and cause vibration of the TM, the thin sheath of tissue that separates the outer ear from the middle ear. Attached to the inside of the TM is the first of three very small bones or ossicles. The ossicular chain is made up of the malleus, incus, and stapes. If the vibration of the TM is of sufficient intensity, the three small bones are vibrated and eventually cause the oval window to vibrate. The stapes, the last of the small bones in the chain, attaches to the oval window, the separation between the middle ear and the inner ear. If the tiny bones become damaged because of chronic fluid, a permanent hearing loss can ensue (Hasentaub, 1987).

The middle ear is actually an extension of the nasopharynx, with the Eustachian tube connecting the two structures (Newby, 1979). The Eustachian tube enters the middle ear at the bottom of the middle ear cavity. Its function is to equalize pressure in the middle ear. Normally, the Eustachian tube lies in a flaccid state and opens when equalizing of air pressure is needed. When there is normal middle ear pressure, the ossicular chain transmits sound adequately. If there is negative pressure, the TM is drawn inward due to an inadequate supply of air. When there is positive pressure, as when there is fluid or infection, the TM bulges outward. When there is excessive negative or positive pressure, the bones cannot perform their vibratory function. Sound waves cannot be transmitted through the middle ear adequately, causing a conductive hearing loss. A conductive loss associated with OM is usually a 20 to 30 dB loss, but it can range from 10 to 50 dB (Eilers, Widen, Urano, Hudson, & Gonzales, 1991; Gravel & Ellis, 1995; Hunter, 1995). Normal hearing is recommended to be 15 dB in young children, 20 dB in older children, and 25 in adults (Eilers et al., 1991; Northern & Downs, 1991).

The posterior wall of the middle ear connects with the air-filled mastoid bone, a part of the temporal bone. Because the mastoid bone is made up of air-filled cells and because of its proximity to the middle ear, it is vulnerable to infection from the middle ear into the mastoid. The superior portion of the middle ear separates the middle ear from the meninges of the brain, posing another vulnerable pathway for infection (Hasentaub, 1987; Newby, 1979).

HYDRAULIC PROCESSES

The footplate of the stapes connects to the oval window, the entrance to the inner ear. The inner ear is comprised of the cochlea, the fluid-filled, snail-shaped organ of hearing, and the semicircular canals, also fluid-filled, which mediate vestibular functions. The end organ of the cochlea is the organ of Corti, the structure containing the microscopic hair cells (cilia) that register, or sense, sound. The cilia are arranged by frequency (tonotopically), with highest pitches on the outside and lower pitches tucked inside the cochlea, where they are less vulnerable to noise-induced hearing loss. When the sound waves are transferred to the cochlea, the fluid in the inner ear causes a shearing action on the cilia. If the oval window becomes damaged, the fluid can leak out of the cochlea and cause a permanent sensorineural hearing loss (Newby, 1979). Likewise, prolonged exposure to loud noise causes an eventual shearing of the cilia, causing a different type of permanent sensorineural loss.

NEUROLOGICAL PROCESSES

The cilia are connected to neurons that eventually make up the auditory portion of the eighth cranial nerve. As the cilia are moved in the fluid-filled cochlea by the sound waves, an electrophysiological response occurs that initiates firing of the neurons. The neural response continues through the auditory pathway to the brainstem and finally on to the cortex in an electrophysiological process.

## CENTRAL AUDITORY PATHWAYS

Once the auditory signal becomes an electrical or neurological signal, it moves quickly through the auditory nerve to various nuclei in the brainstem and on to the cortex. The tonotopic organization is maintained at each level in the auditory pathway. Each nuclei, or relay station, particularly in the brainstem, has specific functions that influence the processing of auditory information and has relevance to the concept of central auditory processing.

### AUDITORY NERVE

Nerve fibers from the vestibular and hearing systems make up the eighth cranial nerve, the vestibuloauditory nerve. The auditory portion originates as axons from the cilia, or sensory receptors, in the cochlea and merge into a nerve bundle. Its primary function is to break down the auditory signal into component parts and to send the information accurately to the central auditory nervous system for further processing (Bellis, 2003).

### COCHLEAR NUCLEUS

The cochlear nucleus is the first of several nuclei and is located between the medulla oblongata and the pons in the brainstem. The cochlear nucleus is considered the first level at which any true processing of auditory information occurs; its purpose is to enhance certain acoustic features of the auditory signal so that the features are more perceptually salient or clear for the listener (Bellis, 2003). The cochlear nucleus is also the first level of the central auditory nervous systems in which decussation or crossover of nerve fibers occurs. If there is any dysfunction below the level of the cochlear nucleus, it will be an ipsilateral pure-tone deficit, involving only one ear, but above the cochlear nucleus, it may be bilateral or contralateral (Chermak & Musiek, 1997). This concept is very important when considering the possibility of a central auditory processing disorder (Bellis, 2003).

### SUPERIOR OLIVARY COMPLEX

Medial to the cochlear nucleus and positioned in the caudal portion of the pons is the superior olivary complex. The superior olivary complex receives and processes binaural auditory information, allowing it to be sensitive to changes in intensity and to time changes (when each signal reaches each ear). Because it can perform these tasks, the superior olivary complex can localize auditory information and facilitate auditory figure-ground functions (Chermak & Musiek, 1997).

### INFERIOR COLLICULUS

The inferior colliculus is located between the pons and midbrain. Most of the fibers that connect with the inferior colliculus are contralateral, but there are bilateral and unilateral fibers as well. The inferior colliculus divides into two main pathways. The *primary* pathway maintains the tonotopic organization, but the *diffuse* pathway interprets a more broad range of frequencies and is not tonotopic.

### LATERAL LEMNISCUS

The lateral lemniscus is the primary ascending nerve bundle that transmits auditory information to the brain. It originates at the superior olivary complex and continues to the lateral lemniscus in the midbrain. Its primary function is to remove unnecessary features of the signal (signal extraction) and make important features more salient for the listener (signal enhancement).

### MEDIAL GENICULATE BODY

The medial geniculate body is located on the thalamus. There are three divisions of the medial geniculate body. The most ventral portion responds to acoustic stimuli and appears to be important in auditory discrimination of speech signals. The others respond to somatosensory and acoustic stimuli and are believed to be important in cross-modality processing (Chermak & Musiek, 1997).

## DEVELOPMENT OF THE AUDITORY SYSTEM

Structurally, the auditory system is mature at birth. A 5-month-old fetus has all the necessary outer, middle, and inner ear features necessary for hearing (Reinis & Goldman, 1980). The inner ear appears at 20 days, and by the end of the 5th week, there is evidence of two lobes in the inner ear that will develop into the semicircular canals of the vestibular system and the cochlea of the auditory system. The temporal lobe begins to develop at 10 to 12 weeks gestation and is well developed by about 20 weeks. Structural asymmetries of the temporal lobe are apparent at 30 weeks gestation (Teeter & Semrud-Clikeman, 1997; Wada, Clark, & Hamm, 1975). At birth, however, the newborn's auditory system is functionally unprepared to process auditory information, partly because myelination is incomplete at birth. Myelination begins when a child is born and continues throughout childhood until the age of 12 or 14 years. The brainstem structures become myelinated first, and the corpus callosum is among the last to become myelinated. Although Roush and Henderson (1995) believe the human auditory system is so well developed at birth that it should be less vulnerable to the effects of sensory deprivation (such as hearing impairment secondary to OM), functional differences are reported in the brainstem functioning of children who experience recurrent OM (Besing, Koehnke, & Goulet, 1993; Hall, Grose, & Drake, 1997; Wellendorf, Hall, Grose, & Pillsbury, 1995) and may lead to maturational differences in the peripheral and central auditory systems (Hurley & Hurley, 1995).

## CENTRAL AUDITORY PROCESSING

The study of auditory processing disorders began in the 1950s, when Bocca and colleagues (Bocca, Calearo, & Cassinari, 1954) noted several patients with normal peripheral hearing but poor understanding of auditory information in noisy situations. They localized lesions in the brainstem and left auditory cortex, which explained the deficits (Bocca et al., 1954). In the 1960s, interest in auditory processing disorders was motivated by the possibility that they could cause language and learning disabilities (Keith, 1984). In the 1970s, scientific interest became more intense, and studies were performed on animals and with humans to learn more about how auditory information is processed. Several test batteries were developed and field-tested in the 1970s and 1980s. The 1990s and the new millennium have seen increased interest in auditory processing, including a consensus statement from the American Speech Language Hearing Association

(ASHA) prescribing a definition of central auditory processing disorders. The focus during these later years has shifted somewhat to the management of the disorder and how to assist the individual to be the best listener possible (Bellis, 2003; Ferre & Bellis, 1999).

In 2000, the Brutton Conference in Dallas addressed screening, differential diagnosis, a minimal test battery, and directions for future research in auditory processing, including a need to investigate normal auditory processing development, the prevalence, types, and efficacy of treatment, and the use of newer tests for diagnosis and treatment recommendations. Along with these issues, the terminology was changed to auditory processing disorders (APD) to reflect that the deficit is auditory in nature and that it involves more than a sequential step-by-step processing of auditory information. This was not the first name change, nor has it been universally accepted.

## Current Definition of Central Auditory Processing Disorders

The term "central auditory processing" was proposed by Keith in 1977 at an ASHA conference to describe an auditory process that happens central to the cochlea (Chermak & Musiek, 1997; Keith, 1984). Keith proposed that auditory perceptual skills are the building blocks of auditory processing skills and that auditory processing skills facilitate language development in a reciprocal manner with neuroanatomy. Keith (1988, 1999) hypothesized that a CAPD represents a subset of language disorders and that the basic problem in CAPD is diminished understanding of the auditory information when the speech signal is presented under less than optimal listening conditions. Individuals with normal auditory processing capabilities can compensate in poor listening conditions because of redundancy in language.

Just as there is no consensus on terminology, there is ongoing debate about what constitutes CAP, whether CAPD is the cause or a symptom of language/learning disorder (Keith, 1984), or whether it even actually exists (Cacace & McFarland, 1998; Kamhi & Beasley, 1985; Rees, 1981). In 1996, the ASHA Task Force proposed the following definition:

> Central Auditory Processes are the auditory mechanisms and processes responsible for the following behavioral phenomena: sound localization and lateralization; auditory discrimination; auditory pattern recognition; temporal aspects of audition, including temporal resolution, temporal masking, temporal integration, and temporal ordering; auditory performance with competing acoustic signals; and auditory performance with degraded acoustic signals. (p. 41)

## Diagnosis of Central Auditory Processing Disorders

Adults as well as children can have a CAPD, and in quiet environments they can often compensate for their disorder. For children, the school environment contains numerous distractions that will impair their ability to sustain attention and perceive the auditory signal in a manner that allows them to comprehend. Typically, teachers will notice that these children cannot sustain their attention, have poor auditory memory skills and poor phonological awareness skills, and cannot follow directions (Bellis, 2003; Friel-Patti, 1999; Keith, 1999; Smoski, Brunt, & Tannahill, 1992). Such children also tend to develop literacy problems and sometimes behavioral problems (Heiervang, Stevenson, & Hugdahl, 2002; Katz & Cohen, 1985).

Data can be gathered by various multidisciplinary team members, including school psychologists and neuropsychologists, but audiologists are uniquely trained and qualified to diagnose CAPD (Ferre & Bellis, 1999; Jerger & Musiek, 2000; Keith & Stromberg, 1985). A comprehensive evaluation includes a thorough medical, developmental, and social history, as well as observation in various acoustic environments. These steps optimally are completed prior to a referral for a CAPD evaluation, and an evaluation should be completed only when there is sufficient data to suspect a CAPD.

*Screening*   One of the outcomes of the Brutton Conference in 2000 was a consensus statement on screening for CAPD. Checklists or questionnaires, electrophysiological techniques, and behavioral measures are used for screening. The purpose of screening is to avoid over- and underidentification and to provide the audiologist with enough information to substantiate a referral. Four popular screening devices are the Children's Auditory Performance Scale (Smoski, Brunt, & Tannahill, 1998), the Screening Instrument for Targeting Educational Risk (Anderson & Matkin, 1996), the Screening Test for Auditory Processing Deficits (Keith, 1986), a behavioral measure of auditory processing, and teacher checklists. The checklists optimally are completed by the teacher and interpreted by the audiologist. Because the audiologist has the training and equipment to conduct the behavioral and electrophysiological tests, the audiologist must be involved with this step.

*Evaluation*   Experts at the Brutton Conference (Jerger & Musiek, 2000) recommended that a CAPD battery should minimally include dichotic listening tests, monoaural low-redundancy speech tasks, binaural interaction, and temporal processing. Subjects should be at least 6 years old (although some batteries have extended down to 3 years) and should have normal hearing acuity and normal cognition to be administered a CAP battery (Bellis, 2003). Behavioral measures, electroacoustic procedures, such as auditory evoked brainstem response, and neuroimaging studies, such as magnetic resonance images, have been used in CAPD test batteries (Chermak & Musiek, 1997; Hood, 1998). Evaluation results can be used to suggest a child's neurodevelopmental status, determine whether compromised auditory functioning may contribute to language and reading problems (Keith, 1988), measure the functional integrity of the right and left cortical regions, provide information regarding the efficiency of the corpus callosum, measure subcortical functioning, provide a picture of auditory strengths and weaknesses, and relate the auditory profile to communication and learning strategies (Ferre & Bellis, 1999).

*Dichotic Listening Tests*   With these tests, different information is simultaneously presented to each ear. The subject is asked to recall what was presented to both ears, primarily measuring the left hemisphere, or to focus on one ear, measuring the ability to suppress the other ear. These types of tests are sensitive to disruption in the interhemispheric transfer of information via the corpus callosum, as well as brainstem structures, and cortical dysfunction (Bellis, 2003). Typically, there is a right ear advantage for verbal information and a left ear advantage for nonverbal auditory information (Asbjornsen et al., 2000; Bryden, 1963; Dirks, 1964; Kimura, 1961). Examples of dichotic tests include the Dichotic Digits Test (Kimura, 1961), Staggered Spondaic Word Test (Katz, 1962), and the Competing Sentence Test (Willeford & Burleigh, 1994).

*Monoaural Low-Redundancy Speech Tests* These tests involve presentation of monosyllable words that are distorted in some way to reduce linguistic redundancy. The purpose is to evaluate the listener's auditory closure ability when the signal is distorted. These tests are sensitive to central disorders, including those in the brainstem and primary auditory cortex (Baran et al., 1985; Bellis, 2003). Tests include the Low Pass Filtered Speech Tests (Willeford, 1977) and the Pediatric Speech Intelligibility Test (Jerger, Jerger, & Abrams, 1983).

*Temporal Patterning Tests* There are two types of temporal patterning tests (Chermak & Musiek, 1997). In each type, the listener hears triads of tone bursts that differ in frequency or duration. First, the listener reports the pattern that is heard (e.g., high-low-low) requiring interhemispheric transfer of information from the right to the left hemisphere. Second, the listener is asked to hum the pattern, which removes the language component and the need to transfer information across hemispheres. This portion is sensitive to cortical and interhemispheric disruption. The tests have also been helpful in separating right hemisphere disorders from interhemispheric and/or left-hemispheric disorders. (Musiek, Kibbe, & Baran, 1984). Two commonly used tests are the Pitch Pattern Sequence Test (Ptacek & Pinheiro, 1971) and the Duration Patterns Test (Pinheiro & Musiek, 1985).

*Binaural Interaction Test* In this test, the input to each ear consists of a portion of the target message so that the interaction between the two ears is required to achieve a unified precept. The listener processes disparate but complementary time and amplitude information to the ears. This type of test is sensitive only to gross brainstem pathology (Musiek, 1983). Two tests in this area are the Tonal and Speech Materials for Auditory Perception Assessment (1992) and the Rapidly Alternating Speech Perception Test (Willeford & Bilger, 1978).

*Electroacoustic Measures* The Auditory Evoked Brainstem Potentials (AEBP) test has been used for years to measure differences in the rate of processing auditory stimuli. Basically, electrodes are strategically placed on the scalp, and the listener is presented with audible clicks. There are five primary waves involved in the AEBP. Wave I is believed to correspond to areas in the acoustic nerve, Wave II also corresponds to the eighth cranial nerve, Wave III to the cochlear nucleus, and Waves IV and V to several sites in the brainstem, including the cochlear nucleus, superior olivary complex, and lateral lemniscus. In addition to AEBP, there is a middle latency response believed to originate in the temporal lobe or thalamic region. Farther down the pathway, there is a late-event related potential, which is considered a response to internally generated events, such as the integration and attention functions of the limbic system and auditory cortex (Bellis, 2003). When the waves are absent, the condition is considered deviant.

## AUDITORY BEHAVIORS

ASHA has recommended that when any one or a combination of auditory behaviors is impaired, there is an auditory processing disorder. To assess these auditory behaviors, audiologists primarily use dichotic listening, monoaural low-redundancy speech, temporal patterning, and binaural interaction tests.

*Sound Localization and Lateralization*   Katz and Cohen (1985) have suggested that brainstem functions are associated with localization and differentiating foreground and background auditory stimuli. In the classroom, a child with difficulty in this area may lack attending skills and may easily misinterpret auditory information.

*Auditory Discrimination*   Researchers have found that every level of the peripheral and central auditory system plays a role in speech sound encoding, or phonemic discrimination (Bellis, 2003; Hall, Grose, & Pillsbury, 1995). Problems with auditory discrimination are considered "pervasively destructive" to children's academic performance because they can interfere with reading, comprehension, spelling, and written language (Young, 1985). Children who perform well on minimal pair discrimination tasks in a soundproof booth or even in a neuropsychological evaluation may lack the ability to discriminate sounds when seated in a classroom with normal background noise. Keith (1981) has reported that it is difficult to recognize phonemes because they are not perceptual units and because there is simultaneous processing of more than one sound. He also indicated that auditory discrimination for speech is a linguistic process that requires intact auditory memory if information is to be processed effectively.

*Auditory Pattern Recognition*   McFarland and Cacace (1997) have studied the influence of short-term memory on visual and auditory pattern recognition tasks. They believe that if the influence is equal for both modalities, it supports the hypothesis of a global disorder responsible for CAPD. If, on the other hand, the influence is unequal, this supports CAPD as a separate disorder. These authors concluded that common resources are needed to perform both the auditory and visual versions of the task (a global influence) and that linguistic, modality-specific, and modality-independent processes are also involved.

*Temporal Aspects*   The temporal aspects of auditory processing are important in the perception of speech and music and occur at every synapse in the auditory nervous system, including the temporal lobe of both hemispheres and the corpus callosum. Because speech perception depends on the sequential analysis of auditory stimuli, several researchers believe that a deficit in processing rapidly changing auditory stimuli is the primary factor in CAPD, language, and learning problems (Anderson, Brown, & Tallal, 1993; Stark & Bernstein, 1984). Both the duration of the actual stimuli and the amount of time in between the sounds (interstimuli interval; ISI) are important in auditory perception. In terms of timing, the first 100 to 200 milliseconds of an auditory signal are the most important in speech perception or for stimuli recognition (Massaro, 1972). Heiervang et al. (2002) found that dyslexic children had difficulty correctly identifying complex tones of short duration when they were presented in rapid succession. In terms of ISI, when transitions between phonemes were lengthened, children with language impairment improved their ability to discriminate the sounds (Katz & Cohen, 1985).

*Auditory Performance with Competing Acoustic Stimuli (Dichotic Listening)*   Dichotic listening is considered by many to be a reliable measure of functional lateralization of the brain and a valid measure for assessing selective auditory attention (Asbjornsen et al., 2000). Because the listener must attend to different auditory stimuli in each ear, the task requires competition for processing resources, and processing may be further limited by linguistic factors (Keith, 1984; McFarland & Cacace, 1997). Age-related changes in auditory skills have been studied using dichotic listening. Bowen and Hynd (1988) compared learning disabled (LD) and normal adults on dichotic listening tasks and found that there is a developmental change in the ability to suppress the nondominant hemisphere and that normal adults were able to switch attention from ear to ear. Research also was reported concerning an age-related decline in the interhemispheric transfer of auditory information (Jerger, Moncrieff, Greenwald, Wambacq, & Seipel, 2000).

*Auditory Performance with Degraded Acoustic Signals (Figure-Ground)*   Auditory figure-ground problems are a nearly universal problem in CAPD (Katz & Cohen, 1985). The anterior regions of the brain along with the auditory pathways are believed to be involved in the ability to identify speech in background noise (Katz & Cohen, 1985). Because of their difficulties, children with auditory figure-ground problems may need more time to monitor their environment in order to focus on important information (Keith, 1984). Some researchers found that with practice, students became desensitized to background noise by listening for words in noisy backgrounds, thus improving their figure-ground listening skills (Katz & Cohen, 1985). In another study (Shapiro & Mistal, 1985), students with a reading disorder received amplified instruction. These students improved their ability to discriminate words in compromised listening situations. They also showed improvement in auditory memory tasks and speech articulation of multisyllabic words. Thus, practice and classroom amplification should be considered appropriate interventions.

SUBPROFILES OF CENTRAL AUDITORY PROCESSING DISORDERS

Generally, CAPD are considered a heterogeneous group of processing deficits that are auditory in nature and involve the processing of verbal and nonverbal acoustic stimuli (Bellis, 2003; Chermak & Musiek, 1997). Although auditory in nature, there can be overlap with other modalities and other disorders. If one accepts CAPD, then it seems logical to consider subtypes of this disorder.

According to Musiek, Gollegly, and Ross (1985), the subprofiles are best conceptualized by etiology (neurological, developmental, maturational, and idiopathic). Neurological subtypes occur in about 2% to 3% of children with LD and CAPD who have an underlying neurological condition impacting their ability to process auditory information. Developmental cases involve children with abnormal brain development not associated with delayed maturation. Maturational cases include children who have lags in development. As their neurological structures mature and become myelinated, their central auditory processing improves. Idiopathic subtypes are those cases with no known etiology or those with a combination of etiologies.

Some authors believe in top-down and bottom-up processing of auditory information (Ferre & Bellis, 1999). They believe that processing spoken language depends in part on the individual's state of arousal and attention (top-down). Any higher-order dysfunction, including attention, memory, cognition, or language deficits, can impair the individual's ability to process or understand auditory information, including spoken language (Bellis, 2003; Ferre & Bellis, 1999; Kolb & Whishaw, 1996). For example, a parietal or frontal lobe lesion can influence the efficiency of auditory processing. Even if the individual accurately encodes auditory information, a higher-order dysfunction can have a significant impact on processing and comprehension of spoken language (Lezak, 1995). In addition, all structures and mechanisms from the bottom up, cochlea through brainstem, must work efficiently to achieve adequate processing (Kolb & Whishaw, 1996; Restak, 2001).

In an effort to develop a CAPD model, Ferre and Bellis (1999) have identified three primary profiles that indicate different lesion sites as well as typical behaviors associated with each lesion. These researchers have also offered treatment recommendations based on the type of CAPD diagnosed. The first profile, the auditory decoding deficit, is believed by some to be the only true CAPD because it is specific to the auditory modality. The auditory processes most likely to be impaired with this type of CAPD include auditory closure, temporal processing, speech sound discrimination, and binaural listening. In the classroom, these children often struggle with phonological awareness, decoding, and spelling. Interventions include classroom management strategies and drills to improve specific skills. The prosodic deficit is often the auditory part of a larger and comorbid processing disorder. Temporal patterning, binaural listening, and auditory discrimination of nonverbal auditory stimuli are often impaired. As a result of these deficits, the child may demonstrate very poor social communication or pragmatic language skills. Phonological awareness skills tend to be unimpaired, and the child may become a proficient reader. Ferre and Bellis have recognized this as a CAPD because the right temporal lobe is often the site of a lesion. Intervention includes direct social skill instruction, such as role-playing and prompting in how to handle social situations and how to interpret nonverbal communication. An integration deficit results from inefficient interhemispheric integration. Temporal patterning and binaural listening tend to be affected. In the classroom, any task requiring cooperation of both hemispheres or several regions of the brain may be impaired, such as note taking, playing a musical instrument, and copying from the board (Bellis, 2003; Ferre & Bellis, 1999; Lezak, 1995). Interventions include providing an enhanced listening environment and training to improve listening. Specific tasks, such as note taking, may need to be addressed as well. With this profile, the use of multimodality instruction is contraindicated (Bellis, 2003; Ferre & Bellis, 1999); a better plan is to provide instruction through one modality at a time to avoid confusion for the student (Bellis, 2003; Ferre & Bellis, 1999).

## School Neuropsychological Intervention

In the public schools, children are generally eligible for special education services to address auditory processing problems under two special education eligibility labels, speech and language disability and learning disability. Students may also be eligible to receive accommodations through the use of a Section 504 plan (an antidiscrimination protection).

The ASHA Task Force (1996) found that there is inadequate evidence of treatment efficacy for CAPD treatment and that intervention should focus on management strategies. The audiologist should be intimately involved in treatment, along with the speech and language pathologist, classroom teacher, parents, school psychologist, school neuropsychologist, and other team members as needed. Every member of the student's team should contribute suggestions for improving the listening environment for the student. School psychologists and school neuropsychologists have a greater knowledge of brain-based behaviors and of the school environment. Because of their knowledge, they should become involved by working closely with the audiologist to ascertain the student's auditory strengths and weaknesses, to identify interfering variables, such as attention and concentration, and to determine how best to accommodate the student's auditory deficiencies and needs at school. Leaders in the field of auditory processing disorders recommend that individualized intervention focus on four areas: (1) teaching the use of environmental modifications, (2) compensatory strategies, (3) counseling, and (4) remedial instruction (Chermak & Musiek, 1997; Ferre, 2002; Friel-Patti, 1999).

## Environmental Modifications

In terms of environmental modifications, preferential seating is often enough to assist students. They need to be seated away from as much extraneous noise as possible and near the source of important auditory and visual information, such as the teacher, overhead, and television monitor (Willeford & Burleigh, 1985; Friel-Patti, 1999). Classroom amplification systems may be an appropriate intervention when students require a greater signal-to-noise ratio to improve their ability to listen in a classroom. This may be more appropriate for lower grades because the student tends to have one teacher and not need to move about the school for subjects. If necessary, personal listening devices, such as desk models, headphones, and ear plugs, can be provided so that the student can listen to the teacher, who wears a microphone and can be mobile. Because listening can be an exhausting task for students with an auditory processing disorder, they may require breaks more frequently than other students.

## Compensatory Strategies

Compensatory strategies (Willeford & Burleigh, 1985) may include allowing students to use a tape recorder to hear the lesson and instructions more than once. Students should be provided lists and taught how to make their own lists. A homework calendar is also useful when the student is unable to accurately remember assignment information. When possible, students with an auditory processing disorder should be encouraged to use a study buddy; this strategy may need to be set up and monitored by the teachers so that the student does not take advantage of his or her buddy. Finally, it is very important for students with a hearing disorder to learn to ask for clarification so that they do not spend time doing work incorrectly and so that they do not misunderstand information.

## COUNSELING

It is important to teach students with an identified auditory processing disorder how to advocate for themselves (Willeford & Burleigh, 1985). Students, their parents, and teachers need to understand the nature of the difficulties and how to adjust for them in various situations, so that they can be involved in treatment throughout the school years. Sadly, the importance of this area of service often is disregarded in the public schools.

## DIRECT INTERVENTION

In terms of direct intervention, several specific types of tasks can be taught or practiced. There are several programs commercially available that promote auditory skills through skill-based practice, but there is no evidence that improving specific auditory skills will allow a student with an auditory processing disorder to function more ably in the classroom (Seats, 1997; Tallal & Merzenich, 1997). Students can be taught how to improve their attending behavior through self-monitoring exercises. They can also be taught strategies to improve their memory skills (e.g., chunking information, using mnemonics and lists). To improve their auditory closure, they can practice phonological awareness skills (e.g., closure, blending). Some students may misunderstand stress or prosody in speech and may benefit from direct instruction in this area. For some students, interhemispheric activities are useful (e.g., identifying differences and similarities in music, practicing note taking skills, and using drawing as an aid to comprehension). Finally, deficient auditory skills will likely interfere with literacy development. Specific reading strategies that may be helpful include teaching prereading strategies (e.g., generate hypotheses about the passage, preteach vocabulary, generate questions about the passage), using outlines and templates to organize, and recognizing and using context cues.

## IS OTITIS MEDIA CONNECTED TO OTHER DISORDERS?

Many researchers have proposed a causal link between OM and CAPD, learning disabilities, language disorders, and emotional/behavioral disorders. Numerous studies have supported differences in the auditory-evoked brainstem potential functioning, language development, auditory behaviors, classroom behavior, and more among children with a history of OM (Asbjornsen et al., 2000; Bjoraker, 2001; Black & Sonnenschein, 1993; Gravel & Wallace, 1992; Hall et al., 1995; Longian et al., 1992; Secord, Erickson, & Bush, 1988). Most studies have pointed out that OM as a *singular cause* of other disorders is untenable. Rather, it is the unique interaction of a child's circumstances that leads to delays or disorders in language, academic, cognitive, or behavioral functioning (Bishop & Edmundson, 1986; Black & Sonnenschein, 1993).

## OTITIS MEDIA AND LANGUAGE

Many experts believe that the hearing loss associated with OM is the core problem because to acquire age-appropriate phonological skills, a child must perceive, store, and analyze the characteristics of sound (Gravel & Ellis, 1995; Gravel & Wallace, 1995; Schwartz et al., 1997; Schwartz & Goffman, 1995). When there is inconsistent auditory acuity (fluctuations in acuity and unilateral or bilateral changes), there is inconsistent auditory input and the child does not hear accurate and consistent representations of concepts (Hasentaub, 1987). For example, the word "cat" may be heard as "at," "ca," "c," and so on (Hasentaub, 1987). The child does not know these are the same concept and that they should sound reasonably similar each time they are produced. Unfortunately, in many studies, the degree of hearing loss is not documented or considered when discussing research results.

Hearing acuity and the degree of loss appear to influence phonological development (Paden et al., 1987). Although researchers assert that there is no single factor that leads to poor phonological development, they have found that hearing threshold was the most important variable in the speech development of children at age 3 (Paden et al., 1987). The second most important variable was the children's speech reception threshold (using a test of discrimination), which is dependent on acuity. The children in the study who had tubes in their ears (and thus consistent hearing acuity) performed better on a phonology task than children who experienced their first OM at a younger age.

Donahue (1993) conducted a case study with a child who had a history of OM. She found that this child learned the phonological system in a manner similar to that of hearing impaired children. Specifically, the child avoided stop consonants (e.g., t, k, d, g) and seemed to prefer consonants that could be prolonged (e.g., l, s), nasal sounds (e.g., m, n), vowels, and bilabials (e.g., p, b, w), likely because they provided more visual and kinesthetic feedback in the absence of adequate auditory information. Early treatment to prevent recurrent OM and hearing impairment is critical for normal speech and language to develop.

A number of studies found that infants with a history of OM had less syllable diversity in their babbling (Schwartz et al., 1997). By school age, however, they had achieved mature phonology. In contrast, Roberts, Burchinal, Koch, Footo, and Henderson (1988) found that the OM children in their study became intelligible more slowly than peers, and their phonological skills had not matured adequately at school age. The authors reasoned that phonological process errors are common with typical preschoolers, but they tend to improve by school age. School psychologists and neuropsychologists working with young children must be vigilant about children's hearing acuity and their listening needs as they relate to speech and language development.

Language development includes development of semantics, syntax, morphology, and pragmatics. Teele et al. (1984) found that a greater number of days with bilateral OM from birth to age 3 was associated with lower vocabulary scores and auditory comprehension scores. In Donahue's (1993) case study, the child demonstrated a regression of vocabulary development from the 60th percentile at 9 months to the 20th percentile at 15 months. The more time spent with OM during the age range of 12 to 18 months was very predictive of delayed expressive language functioning (Lonigan et al., 1992). Morphology involves linguistic features that change meaning, such as word endings for plurality, past tense, and posses-sives. In English, many of these inflectional endings require a higher-pitched sound (such as "s"). These endings and function words (e.g., "is," "a") are vulner-able to omission with OM children because of their sound frequency and because they require more intensity to be heard (Schwartz et al., 1997).

## OTITIS MEDIA AND LEARNING

Studies regarding learning and cognition have been equivocal at best, but global cognitive ability appears to be less influenced by the effects of OM than language-based academic achievement (Gravel & Wallace, 1995; Roberts, Burchinal, & Campbell, 1994; Roberts & Medley, 1995; Secord et al., 1988; Wallace & Hooper, 1997). If a child inaccurately encodes language into his or her database as a result of a hearing impairment, academic achievement is often eventually impaired (Roberts & Medley, 1995; Wallace & Hooper, 1997). Gravel and Wallace found no difference between children with a history of OM and normal controls in math achievement or cognition, but reading scores were significantly weaker for the OM children. Secord et al. (1988) found that LD students with a history of OM had weak auditory verbal abilities involving sequential information processing and a strength in nonverbal spatial abilities involving simultaneous information processing. The authors concluded that early chronic OM led to serious language-based cognitive deficits but not global deficits. There is evidence that the achievement problems could be short-term and that children may overcome aca-demic delays. When children with a history of OM were studied at age 12, there was no difference between their academic skills and that of their non-OM peers (Roberts, Burchinal, & Clark-Klein, 1995). Conversely, Roberts, Burchinal, and Campbell (1994) found that OM was not related to academic achievement or cog-nitive ability.

## OTITIS MEDIA AND CENTRAL AUDITORY PROCESSING DISORDERS

Several theories have attempted to explain a connection between OM and CAPD (e.g., Willeford & Burliegh, 1985). Some theorists have postulated that children with OM do not have the advantage of hearing all auditory cues during critical or sensitive language learning periods (Gravel & Nozza, 1997; Hasentaub, 1987; Schwartz et al., 1997). When the child with a fluctuating hearing loss must listen and attempt to learn in a noisy or poor acoustic environment, learning the lan-guage code becomes especially difficult and the child does not establish an ade-quate auditory base (Gravel & Nozza, 1997; Gravel & Wallace, 1992). From this view, there may be *neural reorganization of the auditory pathways,* such as brainstem changes (Hurley & Hurley, 1995), when there is a chronic conductive hearing loss, as has been found in animal studies (Coleman & O'Connor, 1979; Knudsen, Knudsen, & Esterly, 1984). Besing and Koehnke (1995) found a reduced ability to localize sounds in children with a history of OM. Monoaural listening (the ability to listen with one ear in noisy situations) and binaural listening (the coordinated processing of auditory information from both ears) was deficient in children who had a history of OM (Hall et al., 1995, 1997). Binaural listening is especially criti-cal for developing sustained attention to auditory information. The authors iden-tified the importance of binaural listening in a classroom. If binaural listening is intact and the child must choose between listening to a teacher or to competing noise, the child will listen to the teacher. If impaired, the child cannot make this choice and may be unable to sustain attention on the teacher. Auditory discrimination skills appeared to be deficient with OM 6- and 7-year-olds in two separate studies (Eimas & Clarkson, 1986; Menyuk, 1986). These children could not discriminate voiced/voiceless phonemes in a minimal pair test.

Certainly, impairment at the brainstem and subsequent limitations in various auditory behaviors can impact a child's development. There appears to be adequate support for an OM and CAPD connection, but how the brainstem becomes damaged remains a question.

## Otitis Media and Behavior

Several researchers have found a relationship between children who have a history of OM and subsequent problematic classroom behaviors. When children's hearing fluctuates during critical language learning years, it is hypothesized that they "tune out" or learn not to attend because the stimuli are too confusing (Roberts et al., 1994). Although these children may perform better on comprehension tasks when there is a stronger signal-to-noise ratio to hold their attention, they simply do not develop requisite classroom attending skills (Gravel & Wallace, 1992).

School psychologists and neuropsychologists should be aware of these potential deficiencies as they become involved in referrals. They should investigate the student's auditory background thoroughly and make the appropriate referral to the audiologist if there are questions about central auditory processing skills. They should concurrently assist with developing appropriate classroom accommodations so that the best possible listening environment is promoted for the student.

*Central Auditory Processing Disorders and Attention-Deficit/Hyperactivity Disorder*
Interestingly, the symptoms of CAPD and the diagnostic criteria for children with ADHD are nearly identical (Gascon, Johnson, & Burd, 1986). Three explanations have been offered to clarify the CAPD and ADHD connection. It is possible that the comorbidity reflects two separate and distinct disorders. Riccio, Cohen, Hynd, and Keith (1996) found a greater number of commission errors for students with CAPD/ADHD than students with CAPD on an auditory vigilance task, suggesting they are similar but different disorders. It could also be that the two are in fact one disorder with a similar neurological basis (Gascon et al., 1986; Hagerman & Falkenstein, 1987; Wasserman, Pine, & Bruder, 1999). Evidence for this theory lies in performance increases on auditory processing tasks and behavioral measures after introduction of stimulant medication (Gascon et al., 1986; Keith & Engineer, 1991). Finally, it is possible that the inattention, impulsivity, and hyperactivity are the result of a common underlying disorder. Riccio, Hynd, Cohen, Hall, and Molt (1994) suspected that behavioral problems developed over time as a result of language and learning disability and recommended a thorough speech and language evaluation for any child suspected of having ADHD in order to rule out any auditory-linguistic deficits.

## CONCLUSION

Otitis media is a serious problem for children during language learning years. Although OM is experienced by nearly all children at one time or another, only a small percentage develop auditory processing, language, learning, or behavioral problems. Critical evidence has suggested a connection between OM and later problems for these children. Many theories and studies reviewed have proposed that OM leads to auditory processing problems that in turn influence language, learning, and behavior. Researchers promote various interventions to treat the auditory processing system and processes, but most agree that environmental modification provides the greatest relief for these children and youth.

The field of central auditory processing continues to be a hot topic and a fruitful area for research. There are no clear answers regarding types of CAPD, but there is much discussion that APD is the more appropriate term because when auditory information is processed linguistically, it becomes a receptive language issue rather than an auditory processing issue. Research should continue to identify how CAPDs are specific and isolated disorders and how to differentially diagnose them. This would include developing and evaluating new assessment procedures and instruments. Because assessment is not finished until an appropriate intervention has been implemented and data evaluated, current research must investigate both short- and long-term treatment efficacy. Another vital research area concerns the investigation of the connection between OM and CAPD. At this time, there are many studies suggesting a connection, but the neurodevelopmental path of these disorders remains clouded and uncertain at best. Future research in the areas of auditory processing, language, learning, and behavior should continue to provide evidence-based interventions that will benefit individuals. Research may perhaps even uncover a causal link between OM and CAPD.

## REFERENCES

Alho, O., Oja, H., Koivu, M., & Sorri, M. (1995). Risk factors for chronic otitis media with effusion in infancy. *Archives of Otolaryngology Head Neck Surgery, 121,* 839–843.

Alsarraf, R., & Gates, G. A. (1999). The real cost of otitis media. *Acta Pediatrica, 88,* 487–488.

American Speech Language Hearing Association. (1996). Central auditory processing: Current status of research and implications for clinical practice. *American Journal of Audiology, 5,* 41–54.

Anderson, K., Brown, C. P., & Tallal, P. (1993). Developmental language disorders: Evidence for a basic processing deficit. *Current Opinion in Neurology and Neurosurgery, 6,* 98–106.

Anderson, K., & Matkin, N. H. (1996). *Screening Instrument for Targeting Educational Risk (SIFTER).* Tampa, FL: Educational Audiology Associates.

Arick, D. S. (1995). Diagnosis and treatment of otitis media. *Seminars in Hearing, 16,* 20–27.

Asbjornsen, A., Homefjord, A., Reisaeter, S., Moeller, P., Klausen, O., Prytz, B., et al. (2000). Lasting auditory attention impairment after persistent middle ear infections: A dichotic listening study. *Developmental Medicine and Child Neurology, 42,* 481–486.

Baran, J. A., Verkest, S., Gollegly, K., Kibbe-Michal, K., Rintelmann, W. J., & Musiek, F. (1985). Use of compressed speech in the assessment of central nervous system disorder. *Journal for the Acoustical Society of America, 78*(Suppl. 1), 41.

Bellis, T. J. (2003). *Assessment and management of central auditory processing disorders in the educational setting from science to practice* (2nd ed.). Clifton Park, NY: Delmar Learning.

Besing, J. M., & Koehnke, J. (1995). A test of virtual auditory localization. *Ear and Hearing, 16,* 220–229.

Besing, J. M., Koehnke, J., & Goulet, C. (1993). *Binaural performance associated with a history of otitis media in children.* Paper presented at the 15th Midwinter Research Meeting of the Association for Research in Otolaryngology, St Petersburg Beach, FL.

Bishop, D., & Edmundson, A. (1986). Is OM a major cause of specific developmental language disorders? *British Journal of Communication Disorders, 21,* 321–338.

Bjoraker, K. J. (2001). *An examination of neuropsychological factors in emotionally disabled children.* Unpublished doctoral dissertation, University of Northern Colorado, Greeley, CO.

Black, M. M., & Sonnenschein, S. (1993). Early exposure to otitis media: A preliminary investigation of behavioral outcome. *Developmental and Behavioral Pediatrics, 14,* 150–155.

Bocca, E., Calearo, C., & Cassinari, V. (1954). A new method for testing hearing in temporal lobe tumors. *Acta Otolaryngologica, 45,* 289–304.

Bondy, J., Berman, S., Glazner, G., & Lezotte, D. (2000). Direct expenditures related to otitis media diagnosis: Extrapolations from a pediatric medicaid cohort. *Pediatrics, 105,* 1–7.

Bowen, S. M., & Hynd, G. W. (1988). Do children with learning disabilities outgrow deficits in selective auditory attention? Evidence from dichotic listening in adults with learning disabilities. *Journal of Learning Disabilities, 21,* 623–630.

Bryden, M. (1963). Ear preference in auditory perception. *Journal of Experimental Psychology, 16,* 359–360.

Bylander, A., & Tjernstrom, O. (1983). Changes in Eustachian tube function with age in children with normal ears. *Acta Otolaryngolica* (Stockholm), *96,* 467–477.

Byrd, R. S., & Weitzman, M. L. (1994). Predictors of early grade retention among children in the United States. *Pediatrics, 93,* 481–487.

Cacace, A. T., & McFarland, D. J. (1998). Central auditory processing disorders in school-aged children: A critical review. *Journal of Speech Language Hearing Research, 41,* 355–373.

Chermak, G. D., & Musiek, F. E. (1997). *Central auditory processing disorders: New perspectives.* Albany, NY: Singular Publishing Group.

Coleman, J. R., & O'Connor, P. (1979). Effects of monoaural and binaural sound deprivation on cell development in the anteroventral cochlear nucleus of rats. *Experimental Neurology, 64,* 553–566.

Daly, K. A. (1997). Definition and epidemiology of otitis media. In J. E. Roberts, I. F. Wallace, & F. W. Henderson (Eds.), *Otitis media in young children: Medical, developmental, and educational considerations* (pp. 13–42). Baltimore: Brookes.

Dirks, D. (1964). Perception of dichotic and monoaural verbal material and cerebral dominance for speech. *Acta Otolaryngology, 58,* 78–80.

Donahue, M. L. (1993). Early phonological and lexical development and otitis media: A diary study. *Journal of Child Language, 20,* 489–501.

Eilers, R. E., Widen, J. E., Urbano, R., Hudson, T., & Gonzales, L. (1991). Optimization of automated hearing test algorithms: A comparison of data from simulations and young children. *Ear and Hearing, 12,* 199–204.

Eimas, P., & Clarkson, R. (1986). Speech perception in children: Are there effects of otitis media. In J. F. Kavanaugh (Ed.), *Otitis media and child development* (pp. 139–159). Parkton, MD: York Press.

Ferre, J. M. (2002). Behavioral therapeutic approaches for central auditory problems. In J. Katz (Ed.), *Handbook of clinical audiology* (5th ed., pp. 525–531). New York: Lippincott, Williams, & Wilkins.

Ferre, J. M., & Bellis, T. J. (1999). Multidimensional approach to the differential diagnosis of central auditory processing disorders in children. *Journal of the American Academy of Audiology, 10,* 319–328.

Friel-Patty, S. (1999). Clinical decision-making in the assessment and intervention of CAPD. *Language, Speech, and Hearing Services in the Schools, 30,* 345–352.

Gascon, G. G., Johnson, R., & Burd, L. (1986). Central auditory processing and attention deficit disorders. *Journal of Child Neurology, 1,* 27–33.

Gottlieb, G. (1981). The role of early experience in species-specific perceptual development. In R. M. Aslin, J. R. Alberts, & M. R. Peterson (Eds.), *Development of perception: Vol. 1. Psycho-biological perspectives* (pp. 5–44). New York: Academic Press.

Gravel, J. S., & Ellis, M. A. (1995). The auditory consequences of otitis media with effusion: The audiogram and beyond. *Seminars in Hearing, 16,* 44–59.

Gravel, J. S., McCarton, C. M., & Ruben, R. J. (1988). A prospective study of otitis media in infants born at very-low birthweight. *Acta-Otolaryngolica, 105,* 516–521.

Gravel, J. S., & Nozza, R. J. (1997). Hearing loss among children with otitis media with effusion. In J. E. Roberts, I. F. Wallace, & F. W. Henderson (Eds.), *Otitis media in young children: Medical, developmental, and educational considerations* (pp. 63–92). Baltimore: Brookes.

Gravel, J. S., & Wallace, I. F. (1992). Listening and language at 4 years of age: Effects of early otitis media. *Journal of Speech and Hearing Research, 3,* 588–595.

Gravel, J. S., & Wallace, I. F. (1995). Early otitis media, auditory abilities, and educational risk. *American Journal of Speech Language Pathology, 4,* 89–94.

Hagerman, R. J., & Falkenstein, A. R. (1987). An association between recurrent OM in infancy and later hyperactivity. *Clinical Pediatrics, 26,* 253–257.

Hall, J. W., III. (1992). *Handbook of auditory evoked response.* Boston: Allyn & Bacon.

Hall, J. W., III, Grose, J. H., & Drake, A. F. (1997). Effects of otitis media with effusion on auditory perception. In J. E. Roberts, I. F. Wallace, & F. W. Henderson (Eds.), *Otitis media in young children: Medical, developmental, and educational considerations* (pp. 93–108). Baltimore: Brookes.

Hall, J. W., III, Grose, J. H., & Pillsbury, M. C. (1995). Long-term effects of chronic otitis media in children. *Archives of Otolaryngology Head Neck Surgery, 121,* 847–852.

Hasentaub, M. S. (1987). *Language learning and otitis media.* Boston: College Hill Press.

Heirevang, E., Stevenson, J., & Hugdahl, K. (2002). Auditory processing in children with dyslexia. *Journal of Child Psychology and Psychiatry, 43,* 931–938.

Henderson, F. W., & Roush, J. (1997). Diagnosis of otitis media. In J. E. Roberts, I. F. Wallace, & F. W. Henderson (Eds.), *Otitis media in young children: Medical, developmental, and educational considerations* (pp. 43–59). Baltimore: Brookes.

Hood, L. J. (1998). *Clinical applications of the auditory brainstem response.* San Diego, CA: Singular Publishing Group.

Hunter, L. L. (1995). Hearing loss in young children with otitis media. Paper presented at the Annual convention of the American Speech Language Hearing Association. Orlando, FL.

Hurley, R. M., & Hurley, A. (1995). The auditory brainstem response in children with histories of otitis media. *Seminars in Hearing, 16,* 37–43.

Jerger, J., Jerger, S., & Abrams, S. (1983). Speech audiometry in the young child. *Ear and Hearing, 4,* 56–66.

Jerger, J., Moncrieff, D., Greenwald, R., Wambacq, I., & Seipel, A. (2000). Effect of age on interaural asymmetry of event-related potentials in a dichotic listening task. *Journal of American Academy of Audiology, 11,* 383–389.

Jerger, J., & Musiek, F. (2000). Report of the consensus conference on the diagnosis of CAPD in school-aged children. *Journal of the American Academy of Audiology, 11,* 467–474.

Kamhi, A. G., & Beasley, D. S. (1985). CAP Disorders: Is it a meaningful construct or a twentieth century unicorn? *Journal of Childhood Communication Disorders, 9,* 5–13.

Kaplan, G. J., Gleshman, J. K., Bender, T. R., Baum, C., & Clark, P. S. (1973). Long-term effects of otitis media: A ten-year cohort study of Alaskan Eskimo children. *Pediatrics, 52,* 577–585.

Katz, J. (1962). The use of staggered spondaic words for assessing the integrity of the central auditory nervous system. *Journal of Auditory Research, 2,* 327–337.

Katz, J., & Cohen, C. F. (1985). Auditory training for children with processing disorders. *Journal of Childhood Communication Disorders, 9,* 65–81.

Keith, R. W. (1971). Central auditory dysfunction. New York: Grune & Stratton.

Keith, R. W. (1981). Audiological and auditory-language tests of central auditory function. In R. W. Keith (Ed.), *Central auditory and language disorders in children* (pp. 61–76). San Diego, CA: College Hill Press.

Keith, R. W. (1984). Central auditory dysfunction: A language disorder? *Topics in Language Disorders, 4,* 48–56.

Keith, R. W. (1986). *SCAN: A screening test for auditory processing deficit disorders.* New York: Psychological Corporation.

Keith, R. W. (1988). Tests of central auditory function. In R. J. Roeser & M. P. Downs (Eds.), *Auditory disorders in school children: Identification and remediation* (2nd ed., pp. 83–97). New York: Thieme Medical Publishers.

Keith, R. W. (1999). Clinical issues in central auditory processing disorders. *Language, Speech, and Hearing Services in the Schools, 30,* 339–344.

Keith, R. W., & Engineer, P. (1991). Effects of methylphenidate on the auditory processing abilities of children with attention deficit-hyperactivity disorder. *Journal of Learning Disabilities, 24,* 630–636.

Keith, R. W., & Stromberg, E. (1985). An interdisciplinary approach to the identification and assessment of auditory processing disorders. *Journal of Childhood Communication Disorders, 9,* 15–30.

Kimura, D. (1961). Some effects of temporal lobe damage on auditory perception. *Canadian Journal of Psychology, 15,* 156–165.

Knishkowy, B., Palti, H., Adler, B., & Tepper, D. (1991). Effects of otitis media on development: A community-based study. *Early Human Development, 26,* 101–111.

Knudsen, E. J., Knudsen, P. F., & Esterly, S. D. (1984). A critical period of the recovery of sound localization accuracy following monoaural occlusion in the barn owl. *Journal of Neuroscience, 4,* 1012–1020.

Kolb, B., & Whishaw, I. Q. (1996). *Fundamentals of human neuropsychology.* New York: Freeman and Company.

Lezak, M. D. (1995). *Neuropsychological assessment* (3rd ed.). New York: Oxford Press.

Lim, D. J. (1984). Anatomy, morphology, cell biology, and pathology of the tubotympanum. In D. J. Lim, C. D. Bluestone, J. O. Klein, & J. D. Nelson (Eds.), *Recent advances in otitis media with effusion* (pp. 71–73). Philadelphia: Decker.

Lonigan, C. J., Fischel, J. E., Whitehurst, G. J., Arnold, D. S., & Valdez-Menchaca, M. C. (1992). The role of otitis media in the development of expressive language disorder. *Developmental Psychology, 28,* 430–440.

Marchant, C. D., Shurin, P. A., Turczyk, V. A., Wasikowski, D. E., Tutihasi, M. A., & Kinney, S. E. (1984). Course and outcome of otitis media in early infancy: A prospective study. *Journal of Pediatrics, 104,* 826–831.

Massaro, D. W. (1972). Preperceptual images, processing times, and perceptual units in auditory perception. *Psychological Review, 79,* 124–145.

McFarland, D. J., & Cacace, A. T. (1997). Modality specificity of auditory and visual pattern recognition: Implications for the assessment of central auditory processing disorders. *Audiology, 36,* 249–260.

Menyuk, P. (1986). Predicting speech and language problems with persistent otitis media. In J. Kavanaugh (Ed.), *Otitis media and child development* (pp. 192–208). Parkton, MD: York Press.

Musiek, F. E. (1983). The evaluation of brainstem disorders using A. B. R. & central auditory tests. *Monographs in Contemporary Audiology, 4,* 1–24.

Musiek, F. E., Gollegly, K. M., & Ross, M. K. (1985). Profiles of types of central auditory processing disorders. *Journal of Childhood Communication Disorders, 9,* 43–63.

Musiek, F. E., Kibbe, K., & Baran, J. A. (1984). Neuroaudiological results from split-brain patients. *Seminars in Hearing, 5,* 219–229.

Newby, H. A. (1979). *Audiology* (4th ed.). Englewood Cliffs, NJ: Prentice-Hall.

Northern, J. L., & Downs, M. P. (1991). *Hearing in children* (4th ed.). Baltimore: Williams & Wilkins.

Owen, M. J., Baldwin, C. D., Luttman, D., & Howie, V. M. (1993). Universality of otitis media with effusion detected by tympanometry on frequent home visits in Galveston, Texas. In D. J. Lim, C. D. Bluestone, J. O. Klein, J. D. Nelson, & P. L. Ogra (Eds.), *Recent advances in otitis media* (pp. 17–20). Toronto, Ontario, Canada: Decker Periodicals.

Paden, E., Novak, M., & Beiter, A. (1987). Predictors of phonological inadequacy in young children prone to otitis media. *Journal of Speech and Hearing Disorders, 52,* 232–242.

Pinheiro, M. L., & Musiek, F. (1985). Sequential and temporal ordering in the auditory system. In M. L. Pinheiro & F. E. Musiek (Eds.), *Assessment of central auditory dysfunction: Foundations and clinical correlates* (pp. 219–238). Baltimore: Williams & Wilkins.

Prellner, K. (1995). Factors disposing for otitis media. *Seminars in Hearing, 16,* 1–19.

Prellner, K., Kalm, O., & Pedersen, F. K. (1984). Pneumococal antibodies and complement during and after periods of recurrent otitis media. *International Journal of Pediatric Otorhinolaryngology, 7,* 39–49.

Ptacek, P. H., & Pinheiro, M. L. (1971). Pattern reversal in auditory perception. *Journal of the Acoustical Society of America, 49,* 493–498.

Pukander, J. S., & Karma, P. H. (1988). Persistence of middle-ear effusion and its risk factors after an acute attack of otitis media with effusion. In D. J. Lim, C. D. Bluestone, J. O. Klein, & J. D. Nelson (Eds.), *Recent advances in otitis media with effusion* (pp. 8–11). Philadelphia: Decker.

Rasmussen, F. (1994). Recurrence of otitis media at preschool age in Sweden. *Journal of Epidemiology and Community Health, 48,* 33–35.

Rees, N. (1981). Saying more than we know: Is auditory processing disorder a meaningful concept. In R. W. Keith (Ed.), *Central auditory and language disorders in children* (pp. 94–120). San Diego, CA: College Press.

Reinis, S., & Goldman, J. M. (1980). *The development of the brain: Biological and functional perspectives.* Springield, IL: Charles C Thomas.

Restak, R. (2001). *The secret life of the brain.* Washington, DC: Joseph Henry Press.

Riccio, C. A., Cohen, M. J., Hynd, G. W., & Keith, R. W. (1996). Validity of the auditory continuous performance test in differentiating central auditory processing disorders with and without ADHD. *Journal of Learning Disabilities, 29,* 561–566.

Riccio, C. A., Hynd, G. W., Cohen, M. J., Hall, J., & Molt, L. (1994). Comorbidity of central auditory processing disorders and attention deficit hyperactivity disorder. *Journal of American Academy of Child and Adolescent Psychiatry, 33,* 849–856.

Roberts, J. E., Burchinal, M. R., & Campbell, F. (1994). Otitis media in early childhood and patterns of intellectual development and later academic performance. *Journal of Pediatric Psychology, 19,* 347–367.

Roberts, J. E., Burchinal, M. R., & Clarke-Klein, S. M. (1995). Otitis media in early childhood and cognitive, academic, and behavior outcomes at 12 years of age. *Journal of Pediatric Psychology, 20,* 645–660.

Roberts, J. E., Burchinal, M. R., & Henderson, F. W. (1993). Otitis media and school-age outcomes. In D. J. Lim, C. D. Bluestone, J. O. Klein, & J. D. Nelson (Eds.), *Recent advances in otitis media with effusion* (pp. 561–565). Philadelphia: Decker.

Roberts, J. E., Burchinal, M. R., Koch, M. A., Footo, M. M., & Henderson, F. W. (1988). Otitis media in early childhood and its relationship to later phonological development. *Journal of Speech and Hearing Disorders, 53,* 416–424.

Roberts, J. E., & Medley, L. P. (1995). Otitis media and speech-language sequelae in young children: Current issues in management. *American Journal of Speech Language Pathology, 4,* 15–24.

Roberts, J. E., & Wallace, I. F. (1997). Language and otitis media. In J. E. Roberts, I. F. Wallace, & F. W. Henderson (Eds.), *Otitis media in young children: Medical, developmental, and educational considerations* (pp. 129–161). Baltimore: Brookes.

Roush, J., & Henderson, F. (1995). Medical and audiological management of otitis media: Consensus and controversy. *Seminars in Hearing, 16,* 105–112.

Schwartz, R. G., Mody, M., & Petinou, K. (1997). Phonological acquisition and otitis media. In J. E. Roberts, I. F. Wallace, & F. W. Henderson (Eds.), *Otitis media in young children: Medical, developmental, and educational considerations* (pp. 109–131). Baltimore: Brookes.

Schwartz, R. G., & Goffman, L. (1995). Metrical patterns of words and production accuracy. *Journal of Speech and Hearing Research, 38,* 108–124.

Seats, T. (1997, November). *Treatment efficacy of temporal exercises in habilitating children with central auditory processing disorder.* Paper presented at the annual meeting of the American Speech Language Hearing Association, San Antonio, TX.

Secord, G. J., Erickson, M. T., & Bush, J. P. (1988). Neuropsychological sequelae of otitis media in children and adolescents with learning disabilities. *Journal of Pediatric Psychology, 23,* 532–542.

Shapiro, A. H., & Mistal, G. (1985). ITA auditory training for reading and spelling of disabled children. *Hearing Journal, 38,* 26–31.

Silva, P. A., Chalmers, D., & Stewart, I. (1986). Some audiological, psychological, educational, and behavioral characteristics of children with bilateral otitis media with effusion: A longitudinal study. *Journal of Learning Disabilities, 19,* 165–169.

Smoski, W. J., Brunt, M. A., & Tannahill, J. C. (1992). Listening characteristics of children with central auditory processing disorders. *American Speech Language Hearing Association, 23,* 145–152.

Smoski, W. J., Brunt, M. A., & Tannahill, J. C. (1998). *Children's Auditory Performance Scale (CHAPS).* Tampa, FL: Educational Audiology Associates.

Stark, R. E., & Bernstein, L. E. (1984). Evaluating central auditory processing in children. *Topics in Language Disorders, 4,* 57–70.

Tallal, P., & Merzenich, M. (1997). *Fast ForWard training for children with language-learning problems: National field-test results.* Presented at the annual meeting of the American Speech Language Hearing Association, Boston, MA.

Teele, D. W., Klein, J. O., & Rosner, B. A. (1980). Epidemiology of otitis media in children. *Annals of Otology, Rhinology, and Laryngology, 89* (Suppl. 68), 5–6.

Teele, D. W., Klein, J. O., Rosner, B. A., & the Greater Boston Otitis Media Study Group. (1984). Otitis media with effusion during the first three years of life and development of speech and language. *Pediatrics, 74,* 282–287.

Teeter, P. A., & Semrud-Clikeman, M. (1997). *Child neuropsychology: Assessment and interventions for neurodevelopmental disorders.* Needham Heights, MA: Allyn & Bacon.

Veteran's Administration Central. (1992). *Tonal and speech materials for auditory perception assessment.* Long Beach, CA: Author.

Wada, J. A., Clark, R., & Hamm, A. (1975). Cerebral hemispheric asymmetry in humans. *Archives of Neurology, 32,* 239–246.

Wallace, I. F., & Hooper, S. R. (1997). Otitis media and its impact on cognitive, academic, and behavioral outcomes: A review and interpretation of the findings. In J. E. Roberts, I. F. Wallace, & F. W. Henderson (Eds.), *Otitis media in young children: Medical, developmental, and educational considerations* (pp. 163–194). Baltimore: Brookes.

Wasserman, G. A., Pine, D. S., & Bruder, G. E. (1999). Dichotic listening deficits and the prediction of substance abuse use in young boys. *Journal of American Academy of Child and Adolescent Psychiatry, 38,* 1032–1039.

Wellendorf, T. G., Hall, J. W., Grose, J. H., & Pillsbury, H. C. (1995). Effect of early otitis media on some psychoacoustic measures. *Seminars in Hearing, 16,* 28–36.

Willeford, J. A. (1977). Assessing central auditory behavior in children: A test battery approach. In R. W. Keith (Ed.), *Central auditory dysfunction* (pp. 43–72). New York: Grune & Stratton.

Willeford, J. A., & Bilger, J. M. (1978). Auditory perception in children with learning disabilities. In J. Kart (Ed.), *Handbook of clinical audiology* (2nd ed., pp. 410–425). Baltimore: Williams & Wilkins.

Willeford, J. A., & Burliegh, J. M. (1985). *Handbook of central auditory processing disorders in children.* Orlando, FL: Grune & Stratton.

Willeford, J., & Burleigh, J. M. (1994). Sentence procedures in central testing. In J. Katz (Ed.), *Handbook of clinical audiology* (4th ed., pp. 256–268). Baltimore: Williams & Wilkins.

Young, M. L. (1985). Central auditory processing through the looking glass: A critical look at diagnosis and management. *Journal of Childhood Communication Disorders, 9,* 31–42.

# CHAPTER 22

# Providing Neuropsychological Services to Learners with Chronic Illnesses

JAMES P. DONNELLY

I N 1900, MORE THAN 3% of American children died between their first and twentieth birthdays. One hundred years later, the odds of death in this age range had been reduced to fewer than 2 in 1,000 (Guyer, Freedman, Strobino, & Sondik, 2000). Truly, the recently completed century was witness to an extraordinary change in the prospects for longevity in the United States, particularly in the control of infectious disease.[1]

Most children in the United States now enjoy good health and have health insurance (Centers for Disease Control and Prevention [CDC], 2004). Yet, to the families who anticipate or grieve the death of a child from a chronic illness turned terminal, and to those children who contend with the challenges of survival and illness management, the conquest of childhood disease is far from complete. School psychologists, particularly those with a neuropsychological background and orientation, may play an increasingly important role in efforts to understand and manage the impact of chronic illness in children and adolescents (D'Amato, 1990). This chapter provides an overview of the issues and current knowledge base in this area.

## HISTORICAL FOUNDATIONS

Just over 30 years ago, the first major national conference on outcomes of chronic pediatric health conditions was held in Rochester, New York (Grave & Pless,

---

[1] Unfortunately, the same observation cannot be made on a worldwide basis with regard to the longevity of children. For example, in 1999, an estimated 330,000 HIV-infected children died before age 5 in sub-Saharan Africa (Walker, Schwartlander, & Bryce, 2002), and every day nearly 2,000 African children are infected by their mothers (Dabis & Ekpini, 2002).

1974). Jointly sponsored by the Rochester Child Health Study, the Fogarty International Center, and the National Institutes of Health (NIH), the conference brought together pediatric health care and allied professionals to consider the outcomes of chronic illness. The list of presenters was made up of primary care medical professionals (mainly pediatricians), but included two psychologists, a professor of education, an NIH program officer in child health, and a professor of epidemiology who would later go on to help define the field of health-related quality of life (George Torrance of McMaster University). Review of the volume that came from that conference reveals that the school-related problems of children with chronic illness were at the forefront of concern even when survival rates were modest by today's standards. As the following somber quote from one of the conference organizers suggests, the trade-offs between quantity and quality of life were regarded as very serious challenges with ethical as well as educational implications:

> Children sick with chronic illness must with increasing frequency endure abbreviated lives of costly misery as a result of their double contretemps: the illness and its attempted cure. The technological advances in the past decade dwarf the advances in medical ethics. . . . The walking wounded of childhood represent poignant specimens of losing encounters with medical science, specters whose days of energy and promise have faded into nights of pain and pallor. (Grave, 1974, in Grave & Pless, 1974, p. xiii)

The roots of modern concerns were planted in such dialogue. Thirty years later, the ranks of the "walking wounded of childhood" are far greater in number, and study of illness survivor issues is well under way. The emphasis on the joint matters of achievement, adjustment, and overall quality of life was evident in the record of the 1974 conference and is still central. Specific issues of concern at that time ranged from an emerging methodology of measurement of treatment effects on learning ability, to management of the impact of school absence, to the child's emotional, social, and familial functioning. These issues remain with us today.

In this chapter and this volume, we attempt to define the current perspective on these matters in the context of the driving intellectual and social forces in children's health for the current generation. Detailed consideration of the contextual tensions we now face is beyond the current scope, but a partial list would have to include better educational and health technology with major gaps in access; more and higher standards in educational achievement for children at all levels; greater numbers of survivors of chronic health conditions rooted in genetics, poverty, and behavior; growing sophistication and specialization of support services such as school neuropsychology; and an economic climate that seems particularly challenging in health and education.

## OVERVIEW OF CHRONIC ILLNESS IN CHILDREN

Table 22.1 shows the leading causes of death for children ages 5 to 18 in 2001, the most recent year for which data were available (CDC, 2004, retrieved January 4, 2004).

Most learners with chronic and even end-stage illness remain enrolled in school during the course of their illness. School is often one of the last vestiges of normal childhood for the chronically or terminally ill child. Judgment about appropriate

**Table 22.1**
The Leading Causes of Death for
School-Age Children in 2001

| Rank | Cause of Death | Number of Deaths |
|------|----------------|------------------|
| 1 | Unintentional injury | 7,687 |
| 2 | Homicide | 1,602 |
| 3 | Malignant neoplasm | 1,559 |
| 4 | Suicide | 1,400 |
| 5 | Congenital anomalies | 595 |
| 6 | Heart disease | 535 |
| 7 | Chronic lower respiratory disease | 168 |
| 8 | Benign neoplasms | 142 |
| 9 | Influenza and pneumonia | 141 |
| 10 | Cerebrovascular | 134 |
| Total Deaths | | 13,954 |

*Source:* Centers for Disease Control, National Center for Injury Prevention and Control, http://webapp.cdc.gov/sasweb/ncipc/lendcars10.html. Retrieved January 4, 2004.

learning and school participation goals is a function of what the child and family express as wants or needs, what limits the health condition places on education, and the degree to which the school system can provide individual support.

## DEFINING CHILDHOOD CHRONIC ILLNESS

Older surveys of childhood chronic illnesses often have a perspective that is shaped by categorical classification of children, perhaps giving the impression that an illness is as stable as a statistical snapshot at a particular moment. Yet chronic illness is best characterized by variability within the course of the child's life and across children with similar diagnoses (Stein & Jessop, 1989). During the course of illness, children may move from relatively stable to critically ill and back numerous times, with an accompanying impact on level of functioning that may be temporary or permanent. Individual differences in adaptation will also be evident and influenced by variables including developmental level, family and peer support, culture, personality, coping, and the ability at both general and specific levels of functioning.

Probably the simplest definition of chronic illness is that found in the *Thesaurus of Psychological Index Terms* (American Psychological Association, 2001): "An illness or disorder that persists for a prolonged period of time." This broad definition avoids the difficulty of determining boundaries between conditions that might be labeled primarily physical versus psychological and directs the analyst to common elements of all chronic illnesses. Yet specificity is needed whenever decisions are to be made about which child will receive what kind of diagnosis or service.

The two major approaches to specification of chronic illness have been the disease-specific or categorical and the functional or noncategorical (Ireys, 2001).

As Ireys pointed out, the choice of definition is critical when attempting to estimate the prevalence, cost, or impact of a condition or to plan programs to support children who are thereby considered eligible.

Superficially, the disease-specific approach seems to offer simplicity in defining who will be considered chronically ill. From this perspective, a list of over 200 chronic illnesses can be generated, including cystic fibrosis, sickle cell anemia, hemophilia, diabetes, and asthma (Ireys, 2001). These inclusive chronic illness taxonomies may also include the variety of birth defects, metabolic disturbances, spinal cord and other injuries related to accidents, and both the genetic and acquired organ dysfunctions that many children experience. Additionally, due to the effectiveness of many new treatments, most cancers are considered life-limiting in a functional rather than terminal sense. The set of infectious diseases, many of which (e.g., AIDS) impact the neuropsychological profile of the child, include many chronic and acute illnesses. Altogether, the CDC lists 54 different infectious diseases in the federal government classification of "notifiable diseases." In addition, the concept of chronic illness has been invoked in consideration of other biobehavioral issues of childhood such as oral health and obesity.

The major limit of the categorical approach is that it forces one to decide on which list to consult and ignores the variability within conditions in the course of a disease; the common variance in needs, deficits, and strengths across conditions in many domains; and the similarities in functional impact of the condition that will be the primary concern of anyone seeking consultation of the pediatric or school neuropsychologist. The functional approach to the study of chronic illness considers the consequences of the condition and has been championed by Stein and colleagues (Stein, 1996; Stein, Bauman, Epstein, Gardner, & Walker, 2000; Stein, Bauman, Westbrook, Coupey, & Ireys, 1993; Stein & Jessop, 1989; Stein & Silver, 1999, 2002; Stein, Westbrook, & Bauman, 1997; Stein, Westbrook, & Silver, 1998; Stein et al., 1987), who have studied the implications of various definitions from such matters as prevalence estimates and provision of services. Their definition includes the following elements: the presence of a disorder with a biological, psychological, or cognitive basis of 12 months or more duration (including prognosis) that is likely to require special services, limit functioning, and/or produce a need for supportive services, medication, or technology (Stein et al., 1993). In his comprehensive review of childhood illness epidemiology, Ireys (2001) suggested that an overall estimate of 15% to 20% of children with chronic health conditions with a range of about 6% to 7% with significant limitations in activity is likely to remain relatively stable. Ireys also noted that the condition-specific and noncategorical perspectives are complementary. The present perspective attempts to follow Ireys in providing integration, with some attention to findings in populations defined by diagnosis as well as an attempt to identify cross-cutting issues and a general model.

## SCOPE OF REVIEW AND LITERATURE SEARCH PROCEDURES

The nomological net for the present discussion is multidimensional and multidisciplinary. In some areas, there is a corpus of studies to provide an evidence base in the domain of the school neuropsychology of chronic illness. For example, the literature in cancer with central nervous system (CNS) involvement is near that level. Chronic illnesses impact children in highly individual ways, but awareness of the likelihood of cognitive, affective, or behavioral issues may give the psychologist a head start in assessment, consultation, and intervention. The chapter closes with an attempt to integrate school neuropsychology into the broader conceptual framework of health-related quality of life. Some topics of related interest and great importance, such as the behavioral contributors to chronic illness (e.g., smoking, diet, exercise) are beyond the scope of this discussion.

The literature gathered for this chapter was obtained via primary and secondary search methods. The primary search included separate and combined searches of the following databases: MEDLINE (1966–2004), PsychINFO (1974–2004), HealthSTAR/Ovid HealthSTAR (1975–2004), and the Cochrane Central Register of Controlled Trials. The following keywords were included in separate and then combined searches: chronic illness, intellectual, cognitive, neuropsychological, and neuropsychology. The first combined search produced 765 citations, of which 613 were unique. When the set of 613 citations was limited to human populations less than 18 years of age, 282 items remained (MEDLINE = 147, PsychINFO = 124, Cochrane = 8, and HealthSTAR = 3). Similar searches were also conducted including specific chronic illnesses as keywords. Relevant review articles and books were retrieved as well. The secondary searches involved review of the reference lists in the review articles and selected author searches. Sources were excluded if they were most relevant to another chapter in this volume, outside the range of years searched, beyond the focus of illnesses covered in this chapter, or not in English.

## THEORETICAL CONSIDERATIONS

Anderson (1998) outlined five levels of analysis in behavioral medicine. The levels he identified correspond well with emerging science and practice in school neuropsychology: social/environment, behavioral/psychological, organ systems, cellular, and molecular. With regard to the school or pediatric neuropsychology of chronic illness, there is relatively little specific theory to call on. A small number of studies have attempted to examine multiple levels of analysis.

Moore and colleagues (Moore, Copeland, Ried, & Levy, 1992) examined the correspondence of treatment modalities with neuropsychological and neurophysiological indicators. They reported results that suggested the possibility that cranial radiotherapy may be especially likely to produce white matter lesions that could account for observed deficits via slowing of cortical activity. Such multilevel studies are likely to become increasingly prominent and informative as advances in imaging and genomics continue.

At the behavioral/psychological level, one of the most influential theoretical perspectives is stress and coping theory. Stress and coping theory may be quite useful in the conceptualization of several aspects of the school neuropsychology of chronic illness, including consideration of the individual and systemic stress for families with a chronically ill child. Compas and Boyer (2001) described a dual-process model of stress and coping, proposing a prominent role for attention in stress responses based on differentiation of voluntary and involuntary control of behavior.

Health-related quality of life (Hr-QoL) is a rapidly emerging field in child health studies (Koot & Wallander, 2001). The construct continues to evolve in terms of definition and measurement, but it provides the possibility of a unifying construct in children's health, as is evident in Koot and Wallander's definition: "Quality of life is the combination of objectively and subjectively indicated well-being in multiple domains of life considered salient in one's culture and time, while adhering to universal standards of human rights" (p. 6). The school neuropsychologist might conceptualize the chronically ill learner in terms of both global and specific aspects (e.g., cognitive, affective, motor) of Hr-QoL. Quality of life, in these terms, becomes an overarching concern at both initial assessment and outcome connected to more specific functional domains of achievement and adjustment.

## SPECIFIC CONDITIONS

In the following sections, several of the most frequently encountered chronic illnesses are reviewed. The section concludes with an attempt to identify cross-cutting issues that may be encountered in these and other chronic illnesses of childhood.

### AIDS AND HIV

The emergence of AIDS as a global health threat has been reported and studied on many levels. The most recent CDC estimate was that as of 2002, there are 8,807 children under the age of 13 in the United States with AIDS, and of these, 3,249 are less than 1 year old (CDC, 2004). The annual reported rate of new cases has declined substantially from the 745 new cases seen in 1995 to the most recently reported number of 150 new diagnoses in children under 13 seen in 2002. This remarkable decline in syndrome diagnoses was a result of research showing the profound reduction in transmission of the virus from infected mothers to children as a result of zidovudine (ZVD) therapy (Rausch & Stover, 2001). Yet, as in other conditions where medical treatment has reduced mortality, the burden of chronic illness remains. For children with HIV, this includes a variety of functional, affective, social, and cognitive issues.

The literature in this area is voluminous. For example, a search of MEDLINE on the keywords AIDS and HIV for the period 1980 to November 2003 produced approximately 65,000 hits. Of these studies, about one sixth (9,822) are limited to those age 18 or less. Because the high-risk behaviors associated with HIV transmission are not unusual in adolescent populations, much of the attention in this field has been focused on education and prevention, including some recent well-designed studies (Schonfeld et al., 1995; St. Lawrence, Jefferson, Alleyne, & Brasfield, 1995). In addition, the variety of complex psychological issues associated with children related to the virus or the disease has generated a good deal of interest. For example, communication within families affected (Lester et al., 2002), adjustment of children with infected parents (Forehand et al., 1998), perceptions of classmates of ill children (Cole, Roberts, & McNeal, 1996), and quality of life (Rotheram-Borus et al., 2001) have all been recently studied. When the search for empirical data is narrowed to the area of cognitive functioning, 28 studies that directly assessed neuropsychological or neurodevelopmental aspects of HIV infection and AIDS in infants, children, or adolescents were found.

Rausch and Stover's (2001) recent review of the research noted that concerns about cognitive changes in the course of AIDS were recognized early in the battle with this epidemic, particularly the dementia and delirium that often accompanies the end-stage of the disease. At present, the primary risk with regard to neuropsychological functioning is progressive encephalopathy (PE), which is estimated to be present in up to 23% of infected children in one study (Wolters & Brouwers, 1998). Another study examined both progressive and nonprogressive neurologic signs in HIV-infected children, finding that nearly half of the sample (30/62) showed some neurologic involvement, that most of these cases were classifiable as progressive (83%), and that important differences in symptoms were associated with age (Angelini et al., 2000). The clinical picture presented by the child with PE includes (1) impaired brain growth, (2) progressive motor dysfunction, and (3) loss, plateau, or inadequate acquisition of neurodevelopmental milestones (Rausch & Stover, 2001).

In some of the most recent studies comparing neuropsychological test performance of HIV-infected children to noninfected children, Blanchette and colleagues (Blanchette, Smith, Fernandes-Penney, King, & Read, 2001; Blanchette, Smith, King, Fernandes-Penney, & Read, 2002) reported that overall, the HIV-infected children displayed normal-level abilities on most tests of intellect. They did find subtle differences in motor function and interpreted this in the context of CT imaging studies of infected children showing potential for deficits in visual-motor and spatial abilities. In addition, results of comparisons of infected infants with a sample of noninfected children of HIV+ mothers showed significant deficits on the Bayley Scales of Infant Development. Motor impairment has been found in a sample of 14 Zairian infants (Boivin et al., 1995). The developmental trajectory of these deficits on reaching school age is not known, yet concern about greater impact at early age is clearly warranted. Other investigators have identified deficits in executive function in HIV+ children who are neurologically asymptomatic (Bisiacchi, Suppiej, & Laverda, 2000).

The hypothesis that white matter abnormalities (WMA) could account for some of the variance in cognitive performance observed in HIV+ children was examined in a study that compared neuropsychological test results with CT imaging (Brouwers, Van Der Vlugt, Moss, Wolters, & Pizzo, 1995). The study found that not only were the children with WMA significantly lower on global intellectual functioning, but they also showed specific behavioral problems (attention-deficit/hyperactive- and autistic-type behavior) to a greater degree than HIV+ children with similar atrophy but not WMA.

In summary, although full-blown AIDS has become less likely in children, HIV infection remains a significant issue in terms of prevalence and cognitive, affective, social, and related quality of life manifestations. It appears that variability in course is to be expected as children age, that motor deficits may be seen in infants, and that PE appears in a significant number of cases. In addition, a great range of stressors is likely to be present in the child's life, complicating both adjustment and academic performance.

RESPIRATORY CONDITIONS

Respiratory conditions are the most prevalent of chronic health conditions in children and influence school participation and performance both directly and indirectly. The CDC estimated that 11% of all children under 18 years of age have been diagnosed with asthma at some point in their lives. In addition, 12% of American children less than 18 years of age suffered from respiratory allergies, 10% suffered from hay fever, and an additional 10% suffered from other allergies in the survey period (the past 12 months; CDC, 2004, retrieved January 6, 2004, from http://www.cdc.gov/nchs/fastats/children.htm).

"Asthma is the single, largest public health burden in pediatrics" (Turner-Henson & Johnston, 2002, p. 3). In their recent review, Turner-Henson and Johnston cited findings from epidemiological, medical, psychological, and educational studies to support this profound statement. They noted the recent American Lung Association estimate that approximately 8 million children in the United States have been diagnosed with asthma (ALA as cited in Turner-Henson & Johnston, 2002). Overall, the most recent federal government estimate of asthma incidence is 11.8% (95% CI: 11.6 to 12.0). This translates to more than 25 million cases (CDC, 2004; retrieved December 20, 2003, from http://www.cdc.gov /nceh/airpollution/asthma/brfss/02/lifetime/tableL1.htm). The most recent CDC data are also striking when acute episodes are examined: 55.5% of children up to the age of 14 experienced an asthma episode in the prior year (based on the January through June 2003 National Health Interview Survey). Most severely affected within the population of 14 and under children are Black males; the estimated occurrence of an asthma episode for this group during the survey period was 89.2% (95% CI: 63.7 to 114.8). Although there is evidence of a genetic role in asthma, much of the subgroup variance is most likely related to socioeconomic factors that limit options for residence and preventive health care.

Asthma may have a great impact on school performance because of school absences and other disruptions. For example, the annual number of school absences attributed to asthma is over 10 million (Lozano, Sullivan, Smith, & Weiss, 1999). In addition, investigators have examined the possibility of direct effects of asthma treatments on academic and neuropsychological test performance (Bender, Belleau, Fukuhara, Mrazek, & Strunk, 1987; Bender, Lerner, & Kollasch, 1988; Rachelefsky et al., 1986). Medication is the first line of treatment for asthma, but concern over the side effects of commonly prescribed drugs has included school attendance, school performance, and such neuropsychological parameters as memory, attention, motor steadiness, and visual-spatial planning (Furukawa et al., 1988; Gil, Silveira, Soares, Sole, & Naspitz, 1993; Mansfield, Mendoza, Flores, & Meeves, 2003; Rietveld & Colland, 1999).

The Childhood Asthma Management Program (CAMP) has addressed most of the limitations of prior studies in conducting a longitudinal program of research (Anonymous, 1999). The CAMP research program is as a multicenter, randomized, double-masked clinical trial designed to determine the long-term effects of treatments (budesonide, a glucocorticoid used daily; albuterol, a short-acting beta agonist bronchodilator used as needed; nedocromil, a nonsteroid anti-inflammatory agent used daily; and placebo) for mild to moderate childhood asthma. The sample includes more than 1,000 children with asthma who are participating in this series of studies designed to provide strong evidence related to treatment efficacy and side effects. This highly productive research program included a recent study that incorporated a standardized neuropsychological battery (the Wechsler Intelligence Scale for Children III/Wechsler Preschool and

Primary Scale of Intelligence Revised [WISC-III/WPPSI-R]; the Woodcock-Johnson Psychoeducational Battery Revised; the Wide Range Assessment of Memory and Learning); and the Gordon Diagnostic Systems (Annett, Aylward, Lapidus, Bender, & DuHamel, 2000). The study to date has found no significant relationships between treatment, severity (mild or moderate), or socioeconomic status on any of the neuropsychological measures, suggesting that previous concerns may have been overstated. The authors cautioned that the results generalize only to mild and moderate asthma and that other asthma-related correlates of academic performance, such as school absence, decreased physical activity, and more severe respiratory distress, should not be discounted.

## CANCER

There are many forms of cancer, but the forms most frequently seen in children are brain tumors and leukemia (Ries et al., 2003). Federal government statistics document dramatic improvements in survival for children with cancer. Across all diagnoses, the 5-year survival rate has gone from 20% for the period 1950 to 1954 to 78.7% for the period 1992 to 1999 (Ries et al., 2003). As the mortality pattern has become more consistent with that of other chronic illnesses, quality of life issues have become very important to all concerned with these children.

Because the newer treatments (chemotherapy, radiation, and surgery) were recognized as not only effective but intensive, interest in cognitive sequelae of pediatric cancer treatment has been strong. Koocher and colleagues' original survivor study (Koocher, O'Malley, Gogan, & Foster, 1980) began an active period of research that continues to the present. The following represents a summary of the history of treatment of the most common childhood cancers.

*Brain Tumors*   Anderson (2003) recently reviewed the literature on late effects of treatment for CNS malignancies. He concluded that cognitive abnormalities and endocrine disorders were the most commonly seen long-term side effects of treatment. The primary cause of dysfunction was found to be radiotherapy, followed by chemotherapy (intrathecal methotrexate) and surgery. Craniopharyngioma is a benign tumor, but because of the likelihood of surgery to the brain, becomes a major concern in terms of cognitive impact. A group of 16 such patients treated at a comprehensive cancer center was evaluated with a broad neuropsychological battery (Carpentieri et al., 2001). Globally, the sample was within normal range, but memory deficits were noted.

More recently, Mulhern et al. (2001) presented a new method for calculating the volume of white matter loss that represented an important development in the study of this hypothesis. The MRI levels are classified by tissue type and color coded and the volume of normal-appearing white matter (NAWM) is calculated by determining the number of pixels in each color (multiplied by pixel volume). The three dependent variables included in the study were estimated Wechsler IQ (abbreviated WISC-III or Wechsler Adult Intelligence Scale Revised), verbal memory (California Verbal Learning Test), and sustained attention (Conner's Continuous Performance Test). The analysis included tests of the relationship of age at time of cranial radiation, time since radiation treatment, and NAWM with the cognitive variables. Significant and moderate effect sizes were found for all three independent variables for overall IQ, even when correlations were partialed. However, for verbal memory, only time since radiation was significantly correlated ($r = -.54$, $p < .05$), and for sustained attention, only age at time of treatment was significantly associated ($r = .55$, $p < .005$). In addition to the methodologic demonstration and correlational results, this study found a mean estimated full-scale IQ of 86. The authors pointed out that, in concert with recently reported findings of the Pediatric Oncology Group (Mulhern et al., 1998), the risks of radiation treatment for medulloblastoma are greatest for younger patients receiving standard dosages.

*Leukemia*   Butler and Copeland (1993) conducted a comprehensive review of the neuropsychological effects of radiation and chemotherapy on children with leukemia. Their review identified a number of methodological concerns with prior studies that prevented clear conclusions regarding the duration or intensity of long-term effects. Barr et al. (1993) developed a multidimensional measurement model to study long-term outcomes among childhood leukemia survivors. Their measure includes seven dimensions: sensation, mobility, emotion, cognition, self-care, pain, and fertility. They found that for patients with acute lymphocytic leukemia (ALL), increased morbidity risk was associated with younger age, higher-risk diagnoses, and radiotherapy. Long-term difficulties were particularly notable in emotion and cognition.

Recently, Espy and colleagues (2001) reported the results of a carefully designed prospective study of prophylactic CNS chemotherapy for ALL in 30 cases. The design included follow-up assessments at 2, 3, and 4 years as well as statistical control of demographic variables. Growth curve analyses showed modest declines in several domains, including arithmetic, visual-motor integration, and verbal fluency. The authors noted that both treatment and background variables were related to observed variability and that most domains were not adversely impacted, including reading, spelling, language, and memory. Nonetheless, their analysis supports the recommendation that children treated for ALL with CNS prophylaxis be monitored on sensitive neuropsychological measures and that supportive services such as occupational therapy to assist with motor abilities be made available as needed.

*Comparative Studies*   Copeland et al. (1988) attempted to isolate variance in neuropsychological test performance by comparing a group of leukemia patients ($n = 19$) receiving both CNS and systemic chemotherapy with the same number of patients with osteogenic sarcoma who received only systemic chemotherapy. Their analysis indicated that vincristine was associated with peripheral neuropathies, including deficits in fine motor and tactile perceptual abilities, but there were no other differences or deficits observed. In a later study, Barr and colleagues (2000) compared cross-sectional samples of children who had been treated for neuroblastoma and Wilms' tumor to contrast outcomes of diseases with markedly divergent prognoses. Children with neuroblastoma were at higher risk for hearing and speech deficits, most likely due to the peripheral neuropathy (ototoxicity) known to be associated with platinum-based chemotherapies. Interestingly, in comparing the perceptions of parents and their children, they found strong agreement except in the area of cognitive functioning. On the Health Utilities Index 3 (HUI-3), parents and their children gave concordant ratings about 72% of the time in both diagnostic groups. All other areas of functioning showed levels of agreement over 90%.

Barr and colleagues (2001) have also examined the status of pediatric cancer survivors in Latin America, again using the HUI-3. They examined a sample of 178 parents and 144 physicians with reference to children of various cancer diagnoses. Difficulties in emotion and cognition were noted in the ALL children, consistent with their previous finding in Canada, but in addition, they noted that pain was an issue for ALL survivors. This study also found that non-Hodgkin's lymphoma was associated with the greatest overall set of posttreatment complications. Emotion and pain were the dimensions most affected in the children with Wilms' tumor and Hodgkin's disease.

A recent study in Canada examined the role of self-efficacy in the educational achievement of pediatric cancer patients (Crossland, 2002). Although the results of the study are limited by the sample size ($n = 5$), the author's case for the importance of personal control in this population and provision of academic and personal support regarding the child's own expectations during the course of treatment is quite sensible. One potential role of the pediatric or school neuropsychologist may be monitoring performance, providing feedback, and helping the child with cancer to maintain academic self-efficacy as well as the sense of connection to school.

## Diabetes

Diabetes mellitus is a disorder of glucose metabolism with the potential to significantly disrupt cognitive function and school performance. Type I diabetes, also known as insulin-dependent diabetes, is the most frequent endocrine disorder in children, and incidence rates have been climbing rapidly since the 1950s (Gale, 2002). Gale noted that by the end of the twentieth century in Western countries, approximately 4 children per 1,000 would require insulin treatment by 20 years of age. Risk factors include genetics, environment, and nutrition (Lipman, 2002).

Rovet (2000) recently reviewed the research on neuropsychological aspects of childhood diabetes, including results of her carefully planned prospective studies conducted over the past 15 years. She noted that much of the prior research can be characterized as descriptive and quite limited in most design aspects, but there are some findings that may be interpreted with confidence. It appears that hyperglycemia may affect all of the following domains: attention, visual-spatial processing, eye-hand coordination, and verbal skills. Another review, which included school performance as well as cognitive ability, identified an association with lower global IQ scores as well as increased usage of special services (Holmes, Cant, Fox, Lampert, & Greer, 1999). These authors also noted that these issues are complicated by greater incidence in lower-socioeconomic status populations.

Hypoglycemic episodes may result from insulin therapy and be particularly damaging to younger children, especially because of the possibility of convulsions that may permanently diminish memory and visual-spatial abilities (Rovet, Ehrlich, Czuchta, & Akler, 1993). A recent study of children with Type I diabetes mellitus examined the impact of hypoglycemia on neuropsychological functioning (Hannonen, Tupola, Ahonen, & Riikonen, 2003). The design contrasted three groups of elementary school-age children (diabetes with severe hypoglycemia, diabetes without severe hypoglycemia, and a group of healthy children). Children with a history of severe hypoglycemia were significantly different from both of the comparison groups in terms of neuropsychological impairments, amount of special education received, and parent-reported learning difficulties. The children with hypoglycemic history were twice as likely as the children without this history to have impairment (defined as $\geq 2\ SD$ below the mean) in at least one domain. The authors suggested that severe hypoglycemia is a risk factor for learning difficulties due to deficits in auditory-verbal functioning.

## Sickle Cell Disease

Sickle cell disease (SCD) refers to a set of genetically based blood disorders with the potential to have both direct and indirect effects on school performance and adjustment. The condition originated in Africa and is thought to have provided an evolutionary advantage to populations at high risk of exposure and death from malaria (National Heart, Lung, and Blood Institute, 2004). Currently, about 1 of every 500 U.S. children of African heritage is born with the condition. The disease manifests in hemoglobin defects (a "sickle" rather than the normal disk shape), which produce a number of symptoms ranging in severity from mild to life-threatening. In regard to school-age children, the primary concerns in academic performance are related to direct assaults on the brain via stroke as well as pain and fatigue (Helps, Fuggle, Udwin, & Dick, 2003). The degree of deficit, age-impact trajectory, and specificity of cognitive impact have been studied in recent years (Brandling-Bennett, White, Armstrong, Christ, & DeBaun, 2003; Kral, Brown, & Hynd, 2001; Nabors & Freymuth, 2002; Noll et al., 2001; Schatz, Brown, Pascual, Hsu, & DeBaun, 2001; Schatz, White, Moinuddin, Armstrong, & DeBaun, 2002; Steen et al., 2002; Steen et al., 2003; Thompson et al., 2003; Thompson, Gustafson, Bonner, & Ware, 2002; Wang et al., 2001). A recent meta-analysis addressed the conflicting findings related to whether and how SCD impacts cognitive performance (Schatz et al., 2002).

Schatz and colleagues (2002) collected all published studies of cognitive functioning in children with SCD. Their data set included 18 studies with a variety of test results, including IQ and other, more specific cognitive dimensions. The overall analysis of IQ produced a small to moderate effect size ($d = -.313$, $t(1075) = -5.02$, $p < .01$), which represented an average of 4.3 standard score points. This effect was not related to year of study publication or to the available sample sizes for the SCD and comparison cases. In the analysis of specific domains, they found that significant deficits were most likely for measures of attention and executive skills. An overall estimate of effect size across the specific domains is likely to be in the interval of 0.34 and 0.43, but specific estimates within domains were not given (perhaps because of the small numbers of estimates per domain that were available in the literature).

A recent prospective study completed within the long-term research program known as the Cooperative Study of Sickle Cell Disease examined the relationship of family and other psychosocial variables to disease characteristics and cognitive status (Thompson et al., 2003). Decline was noted in overall intellectual functioning along with stability in the measures of family functioning. Interestingly, the higher the child's baseline intellectual functioning, the lower the long-term risk of behavior problems.

The pathophysiology of SCD effects was investigated in a study hypothesizing roles of both focal deficits due to infarct as well as low hematocrit (Steen et al.,

2003). The analysis produced evidence of significant independent effects on intellectual functioning from both the local injury apparent on MRI as well as the more diffuse pathology indicated by the hematocrit measures. The results were interpreted to suggest that chronic brain hypoxia probably plays an important role in the development of intellectual difficulties for children with SCD.

## CROSS-CUTTING ISSUES

In the following discussion, attention turns to questions that cross diagnostic categories and instead summarize extant knowledge of children with chronic illness in general. The review concludes with presentation of a graphic model of the relationship of potential causes, mediators, moderators, and outcomes as a way of summarizing and integrating the course and consequences of chronic childhood illness.

### Do Children with Chronic Illness Exhibit More Psychosocial Problems?

Lavigne and Faier-Routman (1992) reviewed 87 studies of children's adjustment to physical disorders in the first meta-analysis of this question. Their synthesis suggested that children with physical disorders are at increased risk for overall adjustment problems, especially when comparisons are made with published norms rather than with study controls. Additionally, self-concept of children with physical disorders across all studies appears significant for studies with careful matching or comparisons with norms. Risk for adjustment problems was related to source of report (e.g., parent versus teacher). The authors also highlighted interdisease differences, but the small number of studies within individual disorders limited the conclusions.

### School Absence and Return

Days of school lost is an important statistical indicator of the impact of illness on children. As noted earlier, approximately 18% to 20% of school-age children live with a chronic illness (Ireys, 2001). School absence due to chronic illness impacts several domains central to school-related functioning, and the topic is therefore of considerable importance to the school neuropsychologist. The growing importance of the issue is evident when just one disease (cancer) is considered. Currently, it is estimated that by the year 2010, 10% of the U.S. population will be cancer survivors. This area is ripe for meta-analysis, as no comprehensive review could be found.

One of the most challenging aspects of many chronic illnesses, including cancer, is the return to school following treatment. Children may report that going back to school was worse than the treatment itself because of the social consequences, including loss of friendship, teasing, rejection, and gross misunderstanding of the disease even by teachers and school administrators.

A recent large survey of elementary school children shows that misinformation about causes of cancer is quite widespread (Chin et al., 1998). This study, which included 784 children in kindergarten through sixth grade, revealed that although children's concepts about cancer causes become more sophisticated with age, there is a generally low level of accurate information. Particularly troubling is the finding that about 1 in 5 children believes that cancer is contagious, helping

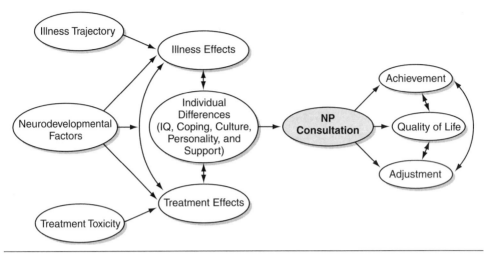

**Figure 22.1**   Conceptual Model of the School Neuropsychology of Chronic Illness

to set the stage for more difficult school adjustment for classmates returning to school following treatment. The school neuropsychologist can play an important role in providing accurate information to school personnel and peers about the functional limits to be expected as well as support of the personal and social connections to school.

AN INTEGRATIVE GENERAL MODEL

To summarize and integrate the issues in the school neuropsychology of chronic illness, a basic conceptual model was developed and is given in Figure 22.1. This model includes distal factors related to the neurodevelopmental history of the child, which should include data on the prenatal, perinatal, and postnatal status of mother and child (D'Amato, 1990). Proximal factors include illness and treatment effects, which may be direct or indirect with regard to impact on neuropsychological functioning. A partial list of these effects is given in Table 22.2. Based

**Table 22.2**
Chronic Illness and Treatment Effects with Potential
Impact on School Functioning

| |
| --- |
| Tissue damage (brain and other vital organs) |
| Perceptual and motor impairment |
| School absence and reduced participation |
| Fatigue |
| Pain |
| Decreased general activity level |
| Changes in affective states |
| Lowered self-esteem and self-efficacy |
| Family stress |
| Dependence |
| Altered attitudes and expectations of others |
| Altered peer relations |

on the literature reviewed, one might hypothesize that most of the impact of illness and treatment factors might be negative. Yet it is possible that illness may bring about a crisis with positive effects, including increasing psychosocial support, individual attention to educational issues, medication benefits as well as toxicities, and the possibility of enhanced self-efficacy via perceived triumph over very significant challenges. The emergence of the positive psychology perspective will likely include a broadening of outcome assessments to capture such possibilities (Chafouleas & Bray, 2004).

## CONCLUSION

The previous discussion is of necessity a time-bounded snapshot of the empirical knowledge base in the emerging school neuropsychology of chronic illness. In addition, we must consider several issues that define the context of these issues: the relationship level of analysis to assessment, the context of consultation, and the prospects for future research.

### A COMMENT ON LEVEL OF ANALYSIS AND ASSESSMENT

For the statistically minded person, it is accurate and efficient to refer to chronic health conditions as correlated with other variables such as socioeconomic status, residence, race, and gender. For the individual learner coping with chronic illness, hunger, poverty, crime, a broken home, limited or no primary health care, and other problems, this analysis might be a source of hopelessness rather than help. Yet, when the school neuropsychologist encounters such a child, he or she must maintain awareness of the multilevel nature of such problems, assessing the interaction of person, illness, and environment. The outcome of the assessment should be clarification of the strengths, limits, and possibilities of the child for all concerned with his or her well-being.

### ASSESSMENT

Perhaps the most important role for the school neuropsychologist concerned with a child with chronic illness will be in the assessment of possible gaps in academic potential versus achievement. As D'Amato (1990) pointed out in his original description of the neuropsychological approach to school psychology, there is a long-standing point of view suggesting that "behavioral and educational data must be reconciled, interpreted, and evaluated in light of the basic *physiological* functioning of the individual" (p. 142). For children with chronic illness, this is often the central concern of the referral source, along with some set of recommendations for support or enhancement of performance or adjustment.

The present review only scratches the surface of the complexity likely to be found in the individual case but should provide an orientation to assessment goals. At the most basic level, assessment requires a sorting out of direct and indirect effects of illness and treatment. In this regard, neuropsychological assessment may reveal both quantitative and qualitative findings to account for observed performance. These findings may include direct and permanent neurophysiological effects of disease or treatment as well as the range of indirect and possibly temporary causes of performance deficits such as school absence, pain, fatigue, worry, depression, lack of peer support, low self-efficacy, and other factors common to chronic illness that may manifest in poor school performance.

Baseline assessment should be a high priority as soon as possible after the diagnosis and should be supplemented by a complete neurodevelopmental history. Supplementary measures may be extremely useful in differentiation of causes and effects, though care must be taken in limiting the testing burden for children, especially those currently in active and intensive treatment. Inclusion of measures of fatigue, pain, and Hr-Qol as part of the baseline and ongoing follow-up with children is recommended as an important source of data on the child's subjective experience of illness and may also become a valuable aspect of evaluation.

## THE MANY FACES OF CONSULTATION

Consultation with medical practitioners and maintenance of one's own knowledge base are critical factors in the degree to which the school neuropsychologist can provide insight and recommendations to help all concerned understand and accommodate the circumstances of the child. The school neuropsychologist is likely to be at the nexus of student, teacher, parent, and physician concerns about school performance and adjustment and will need to be able to translate and communicate at multiple levels. Quite often, the school neuropsychologist is in a prime position to advocate on behalf of the learner with a chronic illness as the expert with the best sense of the child's needs in the school context. As we have seen, chronic illnesses often bring a large team of professionals with diverse skills into the child's life. As perhaps the newest member of that team, the school neuropsychologist will likely find an emerging role. One of the foremost tasks will involve understanding of others' roles and communication about one's own contribution to the well-being of the child. This task may be particularly challenging in that neuropsychology is not widely understood by the public, including health care professionals.

Yet the school neuropsychologist has much to contribute, perhaps most importantly the provision of accurate estimates of ability in the context of an understanding of the child's developmental level and family and school system. Replacing low expectations, inappropriate placements, and exclusion based on fears or stereotypes with concrete and realistic goals for functioning and achievement in school may ultimately make the biggest difference in the long-term outcomes of childhood chronic illness.

## FUTURE RESEARCH

One issue of great importance in the interpretation of statistically significant findings is that of clinical significance. That is, we need to understand the degree to which a measurable deficit relative to a comparison group is not only reliable (i.e., unlikely to be due to chance) but also meaningful in a child's life. In an evolutionary scientific sense, it may be the case that the statistically significant findings of today's studies will lead to increased attention to this issue so that, just as we consider a deviation of 2 degrees in body temperature meaningful, we will have a better idea of how much change on a measure of cognitive ability warrants further monitoring or intervention. In addition, it is hoped the increasing use of interval rather than just point estimates (95% confidence intervals versus reports of means) will provide the practitioner with a better context for interpretation and recommendations. In the long run, school neuropsychology will map the relationship of conditions, diagnostic technology, functional and psychosocial impact, support services, and outcomes in childhood illness on which such judgments will be based.

Programmatic national research efforts and meta-analyses will continue to illuminate the big picture with regard to the needs of children with chronic illness, including educational and neuropsychological profiles. For example, the federal and state-level Children with Special Health Care Needs programs are responsible for planning and developing systems of care for children with special health care needs. An important part of this effort will be a new national survey that will provide standard national and state data on the prevalence and impact of special health care needs among children. This survey was developed and will be administered by the federal Maternal and Child Health Bureau in partnership with the National Center for Health Statistics (van Dyck et al., 2002). For the present review, two meta-analyses and one systematic review from the Cochrane database were identified. The potential for meta-analysis of within- and across-condition effects relevant to school neuropsychology is rapidly growing. The initiation of large multicenter studies with randomized designs that include neuropsychological measures is very encouraging as well.

CONCLUSION

Ruth Stein has been a leading advocate for children with chronic illness over the past quarter century. In 1989, she called for a new paradigm to address the complexities of caring for the growing population of children with serious illness. She may not have anticipated that school neuropsychology might one day become part of such a new paradigm, but her words bear repeating to those who may be assuming this role: "Without normalizing their experiences during their formative years, seriously ill children face considerable handicaps in terms of social and cognitive skills and will have limited opportunities for adult self-sufficiency, independence and competence" (p. xxviii). It is clear that the school neuropsychologist can play a key role in helping to normalize and, in many cases, prevent or minimize the problems related to chronic illness and in the process, significantly impact the quality of life of a growing segment of the school population.

REFERENCES

Anderson, N. B. (1998). Levels of analysis in health science: A framework for integrating sociobehavioral and biomedical research. *Annals of the New York Academy of Sciences—Neuroimmunomodulation: Molecular aspects, integrative systems, and clinical advances, 840,* 563–576.

Anderson, N. E. (2003). Late complications in childhood central nervous system tumour survivors. *Current Opinion in Neurology, 16,* 677–683.

Angelini, L., Zibordi, F., Triulzi, F., Cinque, P., Giudici, B., Pinzani, R., et al. (2000). Age-dependent neurologic manifestations of HIV infection in childhood. *Neurological Sciences, 21*(3), 135–142.

Annett, R. D., Aylward, E. H., Lapidus, J., Bender, B. G., & DuHamel, T. (2000). Neurocognitive functioning in children with mild and moderate asthma in the childhood asthma management program: The Childhood Asthma Management Program (CAMP) Research Group. *Journal of Allergy and Clinical Immunology, 105,* 717–724.

Anonymous. (1999). The Childhood Asthma Management Program (CAMP): Design, rationale, and methods [Childhood Asthma Management Program Research Group]. *Controlled Clinical Trials, 20,* 91–120.

American Psychological Association. (2001). *Thesaurus of psychological index terms* (9th ed.). Washington, DC: American Psychological Association.

Barr, R. D., Chalmers, D., De Pauw, S., Furlong, W., Weitzman, S., & Feeny, D. (2000). Health-related quality of life in survivors of Wilms' tumor and advanced neuroblastoma: A cross-sectional study. *Journal of Clinical Oncology, 18,* 3280–3287.

Barr, R. D., Furlong, W., Dawson, S., Whitton, A. C., Strautmanis, I., Pai, M., et al. (1993). An assessment of global health status in survivors of acute lymphoblastic leukemia in childhood. *American Journal of Pediatric Hematology-Oncology, 15,* 284–290.

Barr, R. D., Gonzalez, A., Longchong, M., Furlong, W., Vizcaino, M. P., Horsman, J., et al. (2001). Health status and health-related quality of life in survivors of cancer in childhood in Latin America: A MISPHO feasibility study. *International Journal of Oncology, 19,* 413–421.

Bender, B. G., Belleau, L., Fukuhara, J. T., Mrazek, D. A., & Strunk, R. C. (1987). Psychomotor adaptation in children with severe chronic asthma. *Pediatrics, 79,* 723–727.

Bender, B. G., Lerner, J. A., & Kollasch, E. (1988). Mood and memory changes in asthmatic children receiving corticosteroids. *Journal of the American Academy of Child and Adolescent Psychiatry, 27,* 720–725.

Bisiacchi, P., Suppiej, A., & Laverda, A. (2000). Neuropsychological evaluation of neurologically asymptomatic HIV-infected children. *Brain and Cognition, 43,* 49–52.

Blanchette, N., Smith, M. L., Fernandes-Penney, A., King, S., & Read, S. (2001). Cognitive and motor development in children with vertically transmitted HIV infection. *Brain and Cognition, 46,* 50–53.

Blanchette, N., Smith, M. L., King, S., Fernandes-Penney, A., & Read, S. (2002). Cognitive development in school-age children with vertically transmitted HIV infection. *Developmental Neuropsychology, 21,* 223–241.

Boivin, M. J., Green, S. D., Davies, A. G., Giordani, B., Mokili, J. K., & Cutting, W. A. (1995). Preliminary evaluation of the cognitive and motor effects of pediatric HIV infection in Zairian children. *Health Psychology, 14,* 13–21.

Brandling-Bennett, E. M., White, D. A., Armstrong, M. M., Christ, S. E., & DeBaun, M. (2003). Patterns of verbal long-term and working memory performance reveal deficits in strategic processing in children with frontal infarcts related to sickle cell disease. *Developmental Neuropsychology, 24,* 423–434.

Brouwers, P., Van Der Vlugt, H., Moss, H., Wolters, P., & Pizzo, P. (1995). White matter changes on CT brain scan are associated with neurobehavioral dysfunction in children with symptomatic HIV disease. *Child Neuropsychology, 1,* 93–105.

Butler, R. W., & Copeland, D. R. (1993). Neuropsychological effects of central nervous system prophylactic treatment in childhood leukemia: Methodological considerations. *Journal of Pediatric Psychology, 18,* 319–338.

Carpentieri, S. C., Waber, D. P., Scott, R. M., Goumnerova, L. C., Kieran, M. W., Cohen, L. E., et al. (2001). Memory deficits among children with craniopharyngiomas. *Neurosurgery, 49,* 1053–1057.

Centers for Disease Control and Prevention. (2004). *Acquired immunodeficiency syndrome (AIDS) cases, according to age at diagnosis, sex, detailed race, and Hispanic origin: United States, selected years: 1985–2002.* Retrieved January 4, 2004, from http://www.cdc.gov /nchs/data/hus/tables/2003/03hus053.pdf.

Chabot, D. R., & Matteis, M. C. (1992). Families facing death and serious illness. In M. E. Procidano & C. B. Fisher (Eds.), *Contemporary families: A handbook for school professionals* (pp. 159–178). New York: Teacher's College Press.

Chafouleas, S. M., & Bray, M. A. (2004). Introducing positive psychology: Finding a place within school psychology. *Psychology in the Schools, 41*, 1–5.

Chin, D. G., Schonfeld, D. J., O'Hare, L. L., Mayne, S. T., Salovey, P., Showalter, D. R., et al. (1998). Elementary school-age children's developmental understanding of the causes of cancer. *Journal of Developmental and Behavioral Pediatric, 19*, 397–403.

Cole, K. L., Roberts, M. C., & McNeal, R. E. (1996). Children's perceptions of ill peers: Effects of disease, grade, and impact variables. *Children's Health Care, 25*, 107–115.

Compas, B. E., & Boyer, M. C. (2001). Coping and attention: Implications for child health and pediatric conditions. *Journal of Developmental and Behavioral Pediatrics, 22*, 323–333.

Copeland, D. R., Dowell, R. E., Fletcher, J. M., Sullivan, M. P., Jaffe, N., Cangir, A., et al. (1988). Neuropsychological test performance of pediatric cancer patients at diagnosis and one year later. *Journal of Pediatric Psychology, 13*, 183–196.

Crossland, A. (2002). Efficacy beliefs and the learning experiences of children with cancer in the hospital setting. *Alberta Journal of Educational Research, 48*, 5–19.

Dabis, F., & Ekpini, E. R. (2002). HIV-1/AIDS and maternal and child health in Africa. *Lancet, 359*, 2097–2104.

D'Amato, R. C. (1990). A neuropsychological approach to school psychology. *School Psychology Quarterly, 5*, 141–160.

Espy, K. A., Moore, I. M., Kaufmann, P. M., Kramer, J. H., Matthay, K., & Hutter, J. J. (2001). Chemotherapeutic CNS prophylaxis and neuropsychologic change in children with acute lymphoblastic leukemia: A prospective study. *Journal of Pediatric Psychology, 26*, 1–9.

Forehand, R., Steele, R., Armistead, L., Morse, E., Simon, P., & Clark, L. (1998). The Family Health Project: Psychosocial adjustment of children whose mothers are HIV infected. *Journal of Consulting and Clinical Psychology, 66*, 513–520.

Furukawa, C. T., DuHamel, T. R., Weimer, L., Shapiro, G. G., Pierson, W. E., & Bierman, C. W. (1988). Cognitive and behavioral findings in children taking theophylline. *Journal of Allergy and Clinical Immunology, 81*, 83–88.

Gale, E. A. (2002). The rise of childhood type 1 diabetes in the 20th century. *Diabetes, 51*, 3353–3361.

Gil, C. A., Silveira, M. L., Soares, F. J., Sole, D., & Naspitz, C. (1993). Study of the effects of treatment with theophylline on the cognitive process and behaviour of children with bronchial asthma. *Allergologia et Immunopathologia, 21*, 204–206.

Grave, G. D., & Pless, I. B. (1974). *Chronic childhood illness: Assessment of outcome* (DHEW Publication No. NIH 76-877). Washington, DC: U.S. Department of Health, Education and Welfare.

Guyer, B., Freedman, M. A., Strobino, D. M., & Sondik, E. J. (2000). Annual summary of vital statistics: Trends in the health of Americans during the 20th century. *Pediatrics, 106*, 1307–1317.

Hannonen, R., Tupola, S., Ahonen, T., & Riikonen, R. (2003). Neurocognitive functioning in children with type-1 diabetes with and without episodes of severe hypoglycemia. *Developmental Medicine and Child Neurology, 45*, 262–268.

Helps, S., Fuggle, P., Udwin, O., & Dick, M. (2003). Psychosocial and neurocognitive aspects of sickle cell disease. *Child and Adolescent Mental Health, 8,* 11–17.

Holmes, C. S., Cant, M., Fox, M. A., Lampert, N. L., & Greer, T. (1999). Disease and demographic risk factors for disrupted cognitive functioning in children with insulin-dependent diabetes mellitus (IDDM). *School Psychology Review, 28,* 215–227.

Ireys, H. (2001). Epidemiology of childhood chronic illness: Issues in definitions, service use, and costs. In H. M. Koot & J. L. Wallander (Eds.), *Quality of life in child and adolescent illness* (pp. 124–150). East Sussex, England: Brunner-Routledge.

Koocher, G. P., O'Malley, J. E., Gogan, J. L., & Foster, D. J. (1980). Psychological adjustment among pediatric cancer survivors. *Journal of Child Psychology and Psychiatry and Allied Disciplines, 21,* 163–173.

Koot, H. M., & Wallander, J. L. (2001). *Quality of life in child and adolescent illness:* New York: Taylor & Francis.

Kral, M. C., Brown, R. T., & Hynd, G. W. (2001). Neuropsychological aspects of pediatric sickle cell disease. *Neuropsychology Review, 11,* 179–196.

Lavigne, J. V., & Faier-Routman, J. (1992). Psychological adjustment to pediatric physical disorders: A meta-analytic review. *Journal of Pediatric Psychology, 17,* 133–157.

Lester, P., Chesney, M., Cooke, M., Whalley, P., Perez, B., Petru, A., et al. (2002). Diagnostic disclosure to HIV-infected children: How parents decide when and what to tell. *Clinical Child Psychology and Psychiatry, 7,* 85–99.

Lipman, T. H. (2002). Type 1 diabetes. In L. L. Hayman, M. N. Mahon, & J. R. Turner (Eds.), *Chronic illness in children* (pp. 217–246). New York: Springer.

Lozano, P., Sullivan, S. D., Smith, D. H., & Weiss, K. B. (1999). The economic burden of asthma in US children: Estimates from the National Medical Expenditure Survey. *Journal of Allergy and Clinical Immunology, 104,* 957–963.

Mansfield, L., Mendoza, C., Flores, J., & Meeves, S. G. (2003). Effects of fexofenadine, diphenhydramine, and placebo on performance of the test of variables of attention. *Annals of Allergy, Asthma, and Immunology, 90,* 554–559.

Moore, B. D., Copeland, D. R., Ried, H., & Levy, B. (1992). Neurophysiological basis of cognitive deficits in long-term survivors of childhood cancer. *Archives of Neurology, 49,* 809–817.

Mulhern, R. K., Kepner, J. L., Thomas, P. R., Armstrong, F. D., Friedman, H. S., & Kun, L. E. (1998). Neuropsychologic functioning of survivors of childhood medulloblastoma randomized to receive conventional or reduced-dose craniospinal irradiation: A Pediatric Oncology Group study. *Journal of Clinical Oncology, 16,* 1723–1728.

Mulhern, R. K., Palmer, S. L., Reddick, W. E., Glass, J. O., Kun, L. E., Taylor, J., et al. (2001). Risks of young age for selected neurocognitive deficits in medulloblastoma are associated with white matter loss. *Journal of Clinical Oncology, 19,* 472–479.

Nabors, N. A., & Freymuth, A. K. (2002). Attention deficits in children with sickle cell disease. *Perceptual and Motor Skills, 95,* 57–67.

National Heart, Lung, and Blood Institute. (2004). *Facts about Sickle Cell disease.* Retrieved December 15, 2003, from http://www.nhlbi.nih.gov/health/public/blood/sickle/sca_fact.pdf.

Noll, R. B., Stith, L., Gartstein, M. A., Ris, M. D., Grueneich, R., Vannatta, K., et al. (2001). Neuropsychological functioning of youths with sickle cell disease: Comparison with non-chronically ill peers. *Journal of Pediatric Psychology, 26,* 69–78.

Rachelefsky, G. S., Wo, J., Adelson, J., Mickey, M. R., Spector, S. L., Katz, R. M., et al. (1986). Behavior abnormalities and poor school performance due to oral theophylline use. *Pediatrics, 78,* 1133–1138.

Rausch, D. M., & Stover, E. S. (2001). Neuroscience research in AIDS. *Progress in Neuro-Psychopharmacology and Biological Psychiatry, 25,* 231–257.

Ries, L. A., Kosary, C. L., Hankey, B. F., Miller, B. A., Clegg, L., Mariotto, A., et al. (2003). *SEER Cancer Statistics Review, 1975–2000.* Bethesda, MD: National Cancer Institute.

Rietveld, S., & Colland, V. T. (1999). The impact of severe asthma on schoolchildren. *Journal of Asthma, 36,* 409–417.

Rotheram-Borus, M. J., Murphy, D. A., Wight, R. G., Lee, M. B., Lightfoot, M., Swendeman, D., et al. (2001). Improving the quality of life among young people living with HIV. *Evaluation and Program Planning, 24,* 227–237.

Rovet, J. F. (2000). Diabetes. In K. O. Yeates, M. D. Ris, & H. G. Taylor (Eds.), *Pediatric neuropsychology: Research, theory, and practice.* (pp. 336–365). New York: Guilford Press.

Rovet, J. F., Ehrlich, R. M., Czuchta, D., & Akler, M. (1993). Psychoeducational characteristics of children and adolescents with insulin-dependent diabetes mellitus. *Journal of Learning Disabilities, 26,* 7–22.

Schatz, J., Brown, R., Pascual, J., Hsu, L., & DeBaun, M. (2001). Poor school and cognitive functioning with silent cerebral infarcts and sickle cell disease. *Neurology, 56,* 1109–1111.

Schatz, J., White, D. A., Moinuddin, A., Armstrong, M., & DeBaun, M. R. (2002). Lesion burden and cognitive morbidity in children with sickle cell disease. *Journal of Child Neurology, 17,* 891–895.

Schonfeld, D. J., O'Hare, L. L., Perrin, E. C., Quackenbush, M., Showalter, D. R., & Cicchetti, D. V. (1995). A randomized, controlled trial of a school-based, multi-faceted AIDS education program in the elementary grades: The impact on comprehension, knowledge and fears. *Pediatrics, 95,* 480–486.

Steen, R., Hu, X., Elliott, V. E., Miles, M. A., Jones, S., & Wang, W. C. (2002). Kindergarten readiness skills in children with sickle cell disease: Evidence of early neurocognitive damage? *Journal of Child Neurology, 17,* 111–116.

Steen, R. G., Miles, M. A., Helton, K. J., Strawn, S., Wang, W., Xiong, X., et al. (2003). Cognitive impairment in children with hemoglobin SS sickle cell disease: Relationship to MR imaging findings and hematocrit. *American Journal of Neuroradiology, 24,* 382–389.

Stein, R. E. (1996). To be or not to be noncategorical. *Journal of Developmental and Behavioral Pediatrics, 17,* 36–37.

Stein, R. E., Bauman, L. J., Epstein, S. G., Gardner, J. D., & Walker, D. K. (2000). How well does the questionnaire for identifying children with chronic conditions identify individual children who have chronic conditions? *Archives of Pediatrics and Adolescent Medicine, 154,* 447–452.

Stein, R. E., Bauman, L. J., Westbrook, L. E., Coupey, S. M., & Ireys, H. T. (1993). Framework for identifying children who have chronic conditions: The case for a new definition. *Journal of Pediatrics, 122,* 342–347.

Stein, R. E., Gortmaker, S. L., Perrin, E. C., Perrin, J. M., Pless, I. B., Walker, D. K., et al. (1987). Severity of illness: Concepts and measurements. *Lancet, 2,* 1506–1509.

Stein, R. E., & Jessop, D. J. (1989). What diagnosis does not tell: The case for a noncategorical approach to chronic illness in childhood. *Social Science and Medicine, 29,* 769–778.

Stein, R. E., & Silver, E. J. (1999). Operationalizing a conceptually based noncategorical definition: A first look at US children with chronic conditions. *Archives of Pediatrics and Adolescent Medicine, 153,* 68–74.

Stein, R. E., & Silver, E. J. (2002). Comparing different definitions of chronic conditions in a national data set. *Ambulatory Pediatrics, 2,* 63–70.

Stein, R. E., Westbrook, L. E., & Bauman, L. J. (1997). The questionnaire for identifying children with chronic conditions: A measure based on a noncategorical approach. *Pediatrics, 99*, 513–521.

Stein, R. E., Westbrook, L. E., & Silver, E. J. (1998). Comparison of adjustment of school-age children with and without chronic conditions: Results from community-based samples. *Journal of Developmental and Behavioral Pediatrics, 19*, 267–272.

St. Lawrence, J. S., Jefferson, K. W., Alleyne, E., & Brasfield, T. L. (1995). Comparison of education versus behavioral skills training interventions in lowering sexual HIV-risk behavior of substance-dependent adolescents. *Journal of Consulting and Clinical Psychology, 63*, 154–157.

Thompson, R. J., Armstrong, F., Link, C. L., Pegelow, C. H., Moser, F., & Wang, W. C. (2003). A prospective study of the relationship over time of behavior problems, intellectual functioning, and family functioning in children with sickle cell disease: A report from the Cooperative Study of Sickle Cell Disease. *Journal of Pediatric Psychology, 28*, 59–65.

Thompson, R. J., Jr., Gustafson, K. E., Bonner, M. J., & Ware, R. E. (2002). Neurocognitive development of young children with sickle cell disease through three years of age. *Journal of Pediatric Psychology, 27*, 235–244.

Turner-Henson, A., & Johnston, J. (2002). Pediatric asthma. In L. L. Hayman, M. M. Mahon, & J. R. Turner (Eds.), *Chronic illness in children* (pp. 3–26). New York: Springer.

van Dyck, P. C., McPherson, M., Strickland, B. B., Nesseler, K., Blumberg, S. J., Cynamon, M. L., et al. (2002). The national survey of children with special health care needs. *Ambulatory Pediatrics, 2*, 29–37.

Walker, N., Schwartlander, B., & Bryce, J. (2002). Meeting international goals in child survival and HIV/AIDS. *360*, 284–289.

Wang, W., Enos, L., Gallagher, D., Thompson, R., Guarini, L., Vichinsky, E., et al. (2001). Neuropsychologic performance in school-aged children with sickle cell disease: A report from the Cooperative Study of Sickle Cell Disease. *Journal of Pediatrics, 139*, 391–397.

Wolters, P. L., & Brouwers, P. (1998). Evaluation of neurodevelopmental deficits in children with HIV infection. In H. E. Gendelman, S. A. Lipton, L. Epstein, & S. Swindells (Eds.), *The neurology of AIDS* (pp. 425–442). New York: Chapman & Hall.

CHAPTER 23

# Providing Neuropsychological Services to Early Childhood Learners

CATHY F. TELZROW, ANDREA BEEBE, and JULIE WOJCIK

SEVERAL OBJECTIVES HAVE been established for this volume: (1) combining the lenses of two major specialties—school psychology and neuropsychology—to increase understanding of children's neurologically based disorders; (2) merging this knowledge with recent clinical and research findings to enhance the provision of educational interventions; and (3) bridging the worlds of theory and practice in a manner that is practical for the authentic settings in which children live and thrive. In an early publication on child neuropsychology, Rourke and colleagues wrote, "Theory, research, and practice in child neuropsychology are not, at present, linked in very many direct ways" (Rourke, Bakker, Fisk, & Strang, 1983, p. vii). Two decades following that publication, the current editors' objectives make it clear that achieving synchrony around these topics is still an important pursuit.

This volume's emphasis on bringing together the specialties of school psychology and neuropsychology is particularly relevant to the early childhood population. During this critical period of development, timely identification of neurologically based risk indicators and special needs, followed by the reliable implementation of evidence-based interventions, can ameliorate learning and behavioral difficulties that may otherwise compromise a child's successful attainment of critical skills. The period of early childhood is generally defined as encompassing the age span of 3 to 8 years; this chapter concentrates on the first half of that period—ages 3 to approximately 6 years—because of the importance of this period for prevention and early intervention for children identified as at risk for educational difficulties.

This chapter begins with a brief overview of the historical foundations and subsequent professional evolutions that are relevant to neuropsychological assessment and intervention in early childhood. This is followed by a description of seven theoretical paradigms in psychology that influence current research and practice and have particular implications for young children. The preponderance of the chapter focuses on the description and illustration of a school neuropsychology approach to assessment and intervention with young children. Basic premises from research and practice that guide the model are identified; a domain-specific, flexible battery approach to assessment of child performance is described; a data-driven, intervention-based method of intervention design, implementation, and evaluation is outlined; and the application of the approach is illustrated through a case study presentation.

## THE LEGACY AND DEVELOPMENT OF NEUROPSYCHOLOGICAL ASSESSMENT AND INTERVENTION IN EARLY CHILDHOOD

Neuropsychology's heritage is one of localization of function through the examination of adults with known brain injury. Early explorations into child neuropsychology involved fairly direct application of adult models, with little appreciation for the notion that children were not simply smaller versions of their grown-up counterparts. This stage of research and practice was characterized by child adaptations of adult neuropsychological test batteries, a traditional emphasis on a blind approach to interpretation of neuropsychological test data, explicit assumptions regarding "compromised cerebral functioning," and a medical model treatment paradigm (Anderson, Northam, Hendy, & Wrennall, 2001; Fletcher & Taylor, 1984; Rourke et al., 1983; Yeates & Taylor, 2001).

Although the application of adult-oriented approaches to children advanced the field in a number of ways, this practice also perpetuated several fallacies (Fletcher & Taylor, 1984). Examples include assumptions that (1) pathognomonic signs of brain impairment in adults can be applied reliably to children, (2) assessments of a given construct in adults measure the same function in children, (3) correlates of identified deficits are diagnostically meaningful, and (4) it is defensible to infer brain dysfunction from behavioral performance. Beginning in the 1980s, the emergence of the first explicitly trained child clinical neuropsychologists, coupled with advances in neuroimaging that de-emphasized the importance of localization of brain impairment, signaled a different type of paradigm, which incorporated developmental and ecological considerations (Williams & Boll, 1997; Yeates & Taylor, 2001). This significant shift in perspective was facilitated by the contributions of clinicians and researchers whose professional orientations encompassed both school psychology and neuropsychology specialties (e.g., D'Amato & Dean, 1988; Hynd & Obrzut, 1981; Reynolds, 1981). The work of these individuals has been instrumental in shaping the science of school neuropsychology portrayed in this volume.

## PSYCHOLOGICAL PARADIGMS WITH IMPLICATIONS FOR THE SCHOOL NEUROPSYCHOLOGY OF ASSESSMENT AND INTERVENTION IN EARLY CHILDHOOD

Seven psychological paradigms of relevance to this chapter are introduced and briefly described in this section. Although some of these conceptual orientations have been discussed extensively in the child clinical neuropsychology literature, others reflect trends in general psychology or school psychology. The authors contend that merging the distinct but complementary orientations of general psychological foundations and the applied specialties of neuropsychology and school psychology helps to establish a contemporary backdrop for the school neuropsy-chology assessment and intervention in early childhood.

## DEVELOPMENTAL PERSPECTIVE

Nearly every publication focused on child neuropsychology for the past 25 years has emphasized the importance of a developmental perspective when conducting assessments and planning and implementing interventions for children. As conceptualized in this chapter, employing a developmental perspective incorporates these critical elements: (1) an understanding of age-related expectations for performance, particularly when interpreting assessment data; (2) a recognition of and appreciation for the complex interaction between the young child's development and the phenotypic expression of neuropsychologically based disorders at different ages; (3) consideration of the manner in which the age-related expectations of caregivers and teachers influence the child's adaptive functioning; and (4) appreciation for ways that nonneurological constructs that are nonetheless critical for child adjustment may change over time and in association with the identified disorders (Anderson et al., 2001; Taylor & Fletcher, 1990).

A developmental perspective is especially critical for the early childhood population because of the dramatic and rapid changes that are associated with this period of development (Anderson et al., 2001; Aylward, 1997). Of particular relevance to this chapter's focus on young children are the keystone behaviors typically associated with these ages, including motor and perceptual motor facility, the acquisition and fluent use of language, preliteracy and early literacy skills, and age-appropriate social and adaptive functioning. Because risks for attaining these developmental objectives have clear implications for successful adjustment, the identification of such impediments in young children, coupled with the implementation of appropriate interventions, represents a major focus of this chapter.

## ECOLOGICAL ORIENTATION

A fundamental premise of the authors is that there is a dynamic and bidirectional relationship between neurological substrates and environmental experiences. Several child clinical psychologists (e.g., Bernstein, 2001; Dennis, 2001; Taylor & Fletcher, 1990) have presented elegant models to illustrate the complex interactions among the cognitive and psychosocial constructs that influence children's functioning, as well as myriad ways in which a manifest disability with confirmed neurological etiology may be ameliorated or exacerbated by biological and environmental factors. An ecological orientation requires clinicians not only to consider a child's presenting concerns, but to examine the influence of other biological traits (e.g., temperament, comorbid conditions) and environmental events (e.g., persistent poverty, chronic family stressors, exposure to early intervention programming) that may represent risk or protective factors, as well as the bidirectional effects of these components (Anderson et al., 2001; Yeates & Taylor, 2001).

## CULTURAL COMPETENCE

Cultural competence involves "the ability to think, feel, and act in ways that acknowledge, respect, and build upon ethnic, sociocultural, and linguistic diversity" (Lynch & Hanson, 1998, p. 50). The increasingly diverse nature of the population of the United States, evidence that intervention outcomes are associated with cultural competence, and the increased prominence given to cultural competence in research and practice (American Psychological Association, 2003; Rogers & Lopez, 2002) warrant the inclusion of cultural competence among the key paradigms shaping the school neuropsychology model of assessment and intervention in early childhood described in this chapter.

Cultural competence has been promoted as an essential element in research and training for school psychologists (National Association of School Psychologists, 2003; Ysseldyke et al., 1997). A national sample of school psychology practitioners, faculty, and supervisors/administrators identified critical cross-cultural competencies in 14 practice domains (Rogers & Lopez, 2002). Several of these are particularly relevant to this chapter's focus, including those associated with assessment (e.g., instrument selection, alternative assessment methods), report writing (e.g., incorporating culturally relevant background information, reporting use of interpreters or translators), and working with parents (e.g., understanding cultural differences in family structure and hierarchy, demonstrating sensitivity to culturally related views of schooling and disability; Rogers & Lopez, 2002).

The intersection of cultural competence and neuropsychology is a fairly recent phenomenon (Fletcher-Janzen, Strickland, & Reynolds, 2000; Whelan, 1999). Wong, Strickland, Fletcher-Janzen, Ardila, and Reynolds (2000) identified several theoretical issues that are relevant to this interface and described conceptual fallacies and gaps between needs and training expectations and approaches. These authors offered nine practical suggestions for providing services to culturally dissimilar clients, including recommendations pertaining to conducting interviews, employing interpreters or translators, and test selection.

## DISABILITY VERSUS REHABILITATION PARADIGM

Consistent with its origins in the study of brain injury, a medical model orientation has traditionally characterized the field of neuropsychology (Long, 1996; McMahon & Shaw, 1996). In this perspective, disabilities are conceptualized as representing individual deficiencies, the terminology employed conveys a disease/disorder model, and approaches to treatment are remedial in nature (Pledger, 2003). In contrast, a habilitation/rehabilitation paradigm adopts a person-first, ecological perspective for conceptualizing disabilities and focuses less on identified deficits than on the contextual factors that represent barriers for an individual. In the latter paradigm, treatment is concerned with facilitating environmental adaptations and interpersonal adjustments that reduce functional limitations (Gill, Kewman, & Brannon, 2003; Whelan, 1999; Yeates & Taylor, 2001).

Several indicators of this changing paradigm in the conceptualization of disability have been evident in school psychology and the broader educational arena over the past 2 decades. For the first time in 1992, the American Association on Mental Retardation (AAMR) emphasized the intensity of needed support over intellectual ability indices as the basis for classification. School psychology's shift from a traditional diagnostic approach to a problem-solving intervention paradigm is a second example of this change in orientation (Reschly & Ysseldyke, 2002). A third indicator is the inclusive education movement and the associated emphasis on improving the delivery of instruction to learners rather than presuming static levels of attainment as a consequence of a specific disability condition (Telzrow, 1999).

Clinicians who embrace a habilitation/rehabilitation paradigm have criticized the field of neuropsychology for being overly focused on the assessment and identification of deficits to the neglect of individuals' assets, employing clinical measures that have questionable treatment validity, and being preoccupied with diagnosis instead of intervention (McMahon & Shaw, 1996). Although these criticisms are historically valid, models of contemporary practice have begun to incorporate more functional and authentic approaches to assessment that can reliably inform interventions (Anderson et al., 2001; Sbordone, 1996).

## TREATMENT UTILITY OF ASSESSMENT

Traditional indices of the technical adequacy of assessment instruments, such as coefficients of reliability and validity, have been supplemented by a more recent construct: the treatment utility of assessment. A test or measurement approach is shown to have acceptable treatment utility when the derived data are useful for informing interventions (Hayes, Nelson, & Jarrett, 1987; Telzrow, 1987). Increasingly, treatment utility is the gold standard for evaluating tests and assessment approaches (Telzrow & McNamara, 2001), and this concept is reflected in the 1997 reauthorization of the Individuals with Disabilities Education Act (IDEA), which "clearly mandates the collection of reliable, valid, and intervention-related assessment information" (Reschly, 2000, p. 95).

A presidential commission charged with examining special education practices identified traditional assessment approaches as an arena for necessary reform, concluding: "The results of these assessments are rarely used to evaluate progress or relate in other meaningful ways to educational need" (President's Council on Special Education Excellence, 2002, p. 24). This report's recommendations include enhanced early identification and intervention, simplification of the identification process, and greater use of intervention-based data to examine children's response to intervention. Although neuropsychology has been criticized for giving insufficient attention to the treatment utility of assessment (McMahon & Shaw, 1996), there is increasing emphasis placed on approaches that can contribute to the design and evaluation of functional performance in actual settings (Anderson et al., 2001).

## EVIDENCE-BASED INTERVENTIONS

During the past decade, practitioners and researchers in the fields of psychology and education have been less concerned with "doing something" than "doing the *right* something" when designing and implementing treatments. The Division of Clinical Psychology's efforts to identify empirically supported psychological interventions represented an early example of this trend (Task Force on Promotion and Dissemination of Psychological Procedures, 1995). Although criticized in some contexts because of potentially negative social policy implications (Chambless & Ollendick, 2001), this work provided an important foundation for subsequent research on empirically supported treatments in related fields. Several years following the commencement of this pioneering activity, an initiative to identify and disseminate information about evidence-based interventions with relevance for school psychologists was undertaken by a task force jointly supported by the Society for the Study of School Psychology and the Division of School Psychology (Division 16) of the American Psychological Association. The work of the Task Force on Evidence Based Interventions in School Psychology (2003) focuses on five major domains: academic intervention programs, comprehensive school health care, family intervention programs, schoolwide and classroom-based programs, and school-based intervention programs for social behavior problems.

A similar emphasis on evidence-based interventions in education is reflected in the No Child Left Behind Act of 2001. This legislation reauthorized the Elementary and Secondary Education Act—the primary federal law governing K–12 education—and incorporated systems, incentives, and consequences that were designed to enhance the educational performance of all learners. One key component of No Child Left Behind is an emphasis on research-based instruction, particularly in the area of reading. The What Works Clearinghouse (2003), a Web-based repository of scientifically supported interventions, was established by the U.S. Department of Education in 2002 to support the dissemination of evidence-based practice strategies.

## EDUCATIONAL ACCOUNTABILITY

One result of the emphasis on evidence-based interventions is an expectation that teachers and support personnel will implement what works and that student performance will be enhanced as a consequence. The significance of the increased attention given to educational accountability during the past decade is indicated most clearly in the No Child Left Behind Act of 2001. As its name suggests, the significance of this legislation is not only its focus on enhancing the academic performance of students, but the maintenance of high expectations for all learners, including those who have traditionally performed poorly on standard indicators of educational success due to poverty, minority status, limited English proficiency, or disabilities. The extension of high expectations to students with disabilities was evident in the 1997 reauthorization of IDEA, which required states to include learners with disabilities in large-scale assessments and to report their progress with the same frequency as for students without disabilities (Ysseldyke, Nelson, & House, 2000).

## INTERSECTION OF PARADIGMS

These paradigms rarely operate in isolation; instead, their influence is exerted via complex interactions between and among them. For example, because cultural background has been associated with an individual's perception of disability, appreciation for how a family's ethnic and cultural heritage influence stress, coping, and adjustment following an acquired brain injury is essential (Marlowe, 2000). Interactions also are evident among the treatment utility of assessment, evidence-based interventions, and accountability paradigms. When considered in combination, these seven paradigms create a contemporary context for the school neuropsychology of assessment and intervention with learners in early childhood.

## THE SCHOOL NEUROPSYCHOLOGY OF ASSESSMENT AND INTERVENTION IN EARLY CHILDHOOD

In this section, the authors' school neuropsychological model of assessment and intervention in early childhood is described. Implementation of this four-step approach is illustrated through a case study involving a young child with a reading and writing learning disorder.

### DESCRIPTION OF APPROACH

The school neuropsychology model of assessment and intervention in early childhood advocated in this chapter combines an adaptation of Taylor and Fletcher's (1990) biobehavioral systems assessment model with a problem-solving approach to intervention design and implementation (Berninger, Stage, Smith, & Hildebrand, 2001; D'Amato, Rothlisberg, & Leu Work, 1999). Taylor and Fletcher's model portrays two major types of child traits, cognitive and psychosocial, which interact in a bidirectional manner. Additionally, biological and environmental factors are conceptualized as directly influencing these child traits positively or negatively. The manifest disability is a consequence of the interacting child traits and the biological and environmental influences.

This model is particularly applicable to a school neuropsychology approach to assessment for several reasons. First, unlike some methods of child neuropsychological assessment, Taylor and Fletcher (1990) eschew the need to infer neurologic impairment as the reason for observed concerns about student functioning in the absence of confirming data for such a conclusion. Consequently, when there is no known neurologic etiology, the focus of the assessment process is on observed patterns of learner performance rather than on inferences about the integrity of the central nervous system. Second, the biobehavioral model of assessment integrates cognitive and psychosocial traits that are meaningful for school-based practitioners, resulting in an emphasis on critical or keystone behaviors that have direct relevance for child adjustment and educational success (Lentz, Allen, & Ehrhardt, 1996). Finally, this model gives consideration to the important ecological influences that may result from biological and environmental factors in the child's life, and as a consequence is consistent with the habilitation/rehabilitation paradigm that is fundamental to educational settings.

The adaptation of the biobehavioral model employed in this chapter divides Taylor and Fletcher's (1990) broad categories of cognitive and psychosocial traits into seven narrower domains of functioning. This adaptation allows for more explicit consideration of areas of performance that are indicative of major developmental targets during the period of early childhood. The seven domains of performance reflected in the school neuropsychology model of assessment and intervention in early childhood are general intellectual ability, communication, nonverbal reasoning, perceptual motor ability, preliteracy and literacy, executive functions, and social and adaptive functioning. These domains were selected for several reasons. First, they encompass the most salient areas of cognitive and psychosocial functioning during the early childhood period. Second, these areas are relevant to common referral concerns in young children, which typically relate to failure to achieve critical competencies associated with these domains of functioning. Finally, these domains were selected because they represent keystone behaviors that are strong predictors of young children's personal, interpersonal, and academic adjustment (Espy, Kaufmann, Glisky, & McDiarmid, 2001; Lentz et al., 1996).

In the school neuropsychology model of assessment and intervention in early childhood outlined in this chapter, information derived from biobehavioral assessment is interpreted in a problem-solving approach to intervention design, implementation, and evaluation. This is "a systematic process that includes the assessment of children and their environments, identification of needs, development and implementation of supports to meet needs, and the monitoring and evaluation of outcomes" (Thomas & Grimes, 2002, p. v). With its foundation in the scientific method and broad-based applications in behavioral consultation, particularly in educational settings, this approach incorporates many of the core paradigms discussed earlier, including an ecological orientation, a rehabilitation/habilitation focus, evidence-based interventions, and educational accountability (Reschly & Ysseldyke, 2002).

The school neuropsychology model of assessment and intervention in early childhood employs a four-stage process that involves problem identification and analysis (the assessment phase framed around Taylor and Fletcher's, 1990, biobehavioral approach), intervention design and implementation, and intervention evaluation. The model's major components are described next.

*Step 1: Problem Identification*   The problem identification phase, which is analogous to identifying the manifest disability in Taylor and Fletcher's (1990) model, involves the clarification and description of the presenting concerns. It requires thoughtful consideration of the critical areas of developmental attainment in the context of information provided by caregivers and educators. The major objective of the problem identification stage is to describe the child excesses or deficits that interfere with age-appropriate functioning and to frame this description so it is behavioral, measurable, and specific. For example, "During story time, Sara rocks back and forth and flicks her hands in front of her face. She does not respond to her name or participate in any classroom activities unless physically prompted."

For many young children, a comprehensive problem identification process will identify multiple excess/deficit areas that are relevant for learning and behavior. In addition to targeting explicit areas of concern for intervention, the problem identification phase should provide a baseline level of performance for anchoring and evaluating responses to intervention over time.

*Step 2: Problem Analysis*   The objective of this phase of the problem-solving assessment/intervention model is to identify the factors that contribute to the expression and maintenance of the manifest disability. In Taylor and Fletcher's (1990) biobehavioral model, this phase employs relevant assessment approaches and measures to identify cognitive and psychosocial traits as well as pertinent biological and environmental variables that exacerbate or ameliorate the expression of the manifest disability via their direct influence on the child traits. These two overarching objectives—assessment of learner traits and analysis of variables that influence them—constitute this stage of the school neuropsychology model of assessment and intervention in early childhood.

The authors recommend the use of a domain-oriented, flexible battery approach for assessing child performance traits during the problem analysis phase (D'Amato et al., 1999; Telzrow, 1989). This approach has several advantages over standard battery models, including that it (1) allows for the selection of instruments and procedures that are developmentally appropriate, technically sound, and sensitive to the referral question; (2) provides for a conceptual framework that is familiar to school psychologists; and (3) facilitates the application of assessment data to educational settings (D'Amato et al., 1999; Taylor & Fletcher, 1990; Telzrow, 1989; Williams & Boll, 1997).

As noted earlier, seven domains of child performance are featured in this model, each representing a critical area of functioning for the early childhood population. Examples of specific instruments and procedures that may be appropriate for assessing these traits in children between the ages of approximately 3 and 6 years are depicted by domain in the Appendix to this chapter. One important caveat regarding the assessment of child traits that is uniquely relevant to this chapter's focus on young children is that standardized norm-referenced tests may be incorporated to a lesser extent than is the case with older children (Anderson et al., 2001; Baron & Gioia, 1998). Several limitations of measures that are commonly employed in the neuropsychological assessment of children have been identified in the literature, including low-interest content, absent or restricted age-based norms, unauthentic task requirements, and insensitivity to subtle changes over time. Furthermore, from a developmental perspective, formal assessment may be negatively impacted by the young child's limited goal orientation, inability to sustain attention, general comfort level, or lack of exposure to a structured educational setting.

Because of the inherent limitations in obtaining reliable and valid findings when testing very young children, the problem analysis process may emphasize a variety of direct and indirect assessment approaches to assist in understanding core cognitive and psychosocial constructs (Baron & Gioia, 1998). Examples of methods that may be particularly helpful for supplementing findings from individually administered tests include direct observations in authentic settings; analogue assessments that examine children's interaction with specifically selected stimuli or under prescribed conditions (Espy et al., 2001; Ylvisaker & Gioia, 1998); interviews of parents, caregivers, and teachers (Taylor et al., 2002); direct measures of early literacy skills (DIBELS, 2003; Good, Simmons, & Kame'enui, 2001); and functional behavioral assessment (Witt, Daly, & Noell, 2000). Several of these are direct assessment approaches, which are preferred over higher-inference standardized norm-referenced measures because of their social validity and treatment utility, their potential for reducing systematic bias, and their usefulness for evaluating intervention effectiveness (Telzrow & McNamara, 2001).

In addition to a thorough assessment of child performance in these seven domains, the problem analysis phase also involves assessment of the biological and environmental factors that influence child traits and may be contributing to the identified concern or manifest disability. Upah and Tilly (2002) employ the acronym ICEL to represent the four major areas that are relevant for problem analysis and are amenable to intervention design: instruction, curriculum, environment, and learner. Examples of instructional factors include engaged time in instruction, incentives for performance, and the availability of corrective feedback. Curricular factors of relevance may include the difficulty level of the material, the type of stimulus to which the child responds, and the requirement for prerequisite skills. Environmental factors may include the physical layout of the classroom or school, the presence of visual or auditory distractions, and interpersonal demands of the setting. Learner characteristics refer to specific knowledge, skills, and dispositions of the child rather than to a diagnosed disorder.

For very young children who are not engaged in a formal instructional setting, developmentally appropriate modifications to the instruction and curriculum components of Upah and Tilly's (2002) model are necessary. In such instances, alternative age- and setting-specific concepts that are analogous to curriculum and instruction could be substituted for these classroom-based terms. For example, parenting practices might represent the "instruction" in the home for a preschool child, and age-appropriate keystone behaviors associated with play or self-care skills could be conceptualized as the young child's "curriculum." Thus, although the foci of the problem analysis phase may differ if young children are not engaged in formal instruction, the model retains its emphasis on modifiable supports and learner characteristics rather than diagnostic outcomes.

Hypotheses and prediction statements are used to summarize the problem analysis phase and guide treatment planning. Using the earlier example of Sara, the following hypothesis might result from the problem analysis: "Sara rocks back and forth, flicks her hands in front of her face, does not respond to her name or participate in classroom activities unless physically prompted because she does not have selective attention skills." A prediction statement derived from this hypothesis clearly signals a specific intervention: "If Sara were taught selective attention skills, then she would attend to classroom activities and engage in learning without physical prompts."

Several of the paradigms discussed earlier are of key importance during the problem analysis phase. For example, assessments should be developmentally suitable, ecologically sound, and culturally competent and possess acceptable levels of treatment utility. The integration of child performance data and information regarding the ecology in which the child functions during the problem analysis phase clearly highlights the habilitation/rehabilitation focus of the school neuropsychology model of assessment and intervention in early childhood. Unlike a medical model paradigm, in which the objective may be to derive a diagnosis ("Sara rocks back and forth, flicks her hands in front of her face, does not respond to her name or participate in classroom activities unless physically prompted *because she has autism*"), this approach emphasizes the ecological factors and learner characteristics that can be modified, which facilitates the design and implementation of interventions.

*Step 3: Intervention Implementation*    Child neuropsychology traditionally has been characterized by considerably more emphasis on assessment than on intervention (Anderson et al., 2001). This phase of the school neuropsychology approach to assessment and intervention in early childhood extends beyond Taylor and Fletcher's (1990) biobehavioral model of child neuropsychological assessment into the arena of intervention design and implementation. It involves (1) selecting an intervention that has a high probability of success because it addresses the biological and environmental factors that are contributing to the concern and is evidence based, (2) incorporating ongoing measures of the child's response to the intervention as part of implementation, and (3) integrating a measure of intervention fidelity to facilitate subsequent evaluation of intervention effectiveness (Telzrow & Beebe, 2002; Upah & Tilly, 2002).

This stage is particularly salient for U.S. school neuropsychology as a consequence of American children's nearly universal access to educational settings.

Anderson et al. (2001) noted that because reintegration into the educational environment frequently is viewed as a critical milestone following acquired brain injuries, "the school becomes a defacto 'rehabilitation' provider" (p. 389). Similarly, in the case of developmental disorders, the evaluation and service provision mandates of IDEA will likely guarantee the child's participation in an educational setting. The school neuropsychologist's availability in the system to coordinate and facilitate the implementation of interventions represents an advantage over external consultants who may be less familiar with certain aspects of curriculum and instruction, as well as the unique culture of educational systems.

*Step 4: Treatment Evaluation*   The final stage of the school neuropsychology model of assessment and intervention in early childhood results in a decision regarding the effectiveness of the intervention. As a consequence of the disappointing history of the search for aptitude-treatment interactions, this process ultimately requires the application of a single case methodology (Reschly & Ysseldyke, 2002). The treatment evaluation stage involves the examination of two types of data: intervention fidelity data and progress monitoring data. Intervention fidelity data, which may be derived from integrity checks obtained through self-assessment or from independent observers, indicate the degree to which the planned intervention was implemented correctly (Telzrow & Beebe, 2002). This provides a context for interpreting progress monitoring data concerning the student's response to the intervention. Possible decisions include termination of treatment if targeted goals were reached, continuation of the intervention and accompanying data collection, and revision of the treatment plan to produce a more favorable outcome.

## Case Study

The following case study illustrates how the four-step school neuropsychological model of assessment and intervention in early childhood is implemented for a young child with a learning disorder in the areas of reading and writing.

### Step 1: Problem Identification

During Cody's kindergarten year, his parents noticed that he was having difficulty recognizing letters and phonemes and forming letters correctly when using a paper and pencil. In November of his 1st-grade year, Cody's parents and teacher discussed his school progress. His mother noted that although he showed facility in learning new information and memorizing facts and building complicated Lego structures at home, his literacy skills were not progressing adequately. Cody's teacher reported that he was often able to provide oral responses to complicated questions during class discussions, but he was behind his class peers in gaining phonics-related skills. His teacher noted that Cody also engaged in avoidance behaviors when it was time to read silently or orally in class and when faced with writing tasks. For example, during group reading, Cody played with items on his desk, spun his pencil between his fingers, and gazed around the room. Cody displayed high anxiety levels in class, as evidenced by excessive worrying about what others thought of his work, repeatedly stating that he was afraid of making mistakes, and frequent somatic complaints (e.g., headaches and stomach aches). Analysis of his written work indicated that he reversed letters and numbers, often wrote from right to left and began letter formations from the bottom, and did not provide spacing between words. His parents noted that homework requiring age-appropriate reading and writing that was intended to take 15 to 20 minutes often required more than an hour to complete and reduced Cody to tears.

Because he was provided small and large group instruction in phonics and literacy in the classroom and was assisted at home by his parents, it was judged that Cody's lack of progress in literacy skills could not be explained by environmental or ecological factors, such as insufficient instruction or limited exposure to printed text.

### STEP 2: PROBLEM ANALYSIS

Observations by the school psychologist confirmed parent and teacher reports that Cody seemed overwhelmed by tasks requiring reading and writing in class, that he often engaged in escape behaviors to avoid these tasks, and that he was relatively more successful with hands-on perceptual tasks such as building a model in the science center or creating a prototype for an item he wanted to "invent." An interview with Cody's parents revealed that his father had had similar problems acquiring reading and writing skills in the early grades and that such activities continued to require a great amount of effort despite successful completion of high school and membership in the National Honor Society.

Scores obtained on individually administered standardized, norm-referenced tests (SNRTs) indicated that Cody's cognitive abilities were in the very superior range and that his long-term memory, verbal abstract reasoning, vocabulary, social judgment, and perceptual organization were all well above average for his age (see Table 23.1). Although Cody's reading and writing skills were in the average to superior range on SNRTs, this was judged to be the result of a limited test floor, such that low raw scores are associated with average standard scores. During the administration of an informal reading inventory, Cody often skipped whole lines or sections of the grade-level passage without appearing to notice; had a difficult time reading linking words such as "to, and, but"; read in a monotone voice; and became very frustrated due to his limited reading fluency. Interviews with Cody's parents revealed that they spent 1 to 2 hours per night reinforcing his early reading skills, including helping with homework completion, engaging in paired reading, and direct phonics instruction using a scripted home-teaching method (Distar Reading Program Adapted for Parent and Child; Engelmann, Haddox, & Bruner, 1986).

A functional behavioral assessment conducted in his classroom revealed that Cody engaged in avoidance behaviors when required to read or write independently and that he became anxious when asked to read aloud in class (including somatic complaints of headache and stomach ache, presenting excuses for being unable to read the requested passage, and often losing his place). Curriculum-based assessments indicated that Cody was able to read 28 out of 41 1st-grade words from a Dolch word list and 125 out of 150 words on a 1st-grade mastery word list that had been directly taught in class. Cody was less successful applying decoding rules to nonsense words; when presented with a list of one-syllable nonsense words, he was able to identify only 3 words correctly out of 20 presented. The examiner noted that Cody was able to answer all comprehension questions correctly when a passage was read to him (including inference and higher-level thinking questions) but had limited comprehension when reading independently due to poor decoding and fluency.

**Table 23.1**
Results of Standardized Norm-Referenced Tests for Cody, Grade 1

| Domain | Test | Standard Score/ T-Score | Percentile Rank |
|---|---|---|---|
| General Intellectual Ability | WISC-III | | |
| | −Full Scale IQ | 133 | 99 |
| | −Verbal IQ | 126 | 96 |
| | −Performance IQ | 136 | 99 |
| | WJ-III Cog | | |
| | −General Intellectual Ability | 133 | 99 |
| | −Verbal Ability | 131 | 98 |
| | −Thinking Ability | 132 | 98 |
| | −Phonemic Awareness | 109 | 72 |
| Pre-Literacy and Literacy | WIAT-II | | |
| | −Word Reading | 106 | 66 |
| | −Pseudoword Decoding | 98 | 45 |
| | −Spelling | 98 | 45 |
| | −Written Expression | 94 | 34 |
| | WJ-III Ach | | |
| | −Reading Composite | 109 | 72 |
| | −Written Expression | 131 | 98 |
| | −Reading Vocabulary | 104 | 60 |
| Communication | PPVT-III | 109 | |
| | TOLD-P:3 | | |
| | −Spoken Lang Quotient | 111 | |
| | −Listening Quotient | 106 | |
| | −Speaking Quotient | 106 | |
| Perceptual Motor Ability | Visual Motor Integration Test | 99 | 47 |
| Social and Adaptive Functioning | BASC: Teacher Rating | | |
| | −Anxiety | 87 | 99 |
| | −Attention Problems | 71 | 97 |
| | −Learning Problems | 69 | 94 |
| | −School Problems Comp. | 71 | 96 |
| | BASC: Parent Rating | | |
| | −Anxiety | 89 | 99 |
| | −Attention Problems | 66 | 83 |

*Note:* BASC = Behavior Assessment Scale for Children; PPVT-III = Peabody Picture Vocabulary Test, third edition; TOLD-P:3 = Test of Language Development-Primary, third edition; VMI = The Beery-Buktenica Test of Visual-Motor Integration; WIAT-II = Wechsler Individual Achievement Test, second edition; WISC-III = Wechsler Intelligence Scale for Children, third edition; WJ-III Ach = Woodcock Johnson Tests of Achievement, third edition; WJ-III Cog = Woodcock Johnson Tests of Cognitive Ability, third edition.

The following hypothesis was derived from the problem analysis: Cody becomes anxious and self-conscious during reading and writing tasks because these skills are less well developed than would be predicted for his age and overall ability because he has not been able to "crack the code" due to a developmental reading disability. A prediction statement derived from this hypothesis is: If Cody learned phonetic decoding and recoding skills through a scripted (direct and specific) phonics-based program including overlearning at his current instructional level, he would increase his reading fluency skills and demonstrate less anxiety.

STEP 3: INTERVENTION IMPLEMENTATION

The team at Cody's school concluded that he was eligible for special education because of a specific learning disability and developed an individualized education program (IEP) to address his needs in March of his 1st-grade year. His IEP included specific interventions to teach decoding strategies for identifying beginning, medial, and ending sounds in order to improve reading fluency. The intervention specialist provided direct phonics instruction (choral reading) at his instructional level in a small group setting for 60 minutes each school day. To improve Cody's writing skills, visual cues and teacher prompts were used to teach correct formation of upper- and lower-case letters, letter/word spacing, and grammar and capitalization when writing beginning sentences.

In addition to these examples of specially designed instruction, other components of Cody's IEP included consultation between his general education teacher and the special education resource teacher, repeated directions and questions in class, shortened assignments, scribing to allow documentation of Cody's mastery of knowledge in content areas, oral tests when appropriate, computer usage with word-prediction software, and daily journaling with assistance from the resource teacher in the general education classroom. At home, Cody's parents continued to provide daily 15-minute lessons in direct phonics instruction using the Distar Reading Program and also engaged in paired reading to enhance his fluency.

STEP 4: TREATMENT EVALUATION

Data were reviewed at the end of Cody's 1st-grade year to determine how much progress he had made toward his individual goals. The following excerpt from Cody's IEP summarizes present levels of performance after 3 months of intervention:

Cody performs with much less anxiety if he is given assignments broken down into smaller groupings, and he is able to check his work before moving on to the next assignment. His handwriting has greatly improved. Although he continues to display some letter and word reversals, when he takes his time and concentrates, he can form his letters correctly, use adequate spacing, and use the left margin while writing. Cody is able to fluently read short passages at the Primer level as assessed by the Brigance Diagnostic. When given short passages at the lower to upper 1st-grade level, he is able to read using correct decoding strategies and with less hesitation. Cody is able to decode beginning, medial, and ending sounds in new words presented to him. When given three words, he was able to write a complete sentence

**Table 23.2**
Progress Monitoring Data for Cody, Grade 2

| Measure | September | February | May |
|---|---|---|---|
| DIBELS Oral Reading Fluency | 67 wcpm | 86 wcpm | 125 wcpm |
| Written Expression Fluency | 8/16 wsc | 33/38 wsc | 36/49 wsc |
| Dolch Sight Word List, Grade 2 | 37/46 correct | 43/46 correct | 46/46 correct |

*Notes:* wcpm = Words correct per minute; wsc = Words spelled correctly.

**Table 23.3**

Standardized Achievement Test Results for Cody, Grade 2

| Iowa Tests of Basic Skills | National Percentile Rank |
| --- | --- |
| Vocabulary | 39 |
| Reading Comprehension | 51 |
| Word Analysis | 82 |
| Spelling | 24 |
| Math Problems | 92 |
| Social Studies | 86 |
| Science | 88 |

correctly adding necessary words and using grade-level grammar skills. He is able to correctly spell at least 9 out of 10 spelling words on a weekly basis and can correctly spell beginning and ending sounds of unfamiliar words; he continues to struggle with letter sequencing in medial sounds when writing. Cody continues to use visual aids such as alphabet strips or classroom posters to help him write letters and words correctly.

*Ongoing Progress Monitoring*   To ensure that Cody continued to make progress and to determine the need for additional interventions, his IEP team monitored his reading and writing fluency through ongoing, informal assessments. The Dynamic Indicators of Basic Early Literacy Skills (DIBELS) was administered at the beginning, middle, and end of his 2nd-grade school year, and these results demonstrated continuing progress, with attainment of age- and grade-appropriate reading fluency by the end of his 2nd-grade year (see Table 23.2). Progress in written expression was evaluated by reviewing his daily journal entries to a verbal prompt provided by the teacher. Review of prompts from the beginning, middle, and end of the year demonstrated a consistent trend of an increase in the number of words written across this period. The Iowa Test of Basic Skills, administered to Cody's 2nd-grade class in September of that year, resulted in average to above-average scores relative to his same-age peers (see Table 23.3).

## CONCLUSION

The school neuropsychology of assessment and intervention in early childhood is guided by several assumptions about children, assessment, and intervention. The authors contend that children's behavior and functioning must be viewed through developmental, ecological, and culturally competent lenses; that assessments must yield results that have utility for intervention planning; that selected treatments must have a high probability of success; and that the actual result for an individual child must be determined through monitoring of performance over time. All of these assumptions are incorporated in the four-stage problem-solving model described in this chapter. The case study of Cody illustrated how this approach facilitates the intersection of the complementary orientations of neuropsychology and school psychology and contributes to timely problem identification and intervention implementation in the key area of literacy.

## Appendix: Selected Test Instruments in Seven Domains of Child Characteristics

| Instrument | Age | Time | Scores | Special Population | Comments |
|---|---|---|---|---|---|
| **General Intellectual Ability** | | | | | |
| Differential Abilities Scale (DAS; Elliott, 1990) | Preschool level 2.6 to 7.11 | 25–65 min. | Standard scores (100/15); AE scores | Hearing impaired, cognitive delay, limited English, communication disorders, gifted, learning disabilities | *Features:* Verbal and nonverbal scores for children ≥ 3–6; General Conceptual Ability score; assessment of conceptual reasoning skills; early literacy and numeracy skills; computer scoring available<br>*Impression:* Nonverbal index for young child is a strength |
| Stanford-Binet Intelligence Scales, 5th edition (SBV; Roid, 2003) | 2.0 to 85+ | 5 min. per subtest | Standard scores (100/15); Subtest scores (10/3); AE scores; Change-sensitivity scores | Cognitive delay, communication disorders, gifted, hearing impaired, limited English, learning disabilities, autistic spectrum disorders | *Features:* Verbal, Nonverbal, and Full Scale scores; factors include: Fluid Reasoning, Knowledge, Quantitative Reasoning, Visual-Spatial Processing, and Working Memory; computer scoring available<br>*Impression:* Important component in a comprehensive early childhood evaluation |
| Wechsler Preschool and Primary Scale of Intelligence, 3rd edition (WPPSI-III; Wechsler, 2002) | 2.6 to 7.3 | 2.6 to 3.11 = 30–45 min.; 4.0 to 7.3 = 45–60 min. | Standard scores (100/15); Subtest scores (10/3); percentile rank; AE scores | Cognitive delay, gifted, autism, language disorders, learning disabilities, ADHD | *Features:* Co-normed with the WIAT-II; Verbal, Nonverbal, and Full Scale scores; computer scoring available<br>*Impression:* Reduced test time over earlier edition; important component in a comprehensive early childhood evaluation |
| Woodcock-Johnson III Tests of Cognitive Abilities (WJ III; Woodcock, McGrew, & Mather, 2001) | 2.0 to 90+ | Standard battery = 35–45 min.; Extended battery = 90–110 min. | Standard scores (100/15); percentile rank; AE/GE scores; discrepancy scores | Cognitive delay, learning disabilities, communication disorders, ADHD | *Features:* Co-normed with WJ III Tests of Achievement; General Intellectual Ability score; broad cognitive areas: Verbal Ability, Thinking Ability, and Cognitive Efficiency<br>*Impression:* Important component in a comprehensive early childhood evaluation |

## Communication

| | | | | | |
|---|---|---|---|---|---|
| Bracken Basic Concept Scale-Revised (Bracken, 1998) | 2.6 to 7.11 | 30 min. | Standard scores (100/15); percentile rank; concept age equivalents | Cognitive delay, autistic spectrum disorders, communication disorders | *Features:* School readiness level; linguistic concept knowledge; Spanish version; linked to Bracken Concept Development Program *Impression:* Self-/Social Awareness subtest helpful when assessing children with PDD; results helpful for intervention design |
| Preschool Language Scale, 4th edition (PLS4; Zimmerman, Steiner, & Pond, 2002) | Birth to 6.11 | 20–45 min. | Standard scores (100/15); percentile rank; AE scores | Cognitive delay, autistic spectrum disorders, communication disorders, reading disorders | *Features:* Scores for Total Language, Auditory Comprehension, and Expressive Communication; Spanish version; includes a caregiver questionnaire; assessment of early literacy and phonological awareness *Impression:* High interest content; results helpful for intervention design |
| Comprehensive Assessment of Spoken Language (CASL; Woolfolk, 1999) | 3.0 to 21.11 | 3–5 = 30 min.; > 5 = 45 min. | Standard scores (100/15); percentile rank; AE scores; NCE; stanines | Cognitive delay, autistic spectrum disorders, language disorders, dyslexia, aphasia | *Features:* Core subtests for ages 3–4: Basic Concepts, Syntax Construction, and Pragmatic Judgment; Core subtests for ages 5–6: Antonyms, Syntax Construction, Paragraph Comprehension, and Pragmatic Judgment *Impression:* Especially helpful for the assessment of a young child's social language |
| Expressive One-Word Picture Vocabulary Test (EOWPVT; Brownell, 2000a) | 2.0 to 18.11 | 15–20 min. | Standard scores (100/15); percentile rank; AE scores | Communication disorders, reading disorder, bilingual | *Features:* Verbal retrieval of nouns, verbs, and categories; co-normed with ROWPVT; Spanish version (ages 4–12) *Impression:* Easy to administer; high interest pictures; limited attention skills required; results helpful for intervention design |
| Receptive One-Word Picture Vocabulary Test (ROWPVT; Brownell, 2000b) | 2.0 to 18.11 | 15–20 min. | Standard scores (100/15); percentile rank; AE scores | Language disorder, bilingual, emotional disturbance, selective mutism, motor impaired | *Features:* Co-normed with EOWPVT; Spanish version (ages 4–12) *Impression:* Easy to administer; high interest pictures; limited attention skills required; results helpful for intervention design |

*(continued)*

Appendix: Selected Test Instruments in Seven Domains of Child Characteristics (*Continued*)

| Instrument | Age | Time | Scores | Special Population | Comments |
|---|---|---|---|---|---|
| Test of Language Competence, expanded edition (Wiig, 1988) | Level 1 5.0 to 9.11 | 30–40 min. | Standard scores (100/15); percentile rank; AE scores; NCE; stanines | Autistic spectrum disorders, language disorders, learning disabilities, cognitive delay | *Features:* Areas include: Inferences, Ambiguity, Figurative Language, Recreating Speech Acts *Impression:* Especially helpful in the assessment of a young child's social language |
| Clinical Evaluation of Language Fundamentals Preschool (CELF-Preschool; Wiig, Secord, & Semel, 1992) | 3.0 to 6.11 | 30–45 min. | Standard scores (100/15); Subtest scores (10/3); percentile rank; AE scores | Autistic spectrum disorders, language disorders, cognitive delay | *Features:* Scores of Total, Expressive and Receptive language; assesses semantics, morphology, and syntax, and auditory memory *Impression:* Primarily picture based; requires sustained attention; results helpful for intervention design |
| **Nonverbal Reasoning** | | | | | |
| Leiter International Performance Scale (LIPS; Leiter, 1979) | 2.0 to adult | 30–45 min. | Revised equivalents (updated) | Hearing impaired, autistic spectrum disorders, ADHD, cognitive delay | *Features:* Demands on language, time, fine motor, and attention are minimized; opportunities for demonstration *Impression:* Despite dated norms and limited psychometrics retains utility; high interest content; manipulative/hands-on approach; helpful when evaluating children with PDD |
| Leiter International Performance Scale-Revised (Roid & Miller, 1997) | 2.0 to 20.11 | 25–40 min. | Standard scores (100/15); percentile rank; AE/GE scores | Hearing impaired, TBI, cognitive delay, limited English, diverse culture, ESL | *Features:* Language demands minimized; includes social-emotional rating scales; domains include: Visualization and Reasoning, Attention, and Memory; growth scores to assess progress; computer scoring available *Impression:* Strong attention component required for the young child |

| Instrument | Age range | Administration time | Scores | Disorders | Features / Impression |
| --- | --- | --- | --- | --- | --- |
| Goodman Lock Box (Goodman, 1981) | 2.0 to 5.11 | 10 min. | percentile rank | Cognitive delay, ADHD, autistic spectrum disorders | *Features:* Language demands minimized; domains include: Competence, Organization, and Aimless Actions. *Impression:* Highly engaging format; challenge to score; opportunity to observe behaviors in a semi-structured format; helpful when evaluating children with PDD |

**Perceptual Motor Ability**

| Instrument | Age range | Administration time | Scores | Disorders | Features / Impression |
| --- | --- | --- | --- | --- | --- |
| The Beery-Buktenica Developmental Test of Visual-Motor Integration, 5th edition (VMI-5; Beery & Beery, 2004) | Short Form 2.0 to 7.0 | 10 min. | Standard scores (100/15); AE scores | Nonverbal LD, dysgraphia, ADHD, executive functions, autistic spectrum disorders | *Features:* Visual Perceptual and Motor Coordination supplemental sections; lists developmental milestones for ages birth to 6; results useful for IEP and IFSP goals. *Impression:* High interest content; physical involvement promotes engagement; results helpful for intervention design |
| Peabody Developmental Motor Scales, 2nd edition (PDMS-2; Folio & Fewell, 2000) | Birth to 5.0 | 45–60 min. | Scaled scores; T-scores; z-scores; AE scores | Motor impairment | *Features:* Total, fine and gross motor scores; link results to Peabody Motor Activities Program (PMAP); computer scoring available. *Impression:* High interest content |
| Bruininks-Oseretsky Test of Motor Proficiency (BOT; Bruininks, 1978) | 4.6 to 14.5 | Short Form = 15–20 min. | Standard scores; percentile rank; stanines | Motor impairment | *Features:* Fine and gross motor scores. *Impression:* High interest content |

**Literacy—Pre-Literacy**

| Instrument | Age range | Administration time | Scores | Disorders | Features / Impression |
| --- | --- | --- | --- | --- | --- |
| Lindamood Auditory Conceptualization Test (LAC; Lindamood & Lindamood, 1979) | Pre-K to adult | 10 min. | Criterion referenced | Reading disorder, spelling disorder | *Features:* Assessment of sound discrimination and word segmentation; Spanish version. *Impression:* High interest content; results helpful for intervention design |
| Comprehensive Test of Phonological Processing (CTOPP; Wagner, Torgesen, & Rashotte, 1999) | Level 1 5.0 to 6.11 | 30 min. | Standard scores (100/15); subtest scaled scores (10/3); percentile rank; AE/GE scores | Reading disorders | *Features:* Composite scores include: Phonological Awareness, Phonological Memory, and Rapid Naming; practice items. *Impression:* Audiotape and picture format requires sustained attention; results helpful for intervention design |

(continued)

Appendix: Selected Test Instruments in Seven Domains of Child Characteristics (*Continued*)

| Instrument | Age | Time | Scores | Special Population | Comments |
|---|---|---|---|---|---|
| Test of Phonological Awareness (TOPA; Torgesen & Bryant, 1994) | Kindergarten version 5.0 to 6.11 | 15–20 min. | Standard scores (100/15); percentile rank; T-scores; z-scores; stanines; NCE | Reading disorders, general class screener | *Features*: Kindergarten and early elementary versions; group or individual administration *Impression*: Physical involvement promotes engagement; practice items helpful; results helpful for intervention design |
| Dynamic Indicators of Basic Early Literacy Skills, 6th edition (DIBELS; Good & Kaminski, 2002) | Preschool through 3rd grade | Brief probes | Benchmark goals | Reading disorders, general class screener | *Features*: Curriculum Based Measurement; assessment of phonological awareness, alphabetic principle, and fluency; free download from Internet; Spanish version *Impression*: Periodic assessment to monitor progress; results helpful for intervention design and evaluation |
| **Executive Functions** | | | | | |
| The Shape School (Espy, 1997) | 32 to 68 months | 45–75 min. | Mean and *SD* | TBI, neurological involvement, impaired executive function | *Features*: Assessment of inhibition and switching processes *Impression*: Engaging storybook format |
| Tower of Hanoi (Welsh, Pennington, & Grossier, 1991) | 3.0 to adult | 20 min. | Mean and *SD* | TBI, neurological involvement, impaired executive function | *Features*: Assessment of problem solving/planning *Impression*: Engaging format |
| NEPSY: A Developmental Neuropsychological Assessment (Korkman, Kirk, & Kemp, 1998) | 3.0 to 12.0 | 3–4 = 45–60 min.; 5–12= 1–2 hours | Standard scores (100/15); subtest scores (10/3); percentile rank | TBI, autistic spectrum disorders, language disorders, cognitive delay, learning disability, ADHD, dyspraxia | *Features*: Core domains: Attention/Executive, Language, Sensorimotor Function, Visuospatial Processing, Memory & Learning *Impression*: Requires sustained attention for the young child; Visuomotor Precision and Imitating Hand Positions subtests helpful when assessing dyspraxia; helpful for intervention design |

| Instrument | Age Range | Time | Scores | Conditions | Features/Impression |
|---|---|---|---|---|---|
| Behavior Rating Inventory of Executive Function (BRIEF; Gioia, Isquith, Guy, & Kenworthy, 2000) | 5.0 to 18.0 | 10–15 min. | T-scores, percentile rank | Impaired executive function, cognitive delay, learning disabilities, autistic spectrum disorders, low birth weight, ADHD, Tourette's disorder | *Features:* Parent and teacher forms; indices of behavior regulation, metacognition, and executive function. *Impression:* Results helpful for intervention design |

**Social and Adaptive Functioning**

| Instrument | Age Range | Time | Scores | Conditions | Features/Impression |
|---|---|---|---|---|---|
| Child Development Inventory (CDI; Ireton, 1992) | 1.0 to 6.0 | 60 min. | AE scores | Cognitive delay, autistic spectrum disorders, communication disorders, motor impairment | *Features:* Completion by parent or caregiver; domains include: Social Development, Self Help, Gross Motor, Fine Motor, Language, Letters & Numbers; audiotape version. *Impression:* Results helpful for intervention design |
| Vineland Adaptive Behavior Scale (Sparrow, Balla, & Cicchetti, 1984) | Birth to adult | 60 min. | Standard scores (100/15); percentile rank; AE scores | TBI, cognitive delay, ADHD, learning disabilities, autistic spectrum disorders | *Features:* Parent Interview—Survey and Expanded versions; teacher completion form; Adaptive Behavior Composite; domains include: Motor Skills for children < 6 years of age, Daily Living Skills, Socialization, and Communications. *Impression:* Updating needed, results helpful for intervention design |
| Scales of Independent Behavior-Revised (SIB-R; Bruininks, Woodcock, Weatherman, & Hill, 1996) | Early Development Form Infant to 6.0 | Early Development = 15–20 min. | Standard scores (100/15); percentile rank; AE scores | TBI, ADHD, learning disability, autistic spectrum disorders, cognitive delay | *Features:* Completion by parent; early development, short and full form; assesses behaviors in multiple settings. *Impression:* Results helpful for intervention design |
| Social Skills Rating System (SSRS; Gresham & Elliott, 1990) | 3.0 to 18.0 | 10–25 min. per questionnaire | Standard scores (100/15); percentile rank | TBI, cognitive delay, ADHD, learning disability, autistic spectrum disorders, emotional disturbance | *Features:* Preschool teacher and parent forms; Preschool areas: Social Skills and Problem Behaviors; computer scoring available. *Impression:* Provides information regarding positive and negative behaviors; results helpful for intervention design |

(continued)

Appendix: Selected Test Instruments in Seven Domains of Child Characteristics (*Continued*)

| Instrument | Age | Time | Scores | Special Population | Comments |
|---|---|---|---|---|---|
| Child Behavior Checklist (CBCL; Achenbach & Rescorla, 2000) | 1.6 to 5.0 | 10–15 min. | T-scores | Autistic spectrum disorders, TBI, emotional disturbance, language disorders | *Features:* Completed by parent/caregiver; *DSM-IV* linked categories; Spanish version; includes a language survey for children 18–35 months; computer scoring available <br> *Impression:* Comprehensive coverage of behaviors; results helpful for intervention design |
| Behavior Assessment System for Children, 2nd ed; Reynolds & Kamphaus, 2004) | Preschool Parent and Teacher Forms 2 to 5 | Preschool Parent Rating Scale = 10–20 min.; Preschool Teacher Rating Scale = 10–15 min. | T-scores; percentile rank | Emotional disturbance, ADHD | *Features:* Teacher and Parent response utilizes a 4-point frequency scale; general and clinical norms; differentiates attention from hyperactivity; Parent form: Spanish version available, 4th grade reading level, audio recording available; Structured Developmental History (completed by clinician or parent): Spanish version available; Student Observation System; Parent Feedback Form; computer scoring available <br> *Impression:* Comprehensive measure to identify behavioral problems at home, in school, and in the community, which may be useful for conducting manifestation determinations, functional behavioral assessments, and developing IFSPs. |
| The Childhood Autism Rating Scale (Schopler, Reichler, & Renner, 1988) | 2.0+ | 15–20 min. | 3 Categories—Not Autistic, Mild/moderate, Severe | Cognitive delay, autistic spectrum disorders, communication disorders, emotional disturbance | *Features:* Based on professional observations <br> *Impression:* Focus on classic autism characteristics; results helpful for intervention design |

| Instrument | Age range | Administration time | Scoring | Disorders considered | Features / Impression |
|---|---|---|---|---|---|
| Asperger Syndrome Diagnostic Scale (ASDS; Myles, Bock, & Simpson, 2001) | 5.0 to 18.0 | 10–15 min. | Standard scores (100/15); subscale score (10/3); percentile rank | Cognitive delay, autistic spectrum disorders, emotional disturbance, communication disorders | *Features:* Ratings completed by familiar adult (e.g., parent, teacher, caregiver); *DSM-IV* and *ICD-10* based criteria; subscale areas: Maladaptive, Social, Sensorimotor, Language, and Cognitive. *Impression:* Rating scale does not acknowledge frequency or intensity of behavior; results helpful for intervention design |
| Gilliam Autism Rating Scale (GARS; Gilliam, 1995) | 3.0 to 22.11 | 5–10 min. | Standard score (100/15); Subscale score (10/3); percentile rank | Cognitive delay, autistic spectrum disorders, emotional disturbance, language disorders | *Features:* Ratings completed by familiar adult (e.g., parent, teacher, caregiver); *DSM-IV* and *ICD-10* based criteria; subscale areas: Communication, Social Interaction, Stereotyped Behaviors, Developmental Disturbances; Communication subtest not completed for nonverbal children |
| Gilliam Asperger's Disorder Scale (GADS; Gilliam, 2001) | 3.0 to 22.0 | 5–10 min. | Standard score (100/15); subscale score (10/3); percentile rank | Cognitive delay, emotional disturbance, language disorders, autistic spectrum disorders | *Features:* Ratings completed by familiar adult (e.g., parent, teacher, caregiver); *DSM-IV* and *ICD-10* based criteria; subscale areas: Pragmatic Skills, Social Interaction, Restricted Patterns of Behavior, Cognitive Patterns. *Impression:* Concrete examples provided; results helpful for intervention design |

## REFERENCES

Achenbach, T., & Rescorla, L. (2000). *Child behavior checklist.* Burlington, VT: University of Vermont.

American Association on Mental Retardation. (1992). *Mental retardation: Definition, classification, and systems of supports.* Washington, DC: Author.

American Psychological Association. (2003). Guidelines on multicultural education, training, research, practice, and organizational change for psychologists. *American Psychologist, 58,* 377–402.

Anderson, V., Northam, E., Hendy, J., Wrennall, J. (2001). *Developmental neuropsychology: A clinical approach.* Hove, East Sussex: Psychology Press Ltd.

Aylward, G. P. (1997). *Infant and early childhood neuropsychology.* New York: Plenum Press.

Baron, I. S., & Gioia, G. A. (1998). Neuropsychology of infants and young children. In G. Goldstein, P. D. Nussbaum, & S. R. Beers (Eds.), *Neuropsychology* (pp. 9–34). New York: Plenum Press.

Beery, K. E., & Beery, N. A. (2004). *The Beery-Buktenica Developmental Test of Visual Motor Integration* (5th ed.). Minneapolis, MN: NCS Pearson, Inc.

Beery, K. E., & Buktenica, N. A. (1997). *Developmental Test of Visual-Motor Integration.* (4th ed.). Minneapolis, MN: Pearson Assessments.

Berninger, V. W., Stage, S. A., Smith, D. R., & Hildebrand, D. (2001). Assessment for reading and writing intervention: A three-tier model for prevention and remediation. In J. J. W. Andrews, D. H. Saklofske, & H. L. Janzen (Eds.), *Handbook of psychoeducational assessment: Ability, achievement, and behavior in children* (pp. 195–223). San Diego, CA: Academic Press.

Bernstein, J. H. (2001). Developmental neuropsychological assessment. In K. O. Yeates, M. D. Ris, & H. G. Taylor (Eds.), *Pediatric neuropsychology: Research, theory, and practice* (pp. 405–438). New York: Guilford Press.

Bracken, B. A. (1998). *Bracken Basic Concept Scale-Revised.* San Antonio, TX: Psychological Corporation.

Brownell, R. (Ed.). (2000a). *Expressive One-Word Picture Vocabulary Test-2000 Edition.* Novato, CA: Academic Therapy Publications.

Brownell, R. (Ed.). (2000b). *Receptive One-Word Picture Vocabulary Test-2000 Edition.* Novato, CA: Academic Therapy Publications.

Bruininks, R. H. (1978). *Bruininks-Oseretsky Test of Motor Proficiency.* Circle Pines, MN: American Guidance Service.

Bruininks, R. H., Woodcock, R. W., Weatherman, R. E., & Hill, B. K. (1996). *Scales of Independent Behavior-Revised.* Itasca, IL: Riverside.

Chambless, D. L., & Ollendick, T. H. (2001). Empirically supported psychological interventions: Controversies and evidence. *Annual Review of Psychology, 52,* 685–716.

D'Amato, R. C., & Dean, R. S. (1988). School psychology practice in a department of neurology. *School Psychology Review, 17,* 416–420.

D'Amato, R. C., Rothlisberg, B. A., & Leu Work, P. H. (1999). Neuropsychological assessment for intervention. In C. R. Reynolds & T. B. Gutkin (Eds.), *Handbook of school psychology* (3rd ed., pp. 452–475). New York: Wiley.

Dennis, M. (2001). Childhood medical disorders and cognitive impairment: Biological risk, time, development, and reserve. In K. O. Yeates, M. D. Ris, & H. G. Taylor (Eds.), *Pediatric neuropsychology: Research, theory, and practice* (pp. 3–22). New York: Guilford Press.

DIBELS. (2003, August 20). Retrieved December 5, 2003, from http://dibels.uoregon.edu/index.php.

Dunn, L. M., & Dunn, L. M. (1997). *Peabody Picture Vocabulary Test–3rd ed.* Circle Pines, MN: American Guidance Service.

Elliott, C. D. (1990). *Differential Abilities Scale.* San Antonio, TX: The Psychological Corp.

Engelmann, S., Haddox, P., & Bruner, E. (1986). *Teach your child to read in 100 easy lessons.* New York: Simon & Shuster.

Espy, K. A. (1997). The Shape School: Assessing executive function in preschool children. *Developmental Neuropsychology, 13,* 495–499.

Espy, K. A., Kaufmann, P. M., Glisky, M. L., & McDiarmid, M. D. (2001). New procedures to assess executive functions in preschool children. *The Clinical Neuropsychologist, 15,* 46–58.

Fletcher, J. M., & Taylor, H. G. (1984). Neuropsychological approaches to children: Towards a developmental neuropsychology. *Journal of Clinical Neuropsychology, 6,* 39–56.

Fletcher-Janzen, E., Strickland, T. L., & Reynolds, C. R. (2000). *Handbook of cross-cultural neuropsychology.* New York: Kluwer Academic/Plenum Press.

Folio, M. R., & Fewell, R. (2000). *Peabody Developmental Motor Scales–2nd ed.* Itasca, IL: Riverside.

Gill, C. J., Kewman, D. G., & Brannon, R. W. (2003). Transforming psychological practice and society: Policies that reflect the new paradigms. *American Psychologist, 58,* 305–312.

Gilliam, J. E. (1995). *Gilliam Autism Rating Scale.* Austin, TX: ProEd.

Gilliam, J. E. (2001). *Gilliam Asperger's Disorder Scale.* Austin, TX: ProEd.

Gioia, G. A., Isquith, P. K., Guy, S. C., & Kenworthy, L. (2000). *Behavior Rating Inventory of Executive Function.* Odessa, FL: Psychological Assessment Resources.

Good, R. H., III., & Kaminski, R. A. (Eds.). (2002). *Dynamic Indicators of Basic Early Literacy Skills–6th Edition.* Eugene, OR: Institute for the Development of Educational Achievement. Available: http://dibels.uoregon.edu.

Good, R. H., III, Simmons, D. C., & Kame'enui, E. J. (2001). The importance and decision-making utility of a continuum of fluency-based indicators of foundational reading skills for third-grade high stakes outcomes. *Scientific Studies of Reading, 5,* 257–288.

Goodman, J. F. (1981). *Goodman lock box.* Wood Dale, IL: Stoelting Company.

Gresham, F. M., & Elliott, S. N. (1990). *Social Skills Rating System.* Circle Pines, MN: American Guidance Service.

Hammill, D. D., & Newcomer, P. L. (1997). *Test of Language Development: Primary* (3rd ed.). Circle Pines, MN: American Guidance Service.

Hayes, S. C., Nelson, R. O., & Jarrett, R. B. (1987). The treatment utility of assessment: A functional approach to evaluating assessment quality. *American Psychologist, 42,* 963–974.

Hynd, G. W., & Obrzut, J. E. (Eds.). (1981). *Neuropsychological assessment and the school-age child: Issues and procedures* (pp. 237–275). San Diego, CA: Grune & Stratton.

Ireton, H. (1992). *Child Development Inventory.* Minneapolis, MN: Behavior Science Systems.

Korkman, M., Kirk, U., & Kemp, S. (1998). *NEPSY: A Developmental Neuropsychological Assessment.* San Antonio, TX: Psychological Corporation.

Leiter, R. G. (1979). *Leiter International Performance Scale.* Wood Dale, IL: Stoelting Company.

Lentz, F. E., Jr., Allen, S. J., & Ehrhardt, K. E. (1996). The conceptual elements of strong interventions in school settings. *School Psychology Quarterly, 11,* 118–136.

Lindamood, C. H., & Lindamood, P. (1979). *Lindamood Auditory Conceptualization Test.* Austin, TX: ProEd.

Long, C. J. (1996). Neuropsychological tests: A look at our past and the impact that ecological issues may have on our future. In R. J. Sbordone & C. J. Long (Eds.), *Ecological
validity of neuropsychological testing* (pp. 1–14). Delray Beach, FL: St. Lucie Press.

Lynch, E. W., & Hanson, M. J. (1998). *Developing cross-cultural competence* (2nd ed.). Baltimore: Brookes.

Marlowe, W. B. (2000). Multicultural perspectives on the neuropsychological assessment of
children and adolescents. In E. Fletcher-Janzen, T. L. Strickland, & C. R. Reynolds (Eds.),
*Handbook of cross-cultural neuropsychology* (pp. 145–165). New York: Kluwer Academic/
Plenum Press.

McMahon, B. T., & Shaw, L. R. (1996). Neuropsychology and rehabilitation counseling:
Bridging the gap. In R. J. Sbordone & C. J. Long (Eds.), *Ecological validity of neuropsychological testing* (pp. 369–386). Delray Beach, FL: St. Lucie Press.

Myles, B., Bock, S., & Simpson, R. (2001). *Asperger Syndrome Diagnostic Scale*. Circle Pines,
MN: American Guidance Service.

National Association of School Psychologists. (2003). *Portraits of children: Culturally competent assessment*. Bethesda, MD: Author.

Pledger, C. (2003). Discourse on disability and rehabilitation issues: Opportunities for
psychology. *American Psychologist, 58,* 279–284.

President's Council on Special Education Excellence. (2002). *A new era: Revitalizing special education for children and their families*. Washington, DC: U.S. Department of
Education.

The Psychological Corporation. (2002). *Wechsler Individual Achievement Test* (2nd ed.). San
Antonio, TX: Author.

Reschly, D. J. (2000). Assessment and eligibility determination in the Individuals with
Disabilities Education Act of 1997. In C. F. Telzrow & M. Tankersley (Eds.), *IDEA
Amendments of 1997: Practice guidelines for school-based teams* (pp. 65–104). Bethesda,
MD: National Association of School Psychologists.

Reschly, D. J., & Ysseldyke, J. E. (2002). Paradigm shift: The past is not the future. In
A. Thomas & J. Grimes (Eds.), *Best practices in school psychology IV* (pp. 3–20). Bethesda,
MD: National Association of School Psychologists.

Reynolds, C. R. (1981). The neuropsychological basis of intelligence. In G. W. Hynd & J. E.
Obrzut (Eds.), *Neuropsychological assessment and the school-aged child: Issues and procedures* (pp. 87–124). New York: Grune & Stratton.

Reynolds, C. R., & Kamphaus, R. W. (1992). *Behavior assessment system for children*. Circle
Pines, MN: American Guidance Service.

Reynolds, C. R., & Kamphaus, R. W. (2004). *Behavior assessment system for children* (2nd
ed.). Circle Pines, MN: American Guidance Service.

Rogers, M. R., & Lopez, E. C. (2002). Identifying critical cross-cultural school psychology
competencies. *Journal of School Psychology, 40,* 115–141.

Roid, G. H. (2003). *Stanford-Binet Intelligence Scales* (5th ed). Itasca, IL: Riverside.

Roid, G. H., & Miller, L. J. (1997). *Leiter International Performance Scale-Revised*. Wood Dale,
IL: Stoelting Company.

Rourke, B. P., Bakker, D. J., Fisk, J. L., & Strang, J. D. (1983). *Child neuropsychology: An introduction to theory, research, and clinical practice*. New York: Guilford Press.

Sbordone, R. J. (1996). Ecological validity: Some critical issues for the neuropsychologist.
In R. J. Sbordone & C. J. Long (Eds.), *Ecological validity of neuropsychological testing*
(pp. 15–41). Delray Beach, FL: St. Lucie Press.

Schopler, E., Reichler, R. J., & Renner, B. R. (1988). *The Childhood Autism Rating Scale*. Circle Pines, MN: American Guidance Service.

Sparrow, S. S., Balla, D. A., & Cicchetti, D. (1984). *Vineland Adaptive Behavior Scales*. Circle Pines, MN: American Guidance Services.

Task Force on Evidence Based Interventions in School Psychology. (2003, November 25). Retrieved December 6, 2003, from http://www.sp-ebi.org.

Task Force on Promotion and Dissemination of Psychological Procedures. (1995). Training in and dissemination of empirically-validated psychological treatments: Report and recommendations. *Clinical Psychology: Science & Practice, 48*, 3–23.

Taylor, H. G., & Fletcher, J. M. (1990). Neuropsychological assessment of children. In G. Goldstein & M. Hersen (Eds.), *Handbook of psychological assessment* (2nd ed., pp. 228–255). New York: Pergamon Press.

Taylor, H. G., Yeates, K. W., Wade, S. L., Drotar, D., Stancin, T., & Minich, N. (2002). A prospective study of short- and long-term outcomes after traumatic brain injury in children: Behavior and achievement. *Neuropsychology, 16*, 15–27.

Telzrow, C. F. (1987). The "So What?" question: Intervention with learning disabled children. In J. M. Williams & C. J. Long (Eds.), *The rehabilitation of cognitive disabilities* (pp. 191–205). New York: Plenum Press.

Telzrow, C. F. (1989). The school psychologist's perspective on testing students with traumatic brain injury. *Journal of Head Trauma Rehabilitation, 7*(1), 23–34.

Telzrow, C. F. (1999). IDEA Amendments of 1997: Promise or pitfall for special education reform? *Journal of School Psychology, 37*, 7–28.

Telzrow, C. F., & Beebe, J. J. (2002). Best practices in facilitating intervention adherence and integrity. In A. Thomas & J. Grimes (Eds.), *Best practices in school psychology IV* (pp. 503–516). Bethesda, MD: National Association of School Psychologists.

Telzrow, C. F., & McNamara, K. (2001). New directions in assessment for students with disabilities. *Work: A Journal of Prevention, Assessment & Rehabilitation, 17*, 105–116.

Thomas, A., & Grimes, J. (Eds.). (2002). *Best practices in school psychology, IV*. Bethesda, MD: National Association of School Psychologists.

Torgesen, J. K., & Bryant, B. R. (1994). *Test of Phonological Awareness*. Austin, TX: ProEd.

Upah, K. R. F., & Tilly, W. D. III. (2002). Best practices in designing, implementing, and evaluating quality interventions. In A. Thomas & J. Grimes (Eds.), *Best practices in school psychology IV* (pp. 483–501). Bethesda, MD: National Association of School Psychologists.

Wagner, R. K., Torgesen, J. K., & Rashotte, C. A. (1999). *Comprehensive Test of Phonological Processing*. Austin, TX: ProEd.

Wechsler, D. (1991). *Wechsler Intelligence Scale for Children* (3rd ed.). San Antonio, TX: Psychological Corporation.

Wechsler, D. (2002). *Wechsler Preschool and Primary Scale of Intelligence–3rd ed*. San Antonio, TX: Psychological Corporation.

Welsh, M. C., Pennington, B. F., & Groisser, D. B. (1991). A normative-developmental study of executive function: A window on prefrontal function in children. *Developmental Neuropsychology, 7*, 131–149.

What Works Clearinghouse. (2003, June 20). Retrieved December 5, 2003, from http://www.w-w-c.org.

Whelan, T. B. (1999). Integrative developmental neuropsychology: A general systems and social-ecological approach to the neuropsychology of children with neurogenetic disorders. In S. Goldstein & C. R. Reynolds (Eds.), *Handbook of neurodevelopmental and genetic disorders in children* (pp. 84–98). New York: Guilford Press.

Wiig, E. H. (1988). *Test of Language Competence-Expanded Edition*. San Antonio, TX: Psychological Corporation.

Wiig, E. H., Secord, W., & Semel, E. (1992). *Clinical evaluation of language fundamentals-preschool.* San Antonio, TX: Psychological Corporation.

Williams, M. A., & Boll, T. J. (1997). Recent advances in neuropsychological assessment of children. In G. Goldstein & T. M. Incagnoli (Eds.), *Contemporary approaches to neuropsychological assessment* (pp. 231–276). New York: Plenum Press.

Witt, J. C., Daly, E. M., & Noell, G. (2000). *Functional assessments: A step-by-step guide to solving academic and behavior problems.* Longmont, CO: Sopris West.

Woodcock, R. W., McGrew, K. S., & Mather, N. (2001). *Woodcock-Johnson III Tests of Achievement.* Itasca, IL: Riverside.

Woodcock, R. W., McGrew, K. S., & Mather, N. (2001). *Woodcock-Johnson III Tests of Cognitive Abilities.* Itasca, IL: Riverside.

Wong, T. M., Strickland, T. L., Fletcher-Janzen, E., Ardila, A., & Reynolds, C. R. (2000). Theoretical and practical issues in the neuropsychological assessment and treatment of culturally dissimilar patients. In E. Fletcher-Janzen, T. L. Strickland, & C. R. Reynolds (Eds.), *Handbook of cross-cultural neuropsychology* (pp. 3–18). New York: Kluwer Academic/Plenum Press.

Woolfolk, E. C. (1999). *Comprehensive Assessment of Spoken Language.* Circle Pines, MN: American Guidance Service.

Yeates, K. O., & Taylor, H. G. (2001). Neuropsychological assessment of children. In J. J. W. Andrews, D. H. Saklofske, & H. L. Janzen (Eds.), *Handbook of psychoeducational assessment: Ability, achievement, and behavior in children* (pp. 415–450). San Diego, CA: Academic Press.

Ylvisaker, M., & Gioia, G. A. (1998). Cognitive assessment. In M. Ylvisaker (Ed.), *Traumatic brain injury rehabilitation: Children and adolescents* (2nd ed., pp. 159–179). Boston: Butterworth-Heinemann.

Ysseldyke, J., Dawson, P., Lehr, C., Reschly, D., Reynolds, M., & Telzrow, C. (1997). *School psychology: A blueprint for training and practice, I. I.* Bethesda, MD: National Association of School Psychologists.

Ysseldyke, J. E., Nelson, J. R., & House, A. L. (2000). Statewide and districtwide assessments: Current status and guidelines for student accommodations and alternate assessments. In C. F. Telzrow & M. Tankersley (Eds.), *IDEA Amendments of 1997: Practice guidelines for school-based teams* (pp. 29–63). Bethesda, MD: National Association of School Psychologists.

Zimmerman, I. L., Steiner, V. G., & Pond, R. E. (2002). *Preschool Language Scale* (4th ed.). San Antonio, TX: Psychological Corporation.

# CHAPTER 24

# Fetal Alcohol Syndrome: Neuropsychological Outcomes, Psychoeducational Implications, and Prevention Models

LeADELLE PHELPS

INTRAUTERINE EXPOSURE TO alcohol has been associated with a variety of negative outcomes referred to as Fetal Alcohol Syndrome (FAS), Fetal Alcohol Effects (FAE), and Alcohol-Related Neurodevelopmental Disorder (ARND; Stratton, Howe, & Battaglia, 1996). The diagnosis of FAS is given when there is (1) prenatal and/or postnatal growth retardation (i.e., weight, length, and/or head circumference below the 10th percentile when corrected for gestational age); (2) evidence of central nervous system involvement (e.g., signs of neurological abnormality, developmental delay, or intellectual impairment); and (3) the characteristic facial dysmorphology (i.e., microcephaly [small head], microphthalmia [small eyes with skin folds at the corners], poorly developed philtrum [vertical ridge between nose and mouth], thin upper lip, and flattening of the midfacial jawbone region). Less severe variations are FAE and ARND. Because FAS/FAE/ARND symptomatology may not be readily evident, underdiagnoses and misdiagnoses are common (for an excellent review on diagnostic pitfalls, refer to Aase, 1995).

The worldwide incidence rate of FAS is now estimated at 0.97 per 1,000 live births (Abel, 1995). This is a twofold increase over previous estimates, the augmentation being related to better sampling procedures. The highest prevalence rates (40 to 46 per 1,000) of FAS worldwide have been reported in the Western Cape region of South Africa (May, Booke, & Gossage, 2000). FAS is viewed as such a major worldwide public health issue that an international meeting representing nine countries was held in Spain to facilitate global collaborative research in diagnosis, neurobehavioral outcomes, and prevention strategies (Riley et al., 2003). South Africa is not alone in having high prevalence rates, for the United States has one of the highest occurrences worldwide, 1.95 per 1,000, compared to only

561

0.08 per 1,000 in Europe (Abel, 1998a). In the United States, poverty is a major factor, with lower socioeconomic status (SES) African American and Native American populations having 10 times higher prevalence rates than middle SES Caucasian samples (Abel, 1995). Given these rates, there are an estimated 2,000 children with FAS born each year in the United States, and FAS-related expenditures per year exceed $250 million (Abel, 1998b).

## NEUROPSYCHOLOGICAL OUTCOMES

Because alcohol ingested by the mother crosses the placenta, the development of a growing fetus's entire central nervous system can be altered when a sufficient amount of alcohol interferes with neurotransmitter production, cell development, cell migration, and brain growth throughout gestation (Kaufman, 1997). Considerable damage can occur before the mother is even aware of her pregnancy. For example, the human brain develops via neurons generated in the ventricles (the innermost brain cavity) that start to migrate to the outer rim of the brain around the *11th* day after gestation, when the embryo is about the size of a grain of rice (Johnson, Swayze, Sato, & Andreasen, 1996). Researchers have documented that alcohol significantly affects the growth and differentiation of these neural cells, resulting in a wide variety of neuroanatomical abnormalities. Likewise, embryonic development of craniofacial features and the forebrain occurs from weeks 4 to 10 (Diewert, Lozanoff, & Choy, 1993). The spectrum of neuropathology related to prenatal alcohol exposure is broad, with no specific *pattern* of brain malformations. Chronicity, severity, and timing of exposure are key variables affecting outcomes (for a review, see Roebuck, Mattson, & Riley, 1998).

### CEREBRAL DYSGENESIS

The reduction in the size of the brain (microcephaly) is one of the hallmark features of FAS and indicative of decreased brain growth or excessive cell death (Roebuck et al., 1998). Early autopsies of children diagnosed with FAS documented severe cerebral dysgenesis (defective or abnormal development) and evidence of abnormal neural and glial migration (e.g., Clarren, Alvord, Sumi, Streissguth, & Smith, 1978; Kinney, Faix, & Braz, 1980). For example, Wisniewski, Dambska, Sher, and Qazi (1983) reported cases with heterotrophic glial clusters (i.e., nonnerve supportive tissue of the brain and spinal cord) in the meninges and white matter of the cerebral cortex. Numerous studies using magnetic resonance imaging (MRI) have documented neuronal migration abnormalities resulting in underdeveloped cerebral hemispheres, fused frontal lobes, and cortical atrophy (Riikonen, Salonen, Partanen, & Verho, 1999; Swayze et al., 1997).

### CALLOSAL DYSGENESIS

The corpus callosum, the major fiber tract connecting the two cerebral hemispheres, starts to develop between weeks 6 and 8 of gestation and is fully formed by 18 to 20 weeks (Barkovich & Norman, 1988). Autopsy studies have documented notable abnormalities in this region, ranging from partial to full agenesis (Clarren et al., 1978; Coulter, Leech, Schaefer, Scheithauer, & Brumbeck, 1993; Kinney et al., 1980; Wisniewski et al., 1983). More recent studies using MRI have reported cases with significantly reduced volume of the corpus callosum (Mattson, Riley, Sowell, & Jennigan, 1997; Riley et al., 1995). In addition, Swayze et al. (1997) reported that patients with more severe facial dysmorphologic characteristics were likely to have more involved callosal abnormalities.

Four recent studies using MRI mapping have compared patients diagnosed with FAS to control participants (Archibald et al., 2001; Bookstein, Sampson, Streissguth, & Connor, 2001; Riikonen et al., 1999; Sowell et al., 2001). All reported callosal area size reduction differences between the groups. Significant displacement was also observed in both the inferior-superior and the anterior-posterior locations on the corpus callosum (Sowell et al., 2001). It has been hypothesized that dysgenesis occurs as a result of (1) arrested growth of the corpus callosum during the first trimester of pregnancy, (2) specific insult to the region of the callosum that was developing at the time of toxic alcohol exposure, and (3) later, more generalized, delayed development related to continued chronic alcohol abuse (Bookstein et al., 2001; Rubinstein, Youngman, & Hiss, 1994). Finally, when comparing MRI results of patients diagnosed with FAS to those with less severe symptoms (i.e., FAE or ARND), subtler dysmorphology was evident (Archibald et al., 2001).

### Hippocampal and Basal Ganglia Dysgenesis

The hippocampal commisure is a thin sheet of fibers passing under the posterior portion of the corpus callosum; the basal ganglia consist of four masses of gray matter (the caudate, lentiform, amygdaloid nuclei, and claustrum) located deep in the cerebral hemispheres. Early autopsy studies reported hypoplasia of the hippocampus and absent or abnormal basal ganglia (Coulter et al., 1993; Peiffer, Majewski, Fischbach, Bierich, & Volk, 1979; Wisniewski et al., 1983). More recent MRI studies have documented reductions in volume of both these anatomical structures (Archibald et al., 2001; Bhatara et al., 2002; Mattson, Riley, et al., 1997; Riikonen et al., 1999).

## PSYCHOEDUCATIONAL IMPLICATIONS

Data generally support the conclusion that intrauterine alcohol exposure results in a broad range of deficits, with chronicity, timing, and severity of the exposure being associated with a corresponding continuum of negative outcomes (Testa, Quigley, & Eiden, 2003). Different profiles of alcohol-related birth defects are related to varying exposures at critical periods of fetal development. For example, numerous large human prospective studies have documented the following:

1. Chronic heavy alcohol consumption (i.e., an average of three or more drinks a day throughout pregnancy) usually results in structural anomalies, growth retardation, and compromised central nervous system functioning (i.e., entire constellation of FAS).
2. Episodic binge drinking (i.e., six or more drinks in a single day) or chronic consumption restricted to the first and second trimesters of pregnancy significantly increases the probability of general fetal developmental deficits, delay in speech acquisition, and skeletal anomalies. Such episodes/abuse

limited to the third trimester can negatively affect future intellectual and behavioral functioning.
3. Frequent moderate social drinking during pregnancy may result in more subtle neurobehavioral effects (e.g., attention difficulties, slow processing speed, memory problems).
4. Definitive outcomes of light consumption are not conclusive (Aronson & Hagberg, 1998; Kaplan-Estrin, Jacobson, & Jacobson, 1999; Larroque & Kaminski, 1998; Sampson et al., 1997; Streissguth, Barr, Bookstein, Sampson, & Olson, 1999; Testa et al., 2003).

Further diversity in FAS/FAE symptomatology is attributed to maternal and fetal alcohol metabolic rates as well as the modulating influence of the genetic makeup of mother and/or fetus. For example, Streissguth and Dehaene (1993) compared the developmental outcomes of monozygotic (MZ) and dizygotic (DZ) twin pairs born to alcoholic mothers and reported that the teratogenic qualities of ethanol could be modified by genetic differences. Although the twin pairs received comparable levels of prenatal alcohol exposure, FAS/FAE symptomatology was more uniformly expressed in MZ than in DZ twins. The authors concluded that fetal genotype affects the susceptibility of the central nervous system to alcohol.

At birth, infants with intrauterine exposure to alcohol frequently have low birthweight (i.e., below the 10th percentile when adjusted for gestational age), preterm delivery, a small head circumference, facial dysmorphology, general developmental delays, psychomotor retardation, and cognitive deficits (Auti-Ramo, Gaily, & Granstrom, 1992; Borges, Lopez, Medina, Tapia, & Garrido, 1993; Jacobson et al., 1993). As children age, researchers have found that, relative to controls, children with FAS and FAE are impaired on tests of intelligence, attention, learning, memory, fine motor speed, visual-motor integration, and academic competencies (Auti-Ramo, 2000; Mattson, Gramling, Delis, Jones, & Riley, 1997; Wass, Simmons, Thomas, & Riley, 2002). In fact, FAS is now accepted as the leading known cause of mental retardation in the Western world, surpassing even Down syndrome, cerebral palsy, and spina bifida (Olson et al., 1997). Even when matched for intellectual competencies, learners with FAS show inadequate judgment and problem solving, significant social deficits, and impaired working memory (Kelly, Day, & Streissguth, 2000; Richardson, Ryan, Willford, Day, & Goldschmidt, 2002; Thomas, Kelly, Mattson, & Riley, 1998). Finally, diagnoses of Attention-Deficit/Hyperactivity Disorder (ADHD) and Oppositional Defiant Disorder (ODD), as well as subclinical levels of other behavior problems, are frequent (Steinhausen & Spohr, 1998). In fact, ADHD has been found in about 85% of such children, cutting across all IQ categories and varying in severity from mild attention deficits to severe management difficulties (Steinhausen & Spohr, 1998). Specific difficulties in the social domain include an inability to respect personal boundaries, demanding of attention, bragging, stubbornness, poor peer relations, and being overly tactile in social interactions (Kelly et al., 2000).

During adolescence, mental retardation or below-average IQ, behavior problems, ADHD symptomatology (i.e., inattention, distractibility, impulsivity), decreased social competence, and poor school performance continue (Olson, Feldman, Streissguth, Sampson, & Bookstein, 1998; Steinhausen & Spohr, 1998). In adulthood, alcohol or drug dependence, depression, and psychotic disorders are not uncommon (Baer, Sampson, Barr, Connor, & Streissguth, 2003; Famy, Streissguth, & Unis, 1998; O'Connor et al., 2002). Even when cognitive deficits are not severe (i.e., IQ scores in low-average to above-average range), difficulties in concentration, verbal learning, and executive functioning are evident (Connor, Sampson, Bookstein, Barr, & Streissguth, 2001; Kerns, Don, Mateer, & Streissguth, 1997).

## NEUROPSYCHOLOGICAL ASSESSMENT

Given the myriad outcomes evidenced with FAS, the pediatric school psychologist has many assessment tools from which to choose. Following is a short list of suggested measures that were selected based on the constructs measured, proven reliability and validity, and norms for a broad age span.

To assess cognitive functioning, the Woodcock-Johnson III Tests of Cognitive Abilities (WJ III COG; Woodcock, McGrew, & Mather, 2001a) is recommended. Used with individuals from 5 to 95 years of age, the WJ III COG is based on the Cattell-Horn-Carroll (CHC; McGrew, 1997) theory of cognitive abilities and provides not only an index of general intelligence (*g*) but also measures of seven CHC broad abilities: crystallized intelligence (Gc), fluid intelligence (Gf), short-term memory (Gsm), long-term retrieval (Glr), visual-spatial processing (Gv), auditory processing (Ga), and processing speed (Gs). Containing 20 subtests, the WJ III COG allows the examiner to select the appropriate measures to administer based on the reason for referral (Schrank, Flanagan, Woodcock, & Mascolo, 2002). This test was selected over other cognitive measures because of its sound theoretical model and measurement of broad abilities key to FAS assessment (Phelps, McGrew, Knopik, & Ford, 2005). That is, the WJ III COG provides standard scores for crystallized competencies, problem solving, short-term and delayed memory, fine motor speed, visual-motor integration, and verbal learning.

For a more refined measure of short-term learning, memory, and retrieval, the Wide Range Assessment of Memory and Learning, Second Edition (WRAML-2; Adams & Sheslow, 2003) is suggested. With norms for ages 5 to 90, the WRAML-2 provides indices of visual, verbal, working, and delayed memory recall. The California Verbal Learning Test-Children's Version (CVLT-C; Delis, Kramer, Kaplan, & Ober, 1994) and the California Verbal Learning Test, Second Edition (CVLT-II; Delis, Kramer, Kaplan, & Ober, 2000), which is used with adolescents and adults, offer an alternative if one seeks a verbal learning test that includes immediate memory and short-delay free recall and cued recall trials preceded by an interference task. Spanning ages 5 to 89, these two CVLT measures provide useful information regarding error types and cued recall abilities.

If assessing a youngster or young adult with limited language skills, the Wisconsin Card Sorting Test (Grant & Berg, 1993) provides a nonverbal measure of deductive problem solving and responsiveness to feedback. This measure is helpful in identifying ineffective learning strategies and perseveration. Likewise, the Halstead Category Test (CT) offers similar insights. CT norms for children ages 5 to 14 (Reitan, 1987) and older adolescents (Reitan & Wolfson, 1985) are available.

For an assessment of attention, concentration, impulsivity, and distractibility, the Connors' Continuous Performance Test, Second Edition (CPT-II; Connors,

2000) is highly recommended. Children and adolescents respond well to the CPT-II computer format. Requiring only 15 minutes of administration time, the test assesses attention to detail and information-processing efficiency in children 4 years and older.

The comprehensive Woodcock-Johnson III Tests of Achievement (WJ III ACH; Woodcock, McGrew, & Mather, 2001b) can measure academic competencies. Developed simultaneously with the WJ III COG, the WJ III ACH supplies both age- and grade-normed measures of reading fluency and comprehension, math calculation and reasoning skills, writing fluency and expression, listening comprehension, and oral expression. Of particular note are subtests that provide a full appraisal of phonological awareness (i.e., rhyming, deletion, substitution, reversals) and word attack competencies.

Teacher and parent rating forms provide broad-spectrum assessments of behavioral and social competencies for children ages 2 to 16. The Achenbach (1991a, 1991b, 1991c) Teacher Report Form, the parent report, referred to as the Child Behavior Checklist, and a self-report checklist for older children and adolescents (Youth Self Report Form) are cross-informant rating scales that are considered to be a foundation for screening internalizing and externalizing behavior problems (Simonian & Tarnowski, 2004). Scores are reported for behavioral issues related to aggression, ADHD, anxiety, depression, ODD, and social difficulties. Another alternative is the Behavior Assessment System for Children (Reynolds & Kamphaus, 1992), which is also a multidimensional report form with parent (Parent Rating Scale), teacher (Teacher Rating Scale), and self-report forms for children 8 to 11 years (Self-Report of Personality-Child) and adolescents 12 to 18 years (Self-Report of Personality-Adolescent). Scores are reported for composite areas (Externalizing, Internalizing, Behavioral Symptoms, Adaptive Skills, School Problems) and subscales (e.g., aggression, anxiety, impulsivity, social skills).

## PREVENTION MODELS

Effective psychosocial prevention programming is dependent on the identification of specific risk and protective factors. Risk catalysts are associated with higher probability of onset, greater severity, and longer duration of the disorder, whereas protective variables are affiliated with improved resistance and resilience. After successful identification of such factors, highly specific strategies can be developed, with the prevailing intent to reduce risk factors while enhancing protective factors.

To prevent prenatal alcohol exposure, we must not only identify such risk and protective factors, but also distinguish which precursors are the strongest predictors, how such variables interact, and which populations are most vulnerable. Obviously, the population to target is females of childbearing age (i.e., to expose a fetus to drugs, one must first be able to conceive). The identification of variables predictive of alcohol usage among females of childbearing age would aid significantly in the development of early prevention programs designed to intervene before any such exposure has occurred. Likewise, there are three subcategories in the realm of prevention programming: (1) universal preclusion activities designed for general populations with no identified risk status; (2) selective programming targeted to meet the needs of individuals or subgroups who, due to biological, psychological, and/or social considerations, are at significantly higher risk than the general population; and (3) specific procedures intended for high-risk persons who have minimal but nonetheless detectable symptoms of the disorder (Mrazek & Haggerty, 1994). Therefore, targeting nonpregnant females of childbearing age who are at significant risk for alcohol abuse or who are already evidencing such abuse would be appropriate. It is generally hypothesized that multilevel (i.e., primary, secondary, and tertiary) comprehensive prevention programs that target specific populations and focus on precise risk/protective factors would be most efficacious in the prevention of intrauterine alcohol exposure.

To date, no intervention programs directed at reducing or eliminating consumption by pregnant women who abuse alcohol have been successful (for a review of this literature, refer to Abel, 1998c; Schorling, 1993). Likewise, knowledge of the negative consequences of prenatal exposure among minority women of childbearing age whose household income is less than $50,000 is alarmingly poor (Dufour, Williams, Campbell, & Aitkens, 1994). It seems evident that prenatal prevention instruction may be more successful if directed toward adolescents and young adults who have yet, or who have only begun, to experiment with alcohol.

Two significant limitations of previously published primary prevention efforts with adolescents/young adult populations are the reliance on didactic presentations of factual information and the exclusive focus on risk factors. For example, alcohol and drug abuse prevention programs have frequently relied on dissemination of factual information in an effort to increase knowledge, change attitudes, and effect behavior change. Often relying on arousal of fear, such didactic approaches have been shown to affect knowledge and attitudes but have little impact on reducing current use, altering projected intentions, or changing future actions (for two excellent reviews of this literature, refer to Burgess, 1997; Kim, Crutchfield, Williams, & Hepler, 1998). As the old adage goes: "Insight seldom changes behavior."

More recent approaches have focused primarily on the social mores and psychological factors presumed to encourage alcohol use. Such activities as increasing student awareness of peer norms promoting drug use (i.e., social influence model), providing specific skills and techniques to resist inappropriate use (i.e., cognitive-behavioral model), and enhancing general self-esteem (i.e., life skills model) have been implemented with limited success. (Only studies that provided longitudinal follow-up data and utilized a control/experimental group design are cited.) A good example of such a program is Project DARE (Drug Abuse Resistance Education), which was designed to affect 6th- through 12th-grade students' attitudes, beliefs, social skills, and drug use behaviors. Using multilevel analyses (i.e., random-effects ordinal regressions) conducted over 6 years, Rosenbaum and Hanson (1998) reported no long-term effects on a wide range of drug use measures and no lasting effects on hypothesized protective factors. Unfortunately, all the previously documented short-term effects had dissipated by the conclusion of the 6-year follow-up.

Other longitudinal studies have had similar outcomes. For example, the Michigan Model for Comprehensive School Health Education utilized a social pressures resistance skills prevention model completed over a 2-year time frame during the 6th and 7th grades. Using a repeated-measures ANOVA intervention/no intervention research design, Shope, Copeland, Kamp, and Lang (1998) reported that by the 5-year follow-up (completed in the 12th grade), all significant effects on alcohol, cigarette, cocaine, and other drug use had dissipated. Likewise, Werch, Pappas,

Carlson, and DiClemente (1998) completed a brief alcohol prevention program that focused on enhancing protective social/personal factors with 6th-grade children. Although a significant difference in alcohol use between the experimental/control groups was noted at 1-month follow-up, no differences were evident by 1-year post-treatment. In conclusion, the high hopes researchers had for the "new generation" of social/psychological protective variable models that were aimed at the general population (i.e., primary prevention) have been dashed. (For a more in-depth discussion, refer to Brown & Kreft, 1998; Gorman, 1998).

On the positive side, a large-scale drug abuse prevention program (Project Towards No Drug Abuse) involving youth who were at high risk for drug abuse did show significant preventive effects for alcohol and hard drug use at 1-year follow-up (Sussman, Dent, Stacy, & Craig, 1998). Likewise, Chou, et al. (1998) reported significant experimental/control differences at 1.5-year follow-up in the use of cigarettes, alcohol, and marijuana among 6th- and 7th-grade students who were active users of these substances at the time of pretesting. Thus, when efforts are targeted at individuals who are at significantly higher risk for alcohol use, or who already evidence minimal but detectable symptoms of alcohol use/abuse (i.e., secondary and tertiary prevention), results are more positive. However, more longitudinal data (e.g., 5 to 6 years posttreatment) are necessary.

Although here is no crystal ball to guide continuing efforts, findings from past unsuccessful attempts suggest that future alcohol prevention programming should move away from global attempts and shift toward more concerted efforts with specified at-risk populations. In fact, Ernest Abel (1998c), a noted researcher in the area, went so far as to state that the focus must be on *reducing abuse* rather than more generalized endeavors. The most successful programs appear to be those that focus on a select subset of the population (i.e., at-risk status) and incorporate a multitude of risk/protective factors in the curriculum. With this in mind, it is recommended that future efforts focus on the unique psychosocial needs of adolescents/young adult females who are experimenting with early alcohol usage, and that the interventions aim at enhancing individual resilience. Such could be accomplished by a critical evaluation of the sociocultural mores of drinking and drug use and encouraging personal values clarification. Interactive activities that include group discussions, problem solving, and cooperative exercises are suggested. Thus, the proposed prevention model would utilize active individual participation and highlight strengthening specific personal attributes and adaptive coping skills that attenuate the sociocultural pressures promoting drug and alcohol use. Such a prevention program could employ group discussions, modeling, behavioral rehearsal, homework assignments, and frequent feedback as techniques to impact current behavior and future behavioral intentions. Finally, the active participation of parents and extended family members may be of benefit (Ma, Toubbeh, Cline, & Chisholm, 1998). Regardless of the specific programming curriculum, sensitivity to local social mores and cultural awareness is imperative.

## CONCLUSION

Children with medical histories of prenatal alcohol exposure are a heterogeneous population, and their functioning is dependent on many diverse factors. Considerable harm can be done when we make assumptions, overgeneralize, or label a child as "alcohol-exposed." Instead, professionals are encouraged to view exposure to teratogenic substances as one of many risk factors that may have a negative impact on development. Recall that the majority of children with such exposure will likely come from poor neighborhoods and be of minority status. Providing appropriate medical, psychosocial, and educational interventions to such children may be necessary. If warranted, services in the regular classroom may be provided under the ADA Section 504 Other Health Impaired category in the context of an integrated, comprehensive full-service school model.

Finally, by facilitating a better understanding of FAS and FAE, professionals may help mitigate common negative stereotypes and overreactions as well as enhance prevention, early identification, and intervention endeavors. Likewise, by functioning as a liaison with medical personnel and, when warranted, assisting in the development of appropriate school- and community-based support services, we may improve the long-term outlook for these children.

## REFERENCES

Aase, J. M. (1995). Clinical recognition of FAS: Difficulties of detection and diagnosis. *Alcohol Health and Research World, 18,* 5–9.

Abel, E. L. (1995). An update on the incidence of FAS: FAS is not an equal opportunity birth defect. *Neurotoxicology and Teratology, 17,* 437–443.

Abel, E. L. (1998a). Fetal alcohol syndrome: The American paradox. *Alcohol and Alcoholism, 33,* 195–201.

Abel, E. L. (1998b). Prevention of alcohol abuse-related birth effects I: Public education efforts. *Alcohol and Alcoholism, 33,* 411–416.

Abel, E. L. (1998c). Prevention of alcohol abuse-related birth effects: II. Targeting and pricing. *Alcohol and Alcoholism, 33,* 417–420.

Achenbach, T. (1991a). *Child behavior checklist.* Burlington, VT: University of Vermont.

Achenbach, T. (1991b). *Teacher report form.* Burlington, VT: University of Vermont.

Achenbach, T. (1991c). *Youth self report.* Burlington, VT: University of Vermont.

Adams, W., & Sheslow, D. (2003). *Wide range assessment of memory and learning* (2nd ed.). San Antonio, TX: Psychcorp.

Archibald, S. L., Fennema-Notestine, C., Gaunt, A., Riley, E. P., Mattson, S. N., & Jernigan, T. L. (2001). Brain dysmorphology in individuals with severe prenatal alcohol exposure. *Developmental Medicine and Child Neurology, 43,* 148–154.

Aronson, M., & Hagberg, B. (1998). Neuropsychological disorders in children exposed to alcohol during pregnancy: A follow-up study of 24 children to alcoholic mothers in Goeteborg, Sweden. *Alcoholism: Clinical and Experimental Research, 22,* 321–324.

Auti-Ramo, I. (2000). Twelve-year follow-up of children exposed to alcohol in utero. *Developmental Medicine and Child Neurology, 42,* 406–411.

Auti-Ramo, I., Gaily, E., & Granstrom, M. L. (1992). Dysmorphic features in offspring of alcoholic mothers. *Archives of Disease in Childhood, 67,* 712–716.

Baer, J. S., Sampson, P. D., Barr, H. M., Connor, P. D., & Streissguth, A. P. (2003). A 21-year longitudinal analysis of the effects of prenatal alcohol exposure on young adult drinking. *Archives of General Psychiatry, 60,* 377–385.

Barkovich, A. J., & Norman, D. (1988). Anomalies of the corpus callosum: Correlations with further anomalies of the brain. *American Journal of Neurological Research, 9,* 493–501.

Bhatara, V. S., Lovrein, F., Kirkeby, J., Swayze, V., Ubruh, E., & Johnson, V. (2002). Brain function in fetal alcohol syndrome assessed by single photon emission computed tomography. *South Dakota Journal of Medicine, 55,* 59–62.

Bookstein, F. L., Sampson, P. D., Streissguth, A. P., & Connor, P. D. (2001). Geometric morphometrics of corpus callosum and subcortical structures in the fetal alcohol affected brain. *Teratology, 64,* 4 –32.

Borges, G., Lopez, M., Medina, M. E., Tapia, R., & Garrido, F. (1993). Alcohol consumption, low birth weight, and preterm delivery in the National Addictions Survey (Mexico). *International Journal of the Addictions, 28,* 355–368.

Brown, J. H., & Kreft, I. G. (1998). Zero effects of drug prevention programs: Issues and solutions. *Evaluation Review, 22,* 3–14.

Burgess, R. (1997). Deconstructing drug prevention: Towards an alternative purpose. *Drug Education Prevention and Policy, 4,* 271–283.

Chou, D., Montgomery, S., Pentz, M., Rohrbach, L. A., Johnson, C., Andersen, F., et al. (1998). Effects of community-based prevention program in decreasing drug use in high-risk students. *American Journal of Public Health, 88,* 944–948.

Clarren, S. K., Alvord, E. C., Sumi, M., Streissguth, A. P., & Smith, D. W. (1978). Brain malformations related to prenatal exposure to ethanol. *Journal of Pediatrics, 92,* 47–64.

Connor, P. D., Sampson, P. D., Bookstein, F. L., Barr, H. M., & Streissguth, A. P. (2001). Direct and indirect effects of prenatal alcohol damage on executive function. *Developmental Neuropsychology, 18,* 331–354.

Connors, C. K. (2000). *Connors' continuous performance test* (2nd ed.). San Antonio, TX: Psychcorp.

Coulter, L., Leech, R. W., Schaefer, G. B., Scheithauer, B. W., & Brumbeck, R. A. (1993). Midline cerebral dysgenesis, dysfunction of the hypothalamic-pituitary axis and fetal alcohol effects. *Archives of Neurology, 50,* 771–775.

Delis, D. C., Kramer, J. H., Kaplan, J., & Ober, B. A. (1994). *California Verbal Learning Test-Children's Version.* San Antonio, TX: Psychcorp.

Delis, D. C., Kramer, J. H., Kaplan, J., & Ober, B. A. (2000). *California Verbal Learning Test.* (2nd ed.).San Antonio, TX: Psychcorp.

Diewert, V. M., Lozanoff, S., & Choy, V. (1993). Computer reconstructions of human embryonic craniofacial morphology showing changes in relations between face and brain during primary palate formation. *Journal of Craniofacial Genetic Developmental Biology, 13,* 193–201.

Dufour, M. C., Williams, G. D., Campbell, K. E., & Aitkens, S. S. (1994). Knowledge of F. A. S., and the risks of heavy drinking during pregnancy: 1985 and 1990. *Alcohol Health and Research World, 18,* 86–92.

Famy, C., Streissguth, A. P., & Unis, A. S. (1998). Mental illness in adults with fetal alcohol syndrome or fetal alcohol effects. *American Journal of Psychiatry, 155,* 552–554.

Gorman, D. M. (1998). The irrelevance of evidence in the development of school-based drug prevention policy. *Evaluation Review, 22,* 118–146.

Grant, D. A., & Berg, W. A. (1993). *Wisconsin Card Sorting Test.* Odessa, FL: Psychological Assessment Resources.

Jacobson, S. W., Jacobson, J. L., Sokol, R. J., Martier, S. S., Ager, J. W., & Kaplan-Estrin, M. G. (1993). Teratogenic effects of alcohol on infant development. *Alcoholism: Clinical and Experimental Research, 17,* 174–183.

Johnson, V. P., Swayze, V. W., Sato, Y., & Andreasen, N. C. (1996). Fetal alcohol syndrome: Craniofacial and central nervous system manifestations. *American Journal of Medical Genetics, 61,* 329–339.

Kaplan-Estrin, M., Jacobson, S. W., & Jacobson, J. L. (1999). Neurobehavioral effects of prenatal alcohol exposure at 26 months. *Neurotoxicology and Teratology, 21,* 503–511.

Kaufman, M. H. (1997). The teratogenic effects of alcohol following exposure during pregnancy, and its influence on the chromosome constitution of the pre-ovulatory egg. *Alcohol and Alcoholism, 32,* 113–128.

Kelly, S. J., Day, N., & Streissguth, A. P. (2000). Effects of prenatal alcohol exposure on social behavior in humans and other species. *Neurotoxicology and Teratology, 22,* 143–149.

Kerns, K., Don, A., Mateer, C. A., & Streissguth, A. P. (1997). Cognitive deficits in nonretarded adults with fetal alcohol syndrome. *Journal of Learning Disabilities, 30,* 685–693.

Kim, S., Crutchfield, C., Williams, C., & Hepler, N. (1998). Toward a new paradigm in substance abuse and other problem behavior prevention for youth: Youth development and empowerment approach. *Journal of Drug Education, 28,* 1–17.

Kinney, H., Faix, R., & Braz, J. (1980). The fetal alcohol syndrome and neuroblastoma. *Pediatrics, 66,* 130–132.

Larroque, B., & Kaminski, M. (1998). Prenatal alcohol exposure and development at preschool age: Main results of a French study. *Alcoholism: Clinical and Experimental Research, 22,* 295–303.

Ma, G. X., Toubbeh, J., Cline, J., & Chisholm, A. (1998). Fetal alcohol syndrome among Native American adolescents: A model prevention program. *Journal of Primary Prevention, 19,* 43–55.

Mattson, S. N., Gramling, L., Delis, D. C., Jones, K. L., & Riley, E. P. (1997). Global-local processing in children prenatally exposed to alcohol. *Child Neuropsychology, 2,* 165–175.

Mattson, S. N., Riley, E. P., Sowell, E. R., & Jennigan, T. L. (1997). A decrease in the size of the basal ganglia in children with fetal alcohol syndrome. *Alcoholism: Clinical and Experimental Research, 20,* 1088–1093.

May, P. M., & Booke, L., & Gossage, J. P. (2000). Epidemiology of fetal alcohol syndrome in a South African community in the Western Cape Province. *American Journal of Public Health, 90,* 1905–1912.

McGrew, K. S. (1997). Analysis of the major intelligence batteries according to a proposed comprehensive Gf-Gc framework. In D. P. Flanagan, J. L. Glenshaft, & P. L. Harrison (Eds.), *Contemporary intellectual assessment: Theories, tests, and issues* (pp. 151–180). New York: Guilford Press.

Mrazek, R. F., & Haggerty, R. J. (Eds.). (1994). *Reducing risk of mental disorders: Frontiers for preventive intervention research.* Washington, DC: National Academy Press.

O'Connor, M. J., Shah, B., Whaley, S., Cronin, P., Gunderson, B., & Graham, J. (2002). Psychiatric illness in a clinical sample of children with prenatal alcohol exposure. *American Journal of Drug and Alcohol Abuse, 28,* 743–754.

Olson, H. C., Feldman, J. J., Streissguth, A. P., Sampson, P. D., & Bookstein, F. L. (1998). Neuropsychological deficits in adolescents with fetal alcohol syndrome: Clinical findings. *Alcoholism, Clinical, and Experimental Research, 22,* 1998–2012.

Olson, H. C., Streissguth, A. P., Sampson, P. D., Barr, H. M., Bookstein, F. L., & Thiede, K. (1997). Association of prenatal alcohol exposure with behavioral and learning problems in early adolescence. *Journal of the Academy of Child and Adolescent Psychiatry, 36,* 1187–1194.

Peiffer, J., Majewski, F., Fischbach, H., Bierich, J. R., & Volk, B. (1979). Alcohol embryo and fetopathy. *Journal of Neurological Science, 41,* 125–137.

Phelps, L., McGrew, K. S., Knopik, S. N., & Ford, L. (2005). The general (*g*), broad and narrow CHC stratum characteristics of the WJ III and WISC-III tests: A confirmatory cross-battery investigation. *School Psychology Quarterly, 20,* 58–66.

Reitan, R. M. (1987). *Neuropsychological assessment of children.* Tucson, AZ: Neuropsychology Press.

Reitan, R. M., & Wolfson, D. (1985). *Halstead-Reitan Neuropsychological Test Battery: Theory and clinical interpretation.* Tucson, AZ: Neuropsychology Press.

Reynolds, C. R., & Kamphaus, R. W. (1992). *Behavior assessment system for children.* Circle Pines, MN: American Guidance Service.

Richardson, G. A., Ryan, C., Willford, J., Day, N. L., & Goldschmidt, L. (2002). Prenatal alcohol and marijuana exposure: Effects on neuropsychological outcomes at 10 years. *Neurotoxicology and Teratology, 24,* 309–320.

Riikonen, R., Salonen, I., Partanen, K., & Verho, S. (1999). Brain perfusion SPECT and MRI in fetal alcohol syndrome. *Developmental Medicine and Child Neurology, 41,* 652–659.

Riley, E. P., Guerri, C., Calhoun, F., Charness, M. E., Foroud, T. M., Li, T. K., et al. (2003). Prenatal alcohol exposure: Advancing knowledge through international collaboration. *Alcoholism: Clinical and Experimental Research, 27,* 118–135.

Riley, E. P., Mattson, S. N., Sowell, E. R., Jennigan, T. L., Sobel, D. F., & Jones, K. l. (1995). Abnormalities of the corpus callosum in children prenatally exposed to alcohol. *Alcoholism: Clinical and Experimental Research, 19,* 1198–1202.

Roebuck, T. M., Mattson, S. N., & Riley, E. P. (1998). A review of the neuroanatomical findings in children with fetal alcohol syndrome or prenatal exposure to alcohol. *Alcoholism: Clinical and Experimental Research, 22,* 339–344.

Rosenbaum, D. P., & Hanson, G. S. (1998). Assessing the effects of school-based drug education: A six-year multilevel analysis of Project DARE. *Journal of Research in Crime and Delinquency, 35,* 381–412.

Rubenstein, D., Youngman, V., & Hise, J. H. (1994). Partial development of the corpus callosum. *American Journal of Neuroradiology, 15,* 869–875.

Sampson, P. D., Kerr, B., Olson, H. C., Streissguth, A. P., Hunt, E., Barr, H. M., et al. (1997). The effects of prenatal alcohol exposure on adolescent cognitive processing: A speed-accuracy tradeoff. *Intelligence, 24,* 329–353.

Schorling, J. B. (1993). The prevention of prenatal alcohol use: A critical analysis of intervention studies. *Journal of Studies on Alcohol, 54,* 261–267.

Schrank, F. A., Flanagan, D. P., Woodcock, R. W., & Mascolo, J. T. (2002). *Essentials of WJ III Cognitive Abilities Assessment.* Hoboken, NJ: Wiley.

Shope, J. T., Copeland, L. A., Kamp, M. E., & Lang, S. W. (1998). Twelfth grade follow-up of the effectiveness of a middle school-based substance abuse prevention program. *Journal of Drug Education, 28,* 185–197.

Simonian, S. J., & Tarnowski, K., J. (2004). Early identification of physical and psychological disorders in the school setting. In R. T. Brown (Ed.), *Handbook of pediatric psychology in school settings.* Mahwah, NJ: Erlbaum.

Sowell, E. R., Mattson, S. N., Thompson, P. M., Jernigan, T. L., Riley, E. P., & Toga, A. W. (2001). Mapping callosal morphology and cognitive correlates. *Neurology, 57,* 235–244.

Steinhausen, H., & Spohr, H. (1998). Long-term outcomes of children with fetal alcohol syndrome: Psychopathology, behavior, and intelligence. *Alcoholism, Clinical, and Experimental Research, 22,* 334–338.

Stratton, K. R., Howe, C. J., & Battaglia, F. C. (Eds.). (1996). *Fetal alcohol syndrome: Diagnosis, epidemiology, prevention, and treatment.* Washington, DC: Institute of Medicine, National Academy Press.

Streissguth, A. P., Barr, H. M., Bookstein, F. L., Sampson, P. D., & Olson, H. C. (1999). The long-term neurocognitive consequences of prenatal alcohol exposure: A 14-year study. *Psychological Science, 10,* 186–190.

Streissguth, A. P., & Dehaene, P. (1993). Fetal alcohol syndrome in twins of alcoholic mothers: Concordance of diagnosis and IQ. *American Journal of Medical Genetics, 47,* 857–861.

Sussman, S., Dent, C. W., Stacy, A. W., & Craig, S. (1998). One-year outcome of project towards no drug abuse. *Preventive Medicine, 27,* 632–642.

Swayze, V. W., Johnson, V. P., Hanson, J. W., Piven, J., Sato, Y., Giedd, J. N., et al. (1997). Magnetic resonance imaging of brain anomalies in fetal alcohol syndrome. *Pediatrics, 99,* 232–240.

Testa, M., Quigley, B. M., & Eiden, R. D. (2003). The effects of prenatal alcohol exposure on infant mental development: A meta-analytic review. *Alcohol and Alcoholism, 38,* 295–304.

Thomas, S. E., Kelly, S. J., Mattson, S. N., & Riley, E. P. (1998). Comparison of social abilities of children with fetal alcohol syndrome to those of children with similar IQ scores and normal controls. *Alcoholism, Clinical, and Experimental Research, 22,* 528–533.

Wass, T. S., Simmons, R. W., Thomas, J. D., & Riley, E. P. (2002). Timing accuracy and variability in children with prenatal exposure to alcohol. *Alcoholism: Clinical and Experimental Research, 26,* 1887–1896.

Werch, C. E., Pappas, D. M., Carlson, J. M., & DiClemente, C. C. (1998). Short- and long-term effects of a pilot prevention program to reduce alcohol consumption. *Substance Use and Abuse, 33,* 2303–2321.

Wisniewski, K., Dambska, M., Sher, J. H., & Qazi, Q. (1983). A clinical neuropathological study of the fetal alcohol syndrome. *Neuropediatrics, 14,* 197–201.

Woodcock, R. W., McGrew, K. S., & Mather, N. (2001a). *Woodcock-Johnson III Tests of Achievement.* Itasca, IL: Riverside.

Woodcock, R. W., McGrew, K. S., & Mather, N. (2001b). *Woodcock-Johnson III Tests of Cognitive abilities.* Itasca, IL: Riverside.

# CHAPTER 25

# Providing Neuropsychological Services to Children Exposed Prenatally and Perinatally to Neurotoxins and Deprivation

LAURA M. ARNSTEIN and RONALD T. BROWN

THERE ARE A variety of prenatal and perinatal circumstances that may be etiologic in neurobehavioral deficits. Although these impairments may sometimes be readily identified very early in development (e.g., neural tube deficits), some may not become apparent until the learner enters school and begins to struggle academically or behaviorally. In this chapter, we review a wide range of factors that may play a role in later neurobehavioral difficulties. These factors range from substances the mother consumes or is exposed to during pregnancy (teratogens) to specific maternal factors (such as nutrition and age) and complications that may occur during delivery.

The prenatal environment plays an important role in fostering healthy development. Unfortunately, in all but the most obvious of cases, making an accurate diagnosis for a child who has been prenatally exposed to (or deprived of) a specific substance may be particularly challenging. There are no specific instruments that currently exist to inform the practitioner that a school-age child has been prenatally exposed to (or deprived of) a specific substance. Further, unless the infant or mother shows obvious symptoms, such tests are rarely performed at birth. As a result, children with neurobehavioral effects secondary to problems in the prenatal environment may be diagnosed with a wide variety of disorders describing the nature, but not the etiology, of the disability. Diagnoses may include mental retardation, Attention-Deficit/Hyperactivity Disorder (ADHD), learning disabilities, and delayed speech. From an interventionist standpoint, the etiology of a disability is rarely as relevant to management as is the nature of the disability. However, the identification of the etiology of a disability can be extremely important in the possible identification of public health hazards. One example is the consumption of fish that is high in mercury content, which may serve as a teratogen to offspring. Further, in certain cases, identification of prenatal factors can be essential in helping the family access needed services. For example, some states and agencies provide specific services for children with Fetal Alcohol Syndrome that may not be available to a child with a disorder that does not have an associated teratogen.

The first three sections of this chapter are concerned with specific teratogens (substance abuse, psychotropic medications, environmental agents). A teratogen is a substance that negatively affects typical development. In the most severe cases, gestational exposure to teratogenic substances results in fetal death. In other cases, exposure to neurotoxins may result in structural abnormalities and growth deficiencies. In less severe circumstances, more subtle functional systems such as attention, learning, and memory may be affected. According to Streissguth (1997), several factors play a role in the way fetal development is affected by teratogens. First, in most cases, more exposure to the substance results in greater teratogenic effects; this is known as a "dose response relationship." Second, the timing of the exposure may have drastically different effects on development. Abuse during the first trimester is typically associated with physical effects to the fetus. For example, during the first trimester, prenatal substance exposure can result in gross organ malformations, such as congenital heart defects. Exposure during the second and third trimesters can result in growth retardation and microcephaly. The developing central nervous system is vulnerable to teratogenic effects throughout gestation. Third, genetic variability among mothers and offspring can influence the effect of a specific teratogen on development.

The fourth section of the chapter is devoted to maternal characteristics that may impact development. These include abnormalities in maternal diet and nutrition as well as maternal age. Finally, we review perinatal factors that may influence later outcome. These factors include complications that occur during delivery, premature delivery, and low birthweight. We conclude with recommendations for evaluation and treatment.

## SUBSTANCE ABUSE

The relationship between maternal substance abuse during pregnancy and later childhood outcome has been well investigated. After birth, the exposed infant may suffer from withdrawal (neonatal toxicity). In addition to these immediate effects, there are often long-term neurodevelopmental consequences of exposure that may become evident as the child develops (Walker, Rosenberg, & Balaban-Gil, 1999). Although a great deal of research has been conducted in the area of prenatal substance abuse, the research is particularly subject to confounding factors that make interpretation of results difficult. First, the use of one substance may be associated with the use of other common substances such as nicotine, caffeine, and alcohol, and it is often difficult to disentangle the effects on offspring of multiple substance use. Second, substance use is often linked with poor prenatal nutrition and maternal stress, which can also negatively affect the developing fetus. It is important to note whether studies attempt to control for these factors as well as for socioeconomic status. Third, many investigators must rely on self-report of substance use, which may lead to underreporting. The use of biological markers of maternal substance use (e.g., urine screens, blood plasma levels) is helpful, but not always possible, depending on the substance of interest. Fourth, the timing of exposure may also have differential effects as fetal systems and functions develop at different times throughout gestation. Children exposed to substances throughout pregnancy may have a different developmental profile than those exposed only in the first trimester. Therefore, it is important that studies address the timing of exposure. In human research, this can be very challenging as mothers often deny or minimize substance abuse. Finally, it is often difficult to determine the teratogenic effects of a specific substance versus the negative effects of an environment in which caregivers are substance abusers. In the following sections, the individual effects of four commonly abused substances are reviewed: alcohol, nicotine, cocaine, and marijuana.

## ALCOHOL

Prenatal alcohol exposure is one of the leading causes of cognitive impairment in children. Children who have been regularly exposed to large amounts of alcohol during gestation may develop Fetal Alcohol Syndrome (FAS). FAS corresponds to a syndrome of growth retardation (pre- and/or postnatal), central nervous system dysfunction, and at least two specific morphological abnormalities (microcephaly, short palpebral fissures, hypoplastic maxillary area) following heavy prenatal alcohol exposure (Zevenbergen & Ferraro, 2001). However, many children suffer from the effects of fetal alcohol exposure despite their failing to manifest the full syndrome. FAS is considered to be only part of the Fetal Alcohol Spectrum Disorders (FASD). The term FASD can be used to describe both severely and subtly affected individuals (Sokol, Delaney-Black, & Nordstrom, 2003). There are many other terms that are sometimes used for less severely affected children. For example, individuals with only two symptoms may be diagnosed with Fetal Alcohol Effects (FAE) or alcohol-related birth defects. Although this group has not been studied as extensively as those with FAS, it appears that they may have many of the same difficulties as those with the full syndrome. For example, Mattson, Riley, Gramling, Delis, and Jones (1998) found that children with high doses of prenatal alcohol exposure were impaired on tests of language, verbal learning and memory, academic skills, fine motor speed, and visual-motor integration, regardless of whether they met criteria for a diagnosis of FAS based on physical features. However, because the vast majority of the research has focused on children with the full-blown syndrome, we focus on these individuals.

Children with FAS typically demonstrate significant impairment in overall cognitive ability. Janzen, Nanson, and Block (1995) found that children with FAS had an average IQ of 65 (impaired range of cognitive functioning). A specific pattern of cognitive impairment has not emerged across studies. Rather, it appears that children with FAS have difficulties in multiple cognitive areas. Korkman, Autti-Ramo, Koivulehto, and Granstrom (1998) conducted neuropsychological evaluations on children known to have been prenatally exposed to alcohol. Cognitive deficits were found in the areas of naming, receptive language, attention, and visual-motor abilities. Memory and motor precision were spared. Academically, children with FAS most frequently have been found to have math disorders. However, disorders of reading and spelling also have been demonstrated (Streissguth, 1997).

In addition to the dysmorphic syndrome, cognitive deficits, and academic difficulties, children with FAS tend to have behavioral comorbidities that may further impair their functional outcomes. Many children with FAS also meet diagnostic criteria for ADHD (Nanson & Hiscock, 1990). Brown and colleagues (1991) found significant deficits in sustained attention among children prenatally exposed to alcohol throughout pregnancy. Steinhaussen and Spohr (1998) followed more than 150 children with FAS during preschool, early school age, and late school age. These investigators found that attentional deficits and hyperactivity were persistent over time. They also found increased rates of emotional disorders, sleep disorders, and abnormal habits that were particularly prevalent among school-age children. Finally, Steinhaussen and Spohr found that an array of behavior problems occurred that were age-dependent.

FAS is not just a childhood disorder; the intellectual and behavioral effects of FAS persist into adolescence and adulthood (Streissguth, 1994). In follow-up studies of adolescents and adults with FAS, findings have revealed short stature in this population. Although the average IQ is in the impaired range, significant variability has been demonstrated in intellectual functioning. Findings also have revealed a severe arithmetic disability, poor judgment, difficulty with independent living and adaptive behavior, and dysfunctional lives. According to Connor and Streissguth (1996), rather than simply affecting academic achievement, the deficiencies associated with FAS tend to be pervasive in all functional areas of the individual's life, such as school, work, and social functioning. Further, individuals with FAS may have higher rates of substance abuse and problems with the law than individuals with other syndromes associated with mental retardation (Streissguth, 1997). In fact, Streissguth, Moon-Jordon, and Clarren (1995) suggest that a diagnosis of FAS be considered at the time of admission for alcohol treatment to help avoid treatment failure due to these individuals' inability to profit from traditional treatment approaches.

Not surprisingly, the amount of alcohol consumed (dose), timing of exposure during pregnancy (i.e., first, second, or third trimester), and duration of exposure each appears to influence outcome. In a study conducted by Korkman et al. (1998), children whose mothers stopped drinking during the first trimester of pregnancy were unaffected, whereas those whose mothers continued to drink throughout the pregnancy had the highest frequency of features associated with FAS. In a related investigation, Aronson and Hagburg (1998) found an association between the degree of alcohol exposure and the severity of neuropsychological problems. Children whose mothers stopped abusing alcohol by the 12th week of gestation evidenced normal development. Similarly, Autti-Ramo (2000) found that children of mothers who drank throughout pregnancy were more likely to require special education and to have behavior problems than were those children whose mothers stopped drinking during the first trimester. However, Coles and colleagues (1991) demonstrated measurable deficits in academic skills and growth in children exposed only during the first part of pregnancy (mothers who stopped drinking during the second trimester). It is unclear how much, if any, alcohol is safe to consume during pregnancy. Although much of the research has focused on children exposed to high levels of alcohol, recent research suggests that even relatively small amounts of alcohol (half a drink per day) may result in poor outcomes (Sood et al., 2001). For this reason, the American Academy of Pediatrics

(2000) recommends complete abstinence from alcohol before conception and during pregnancy.

Although FAS is a completely preventable syndrome, incidence rates of the disorder continue to be significant and represent a national public health concern. FAS and FASD are often misdiagnosed or, in some cases, purposefully left undiagnosed. According to Astley, Bailey, Talbot, and Clarren (2000), this may result from physicians' lack of familiarity with the disorder itself, the role an accurate diagnosis plays in obtaining appropriate treatment, or the lack of services available to children with this diagnosis. Very early identification may be difficult because the facial features associated with FAS may not be easily discriminated in newborns and neurodevelopmental problems are difficult to measure in infants (Coles, Kable, Drews-Botsch, & Falek, 2000). Further, growth deficits associated with FAS also are common to many disorders. Interestingly, identification of FAS may become more difficult as the individual ages, as people with FAS tend to lose the characteristic facial features after puberty (Streissguth, 1994).

## NICOTINE

Despite massive public health campaigns regarding the dangers of smoking during pregnancy, the rate of smoking among pregnant women has remained surprisingly high. In 2002, 11.4% of women giving birth reported that they smoked during their pregnancy (Martin et al., 2003). Adolescent mothers had the highest smoking rate of all age groups. Among racial and ethnic groups, American Indian, non-Hispanic White, and Hawaiian women were the most likely to smoke during pregnancy (Martin et al., 2003).

Smoking during pregnancy exposes the developing fetus to thousands of chemicals, most notably carbon monoxide and nicotine. Clear associations have been demonstrated between smoking and infertility, miscarriages, stillbirths, and low birthweight babies (Olds, 1997). However, the relationship between maternal smoking and children's long-term neurobehavioral outcome is less clear. Many studies have found associations between maternal smoking and cognitive and academic problems in learners (Rush & Callahan, 1989). However, in more recent studies, when the effects of alcohol and rearing environment are controlled statistically, these associations often disappear (Olds, 1997). There is more compelling evidence to suggest that maternal smoking is associated with behavior problems and symptoms of ADHD. A review by Olds indicates that after controlling for variables such as prenatal alcohol exposure and quality of caregiving, almost all studies in this area have found an association between maternal smoking and child behavior problems, including conduct problems and symptoms related to ADHD. In a review of studies on various lifestyle factors in pregnancy (smoking, alcohol use, caffeine use, and stress), studies on nicotine exposure revealed the clearest and greatest risk of attentional-related problems (Linnet at al., 2003). Importantly, there also appears to be an effect from amount of nicotine consumed; children exposed to more than one pack per day developed more behavior problems than those exposed to less than one pack per day (Weitzman, Gortmaker, & Sobel, 1992). In a prospective investigation, Brennan, Grekin, and Mednick (1999) found a compelling relationship between the amount of prenatal smoking exposure and number of arrests among 34-year-old men. Findings revealed an association between fetal smoking exposure and persistent criminal behavior that was independent of demographic and other potentially confounding variables.

## COCAINE

Over the past few decades, there has been significant controversy over the effects of cocaine (including crack cocaine) on the developing fetus. It was commonly believed that prenatal cocaine exposure led to lifelong, catastrophic developmental, behavioral, and/or cognitive difficulties (Frank, Augustyn, Knight, Pell, & Zuckerman, 2001). These prenatally exposed infants were once termed "crack babies," a stigmatizing and misleading descriptor that often followed the child into the school system and beyond. Interestingly, recent empirical evidence suggests that cocaine's effects on developmental outcomes are minimal. In a review of the literature, Frank and colleagues conclude that cocaine exposure does not seem to be associated with specific developmental effects. Among children age 6 years or less, there were no effects of cocaine on physical growth. For children under the age of 3, no effects on language were found. Some studies found suboptimal motor development prior to 7 months, but not after infancy, and even this finding may reflect other confounding factors, such as having been raised in an impoverished environment characterized by substance abuse. Finally, there is only minimal evidence for any behavioral effects of exposure. The review of literature concludes that effects once believed to be attributable to cocaine exposure could be explained by exposure to other substances, such as tobacco, marijuana, and alcohol, as well as by the quality of the rearing environment.

## MARIJUANA

Marijuana is one of the most commonly abused substances among women of childbearing age. Use of marijuana during pregnancy exposes the developing fetus to high carbon monoxide levels as well as to THC, the active component of the drug. Despite the frequency with which this substance is used, the literature regarding the neurobehavioral consequences of prenatal exposure remains inconclusive (Walker et al., 1999). In a review of the literature, Fried and Simon (2001) conclude that there is little evidence for adverse influence of marijuana use on the course of pregnancy or on early development. However, there is growing evidence that early exposure may result in later cognitive difficulties and attentional deficits. In particular, it appears that executive functions such as attention and visual analysis/hypothesis testing are affected by prenatal exposure (Fried & Simon, 2001).

## PSYCHOTROPIC MEDICATIONS

The number of pregnant women receiving psychotropic medications (those that affect the central nervous system) is increasing every year. Unfortunately, very little is known about the effects of many medications when used during pregnancy. Because of practical and ethical barriers, few controlled studies investigating the effect of psychotropic drug exposure on the developing fetus have been conducted. Most of the available evidence regarding the safe use of these agents during pregnancy comes from case studies and national registries. As a result, most psychotropic drugs are classified by the Food and Drug Administration as Category B (i.e., either evidence of risk from animal studies or no human studies have been completed) or Category C (i.e., risk cannot be ruled out) for use during pregnancy.

Short-term concerns of exposure to psychotropic agents include the possibility of miscarriage and fetal malformation. Additionally, some neonates born to women taking psychotropic medications may display withdrawal symptoms in the days and weeks following birth. Over the long term, concerns arise regarding potential damage to the fetus's developing central nervous system that may manifest in subsequent learning or behavioral problems throughout childhood. Because so little is known about the long-term effects of these medications, the American Academy of Pediatrics, Committee on Drugs (2000) has made two specific recommendations for cases in which psychotropic medication must be used during pregnancy: (1) The mother should be prescribed the lowest possible dose to manage her symptoms; (2) exposed newborns should be monitored for withdrawal symptoms and potential developmental disabilities. Currently, there are no recommendations regarding the monitoring of exposed children throughout early childhood and the school years, although such monitoring seems prudent given the potential deleterious effects of these agents on central nervous system development.

There are four primary categories of psychotropic medications for which evidence of their teratogenic effects is available: antidepressants, anxiolytics, antimanic agents including anticonvulsants, and antipsychotic agents.

Antidepressants

Specific serotonin reuptake inhibitors (SSRIs; e.g., fluoxetine, Prozac) are currently the most commonly prescribed antidepressants. To date, no studies suggest that SSRIs are associated with spontaneous loss of pregnancy or with major fetal anomalies (Cohen & Rosenbaum, 1998). However, one study has revealed that infants exposed to SSRIs during the third trimester of pregnancy were more likely to be born premature and had a higher rate of admission to high-risk nurseries (Ahluwalia & Meyer, 1998). There is currently little evidence to suggest that SSRI exposure affects long-term neurobehavioral outcome, although more research is needed in this area prior to formulating any definitive conclusions. Nulman and colleagues (1997) reported normal language and intellectual development among preschoolers exposed to fluoxetine in utero.

With regard to the older class of antidepressants known as tricyclic antidepressants, there is no evidence linking the use of these agents during pregnancy with congenital abnormalities, miscarriage, or premature births (Craig & Abel, 2001). There is also no available evidence for long-term cognitive or behavioral effects of tricyclic exposure. Mirsi and Siveretz (1991) followed a group of children exposed to tricyclics at some time during gestation or early infancy. Three-year-old children in this group were within normal limits developmentally in all areas. Nulman et al. (1997) also failed to find differences in intellectual functioning, language development, or behavior among children exposed to trycyclics prenatally versus their peers who had no exposure.

Finally, atypical antidepressants (e.g., monoamine oxidase inhibitors) are sometimes prescribed for individuals who are refractory to other antidepressant agents. There are no data available to support the safe use of atypical antidepressants during pregnancy.

## ANXIOLYTICS

Occasionally, benzodiazepines (e.g., diazepam) are used when an immediate anxiolytic (anti-anxiety) effect is desired. The use of benzodiazapines during pregnancy has been associated with "floppy infant syndrome" (i.e., hypotonia, lethargy, sucking difficulties, cyanosis, and hypothermia) and symptoms associated with withdrawal (i.e., tremors, irritability, mypertonia, hypertonia, and hyperflexia; Ahluwalia & Meyer, 1998). Although studies to date have been inconclusive, there also is evidence linking the use of diazepam (Valium) during pregnancy to an increased incidence of cleft lip and palate (Ahluwalia & Meyer, 1998). In light of this body of literature, the use of anxiolytic agents for pregnant women is clearly discouraged given the teratogenic effects of these agents.

## ANTIMANIC AGENTS

Lithium carbonate is typically used to manage individuals with Bipolar Disorder. Use of lithium during the first trimester of pregnancy has been associated with Epstein's anomaly, a congenital cardiac malformation of the tricuspid valve (Ernst & Goldberg, 2002). Moreover, use of lithium during the second and third trimesters of pregnancy has been associated with premature delivery, thyroid abnormalities, nephrogenic diabetes insipidus, and floppy baby syndrome. Data regarding the long-term outcome for children exposed prenatally to lithium are limited. However, Schou (1976) has reported no differences in behavior and development between lithium-exposed 5-year-olds with no congenital malformations in relation to sibling controls who were not exposed to lithium. Despite the findings presented by Schou, given the literature reviewed previously, the practitioner must be especially judicious in using these agents with pregnant women.

Anticonvulsant agents are frequently used as antimania treatments as well as for the management of seizure disorders. Phenytoin (Dilantin) use during pregnancy can result in a variety of abnormalities, and, in more severe cases, it may result in a pattern of malformation known as Fetal Hydantoin Syndrome. These abnormalities may include pre- and postnatal growth deficiency, cognitive impairments, and malformations of the craniofacial area and limbs (Jones, 1997). Nearly 50% of exposed children are likely to have some effects, and approximately 10% will show the full Fetal Hydantoin Syndrome (Jones, 1997). Similarly, the use of valproate (Depakote) and carbamazepine (Tegretol) during pregnancy is associated with increased risks for major congenital malformations such as skeletal abnormalities, spina bifida, congenital heart defects, developmental disabilities, and intrauterine growth retardation. Jones, Lacro, Johnson, and Adams (1989) found that about 20% of children exposed to carbamazepine had some form of developmental delay, although this delay was minor in many cases. However, Gaily and Granstrom (1989) failed to find a similar association. Risks associated with the use of anticonvulsants can be minimized by using supplements of folic acid and vitamin K (Ernst & Goldberg, 2002). However, there is no "safe" dose, nor has a dose response relationship ever been demonstrated (Jones, 1997).

ANTIPSYCHOTICS

The antipsychotic or neuroleptic agents are frequently employed for psychiatric disorders such as Schizophrenia, severe aggression, and Tourette's Disorder. There is no documented evidence that there are specific teratogenic effects associated with low doses of traditional antipsychotic agents, including chlorpromazine (Thorazine), thioridazine (Mellaril), and haloperidol (Haldol; Craig & Abel, 2001). More recently, there has been a trend for an increase in use of the atypical antipsychotic agents because these are associated with fewer adverse effects, such as tardive dyskinesia (a sometimes irreversible syndrome of abnormal involuntary movements that occurs after long-term use of antipsychotics) and extrapyramidal effects (medication side effects causing odd muscular reactions). However, animal studies have revealed potential teratogenic effects of these agents on the developing fetus, including pup death, stillbirths, and developmental delays. Although studies with humans are needed, given the associated adverse effects in animals, judicious use of these medications with pregnant women is clearly warranted. A case registry of infants born to mothers taking olanzapine (Zyprexa) is available, and to date there have been few reported teratogenic effects, suggesting the possible feasibility of this agent for pregnant women in need of antipsychotic management (Ernst & Goldberg, 2002). However, there are no published studies regarding neurobehavioral sequelae of olanzapine, clozapine, risperidone, and quetiapine.

## ENVIRONMENTAL FACTORS

In addition to drugs of abuse and prescription medications, pregnant women may be exposed to a wide variety of environmental factors that can have harmful effects on fetal development. With the worldwide rise in industry have come massive problems with environmental pollution from industrial accidents and from standard industry practices. Children today are exposed to thousands of chemicals that were not present in the environment 50 years ago. Some of these pollutants, such as polychlorinated biphenyls (PCBs), lead, and methylmercury (MeHg), are known to interfere with development. However, the effects of many other chemicals such as pesticides are currently unknown. In this section, we review the effects of prenatal exposure to seafood neurotoxins (PCBs and MeHg) and lead. In addition, maternal exposure to radiation, which can occur in the environment following disasters such as at Chernobyl or during medical diagnostic procedures and treatment, also is reviewed.

SEAFOOD NEUROTOXINS

Exposure to PCBs and MeHg through maternal seafood consumption has been linked to long-term developmental difficulties (Stewart, Reihman, Lonsky, Darvill, & Pagano, 2003). Together with a variety of other potential pollutants, both substances are present in fish. Therefore, the separate and combined effects of PCBs and MeHg can be difficult to dismantle and identify.

A cohort of children born to women who consumed fish from Lake Michigan has been studied extensively (e.g., Jacobson & Jacobson, 1996). Consumption of fish and subsequent elevated cord serum PCB levels were associated with low birthweight and small head circumference. At 4 years of age, PCB-exposed children evidenced poorer short-term memory and visual discrimination than did nonexposed children (Jacobson, Jacobson, Padgett, & Brumitt, 1992). At a follow-up evaluation of these children at 11 years of age, they evidenced decreased intellectual functioning, memory, achievement, and attention (Jacobson & Jacobson, 1996). More important, across studies a dose response relationship has been noted; specifically, higher levels of PCB exposure were associated with a greater frequency of problems. Stewart and colleagues (2003) found that cord blood PCBs were associated with poorer developmental performance at 38 months, but not at 54 months, suggesting some level of recovery between the ages of 3 and 4½ years.

High levels of prenatal MeHg exposure have been associated with cerebral palsy and mental retardation (Myers, Davidson, & Shamlaye, 1998). However, the effects of low-level exposure, such as might be found in fish from nonpolluted areas, is still unclear. Populations of people living on islands in the North Atlantic (Faroe Islands) eat a diet that is rich is seafood. A prospective study of a group of children from these islands revealed deficits in several areas of cognitive functioning following prenatal exposure to MeHg (Grandjean et al., 1997). However, a prospective study using participants from a group of islands in the Indian Ocean (the Seychelles) failed to find deficits in children exposed to MeHg (Pulumbo et al., 2000).

## MATERNAL LEAD EXPOSURE

Lead is well recognized as an environmental toxin. Extensive legislation has been in place since the late 1960s to prevent, detect, and treat lead poisoning in children (Pueschel, Linakis, & Anderson, 1996). The neurobehavioral consequences of lead exposure in early childhood have been well documented and are covered in another chapter in this book (see Chapter 18). However, it is less well recognized, although equally well documented, that maternal lead exposure can have serious deleterious consequences for fetal development. Women living near smelters or in countries using leaded fuels are at risk for exposure. Lead exposure also occurs through contact with lead-based paint, through occupational exposure (such as fabrication of lead-based jewelry), and through diet (including consumption of food from lead-soldered cans and water from lead pipes; Pueschel, Linakis, & Anderson, 1996). In one documented case, an infant was born with elevated lead levels due to maternal pica behavior (Hamilton, Rothenberg, Khan, Manalo, & Norris, 2001).

Although the negative consequences of high levels of prenatal lead exposure have been recognized for a long time, it is only in the past 10 years that even low maternal lead levels became a concern. It is well documented that there is an increased incidence of miscarriage and stillbirth among lead-exposed pregnant women. There also is a risk of low birthweight and prematurity associated with even low levels of lead exposure (Dietrich, 1996). Although serious malformations have not been associated with maternal lead exposure, more minor malformations have been noted, such as skin tags and papillae, hydroceles, hemangiomas, lymphangiomas, and undescended testicles in males.

Prenatal exposure to low levels of lead has been demonstrated to be associated with low intellectual functioning and learning disabilities (Dietrich, 1996). For example, Wasserman and colleagues (2000) followed a group of children born in a smelter town in Yugoslavia until 7 years of age. Findings revealed that prenatal blood levels of lead were associated with small decrements in intellectual functioning throughout early childhood. In addition to subtle cognitive effects of early lead exposure, externalizing behavioral problems also have been identified. Prenatal lead exposure has been associated with greater delinquent and antisocial behaviors in adolescence as measured by parent report (Dietrich, Ris, Succop, Berger, & Bornschein, 2001).

MATERNAL RADIATION EXPOSURE

Radiation exposure during pregnancy may occur in a variety of circumstances, including warfare, power plant disaster, medical diagnosis, and medical treatment. Data gathered from prenatally exposed victims of the atomic bombings of Hiroshima and Nagasaki in 1945 indicated that maternal radiation exposure is associated with congenital and developmental abnormalities. These studies have shown that early prenatal exposure (0 to 16 weeks) is associated with small head circumference. Exposure between 8 and 25 weeks is associated with decrements in intellectual functioning and seizures.

In 1986, an explosion at the Chernobyl nuclear power plant in the Ukrainian Republic of the Union of Soviet Socialist Republics resulted in the spread of radioactive debris over parts of the western USSR, Eastern Europe, and Scandinavia. Data from the Chernobyl disaster were much less dire than that from the atomic bomb studies in Japan. Litcher and colleagues (2000) compared school-age learners (10 to 12 years) who were exposed prenatally to radiation (but evacuated shortly after the Chernobyl accident) to classmates who were not exposed, and found no significant differences on measures of cognitive and academic performance and behavior. However, Loganovskaja and Loganovsky (1999) did find more disorganized EEG patterns, a higher frequency of borderline IQs, and more behavioral/emotional problems among children prenatally exposed to Chernobyl radiation.

The base rate of risk of exposure due to warfare and accidents is fairly low; medical exposure to radiation is more common. Without proper preventive measures, medical workers may be exposed to radiation on a regular basis during routine procedures. Pregnant women also are exposed to radiation during regular diagnostic procedures (x-ray) and therapeutic procedures, such as radiation therapy used for cancer treatment. The risk from exposure during regular diagnostic procedures appears to be minimal. A study by Ornoy, Patlas, and Schwartz (1996) failed to identify differences in motor and cognitive functioning of children exposed to mothers' abdominal and nonabdominal x-ray during gestation. Conversely, Bohnen, Ragozzino, and Kurland (1996) found decreased head circumference at birth among children exposed during the second and third trimesters. Of course, higher doses of radiation employed in therapeutic procedures (e.g., radiation therapy used for cancer) can have serious consequences for the developing fetus, including fetal death, childhood cancer, and impairments in intellectual functioning. In many cases, treatment with radiation therapy may be delayed until after delivery, or termination of pregnancy is considered. Cancers that are remote to the pelvis can sometimes be treated safely (International Commission on Radiological Protection, 2000).

## MATERNAL FACTORS

Maternal lifestyle and personal factors can have significant effects on fetal development. As noted in previous sections, exposure to street drugs, prescription drugs, and legal substances (caffeine, nicotine, etc.) can have teratogenic effects. Other specific factors such as maternal age and maternal nutrition may place women at risk for adverse pregnancy outcome. We consider each of these factors in the following sections.

## MATERNAL AGE

In 1997, the overall teenage pregnancy rate was 91 per 1,000 (Elford & Spence, 2002). Among high school learners, almost 5% reported that they had been pregnant or had gotten someone else pregnant (Grunbaum et al., 2002). Compared to women who deliver as adults, teenage mothers are more likely to be African American, to be single mothers, and to be diagnosed with a sexually transmitted disease (Eure, Lindsay, & Graves, 2002).

Teenage pregnancy is associated with significant health risks for both mother and baby. Pregnant teenagers frequently do not present for prenatal care until late in pregnancy and, as a result, receive less prenatal care than do adult mothers (Elford & Spence, 2002). Women who give birth as teenagers are more likely to experience complications during pregnancy or delivery. Teenage mothers are more likely to deliver babies with more health problems (Elford & Spence, 2002). Younger adolescents who give birth also are at greater risk for complications such as preeclampsia, eclampsia, and preterm delivery (Eure et al., 2002). Moreover, babies born to young adolescent mothers are more likely to have low birthweight (Eure et al., 2002).

In addition to medical risks, teenage pregnancy is associated with a host of other difficulties. Among teenagers who give birth, about 90% keep their babies (Elford & Spence, 2002). Children of teenage parents are often faced with social, educational, and economic difficulties. For example, adolescent mothers are more likely to drop out of high school, to be unmarried, and to be welfare dependent (Elford & Spence, 2002).

## MATERNAL NUTRITION

Proper maternal nutrition during pregnancy is important in promoting fetal development. Even healthy women may be at risk for specific nutritional deficits that may affect prenatal development. The most dramatic association between maternal nutrition and fetal development can be seen in the case of folic acid. Folic acid deficiency is linked to neural tube deficits (NTDs). NTDs are malformations of the spinal cord, brain, and vertebrae. For example, spina bifida, the most common NTD, involves a failure in spinal cord closure during the first month of gestation. As a result, the child may be born with a partially exposed spinal cord that may be susceptible to injury or infection. Folic acid supplementation before and during pregnancy can drastically reduce the risk of NTDs (Honein, Paulozzi, Matthews, Erickson, & Wong, 2001). However, because relatively few women (29%) follow the recommendation for folic acid supplementation, in 1998 the U.S. Food and Drug Administration made folic acid fortification mandatory in enriched grain products.

Cobalamin (vitamin B12) and iron also have been shown to be important for early development. Mothers following a vegetarian diet may be at risk for dietary deficiency of cobalamin. Breast-fed infants may also develop this deficiency. Symptoms of cobalamin deficiency in children may include failure to thrive, delayed development, behavioral difficulties, and a variety of other physical, neurological, and hematologic problems (Rosenblatt & Whitehead, 1999).

Of particular interest are data to suggest that poor prenatal nutrition during pregnancy is associated with later personality disorders in offspring. Prenatal nutrition may play a role in the development of antisocial personality traits later in life. A study of men born in the Netherlands during World War II divided participants into those born in a famine region (due to German blockade), where severe nutritional deficiency was suffered, and those born in nonfamine regions, where moderate nutritional deficiency was suffered (Neugebauer, Hoek, & Susser, 1999). The investigators found that men exposed to severe deficiency in prenatal nutrition during the first and/or second trimester were at increased risk for Antisocial Personality Disorder.

Certain maternal disorders that result in nutritional imbalances may also play a negative role in prenatal outcome. For example, untreated maternal phenylketonuria (PKU) may result in abnormalities in cognitive performance and physical development. PKU is an autosomal recessive abnormality that results in markedly reduced activity of an enzyme that metabolizes phenylalanine. Babies who have PKU and are not treated can develop microcephaly, mental retardation, and behavioral difficulties. However, when PKU is diagnosed at birth, dietary restriction (especially very early in life) can allow for normal cognitive development. As this disorder is better recognized and managed, more women with PKU develop without major cognitive deficits and may become pregnant during their childbearing years. However, without proper dietary control before conception and during pregnancy, maternal PKU can result in fetal microcephaly, mental retardation, prenatal growth retardation, heart defects, and craniofacial abnormalities (Jones, 1997). In a 4-year follow-up investigation of children born to women with PKU, metabolic control earlier in pregnancy was associated with higher scores on a number of cognitive indices (Waisbren et al., 2000). Although findings suggest that treatment at any time during pregnancy can reduce risk, the best outcomes occur when metabolic control is established before pregnancy. The investigators note that every week of maternal metabolic control counts toward a more favorable outcome and therefore recommend interventions aimed at preventing unplanned pregnancies in this population.

## PERINATAL FACTORS

A number of factors associated with the timing of delivery, the child's development at delivery, and the ease of delivery have been associated with long-term developmental outcomes. Some factors, such as birthweight and prematurity, are linked to factors already addressed in this chapter (substance use/abuse, maternal nutrition). Similar to many of the factors reviewed in this chapter, the effects of separate perinatal factors can be difficult to disentangle. For example, about 12% of total births are preterm (less than 38 weeks) and about 8% are low birthweight (Martin et al., 2003). However, there is not a linear relationship between birthweight and prematurity. Some premature infants are not low birthweight, and low birthweight infants may be born prematurely or at term. We next consider the effects of obstetric complications, low birthweight, and premature birth.

## OBSTETRIC COMPLICATIONS

Obstetric complications include a wide variety of abnormalities during pregnancy and delivery: preeclampsia (i.e., high blood pressure, protein in the urine, swelling), eclampsia (preeclampsia with seizures), hypoxic injury (failure to receive sufficient oxygen during delivery leading to brain damage), and fetal asphyxia. Schizophrenia in offspring has been linked with obstetric complications. In a meta-analysis of studies in this area, Geddes and Lawrie (1995) concluded that there is an overall odds ratio of 2.03 for Schizophrenia following obstetric complications. In other words, the odds of developing Schizophrenia among individuals who had complications during the birth process is more than twice that of those who did not suffer similar complications. Among the factors that have been shown to be associated with risk are preeclampsia, small head circumference, low birthweight, Rh incompatibility, fetal distress, and body weight heavy for length (Dalman, Allebeck, Cullberg, Grunewald, & Koster, 1999). In a large-sample longitudinal investigation, Dalman and colleagues found that complications during pregnancy and delivery were associated with an increased risk of later development of Schizophrenia. They also found that preeclampsia was the strongest risk factor. Although the exact nature of this relationship is still unknown, it is believed that prenatal asphyxia may impede the development and functioning of certain neurotransmitter mechanisms.

Similarly, some investors have posited an association between obstetric complications and later criminal behavior. Support for this association has yielded equivocal findings. A very large study conducted on a cohort of over 15,000 Swedish residents born in 1953 and followed to the age of 30 indicated that low socioeconomic status and inadequate parenting are strongly associated with later offending (Hodgkins, Kratzer, & McNeil, 2001). The researchers found that inadequate parenting along with pregnancy complications slightly increased the risk of law-violating behavior but doubled the risk of violent offending.

## LOW BIRTHWEIGHT

It has been well documented that low birthweight babies are at greater risk for developmental problems, including cognitive impairments, developmental delays, and significant health problems. Low birthweight (<2,500 g) and very low birthweight (<1,500 g) children are at increased risk for attention problems, behavioral difficulties, academic failure, and cognitive impairment. African American women, women under 19, women over 30, unmarried women, and women without a high school education are more likely to deliver a low birthweight baby.

Although low birthweight babies are at initial risk for serious health complications, many of the neurodevelopmental sequelae of prematurity and low birthweight do not become apparent until the child is school-age. Specifically, low birthweight has been associated with visual-motor integration problems. Many studies have suggested that fine motor and visual-motor integration deficits are relatively common among low birthweight infants (Gabbard, Goncalves, & Santos, 2001). These deficits can also lead to poor academic and functional outcomes.

Among very low birthweight children, there is a very high incidence of disabilities. However, there is some evidence to suggest that some level of recovery may occur over time for this population. Ment and colleagues (2003) followed longitudinally almost 300 children up to 96 months of age who were born weighing less than 1,250g at birth. Findings revealed significantly improved intellectual functioning and language over time. It should be noted, however, that very low birthweight children with early intraventricular hemorrhage with subsequent central nervous system injury declined on language scores as they developed.

Although there is clear evidence for neurobehavioral difficulties among low birthweight children, there is some controversy in the extant literature as to whether babies born small for gestational age (less than 5th percentile on growth charts) also are at risk for cognitive impairments. Some studies have demonstrated cognitive dysfunction in this population, but other investigations have been less conclusive. In a 26-year follow-up of individuals born small for gestational age, Strauss (2000) reported that they had significant differences in academic and vocational achievement than did their normally developing birthweight peers. Children born small for gestational age were less likely to achieve academically and more likely to require special education services throughout childhood and adolescence compared to their normally developing birthweight peers. As adults, they had lower incomes and were less likely to have professional or managerial jobs. No differences were found between the two groups for amount of education, marital status, employment status, and life satisfaction.

## PREMATURITY

There is an increased risk of infant death among babies delivered prematurely. However, advances in medical technology now allow many of these infants to survive. In fact, 85% of babies weighing less than 1,500g at birth survive (Hack, Friedman, & Fanaroff, 1996). Among those babies who survive past early infancy, children born prematurely are subject to a wide range of difficulties, including cerebral palsy, blindness, and deafness. There also is compelling evidence to suggest that these children are at risk for neurobehavioral problems, including cognitive delays and learning problems.

Premature birth can have an enduring impact on brain development and maturation. Peterson and colleagues (2000) conducted a longitudinal follow-up study of preterm children. Using MRI scans of the children at 8 years of age, these researchers found that preterm children had significantly smaller regional cortical volumes than full-term comparison controls. Particular abnormalities were found in the sensorimotor cortex. Findings also revealed that reductions in brain volume were associated with deficits in intellectual functioning. In a meta-analysis of studies investigating the cognitive and behavioral outcomes of children born prematurely, Bhutta, Cleves, Casey, Cradock, and Anand (2002) found that preterm children were at risk for cognitive impairments, attentional problems, and behavioral difficulties. Not surprisingly, amount of prematurity was directly associated with cognitive impairment among school-age children. Prematurity has been linked with poor language skills (Briscoe, Gathercole, & Marlow, 1998) and slightly decreased intellectual ability (Aylward, Pfeiffer, Wright, & Verhulst, 1989). There is some evidence to suggest that children born prematurely have memory deficits (e.g., Briscoe et al., 1998) that may be responsible for lower intellectual functioning and poorer academic achievement.

A complicating factor in this area of research is that deficits and difficulties seem to change over time. A number of studies have demonstrated intellectual and cognitive deficits among preterm children under the age of 3 years. However, Menyuk, Liebergott, Schultz, Chesnick, and Ferrier (1991) found that these differences dissipated when chronological age was corrected for prematurity. Alternatively, there is some evidence that the negative effects of prematurity may not be detected until the child reaches later school age. A longitudinal study found small differences between premature and full-term children at the age of 5 years, but more significant differences at the age of 8 years. In particular, children born prematurely who were followed for 8 years showed deficits in verbal comprehension, freedom from distractibility, and perceptual organization. Similarly, in the area of language development, more pronounced deficits have been noted among older children relative to their younger counterparts (Robinson & Gonzalez, 1999). These results suggest that premature delivery may have lasting consequences that may not be readily apparent until the child is school age.

## CONCLUSION

In summary, there are a wide variety of events and conditions during the preconception, gestation, and birth periods that may impact a child's development and later neurobehavioral outcomes. These include maternal substance use (both legal and illegal), environmental exposure to neurotoxins, maternal nutritional deficiencies, and obstetric complications. There are no specific instruments or measures that will alert a professional to prenatal conditions or teratogens that may be etiologic in the development of school-age difficulties. However, when evaluating a learner who is struggling academically or behaviorally, an interview regarding the learner's early developmental history can be important in helping to answer the referral questions. To determine most prenatal and perinatal factors, a comprehensive history conducted with the biological parents is most helpful. A comprehensive interview may include the following questions:

- Was the mother exposed to any viruses during her pregnancy? Was she treated for any illnesses during her pregnancy? It is important to note both the viruses she was exposed to and the method of treatment employed.
- Was there any exposure to tobacco or alcohol? How much and at what point in the pregnancy? Many women cease drinking and smoking in the first few weeks of pregnancy. This is much less dangerous for fetal development than a mother who has continued to use substances throughout her pregnancy.
- Was there any exposure to prescription drugs? It is important to note the exact medication used as well as the reason for use?
- Was there any exposure to street drugs (illegal substances)? How much and when? Note the exact substance used and the method or route by which it was used (smoked, injected, snorted).
- Was the baby born on time? How much did he or she weigh? A gestational age of at least 38 weeks and a birthweight of at least 6 pounds are considered to be within normal limits.
- Were there any complications during the pregnancy or delivery? Did the baby require resuscitation? Did the baby go to the neonatal intensive care unit? Did the baby have to stay in the hospital longer than the mother? Infants are typically discharged from the hospital at the same time as their mother.

- How old were the child's parents at the time of his or her birth? Were either exposed to any occupational hazards? Did either parent live in an older house that was being remodeled?

It is important to note that some questions, such as those regarding use of illegal substances, must be asked with sensitivity as many women are hesitant to provide this type of information. A woman who consumed alcohol during the first weeks of pregnancy should not be made to feel responsible for her child's current difficulties. Further, consideration must be given to the ethical problems that might be posed if the parent admits to continued substance use and has custody of the child or is at risk of again becoming pregnant. In some states and organizations, the interviewer may be ethically or legally bound to report this type of information.

A learner who is struggling in school and has a known prenatal or perinatal risk factor should be comprehensively evaluated. Because the child's difficulties in these cases may be quite broad and may involve deficits in a number of areas (cognitive, physical, and emotional), the school psychologist should work with a multidisciplinary team to identify all relevant areas of need and to provide an appropriate and comprehensive treatment plan. With all syndromes, assessment may be used to identify specific cognitive strengths and weaknesses and to develop a relevant plan of action.

Management of symptoms is typically not syndrome specific but rather is based on symptoms. Depending on the nature of the child's difficulties, he or she may be eligible for services under the federal classifications of Other Health Impairment, Physical Disability, specific Learning Disability, Emotional Disturbance, or Mental Retardation. Of the syndromes and factors discussed in this chapter, only FAS has a significant body of literature regarding treatment recommendations. However, even in this area, there are virtually no studies to provide empirical support for treatment interventions (Zevenbergen & Ferraro, 2001). Due to the heterogeneous nature of these disorders, it is unlikely that syndrome-specific treatment protocols will ever be devised. Instead, treatment is likely to be based on the individual needs of the child. Learners with physical limitations will necessitate special assistance as well as occupational therapy, physical therapy, and adapted physical education. Learners with cognitive and learning difficulties may require special assistance to remain in a mainstream class, such as special education resource services and itinerant consultants. More severely affected learners may require self-contained classrooms designed for learners with cognitive, behavioral, or learning problems. Speech therapy may also be necessary in these cases. Occupational therapy can be helpful in building adaptive self-help skills such as dressing, feeding, and self-care.

Many syndromes are associated with comorbid behavioral difficulties. Treatment may include psychotropic medication (such as medication used to manage symptoms of inattention and overactivity, seen in FAS), behavioral parent training, and structured classroom behavioral management plans. Family interventions may include assisting parents or caregivers in establishing realistic expectations for their children's academic achievement and behavior.

Although there is a dearth of empirically validated literature on specific applications to learners with developmental impairments, strategies derived from the literature on cognitive rehabilitation may be useful in some cases. These include teaching the child compensatory strategies to circumvent areas of weakness. Regardless of the specific cause of the child's difficulties, applied behavior analysis can be used to determine the function of problem behavior and to create individualized treatment plans. Finally, some psychotropic agents (e.g., methylphenidate, Ritalin) show potential efficacy in managing symptoms of hyperactivity and inattention in children with documented FAS (Oesterheld et al., 1998). According to a review by Hagerman (1999), stimulants appear to be effective in managing hyperactivity but not impulsivity or attentional deficits in learners with FAS. Currently, the National Institutes of Health, National Institute of Alcohol Abuse and Alcoholism is sponsoring a clinical trial designed to examine the efficacy of methylphenidate in children with FAS.

In most cases, prognosis depends not only on the specific syndrome, but also on the severity of the effect on the child. As with any disability, proper classroom placement, adjunct services, and intervention plans promote optimal outcomes.

## REFERENCES

Ahluwalia, Y. K., & Meyer, B. E. B. (1998). Psychiatric disorders. In N. Gleicher (Ed.), *Principles and practice of medical therapy in pregnancy* (pp. 1417–1425). New York: Appleton and Lange.

American Academy of Pediatrics, Committee on Drugs. (2000). Use of psychoactive medication during pregnancy and possible effects on the fetus and newborn (RE9866). *Pediatrics, 105,* 880–887.

Aronson, M., & Hagberg, B. (1998). Neuropsychological disorders in children exposed to alcohol during pregnancy: A follow-up study of 24 children to alcoholic mothers in Goteborg, Sweden. *Alcoholism: Clinical and Experimental Research, 22,* 321–324.

Astley, S. J., Bailey, D., Talbot, C., & Clarren, S. K. (2000). Fetal alcohol syndrome (FAS) primary prevention through FAS diagnosis: I. Identification of high-risk birth mothers through the diagnosis of their children. *Alcohol and Alcoholism, 35,* 499–508.

Autti-Ramo, I. (2000). Twelve-year follow-up of children exposed to alcohol in utero. *Developmental Medicine and Child Neurology, 42,* 406–411.

Aylward, G. P., Pfeiffer, S. I., Wright, A., & Verhulst, S. T. (1989). Outcome studies in low birthweight infants published in the last decade: A meta-analysis. *Journal of Pediatrics, 115,* 515–520.

Bhutta, A. T., Cleves, M. A., Casey, P. H., Cradock, M. M., & Anand, K. J. S. (2002). Cognitive and behavioral outcomes of school-aged children who were born premature: A meta-analysis. *Journal of the American Medical Association, 288,* 728–737.

Bohnen, N. I., Ragozzino, M. W., & Kurland, L. T. (1996). Brief communication: Effects of diagnostic irradiation during pregnancy on head circumference at birth. *International Journal of Neuroscience, 87,* 175–180.

Brennan, P. A., Grekin, E. R., & Mednick, S. A. (1999). Maternal smoking during pregnancy and adult male criminal outcomes. *Archives of General Psychiatry, 56,* 215–219.

Briscoe, J., Gathercole, S. E., & Marlow, N. (1998). Short-term memory and language development in preterm children. *Journal of Speech and Hearing Research, 41,* 654–666.

Brown, R. T., Coles, C. D., Smith, I. E., Ptaxman, K. A., Silverman, J., Erikson, S., et al. (1991). Effects of prenatal alcohol exposure at school age, II. Attention and behavior. *Neurotoxicology and Teratology, 13,* 369–376.

Cohen, L., & Rosenbaum, J. (1998). Psychotropic drug use during pregnancy: Weighing the risks. *Journal of Clinical Psychiatry, 59,* 18–28.

Coles, C. D., Brown, R. T., Smith, I. E., Platzman, K. A., Erikson, S., & Falek, A. (1991). Effects of prenatal alcohol exposure at school age I: Physical and cognitive development. *Neurotoxicology and Teratology, 13,* 357–367.

Coles, C. D., Kable, J. A., Drews-Botsch, C., & Falek, A. (2000). Early identification of risk for effects of prenatal alcohol exposure. *Journal of Studies on Alcohol, 61,* 607–616.

Connor, P. D., & Streissguth, A. P. (1996). Effects of prenatal exposure to alcohol across the life-span. *Alcohol Health and Research World, 20,* 170–174.

Craig, M., & Abel, K. (2001). Prescribing for psychiatric disorders in pregnancy and lactation. *Best Practice and Research in Clinical Obstetrics and Gynecology, 15,* 1012–1030.

Dalman, C., Allebeck, P., Cullberg, J., Grunewald, C., & Koster, M. (1999). Obstetric complications and risk of schizophrenia. *Archives of General Psychiatry, 56,* 234–240.

Dietrich, K. N. (1996). Low level lead exposure during pregnancy and its consequences for fetal and child development. In S. M. Pueschel, J. G. Linakis, & A. C. Anderson (Eds.), *Lead poisoning in childhood.* Baltimore: Brookes.

Dietrich, K. N., Ris, M. D., Succop, P. A., Berger, O. G., & Bornschein, R. L. (2001). Early exposure to lead and juvenile delinquency. *Neurotoxicology and Teratology, 23,* 511–518.

Elford, K. J., & Spence, J. E. H. (2002). The forgotten female: Pediatric and adolescent gynecological concerns and their reproductive consequences. *Journal of Pediatric and Adolescent Gynecology, 15,* 7–77.

Ernst, C. L., & Goldberg, J. F. (2002). The reproductive safety profile of mood stabilizers, atypical antipsychotics, and broad-spectrum psychotropics. *Journal of Clinical Psychiatry, 63,* 42–53.

Eure, C. R., Lindsay, M. K., & Graves, W. L. (2002). Risk of adverse pregnancy outcomes in young adolescent parturients in an inner-city hospital. *American Journal of Obstetrics and Gynecology, 186,* 918–920.

Frank, D. A., Augustyn, M., Knight, W. G., Pell, T., & Zuckermam, B. (2001). Growth, development, and behavior in early childhood following prenatal cocaine exposure. *Journal of the American Medical Association, 285,* 1613–1625.

Fried, P. A., & Simon, A. M. (2001). A literature review of the consequences of prenatal marijuana exposure: An emerging theme of a deficiency of executive function. *Neurotoxicology and Teratology, 23,* 1–11.

Gabbard, C., Goncalves, V. M., & Santos, D. C. (2001). Visual-motor integration problems in low birth weight infants. *Journal of Clinical Psychology in Medical Settings, 8,* 199–204.

Gaily, E., & Granstrom, M. L. (1989). A transient retardation of early postnatal growth in drug-exposed children of epileptic mothers. *Epilepsy Research, 4,* 147–155.

Geddes, J. R., & Lawrie, S. M. (1995). Obstetric complications and schizophrenia: A meta-analysis. *British Journal of Psychiatry, 167,* 786–793.

Grandjean, P., Weihe, P., White, R. F., Debes, F., Araki, S., Yokoyama, K., et al. (1997). Cognitive deficit in 7-year-old children with prenatal exposure to methylmercury. *Neurotoxicology and Teratology, 19,* 417–428.

Grunbaum, J. A., Kann, L., Kinchen, S. A., Williams, B., Ross, J. G., Lowry, R., et al. (2002). Youth risk behavior surveillance—United States, 2001. *Morbidity and Mortality Weekly Report, 51*(SS04), 1–64.

Hack, M., Friedman, H., & Faranoff, A. A. (1996). Outcomes of extremely low birthweight infants. *Pediatrics, 98,* 931–937.

Hagerman, R. J. (1999). Psychopharmacological interventions in fragile X syndrome, fetal alcohol syndrome, Prader-Willi syndrome, Angelman syndrome, Smith-Magenis syndrome, and velocardiofacial syndrome. *Mental Retardation and Developmental Disabilities Research Reviews, 5,* 305–313.

Hamilton, S., Rothenberg, S. J., Khan, F. A., Manalo, M., & Norris, K. C. (2001). Neonatal lead poisoning from maternal pica during pregnancy. *Journal of the National Medical Association, 93,* 317–319.

Hodgkins, S., Kratzer, L., & McNeil, T. F. (2001). Obstetric complications, parenting, and risk of criminal behavior. *Archives of General Psychiatry, 58,* 746–752.

Honein, M. A., Paulozzi, L. J., Matthews, T. J., Erickson, J. D., & Wong, L. C. (2001). Impact of folic acid fortification of the U.S. food supply on the occurrence of neural tube defects. *Journal of the American Medical Association, 23,* 2981–2986.

International Commission on Radiological Protection. (2000). *Pregnancy and Medical Radiation, ICRP Publication 84,* 1–39.

Jacobson, J. L., & Jacobson, S. W. (1996). Intellectual impairment in children exposed to polychlorinated biphenyls in utero. *New England Journal of Medicine, 335,* 783–789.

Jacobson, J. L., Jacobson, S. W., Padgett, R. J., & Brumitt, G. A. (1992). Effects of prenatal PCB exposure on cognitive processing efficiency and sustained attention. *Developmental Psychology, 28,* 297–306.

Janzen, L. A., Nanson, J. L., & Block, G. W. (1995). Neuropsychological evaluation of preschoolers with fetal alcohol syndrome. *Neurotoxicology and Teratology, 17,* 273–279.

Jones, K. L. (1997). *Smith's recognizable patterns of human malformation* (5th ed). Philadelphia: Saunders.

Jones, K. L., Lacro, R. V., Johnson, K. A., & Adams, J. (1989). Pattern of malformations in the children of women treated with carbamazepine during pregnancy. *New England Journal of Medicine, 320,* 1661–1666.

Korkman, M., Autti-Ramo, I., Koivulehto, H., & Granstrom, M. L. (1998). Neuropsychological effects at early school age of fetal alcohol exposure of varying duration. *Child Neurology, 4,* 199–212.

Litcher, L., Bromet, E. J., Carlson, G., Squires, N., Goldgaber, D., Panina, N., et al. (2000). School and neuropsychological performance of evacuated children in Kiev 11 years after the Chernobyl disaster. *Journal of Child Psychology, Psychiatry, and Allied Disciplines, 41,* 291–299.

Linnet, K. M., Dalsgaard, S., Obel, C., Wisbord, K., Henriksen, T. B., Rodriguez, A., et al. (2003). Maternal lifestyle factors in pregnancy risk of attention deficit hyperactivity disorder and associated behaviors: Review of current evidence. *American Journal of Psychiatry, 160,* 160–166.

Loganovskaja, T. K., & Loganovsky, K. N. (1999). EEG, cognitive and psychopathological abnormalities in children irradiated in utero. *International Journal of Psychophysiology, 34,* 213–224.

Martin, J. A., Hamilton, B. E., Sutton, P. D., Ventura, S. J., Menacker, F., & Munson, M. L. (2003). Births: Final data for 2002. *National Vital Statistics Reports, 5210.* Hyattsville, Maryland: National Center for Health Statistics.

Mattson, S. N., Riley, E. P., Gramling, L., Delis, D. C., & Jones, K. L. (1998). Neuropsychological comparison of alcohol-exposed children with or without physical features of fetal alcohol syndrome. *Neuropsychology, 12,* 146–153.

Ment, L. R., Vohr, B., Allan, W., Katz, K., Schneider, K. C., Westerveld, M., et al. (2003). Change in cognitive function over time in very low birth weight infants. *Journal of the American Medical Association, 289,* 705–711.

Menyuk, P., Liebergott, J., Schultz, M., Chesnick, M., & Ferrier, L. (1991). Patterns of early lexical development in premature and full-term infants. *Journal of Speech and Hearing Research, 50,* 195–207.

Mirsi, S., & Siveretz, A. (1991). Tricyclic drugs in pregnancy and lactation: A preliminary report. *International Journal of Psychiatry in Medicine, 21,* 157–171.

Myers, G. J., Davidson, P. W., & Shamlaye, C. G. (1998). A review of methylmercury and child development. *Department of Neurology, 19,* 313–328.

Nanson, J. L., & Hiscock, M. (1990). Attention deficits in children exposed to alcohol prenatally. *Alcoholism: Clinical and Experimental Research, 14,* 656–661.

Neugebauer, R., Hoek, H. W., & Susser, E. (1999). Prenatal exposure to wartime famine and development of antisocial personality disorder in early adulthood. *Journal of the American Medical Association, 281,* 455–462.

Nulman, I., Rovet, J., Stewart, D. E., Wolpin, J., Gardner, H. A., Theis, J. G., et al. (1997). Neurodevelopment of children exposed in utero to antidepressant drugs. *New England Journal of Medicine, 336,* 258–262.

Olds, D. (1997). Tobacco exposure and impaired development: A review of the evidence. *Mental Retardation and Developmental Disabilities, 3,* 257–269.

Oesterheld, J. R., Kofoed, L., Tervo, R., Fogas, B., Wilson, A., & Fiechtner, H. (1998). Effectiveness of methylphenidate in Native American children with fetal alcohol syndrome and attention deficit/hyperactivity disorder: A controlled pilot study. *Journal of Child and Adolescent Psychopharmacology, 8,* 39–48.

Ornoy, A., Patlas, N., & Schwartz, L. (1996). The effects of in utero diagnostic X-irradiation on the development of preschool-age children. *Israel Journal of Medical Sciences, 32,* 112–115.

Palumbo, D. R., Cox, C., Davidson, P. W., Myers, G. J., Choi, A., Shamlaye, C., et al. (2000). Association between prenatal exposure methylmercury and cognitive functioning in Seychellois children: A reanalysis of the McCarthy Scales of Children's Ability from the main cohort study. *Environmental Research, 84,* 81–88.

Peterson, B. S., Vohr, B., Staib, L., Cannistraci, C. J., Dolberg, A., Schneider, K. C., et al. (2000). Regional brain volume abnormalities and long-term cognitive outcomes in preterm infants. *Journal of the American Medical Association, 284,* 1939–1947.

Pueschel, S. M., Linakis, J. G., & Anderson, A. C. (1996). *Lead poisoning in childhood.* Baltimore: Brookes.

Rosenblatt, D. S., & Whitehead, V. M. (1999). Cobalamin and folate deficiency: Acquired and hereditary disorders in children. *Seminars in Hematology, 36,* 19–34.

Robinson, D., & Gonzalez, L. S. (1999). Children born premature: A review of linguistic and behavioral outcomes. *Infant-Toddler Intervention, 9,* 373–390.

Rush, D., & Callahan, K. (1989). Exposure to passive cigarette smoking and child development. A critical review. *Annals of the New York Academy of Sciences, 562,* 74–100.

Schou, M. (1976). What happened later to the lithium babies? A follow-up study of children born without malformations. *Acta Psychiatrica Scandinavica, 54,* 193–197.

Sokol, R. J., Delaney-Black, V., & Nordstrom, B. (2003). Fetal alcohol spectrum disorder. *Journal of the American Medical Association, 290,* 2996–2999.

Sood, B., Delaney-Black, V., Covington, C., Nordstrom-Klee, B., Ager, J., Templin, T., et al. (2001). Prenatal alcohol exposure and childhood behavior at age 6 to 7 years: Dose-response effect. *Pediatrics, 108,* E34.

Stewart, P. W., Reihman, J., Lonky, E. I., Darvill, T. J., & Pagano, J. (2003). Cognitive development in preschool children parentally exposed to PCBs and MeHg. *Neurotoxicology and Teratology, 25,* 11–22.

Strauss, R. S. (2000). Adult functional outcome of those born small for gestational age. *Journal of the American Medical Association, 283,* 625–632.

Steinhaussen, H. C., & Spohr, H. L. (1998). Long term outcome of children with fetal alcohol syndrome: Psychopathology, behavior, and intelligence. *Alcoholism: Clinical and Experimental Research, 22*, 334–338.

Streissguth, A. P. (1994). A long-term perspective of FAS. *Alcohol Health and Research World, 18*, 74–81.

Streissguth, A. P. (1997). *Fetal alcohol syndrome.* Baltimore: Brookes.

Streissguth, A. P., Moon-Jordon, A., & Clarren, S. K. (1995). Alcoholism in four patients with fetal alcohol syndrome: Recommendations for treatment. *Alcoholism Treatment Quarterly, 13*, 89–103.

Waisbren, S. E., Hanley, W., Levy, H. L., Shifrin, H., Allred, E., Azen, C., et al. (2000). Outcome at age 4 years in offspring of women with maternal phenylketonuria. *Journal of the American Medical Association, 283*, 756–762.

Walker, A., Rosenberg, M., & Baladan-Gil, K. (1999). Neurodevelopmental and neurobehavioral sequelae of selected substances of abuse and psychiatric medications in utero. *Neurologic Disorders, 8*, 845–866.

Wasserman, G. A., Liu, X., Popovac, D., Factor-Litvak, P., Kline, J., Waternaux, C., et al. (2000). The Yugoslavia prospective lead study: Contributions of prenatal and postnatal lead exposure to early intelligence. *Neurotoxicology and Teratology, 22*, 811–818.

Weitzman M., Gortmaker S., & Sobol A. (1992). Maternal smoking and behavior problems of children. *Pediatrics, 90*, 42–49.

Zevenbergen, A. A., & Ferraro, F. R. (2001). Assessment and treatment of fetal alcohol syndrome in children and adolescents. *Journal of Developmental and Physical Disabilities, 13*, 123–136.

# CHAPTER 26

# Understanding the
# Neuropsychology of Drug Abuse

ARTHUR MacNEILL HORTON JR. and ARTHUR MacNEILL HORTON III

D RUG ABUSE PROBLEMS have a history as old as humankind. Since the earliest recorded time, substances to modify moods, behaviors, and perceptions have been used by large groups of persons. Since the beginning of recorded history, human beings have used alcohol and natural substances such as peyote from the cactus and leaves from the opium plant to change their emotions. In the twentieth century, technology enabled raw materials to be processed to produce heroin and cocaine; chemical advances have included LSD, PCP, designer drugs, and "ice," among others. What new drugs of abuse will be developed in the future is unknown, but it is almost certain that new drugs of abuse will be developed.

Prohibition of the use of addictive substances, though widespread, has rarely been successful. Tobacco use in England in the early 1600s was discouraged by the government of King James I without effect. In the 1700s, chocolate was made illegal in England for a period of time. Moreover, the British Empire fought two wars to allow opium to be sold in China in the 1700s and 1800s over the very vigorous objections of the Chinese emperor. The United States' attempt to prohibit alcohol use was a complete failure and was reversed by a constitutional amendment in 1933. Contemporary efforts to prohibit drug use also have been less than entirely successful (Substance Abuse and Mental Health Services Administration [SAMHSA], 2003).

Survey data indicate that in 2002 (the most recent available findings), 19.5 million Americans, or 8.3% of the U.S. population age 12 or older, were illicit drug users (SAMHSA, 2003). Of illicit drugs, marijuana is the most commonly used, with 14.6 million users or 6.2% in 2002 (SAMHSA, 2003). Among other commonly used illicit drugs in 2002, 2 million persons (0.9%) were current cocaine abusers,

---

Sections of this chapter have been adapted and updated from an earlier chapter: "Neuropsychology of Drug Abuse" (pp. 357–368), by A. M. Horton Jr. in *Ecological Validity of Neuropsychological Testing*, R. J. Sbordone and C. J. Long (Eds.), 1996, Delray Beach, FL: GR Press/St. Lucie Press.

1.2 million used hallucinogens (including 676,000 users of Ecstasy), 166,000 used heroin, and 6.2 million (2.6%) used psychotherapeutic drugs nonmedically (SAMHSA, 2003). Of the psychotherapeutic drug users, 4.4 million used pain relievers, 1.8 million used tranquilizers, 1.2 million used stimulants, and 0.4 million used sedatives (SAMHSA, 2003). Among youths age 12 to 17, 11.6% were illicit drug users (SAMHSA, 2003). The rate of illicit drug use was the highest for young adults, age 18 to 25, at 20.2% in 2002 (SAMHSA, 2003).

Alcohol use in the United States is even higher. In 2002, it was estimated that 120 million Americans age 12 or older were current alcohol drinkers (51.0%; SAMHSA, 2003). Of those current alcohol users, 54 million (22.9%) were monthly binge drinkers and 15.9 (6.7%) were heavy drinkers (SAMHSA, 2003). Among learners age 12 to 20, 10.7 million (28.8%) reported monthly drinking in 2002 (SAMHSA, 2003). As might be expected, the rate of alcohol use increased with age: At age 12, 2.0% used alcohol; at age 13, 6.5%; at age 14, 13.4%; at age 15, 19.9%; at age 16, 29.9%; at age 17, 36.2% (SAMHSA, 2003).

Numbers do not capture the extent of damage to society caused by drugs of abuse. Drug abuse has been estimated to cost the United States at least $275 billion a year (in 1992 dollars; Harwood et al., 1998). Drug abuse affects society through greatly increased health costs as well as costs from the results of domestic violence, traffic accidents, crime, and lost time from work (Hubbard et al., 1989). In addition, there are negative psychological, social, and emotional effects on drug abusers and their spouses and children that produce delayed emotional damage and affect later generations.

On the other hand, the use of certain substances to modify moods and behaviors may be regarded under some circumstances as normal and appropriate. It is clear that social norms influence decisions as to whether the use of a drug is pathological. For example, Native American tribes in the southwestern United States use peyote in religious rites. Similarly, the majority of adults in the United States use caffeine in the form of coffee, tea, or cola drinks. The limited use of marijuana for certain diseases has been allowed by legal authorities for selected individuals in the United States. Indeed, marijuana use has been substantially decriminalized in a number of states in the western United States. In Nevada, a measure to make the use of marijuana legal and a state monopoly was narrowly defeated in recent years. As is well known, narcotics may be used for the alleviation of pain in medically ill individuals when a physician's prescription has been obtained.

It is important to realize that society's views regarding the use of addictive substances may change over time. The first use of many substances abused today, of course, was for therapeutic purposes. Early in his career, Sigmund Freud advocated the use of cocaine as a pain medication. When a colleague became addicted to cocaine, Freud changed his mind. As mentioned earlier, some substances that were previously prohibited are legal and accepted today. What the future will bring is unknown, but it will be important for all citizens to be aware of the nature of the problem of drug abuse as they should be involved in the decisions of which substances should be prohibited and which should be made legal and accepted. Among other factors, the effects of drugs of abuse on the human brain should be considered in making decisions regarding these drugs. The effects on the human brain is, of course, not the only factor to consider in formulating U.S.

drug abuse policy, but it is an area regarding which school psychologists and neuropsychologists have unique expertise that can be used to inform national and state policymakers.

The use of drugs of abuse by learners in the school is a very important concern. Because children are in a developmental phase and still maturing, the effects of drugs of abuse may be more impairing than when adults abuse drugs. Also, drug abuse by schoolchildren interferes with the purpose of school: the effective education of children and youth. It is expected that the use of drugs of abuse by school-age children may interfere with learning and memory processes. The purpose of this chapter is to review what is currently known about drug abuse and discuss approaches to the neuropsychological assessment of learners who have been exposed to drugs of abuse, with special attention to the role of school psychologists.

## OVERVIEW

Research literature has documented, convincingly, neuropsychological effects from certain drugs of abuse (Allan & Landis, 1998; Parson & Farr, 1981; Reed & Grant, 1990). Although this literature is at an early stage of development, given the extent of drug abuse in the United States there are important implications for the assessment and treatment of drug abusers (Spencer & Boren, 1990). Tarter and Edwards (1987) were among the first researchers to note that little attention had been devoted to the functional adaptive capacity of individuals with substance abuse problems. They proposed that use of neuropsychological assessment to measure an individual's organic integrity would provide a basis for estimating that individual's potential for recovery as well as determining a prognosis. In the school setting, the degree and pattern of neuropsychological impairment can provide important information to guide classroom placement and educational accommodation decisions.

An agreement that drug abuse causes residual neuropsychological damage has been reached only recently for selected drugs, studies to assess the neuropsychological treatment implications in populations of drug abusers for the most part remain to be done. The fact that residual neuropsychological effects of abused drugs are a reality is a recent advance (Spencer & Boren, 1990), and researchers are only beginning to address treatment implications. This chapter, however, can serve to set the stage for the planning of future neuropsychological studies in this important and exciting area of clinical and scientific interest.

This chapter postulates that selected drugs of abuse cause neuropsychological deficits and that these deficits are relatively enduring (Spencer & Boren, 1990). For example, certain drug-related states such as intoxication, withdrawal, and delirium are considered to be relatively transient. Although the effects on learning and memory from intoxication and delirium are serious, it is expected that with most individuals these effects are state dependent rather than enduring after withdrawal from the abused substances. The neuropsychological effects of abused drugs to be examined in this chapter are organic syndromes of greater duration.

Other than those related to alcohol, the major syndromes associated with organic deficits recognized by the *Diagnostic and Statistical Manual of Mental Disorders,* text revision (*DSM-IV-TR;* American Psychiatric Association, 2000) include Post-Hallucinogen Perception Disorder, PCP Organic Mental Disorder Not Otherwise Specified, and Amnesic Disorder caused by sedative hypnotic drugs.

## BRAIN STRUCTURES AND PROCESSES
## UNDERLYING ADDICTIVE BEHAVIORS

A basic understanding of the brain structures and processes underlying addictive behavior can help those suffering from substance use and abuse as well as those confronted with it. Neurologically speaking, addiction occurs in large part from changes to the reward pathway of the brain when exposed to drugs such as cocaine, heroin, and marijuana (Figure 26.1).

For general functioning, the reward pathway performs positive conditioning whereby evolutionarily beneficial behaviors precipitate the experience of pleasure. The brain connects the behavior to the pleasurable feeling, and the individual becomes more likely to perform the behavior again to attain the same experience again. A brief exposition of neurophysiology followed by examples of drug-brain interaction provides a useful understanding of the diseases of use and abuse (Figure 26.2 on p. 600).

The brain is composed of 100 billion cells, neurons functioning as an integrated whole through intracellular communication. Messages are transmitted via chemical and electrical signals. Though diversity is the rule, the parts of a given individual neuron do permit classification relevant to the transmission of information (Figure 26.3 on p. 601).

Reception of information from other neurons occurs at the dendrites and soma, the response to which yields the initiation of chemical processes in the

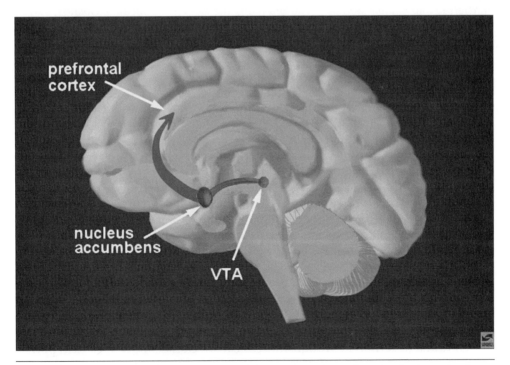

**Figure 26.1**   The Reward Pathway and Its Constituent Parts Showing Its Location in the Brain. *Source:* "The Brain and the Actions of Cocaine, Opiates, and Marijuana," n.d., retrieved August 23, 2004, from http://www.drugabuse.gov/pubs/teaching /Teaching.html.

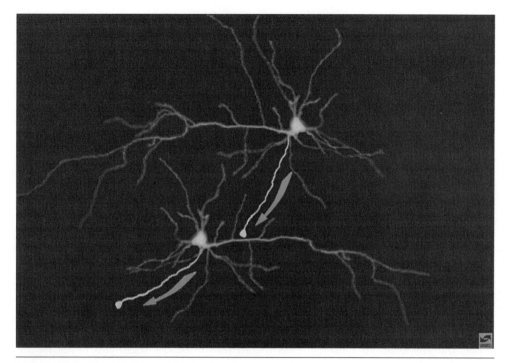

**Figure 26.2**  Two Neurons Able to Communicate. The arrows designate the route of transferred information. *Source:* "The Brain and the Actions of Cocaine, Opiates, and Marijuana," n.d., retrieved August 23, 2004, from http://www.drugabuse.gov/pubs /teaching/Teaching.html.

neuron. Each neuron's membrane regulates the internal chemical environment of the cell. Compared to their external surroundings, membranes actively maintain an electrical potential that is the difference of the electrical charge between the inside of the neuron and the outside. The difference results from the numbers or, more specifically, concentrations of positively and negatively charged ions on each side of the membrane. Laws of physics (the Second Law of Thermodynamics) tell us that such differences seeks a balance (equilibrium) where the concentrations of ions and thus electrical charge do not differ, similar to mixing hot and cold water, which over time produces a uniform temperature. Membranes inhibit this tendency, impeding the flow of ions between the two areas. Ions are allowed to transverse the membrane only through channels in the membrane specific for that ion and/or charge. These channels may open and close through a variety of mechanisms (The Brain and the Actions of Cocaine, n.d.).

At baseline prior to receiving signals from other neurons, a neuron is said to be at resting potential. The membrane of dendrites and soma contains receptors that bind selectively with neurotransmitters, the chemical signals sent between neurons. Binding of certain neurotransmitters causes change in the electrical potential through the opening and closing of ion channels nearby. When inundated with signals from surrounding neurons that excite (depolarize the neuron, or become less negative inside), an action potential is produced. An electrical current travels from the dendrites or soma to the axon of the neuron as ion channels sensitive to electrical charge open. Instead of settling, however, the cascading effect

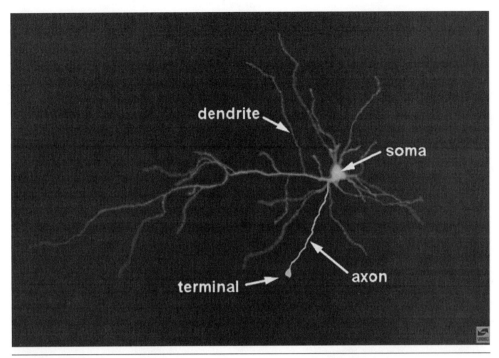

**Figure 26.3** The Characteristic Parts of a Neuron Involved in Its Ability to Receive and Send Messages. *Source:* "The Brain and the Actions of Cocaine, Opiates, and Marijuana," n.d., retrieved August 23, 2004, from http://www.drugabuse.gov/pubs/teaching/Teaching.html.

of the flow of ions pushes the electrical potential past the equilibrium in a manner similar to the release of a compressed spring. The current generated reaches the end of the axon at the terminal. There, vesicles fuse with the neuron's membrane, causing the release of the stored neurotransmitters into the external cellular wall (The Brain and the Actions of Cocaine, n.d.).

The membrane at the terminal is referred to as the presynaptic membrane; in combination with the postsynaptic membrane of another neuron, it forms the synapse. The space between the two neurons that the neurotransmitters travel is the synaptic cleft. Once the synaptic cleft is crossed, the neurotransmitters bind to receptors on the postsynaptic membrane. The response of the neuron to the occupation of a receptor depends on the type of neurotransmitter and the type of receptor. Enzymes may be activated or inhibited. Ion channels may open or close, allowing for the entering or exiting of ions. Neurotransmitters dissociate from the receptor after binding and then are removed from the synaptic cleft by uptake pumps on the terminal of the presynaptic membrane or by enzymes that deactivate neurotransmitters, breaking them apart so that they can no longer link up to receptors. This process of communication is repeated as information travels through the brain (Figure 26.4 on p. 602).

Specifically relevant to the reward pathway and addiction is the neurotransmitter dopamine because of its prevalence in the reward pathway. Additionally, neuromodulators known as endorphins play a role by binding to both pre- and postsynaptic receptors to modify neuronal responses to activity already happening in the synapse (The Brain and the Actions of Cocaine, n.d.).

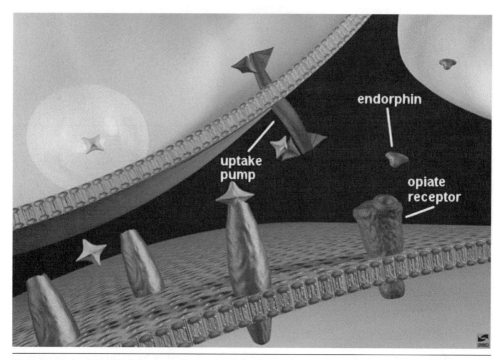

**Figure 26.4**   The Activity in a Synapse When Chemical Signals Are Being Sent between Neurons. *Source:* "The Brain and the Actions of Cocaine, Opiates, and Marijuana," n.d., retrieved August 23, 2004, from http://www.drugabuse.gov/pubs/teaching /Teaching.html.

The brain as a vast network of communication is also subdivided structurally. The different structures produce specific functions and interact with one another to yield more functions and behaviors. Examples of structures related to function are the hippocampus and memory, the visual cortex and sight, and the hypothalamus and homeostasis. Routes of communication between structures, like the structures themselves, rely on neuronal interaction. These connections, termed pathways, allow for the sending and integration of information between brain regions. The reward pathway is one such example. It progresses from the ventral tegmental area (VTA) to the nucleus accumbens to the prefrontal cortex and is activated when positive reinforcement—reward—occurs with a certain behavior (http://www.nida.nih.gov/pubs/Teaching). The behavior thus becomes associated with the reward. Both humans and animals will continue to perform the behavior so long as the reward accompanies the behavior. From experimental results, we know that stimulation of the nucleus accumbens or VTA with cocaine activates the reward pathway. Activation did not occur with cocaine administered to other parts of the brain, even those in close proximity to the reward pathway (The Brain and the Actions of Cocaine, n.d.).

Addictive drugs possess the capacity to produce strong relationships between intense feelings of pleasure and the drug-taking behavior through intense and/or frequent activation of the reward pathway. In extreme cases, this activation can cause drug-taking behavior to be selected over behaviors fundamental to survival.

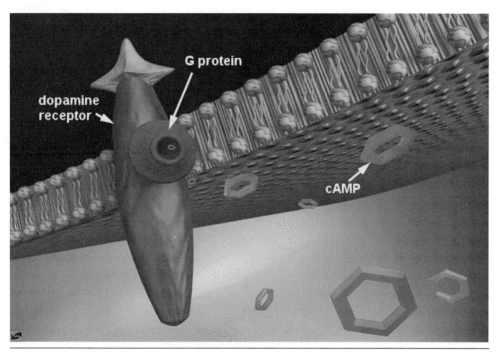

**Figure 26.5**   The Normal Effects of Dopamine Bound to a Neuron Causing Activities inside the Neuron to Change. *Source:* "The Brain and the Actions of Cocaine, Opiates, and Marijuana," n.d., retrieved August 23, 2004, from http://www.drugabuse.gov/pubs /teaching/Teaching.html.

Changes in brain function resulting from drug-brain interaction can be shown through the examples of cocaine, heroin, and marijuana. Many other drugs affect the brain in analogous ways to these three examples. Cocaine smoked, snorted, or injected yields high concentrations in the VTA and nucleus accumbens, where dopamine is heavily used in transmissions between neurons. Cocaine in these areas binds to dopamine's uptake pump, blocking its ability to remove dopamine from the synapse (Figure 26.5).

Synaptic dopamine levels rise and dopamine receptors become more active than normal. The binding of dopamine and its receptors attracts a G-protein to the site. At this point, the G-protein, with the inclusion of an enzyme, forms a dopamine receptor-G-protein/adenylate cyclase complex. In this combination, the enzyme is turned on and produces cAMP (cyclic adenosine monophosphate) molecules that regulate the neuron's ability to generate action potentials as well as many other important functions (Figures 26.6 and 26.7).

Cocaine therefore increases cAMP in the postsynaptic neuron, with the net effects of increased abnormal firing patterns and increased activation of the reward pathway. The use of cocaine becomes strongly linked to the reward, the experience of intense pleasure. Maintenance of the reward requires further use that in turn strengthens the association. Although the effects on the reward pathway are primarily responsible for the addictiveness of cocaine, the drug makes its way to all areas of the brain. In particular, cocaine disrupts the brain's ability to utilize glucose (its metabolic activity). Glucose is the fuel of the brain, providing energy

**Figure 26.6** The Way Cocaine Increases the Amount of Dopamine Going between the Neurons. *Source:* "The Brain and the Actions of Cocaine, Opiates, and Marijuana," n.d., retrieved August 23, 2004, from http://www.drugabuse.gov/pubs/teaching /Teaching.html.

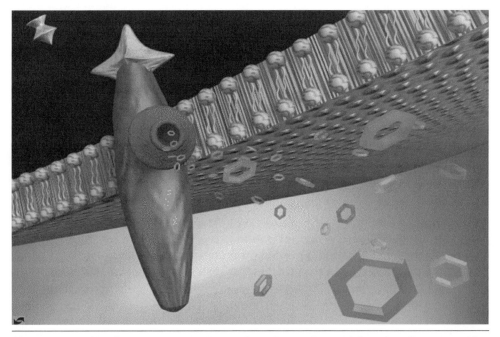

**Figure 26.7** The Change inside a Neuron from Dopamine and Cocaine. Contrast with Figure 26.5 to See Difference in Activity and Production of cAMP. *Source:* "The Brain and the Actions of Cocaine, Opiates, and Marijuana," n.d., retrieved August 23, 2004, from http://www.drugabuse.gov/pubs/teaching/Teaching.html.

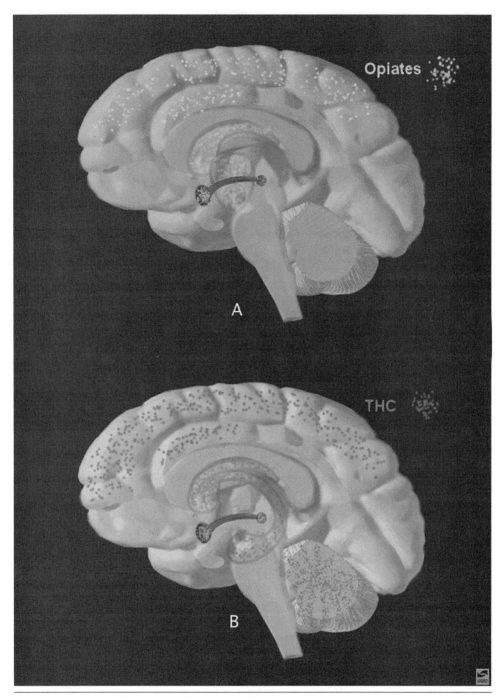

**Figure 26.8** (A) A Side View of the Brain Showing Where Opiates Marked by White Dots Are Found and Active in the Brain. (B) Areas of the Brain Where THC Is Found and Active Shown by Black Dots. *Source:* "The Brain and the Actions of Cocaine, Opiates, and Marijuana," n.d., retrieved August 23, 2004, from http://www.drugabuse.gov/pubs/teaching /Teaching.html.

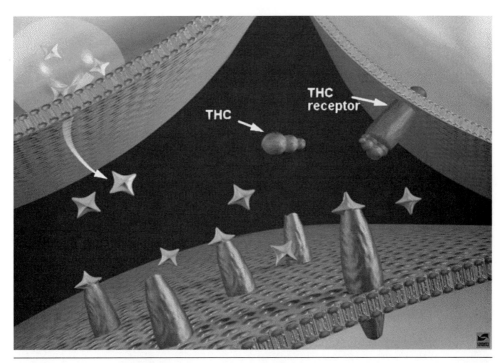

**Figure 26.9**   Increased Dopamine Levels from the Presence of THC. *Source:* "The Brain and the Actions of Cocaine, Opiates, and Marijuana," n.d., retrieved August 23, 2004, from http://www.drugabuse.gov/pubs/teaching/Teaching.html.

for its function. The brain's ineffective use of glucose can cause degradation of multiple brain functions (The Brain and the Actions of Cocaine, n.d.).

Heroin and other opiates, in a manner similar to cocaine, concentrate in the VTA and nucleus accumbens of the reward pathway, producing a net result of increased dopamine release. The cellular mechanisms differ from those of cocaine. Opiates bind to opiate receptors, which are found on neither the presynaptic neuron nor the postsynaptic neuron, but on a third, neighboring neuron. This binding makes the neuron send signals to the dopamine terminals to release more dopamine. Again like cocaine, higher levels of synaptic dopamine lead to greater production of cAMP in the postsynaptic neuron and the reward pathway is activated, associating the drug behavior with an intense reward characteristic of addiction (Figure 26.8 on p. 605).

Least understood in terms of drug-reward pathway interaction of the three examples is marijuana, with its active ingredient cannabinoids or THC (delta-9-tetrahydrocannabinol). Regions of the reward pathway, the VTA and nucleus accumbens, contain concentrations of THC receptors. One theory holds that THC activation of the reward system is a process like that of the opiate with a neighboring neuron, yielding more production of cAMP in the postsynaptic neuron (Figure 26.9).

Here, too, the reward pathway is activated by impulses sent from the nucleus accumbens to the prefrontal cortex. The long-term effect of marijuana use on the reward pathway is still unknown. Other areas of the brain affected by the presence of THC are the hippocampus, where it reduces normal memory function, and the cerebellum, where it can cause lack of coordination and loss of balance (The Brain and the Actions of Cocaine, n.d.).

## PSYCHOACTIVE SUBSTANCE ABUSE RESEARCH ISSUES

To understand the effects of different substances of abuse, some discussion of specific effects will be helpful. The following sections present brief and very selective mini-reviews of the neuropsychological test data currently available regarding the residual effects of various psychoactive substances. There are, however, many very serious methodological difficulties involved with measuring residual drug abuse effects in human beings. A review by Reed and Grant (1990) addressed many of these issues. For example, age, gender, and education present methodological confounds, yet many neuropsychological tests are correlated with age, gender, and education. It is hoped that the recent availability of more accurate and comprehensive age and education norms for a number of neuropsychological tests will address this problem area (Heaton, Miller, Taylor, & Grant, 2004). In addition, use of multiple substances of abuse is difficult to control in research investigations. For the purposes of research, substance abusers may be characterized as having a preference for one substance; in reality, their daily consumption of addictive substances is primarily a product of drug availability. Thus, the majority of drug addicts are "garbage can" abusers, who use a wide variety of psychoactive substances.

The amount of drugs taken by patients is also difficult to measure. Research studies ask patients retrospectively how much of a drug or drugs they have abused. The self-report may be solicited quite some time after the episode of substance abuse. Many substance abusing patients may have impaired short-term memory, and recall of what drugs were abused can be confounded with the type and pattern of cognitive deficits.

The methods for assessing residual drug effects based on the mode of consumption are poorly developed. Ingestion of drugs through needle injection, orally, or through the nose produce different effects with respect to the action of the drug and possibly the residual neuropsychological impairment. Also, premorbid and concurrent medical risk factors can be of great significance. Tarter and Edwards (1987) discuss a number of these risk factors that influence a person's reactions to various drugs, such as learning disabilities and Attention-Deficit/Hyperactivity Disorder symptoms in childhood. Mental disorders that may be present are difficult to diagnose in an addict population. It has been clearly demonstrated that the lack of certain nutrients can play havoc on cognitive functioning. Various organ systems can be impaired and thus have secondary effects on a person's mental ability. In short, multiple psychological, psychiatric, medical, and nutritional factors can obscure the residual neuropsychological effects of drugs of abuse in human beings.

### Marijuana/Cannabis

Early research studies (Carlin & Trupin, 1977; Grant, Rochford, Fleming, & Stunkard, 1973; Mendelson & Meyer, 1972) failed to find significant neuropsychological deficits in marijuana users. Later well-controlled research studies, however, have suggested that memory functions may be impaired after consistent marijuana use (Page, Fletcher, & True, 1988; Schwartz, Gruenewald, Klitzner, & Fedio, 1989). Many earlier neuropsychological test batteries contained poor measures of short-term memory functioning and could be the reason for the earlier negative results. More recent research (Pope & Yurgelun-Todd, 1996) suggested residual neuropsychological effects on memory and executive functioning.

Grant, Gonzales, Carey, Natarajan, and Wolfson (2003) conducted a quantitative synthesis of empirical research (meta-analysis) pertaining to the residual effects of cannabis on the neurocognitive performance of adult human subjects. They examined 15 studies, after screening 1,014 studies for methodological flaws, which provided data on 704 cannabis users and 484 nonusers. Grant et al. calculated effect sizes for eight neuropsychological ability domains and found small but significant effect sizes only for learning and forgetting domains. Grant et al. go on to speculate that the small effect sizes suggest that where cannabis compounds are found to have therapeutic value, the compounds might have an acceptable margin of safety in medical settings. It should be noted that this meta-analysis was limited to adults.

Children and adolescents who are undergoing neuropsychological developmental changes may be more vulnerable than adults to the neurocognitive effects of cannabis. For example, Fried and Smith (2001) suggested that executive dysfunction was found in children of mothers who abused cannabis in a sample in Canada. Goldschmidt, Day, and Richardson (2000) found similar neurocognitive results in a U.S. sample of children of mothers who used cannabis.

## Hallucinogens/LSD/Ecstasy

Research studies of hallucinogens/LSD have noted only selective deficits. McGlothlin, Arnold, and Freedman (1969) and Acord and Barker (1973) in early studies found visual abstraction and concept formation deficits. These subtle deficits were very mild and could have been related to the comorbid factors mentioned previously by Tarter and Edwards (1987). Additional well-controlled research is needed to address this issue. Interestingly, 3,4-methylenedioxymethamphetamine (MDMA), or Ecstasy, has been considered a stimulant, but its hallucinogenic properties have been appreciated more recently. Ecstasy is different from other hallucinogens; recent research has clearly demonstrated that Ecstasy impairs memory weeks after drug use has stopped (Bolla, McCann, & Ricaurte, 1998: Zakzanis & Young, 2001).

## Opiates

The case of opiates and neuropsychological impairment is somewhat confusing. Fields and Fullerton (1975) in an early study found no evidence for neuropsychological deficits with heroin addicts. A later study (Rounsaville, Novelly, Kleber, & Jones, 1980) suggested that heroin addicts who also were polydrug users had neuropsychological deficits. Heroin addicts with the most impairment tended to have a childhood history of hyperactivity and a poorer academic record. The confusing part is that the same group of investigators, Rounsaville, Jones, Novelly, and Kleber (1982), who earlier found neuropsychological impairment conducted a follow-up study (using the same addict subjects as in the Rounsaville et al., 1980, study) and found their drug users to perform better than demographically similar controls on neuropsychological tests. Exactly what happened is unclear, but there has been little subsequent research on neuropsychological impairment in heroin addicts. One possibility is that heroin addicts, like boxers, are a physiologically superior group and even with a degree of neuropsychological impairment are more able than normal individuals.

## SEDATIVES

Judd and Grant (1975) reported neuropsychological deficits among sedative abusers. However, a number of their subjects had also been abusers of stimulants, alcohol, and opiates. Bergman, Borg, and Holm (1980) also found neuropsychological impairments in subjects who were treated only for illicit sedative abuse and better controlled for polydrug abuse. The evidence is so well accepted that the *DSM-IV* contains a category for sedative-hypnotic, amnesic impairment.

## PHENCYCLIDINE

Phencyclidine (PCP), or angel dust, has been reported to evoke uncontrollable psychotic outbursts. Neuropsychological research studies have not overwhelmingly demonstrated the presence of organic mental disorder in PCP users, and a PCP organic mental disorder category that existed in *DSM-III-R* was dropped from *DSM-IV*. Carlin, Grant, Adams, and Reed (1979) found only subtle neuropsychological deficits. At this time, however, few conclusions can be confidently drawn regarding the potential effects of PCP use on neuropsychological functioning, as the study used a small sample size and hasn't been replicated.

## COCAINE/STIMULANTS

O'Malley and Gawin (1990) found a mild degree of neuropsychological impairment in chronic cocaine users. The level of deficits found was mild and similar to the level of deficits found in research studies with polydrug users. A landmark study of neuropsychological deficits with respect to cocaine abusers (Strickland et al., 1993) correlated the results with single photon emission computerized tomography (SPECT) findings. Neurocognitive deficits in cocaine users are likely to be due to strokes and seizures (Volkow, Mullani, Gould, Adler, & Krajewski, 1988). There is considerable animal research suggesting possible neuropsychological deficits due to stimulants (Reed & Grant, 1990). Recent studies (Kalechstein, Newton, & Green, 2003: Nordahl, Salo, & Leamon, 2003) indicate that neuropsychological deficits are related to methamphetamine use.

Future studies in this area could use tools such as positron emission tomography (PET; Volkow, Fowler, & Wolf, 1991) in conjunction with neuropsychological testing (Reitan & Wolfson, 1993; Roberts & Horton, 2001).

## INHALANTS/SOLVENTS

The evidence for neuropsychological impairment from use of inhalants/solvents is at the level of the television ad showing an egg in a frying pan and saying "This is your brain on drugs." One of the first studies was published by Bigler (1979) and demonstrated a generalized pattern of neuropsychological deficits. A subsequent study by Korman, Matthews, and Lovitt (1981) demonstrated clear neuropsychological impairment by inhalant abusers. Tsushina and Towne (1977) found that glue sniffers were neuropsychologically impaired. Berry, Heaton, and Kirley (1977) found a group of chronic abusers impaired on neuropsychological tests. It is clear that inhalants/solvents cause neuropsychological impairment.

POLYDRUG ABUSE

Neuropsychological impairment in polydrug abusers has been amply demonstrated. In an early study, Grant, Mohns, Miller, and Reitan (1976) demonstrated neuropsychological impairment in a population of polydrug users. In addition, Reed and Grant (1990) provided evidence for impairment of neuropsychological functioning. The studies suggesting polydrug users are suffering neuropsychological impairment, however, suffer from possible confounds with respect to risk factors that are medical and psychiatric in nature. Some of the polydrug users studied also abused alcohol, and the effects seen are due more to alcohol consumption than specific drug effects.

## CONCLUSION

The weight of evidence (Spencer & Boren, 1990) indicates there are residual effects on behavior from repeated drug abuse; nonetheless, the magnitude of effects is subtle. Indeed, future research might consider assessing subcortical effects of the action of drug abuse on the brain rather than use instruments that are primarily focused on cortical functioning. Very sensitive assessments of memory, attention, and abstraction are needed (Horton, 1979, 1980, 1993, 1996; Horton & Anilane, 1986; Mezzich & Moses, 1980; Norton, 1978).

Individuals who are impaired from inhalant/solvent abuse (cocaine, marijuana, ecstasy, stimulants) and polydrug abuse clearly demonstrate impairment in terms of neuropsychological functioning. It is clear that (1) these deficits are often subtle; (2) they do not impair gross language or motor functioning or, in most cases, gross sensory-perceptual functioning; but, rather, (3) they involve higher levels of neurocognitive abilities such as short-term memory, visually abstract problem solving, and complex concept formation. It may very well be that some drug abusers can perform relatively well at low-level positions or relatively nondemanding social situations, yet show pronounced problems with mentally demanding employment tasks or in complex social situations (Heaton & Pendleton, 1981).

This chapter reviewed definitions of substance abuse and organic mental functioning, and briefly discussed brain structures and processes underlying addictive behaviors. Difficulties involved in assessing the residual neuropsychological effects of various psychoactive substances were presented. Neuropsychological test results with drug addicts were reviewed. The current research with respect to the neuropsychological effects of abused drugs is composed of a small number of studies, many of which are flawed. In brief, the neuropsychology of drug abusers is an area requiring much additional work. The hope and expectation is that this chapter has been a small step in the direction of better understanding this important area.

# REFERENCES

Acord, L. D., & Barker, D. D. (1973). Hallucinogenic drugs and cerebral deficit. *Journal of Nervous and Mental Diseases, 156,* 281–283.

Allen, D. N., & Landis, R. K. B. (1998). Neuropsychological correlates of substance abuse disorders. In P. J. Snyder & P. D. Nussbaum (Eds.), *Clinical neuropsychology: A pocket handbook for assessment* (pp. 591–612). Washington, DC: American Psychological Association.

American Psychiatric Association. (2000). *Diagnostic and statistical manual of mental disorders* (4th ed., rev.). Washington, DC: Author.

Benedict, R. H. B., & Horton, A. M., Jr. (1992). Reuropsychology of alcohol induced brain damage: Current perspectives on diagnosis, recovery, and prevention. In D. Templer, L. Hartlage, & W. G. Cannon (Eds.), *Preventable brain damage: Brain vulnerability and brain health* (pp. 146–160). New York: Springer.

Bergman, H., Borg, S., & Holm, L. (1980). Neuropsychological impairments and the exclusive abuse of sedatives or hypnotics. *American Journal of Psychiatry, 137,* 215–217.

Berry, G., Heaton, R., & Kirley, M. (1977). Neuropsychological deficits of chronic inhalant abusers. In B. Rumaek & A. Temple (Eds.), *Management of the prisoned patient* (pp. 59–83). Princeton, NJ: Sciences.

Bigler, E. D. (1979). Neuropsychological evaluation of adolescent patients hospitalized with chronic inhalant abuse. *Clinical Neuropsychology, 1,* 8–12.

Bolla, K. I., McCann, D. U., & Ricaurte, G. A. (1998). Memory impairment in abstinent MDMA ("ecstasy") users. *Neurology, 51,* 1532–1537.

The Brain & the Actions of Cocaine, Opiates, and Marijuana. (n.d.). Retrieved August 23, 2004, from http://www.nida.nih.gov/pubs/Teaching.

Carlin, A., Grant, I., Adams, K., & Reed, R. (1979). Is phencyclidine (PCP) abuse associated with organic mental impairment? *American Journal of Drug and Alcohol Abuse, 6,* 273–281.

Carlin, A. S., & Trupin E. (1977). The effects of long-term chronic cannabis use on neuropsychological functioning. *International Journal of Addiction, 12,* 617–624.

Fields, F. S., & Fullerton, J. (1975). Influences of heroin addiction on neuropsychological functioning. *Journal of Consulting and Clinical Psychology, 43,* 114.

Fried, P. A., & Smith, A. M. (2001). A literature review of the consequences of prenatal marijuana exposure: An emerging theme of a deficiency in executive functioning. *Neurotoxicology and Teratology, 23,* 1–11.

Goldschmidt, L., Day, N. L., & Richardson, G. A. (2000). Effect of prenatal marijuana exposure on child behavior problems at age 10. *Neurotoxicology and Teratology, 22,* 325–336.

Grant, I., Gonzales, R., Carey, C., Natarajan, L., & Wolfson, T. (2003). Non-acute (residual) neurocognitive effects of cannabis use: A meta-analytic study. *Journal of the International Neuropsychological Society, 9,* 679–689.

Grant, I., Mohns, L., Miller, M., & Reitan, R. (1976). A neuropsychological study of polydrug users. *Archives of General Psychiatry, 33,* 973–978.

Grant, I., Rochford, J., Fleming, A., & Stunkard, A. (1973). A neuropsychological assessment of the effects of moderate marijuana use. *Journal of Nervous and Mental Diseases, 156,* 278–280.

Harwood, H. J., Fountain, D., Livermore, G., et al. (1998). *Economic costs to society of alcohol and drug abuse and mental illness: 1992.* Washington, DC: National Institute on Drug Abuse and National Institute on Alcohol and Alcohol Abuse.

Heaton, R. K., Miller, S. W., Taylor, M. J., & Grant, I. (2004). *Revised comprehensive norms for an expanded Halstead-Reitan Battery: Demographically adjusted neuropsychological norms for African American and Caucasian adults.* Lutz, FL: Psychological Assessment Resources.

Horton, A. M., Jr. (1979). Some suggestions regarding the clinical interpretation of the Trail Making Test. *Clinical Neuropsychology, 1,* 20–23.

Horton, A. M., Jr. (1980). Cutting scores on the Trail Making Test. *Clinical Neuropsychology, 2*(3), 99.

Horton, A. M., Jr. (1993). Future directions in the development of addiction assessment instruments. In B. J. Rounsaville, F. M. Tims, A. M. Horton, Jr., & B. J. Sowder (Eds.), *Diagnostic source book on drug abuse research and treatment* (pp. 87–92). Rockville, MD: U.S. Department of Health and Human Services.

Horton, A. M., Jr. (1996). Neuropsychology of drug abuse. In R. J. Sbordone & C. J. Long (Eds.), *Ecological validity of neuropsychological testing* (pp. 357–368). Delray Beach, FL: St. Lucie Press.

Horton, A. M., Jr., & Anilane, J. (1986). Relationship of Trail Making Test-Part B., & brain age quotients: Long and short forms. *Psychotherapy in Private Practice, 21,* 39–43.

Hubbard, R. L., Marsden, M. E., Rachal, J. V., Harwood, H. J., Cavanaugh, E. R., & Ginzburg, H. M. (1989). *Drug abuse treatment: A national study of effectiveness.* Chapel Hill, NC: University of North Carolina Press.

Judd, L. L., & Grant, I. (1975). Brain dysfunction in chronic sedative users. *Journal of Psychedelic Drugs, 7,* 143–149.

Kalechstein, A. D., Newton, T. F., & Green, M. (2003). Methamphetamine dependence is associated with neurocognitive impairment in the initial phases of abstinence. *Journal of Neuropsychiatry and Clinical Neurosciences, 15,* 215–220.

Korman, M., Matthews, R. W., & Lovitt, R. (1981). Neuropsychological effects of abuse on inhalants. *Perceptual and Motor Skills, 53,* 547–553.

Mack, A. H., Franklin, J. E., & Francis, R. J. (2001). *Concise guide to the treatment of alcohol and addictions* (2nd ed.). Washington, DC: American Psychiatric Association.

McCaffrey, R. J., Krahula, M. M., Heimberg, R. G., Keller, K. E., & Purcell, M. J. (1988). A comparison of the Trail Making Test, Symbol Digit Modalities Test and the Hooper Visual Organization Test in an inpatient substance abuse population. *Archives of Clinical Neuropsychology, 3,* 181–187.

McGlothlin, W. H., Arnold, D. D., & Freedman, D. X. (1969). Organicity measures following repeated LSD ingestion. *Archives of General Psychiatry, 21,* 704–709.

Mendelson, J. H., & Meyer, R. E. (1972). Behavioral and biological concomitants of chronic marijuana smoking by heavy and casual users. In *Marijuana: A signal of misunderstanding* (Vol.1). Washington, DC: U.S. Government Printing Office.

Mezzich, J. E., & Moses, J. A. (1980). Efficient screening for brain-dysfunction. *Biological Psychiatry, 15,* 333–337.

Nordahl, T. E., Salo, R., & Leamon, M. (2003). Neuropsychological effects of chronic methamphetamine use on neurotransmitters and cognition: A review. *Journal of Neuropsychiatry and Clinical Neurosciences, 15,* 317–325.

Norton, J. (1978). The Trail Making Test and Bender Background Interference Procedure as screening devices. *Journal of Clinical Psychology, 34,* 916–922.

O'Malley, S. S., & Gawin, F. H. (1990). Abstinence symptomatology and neuropsychological deficits in chronic cocaine abusers. In J. W. Spencer & J. J. Boren (Eds.), *Residual effects of abused drugs on behavior* (National Institute on Drug Abuse Research Monograph No. 101, OHHS Pub. No. ADM 90-1719, pp. 179–190). Washington, DC: Government Printing Office.

Page, J. B., Fletcher, J., & True, W. P. (1988). Psychosociocultural perspectives on chronic cannabis use: The Costa Rican followup. *Journal of Psychoactive Drugs, 20,* 57–65.

Parson, O. A., & Farr, S. P. (1981). The neuropsychology of alcohol and drug use. In S. Filskov & T. J. Boll (Eds.), *Handbook of clinical neuropsychology* (pp. 320–365). New York: Wiley.

Pope, H. G., & Yurgelun-Todd. (1996). The residual cognitive effects of heavy marijuana use in college students. *Journal of the American Medical Association, 275,* 521–527.

Reed, R., & Grant, I. (1990). The long term neurobehavioral consequence of substance abuse: Conceptual and methodological challenge for future research. In J. W. Spencer & J. J. Boren (Eds.), *Residual effects of abused drugs on behavior* (Research Monograph No. 101, pp. 10–56). Rockville, MD: National Institute on Drug Abuse.

Reitan, R. M., & Wolfson, D. (1993). *The Halstead-Reitan Neuropsychological Battery* (2nd ed.). Tucson, AZ: Neuropsychology Press.

Roberts, C., & Horton, A. M., Jr. (2001). Using the Trail Making Test to screen for cognitive impairment in a drug abuse treatment sample. *International Journal of Neuroscience, 109,* 273–280.

Rounsaville, B. J., Novelly, R. A., Jones, C. C., & Kleber, H. D. (1980). Neuropsychological impairments in opiate addicts: Risk factors. *Annuals of the New York Academy of Science, 362,* 79–80.

Rounsaville, B. J., Jones, C. C., Novelly, R. A., & Kleber, H. D. (1982). Neuropsychological functioning in opiate addicts. *Journal of Nervous and Mental Diseases, 170,* 209–216.

Sbordone, R. J. (1993). Personal communication.

Schwartz, R. H., Gruenewald, P. J., Klitzner, M., & Fedio, P. (1989). Short-term memory impairment in cannabis-dependent adolescents. *American Journal of Diseases of Children, 143*(100), 1214–1219.

Spencer, J. W., & Boren, J. (1990). *Residual effects of abused drugs in behavior* (Research Monograph No. 101). Rockville, MD: National Institute on Drug Abuse.

Strickland, T. L., Mena, I., Villanueva-Meyer, J., Miller, B., Mehringer, C. M., Satz, P., et al. (1993). Cerebral perfusion and neuropsychological consequences of chronic cocaine use. *Journal of Neuropsychiatry and Clinical Neurosciences, 5,* 419–427.

Substance Abuse and Mental Health Services Administration. (2003). *Overview of Findings from the 2002 National Survey on Drug Use and Health* (Office of Applied Studies, NHSDA Series H-21, DHHS Publication No. SMA 03-3774). Rockville, MD: Author.

Tarter, R. E., & Edwards, K. L. (1987). Brief and comprehensive neuropsychological assessment of alcohol and substance abuse. In L. C. Hartlage, J. L. Hornsby, & M. J. Asken (Eds.), *Essentials of neuropsychological assessment* (pp. 138–162). New York: Springer.

Tsushina, W., & Towne, W. (1977). Effects of paint sniffing on neuropsychological test performance. *Journal of Abnormal Psychology, 86,* 402–407.

Volkow, N. D., Fowler, J. S., & Wolf, A. P. (1991). Use of positron emission tomography to study cocaine in the human brain. In R. S. Rapaka, A. Makriyhnnis, & M. J. Kuhar (Eds.), *Emerging technologies and new direction in drug abuse research* (National Institute on Drug Abuse Research Monograph No. 112, DHHS Pub. No. ADM 91-1812, pp. 168–179). Washington, DC: Government Printing Office.

Volkow, N. D., Mullani, N., Gould, K. L., Adler, S., & Krajewski, K. (1988). Cerebral blood flow in chronic cocaine users: A study with positron omission tomography. *British Journal of Psychiatry, 152,* 641–648.

Zakzanis, K. K., & Young, D. A. (2001). Memory impairment in abstinent MDMA ("ecstasy") users: A longitudinal investigation. *Neurology, 56*(7), 966–969.

CHAPTER 27

# Providing Neuropsychological Services to Learners with Low-Incidence Disabilities

LAWRENCE LEWANDOWSKI

THE FIELD OF school neuropsychology has devoted most of its attention to the more common and popular childhood disorders, learning disabilities (LD), and Attention-Deficit/Hyperactivity Disorder (AD/HD). These disorders, while well recognized in the schools as distinct categories, are quite heterogeneous in nature and comprise many less common, low-incidence disorders. For example, there are various developmental/genetic disorders that manifest with LD and/or ADHD, among other neuropsychological characteristics. These include Down syndrome (DS), Gilles de la Tourette syndrome (GTS), Turner syndrome (TS), velocraniofacial syndrome (VCFS), Klinefelter syndrome (KS), neurofibromatosis (NF-1), fragile X syndrome (FXS), tuberous sclerosis complex (TSC), and Sturge Weber syndrome (SWS). The incidence rates for these disorders range between 1 per 1,000 to 1 per 5,000 (except SWS). Although these are considered to be low-incidence disorders, collectively there is a strong likelihood that school neuropsychologists serving more than 500 learners will encounter one or more children with one of these disorders.

Each of these nine disorders has unique medical, developmental, and psychological features that require separate knowledge bases. The purpose of this chapter is to equip the school psychologist or school neuropsychologist with some core knowledge about each disorder that will help with identification and assessment, thorough understanding, and implications for treatment. Unlike other disorders reviewed in this book, there are no group, school-based studies of these low-incidence disorders. One cannot easily point to evidence-based treatment protocols for the academic problems of learners with TS, for example. However, knowledge about the characteristics of the syndrome along with research findings about psychological functioning will permit us to make informed suggestions regarding assessment and interventions. The remainder of this chapter reviews the relevant background and psychological information for each of the nine disorders and addresses developmental, family, and school concerns. The medical aspects of these disorders, which are considerable for each, are abbreviated so that we can focus on educational, cognitive, and psychosocial facets of each disorder.

Before separately reviewing each disorder, there are some general points that should be noted pertinent to all of the disorders. An important link across these disorders is that most of them are considered to be genetic disorders (except SWS). Certainly, disorders such as LD, ADHD, and Autism have genetic components. However, the genetic contributions to these disorders are not well understood and may not be as etiologically significant as they are in the aforementioned disorders. Additionally, the syndromes reviewed in this chapter all express neurodevelopmental disturbances, with known brain dysfunction accompanying most of them. Typically, these disorders manifest with anomalies in other developmental systems, such as muscular, skeletal, cutaneous, endocrine, and metabolic. In short, a person with one of these syndromes is likely to have myriad problems that could affect physical, mental, educational, emotional, and behavioral development. It is important to keep the issue of comorbidity in mind as each syndrome is reviewed.

## DOWN SYNDROME

Credit for the discovery of DS is given to H. Langdon Down, a British physician who described a set of individuals with a broad face, thick tongue, epicanthal folds around the eyes, language problems, and a shortened life expectancy. Down felt that people with this condition showed a retrogression of European heritage similar to the Mongolian race. He termed the condition Mongolian idiocy, later known as mongolism (Zellweger, 1977). In 1959, researchers identified the chromosomal abnormality that underlies DS (Lejeune, Gautier, & Turpin, 1959).

DS is caused by the presence of an extra copy of chromosome 21 (whole or partial). Of the variants of DS, trisomy 21 accounts for about 95% of the cases. A majority of trisomy 21 conceptions results in stillbirth or miscarriage. It is believed that DS occurs in 1 of every 700 to 1,000 live births (Roizen, 2002). The risk of DS seems to increase with maternal age, particularly after age 45. In addition to the features originally described by Down, DS is linked with medical problems across the organ systems. There is high risk (50% to 100% of those with DS) of heart defects, endocrine abnormalities, compromised vision and hearing, skin conditions, dental problems, orthopedic problems, hypotonia, and infertility or reduced fertility.

### CHARACTERISTICS

Some regard DS as the prototype for mental retardation. The characteristic facial features make the disorder easy to identify, and virtually all individuals with DS have some degree of cognitive limitation, with the majority experiencing a moderate degree of retardation. For many with DS, mental development is closer to normal during infancy, but the rate of intellectual development does not keep pace with age. As intellectual development slowly progresses, declines in IQ scores often are observed (see Evans & Gray, 1999; Hodapp, 1997, for review). Analysis of the IQ profiles indicates that learners with DS tend to perform better on visual-spatial than auditory-verbal tasks (e.g., Powell, Houghton, & Douglas,

1997). Numerous studies have documented the language difficulties associated with DS, particularly with expressive language (J. Miller, 1992). Speech articulation is a problem for virtually all those with DS, particularly in light of problems with hearing, low muscle tone, and oral structure abnormalities. Beside the medical and cognitive characteristics, DS is associated with low muscle tone and poor motor coordination. The high proportion of obesity is not helpful to mobility. In contrast to declines in intellectual functioning, the adaptive skills of DS individuals may not deteriorate, particularly with proper stimulation (Loveland & Kelley, 1991).

A host of studies document brain anomalies in samples of learners with DS. Findings have included less than normal cerebral volume, underdeveloped temporal and frontal lobes, and thinning and widening of the corpus callosum (see Wang, 1996, for review). One of the intriguing features of DS is its association with Alzheimer's disease (AD). Estimates of AD in DS range from 15% to 40%, with the incidence increasing dramatically after age 40. Scientists have found the classic brain anomalies of plaques and neurofibrillary tangles known to accompany AD (Wisniewski, Wisniewski, & Wen, 1985). These brain changes may account for some of the cognitive, adaptive, and personality deterioration that is frequently noted in DS individuals even as young as adolescence.

Children with DS are known for their tendencies toward a pleasant disposition, occasional obstinacy, and a habit of imitation. It is clear that such stereotypes do not apply to all those with DS. It does appear, with the exception of AD, that they are at no greater risk for psychiatric disorders. However, approximately 20% have some type of emotional or behavioral problems that impair learning or adjustment (Dykens & Kasari, 1997).

Whether it is the DS personality, the visibility of the disorder, or its wide acceptance and support, it appears that families with a DS member cope better than families with other disabilities. Various studies have shown positive family relationships involving a child with DS, including close sibling relationships (see Hodapp, 1996).

## Assessment Considerations

The diagnosis of DS is made at birth or determined by amniocentesis, so early intervention is quite common. Assessment then is used to describe and monitor functioning across developmental domains. Neuropsychological evaluations should first adjust procedures to any medical or sensory difficulties of the child. Cognitive and adaptive testing is typically conducted to determine general levels of development and functioning. Assessment of speech/language functions is particularly important. Memory, spatial, and motor performances will inform treatment and management at home and school. Educational testing is usually rudimentary. It is estimated that over half of those with DS will be able to read 50 or more words, but few will be able to read beyond a 4th-grade level (Pueschel & Hopmann, 1993). Most students with DS will not reach functional levels of reading, writing, or math.

The psychologist is likely the professional who will check the student's behavior as well as emotional status at home and school. As functioning may decline with age, the psychologist needs to document and explain this to family and school staff. Together with a team of professionals, the psychologist can help generate educational, adaptive, and vocational plans that are optimal for the student.

As mentioned, early intervention is usually put in motion during the preschool years. In addition to medical care, occupational therapy, physical therapy, and speech therapy are commonly delivered services. Early stimulation programs and/or home consultation services are common in most states. Education in inclusive settings is often possible and preferred by families, at least through the early grades. This is particularly viable for higher-functioning students with no behavior problems. Among the specialized interventions for students with DS is sign language. Given problems with expressive speech yet with reasonably good imitation and memory skills, sign language can be a useful alternative for some DS children.

Any treatment program is likely to focus a good bit of attention on adaptive and vocational skills. Hodapp (1997) noted that stimulating environments aid the development of adaptive functioning through adolescence. Vocational training along with job coaching and internships become increasingly important as the child ages and becomes more independent. Most individuals with DS will require some degree of supervision and assistance with life management, ranging from total care to near independence. There are many support services for those with DS and their families that facilitate positive social and vocational outcomes. Perhaps the toughest psychological adjustment for everyone is the management of dementia if Alzheimer's disease appears, although this usually occurs after school age.

## FRAGILE X SYNDROME

The history of FXS dates back to 1943, when Martin and Bell described a form of mental retardation that was X-linked. By 1969, a chromosomal test was developed to detect FXS. In the early 1990s, scientists isolated and mapped the FMR1 gene that causes FXS. It appears that some individuals carry a premutation (unstable or incomplete version) of FMR1. Usually, premutation is not observable; however, it can increase with successive generations until an abnormality in the structure of the X chromosome becomes evident and fragile X symptoms occur. Although more people carry the premutation, it is estimated that 1 in 3,600 males and 1 in 5,000 females receive the full mutation (National Fragile X Foundation, 2003).

The major characteristics of the disorder include mental retardation, particularly in males, a long face with prominent chin and ears, hyperextensible joints, poor language and motor development, short attention span and hyperactivity, tactile defensiveness, autistic-like behaviors (e.g., poor eye contact, fascination with spinning objects), and behavioral problems (e.g., hand biting, aggression, impaired social skills). There are some key differences between males and females with this disorder. Boys are likely to have retardation marked by early developmental delays. Approximately 50% of girls with FXS have mental retardation (MR). Boys tend to manifest more symptoms of ADHD and Autism than girls, and they tend to be more sensitive to touch and react aggressively. On the other hand, girls seem to be more shy and withdrawn and tend to experience learning problems, particularly in math. Speech and language problems are more common in boys with FXS, including perseveration and echolalia. Boys seem to be most at risk for MR, Autism, and ADHD, whereas girls are at greater risk for LD, ADD without hyperactivity, and possible anxiety and depression. Certainly, this is one disorder in which sex differences require very different considerations.

## ASSESSMENT CONSIDERATIONS

The range of symptom expression in FXS is quite wide. For example, most boys have IQs that range from borderline to severely retarded, whereas girls range from normal to mildly retarded. Language problems range from subtle to pervasive communication deficits, as seen in severe Autism. Problems with executive functions range from inattention to ADHD combined type, including problems of inhibitory control. Also, behavior patterns range from within normal limits to self-stimulation, hyperactivity, and aggression.

It seems obvious that virtually all areas of functioning can be affected by the disorder and must be considered in a comprehensive assessment. Such testing would include assessment of cognitive and language abilities, symptoms of ADHD and Autism, educational achievement, adaptive and social behavior, and sensorimotor functioning. It is important when working with the FXS learner to be aware of any hypersensitivity to touch or other stimuli, as well as possible reactivity to changes in the environment. The diagnostic picture is sometimes further complicated by issues such as seizures, tremors, abnormal sleep patterns, proneness to ear infections, oculomotor dysfunction, and gastrointestinal disorders. In the extreme, the combination of symptoms can be a huge challenge to the child, parents, and support professionals. It should be noted that children with FXS also have positive behavioral and emotional characteristics, including being warm and loving and having a good sense of humor.

Typically, diagnosis is based on medical evidence. The role of psychological assessment is to provide the most comprehensive overview of all areas of functioning and its impact on the child, home, and school. With this comprehensive profile the psychologist can inform and assist with educational, cognitive, psychosocial, and behavioral programming.

## TREATMENT CONSIDERATIONS

Following from the discussion of characteristics and assessment, the treatment of FXS must be multifaceted. There is no medical treatment, although cytogenetic testing in some cases can determine carriers of the premutation and detect FXS in the fetus. Some children with FXS receive medication treatment for seizures, ADHD, or behavior control. A majority of these learners will require special education services ranging from tutoring and resource support to intensive supervision and multiple therapies. In extreme cases, learners have needed one-to-one instruction for part of the school day. Speech and language therapy is frequently an accompanying service, often focusing on oral-motor control and pragmatics. Occupational therapy also is commonly provided; this ranges from basic movement and positioning goals to sensory-integration therapy. Social and adaptive skills are usually problematic for these youngsters, so interventions in these areas are often required.

School neuropsychologists may be consulted on issues of impulsive, defiant, self-injurious, and/or aggressive behavior. A functional assessment likely will be helpful in determining the environmental factors that trigger the behavior(s). Some proactive strategies for working with FXS learners include small group instruction, structure and predictability, avoiding crowding and confusion, reducing extraneous stimuli, providing nonverbal cues and feedback, allowing escape from stressful situations and overstimulation, providing calming activities, and assisting with transitions.

The school psychologist should be in a good position to understand the various difficulties faced by the FXS learner and convey this knowledge in a developmental and educational context to teachers and staff. Together they can develop an informed individualized educational plan. The neuropsychologist can then serve as a consultant regarding academic, behavioral, and social concerns of the teachers and parents. It is important that the psychologist and/or social worker be a support to the family. Some research has noted that, particularly in cases with severe symptoms (i.e., MR, Autism), the stress on the mother is considerable (Johnston et al., 2003). Extending behavioral and other treatment strategies to the family could make a difference in reducing stress in the home and improving overall outcomes for the child.

Parents and professionals have been working feverishly in this area to develop information and support systems as well as intervention approaches for FXS children. Given the heterogeneity of this low-incidence disorder, it is difficult to conduct systematic treatment research. Most of the earlier suggestions have not been empirically driven; they accrue from clinical experience. This field surely could benefit from single-subject treatment research. Perhaps in the near future evidence-based interventions will be delineated for FXS.

## GILLES DE LA TOURETTE SYNDROME

Gilles de la Tourette was a contemporary of Freud, both working in France in the late 1880s. Tourette became acquainted with a princess who displayed motor and colorful verbal tics. He described this case in 1885, and this became the basis for the syndrome that carries his name. Since that time, considerable research and writing has addressed this fascinating and perplexing disorder.

GTS is an inherited disorder in most cases. It is the result of single-gene transmission of the GTS gene. This genetic vulnerability is thought to disrupt the balance of neurotransmitters (dopamine, norepinephrine, and serotonin) in the basal ganglia, thalamus, and frontal striatal projections (Murray, 1997). Approximately 1 in 83 persons carry this gene. Incidence rates are estimated between 1 and 3 per 1,000 children, with boys 5 to 10 times more susceptible than girls (Scahill, Tanner, & Dure, 2001). There are other tic disorders that confound the diagnosis of GTS and may affect the accuracy of the estimates. Onset of the disorder must be present before age 18, but the modal age for the onset is 7.

### CHARACTERISTICS

GTS is marked by the presence of recurring, repetitive, and involuntary motor and vocal expressions referred to as tics (Muller et al., 2003). Motor tics typically involve the head and face, including such expressions as blinking, squinting, grimacing, mouth opening, licking lips, and head and neck movements (Comings, 1990). In addition, there may be purposeless behaviors such as smelling fingers,

picking skin, touching, flapping, grooming, chewing, and making obscene gestures. These stereotyped behaviors are similar to compulsive rituals expressed by
persons with Obsessive-Compulsive Disorder (OCD). Various studies indicate comorbidity rates of GTS and OCD between 20% and 70% (King, Leckman, Scahill,
& Cohen, 1999). Vocal tics add to the uniqueness of this disorder. Common vocal
tics include throat clearing, grunting, yelling, sniffing, barking, swearing, and
snorting, as well as repetitions of one's own words (Comings, 1990). The severity
of tics varies across individuals, and the tics are often exacerbated by stressful situations. It is an understatement to say that GTS behavior is often misunderstood
by observers, and those with GTS may pay a huge social cost for something they
have no control over.

Besides OCD, ADHD and LD are common accompaniments to GTS. Estimates
of comorbidity suggest that GTS and ADHD overlap in 40% to 70% of cases, and
LD may exist in 10% to 25% of GTS patients (Walkup et al., 1999). Such estimates
are variable across studies and subject to definitional differences employed. GTS
is also known to co-occur with Autism, Asperger's syndrome, and Schizophrenia. Those with GTS also are at increased risk for anxiety, depression, speech
deficits, motor problems, and sleep disorders.

Learners with GTS typically have normal intelligence, although scores fall
below the general population. Those with more severe forms of GTS tend to have
lower IQ scores, although it may be that LD, ADHD, and other co-occurring disorders account for the lower test scores (Ozonoff, Strayer, McMahon, & Filloux,
1998). Neuropsychological testing has revealed deficits in executive functioning,
particularly response inhibition, as well as in visuomotor integration, visuospatial functions, mathematics, and motor coordination (Bradshaw, 2001; Muller
et al., 2003; Schultz, Carter, Scahill, & Leckman, 1999). Bornstein (1990) suggests
that approximately 20% of GTS patients perform abnormally on neuropsychological assessments. It has been noted that individuals with "pure" GTS tend to perform more normally on neuropsychological measures and tests of executive
functioning (Goh, Bradshaw, Bradshaw, & Georgiou-Kalistianis, 2002; Shin et al.,
2001), suggesting that comorbid ADHD and LD may contribute to weaknesses in
neuropsychological or executive function performances.

Academic casualty also seems dependent on the severity of the symptom complex and presence of comorbid conditions. Students with multiple problems have
difficulties in school with behavioral control, attention, and concentration, as well
as social competence. Learning difficulties are seen across all areas; however,
writing and math difficulties tend to be more prevalent with GTS as compared to
the rest of the population (Walkup et al., 1999). Adjustment in the school setting
goes beyond academic skill deficits. Students with GTS spend considerable energy trying to control tics, stereotyped behaviors, and impulsivity. Their behaviors may draw attention, laughter, and ridicule from peers and interfere with
learning. Due to this chain of behavioral events, GTS students often experience
stress and anxiety in school. This only exacerbates the tics and further interferes
with learning.

ASSESSMENT CONSIDERATIONS

In cases of "pure" GTS, there may be just motor and vocal tics with little disturbance in neurocognitive and behavioral functioning. In many cases, however, the

diagnostic picture is complicated by comorbid conditions such as OCD, ADHD, LD, anxiety, and depression. Such differential diagnosis requires a comprehensive assessment. In addition to the standard psychoeducational battery, the school psychologist may need to specifically assess for ADHD, OCD, anxiety, self-esteem, social skills, and family functioning. Due to the observable nature of many of the symptoms, classroom observations and perhaps a complete behavioral assessment are recommended. Neuropsychological testing, at least in limited form, could be essential in delineating strengths and weaknesses across areas of functioning (e.g., visuomotor, spatial, executive, language, and processing speed), and these findings could inform academic and other interventions. A comprehensive assessment of GTS likely will involve a team of professionals who ultimately integrate medical, developmental, behavioral, social, educational, and neuropsychological findings. Investigators at Yale University offer a model for such an assessment approach (see Leckman et al., 1999).

## TREATMENT CONSIDERATIONS

Medication is commonly used in conjunction with educational, behavioral, and psychosocial interventions. Traditionally, haloperidol, clonidine, and guanfacine have been used to control tic symptoms. Other medications are commonly used to control OCD, anxiety, and ADHD symptoms. Therefore, some GTS patients are on a combination of medications (Comings, 1990). Behavioral treatment techniques (i.e., self-monitoring, contingency management) are widely applied to this population in controlling tics, compulsivity, and impulsivity. On occasion, a plan is necessary to deal with rage reactions. Environmental engineering can be helpful in preventing some behaviors; a structured environment with seating away from doors and windows may be preferable. Some suggest testing in private to avoid the tension around maintaining quiet. Teachers have found it helpful to allow some flexibility in class rules, perhaps allowing a GTS student to escape an anxious situation, not having the student read or present to the class, and not reprimanding or drawing attention to the student for unusual behaviors.

Depending on the learner, it may be helpful to reduce workload, break tasks down, and provide visual with auditory cues. Academic support is commonly needed with writing and math tasks. Modifications of assignments, particularly visuomotor tasks such as drawing, writing, and worksheets, should be considered. Test accommodations may involve a separate location as well as extended time and alternative response modes. Sensitivity to the various symptom areas will typically result in positive changes that promote success in school and a preserved self-esteem (see Tourette Syndrome Association, 2003).

Despite best efforts by the school, the child with GTS still has to cope with psychosocial adjustment. Individual and family therapies are recommended to deal with the stress, conflict, and confusion associated with GTS. These students often need help with social skills and peer interactions and help dealing with peer rejection. There are no specialized treatment programs for GTS individuals, although there are treatment clinics with expertise in this area. Even these specialty clinics borrow best treatment practices across domains (i.e., behavior control, inattention and impulsivity, specific learning disabilities, social skills). The Yale Child Study Center has such a clinic and provides multifaceted treatment (see Leckman & Cohen, 1999).

## KLINEFELTER SYNDROME

Klinefelter syndrome gets its name from Dr. Harry Klinefelter, who published a report in 1942 describing nine men who had infertility, small testes, enlarged breasts, and other symptoms. Approximately 10 years later, the chromosomal basis for the disorder was determined. KS results from a sex chromosome abnormality in which a male receives a 47, XXY instead of XY pattern. There are other versions of KS in which the sex chromosome pattern has more than one extra X chromosome. Estimates of incidence vary between 1 in 500 to 1 in 1,000 newborns (Abramsky & Chapple, 1997; Hynd & Willis, 1988). These incidence rates are quite similar to those for DS; however, a majority of men with the KS karyotype do not present with any symptoms and have no awareness of the aberration. Consequently, relatively few men with the 47, XXY karyotype have the actual Klinefelter syndrome (Bock, 1993).

KS is not an inherited disorder. KS males are sterile and not capable of fathering children. It appears that the cause of KS involves an error of nondisjunction during parental gametogenesis. Although KS is a chromosome disorder, many consider it an endocrine disorder that results from hyposecretion of sex hormones, hence the number of endocrine anomalies and treatment with testosterone replacement.

Although most symptoms involve the endocrine system, the central nervous system has been implicated. Some studies have noted structural brain difference between KS and normal individuals. For example, Warwick et al. (1999) found smaller whole brain volumes and enlarged lateral ventricles in a KS sample. Both brain and neuropsychological studies have implicated the left temporal lobe as an area of vulnerability, perhaps responsible for impaired auditory-verbal processing and language dysfunction. The neurohormonal mechanisms involved in such brain dysfunction are not known at this time.

### CHARACTERISTICS

The common symptoms of KS include infertility, small testes, enlarged breasts, sparse facial and body hair, above average height, lower sex drive, rounded body type, lack of motor coordination, and overweight (Bock, 1993). In addition to the physical differences, language development is often delayed (Ratcliffe, 1999), and this is likely a precursor to learning disabilities in reading and writing. It is possible that the psychoeducational symptoms are noted before the endocrine changes. There are cases in which school evaluations have precipitated the KS diagnosis. It should be noted that most of the physical symptoms are not readily identifiable until puberty, although the chromosomal abnormality can be detected before birth through amniocentesis or chorionic villus sampling.

In addition to language and learning difficulties, individuals with KS may experience other cognitive deficiencies. Although IQs tend to be in the average range (Pennington, Bender, Puck, Salbenblantt, & Robinson, 1982), slightly lower IQs are found in comparison to normal groups (see Mandoki, Sumner, & Hoffman, 1991; Ratcliffe, Masera, Pan, McKie, 1994). IQ scores tend to be lower with each additional X chromosome in the KS pattern (i.e., 48, XXXY). More specifically, there is some indication that individuals with KS have problems with verbal working memory and related executive functions (Fales et al., 2003). A recent study suggests that problems with verbal processing speed and verbal executive skills tend to be found in those KS patients with VIQ < PIQ (Brauer Boone et al., 2001).

The psychosocial concerns for KS patients are significant. Many KS children tend to be shy, passive, and withdrawn. Low self-esteem and feelings of inadequacy are understandable given the symptoms. Low levels of activity, immaturity, and poor peer relations are not uncommon. Externalizing behavioral problems such as impulsivity and aggressiveness also can accompany the syndrome (Sandberg & Barrick, 1995), as well as increased risk for depression and Schizophrenia (Miyamoto, Kitawaki, Koida, & Nagao, 1993).

### Assessment Considerations

A comprehensive assessment of KS involves thorough medical/physical examinations. The school evaluation should focus on cognitive and academic strengths and weaknesses, including thorough testing of language and executive functions. Problems of verbal fluency, reading comprehension, written and oral expression, and verbal memory are not uncommon. Therefore, some neuropsychological testing may be a useful supplement to psychoeducational assessment. Because KS develops/evolves with age, evaluation and monitoring must consider developmental progression of symptoms. Certainly, psychosocial assessment is recommended, given the risk of self-esteem and depression issues. School and home observations regarding social interactions are crucial. Measures of personality, self-esteem, and peer relations, along with teacher and parent reports, are helpful in delineating the psychological effects of the syndrome.

### Treatment Considerations

The most specific treatment for KS is testosterone replacement therapy. This involves a regular schedule of testosterone injections (androgen), typically initiated at the beginning of puberty. Such treatment has been shown to increase strength, muscle mass, and hair growth, making the patient more masculine in appearance. This treatment has been known to have far-reaching effects, such as improving concentration, sleep patterns, and self-confidence.

From a school neuropsychology standpoint, the earliest problems will likely involve language delay, particularly expressive language problems. Language therapy is an essential adjunct service in the school. A majority of students with KS will have language-based learning disabilities. Thus, special education services for LD are recommended, including tutoring, resource help, modifications, and accommodations. An important goal in the therapeutic regimen is normalization. These students want to fit into the mainstream rather than be targeted as different. Sensitivity is needed regarding their physical features (i.e., adaptive physical education), immaturity and peer relations (i.e., social skills training), and their knowledge and acceptance of their condition (i.e., counseling or coaching). Parents may need help in discussing the implications of KS with their child, particularly the sexual characteristics and sterility. The role of the psychologist in assessment and intervention can be extremely significant with KS. Working knowledge of this syndrome may enable a psychologist to spot the symptoms before anyone else or anticipate areas of need in identified individuals.

## TURNER SYNDROME

TS is a genetic disorder based on a chromosome anomaly in which females are missing a second sex chromosome, possibly the result of meiotic nondisjunction. The condition was first discovered in 1938 by Harry Turner, who noticed short stature and sexual infantilism in a group of women. Between 1% and 2% of all pregnancies are estimated to have this 45,X chromosome constitution; however, approximately 99% of these fetuses spontaneously abort. The incidence of the disorder is estimated at between 1 in 2,000 to 1 in 5,000 live female births. The prevalence is approximately 60,000 females in the United States, with 800 new cases per year (Turner Syndrome Society, 2003). Although a majority of girls with TS show the 45,X karyotype, a wide variety of karyotypic abnormalities are possible.

TS is associated with a number of physical anomalies, including short stature, gonadal dysgenesis, webbed neck, shield chest, low hairline, prominent ears, high arched and narrow palate, swelling of hands and feet, renal anomalies, cardiac problems, hearing loss, and various skeletal abnormalities. TS women also are at risk for visual/ocular problems such as strabismus, amblyopia, ptosis, color blindness, and congenital glaucoma (Rieser & Davenport, 2003).

TS is relatively easy to diagnose and has been the target of considerable research. Although it is not exactly clear how the brain becomes affected in TS, various studies have demonstrated brain irregularities associated with the syndrome. For example, aberrant brain wave patterns have been found in the temporal cortex (Brown et al., 2002); other studies implicate the parietal lobes. There have been reports of reduced glucose metabolism in the bilateral parietal and occipital cortices, along with increased bilateral cerebrospinal fluid volume in the ventricles and decreased gray matter (Murphy et al., 1997). Brown et al. reported bilateral decrease in white matter of the occipital and parietal lobes. Besides cortical findings, other reported brain effects are reduced size of the hippocampus, pons, thalamus, and vermis of the cerebellum (Bishop et al., 2000). Some early investigators proposed right parietal lobe involvement based on the neuropsychological symptoms; however, more recent neuroscientific evidence suggests that more than the right parietal lobe is likely affected by the disorder.

The neuopsychological profile of girls with TS is quite distinctive and fairly well established. TS is not associated with mental retardation, but it is noted for spatial, visual-motor, motor, and mathematical difficulties (O'Connor, Fitzgerald, & Hoey, 2000). Typically, the verbal IQ is significantly greater than the nonverbal IQ score. Girls with TS have difficulty with drawing and copying tasks, handwriting, mental rotation tasks, right-left orientation, directionality, and visual memory. There is some thought that a visuospatial working memory deficit underlies some of the visual-perceptual problems noticed with TS (Buchanan, Pavlovic, & Rovet, 1998). These various neuropsychological deficiencies certainly may affect academic achievement, and in particular may result in math disabilities (Mazzocco, 2001).

The psychosocial affects of TS also have been well delineated. Consistent with their visuoperceptual deficiencies, girls with TS seem to have some difficulty reading social cues and inferring facial affect (Lesniak-Karpiak, Mazzocco, & Ross, 2003; McCauley, Kay, Ito, & Treder, 1987). They seem to be less socially competent and have fewer friends than normals (McCauley, Feuillan, Kushner, & Ross, 2001). In fact, peer ridicule seems to be one of the major sources of discontent for girls with TS, leading to negative body perception and self-image. This all seems to be related to decreased feelings of self-worth and increased risk of de-pression (McCauley, Ross, Kushner, & Cutler, 1995; Rickert, Hassed, Hendon, & Cunniff, 1996). Other findings note more adjustment problems, somatic symp-toms, anxiety, and social immaturity in TS girls (Skuse, Cave, O'Herlihy, & South, 1998). Clearly, there are physical and neurocognitive features of TS that make for difficult psychosocial adjustment.

### ASSESSMENT CONSIDERATIONS

Psychologists are not called on to diagnose TS, but they will be instrumental in de-lineating a neuropsychoeducational profile, including possible learning disabilities and emotional problems. Besides cognitive and educational testing, a comprehen-sive assessment should include additional tests of visual-perceptual and spatial functioning, visual memory including nonverbal working memory, visual-motor coordination, and mathematics. Any evaluation should include measures of per-sonality and emotionality, including measures of self-esteem, anxiety, and social relationships. Family functioning is another area that warrants attention, espe-cially given the unusual combination of medical, physical, and psychological symp-toms confronting girls with TS. Skuse et al. (1998) emphasize a comprehensive understanding of all quality of life issues.

### TREATMENT CONSIDERATIONS

Treatment interventions typically begin with medical management. Hormone therapy is typical to enhance growth and development of secondary sex charac-teristics. Renal, cardiac, and thyroid function may need to be treated as well. Au-ditory and ophthalmic care tends to be ongoing. Special education services are often necessary for students with TS. Fine and gross motor problems warrant physical and/or occupational therapy. Mathematics and writing disorders are common learning disabilities that require academic interventions (i.e., math tu-toring, resource assistance), modifications of assignments (i.e., reduced math problems on a page), and test accommodations (i.e., avoiding drawing, use of com-puter for writing). Psychological services likely will stem from a comprehensive assessment that informs parents and school staff of the learning needs of the child. The psychologist also may play a role in minimizing the social costs to the child with TS and helping to promote self-esteem, social competence, and peer relationships. Girls with TS tend to have strengths in verbal cognitive skills, mak-ing them good candidates for both counseling and academic success.

## NEUROFIBROMATOSIS

NF-1 is a progressive, multisystem disorder based on an autosomal dominant mode of inheritance. The disorder also is referred to as von Recklinghausen disease, named after the physician who first delineated the disorder in 1882. NF-1 results from abnormalities in the autosomal dominant chromosome 17 at band q 11.2 (Led-better, Rich, O'Connell, Leppert, & Carey, 1989). In half the cases, the abnormality is the result of a new mutation. The mutant NF-1 gene has high penetrance, so vir-tually everyone with this genotype will show clinical manifestations. Chromosome

17 is a facilitator of the protein neurofibromin, important for suppressing tumors. Dysfunction of this process results in the occurrence of multiorgan neurofibromas. Diagnostic criteria for NF-1, according to the National Institute of Neurological Disorders and Stroke (2004), includes two or more of the following: six or more café-au-lait spots over 5mm in diameter; two or more neurofibromas of any type or one plexiform neurofibroma; freckling in the axillary or inguinal region; optic glioma; two or more iris hamaratomas; a distinctive osseous lesion; or a first-degree relative with NF-1. The estimate of incidence is 1 per 3,000 births, and the prevalence is approximately 100,000 in the United States alone.

## CHARACTERISTICS

Clinical manifestations of this disorder can vary widely based on the expression of the gene. Severity is graded (1 to 4) based on severity of presentation. Freckles, spots, and neurofibromas can occur anywhere on the skin, and the neurofibromas attack any organ, including the nervous system. The neurofibromas cause focal lesions in the cerebellum, brain stem, basal ganglia, and subcortical structures. These aberrant growths can compromise organs, trigger seizures, and disrupt brain function. Although mental retardation is present in only severe cases, NF-1 increases the risk for speech problems, learning disabilities, motor incoordination, and ADHD symptoms (Kayl & Moore, 2000; North, Joy, Yuille, Cocks, & Hutchins, 1995). Group IQ scores tend to be lower in NF-1 than in the normative population, and a decline in IQ score seems to correlate with severity of the disease (Varnhagen et al., 1988). Estimates of learning disabilities in NF-1 samples range between 30% and 65% (North, 1999). North and colleagues (1995) studied a sample of 40 children with NF-1 and found that nearly 50% had significant reading difficulties, and 27.5% were deficient in math. It appears that both language-based and nonverbal learning deficits appear with NF-1 (Cutting et al., 2002).

Neuropsychological findings have implicated a variety of deficiencies: linguistic (Mazzocco et al., 1995), visuospatial (Legius, Descheemaeker, Spaepen, Casaer, & Fryns, 1994), motor (North et al., 1995), and executive functions (Hofman, Harris, Bryan, & Denckla, 1994). Test-specific problems have been noted with judgment of line orientation, vocabulary and verbal reasoning, and fine motor control. Given that lesions can occur throughout the brain, it is no wonder that neuropsychological dysfunction is diffuse.

NF-1 can cause a host of medical problems, including blindness, seizures, and pulmonary, skeletal, and gastrointestinal dysfunction. These issues along with physical disfigurement make for a challenging psychosocial development. It is understandable that those NF-1 children with obvious deformities may have difficulty making friends. Social isolation and feelings of inadequacy may lead to anxiety and/or depression (Benjamin et al., 1993). The progressive nature of the disease also makes coping difficult for the patient and family.

## ASSESSMENT CONSIDERATIONS

Because of the varying severity and diffuse neurocognitive symptoms, neuropsychological assessments of NF-1 need to be multifaceted. As with the other genetic disorders already discussed, a team evaluation makes the most sense. Input from parents, physicians, teachers, psychologist, and various therapists are essential in composing a comprehensive profile of the child with NF-1. These children are at risk for learning disabilities, so the psychologist would perform comprehensive psychoeducational testing and supplement this with neuropsychological tests. Equally important is the assessment of socioemotional functioning, given the mental health needs of the child and family. Integration of test data, observations, interviews, brain scans, and records and reports from all professionals will be crucial for developing educational and management plans. Because NF-1 can worsen and seizure activity can increase, it is important to monitor performance and perhaps test more regularly than every 3 years.

TREATMENT CONSIDERATIONS

There is no cure for NF-1, and the prognosis can vary from excellent to serious physical and mental compromise. Medical intervention may be necessary for various system compromises, seizure control, tumor surgery, and other health problems. The school neuropsychologist can play a critical role in delineating learning strengths and weaknesses, monitoring neuropsychological functioning, and developing interventions to meet academic and psychosocial needs. Supportive counseling is another natural role for the school psychologist. As always, the psychologist can be an information resource and consultant to family and school staff.

## TUBEROUS SCLEROSIS COMPLEX

Dr. Friedrich von Recklinghausen (1862) was one of the first to present information on a TSC case. However, most of the credit for describing the disorder goes to Dr. D. M. Bourneville (c. 1880). Similar to NF-1, TSC is a genetic disorder affecting the neurocutaneous system. It is an autosomal dominant inherited condition caused by a mutation of two genes, TSC1 and TSC2. The mutations disrupt the regulation of tumor suppression and cell proliferation. This results in unwanted growths such as tubers and focal dysplasias in the brain and other organs (i.e., heart, lungs, kidney, skin, and various glands). The brain tubers occur in the lateral ventricles, subcortical white matter, and cortical convolutions. Lesions of the kidneys, heart, and lungs usually develop or increase in size with age. This is a rare disorder with widely ranging estimates of incidence. Early estimates were as low as 1 per 150,000. More recent estimates are as high as 1 per 6,000 (TS Alliance, 2003).

CHARACTERISTICS

Present in virtually all cases of TSC are seizure disorder, intellectual impairment, and adenoma sebaceum (facial lesions that often form a "butterfly patch" across the bridge of the nose). It is common for an affected individual to experience infantile spasms. Later, these spasms progress to a seizure disorder, thought to occur in 90% of TSC patients (Hynd & Willis, 1988). Typically, the number and topography of the brain lesions influence the degree of seizure disorder, mental impairment, and behavior control problems. In the case of intractable seizures, hemispherectomies have been performed, resulting in hemiplegia and neurocognitive deficits.

Two psychiatric conditions have been associated with TSC and frontal brain involvement: Autism and ADHD (Hunt, 1998). Group studies of TSC have been limited due to its rare occurrence. Neuropsychological studies have shown this population to have deficiencies across all domains of brain functioning consistent with the diffuse nature of brain lesions in TSC (Jambaque et al., 1991; V. S. Miller & Bigler, 1982). Academic problems are directly related to severity of the brain disease and mental impairment, and likely will cut across all areas of learning. School personnel must keep in mind that deterioration in performance and behavior is possible.

## ASSESSMENT CONSIDERATIONS

TSC is a condition that warrants a neuropsychological assessment. Most of the cognitive, academic, and behavioral problems of a person with TSC are related to the presence and location of brain lesions. A neuropsychological assessment can delineate brain-behavior strengths and weaknesses that likely map areas of the brain that are affected and unaffected. A neuropsychological assessment at a young age can serve as a baseline for comparison to later assessments for determining progression of the disorder. Once again, a team approach is highly encouraged. Medical, motor, and speech concerns accompany the intellectual, academic, and behavioral problems usually seen. A team evaluation will best capture the unique expression of this rare disorder.

## TREATMENT CONSIDERATIONS

Unfortunately, there is no cure and no treatment that will arrest the progression of the disorder. This is not a "one size fits all" disorder. Intervention efforts start with good medical care, ongoing assessment across all areas of functioning, and appropriate treatment of cognitive, speech, motor, academic, behavioral, and psychosocial needs. There is no treatment package for TSC and no outcome research on intervention effectiveness. An important role of the psychologist is to monitor functioning over time so as to inform the academic and behavioral planning process.

# VELOCARDIOFACIAL SYNDROME

VCFS was recognized by Dr. Robert Shprintzen (1978), who identified a cluster of symptoms in 12 children. The key symptoms included cleft palate, pharyngeal hypotonia, cardiac anomalies, and flat nasal bridge, although over 180 clinical features have been identified (Batshaw, 2002; Velocardiofacial Syndrome Educational Foundation, 2003). VCFS is an autosomal dominant inherited disorder associated with deletions on the long arm of chromosome 22, denoted as del22q11. Incidence is estimated at approximately 1 per 4,000 live births.

## CHARACTERISTICS

In addition to the identifying features of the syndrome, there are many clinical concerns associated with VCFS (see Shprintzen, 2000). Respiratory illnesses are common in infancy, and along with cardiac problems may lead to hospitalizations. Early developmental milestones tend to be delayed and hypotonia is common. Hypernasality is present in a majority of cases, which may contribute to the high proportion of speech and language deficits. Intellectual impairment is typical, with mean IQ scores in the borderline range of intelligence and Performance IQ approximately 10 points lower than Verbal IQ (Gothelf & Lombroso, 2001). All children with VCFS seem to have learning difficulties, particularly as they get older and academic demands increase. Behavioral characteristics include shyness, dependency, impulsivity, irritability, and poor concentration (Prinzie et al., 2002). Children with VCFS are at risk for ADHD, anxiety, and depression; there is a particularly high co-occurrence of Schizophrenia.

Neuropsychological studies have indicated specific deficits in individuals with VCFS. Both Swillen et al. (2000) and Henry et al. (2002) found evidence of visuoperceptual impairment, supporting the notion of a nonverbal learning disability. Other deficits were noted with problem solving and planning as well as abstract and social thinking. These deficits likely are related to abnormalities in brain morphology noted bilaterally in white matter, the left cerebellum, and frontal and temporal lobes (Mitnick, Bello, & Shprintzen, 1994; van Amelsvoort et al., 2001).

### ASSESSMENT AND TREATMENT CONSIDERATIONS

Medical attention occurs early with VCFS, and ongoing monitoring and care are important. Physical deformities of the mouth, nose, and face affect speech production and appearance, making these children observably different. Early assessment and intervention is common practice for speech and motor concerns. Cognitive and adaptive delays also should be addressed. As the children reach school age they invariably require special services for learning disorders. Periodic IQ and achievement testing are necessary to document levels of performance and watch for possible declines in functioning. Specific areas that merit assessment and programming are visuoperceptual, expressive language, planning, reading comprehension, math reasoning, and behaviors associated with ADHD (Shprintzen, 2000). Psychologists need to keep a watchful eye on later-developing psychiatric problems. Behavioral concerns to be aware of are shyness, withdrawal, anxiety, and depression. A major concern for VCFS is the development of Schizophrenia. The degree of comorbidity is unclear; however, it is clear that Schizophrenia occurs far more than usual with VCFS. Given the psychiatric concerns, psychological support for the learner is essential and support for the family is often needed.

VCFS is one of the most common genetic disorders, yet it was identified just 25 years ago and is comparatively understudied. National studies are currently under way to investigate the neuropsychological and psychosocial functioning of children with VCFS, hopefully leading to targeted treatment interventions.

## STURGE WEBER SYNDROME

Sturge first described this disorder in 1879 by noting a youngster with a facial nevus and partial epilepsy. In 1922, Weber described a similar case with the term "encephalotrigeminal angiomatosis." This disorder is now referred to as Sturge Weber syndrome. It is a congenital disorder of unknown origin that typically involves brain calcifications, leptomeningeal angiomas, facial nevus (port wine stain), seizures, hemiparesis, visual anomalies (glaucoma and hemianopia), and neurocognitive deficits. It is believed that the problems originate from residual vascular tissue that interferes with the cephalic portion of the neural tube in early development (Garcia, Roach, & McLean, 1981). This is the most rare of the disorders discussed in this chapter, with estimates of incidence at 1 in 50,000.

## CHARACTERISTICS

The trademark symptom of SWS is the port wine stain on one side of the face. Stains that involve upper and lower eyelids are more likely to correlate with SWS and brain involvement (Tallman, Tan, & Morelli, 1991). Another common characteristic is seizure disorder. This occurs in approximately 75% of the cases and is usually localized to the hemisphere contralateral to the stain. In some cases, seizures are bilateral; this factor is correlated with a greater number of seizures and lower IQ. More commonly, there are unilateral seizures and a corresponding hemiparesis (weakness on the side of the body opposite the hemisphere of the seizures). There have been many cases in which the seizures are intractable and hemispherectomies were performed. In most cases, the children survive seizure free; however, the degree of intensity of the seizures tends to predict the cognitive outcome of these children (Kossoff, Buck, & Freeman, 2002). Brain calcifications can be an ongoing problem that worsens with age, and these individuals are at risk for future cerebrovascular problems (Sujansky & Conradi, 1995).

Cognitive deficits are often associated with SWS, whether a child has had surgery or not. In comparison to siblings, Chapieski, Friedman, and Lachar (2000) found children with SWS to have more cognitive, academic, social, mood, and compliance problems. The cognitive deficiencies can vary widely based on the expression of the disorder. The lateralized brain involvement in some cases yields classic patterns of right or left hemisphere dysfunction.

## ASSESSMENT CONSIDERATIONS

Obviously, early concerns will focus on seizures, visual complications, and motor problems. Brain MRI, EEG, and ophthalmologic tests are common. Neuropsychological assessment at young ages will focus on developmental progress across domains and adaptive functioning. By the time the child reaches school age the psychologist should be monitoring neurocognitive and academic performance for possible regression due to seizures, brain calcifications, or vascular changes. Approximately half of those with SWS will have significant cognitive delays and mental retardation. The neurocognitive profile should help inform classroom setting, modifications, accommodations, and academic interventions. In addition to neuropsychological profiling, the psychologist certainly should assess social-emotional domains. Learners with SWS are at risk for being teased and bullied (Lee, 1990), as well as experiencing emotional distress. There also is considerable stress on the family (Hilbert, Walker, & Rinehart, 2002), particularly with the concerns associated with ongoing seizures and possible deterioration of function.

## TREATMENT CONSIDERATIONS

SWS is another disorder that requires a support team. Obviously, medical intervention is of utmost importance right from birth. Depending on the level of complications, cognitive, motor, and visual problems will require early intervention to some degree. Various therapists may be involved to support parents and classroom teachers. Special education services and academic interventions may have to consider specific patterns of neurocognitive problems (i.e., MR, dyslexia, nonverbal LD). If the child has a hemianopia and hemiplegia, school staff will need to be strategic in working with learning materials. The school should work closely and collaboratively with parents from preschool on, especially given the possible changes in functional status over time. Most individuals with SWS have a normal life expectancy, and a sizable percentage will function within normal limits given appropriate support.

## CONCLUSION

As noted throughout the chapter, these disorders are rare and complicated. The field of psychology does not have educational "treatment packages" for such low-incidence disorders. Clearly, this is an area in need of research and development. Despite a lack of empirically validated treatment approaches specific to each disorder, neuropsychologists can use their existing assessment and intervention tool kits to assist youngsters with these disorders. Some of the characteristics of these disorders are so unique (i.e., tics, skin stain, short stature) that a thorough understanding of all aspects of each disorder is a necessary starting point. It is hoped that the knowledge provided in these few pages will equip school psychologists with that starting point, so that they can provide the best possible services to learners with low-incidence disorders.

## REFERENCES

Abramsky, L., & Chapple, J. (1997). 47XXY and 47XYY: Estimated rates of and indication for postnatal diagnosis with implications for prenatal counseling. *Prenatal Diagnosis, 17*, 363–368.

Batshaw, M. L. (2002). *Children with disabilities* (5th ed.). Baltimore: Brookes.

Benjamin, C. M., Colley, A., Donnai, D., Kingston, H., Harris R., & Kerzin-Storrar, L. (1993). Neurofibromatosis type 1 (NF1): Knowledge, experience, and reproductive decisions of affected patients and families. *Journal of Medical Genetics, 30*, 567–574.

Bishop, D. V. M., Canning, E., Elgar, K., Morris, E., Jacobs, P. A., & Skuse, D. H. (2000). Distinctive patterns of memory function in subgroups of females with Turner syndrome: Evidence for imprinted loci on the X-chromosome affecting neurodevelopment. *Neuropsychologia, 38*, 712–721.

Bock, R. (1993). *Understanding Klinefelter syndrome: A guide for XXY males and their families.* (NIH Publication No. 93-3202, pp. 1–14). Washington, DC: U.S. Department of Health and Human Services.

Bornstein, R. A. (1990). Neuropsychological performance in children with Tourette's syndrome. *Psychiatry Resources, 33*, 73–81.

Bradshaw, J. L. (2001). *Developmental disorders of the frontostriatal system: Neuropsychological, neuropsychiatric, and evolutionary perspectives.* Philadelphia: Taylor & Francis.

Brauer Boone, K., Swerdloff, R. S., Miller, B. L., Geschwing, D. H., Razani, J., Lee, A., et al. (2001). Neuropsychological profiles of adults with Klinefelter syndrome. *Journal of the International Neuropsychological Society, 7*, 446–456.

Brown, W. E., Kesler, S. R., Eliez, S., Warsofsky, I. S., Haberecht, M., Patwardhan, A., et al. (2002). Brain development in Turner syndrome: A magnetic resonance imaging study. *Psychiatry Research: Neuroimaging, 116*, 187–196.

Buchanan, L., Pavlovic, J., & Rovet, J. (1998). A reexamination of the visuospatial deficit in Turner syndrome: Contributions of working memory. *Developmental Neuropsychology Special Issue: Gonadal Hormones and Sex Differences in Behavior, 14*, 341–367.

Chapieski, L., Friedman, A., & Lachar, D. (2000). Psychological functioning in children and adolescents with Sturge-Weber syndrome. *Journal of Child Neurology, 15,* 660–665.

Comings, D. E. (1990). *Tourette syndrome and human behavior.* Durante, CA; Hope Press.

Cutting, L. E., Huang, G., Zeger, S., Koth, C. W., Thompson, R. E., & Denckla, M. B. (2002). Growth curve analyses of neuropsychological profiles in children with neurofibromatosis type 1: Specific cognitive tests remain "spared" and "impaired" over time. *Journal of Clinical and Experimental Neuropsychology, 18,* 784–792.

Dykens, E. M., & Kasari, C. (1997). Maladaptive behavior in children with Prader-Willi syndrome, Down syndrome, and non-specific mental retardation. *American Journal of Mental Retardation, 102,* 228–237.

Fales, C. L., Knowlton, B. I., Holyoak, K. J., Geschwind, D. H., Swerdloff, R. S., & Gonzalo, I. G. (2003). Working memory and relational reasoning in Klinefelter syndrome. *Journal of the International Neuropsychological Society, 9,* 839–846.

Garcia, J., Roach, E., & McLean, W. (1981). Recurrent thrombotic deterioration in the Sturge-Weber syndrome. *Childs Brain, 8,* 427–433.

Goh, A. M. Y., Bradshaw, J. L., Bradshaw, J. A., & Georgiou-Kalistianis, N. (2002). Inhibition of expected movements in Tourette's syndrome. *Journal of Clinical and Experimental Neuropsychology, 24,* 1017–1031.

Gothelf, D., & Lombroso, P. J. (2001). Genetics of childhood disorders: Velocariofacial syndrome. *Journal of the American Academy of Child and Adolescent Psychiatry, 40,* 489–491.

Henry, J. C., Amelsvoort, T. V., Morris, R. G., Owen, M. J., Murphy, D. G., & Murphy, K. C. (2002). An investigation of the neuropsychological profile in adults with velo-cardiofacial syndrome (VCFS). *Neuropsychologia, 40,* 471–478.

Hilbert, G. A., Walker, M. B., & Rinehart, J. (2002). "In for the long haul": Responses of parents caring for children with Sturge-Weber syndrome. *Journal of Family Nursing, 6,* 157–179.

Hodapp, R. M. (1996). Down syndrome: Developmental, psychiatric, and management issues. *Child and Adolescent Psychiatric Clinics of North America, 5,* 881–894.

Hodapp, R. M. (1997). Cognitive functioning in adolescents with Down syndrome: Theoretical and practical issues. In S. M. Pueschel & M. Sustrova (Eds.), *Adolescents with down syndrome: Toward a more fulfilling life* (pp. 91–98). Baltimore: Brookes.

Hodapp, R. M., Dykens, E. M., Hagerman, R. J., Schreiner, R., Lachiewics, A. M., & Leckman, J. F. (1990). Developmental implications of changing trajectories of IQ in males with fragile X syndrome. *Journal of the American Academy of Child and Adolescent Psychiatry, 29,* 214–219.

Hofman, K. J., Harris, E. I., Bryan, R. N., & Denckla, M. B. (1994). Neurofibromatosis type 1: The cognitive phenotype. *Journal of Pediatrics, 124,* 51–58.

Hunt, A. (1998). A comparison of the abilities, health and behavior of 23 people with tuberous sclerosis at age 5 and as adults. *Journal of Applied Research in Intellectual Disabilities, 11,* 227–238.

Hynd, G. W., & Willis, W. G. (1988). *Pediatric neuropsychology.* Orlando, FL: Grune & Stratton.

Jambaque, I., Cusmai, R., Curatolo, P., Cortesi, F., Perrot, C., & Dulac, O. (1991). Neuropsychological aspects of tuberous scelerosis in relation to epilepsy and MRI findings. *Developmental Medicine and Child Neurology, 33,* 698–705.

Johnston, C., Hessl, D., Blasey, C., Eliez, S., Erba, H., Dyer-Friedman, J., et al. (2003). Factors associated with parenting stress in mothers of children with fragile X syndrome. *Journal of Developmental & Behavioral Pediatrics, 24,* 267–275.

Kayl, A. E., & Moore, B. D. (2000). Behavioral phenotype of neurofibromatosis type 1. *Mental Retardation and Developmental Disabilities, 6,* 117–124.

King, R. A., Leckman, J. F., Scahill, L., & Cohen, D. J. (1999). Obsessive-compulsive disorder, anxiety, and depression. In J. F. Leckman & D. J. Cohen (Eds.), *Tourette's syndrome: Tics, obsessions, compulsions* (pp. 43–62). New York: Wiley.

Kossoff, E., Buck, C., & Freeman, J. (2002). Outcomes of 32 hemispherictomies for Sturge-Weber syndrome worldwide. *Neurology, 59*, 1735–1738.

Leckman, J. F., & Cohen, D. J. (Eds.). (1999). *Tourette's syndrome: Tics, obsessions, compulsions.* New York: Wiley.

Leckman, J. F., King, R. A., Scahill, L., Findlley, D., Ort, S. I., & Cohen, D. J. (1999). Yale approach to assessment and treatment. In J. F. Leckman & D. J. Cohen (Eds.), *Tourette's syndrome: Tics, obsessions, compulsions* (pp. 285–309). New York: Wiley.

Ledbetter, D. H., Rich, D. C., O'Connell, P., Leppert, M., & Carey, J. C. (1989). Precise localization of NF1 to 17q11.2 by balanced translocation. *American Journal of Human Genetics, 44*, 20–24.

Lee, Sing. (1990). Psychopathology in Sturge-Weber syndrome. *Canadian Journal of Psychiatry, 35*, 674–678.

Legius, E., Descheemaeker, M. J., Spaepen, A., Casaer, P., & Fryns, J. P. (1994). Neurofibromatosis type 1 in childhood: A study of the neuropsychological profile in 45 children. *Genetic Counseling, 5*, 51–60.

Lejeune, J., Gautier, M., & Turpin, R. (1959). Etude des chromosomes somatiques de neuf enfants mongoliens. *Comptes Rendus de l'Academie de Sciences, 248*, 1721–1722.

Lesniak-Karpiak, K., Mazzocco, M. M., & Ross, J. L. (2003). Behavioral assessment of social anxiety in females with Turner or fragile X syndrome. *Journal of Autism and Developmental Disorders, 33*, 55–67.

Loveland, K. A., & Kelley, M. L. (1991). Development of adaptive behavior in preschoolers with autism or Down syndrome. *American Journal on Mental Retardation, 96*, 13–20.

Mandoki, M. W., Sumner, G. S., & Hoffman, R. P. (1991). A review of Klinefelter's syndrome in children and adolescents. *Journal of the American Academy of Child and Adolescent Psychiatry, 30*, 167–172.

Mazzocco, M. M. (2001). Math learning disability and math, L.D. subtypes: Evidence from studies of Turner syndrome, fragile X syndrome, and neurofibromatosis type 1. *Journal of Learning Disabilities, 34*, 520–533.

Mazzocco, M. M., Turner, J. E., Denckla, M. B., Hofman, K. J., Scanlon, D. C., & Vellutino, F. R. (1995). Language and reading deficits associated with neurofribromatosis type 1: Evidence for a not-so-verbal learning disability. *Developmental Neuropsychology, 11*, 503–522.

McCauley, E., Feuillan, P., Kushner, H., & Ross, J. L. (2001). Psychosocial development in adolescents with Turner syndrome. *Developmental and Behavioral Pediatrics, 22*, 360–365.

McCauley, E., Kay, T., Ito, J., & Treder, R. (1987). The Turner syndrome: Cognitive deficits, affective discrimination, and behavior problems. *Child Development, 58*, 464–473.

McCauley, E., Ross, J. L., Kushner, H., & Cutler, G. (1995). Self-esteem and behavior in girls with Turner syndrome. *Journal of Developmental and Behavioral Pediatrics, 16*, 82–88.

Miller, J. (1992). Lexical development in young children with Down syndrome. In R. Chapman (Ed.), *Processes in language acquisition and disorders* (pp. 202–216). St. Louis, MO: Mosby.

Miller, V. S., & Bigler, E. D. (1982). Neuropsychological aspects of tuberous sclerosis. *Clinical Neuropsychology, 4*, 26–34.

Mitnick, R. J., Bello, J. A., & Shprintzen, R. J. (1994). Brain anomalies in velocardio-facial syndrome. *American Journal of Medical Genetics, 54*, 100–106.

Miyamoto, A., Kitawaki, K., Koida, H., & Nagao, K. (1993). MRI and SPECT of Klinefelter's syndrome with various neuropsychiatric symptoms: A case report. *Japanese Journal of Psychiatry and Neurology, 47,* 863–867.

Muller, S. V., Johannes, S., Wieringa, B., Weber, A., Muller-Vahl, K., Matzke, M., et al. (2003). Disturbed monitoring and response inhibition in patients with Gilles de la Tourette syndrome and co-morbid obsessive compulsive disorder. *Behavioral Neurology, 14,* 29–37.

Murphy, D. G. M., Mentis, M. J., Pietrini, P., Grady, C., Daly, E., Haxby, J. V., et al. (1997). A PET study of Turner's syndrome: Effects of sex steroids and the X chromosome on brain. *Biological Psychiatry, 41,* 285–298.

Murray, J. B. (1997). Psychophysiological aspects of Tourette's syndrome. *Journal of Psychology, 131,* 615–626.

National Fragile X Foundation. (n.d.). Retrieved July 8, 2004, from http://www.fragilex.org/html/characteristics.htm.

National Institute of Neurological Disorders and Stroke (n.d.). Retrieved July 11, 2004, from http://www.ninds.nih.gov/disorders/neurofibromatosis/neurofibromatosis.htm.

Netley, C., & Rovet, J. (1982). Verbal deficits in children with 47, XXY and 47, XXX karyotypes: A descriptive and experimental study. *Brain and Language, 17,* 58–72.

North, K. (1999). Cognitive function and academic performance. In J. M. Friedman, D. H. Gutmann, M. Maccollin, & V. M. Riccardi (Eds.), *Neurofibromatosis: Phenotype, natural history, and pathogenesis* (pp. 162–189). Baltimore: Johns Hopkins University Press.

North, K., Joy, P., Yuille, D., Cocks, N., & Hutchins, P. (1995). Cognitive function and academic performance in children with neurofibromatosis type 1. *Developmental Medicine and Child Neurology, 37,* 427–436.

O'Connor, J., Fitzgerald, M., & Hoey, H. (2000). The relationship between karyotype and cognitive functioning in Turner syndrome. *Irish Journal of Psychiatry, 17,* 82–85.

Ozonoff, S., Strayer, D. L., McMahon, W. M., & Filloux, F. (1998). Inhibitory deficits in Tourette syndrome: A function of comorbidity and symptom severity. *Journal of Child Psychiatry, 39,* 1109–1118.

Pennington, B., Bender, B., Puck, M., Salbenblantt, J., & Robinson, A. (1982). Learning disabilities in children with sex chromosome anomalies. *Child Development, 53,* 1182–1192.

Powell, L., Houghton, S., & Douglas, G. (1997). Comparison of etiology-specific cognitive functioning profiles for individuals with fragile X., and individuals with Down syndrome. *Journal of Special Education, 31,* 362–376.

Prinzie, P., Swillen, A., Vogels, A., Kockuyt, V., Curfs, L., Haselager, G., et al. (2002). Personality profiles of youngsters with velo-cardio-facial syndrome. *Genetic Counseling, 13,* 265–280.

Pueschel, S. M., & Hopmann, M. R. (1993). Speech and language abilities of children with Down syndrome: A parent's perspective. In A. P. Kaiser & D. B. Gray (Ed.), *Enhancing children's communication: Vol. 2. Research foundations for intervention* (pp. 335–362). Baltimore: Brookes.

Ratcliffe, S. G. (1999). Long-term outcome in children of sex chromosome abnormalities. *Archives of Disease in Childhood, 80,* 192–195.

Ratcliffe, S. G., Masera, N., Pan, H., & McKie, M. (1994). Head circumsference and IQ of children with sex chromosome abnormalities. *Developmental Medicine and Child Neurology, 36,* 533–544.

Rickert, V. I., Hassed, S. J., Hendon, A. E., & Cunniff, C. (1996). The effects of peer ridicule on depression and self-image among adolescent females with Turner syndrome. *Journal of Adolescent Health, 19,* 34–38.

Rieser, P., & Davenport, M. (2003). Turner syndrome: A guide for families. www.turner-syndrome.org.

Roizen, N. J. (2002). Down syndrome. In M. L. Batshaw (Ed.), *Children with disabilities* (pp. 307–320). Baltimore: Brookes.

Rovet, J., & Netley, C. (1982). Processing deficits in Turner's syndrome. *Developmental Psychology, 18,* 77–94.

Sandberg, D., & Barrick, C. (1995). Endocrine disorders in childhood: A selective survey of intellectual and educational sequelae. *School Psychology Review, 24,* 146–170.

Scahill, L., Tanner, C., & Dure, L. (2001). The epidemiology of tics and Tourette syndrome in children and adolescents. *Advances in Neurology, 85,* 261–171.

Schultz, R. T., Carter, A. S., Scahill, L., & Leckman, J. F. (1999). Neuropsychological findings. In J. F. Leckman & D. J. Cohen (Eds.), *Tourette's syndrome: Tics, obsessions, compulsions* (pp. 80–103). New York: Wiley.

Shin, M. S., Chung, S. J., Hong, K. E. M. (2001). Comparative study of the behavioral and neuropsychologic characteristics of tic disorder with or without attention deficit/hyperactivity disorder (ADHD). *Journal of Child Neurology, 16,* 719–726.

Shprintzen, R. J., Goldberg, R. B., Lewin, M. L., Sidoti, E. J., Berkman, M. D., Argamaso, R. V., et al. (1978). A new syndrome involving cleft palate, cardiac anomalies, typical facies, and learning disabilities: Velo-cardio-facial syndrome. *Cleft Palate Journal, 15,* 56–62.

Shprintzen, R. J. (2000). Velo-cardio-facial syndrome: A distinctive behavioral phenotype. *Mental Retardation and Developmental Disabilities Research Reviews, 6,* 142–147.

Skuse, D. H., Cave, S., O'Herlihy, A., & South, R. (1998). Quality of life in children with Turner Syndrome: Parent, teacher, and individual perspectives. In D. Drotar (Ed.), *Measuring health-related quality of life in children and adolescents: Implications for research and practice* (pp. 313–326). Mahwah, NJ: Erlbaum.

Sujansky, E., & Conradi, S. (1995). Outcome of Sturge-Weber syndrome in 52 adults. *American Journal of Medical Genetics, 57,* 35–45.

Swillen, A., Vandeputte, L., Cracco, J., Maes, B., Ghesquiere, P., Devriendt, K., et al. (2000). Neuropsychological, learning and psychosocial profile of primary school aged children with velo-cardio-facial syndrome (22q11 deletion): Evidence for a nonverbal learning disability? *Child Neuropsychology, 6,* 1–12.

Tallman, B., Tan, O., & Morelli, J. (1991). Neuroradiological findings in Sturge-Weber syndrome. *Neuropediatrics, 22,* 115–120.

Tourette Syndrome Association. (n.d.). Retrieved July 15, 2004, from http://www.tsa-usa.org.

Tuberous Sclerosis Alliance. (n.d.). Retrieved online June 6, 2004, from http://tsalliance.easycgi.com/pages.aspx?content=2.

Turner Syndrome Society of the U.S. (n.d.). Retrieved July 8, 2004, from http://www.turner-syndrome-us.org/resource/faq.html.

van Amelsvoort, T., Daly, E., Roberston, D., Suckling, J. N. G., Critchley, H., Owen, M. C., et al. (2001). Structural brain abnormalities associated with deletion at chromosome 22q11. *British Journal of Psychiatry, 178,* 412–419.

Varnhagen, C. K., Lewin S., Das, J. P., Bowen, P., Ma, K., & Klimek, M. (1988). Neurofibromatosis and psychological processes. *Journal of Developmental and Behavioral Pediatrics, 9,* 257–265.

Velocardiofacial Syndrome Educational Foundation (n.d.). Retrieved June 13, 2004, from http://www.vcfsef.org.

Walkup, J. T., Khan, S., Schuerholz, L., Paik, Y. S., Leckman, J. F., & Schultz, R. T. (1999). Phenomenology and natural history of tic-related ADHD and learning disabilities. In

J. F. Leckman & D. J. Cohen (Eds.), *Tourette's syndrome: Tics, obsessions, compulsions* (pp. 63–79). New York: Wiley.

Wang, P. P. (1996). A neuropsychological profile of Down syndrome: Cognitive and brain morphology. *Mental Retardation and Developmental Disability Research Reviews, 2,* 102–108.

Warwick, M. M., Doody, G. A., Lawrie, S. M., Kestelman, J. N., Best, J. J., & Johnstone, E. C. (1999). Volumetric magnetic resonance imaging study of the brain in subjects with sex chromosome aneuploidies. *Journal of Neurology, Neurosurgery, and Psychiatry, 66,* 628–632.

Wisniewski, K. E., Wisniewski, H. M., & Wen, G. Y. (1985). Occurrence of Alzheimer's neuropathology and dementia in Down syndrome. *Annals of Neurology, 17,* 278–282.

Zellweger, H. (1977). Down syndrome. In P. J. Vinker & G. W. Bruyn (Eds.), *Handbook of clinical neurology* (Vol. 31, pp. 367–469). Amsterdam: North Holland.

# CHAPTER 28

# Providing Neuropsychological Services to Culturally and Linguistically Diverse Learners

ROBYN S. HESS and ROBERT L. RHODES

T HE CULTURAL AND linguistic composition of the United States school-age population is more diverse today than ever before. More parents and children have immigrated to this country during the past decade than any other time since the turn of the twentieth century (U.S. Immigration and Naturalization Service, 2002). In fact, of the nearly 54 million learners in kindergarten through grade 12, 1 in 5 has a parent who was born outside of the United States and 1 out of every 10 students was born in another country (U.S. Census Bureau, 2002). This tremendous rate of immigration and the high rate of growth for many established minority populations are steadily changing the student population served through educational and school neuropsychology practice.

## GROWTH OF CULTURALLY AND LINGUISTICALLY DIVERSE POPULATION NATIONWIDE

The focus of this chapter is on four of the five major ethnic groups in the United States: African American, Asian American, Hispanic-Latino, and Native American. These four groups are among the largest minority groups with the longest period of residence in the United States, and there are great variations within each based on immigration history, socioeconomic status (SES), language, acculturation status, and values (Gibbs & Huang, 2003).

The Hispanic school-age population is increasing rapidly, recently becoming the largest minority children's group in the United States, with 17% under the

---

Slightly different terms (e.g., Latino/Hispanic and African American/Black) are used throughout this document to reflect the term used in the original source.

age of 18 (Kent, Pollard, Haaga, & Mather, 2001). This diverse group includes children of Central and South American, Puerto Rican, and Cuban origin, although the largest subgroup of the Hispanic population is composed of individuals of Mexican origin. The second largest group, African Americans or Blacks, is also a generally young group, with 33% of all Black individuals reported to be under the age of 18, compared to 23% of the non-Hispanic White population (McKinnon, 2003). The Black school-age population in the United States represents 16% of the total student population (U.S. Census Bureau, 2002).

Asian/Pacific Islanders and Native Americans, groups that are mainly clustered in the western United States, represent a much smaller proportion of the total U.S. population (4.4% and 0.9%, respectively), but are also characterized by great diversity and a relatively youthful population (Kent et al., 2001). Asian/Pacific Islanders have increased at more than triple the growth rate of the U.S. population (Reeves & Bennett, 2003), largely due to patterns of immigration. Within the Asian/Pacific Islander population, 88% were born outside of the United States or had at least one parent who was born in another country (Reeves & Bennett, 2003). There are 1.4 million American Indian, Eskimo, and Aleut children in the United States; 29% live on reservations or in Alaska Native villages, and the rest live in urban areas (Snipp, 2002).

Represented among the culturally and linguistically diverse school-age population is a growing number of learners with limited English proficiency (LEP). From 1990 to 2000, the student population with LEP in the United States increased approximately 105%; the general student population increased slightly less than 25% during the same period (National Clearinghouse for English Language Acquisition and Language Instruction Educational Programs [NCELA], 2002). The LEP student population in the United States includes speakers of over 400 different languages (Kindler, 2002). Of the students who are English-language learners, the 10 most common native languages include a majority of Spanish speakers (77%), followed by Vietnamese (2.3%), Hmong (2.2%), Haitian Creole (1.1%), Korean (1.1%), Cantonese (1.0%), Arabic (0.9%), Russian (0.9%), Navajo (0.9%), and Tagalog (0.8%; NCELA, 2002).

## UNIQUE EXPERIENCES AND CHARACTERISTICS OF CULTURALLY AND LINGUISTICALLY DIVERSE STUDENTS

It has long been recognized that learners from ethnically diverse groups are overrepresented in certain high-incidence categories in special education, including mild mental retardation, emotional disturbance, and, to a lesser degree, learning disabilities (Artiles & Trent, 1994; National Research Council, 2002). A component of this finding might be expected given that minority children are disproportionately poor, and poverty is associated with higher rates of low birthweight, poorer nutrition, less supportive home environments for early cognitive and emotional development, and exposure to harmful toxins (McLoyd, 1998b; National Research Council, 2002). The negative impact of poverty increases significantly when children are both poor and have minority status (Farley, 1997). Among all children in the United States less than 18 years old, the poverty rate is 16%, and it is three times as high for Black children (30%) as for non-Hispanic White children (10%; McKinnon, 2003). Likewise, approximately 26% of all American Indians and Alaska Natives live in poverty, as do nearly 23% of Hispanics (Bishaw & Iceland, 2003).

There is considerable evidence to suggest that poverty exposes children to a number of potentially harmful, neuropsychologically related incidents, substances, and conditions (Bradley & Whiteside-Mansell, 1997; National Research Council, 1993). Poor children experience higher rates of disease and injury than children from more affluent backgrounds (Durkin, Davidson, Kuhn, O'Conner, & Barlow, 1994). For example, the rate of head injury among minority youth is significantly higher than for nonminority population members (Bruns & Hauser, 2003). Likewise, ethnic and racial disparities in posttraumatic brain injury emergency treatment (Bazarian, Pope, McClung, Cheng, & Flesher, 2003) and racial group differences among parent and family outcomes following pediatric traumatic brain injury (Yeates et al., 2002) potentially magnify already unusually high rates of injury among minority youth.

Substance abuse is also a critical issue among many minority youth, from prenatal exposure through later use. The rates of Fetal Alcohol Syndrome (FAS) in Native American populations range from 1.3 per 1,000 births among Navajo women to 10.3 per 1,000 in Plains women (Myers, Kagawa-Singer, Kumanyika, Lex, & Markides, 1995). Among the Native American adolescent population, the death rate attributable to suicide and unintentional injuries (both frequently related to substance abuse) is twice that of youths from other ethnic groups and accounts for nearly 75% of the total death rate for this age group (Bagley, Angel, Dilworth-Anderson, Liu, & Schinke, 1995).

The serious risk factors that may be experienced by culturally and linguistically diverse children are sometimes further compounded when they begin school. In schools that high numbers of low-income, minority children attend, per pupil expenditures are frequently lower, leading to fewer resources and teachers with less training and experience (Darling-Hammond & Post, 2000; National Research Council, 2002). Thus, the resources are not available to ameliorate these sources of risk. Furthermore, there are an extremely limited number of culturally and linguistically diverse practitioners. Fewer than 6% of general school psychologists are members of a minority population (Curtis, Hunley, Walker, & Baker, 1999). Similar disproportionate representation is present in neuropsychology, with only 7% of the American Psychological Association Division of Clinical Neuropsychology reporting minority status (American Psychological Association Research Office, 1998).

Given these multiple factors that impact the healthy development of ethnically and linguistically diverse children, it is critical that we implement assessment models that lead to empirically supported interventions that are sensitive to these ecological contexts. Neuropsychology represents an excellent model for this work as it has historically embraced both individualized clinical approaches and large, empirical studies, allowing the practitioner to develop a scientifically based clinical practice that has the flexibility to address the needs of diverse populations (Lamberty, 2002).

## NEUROPSYCHOLOGY AND CULTURALLY AND LINGUISTICALLY DIVERSE PEDIATRIC POPULATIONS

Since the 1940s, information about brain-behavior relationships gathered from adult models of brain function and assessment has been applied to our understanding and practice with children (Reitan & Davidson, 1974). Unfortunately, although this work facilitated our study of the developing brain, it did not provide a better explanation for how these systems function together in the immature brain. Profound differences exist between the *developing* brain of the child and the fully *developed* brain of an adult (Marlowe, 2000).

Just as the neuropsychological work with adults has been applied to children, so has the work with majority culture individuals been applied to individuals from ethnically and culturally diverse backgrounds. An individual's performance on neuropsychological tests was thought to be a reflection of the integrity of that person's cerebral functioning. It was not until the 1960s that research began to emerge suggesting that demographic variables such as age, educational attainment, and gender impacted performance on measures of attention, memory, language, executive functioning, and sensory and motor functions (Marlowe, 2000; Miles, 2002). By the mid-1980s, consideration of demographic variables became more common in clinical research and practice. However, the methodology was often comparative rather than through intragroup research, and this work did not allow characteristics unique to a particular group to emerge (Lamberty, 2002).

Neuropsychologists have continued to explore new ways to adapt their practices to meet the needs of a changing population (Ardila, Rodríguez-Menéndez, & Rosselli, 2002; Marlowe, 2000). One adaptation has been to make demographic corrections based on education and ethnicity to established instruments (Lamberty, 2002); another effort has been the creation of a neuropsychological test battery that can be used across diverse populations (e.g., Cross-Cultural Neuropsychological Test Battery; Dick, Teng, Kempler, Davis, & Taussig, 2002). Other approaches, such as translating instruments, have been met with resistance, especially when these efforts occur without understanding the culture or the language in which the test will be used (Artiola i Fortuny & Mullaney, 1997). For example, Dick et al. suggested that Hispanics achieve significantly lower scores on translated versions of the Wechsler Adult Intelligence Scale-Revised (WAIS-R) Digit Span tests than other ethnically diverse groups because of the complexity of the language of administration. The Digit Span tests may be more difficult for Spanish-speaking individuals than other participants because seven of the numbers from 1 to 9 are multisyllabic in Spanish, whereas all are monosyllabic in Chinese and Vietnamese, and only one digit (7) has two syllables in English. In general, there has been a limited focus in the neuropsychological literature on the impact of cultural and linguistic differences and language acquisition on assessment, and this research has been even more limited with child populations. Just as adult neuropsychological practice trickled down to become more child-focused and expanded to incorporate a culturally sensitive approach, it now appears that the borders of neuropsychological assessment and intervention will need to flex once again to apply to culturally and linguistically diverse children.

## INFLUENCE OF CURRENT THEORETICAL PARADIGMS IN PSYCHOLOGY

Neuropsychological assessment for intervention with children who are culturally and linguistically diverse calls for the merging of developmental, ecological, and cross-cultural perspectives within a neuropsychological context. Not only are children unique in their central nervous system composition but also in the infinite number of ways that damage and recovery can occur (Gaddes & Edgell, 1994). A neuropsychological perspective relies on a systematic assessment and integration of internal (e.g., ability, executive functioning) and external (e.g., educational opportunities, language spoken in the home) systems to understand the cognitive processes underlying behavior (D'Amato, Rothlisberg, & Leu Work, 1999).

A developmental perspective acknowledges the interrelationship between biology and culture as individuals work to master basic developmental tasks. This perspective provides a framework for examining the influence of race, ethnicity, language, and SES on the psychosocial tasks of growing up in a complex physical and social environment. Although certain aspects of maturation are universal, there is great variation in the behavior associated with and the emphasis placed on certain developmental outcomes (Berk, 1996). Furthermore, caution must be used when applying these cognitive and psychosocial developmental theories as much of our current understanding is based on outcomes of research with non-Latino, White, middle-class children and families (McLoyd, 1998a). Many researchers in the field of child development are proponents of an ecological framework that allows for a better understanding of the sociological influences on normative development in culturally diverse children and adolescents (e.g., McLoyd, 1998a; Mistry, Vandewater, Huston, & McLoyd, 2002).

There are two helpful models to use when considering the contextual or sociological influences on a child: ecological and cross-cultural. Bronfenbrenner's (1979) ecological model of human development has provided an effective framework for organizing our knowledge in the assessment for intervention process. This perspective also highlights the importance of the interactions between the individual and the multiple, interrelated contexts within which the child functions (Bronfenbrenner, 1979). The ecological model includes four components beyond the individual that operate on the following levels: *microsystem* (daily contexts; e.g., home), *mesosystem* (interactions between daily contexts; e.g., home and school), *exosystem* (indirect contexts; e.g., neighborhood), and *macrosystem* (e.g., larger institutions and culture). From an ecological perspective, the individual possesses characteristics that are neither positive nor negative; they are instead viewed in terms of their appropriateness within the individual settings or environments (Bronfenbrenner, 1979; Conoley & Haynes, 1992).

A cross-cultural perspective also provides a contextual framework from which to view children and their families. This perspective assumes that all behavior serves some adaptive function and is directed by a set of cultural rules and norms that help to socialize and shape group behavior (Gibbs & Huang, 2003; Gopaul-McNicol & Armour-Thomas, 2002). This cross-cultural perspective has been used by mental health researchers to provide a comparative context for understanding psychological phenomena (Green, 1999). This line of research has naturally evolved into consideration of culturally responsive or sensitive practice, especially as related to assessment, consultation, and intervention with culturally diverse individuals.

## A SCHOOL NEUROPSYCHOLOGICAL APPROACH TO CULTURALLY AND LINGUISTICALLY DIVERSE CHILDREN

School neuropsychology, a recently developed area of training and practice in psychology, provides a model that is consistent with these perspectives in that it combines neuropsychology, school psychology, and a broad contextual approach

(D'Amato et al., 1999). The focus of this field is to address the needs of children and adolescents who have neuropsychological and neuropsychiatric issues through assessment that leads to practical, effective school interventions. As a result, this chapter primarily focuses on research and interventions appropriate for school-age children between the ages of 6 and 18.

Neuropsychological assessment does not represent a set procedure but is largely governed by the particular orientation of the individual clinician; the majority of practitioners report the use of a flexible battery approach where a specific collection of tests and procedures are chosen on an individualized basis. For example, Sweet, Moberg, and Suchy (2000) found that 90% of board-certified neuropsychologists use a flexible battery approach. An approach that emphasizes multiple sources of data and use of a variety of approaches is consistent with the assessment and treatment of a culturally diverse population. Additionally, this approach is also practical for a school setting where a team approach to assessment for intervention planning is applied. Although certain aspects of the neuropsychological perspective will be the same across ethnic groups (e.g., locus of injury, neurobiology), the resulting behaviors that are expressed will likely vary based on the child's ethnicity and personal history. Therefore, it is critically important to conduct a thorough investigation of the child's and family's language and culture because of the potential attitudinal, behavioral, and social implications of membership in a particular ethnic or racial group.

## ASSESSING CULTURAL AND LINGUISTIC FACTORS IN THE CLINICAL INTERVIEW AND RECORD REVIEW

A neuropsychological assessment is best considered a procedural continuum beginning with a comprehensive interview. Given the scarcity of reliable and valid instruments for measuring neuropsychological functioning with culturally and linguistically diverse children, it may also be the best source of information. Throughout the interview, the practitioner must remain aware that the data collected are subject to the biases of both the interviewer and the unique cultural experiences of the family and child (Takushi & Uomoto, 2001).

One more complexity of the clinical interview includes language and use of interpreters. This is an extremely important, though often underdeveloped, competency for all psychologists. The limited number of culturally and linguistically diverse school personnel often necessitates extensive use of interpretation services. The interpreter frequently becomes the voice for the process; thus, skill in the selection and appropriate use of an interpreter is critical. School psychologists should review the skills and competencies recommended for school-based interpreters (e.g., equally fluent in both languages, knowledgeable about school settings, trained in issues of confidentiality). See Rhodes (2000) for a practical guide for using interpreters in a school-based setting.

Because of the complexity in gathering and organizing information on minority clients, Gibbs and Huang (2003) proposed an ecological model that considers the impact of ethnicity, social class, and adaptation on the five major domains of functioning: (1) *individual* level of psychosocial adjustment, (2) relationships with *family*, (2) *school* adjustment and achievement, (4) relationships with *peers*, and (5) adaptation to the *community*. An underlying variable that affects child and family functioning at each of these levels is the SES of the family. At the most basic level, a family's income affects the degree of prenatal and ongoing medical care as well as the nutrition of a child. At more indirect levels, socioeconomic variables impact the quality of education that the child receives and the accessibility of resources in the community (Echemendía & Julian, 2002; Mistry et al., 2002).

From a neuropsychological perspective, the *individual* level includes such variables as cognitive ability, sensory and perceptual functioning, and attention and memory. When interviewing the family, it is especially important to ask specific questions related to the child's health history, including any potential head injury. This domain also includes appearance, affect, interpersonal competence, and attitudes toward school as variables that impact a child's functioning and have implications related to ethnicity. For example, lack of eye contact and reserved affect may be culturally appropriate norms and should not be misconstrued as lack of attention or a symptom of depression (Canino & Spurlock, 1994; Wong, 2000).

Another critical aspect of psychosocial adaptation includes a consideration of the acculturation level of the child and family (Horton, Carrington, & Lewis-Jack, 2001; Marlowe, 2000). Six areas in which acculturation can affect psychological functioning include: language, cognitive styles, personality, identity, attitudes, and acculturative stress (Berry, Trimble, & Omedo, 1988). Historically, acculturation has been measured by simple indicators such as language spoken or amount of time in the United States. Although a comprehensive interview will provide an indication of the individual and family acculturation level, there are also a small number of instruments available, typically with small sample sizes and limited generalizability. For example, the Psychological Acculturation Scale (Tropp, Erkut, García Coll, Alarcón, & Vásquez-García, 1999) was designed to measure acculturation in Puerto Rican adolescents and adults and includes both behavioral and psychological aspects of acculturation. Some researchers believe that U.S.-born African Americans who speak English also have different levels of acculturation (Landrine & Klonoff, 1996). In fact, Manly et al. (1998) found that African Americans reporting less acculturation obtained lower scores on the WAIS-R Information subtest and the Boston Naming Test than did more acculturated individuals. No similar studies including child/adolescent populations were found, suggesting that that this is an important area for future research.

Assessment of *family* roles should take into account family structure, size, tradition, and communication patterns and expectations. All of these variables are influenced by the ethnicity and social class of the family. For example, it has been noted that Asian American populations experience more shame and stigmatization related to emotional problems than the general population (Sue & Sue, 1987), possibly resulting in a reduced likelihood of pursuing outside assistance (Wong, 2000). Once the Asian family does seek help, it is important to present a clear definition of neuropsychology and the purpose of the assessment, such as measuring aspects of brain functioning, as this perspective may be more acceptable to less acculturated families because it is perceived as medical rather than psychological (Wong, 2000). Conversely, among African American families, the idea of a neuropsychological evaluation may arouse mistrust due to the historical misuse of test results for this population (Miles, 2002).

One of the major domains of a child's life is adjustment to and achievement within the *school* setting. Ochoa and Rhodes (in press) provide an overview of student-specific information that should be gathered or reviewed by practitioners to determine the effect of life experience and language exposure on present levels of functioning. Recommended areas of investigation include the individual's educational and language history as well as current language proficiency. Practitioners should determine the country in which the child has been educated, the language(s) of instruction, previous bilingual education services, reason for termination or exit from bilingual education services, grades repeated, number of schools attended, areas of academic success, and areas of academic difficulty or concern. Because education can account for up to 15% of variance in scores on some neuropsychological assessments among adult populations (Dick et al., 2002), practitioners should use extra caution when interpreting the results of students who have experienced educational gaps.

Record review (e.g., type of language support provided) and parent interview (including home language surveys) should be utilized to examine the language history of the child and family. What language or languages are currently used at home? What language or languages have been used at home during the life of the student? What language appears to be preferred by the student? In what language does the student prefer to read? In what language does the student watch TV or listen to music? Likewise, the current language proficiency of the student should be examined through record review, teacher interview, and formal and informal assessment. *The mere fact that a child appears to use a particular language more frequently should not serve as an indicator of language proficiency.* The results of recently administered language proficiency measures provide insight into the student's level of language proficiency across both languages. The results should be no more than 6 months old and should be the product of a trained examiner using age- and language-appropriate measures.

To understand and effectively integrate information related to language history, it is important that school psychologists understand the unique nature and developmental pattern of the second-language acquisition process. For example, children may experience a decreased ability to speak their first language as they are exposed to English. If school language-dominance records indicate this phenomenon, the child's communicative abilities in both languages may be impaired. Key sources of information include Cummins (1984) and Thomas and Collier (2002). These and other studies examine the expected rate of second-language acquisition, the multiple factors that may influence language acquisition, the difference between basic communication skills and academic language, and the potential impact of second-language acquisition on academic achievement.

An informal assessment of *peer* and *community* relationships can also provide an indication of the child's or adolescent's adaptive functioning. In working with minority youth, it is important to consider friendships both within and outside the school, as these relationships may vary (Gibbs & Huang, 2003). For example, a Black adolescent may seem isolated and withdrawn when attending a predominantly White high school but have a large group of friends in the neighborhood setting. Additionally, it is important to consider the degree of involvement of the family in their community and the types of activities and resources that are available. This component will be especially important in comprehensive treatment planning.

Beyond community influences are the broad societal factors (e.g., legislation, political/societal movements) that impact assessment and intervention practice with culturally and linguistically diverse children. Consent decrees and case law established over the past 3 decades serve as the foundation for public law regulations related to the assessment of students who are culturally and linguistically diverse (e.g., *Diana v. State Board of Education,* 1970; *Larry P. v. Riles,* 1984). The Individuals with Disabilities Education Act, Revisions of 1997 (IDEA 97; 1997) expanded on previous requirements for these students with the establishment of the Procedures for Evaluation and Determination of Eligibility (PEDE). The PEDE requires that tests and other evaluation materials be selected so as not to be discriminatory on a racial or cultural basis and be provided and administered in the child's native language or other mode of communication unless it is clearly not feasible to do so. The PEDE also requires the careful selection and utilization of a variety of assessment strategies and tools when assessing students with limited English proficiency to ensure that they measure the extent to which a child has a disability rather than measuring the student's English-language skills.

Use of a Flexible Neuropsychology Battery in the Schools

A variety of approaches and guidelines have been introduced to assist practitioners in best practices in multicultural assessment (e.g., Gopaul-McNicol & Armour-Thomas, 2002; Sattler, 2002), and these may be applied to school neuropsychological assessment as well. It is important to note that multicultural assessment does not advocate deviation from standardized procedures with ethnic minorities. When "testing the limits" is conducted, it should be done only after the entire test has been administered under standard conditions (Cuéllar, 1998; Gopaul-McNicol & Armour-Thomas, 2002). Furthermore, whenever the tests are unable to control for specific cultural variables such as language or acculturation, consider evaluating the child or adolescent using measures that have been specifically adapted and renormed for a given population (Lopez et al., 1989). Despite careful attention to test selection, children from varying cultural backgrounds bring different experiences, knowledge, expectations, and sociolinguistic norms to the assessment setting, and these variables may contribute to different interpretations of test items and a pattern of lower performance than among members of the majority culture (Gopaul-McNicol & Armour-Thomas, 2002).

The impact of language cannot be underestimated as it will have a profound impact on all aspects of assessment. For some Hispanics, both Spanish and English may be active languages, and the individual's functional language may be a mixture of both, creating a high degree of interference (Ardila et al., 2002). Therefore, if the comprehensive interview suggests that any language other than English is present in the student's life, it is best to begin the neuropsychological assessment with a test of receptive language ability in each language. It is easier to make incorrect assumptions about language dominance in children than in adult populations (Ardila et al., 2002).

*Communication/Language Skills* The Woodcock-Muñoz Language Survey (Woodcock & Muñoz-Sandoval, 2001) is one of the most frequently used measures of language proficiency for Spanish-and-English-speaking students and is one of the few measures that provides information about the student's academic language development in the student's first language and in English. Another instrument that shows promise is the Bilingual Verbal Ability Test (BVAT; Muñoz-Sandoval, Cummins, Alvarado, & Ruef, 1998), which is available in 18 languages in addition to English. Frequently spoken languages assessed by the BVAT include Vietnamese, Hmong, Haitian-Creole, Chinese, Arabic, Russian, and Navajo.

Rhodes, Kayser, and Hess (2000) have suggested procedures to aid in the differential diagnosis of a language impairment and normal language development among LEP children during the neuropsychological assessment process. Information gathered from the comprehensive interview (e.g., parental concerns, language use) can be combined with teacher interviews and observations from the speech-language pathologist to develop a complete picture of the child's language use and skills. Children with language impairments typically have restricted abilities related to forms (syntax and phonology), use, and content (semantics) in both languages regardless of the context. Additionally, the practitioner will want to consider data related to sequencing, memory, and attention span. Language-impaired children often have difficulty in these areas in both languages. These data should all support the diagnosis of language impairment. The characteristics of acquired aphasia, dysarthria, apraxia, and traumatic brain injury will be present in both languages.

It is easy to recognize the impact of language when a child clearly speaks a language other than English as his or her first language. However, it is critical to consider the more subtle effects of language when a child speaks nontraditional English (e.g., Black English) or has specific culturally determined patterns of usage. For example, Manly et al. (1998) has found that Black English use among African American adults was correlated with performance deficits on the Trail Making B test and the Information subtest on the WAIS-R. Furthermore, Native American children scored lower on tests of language (Dauphinais & King, 1992) and verbal ability as measured by the Wechsler Intelligence Scale for Children III (WISC-III; Tanner-Halverson, Burden, & Sabers, 1993), leading some to propose that for this population there is a cultural mismatch between the decontextualized format of test taking and the culturally determined patterns of language use (Gopaul-McNicol & Armour-Thomas, 2002). Once the level of language skill has been determined, practitioners can make better decisions about which instruments to use and how to interpret the results to obtain the best information about the child's strengths and weaknesses.

*Intelligence/Cognitive*   Several researchers have reviewed the difficulties in using IQ and other cognitive ability tests to assess culturally and linguistically diverse children (e.g., Dent, 1996; Gopaul-McNicol & Armour-Thomas, 2002; Marlowe, 2000). The inclusion of children from diverse backgrounds in normative samples for a test *does not justify* its use with those populations, because the minority group norms will not cluster within the distribution in large enough numbers to have any influence on the norms (Dent, 1996). On the Wechsler scales, African American, Hispanic, and Native American populations all have mean scores that are approximately 10 points to 1 standard deviation below the mean (Tanner-Halverson et al., 1993; Wasserman & Becker, 1999). Although mean score differences do not necessarily constitute test bias (Reynolds & Kaiser, 1992), the overrepresentation of minority children in special education classrooms has led some to discourage the use of verbally weighted measures of intelligence such as the Wechsler scales and instead use alternative approaches such as the Cognitive Assessment System (CAS; Naglieri & Das, 1997a) or a triarchic theory of intelligence (Sternberg, 1999).

Despite these cautions, the Wechsler scales remain one of the most widely used instruments in assessing cognitive ability (Marlowe, 2000). There are at least two translated versions of the WISC-III, the Escala de Inteligencia Wechsler par Ninos-Revisada (Psychological Corporation, 1983) and the Escala de Inteligencia Wechsler para Ninos-Revisada de Puerto Rico (Psychological Corporation, 1993). The former is considered a research edition and was published without normative data; the latter has a narrow norming base (Puerto Rican children) and may not be appropriate for most Hispanic groups in the United States (Echemendía & Julian, 2002). It is also important to note that these translated and normed instruments are now dated, given the publication of the WISC-IV and the soon to be published WISC-IV-Spanish.

Two alternatives to translated versions of traditional ability tests are comprehensive nonverbal assessments, such as the Universal Nonverbal Intelligence Test (UNIT; Bracken & McCallum, 1998), and measures reportedly based on neuropsychological theory, such as the Kaufman Assessment Battery for Children-II (K-ABC-II; Kaufman & Kaufman, 2004) and the CAS. The UNIT was designed to be totally nonverbal and to measure memory and reasoning through symbolic (language-mediated) and nonsymbolic modalities. Additionally, the psychometric properties of the instrument appear to be sound, although further research is needed (Sattler, 2001).

The K-ABC-II, was developed along two theoretical perspectives, a Lurian model and a Cattell-Horn-Carroll model, so that practitioners can interpret their results based on the referral question and the child's background. The test offers an expanded age range (3–18) and, like the original, a nonverbal battery option and answers in Spanish for those items that require an oral response. As part of an intensive, prepublication process to establish the cultural fairness of the new edition, a study with 46 Taos Pueblo Indian children was conducted; the researchers found that although the children were very different in language and culture from the mainstream population, they scored in a very similar manner to the national standardization sample (Fletcher-Janzen, 2003). The CAS offers an alternative framework for examining and interpreting ability based on the Planning, Attention, Simultaneous, Successive (PASS) model of cognitive processing theory (Naglieri & Das, 1997b). A review of preliminary data suggested that there is less discrepancy between the scores of White and African American children on this measure and that fewer African American children were identified as mentally retarded using the CAS rather than the WISC-III (Naglieri & Rojahn, 2001). This instrument is also promising because its emphasis on processing strengths and weaknesses facilitates academic intervention planning, although the interpretation of the Planning and Attention factors remains questionable (Sattler, 2001).

A new instrument, the Dean-Woodcock Neuropsychological Battery (Dean & Woodcock, 2003), is a comprehensive assessment tool for sensorimotor functioning that is aligned with the Woodcock-Johnson III Tests of Cognitive Abilities and Tests of Achievement. This newest measure represents the efforts of Dean and Woodcock (1999) to align a neuropsychological approach with the Gf-Gc perspective on intelligence. All of the components of this instrument are available in Spanish. Because this instrument is so ne p 646-w, there are no published data available related to potential cultural, educational, or income differences, but this tool may represent a promising instrument for practitioners and researchers alike.

*Achievement* Common areas of academic achievement measurement include reading, mathematics, spelling, and writing. Because academic performance is based on experientially dependent skills and abilities, the assessment of achievement can be an exceedingly complex process with children from culturally and linguistically diverse backgrounds who may have educational and life experiences that are unique in comparison to the normative population of many commonly used measures. As noted by Duran (1989), until a student is proficient in English, measures of academic achievement may really only be a crude test of English competence rather than an accurate assessment of academic growth and development.

Standardized measures of academic achievement, curriculum-based measurement, or a combination of these are common methods of assessing the academic achievement of students who are culturally and linguistically diverse. Frequently used standardized measures of academic achievement include the Woodcock-Johnson III Tests of Achievement (Woodcock, McGrew, & Mather, 2001); the Batería Woodcock-Muñoz-Revisada: Pruebas de Aprovechamiento (Woodcock & Muñoz-Sandoval, 1996), a parallel Spanish version of the Woodcock-Johnson Psychoeducational Battery-Revised; and the Aprenda: La Prueba de Logros en Español, Segunda Edición (Psychological Corporation, 1997), a measure of academic achievement for Spanish-speaking students in the areas of reading, language arts, and mathematics. Unfortunately, there are not many options available if the child's first language is not Spanish. Curriculum-based measurement is one of the most widely used methods of curriculum-based assessment and has been suggested as a potential strategy for making educational decisions with bilingual Hispanic students (Baker & Good, 1995; Shinn, 1989). Several good sources are available that provide an overview of the fundamentals of curriculum-based measurement administration, sampling, and scoring procedures (e.g., Fuchs & Fuchs, 1990; Shinn, 1989).

*Executive Functions and Problem Solving*   In nearly all measures of neuropsychological functioning, the amount of schooling that an individual has experienced will play a role in his or her functioning (Rosselli, 1993). Some tests have been observed to be more sensitive to educational variables (e.g., language tests) than others (e.g., Wisconsin Card Sorting Test; Heaton, 1981), as exemplified in the work of Rosselli and Ardila (1993). Furthermore, research has demonstrated that the educational effect on neuropsychological test performance is not linear. That is, differences between 0 and 3 years of education are usually significant, whereas there are virtually no differences found between individuals with 12 and 15 years of education (Puente & Ardila, 2000). It has been suggested that the process of education actually changes how the brain organizes information, thus impacting performance on items that seemingly would not be related to one's educational experiences (e.g., visuospatial skills; Ardila, Rosselli, & Rosas, 1989; Rosselli, 1993). With this caution in mind, there are a few promising instruments available that provide comprehensive assessments of individual functioning.

The NEPSY: A Developmental Neuropsychological Assessment (Korkman, Kirk, & Kemp, 1998) is a developmental neuropsychological test that was developed to identify neuropsychological problems in children (see Chapter 11 for a review). The NEPSY measures five core domains: (1) attention and executive functioning, (2) sensorimotor, (3) visuospatial, (4) language, and (5) memory. A review of two preliminary studies has suggested the utility of the NEPSY with diverse populations. Mulenga, Ahonen, and Aro (2001) tested 45 literate schoolchildren in Zambia with the NEPSY and concluded that although there were differences between the norm group and the Zambian group of children (e.g., lower Language and Attention and Executive Functioning scores and higher Visuospatial scores for the Zambian population), the NEPSY did not appear to be overly sensitive to language and cultural differences. Additionally, McCloskey (2001) found support for use of the NEPSY with a group of 55 low-income Hispanic children based on the similarities between the correlations for this group and for the standardization sample. Obviously, the practitioner would want to use care in selecting the subtests that would be least impacted by the child's language and/or schooling history as well as using caution in the interpretation of the results pending additional research support.

An exciting development in the field is the application of the Cambridge Neuropsychological Testing Automated Battery to pediatric populations. The battery emphasizes executive functioning, including measures of planning, set shifting, spatial working memory, and nonverbal memory span (Luciana, 2003). More important, because of the nonverbal nature of the tasks, empirical data support comparable task performance between children who are native versus nonnative English speakers when English is the language used to present each task (Luciana & Nelson, 2002). Only preliminary data exist on the reliability of the instrument with pediatric populations, but early findings have suggested that the internal consistency coefficients of this measure are strong (.73 to .95) in 4- to 12-year-old children (Luciana, unpublished data in Luciana, 2003). Unfortunately, the cost of this instrument at this time is prohibitive for most school districts and private clinics.

*Attention/Memory/Learning*   One of the key components to memory and learning is the ability to selectively attend to relevant information that is presented during the course of daily functioning. Unfortunately, attention and memory also appear to be sensitive to factors of SES and schooling (e.g., Ardila et al., 1989; Rosselli & Ardila, 1993). For example, the commonly used Gordon Diagnostic System, a computerized program that measures inhibition, vigilance, and errors of commission, has been studied with Puerto Rican children (Bauermesiter, Berríos, Jiménez, Acevedo, & Gordon, 1990). The authors compared the norms between a U.S. sample and a Puerto Rican sample and found significant differences, especially for younger children, suggesting the importance of creating local norms.

Memory should be measured using both verbal and nonverbal stimuli because of language differences. It is important to recognize that even if the child speaks the dominant language, he or she may be limited in English proficiency. Harris, Cullum, and Puente (1995) found that nonbalanced (proficient in conversational English, but not equally adept in both languages) Spanish-English bilinguals learned fewer words and had poorer retention scores when tested in English as compared to Spanish on the California Verbal Learning Test (Delis, Kramer, Kaplan, & Ober, 1987). The results of this study suggested that the relative degree of bilingualism was significant and that it systematically altered the learning and retention of verbal information. When assessed in their dominant language, no significant differences were found in groups. Therefore, when possible, the practitioner should assess the child in both the *first* and *second* languages.

*Sensory, Perceptual, and Motor*    In general, measures used to assess gross and fine motor skills will be similar across cultures. However, it is important to keep in mind the degree of familiarity an individual might have with the tools used to measure fine motor skills (e.g., pencil use, scissors). This type of information can be gathered during the interview to determine the most appropriate measures as well as how to interpret individual items. Cultural differences might also impact test behaviors. For example, Puente and Ardila (2000) have cautioned that Hispanic children often respond differently on timed tests in that they tend to work at their own pace rather than compete with a clock.

As with other aspects of neuropsychological functioning, measures of visual-spatial abilities are vulnerable to factors related to SES and education level. Although nonverbal measures like the Rey-Osterrieth Complex Figure (ROCF; Osterrieth, 1944; Rey, 1941) and the Developmental Test of Visual-Motor Integration (Beery, Buktenica, & Beery, 2004) might be considered appropriate to assist with the diagnosis of non-English-speaking children who are suspected of having learning problems due to visual-motor difficulties, it is important to note the cultural differences and negative impact of lower SES and educational level on these types of instruments (e.g., Ardila & Rosselli, 1994; Frey & Pinelli, 1991). For example, Ardila and Rosselli compiled normative data on 5- to 12-year-old Colombian children using a variety of common neuropsychological instruments, including the ROCF task: copy and immediate reproduction and recognition of superimposed figures. These authors found that children showed increasing patterns of scoring with age similar to those presented by Kolb and Whishaw (1985), although the results were slightly lower due to differing levels of SES in the two groups. The task for recognition of superimposed figures was significantly impacted by educational level (Ardila & Rosselli, 1994).

*Behavior and Personality*    An important component of any neuropsychological assessment includes an evaluation of individual behavior. The Behavior Assessment System for Children (BASC; Reynolds & Kamphaus, 1992) and now its revision, BASC-II (BASC-II; Reynolds & Kamphaus, 2004), is a well-supported, frequently used instrument to identify behavioral and emotional disorders in children and adolescents (e.g., Merydith, 2001). Although a Spanish version, El Sistema Multidimensional de Evaluación de la Conducta de los Niños (el Sistema) was available with the original version, there was very limited research using the Spanish translation with the exception of a study by McCloskey, Hess, and D'Amato (2003). McCloskey et al. generally supported the use of the Escalas Evaluativas de los Padres, the Spanish version of the BASC-Parent Rating Scales (BASC-PRS), with low-income Hispanic children, particularly with the Internalizing, Externalizing, and Adaptive Composites. However, there were differences between this sample and the normative sample in that significant differences were noted between the Adaptive Composite and scales from other composites. The BASC-II provides a Spanish translation of the Parent Rating Scales, Self-Report of Personality (SRP), and the Structured Developmental History. Preliminary data presented in the manual suggest that the internal reliability for the Spanish PRS and SRP are adequate but lower than the reliabilities for the general norming sample. Ongoing research on the use of the BASC-II with non-majority populations is needed to assist practitioners in interpreting their findings.

If more detailed information regarding social problem solving and task compliance is required, Tell-Me-A-Story (Constantino, 1987) provides the school practitioner with an instrument that shows good validity when used with other cultures (Costantino, Malgady, Casullo, & Castillo, 1991). It is one of the only comprehensive personality measure that offers nonminority and minority norms for four groups (African American, Puerto Rican, other Hispanic, and White; Constantino, Flanagan, & Malgady, 2001).

## SCHOOL INTERVENTION APPROACHES WITH CULTURALLY AND LINGUISTICALLY DIVERSE CHILDREN

Psychology has made many new inroads into understanding the learning process and the subsequent development of corrective or adaptive programs for students with learning disorders and traumatic brain injuries. School practitioners must quickly and accurately filter through the accumulated data to develop the most likely hypothesis to explain the findings and offer effective interventions (D'Amato et al., 1999). In doing so, the practitioner must also consider the appropriateness of the interventions based on the cultural and linguistic diversity of the child and family.

After completing a thorough neuropsychological assessment of the child, the practitioner will want to utilize an ecological perspective to develop a working hypothesis. The school practitioner must consider the various contexts (e.g., family, school, community) of the child's life and how the interactions within those domains may have impacted the results. There is not a specific formula for how to modify one's interpretation, but those results that are most vulnerable to external variables (e.g., SES, language differences) may be afforded less emphasis unless there is convincing evidence to suggest that an area truly represents a deficit. The most weight should be given to those results that directly link to the referral question, represent a concern for the family and school, and represent an area of weakness according to the assessment results. As noted by Sattler (2002), the examiner should use a multimethod assessment approach and then weave together the various pieces of information to create a cohesive, consistent picture of the child or adolescent and resolve any major discrepancies before developing a hypothesis.

Once this careful evaluation of the results has occurred and a preliminary hypothesis is developed, the practitioner is ready to work with the school and the family to develop an intervention plan. On the individual level, the school practitioner will want to use the strengths of the child to address his or her needs. Additionally, the practitioner should consider the broader contexts of the child's life. When the family and school work together, it leads to better outcomes and higher academic achievement for children (Christenson, 2003). Furthermore, by helping connect the child's family to resources, the practitioner is helping to build a more positive relationship with the family and helping the family build a broader base of community support.

The field of school psychology has made the integration of evidence-based interventions a priority. Unfortunately, there currently appears to be little connection between clinical and school practice and empirically supported interventions (Kratochwill & Stoiber, 2000). School neuropsychologists face an

additional dilemma when attempting to implement these evidence-based practices because of the scarcity of research with culturally and linguistically diverse students. (A thorough description of evidence-based practices is provided
in Chapter 37.) Although minority children are often included in intervention
research, the findings are rarely disaggregated by ethnicity and comparisons
made between these students and majority population students (National Research Council, 2002). The lack of data specific to ethnically diverse groups was
consistent with the findings of Swanson, Hoskyn, and Lee (1999), who found in
a meta-analysis of 180 intervention studies in students with LD, that the majority of studies did not report ethnicity.

Adding to the difficulty in developing successful interventions is the lack of
overlap between the various fields of research that apply to culturally diverse students (who may speak another language) and who suffer from neurological
deficits. In effect, a school psychologist working with a diverse population must be
familiar with the literature related to culturally appropriate interventions for the
specific population, effective instructional strategies for linguistically diverse or
English-language learners, and appropriate interventions specific to the neuropsychological problem (e.g., learning disability, traumatic brain injury, attention
deficit/hyperactivity disorder). Because of the breadth of knowledge required, it
is recommended that intervention planning take place within a multidisciplinary
framework that includes family members (and the child), a family advocate who is
familiar with (and perhaps a member of) the family's ethnic/racial/linguistic
group, a representative of the school's English-language learners program, a regular and special education teacher, the school psychologist, and other representatives as appropriate.

Another challenge related to establishing and implementing evidence-based
interventions with culturally and linguistically diverse children is related to
treatment initiation and follow up among diverse populations due to population
mobility, differences in language and cultural perspectives, and opportunities to
access resources (Echemendía & Julian, 2002; Mistry et al., 2002; Wong, 2000). Finally, there is also the complexity of the school setting that stands as a challenge
to those who want to implement evidence-based interventions. These challenges
highlight the importance of adopting a flexible model that incorporates contextual approaches that consider the classroom, school, and community of the child.
Gersten and Baker (2000) offered a unique approach for exploring effective instructional strategies with English-language learners in which they combined interviews with recognized experts with findings from the empirical literature to
articulate directions for improving current practice and conducting future research. This type of combined approach is consistent with developing effective
interventions for culturally and linguistically diverse children.

A contextual perspective (as discussed in Chapter 2) requires that a neuro-
psychologically-oriented school psychologist engage in a wide variety of consultative and interdisciplinary activities with teachers, parents, and support staff
(Kratochwill & Stoiber, 2000). Ingraham (2000) has advocated for the adoption of
a comprehensive, multicultural framework in school psychology consultation so
that practitioners can better meet the needs of culturally diverse students, teachers, and family members. Through the use of this model, school practitioners recognize and discuss the role of culture in the consultation and intervention
process and make adaptations as needed to enhance the effectiveness of the consultative relationship and the resulting intervention plan.

Another trend in the field of school psychology is the incorporation of technology into daily practice. Although most practitioners frequently use computers for communication, report writing, and perhaps scoring of tests, it is much less common for these individuals to use technology resources for test administration, for collecting and tracking data, and as an integral component of intervention programs (e.g., instructional software, assistive technology; Hess, Goetz, Martin-Delaney, & Hutaff, 2004). Expanded technology use could facilitate the tracking intervention effectiveness over time, allowing the practitioner to maintain ongoing data on student progress. This type of careful data collection facilitates flexible and timely decision making around needed program changes. Furthermore, it is helpful if an individual is working with a unique population to assist in establishing local norms on commonly used assessments, allowing for more appropriate interpretation of assessment findings.

## CONCLUSION

There is little agreement on the best way to adapt assessment to meet the needs of an increasingly diverse population. Some do not believe that any one instrument designed for the majority group can adequately tap the neuropsychological skills of diverse groups without being impacted by ethnicity, age, education, and socioeconomic level. As a result, these researchers advocate for new instruments or approaches that draw on the unique abilities of individuals from different ethnic groups (Gopaul-McNicol & Armour-Thomas, 2002; Manly & Jacobs, 2002). This approach may represent a long-term solution, but school practitioners also require short-term answers.

Given the complexity of the different issues related to neuropsychological assessment of children who are culturally and linguistically diverse, school practitioners should keep a singular focus on developing the best understanding of the child's (and family's) strengths and needs, and not on the tests alone. It is important that the practitioner develop an increased awareness of the impact of culture, language, SES, and education on the instruments used in a neuropsychological battery and incorporate these in a flexible, individualized approach. Additionally, practitioners should use extreme caution in their interpretation when using instruments that are not well matched to the child's background or alternative assessments that have limited norms. Interventions that result from the assessment should be contextually and culturally relevant and frequently monitored to determine whether they are having a positive effect on the child's subsequent skill acquisition. In recognition of the tentative nature of the original hypothesis, all members of the evaluation and intervention team must promote an open mind toward ongoing modification of treatment plans if the strategies are not effective.

In addition to these short-term approaches, the field of school neuropsychology must also look to long-term solutions. Much of our effort should be directed toward increasing the number of culturally and linguistically diverse practitioners who will potentially have a better understanding of the subtle linguistic and cultural variations that permeate everyday life for diverse families and can incorporate this knowledge into their clinical work. Practitioners can also work to create local norms for specific groups that allow for different levels of comparison of student functioning and identify potential differences that will facilitate more accurate interpretation of neuropsychological results. Finally, as a field, we must continue to research the effectiveness of evidence-based neuropsychological interventions across various ethnic and linguistic groups.

## REFERENCES

American Psychological Association Research Office. (1998). *1997 APA directory survey, with new member updates for 1998.* Washington, DC: American Psychological Association.

Ardila, A., Rodríguez-Menéndez, G., & Rosselli, M. (2002). Current issues in neuropsychological assessment of Hispanics/Latinos. In F. R. Ferraro (Ed.), *Minority and cross-cultural aspects of neuropsychological assessment* (pp. 161–179). Lisse, The Netherlands: Swets & Zeitlinger.

Ardila, A., & Rosselli, M. (1994). Development of language, memory and visuospatial abilities in 5 to 12 year old children using a neuropsychological battery. *Developmental Neuropsychology, 10,* 97–120.

Ardila, A., Rosselli, M., & Rosas, P. (1989). Neuropsychological assessment in illiterates: Visuospatial and memory skills. *Brain and Cognition, 11,* 147–166.

Artiles, A. J., & Trent, S. C. (1994). Overrepresentation of minority students in special education: A continuing debate. *Journal of Special Education, 27,* 410–437.

Artiola i Fortuny, L., & Mullaney, H. A. (1997). Neuropsychology with Spanish speakers: Language use and proficiency issues for test development. *Journal of Clinical and Experimental Neuropsychology, 19,* 615–622.

Bagley, S. P., Angel, R., Dilworth-Anderson, P., Liu, W., & Schinke, S. (1995). Adaptive health behaviors among ethnic minorities. *American Psychologist, 45,* 390–395.

Baker, S. K., & Good, R. (1995). Curriculum based measurement of English reading with bilingual Hispanic students: A validation study with second-grade students. *School Psychology Review, 24,* 561–578.

Bauermesiter, J. J., Berríos, V., Jiménez, A. L., Acevedo, L., & Gordon, M. (1990). Some issues and instruments for the assessment of attention-deficit hyperactivity disorder in Puerto Rican children. *Journal of Clinical Child Psychology, 19,* 9–16.

Bazarian, J. J., Pope, C., McClung, J., Cheng, Y. T., & Flesher, W. (2003). Ethnic and racial disparities in emergency department care for mild traumatic brain injury. *Academic Emergency Medicine, 10*(11), 1209–1217.

Beery, K. E., Buktenica, N. A., & Beery, N. A. (2004). *The Beery-Buktenica Test of Visual-Motor Integration* (5th ed.). Bloomington, MN: Pearson.

Berry, J. W., Trimble, J., & Olmedo, E. L. (1988). Assessment of acculturation. In W. J. L., & J. W. Bern (Eds.), *Field methods in cross-cultural research* (pp. 291–324). Beverly Hills, CA: Sage.

Berk, L. (1996). *Infants, children, and adolescents* (2nd ed.). Boston: Allyn & Bacon.

Bishaw, A., & Iceland, J. (2003). *Poverty 1999* [Current population reports]. Washington, DC: U.S. Census Bureau.

Bracken, B., & McCallum, S. (1998). *Universal nonverbal intelligence test.* Itasca, IL: Riverside.

Bradley, R. H., & Whiteside-Mansell, L. (1997). Children in poverty. In R. T. Ammerman & M. Hersen (Eds.), *Handbook of prevention and treatment with children and adolescents: Intervention in the real world context* (pp. 13–58). New York: Wiley.

Bronfenbrenner, U. (1979). *The ecology of human development: Experiments by nature and design.* Cambridge, MA: Harvard University Press.

Bruns, J., & Hauser, W. A. (2003). The epidemiology of traumatic brain injury: A review. *Epilepsia, 44*(10), 2–10.

Canino, I. A., & Spurlock, J. (1994). *Culturally diverse children and adolescents: Assessment, diagnosis, and treatment.* New York: Guilford Press.

Christenson, S. L. (2003). The family-school partnership: An opportunity to promote the learning competence of all students. *School Psychology Quarterly, 18,* 454–482.

Conoley, J. C., & Haynes, G. (1992). An ecological approach to intervention. In R. C. D'Amato & B. A. Rothlisberg (Eds.), *Psychological perspectives on intervention: A case study approach to prescriptions for change* (pp. 177–189). New York: Longman.

Constantino, G. (1987). *Picture cards: The TEMAS (Tell-Me-A-Story) test.* Los Angeles, CA: Western Psychological Services.

Constantino, G., Flanagan, R., & Malgady, R. G. (2001). Narrative assessments: TAT, CAT, and TEMAS. In L. A. Suzuki, J. G. Ponterotto, & P. J. Meller (Eds.), *Handbook of multicultural assessment* (2nd ed., pp. 217–236). San Francisco, CA: Jossey-Bass.

Constantino, G., Malgady, R., Casullo, M. M., & Castillo, A. (1991). Cross-cultural standardization of TEMAS in three Hispanic subcultures. *Hispanic Journal of Behavioral Sciences, 13,* 48–62.

Cuéllar, I. (1998). Cross-cultural clinical psychological assessment of Hispanic Americans. *Journal of Personality Assessment, 70,* 71–86.

Cummins, J. (1984). *Bilingual special education issues in assessment and pedagogy.* San Diego, CA: College-Hill.

Curtis, M. J., Hunley, S. A., Walker, K. J., & Baker, A. C. (1999). Demographic characteristics and professional practices in school psychology. *School Psychology Review, 28,* 104–116.

D'Amato, R. C., Rothlisberg, B. A., & Leu Work, P. H. (1999). Neuropsychological assessment for intervention. In C. R. Reynolds & T. B. Gutkin (Eds.), *The handbook of school psychology* (pp. 452–475). New York: Wiley.

Darling-Hammond, L., & Post, L. (2000). Inequality in teaching and schooling: Supporting high quality teaching and leadership in low income schools. In R. D. Kalenberg (Ed.), *A notion at risk: Preserving public education as an engine for social mobility* (pp. 127–168). New York: Century Foundation.

Dauphinais, P. L., & King, J. (1992). Psychological assessment with American Indian children. *Applied and Preventive Psychology, 1,* 97–110.

Dean, R. S., & Woodcock, R. W. (1999). *The WJ-R and Batería R in neuropsychological assessment: Research report number 3.* Retrieved March 28, 2004, from http://www.riverpub.com/products/clinical/wj3/pdf/DeanWoodcockRR3.pdf.

Dean, R. S., & Woodcock, R. W. (2003). *Dean-Woodcock Neuropsychological Battery.* Itasca, IL: Riverside.

Delis, D. C., Kramer, J. H., Kaplan, E., & Ober, B. A. (1987). *California Verbal Learning Test: Manual.* San Antonio, TX: Psychological Corporation.

Dent, H. E. (1996). Non-biased assessment or realistic assessment. In R. Lewis (Ed.), *Handbook of tests and measurements for Black populations* (Vol. 1, pp. 103–122). Hampton, VA: Cobb & Henry.

Diana v. State Board of Education, Civ. Act. No. C-70-37 (N.D. Cal., 1970).

Dick, M. B., Teng, E. L., Kempler, D., Davis, D. S., & Taussig, I. M. (2002). The Cross-Cultural Neuropsychological Test Battery (CCNB): Effects of age, education, ethnicity, and cognitive status on performance. In F. R. Ferraro (Ed.), *Minority and cross-cultural aspects of neuropsychological assessment* (pp. 18–41). Lisse, The Netherlands: Swets & Zeitlinger.

Duran, R. P. (1989). Assessment and instruction of at-risk Hispanic students. *Exceptional Children, 56,* 154–158.

Durkin, M. S., Davidson, L. L., Kuhn, L. O'Conner, P., & Barlow, B. (1994). Low-income neighborhoods and the risk of severe pediatric injury: A small area analysis in northern Manhattan. *American Journal of Public Health, 84,* 587–592.

Echemendía, R. J., & Julian, L. (2002). Neuropsychological assessment of Latino children. In F. R. Ferraro (Ed.), *Minority and cross-cultural aspects of neuropsychological assessment* (pp. 181–203). Lisse, The Netherlands: Swets & Zeitlinger.

Farley, R. (1997). Racial trends and differences in the United States 30 years after the civil rights decade. *Social Science Research, 26,* 235–262.

Fletcher-Janzen, E. (2003). *A validity study of the Kaufman Assessment Battery for Children, Second Edition (KABC-II) and the Taos Pueblo Indian Children of New Mexico.* Retrieved March 28, 2004, from www.psychologicalforum.com/articles/nov03.asp.

Frey, P. D., & Pinelli, B. (1991). Visual discrimination and visuomotor integration among two classes of Brazilian children. *Perceptual and Motor Skills, 72,* 847–850.

Fuchs, L. S., & Fuchs, D. (1990). Curriculum-based measurement: A standardized long-term goal approach to monitoring student progress. *Academic Therapy, 25,* 615–632.

Gaddes, W. H., & Edgell, D. (1994). *Learning disabilities and brain function: A neuropsychological approach* (3rd ed.). New York: Springer-Verlag.

Gersten, R., & Baker, S. (2000). What we know about effective instructional practices for English-language learners. *Exceptional Children, 66,* 454–470.

Gibbs, J. T., & Huang, L. N. (2003). *Children of color: Psychological interventions with culturally diverse youth.* San Francisco, CA: Jossey-Bass.

Gopaul-McNicol, S., & Armour-Thomas, E. (2002). *Assessment and culture: Psychological tests with minority populations.* San Diego, CA: Academic Press.

Green, J. W. (1999). *Cultural awareness in the human services: A multi-ethnic approach* (3rd ed.). Boston: Allyn & Bacon.

Harris, J. G., Cullum, C. M., & Puente, A. E. (1995). Effects of bilingualism on verbal learning and memory in Hispanic adults. *Journal of the International Neuropsychological Society, 1,* 10–16.

Heaton, R. K. (1981). *A manual for the Wisconsin Card Sorting Test* Odessa, FL: Psychological Assessment Resources.

Hess, R. S., Goetz, J., Martin, A., & Hutaff, C. (2004). *Technology use, proficiency and access among school psychologists.* Manuscript in preparation.

Horton, A. M., Carrington, C. H., & Lewis-Jack, O. (2001). Neuropsychological assessment in a multicultural context. In L. A. Suzuki, J. G. Ponterotto, & P. J. Meller (Eds.), *Handbook of multicultural assessment: Clinical, psychological, and educational applications* (2nd ed., pp. 433–460). San Francisco, CA: Jossey-Bass.

Individuals with Disabilities Education Act (1997) Pub. L. No. 105-17, Sec. 615.

Ingraham, C. L. (2000). Consultation through a multicultural lens: Multicultural and cross-cultural consultation in schools. *School Psychology Review, 29,* 320–343.

Kaufman, A. S., & Kaufman, N. L. (2004). *Kaufman Assessment Battery for Children* (2nd ed.). Circle Pines, MN: American Guidance System.

Kent, M. M., Pollard, K. M., Haaga, J., & Mather, M. (2001). First glimpses from the 2000 U.S. Census. *Population Bulletin, 56*(2), 3–39.

Kindler, A. L. (2002). *Survey of the states' limited English proficient students and available educational programs and services 1999–2000 summary report.* Washington, DC: National Clearinghouse for English Acquisition and Language Instruction Educational Programs.

Kolb, B., & Whishaw, I. (1985). *Fundamentals of human neuropsychology* (2nd ed.). New York: Freeman.

Korkman, M., Kirk, U., & Kemp, S. (1998). *NEPSY: A developmental neuropsychological assessment manual.* San Antonio, TX: Harcourt Brace.

Kratochwill, T. R., & Stoiber, K. C. (2000). Empirically supported interventions and school psychology: Conceptual and practice issues—Part II. *School Psychology Quarterly, 15,* 233–253.

Lamberty, G. J. (2002). Traditions and trends in neuropsychological assessment. In F. R. Ferraro (Ed.), *Minority and cross-cultural aspects of neuropsychological assessment* (pp. 3–15). Lisse, The Netherlands: Swets & Zeitlinger.

Landrine, H., & Klonoff, E. A. (1996). The African American acculturation scale: Origin and current status. In R. L. Jones (Ed.), *Handbook of tests and measurements for Black populations* (Vol. 2, pp. 119–138). Hampton, VA: Cobb & Henry.

Larry P. V. Riles, 343 F. Supp. 1306 (D.C.N.D. Cal., 1972), aff'd., 502 F.2d 963 (9th Cir. 1974), further proceedings, 495 F. Supp. 926 (D.C.N.D. Cal., 1979), aff'd, 502 F.2d 693 (9th Cir. 1984).

Lopez, S. R., Grover, K. P., Holland, D., Johnson, M. J., Kain, C. D., Kanel, K., et al. (1989). Development of culturally sensitive psychotherapists. *Professional Psychology: Research and Practice, 20,* 369–376.

Luciana, M. (2003). Practitioner review: Computerized assessment of neuropsychological function in children: Clinical and research applications of the Cambridge Neuropsychological Testing Automated Battery (CANTAB). *Journal of Child Psychology and Psychiatry, 44*(5), 649–663.

Luciana, M., & Nelson, C. A. (2002). Assessment of neuropsychological functioning in children using the Cambridge Neuropsychological Testing Automated Battery (CANTAB): Normative performance in 4–12-year-olds. *Developmental Neuropsychology, 22,* 595–624.

Manly, J. J., & Jacobs, D. M. (2002). Future directions in neuropsychological assessment with African Americans. In F. R. Ferraro (Ed.), *Minority and cross-cultural aspects of neuropsychological assessment* (pp. 79–96). Lisse, The Netherlands: Swets & Zeitlinger.

Manly, J. J., Miller, S. W., Heaton, R. K., Byrd, D., Reilly, J., Velasquez, R. J., et al. (1998). The effect of African-American acculturation on neuropsychological test performance in normal and HIV-positive individuals. *Journal of the International Neuropsychological Society, 4,* 291–302.

Marlowe, W. B. (2000). Multicultural perspectives on the neuropsychological assessment of children and adolescents. In E. Fletcher-Janzen, T. L. Strickland, & C. R. Reynolds (Eds.), *Handbook of cross-cultural neuropsychology* (pp. 145–168). New York: Kluwer Academic/Plenum Press.

McCloskey, D. (2001). Evaluating the neuropsychological and behavioral abilities of migrant child and non-migrant children of Hispanic background. *Dissertation Abstracts International, 61,* 12-B. (UMI No. 6755)

McCloskey, D., Hess, R. S., & D'Amato, R. C. (2003). Evaluating the utility of the Spanish version of the behavior assessment system for children: Parent report system. *Journal of Psychoeducational Assessment, 21,* 325–337.

McLoyd, V. C. (1998a). Changing demographics in the American population: Implications for research with minority children and adolescents. In V. C. McLoyd & L. Steinberg (Eds.), *Studying minority adolescents: Conceptual, methodological and theoretical issues* (pp. 3–28). Mahwah, NJ: Erlbaum.

McLoyd, V. C. (1998b). Socioeconomic disadvantage and child development. *American Psychologist, 53,* 185–201.

McKinnon, J. (2003). *The Black population in the United States: March 2002.* U.S. Census Bureau, Current Population Reports, Series P20-541. Washington, DC: Government Printing Office.

Merydith, S. P. (2001). Temporal stability and convergent validity of the behavior assessment system for children. *Journal of School Psychology, 30,* 253–265.

Miles, G. T. (2002). Neuropsychological assessment of African Americans. In F. R. Ferraro (Ed.), *Minority and cross-cultural aspects of neuropsychological assessment* (pp. 63–77). Lisse, The Netherlands: Swets & Zeitlinger.

Mistry, R. S., Vandewater, E. A., Huston, A. C., & McLoyd, V. C. (2002). Economic well-being and children's social adjustment: The role of family process in an ethnically diverse low-income sample. *Child Development, 73,* 935–951.

Mulenga, K., Ahonen, T., & Aro, M. (2001). Performance of Zambian children on the NEPSY: A pilot study. *Developmental Neuropsychology, 20,* 375–383.

Muñoz-Sandoval, A. F., Cummins, J., Alvarado, C. G., & Ruef, M. L. (1998). *Bilingual verbal ability tests.* Itasca, IL: Riverside.

Myers, H. F., Kagawa-Singer, M., Kumanyika, S. K., Lex, B. W., & Markides, K. S. (1995). Behavioral risk factors related to chronic diseases in ethnic minorities. *American Psychologist, 14,* 613–621.

Naglieri, J. A., & Das, J. P. (1997a). *Cognitive assessment system.* Itasca, IL: Riverside.

Naglieri, J. A., & Das, J. P. (1997b). *Cognitive assessment system interpretive handbook.* Itasca, IL: Riverside.

Naglieri, J. A., & Rojahn, J. (2001). Intellectual classification of Black and White children in special education programs using the WISC-III and the Cognitive Assessment System. *American Journal on Mental Retardation, 106,* 359–367.

National Clearinghouse for English Language Acquisition and Language Instruction Educational Programs. (2002). *United States most commonly spoken languages.* Retrieved October 17, 2003, from http://www.ncela.gwu.edu/askncela/01leps.htm.

National Research Council. (1993). *Measuring lead exposure in infants, children, and other sensitive populations.* Washington, DC: National Academy Press.

National Research Council. (2002). *Minority students in special and gifted education.* Washington, DC: National Academy Press.

Ochoa, S. H., & Rhodes, R. L. (in press). Assisting parents of bilingual students achieve equity in public schools. *Journal of Educational and Psychological Consultation.*

Osterrieth, P. A. (1944). Le test de copie d'une figure complexe [Test of copying a complex figure: Contributions to the study of perception and memory]. *Archives de Psychologie, 30,* 206–356.

Psychological Corporation. (1983). *Escala de inteligencia Wechsler para Niños—Revisada* [Wechsler Intelligence Scale for Children-Revised]. San Antonio, TX: Psychological Corporation.

Psychological Corporation. (1993). *Escala de inteligencia Wechsler para Niños—Revisada de Puerto Rico* [Wechsler Intelligence Scale for Children-Puerto Rican Revision]. San Antonio, TX: Psychological Corporation.

Psychological Corporation. (1997). *Aprenda: La Prueba de Logros en Español, Segunda Edición* [Learn: Spanish Test of Achievement, Second Edition]. San Antonio, TX: Psychological Corporation.

Puente, A. E., & Ardila, A. (2000). Neuropsychological assessment of Hispanics. In E. Fletcher-Janzen, T. Strickland, & C. R. Reynolds (Eds.), *The handbook of cross-cultural neuropsychology* (pp. 87–104). New York: Plenum Press.

Reeves, T., & Bennett, C. (2003). *The Asian and Pacific Islander population in the United States: March 2002.* U.S. Census Bureau, Current Population Reports, Series P20–540. Washington, DC: Government Printing Office.

Reitan, R. M., & Davidson, L. (Eds.). (1974). *Clinical neuropsychology: Current status and applications.* Washington, DC: Winston.

Rey, A. (1941). L'examen psychologique dans les cas l'encephalopathie traumatic [The psychological examination in cases of traumatic encephalopathy]. *Archives de Psychologie, 28,* 215–285.

Reynolds, C. R., & Kaiser, S. (1992). Test bias in psychological assessment. In T. B. Gutkin & C. R. Reynolds (Eds.), *The handbook of school psychology* (2nd ed., pp. 487–525). New York: Wiley.

Reynolds, C. R., & Kamphaus, R. W. (1992). *Manual for the Behavioral Assessment System for Children (BASC).* Circle Pines, MN: American Guidance Service.

Reynolds, C. R., & Kamphaus, R. W. (2004). *Manual for the Behavioral Assessment System for Children* (2nd ed.). Circle Pines: MN: American Guidance Service.

Rhodes, R. L. (2000). Legal and professional issues in the use of interpreters: A fact sheet for school psychologists. *Communiqué, 29*(1), 28.

Rhodes, R. L., Kayser, H., & Hess, R. S. (2000). Neuropsychological differential diagnosis of Spanish-speaking preschool children. In E. Fletcher-Janzen, T. L. Strickland, & C. R. Reynolds (Eds.), *Handbook of cross-cultural neuropsychology* (pp. 317–333). New York: Kluwer Academic/Plenum Press.

Rosselli, M. (1993). Neuropsychology of illiteracy. *Behavioral Neuropsychology, 6,* 107–112.

Rosselli, M., & Ardila, A. (1993). Developmental norms for the Wisconsin Card Sorting Test in 5- to 12-year-old children. *Clinical Neuropsychologist, 7,* 145–154.

Sattler, J. M. (2001). *Assessment of children: Cognitive applications* (4th ed.). San Diego, CA: Sattler.

Shinn, M. R. (1989). *Curriculum-based measurement: Assessing special children.* New York: Guilford Press.

Snipp, C. M. (2002). *American Indian and Alaska Native children in the 2000 census.* The Annie E. Casey and The Population Reference Bureau. Retrieved February 7, 2004, from http://www.aecf.org/kidscount/indian_alaska_children.pdf.

Sternberg, R. J. (1999). A triarchic approach to the understanding and assessment of intelligence in multicultural populations. *Journal of School Psychology, 37,* 145–160.

Sue, D. W., & Sue, D. (1987). Barriers to effective cross-cultural counseling. *Journal of Counseling Psychology, 24,* 420–429.

Swanson, H. L., Hoskyn, M., & Lee, C. (1999). *Interventions for students with learning disabilities: A meta-analysis of treatment outcomes.* New York: Guilford Press.

Sweet, J. J., Moberg, P. J., & Suchy, Y. (2000). Ten-year follow-up survey of clinical neuropsychologists: Part I. Practices and beliefs. *The Clinical Neuropsychologist, 14,* 18–37.

Takushi, R., & Uomoto, J. M. (2001). The clinical interview from a multicultural perspective. In L. A. Suzuki, J. G. Ponterotto, & P. J. Meller (Eds.), *Handbook of multicultural assessment* (2nd ed., pp. 47–66). San Francisco, CA: Jossey-Bass.

Tanner-Halverson, P., Burden, T., & Sabers, D. (1993). WISC-III normative data for Tohono O'odham Native American Children. *Journal of Psychoeducational Assessment. Monograph Series: Wechsler Intelligence Scale for Children-III,* 125–133.

Thomas, W. P., & Collier, V. P. (2002). *A national study of school effectiveness for language minority students' long-term academic achievement.* Retrieved September 4, 2002, from http://www.crede.uscu.edu/research/llaa1.html.

Tropp, L. R., Erkut, S., García Coll, C. G., Alarcón, O., & Vásquez-García, H. A. (1999). Psychological acculturation: Development of a new measure for Puerto Ricans on the U.S. mainland. *Educational and Psychological Measurement, 59,* 351–367.

U.S. Census Bureau. (2002). *School enrollment: Social and economic characteristics of students.* Retrieved February 7, 2004, from http://www.census.gov/population/www/socdemo/school/cps2002.html.

U.S. Immigration and Naturalization Service. (2002). *Immigration fact sheet.* Washington, DC: U.S. Department of Justice.

Wasserman, J. D., & Becker, K. A. (1999). *Recent advances in intellectual assessment of children and adolescents: New research on the Cognitive Assessment System (CAS).* Itasca, IL: Riverside Research Report.

Wong, T. M. (2000). Neuropsychological assessment and intervention with Asian Americans. In E. Fletcher-Janzen, T. L. Strickland, & C. R. Reynolds (Eds.), *Handbook of cross-cultural neuropsychology* (pp. 43–53). New York: Kluwer Academic/Plenum.

Woodcock, R. W., McGrew, K. S., & Mather, N. (2001). *The Woodcock-Johnson III.* Itasca, IL: Riverside.

Woodcock, R. W., & Muñoz-Sandoval, A. F. (1996). *Batería Woodcock-Muñoz-Revisada* [Woodcock-Muñoz Battery-Revised]. Itasca, IL: Riverside.

Woodcock, R. W., & Muñoz-Sandoval, A. F. (2001). *Woodcock-Muñoz language survey.* Itasca, IL: Riverside.

Yeates, K. O., Taylor, H. G., Woodrome, S. E., Wade, S. L., Stancin, T., & Drotar, D. (2002). Race as a moderator of parent and family outcomes following pediatric traumatic brain injury. *Journal of Pediatric Psychology, 27,* 393–403.

# NEUROPSYCHOLOGICAL INTERVENTIONS IN THE SCHOOLS

# CHAPTER 29

# Developing Classroom and Group Interventions Based on a Neuropsychological Paradigm

PATRICIA H. L. WORK and HEE-SOOK CHOI

Historically, a neuropsychological approach has been found useful in clinics and other settings where the focus is on an individual child or adult with brain dysfunction (Luria, 1973; Teeter & Semrud-Clikeman, 1997). Although this approach continues to be highly appropriate in clinical settings, academic settings are increasingly calling for strength-based programming that acknowledges a child's assets while providing an avenue for improving areas of deficit. The use of a neuropsychological approach is logical given that the underlying principles that guide interventions for children with brain dysfunction may also be applied to students with learning difficulties. This approach creates an excellent foundation for programs that serve students in a school or group setting who exhibit a wide array of abilities and needs. The school neuropsychology approach allows practitioners the opportunity to link current research to practice in ways that benefit children and respond to a variety of needs and abilities.

This chapter provides an overview of the important principles that form the basis of intervention approaches found in clinical and school neuropsychology. Clearly researched interventions and techniques that may be used with individuals and groups of students are discussed, including strategies that are linked to specific learning and attention difficulties. Then models designed specifically for using a neuropsychological approach are offered that have shown promise in group or classroom settings. Following these models, case examples of programs developed to assist with learning and attention problems are provided.

## NEUROPSYCHOLOGICAL PRINCIPLES

A review of the underlying tenets found in neuropsychological interventions and practice is needed to aid service providers in the development of program or classroom interventions using a neuropsychological approach. Although the field utilizes a wide array of theoretical approaches and freely integrates them (Teeter & Semrud-Clikeman, 1997), there are several principles that appear to be consistent throughout the field and across both clinical and school settings.

## DEVELOPMENTAL EMPHASIS

Programs guided by neuropsychological principles have a developmental emphasis. There is an expectation of growth and maturation over time in the child's brain based on the assumption that the brain develops in a sequential and predictable manner. A developmental focus assures that classrooms and programs seeking to help children reflect an understanding of maturational levels of children. Thus, learners are presented with material appropriate to their level of cognitive development.

As the normal brain matures, it is capable of increasingly differentiated abilities (e.g., more complex motor movements). However, when a child is asked to learn a skill without the prerequisite maturation, a functional deficit is likely to occur that will result in academic difficulty. If we use as an example a child who has not developed the fine motor coordination required for holding a pencil, it is easy to see that this difficulty will likely result in impaired functioning in written work, art, and other activities in the school setting that require fine motor abilities.

A developmental approach becomes increasingly important when higher-order mental functions (e.g., attention, planning) have been compromised by underlying lesions or immaturity of the developing brain (Semenova, Machinskaya, Akhutina, & Krupskaya, 2001). These skills are needed for all aspects of education and social interaction. For example, if a child wishes to engage in a conversation with peers, a lack of planning may result in impulsive actions or inappropriate topics of conversation. This same difficulty with planning may also be seen when the child is required to organize himself or herself for completing an assignment. Compared to the previous example of fine motor delays, the planning difficulty becomes much more difficult to isolate and treat because it permeates all areas of the child's life. Hence, as the child matures, a developmental focus becomes even more important in understanding the broad reach of delays.

## DYNAMIC LOCALIZATION

The second principle that is often used in programs and classrooms with a neuropsychological emphasis is dynamic localization (Luria, 1973). Dynamic localization suggests that development and maturation are dynamic and interactive processes that depend on both specific localized regions of the brain and functional systems within the brain operating smoothly in conjunction with each other. Hence, when a child suffers a lesion in a particular area of the brain (the localized region), the other areas that have remained intact will continue to function depending on the action required and the systems in the brain that are required to function in carrying out the action. Thus, the effects of the lesion may or may not be evident depending on how well other areas of the brain are functioning and the exact nature of the lesion. In a study of the acquisition of written language, for example, it was found that an interaction of the frontal cortical regions with deep regulatory structures, including the thalamus, was required for planning and control needed for written language among 7- to 8-year-olds. When there was a mismatch between a child's maturity of the frontal-thalamic regulatory system and the child's ability to voluntarily regulate activity needed for the acquisition of written language, learning problems were evident (Semenova et al., 2001). Thus, the principles of developmental appropriateness and dynamic localization are highly interdependent and form the foundation for the approaches outlined in this chapter.

*Luria's Zones*   To better understand dynamic localization, it is helpful to review the three neuropsychological zones described by Luria (1973). He suggested that the brain function may be best understood by dividing the brain into zones that include various processes and functional behaviors. In the (first) primary projection zone, sensory input is received and sensations are transferred to the cerebral cortex. The second set of zones, or the secondary association zones, are used for analyzing, interpreting, and storing information. The third zones are responsible for integration of information from a variety of sources (Obrzut & Hynd, 1990; Reynolds & French, 2003). In particular, the second and third zones are implicated in acquisition of information and learning difficulties. The second zone is implicated in understanding a child's strengths and weaknesses in the serial organization of speech and movement, processing of kinesthetic information, processing of acoustic information, and visual information processing. Then areas of the tertiary zones of the brain are used in polymodal information processing and executive or supervisory functions (Akhutina, 1997). Because the tertiary zones are the last to develop, they are the most likely to demonstrate areas of deficit in children, especially in regard to planning, spatial organization, and information processing (including auditory processing and phonemic awareness).

VYGOTSKY'S STAGES

When designing interventions and programs, it is important to consider the appropriate level of difficulty of the material presented and how the adults provide structure and support. Creating child-adult interactions that are organized in accordance with Vygotsky's (1986) three stages includes giving the child guidance, first, from an external source (e.g., a teacher). This allows the child to respond to an adult or external model who guides the new behavior or learning. The second stage moves the child toward increased independence when the child begins to guide himself or herself while the adult is still available for correction and guidance. The third stage is implemented when the internalization of a new behavior begins and the child is able to provide his or her own model or guidance for performing the task correctly. To effectively execute the first stage the adult must enter the child's zone of proximal development to strengthen the child's areas of difficulty. After a child's weaknesses and strengths are evaluated and a strategy is created to assist the child in moving from the dependent learning stage to the independent learning stage, tasks must be developed and selected that rely on the child's strengths while allowing the child to receive assistance in addressing the areas of difficulty or weakness (Akhutina, 1997).

## ESTABLISHING A FOUNDATION FOR INTERVENTIONS

The following suggestions have been provided specifically for use in classroom settings designed to facilitate program planning for students using a neuropsychological approach to improve cognitive functioning. Ylvisaker, Szekeres, and

Hartwick (1994) proposed eight principles to guide classroom learning. They suggest that students must first be provided with opportunities for success in the classroom. This success will occur when students are given appropriate expectations and planned compensation (i.e., determining what supports a student will need prior to failure). Second, the sequential gradation of activities is recommended to assure that students are progressing at their own level. This assures that students are not over- or underchallenged by academic tasks. Third, generalization of skills must be planned into programming to assure that skills are not learned in one setting only. The generalization of skills has been particularly important in teaching skills needed for appropriate social interaction. The fourth principle is the need for student motivation, initiative, and problem solving. Overcoming emotional disengagement may be one of the more challenging tasks for educators. However, it is necessary for transfer of skills to new settings. The fifth principle is the integration of interventions among all staff. This assures that students will practice new skills or approaches in various settings throughout the day. Considering chronological age along with developmental and academic levels is the sixth principle. This is needed to assure that students are not given material that may be insulting because it is designed for a specific level of development without consideration of the student's age. The seventh principle includes both individual and group interventions to provide various contexts for social and cognitive skill development. The eighth principle requires that improvements be measured in functional contexts and activities as well as in more formal settings. This assures that learning is shown across environments. It also requires psychologists and teachers to pay attention to real-world performance as well as more formalized approaches to assessment. These principles provide guidance to teachers and psychologists who want to assure that students are learning and applying new information and skills.

## LINKING RESEARCH TO EDUCATIONAL PRACTICE

The shift in scientific research in the 1990s "from an emphasis on mind to an emphasis on brain" (p. 398) has resulted in a growing interest among educators in how the research findings in neuroscience may be incorporated into classroom interventions (O'Boyle & Gill, 1998). This growing interest in brain-based intervention in education appears to have been galvanized by the converging evidence of the plasticity of the brain and the contribution of environmental factors to the developing brain. Though much of the structural development of the brain is completed early on, its maturation continues until late adolescence (e.g., through cell death, choosing neurons, pruning, and selecting neuronal connections; Kolb & Fantie, 1997). The process of cell death and pruning synapses is believed to be impacted by environmental and experiential factors to a considerable degree; therefore, it is assumed that appropriate interventions in education may alter the functional organization of the developing brain of children.

However, neuroscientific findings may not always be clearly and easily translatable into classroom learning techniques. It is not uncommon to encounter in the literature a surfeit of postulations rather than supporting data, attesting to the complexity of the brain-behavior relationships and our limited understanding of these relationships, especially in children. Efforts are under way, however, to bridge the gap between neuroscience and educational practice (e.g., Byrnes & Fox,

1998; Jepsen & VonThaden, 2002). Educational programs using brain-based principles, albeit experimental, abound, and with promising results (e.g., Caulfield, Kidd, & Kocher, 2000; Simpson, 1994; Wagmeister & Shifrin, 2000; Westwater & Wolfe, 2000).

## USING A NEUROPSYCHOLOGICAL APPROACH FOR CLASSROOM INTERVENTION

A comprehensive neuropsychological assessment is a prerequisite to developing effective intervention strategies. Neuropsychological assessment quantitatively and qualitatively examines sensory and perceptual systems, motor functions, intellectual/cognitive abilities, memory/learning/processing, communication/language skills, academic achievement, personality/behavior/family, and environmental fit (D'Amato, Rothlisberg, & Leu Work, 1999). A complete neuropsychological profile developed for an individual child, containing information from all desired domains, helps practitioners to plan strategies based on each child's strengths and needs. A thorough and comprehensive evaluation is essential prior to treatment because each human brain is unique in terms of its neural structure and growth patterns. Moreover, if brain damage has occurred in young children, it may produce very different behavioral effects than in adults due to the plasticity of the immature brain. Even identical lesions could result in different deficits depending on the developmental state of the brain at the time of injury (Kolb & Fantie, 1997). Thus, a thorough assessment addressing the pattern of neuropsychological strengths and weaknesses is the first step to planning an integrated intervention program for addressing specific problems. Specific strategies are then selected based on the child's unique pattern of neurocognitive and psychosocial strengths and weaknesses. Monitoring and evaluating the effectiveness of the intervention is also an integral part of the intervention, along with ongoing modifications as needed.

Broadly, three neuropsychological approaches to rehabilitation or intervention have been identified: a strength-based focus (compensatory), a deficit-based focus (remedial), and a combination approach focusing on both strengths and deficits (D'Amato et al., 1999; Teeter & Semrud-Clikeman, 1997). The strength-based intervention programs focus on the child's neurocognitive strengths and assets and draw on the child's intact or more efficient brain systems. Conversely, deficit-based programs are designed to improve the child's weaknesses via remediation of neurocognitive deficits. Most neuropsychologists and educators, however, would agree that neither the strength-based approach nor the deficit-based approach alone is sufficient. A unified approach should utilize the child's unique strengths to remedy the child's individual deficits (D'Amato et al., 1999). Often, instruction must be both compensatory and remedial in nature to consider individual variability in development (Rourke, 1994). This approach is in keeping with the emphasis in education on the importance of developmental and individual variability in learning, and the reading and writing acquisition process in particular (Molfese & Molfese, 2002).

## CLASSROOM INTERVENTIONS FOR LEARNING AND BEHAVIOR PROBLEMS

With recent technological advances (e.g., brain imaging techniques), along with promising research findings in the fields of neuropsychology, neurophysiology, learning disabilities, and cognitive psychology, consistent patterns of neural correlates of childhood learning and behavior problems have begun to emerge. These findings have demonstrated *effective* neuropsychological intervention with children and adults (Shaywitz, 2004). The following sections address neurological and neurocognitive bases of common learning and behavior disorders and highlight those classroom interventions that have been shown to be effective with substantial empirical support. Where appropriate, attempts are made in linking neurological correlates to empirically proven educational practice.

### LEARNING DISORDERS

The prevalence of learning disorders among school-age children has been reported to be as high as 20% (Smith, 1998), and various learning problems are commonly categorized under the umbrella term "learning disabilities." Numerous definitions of learning disabilities have been put forth by researchers, educators, and advocacy groups, leading to confusion in the field as to what precisely a learning disability is. The most widely accepted legal definition of learning disability in the field of education is that found in the Individuals with Disabilities Education Act (IDEA), which also has been criticized for being too broad and vague to be informative. However, what is consistently implied in these various definitions and accepted by the field of learning disabilities is a focus on neurological involvement: The disorder is presumed to be neurologically based.

Researchers have also attempted to subtype the disabilities, resulting in a plethora of learning disability subtypes (e.g., D'Amato, Dean, & Rhodes, 1998). Given the definitional problems and heterogeneity of the disorders, it is no surprise that there are multiple functional subtypes of learning disabilities. Nevertheless, the literature in learning disabilities has generally categorized the disorders into two broad types: verbal learning disabilities and nonverbal learning disabilities. Children with verbal learning disabilities have difficulties in the areas of reading, spelling, and writing, the skills of which are believed to be subsumed by the hemisphere dominant for language. Thus, verbal learning disabilities are commonly referred to as left hemisphere-mediated learning disabilities. Children with nonverbal learning disabilities, on the other hand, are more likely to experience difficulties in visual-spatial, arithmetic, and social perception skills. These difficulties are believed to be mediated by the hemisphere that is nondominant for language and are sometimes called right hemispheric learning disabilities (James & Selz, 1997).

In addition, studies looking into comorbidity with other disorders abound in the learning disorders literature. Many children with learning disabilities exhibit characteristics of other disorders, such as Attention-Deficit/Hyperactivity Disorder (ADHD) or depression (e.g., Heath & Ross, 2000; Kronenberger & Meyer, 2001). ADHD, in particular, has been identified as a condition that frequently co-occurs with learning disabilities. This disorder is addressed in a later section.

*Verbal Learning Disabilities*   There is no shortage of neuroanatomical and neuropsychological explanations of the possible etiology of reading disorders. Abnormal brain asymmetry (Hynd & Hooper, 1992), prefrontal and parietal lobe involvement (Tallal, Galaburda, Llinas, & Von Euler, 1993), anomalies in the left temporal regions (Semrud-Clikeman, Hynd, Novey, & Eliopulous, 1991), and dysfunctional interhemispheric processing (Banich & Shenker, 1994), to name a few, are hypothesized to be implicated. Though reading disabilities are believed to be primarily mediated by the left hemisphere, more recent research postulates that both inter- and intrahemispheric communication are necessary to handle the complicated processes involved in reading and language and that neither hemisphere alone is functionally sufficient (James & Selz, 1997). Additional supporting data for such a conceptualization come from neuroscientific studies with average and gifted learners. For example, O'Boyle and his colleagues (O'Boyle, Alexander, & Benbow, 1991; O'Boyle, Gill, Benbow, & Alexander, 1994), through a series of experiments with intellectually precocious students, have found much greater involvement of the right hemisphere in processing language-related stimuli compared to average students and that for the intellectually precocious students, both hemispheres were equally effective in engaging in any cognitive skill, be it linguistic, mathematical, or otherwise.

Research in neuroscience and neuropsychology appears to point to developmental anomalies in the left temporal-parietal regions for language-based difficulties. There is also a large body of research suggesting the involvement of the right hemisphere in processing language-related stimuli (Zera, 2001). Given these findings, it is not surprising that classroom interventions in phonological awareness and the programs using a multisensory approach have consistently proven to be effective.

*Intervention Strategies for Children with Verbal Learning Disabilities*   Over the past two decades, an impressive number of research studies have converged to indicate that phonological awareness deficits may be a primary cause of reading difficulties (e.g., Hurford et al., 1993; Lyon, 1995; Mann, 1993; National Institute of Child Health and Human Development, 2000). Phonological awareness involves the ability to hear and manipulate sounds and is part of a larger construct known as phonological processing. These terms have been used interchangeably with the term "phonemic awareness." Phonemes represent individual sounds, the smallest functional unit of sound. The distinction between the two terms, phonological awareness and phonemic awareness, basically refers to the *size* of the phonological units.

The efficacy studies on phonological awareness instruction have unequivocally shown that explicit instruction in phonological awareness made a significant difference across all learners, whether normally achieving or learning disabled, and that phonological awareness can be taught across abilities. More specifically, intervention studies have shown that teaching phonological awareness had significantly positive effects on various measures of phonological awareness, reading, and spelling (Ball & Blachman, 1991; Byrne & Fielding-Barnsley, 1989; Cunningham, 1990; Vellutino & Scanlon, 1987) as well as long-term transfer effects on reading and spelling (Lie, 1991; Lundberg, Frost, & Petersen, 1988). Several of these studies also addressed the utility of letter-sound correspondence instruction and instruction in rapid naming (phonological recoding) and list learning (phonetic recoding), specifically for students with learning disabilities, in conjunction with phonological awareness instruction. Research (e.g., Vellutino, 1992) has supported combining phonological awareness instruction with letter-sound instruction.

Multisensorial specialized instructional programs such as Lindamood-Bell Learning Processes (LBLP), Scientific Learning's Fast ForWord prereading phonemic awareness, a computer-based program, and variations of the Orton-Gillingham approach have also shown to be effective (Kennedy & Backman, 1993; Lindamood, Bell, & Lindamood, 1997; Torgesen et al., 2001; Wagmeister & Shifrin, 2000). Multisensory teaching methods use a combination of the child's sensory systems—visual, auditory, and kinesthetic-tactile pathways—in learning to read and write. The assumption is that the child will be more likely to learn if more than one sensory pathway is involved in learning experiences. By activating all sensory inputs, these teaching methods increase the involvement of both cerebral hemispheres. Most of the multisensorial programs also include direct instruction in phonological awareness, which may be, in part, attributable to their success. For example, the LBLP, including Lindamood Phonemic Sequencing, Visualizing and Verbalizing for Language Comprehension and Thinking, and Program Seeing Stars: Symbol Imagery for Phonemic Awareness, Sight Words, and Spelling, have been shown to help increase learners' phonological awareness and oral and written language skills.

Though there is ample evidence to suggest the superiority of explicit code instruction such as phonological awareness instruction, whole language instructional programs also deserve recognition. Whole language programs tend to be inductive and meaning-based and stress the importance of teaching reading as a language activity, linking reading to writing (Berninger & Abbott, 2002). Reviews of studies comparing the two instructional approaches, whole language versus basal approaches for both beginning reading and writing instruction, have concluded that both instructional approaches seem to produce similar effects on reading and writing achievement (Graham & Harris, 1996; Stahl, McKenna, & Pagnucco, 1994; Swanson & Hoskyn, 1998). These findings underscore the notion of individual differences in brain functioning and difficulties in drawing universal conclusions. Consequently, from a neuropsychological paradigm, there is more than one way to learn how to read and write.

*Nonverbal Learning Disabilities*   As with verbal learning disabilities, studies investigating the brain structure and function relationships in individuals identified as having nonverbal learning disabilities have resulted in various postulations regarding the possible neuroanatomical implications, including left parietal lobe dysfunction, right hemisphere dysfunction, bilateral dysfunction, occipital lobe lesions, white matter dysfunction, and involvement of subcortical structures (James & Selz, 1997). Based on their review of these studies, James and Selz concluded that nonverbal learning disabilities are mediated by a right hemisphere dysfunction, coupled with the likelihood of subcortical-level involvement. They also pointed out the evidence of both hemispheres contributing to nonverbal learning disabilities, which supports the notion that visual-spatial, language, reading, and working memory skills all play a part in success in arithmetic performance (Wilson & Swanson, 2001; Zera, 2001).

In addition to academic difficulties in the area of arithmetic in children with nonverbal learning disabilities, numerous studies (Bigler, 1989; Hynd & Hooper, 1992) have posited that children with nonverbal learning disabilities are more likely to experience emotional problems than children with language-based disorders. Given that these children have difficulties in nonverbal problem solving, cause-effect relationships, social perception, social judgment, ability to benefit from feedback, and adaptive behavior (Rourke, Young, & Leenaars, 1989), it is not surprising that they are at greater risk for depression and suicide due to social alienation and peer rejection (Hynd & Hooper, 1992; Voeller, 1986). Therefore, classroom interventions targeting academic rehabilitation for children with non-verbal learning disabilities must also include treatment programs geared to alle-viating their emotional difficulties and social problems as well.

*Intervention Strategies for Children with Nonverbal Learning Disabilities*   Although a number of intervention techniques to enhance mathematics problem-solving and calculation skills have been suggested (Rourke, 1994; Rourke et al., 1989; Strang & Rourke, 1985), there is scant information regarding the efficacy of these rehabili-tation techniques. Moreover, there seems to be a disconnect between established knowledge in neuroscience and educational practice in the area of arithmetic. Despite an extensive body of literature describing neuropsychological correlates of nonverbal learning disabilities, very few intervention studies of children with arithmetic problems have adequately taken into consideration the neuropsycholog-ical characteristics of these children (Fleischner, 1994). Of those suggested inter-vention techniques in mathematics, problem-solving strategy instruction has been empirically shown to be effective in a number of studies, particularly with adoles-cents with learning disabilities (Maccini & Hughes, 1997; Montague & Boss, 1986). This cognitive approach generally targets executive functions and/or metacogni-tion. Instruction emphasizes increased awareness of task demands, the selection and use of appropriate strategies, evaluation of the strategies, and switching to al-ternative strategies when necessary.

The limited number of empirical studies on classroom interventions based on neuropsychological findings in the area of mathematics stands in sharp contrast to those demonstrated to be effective in the language-based areas, reflecting per-haps the long-standing emphasis on reading in education. However, with a re-newed emphasis on science and math education with the passage of the No Child Left Behind Act (NCLB) of 2001, more research may begin to emerge. NCLB may serve as an impetus for scientific research in this area, as the law calls for in-structional techniques that are empirically proven to be effective through scien-tifically based research.

As discussed earlier, children with nonverbal learning disabilities also experi-ence psychosocial problems. Due to the growing awareness of social skills deficits associated with learning disabilities, social skills training has been a routine rec-ommendation as part of individualized educational programming for children with learning disorders. There are a number of social skills training programs, in-cluding, for example, McGinnis and her colleagues' (McGinnis, E., & Goldstein, 1990; McGinnis, Goldstein, Sprafkin, & Gershaw, 1984) Skillstreaming the Ele-mentary School Child and Skillstreaming in Early Childhood and Walker and his colleagues' (Walker, Homes, Todis, & Horton, 1988; Walker, McConnell, Todis, Walker, & Golden, 1988) ACCEPT and ACCESS programs for elementary children and adolescents. Effectiveness of these and other social skills training programs has been demonstrated in numerous studies (for a review, see Zaragoza, Vaughn, & McIntosh, 1991). The issues of transfer and generalization outside the training en-vironment has also been addressed by more recent research (Choi & Heckenlaible-Gotto, 1998; Haak, 1993), demonstrating that social skills training delivered in the regular classroom by the regular classroom teacher promotes generalizability because the teacher can readily reinforce the skills taught on a daily basis and over a longer period of time.

## Behavior Disorders

As previously mentioned, many children identified as having learning disabilities exhibit the behaviors characteristic of children with ADHD. By the same token, the vast majority of children with ADHD also display academic problems (Barkley, 1996, 1998), and many of them are identified as having learning disabilities. Co-occurrence of ADHD and LD is widely reported, with the rates varying considerably. In clinic populations, the rates have been reported to be 20% to 50%, as compared to 9% to 11% in the general population (Anastopoulos & Barkley, 1992). In addition, ADHD is one of the most common psychiatric disorders in children and is often comorbid with disruptive behavior disorders such as Oppositional Defiant Disorder and Conduct Disorder (Barkley, 1996; Boliek & Obrzut, 1997). The following section specifically addresses children and youth with ADHD and its neurological and neuropsychological aspects as well as classroom and home interventions.

*Attention-Deficit/Hyperactivity Disorder*   Children with ADHD are typically characterized as having three core symptoms: inattention, impulsivity, and hyperactivity. There are associated neurocognitive deficits in many areas, including motor coordination and sequencing, working memory and mental computation, planning and anticipation, verbal fluency and confrontational communication, effort allocation, applying organizational strategies, the internalization of self-directed speech, adhering to restrictive instructions, self-regulation of emotional arousal, and immature or diminished moral reasoning (Barkley, 1996). Most, if not all, of the foregoing neuropsychological correlates are considered to fall under the domain of executive functioning subsumed by the frontal lobes.

However, the literature concerning the neurological basis of children with ADHD is filled with numerous inconsistencies due to methodological differences across studies and the heterogeneity of the disorder in general. Moreover, Boliek and Obrzut (1997) have pointed out "there are hypotheses implicating dysfunctions at nearly every neuroanatomical level of the brain from the brain stem to the frontal lobes" (p. 621). Although it is well accepted that ADHD is a neurologically based disorder, many children with ADHD do not show "hard" signs or histories of brain damage (Barkley, 1998). Not surprisingly, the early literature linked children with ADHD to children with minimal brain dysfunction, which was also assumed to be responsible for learning disabilities (Barkley, 1996).

Though the precise mechanisms are far from certain, evidence pointing to frontal lobe dysfunction seems to be the strongest. Damage to the frontal lobes has long been associated with the symptoms found in ADHD, and the frontal lobe areas are commonly thought to be involved in attention, executive functions, and motor functions. Brain imaging studies have also implicated abnormalities in the subcortical striatal areas (e.g., caudate nucleus and globus pallidus) and the cerebellum, in addition to the frontal lobes (Castellanos, 2001; Voeller, 2001). Indeed, using brain scans, abnormal functioning of the frontal-striatal areas has been found as well, in terms of decreased blood flow and decreased glucose utilization (Rapport & Chung, 2000). This suggests underactivity in those areas. A deficiency in the metabolism of neurotransmission is also thought to be related to children with ADHD. Psychopharmacological studies have implicated norepinephrine and dopamine to be possible neurotransmitter markers for children with ADHD (Boliek & Obrzut, 1997). These neurotrasmitters are posited to be important in the functioning of the frontal-striatal and related areas of the brain (Biederman & Spencer, 2000).

*Intervention Strategies for Children with Attention-Deficit/Hyperactivity Disorder*
Numerous treatment strategies (e.g., individual counseling, cognitive therapy, behavior therapy, parent training) have been attempted and evaluated with children with ADHD. However, two broad approaches to intervention that have shown positive results are stimulant medication and behavior management. Stimulant medications are the psychotropic drugs most frequently prescribed to children in the United States, primarily for ADHD (Riddle, Kastelic, & Frosch, 2001). The most commonly prescribed stimulants include methylphenidate (Ritalin, Concerta), dextroamphetamine (Dexedrine), and the combination of amphetamine and dextroamphetamine (Adderall). The stimulants increase the arousal and activity of the central nervous system and affect the neurotransmitters dopamine and norepinephrine, likely in the frontal cortex or in the midbrain (Biederman & Spencer, 2000), resulting in increased attention and decreased impulsivity and activity levels. Stimulant medications have also shown to reduce related symptoms such as aggressive, noncompliant, and oppositional behaviors (Hinshaw, Henker, Whalen, Erhardt, & Dunnington, 1989).

Though an extensive body of research has demonstrated the effectiveness of a stimulant medication across settings and measures, it is well established that not all children with ADHD respond to stimulant medications. An estimated 20% to 25% of these children do not show improvement, and there are other concerns regarding the medications, including side effects, overprescription, and possible abuse (Beck, Silverstone, Glor, & Dunn, 1999; Kollins, MacDonald, & Rush, 2001).

The success of behavior management with children with ADHD has also been well documented as it has been frequently implemented as an alternative to medication. The behavior modification procedures most often utilized in the classroom include token reinforcement, time-out, and response cost (Kronenberger & Meyer, 2001). Research also has suggested that the structure and organization of the classroom and of educational tasks are important factors for enhancing learning in children with ADHD. Though empirical investigations show increased on-task and other appropriate behaviors through classroom-based interventions, behavior management programs often require much effort and time, sometimes beyond what is feasible for teachers. In addition, cognitive-behavioral interventions, which primarily focus on the enhancement of self-control and self-regulation, have not proven successful (Pelham, Wheeler, & Chronis, 1998). Limited success for cognitive-behavioral treatment for children with ADHD is rather disappointing in that increasing self-control or self-regulation (i.e., executive functions) seems a logical target in treating ADHD. Continued research is needed in this area.

By far, a combined approach, both medication and behavior management, known as multimodal intervention, has been the treatment of choice for children with ADHD. Combined treatment approaches tend to be more effective than any single approach due to the multifaceted nature of the problems these children manifest. The results of the extensive Multimodal Treatment Study of Children with ADHD (MTA) initiated by the National Institute of Mental Health (MTA Cooperative Group, 1999) over a period of 14 months has indicated that all treatment groups—medication treatment, behavioral treatment, combined treatment (i.e., both medication and behavioral treatments), and community care treatment—show positive effects in reducing core ADHD symptoms, but that the amount of improvement varied with the type of treatment. For most core ADHD symptoms, the medication and combined treatments were superior to behavioral and community care treatments. It appears that the behavioral approach alone may not be as effective as the medication or the combined approach, which again underscores the necessity of collaboration and communication between educators and medical professionals.

## MODELS FOR NEUROPSYCHOLGICAL INTERVENTION

The use of a model to guide the development of an intervention plan for an individual or group of students assures that key elements of the intervention are not overlooked. Although several models have been developed to guide the use of a neuropsychological approach when working with children (D'Amato et al., 1999; Reitan & Wolfson, 1992; Rourke, 1994; Teeter & Semrud-Clikeman, 1997), two models in particular will be detailed, which appear to be most appropriate for working with children in a group or classroom setting.

The Developmental Neuropsychological Remediation/Rehabilitation Model was originally created for use with students who had learning disabilities (Rourke, 1994). In brief, it encourages participants to envision an ideal intervention plan and then look at resources and environments that can accommodate the ideal vision and synthesize it with the reality of the student's environment. It is helpful for working with a variety of children and assures that several options have been considered prior to implementation of a set of interventions for individuals and groups.

Using this model, *step 1* requires an academic and psychosocial assessment of the student's neuropsychological assets and needs. These are addressed through a neuropsychological profile and an ecological evaluation. In this way, the student's internal strengths and weaknesses as well as those of the environment are assessed (Leu Work & D'Amato, 1994). Often in school settings, informal information may be highly useful for estimating a child's functioning in areas that are not typically measured in traditional psychological evaluations. *Step 2* evaluates the demands of the environment: What is the expectation of a particular environment? Is a student required to navigate long hallways? Does the student have the social support needed to make progress academically? The answers to these questions provide an understanding of what is required for success in a particular setting. *Step 3* is the estimation of short- and long-term prognosis. This step reveals many preconceived ideas about the limitations and expectations for an individual or group of students. These limiting beliefs may be useful in understanding the expectations of the various participants in the intervention. In *step 4*, an ideal remediation plan is outlined by the group, allowing participants to think outside of the box and create solutions that might not be thought of when the limitations of the environment are the focus. It should be emphasized that the ideal plan is used to assist in generating solutions and interventions that may have been overlooked. It is not an assurance that the ideal plan is in fact actually the best for the student or that it will be implemented over time. In *step 5*, the ideal plan is brought into the light of the available resources. This step is needed to begin to bring the plan into reality. Again, by looking at the ideal plan first and then looking at resources, the group members can evaluate resources from new perspectives and create innovative solutions to sometimes difficult problems. In *step 6*, a plan that can be implemented (i.e., a realistic plan) is developed. It is important that the plan is implementable and grounded in the reality of the situation and should include the whole environment of the child or group of children. The sixth step is important to gain a set of goals or strategies that are realistic and have examined several alternative allocations of resources and strategies.

The Structure, Organization, and Strategies (SOS) Model provides a dynamic and interactive approach that addresses limitations and strengths of the structure while assisting students in a group setting (D'Amato et al., 1999). This model is child-centered and requires that the child's perceptions, memory, affect, and problem-solving skills be the center of the intervention approaches. The child is viewed as influencing and being influenced by environmental factors (e.g., support, family, nutrition, health care), biogenetic factors (e.g., intactness of the central nervous system and processing efficiency), and the outcome behaviors that are observable in social and academic settings. The child-centeredness of this model makes it particularly appropriate for educational settings. Although developed initially for individual children, this model has been useful in the development of a program designed for a group (Work & Beedy, 2001).

The SOS Model requires participants to evaluate the setting or structure of service delivery and alter it if needed to benefit the outcome for a student or group of students. After determining that a setting is limited, often simple alterations can make a large difference. For example, creating a space with less clutter can reduce distractions for students and encourage on-task behaviors. Next, the organization of the setting is established to maximize student success. This entails making sure structures that encourage positive behavior and academic success are in place for student success. If a group of children have great difficulty with transitions from one academic subject to another, it is easier to provide structured transitions between subjects rather than reacting to the chaos that can ensue in the classroom during subject transitions. By changing the organization of the environment, students are able to experience the success needed for independence at a more structured level prior to success at a more independent level.

After the structure and organization of the setting are addressed, students need to be provided with strategies for learning. Such strategies might include memory techniques, notebook systems, or reading strategies that have been shown to be effective in enhancing student success. This model is unique because it is child-focused and directly addresses the environmental demands placed on a child or group of children. It also assures that children are given the specific skills needed for academic success. As previously noted, because this is a dynamic approach, assessment is ongoing and interactive. Thus, it must be adapted as the student interacts with the environment (context), method, and content of new learning.

## CASE EXAMPLES USING A NEUROPSYCHOLOGICAL APPROACH IN A SCHOOL SYSTEM

Two case examples are provided to illustrate the use of a neuropsychological approach on both the individual and systemic levels. First, a case is presented considering a child with neuropsychologically related difficulties in an inclusive classroom. Then a program created at a private school for high school students in New Hampshire is reviewed to demonstrate the systemic use of a neuropsychological approach.

### Using School Neuropsychology at the Individual Level: The Case of Emma

Emma, a 4th-grader, had a history of doing well in school. She began having some difficulty in reading and math at the end of 3rd grade. In particular, although she read words easily, she began to demonstrate difficulty comprehending what she had read. Likewise, in math, Emma found the problem-solving approaches required in the newly adopted math program particularly troublesome. Her parents and teachers were quite concerned that, although she had always attended the same school and lived about four blocks away on the same street, she had become lost on her way to school, apparently forgetting to stop when she arrived and simply continuing down the same street into an entirely different section of the city. When required to participate in any team sports, such as soccer, Emma appeared lost and unable to play a position.

Emma was referred for an evaluation by a district school psychologist. In interviewing her parents, the school psychologist learned that Emma had had a severe illness when she was 18 months old. During the illness, she was in a coma for 28 hours due to a high fever. In spite of the severity of the illness, Emma's parents were convinced that the coma had no ill effects because their family doctor had told them "her brain would heal because she was so young." After a preliminary assessment, the school psychologist consulted with a district school neuropsychologist, who agreed to conduct a few supplemental measures and collaborate on the case.

The school psychologist found Emma to have overall ability in the low-average range. However, Emma had significant delays in her ability to use abstract thinking for problem solving in both verbal and spatial problem-solving tasks. In particular, spatial problem solving was tremendously difficult for her, and she exhibited extreme frustration when trying to manipulate blocks to find solutions. Emma demonstrated particular difficulty with starting and stopping behaviors, planning, and abstract thinking, especially when attempting to find solutions to nonverbal problems. Her math computation was average, but problem solving in math was extremely difficult. Emma took much longer than other children to complete written tasks. The school neuropsychologist evaluated Emma's ability to solve problems using tactile information alone and found that it was almost impossible for her to complete any of the requested tasks. Mental flexibility was another area of difficulty for her. On the positive side, Emma was able to read words easily, compute math problems accurately, and willingly tried everything that was asked of her. Her short-term auditory memory was a strength for her.

A program was developed for Emma that included her family and the school. At home, her parents planted a special tree in the yard to help Emma identify when she was home. Because this intervention was not effective, her parents also added a stop sign in the yard. The stop sign was more effective, and Emma's ability to walk home improved. The school crossing guard placed a stop sign on the school lawn in the morning to help Emma know when to stop at the school. For written language, Emma's keyboarding program at school was supplemented with a small word processing program that she kept at her desk. Emma was taught to use a simple graphic organizer when the word processing program was not practical. The teacher agreed to use two-column note taking with the whole class to help give Emma the structure she needed for beginning note taking. Emma also used a template on her word processing program to help in her studies.

Because her skills and deficits were similar to theirs, Emma began receiving supplemental reading instruction in a small group designed for students with nonverbal learning disabilities. The special education teacher focused on targeting specific executive functions. Instruction was designed to increase awareness of task demands, the selection and use of appropriate strategies, evaluation of the strategies, and switching to alternative strategies to help Emma understand what she was reading.

The highly tactile math program was altered for Emma so she could talk her way through problems with a paraprofessional. This adaptation reduced the confusion Emma experienced when using manipulatives and abstract thinking. Emma's excellent auditory short-term memory helped her to recall information using this approach to math.

Other interventions included a peer helper to cue Emma to begin a task. In addition, her teacher assisted by alerting Emma to an egg timer that was turned on about 3 minutes before the end of a task. This reduced the number of times Emma continued to work when her peers had moved on to another activity.

The school psychologist agreed to meet with Emma and her parents to assist with the loss, grief, and frustration her family experienced as they adapted to Emma's strengths and areas of difficulty. Emma's family continued to adapt to the loss of the child they believed Emma was and their new role as advocates for her. They expressed appreciation for the committed, concerned, and knowledgeable practitioners at the school Emma attends and for the collaborative approach to finding interventions that were effective for their daughter.

## Using School Neuropsychology on the Systemic Level

Relying on the SOS Model and the principles found in school neuropsychology, New Hampton School designed a teaching/coaching program to assist students with attention difficulties in a high school setting. Because most students in the program were on medication to assist with behavior, the program utilized a multimodal approach to assist students in learning new behaviors that would help them achieve the academic and social skills needed for success.

The Center for Creative Intelligence Teacher/Coaching Program was designed to serve a group of 50 students in 9th grade. To assure a student focus, students were involved in planning their own goals, monitoring progress, and designing strategies that were most useful in meeting their individual goals. Training of teachers began during the winter term of the previous year. Teachers volunteered to participate in approximately 40 hours of training to help students find areas for potential goal setting through formal and informal evaluation of individual strengths and weaknesses. Because a majority of the students had documented attention difficulties, teachers were also trained to help students create new behavior patterns using Vygotsky's three stages.

Students attended an extended 9th-grade orientation that was created to help them become familiar with each other prior to the start of school. This orientation was designed to increase student engagement with peers and meet the social needs of students entering a new learning environment. By participating in activities designed to build teams and help students engage in group problem solving, relationships were established and group bonding began prior to the beginning of school. Because teachers/coaches participated in the orientation they could begin to identify group needs and strengths early on. This time together also gave students the opportunity to begin to create friendships and meet social needs typical of students entering a high school setting. In addition, during the orientation period, students also followed a shortened class schedule. This was designed to provide them with opportunities to begin to establish organizational routines and study habits.

Once school began, teachers/coaches worked with students to help them identify personal and group strengths. Students were also encouraged to use strengths and engage in extracurricular activities that would allow them success in a nonacademic setting if that was where their strength or interest was. For example, several students found football to be highly motivating, and others participated in pottery classes or photography outside of the academic day. Teachers/coaches also encouraged students to participate in activities and tasks that allowed them to utilize their strengths while practicing new skills such as note taking and backpack organization.

Engaging students emotionally in learning academic skills was perhaps the most difficult task for the teachers/coaches. Most students needed intense guidance to establish that they could be successful in areas in which they had previously only met failure. Often, this guidance and encouragement lasted several months before students began to internalize new learning. Although students progressed through Vygotsky's stages toward independent functioning, it often was *not* a linear process. In fact, students with a long history of failure appeared to fail after an initial period of success. By training teachers/coaches to expect this nonlinear progress, they were able to maintain consistency for students.

One of the greatest benefits students experienced from participating in this program was the development of social connections that lasted into their sophomore year. These students also exhibited a higher grade point average throughout the year compared to students of the previous years who had not participated in the program. Although the program was relatively new, the use of a neuropsychological approach appeared to provide a framework that was pedagogically and neuropsychologically sound and able to assist students in group as well as individual settings (Work, 2002; Work & Beedy, 2001).

## CONCLUSION

A neuropsychological approach in the schools is a promising avenue for practitioners to use while helping students with a variety of backgrounds and needs. The principles of this approach can assist in establishing interventions that are appropriate and effective. It is important to remember that practitioners as well as others working with children should initiate strategies that are evidence-based and developmentally appropriate. The neuropsychological approach is one of the only paradigms that clearly establishes the importance of addressing deficits while building strengths. This approach offers an extensive variety of instructional and behavioral techniques for professionals who want to understand students and help them develop appropriate educational and psychological life skills. The neuropsychological approach has been extremely effective in helping practitioners, families, and community members assist students with learning problems and emotional difficulties.

## REFERENCES

Akhutina, T. V. (1997). The remediation of executive functions in children with cognitive disorders: The Vygotsky-Luria neuropsychological approach. *Journal of Intellectual Disability Research, 41,* 144–151.

Anastopoulos, A. D., & Barkley, R. A. (1992). Attention-deficit hyperactivity disorder. In C. E. Walker & M. C. Roberts (Eds.), *Handbook of clinical child psychology* (pp. 413–430). New York: Wiley.

Ball, E. W., & Blachman, B. A. (1991). Does phoneme awareness training in kindergarten make a difference in early word recognition and developmental spelling? *Reading Research Quarterly, 24,* 49–66.

Banich, M. T., & Shenker, J. I. (1994). Investigation of inter-hemispheric processing: Methodological considerations. *Neuropsychology, 8,* 263–277.

Barkley, R. A. (1996). Attention deficit/hyperactivity disorder. In E. J. Mash & R. A. Barkely (Eds.), *Child psychopathology* (pp. 63–112). New York: Guilford Press.

Barkley, R. A. (1998). *Attention deficit/hyperactivity disorder: A handbook for diagnosis and treatment.* New York: Guilford Press.

Beck, C., Silverstone, P., Glor, K., & Dunn, J. (1999). Psychostimulant prescriptions by psychiatrists higher than expected: A self-report survey. *Canadian Journal of Psychiatry, 44,* 680–684.

Berninger, V. W., & Abbott, R. D. (2002). Modeling developmental and individual variability in reading and writing acquisition: A developmental neuropsychological perspective. In D. L. Molfese & V. J. Molfese (Eds.), *Developmental variations in learning: Applications to social, executive function, language, and reading skills* (pp. 275–308). Mahwah, NJ: Erlbaum.

Biederman, J., & Spencer, T. J. (2000). Genetics of childhood disorder: XIX. ADHD, Part 3: Is ADHD a noradrenergic disorder? *Journal of the American Academy of Child and Adolescent Psychiatry, 39,* 1330–1333.

Bigler, E. R. (1989). On the neuropsychology of suicide. *Journal of Learning Disabilities, 22,* 180–185.

Boliek, C. A., & Obrzut, J. E. (1997). Neuropsychological aspects of attention deficit/hyperactivity disorder. In C. R. Reynolds & E. Fletcher-Janzen (Eds.), *Handbook of clinical child neuropsychology* (2nd ed., pp. 619–633). New York: Plenum.

Byrne, B., & Fielding-Barnsley, R. (1989). Phonemic awareness and letter knowledge in the child's acquisition of the alphabetic principle. *Journal of Educational Psychology, 81,* 313–321.

Byrnes, J. P., & Fox, N. A. (1998). The educational relevance of research in cognitive neuroscience. *Educational Psychology Review, 10,* 297–342.

Caulfield, J., Kidd, S., & Kocher, T. (2000, November). Brain-based instruction in action. *Educational Leadership,* 62–65.

Castellanos, F. X. (2001). Neuroimaging studies of ADHD. In M. V. Solanto & A. F. Arnsten (Eds.), *Stimulant drugs and ADHD: Basic and clinical neuroscience* (pp. 243–258). New York: Oxford.

Choi, H., & Heckenlaible-Gotto, M. J. (1998). Classroom-based social skills training: Impact on peer acceptance of first-grade students. *Journal of Educational Research, 91,* 209–214.

Cunningham, A. (1990). Explicit vs. implicit instruction in phonemic awareness. *Journal of Experimental Child Psychology, 50,* 429–444.

D'Amato, R. C., Dean, R. S., & Rhodes, R. L. (1998). Subtyping children's learning disabilities with neuropsychological, intellectual, and achievement measures. *International Journal of Neuroscience, 96,* 107–125.

D'Amato, R. C., Rothlisberg, B. A., & Leu Work, P. H. (1999). Neuropsychological assessment for intervention. In T. B. Gutkin & C. R. Reynolds (Eds.), *Handbook of school psychology* (3rd ed., pp. 452–475). New York: Wiley.

Fleischner, J. E. (1994). Diagnosis and assessment of mathematics learning disabilities. In G. R. Lyon (Ed.), *Frames of reference for the assessment of learning disabilities: New views on measurement issues* (pp. 441–458). Baltimore: Brookes.

Haak, T. A. (1993). *Establishing social skills for exceptional needs students and their nonhandicapped peers in the elementary classroom utilizing a social skills training program.* Practicum Report, Nova University. (ERIC Document Reproduction Service No. ED 375 579).

Heath, N. L., & Ross, S. (2000). Prevalence and expression of depressive symptomatology in students with and without learning disabilities. *Learning Disability Quarterly, 23,* 24–36.

Hurford, D. P., Darrow, L. J., Edwards, T. L., Howerton, C. J., Mote, C. R., & Schauf, J. D., et al. (1993). An examination of phonemic processing abilities in children during their first-grade year. *Journal of Learning Disabilities, 26,* 167–177.

Graham, S., & Harris, K. (1996). The effects of whole language on children's writing: A review of literature. *Educational Psychologist, 19,* 187–192.

Hinshaw, S. P., Henker, B., Whalen, C. K., Erhardt, D., & Dunnington, R. E. (1989). Aggressive, prosocial, and nonsocial behavior in hyperactive boys: Dose effects of methylphenidate in naturalistic settings. *Journal of Consulting and Clinical Psychology, 57,* 636–643.

Hynd, G. W., & Hooper, S. R. (1992). *Neurological basis of childhood psychopathology.* London: Sage.

James, E. M., & Selz, M. (1997). Neuropsychological bases of common learning and behavior problems in children. In C. R. Reynolds & E. Fletcher-Janzen (Eds.), *Handbook of clinical child neuropsychology* (2nd ed., pp. 157–179). New York: Plenum.

Jepsen, R. H., & VonThaden, K. (2002). The effect of cognitive education on the performance of students with neurological developmental disabilities. *NeuroRehabilitation, 17,* 201–209.

Kennedy, K., & Backman, J. (1993). Effectiveness of the Lindamood Auditory Discrimination in Depth Program with students with learning disabilities. *Learning Disabilities Research and Practice, 8,* 253–259.

Kolb, B., & Fantie, B. (1997). Development of the child's brain and behavior. In C. R. Reynolds & E. Fletcher-Janzen (Eds.), *Handbook of clinical child neuropsychology* (2nd ed., pp. 157–179). New York: Plenum.

Kollins, S. H., MacDonald, E. K., & Rush, C. R. (2001). Assessing the abuse potential of methylphenidate in nonhuman and human subjects: A review. *Pharmacology, Biochemistry and Behavior, 68,* 611–627.

Kronenberger, W. G., & Meyer, R. G. (2001). *The child clinician's handbook* (2nd ed.). Boston: Allyn & Bacon.

Leu Work, P., & D'Amato, R. C. (1994). Right children, wrong teachers? Using an ecological assessment for placement decisions. *26th Proceedings of the National Association of School Psychologists.* Washington, DC: NASP.

Lie, A. (1991). Effects of a training program for stimulating skills in word analysis in first-grade children. *Reading Research Quarterly, 26,* 234–250.

Lindamood, P., Bell, N., & Lindamood P. (1997). Sensory-cognitive factors in the controversy over reading instruction. *Journal of Developmental and Learning Disorders, 1,* 143–182.

Lundberg, I., Frost, J., & Petersen, O. P. (1988). Effects of an extensive program for stimulating phonological awareness in preschool children. *Reading Research Quarterly, 23,* 263–284.

Luria, A. R. (1973). *The working brain.* Harmonds-Worth, England: Penguin Books.

Lyon, G. R. (1995). Toward a definition of dyslexia. *Annals of Dyslexia, 45,* 3–27.

Maccini, P., & Hughes, C. A. (1997). Mathematics interventions for adolescents with learning disabilities. *Learning Disabilities Research and Practice, 12,* 168–176.

Mann, V. (1993). Phonemic awareness and future reading ability. *Journal of Learning Disabilities, 26,* 259–269.

McGinnis, E., Goldstein, A. P., Sprafkin, R. P., & Gershaw, N. J. (1984). *Skillstreaming the elementary school child: A guide for teaching prosocial skills.* Champaign, IL: Research Press Company.

McGinnis, E., & Goldstein, A. P. (1990). *Skillstreaming in early childhood: A guide for teaching prosocial skills.* Champaign, IL: Research Press Company.

Molfese, D. L., & Molfese, V. J. (Eds.). (2002). *Developmental variations in learning: Application to social, executive function, language, and reading skills.* Mahwah, NJ: Erlbaum.

Montague, M., & Boss, C. (1986). The effect of cognitive strategy training on verbal math problem solving performance of learning disabled adolescents. *Journal of Learning Disabilities, 19,* 26–33.

MTA Cooperative Group. (1999). A 14-month randomized clinical trial of treatment strategies for attention-deficit/hyperactivity disorder. *Archives of General Psychiatry, 56,* 1073–1086.

National Institute of Child Health and Human Development. (2000). *Report of the national reading panel: An evidence-based assessment of the scientific research literature on reading and its implications for reading instruction.* Bethesda, MD: NICHD Clearinghouse.

O'Boyle, M. W., Alexander, J. E., & Benbow, C. P. (1991). Enhanced RH activation in the mathematically precocious: A preliminary EEG investigation. *Brain Cognition, 17,* 138–153.

O'Boyle, M. W., & Gill, H. S. (1998). On the relevance of research findings in cognitive neuroscience to educational practice. *Educational Psychology Review, 10,* 397–409.

O'Boyle, M. W., Gill, H. S., Benbow, C. P., & Alexander, J. E. (1994). Concurrent finger-tapping in mathematically gifted males: Evidence for enhanced right hemisphere involvement during linguistic processing. *Cortex, 30,* 519–526.

Obrzut, J. E., & Hynd, G. W. (1990). Cognitive dysfunction and psychoeducational assessment in traumatic brain injury. In E. Bigler (Ed.), *Traumatic brain injury: Mechanisms of damage, assessment, intervention and outcome* (pp. 165–180). Austin, TX: ProEd.

Pelham, W. E., Wheeler, T., & Chronis, A. (1998). Empirically supported psychosocial treatments for attention deficit hyperactivity disorder. *Journal of Clinical Child Psychology, 27*, 190–205.

Rapport, M. D., & Chung, K.-M. (2000). Attention deficit hyperactivity disorder. In M. Hersen & R. T. Ammerman (Eds.), *Advanced abnormal child psychology* (pp. 146–173). Mahwah, NJ: Erlbaum.

Reitan, R. M., & Wolfson, D. (1992). *Neuropsychological evaluation of older children.* Tuscon, AZ: Neuropsychology Press.

Reynolds, C. R., & French, C. L. (2003). The neuropsychological basis of intelligence revised: Some false starts and a clinical model. In A. M. Horton, Jr., & L. C. Hartlage (Eds.), *Handbook of forensic neuropsychology* (pp. 23–56). New York: Springer.

Riddle, M. A., Kastelic, E. A., & Frosch, E. (2001). Pediatric psychopharmacology. *Journal of Child Psychology and Psychiatry, 42*, 73–90.

Rourke, B. (1994). Neuropsychological assessment of children with learning disabilities: Measurement issues. In C. R. Lyon (Ed.), *Frames of reference for the assessment of learning disabilities: New views on measurement issues* (pp. 475–514). Baltimore: Brookes.

Rourke, B., Young, G. C., & Leenaars, A. A. (1989). A childhood learning disability that predisposes those afflicted to adolescent and adult depression and suicide risk. *Journal of Learning Disabilities, 22*, 169–175.

Semenova, O. V., Machinskaya, R. I., Akhutina, T. V., & Krupskaya, E. V. (2001). Brain mechanisms of voluntary regulation of activity during acquisition of the skill of writing in seven to eight year old children. *Human Physiology, 27*, 405–412.

Semrud-Clikeman, M., Hynd, G. W., Novey, E. S., & Eliopulous, D. (1991). Dyslexia and brain morphology: Relationship between neuroanatomical variation and neurolinguistic tasks. *Learning and Individual Differences, 3*, 225–242.

Shaywitz, S. (2004). *Overcoming dyslexia: A new and complete science-based program for reading at any level.* New York: Alfred Knopf.

Simpson, M. S. (1994). Neurophysiological considerations related to interactive multimedia. *Educational Technology Research and Development, 42*(1), 75–81.

Smith, C. R. (1998). *Learning disabilities: The interaction of learner, task, and setting* (4th ed.). Boston: Allyn & Bacon.

Stahl, S., McKenna, M., & Pagnucco, J. (1994). The effects of whole language instruction: An update and a reappraisal. *Educational Psychologist, 29*, 175–185.

Strang, J. D., & Rourke, B. (1985). Adaptive behavior of children with specific arithmetic disabilities and associated neuropsychological abilities and deficits. In B. P. Rourke (Ed.), *Neuropsychology of learning disabilities: Essentials of subtype analysis* (pp. 302–328). New York: Guilford Press.

Swanson, H. L., & Hoskyn, M. (1998). Experimental intervention research on students with learning disabilities: A meta-analysis of treatment outcomes. *Review of Educational Research, 68*, 277–321.

Tallal, P., Galaburda, A. M., Llinas, R. R., & Von Euler, C. (1993). *Temporal information processing in the nervous system: Special reference to dyslexia and dysphasia.* New York: New York Academy of Sciences.

Teeter, P. A., & Semrud-Clikeman, M. (1997). *Child neuropsychology: Assessment and interventions for neurodevelopmental disorders.* Needham Heights, MA: Allyn & Bacon.

Torgesen, J., Alexander, A., Wagner, R., Rashoutte, C., Voeller, K., & Conway, T., et al. (2001). Intensive remedial instruction for children with severe reading disabilities: Immediate and long-term outcomes from two instructional approaches. *Journal of Learning Disabilities, 34*, 33–58.

Vellutino, F. R. (1992). Afterword. In S. Templeton & D. Bear (Eds.), *Development of ortho-graphic knowledge and the foundations of literacy* (pp. 353–357). Hillsdale, NJ: Erlbaum.

Vellutino, F. R., & Scanlon, D. M. (1987). Phonological coding, phonological awareness and reading ability: Evidence from a longitudinal and experimental study. *Merrill-Palmer Quarterly, 33,* 321–363.

Voeller, K. S. (1986). Right hemisphere deficit syndrome in children. *American Journal of Psychiatry, 143,* 1004–1011.

Voeller, K. S. (2001). Attention-deficit/hyperactivity disorder as frontal-subcortical disorder. In D. G. Lichter & J. L. Cummings (Eds.), *Frontal-subcortical circuits in psychiatric and neurological disorders* (pp. 334–371). New York: Guilford Press.

Vygotsky, L. (1986). *Thought and language* (A. Kozulin, Trans.). Cambridge, MA: MIT Press.

Wagmeister, J., & Shifrin, B. (2000, November). Thinking differently, learning differently. *Educational Leadership,* 45–48.

Walker, H. M., McConnell, S. R., Todis, B., Walker, J., & Golden, H. (1988). *The Walker social skills curriculum: The ACCEPTS program.* Austin, TX: ProEd.

Walker, H. M., Homes, D., Todis, B., & Horton, G. (1988). *The Walker social skills curriculum. The ACCESS Program: Adolescent curriculum for communication and effective social skills.* Austin, TX: ProEd.

Westwater, A., & Wolfe, P. (2000, November). The brain-compatible curriculum. *Educational Leadership,* 49–52.

Wilson, K. M., & Swanson, H. L. (2001). Are mathematics disabilities due to a domain-general or domain-specific working memory deficits? *Journal of Learning Disabilities, 34,* 237–248.

Work, P. (2002, October). *New Hampton school's support programs.* Paper presented at the meeting of the New England Association of Learning Specialists, Tilton School. Tilton, NH.

Work, P., & Beedy, J. (2001, November). *Creating a culture of character and creativity in a private boarding school.* Paper presented at the Association of Boarding Schools 5th National Conference, Chicago.

Ylvisaker, M., Szekeres, S. F., & Hartwick, P. (1994). A framework for cognitive intervention. In R. C. Savage & G. F. Wolcott (Eds.), *Educational dimensions of acquired brain injury* (pp. 35–67). Austin, TX: ProEd.

Zaragoza, N., Vaughn, S., & McIntosh, R. (1991). Social skills interventions and children with behavior problems: A review. *Behavioral Disorders, 16,* 260–275.

Zera, D. A. (2001). A reconceptualization of learning disabilities via a self-organizing systems paradigm. *Journal of Learning Disabilities, 34,* 79–94.

# CHAPTER 30

# Translating Neuropsychological Evaluation Information into the Individualized Education Plan, School Discipline Plan, and Functional Assessments of Behavior

LORA TUESDAY HEATHFIELD, JANIECE L. POMPA, and ELAINE CLARK

THE INCIDENCE OF neuropsychological deficits in children and adolescents is on the rise. Much of this increase is due to advances in medical technology that serve to prolong the lives of those who may not have survived their injuries or congenital anomalies without such advancements. For example, there has been an increasing survival rate of infants born preterm and of very low birthweight due to improved medical technology, which in turn increases the incidence of neurological impacts on the growth and development of these children's central nervous system (CNS). There also has been increasing evidence that many children and adolescents who experience learning or behavioral difficulties, such as learning disabilities and Attention-Deficit/Hyperactivity Disorder (ADHD), have known CNS impairment (Gaddes & Edgell, 1994; Teeter & Semrud-Clikeman, 1997). Some of these cases include children with traumatic brain injury (TBI). In the United States, TBI has been identified as the number one cause for death and disability in children and adolescents due to falls, firearms, domestic abuse, and motor vehicle crashes (Centers for Disease Control and Prevention, 1999). Even subtle brain-based sequelae can potentially impact a learner's academic performance. Currently, more than five million learners in the United States receive special education services in our nation's schools, and over half of those students are identified as learning disabled (U.S. Department of Education, 2002). Many of these learners will potentially benefit from the information a school-based neuropsychological evaluation can add to a traditional psychoeducational evaluation. The field of neuropsychology combines knowledge in the fields of psychology and medicine to identify those behaviors linked to brain functioning. With the goal of improving educational outcomes for these students, neuropsychology in the context of schools has much to offer.

Section V of this volume is devoted to the nuances of the neuropsychological approach to the assessment of learners in a school environment. The ultimate goal of such an assessment is to generate interventions that can be utilized in the school environment to effect behavior change that results in improved academic and social functioning. In essence, neuropsychological assessments can be useful to school personnel only if they result in the application of effective treatment strategies (Long, 1996). Brain-behavior relationships are not observed directly during assessment, but rather are inferred through both quantitative (i.e., neuropsychological test and subtest results) and qualitative (i.e., behaviors observed during assessment and in the classroom) information. One advantage a school-based neuropsychological assessment has over traditional psychoeducational assessment is the neuropsychologist's ability to focus a portion of the assessment on behaviors that are known to be linked to specific brain functioning; this includes memory, attention, and processing speed. Accurate interpretation of these brain-behavior relationships is thought to be important in increasing the accuracy of predicting future functioning. This is also considered to be fundamental to the process of formulating appropriate interventions for students experiencing learning difficulties. How one then translates this information into effective intervention strategies is possibly the most pivotal step in the process of applying neuropsychology in the context of the schools for the purpose of enhancing students' educational performance.

## HISTORY AND THEORETICAL FOUNDATIONS FOR INTERVENTIONS IN NEUROPSYCHOLOGY

A variety of theoretical approaches abound in the history of psychology and its application to understanding human behavior and individual differences. All too often, psychological assessment and treatment approaches are grounded in only one of these theories despite the documented efficacy of a variety of theoretical approaches. The field of neuropsychology is no exception to this phenomenon, but debates continue as to which theoretical model is most appropriate (Teeter & Semrud-Clikeman, 1995). Historically, the field of neuropsychology has been grounded primarily in biologically based theories, with more recent efforts to integrate behavioral theories (Teeter & Semrud-Clikeman, 1997). However, some in the field of clinical neuropsychology have cited a need for an even more integrative approach to assessment, interpretation, and treatment (e.g., D'Amato & Rothlisberg, 1992; Teeter & Semrud-Clikeman, 1995). It is thought that a more integrated theoretical approach better represents the complex two-way interactions between neurocognition and other factors, such as environmental elements and psychosocial variables, that impact a child's development and subsequent neurocognitive sequelae (Gaddes & Edgell, 1994). Teeter and Semrud-Clikeman (1997) argue that this transactional model facilitates the design of effective interventions for learners with neurocognitive disorders by addressing interrelated cognitive, behavioral, and psychosocial factors.

## A SCHOOL-BASED NEUROPSYCHOLOGICAL
## APPROACH TO INTERVENTIONS

A school-based neuropsychological approach takes an interactional model even further by combining the multitheoretical and interactional model of neuropsychology with the learning process. The neuropsychologist in the schools has the unique advantage of integrating what is known about CNS development and related behaviors with those factors that promote successful educational outcomes for learners. This integrated approach facilitates linking assessment results with empirically validated interventions and there is some research evidence that consideration of a child's neuropsychological functioning can lead to more appropriate interventions (Teeter & Semrud-Clikeman, 1997). Historically, there have been significant challenges to accomplishing this due to the emphasis in neuropsychology on standard battery assessment; determination of diagnosis, etiology, and location of brain damage; and the identification of associated functional deficits (Fletcher-Janzen & Kade, 1997; Teeter & Semrud-Clikeman, 1997). Fortunately, improved technology that has resulted in better understanding of brain functions and their relationship to observed behaviors, such as neuropsychological test performance (Bigler, 1990), has allowed a shift in focus. The neuropsychology field's knowledge of these brain-behavior relationships has increased substantially because of advances in neuroimaging technology such as magnetic resonance imaging, allowing the field to now focus on the identification of subtle cognitive dysfunctions and their associated deficits. Thus, child neuropsychology in the context of schools can offer a more applicable assessment approach to traditional psycho- educational assessment. Such an assessment approach results in information pertinent to the development of effective interventions to improve the academic, behavioral, and social functioning of learners experiencing educational difficulties that are related to cognitive dysfunction.

Understanding how neuropsychological deficits impact children's development can be essential in the planning of appropriate educational interventions. The CNS and cognitive skills of children continue to develop and change over time as children progress through developmental stages (Rodier, 1994). Cognition is the primary mode of development impacted by CNS impairment; however, brain function and cognitive development also significantly impact other aspects of children's development, such as social and emotional development (Majovski, 1997). Subsequently, the overall development of a child who experienced a brain insult at birth (e.g., hypoxia) will differ substantially from that of a child whose brain injury was sustained at school age (e.g., closed head injury; Spreen, Risser, & Edgell, 1995). Specific developmental skills are likely to be differentially affected depending on whether the CNS disorder or dysfunction occurred prior to or during skill acquisition or after a skill had already been well established (Yeates et al., 2002). Clinical child neuropsychologists can facilitate a better understanding of brain-behavior relationships in relation to children's development and specific intervention strategies; school psychologists with child neuropsychology training have an additional advantage due to their understanding of the interrelationships between brain function, behavior, developmental factors, and educational outcomes. This can be especially critical for a complex disorder such as lead toxicity, which to date has not been found to have any identifiable pattern of neurocognitive sequelae (Dietrich, 1999). Consideration of the interaction between all these factors can result in a more comprehensive assessment of students with learning difficulties and consequently more applicable educational interventions.

Specific diagnoses associated with brain dysfunction do not present as the same behavioral symptoms across individuals. Conversely, a particular pattern of deficits does not necessarily imply a specific neurologically based diagnosis, and deficits demonstrated on neuropsychological assessment instruments do not in and of themselves reflect brain abnormalities (Fennell & Bauer, 1997). Neuropsychological deficits can be reflective of delays in maturation, gaps in functioning, or differences in brain development (Levine, 1994). Other factors, such as emotional issues or lack of appropriate instruction, can also significantly impact a child's performance on neuropsychological measures. Typically, the behavioral symptomatology exhibited by children and adolescents with neurologic dysfunction is unique to the individual. Additionally, the school-based neuropsychologist needs to consider whether an identified deficit represents a true skill deficit (i.e., the learner cannot perform the skill) or a performance deficit (i.e., the learner can perform the skill but does not). It is also critical to ascertain whether the perceived cognitive deficit is even directly related to the learning difficulties experienced by the learner (Taylor, 1988). For example, a learner who has a visuospatial deficit may have difficulty with math concepts due to performance anxiety rather than the cognitive deficit itself. Assessment data regarding neuropsychological deficits need to be considered along with other behavioral or test performance data in the process of identifying neuropathology as well as in the context of the reported educational difficulties. Identification of any cerebral impairments at the earliest possible point in a child's developmental course is critical for minimizing associated learning and behavioral deficits through the implementation of early intervention strategies. For example, identifying a verbal memory deficit in kindergarten when formal reading instruction is introduced can result in modifications to reading instruction prior to the student experiencing years of reading failure that might occur if the deficit was not identified until 3rd grade. The ultimate goal of school-based neuropsychological assessments, however, is the design of effective treatment strategies that address the specific referral questions and result in better educational outcomes for learners.

Traditional psychoeducational assessment tools, such as standardized measures of intelligence, can reveal some important information about a child's neuropsychological abilities; however, the information generated is often limited in scope (Fletcher & Levin, 1988). Results of these standard psychoeducational measures also may be interpreted differently by neuropsychologists due to their knowledge of brain-behavior relationships. Also, it is thought that learning is based on multiple neuropsychological functions that traditional psychoeducational assessments do not typically address. Neuropsychological assessment measures have been shown to generate additional detailed information about child cerebral functioning, resulting in a comprehensive profile of cognitive strengths and weaknesses that may potentially result in more effective treatment recommendations (Whitten, D'Amato, & Chittooran, 1992). Neuropsychological assessment information can be used to develop effective interventions for a variety of neurocognitive disorders (Gaddes & Edgell, 1994; Teeter & Semrud-Clikeman, 1997), lending support to using a school-based neuropsychological model.

## TRANSLATING NEUROPSYCHOLOGICAL ASSESSMENT RESULTS TO TREATMENT RECOMMENDATIONS

Traditional psychoeducational assessments have been criticized for a lack of evidence that the resulting assessment information contributes to the formulation of effective treatment outcomes (Braden & Kratochwill, 1997). However, others strongly support the utility of traditional psychoeducational assessment in designing appropriate treatments (e.g., Sattler, 2003). The development of effective interventions ultimately relies on the information derived from the assessment, taking into consideration both child and environmental influences. Functioning in the areas of language, memory, attention, and concentration, executive functioning, sensorimotor ability, visuospatial ability, emotion, and behavior all may be impacted by neuropsychological dysfunction and thereby affect school performance. Also, learning tasks vary in terms of the cognitive skills required, so specific strengths or deficits can impact academic performance differentially (Telzrow, 1981). Neuropsychological assessment of these specific cognitive and related skills results in information about the learner's strengths and weaknesses in the context of neuropsychological development and how that student best processes information to learn, which can be utilized in the formulation of appropriate interventions for that individual (D'Amato, 1990). For example, using a verbal mediation strategy such as mnemonic rhymes to enhance remembering spelling rules is likely to be a more effective intervention if a learner has strong auditory processing skills. In the end, the most critical outcome of a psychoeducational or neuropsychological assessment is the identification of specific intervention strategies that explicitly address the particular referral questions and ultimately help the individual learner experience academic and social success, not simply differential diagnosis or determination of special education eligibility.

### Promoting Ecologically Valid Assessment Results

It is important to consider that formal neuropsychological assessment measures are usually administered to the learner in a very structured, quiet environment, which is nothing like the typical classroom. Subsequently, formal test results may not accurately reflect a student's potential for learning (Telzrow, 1991). Assessment activities that closely resemble actual functioning in the school environment are preferable in order to facilitate translation to applicable recommendations (Haak & Livingston, 1997). Functional assessments conducted in the child's natural environments are strongly advocated in order to understand how any identified neuropsychological deficits impact the child's functioning in actual academic and social situations. For example, results of a formal neuropsychological assessment suggesting a deficit in auditory attention certainly can be helpful in formulating recommendations for intervention. However, determining that the child has auditory attention difficulties that manifest as problems following the teacher's verbal instructions in the classroom, but the child's performance improves when instructions are shortened and the child repeats the instructions aloud, translates directly into an applicable and functional intervention strategy that is likely to positively impact school performance.

There are several models for developing neuropsychological interventions (see Teeter, 1997); however, one distinction between the various models seems to be whether the focus is on developing compensatory skills and/or adjusting task requirements (accommodation) or remediation (rehabilitation) of deficient neuropsychological skills, or a combination of the two. A school-based neuropsychological intervention model predominantly focuses on the development of compensatory skills or environmental adjustments within the constraints of the educational system, but also considers under what conditions a rehabilitative approach might be more appropriate, such as in very young children (Whitten et al., 1992). Remedial interventions for slow reading fluency due to processing speed deficits might be beneficial for a learner in 3rd grade, but more compensatory strategies, such as using audio recordings of textbooks to minimize reading demands, would be more advantageous for a high school student. Factors to consider in addition to the student's age and developmental level include the severity of the deficit, the student's level of frustration and resulting impact on self-esteem, and the outcome of remedial interventions attempted previously. In their design of intervention strategies, school psychologists with child neuropsychology training can utilize their knowledge of a child's individual neuropsychological strengths and weaknesses exhibited in their natural environments, the course of typical child development, and aspects of learning theories in the educational system. The school-based neuropsychologist must consider not only a child's developmental status and the severity of primary neurocognitive dysfunctions, but also associated deficits such as academic performance. It is then possible to determine appropriate compensatory strategies designed to utilize and build on strengths while circumventing or accommodating weaknesses (Teeter, 1997; Telzrow, 1986).

Neuropsychological treatment for individuals who sustained brain injury and subsequently suffered functional impairments gave rise to the practice of cognitive rehabilitation in the 1980s, which is a subject of continued controversy due to its questionable efficacy (Fletcher-Janzen & Kade, 1997). Cognitive rehabilitation typically focuses on teaching specific cognitive processes but may also include compensatory strategies (McCoy, Gelder, VanHorn, & Dean, 1997). Whether cognitive rehabilitation results in improved cognitive functioning is still debated in the literature. Cognitive rehabilitation has also been criticized for focusing solely on cognitive function at the expense of socioemotional functioning (McCoy et al., 1997), which is problematic given the interrelatedness of these domains and the incidence of emotional difficulties associated with neurological impairment.

Another mode of treatment is neuropsychological or neuroeducational programming, which utilizes brain-based teaching strategies (Savage & Mishkin, 1994). According to Savage and Mishkin, neuroeducational treatment considers needed environmental changes and the influence of developmental factors. This model focuses on teaching and learning that is based on what is known about brain functioning. The development of an individualized education plan (IEP) follows from this neuroeducational model.

## THE DEVELOPMENT OF THE INDIVIDUALIZED EDUCATION PLAN

Like the assessment process, IEP development is an ongoing and continuous process. The IEP process involves not only planning, but implementation and evaluation. The goal, of course, is effective programming geared to the specific needs of the identified student. Students with learning difficulties linked to underlying cerebral impairment can often present a unique set of needs.

REQUIREMENTS OF THE INDIVIDUALS WITH DISABILITIES EDUCATION ACT

The Individuals with Disabilities Education Improvement Act (IDEA) of 2004 mandates IEPs for each student in the schools identified as having a disability. An IEP is the main tool for ensuring individualized services for each student with a disability who is identified as eligible for special education. By law, an IEP requires a team effort, but more important, each team member is considered to have specific areas of expertise and can provide important information regarding the student's educational and social needs. The school-based neuropsychologist can be a crucial member of this team both in the process of determining possible special education eligibility and, more important, in the development of appropriate long-term and short-term goals, particularly for students with learning difficulties related to brain dysfunction. Parents are also important participants in the IEP process. The IEP is considered a joint collaboration designed to build consensus among the team members on how to best meet the individual student's learning needs.

Interpretation of a student's instructional needs based on neuropsychological assessment results is a primary role of the school-based neuropsychologist on the IEP team. One of the required components of an IEP is a description of present levels of educational performance, which is directly associated with the comprehensive neuropsychological assessment results. Another required component is information on how the identified disability interferes with that student's progress in the general education curriculum. The IEP also must include measurable annual goals and short-term objectives, information as to how the student's progress toward these goals will be measured, and the specific services, supports, and program modifications needed to help the student achieve the identified goals and participate in the general curriculum.

The expertise of the school-based neuropsychologist can aid in the development of each of these IEP components. To facilitate the process of developing the IEP, the school-based neuropsychologist can present information from the neuropsychological assessment in an organized fashion. This can include discussing the student's current levels of functioning and associated needs in the various relevant domains (e.g., memory, attention, and concentration) and how they relate to the student's academic and social functioning, while at the same time avoiding the use of technical jargon. Functional skill levels and specific needs in related areas such as emotion, behavior, and social skills should also be addressed. Ultimately, the IEP goals established for an individual student are only as good as the information that is provided during the development of the IEP.

CONSIDERATIONS IN IDENTIFYING INDIVIDUALIZED EDUCATION PLAN GOALS

The complexity of the learning needs for many students with neuropsychological deficits is at times overwhelming. Subsequently, many of these students can have difficulty generalizing skills learned in one context to another. To avoid the possibility of context-dependent skill development, it is important to plan for generalization of skill development in the IEP. Annual goals and short-term objectives should ensure that instruction takes place in functional situations rather than through isolated learning trials (e.g., Sohlberg & Raskin, 1996) and that supported instruction is applied across all critical environments, including the home and community environments whenever possible. Additionally, because of the numerous learning needs of students with neuropsychological deficits, the IEP team may consider narrowing the focus of IEP goals in terms of number while ensuring that intervention is provided at an adequate intensity to facilitate progress toward each of these goals.

Due to the complex needs of students with specific neurodevelopmental disorders, often multiple agencies and individuals are involved in a student's care. Coordination of information and services between family and school, as well as any outside agencies such as medical personnel or rehabilitative staff, is critical to providing effective care. Having an identified contact person at the school who is the primary communicator can facilitate a smooth transition of information (Mira, Tucker, & Tyler, 1992). This role becomes especially critical in the case of school reentry of a student who was hospitalized after sustaining a TBI and is still in the process of recovery. Because of their training background in psychology, medicine, and education, neuropsychologists functioning in the school context can ideally serve in this capacity.

The learning difficulties experienced by many students with neuropsychological deficits are likely to impact multiple areas of their lives, including aspects of their lives outside of the school environment. Various aspects of a child's functioning may be directly or indirectly impacted by those learning difficulties as well as across multiple environments. This suggests the need to consider the individual from a holistic perspective when developing IEP goals. Mira et al. (1992) have specified several areas to consider for students with TBI that could easily be applied to other students who are experiencing learning difficulties related to neuropsychological dysfunction. These include issues that are contextual, physical, cognitive, instructional, psychosocial, and behavioral (see p. 53). Each of these areas is addressed next in terms of its application to the development of relevant IEP goals for students with neurocognitive deficits.

*Contextual Issues*   There are various aspects of the student's learning environment that should be considered when identifying appropriate IEP goals. Although identification of learning difficulties that are neurologically based certainly implies deficits that are primarily child-centered, simple adjustments to the educational environment often can promote more effective learning. Ecological changes such as adjusting the length of instructional sessions to coincide with any attentional limitations, the size of the classroom (teacher-student ratio), the accessibility to needed adaptive equipment, and the noise level of the classroom environment should be considered in the development of IEP goals. Increasing the consistency of the classroom routine, providing short breaks during long tasks, and decreasing the amount of copying from the chalkboard are all fairly easy environmental changes to implement. Such seemingly minor changes could significantly impact the effectiveness of planned instructional interventions.

*Physical Issues*   Although many identified neurological disorders do not necessarily result in specific physical limitations (e.g., ADHD), some disorders may significantly impact an individual's motor or sensory functioning (e.g., seizure disorders). Consideration of the physical effects of these disorders is critical in the IEP development process. Limitations in physical stamina, slowed motor output (such as writing speed), speech deficits, or difficulty with motor dexterity or visual tracking need to be considered when developing goals. Providing periods of rest for a student who has generalized seizures may facilitate an improvement in that student's academic performance. Also, the need for physical accommodations, such as access to a microcomputer or AlphaSmart because of illegible handwriting, is important to consider in the IEP development process. Relatedly, any visual acuity, hearing acuity, or other sensory deficits (such as sound discrimination) identified prior to assessment should be considered when establishing relevant goals. For example, using a device that vibrates at regular intervals would be preferable to a beep tape for a student who has problems with hearing acuity in addition to attention and concentration difficulties. Disregard for any of these associated physical issues could potentially impact the effectiveness of educational or other intervention strategies.

*Cognitive Issues*   Deficits in cognitive functioning are likely the primary issue to address when formulating IEP goals for students with neuropsychological deficits. Aspects of cognitive functioning that might be impacted include information-processing speed, sustained or divided attention, memory skills (verbal or visual, immediate or delayed, retrospective or prospective), problem-solving strategies, organizational skills, and the ability to transition between tasks or initiate tasks. All of these cognitive skills are considered crucial to the learning process, and any limitations can significantly impact not only a student's ability to learn but, ultimately, that student's educational performance as well.

Further analysis of these broad cognitive skills also should be considered in the development of relevant goals because some cognitive skills are composed of many subskills. For example, memory skills can be further analyzed in terms of verbal or visual memory, immediate or delayed memory, retrospective or prospective memory, or any combination thereof. Cognitive skill deficits can also be interrelated, such as memory and attention. For instance, a deficit in sustained attention may present difficulties with delayed memory, and working memory deficits can affect performance on tasks requiring divided attention.

A student's cognitive strengths and limitations are the most meaningful factors to consider in the process of determining relevant IEP goals. Many interventions can be designed to capitalize on a student's cognitive strengths while circumventing cognitive deficits.

*Instructional Issues*   Even if the learner has not met the specific criteria necessary to be eligible for special education services and the development and implementation of an IEP, many effective instructional strategies can easily be applied in regular classrooms. The primary aspect to consider in designing effective instructional strategies is determining which specific areas of academic achievement are impacted (e.g., math computation, reading decoding), which associated academic skills are impacted (e.g., organizational skills, memory skills, attending skills), and which instructional strategies have been either effective or ineffective in the past. The majority of information about potentially effective teaching strategies can be gleaned from informal experimentation or probes done during the neuropsychological assessment. For example, an assessment task simulating individual seat work can be interspersed with short breaks to determine if a student who has difficulty sustaining attention in the classroom might attend and perform better with shorter work sessions, such as 5 or 10 minutes. Repeating the same intervention during different tasks (e.g., silent reading and arithmetic worksheets) can yield critical information about whether this intervention might be task-specific or more broadly effective across academic tasks. Similarly, does the same intervention also work for adult-led learning activities, or would an alternative intervention be more effective in this context (e.g., cuing to attend with a beep tape). Readministration of some assessment tasks using slight modifications (e.g., limits testing) can also yield meaningful information regarding how to utilize a student's cognitive strengths to circumvent his or her cognitive weaknesses. For instance, does a learner's retention of new verbal information improve when paired with a visual cue? Is math fluency increased when provided access to a printed number line? Obviously, these types of informal probes greatly facilitate the development of interventions appropriate to specific individuals, thus enhancing the likelihood of progressing toward and achieving identified IEP goals.

*Psychosocial Issues*   There is increasing evidence that those children who experience CNS deficits are at an increased risk for psychopathology whether the neurological deficit is mild or severe (Majovski, 1997). For example, research indicates that psychopathology is linked to the presence of a variety of neurological disorders, such as epilepsy (Tramontana & Hooper, 1997). Additionally, individuals who sustain a TBI are often more functionally impaired from the resulting emotional difficulties and personality changes than from the associated cognitive deficits (Lezak & O'Brien, 1990). A neuropsychological approach to assessment and intervention in the schools may result in earlier identification of these social-emotional impairments to reduce the risk of more severe psychopathology. School-based neuropsychologists also can utilize their knowledge about the social-emotional correlates of various neurocognitive disorders to plan interventions. Knowing that social relatedness difficulties are associated with ADHD, for example, can lead to proactive intervention strategies designed to minimize the risk for social isolation. Some disorders with neuropsychological correlates, such as HIV infection, can result in a significant emotional burden for the student as well as family members. The need for psychotherapeutic interventions (individual, group, or family counseling) or skills training to address relevant psychosocial variables (e.g., depressive or anxious symptomatology, low frustration tolerance, low self-esteem, becoming easily upset) also should be considered in IEP goal development.

*Behavioral Issues*   A high percentage of learners with underlying cerebral impairments experience significant behavioral problems associated with academic failure. Problematic behaviors can be presented either as excesses (e.g., aggression) or deficits (e.g., social withdrawal) or both in the same individual. Typically, these challenging behaviors require specific interventions designed to either increase or decrease the behavior's frequency, duration, or intensity. School-based neuropsychologists can aid considerably in the development of effective behavioral interventions for this population due to their knowledge of behaviors that are associated with specific neuropsychological deficits. To design effective behavioral interventions, however, there is a strong consensus that identification of the environmental antecedent and consequent events that control or maintain the behavior is essential. The process of determining the relevant controlling variables is achieved by conducting a functional behavior assessment (FBA). Utilizing FBA with students who have neuropsychological deficits is described in more detail later in this chapter.

*Other Related Issues*   Mira et al. (1992) identified these five classes of issues to consider when designing intervention plans, however, there are related issues to consider as well. Issues discussed here include medical issues, community issues, and family issues. To better understand the broad range of a specific child's needs, the psychoeducational needs of others in the child's life should also be considered. It may be necessary to arrange for school personnel or family members to access relevant educational information regarding a child's disability or neurological disorder. Even providing information about appropriate support groups and parent associations can be very relevant. There also may be a compelling need to acquire additional medical information regarding a specific student, so referral for medical evaluations, such as an updated neurological exam or a psychiatric evaluation to consider the use of pharmacological interventions, may be necessary.

Because neuropsychological deficits can impact a child's functioning outside the educational environment, consideration of the child's functioning in the community can be incorporated into the IEP goals, particularly in planning for the generalization of skill development. More severe deficits might ultimately limit an adolescent's employment options or potential for independent living as an adult, and related interventions can be instituted in the IEP if necessary. Family members should be encouraged to participate in the development of a student's IEP, but not simply by attending the formal IEP meeting and signing necessary permission forms. The family has considerable knowledge of the child's functional skills and deficits, historical information about any past intervention efforts, and relevant medical information, and they should be active team participants in the development of IEP goals.

It is also necessary to consider that cultural factors can influence how a child performs in academic and social contexts. First, language and cultural variables directly impact the learning experiences that children are exposed to, ultimately affecting each child's neurodevelopmental functioning and growth. Social and environmental experiences influence a child's development in many ways and are inextricably related to development of the CNS (Majovski, 1997). These experiential variables are thought to play an even larger role in the neuropsychological development of children than of adults (Fennell & Bauer, 1997). Second, the neuropsychological assessment process itself must be nondiscriminatory with regard to culture, language, and ethnicity as mandated in IDEA. However, standardized neuropsychological assessment instruments typically demand a fairly good understanding of language (usually English), and the normative groups are sometimes based on restrictive samples. It is therefore imperative that these caveats are considered when interpreting assessment results to avoid misinterpreting what may be normal cultural variations. Cultural factors also play a substantial role in the formulation of recommendations, particularly in terms of the family's worldviews and family members' experiences with the special education system. Considering an individual's and a family's preferences is essential for developing IEP goals that are not contradictory to their cultural beliefs and that they perceive will result in functional changes in the student's life.

## FUNCTIONAL BEHAVIOR ASSESSMENT AND INDIVIDUALIZED EDUCATION PLAN GOAL DEVELOPMENT

The National Association of School Psychologists (NASP, 1999) has endorsed the use of FBA procedures in schools and FBA is mandated in IDEA under certain conditions. Additionally, the use of an individualized assessment approach for the selection of interventions in educational settings has been recommended by many in the field of school psychology (DuPaul & Ervin, 1996; Kratochwill & McGivern, 1996). Although the basic definition of individualized FBA techniques is not specified in IDEA, typically, FBA involves identifying the relationships between challenging behaviors and various child and environmental factors to determine the environmental events controlling the behavior of concern (Kratochowill & McGivern, 1996). Designing an effective treatment plan is the goal of an individualized FBA, but this process can become complex given that multiple factors can trigger or maintain problematic behaviors; that is, students often demonstrate multiple challenging behaviors that can be interrelated, and causal factors can change over time (Haynes & Williams, 2003). However, once these contingency factors are identified, it is possible to manipulate them to reduce the likelihood of the problematic behaviors occurring. Unfortunately, there are few practical approaches linking the results of FBA to feasible intervention strategies (Ervin et al., 2001), so it is generally incumbent upon the school-based neuropsychologist or other practitioner to identify any specific interventions for implementation.

The process of conducting a thorough FBA and linking those results to effective intervention strategies becomes even more challenging if a student with learning difficulties has an underlying neuropsychological deficit that is associated with problematic behaviors. Any underlying cerebral impairment identified during the neuropsycholgical assessment suggests that there also may be biological or neurological factors that contribute to or trigger the challenging behaviors. Because of their knowledge of the emotional and behavioral components affiliated with neuropsychological deficits, school-based neuropsychologists may have an advantage in designing appropriate intervention plans. For example, determining that a learner's aggression is related to cognitive dysfunction from frontal lobe epilepsy rather than avoidance of challenging academic tasks would result in very different intervention strategies and, consequently, very different outcomes. Similarly, educational personnel may mistakenly attribute a student's lack of homework completion to apathy or defiance, when in fact a prospective memory deficit interferes with the student's ability to remember to turn in homework. Although these underlying biological factors can be difficult to identify because they are not readily observable and may not be as modifiable as other causal variables, FBA is an effective assessment strategy that can be used by school-based neuropsychologists to design effective IEP goals.

IDEA mandates the use of an individualized FBA for any student identified with a disability who has been suspended for more than 10 consecutive days for a safe schools violation (i.e., violations involving weapons or controlled substances; Drasgow & Yell, 2001). The FBA is part of the process designed to determine whether the safe schools violation was a manifestation of the student's disability. Frequently, the student's disability is considered to be related to the behavioral incident unless the disability is determined to not have impaired the student's ability to understand the consequences of the behavior or to control the behavior. Students with learning difficulties may be at increased risk for such safe schools violations if they exhibit deficits in executive functioning, which may impair a student's ability to control impulsive behaviors or understand the consequences of such behavior. This highlights the need for a more proactive approach to the design and implementation of behavioral interventions to reduce the potential for these types of impulsive behaviors that often have dire consequences, particularly for students with specific cognitive deficits, such as in executive functioning.

IDEA also encourages FBA in determining the need for any behavioral supports prior to the development of the IEP. Specific interventions that address behaviors that impede the learning of the student or others should be included directly in the student's IEP. Accurate identification of any underlying cognitive deficits can be critical to the FBA process, resulting in more effective educational and social outcomes for the student.

## School Discipline Plans and Individualized Education Plan Goal Development

School discipline plans can also serve a proactive function by ensuring that students with disabilities are not disciplined differentially from those without disabilities. Disciplinary action involving the cessation of support services identified in a student's IEP is not permitted. However, if it ever becomes necessary to remove a student from his or her current placement due to considerable risk of injury to the student or others, a hearing officer rather than school personnel determines this. Behavior that is related to a student's underlying cognitive dysfunction presents a unique challenge to the application of disciplinary strategies. In such a case, the additional information gained from a school-based neuropsychological assessment can greatly contribute to the team's development of more effective IEP goals. For example, including IEP goals that promote self-monitoring strategies may be more effective than discipline involving punitive consequences for impulsive behaviors that are attributable to a frontal lobe tumor. Similarly, a student with Autism whose social judgment is impaired will likely benefit more from IEP goals focusing on the development of peer relationship skills as opposed to discipline plans that result in a meeting with the student and the student's caregivers to discuss the consequences of the student's behavior.

Inclusion of proactive discipline strategies that are consistent with schoolwide discipline plans also can be incorporated as IEP goals. Preferably, schoolwide positive behavior support can be implemented, which has been shown to significantly reduce the frequency of discipline referrals (see Crone & Horner, 2003). This strategy corresponds well with the concept of errorless learning (Baddeley & Wilson, 1994), which seeks to promote success in the learning of new skills and therefore reduces the need to unlearn incorrect responses, such as attending to irrelevant stimuli. This strategy is particularly critical for students with underlying neuropsychological deficits, who may be at risk for overlearning incorrect responses.

## INDIVIDUALIZED EDUCATION PLAN IMPLEMENTATION AND EVALUATION

Implementation of the IEP involves actually providing the identified services, supports, and modifications necessary for the student to achieve the established long- and short-term goals (Blosser & DePompei, 1994). This implies the need for ongoing assessment and evaluation of treatment effectiveness to verify that the recommended interventions actually facilitate the intended behavioral changes. This evaluation should be ongoing to promptly make revisions or even devise new intervention strategies if they are not effective and avoid the prolonged use of interventions when they are no longer needed (Teeter & Semrud-Clikeman, 1997). Curriculum-based measurement can be used in this regard to monitor small changes in a student's performance on a specific academic task, such as reading fluency. Thus, neuropsychological assessment and intervention are inextricably interconnected, and both are essentially ongoing processes.

### APPLICATIONS OF SCHOOL-BASED NEUROPSYCHOLOGY TO INDIVIDUALIZED EDUCATION PLAN DEVELOPMENT

School personnel, including most practicing school psychologists, typically do not receive extensive training in neuropsychology, so their knowledge of the developmental and behavioral sequelae of various neurocognitive disorders is understandably limited. School personnel with training in both school psychology and neuropsychology can serve as an important member of the IEP team in this regard. They can convey important information not only to other school personnel on the team but to family members as well. A school-based neuropsychologist also can bridge the gap between the fields of medicine and education and facilitate cohesive team building in the process. As more is learned about learning difficulties and their association to specific brain functions, children who are struggling in school stand to benefit the most, along with their families. Despite the fact that educator hypotheses about student behavior are sometimes accurate, an understanding of the link between student behavior in the academic setting and brain function is clearly limited to a few specialized medical professions. A school-based neuropsychologist can be a valuable member of IEP teams as team members work together to develop appropriate goals for individual learners. Direct contact between medical personnel and families or school personnel is often limited, so there is a considerable need to merge the expertise in both education and medicine. School-based neuropsychologists can fulfill a critical need for schools that serve many students with multiple learning problems.

## CONCLUSION

A more direct linkage between assessment results and treatment recommendations can ensure more efficient outcomes by avoiding a trial-and-error approach.

Knowledge of a learner's specific cognitive strengths and weaknesses can be applied to treatment recommendations to enhance the likelihood of treatment success. The goal is to tailor recommendations to be pragmatic and result in functional life improvements. For those learners struggling in school, this translates to improvements in their lives that allow them to succeed academically and socially. Neuropsychologists functioning in a school context can contribute immensely toward this goal.

## REFERENCES

Baddeley, A., & Wilson, B. A. (1994). When implicit learning fails: Amnesia and the problem of error elimination. *Neuropsychologia, 32,* 53–68.

Bigler, E. (1990). *Traumatic brain injury.* Austin, TX: ProEd.

Blosser, J. L., & DePompei, R. (1994). Creating an effective classroom environment. In R. C. Savage & G. F. Wolcott (Eds.), *Educational dimensions of acquired brain injury* (pp. 413–451). Austin, TX: ProEd.

Braden, J. P., & Kratochwill, T. R. (1997). Treatment utility of assessment: Myths and realities. *School Psychology Review, 26,* 475–485.

Centers for Disease Control and Prevention. (1999). *Traumatic brain injury in the United States: A report to Congress.* Atlanta, GA: Author.

Crone, D. A., & Horner, R. H. (2003). *Building positive behavior support systems in schools: Functional behavioral assessment.* New York: Guilford Press.

D'Amato, R. C. (1990). A neuropsychological approach to school psychology. *School Psychology Quarterly, 5,* 141–160.

D'Amato, R. C., & Rothlisberg, B. A. (1992). Introduction: Foundations of psychological intervention. In R. C. D'Amato & B. A. Rothlisberg (Eds.), *Psychological perspectives on intervention: A case study approach to prescriptions for change* (pp. 1–5). New York: Longman.

Dietrich, K. N. (1999). Environmental neurotoxicants and psychological development. In K. O. Yeates, M. D. Ris, & H. G. Taylor (Eds.), *Pediatric neuropsychology: Research, theory, and practice* (pp. 206–234). New York: Guilford Press.

Drasgow, E., & Yell, M. L. (2001). Functional behavior assessments: Legal requirements and challenges. *School Psychology Review, 30,* 239–251.

DuPaul, G. J., & Ervin, R. A. (1996). Functional assessment of behaviors related to attention-deficit/hyperactivity disorder: Linking assessment to intervention design. *Behavior Therapy, 27,* 601–622.

Ervin, R. A., Radford, P. M., Bertsch, K., Piper, A. L., Ehrhardt, K. E., & Poling, A. (2001). A descriptive analysis and critique of the empirical literature on school-based functional assessment. *School Psychology Review, 30,* 193–210.

Fennell, E. B., & Bauer, R. M. (1997). Models of inference in evaluating brain-behavior relationships in children. In C. R. Reynolds & E. Fletcher-Janzen (Eds.), *Handbook of clinical child neuropsychology* (2nd ed., pp. 204–215). New York: Plenum Press.

Fletcher, J. M., & Levin, H. S. (1988). Neurobehavioral effects of brain injury in children and adolescents. In D. Routh (Ed.), *Handbook of pediatric psychology* (pp. 258–295). New York: Guilford Press.

Fletcher-Janzen, E., & Kade, H. D. (1997). Pediatric brain injury rehabilitation in a neurodevelopmental milieu. In C. R. Reynolds & E. Fletcher-Janzen (Eds.), *Handbook of clinical child neuropsychology* (2nd ed., pp. 452–481). New York: Plenum Press.

Gaddes, W. H., & Edgell, D. (1994). *Learning disabilities and brain function: A neuropsychological approach* (3rd ed.). Berlin, Germany: Springer-Verlag.

Haak, R. A., & Livingston, R. B. (1997). Treating traumatic brain injury in the school. In C. R. Reynolds & E. Fletcher-Janzen (Eds.), *Handbook of clinical child neuropsychology* (2nd ed., pp. 482–505). New York: Plenum Press.

Haynes, S. N., & Williams, A. E. (2003). Case formulation and design of behavioral treatment programs: Matching treatment mechanisms to causal variables for behavior problems. *European Journal of Psychological Assessment, 19*, 164–174.

Kratochwill, T. R., & McGivern, J. E. (1996). Clinical diagnosis, behavioral assessment, and functional analysis: Examining the connection between assessment and intervention. *School Psychology Review, 25*, 342–355.

Levine, M. D. (1994). *Educational care*. Cambridge, MA: Educators Publishing Service.

Lezak, M. D., & O'Brien, K. P. (1990). Chronic emotional, social, and physical changes after traumatic brain injury. In E. Bigler (Ed.), *Traumatic brain injury* (pp. 365–380). Austin, TX: ProEd.

Long, C. J. (1996). Neuropsychological tests: A look at our past and the impact that ecological issues may have on our future. In R. J. Sbordone & C. J. Long (Eds.), *Ecological validity of neuropsychological testing* (pp. 1–14). Delray Beach, FL: St. Lucie Press.

Majovski, L. V. (1997). Development of higher brain functions in children: Neural, cognitive, and behavioral perspectives. In C. R. Reynolds & E. Fletcher-Janzen (Eds.), *Handbook of clinical child neuropsychology* (2nd ed., pp. 63–101). New York: Plenum Press.

McCoy, K. D., Gelder, B. C., VanHorn, R. E., & Dean, R. S. (1997). Approaches to the cognitive rehabilitation of children with neuropsychological impairment. In C. R. Reynolds & E. Fletcher-Janzen (Eds.), *Handbook of clinical child neuropsychology* (2nd ed., pp. 439–451). New York: Plenum Press.

Mira, M. P., Tucker, B. F., & Tyler, J. S. (1992). *Traumatic brain injury in children and adolescents*. Austin, TX: ProEd.

National Association of School Psychologists. (1999). *Position statement on school psychologists' involvement in the role of assessment*. Bethesda, MD: Author.

Rodier, P. M. (1994). Vulnerable periods and processes during central nervous system development. *Environmental Health Perspectives, 102*(Suppl. 2), 121–124.

Sattler, J. M. (2003). *Assessment of children: Cognitive applications* (4th ed.). San Diego, CA: Author.

Savage, R. C., & Mishkin, L. (1994). A neuroeducational model for teaching students with acquired brain injuries. In R. C. Savage & G. F. Wolcott (Eds.), *Educational dimensions of acquired brain injury* (pp. 393–411). Austin, TX: ProEd.

Sohlberg, M. M., & Raskin, S. A. (1996). Principles of generalization applied to attention and memory interventions. *Journal of Head Trauma Rehabilitation, 11*, 65–78.

Spreen, O., Risser, A. T., & Edgell, D. (1995). *Developmental neuropsychology*. New York: Oxford.

Taylor, G. H. (1988). Neuropsychological testing: Relevance for assessing children's learning disabilities. *Journal of Consulting and Clinical Psychology, 56*, 795–800.

Teeter, P. A. (1997). Neurocognitive interventions for childhood and adolescent disorders: A transactional model. In C. R. Reynolds & E. Fletcher-Janzen (Eds.), *Handbook of clinical child neuropsychology* (2nd ed., pp. 387–417). New York: Plenum Press.

Teeter, P. A., & Semrud-Clikeman, M. (1995). Integrating neurobiological, psychosocial, and behavioral paradigms: A transactional model for the study of ADHD. *Archives of Clinical Neuropsychology, 10*, 433–461.

Teeter, P. A., & Semrud-Clikeman, M. (1997). *Child neuropsychology: Assessment and interventions for neurodevelopmental disorders*. Boston: Allyn & Bacon.

Telzrow, C. F. (1981). Brain development and the curriculum. *Educational Forum, 64*, 477–483.

Telzrow, C. F. (1986). The science and speculation of rehabilitation in developmental neuropsychological disorders. In L. C. Hartlage & C. F. Telzrow (Eds.), *The neuropsychology of individual differences: A developmental perspective* (pp. 271–307). New York: Plenum Press.

Telzrow, C. F. (1991). The school psychologist's perspective on testing students with traumatic brain injury. *Journal of Head Trauma Rehabilitation, 6,* 23–34.

Tramontana, M. G., & Hooper, S. R. (1997). Neuropsychology of child psychopathology. In C. R. Reynolds & E. Fletcher-Janzen (Eds.), *Handbook of clinical child neuropsychology* (2nd ed., pp. 120–139). New York: Plenum Press.

U.S. Department of Education. (2002). *Twenty-fourth annual report to Congress on the implementation of the Individuals with Disabilities Education Act (IDEA).* Washington, DC: US Government Printing Office.

Whitten, J. C., D'Amato, R. C., & Chittooran, M. M. (1992). A neuropsychological approach to intervention. In R. C. D'Amato & B. A. Rothlisberg (Eds.), *Psychological perspectives on intervention: A case study approach to prescriptions for change.* (pp. 112–136). New York: Longman.

Yeates, K. O., Wade, S. L., Stancin, T., Taylor, H. G., Drotar, D., & Minich, N. (2002). A prospective study of short- and long-term neuropsychological outcomes after traumatic brain injury to children. *Neuropsychology, 16,* 514–523.

# CHAPTER 31

# Understanding and Implementing Cognitive Neuropsychological Retraining

DONGHYUNG LEE and CYNTHIA A. RICCIO

T RADITIONALLY AND HISTORICALLY, school psychologists have focused their energy and efforts in assessment for identification and eligibility for special education services. In the past 20 years, increased attention has been focused on the need for assessment to inform the intervention planning process. In the school setting, behavioral techniques are most frequently employed (DeBonis, Ylvisaker, & Kundert, 2000); behavioral methods (e.g., reinforcement of appropriate behavior with a token economy) are the most studied of the intervention approaches. In the field of neuropsychology, there has been an increase in the activities related to neuropsychological rehabilitation that are multidimensional in nature and expand on behavioral approaches (Eslinger & Oliveri, 2002). Neuropsychological rehabilitation most often is directed at remediating or rehabilitating deficits in cognitive, emotional, and behavioral domains due to traumatic brain injury (TBI) in adults. These approaches are, by definition, very individualized to meet the needs, recovery patterns, wide array of deficits, and goals of a given person (Eslinger & Oliveri, 2002).

Previous attempts to address deficits (i.e., the deficit approach) in school psychology and special education have met with less than optimistic results based on treatment validity studies (e.g., Kavale, 1990; Kavale & Forness, 1987). In part because of the lack of empirical support for interventions based solely on a deficit model that focused on remediating the deficit, there has been a shift to examining variables beyond the usual cognitive ability and achievement realms in order to best meet the needs of individual learners, as well as to identify underlying strengths and weaknesses that inform intervention development. In conjunction with this paradigm shift, there is a need for research to shift from a focus on diagnostic categories to the identification of underlying characteristics (Weinberg & Glantz, 1999). In contrast to the body of literature that argued against the use of neuropsychologically based interventions, there is a growing body of evidence that provides empirical support for cognitive training, including case studies and randomized controlled trials (Eslinger & Oliveri, 2002).

Although the terms "cognitive retraining" and "cognitive rehabilitation" sometimes appear to be used interchangeably, cognitive rehabilitation is somewhat broader and encompasses multimodal intervention approaches for individuals with neurocognitive problems. Historically, cognitive retraining has been considered in the context of intense program development in head injury rehabilitation. In this context, both cognitive rehabilitation and cognitive retraining are associated with restoration of function through process-specific interventions. One definition of cognitive retraining focuses on hierarchically organized sets of exercises designed to restore, or at least improve, impaired components of cognitive processing (Diller, 1976 as cited in Ylvisaker & Szekeres, 1996). For the purposes of this chapter, cognitive retraining, or cognitive training, is used in the broadest sense (i.e., includes cognitive rehabilitation) to describe various intervention and treatment efforts that are intended to promote positive adaptive functioning in individuals with neurologically based cognitive deficits (Barrett & Gonzalez-Rothi, 2002). As related to school psychology, the objectives of cognitive approaches involve restoration or development of specific skills and abilities or compensatory training with the ultimate goal of optimizing adjustment and outcome (Eslinger & Oliveri, 2002).

Cognitive training programs have received the most attention in the context of rehabilitation for individuals who have sustained TBI (Mateer & Mapou, 1996; Park & Ingles, 2000; Sbordonne, 1986). The underlying rationale for the rehabilitation of neurologically based disorders such as TBI is the premise that behavior results from the action and interaction of neurons (Kolb, 1995) and the related presumption that this action and interaction can be altered (or bypassed) by changing the associated neurological processes (see Barrett & Gonzalez-Rothi, 2002, for additional details).

Many other disorders of interest to school psychologists are presumed to have a neurological basis, including Attention-Deficit/Hyperactivity Disorder (ADHD; Riccio, Hynd, Cohen, & Gonzalez, 1993) and learning disabilities (Ingalls & Goldstein, 1999). As such, it is not surprising that the use of cognitive interventions has been recommended for children with ADHD (e.g., Ervin, Bankert, & DuPaul, 1996; Van der Kroll, Oosterbaan, Weller, & Konig, 1998; Wilens et al., 1999; Young, 1999) and children with learning disabilities (Graham & Harris, 2003; Pressley et al., 1995). Given the nature of neurocognitive deficits and their relation to a wide variety of clinical conditions, many of the children who manifest these disorders are likely to experience significant problems in school. Depending on the nature of their difficulties, neurocognitive deficits often will extend to the home and other environments, affecting not only academic but everyday functioning as well. Cognitive approaches may focus on attention and vigilance, unilateral neglect, memory, language, problem-solving, or vocational skills; goals of training may include behavioral and cognitive domains.

Despite a growing interest in neuropsychology among school psychologists, relatively little has been written about related interventions (Marlowe, 2000). In fact, the research specific to cognitive retraining is done in the fields of pediatric neuropsychology, rehabilitation psychology, and cognitive psychology as opposed to school psychology. Although potentially beneficial to all children with underlying neurocognitive deficits, these methods are most often used in settings other than schools. The purpose of this chapter is to provide a bridge between the existing research in related fields and school psychology.

## APPROACHES TO COGNITIVE RETRAINING

Rehabilitation approaches generally either target underlying impairments as in deficit models or use intact processes or external means to address those functional areas affected (Glisky & Glisky, 2002). From a deficit approach, restoration and optimization approaches target the deficit or underlying impairment for remediation (see Table 31.1 on p. 704). For example, if memory deficits are the target, the intervention might include repetition and drill of the skill area. Repeated drill and practice to restore or develop an ability is not based on a theoretical premise. From a neuropsychological perspective, it is based on the assumption that repeated stimulation of neuronal connections through drill and practice may potentially result in establishing alternate neuronal pathways or regeneration of damaged structures or pathways. There is, however, insufficient evidence that this occurs (Glisky & Glisky, 2002). Further, the exclusive emphasis on the underlying impairment ignores those intact functions of the individual. Finally, as suggested by the aptitude of treatment interaction studies, there is no evidence that any progress made through drill and practice generalizes beyond the training situation.

A second approach that also focuses on the underlying impairment focuses on optimizing the remaining function in the area of the deficit. Although there is a continued goal of restoring or developing that functional ability to the extent feasible, there is more of a focus on refining how the functional capacities that remain can be used (S. W. Anderson, 2002). Instead of drill and practice, the emphasis is on strategy instruction and metacognitive training. These methods may be most appropriate for individuals with mild to moderate impairments who have sufficient intact abilities to master the strategies.

In contrast to deficit models, compensatory models focus not on the underlying impairment, but on the functional deficits that result from the impairment and how to compensate for the impairment to improve everyday living (Glisky & Glisky, 2002). Compensation approaches identify methods to bypass deficit skills through the use of intact functions or external aids or substitute methods of reaching the same goal (S. W. Anderson, 2002). Compensation approaches may include strategy instruction that incorporates intact functions. Approaches that use external aids may be better suited for individuals with severe impairment (i.e., less intact functions) but may require intensive training. These approaches include the use of electronic reminders or use of lists to decrease the memory demands of daily life. Although the framework provided by Glisky and Glisky was specific to memory, the same conceptualization applies across cognitive domains (see Table 31.1).

All too often, proponents of one approach to intervention do not consider the potential for additive effects of multiple methods in the intervention process. Freund and Baltes (1998) developed a model of selective optimization with compensation to address the gradual decline associated with aging. The novel component of this model is that it incorporated the restoration or development components of the deficit model with the use of external aids and environmental supports of the compensatory model. As noted earlier, many of the interventions discussed here can be applied to problems encountered in school settings and, in practice, work

**Table 31.1**

Approaches and Methods of Cognitive Retraining

| Approach | Goal | Method | Examples | Limits |
|---|---|---|---|---|
| Deficit models (target underlying impairment) | Restore/develop impaired area | Drill and practice | Computer-assisted training | Ignores intact functions; lack of generalization |
| | Optimize function | Metacognitive training | Self-instructional training strategy instruction | Useful for individuals with mild to moderate impairments; lack of generalization; programs exist for limited foci |
| Compensatory models (focus on functional deficits) | Solve everyday problems | External aids; environmental supports | Organizers, calendars | Extensive training may be required; may be appropriate for moderate to severe impairments |
| | Improve everyday life | Specific knowledge or skill | Domain-specific learning, errorless learning | Lack of generalization; useful only for most severe impairment and rote tasks |

best when initially coupled with behavioral methods more frequently used in school settings. General considerations in developing cognitive intervention programs are discussed next.

## General Considerations in Cognitive Retraining

No matter which approach is emphasized (deficit or compensation) in cognitive retraining activities, the ultimate aim is to enable individuals to achieve goals that may be impeded by cognitive impairment and to promote successful performance of real-world tasks, but not necessarily to improve "cognition" (Ylvisaker & Szerekes, 1996). Intervention activities are designed in a way that assists the individual in moving from a more dependent, externally monitored or supported state to a more independent, internally supported and self-regulated state. The selection of specific intervention strategies should be based on the individual's level of environmental dependency, the constellation of preserved and impaired functions, and the individual's level of awareness (Mateer, 1999).

Ylvisaker and Szerekes (1996) identified additional goals of cognitive approaches to intervention that should be considered when the intervention plan is developed for a given individual: (1) the restoration or development of cognitive processes or systems that were delayed or impaired by the injury or disorder; (2) acquisition of new knowledge that increasingly facilitates effective information processing; (3) increasing the strategic approaches of individuals and equipping them with strategic procedures that enable them to accomplish goals; (4) identification of ways in which academic, social, and vocational environments can be modified to promote success despite ongoing cognitive challenges; (5) identification of instructional strategies that are consistent with the child's profile of cognitive strengths and weaknesses that can be used with greatest effectiveness in school; and (6) heightening children's understanding of their needs so that they are increasingly active participants in the process of solving the many problems caused by their cognitive deficits. Regardless of whether the child has sustained a head injury, has a learning disability, or has some other neurological disorder, these goals would be appropriate and would improve the overall adjustment and functioning of the child.

To develop a cognitive retraining program that will improve the adaptive functioning of individuals where they live and work, the school psychologist needs to conduct a preintervention evaluation, including an evaluation of the individual's neurocognitive and behavioral profile and the real-world impact of their deficits. For children, evaluation needs to include assessment of the contexts in which the child currently resides, as well as the increasing demands of the academic context, present and future. Given the evaluation data on the child, various contexts, and current as well as anticipated future circumstances, specific goals are formulated. For each goal, an adequate approach to intervention is selected and implemented with data kept on performance (i.e., outcome-based measures) to monitor the ongoing effects of the treatment. Generalization strategies also should be developed and implemented from the onset of treatment. Finally, there should be an evaluation of the efficacy of the intervention and determination made about the impact of functioning in natural contexts (Mateer, 1999; Sohlberg & Mateer, 1989). This is not unlike the familiar process of developing an individualized educational plan; however, the goals and alternatives for intervention are expanded beyond the immediate academic or curricular demands.

Typically, the process of intervention involves the implementation of environmental manipulations, training in compensatory activities that allow the individual to function more effectively despite the impairment, and the application of activities designed to restore or improve underlying abilities. Environmental manipulation, behavioral contingency, and the use of external cues and prompts may be most useful in increasing the initiation of activities and in motivating the individual in the earlier stages of training. More internally focused strategies and self-monitoring approaches would become more effective as gains are realized and behavioral flexibility, initiative, and insight improve (Mateer, 1999). The major methods used in cognitive retraining are (1) metacognitive interventions, (2) strategy instruction, (3) computer-assisted training, (4) biofeedback, (5) use of external aids and environmental supports, and (6) domain-specific learning. Each of these are discussed further.

## METACOGNITIVE INTERVENTIONS

Metacognitive interventions involve many procedures that have as a goal the restoration or improvement of some underlying abilities or cognitive capacities; these likely would be considered "optimizing" interventions. Metacognition is considered to have both a static and a dynamic component (Parente & Herrmann, 1996). The static component is the individual's awareness of his or her cognitive processes and the appropriate procedures for improving performance; the dynamic component is the ability to exercise control of one's cognitions and to initiate appropriate actions (Sternberg, 1985). Therefore, metacognitive retraining involves not only facilitating individuals' awareness of their deficits, but also teaching them how to regulate their thoughts and actions. Metacognitive intervention procedures include but are not limited to self-instructional strategy training, strategy instruction, cognitive modeling, self-monitoring, and self-evaluation (Mateer, 1999; Mateer, Kerns, & Eso, 1996). Metacognitive intervention programs commonly involve teaching of systematic problem-solving processes as well as monitoring and regulating behavior via self-talk. These intervention strategies can incorporate behavioral contingencies (e.g., extrinsic rewards).

Ylvisaker, Szekeres, and Feeney (1998) described an ecological metacognitive approach to intervention. Even though their procedures are in the same vein as more traditional metacognitive training, Ylvisaker et al. emphasized ecological elements in the training process. For example, they incorporated everyday tasks as the context for exercising self-regulation as opposed to relying on decontextualized remedial training. Further, they enlisted the people in the child's environment to create a "culture" that facilitates development of the desired functional goal, in this case executive function. Ylvisaker et al. asserted that creating a culture in which the individual routinely seeks out opportunities to stimulate the targeted process (i.e., executive problem solving) is critically important to the development of the process. Typically, the goals of the ecological metacognitive interventions are to help children (1) identify what they are good at as well as what is difficult for them, (2) know that there are special things that can be done by them when they are faced with more difficult tasks, (3) make plans for accomplishing the task, (4) pay attention to how well they are doing, and (5) try a new approach if they are being unsuccessful. Modeling and coaching are used in the context of everyday routines and everyday conversational interactions, including classroom, therapeutic, and recreational activities, as well as in the context of daily living at home. All adults, and possibly older children, who regularly inter-act with the child can function as coaches. The implementation of the self-instruction training in multiple contexts with multiple interventionists, as well as the incorporation of everyday tasks, increases the likelihood of generalization.

Ylvisaker and DeBonis (2000) described a 5-step general intervention sequence in organizing everyday, routine-based interventions. The first step involves collab-oratively identifying what is working and what is not working for the individual in completing the everyday routine being targeted. Written surveys; interviews with the child, parents, and teacher; and group discussions can be used to iden-tify successful and unsuccessful routines (e.g., difficulty in completing homework or chores). Second, changes that are needed to be made by the individual, by oth-ers, or in the environment in order to change negative, unsuccessful routines into positive, successful routines are identified, and repertoires of positive behavior can be built. For example, a parent-child dyad may experiment with alternative plans (e.g., doing homework or chores before playing video games) to achieve their goals (e.g., completing homework or chores without conflict) and report on what worked and what didn't work. Third, parent-child-teacher triads may experiment with a plan (e.g., using an assignment sheet) to achieve the same goal and report on the success or lack of it. The role of the school psychologist in this process is to keep track of the successful and unsuccessful plans and to generate additional strategies that can be tried by the parent, the child, the teacher, or some combina-tion. Working with all critical people involved collaboratively and ensuring that these changes are motivating and reinforcing to all who are identified is impor-tant. Ylvisaker and DeBonis emphasized the importance of ensuring collaborative analysis of the difficulties and the potential intervention plans; they also cau-tioned that this step in the intervention process can be the most serious obstacle or challenge to the school psychologist.

The fourth step in the process extends the intervention to implementation of supports for intensive practice of positive routines and implementation of self-instructional procedures in real-world contexts. The school psychologist or inter-ventionist engages the individual in role-plays of positive routines of interaction and problem solving, provides direct feedback, and offers suggestions regarding supports that may be necessary to maintain the routines at home (e.g., posting re-minders, monitoring success using the routine). The final step involves systemat-ically withdrawing the support (i.e., fading out cues and prompts) as it becomes possible to do so. At the same time, the school psychologist or interventionist fa-cilitates discussions among the critical people involved (i.e., parent, teacher, child) about additional contexts or tasks for which the new routines or procedure might be useful.

## Self-Instructional Training

The foundation of self-instructional training lies in the early work of Vygotsky and Luria. Luria (1966 as cited in Sohlberg & Mateer, 2001) postulated that, in a young child, external speech serves to regulate behavior. With development, this external speech is eventually transformed into the adult regulative practice of in-ternal self-talk. He further hypothesized that the frontal lobes are integral to inner speech processes and that syndromes characterized by poor self-regulation result when there is damage to frontal systems. From a cognitive perspective, Vygotsky (1962) conceptualized that higher levels of cognition and self-regulation occur as a result of gradual internalization of verbal interaction between children and their caregivers and teachers.

The Vygotskian perspective and Luria's writings led cognitive and developmental psychologists to apply verbal self-instruction and self-regulation techniques to the remediation of planning and problem-solving deficits and impulsivity in children and adults. A classic example is a study with five young participants with poor impulse control reported by Meichenbaum and Goodman (1971). In this study, the experimenter modeled verbal self-instruction and error correction while completing tasks, followed by coaching the subjects to perform the verbal instruction elements that had been modeled. This was faded to a "whisper," and self-instruction was eventually performed covertly. Meichenbaum and Goodman reported that this self-instruction training resulted in improved performance on neuropsychological tests of planning and problem solving at a 1-month follow-up. Self-instructional strategies have been applied successfully in managing impulsivity, poor planning and organization, difficulty shifting tasks, and poor problem solving (Sohlberg & Mateer, 2001).

Reviewing several self-instructional programs, Sohlberg and Mateer (2001) summarized a series of overriding steps or components of self-instructional training. The first step is to identify the tasks or problems where impairments interfere, such as specific schoolwork (e.g., reading comprehension), specific vocational tasks, homework management, and home management tasks. Selecting activities that will improve the individual's daily functioning is important, even if training effects are too specific or do not generalize beyond the training tasks. Once the problem area is identified, the nature of the dysfunction or impairment should be identified. Examples may include impulsivity, perseverative responding, lack of planning, difficulty in initiation, poor problem solving, and lack of error detection. The third step involves designing a self-instructional procedure or choosing a metacognitive strategy that will assist with the issue. For example, if there is a need for improvement in error recognition and correction, a self-monitoring training program can be considered. In the next step, the school psychologist or interventionist models implementing the procedure or strategy. Each element in the self-instructional procedure is modeled and the child then practices completing the task while stating the elements of the self-instructional process aloud (i.e., overt verbalization). In a Goal Management Training described by Levine and colleagues (2000), individuals were trained to consider deliberately each of the six stages (i.e., STOP, DEFINE main task, LIST steps, LEARN steps, EXECUTE tasks, and CHECK) while completing multistep tasks.

When appropriate, cue cards can be used to prompt the child to use the self-instructional strategy. Once the child becomes more independent in performing self-instructional procedures, the individual is assisted with the goal of performing the tasks on his or her own while whispering the self-instruction. The individual is provided multiple opportunities to practice the implementation of the self-instruction process. Gradually, the school psychologist or interventionist fades the whispering to inner speech (i.e., covert verbalization). The individual is helped to keep a log of times when he or she uses the self-instruction, as well as those incidences when the individual realizes that the self-instruction might have been useful if he or she had remembered to implement it. Finally, the school psychologist or interventionist considers the generalizability of the self-instructional procedures to other tasks. If it is determined that the mastered procedure is generalizable, the individual is further helped to begin using the same procedures with other types of tasks or in other settings.

Over the past 20 years, self-instructional training has been successfully applied to the remediation of various cognitive impairments. This approach has been widely espoused by many researchers and clinicians in cognitive rehabilitation to address executive function impairments in individuals with TBI (e.g., Alderman, Fry, & Youngson, 1995; Cicerone & Wood, 1986; Duke, Weathers, Caldwell, & Novack, 1992; Levine et al., 2000; Sohlberg, Mateer, & Stuss, 1993). Self-instructional techniques also have been successfully employed in the remediation of attention deficits (Webster & Scott, 1983), verbal memory problems (Lawson & Rice, 1989), and motor impersistence (Stuss, Delgado, & Guzman, 1987).

## Strategy Instruction

Strategy instruction is not dissimilar from self-instructional or other metacognitive procedures. It is another group of interventions that seeks to optimize functioning by reliance on intact functions (Glisky & Glisky, 2002). Individuals with and without impairments use strategies every day. For example, children frequently learn a mnemonic to remember the lines and spaces of music (i.e., Every Good Boy Does Fine, FACE) or to ensure that all parts of the quadratic expression were accounted for (i.e., FOIL). Most commonly applied to memory and the use of mnemonic strategies, strategy instruction is not limited to memory, behavioral regulation, or attentional problems. Strategies can also be applied to multiple instructional areas and problem solving (Pressley et al., 1995). Strategy instruction and strategy use rely on individuals' understanding of the way they learn, remember, and process information (i.e., metacognition). Pressley and colleagues asserted that good information processing includes (1) the use of efficient processes to accomplish tasks, (2) knowledge of strategies that facilitate those processes, (3) automatic and integrated use of multiple strategies for complex tasks, (4) general knowledge, (5) motivational beliefs that foster learning and thinking, and (6) reflective and attentive thinking. Through strategy instruction and use, students can learn to manage and monitor their own cognitive processes, including their ability to select information for further attention and to encode, rehearse, and retrieve appropriate information through internal and external connections and associations (Mayer, 1988).

As with self-instructional training, teacher (or parent) explanations and modeling are part of the process (Pressley et al., 1995). At the same time, however, the child is taught when and where to use the strategies, the positive gains from strategy use in general are discussed with the child, motivational beliefs about learning are addressed, and the child's ability to use a given strategy is demonstrated. The number of strategies taught at a given time to a given child should be limited; these can be gradually increased once the initial strategies have become more automatic. To increase the likelihood of autonomous use, automaticity of use, and appropriate use, it is recommended that initial strategy instruction be intense, explicit, and extensive. Students also are taught to engage in self-monitoring and self-evaluation of strategy use so that they are self-reinforcing. Pressley and colleagues lamented the fact that curricula did not incorporate explicit strategy instruction for all students. Lenski and Niersheimer (2002) also discussed the importance of strategy instruction, in addition to the more directed instruction of curricular material, pointing out that the most proficient readers and writers use multiple strategies and are flexible in their ability to use strategies.

Evaluation of the effectiveness of strategy instruction is complicated by the vast number of potential strategies that have been developed as well as the lack of published research on strategy instruction effectiveness. For elementary school students (with and without disabilities), strategy instruction has been studied in areas of mnemonics, written expression, and mathematics (Wong, Harris, Graham, & Butler, 2003). Some of the studies use strategies based on specific theoretical models (e.g., Naglieri & Johnson, 2000), and others do not. One study examined the use of a metacognitive strategy as a supplement to the traditional approach for teaching math skills to 3rd-graders (Desoete, Roeyers, & De Clerca, 2003). The children were randomly assigned to one of five conditions. At follow-up, the children in the metacognitive program demonstrated better performance than the children in any of the other four conditions (Desoete et al., 2003).

In another study with students in second grade with ($n = 42$) and without ($n = 42$) learning disabilities, Tournaki (2003) compared outcomes across conditions of control (i.e., regular classroom instruction), additional strategy instruction, and additional drill and practice. Results indicated that students with learning disabilities made the most progress (i.e., had the most positive outcome) from the addition of the strategy instruction. For students without learning disabilities, however, the addition of either the strategy instruction or the drill and practice netted the same improvement over the control condition. Other studies have yielded similarly positive results in the area of mathematics (e.g., Owen & Fuchs, 2002).

In the area of written expression, Troia and Graham (2002) reported on the outcomes for 4th- and 5th-grade students taught a three-step strategy (goal setting, brainstorming, organizing) for composition as compared to a control group. The group that received the threefold strategy training was found to engage in more preplanning time and to produce qualitatively better stories. These differences were maintained over time (1-month follow-up); however, there was no generalization of strategy use when the type of writing task changed. A meta-analysis of self-regulated strategy development (SRSD) in written expression for students with and without learning disabilities (Graham & Harris, 2003) yielded positive results as well. Using the SRSD strategy instruction model, the authors found large, positive effects on quality, structure, and length of written product with generalization evident. Studies related to strategy instruction and computer skills also have been positive (McInerney, McInerney, & Marsh, 1997).

## Computer-Assisted Cognitive Retraining

In the 1970s, video games were first used as part of rehabilitation programs for individuals with TBI (B. Lynch, 2002). With advances in computer technology, various rehabilitation therapists developed software for use in cognitive retraining. Although predominantly studied following TBI, computer-assisted cognitive rehabilitation has been used with adults with other disorders, including stroke, Alzheimer's disease, and anoxia (e.g., Gouvier et al., 1997; Kado, Ouellette, & Summers, 2002). These programs focus on deficits in "thinking, memory, and information processing" (B. Lynch, 2002, p. 446). The availability of educational software, both commercially produced and clinician produced, has increased dramatically in the past 30 years. Many of the commercially available programs (e.g., the Carmen San Diego series) are very popular and entertaining (B. Lynch, 2002). In contrast, software designed specifically for rehabilitation purposes may not have the extensive graphics and sound effects and may target only a narrow band of functional skills. Although no published research studies were found on the myriad commercially initiated software programs, reviews have been completed on some of the rehabilitation-specific programs (e.g., Carney et al., 1999; Cicerone, Dahlberg, & Kalmar, 2000).

The number and variety of software and microcomputer programs designed to remediate attention deficits, for example, has increased (Burda, Starkey, & Dominguez, 1991; Gianutsos, 1992; Larose, Gagnon, Ferland, & Pepin, 1989; Podd & Seelig, 1992). Some of the methods reported in the literature to address deficits in attention include the Attention Training System (Gordon Systems, Inc., 1987; Rapport & Gordon, 1987), the Captain's Log (Sanford & Browne, 1988), neurXercise (Podd, Mills, & Seelig, 1987; Podd & Seelig, 1989), Open Focus Attention Training (Fehmi, 1987), Attention Training (Wells, 1990), Attention Process Training (Sohlberg & Mateer, 1989), Pay Attention (Thomson, Seidenstrang, Kerns, Sohlberg, & Mateer, 1994), THINKable (Psychological Corporation, 1991), and Orientation Remedial Module (Ben-Yishay, Diller, & Rattok, 1978; Ben-Yishay et al., 1980). These programs are intended to remediate attention problems or to optimize attention monitoring through repeated drill and practice, provision of prompts, and incorporation of immediate and consistent feedback.

Although software programs for rehabilitation initially focused on deficit areas and remediation of a specific aptitude (e.g., visual memory), the current trend is a focus on more functional skills such as math and driving (B. Lynch, 2002). The range of task types and target skills is extensive and can include action games requiring strategy and/or problem-solving skills, simulation of a specific skill (e.g., driving), and more academically oriented tasks of reading, math, finance, history, and more (W. Lynch, 1992, 1998). As noted by W. Lynch (1992), the same considerations and evaluation of software need to be conducted as for any other method used in psychological practice. Software should be subjected to the same type of clinical trials and evaluation as any other type of intervention prior to the software producer's being able to make claims regarding the efficacy of the product.

BIOFEEDBACK

Based on the assumption that attentional deficits result from dysfunction of the central nervous system (CNS), the use of neurofeedback or biofeedback with electroencephalography (EEG) training to address attentional deficits has been studied in children with ADHD as well as for attentional problems associated with other disorders. The use of EEG biofeedback is derived from the hypothesis that children with ADHD exhibit behaviors suggestive of a low state of CNS arousal (Satterfield & Dawson, 1971; Satterfield, Lesser, Saul, & Cantwell, 1973). The general focus of the training is to decrease the proportion of theta and to increase both the duration and amplitude of beta (Lubar, 1991), thus, raising the level of arousal. From case studies, and using direct observations as outcome measures, it has been asserted that EEG biofeedback training can result in changes in attention (see Lubar, 1991, for a review). Duffy (2000) argued that in the absence of any negative findings in the literature, EEG biofeedback should have a major role in the treatment of many disorders. A number of studies using EEG biofeedback have been conducted (e.g., Alhambra, Fowler, & Alhambra, 1995; J. Anderson, 1997, 1998; Boyd & Campbell, 1998; Rasey, Lubar, McIntyre, Zoffuto, & Abbott, 1996; Rossiter, 1998; Rossiter & LaVaque, 1995; Thompson & Thompson, 1998). The majority of the studies with biofeedback, however, are case studies; there are no studies that incorporate clinical trials or control groups. Thus, the state of the literature suggests a need for more empirical documentation (e.g., randomized clinical trials) of the effectiveness of EEG biofeedback training as a treatment component (French & Riccio, 2005).

## External Aids and Environmental Supports

For some individuals, the methods described earlier may not prove to be sufficient, or the results, though positive, may not provide immediate or sufficient relief. In either case, the group of approaches that target external supports and aids, or cues, may be appropriate. External aids can enable individuals to meet the everyday demands that facilitate their ability to function in important contexts, thereby improving their overall outcome (Glisky & Glisky, 2002). For example, individuals with organizational or memory problems may be able to compensate for their problems if they can be trained to use a PDA or other electronic organizer effectively. Other devices (e.g., pagers, calendars, diaries) also can be incorporated into the treatment options to increase the ability of the child to function independently. Similarly, an electronic dictionary was found useful in the treatment of dysgraphia (Fluharty, 1993). As pointed out by Glisky and Glisky, however, the individual must be trained to use the aids successfully, and initially their use should be reinforced and monitored. For example, use of a PDA to keep track of assignments, appointments, and so on can only be effective if the person remembers to enter those items, remembers to check the PDA, or remembers where he or she left the PDA. With advances in technology, the availability of external aids continues to increase, and these aids serve a variety of functions.

Environmental supports and aids can also include labels, pictograms of what needs to be accomplished or one's schedule (e.g., as used with children with Autism), and written instructions. For individuals with mild to moderate impairment, environmental supports such as these may be needed only at the onset of the treatment program and gradually can be faded, as with other types of cues or prompts. For those individuals with moderate to severe impairment, the external aid or environmental cues may continue to be needed over time. Because of the very specific nature of the external aids and the environmental supports, there is no generalization across settings; at the same time, if external aids or supports work in one setting, they can be incorporated into other settings to maximize functioning.

## Domain-Specific Learning

Domain-specific learning refers to the development of techniques that tap into memory and learning abilities that might be intact even in those individuals with more severe impairments (Glisky & Glisky, 2002). These techniques rely on the fact that even among individuals with severe memory loss, implicit memory often is preserved. With the use of a faded cuing technique or method of vanishing cues, Glisky, Schacter, and Tulving (1986) sought to capitalize on intact memory functions. With this technique, the individual is initially provided with extensive cuing for correct responding to facilitate the learning of domain-specific routines, including computer operations (Glisky & Schacter, 1989). The extent to which the cues are provided is gradually decreased, with the underlying assumption that the individual's implicit memory of the previously provided cues will continue to support the performance of the task.

Related to the vanishing cues approach, errorless learning is another method for domain-specific learning. With this technique, the individual is guided through task completion (e.g., use of a PDA) multiple times. In fact, it has been suggested that the success of the vanishing cue approach is due to the lack of errors made in the initial training in that errors were prevented as a result of the multiple cues provided (Baddeley & Wilson, 1994). Errorless learning has been used to teach a number of specific skills to adults with memory impairments; however, additional research specific to both the vanishing cues and errorless learning is needed. The specificity of these approaches also limits the tasks for which they are appropriate.

## DEVELOPMENTAL CONSIDERATIONS

When impairments or disabilities are viewed in the context of cognitive deficits, it seems logical to make use of interventions that are devised to improve the underlying cognitive process (Mateer et al., 1996). Many of the problems encountered by learners in schools relate to cognitive or executive functions (i.e., planning, problem solving); it has been suggested that prevention and intervention efforts should include strengthening of executive functions for some learners (e.g., Giancola & Parker, 2001). Dowsett and Livesey (2000) exposed 3- to 5-year-olds to tasks requiring executive function; repeated exposure was found to facilitate the development of strategies/rule structures that are associated with inhibitory control. Tasks required the use of response control, representational flexibility, working memory, selective attention, and proficiency in self-correction. Results suggest that there is an interactive effect between neural development and task demands in the early years. For example, the effects of formal schooling on development of cognition and executive function were found to be both task- and age-dependent (McCrea, Mueller, & Parrila, 1999). This finding suggests that intervention for executive function deficits can have positive results; however, the design of the intervention needs to take developmental factors into consideration. As such, cognitive mechanisms such as working memory capacity, inhibition, and strategic problem solving may underlie age-related improvements in a broad range of intellectual and social behaviors (Welsh, 2002). Also, it has been suggested that efficient processing of information may be dependent on the child's ability to execute cognitive operations automatically (Bogler, 1981). Thus, remediation efforts must reestablish and progressively build on automaticity of rudimentary functions. Further, the cognitive demands of the intervention must match the developmental trajectory of the child.

## CONCLUSION

This chapter reviewed major approaches to cognitive retraining with an emphasis on their relevance to school neuropsychology. Although the field of cognitive rehabilitation or cognitive retraining made constant progress in the past decade, its application to learners in school is in its infancy. Since the 1990 IDEA designated

TBI as a new disability category for students requiring special education, the public schools have been forced to assume much of the responsibility for TBI children's rehabilitation and reintegration into schools. In addition, given that more children with neurological disorders (TBI and others) are attending school and often face a great many challenges and obstacles in learning and adjustment in school, school psychologists need to be equipped with effective tools to address the needs and challenges of this population. School psychologists need to consider the constructs of neurocognitive deficits and cognitive retraining in an ecological framework—it is only one piece in the conceptualization and treatment of the behaviors that lead to referral. Cognitive retraining approaches described in this chapter have the potential to be an effective component to rehabilitation of children with neurocognitive problems.

Given multiple approaches, one important question that arises relates to the empirical support available for the various approaches. Regardless of the theoretical perspective underlying the intervention, or whether the behavioral or cognitive intervention is used in conjunction with or in place of medication, empirical evaluation of treatment outcomes is imperative. Across methods, there is a need for increased research in the efficacy of the various programs available. At the present time, critical evaluation of cognitive retraining or training programs is limited to general reviews and discussions of methodological problems specific to a given population (e.g., see McCaffrey & Gansler, 1992, for strategies with TBI; Suslow, Schonauer, & Arolt, 2001, for strategies with Schizophrenia).

Park and Ingles (2000) asserted that their meta-analysis of both specific functional training and more general attentional training programs used with adults with TBI or stroke was the first such review. They noted that the majority of studies that included a control group were found to have small effect sizes (−.01 to .41; mean = .15). Suslow and colleagues (2001) concurred with regard to small effect sizes and also pointed to the low power and contradictory results of available studies. More extensive research is needed to determine the extent of generalizability, maintenance, and efficacy of the varying cognitive approaches for specific populations and neurocognitive profiles. In particular, questions have been raised with regard to the extent of transfer of training and generalization of the skills taught through cognitive retraining (B. Lynch, 2002).

Research efforts should include identification of those characteristics that help to predict the success of a specific treatment for a specific individual (i.e., based on cognitive characteristics, behavioral variables, psychopathology, demographic variables, etiology, and severity) as well as the deficits (functional and attentional) that are to be targeted. The methods of intervention need to be at the appropriate developmental level of the individual and in accord with the individual's values (i.e., culture) and belief system, as well as available without undue hardship. At the same, there is a need to look at the extent of generalization and transfer of training of the method over the long term as well as the short term.

To maximize the usefulness of the data generated and the generalizability of findings across studies, it is important that researchers employ similar (e.g., standardized) treatment protocols and to maintain at least some core, consistent outcome measures across studies. Treatment programs and outcomes measures may need to be modified for use with children (Mateer et al., 1996); these modifications need to be identified and standardized to ensure treatment integrity and comparability of results across studies. It is important that studies be conducted that provide sufficient information to attest to treatment integrity and provide for the possibility of study replication by other investigators as well as clinicians. Most important, there is a need for studies of interventions as applied to a school setting, using academic-related tasks to maximize generalization from training across settings. School psychologists need to take a more active role in bridging the gap between school-based and rehabilitation-based interventions.

In the school setting, the focus may be on single case studies or series; for case studies or series, it is important that the school psychologist provide sufficient objective and reliable data to apply current single-subject design methodologies (see Franklin, Allison, & Gorman, 1996; Kratochwill & Levin, 1992; Reynolds & Willson, 1985). Finally, often, studies that yield no significant differences or negative results are not published; results of these studies provide information that is critical in the development and evaluation of interventions (Kratochwill, Stoiber, & Gutkin, 2000).

## REFERENCES

Alderman, N., Fry, R. K., & Youngson, H. A. (1995). Improvement of self-monitoring skills, reduction of behavior disturbance and the dysexecutive syndrome: Comparison of response cost and a new program of self-monitoring training. *Neuropsychological Rehabilitation, 5,* 193–221.

Alhambra, M. A., Fowler, T. P., & Alhambra, A. A. (1995). EEG biofeedback: A new treatment option for ADD/ADHD. *Journal of Neurotherapy, 1,* 39–43. Retrieved September 20, 2000, from http://www.snr-njt.org/JournalNT/JNT(1-2)3.html.

Anderson, J. (1997). Program evaluation of EEG neurofeedback at New Visions School: 1996–1997. Retrieved September 20, 2000, from http://www.eegspectrum.com/school /anders97.html.

Anderson, J. (1998). Program evaluation EEG neurofeedback at New Visions School: 1997–1998. Retrieved September 20, 2000, from http://www.eegspectrum.com/school /anders98.htm.

Anderson, S. W. (2002). Visuospatial impairments. In P. J. Eslinger (Ed.), *Neuropsychological interventions: Clinical research and practice* (pp. 163–181). New York: Guilford Press.

Baddeley, A. D., & Wilson, B. A. (1994). When implicit learning fails: Amnesia and the problem of error elimination. *Neuropsychologia, 32,* 53–68.

Barrett, A. M., & Gonzalez-Rothi, L. J. (2002). Theoretical bases for neuropsychological interventions. In P. J. Eslinger (Ed.), *Neuropsychological interventions: Clinical research and practice* (pp. 16–37). New York: Guilford Press.

Ben-Yishay, Y., Diller, L., & Rattock, J. (1978). A modular approach to optimizing orientation, psychomotor alertness, and purposive behavior in severe head trauma patients. In *Working approaches to cognitive deficits in brain damage* (Rehabilitation Monograph No. 59). New York: New York University Medical Center, Institute of Rehabilitation Medicine.

Ben-Yishay, Y., Rattok, J., Ross, B., Lakin, P., Cohen, J., & Diller, L. (1980). A remedial module for the systematic amelioration of basic attentional disturbances in head trauma patients. In *Working approaches to cognitive deficits in brain damage* (Rehabilitation Monograph No. 61). New York: New York University Medical Center, Institute of Rehabilitation Medicine.

Bogler, J. P. (1981). Cognitive retraining: A developmental approach. *Clinical Neuropsychology, 4,* 66–70.

Boyd, W. D., & Campbell, S. E. (1998). EEG biofeedback in the schools: The use of EEG biofeedback to treat ADHD in a school setting. *Journal of Neurotherapy, 2*, 65–71.

Burda, P. C., Starkey, T. W., & Dominguez, F. (1991). Computer administered treatment of psychiatric inpatients. *Computers in Human Behavior, 7*, 1–5.

Carney, N., Chestnut, R. M., Maynard, H., Mann, N. C., Patterson, P., & Helfand, M. (1999). Effect of cognitive rehabilitation on outcomes for persons with traumatic brain injury: A systematic review. *Journal of Head Trauma Rehabilitation, 14*, 277–307.

Cicerone, K. D., Dahlberg, C., & Kalmar, K. (2000). Evidence-based cognitive rehabilitation on outcomes for persons with traumatic brain injury: A systematic review. *Journal of Head Trauma Rehabilitation, 81*, 1596–1615.

Cicerone, K. D., & Wood, J. C. (1986). Remediation of executive function deficits after traumatic brain injury. *Neurorehabilitation, 2*, 73–83.

DeBonis, D. A., Ylvisaker, M., & Kundert, D. K. (2000). The relationship between ADHD theory and practice: A preliminary investigation. *Journal of Attention Disorders, 4*(3), 161–173.

Desoete, A., Roeyers, H., & DeClerca, A. (2003). Can offline metacognition enhance mathematical problem-solving? *Journal of Educational Psychology, 95*, 188–200.

Diller, L. (1976). A model for cognitive retraining in rehabilitation. *Clinical Psychology, 29*, 13–15.

Dowsett, S. M., & Livesey, D. J. (2000). The development of inhibitory control in preschool children: Effects of "executive skills" training. *Developmental Psychobiology, 36*, 161–174.

Duffy, F. H. (2000). The state of EEG biofeedback therapy (EEG operant conditioning) in 2000: An editor's opinion. *Clinical Electroencephalography, 31*, V-VIII.

Duke, L. W., Weathers, S. L., Caldwell, S. G., & Novack, T. A. (1992). Cognitive rehabilitation after head trauma. In C. J. Long & L. K. Ross (Eds.), *Handbook of head trauma* (pp. 165–190). New York: Plenum Press.

Ervin, R. A., Bankert, C. L., & DuPaul, G. J. (1996). Treatment of attention deficit/hyperactivity disorder. In M. A. Reinecke, F. M. Dattilio, & A. Freeman (Eds.), *Cognitive therapy with children and adolescents: A casebook for clinical practice* (pp. 38–61). New York: Guilford Press.

Eslinger, P. J., & Oliveri, M. V. (2002). Approaching interventions clinically and scientifically. In P. J. Eslinger (Ed.), *Neuropsychological interventions: Clinical research and practice* (pp. 3–15). New York: Guilford Press.

Fehmi, L. (1987). Biofeedback assisted attention training: Open focus workshop. *Psychotherapy in Private Practice, 5*, 47–49.

Fluharty, G. (1993). Use of an electronic dictionary to compensate for surface dysgraphia. *Journal of Cognitive Rehabilitation, 11*, 28–30.

Franklin, R. D., Allison, D. B., & Gorman, B. S. (1996). *Design and analysis of single-case research.* Hillsdale, NJ: Erlbaum.

French, C. L., & Riccio, C. A. (2005). The status of empirical support for treatments of attention deficits. *Clinical Neuropsychologist, 18*, 528–558.

Freund, A. M., & Baltes, P. B. (1998). Selection, optimization, and compensation as strategies of life management: Correlations with subjective indicators of successful aging. *Psychology and Aging, 13*, 531–543.

Giancola, P. R., & Parker, A. M. (2001). A six-year prospective study of pathways toward drug use in adolescent boys with and without a family history of substance use disorder. *Journal of Studies on Alcohol, 62*, 166–178.

Gianutsos, R. (1992). The computer in cognitive rehabilitation: It's not just a tool anymore. *Journal of Head Trauma Rehabilitation, 7*, 26–35.

Glisky, E. L., & Glisky, M. L. (2002). Learning and memory impairments. In P. J. Eslinger (Ed.), *Neuropsychological interventions: Clinical research and practice* (pp. 137–162). New York: Guilford Press.

Glisky, E. L., & Schacter, D. L. (1989). Extending the limits of complex learning in organic amnesia: Computer training in a vocational domain. *Neuropsychologia, 27*, 107–120.

Glisky, E. L., Schacter, D. L., & Tulving, E. (1986). Learning and retention of compluter related vocabulary in memory-impaired patients: Method of vanishing cues. *Journal of Clinical and Experimental Neuropsychology, 8*, 292–312.

Gordon Systems, Inc. (1987). *Attention training system.* DeWitt, NY: Author.

Gouvier, W. D., Ryan, L. M., O'Jile, J. R., Parks-Levy, J., Webster, J. S., & Blanton, P. D. (1997). Cognitive retraining with brain-damaged patients. In A. M. Horton, Jr., D. Wedding, & J. Webster (Eds.), *The neuropsychology handbook: Vol. 2. Treatment issues and special populations* (2nd ed., pp. 3–46). New York: Springer.

Graham, S., & Harris, K. R. (2003). Students with learning disabilities and the process of writing: A meta-analysis of SRSD studies. In H. L. Swanson, K. R. Harris, & S. Graham (Eds.), *Handbook of learning disabilities* (pp. 323–344). New York: Guilford Press.

Ingalls, S., & Goldstein, S. (1999). Learning disabilities. In S. Goldstein & C. Reynolds (Eds.), *Handbook of neurodevelopmental and genetic disorders in children* (pp. 101–153). New York: Guilford Press.

Kado, R. F., Ouellette, T., & Summers, T. (2002). Computer-assisted cognitive rehabilitation treatment and outcomes. *Journal of Cognitive Rehabilitation, 20*, 20–27.

Kavale, K. A. (1990). Effectiveness of special education. In T. B. Gutkin & C. R. Reynolds (Eds.), *The handbook of school psychology* (2nd ed., pp. 868–898). New York: Wiley.

Kavale, K. A., & Forness, S. R. (1987). A matter of substance over style: A quantitative synthesis assessing the efficacy of modality testing and teaching. *Exceptional Children, 54*, 228–239.

Kolb, B. (1995). *Brain plasticity and behavior.* Hillsdale, NJ: Erlbaum.

Kratochwill, T. R., & Levin, J. R. (1992). *Single-case research design and analysis: New directions for psychology and education.* Hillsdale, NJ: Erlbaum.

Kratochwill, T. R., Stoiber, K. C., & Gutkin, T. B. (2000). Empirically supported interventions in school psychology: The role of negative results in outcome research. *Psychology in the Schools, 37*, 399–413.

Larose, S., Gagnon, S., Ferland, C., & Pepin, M. (1989). Psychology of computers: XIV. Cognitive rehabilitation through computer games. *Perceptual and Motor Skills, 69*, 851–858.

Lawson, M. J., & Rice, D. N. (1989). Effects of training in use of executive strategies on a verbal memory problem resulting from closed head injury. *Journal of Clinical and Experimental Neuropsychology, 6*, 842–854.

Lenski, S. D., & Nierstheimer, S. L. (2002). Strategy instruction from a sociocognitive perspective. *Reading Psychology, 23*, 127–143.

Levine, B., Robertson, I. H., Clare, L., Carter, G., Hong, J., Wilson, B. A., et al. (2000). Rehabilitation of executive functioning: An experimental-clinical validation of goal management training. *Journal of International Neuropsychological Society, 6*, 299–312.

Lubar, J. F. (1991). Discourse on the development of EEG diagnostics and biofeedback for attention deficit hyperactivity disorders. *Biofeedback and Self-Regulation, 16*, 201–225.

Luria, A. R. (1966). *Higher cortical functions in man.* New York: Basic Books.

Lynch, B. (2002). Historical review of computer-assisted cognitive retraining. *Journal of Head Trauma Rehabilitation, 17*, 446–457.

Lynch, W. (1998). Software update 1998: Commercial programs useful in cognitive retraining. *Journal of Head Trauma Rehabilitation, 13*, 91–94.

Lynch, W. (1992). Ecological validity of cognitive rehabilitation software. *Journal of Head Trauma Rehabilitation, 7,* 36–45.

Marlowe, W. B. (2000). An intervention for children with disorders of executive functions. *Developmental Neuropsychology, 18*(3), 445–454.

Mateer, C. A. (1999). The rehabilitation of executive disorders. In D. T. Stuss, G. Winocur, & I. H. Robertson (Eds.), *Cognitive rehabilitation* (pp. 314–322). Cambridge, England: Cambridge University Press.

Mateer, C. A., Kerns, K. A., & Eso, K. L. (1996). Management of attention and memory disorders following traumatic brain injury. *Journal of Learning Disabilities, 29,* 618–632.

Mateer, C. A., & Mapou, R. L. (1996). Understanding, evaluation, and managing attention disorders following traumatic brain injury. *Journal of Head Trauma Rehabilitation, 11,* 1–16.

Mayer, R. E. (1988). Learning strategies: An overview. In C. E. Weinstein, E. T. Goetz, & P. A. Alexander (Eds.), *Learning and study strategies: Issues in assessment, instruction, and evaluation* (pp. 11–24). New York: Academic Press.

McCaffrey, R. J., & Gansler, D. A. (1992). The efficacy of attention-remediation programs for traumatically brain-injured survivors. In C. J. Long & L. K. Ross (Eds.), *Handbook of head trauma: Acute care to recovery* (pp. 203–217). New York: Plenum Press.

McCrea, S. M., Mueller, J. H., & Parrila, R. K. (1999). Quantitative analyses of schooling effects on executive function in young children. *Child Neuropsychology, 5,* 242–250.

McInerney, V., McInerney, D. M., & Marsh, H. W. (1997). Effects of metacognitive strategy training within a cooperative group learning context on computer achievement and anxiety: An aptitude-treatment interaction study. *Journal of Educational Psychology, 89,* 686–695.

Meichenbaum, D. H., & Goodman, J. (1971). Training impulsive children to talk to themselves: A means of developing self-control. *Journal of Abnormal Psychology, 77,* 115–126.

Naglieri, J. A., & Johnson, D. (2000). Effectiveness of a cognitive strategy intervention in improving arithmetic computation based on the PASS theory. *Journal of Learning Disabilities, 33,* 591–597.

Owen, R. L., & Fuchs, L. S. (2002). Mathematical problem-solving strategy instruction for third-grade students with learning disabilities. *Remedial and Special Education, 23,* 268–278.

Parente, R., & Herrmann, D. (1996). *Retraining cognition: Techniques and applications.* Gaithersburg, MD: Aspen.

Park, N. W., & Ingles, J. L. (2000). Effectiveness of attention training after an acquired-brain injury: A meta-analysis of rehabilitation studies. *Brain Cognition, 44,* 5–9.

Park, N. W., & Ingles, J. L. (2001). Effectiveness of attention rehabilitation after an acquired brain injury: A meta-analysis. *Neuropsychology, 15,* 199–210.

Podd, M. H., Mills, M. W., & Seelig, D. P. (1987). *NeurXercise software for cognitive remediation* (Apple II platform). Fort Washington, MD: Authors.

Podd, M. H., & Seelig, D. P. (1989). *NeurXercise software for cognitive remediation.* Fort Washington, MD: Authors.

Podd, M. H., & Seelig, D. P. (1992). Computer-assisted cognitive remediation of attention disorders following mild closed head injuries. In C. J. Long & L. K. Ross (Eds.), *Handbook of head trauma: Acute care to recovery* (pp. 231–244). New York: Plenum Press.

Pressley, M., Woloshyn, V., Burkell, J., Cariglia-Bull, T., Lysynchuk, L., McGoldrick, J. A., et al. (1995). *Cognitive strategy instruction that really improves children's academic performance.* Cambridge, MA: Brookline Books.

Psychological Corporation. (1991). *THINKable rehabilitation system* [computer program]. San Antonio, TX: Author.

Rasey, H. W., Lubar, J. F., McIntyre, A., Zoffuto, A. C., & Abbott, P. L. (1996). EEG biofeedback for the enhancement of attention processing in normal college students. *Journal of Neurotherapy, 1,* 15–21.

Rapport, M. D., & Gordon, M. (1987). *The attention training system (ATS).* DeWitt, NY: Gordon Systems.

Reynolds, C. R., & Willson, V. (1985). *Methodological and statistical advances in the study of individual differences.* New York: Plenum Press.

Riccio, C. A., Hynd, G. W., Cohen, M. J., & Gonzalez, J. J. (1993). Neurological basis of attention deficit hyperactivity disorder. *Exceptional Children, 60,* 118–224.

Rossiter, T. R. (1998). Patient directed neurofeedback for AD/HD. *Journal of Neurotherapy, 2,* 54–63.

Rossiter, T. R., & La Vaque, T. J. (1995). A comparison of EEG biofeedback and psychostimulants in treating attention deficit/hyperactivity disorders. *Journal of Neurotherapy, 1,* 48–59.

Sanford, J. A., & Browne, R. J. (1988). *Captain's Log* [Computer program]. Richmond, VA: BrainTrain.

Satterfield, J. H., & Dawson, M. E. (1971). Electrodermal correlates of hyperactivity in children. *Psychophysiology, 8,* 191.

Satterfield, J. H., Lesser, L. I., Saul, R. E., & Cantwell, D. P. (1973). Response to stimulant drug treatment in hyperactive children: Prediction from E.E.G. & neurological findings. *Journal of Autism and Childhood Schizophrenia, 3,* 36–48.

Sbordonne, R. (1986). Does computer assisted cognitive rehabilitation work? A case study. *Psychotherapy in Private Practice, 4*(4), 51–61.

Sohlberg, M. M., & Mateer, C. A. (2001). Management of dysexecutive symptoms. In M. M. Sohlberg & C. A. Mateer (Eds.), *Cognitive rehabilitation: An integrative neuropsychological approach* (pp. 230–268). New York: Guilford Press.

Sohlberg, M. M., & Mateer, C. A. (1989). *Introduction to cognitive rehabilitation.* New York: Guilford Press.

Sohlberg, M. M., Mateer, C. A., & Stuss, D. T. (1993). Contemporary approaches to the management of executive control dysfunction. *Journal of Head Trauma Rehabilitation, 8*(1), 45–58.

Sternberg, R. J. (1985). *Beyond IQ: A triarchic theory of intelligence.* New York: Cambridge University Press.

Stuss, D. T., Delgado, M., & Guzman, D. A. (1987). Verbal regulation in the control of motor impersistence. *Journal of Neurological Rehabilitation, 1,* 19–24.

Suslow, T., Schonauer, K., & Arolt, V. (2001). Attention training in the cognitive rehabilitation of schizophrenic patients: A review of efficacy studies. *Acta Psychiatrica Scandinavica, 103,* 15–23.

Thompson, L., & Thompson, M. (1998). Neurofeedback combined with training in metacognitive strategies: Effectiveness in students with ADD. *Applied Psychophysiology and Biofeedback, 23,* 243–263.

Thomson, J. B., Seidenstrang, Kerns, K. A., Sohlberg, M. M., & Mateer, C. A. (1994). *Pay attention!* Puyallup, WA: Association for Neuropsychological Research and Development.

Tournaki, N. (2003). The differential effects of teaching addition through strategy instruction versus drill and practice to students with and without learning disabilities. *Journal of Learning Disabilities, 36,* 449–458.

Troia, G. A., & Graham, S. (2002). The effectiveness of a highly explicit, teacher-directed strategy instruction routine: Changing the writing performance of students with learning disabilities. *Journal of Learning Disabilities, 35,* 290–305.

Van der Kroll, R. J., Oosterbaan, H., Weller, S. D., & Konig, A. E. (1998). Attention deficit hyperactivity disorder. In P. J. Graham (Ed.), *Cognitive behaviour therapy for children and families* (pp. 32–44). New York: Cambridge University Press.

Vygotsky, L. S. (1962). *Thought and language.* Cambridge, MA: MIT Press.

Webster, J. S., & Scott, R. R. (1983). The effects of self-instructional training on attentional deficits following head injury. *Clinical Neuropsychology, 5,* 69–74.

Weinberg, N. Z., & Glantz, M. D. (1999). Child psychopathology risk factors for drug abuse: Overview. *Journal of Clinical Child Psychology, 28,* 290–297.

Wells, A. (1990). Panic disorder in association with relaxation-induced anxiety: An attentional training approach to treatment. *Behavior Therapy, 21,* 273–280.

Welsh, M. C. (2002). Developmental and clinical variations in executive functions. In D. L. Molfese & V. J. Molfese (Eds.), *Developmental variations in learning: Applications to social, executive function, language and reading skills* (pp. 139–185). Mahwah, NJ: Erlbaum.

Wilens, T. E., McDermott, S. P., Biederman, J., Brantes, A., Hahesy, A., & Spencer, T. J. (1999). Cognitive therapy in the treatment of adults with ADHD: A systematic chart review of 26 cases. *Journal of Cognitive Psychotherapy, 13,* 215–226.

Wong, B. Y. L., Harris, K. R., Graham, S., & Butler, D. L. (2003). Cognitive strategies instruction research in learning disabilities. In H. L. Swanson, K. R. Harris, & S. Graham (Eds.), *Handbook of learning disabilities* (pp. 383–402). New York: Guilford Press.

Ylvisaker, M., & DeBonis, D. A. (2000). Executive function impairment in adolescence: TBI and ADHD. *Topics in Language Disorders, 20,* 29–57.

Ylvisaker, M., & Szekeres, S. F. (1996). Cognitive rehabilitation for children with traumatic brain injury. In P. W. Corrigan & S. C. Yudkfsky (Eds.), *Cognitive rehabilitation for neuropsychiatric disorders.* Washington, DC: American Psychiatric Press.

Ylvisaker, M., Szekeres, S. F., & Feeney, T. J. (1998). Cognitive rehabilitation: Executive functions. In M. Ylvisaker (Ed.), *Traumatic brain injury: Children and adolescents* (2nd ed., pp. 221–269). Boston: Butterworth-Heinemann.

Young, S. (1999). Psychological therapy for adults with attention deficit hyperactivity disorder. *Counseling Psychology Quarterly, 12,* 183–190.

# CHAPTER 32

# Understanding and Implementing School-Family Interventions after Neuropsychological Impairment

JANE CLOSE CONOLEY and SUSAN M. SHERIDAN

C HILDREN WHO HAVE suffered traumatic brain injury (TBI) or have neurological impairments due to disease, toxins, or genetic makeup present challenges that are best addressed by coordinated treatment and support activities among all their caregivers. Such systematic approaches to treatment, rehabilitation, teaching, and parenting are both complex to describe and difficult to create and maintain.

The goal of this chapter is to focus on one of the key systems that affects children's learning and behavioral adjustments: the interface between schools and families. Other *Handbook* authors have described specialized consultation to teachers needed to support their efficacy with children. This chapter offers information that psychologists can share with educators to inoculate educators to the unique stresses that families endure. Further, a particular approach to shared needs identification, goal setting, and problem solving is described so that educators and families can form a supportive team that enhances students' success. Finally, some of the other activities that school and families can share, such as advocacy and family education and counseling, are explored.

The etiology of a learner's neurological challenge is sometimes relevant to highlight given the different influences on recovery and on family functioning. Often, however, the educator is dealing with a child and family in need of help and support, wherein the etiology of the difficulty is unimportant. For this reason, we use the term "affected child" to refer to a child with neurological difficulties from any cause. If etiology does moderate intervention or outcomes, it is described specifically.

## THE AFFECTED CHILD: THE AFFECTED FAMILY SYSTEM

Educators faced with programming for special learning requirements may benefit from knowing some of the history of the affected child's difficulties, the level of family organization around the difficulty, and the phase of acceptance or denial being experienced by the parents. The teacher is confronted with both a special needs child and a family system that has suffered the trauma of a child with disabilities.

Parents report an array of stresses when they first learn of their child's neurological difficulties. Family members display a sequence associated with their experiences. Both the difficulties and the sequence are instructive for care providers (Brooks, Campsie, Symington, Beattie, & McKinlay, 1987; Leaf, 1993; Lezak, 1988; Livingston & Brooks, 1988; Livingston, Brooks, & Bond, 1985a, 1985b; Slater & Rubenstein, 1987). Although the educator cannot protect the parents from the stresses of raising a special needs child, understanding the parents' experience may assist the educator to be patient and supportive.

## Recovery Milestones

After serious injuries, parents report that their initial concern is the survival of their child (Rosenthal & Young, 1988). If the child is in a coma, parents focus almost exclusively on assisting the medical team in rousing the child. This process may be brief or may take many months.

When survival seems assured, parents turn their attention to acquiring information about the possible long-term consequences of the injury. Although many parents report high satisfaction with the acute care their child received, they often are dissatisfied with the vagueness of the information received from medical professionals about the effects of the injury. Understandably, parents want a specific listing of expected symptoms and a timetable for recovery. Medical professional tend to share the entire range of possible injury effects, from the most serious to the most trivial, and they resist giving rigid recovery schedules (Bond, 1983; Panting & Mercy, 1972).

Parents describe serious concerns about the physical disabilities their child may suffer because of the injury, disease, or developmental disability. This concern abates as they either access information on how to accommodate the physical challenges or realize that their child shows few or no obvious impairments. In the process of raising a child with neurological problems, parents often say that the psychological, behavioral, and emotional challenges their child presents are far more disturbing than the physical limitations (Allen, Linn, Gutierrez, & Willer, 1994; Chadwick, 1985; Fletcher, Ewing-Cobbs, Milner, Levin, & Eisenberg, 1990; McGuire & Rothenberg, 1986).

Educators will encounter differences in parents' readiness to engage in home and school programming depending on the course of the neurological or neuropsychological problem. Parents who have had the child's lifetime to organize around their child's impairments may be immediately ready to engage, realistic about possible outcomes, and patient with small victories. On the other hand, depending on how the family is being served through other systems of care, the teacher may experience the brunt of a family's frustration with the affected child's slow progress or because of other family dynamics described later in the chapter.

In contrast, some pediatric recoveries from moderate and even serious injuries occur rather quickly at first. In these cases, parents are euphoric at the obvious improvements in their children's language, attention, and motor skills (Gardner, 1973; Romano, 1974). They may, in fact, deny the extent or permanence of likely disabilities (Martin, 1988). The optimism associated with early signs of rapid recovery may give way to sadness as recovery progress slows down significantly 10 to 12 months postinjury.

When the injury has been severe, parents begin to experience what some have called "partial death" and "mobile mourning" (Rosenthal & Muir, 1983): Their child is alive but is not the child they knew before the injury. Although they thought they had grieved at the time of the accident, they tend to grieve again and again as their son or daughter misses usual developmental or social milestones. These may include starting school, playing sports, going to a prom, and graduating from high school. When the injury has been rather minor, leaving no physical sequelae, the children can suffer the pressures of being what might be termed "almosters"—they can almost learn like they used to, or they are *almost* as agile as they used to be (Jackson & Haverkamp, 1991).

Educators who are sensitive to the struggles being experienced by the students and families provide a safe haven of understanding for the family. Although interventions for change may be limited for some affected children, families benefit from valid information and from caregivers who are empathic to their despair and their hopes. Trusting relationships are the key to all therapeutic success. Understanding and empathy are cornerstones to trust.

### SPECIAL FAMILY STRESSORS

A truism of family intervention is that all families have problems. What differentiates functional from dysfunctional families is not the number of challenges they face, but their skills in problem solving. Although there is likely much truth in this observation, there is little doubt that families dealing with a child's difficulties are challenged by the number and duration of some of the stressors. Some of these are described next.

*Multiple Treatment Settings*   Depending on the seriousness or recovery time of an injury or other impairment, parents may have to find alternative placements for their son or daughter. Short- and long-term residential care is not easily accessible to many families because of either its cost or its distance from their home (Jackson & Haverkamp, 1991). Such inaccessibility puts enormous stress on a family. Many families experience both challenges; that is, they must find ways to fund the rehabilitation process and travel long distances to be with their child during the first stages of rehabilitation (Brooks, 1991a). Even when a child can come home (or parents experiment with home placement), the young person's special needs may force one parent to give up a job or demand a new network of support that includes medical care, supervision, and rehabilitation (Hall, Karzmark, Stevens, Englander, O'Hare, & Wright, 1994).

*Financial Stresses*   The family's problem-solving and coping resources are sometimes taxed because of the sheer number of tasks that demand attention (Bragg, Klockars, & Berninger, 1992). Financial strain due to medical costs associated with injury or disease is common (Hall et al., 1994). Financial demands include medical and often legal costs, as well as ongoing rehabilitation costs (e.g., assistive and augmentative devices, residential or partial hospitalization costs, and respite care) and costs related to modifying their home environment (e.g., ramps for wheelchairs). Although families may be eligible for some insurance or state or federal (e.g., Social Security) financial assistance, accessing these funds can be difficult and time-consuming.

*Effects on Siblings*   When the affected child is in an alternative treatment facility and educators are not directly involved with that child, the educator may still observe significant family difficulties. Other family members, especially siblings of the affected child, may vie for some of the attention lavished on the child with the disability (Dyson, Edgar, & Crnic, 1989; Simeonsson & Bailey, 1986). These attempts are tinged with guilt about their resentment toward their disabled sibling and with a sense of futility. Siblings report the perception that they will never do anything as significant as living with a neurological challenge.

In the case of TBI, Orsillo, McCaffrey, and Fisher (1993) suggest that siblings of individuals with severe head injuries experience psychological distress for up to 5 years postinjury. As siblings grow older, they also report realizing that the burden of care for their disabled brother or sister may fall on them. This is an anxiety-producing and sometimes anger-producing realization (Rivara et al., 1992). Although not a great deal is known about the relationship between psychopathology and having a sibling with a head injury, some studies have documented that siblings of children with other handicaps are at risk for developing behavioral problems (Breslau, 1982), anxiety (Breslau, 1983), social withdrawal (Lavigne & Ryan, 1979), feelings of guilt and anger (Chinitz, 1981), reduced self-esteem (Ferrari, 1984; Harvey & Greenway, 1984), and feelings of inferiority (Taylor, 1980). Generally speaking, siblings who are young, male, and close in age to the child with a disability experience the greatest difficulty.

It should be noted, however, that positive and constructive reactions to the presence of a disabled sibling are possible (Parke, 1986). Such resilient families, if identified by school personnel, may be a great support to other families dealing with similar challenges. Parent-to-parent networks have been shown to be excellent resources in many disability arenas.

*Managing Support Networks*   Friends and extended family tend to be helpful in the first few months following a trauma or birth or diagnosis of a child with disabilities, but their attention and support drift as the long-term recovery and development processes continue. They may add stress to the nuclear family by offering irrelevant advice or even criticism to the family caretakers (Miller, 1993).

The family's skills in managing the systems that make up their world become critical. Parents often report disillusionment with medical and rehabilitation teams. Adversarial relationships are a constant threat to treatment progress. This adversarial stance, often developed during the medical and short-term rehabilitation stages of recovery following injuries, can set the stage for difficulties between families and schools (Martin, 1988). Parents may approach educators with a combative attitude, believing that only aggressive and demanding interactions will create service options for their child. Threats of legal action are common.

*Family Dysfunction*   Many families report significant role strain or overload because of the special demands of parenting the affected child. These stresses can precipitate negative emotional reactions among family members, especially depression, blame, and anger (Zarski, DePompei, & Zook, 1988; Zarski, Hall, & DePompei, 1987).

Mothers and fathers frequently differ in the ways they react to their affected child. These differences (e.g., one parent is protective, concerned, and anxious, and the other parent is demanding and aloof) may be the source of considerable conflict among family members as the rehabilitation process progresses (Miller, 1993).

Family members may be separated for significant periods of time to assist in the rehabilitation process. This separation also contributes to role strain in remaining family members, as well as to potentially significant role changes. For example, older children may have to take on major responsibilities for child care and homemaking tasks. If the family has difficulty supporting each other during these stressful times, depression, substance abuse, and even divorce are possible outcomes (Hall et al., 1994).

The premorbid functioning of the family is a strong predictor of its members' success in coping with the affected child. Well-functioning families are especially helpful in promoting growth in their affected child's emotional and behavioral skills (Rivara et al., 1992; Rivara et al., 1993). The strong effect that families have on a learner's long-term outcomes is the reason coordinated home-school intervention is so critical. Educators and families working together are a powerful treatment for affected children.

## ANALYSIS

Following their child's injury or the family's notification of their child's disability, family members can experience a dramatic swing of emotions, ranging from terror to euphoria, from dependency and bewilderment to anger, and through all levels of discouragement, depression, mourning, and, finally—ideally—reorganization. Family members move from being relieved the child will live to finding the child somewhat or very difficult. They can be blaming toward the child for not trying hard enough to learn or behave or recover from injury. Families can project their own feelings of lack of control on the child and other caregivers. Anger may be turned toward educators, therapists, or medical personnel if the child's condition fails to improve or worsens. Accepting that their child may not be the one they dreamed about before birth or experienced before an accident is very difficult. Family members may have to adjust their expectations from normalcy or full recovery to accepting that little or no change is likely. All parents have many dreams associated with their children. These must sometimes give way to new goals that involve a lifetime of dependency on the part of the affected child (Allen et al., 1994). The entire family system is traumatized by perceptions of the affected child's challenges.

## CONJOINT FAMILY-SCHOOL CONSULTATION

Sheridan and her colleagues (e.g., Christenson & Sheridan, 2001; Sheridan & Kratochwill, 1992; Sheridan, Kratochwill, & Bergan, 1996; Welch & Sheridan, 1995) have described a powerful process through which school psychologists as well as other educators and families can join forces to assist children's positive adjustment to learning, behavioral, emotional, vocational, and social challenges. This process, conjoint family-school consultation, is described in some detail in the following paragraphs. It holds the best and best documented promise of forging a working alliance among educators, school mental health providers, and parents (Guli, in press; Sheridan, Eagle, Cowan, & Mickelson, 2001).

A key element of family coping and involvement in a learner's recovery is a strong partnership between families and schools (Power, DuPaul, Shapiro, & Kazak, 2003). Reentry into the school setting following an injury or initial entry into a public school by an affected child may pose significant challenges for the child, the family, and the school. Families need the continued support of experts who can provide them with information, skills, and emotional support. Educators must rely on parents to continue educational programs in the home to improve their students' chances for optimal achievement. Frequent communication and shared decision making across home and school are critical for consistent and effective services. Cooperative consultative relationships between families and educators are essential to maximizing a child's education and treatment program (Sheridan & Cowan, 2004).

Establishing supportive, conjoint teams of parents, school psychologists or school neuropsychologists, and educators is a complex task. Education, medical, and rehabilitation experts often disappoint parents because the professionals simply lack the solutions the parents want so much. Professional teams often report that parental dissatisfaction with their work leads them to blame each other and weakens the team's functioning. These realities highlight the importance of working to develop constructive, trusting relationships among all caregivers, including family members, educators, and specialists (Christenson & Sheridan, 2001). Only in the presence of positive relationships are effective partnerships possible.

Well-informed school psychologists can be the critical link between families and school personnel. The families and the schools must engage in a mutual process that leads to reorganization around the affected child. An *empowerment* model is preferred over one that provides families with prescriptions for challenges the child may encounter on school entry or reentry (Dunst, Trivette, & Deal, 1994). In such a model, there is a focus on the strengths and problem-solving abilities of the family as a unit. Emphasis is placed on building support networks and engaging in collaborative decision making (Sheridan, Dowd, & Eagle, in press; Sheridan, Warnes, Brown, Schemm, & Cowan, 2004). Parents are considered an active and central component of educational programming for their child (including programs to meet their child's academic, social-emotional, behavioral, and vocational needs). For example, in a conjoint consultation model (Sheridan & Kratochwill, 1992; Sheridan et al., 1996), parents and school personnel share equally in the identification and prioritization of concerns to be addressed through individualized intervention. Parents, teachers, and school specialists work together to develop and implement a strategy or set of strategies to deal with the most pressing issues facing the child. Further, they continue with this dialogue as interventions are implemented and monitor the need for modifications to ensure the best possible treatment regimen for their child.

In situations that involve collaborative problem solving and decision making for a child affected with head injury, expertise related to medical concerns is necessary for coordinated care. Specialists from other disciplines (e.g., pediatrics, neurology, occupational therapy, physical therapy, speech-language therapy) are often important members of the conjoint team (Power et al., 2003; Sheridan, Warnes, Ellis, et al., 2004), and collaboration among relevant parties is important in the overall care of and planning for the learner (Drotar, Palermo, & Barry,

2004). The school psychologist or neuropsychologist can serve an instrumental, proactive role in maintaining contact with and inviting cooperation from these specialists (Shapiro & Manz, 2004).

A structured approach to collaboration is useful to ensure comprehensive and effective services. Four stages characterize conjoint family-school consultation, with three of the four stages involving structured interviews wherein the child's parents, the teacher, the school psychologist, and other relevant individuals (e.g., specialists) come together to address prominent concerns.

### Problem/Needs Identification

In the first stage of consultation, problem or needs identification, participants identify specific academic, behavioral, or social-emotional issues to be addressed. In the problem/needs identification interview (Kratochwill & Bergan, 1990; Sheridan et al., 1996), participants work together to discuss the child's strengths, identify shared concerns, and prioritize one or two specific needs to address as a consultation team. Relevant goals are established for the child, and strategies for collecting behavioral data are determined. In general, specific data should be collected to determine the actual severity of the affected child's difficulties in adjusting to classroom norms and to assess possible environmental conditions that may be contributing to the child's difficulties (e.g., seating arrangements, group size and expectations, classroom transition schedules). To obtain a comprehensive picture of the child's behaviors, data should be collected at both school and home.

### Problem/Needs Analysis

The second stage of conjoint consultation is problem or needs analysis, during which the team (including parents, teachers, and school psychologist) reconvene for a problem/needs analysis interview (Kratochwill & Bergan, 1990; Sheridan et al., 1996). In this meeting, participants discuss the data that have been collected and explore conditions that may be related to the behavioral occurrence (i.e., antecedents and consequences). An intervention plan is then developed collaboratively, with all team members contributing their ideas and expertise (Jacobs, 2004). Emphasis is placed on procedures and strategies that are effective and acceptable in natural home and school contexts. Specific tactics are determined for addressing the affected child's difficulties at both home and school. It is imperative that all key individuals involved with the child be knowledgeable about and active in the implementation of the intervention. This will ensure consistency and continuity among care providers and maximize the child's chances for success.

### Plan Implementation

During plan implementation, the third stage of conjoint consultation, the intervention is put into place across home and school settings. All individuals who play an active part in the plan should be familiar with their specific roles and responsibilities. The school psychologist consultant is in a good position to monitor each aspect of the program to assist parents and teachers, ensuring that the plan is being implemented as intended in both home and school. In some cases, direct training or modeling of some of the treatment components will be necessary for consultees who are unfamiliar with certain strategies. It is also important that data continue to be collected during this stage to assess the child's responsiveness to the intervention and movement toward consultation goals.

## Plan Evaluation

The final stage of conjoint consultation, plan evaluation, involves determining whether the child is making progress on the specific behaviors or concerns targeted for consultation. In the treatment evaluation interview (Kratochwill & Bergan, 1990; Sheridan et al., 1996), all consultation participants meet to review the data collected prior to and during the implementation of the treatment plan. The intervention program often will require some modification; indeed, in some situations, an entirely new plan will be developed. If the initial goals for the child have been met, team members will typically recycle back through the consultation stages and address another concern facing the child. This stage is especially critical when a child's recovery or developmental progress is variable. Continuous evaluation of the appropriateness of goals for the child, and of improvement or regression surrounding those goals, is critical. It is very important at this stage to ensure that strategies are put into place to help the child maintain treatment gains that have been made.

## Analysis

Parents are often the persons most knowledgeable on issues regarding their family and their child's condition, particularly if they have been active in the recovery process following an injury or engaged with other caregiving medical or social systems. They have firsthand information about their child's temperament, motivation, responsiveness, tolerance levels, and degree of adaptation. They can provide necessary background information on the nature and course of the injury, disease, or congenital condition, adjunct services being provided, family adjustment, and their child's strengths. Partnerships with the school, particularly via consultation models that include home, school, and medical expertise, is critical to ensure consistency across caregivers and maximize achievement toward shared goals.

## FAMILY EDUCATION, ADVOCACY, AND THERAPY

In addition to supporting extensive consultation programs for families with children with neuropsychological or neurological disabilities, schools can mount a number of other helpful family-oriented programs (Livingston et al., 1985a, 1985b; Miller, 1993). Several approaches are described next. Also mentioned is the critical need for case management.

## Education

Many families will benefit from educational programs that describe what is currently known about the learning, behavioral, social, emotional, and vocational needs of children with disabilities. The goal of educational programs is to increase family understanding and knowledge of their affected child's situation.

Knowledge is power. Although general educational sessions are not a substitute for the specific informational needs a family has following their child's head injury or diagnosis of neurological anomaly, the availability of regular programs sponsored by schools offers parents a chance to form relationships with educators and other related professionals.

When providing educational information, it is important that the information is shared in a manner that makes sense to nonmedical personnel, using nontechnical terms and language. Often, schools use medical-based neuropsychologists or physicians as presenters for family workshops or programs. These presenters add credibility but often speak in jargon, which defeats the goal of education as enlightenment. A well-prepared school psychologist consultant is often a great help in suggesting language that respects the family's knowledge while not overloading their ability to absorb and use information (Hamaguchi, 1995; Savage & Wolcott, 2004).

Further, all information must be shared in a manner that is sensitive to the family's vulnerability. Care should be taken not to overwhelm the family with too many facts and details about the affected child's disabilities early in the family's exploration stage. The amount of information first presented should be limited to allow family members sufficient time to process the newly acquired knowledge (DePompei & Zarski, 1989). Details about the disability and predicted course of the disorder and treatment options often need to be repeated several times. Anxiety may interfere with learning, so multiple opportunities for learning are necessary.

Lezak (1978, 1986) suggests that the following key points should be conveyed to families:

- Anger, frustration, and sorrow are natural reactions of family members when a relative is diagnosed with a disability or suffers an injury.
- Caretakers should preserve their own emotional health, physical well-being, and sanity to be of benefit to the affected child.
- Families should be informed and helped to process details surrounding the organic limitations to development or recovery.
- Recovery and development are not continuous and reliable processes. A child may show rapid recovery or achievement in some areas and during some phases of rehabilitation; in other cases, recovery or growth may be slow or absent. Accepting these realities can help families resist blaming treatment staff, medical facilities, or school personnel when their dreams for their child are not met.
- Conflict and disagreements between family members and the affected child are inevitable. Caretakers must rely on their own judgment in making decisions regarding care.
- The family role changes that are concomitant to a relative's disability can be stressful to all.
- Real limits exist pertaining to what family members can do to change the affected child's behaviors and personality. Feelings of guilt or ineptitude are normal but not realistic.

- The family ultimately may be faced with decisions about alternative living or care arrangements for the affected child.
- The family should review legal documents,and financial arrangements concerning the care of the affected child.

Families report not knowing enough about the rehabilitation process, for example, their role and appropriate expectations. If the affected child is being served by both the school system and another medical or rehabilitative system, educational events that integrate information about the multiple systems are helpful. This integration is vital for both parents and the professionals in each system. Educators express concerns similar to those of parents when they realize their students are being served in multiple systems. They want to be supportive of an array of interventions but are often uninformed as to their unique role or how their expectations support or undermine the expectations of others.

The development of a conjoint consultation plan is a good basis for introducing critical information to families and schools. For example, information on how to structure the child's leisure time, what to expect in terms of sexuality from the affected adolescent, or how to deal with externalizing behavior problems may be useful (Asarnow, Lewis, & Neumann, 1991; Black, Jeffries, Blumer, Wellner, & Walker, 1969; Slater & Rubenstein, 1987). In schools, the individualized educational planning development process can serve and support the conjoint consultation process (see Chapter 31, this volume). School psychologists with neuropsychological training or school neuropsychologists must be active and instrumental in helping the team (including parents) develop appropriate educational goals and acquire the necessary information to adequately address each child's unique difficulties.

Although workshops and regular consultations from area professionals are extremely valuable educational opportunities, schools must not overlook the importance of measuring the yearly progress of all children, and neurologically impaired children in particular. Annual meetings with parents or groups of parents allow schools to tailor educational events to both the current educational needs of the child and the developmental expectations of the parents. Although a 16-year-old may still require educational programming that is more common to elementary students, his or her parents can benefit from information about vocational possibilities and opportunities. A common failure of caregiving systems occurs when they become identified with a sole, particular focus and lose sight of an integrated understanding of family system needs.

## FAMILY SUPPORT AND ADVOCACY

Parents face frightening burdens associated with their child's special needs. They require information about the legal and financial situations they face. They benefit from direction regarding insurance, other funding sources, and the legal help they may need to manage personal injury or compensation suits. Ongoing assistance throughout the rehabilitation period is often necessary.

Families often require a case manager to assist them in identifying and accessing all the community and educational services for which they qualify. Case managers may be effective advocates responsible for educating parents about the scope of their child's rights under the Individuals with Disabilities Education Act. Similarly, they may serve as mediators to assist families in the procurement of necessary services. Because service needs change with the age of the child (e.g., from preschool early intervention programs to vocational rehabilitation), it is important that case managers be knowledgeable about child development and transition programs and available to families over time. Case managers are especially helpful if they also know physicians, lawyers, and rehabilitation professionals who are well-informed about neurological impairments.

Linking families with local or national organizations, such as the National Dissemination Center for Children and Youth with Disabilities (nichcy.com; 800-695-0285), the Brain Injury Association of America (biasua.org; family helpline: 800-444-6443), and Disability Resources, Inc. (in Abilene, Texas; drifolks.org), is also a very helpful way to provide them opportunities to access information about their affected child. Further, such linkages can help families cope via their own actions and through more systemic efforts, such as legislation, advocacy with school districts, or regulations affecting disabled people (Savage & Wolcott, 2004). Some settings, such as Disability Resources, Inc., are connected to faith-based efforts that are attractive to some families.

Local organizations are a source for self-help and parent support groups. Almost all families feel guilt, sadness, loss, anguish, and anger associated with their child's disabilities. Although there is no empirical research associated with self-help groups of this type, family groups can play an important role in offering support and normalizing these emotional states. Such support may serve to prevent the development of more serious family dilemmas—especially child abuse (Cross, 2004; Rosenthal & Young, 1988).

Depending on the severity of the affected child's disability, including him or her in educational sessions may be warranted. Some guidelines for this practice have been offered by DePompei and Zarski (1989) and include:

- Cover no more than two new topics in a session.
- Repeat main points on several occasions (and encourage family members to do the same) and ask the affected child for verification.
- Review the same information in more than one session.
- Model responses to the affected child for the family.

## FAMILY COUNSELING

Family counseling is both a preventive and a remedial strategy to consider, especially if it focuses on fostering emotional resources and coping skills and if the therapist can also teach the family strategies for dealing with their child. Family members often neglect their own needs and those of other family members because of the demands of the affected child. Already mentioned is the high rate of marital disruption following the birth of a child with a disability or the injury of a child. Parents may lose sight of the call to nurture their marriage with the same intensity required by their affected child. Parents who are given this advice often agree sadly that their days are not long enough to meet everyone's needs. Romance and shared recreational times for the parents are often the first casualties in a family caring for a child with disabilities.

There is a compelling need for more empirically derived information about the effects of pediatric neurological disorders on families and about designing therapeutic interventions helpful to families (Lehr, 1990; Waaland, 1990; Waaland & Kreutzer, 1988). Much of the research literature concerning neurological disorders and families is based on adult male participants (e.g., Allen et al., 1994). Often, the reports of family reorganization after the injury relate the experiences of wives and children coping with injury of a husband, or of parents (especially mothers) coping with the injury of their unmarried adult child. Results from these studies may not be directly comparable to families with pediatric clients, given the different role expectations for children in contrast to adults.

Counseling or therapy can also focus on strategies that family members can use over time to deal with the child's neurological impairment and behavioral sequelae. Families with TBI survivors often experience a rather rapid initial recovery phase, when they experience a "honeymoon" period and believe that their lives will soon be back to normal (Miller, 1993). Many find, however, that they need to acquire new skills, especially ones related to teaching and goal-setting strategies, to work with their injured son or daughter. They may have to teach their adolescent how to use the toilet and brush his or her teeth. They may have to be involved in language training. Of special importance is the family's need for strategies to cope with aggressive outbursts from the TBI survivor, as aggressiveness is a significant stressor on families (Brooks, 1984).

Counseling for siblings of children with head injuries is often recommended. For example, they can benefit from education about the possible negative effects of prolonged caretaking on themselves and on the rest of the family. Siblings have been shown to display inadequate problem solving and dysfunctional attitudes (Orsillo et al., 1993), using coping strategies such as wishful thinking, self-blame, and avoidance at least as often as more effective, problem-focused or social support coping strategies. Depending on their age, siblings may not be verbally or emotionally mature enough to express their feelings and confusions. If this goes unrecognized, the sibling may endure significant psychological hardship.

It may also be useful to involve the affected child in family counseling sessions to the greatest extent possible. Therapeutic indications for involving the child will likely be related to his or her developmental status, level of injury, and degree of physical, cognitive, and behavioral functioning. Specific therapeutic goals might focus on helping all family members to express thoughts and concerns regarding the affected child's influence on family dynamics and exploring alternative coping skills.

## CONCLUSION

The objectives of this chapter were to outline:

- What families report to be their experiences in coping with a child with neurological difficulties
- The tasks families must navigate to promote a positive family life
- Effective and efficient consultation, education, advocacy, and counseling services that a school-based consultant might offer
- The special role the psychologist plays in meeting family needs, coordinating school and family interventions, and contributing to the cohesiveness and effectiveness of the school-based team (Barry & O'Leary, 1989)

When planning programs for neurologically impaired learners, care providers must keep in mind that the affected child is only one member of a family system (Brooks, 1991b). A growing literature of research and clinical reports documents not only the massive effects children's disabilities can have on parents, siblings, and extended family, but also the critical role a well-functioning family plays in the affected child's eventual adjustment (Jackson & Haverkamp, 1991; Kaplan, 1988; Kreutzer, Marwitz, & Kepler, 1992; Martin, 1988; Rivara et al., 1992; Rivara et al., 1993; Testani-Dufour, Chappel-Aiken, & Gueldner, 1992).

Families of learners with disabilities may experience major psychological, financial, role, and relationship risks. Difficulties for the family stem from both objective and subjective burden. Objective burden refers to objectively observable symptoms and conditions of the affected child, such as language, speech, and memory impairments. Subjective burden concerns the level of distress experienced by family members that is related to both the severity of the child's disability and features of the relative himself or herself. This may be mediated by social variables, such as the presence or absence of support networks, or the relationship between the relative and the affected child (Brooks, 1991b; Brooks et al., 1987). In general, female caregivers of persons with brain impairment report higher levels of burden. Subjective burden is more highly related to the presence of social aggression and cognitive disability in the child than to factors associated with physical disability. Further, the extent of the learner's emotional and behavioral difficulties appears to be more important than the severity of the physical impairments in predicting family members' levels of burden (Allen et al., 1994).

The difficulties experienced by the families of individuals with neuropsychological or neurological disorders are usually long lasting, and some may actually increase over time (Bigler, 1989; Bragg et al., 1992; Hall et al., 1994), especially those associated with subjective burden (Brooks, Campsie, Symington, Beattie, & McKinlay, 1986, 1987; Brooks & McKinlay, 1983). Divorce, family conflict, substance abuse, and social isolation are possible outcomes. According to research by Mauss-Clum and Ryan (1981), the most frequently reported maternal reactions to closed-head injuries are frustration, irritability, arrogance, depression, anger, and feeling trapped. Other common responses include denial (albeit sometimes functional or misunderstood denial), anger, and overprotection (Brooks, 1991b).

It is of some importance that what families report to be valuable as they adjust to their son's or daughter's disability is valid information from caring school psychologists or school neuropsychologists as well as from other educational professionals. Although the child's disability cannot be undone, families benefit from consultation about an array of issues pertinent to coping with the child, health and educational systems, and community agencies (Miller, 1993). Consultation can greatly assist families in their continuing efforts to reorganize around the effects of meeting the needs of a special child (Katz & Deluca, 1992).

## REFERENCES

Allen, K., Linn, R. T., Gutierrez, H., & Willer, B. S. (1994). Family burden following traumatic brain injury. *Rehabilitation Psychology, 39,* 30–48.

Asarnow, R. F., Lewis, R., & Neumann, E. (1991). Behavior problems and adaptive functioning in children with mild and severe closed head injury. *Journal of Pediatric Psychology, 16*, 545–555.

Barry, P., & O'Leary, J. (1989). Roles of the psychologist on a traumatic brain injury rehabilitation team. *Rehabilitation Psychology, 34*(2), 83–90.

Bigler, E. E. (1989). Behavioral and cognitive changes in traumatic brain injury: A spouse's perspective. *Brain Injury, 3*, 73–78.

Black, P., Jeffries, J. J., Blumer, D., Wellner, A., & Walker, A. E. (1969). The post-traumatic syndrome in children. In A. E. Walker, E. E. Caveness, & M. Critchley (Eds.), *The late effects of head injury* (pp. 187–201). Springfield, IL: Thomas Books.

Bond, M. R. (1983). Effects on the family system. In M. Rosenthal, E. R. Griffith, & M. R. Bond (Eds.), *Rehabilitation of the head injured adult* (pp. 209–217). Philadelphia: Davis.

Bragg, R. M., Klockars, A. J., & Berninger, V. W. (1992). Comparison of families with and without adolescents with traumatic brain injury. *Journal of Head Trauma Rehabilitation, 7*(3), 94–108.

Breslau, N. (1982). Siblings of disabled children: Birth order and age-spacing effects. *Journal of Abnormal Child Psychology, 10*, 85–96.

Breslau, N. (1983). The psychological study of chronically ill and disabled children: Are healthy siblings appropriate controls? *Journal of Abnormal Child Psychology, 11*, 379–391.

Brooks, D. N. (1984). Head injury and the family. In D. N. Brooks (Ed.), *Closed head injury: Psychological, social and family consequences* (pp. 123–147). Cambridge, England: Oxford University Press.

Brooks, D. N. (1991a). The effectiveness of post-acute rehabilitation. *Brain Injury, 1*, 5–19.

Brooks, D. N. (1991b). The head-injured family. *Journal of Clinical Experimental Neuropsychology, 13*, 155–188.

Brooks, D. N., Campsie, L., Symington, C., Beattie, A., & McKinlay, W. (1986). The five-year outcome of severe blunt head injury: A relative's view. *Journal of Neurology, Neurosurgery, and Psychiatry, 49*, 764–800.

Brooks, D. N., Campsie, L., Symington, C., Beattie, A., & McKinlay, W. (1987). The effects of sever-head injury on patient and relatives within seven years of injury. *Journal of Head Trauma Rehabilitation, 2*(2), 1–13.

Brooks, D. N., & McKinlay, W. (1983). Personality and behavioral changes after severe blunt head injury: A relative's view. *Journal of Neurology, Neurosurgery, and Psychiatry, 46*, 336–344.

Chadwick, O. (1985). Psychological sequelae of head injury in children. *Developmental Medicine and Child Neurology, 27*, 69–79.

Chinitz, S. P. (1981). A sibling group for brothers and sisters of handicapped children. *Children Today, 15*, 21–23.

Christenson, S. L., & Sheridan, S. M. (2001). *Schools and families: Creating essential connections for learning.* New York: Guilford Press.

Cross, M. (2004). *Proud child, safer child: A handbook for parents and caretakers of disabled children.* Toronto, Ontario, Canada: Women's Press.

DePompei, R., & Zarski, J. J. (1989). Families, head injury, and cognitive-communicative impairments: Issues for family counseling. *Topics in Language Disorders, 9*, 78–89.

Drotar, D., Palermo, T., & Barry, C. (2004). Collaboration with schools: Models and methods in pediatric psychology. In R. Brown (Ed.), *Handbook of pediatric psychology in school settings* (pp. 21–36). Mahweh, NJ: Erlbaum.

Dunst, C. J., Trivette, C. M., & Deal, A. G. (1994). Enabling and empowering families. In C. J. Dunst, C. M. Trivette, & A. G. Deal (Eds.), *Supporting and strengthening families* (pp. 1–11). Cambridge, MA: Brookline Books.

Dyson, L., Edgar, E., & Crnic, K. (1989). Psychological predictors of adjustment by siblings of developmentally disabled children. *American Journal of Mental Retardation, 94,* 292–302.

Ferrari, M. (1984). Chronic illness: Psychosocial effects on siblings—I. Chronically ill boys. *Journal of Child Psychology and Psychiatry, 25,* 459–476.

Fletcher, J. M., Ewing-Cobbs, L., Miner, M. E., Levin, H. S., & Eisenberg, H. M. (1990). Behavioral changes after closed head injury in children. *Journal of Consulting and Clinical Psychology, 58,* 93–98.

Gardner, R. A. (1973). *The family book about minimal brain dysfunction.* New York: Aronson.

Guli, L. A. (2004, July). Parent consultation with school-related outcomes: A review. In C. Carlson (Chair), *Evidence-supported parent and family interventions in school psychology.* Symposium presented at the annual conference of the American Psychological Association, Honolulu.

Hamaguchi, P. M. (1995). *Childhood speech, language, and listening problems: What every parent should know.* New York: Wiley.

Hall, K. M., Karzmark, P., Stevens, M., Englander, J., O'Hare, P., & Wright, J. (1994). Family stressors in traumatic brain injury: A two-year follow-up. *Archives of Physical Medicine and Rehabilitation, 75,* 876–884.

Harvey, D. H. P., & Greenway, A. P. (1984). The self concept of physically handicapped children and their non-handicapped siblings: An empirical investigation. *Journal of Child Psychology and Psychiatry, 25,* 273–284.

Jacobs, H. E. (2004). *Behavior analysis guidelines and brain injury rehabilitation: People, principles, and programs.* Aspen, CO: Aspen Publishing.

Jackson, A., & Haverkamp, D. E. (1991). Family response to traumatic brain injury. *Counseling Psychology Quarterly, 4,* 355–356.

Kaplan, S. P. (1988). Adaptation following serious brain injury: An assessment after one year. *Journal of Applied Rehabilitation Counseling, 19*(3), 3–7.

Katz, R. T., & Deluca, J. (1992). Sequelae of minor traumatic brain injury. *American Family Physician, 46,* 1491–1498.

Kratochwill, T. R., & Bergan, J. R. (1990). *Behavioral consultation in applied settings: An individual guide.* New York: Plenum Press.

Kreutzer, J. S., Marwitz, J. H., & Kepler, K. (1992). Traumatic brain injury: Family response and outcome. *Archives of Physical Medicine and Rehabilitation, 73,* 771–778.

Lavigne, J. V., & Ryan, M. (1979). Psychological adjustment of siblings of children with chronic illness. *Pediatrics, 63,* 616–622.

Leaf, L. E. (1993). Traumatic brain injury: Affecting family recovery. *Brain Injury, 7,* 543–546.

Lehr, E. (1990). *Psychological management of traumatic brain injuries in children and adults.* Rockville, MD: Aspen.

Lezak, M. D. (1978). Living with a characterologically altered brain injured patient. *Journal of Clinical Psychiatry, 39,* 595–598.

Lezak, M. D. (1986). Psychological implications of traumatic brain damage for the patient's family. *Rehabilitation Psychology, 31,* 241–250.

Lezak, M. D. (1988). Brain damage is a family affair. *Journal of Clinical and Experimental Neuropsychology, 10,* 111–123.

Livingston, M. G., & Brooks, D. N. (1988). The burden on families of the brain injured: A review. *Journal of Head Trauma Rehabilitation, 2*(4), 6–15.

Livingston, M. G., Brooks, D. N., & Bond, M. R. (1985a). Patient outcome in the year following severe head injury and relatives' psychiatric and social functioning. *Journal of Neurology, Neurosurgery, and Psychiatry, 48,* 527–533.

Livingston, M. G., Brooks, D. N., & Bond, M. R. (1985b). Three months after severe head injury: Psychiatric and social impact on relatives. *Journal of Neurology, Neurosurgery, and Psychiatry, 48,* 870–875.

Martin, D. A. (1988). Children and adolescents with traumatic brain injury: Impact on the family. *Journal of Learning Disabilities, 21,* 464–470.

Mauss-Clum, N., & Ryan, M. (1981). Brain injury and the family. *Journal of Neurosurgical Nurses, 13,* 165–169.

McGuire, T. L., & Rothenberg, M. B. (1986). Behavioral and psychosocial sequelae of pediatric brain injury. *Journal of Head Trauma Rehabilitation, 1*(4), 16.

Miller, L. (1993). Family therapy of brain injury: Syndromes, strategies, and solutions. *American Journal of Family Therapy, 21,* 111–121.

Savage, R. C., & Wolcott, G. F. (Eds.). (2004). *An educator's manual: What educators need to know about students with traumatic brain injury* (3rd ed.). Framingham, MA: Brain Injury Association.

Orsillo, S. M., McCaffrey, R. J., & Fisher, J. M. (1993). Siblings of head-injured individuals: A population at risk. *Journal of Head Trauma Rehabilitation, 8,* 102–115.

Panting, A., & Mercy, P. (1972). The long term rehabilitation of severe head injuries with particular reference to the need for social and medical support for the patient's family. *Rehabilitation, 38,* 33–37.

Parke, R. D. (1986). Fathers, families, and support systems: Their role in the development of at-risk and retarded infants and children. In J. J. Gallagher & P. M. Vietze (Eds.), *Families of handicapped persons: Research, programs, and policy issues* (pp. 101–113). Baltimore: Brookes.

Power, T. J., DuPaul, G. J., Shapiro, E. S., & Kazak, A. E. (2003). *Promoting children's health: Integrating school, family, and community.* New York: Guilford Press.

Rivara, J. B., Fay, G. C., Jaffe, K. M., Pollissar, N. L., Shurtleff, H. A., & Martin, K. M. (1992). Predictors of family functioning one year following traumatic brain injury in children. *Archives of Physical Medicine and Rehabilitation, 73,* 899–910.

Rivara, J. B., Jaffe, K. M., Fay, G. C., Pollissar, N. L., Martin, K. M., Shurtleff, H. A., et al. (1993). Family functioning and injury severity as predictors of child functioning one year following traumatic brain injury. *Archives of Physical Medicine and Rehabilitation, 74,* 1047–1055.

Romano, M. D. (1974). Family response to traumatic head injury. *Scandinavian Journal of Rehabilitation Medicine, 6,* 1–5.

Rosenthal, M., & Muir, C. A. (1983). Methods of family intervention. In M. Rosenthal, E. R. Griffith, & M. R. Bond (Eds.), *Rehabilitation of the head injured adult* (pp. 407–419). Philadelphia: Davis.

Rosenthal, M., & Young, T. (1988). Effective family intervention after traumatic brain injury: Theory and practice. *Journal of Head Trauma Rehabilitation, 3,* 42–50.

Savage, R. C., & Wolcott, G. F. (Eds.). (2004). *An educator's manual: What educators need to know about students with traumatic brain injury* (3rd ed.). McLean, VA: Brain Injury Association.

Shapiro, E. S., & Manz, P. H. (2004). Collaborating with schools in the provision of pediatric psychological services. In R. Brown (Ed.), *Handbook of pediatric psychology in school settings* (pp. 49–64). Mahweh, NJ: Erlbaum.

Sheridan, S. M., & Cowan, R. J. (2004). Consultation with school personnel. In R. Brown (Ed.), *Handbook of pediatric psychology in school settings* (pp. 599–616). Mahweh, NJ: Erlbaum.

Sheridan, S. M., Dowd, S. E., & Eagle, J. W. (in press). Families as contexts for children's adaptation. In S. Goldstein & R. Brooks (Eds.), *Handbook of resiliency in children.* New York: Kluwer/Plenum Press.

Sheridan, S. M., Eagle, J. W., Cowan, R. J., & Mickelson, W. (2001). The effects of conjoint behavioral consultation: Results of a four-year investigation. *Journal of School Psychology, 39,* 361–385.

Sheridan, S. M., & Kratochwill, T. R. (1992). Behavioral parent-teacher consultation: Conceptual and research considerations. *Journal of School Psychology, 30,* 117–139.

Sheridan, S. M., Kratochwill, T. R., & Bergan, J. R. (1996). *Conjoint behavioral consultation: A procedural manual.* New York: Plenum Press.

Sheridan, S. M., Warnes, E., Brown, M., Schemm, A., & Cowan, R. J. (2004). Family-centered positive psychology: Building on strengths to promote student success. *Psychology in the Schools, 41,* 7–17.

Sheridan, S. M., Warnes, E. D., Ellis, C., Schnoes, C., Burt, J., & Clarke, B. (2004, July). *Efficacy of conjoint behavioral consultation in developmental-behavioral pediatric services.* Paper presented at the annual conference of the American Psychological Association, Honolulu.

Simeonsson, R. J., & Bailey, D. B. (1986). Siblings of handicapped children. In J. J. Gallagher & P. M. Vietze (Eds.), *Families of handicapped persons: Research, programs, and policy issues* (pp. 67–77). Baltimore: Brookes.

Slater, E. J., & Rubenstein, E. (1987). Family coping with trauma in adolescents. *Psychiatric Annuals, 17,* 786–794.

Taylor, S. C. (1980). The effect of chronic childhood illness upon well siblings. *Maternal-Child Nursing Journal, 9,* 109–116.

Testani-Dufour, L., Chappel-Aiken, L., & Gueldner, S. (1992). Traumatic brain injury: A family experience. *Journal of Neuroscience Nursing, 24,* 317–323.

Waaland, P. K. (1990). Family response to childhood brain injury. In J. S. Kreutzer & P. H. Wehman (Eds.), *Community integration following traumatic brain injury* (pp. 224–247). Baltimore: Brookes.

Waaland, P. K., & Kreutzer, J. S. (1988). Family response to childhood traumatic brain injury. *Journal of Head Trauma Rehabilitation, 3*(4), 51–63.

Welch, M., & Sheridan, S. M. (1995). *Educational partnerships: Serving children at risk.* San Antonio, TX: Harcourt-Brace Jovanovich.

Zarski, J. J., DePompei, R., & Zook, A. (1988). Traumatic head injury: Dimensions of family responsivity. *Journal of Head Trauma Rehabilitation, 3*(4), 31–41.

Zarski, J. J., Hall, D. E., & DePompei, R. (1987). Closed head injury patients: A family therapy approach to the rehabilitation process. *American Journal of Family Therapy, 15*(1), 62–68.

# CHAPTER 33

# Understanding and Implementing Neuropsychologically Based Literacy Interventions

LAURICE M. JOSEPH

$H$OW DID YOU LEARN to read? For most people, learning to read seems as automatic as acquiring language. However, the development of literacy skills is complex, involving the reciprocal relationship between neurological and environmental factors (Pennington, 1991). The field of neuropsychology explores the interaction between functions of the brain and the conditions of the environment, which has contributed greatly to understanding underlying processes associated with acquiring literacy, understanding characteristics of learners who struggle with acquiring literacy, and designing interventions that facilitate the development of literacy. This chapter presents a discussion about the critical components of literacy development, a brief discussion about the characteristics of children who struggle with acquiring literacy, and a lengthy section on evidence-supported interventions for facilitating the development of critical component processes of literacy.

## CRITICAL COMPONENT PROCESSES OF LITERACY DEVELOPMENT

The critical components of literacy include those associated with neurological functions. There are critical literacy skills not described in this section because of the lack of information linking them to neurological functions. Research continues to evolve in relation to literacy development and neurological functions.

### PHONOLOGICAL PROCESSING

Phonological processing encompasses all activities related to encoding and executing sounds of spoken language (Adams, 1990). According to Pennington (1991), the area of the brain responsible for phonological processing in normally developing individuals is the perisylvian area of the left hemisphere. This includes Wernike's area in the posterior left temporal lobe and Broca's area in the premotor portion of the left frontal lobe. One of the most important phonological processes is the development of phonemic awareness skills. Explicit teaching of phoneme awareness has consistently been found to relate to word recognition and spelling achievement (Ball & Blachman, 1991; Bentin & Leshem, 1993; Byrne & Fielding-Barnsley, 1991; Foorman, Francis, Fletcher, Schatschneider, & Mehta, 1998; Griffith, 1991; Hatcher, Hulme, & Ellis, 1994; Stahl & Murray, 1994; Vellutino, Scanlon, & Tanzman, 1998; Wagner & Torgesen, 1987).

*Phonemic Awareness* Phonemic awareness is the alertness to and operation of individual sounds in spoken language. A phoneme is an individual sound unit in spoken language. Being aware of phonemes means hearing and attending to individual sounds in words. It involves recognizing sounds in words that are the same (phoneme identity) and distinguishing among those that are different. For instance, it is being aware that the words "apple" and "ant" begin with the same beginning /a/ sound. It is also being aware that the middle sound in the word "sit" is different from the middle sound in the word "set." Children may engage in phoneme categorization and oddity tasks to make comparisons among sounds in words.

Individuals can operate on the sounds of words in spoken language through phoneme segmentation, phoneme blending, phoneme deletion, phoneme addition, and phoneme substitution exercises. Phoneme segmentation activities involve conducting an analysis of the sounds of a word, which includes segmenting syllables and segmenting individual sounds in words. For instance, as a word is slowly articulated, children clap once for each syllable they hear in a word. Another activity involves the instructor saying a word and asking the children to say each individual sound in the word; children would say /c/, /a/, and /t/ after the word "cat" was presented. Among various phoneme awareness tasks, phoneme segmentation was the best predictor of word recognition performance of 1st-grade learners (Nation & Hulme, 1997).

Similar to phoneme segmentation activities are phoneme positional analysis activities, involving identifying the beginning, medial, or final sounds of a word. This is referred to as phoneme isolation when children recognize individual sounds in a word. For instance, children are able to identify that the /i/ sound is the middle of the word "sip."

Phoneme blending involves synthesizing the individual sounds of a word to form a whole word, which includes blending syllables or individual sounds together to form a whole word. For instance, children blend the syllables /can/ and /dle/ to make the word "candle." Children may also blend individual sounds such as /s/, /u/, and /n/ to form the word "sun." Phoneme deletion involves saying the sounds of a word after a phoneme has been deleted from the word, such as saying "at" after the /s/ sound has been removed in the word "sat." Phoneme substitution involves substituting a sound for another sound and forming a different word, such as substituting the /s/ sound in the word "sat" for the /h/ sound and forming the word "hat." Phoneme addition refers to adding a phoneme to an existing word to make a new word, such as adding a /p/ to the beginning of "lot" to make the word "plot."

*Phonological Memory* Phonological processing involves phonological memory or memory span, the ability to hold syllables or individual sounds of words in working, short-term, or long-term memory (Torgesen, 1996). Children need to be able to hold the sounds of words in their working memory when they are asked to operate on and reproduce sounds of a word immediately after hearing it. In other words, production of sounds requires the ability to store the sounds in memory. Gathercole and Baddeley (1990) found that deficits in phonological memory did not affect elementary school-age children's ability to speak and read known words but did affect their ability to speak and read words that were unknown to them. Phonological memory becomes more crucial as children grow older and confront new, complex words such as multisyllabic words. If children are unable to store all of the sounds or chunks of sounds in their immediate memory, they may have difficulty blending all of the sounds to form a whole word. Thus, phonological memory is a characteristic that distinguishes good readers from poor readers (Muter & Snowling, 1998; Torgesen, 1988; Velluntino et al., 1996).

## RAPID AUTOMATIZED NAMING

Rapid automatized naming, sometimes referred to as naming speed, is the efficient retrieval of phonological information (McDougall, Hulme, Ellis, & Monk, 1994). In other words, rapid automatized naming is the ability to speak and read fluently. According to Wolf and Bowers (1999), children experienced the greatest difficulty learning to read if they had deficits in both rapid naming and phonological processing. Rapid automatized naming has been found to be related to early literacy skills such as phonological awareness, letter-name knowledge, and early decoding skills (Compton, 2003) as well as orthographic and comprehension performance (Bowers, 1995; Cutting & Denkla, 2001; Manis, Doi, & Bhadha, 2000). Rapid automatized naming requires the naming of a series of objects, numbers, letters, words, and pseudowords as quickly as possible or within a specified time. The relationship between rapid automatized naming and reading performance has been found to be weaker in the early grades but stronger in the intermediate grades (Kirby, Pfeiffer, & Parrila, 2000). Rapid automatized naming activities can involve rapidly reading a series of words presented on index cards or listed on paper or reading a series of words contained in a reading passage. Thus, rapid naming skills can be taught in and out of connected text.

## ORTHOGRAPHIC PROCESSING

Orthographic processing refers to noting the letter sequences in words or spelling patterns of words. It requires lexical processing, or analyzing the visual or graphic structures of letters and words, and storing these lexical features in memory (Olson, Fosberg, Wise, & Rack, 1994). Discriminating orthographic features of words can be challenging, particularly when words sound alike but are spelled differently, such as "pane" and "pain."

As children advance in their reading and spelling skills, they must also attend to morphemic units of words, such as words containing prefixes and suffixes and compound words. Morphemic understanding contributes to articulating and recognizing spelling patterns of words (Frith, 1985). In a recent investigation, Nagy, Berninger, Abbot, Vaughan, and Vermeulen (2003) found that morphology contributed uniquely to reading comprehension, and oral vocabulary and orthography contributed uniquely to word reading skills for 2nd-grade students. These investigators also found that orthography and phonology contributed uniquely to decoding words with affixes for 4th-graders.

ALPHABETIC PRINCIPLE AND PHONOLOGICAL RECODING

The alphabetic principle states that a letter or letter patterns represent a sound or sounds, respectively. Essentially, it is the understanding that written language is a representational system of spoken language. Children need to be able to associate print with sound in order to decode words. Thus, as children begin to make connections between phonological and orthographic features of language, word identification skills develop.

Initially, when children are beginning to make links between sound and print, they go through a process called phonological recoding (McCormick, 1999; Share, 1995). Most of the words children initially encounter in print are words that have already been a part of their speaking vocabulary. As they encounter a printed word, they recode the orthographic pattern of the word back into its phonological pattern. In other words, phonological recoding is the process by which children examine the printed word, attempt to decode it, and check to see if their pronunciation of the written word matches the spoken word that is already stored in their memory or a part of their speaking vocabulary repertoire.

Many of the basic words that children initially encounter in kindergarten and 1st grade are words with consonant-vowel-consonant patterns. These words often require a sequential decoding of letters to sounds because there is a one-to-one letter-sound correspondence, such as in "cat," "dog," "put," and "did." By the middle of 1st grade and into the 2nd grade, children need to engage in hiearchical decoding of words because not all words contain letter patterns that have a direct one-to-one correspondence with sounds. When children use hiearchical decoding, they allow some letters to cue the sounds of other letters, such as words that end with the silent "e." For example, words such as "came," "joke," "cute," and "kite" require hiearchical decoding because the "e" at the end of the word cues children to pronounce the vowel in the word as a long vowel sound rather than a short vowel sound. Other letter patterns such as vowel diagraphs (e.g., "boil," "loud," "mail," and "seal") also require hiearchical decoding because the combination of two vowels produces its own unique sound.

Plausibly, a reciprocal or bidirectional relationship exists between the development of spoken and of written language. Speaking vocabulary and the awareness of sounds in spoken language contribute to decoding written language; likewise, developing written language contributes to further growth in spoken language skills (Chase & Tallal, 1991). For instance, investigations have reported that individuals' growth in word recognition strengthens their phonological awareness skills (Perfetti, Beck, Bell, & Hughes, 1987).

## CHARACTERISTICS OF CHILDREN WHO STRUGGLE TO ACQUIRE LITERACY

Children with reading and spelling problems are often characterized as either having garden types of reading difficulties or having dyslexia (Stanovich, 1988). Garden types of reading problems lead to below-average reading achievement and also indicate below-average intelligence and spoken, receptive, and written language as well as below-average performance across other academic domains, such as math, social studies, and science. Children with these problems are often referred to as at risk but may not be eligible for special education services, depending on state diagnostic criteria for identifying children with learning disabilities.

Learners with neurologically based reading disabilities are referred to as dyslexics or as children with severe reading and spelling problems that cannot be explained by lack of instruction or poor instruction, mental retardation, or limited environmental conditions. These children tend to have average or above-average intellectual abilities, receptive language abilities, and achievement skills in areas such as math, social studies, and science as long as the criteria for success in those courses demand limited literacy skills, which is typical of the curriculum in the primary grades. Pennington (1991) found that electroenaphalographs (EEGs), evoked potentials, and positron emission tomography (PET) scans have indicated an anomaly of left hemisphere development of dyslexics. Other researchers have found that dylexics have shorter left planum lengths (Hynd, Semrud-Clikeman, Lorys, Novey, & Eliopulos, 1990). The planum temporale is the superior posterior surface of the temporal lobe. In the left hemisphere, the planum temporale is part of Wernike's area, which is responsible for phonological processing. Moreover, Semrud-Clikeman, Hynd, Novey, and Eliopulos (1991) discovered that word attack skills, rapid naming, and passage comprehension difficulties were related to atypical patterns of symmetry in the planum temporale.

Characteristics of the majority of children with dyslexia include slow working memory processes, such as phonological memory difficulties (Breznitz, 1997), speech production difficulties, slow word retrieval (Breznitz, 1997), rapid naming difficulties (Bowers & Wolf, 1995), phonological awareness deficits, and phonological decoding deficits. Fewer children with dyslexia have adequate phonological skills but have difficulties processing orthographic features of written words (Stanovich, 1992). A growing body of recent research using electrophysiological and behavioral measures claims that dyslexics exhibit asynchromatic processing rates between visual-orthographic and auditory-phonological information, which means that some children process visual-orthographic information at slower rates than auditory-phonological linguistic stimuli and vice versa (Breznitz, 2002). An underlying cause of dyslexia may be a physiologically based reduction in speed of processing the connection between phonological and orthographic features of language, which manifests in slow rates of print-to-sound conversions (Breznitz & Berman, 2003). Therefore, children with severe reading disabilities should work on improving their speed of processing phonological and orthographic information, which is strongly related to word reading rates (Breznitz, 2002). According to Henry (1998), individuals with dyslexia may also have disorders in social adjustment, attention, and written expression.

Despite some of the differences in characteristics between garden-variety types of poor readers and dyslexics or specific learning disabilities in reading, both types of poor readers exhibit deficits in phonological processing (Stanovich & Siegal, 1994). Moreover, children who have deficits in both phonological awareness and rapid automatized naming exhibit lower performance in reading than children who have a deficit in only one area (Kirby, Pfeiffer, & Parrila, 2000). Therefore, type of reading and spelling instruction is likely to be very similar for various types of children with reading problems.

## INTERVENTIONS FOR FACILITATING
## LITERACY DEVELOPMENT

Children with severe reading and spelling difficulties need explicit and systematic teaching of strategies (Brady & Moats, 1997). Effective cognitive-behavioral principles of teaching and learning should be incorporated in any teaching technique or program designed to teach children reading and spelling, especially those who struggle with obtaining literacy skills (Joseph, 2002b). These principles include positive reinforcement for successive approximations, repeated exposures, opportunities to practice, corrective feedback, learning strategies that foster independent problem-solving skills, and the use of multisensory stimuli or manipulatives. There are vast amounts of reading and spelling interventions, and the interventions described in this section are certainly not exhaustive. The interventions selected for discussion in this chapter are those that purport to address the spoken and written language processing difficulties associated with neurological dysfunctions. These techniques also encompass effective principles of teaching and learning.

### Word Level Reading and Spelling Intervention Techniques

The following interventions are examples of word reading and spelling interventions and not exhaustive of all effective interventions.

*Sound Boxes*   A technique called sound boxes was created by D. B. Elkonin, a colleague of A. R. Luria, to be used with preschool children who had difficulty discriminating the sequential sound structure of spoken words. Most scholars and teachers refer to sound boxes as Elkonin boxes. Sound boxes consist of a drawn rectangle divided into sections according to the number of sounds heard in a given word. Thus, the divided rectangle transforms into connected boxes (i.e., squares). Tokens or counters are placed below each of the connected boxes, and children are asked to slide the tokens into the boxes while slowly articulating the beginning, middle, and ending sounds of the word. That is, children slide a token into the first box as the first sound is articulated slowly, slide a token into the next box as the next sound is articulated, and slide a token into the last box as the final sound of a word is articulated. For instance, for the word "cat," children are asked to slowly articulate the /c/ sound as they place a token in the first connected box. As they slowly articulate the /a/ sound, they place the token in the middle box, and they place a token in the final box as they slowly articulate the /t/ sound. Thus, this technique has a visual structure and demands physical movement of objects to aid children in segmenting sounds of spoken words. Elkonin (1973) observed children using this technique and found that it helped them become aware that spoken words were made up of discrete sounds and that when sounds were sequentially blended together, they formed a word.

*Word Boxes*   Marie Clay (1993) expanded on Elkonin's boxes and created word boxes to be used in the Reading Recovery Program. Word boxes are an intervention technique designed to help children make one-to-one correspondences with letters and sounds. Whereas sound boxes involve using tokens or counters to aid in the segmentation of sounds of words, word boxes involve using plastic or magnetic letters and writing letters to aid in creating a printed word.

Similar to sound boxes, a rectangle is drawn and divided by vertical lines according to the number of sounds heard in a word. Plastic letters are placed below the connected boxes of the rectangle. Children are asked to articulate the sounds of a given word slowly while they simultaneously place the letters in their respective boxes. If children were articulating the word "boat," they would slide the letter "b" into the first section of the rectangle, slide the letters "oa" into the middle section, and slide the letter "t" into the last section.

Word boxes have been examined in several studies with various types of children. Joseph (1998–1999) explored the effectiveness of this technique with 2nd- and 3rd-grade children with learning disabilities. She found that word boxes were effective for helping this sample of children improve on word recognition and spelling performance. Findings also revealed that children were able to maintain word recognition and spelling performance after lessons ended. In another study, 1st-graders were randomly assigned to either the word boxes instruction condition or a traditional phonics instruction condition that used workbooks (Joseph, 2000b). Children in the word boxes condition outperformed children in the traditional phonics instruction condition on word recognition and spelling. Additional findings revealed that children in the word boxes condition were also able to transfer word recognition and spelling skills to words that were similar to but not directly taught during the instructional sessions.

In a recent study, Shaia, Joseph, and Siegal (in review) found that kindergarten children who struggled to obtain basic emergent literacy skills improved from baseline to intervention sessions on phoneme segmentation fluency and word recognition performance as a function of using word boxes but did not demonstrate any differences, and in some cases demonstrated a decrease in performance, on letter naming fluency. Although the word boxes technique was useful for helping this sample of children segment sounds and decode words, it was not the technique of choice for rapid naming of letters. In many respects, this finding should have come as no surprise because letter naming is not a skill directly taught using the word boxes technique, and for this sample, direct teaching of letter naming skills was needed.

Variations of sound boxes and word boxes have been used as part of more comprehensive phonemic awareness training programs for preschoolers and kindergartners in several seminal investigations (Ball & Blachman, 1991; Bentin & Leshem, 1993; Bryne & Fielding-Barnsley, 1991; Hohn & Ehri, 1983). One variation is the say-it-move-it activity, which uses blank tiles and tiles with printed letters. Each tile represents a sound, and the children place the tiles together as each sound of a word is articulated, thus creating connected boxes. The blank tiles are eventually replaced with tiles with printed letters on them. Each tile contains one letter, and the children move them and place them together as they articulate each sound in a word.

*Sound Sorts*   Sound sorts are an activity that involves sorting pictures according to common beginning or ending sounds of words (Bear, Invernizzi, Templeton, & Johnston, 1996). The instructor designates categories of beginning sounds such as /b/ and /d/, and children are given pictures that represent objects that begin with a /b/ sound or a /d/ sound; they then place the pictures in the /b/ category or the /d/ category. Another variation of the sound sorts activity is to designate two, three, or more words as category words and have these words printed on index cards. The index cards are placed across a table, and children are given tokens or counters. The instructor says a word and the children place the tokens below the category word that shares sounds with the word orally presented.

Sound sorts have been examined in empirical investigations with preschoolers. Maslanka and Joseph (2002) randomly assigned a sample of preschool children to a sound sort or a sound box condition to determine differential effects on phoneme segmentation, phoneme blending, rhyming, and identification of beginning, middle, and ending sounds. Findings suggested that children who received sound box instruction performed better on phoneme segmentation and identifying middle sounds. However, children in both groups improved considerably from pretests to posttests on all skills that were assessed in this study. Sound categorization exercises have also been included as part of comprehensive phoneme awareness training programs.

*Word Sorts*   Word sorts are similar to sound sorts except that they involve sorting printed words below designated categories (Bear et al., 1996). Word sorts are also considered to be a spelling-based phonics technique. Category words are established by the instructor and are printed on index cards, which are placed on a table. A stack of index cards with printed words is shuffled and given to the children, and the children examine each card and place the card below its respective category card according to similar phonological or orthographic features. This technique can be used when teaching word family or phonogram words that share similar sound and spelling patterns. Words may also be sorted according to morphemic patterns or sorted based on shared meaning (Zutell, 1998). For instance, words ending in "ian" (e.g., pediatrician, magician, musician) may be sorted below the category "people," and words ending in "ion" (e.g., institution, education, constitution) may be sorted below the category "things." Word sorting techniques are often referred to as word study approaches for teaching reading and spelling because they involve the examination of spelling and sound patterns of words for the purposes of classifying common characteristics and making distinctions among sound and spelling patterns of words.

The effectiveness of word sorts has been explored in several investigations. Joseph (2000a) randomly assigned 1st-grade students to a word sort instruction condition, a word boxes instruction condition, or a control condition. Results indicated that learners who received word sort instruction performed better in spelling than the other two groups. Learners in the word sorts and word boxes conditions performed better on phoneme segmentation, phoneme blending, and word recognition than the control group. There were no significant differences between the word sorts group and the word boxes group on phoneme segmentation, phoneme blending, and word recognition. A combination of word sorts and word boxes was examined with a sample of children with mental retardation; results revealed that children improved on basic word recognition and spelling performance as a function of using the combination (Joseph, 2002a). In another study, learners with mental retardation were compared to learners not identified with disabilities on word recognition and spelling performance after using word sorts (Joseph & McCachran, 2003). Findings revealed variation in performance in both groups, indicating that some children improved on their word recognition and spelling performance between pretest and posttest measures, and others did not make significant gains. There were no significant differences between the groups of children, but it should be noted that the children with mental retardation were 3rd-graders and the children not identified with disabilities were 1st-graders.

Word sorts have also been included as part of comprehensive literacy programs, such as Early Steps (Santa & Hoien, 1999), Howard Tutoring Program (Morris, Shaw, & Perney, 1990), and Four Blocks Program (Cunningham, 1999). Word sorts have also been compared with other spelling techniques, such as copy-cover-check and traditional spelling instruction (Dangel, 1989). Findings from this study revealed that participants who were taught a combination of word sorts and copy-cover-check outperformed participants who either were provided with word sorts alone or traditional spelling instruction. Participants who were provided with word sorts alone performed better than participants who were provided traditional spelling instruction.

*Copy-Cover-Check*   This technique is designed to help children who have difficulty learning weekly spelling words and who may need additional practice and feedback. Children are asked to copy one of their spelling words. They are asked to cover up the copied version of the word and attempt to spell the word on their own. The students then uncover the copied version to check if their spelling of the word matches the copied version, and they make corrections if they spelled the word incorrectly. This procedure is repeated until an established criterion level of mastery is met.

A version of this technique is add-a-word spelling practice. This procedure has been found to be most helpful for children who consistently achieve a score below 70% on their weekly spelling tests. Students copy 10 spelling words to practice on a copy column of their worksheet. They then cover the words and write the words from memory in a different column. Next, students uncover the copied words and compare their responses with the correct spelling list of words. This process should be repeated at least twice a day for children who have difficulty. After two trials, students may drop the words spelled correctly from the list, retain those spelled incorrectly, and add a new word for every word that is dropped. Students can record their progress on a chart. This procedure has been found to be effective in helping children improve their spelling performance (Pratt-Struthers, Struthers, & Williams, 1983).

*Response Cards*   The strategy allows every student in a classroom to practice spelling words and to learn from each other. Thus, it provides all students with opportunities to practice spelling words and receive feedback. Students are provided with dry-erase boards, small chalkboards, or small poster boards. The teacher says a word, and the children are required to write the word on their response cards and hold them up. Teachers check students' responses and provide corrective feedback if needed. Children also observe their classmates' responses and compare them with their responses. Students can also use preprinted response cards with multiple responses on them and a clothespin to attach the correct spelling of the word to the card. Heward et al. (1996) provide a summary of studies and variety of uses of response cards for learning academic skills.

*Incremental Rehearsal*   Incremental rehearsal is a drill rehearsal technique designed to teach unknown items using a ratio of 90% known and 10% unknown items (Tucker, 1988). This technique can be used to teach fluent reading of words. Nine known words and one unknown word are written on 3 x 5 index cards. The first unknown item is visually presented to the student while the instructor provides the verbal pronunciation. The first unknown is interspersed with the known words nine times throughout the process. The child is asked to verbally state the word each time it is presented. After completing this sequence, the first unknown word will be treated as the first known, the previous ninth known will be removed, and a new unknown word will be rehearsed. Therefore, the number of cards used will always remain at 10. MacQuarrie, Tucker, Burns, and Hartman (2002) compared Tucker's (1989) incremental rehearsal drill model, which involves rehearsing one unknown word with nine known, to more challenging ratios of known to unknown, including a traditional condition that used only unknown words. Results found significantly better retention for incremental rehearsal than for the other conditions. Recently, a comparison of less and more challenging ratios of known to unknown words used to teach spelling words was investigated; findings reported that more words were learned in a shorter amount of time using more challenging ratios of known to unknown words (Cates et al., 2003).

*Repeated Readings*   Repeated readings are a very effective whole word recognition strategy for building fluency with reading words in connected text (Rasinski, 1990). Essentially, children read the same passage several times for 1 minute until mastery of the passage has been achieved. Mastery usually means reading the passage fluently, which means reading all of the words accurately and quickly. Reading fluency is highly correlated with reading comprehension. Children are considered to be reading at grade level if they are reading between 75 and 100 words per minute correctly on a grade-level passage with 3 to 5 errors (Shinn, 1989).

## PHONICS

Phonics is the system by which one learns to link print (graphemes) to sound (phonemes), which is crucial to learning how to read words (Ehri, 1998). There are several comprehensive phonics programs that school districts may implement on a classroomwide, buildingwide, or districtwide level. Some of these programs have been around for many years but are reemerging, especially due to an emphasis on teaching phonics and the synthesis of research reported in the National Reading Panel (2000) report. There are strengths and weaknesses of each program, and more research is needed to demonstrate the efficacy of phonics programs in general.

Some scholars have offered guidelines for selecting phonics programs. For instance, Stahl, Duffy-Hester, and Stahl (1998) suggested that good phonics instruction includes fast-paced lessons, explicit teaching of linking print to sound, systematic procedures, incorporates phoneme awareness and spelling instruction, and does not last more than 20 minutes per day. Through a meta-analysis of treatment outcome studies with students with learning disabilities, Swanson and Hoskyn (1998) found that intervention programs that used a combined model of direct instruction and strategy instruction methods were the most efficacious, especially in regard to helping children generalize skills to words unknown to them.

*Orton-Gillingham Approach*   One of the oldest phonics programs designed to teach children with reading disabilities is the Orton-Gillingham Phonics Program. This program was conceived by Sam Orton and Anna Gillingham at the New York Neurological Institute. Orton directed Gillingham to create an organized set of instructional materials and lessons, and now the Orton-Gillingham Program is in its eighth edition (Gillingham & Stillman, 1997). This instructional program was developed based on Orton's neuropsychological hypothesis about dyslexia. The program emphasizes teaching phonics through multisensory stimuli to provide children with opportunities to link visual, auditory, and kinesthetic senses. It also helps children think about the logic of language as they use language. Students learn to say words as they write them using auditory and visual channels. Kinesthetic-tactile channels are accessed by having the children feel the muscles of their throat and mouth while producing a sequence of sounds and also writing words as they sound them out. The program is designed to teach very basic, decodable words and progresses to teaching more complex, multisyllabic words. Several programs are considered offspring of the Orthon-Gillingham approach to reading: Alphabetic Phonics, Project Read, and Slingerland, Spalding, and Wilson (Henry, 1998). Several investigations have supported the use of these programs (e.g., Foorman, Francis, Beeler, Winikates, & Fletcher, 1997; Stoner, 1991).

*Wilson Reading System*   The Wilson Reading System was designed by Barbara Wilson, who was an Orton-Gillingham teacher. This program encompasses multisensory methods to teaching phoneme segmentation, alphabetic principle, decoding, spelling, advanced word analysis, vocabulary development, sight words, fluency, and comprehension with visualization and metacognition in a one-to-one or small group instruction format. In the late 1980s, the Wilson Reading System was developed at the Massachusetts Center for Students with Language/Learning Disabilities, including individuals with dyslexia. The main goal of the Wilson Reading System is to teach children the structure of the English language as an organized system that also contains irregularities. It is now used in school districts throughout the country. It incorporates effective components of teaching and learning, including direct instruction in language analysis, integration of reading and spelling skills, intensive instruction, and teaching for mastery. Although more research is needed, there have been some investigations reporting the effects of the Wilson Reading System for children at risk for reading failure in rural and middle-class school districts (Bursuck & Dickson, 1999), for college students with dyslexia who needed assistance with spelling (Banks, Guyer, & Guyer, 1993), and for students with language learning disabilities who needed to improve on their word attack and passage comprehension skills (Clark & Uhry, 1995).

*Direct Instruction Reading Mastery*   The Direct Instruction Reading Mastery program (Englemann & Bruner, 1988), derived from the principles and lessons in the Direct Instruction System for Teaching and Remediation (DISTAR) program, involves explicit, systematic, fast-paced instruction on teaching sounds in isolation, teaching blending sounds, and teaching reading vocabulary words that have regular, decodable spellings. The scripted lessons include choral responding, corrective feedback, and opportunities to practice until mastery is obtained. Earlier investigations of DISTAR reported that it was more effective for teaching reading to economically disadvantaged children (Meyer, Gersten, & Gutkin, 1983) and children with brain damage (L'E. Stein & Goldman, 1980). However, another investigation found comparable outcomes in reading achievement between children who received the Direct Instruction Reading Mastery and another type of phonics program (O'Connor, Jenkins, Cole, & Mills, 1993). Although more research is needed to determine the effectiveness of Direct Instruction Reading Mastery with children with disabilities, the program does encompass explicit and systematic instruction, which are components found to be effective for children who struggle to achieve literacy skills (Carnine, Silbert, & Kameenui, 1990).

*Scott Foresman Early Reading Intervention*   The Scott Foresman Early Reading Intervention program, formerly called Project Optimize, is based on a 5-year longitudinal investigation conducted by Simmons and Kameenui (1998). This program is designed for children who need early, intensive phonological awareness, letter names, letter sounds, word reading, spelling, and simple sentence reading instruction. The lessons are based on direct instruction principles of teaching and learning and last a total of 30 minutes. The first 15 minutes are devoted to developing phonological awareness and alphabetic understanding. Some of the tasks that children are asked to complete involve phoneme segmentation, blending, sound discrimination, and reading consonant-vowel-consonant words in connected texts. The second 15 minutes involve teaching children spelling skills, thereby reinforcing phonological and alphabetic skills. Children are asked to initially trace words, write initial and final letters corresponding to sounds of words, and then write all the letters in consonant-vowel-consonant sounding words.

*Success for All*   Success for All is a comprehensive reading program designed for students who are at risk for developing adequate literacy skills. Success for All is divided into smaller programs and consists of the preschool or early kindergarten program, the beginning reading or Reading Roots program, and Beyond the Basics or Reading Wings program (Slavin, Madden, Karweit, Dolan, & Wasik, 1992). This program incorporates phonics instruction with other literacy skills. The preschool or early kindergarten program entails storytelling and retelling, emergent writing, phoneme awareness activities, shared book experience, receptive and expressive vocabulary skills, and alphabetic activities. The beginning reading program involves reading rehearsals, metacognitive strategies, sound, letter, and word development activities, and story reading activities. The Beyond the Basics program includes a variety of story-related activities, direct instruction in comprehending text, independent reading, and listening comprehension. Instructional components of the program include continuous progress monitoring of performance, research-based reading techniques, one-to-one tutoring, and family support.

Ross, Smith, Slavin, and Madden (1997) provide a review of investigations reporting the effectiveness of Success for All for minority students in urban school settings. The program appears to be most effective for helping students who were considered to be performing at the lowest 25% on reading in school, especially helping these children improve on word identification and word attack at the kindergarten and 1st-grade levels (Ross & Smith, 1994).

*Four Blocks Approach*   The Four Blocks reading instruction program is a multilevel, multimethod program that was developed over 8 years ago to meet the needs of children at various reading levels (Cunningham, Hall, & Defee, 1998). There are four blocks of reading instruction time: the guided reading block, the self-selected reading block, the writing block, and the working with words block. The working with words block consists of phonics instruction techniques such as completing a word wall of words that share common spelling patterns and engaging in word sort activities. Although there has been some research exploring the utility of this program with children with disabilities (Katims, 2000), more investigations are needed with samples of children at various reading levels.

*Phast Program*   The Phast (phonological and strategy training) Program presents five strategies in a metacognitive organizational structure called the game plan (Lovett, Lacerenza, & Borden, 2000). The sounding-out strategy involves systematic training in letter-sound correspondences, phonological remediation of sound segmentation and sound blending difficulties, and phonologically based teaching of word identification skills. This phase incorporates many of the components and lessons contained in the Direct Instruction Reading Mastery program. The focus of the rhyming strategy is to teach children words that share common spelling patterns or word family words (sometimes referred to as phonograms). Children learn that many of these words serve as keywords for learning other, more complex words such as learning that the word "cat" may one day help them pronounce the word "catastrophe." Children are guided toward making word analogies through explicit dialogue with their instructor. The peeling-off strategy is used to teach students prefixes and suffixes by segmenting affixes at the beginning (e.g., "re") and end (e.g., "ing") of a word. The students "peel off" the affixes to identify the root word. The vowel alert strategy involves having students attempt different vowel pronunciations in an unknown word until they say the word correctly. Single short or long vowel sounds are taught initially using this strategy, and then vowel combinations such as "ou" and "ea" are taught. I spy strategy involves looking for small familiar parts of a longer unknown word. This strategy is mostly used when teaching compound words. For the word "handshake," for example, the children would say "I spy the word hand, so I will put a box around the word hand. I spy the word shake, so I will put a box around the word shake."

Children are taught when to use the various strategies (depending on the types of words they are learning) through a "game plan." The game plan might consist of planning to use the rhyming strategy and then the I spy strategy. The children are encouraged to monitor their strategy use by checking to see if they are using the strategy appropriately and by determining if the strategy is helping them identify the word. Children record correct responses by giving themselves a score and not giving themselves a score if the strategy did not yield successful results. If a strategy did not yield desirable results, the students are encourage to choose another strategy in the program. In a recent investigation, Lovett, Lacerenza, Borden, Frijters, et al. (2000) found that demonstrable outcomes were observed in word identification, passage comprehension, and nonword reading for a sample of children who received a combination of phonological and strategy training (PHAST program) in contrast to children who only received either phonological or strategy training.

## VOCABULARY AND PASSAGE COMPREHENSION TECHNIQUES

Instruction aimed at developing vocabulary should consist of teaching a small number of words intensively in any given lesson, exposing the student to the same word in various contexts and in a systematic and continuous fashion, game-like activities to stimulate interest in learning concepts and teaching morphological units (e.g., prefixes and suffixes), and explicitly teaching derivations of words through exercises using the dictionary (McCormick, 1999). For instance, categorization activities help children group words that share similar meanings and helps them make distinctions about words that are not similar. Cloze procedure exercises involving a passage with every nth word missing can be used to help children build vocabulary by determining where words are placed contextually within a passage.

Learning strategies instruction approaches were found to be effective for helping children with learning problems understand concepts and improve on their reading comprehension performance of narrative and expository text (see Pressley, 1998, for a review). Learning strategy instruction for comprehending reading passages should consist of self-questioning, retellings and parapharasing, constructing mental representations to integrate information from text, identifying text consistencies, and summarizing the main ideas. Examples of these approaches include semantic mapping, PQ4R (preview, question, read, reflect, recite, and review), and reciprocal teaching.

*Semantic Mapping* Semantic mapping typically involves developing word webs that reflect students' understanding of concepts and constructing a diagram connecting events of a story or connecting facts taken from content area textbooks. Students who struggle with grasping conceptual relationships may find developing maps or diagrams to be helpful visual aids (Novak & Musonda, 1991). Semantic maps can be either process oriented or product oriented. Process-oriented maps usually are completed before students read assigned material to help them establish some background knowledge (McCormick, 1999). This type of mapping requires teacher facilitation of student responses. For example, a teacher may write a concept (e.g., satire) in a drawn box and ask the class to give examples of when they experience it. As the class responds, the teacher writes their comments below the concept. The teacher may then ask students how it feels when they witness the concept and write their responses, drawing connecting lines to the other comments, and so forth. Product-oriented maps, on the other hand, are produced by students as an outcome activity after they have read material. Students generally work independently or with peers and construct a map connecting ideas presented in text.

*PQ4R* The PQ4R method of comprehending reading material is an extension of SQ3R (survey, question, read, recite, and review; Thomas & Robinson, 1972). This method involves previewing the reading material, questioning the reading, reading to answer the questions, reflecting on the reading, reciting the reading, and reviewing the material. Previewing the material means surveying the chapter titles, main topics, and subheadings of the text. Students can turn the headings and subheadings into questions, which are answered by reading the text. Reflections about the content can occur as the material is being read if the students pause to form connections and create images. Reciting is retelling from memory what was read. This form of retelling helps students monitor the information they are obtaining from the reading. If some information is not being retained, students may need to read sections of the text again. Last, students review the material by answering questions and referring back to the text for clarification of mistaken responses to questions.

*Reciprocal Teaching*   Reciprocal teaching is a reading comprehension approach that has helped delayed readers catch up with and even exceed typically developing readers (Palinscar & Brown, 1984). This approach places heavy emphasis on teacher-student interactions in a cognitive apprenticeship fashion. After students and teacher read from common text, they discuss the reading material. Initially, the teacher leads the dialogue by modeling strategies of predicting, question generating, summarizing, and clarifying text. The students are then asked to lead the discussions and apply the strategies that were demonstrated by the teacher. Guided practice is provided until students can use the strategies effectively. The goal of these reciprocal teaching interactions is to construct meaning from texts.

In general, comprehension instruction like the approaches just described produces the best outcomes for students (Gaskins, Anderson, Pressley, Cunicelli, & Satlow, 1993). Strategies that need to be directly facilitated include connecting text to prior knowledge, questioning and predicting events, clarifying information and checking for understanding, paraphrasing or retelling information, and summarizing information from text. Good readers are reported to monitor themselves while reading and determine if they are gaining meaning from the text. In other words, good readers know when they need to reread a section or read a section more slowly (Pressley, 1999).

## CONCLUSION

School psychologists play one of the most unique roles in the schools because they have an understanding about the interaction between the physiological, cognitive, and behavioral characteristics of children and the ecological context of the school, home, and community. This places school psychologists in a unique position to facilitate the understanding of these interactions with other professionals and families who have an interest in helping children develop academically. As has been described in this chapter, reading and spelling performance is the result of appropriate interactions between instruction and the physiological, cognitive, and behavioral characteristics of children. The instructional techniques described in this chapter have been found to be effective for children, and research continues to evolve in discovering best approaches for teaching literacy skills to those most challenged. It is imperative that school psychologists continually engage in the literature regarding literacy instruction so they remain in a position to facilitate understandings of the interaction between instruction and children's learning characteristics and to aid in the selection of appropriate instruction to meet the literacy needs of children.

# REFERENCES

Adams, M. J. (1990). *Beginning to read: Thinking and learning about print.* Cambridge, MA: MIT Press.

Ball, E., & Blachman, B. (1991). Does phonemic awareness training in kindergarten make a difference in early word recognition and developmental spelling? *Reading Research Quarterly, 26,* 49–66.

Banks, S. R., Guyer, B. P., & Guyer, K. E. (1993). Spelling improvement by college students who are dyslexic. *Annals of Dyslexia, 43,* 186–193.

Bear, D. R., Invernizzi, M. A., Templeton, S., & Johnston, F. (1996). *Words their way: Word study for phonics, vocabulary, and spelling.* Englewood Cliffs, NJ: Prentice-Hall.

Bentin, S., & Leshem, H. (1993). On the interaction between phonological awareness and reading acquisition: It's a two-way street. *Annals of Dyslexia, 43,* 125–148.

Bowers, P. G. (1995). Tracing symbol naming speeds unique contributions to reading disabilities over time. *Reading and Writing: An Interdisciplinary Journal, 7,* 189–216.

Brady, S., & Moats, L. (1997). *Informed instruction for reading success: Foundations for teacher preparation.* Baltimore: Orton Dyslexia Society.

Breznitz, Z. (1997). The effect of accelerated reading on memory for text among dyslexic readers. *Journal of Educational Psychology, 89,* 287–299.

Breznitz, Z. (2002). Asynchrony of visual-orthographic and auditory-phonological word recognition processes: An underlying factor in dyslexia. *Reading and Writing: An International Quarterly, 15*(1/2), 15–42.

Breznitz, Z., & Berman, L. (2003). The underlying factors of word reading rate. *Educational Psychology Review, 15*(3), 247–265.

Bursuck, W., & Dickson, S. (1999). Implementing a model for preventing reading failure: A report from the field. *Learning Disabilities Research and Practice, 14*(4), 191–202.

Byrne, B., & Fielding-Barnsley, R. (1991). Evaluation of a program to teach phonemic awareness to young children. *Journal of Educational Psychology, 83,* 451–455.

Carnine, D., Silbert, J., & Kameenui, E. (1990). *Direct instruction reading.* Columbus, OH: Merrill.

Cates, G. L., Skinner, C. H., Watson, S., Meadows, T. J., Weaver, A., & Jackson, B. (2003). Instructional effectiveness and instructional efficiency as considerations for data-based decision making: An evaluation of interspersing procedures. *School Psychology Review, 31*(4), 601–616.

Chase, C. H., & Tallal, P. (1991). Cognitive models of developmental reading disorders. In J. Obrutz & G. W. Hynd (Eds.), *Neuropsychological foundations of learning disabilities* (pp. 199–240). San Diego, CA: Academic Press.

Clark, D., & Uhry, J. (1995). *Dyslexia theory and practice remedial instruction.* Baltimore: York Press.

Clay, M. (1993). *Reading recovery: A guidebook for teachers in training.* Portsmouth, NH: Heinemann.

Compton, D. L. (2003). Modeling the relationship between growth in rapid naming speed and growth in decoding skill in first-grade children. *Journal of Educational Psychology, 95*(2), 225–239.

Cunningham, P. M. (1999). What should we do about phonics. In L. B. Gambrell, L. M. Morrow, S. B. Neuman, & M. Pressley (Eds.), *Best practices in literacy instruction* (pp. 66–89). New York: Guilford Press.

Cunningham, P. M., Hall, D. P., & Defee, M. (1998). Nonability-grouped multilevel instruction: Eight years later. *Reading Teacher, 51*(8), 652–664.

Cutting, L. E., & Denkla, M. B. (2001). The relationship of rapid serial naming and word reading in normally developing readers: An exploratory model. *Reading and Writing: An Interdisciplinary Journal, 14*, 673–705.

Dangel, H. L. (1989). The use of student directed spelling strategies. *Academic Therapy, 25*, 43–51.

Ehri, L. (1998). Grapheme-phoneme knowledge is essential for beginning to read words in English. In J. Metsala & L. Ehri (Eds.), *Word recognition in beginning literacy* (pp. 3–40). Mahwah, NJ: Erlbaum.

Elkonin, D. B. (1973). USSR. In J. Downing (Ed.), *Comparative reading* (pp. 551–579). New York: Macmillan.

Englemann, S., & Bruner, E. (1988). *Reading mastery I: DISTAR reading.* Chicago: Science Research Associates.

Frith, V. (1985). Beneath the surface of developmental dyslexia. In K. E. Patterson, J. C. Marshall, & M. Colheart (Eds.), *Surface dyslexia* (pp. 301–330). London: Erlbaum.

Foorman, B., Francis, D., Beeler, T., Winikates, D., & Fletcher, J. M. (1997). Early interventions for children with reading problems: Study designs and preliminary findings. *Learning Disabilities, 8*, 63–71.

Foorman, B., Francis, D., Fletcher, J., Schatachneider, C., & Mehta, P. (1998). The role of instruction in learning to read: Preventing reading failure in at-risk children. *Journal of Educational Psychology, 90*, 37–55.

Gaskins, I. W., Anderson, R. C., Pressley, M., Cunicelli, E. A., & Satlow, E. (1993). Six teachers' dialogue during cognitive process instruction. *Elementary School Journal, 93*, 277–304.

Gathercole, S. E., & Baddeley, A. D. (1990). Phonological memory deficits in language disordered children: Is there a causal connection? *Journal of Memory and Language, 29*, 336–360.

Gillingham, A., & Stillman, B. W. (1997). *The Gillingham manual: Remedial training for children with specific disability in reading, spelling, and penmanship* (8th ed.). Cambridge, MA: Educators Publishing Service.

Griffith, P. (1991). Phonemic awareness helps first graders invent spellings and third graders remember correct spellings. *Journal of Reading Behavior, 23*, 215–233.

Hatcher, P., Hulme, C., & Ellis, A. W. (1994). Ameliorating reading failure by integrating the teaching of reading and phonological skills: The phonological linkage hypothesis. *Child Development, 65*, 41–57.

Henry, M. K. (1998). Structured, sequential, multisensory teaching: The Orton legacy. *Annals of Dyslexia, 48*, 3–26.

Heward, W. L., Gardner, R., III, Cavanaugh, S. S., Courson, F. H., Grossi, T. A., & Barbetta, P. M. (1996). Everyone participates in this class: Using response cards to increase active student response. *Teaching Exceptional Children*, 4–10.

Hohn, W. E., & Ehri, L. C. (1983). Do alphabet letters help prereaders acquire phonemic segmentation skill? *Journal of Educational Psychology, 75*, 752–762.

Hynd, G. W., Semrud-Clikeman, M., Lorys, A. R., Novey, E. S., & Eliopulas, D. (1990). Brain morphology in developmental dyslexia and attention deficit disorder/hyperactivity. *Archives of Neurology, 47*, 919–926.

Joseph, L. M. (1998–1999). Word boxes help children with learning disabilities identify and spell words. *Reading Teacher, 52*(4), 348–356.

Joseph, L. M. (2000a). Developing first-graders' phonemic awareness, word identification, and spelling: A comparison of two contemporary phonic approaches. *Reading Research and Instruction, 39*(2), 160–169.

Joseph, L. M. (2000b). Using word boxes as a large group phonics approach in a first grade classroom. *Reading Horizons, 41*, 117–127.

Joseph, L. M. (2002a). Facilitating word recognition and spelling using word boxes and word sort phonic procedures. *School Psychology Review, 31*, 122–129.

Joseph, L. M. (2002b). Planning interventions for students with reading problems. In A. Thomas & J. Grimes (Eds.), *Best practices in school psychology* (Vol. 4, pp. 803–816). Bethesda, MD: National Association of School Psychologists.

Joseph, L. M., & McCachran, M. (2003). Comparison of a word study phonics technique between students with moderate to mild mental retardation and struggling readers without disabilities. *Education and Training in Developmental Disabilities, 38*(2), 192–199.

Katims, D. S. (2000). Literacy instruction for people with mental retardation: Historical highlights and contemporary analysis. *Education and Training in Mental Retardation and Developmental Disabilities, 35*, 3–15.

Kirby, J. R., Pfeiffer, S. L., & Parrila, R. K. (2000). Naming speed and phonological awareness as predictors of reading development. *Journal of Educational Psychology, 95*(3), 453–464.

L'E. Stein, C., & Goldman, J. (1980). Beginning reading instruction for children with minimal brain dysfunction. *Journal of Learning Disabilities, 13*, 219–222.

Lovett, M. W., Lacerenza, L., & Borden, S. L. (2000). Putting struggling readings on the PHAST track: A program to integrate phonological and strategy-based remedial reading instruction and maximize outcomes. *Journal of Learning Disabilities, 33*(5), 458–476.

Lovett, M. W., Lacerenza, L., Borden, S. L., Frijters, J. C., Steinbach, K. A., & De Palma, M. (2000). Components of effective remediation for developmental reading disability: Combining phonological and strategy-based instruction to improve outcomes. *Journal of Educational Psychology, 92*(2), 263–283.

MacQuarrie, L. L., Tucker, J. A., Burns, M. K., & Hartman, B. (2002). Comparison of retention rates using traditional, drill sandwich, and incremental rehearsal flash card methods. *School Psychology Review, 31*(4), 584–595.

Manis, F. R., Doi, L. M., & Bhadha, B. (2000). Naming speed, phonological awareness, and orthographic knowledge in second graders. *Journal of Learning Disabilities, 33*, 325–333.

Maslanka, P., & Joseph, L. M. (2002). A comparison of two phonological awareness techniques between samples of preschool children. *Reading Psychology: An International Quarterly, 23*, 271–288.

McCormick, S. (1999). *Instructing students who have literacy problems* (3rd ed.). Upper Saddle River, NJ: Prentice-Hall.

McDougall, S., Hulme, C., Ellis, A., & Monk, A. (1994). Learning to read: The role of short-term memory and phonological skills. *Journal of Experimental Child Psychology, 58*, 112–133.

Meyer, L. A., Gersten, R. M., & Gutkin, J. (1983). Direct instruction: A project follow through success story in an inner-city school. *Elementary School Journal, 84*, 241–252.

Morris, D., Shaw, B., & Perney, J. (1990). Helping low readers in grades 2 and 3: An after school volunteer tutoring program. *Elementary School Journal, 91*, 133–150.

Muter, V., & Snowling, M. (1998). Concurrent and longitudinal predictors of reading: The role of metalinguistic and short-term memory skills. *Reading Research Quarterly, 33*, 320–337.

Nagy, W., Berninger, V., Abbot, R., Vaughan, K., & Vermeulen, K. (2003). Relationship of morphology and other language skills in at-risk second-grade readers and at-risk fourth-grade writers. *Journal of Educational Psychology, 95*(4), 730–742.

Nation, K., & Hulme, C. (1997). Phonemic segmentation, not onset-rime segmentation, predicts early reading and spelling skills. *Reading Research Quarterly, 32*, 154–167.

National Reading Panel. (2000). *Teaching children to read: An evidence-based assessment of the scientific literature on reading and its implications for reading instruction.* Bethesda, MD: National Institute of Child Health and Human Development.

Novak, J. D., & Musonda, D. (1991). A twelve-year longitudinal study of science concept learning. *American Educational Research Journal, 28*, 117–154.

O'Connor, R. E., Jenkins, J. R., Cole, K. N., & Mills, P. E. (1993). Two approaches to reading instruction with children with disabilities: Does program design make a difference? *Exceptional Children, 59*(4), 312–323.

Olson, R., Fosberg, H., Wise, B., & Rack, J. (1994). Measurement of word recognition, orthographic, and phonological skills. In G. R. Lyon (Ed.), *Frames of reference for the assessment of learning disabilities: New views of measurement issues* (pp. 243–278). Baltimore: Brookes.

Palinscar, A. S & Brown, A. L. (1984). Reciprocal teaching of comprehension-fostering and comprehension-monitoring activities. *Cognition and Instruction, 1*, 117–175.

Pennington, B. F. (1991). *Diagnosing learning disorders: A neuropsychological framework.* New York: Guilford Press.

Perfetti, C., Beck, I., Bell, L., & Hughes, C. (1987). Phonemic knowledge and learning to read are reciprocal: A longitudinal study of first-grade children. *Merrill-Palmer Quarterly, 33*, 283–319.

Pratt-Struthers, J., Struthers, J., & Williams, R. (1983). The effects of the add-a-word spelling program on spelling accuracy during creative writing. *Education and Treatment of Children, 6*, 277–283.

Pressley, M. (1998). *Reading instruction that works: The case for balanced teaching.* New York: Guilford Press.

Pressley, M. (1999). Self-regulated comprehension processing and its development through instruction. In L. B. Gambrell, L. M. Morrow, S. Neuman, & M. Pressley (Eds.), *Best practices in literacy instruction* (pp. 90–97). New York: Guilford Press.

Rasinski, T. (1990). Effects of repeated reading and listening while reading on reading fluency. *Journal of Educational Research, 83*, 147–150.

Ross, S. M., & Smith, L. J. (1994). Effects of the Success for All model on kindergarten through second-grade reading achievement, teachers' adjustment, and classroom-school climate at an inner-city school. *Elementary School Journal, 95*(2), 121–138.

Ross, S. M., Smith, L. J., Slavin, R. E., & Madden, N. A. (1997). Improving the academic success of disadvantaged children: An Examination of Success for All. *Psychology in the Schools, 34*(2), 171–180.

Santa, C. M., & Hoien, T. (1999). An assessment of Early Steps: A program for early intervention of reading problems. *Reading Research Quarterly, 34*, 54–79.

Semrud-Clikeman, M., Hynd, G. W., Novey, E. S., & Eliopulos, D. (1991). Dyslexia and brain morphology: Relationships between neuroanatomical variation and neurolinguistic tasks. *Learning and Individual Differences, 3*, 225–242.

Shaia, R., Joseph, L. M., & Siegal, B. (in review). Exploring the effectiveness of word boxes phonics technique on kindergartners' phonemic segmentation, letter-naming, and word Recognition Skills.

Share, D. L. (1995). Phonological recoding and self-teaching: Sin qua non of reading acquisition. *Cognition, 55*, 151–218.

Shinn, M. R. (Ed.). (1989). *Curriculum-based measurement: Assessing special children.* New York: Guilford Press.

Simmons, D. C., & Kameenui, E. J. (1998). *What reading research tells us about children with diverse reading needs: Bases and basics.* Mahwah, NJ: Erlbaum.

Slavin, R. E., Madden, N. A., Karweit, N. L., Dolan, L. J., & Wasik, B. A. (1992). *Success for All: A relentless approach to prevention and early intervention in elementary schools.* Arlington, VA: Educational Research Service.

Stahl, S. A., Duffy-Hester, A., & Stahl, K. A. (1998). Theory and research into practice: Everything you wanted to know about phonics (but were afraid to ask). *Reading Research Quarterly, 33,* 338–355.

Stahl, S. A., & Murray, B. A. (1994). Phonological awareness and its relationship to early reading. *Journal of Educational Psychology, 86,* 221–234.

Stanovich, K. E. (1988). The right and wrong places to look for the cognitive locus of reading disability. *Annals of Dyslexia, 38,* 154–177.

Stanovich, K. E. (1992). Speculations on the causes and consequences of individual differences in early reading acquisition. In P. Gough, L. Ehri, & R. Trieman (Eds.), *Reading acquisition* (pp. 307–342). Hillsdale, NJ: Erlbaum.

Stanovich, K. E., & Siegal, L. S. (1994). Phenotypic performance profile of children with reading disabilities: A regression-based test of the phonological-core variable-difference model. *Journal of Educational Psychology, 86,* 24–53.

Stoner, J. (1991). The potential for at-risk students to learn to read in groups contrasted under traditional and multisensory reading instruction. *Reading and Writing: An Interdisciplinary Journal, 3,* 19–30.

Swanson, H. L., & Hoskyn, M. (1998). Experimental intervention research on students with learning disabilities: A meta-analysis of treatment outcomes. *Review of Educational Research, 68,* 277–321.

Thomas, E. L., & Robinson, H. A. (1972). *Improving reading in every class: A sourcebook for teachers.* Boston: Allyn & Bacon.

Torgesen, J. K. (1988). Studies of children with learning disabilities who perform poorly on memory span tasks. *Journal of Learning Disabilities, 21,* 605–615.

Torgesen, J. K. (1996). A model of memory from an information processing perspective: The special case of phonological memory. In G. R. Lyon & N. A. Krasnegor (Eds.), *Attention, memory, and executive function* (pp. 157–184). Baltimore: Brookes.

Tucker, J. A. (1988). *Basic flashcard technique when vocabulary is the goal.* Unpublished teaching material, Andrews University, Berrien Springs, MI.

Vellutino, F. R., Scanlon, D. M., Sipay, E. R., Small, S. G., Pratt, A., Chen, R., et al. (1996). Cognitive profiles of difficult to remediate and readily remediated poor readers: Early intervention as a vehicle for distinguishing between cognitive and experiential deficits as basic causes of specific reading disability. *Journal of Educational Psychology, 88,* 601–638.

Vellutino, F. R., Scanlon, D., & Tanzman, M. (1998). The case for early intervention in diagnosing specific reading disabilities. *Journal of School Psychology, 36,* 367–397.

Wagner, R. K., & Togesen, J. K. (1987). The nature of phonological processing and its causal role in the acquisition of reading skills. *Psychological Bulletin, 101,* 192–212.

Wolf, M., & Bowers, P. G. (1999). The double deficit hypothesis for the development of dyslexias. *Journal of Educational Psychology, 91,* 415–438.

Zutell, J. (1998). Word sorting: A developmental spelling approach to word study for delayed readers. *Reading and Writing Quarterly: Overcoming Learning Difficulties, 14,* 219–238.

# CHAPTER 34

# Understanding and Implementing Neuropsychologically Based Arithmetic Interventions

CHERISE D. LEREW

## Case Study: Dan

Dan is a 5th grader who receives special education services for a learning disability according to his state's criteria for identification. This criteria indicated that he has a disorder in psychological processes that affected language and/or learning. A medical doctor has also diagnosed Dan as having Attention-Deficit/Hyperactivity Disorder (ADHD).

A neuropsychological evaluation determined that he was significantly impaired in the following achievement areas: reading skills, reading comprehension, written language expression, and comprehension, application, and retention of math concepts. Dan's performance on the evaluation indicated that he fell in the low-average range on nonverbal measures of intellectual abilities and in the borderline range on verbal measures of intellectual abilities. He displayed strengths on measures of processing speed, visual-motor coordination, and short-term visual memory. Similar to most children with ADHD, Dan performed poorly on measures of attention and planning skills. On a behavior rating scale, he achieved scores in the clinically significant range for attention, hyperactivity, anxiety, and depression. On a measure of neuropsychological functioning, Dan's scores fell in the below-expected range on measures of attention, executive functions, and phonological processing.

A 4-week meta-cognitive intervention was implemented with Dan to improve his performance in mathematics. Dan participated in a small group of 3 students for 30 minutes, 3 times per week. During each session, a staff member facilitated a discussion on strategy use. The students were encouraged to discuss what strategies worked, what strategies were ineffective, and what strategies they would use the next time. At the end of the intervention, Dan's math performance increased 185% when compared to the number correct on the first math assignment. There was an evident trend upward in the data.

This case study is an example of an intervention that was based on a comprehensive neuropsychological evaluation and required a minimal amount of staff involvement and effort. In a reasonable amount of time, the student made large improvements in mathematical performance. With the current push toward literacy proficiency, many students with math difficulties are not getting the extra instruction and intervention they need (e.g., No Child Left Behind, 2004). There are several reasons for this lack of support, one of these being a shortage of staff to work individually or in small groups with the students in need. With inclusion, teachers are already spending a significant amount of their time trying to differentiate instruction to meet the needs of the wide variety of skills demonstrated in their classrooms (Kirby & Williams, 1991; Lerner, 2000). It is very difficult for teachers to concentrate a significant amount of energy on one small group without neglecting the rest of the class. Moreover, due to the push to have all children read, extra support is generally provided during literacy instruction, not mathematics.

The current research on reading is much more extensive than the research on mathematics (Ashman & Conway, 1993; Das, Naglieri, & Kirby, 1994; Fleischner & Manheimer, 1997; also see Chapter 33 of this volume). This unbalanced emphasis is due to the value of reading over mathematics performance in the classroom. At present, pedagogy skills are much stronger in literacy instruction when compared to mathematics competency (Fleischner & Manheimer, 1997). School district inservices often provide more instruction for teachers in reading and written language at the expense of expertise in math. Although teachers may have competent math skills themselves, their knowledge base and ability to teach needed skills to students is more limited.

Failure to match instruction and strategies to a student's learning profile results in an imbalance, which ultimately affects the value of the education system and the training of our teachers. The lack of research in mathematics also causes professionals to ask for answers about how to best intervene with learners who struggle in mathematics. The purpose of this chapter is to discuss the use of neuropsychologically based interventions that may be used with children who have mathematical difficulties. Berninger and Abbott (1994) have reported that with many students, learning problems may be the outcome of a mismatch of instruction with a learner's profile of processing capabilities and disabilities. This chapter begins with a discussion of the various terms used to describe mathematical difficulties in children, as well as a summary of the neuropsychological deficits found to be associated with difficulties in mathematics. A few popular intervention models in the field of neuropsychology are described. The chapter concludes with a brief review of the literature that has been conducted on mathematical interventions.

## MATHEMATICS DIFFICULTIES

In the existing literature, several different terms are used to describe mathematics difficulties. Often, students who struggle in this area are considered to have a Mathematics Disorder. The *Diagnostic and Statistical Manual of Mental Disorders*, fourth edition, text revision (*DSM-IV-TR*; American Psychiatric Association, 2000, p. 54) offers the following criteria for diagnosing a Mathematics Disorder:

A. Mathematical ability, as measured by individually administered standardized tests, is significantly below that expected given the person's age, intelligence, and age- appropriate education.

B. The difficulties in Criterion A significantly interfere with academic performance or activities of daily living that require mathematic skills.

C. If a sensory deficit also exists, the problems in mathematics are in excess of those usually associated with the sensory issue.

Another expression that may be used to describe children with weaknesses in mathematics is dyscalculia. The National Center for Learning Disabilities (2003) defines dyscalculia as "a term referring to a wide range of lifelong learning disabilities involving math" (http://www.ncld.org/LDInfoZone/InfoZone _FactSheet_Dyscalculia.cfm). In the education setting, students who struggle with math problems may be identified as having a learning disability. The exact term differs from state to state; however, federal guidelines require documentation of a significant discrepancy between intellectual abilities and achievement performance in one or more of the following areas: oral expression, listening comprehension, written expression, basic reading skill, reading comprehension, mathematics calculation, and mathematical reasoning. Identification of a processing deficit is essential to the qualification of a learning disability. However, many argue that the discrepancy model will soon be replaced (e.g., Berninger & Abbott, 1994; National Center for Learning Disabilities, 2003).

There is no single form of math disability, and impairments vary from individual to individual (National Center for Learning Disabilities, 2003). Difficulties with numerical relationships often start at an early age (Lerner, 2000). If children do not acquire the critical foundation skills for mathematics development, ultimately they will struggle with the increasingly difficult academic expectations as they get older. For example, a learner who struggles with attention problems, perceptual skills, or motor skills may lack the experiences necessary to understand spatial, sequential, or quantitative concepts (Lerner, 2000). Unfortunately, mathematical difficulties may not be discovered until after 1st grade because students usually don't receive structured mathematics instruction until this point (American Psychiatric Association, 2000).

The estimated prevalence of Mathematics Disorder varies from 1% to 6% depending on the source. This statistic is difficult to isolate, as many of the research studies explored learning disabilities as a broad category rather than specifically examining mathematics disorders. The *DMS-IV-TR* estimates that 1% of school-age students have a Mathematics Disorder (American Psychiatric Association, 2000). Students with mathematics problems may also struggle with other educational and psychological issues, such as ADHD and nonverbal learning disabilities.

## NEUROPSYCHOLOGICAL IMPAIRMENTS

There is a wide range of neuropsychological deficits that could lead to a situation in which a student struggles with the acquisition or application of arithmetic skills (Strang & Rourke, 1985). There is some controversy over the idea that different subtypes of mathematical disabilities exist. Experts in the field continue to debate this issue and have not yet come to a consensus (D'Amato, Rothlisberg, &

Leu Work, 1999; Strang & Rourke, 1985). Some believe that there are two basic subtypes: the learner who has primary math problems and the learner who has problems in math performance related to verbal learning disabilities or reading disorders (Fleischner & Manheimer, 1997; Rourke & Finlayson, 1978; Rourke & Strang, 1978, 1983; Strang & Rourke, 1985).

Rourke and his colleagues conducted a series of studies to explore the patterns of neuropsychological strengths and weaknesses in students who struggle with arithmetic (Rourke & Finlayson, 1978; Rourke & Strang, 1978, 1983; Strang & Rourke, 1985). The studies divided the participants into three groups. Group 1 consisted of students with low scores (2 years below expected grade level on the Wide Range Achievement Test [WRAT]; Jastak & Jastak, 1965) in reading, spelling, and math. Group 2 comprised students who performed poorly in math compared to their same-age group; however, the students in this group displayed adequate math skills compared to reading and spelling performance (reading and spelling scores were 1.8 years below math scores). Individuals in Group 3 displayed average reading and spelling scores compared to very low math scores (reading and spelling scores exceeded arithmetic scores by 2 years). Groups 2 and 3 were of particular interest to researchers studying mathematics due to the contrasting patterns of academic skills despite the fact that the two groups had nearly equally impaired levels of performance on the WRAT Arithmetic subtest (Rourke & Finlayson, 1978; Rourke & Strang, 1978, 1983; Strang & Rourke, 1985).

The study conducted by Rourke and Finlayson (1978) indicated that individuals who displayed poor achievement in mathematics compared to their performance in reading and spelling (Group 3) had strengths in auditory-perceptual and verbal skills and weaknesses in visual-perceptual-organizational skills. The students with stronger arithmetic skills than reading and spelling skills (Group 2) performed well on tests of visual-perceptual-organizational skills and poorly on tasks of verbal and auditory-perceptual abilities. Rourke and Strang (1978) found that Group 2 performed in the average range on measures of psychomotor abilities, and Group 3 displayed bilateral impairment on these measures. In the third study of the series, Strang and Rourke (1985) discovered that when compared to Group 2, Group 3 made significantly more errors on a nonverbal problem-solving measure, which required visual-spatial skills and analysis.

The results of this series of experiments indicated that students who exhibited adequate performance on arithmetic skills when compared to reading and spelling skills displayed strengths in right-hemisphere and weakness on left-hemisphere tasks. The opposite was found for students who demonstrated adequate performance in reading and spelling and poor performances in arithmetic (Rourke & Finlayson, 1978; Rourke & Strang, 1978, 1983; Strang & Rourke, 1985).

Regardless of whether subtypes of mathematics disabilities exist, research supports the link between neuropsychological abilities and academic achievement in the area of mathematics. Some of the primary neuropsychological deficits related to math performance are briefly discussed next.

## MOTOR

Learners who struggle with mathematics may not perform well on visual-motor tasks such as copying geometric shapes or numbers or letters. This difficulty with writing may also affect the learner's ability to read and line up numbers correctly.

## MEMORY

To be successful at mathematics, automatically recalling number facts is important (Lerner, 2000). Learners with memory problems often struggle with remembering basic facts necessary for adding, subtracting, multiplying, and dividing. Individuals who have weak memory skills may also have a difficult time remembering and using the steps to a problem as well as related abilities such as reading clocks.

## VISUAL-SPATIAL PROCESSING

Although individuals normally learn spatial relationship concepts by preschool, children with math difficulties often struggle with such concepts as up-down, near-far, and other spatial concepts that are crucial to the development and understanding of our number system (Lerner, 2000). Deficits in this type of processing can lead to a poor understanding of numbers and difficulties with pictorial representations.

## AUDITORY PROCESSING

Learners who struggle with auditory processing have a difficult time following oral directions and teacher and peer requests. Memorizing verbal information, such as timetables and abbreviations, is most often extremely difficult for learners struggling with these issues.

## LANGUAGE PROCESSING

Language is defined as the use of a symbol system to represent meaningful ideas. Language skills are important to math performance because math symbols signify a way to convey numerical concepts (Mercer & Miller, 1992). Language is important for a great variety of abilities, including calculations, word problems, problem solving, and computing.

## REASONING

At times, learners knowingly attempt questions that are beyond their capabilities, which may ultimately lead to solutions that are erroneous (Rourke, 1989). In other situations, the student is unsuccessful in generalizing one particular skill that he or she has mastered to a slightly different procedure (Rourke, 1989).

## ATTENTION

Another problem that children with math difficulties often display is inattention. Learners who struggle to remain focused on activities that are long, repetitive, or tedious may be unable to display sustained attention during instruction time. This can strongly affect students' math performance because they may have missed critical components of instruction as well as the directions for completing specific assignments.

### EXECUTIVE FUNCTIONS

Executive functions involve the ability to regulate, integrate, and coordinate several cognitive processes with the purpose of working toward a goal (Welsh, 1994). This represents one of the often researched but little understood areas of neuropsychology (Lezak, 1995). This process includes attending, planning, self-monitoring, and decision making (Teeter & Semrud-Clikeman, 1997).

### PLANNING

Ashman and Conway (1993) have conceptualized planning as the need to organize information in a way that allows one to pay attention to necessary information and understand the relationship between what is presented and what is already known. The process of planning involves understanding how we learn and that learning has taken place (Ashman & Conway, 1993). Kirby and Williams (1991) believe that problems in the execution of planning can influence learning. For example, they have argued that planning deficits can influence achievement in reading and mathematics. In mathematics, a random attempt at a solution or a failure to switch strategies could be due to planning problems. Polya (1957), a mathematician, supported this theory by his outline of a 4-step process to solving a math problem: (1) First understand the problem; (2) develop a plan involving a series of moves for solving the problem; (3) carry out the plan; and (4) check to see whether the problem was solved correctly. Polya acknowledged the need to do additional planning if the problem was not solved. A person who displays executive function impairments in planning may have a difficult time following the important steps needed to solve math problems.

In summary, learners with mathematical difficulties display strengths and weaknesses in several different areas of neuropsychological functioning; therefore, a comprehensive evaluation is essential to identifying the individual profiles of each learner (see Table 34.1 on p. 764).

## MATHEMATICS DIFFICULTIES FOR LEARNERS WITH ADHD

Learners with ADHD often have a difficult time functioning in an academic setting. Many students with ADHD are underachieving compared to their level of intellectual abilities (Barkley, 1990; Frick et al., 1992). There are several reasons for these difficulties. Deficits in sustained attention make it difficult to pay attention to the teacher and focus on the assigned tasks. Hyperactivity makes it nearly impossible for these individuals to sit in their seats without being disruptive to others by fidgeting and squirming. Impulsivity leads to interrupting others or blurting out answers before hearing the question. Due to their variability in task performance, these children are often referred to as lazy and unmotivated. Problems with organization can lead to negative consequences due to lost assignments and materials, messy desks, and problems following schedules. As the children get older, they struggle with the increasingly difficult requirement to function independently with little structure. Successful homework, of course, requires systematic planning, organization, and sustained effort (Anastopoulos & Shelton, 2001).

**Table 34.1**
Neuropsychological Areas That Should Be Evaluated
in Learners with Mathematical Problems

| Neuropsychological Impairments | Problems in Mathematics |
| --- | --- |
| Motor | |
| Graphomotor | Numbers poorly formed and inaccurate |
| | Difficulty copying geometric shapes and letters |
| Cognitive Processing | |
| Memory | Retention and retrieval of number facts and tables |
| | Forgets steps when doing a problem |
| Visual-Spatial Processing | Misalignment of numbers in columns |
| | Confusion with carrying or borrowing |
| | Misreading math signs |
| | Problems with direction: up-down, left-right, near-far, across |
| Auditory Processing | Difficulty with oral drills |
| Linguistic-Verbal Processing | Problems with concepts such as "less than" or "more than" |
| Reasoning | Unreasonable solutions |
| Attention | Difficulty sustaining attention during instruction and directions |
| Executive Functions | |
| Planning and organization | Difficulties with problem solving |
| Shift in psychological set | Applying the practiced procedure |

In regard to academic interventions, it is especially important to try to understand the relationship between the diagnosis of ADHD and a learning disability (LD). Compared to peers without problems in attention, children with ADHD have a higher prevalence of academic problems. In a sample of hyperactive children, Lambert and Sandoval (1980) found that 53% of the participants were underachieving in reading or math. More recently, Shaywitz and Shaywitz (1991) discovered that 11% of a sample of children with ADHD had a learning disability (LD), but roughly 33% of the children with LD also could be diagnosed with ADHD. Although the statistics support a link between the two disorders, the nature of the relationship between ADHD and LD has not been well defined. This could be due to inconsistencies across studies related to methodological issues such as sample and assessment of learners with LD (Shaywitz & Shaywitz, 1991).

One theory is that the two disorders are separate entities that co-occur on a frequent basis. Another explanation for the comorbidity of these disorders is that LD is the primary disability and ADHD symptoms are secondary issues resulting from the learning problems. LD could produce just the behavioral symptoms of ADHD without having the cognitive characteristics of ADHD (Pennington, Groisser, & Welsh, 1993). Conversely, ADHD could be the primary disorder and the learning problems could be secondary resulting from problems with attention and self-regulation (Douglas & Peters, 1979). The existing research has found variable results when it comes to the comorbidity of these two disorders. Regardless of the label given to the cluster of symptoms in children, these issues must be considered when assessing and developing an intervention plan for those with academic difficulties.

## MATHEMATICAL INTERVENTION MODELS FOR STUDENTS WITH NONVERBAL LEARNING DISABILITIES

Children with nonverbal learning disabilities (NLD) also display poor academic achievement in mathematical reasoning and computation (Rourke, 1989). These children often struggle with concept formation, understanding cause-and-effect relationships, and problem-solving abilities (Rourke, 1989). Rourke encourages the use of *rote memory strategies* as an intervention for students with NLD.

There are several different evidence-based mathematical intervention models. This chapter discusses some models that frequently appear in the literature.

### THE CONCRETE-REPRESENTATIONAL-ABSTRACT MODEL

Some researchers have used a method for teaching math called the Concrete-Representational-Abstract (CRA) model. The sequence of the model moves from concrete to representational to abstract activities (Harris, Miller, & Mercer, 1995; Mercer & Miller, 1992). At the concrete level, students use three-dimensional objects to solve computation problems. Next is the representational level, which uses activities like drawings to solve problems. At the abstract level, the individual attempts to solve the computation problems without objects or drawings (Mercer & Miller, 1992). These researchers have concluded that the CRA model was effective in helping students with learning problems acquire place value and basic math facts (Mercer & Miller, 1992) and show improvements in multiplication facts (Harris et al., 1995).

### APTITUDE-TREATMENT INTERACTION

For decades, researchers and educators have investigated the process of matching instruction to the student's individual characteristics. This practice is known as the aptitude-treatment interaction (ATI) approach. The goal of ATI research has been to identify unique client aptitudes or features that can be linked to treatments so that the most effective intervention can be used to meet the needs of each individual (Braden & Kratochwill, 1997). Unfortunately, initial ATI research has not proven empirically promising (Reynolds, 1988). Several researchers have proposed theories regarding the unsuccessful outcomes of ATI research, suggesting several methodological and conceptual problems. For example, Reynolds commented on the unsophisticated nature of the research, which generally looked at one or two aptitudes rather than the complex patterns individuals display. Moreover, Reynolds pointed out the tendency for the existing research to focus on broad characteristics using groups rather than the individual's unique pattern of aptitudes. According to Reynolds, "Only through putting the individual into the ATI can effective matching of instruction techniques to students take place" (p. 325).

One of the main approaches for measuring aptitudes has been the use of traditional psychoeducational assessments, such as a cognitive/intellectual battery

(Braden & Kratochwill, 1997; D'Amato, Rothlisberg, & Rhodes, 1997; Hald, 2000). Researchers have argued that a child's performance on a cognitive measure will influence how each child should be taught (Braden & Kratochwill, 1997). Profile analysis is a common procedure in this process (Kaufman, 1979; Sattler, 1992). Profile analysis is the development of a graphic display to describe an individual's learning pattern based on each child's performance on the assessment measure.

Even though there appears to be a lack of support for the link between aptitude profiles and interventions, this does not necessarily indicate that cognitive batteries are not useful in producing meaningful ATIs (Kaufman & Kaufman, 1983). It is true that some of the more commonly used cognitive assessment manuals provide no evidence for the link between cognitive performance and academic interventions (Braden & Kratochwill, 1997). However, one exception to this is a few studies using the Kaufman Assessment Battery for Children (K-ABC; Kaufman & Kaufman, 1983). The K-ABC was developed to plan instructional programs for children with academic problems following an ATI approach (Kaufman & Kaufman, 1983). The expectation was the matching of instruction to the student's aptitude related to simultaneous and sequential processing. However, Good, Vollmer, Creek, Katz, and Chowdhri (1993) did not find support for the treatment utility of the K-ABC. It has been suggested that these findings could be due to the incomplete representation of the model the K-ABC was based on, which is Luria's model (Das et al., 1994). Luria's (1980) theory proposed three main cognitive functions (planning, attention, and coding), but the K-ABC was designed to measure only the coding aspect of the process (Das et al., 1994).

Some believe that ATIs will never be successful. In contrast, a growing body of research has indicated that cognitive processes and mathematical achievement can be improved with instruction (Cormier, Carlson, & Das, 1990; Das et al., 1994; Hald, 2000; Kar, Dash, Das, & Carlson, 1992; Kirby & Williams, 1991; Luria, 1980). The previously discussed studies have found promising results linking the planning processes of the Planning, Attention, Simultaneous, and Successive (PASS) theory to improvement in the area of math (Cormier et al., 1990; Das et al., 1994; Hald, 2000; Kar et al., 1992; Naglieri & Gottling, 1995). These findings also suggest that the individual's cognitive processing abilities determine how the students would benefit from the instruction (Hald, 2000). This link between instruction and the student's cognitive profile appears to be indicative of an aptitude-treatment interaction.

## Multistage Neuropsychological Model

Teeter and Semrud-Clikeman (1997) developed the multistage neuropsychological model (MNM) as a structure for linking neuropsychological assessment to intervention. These authors have indicated that effective interventions at early stages of the model may remove the need for further evaluation. However, the 8-stage model requires continuing evaluation of the treatment to ensure the effectiveness of the assessment-intervention connection on an ongoing basis.

*Stages 1 to 4*   Problem identification occurs through an initial evaluation that uses behavioral or curriculum-based assessment measures during the first stage of the MNM (Teeter & Semrud-Clikeman, 1997). The next stage involves educational professionals developing treatment strategies based on the data from the initial evaluation. The authors suggest that ongoing monitoring, evaluating, and modifying of the intervention is important at this time. If the intervention appears to be effective at this level, there may not be a need for additional in-depth evaluation; however, if problems continue, further evaluations and interventions may be necessary (Teeter & Semrud-Clikeman, 1997). The first 4 stages can be completed using school-based professionals. Issues such as math difficulties may call for a more comprehensive evaluation. In Stage 3, assessments may be completed in the areas of intelligence, academic achievement, and psychosocial functioning.

*Stages 5 to 6*   Students with severe difficulties may require a neuropsychological evaluation at Stage 5. This may be especially important for individuals who have not responded to previous treatments or display neurological symptoms (Teeter & Semrud-Clikeman, 1997). In Stage 6, interventions are developed based on findings from the neuropsychological evaluation. The interventions are often compensatory or pharmacological in nature (Teeter & Semrud-Clikeman, 1997). Clinical neuropsychologists in private practice or at university or medical clinics typically conduct Stage 5 and 6 assessments for interventions.

*Stages 7 to 8*   In Stage 7, some individuals need extensive medical or neuroradiological assessments (Teeter & Semrud-Clikeman, 1997). For children with certain medical conditions, neurological interventions may be necessary, which would occur at Stage 8. This intervention may involve treatment in a rehabilitation facility (Teeter & Semrud-Clikeman, 1997).

## COMMON MATHEMATICAL INTERVENTIONS

Numerous intervention programs and strategies are available to help students improve on mathematics performance. Unfortunately, many of these interventions have not been researched. School districts spend thousands of dollars each year to follow the latest trend in teaching programs or remediation activities; however, a majority of these programs use anecdotal evidence rather than evidence-based data to support the effectiveness of the intervention. Experts agree that there is a need for further research on successful interventions in mathematics; nonetheless, some exciting research has taken place, and this important literature is reviewed next.

### STRATEGY TRAINING

Students with learning disabilities are required to take an active role in their instruction by mastering the information and applying this knowledge when solving complex mathematical problems (Jones, Wilson, & Bhojwani, 1997). This process is difficult for students who do not use effective learning strategies and struggle with generalizing skills outside of the instructional setting (Jones et al., 1997). However, with the appropriate strategy training, children who struggle with mathematical skills can improve in academic performance. The strategy training approach includes interventions using direct instruction, cognitive, or meta-cognitive procedures (Xin & Jitendra, 1999).

*Direct Instruction*   One approach to strategy training is that of direct instruction. This is a teacher-directed method that aids individuals in the mastery of mathematics skills through instruction that is structured, explicit, and carefully planned (Lerner, 2000). Explicit instruction is the clear-cut presentation of important concepts and skills (Woodward, 1991). Research indicates that highly explicit math instruction leads to more growth in student achievement than less explicit instruction (Jitendra, Kameenui, & Carnine, 1994). Nelly (2003) compared direct strategy instruction to drill-and-practice instruction for students with and without learning disabilities. The author concluded that when instructing students with learning disabilities, direct strategy instruction was significantly more effective when the student was required to complete a transfer task.

Jones and colleagues (1997) have summarized the direct instruction literature by identifying five recommendations: attaining dynamic responses from the students on a regular basis, keeping an upbeat rate of instruction, assessing the students' attention and precision, providing feedback for accurate responding, and correcting students' mistakes as they happen.

*Cognitive/Meta-Cognitive Procedures*   Mayer (1987) proposed a model for solving mathematical problems that involved four types of mental processes: translation, integration, planning, and solution execution. In an effort to explain their lack of progress, Sternberg (1986) proposed that low-ability children usually lack strong meta-cognitive skills.

A meta-cognitive strategy was investigated in a study conducted by Shimabukuro, Prater, Jenkins, and Edelen (1999). The researchers explored the effects of self-monitoring on academic performance and on-task behaviors. Students were required to self-monitor and self-graph their academic performance in the areas of math, reading comprehension, and written expression. Shimabukuro et al. found that these students made gains in academic performance and their on-task behavior improved in all academic areas. These results suggest that the use of self-monitoring strategies can be extremely effective in helping children with ADHD and learning disabilities improve academic productivity and attending behaviors.

Often, learners who struggle with math difficulties display difficulties with planning and organizational skills. Numerous studies have validated the use of planning interventions with learners who have low planning scores (Hald, 2000; Lerew, 2003; Naglieri & Gottling, 1995, 1997; Naglieri & Johnson, 1998). Cormier et al. (1990) investigated the use of planning facilitation by requiring learners to verbalize the problems as they solved progressive matrices. The learners were then asked to defend their choice and explain why the other options were incorrect. Cormier et al. discovered that learners who were low in the area of planning scored significantly higher after this intervention than students who were high on planning measures. Kar et al. (1992) conducted two studies that examined the effect of a similar intervention on learners with good and poor planning skills. The purpose of this study was to explore the benefits of verbalization on search performance in a number-finding activity. One group completed the task and then had a 5-minute break during which they discussed school activities and family. The second group spent the discussion time talking about how they would conduct the number search and the reasons they would use those strategies. The authors concluded that the strategy of verbalization was related to higher performance on planning tasks when compared to the group that discussed school and families. Kar and colleagues conducted a second part to their study in which they found that high planners did not improve as much as the participants who were low in planning.

As can be seen, the results from a variety of studies indicate that facilitation of planning instruction improves the performance of learners with low planning scores (Cormier et al., 1990; Kar et al., 1992). It is significant that even though these researchers found important implications for the improvement of cognitive processing in the area of planning, their work did not involve academic tasks, although it impacted them.

Similarly, Naglieri and Gottling (1995, 1997) provided planning facilitation using the same procedure as the previous studies. However, Naglieri and Gottling sampled students with learning disabilities and implemented the planning intervention during math instruction. The facilitators encouraged the students to be self-reflective and think about what they would do the next time they completed a math worksheet. The authors discovered that the planning training benefited those with low planning scores more than those with high planning scores on math performance. Both studies consisted of small sample sizes; however, the results were critical because these authors were the first to explore the benefit of planning facilitation as part of math instruction for students with learning disabilities. Naglieri and Johnson (1998) replicated this procedure; this time, 21 students with disabilities were sampled and the purpose was to determine if children with specific PASS profiles would show different rates of improvement. Once again, the researchers reported that those with low planning scores improved more than those who did not need the training.

With the intention of replicating and extending the previous studies, Hald (2000) examined the differential effects of planning facilitation and additional mathematics error instruction with students known to have difficulties in math. Hald's sample consisted of 19 students known to score low in math performance. The students were split into two groups. One group received just the planning facilitation method, and the second group received both the planning facilitation method and additional math instruction on calculation errors. Hald's findings suggested that students low in math and planning benefited more from the planning intervention alone. Students low in math but higher in planning skills benefited more from the combined treatment. All of these results lend support for the benefit of an intervention targeting planning skills. At this point, planning intervention appears quite promising for math instruction, but research using this method in other settings and with other students is lacking.

The findings resulting from this series of research lend support to the link between cognitive processing profiles and instruction (Cormier et al., 1990; Das et al., 1994; Hald, 2000; Kar et al., 1992; Lerew, 2003; Naglieri & Gottling, 1995, 1997; Naglieri & Johnson, 1998). Indeed, planning-based interventions have been found successful when working with children low in planning scores on the Cognitive Assessment System (CAS; Das & Naglieri, 1997; Lerew, 2003; Naglieri & Gottling, 1995, 1997; Naglieri & Johnson, 1998). This leads to the question of whether this holds true for children with ADHD who struggle in math. The cognitive profile of children with ADHD on the CAS shows that they display very low planning scores compared to other cognitive abilities. This issue was explored in a study conducted by Lerew, which utilized a multiple-baseline research design that involved 6 elementary school-age children. These children were classified as ADHD using the current *DSM-IV* (American Psychiatric Association, 2000) criteria. This research also used the CAS and the Behavior Rating Inventory of Executive Function (Gioia, Isquith, Guy, & Kenworthy, 2000) as measures of planning. The math intervention was based on a method designed by Naglieri and Gottling (1997) and described by Naglieri (1998) as the planning facilitation method (PFM).

Hald (2000) utilized this same intervention system with students low in math calculation skills. The math intervention sessions lasted 30 minutes and consisted of 3 steps. In Step 1, the participants worked on math problems for 10 minutes. In Step 2, the researcher facilitated a discussion for 10 minutes. Step 3 consisted of the participants again working on math problems for 10 minutes. The results from an analysis of the baseline information suggested that all participants displayed a horizontally stable baseline. All four of the students with low planning scores demonstrated trends when the baseline data was combined with the intervention data. This indicated that they significantly benefited from the planning facilitation intervention. When examining the percentage of change from baseline to intervention, the mean for the low planners (75% change) was higher than the mean for the high planners (47% change). The findings indicate that all participants benefited from the intervention, but the children with lower planning skills profited more than the students with good planning skills. The overall findings in regard to math achievement appeared to be consistent with the existing research (Hald, 2000; Naglieri & Gottling, 1995, 1997; Naglieri & Johnson, 1998).

In conclusion, meta-cognitive strategies appear to be fairly quick and effective interventions for students who struggle in mathematics. McDougall and Brady (1998) have noted that the initial training does entail staff time and expertise; therefore, the intervention facilitator should be provided with consultation when first using this intervention with a student.

## Computer-Aided Instruction

Advances in computer technology have made computer applications a common tool for teaching mathematics (Lerner, 2000). Computer-aided instruction (CAI) is a popular technological option because computer programs present students with strategically sequenced, individualized tasks and immediate feedback on the quality of their responses (Lewis, 1998). The existing literature on the value of CAI is inconsistent. Some researchers have determined that well-designed computer instruction programs seem to be effective in increasing students' knowledge of math facts (Woodward & Carnine, 1993). Some types of retraining are also discussed in Chapter 32 of this text.

Xin and Jitendra (1999) conducted a meta-analysis exploring the effectiveness of word-problem-solving instruction on the performance of students with learning problems. They found that the largest effect size resulted from studies that utilized CAI. However, in a meta-analysis conducted by Kroesbergen and Van Luit (2003), these authors concluded that studies using CAI showed lower effect sizes than studies where the students received direct instruction. The authors acknowledged the discrepancy between the two findings and suggested that the difference may be due to the studies in Xin and Jitendra's research that used some form of direct instruction. Other studies have discovered CAI and direct instruction to be comparably effective (e.g., Koscinski, 1995; Nwaizu, 1991).

## REPRESENTATION TECHNIQUES

The representation technique uses the representation of ideas or information to solve the problem (Xin & Jitendra, 1999). Representation approaches include pictorial (diagramming), concrete (manipulatives), verbal (linguistic training), and mapping (schema based) instruction. Fleischner and Manheimer (1997) have suggested using manipulatives to introduce novel topics or operations. The authors recommend using manipulatives beyond the traditional time frame because students with learning problems struggle with abstract concepts.

## COMPENSATORY INTERVENTIONS

For individuals with severe neuropsychological deficits that may not be remediable, the most helpful approach to intervention may be to help the individual compensate for his or her impairments. When an individual lacks the ability to acquire a skill, compensatory methods are often utilized (D'Amato et al., 1999). Some examples of compensatory strategies are using calculators, recording lectures with tape recorders, and enlarging the math operation symbols. For students with verbal memory deficits, Strang and Rourke (1985) recommend providing a chart containing common arithmetic tables. Some authors have offered a comprehensive intervention model that could also be applied to mathematics (D'Amato & Rothlisberg, 1996).

## OTHER INTERVENTION FACTORS

Other factors should be considered when developing mathematical interventions. These factors include the method of instruction and the length of instruction.

*Teacher-Directed versus Student-Directed Intervention* Kroesbergen and Van Luit's (2003) study found self-instruction to be the most effective method overall; however, direct instruction seems to be the most effective when teaching basic math skills.

*Length of Intervention* In the meta-analysis conducted by Xin and Jitendra (1999), the authors discovered that long-term interventions (more than 1 month) were more effective than short-term interventions (fewer than 7 sessions) in both group and single-subject designs. The researchers found short-term interventions to be more effective than the intermediate-length interventions (more than 7 sessions but less than 1 month) when examining group designs. Conversely, the researchers found the intermediate-term to be more effective than the short-term when investigating single-case research designs. The investigators attributed this discrepancy to some of the successful interventions that were found in group designs, but not in the single-case designs, producing quick improvements after a short amount of time. Kroesbergen and Van Luit's (2003) meta-analysis also found that the length of the intervention correlated negatively with effect size. The

**Table 34.2**
Learner's Neuropsychological Needs Matched to Commonly Used Interventions

| Neuropsychological Needs | Commonly Used Interventions |
| --- | --- |
| Motor | |
|   Graphomotor | Tape recorder for notes |
| | Teach keyboarding skills and use instead of writing |
| | Use oral-input software for composing |
| Cognitive Processing | |
|   Memory | Use multisensory strategies with repetition |
| | Use graphic organizers |
| | Tape record lectures |
|   Visual-Spatial Processing | Offer precise and clear verbal instructions |
| | Offer verbal repetition |
| | Use highlighting for a visual focus (operation signs) |
|   Auditory Processing | Slow down the pace of instruction |
| | Use pictures and other visual material |
| | Focus on nonverbal cues |
|   Linguistic-Verbal Processing | Slow down the pace of instruction |
| | Ask students to verbalize what they are doing |
|   Reasoning | Use graphic organizers to show relationships |
| | Teach generalization and application across contexts |
|   Attention | Create routines with frequent breaks |
| | Create cue sheets and mnemonics |
| Executive Functions | |
|   Planning and organization | Create flow charts/graphs/cognitive webs |
| | Highlight and color-code important information |

authors theorized that short-term interventions may focus on small and specific areas of knowledge, which could lead to full acquisition after a short period, whereas long-term interventions tended to concentrate on a broad range of knowledge and therefore may be complicated by more variables and lead to smaller effect sizes.

Research has been conducted on a wide variety of mathematical interventions. These interventions include strategy training, CAI, representation techniques, and compensatory interventions. Table 34.2 is a brief list of strategies that can be used with students who display various neuropsychological difficulties. However, when planning interventions for students, it is important to consider their strengths as well as their needs.

## CONCLUSION

D'Amato et al. (1999) showed the importance of neuropsychologically based interventions when they advocated that "providing effective interventions should be the cornerstone of any evaluation" (p. 463). The first step in developing an effective intervention program for students who struggle with mathematical skills involves increasing the research literature that evaluates the different neuropsychologically based mathematical treatments. Educators and researchers are beginning to recognize the need for further exploration of evidenced-based mathematical interventions. However, the existing literature in this area is minimal compared to the research on reading disabilities.

The next step to designing successful neuropsychologically based intervention programs is to gather information regarding the students' neuropsychological strengths and needs based on a comprehensive evaluation. It is not uncommon for a student with mathematical problems to have a comprehensive evaluation conducted that never leads to successful interventions. Several factors may contribute to this detrimental situation. For example, a student might be assessed at a neuropsychological clinic or a children's hospital, and the results of the evaluation are never shared with the necessary school personnel or the examination does not focus on achievement interventions. There are also times when students with mathematical difficulties go through the special education assessment process at the student's school, but due to strict qualification eligibility guidelines the student may not qualify for special services. Examples of this include students with ADHD or NLD. These disorders alone do not necessarily qualify a student for special services, but the child may still exhibit mathematical impairments. In these situations, the evaluation does not necessarily lead to interventions, which is unfortunate for all individuals involved. On a more positive note, more school districts are beginning to develop teams that have expertise in the field of neuropsychology applied to education. Such professionals are crucial to diversifying the teams in the school setting. Hopefully, this trend will continue in educational settings. Until this is standard practice, these students may need to be evaluated in a hospital, clinic, or university setting that has clinicians with knowledge and expertise in this area.

The third step involves the actual design of the intervention. Themes from the neuropsychological findings should be utilized to develop appropriate, individualized interventions for each child. Evidence-based interventions should be implemented that are appropriate for the child's neuropsychological profile. The last step is to evaluate the effectiveness of the intervention. The intervention should be under ongoing evaluation and modified as needed. Commonly, a continuing evaluation of the intervention is not conducted, which ultimately compromises the entire process. Teeter and Semrud-Clikeman (1997) have warned that problems with intervention effectiveness tend to occur when treatment plans continue after they are no longer working. Professionals agree that it is essential for intervention plans to be evaluated frequently through individual assessments such as curriculum-based measures (Jones et al., 1997).

Ongoing research is crucial to the continuation of effective neuropsychologically based mathematical interventions. Current researchers have discovered some exciting results that link assessment to intervention, but continuing evidence is needed. Mathematical interventions have been successfully used to facilitate the development of self-confidence and achievement in the educational setting. Neuropsychologically based math interventions are providing learners with the skills to compensate for and remediate their math challenges and ultimately reach their true potential.

## REFERENCES

American Psychiatric Association. (2000). *Diagnostic and statistical manual of mental disorders* (4th ed., rev.). Washington, DC: Author.

Anastopoulos, A. D., & Shelton, T. L. (2001). *Assessing attention-deficit/hyperactivity disorder*. New York: Kluwer Academic/Plenum Press.

Ashman, A. F., & Conway, R. N. F. (1993). *Using cognitive methods in the classroom*. London: Routledge.

Barkley, R. A. (1990). *Attention deficit hyperactivity disorder: A handbook for diagnosis and treatment*. New York: Guilford Press.

Berninger, V. W., & Abbott, R. D. (1994). Redefining learning disabilities: Moving beyond aptitude-achievement discrepancies to failure to respond to validated treatment protocols. In G. R. Lyon (Ed.), *Frames of reference for the assessment of learning disabilities: New views on measurement issues* (pp. 163–184). Baltimore: Brookes.

Braden, J. P., & Kratochwill, T. R. (1997). Treatment utility of assessment: Myths and realities. *School Psychology Review, 26*, 475–485.

Cormier, P., Carlson, J. S., & Das, J. P. (1990). Planning ability and cognitive performance: The compensatory effects of a dynamic assessment approach. *Learning and Individual Differences, 2*, 437–449.

D'Amato, R. C., & Rothlisberg, B. A. (1996). How education should respond to students with traumatic brain injuries. *Journal of Learning Disabilities, 29*, 670–683.

D'Amato, R. C., Rothlisberg, B. A., & Leu Work, P. H. (1999). Neuropsychological assessment for intervention. In C. R. Reynolds & T. B. Gutkin (Eds.), *The handbook of school psychology* (3rd ed., pp. 452–475). New York: Wiley.

D'Amato, R. C., Rothlisberg, B. A., & Rhodes, R. L. (1997). Utilizing neuropsychological paradigm for understanding common educational and psychological tests. In C. R. Reynolds & E. Fletcher-Janzen (Eds.), *Handbook of clinical child neuropsychology* (2nd ed., pp. 270–295). New York: Plenum Press.

Das, J. P., & Naglieri, J. A. (1997). *Cognitive assessment system interpretive handbook*. Chicago: Riverside.

Das, J. P., Naglieri, J. A., & Kirby, J. R. (1994). *Assessment of cognitive processes: The PASS theory of intelligence*. Boston: Allyn & Bacon.

Douglas, V. I., & Peters, K. G. (1979). Toward a clearer definition of the attentional deficit of hyperactive children. In G. A. Hale & M. Lewis (Eds.), *Attention and the development of cognitive skills*. New York: Plenum Press.

Frick, P. J., Lahey, B. B., Loeber, R., Stouthamer-Loeber, M., Christ, M. A. G., & Hanson, K. (1992). Familial risk factors to oppositional defiant disorder and conduct disorder: Parental psychopathology and maternal parenting. *Journal of Consulting and Clinical Psychology, 60*, 49–55.

Fleischner, J. E., & Manheimer, M. A. (1997). Math interventions for students with learning disabilities: Myths and realities. *School Psychology Review, 26*, 397–414.

Gioia, G. A., Isquith, P. K., Guy, S. C., & Kenworthy, L. (2000). *Behavior rating inventory of executive functions interpretive manual*. Odessa, FL: Psychological Assessment Resources.

Good, R. H., Vollmer, M., Creek, R. J., Katz, L. I., & Chowdhri, S. (1993). Treatment utility of Kaufman Assessment Battery for Children: Effects of matching instruction and student processing strength. *School Psychology Review, 22*, 8–26.

Hald, M. (2000). *A PASS cognitive processes intervention study in mathematics*. Unpublished doctoral dissertation, University of Northern Colorado.

Harris, C. A., Miller, S. P., & Mercer, C. D. (1995). Teaching initial multiplication skills to students with disabilities in general education classrooms. *Learning Disabilities Research and Practice, 10*, 180–195.

Jastak, K. F., & Jastak, S. R. (1965). *Wide range achievement test*. Wilmington, DE: Guidance Associates.

Jitendra, A. K., Kameenui, E., & Carnine, D. (1994). An exploratory evaluation of dynamic assessment of the role of basals on comprehension of mathematical operations. *Education and Treatment of Children, 17,* 139–162.

Jones, E. D., Wilson, R., & Bhojwani, S. (1997). Mathematics instruction for secondary students with learning disabilities. *Journal of Learning Disabilities, 30,* 151–163.

Kar, B. C., Dash, U. N., Das, J. P., & Carlson, J. S. (1992). Two experiments on the dynamic assessment of planning. *Learning and Individual Differences, 5,* 13–29.

Kaufman, A. S. (1979). *Intelligent testing with the WISC-R.* New York: Wiley.

Kaufman, A. S., & Kaufman, N. L. (1983). *Interpretive manual for the Kaufman Assessment Battery for Children.* Circle Pines, MN: American Guidance Service.

Kirby, J. R., & Williams, N. H. (1991). *Learning problems: A cognitive approach.* Toronto, Ontario, Canada: Kagan & Woo.

Koscinski, S. T. (1995). Comparison of teacher-assisted and computer-assisted instruction using constant time delay to teach multiplication facts to students with mild disabilities. *Dissertation Abstracts International, 55,* 3810.

Kroesbergen, E. H., & Van Luit, J. E. (2003). Mathematical interventions for children with special education needs. *Remedial and Special Education, 24,* 97–115.

McDougall, D., & Brady, M. P. (1998). Initiating and fading self-management interventions to increase math fluency in general education classes. *Exceptional Children, 64,* 151–166.

Lambert, N., & Sandoval, J. (1980). The prevalence of learning disabilities in a sample of children considered hyperactive. *Journal of Abnormal Child Psychology, 8,* 33–50.

Lerew, C. D. (2003). *The use of a cognitive strategy as an academic and behavioral intervention for children with attention-deficit/hyperactivity disorder.* Unpublished doctoral dissertation, University of Northern Colorado, Greeley.

Lerner, J. W. (2000). *Learning disabilities: Theories, diagnosis, and teaching strategies* (8th ed.). Boston: Houghton Mifflin Company.

Lezak, M. D. (1995). *Neuropsychological Assessment* (3rd ed.). New York: Oxford Press.

Lewis, R. (1998). Assistive technology and learning disabilities: Today's realities and tomorrow's promises. *Journal of Learning Disabilities, 31,* 16–26.

Luria, A. R. (1980). *Higher cortical functions in man.* New York: Basic Books.

Mayer, E. R. (1987). *Educational psychology.* Boston: Little, Brown.

Mercer, C. D., & Miller, S. P. (1992). Teaching students with learning problems in math to acquire, understand, and apply basic math facts. *Remedial and Special Education, 13,* 19–35.

Naglieri, J. A., & Gottling, S. H. (1995). A cognitive education approach to math instruction for the learning disabled: An individual study. *Psychological Reports, 76,* 1343–1354.

Naglieri, J. A., & Gottling, S. H. (1997). Mathematics instruction and PASS cognitive processes: An intervention study. *Journal of Learning Disabilities, 30,* 513–520.

Naglieri, J. A., & Johnson, D. (1998). Improving math calculation: A cognitive intervention based on the PASS Theory. *Communiqué, 27,* 23.

National Center for Learning Disabilities. (2003). http://www.ncld.org.

Nelly, T. (2003). The differential effects of teaching addition through strategy instruction versus drill and practice to students with and without learning disabilities. *Journal of Learning Disabilities, 36,* 449–459.

No Child Left Behind. (2004). Retrieved on December 16, 2004, from http://www.ed.gov/nclb/landing.jhtml.

Nwaizu, P. C. I. (1991). Using teacher-assisted and computer-assisted instruction to teach multiplication skills to youths with specific learning disabilities. *Dissertation Abstracts International, 51,* 3041.

Pennington, B. F., Groisser, D., & Welsh, M. C. (1993). Contrasting cognitive deficits in attention deficit hyperactivity disorder versus reading disabilities. *Developmental Psychology, 29*, 511–523.

Polya, G. (1957). *How to solve it.* New York: Doubleday.

Reynolds, C. R. (1988). Putting the individual into aptitude treatment interaction. *Exceptional Children, 54*, 324–331.

Rourke, B. P. (1989). *Nonverbal learning disabilities: The syndrome and the model.* New York: Guilford Press.

Rourke, B. P., & Finlayson, M. A. J. (1978). Neuropsychological significance in patterns of academic performance: Verbal and visual-spatial abilities. *Journal of Abnormal Child Psychology, 6*, 121–133.

Rourke, B. P., & Strang, J. D. (1978). Neuropsychological significance of variations in patterns of academic performance: Motor, psychomotor, and tactile perception abilities. *Journal of Pediatric Psychology, 3*, 212–225.

Rourke, B. P., & Strang, J. D. (1983). Subtypes of reading and arithmetical disabilities: A neuropsychological analysis. In M. Rutter (Ed.), *Developmental neuropsychiatry.* New York: Guilford Press.

Sattler, J. M. (1992). *Assessment of children* (3rd ed.). San Diego, CA: Jerome M. Sattler.

Shaywitz, S. E., & Shaywitz, B. A. (1991). Introduction to the special series on Attention Deficit Disorder. *Journal of Learning Disabilities, 24*, 68–71.

Shimabukuro, S. M., Prater, M. A., Jenkins, A., & Edelen, P. (1999). The effects of self-monitoring of academic performance on students with learning disabilities and ADD/ADHD. *Education and Treatment of Children, 22*, 397–414.

Strang, J. D., & Rourke, B. P. (1985). Arithmetic disability subtypes: The neuropsychological significance of specific arithmetical impairment in childhood. In B. P. Rourke (Ed.), *Neuropsychology of learning disability: Essentials of subtype analysis* (pp. 167–182). New York: Guilford Press.

Sternberg, R. J. (1986). *Intelligence applied.* Orlando, FL: Harcourt Brace Jovanovich.

Teeter, P. A., & Semrud-Clikeman, M. (1997). *Child neuropsychology: Assessment and interventions for neuropsychological disorders.* Boston: Allyn & Bacon.

Welsh, M. C. (1994). Executive function and the assessment of attention deficit hyperactivity disorder. In N. C. Jordan & J. Goldsmith-Phillips (Eds.), *Learning disabilities: New directions for assessment and intervention* (pp. 21–42). Boston: Allyn & Bacon.

Woodward, J. (1991). Procedural knowledge in mathematics: The role of the curriculum. *Journal of Learning Disabilities, 24*, 242–251.

Woodward, J., & Carnine, D. (1993). Use of technology for mathematics assessment and instruction: Reflection on a decade of innovations. *Journal of Special Education Technology, 12*, 38–48.

Xin, Y. P., & Jitendra, A. K. (1999). The effects of instruction in solving mathematical word problems for students with learning problems: A meta-analysis. *Journal of Special Education, 37*, 207–225.

# CHAPTER 35

# Understanding and Implementing Neuropsychologically Based Written Language Interventions

MARY M. CHITTOORAN and RAYMOND C. TAIT

S CHOOL NEUROPSYCHOLOGY, a subspecialty of neuropsychology, applies principles derived from the study of brain-behavior relationships to learning problems experienced by children and adolescents with neurological and neuropsychological deficits (Hebben & Milberg, 2002; Teeter & Semrud-Clikeman, 1997). There has been substantial progress in understanding the impact of neuropsychological impairment on academic performance in reading and mathematics, yet there has been relatively little progress in understanding the neuropsychology of writing and in developing interventions for writing disorders. This is due both to the complex, multifactorial nature of writing (Rapcsak, 1997; Snyder & Nussbaum, 1998) and to the lack of adequate diagnostic methods. While much remains to be learned, understanding the relationship between neuropsychological impairment and written language deficits is necessary for the effective management of such disorders in the classroom, where writing is often essential to learning. This chapter briefly reviews the relevant history of clinical neuropsychology and then examines the roles of school psychologists and school neuropsychologists in the assessment and treatment of written language disorders (Power, 2002).

## HISTORICAL FOUNDATIONS

Clinical neuropsychology traces its foundations to nineteenth-century studies that demonstrated the relationship between damage in certain areas of the brain

We would like to thank Bethany Hill-Anderson, graduate research assistant, for her help with our literature review.

and adaptive behaviors (Hartlage, Asken, & Hornsby, 1987). Although early efforts distinguished between individuals with and without brain damage, little attempt was made to localize problems to particular areas of the brain. Subsequent advances led to improved assessment of the severity and specificity of brain damage; however, these improvements did not translate into treatment. Two factors, however, have advanced the discipline of clinical neuropsychology: the number of head injuries consequent to World War II and the emergence of clinical psychology as a legitimate profession (Hartlage, Asken, & Hornsby, 1987). Subsequent developments have improved our ability to identify and describe the location of brain lesions and their impact on behavior. Further, advances in neuroimaging procedures have facilitated an improved understanding of the neurological bases of learning that was not possible in the early years of the field.

Although clinical neuropsychologists continue to be active in traditional medical settings, they have begun to expand their influence to areas that include the behavior of children and adolescents in school settings. Hence, clinical child neuropsychologists today are better able to integrate the assessment of brain-behavior relationships with interventions to address functional deficits in the home, school, and community. This has resulted in a change in public perception regarding the usefulness of neuropsychology across a wide range of ages and impairments, as well as changes in the training and credentialing of clinical and school neuropsychologists. Despite these improvements, there are lingering concerns about the ecological validity of neuropsychological measures and the reliable measurement of behavioral outcomes, particularly with children (Bauer, 2002; Farmer & Brazeal, 1998).

School neuropsychology offers a new perspective on writing by maintaining a dual focus: outwardly, on behavior in academic settings, and inwardly, on the neurological and neuropsychological structures that control such behavior. Indeed, neuropsychological explanations for *all* types of learning and behavior disorders, not just those of neurological or neuropsychological origin, are increasingly evident in the literature (Hooper, 2002: Lezak, 1995; Reynolds & Fletcher-Janzen, 1997). The field provides novel insights that are not possible through the use of psychoanalytic or behavioral paradigms. It moves away from purely standardized, quantified assessments of behavior to a more comprehensive approach that also includes qualitative, clinical explanations for language impairments. It parallels trends in other disciplines toward interdisciplinary efforts directed at particular impairments; such collaboration offers the potential for more effective answers to referral questions than the one-dimensional explanations for behavior that have, so far, been the only recourse for school psychologists. One relatively recent example of this interdisciplinary focus is Teeter and Semrud-Clikeman's (1997) integrated transactional neuropsychological paradigm, which considers the impact, both directly and interactively, of biogenetic, neurological, environmental, cognitive, psychosocial, and academic variables.

## WRITING: DEVELOPMENT AND PROCESS

Before we examine written language disorders, it is important to examine the normal development of written language. Writing has been defined as a complex act of problem-solving that uses graphic symbols to communicate thoughts and meaning (Hooper, 2002; Hooper, Swartz, Wakely, de Kruif, & Montgomery, 2002; Rapcsak, 1997). From an evolutionary perspective, written language in humans is a fairly recent accomplishment, having emerged only about 5,000 years ago in Asia (Feifer & De Fina, 2002). When viewed along a continuum of language expression skills, writing represents "the final stage in the ontogeny of language" (Snyder & Nussbaum, 1998, p. 157); it is dependent on, and grows out of, already established oral language skills. As a form of communication, written language poses additional challenges because it lacks the immediacy, contextual cues, negotiated meaning, and reciprocal feedback that are characteristic of oral language exchanges. Although pragmatic, semantic, and syntactic elements are shared by oral and written language, these two systems diverge at the point of lexical representation for spoken and written words. In fact, there is some evidence that writing is based on cognitive elements that are not shared by speech or reading (Berninger, Abbott, Abbott, Graham, & Richards, 2002; Mather, 2003; Weekes, 1996). Many elements, some language-related, but others independent of language, can influence writing ability (Benson & Ardila, 1996). For instance, written expression is naturally dependent on the writer's mastery of oral language and reading skills but is also heavily influenced by background knowledge and social experiences.

Perhaps the most complete perspective available on written language is the cognitive, information-processing model proposed by Ellis (1982, 1988) and elaborated on by others (e.g., Margolin, 1984; Margolin & Goodman-Schulman, 1992; Rapcsak, 1997). According to this model, written language is composed of two distinct processes: central/linguistic, which focuses on the selection of appropriate words and spellings, and peripheral/motor, which controls the mechanisms by which linguistic information is converted to motor control of arm and hand movements during writing tasks (Lorch, 1995). These central and peripheral language processes interact reciprocally with spelling, visual-spatial components, and behavioral skills to result in a written product (Rapcsak, 1997).

Central processes initiate the writing sequence. Familiar words are spelled by retrieving the selected word from the graphemic output lexicon, and plausible spellings for unfamiliar words use a non-lexical, phoneme-grapheme conversion procedure (Rapcsak, 1997). Strings of graphemes are transmitted to, and stored in, the graphemic buffer, a working memory system that provides temporary storage. At this point, peripheral processes take over. Before the graphemes are converted into writing movements, however, the writer must select the appropriate allographs (various physical forms for each grapheme) from storage in long-term memory (Ellis, 1982) and make additional choices between uppercase and lowercase and print or script (Margolin & Goodman-Schulman, 1992; Rapscak, 1997). Spatial descriptions of letter shapes are then used to activate stored graphic motor programs that guide writing movements. These programs specify the sequence, direction, and relative size of the strokes necessary to create a specific allograph but do not specify absolute stroke size, duration, or force. Information encoded in graphic motor programs is next translated into graphic innervatory patterns that provide sequences of motor commands to specific muscle effector systems, accompanied by information about absolute stroke size, duration, and force (Ellis, 1982). Once all the parameters for the writing task have been established, the motor system executes the necessary strokes to produce written output. During writing, afferent control systems provide continuing sensory feedback to graphic motor programs about strokes that have already been executed, slope of the line of writing, spacing, and orientation to the paper (Margolin, 1984; Margolin & Goodman-Schulman, 1992). Neurological injury can cause breakdowns in the writing process at one or more of these stages, and difficulties at one stage can seriously hinder, or even prevent, the successful completion of tasks at other stages.

Gould (2001) and others describe a 3-stage model of the progression of writing skills that provides a useful way to discuss writing in a school setting. Stage 1, prewriting, includes behaviors such as drawing, tracing, and coloring that provide a foundation for the writing tasks of 1st grade. Stage 2, graphic presentation, involves the refinement of basic orthographic skills as well as the establishment of greater motor control. Stage 3, a 3-phase process beginning at the end of the 2nd grade, is characterized by improved ability to use capitalization, punctuation, syntax, and grammar and an introduction to cursive writing. During the automatization phase of Stage 3, continued mastery of writing skills leads to a greater capacity for self-monitoring, increases in the length of written output, a growing sophistication in the use of language rules and structures, and enhanced planning and organization skills. During the elaboration phase, typically in grades 7 though 9, writing becomes even more automatic, so that children can concentrate on advanced skills such as generating ideas, summarizing, developing, and expressing viewpoints. In the final phase, in grade 9 and beyond, children display distinctive writing styles, so that writing is used as a medium to support play, reasoning, and creativity.

## WRITTEN LANGUAGE DISORDERS

Whereas most children learn to write normally, some children exhibit disorders of written language that significantly affect the quality of their academic experiences. Although information about the prevalence and gender distribution of such disorders is lacking, expression of writing disorders varies functionally as a result of impairment in one or more of the following areas: (1) handwriting, (2) spelling, (3) language, (4) attention and memory, (5) written narrative organizational skills, and (6) metacognitive abilities (Hooper, 2002; Snyder & Nussbaum, 1998). Written language disorders can be classified according to type of disorder or etiology. Four types of writing disorders have been identified: (1) linguistic and fine motor deficits that are associated with errors in phonetic spelling, punctuation, and capitalization, impoverished vocabulary, effortful writing, awkward pen/pencil grip, and slow production; (2) spatial organization problems that affect legibility but not language and reading skills; (3) disorders of visual attention/memory associated primarily with word retrieval deficits, spelling problems, and, to a lesser extent, inadequate self-monitoring during writing tasks; and (4) letter and word sequencing problems (Feifer & De Fina, 2002; Hooper, 2002; Teeter & Semrud-Clikeman, 1997).

Written language disorders may also be classified into two groups based on etiology. The first group, Expressive Language Disorders or speech language impairments, depending on whether one uses a *DSM-IV* or educational classification, are delays in language acquisition or problems with language use. These may be congenital, of idiopathic origin, or the result of other conditions such as mental retardation, although they often manifest only when children enter school. Agraphias, defined as "a loss or impairment of the ability to produce written language caused by (neurological) damage" (Benson & Ardila, 1996, p. 212), constitute the second group of written language disorders. These deficits may manifest at any time during life, tend to persist long after the injury, and are generally slower to recover than oral language deficits (Murdoch, 1990). There is confusion regarding the terms used to describe written language disorders, with agraphia and dysgraphia often used interchangeably and inconsistently. Although some researchers use the term agraphia to refer to a loss of writing abilities and the term dysgraphia to refer to an impairment of writing abilities, this chapter uses the term agraphia to refer to all written language disorders caused by neurological and neuropsychological impairments. The remainder of this chapter focuses on agraphias in the school setting.

The term *agraphia* was introduced by Ogle (1867) to describe acquired impairment in writing resulting from brain damage. Since then, there have been various, often overlapping, classifications of agraphia, including several cognitive typologies. Agraphias typically follow some form of head trauma, brain tumor, cerebrovascular accident, and/or infection (Owens, 1999). Although they can occur in isolation, they are usually seen as part of a general language disorder that affects other linguistic processes such as reading and speaking. Written language is particularly susceptible to neurological or neuropsychological impairment because writing skills are acquired late in life and are used infrequently in daily activities. Although significant brain damage, regardless of location, usually produces some degree of written language deficit, agraphias are most likely to occur with lesions in the left cerebral hemisphere, particularly in the frontal, parietal, and temporal areas. Some children with right hemisphere lesions, however, may show visuospatial disorganization that affects writing; those with more diffuse pathology may experience difficulty in planning. The wide range of etiologies associated with writing deficits derives from the multiple processes that contribute to successful written language. Agraphias can be grouped into central agraphias and peripheral agraphias (Ellis, 1982, 1988). Central, or linguistic, agraphias, described next, are problems in written language that involve spelling and selecting appropriate words for writing tasks.

*Aphasic agraphia* is caused by transcortical lesions or injury to Broca's or Wernicke's area. Aphasia is almost always associated with writing disorders, and this kind of agraphia often causes the most impairment in writing tasks, relative to oral and gestural tasks. In Broca's and transcortical motor aphasia, writing tends to be "spare, effortful, clumsy in calligraphy, abbreviated, agrammatical, and poorly spelled" (Lorch, 1995, p. 298). In conduction and Wernicke's aphasia, however, patients exhibit better written than spoken production of language. The existence of this kind of agraphia has been questioned by researchers (e.g., Beeson & Rapcsak, 1998; Rapcsak & Beeson, 2000) and used as an umbrella term for other types of dysgraphias (e.g., Feifer & De Fina, 2002).

*Lexical (surface) agraphia* is caused by temporal-parietal-occipital area lesions, especially at the junction of the posterior angular gyrus and the parietal-occipital lobe (Roeltgen & Blaskey, 1992). Novel words or nonwords are spelled correctly in naming tasks, dictation, or spontaneously, but familiar words, particularly those with ambiguous phoneme-to-grapheme correspondence, are spelled incorrectly (e.g., flud for flood). Ardila (2001) has recommended caution in applying this category to Spanish-speaking children, who may display written products that are uncommon in the English language but are appropriate in their own.

*Phonological agraphia* is a spelling impairment that is caused most often by lesions in the left supramarginal gyrus or underlying insula. Phonological agraphia may also be associated with Broca's, conduction, Wernicke's, or anomic aphasia. Clinically, this agraphia is characterized by an inability to spell nonwords (distinguishing it from lexical agraphia), with relatively well-preserved spelling of real words. Words that are not in the premorbid vocabulary are not accurately spelled, although there is visual or phonological similarity to target nonwords (e.g., flip for flup) and visual, but not phonological, resemblance to real words (e.g., guilat for guitar; Ellis, 1982).

*Semantic agraphia* is associated with left hemisphere, extraperisylvian lesions (both cortical and subcortical) and with transcortical aphasia. It is characterized by the loss of ability to spell and to write with meaning. Children with semantic agraphia are able to correctly spell irregular words and nonwords, however, they may confuse homophones in writing to dictation (e.g., not for knot), even if a context is provided. Writing to dictation without comprehension is often spared. Children with semantic agraphia may also exhibit impaired spontaneous writing and written naming.

*Deep agraphia (dysgraphia),* which is sometimes seen as a subtype of semantic agraphia (Feifer & De Fina, 2002), is usually associated with extensive left hemisphere lesions that involve most of the perisylvian language zone. Lesions are typically found in the left posterior cortex, including the supramarginal gyrus or insula. Deep agraphia is distinguishable from lexical agraphia because of a preponderance of semantic errors (e.g., igloo-Eskimo; Rapcsak & Beeson, 2000, p. 193) and almost nonexistent spelling of nonsense words. Children with this disorder experience greater difficulty with syntactical words (e.g., prepositions and conjunctions) than with semantic ones (nouns and adjectives) and may spell words with visual similarity to the target word (e.g., sead for soul). Words that have high imageability and concreteness are spelled correctly, as are content, high-frequency, and regular words (Rapcsak & Beeson, 2000). Children with deep agraphia seem unable to appropriately sequence letters within a word, although they may be able to produce all the letters that make up that word.

*Mixed (agraphia) dysgraphia* is typically associated with lesions to the inferior parietal lobes and is characterized by misspellings with reversals, omissions, and substitutions (Feifer & De Fina, 2002). Children with mixed dysgraphia display an inability to sequence letters in a word, especially phonetically irregular ones, and may occasionally produce mirror or backward writing. There is no difficulty copying from text or forming neat letters; however, spontaneously written text often has extra spaces or font changes within words.

*Agraphia due to impairment of the graphemic buffer* tends to be associated with variable localization of lesions (Rapp & Beeson, 2003), although involvement of the left hemisphere, possibly in the frontal-parietal cortical areas, is most common. This agraphia is marked by an inability to store graphemic information in short-term memory and results in errors of grapheme identity and order that are observed in all spelling tasks and that affect all output modalities (Rapcsak &

Beeson, 2000). Characteristic errors include letter substitutions, deletions, additions, and transpositions.

As noted, agraphias can also involve peripheral processes (*peripheral agraphias*) that are associated with problems in translating linguistic information into motor movements. A brief discussion of the types of peripheral agraphias typically found in school settings follows.

*Allographic (ideational) agraphia* is invariably due to a lesion in the left parieto-occipital region and is related to difficulties with the allographic conversion process. Children with allographic agraphia often display intact oral spelling, typing, and spelling with anagram letters. Word writing results in neat letter formation, with letter omissions, substitutions, insertions, and reversals and often a mixture of uppercase and lowercase and print and cursive writing. Both central and peripheral agraphias can result in allographia.

*Apraxic agraphia* is occasionally referred to as pure agraphia and is sometimes used as an umbrella term that includes ideational apraxia and constructional apraxia (Feifer & De Fina, 2002). Apraxic agraphia is caused by lesions in the hemisphere contralateral to the preferred writing hand, usually involving the parietal lobe and the premotor cortex (Lorch, 1995). It is characterized by poor letter formation that is probably due to motor deficits rather than defective letter knowledge or cerebellar dysfunction. Oral spelling, spelling with anagram letters, typing, and copying are generally unaffected, although comprehension may be impaired (Benson & Ardila, 1996). Writing movements and strokes are typically awkward and jerky.

*Constructional (afferent, spatial) agraphia* is typically caused by lesions in the right parietal lobe that affect the motor programs that control letter production. Clinical indicators include inaccurate writing of letters, repetition of letter strokes, wildly wavering or slanting base lines, extra loops, and the use of extra blank space between letters that seriously obscures meaning (e.g., Themanwal ksint hes treet instead of The man walks in the street; Benson & Ardila, 1996, p. 226). Oral spelling and spelling with anagram letters, on the other hand, are relatively intact. The so-called *cascade phenomenon*, frequently associated with constructional agraphia, is characterized by an increasingly wide left margin used in successive lines or, in the case of typing tasks, neglect of the left side of the keyboard (Lorch, 1995). Problems are seen most often at the beginning of words and in letters (e.g., /m/, /u/, and /e/) that require recursive movements. Writing may improve with eyes closed, suggesting that visual and kinesthetic feedback may be implicated. Constructional agraphia has been inconsistently identified by researchers (e.g., Feifer & De Fina, 2002; Gregg, 1995).

*Pure agraphia* is very rare, occurs in the absence of any other language, speech, or reading disorder, and is the result of a focal lesion, most probably in the posterior, temporal-parietal area (Lorch, 1995). A disproportionate number of left-handers are affected by pure agraphia, although it has been seen in right-handed patients with left hemisphere strokes. Pure agraphias involve difficulties with cursive writing, semantic paragraphias, neologisms, misspellings, and, sometimes, mirror writing. The existence of this agraphia has been hotly debated (Benson & Ardila, 1996; Gregg, 1995).

*Gerstmann's syndrome* is caused by lesions to the dominant inferior parietal lobe and includes a constellation of symptoms that include agraphia, dyscalculia, right-left confusion, and finger agnosia. The agraphia is characterized by significant spelling miscues in writing that are associated with an inability to correctly sequence letters in words (Feifer & De Fina, 2002). Gerstmann's syndrome is identified as a peripheral agraphia by Lorch (1995) but is not listed as an agraphia at all by other researchers (e.g., Rapcsak & Beeson, 2000).

*Hemiagraphia (unilateral, disconnection agraphia)* is associated with lesions in the middle to posterior portion of the trunk of the corpus callosum, the bundle of neural fibers that connects the two cerebral hemispheres. Because hemispheric specialization for spelling and writing is not consistent or predictable, the impact of neurological injury in one of the hemispheres cannot be easily described. For example, left-handers with left unilateral agraphia may produce neat, legible writing (Lorch, 1995), whereas right-handers with left hemispheric lateralization of written language and left unilateral agraphia may produce scrawled, unintelligible writing. There is considerable variation in the way this agraphia is described. For example, Lorch lists it as a central agraphia, Gregg (1995) describes it as a type of aphasic agraphia, Benson and Ardila (1996) question its link to the agraphias, and Rapcsak and Beeson (2000) exclude it from the peripheral agraphias.

*Nonpraxic disorders of motor execution,* another agraphia that is controversial with regard to description and membership (Rapcsak & Beeson, 2000), is associated with lesions to the basal ganglia or the cerebellum. It results in inadequate regulation of motor movements that translate to problems with force, speed, and amplitude in handwriting tasks. Micrographia is often seen, as are disjointed and irregular, awkward writing movements.

There are other agraphias inconsistently described by researchers, including isolated agraphia, hypergraphia, micrographia, mechanical agraphia, and mirror writing. All of these share elements of disordered writing but do not clearly fit the criteria for central or peripheral agraphias and therefore are not discussed here.

## NEUROPSYCHOLOGICAL ASSESSMENT OF AGRAPHIAS IN CHILDREN

Neuropsychological assessment is defined as a noninvasive method of examining brain function by studying its behavioral product (Lezak, 1995). It differs from traditional psychoeducational approaches to assessment in its assumption that all behavior is the direct result of, or at least mediated by, brain function (Whitten, D'Amato, & Chittooran, 1992) and in its planned comparisons between premorbid and postmorbid functioning (Teeter & Semrud-Clikeman, 1997). Although the neuropsychological assessment of agraphias in adults is well established, it is relatively recent in children. The assessment of agraphias, difficult under any conditions, is particularly problematic in learner populations, not only because of the dearth of technically sound measures, but because normal developmental changes complicate the assessment process.

To be useful, a neuropsychological assessment of language must identify not only the neurological or neuropsychological impairment, but also its associated functional disability (Ylvisaker, 1998). Such assessment must address the issue of causality and distinguish between written language deficits that are the result of neurological or neuropsychological damage and those that occur as a result of environmental insult or limited intellectual capacity. Assessment also requires a comparison between postmorbid and premorbid functioning as well as with written language in normally functioning peers. It must address a child's deficits as well as strengths and resources and must consider the enormous interindividual as well as intraindividual variability of the effects of neurological or neuropsychological impairment on written language. It must be periodic and ongoing because a child's level of functioning can change so rapidly during the recovery process (Havey, 2002). Finally, it must be a collaborative venture that involves medical and school professionals, families, and, if possible, the child.

A complete neuropsychological assessment of language should be comprehensive enough to answer referral questions while integrating cognitive, academic, behavioral, psychosocial, and environmental variables within a developmental framework (D'Amato & Rothlisberg, 1996; Teeter & Semrud-Clikeman, 1997). The task becomes more difficult because of legal mandates stemming from the Individuals with Disabilities Education Act, amendments of 1997, that call for an increased focus on functional assessments that use multimethod, multisource, and multisetting methodologies wherever possible (D'Amato & Rothlisberg, 1996). Though laborious, a thorough neuropsychological assessment of written language yields a number of advantages. It provides quantifiable results that can aid in both diagnosis and treatment, facilitates the identification of subtle deficits, and provides information that can be used as a baseline for interventions.

Neuropsychological evaluation begins with a complete history and medical evaluation/testing to identify sensory deficits (e.g., vision, hearing) that could influence test results. Functional MRIs may be used to provide information about brain activity during actual writing performance but are, at present, limited to use with children age 5 and older (Gaillard, Xu, & Balsamo, 2002). The selection of appropriate measures for a neuropsychological assessment of written language is of critical importance. The minimum requirement for neuropsychological tests is "sensitivity to the presence of brain damage and the ability to distinguish correctly between the presence of brain damage and normal brain functioning" (Hebben & Milberg, 2002, p. 4). A superior measure can specify the site and severity of brain damage and, perhaps, even its specific etiology. Actuarial or standardized approaches to the assessment of intellectual ability may include the *Wechsler Intelligence Scale for Children, Fourth Edition* (WISC-IV) for children up to age 17, the Cognitive Assessment System, or the *Stanford-Binet, Fourth Edition,* to identify cognitive deficits that contribute to writing problems. Academic achievement in major content areas may be assessed using the *Woodcock-Johnson Psychoeducational Battery-III* (WJ-III), Tests of Achievement, or the Wechsler Individual Achievement Test, second edition (WIAT-II). Written language may be assessed using the Writing Fluency subtest from the WJ-III, Supplemental Battery, the Written Expression subtest of the WIAT-II, the Written Language subtest of the *Kaufman Test of Educational Achievement,* the Test of Written Language (TWEL-3) for school-age children, the Test of Early Written Language (TEWL-2) for young children, or the Test of Adolescent and Adult Language, Third Edition (TOAL-3). Actuarial measures of spelling include the Spelling subtest of the Wide Range Achievement Test II, the Johns Hopkins Dysgraphia Battery, and the Real World Spelling Test. Neuropsychological measures such as the Halstead-Reitan Battery Aphasia Screening Test, Written Language Sections, the Luria-Nebraska, Section K, and the Boston Diagnostic Aphasia Examination, Written Language Sections can be used for explicit assessment of written language. Writing samples can be elicited with the Cookie Theft Picture from the Boston Diagnostic Aphasia Exam and the Picnic Scene from the Western Aphasia Battery. Written naming of objects may be assessed with the

Boston Naming Test and may be compared to oral naming of the same stimuli. Other commonly used measures of language include the Western Aphasia Battery, Written Language Section, the Battery of Adult Reading Function, Subtests 1 to 4 and Appendices A and B, the NEPSY, and the Dean-Woodcock.

Executive functions, memory, and attention are increasingly seen as important in neuropsychological assessments of written language and may be assessed using a variety of measures, such as the Category Test, the Tower of Hanoi, the Wisconsin Card Sort Test, the Trail Making Test, and the Continuous Performance Test. Constructional dyspraxia may be assessed using the Bender Gestalt, the Beery Visual-Motor Integration Test, or the Design Copying test from the NEPSY.

Although actuarial, norm-referenced assessments allow for useful comparisons with same-age or same-grade peers, their detractors have argued that such assessments discriminate against culturally diverse populations, that their administration and interpretation are time-consuming, and that test results are not easily translated into useful classroom interventions. They propose process approaches as an alternative to actuarial tests. Such approaches to assessment rely on a variety of measures used flexibly, depending on the presenting problem and the unique needs of the child. For example, Berninger's (1994) Core Battery for Writing Assessment uses both formal and informal measures that are tailored to the needs of the child. Actuarial measures of written language can also be supplemented by criterion-referenced measures (e.g., Brigance, Clinical Evaluation of Language Fundamentals-Revised) and clinical approaches (e.g., writing samples, behavioral observations, and clinical interviews) that allow for the assessment of a wide range of writing skills and behaviors (Havey, 2002; Teeter & Semrud-Clikeman, 1997). Another useful approach, curriculum-based assessment, allows for ongoing measurement of small, discrete changes not identifiable with actuarial approaches (Havey, 2002). Task analysis and error pattern analysis, dynamic assessments of language learning potential, authentic assessments to evaluate real-world use of language, and "testing the limits" have also been offered as adjuncts to standardized assessments (Teeter & Semrud-Clikeman, 1997).

Tests of written language should include at least the following: (1) signing one's name; (2) copying numbers, letters, words, and sentences; (3) transcoding script into print, cursive, uppercase, and lowercase letters and roman and arabic numerals; (4) writing to dictation of numbers, letters, words, and sentences; (5) writing the names of objects presented and actions demonstrated; and (6) spontaneous narrative writing of sequences and information (e.g., Write three sentences that describe how you brush your teeth in the morning; Lorch, 1995; Rapczak & Beeson, 2000). Writing samples during testing can yield valuable data about grammatical usage, apraxia, and visual perceptual/spatial functioning (Lezak, 1995). Copying tasks, both immediate and delayed, may provide information about short-term memory and the functional status of the graphemic buffer. Comparisons of spoken and written language as well as oral and written fluency are also recommended (Lezak, 1995). Classroom samples, such as first drafts of expository writing, narrative fiction, and nonfiction, can yield useful information about typical writing performance, and portfolios and brief "serial evaluations" (Baron, 2004; Crawford, Helwig, & Tindal, 2004) can provide information about changes in written production over time.

Clinical interviews with the child, family, and teachers also yield important information about other factors that may influence performance, such as lack of interest or reluctance to write (Baron, 2004; Feifer & De Fina, 2002). Although interviews are generally underutilized in neuropsychological assessments of academic functioning (Baker & Hubbard, 2002), teachers and family members may be particularly helpful when comparing postmorbid and premorbid functioning. They may also offer valuable insight into *moderator variables* (Telzrow, 1991), the social, environmental, and motivational factors that affect a child's ability to adjust to the impairment and to benefit from intervention.

Direct observations can provide additional information about behaviors that influence written language (Baker & Hubbard, 2002; Havey, 2002). Observations should be made in the following areas: grasp, dominant hand, letter height and size, placement of writing on the page, consistency in letter formation, spacing between letters, words, and sentences, overwriting, and erasures (Baron, 2004), as well as rate of writing (Lezak, 1995). Observations can also be useful when comparing performance across modalities; oral spelling, typing, and spelling with anagram letters that vary markedly from spelling by dictation yield additional insights that may be used in setting up interventions.

The general adaptational capacities of the child's brain, defined as the "brain's capacity for structural and functional change" (Rourke, Bakker, Fisk, & Strang, 1983, p. 162), are an important part of a neuropsychological assessment. Indicators include intelligence test scores, the absence of pathological signs in a child's neuropsychological profile, and good performances on both sides of the body for measures of motor, psychomotor, and tactile-perceptual abilities. The absence of such signs, however, does not necessarily indicate that the child's brain is intact. Other signs include the ability of the brain to benefit from feedback (which can be assessed using the Category and the Tactual Performance tests on the Halstead-Reitan), vigilance (which can be assessed using the Seashore Rhythm Test or the Underlining Tests), the use of adaptive strategies, and patterns of neuropsychological strengths and weaknesses.

Once agraphia has been established, it is important to determine its type so as to identify the impaired processing component and residual or compensatory strategies used by the learner. It has been suggested that consistent difficulties across different modalities are diagnostic of central agraphia, whereas modality-specific deficits suggest peripheral agraphia (Rapcsak & Beeson, 2000). Evaluations of central agraphias should also examine the impact on written language of lexical status (words versus nonwords), imageability/concreteness (high versus low), word class (content words versus functional, nouns versus verbs), frequency (high versus low), orthographic regularity (regular versus ambiguous or irregular), word length (short versus long), and morphology (monomorphemic versus affixed; Rapcsak & Beeson, 2000). The assessment of peripheral agraphias requires an evaluation of the child's ability to write in uppercase and lowercase forms, in print or cursive, and to shift between various allographic forms (e.g., upper- to lowercase). Legibility, letter size, and morphology should be assessed and evidence of impaired afferent control and defective spatial organization should be noted. Behavioral observations during writing tasks can provide the examiner with important information regarding speed of writing, force of strokes, and amplitude. It may also be helpful to ask the child to write separately with each hand to compare written productions and to determine the presence of limb apraxia.

Finally, assessment of written language disorders in children requires an evaluation of changes in personality and behavioral functioning that may occur subsequent to neuropsychological damage and that may affect the successful completion of writing tasks. For example, frontal lobe damage has been found to affect self-control, impulsivity, social skills, conceptual thinking, emotional lability, and attitude toward the writing task, including frustration, reluctance, and requests for adult help. Such behaviors can have a deleterious impact on the child's writing performance.

## WRITTEN LANGUAGE INTERVENTIONS WITH CHILDREN

Academic interventions in general, and written language interventions in particular, are most successful when they are based on a comprehensive assessment of children's strengths and weaknesses. Multiple intervention models and strategies are available for use with children who exhibit problems in written language. However, the planning and implementation of such interventions must be informed generally, by issues related to rehabilitation in children, and specifically, by principles of neuropyschological interventions with children. A discussion of these issues is offered in the following sections.

### GENERAL ISSUES RELATED TO REHABILITATION IN CHILDREN

Recovery from neuropsychological or neurological damage in children is influenced by a number of factors. Generally, a prognosis is better when the period of unconsciousness and/or amnesia is shorter and when the posttraumatic residual abilities are greater (Owens, 1999). The child's age at the time of injury predicts recovery somewhat, as young children tend to recover faster than older children. Other factors that have an impact on recovery include premorbid levels of functioning, age and extent of the injury, rate of growth of lesion, socioeconomic status (including access to health care, parental income and education), child-rearing practices, and gender (Ardila, 2001; Gaillard et al., 2002; Lorch, 1995; Ylvisaker, Szekeres, & Haarbauer-Krupa, 1998).

Researchers have offered competing hypotheses about the brain's ability to compensate for language deficits subsequent to neurological damage in childhood (Gaillard et al., 2002). The traditional view describes the young child's brain as pluripotent and suggests that, in the event of direct injury, extensive areas of the brain can sustain language function. The other, more contemporary view states that language networks are firmly established by the age of 4 or 5, certainly by the time children enter school, and that language in both children and adults is highly lateralized and regionally specific. Children with neurological and/or neuropsychological injuries show a remarkable ability to regain premorbid function, although the reorganization of neurological structures subsequent to injury appears to be limited by a critical period that extends from early childhood into adolescence and, occasionally, into adulthood (Gaillard et al., 2002). Although children generally have an advantage over adults with regard to recovery because of the plasticity of the brain, there are occasional paradoxical effects found in young children. For example, an injury may result in long-term deficits that become evident only when academic demands increase and cause an unexpected breakdown in functioning. Hence, predictions as to the efficacy of long-term outcomes in learners must be undertaken with caution because of a multitude of factors that may not have been clearly identified (Lord-Maes & Obrzut, 1996).

Developmental issues also greatly complicate the planning and delivery of interventions for written language disorders in children. First, the psychologist must consider the impact of normal, developmental changes on children's functioning and be able to differentiate between these and other changes that are attributable to intervention (Lord-Maes & Obrzut, 1996). Treatment approaches have to be modified as improvement occurs and as children's needs change over time. Although such changes can make it difficult to predict the rate and direction of recovery, one solution is to develop short-term, individual therapies that proceed in a graduated manner and are evaluated continuously, so that they are sensitive to the changing needs of the child (Havey, 2002). Developmental changes are particularly critical for adolescents who, in addition to their disability, experience adjustment issues related to identity, separation-individuation, body image, and peer interactions (Turkstra, 2000). For this age group, therefore, cognitive-behavioral models that emphasize self-awareness, independence, and self-regulation may be especially helpful (Naglieri, 2002). Other developmental factors must be considered in designing interventions. For example, writing interventions with young learners, for whom writing skills may not be well established, are generally less effective than similar interventions with older learners for whom functional mechanisms for writing have been established.

Ecological, systems-based models of intervention are increasingly used with pediatric populations due to a growing recognition that neuropsychological impairments affect not only children but also their families, schools, and communities (Benson & Ardila, 1996; D'Amato & Rothlisberg, 1996; Ylvisaker, 1998). Indeed, a child's long-term outcome is significantly influenced by the quality of home life as well as interactions with family members during the recovery period. Further, because a sizable proportion of a child's waking day is spent in school, all interventions must also include a focus on improving school functioning. Neuropsychological rehabilitation in children and adolescents, then, is "a method of restructuring lives in a social context" (Uzzell, 1998, p. 41) and requires a comprehensive, integrative approach that includes input from fields such as neurology, psychology, neuropsychology, occupational therapy, speech/language therapy, regular education, and special education.

Developmental and ecological factors are important in rehabilitation; however, some issues cut across developmental stages. The main goal of any intervention with children and adolescents who have neuropsychological impairments is to develop realistic treatments that aim to restore premorbid functioning and that "promote the utilization of preserved abilities to substitute for lost or impaired functions" (Rapcsak & Beeson, 2000, p. 207). Further, neuropsychological rehabilitation should help children become aware of both their strengths and their limitations and the functional implications of their disability (Eslinger & Oliveri, 2002). Life goals are also important, including follow-up care that addresses patient and family education, individual or family counseling to facilitate psychological adjustment, and vocational and career counseling for older children and adolescents (Eslinger & Oliveri, 2002). Goals must take into account the child's age, interests, and associated problems, such as memory skills deficits and visual perceptual problems, that may have an impact on performance. Goals must also be part of a larger plan that includes frequent, relatively short treatment sessions that circumvent the short attention span and easy fatigue that are the hallmark of children in recovery. Sessions can be lengthened once treatment methods become familiar and children show improvement. Ideally, academic and behavioral goals of peers should be modified for children with neurological or neuropsychological impairments so that language and academic skills that are important in the classroom will be reinforced during treatment. Methods, materials, and activities should be both functional and of high interest to learners. There is a general belief that motivation to produce written language is the single most important contributor to success; indeed, the degree to which teachers are effective reflects the degree to which they are able to use the child's desire for communication as a motivator (Feifer & De Fina, 2002).

## PRINCIPLES OF NEUROPSYCHOLOGICAL INTERVENTION WITH CHILDREN

Four areas must be considered in neuropsychological treatment planning (Rourke et al., 1983). The first involves the child's specific neuropsychological profile, including the number and types of systems that are impaired and the degree of impairment, the neuropsychological strengths, and the premorbid engrams (stored systems of information or isolated skills that may be used as a starting point for therapy). A second area has to do with information about known or hypothesized brain lesions, including their extent and chronicity, the child's age at onset, and the development of any secondary problems such as hydrocephalus or meningitis. A third area has to do with the environmental demands of the child's school setting and family interactions. Armed with this information, the clinician can then determine availability of resources, such as intrapersonal strengths, accessibility of experienced clinicians, and potential for family involvement. A fourth area has to do with the child's motivation for treatment.

Rourke et al. (1983) provide a convenient overview of a 6-stage treatment planning model. Though a bit dated, it remains quite useful for school neuropsychologists today. Step 1 is a detailed evaluation of a child's neuropsychological abilities and other variables related to the impairment. Step 2 is an evaluation of the child's immediate and long-term environmental demands so that a set of short-term and long-term behavioral outcomes can be identified in Step 3. In Step 4, two detailed short- and long-term treatment plans are developed, one ideal, the other realistic. Step 5 involves checking on the availability of rehabilitation resources. Following these steps, a realistic treatment plan can be formulated in Step 6.

School neuropsychological interventions are collaboratively designed, implemented, and evaluated by school and nonschool personnel instead of being limited to the medical professionals whose domain they once were (Havey, 2002; Sattler & D'Amato, 2002; Ylvisaker et al., 1998). It has been estimated that more than half of all currently practicing neuropsychologists are involved in cognitive rehabilitation or retraining activities, many of them in school settings. Most school neuropsychologists provide services to schoolchildren with neurological impairments and written language deficits through the Individuals with Disabilities Education Improvement Act of 2004, under the category of Traumatic Brain Injury

(D'Amato & Rothlisberg, 1996). They may, however, also provide special educational services to children with written language problems that are not the result of neurological or neuropsychological injury. Learners are eligible for such services through their 22nd birthday.

School neuropsychologists typically use one of three approaches to treatment: (1) directly addressing a child's weaknesses, (2) capitalizing on strengths identified during assessment, or (3) a combination of the two (D'Amato & Rothlisberg, 1996). Superior outcomes have been reported for interventions that used the child's strengths as a basis for remediation (Teeter & Semrud-Clikeman, 1997). Such an approach allows for choices between remedial or compensatory rehabilitative therapy that builds on identified strengths to compensate for weaknesses. In some instances, of course, remediation is appropriate (e.g., in the case of children under the age of 5, who have not developed the requisite skills, or in the case of older children with emotional problems).

Arguably the most important aspect of an intervention is its relevance for the individual student. Because behavioral self-management is an important precursor to rehabilitative success, learners must have a mind-set for the work ahead and understand that attention, interest, cooperation, and motivation are key ingredients of a successful treatment program. It is also important that intervention be set up in small increments, with basic skills leading to more difficult ones, so that the child has the opportunity to experience immediate success. This is particularly important in the case of young children. Effective rehabilitation programs usually begin with reading and listening and only later progress to writing. Generally, children with neuropsychological impairments should be provided with a variety of writing experiences. Early attempts at writing should be based on familiar experiences and should gradually move toward more advanced kinds of writing. The classroom teacher can act as facilitator, coach, and model. For example, the teacher and learner can collaboratively create a written product with the adult modeling the writing cycle and assuming the responsibility for the mechanics of writing so that the learner is relieved of this pressure. At the upper elementary level, bypass strategies to avoid deficits are often recommended. Examples of such an approach include shortened assignments, gradually increasing performance standards (first on the content and later on the quality and the mechanics), avoiding punishment, offering oral exams rather than written ones, and giving untimed tests. Keyboarding skills can be taught, preferably on a manual typewriter before moving to word processing software, so that the mechanics of writing become automatic. Other bypass or compensatory strategies that include the use of computer word processing and spelling and grammar checking are strongly encouraged so that children can invest their time and energy in the writing process instead of the mechanics of writing.

There are a number of factors that influence treatment outcomes for individuals with impairments and language dysfunction. Generally, outcomes will be more positive if therapy is initiated early and maintained longer. Intensive therapy can have a positive effect on recovery, especially if the learner is young and if language loss is relatively minor. The etiology of language disorders can affect outcome, as can the absence of associated disorders. A child with well-developed adaptational capacities has a much better prognosis than one without and can benefit from a wider range of rehabilitation approaches and strategies. Further, such a child has the capacity to be actively involved in the rehabilitation process and may be able to provide information regarding the impact of the injury on daily life. Intrapersonal factors such as morale and resilience can also have a significant effect on treatment outcomes. Cultural variations in the acceptance of injury, behavior following injury, and receptivity to treatment must also be considered (Ponton & Monguio, 2001). Finally, interdisciplinary treatments that are implemented in a context of functional daily living activities tend to have superior outcomes.

## Intervention Models and Strategies for Writing Disorders

A variety of theoretical approaches to intervention may be employed, depending on the experience and preference of the therapist, the goals of the treatment program, and the individual learner's neurodevelopmental profile (Feifer & De Fina, 2002; Hinckley, 2002; Margolin & Goodman-Schulman, 1992). Behavioral interventions that use operant conditioning techniques and immediate, rather than delayed, feedback may be useful for children, particularly younger learners. Computer technology that uses behavioral principles to teach and reinforce writing skills is especially useful and appealing to learners; in fact, there are several software programs that have been developed for just this purpose. Cognitive neuropsychological approaches tend to examine task performance on selected measures of knowledge and skills and then use it to infer impairment in the relevant neuropsychological component. Cognitive and cognitive-behavioral models, which have primary application in educational settings, focus on various cognitive abilities such as attention, memory, and executive functions as key components of the rehabilitation process. They also utilize strategy instruction, self-talk, self-regulation, and other metacognitive techniques that encourage self-reliance and independence (Bain, Bailet, & Moats, 2001). Compensatory approaches tend to be practical and functional and use the child's residual cognitive capacities to accomplish tasks using alternative strategies. Linguistic approaches apply aspects of linguistic theory to the understanding of written language deficits and to the development of appropriate treatments. Social approaches focus on psychosocial aspects of neurological or neuropsychological impairment and incorporate learners' social networks in treatment. For instance, exchanges of e-mail messages, short notes, and pen-pal letters help learners see both the appeal and the usefulness of writing as a means of communication. Finally, neurological approaches, most similar to parts of the medical model, emphasize discovery of brain impairment (answering the why question) as well as intact areas of the brain and use those as a starting point for rehabilitation. According to Hinckley, the cognitive/learning and neurological approaches may offer the best hope for the treatment of children with neurological impairment.

Writers have also proposed numerous, specific treatment models, some of which are described in the following section. The most prevalent model of rehabilitation is based on Luria's work, which links recovery of function to newly learned connections developed through mental retraining exercises specifically targeted at disrupted processes. Such a model presupposes that direct intervention is essential to the recovery and reorganization of the brain (Uzzell, 1998). The multistage neuropsychological model (Teeter & Semrud-Clikeman, 1997) proposes 8 stages, beginning with behavioral-observational assessment and proceeding to more extensive cognitive, psychosocial, neuropsychological, and/or neurological evaluations at succeeding stages. At each level, assessment results lead to new goals, new interventions, and, subsequently, new evaluations.

The REHABIT model of intervention, the Reitan Evaluation of Hemispheric Abilities and Brain Improvement Training (Teeter & Semrud-Clikeman, 1997), includes 3 stages: assessment, training with Halstead-Reitan test items, and rehabilitation with REHABIT materials. Training is conducted in five major areas: (1) verbal-language deficits, (2) abstract reasoning, (3) logical deficits, (4) visual-spatial problems, and (5) right-left hemisphere deficits.

Owens (1999) has described a process-oriented, functional model of intervention and compares it with traditional therapeutic approaches to language problems. In this approach, therapy is conducted in individual, small, or large groups in a contextually appropriate setting such as the home or school instead of in an artificially managed setting such as a clinic. Children are taught about the interrelationships of linguistic skills instead of learning isolated skills. Writing is described as an opportunity to transmit messages instead of focusing on skill acquisition, practice, and drill. The use of writing as a social tool of communication is also stressed during intervention. Learners are given numerous opportunities to use written language and to develop their skills by using language with a variety of purposes and partners.

Another approach to rehabilitation is offered by Fryburg (1997), using the Whole Brain Interactive Approach to Reading, Writing, and Language Instruction. The program is based on a neuropsychological profile of children's strengths and weaknesses so that "teaching procedures utilize the student's [intact functional systems] and limit the debilitating effect of the student's disabilities" (p. 274). The learner participates collaboratively in all stages of the rehabilitation process, with the focus of instruction being adjustment to school and community. Learning objectives are designed to integrate the functional systems of listening, speaking, reading, and writing instead of treating them as isolated systems. Typically, stronger abilities in one or more areas are used to build competence in weaker areas. Continuous monitoring and sequential progress from basic to complex skills are cornerstones of the program. Finally, concepts such as Vygotsky's *zone of proximal development* and Bruner's *scaffolding* are used to help the teacher or clinician with intervention goals and implementation. Numerous other models exist that have varying degrees of acceptance, including Sohlberg and Mateer's Process-Specific Approach and the Stimulation Model (described in Bain et al., 2001), and the No-Transfer-of-Training Model (Uzzell, 1998).

The following section outlines specific strategies that have been suggested for children who exhibit central and peripheral agraphias; however, they may also be used with children who have developmental disorders of writing. Treatment for central agraphias is aimed at strengthening the lexical-semantic route, facilitating use of the non-lexical route, or a combination of the two. Some approaches try to build writing skills in an item-specific manner (i.e., word by word); others target the remediation of processes that influence the spelling for more than one item. Treatments for central agraphias are discussed as though they were process specific, but in actual fact, there is a dynamic interaction between damaged and intact functions that influences both treatment and writing ability. Semantic agraphia can be remediated by using programs such as Writing Skills for the Adolescent, Sentence Combining, or Sopris West's Step Up to Writing (Feifer &

De Fina, 2002). Mixed agraphia can be addressed using the Language Experience Approach, CAST: Universal Design for Learning, and Musical Spelling. Surface agraphia might be treated successfully with approaches like the Cover-Write Method, the Fernald Method, and Visual Spelling. Finally, phonological agraphia can be addressed with the use of Alphabetic Phonics, Making Words, and Writing to Read (Feifer & De Fina, 2002). Partial lexical knowledge or relatively preserved phonological knowledge (characteristic of central agraphias) may allow children to self-correct using an electronic pocket dictionary with a spelling option. For children who use word processors, the spell-check function allows for identification of misspelled words and the provision of plausible options (Rapcsak & Beeson, 2000).

Unlike interventions for central agraphias, often planned and implemented solely by classroom teachers, interventions for peripheral agraphias may require the involvement of occupational therapists or other special education personnel. There has been relatively little research in this area, possibly due to the fact that intact central processes allow children to use mechanical aids, such as typewriters or word processors, to circumvent motor problems. It has been speculated that some of the approaches used for the treatment of central agraphias (e.g., tracing, copying, transcribing, and delayed copying) may facilitate retraining of the allographic conversion process and help with the execution of the appropriate motor programs. The main focus of treatment for children with peripheral agraphias is to teach them to write letters and words. Although the process is slow and painstaking, once mastery is achieved, the therapist can work on helping the learner develop automaticity. Micrographia, for instance, can be helped by using parallel lines or a template to help the writer form larger letters and words. Other successful treatments have included fading of external cues, verbal reminders, continual self-monitoring, and self-talk (Feifer, 2004).

There are two broad curricular choices available to teachers undertaking classroom interventions, the product and the process approaches (Bain et al., 2001). The former focuses on the end product of writing or the teaching of isolated skills that contribute to that final product. Such an approach usually organizes writing strategies into four groups: (1) background knowledge, (2) semantics, (3) syntax, and (4) grapho-symbolics (Gould, 2001). The newer, holistic, or process, approach sees writing as a process-oriented task and considers both the development of skills and the intrinsic value of the writing activity itself. Both approaches are concerned with developing competent writers, but they address the issue in different ways. The product approach has been soundly criticized on the grounds that such teaching obscures the communicative intent of writing and reduces it simply to a set of discrete skills without purpose or meaning (Gould, 2001). On the other hand, opponents of the process approach argue that an overemphasis on context and meaning prevents children from learning the basic skills that are fundamental to good communication. As is usually the case, the best approach, probably, is a combination of the two (Gould, 2001).

Successful interventions that address the writing process typically use a framework that includes some variation of three essential steps: planning, writing, and revising (Baker & Hubbard, 2002). More comprehensive interventions target the skills necessary at each of these phases (i.e., prewriting, drafting, revision, editing, and publishing). At each stage, the school neuropsychologist can work on correcting weaknesses until normal function returns or until additional efforts result in no further improvement. A strengths-based approach is preferred during intervention; if a child relies on auditory cues, such stimuli could be used to provide access to written material. Similarly, if a child is unable to use the visual modality effectively, interventions that rely on that modality must be avoided (Reynolds, 1986; Reynolds & French, 2003). The axiom certainly is true: Dead tissue will not learn. According to Baker and Hubbard, explicit instruction in the writing process and in different genres of writing, as well as guided feedback from teachers or peers, led to the most positive outcomes, both for good writers and those with writing problems.

Several authors have emphasized the importance of explicitly teaching writing skills instead of assuming that children will pick up those skills on their own. For example, Baker, Gersten, and Graham (2003) discussed the need to carefully outline and systematically teach the steps in the process of writing an essay or narrative and to avoid taking background knowledge or skills acquisition for granted. Important aspects of the process include ensuring mastery of the mechanics of writing, improving quality through feedback and elaborated dialogue (similar to the approach advocated by Robertson, 2000), and teaching students to understand different text structures and their relationship to writing genres. Cognitive techniques such as think sheets, planning sheets, and mnemonic aids could be useful at any age and could be modified for all ages. Baker and his colleagues have suggested examining a typical sequence of writing development and trying to match student performance with those steps. Unlike other writers in the field, they believe that encouraging students to observe and model the performance of skilled writers could be counterproductive, as these students probably lack the necessary resources and skills to do so effectively.

Bain et al. (2001), also process-oriented theorists, discussed interventions that could be used at each stage of writing. At the prewriting stage, students could be encouraged to participate in peer and teacher conferences or to use journals to brainstorm ideas for writing. At the drafting stage, students could be urged to write daily in private, ungraded journals, to dictate their work to peers or teachers, and to view their first draft as a work in progress instead of a flawless product. To this end, students could be encouraged simply to get ideas down on paper and to guess at spellings. At the revision stage, the emphasis is on content, refining meaning, and improving the communicative aspect of the written word. At this stage, useful techniques include peer and teacher feedback on writing, group conferences to discuss progress, and teaching ways to rearrange material for maximum comprehension. At the editing stage, students are ready to focus on the mechanics of writing by proofreading and editing their work. One strategy that might be used at this stage is COPS: Capital letters, Overall appearance, Punctuation, and Spelling. Once again, students are encouraged to focus on gradual but steady improvement. When they have done as much as they can independently, they may turn their work over to a peer or a teacher for further assistance. At the publishing stage, students could focus on recopying their work or typing it in publishable form. Publication outlets for student work include school newspapers, literary magazines, and commercial publications targeted to student populations.

Other process approaches provide assistance to students who lack the metacognitive skills to monitor their own writing process. The acronym POWER is used to help the student Plan, Organize, Write, Edit, and Revise (Englert, 1990;

Feifer & De Fina, 2002). Teachers think aloud the steps of the process and use scaffolding and graduated prompts that are eventually replaced by student self-talk and self-monitoring. Cognitive Strategy in Writing, a process approach proposed by Englert and Raphael (1988), can be used for children with special needs and includes a series of think sheets and incorporates teacher modeling and think aloud techniques. Harris and Graham (1996) have offered the mnemonic PLANS to Pick goals, List ways of meeting those goals, And make Notes, and Sequence the notes. Peer editing and peer revision (Baker & Hubbard, 2002) are other techniques that currently are growing in popularity. Such techniques allow neuropsychologically impaired children to work in teams with one or more peers who provide them with coaching, teaching, and monitoring of written products. Such approaches can be helpful not only to the child with the impairment but to the helper, as well. A number of additional methods of peer assistance are discussed in Bain et al. (2001).

The K-W-L Plus method is a charting strategy that is an adaptation of a popular strategy designed to help students read for meaning (Carr & Ogle, 1987). Students develop a chart with four columns, with the first column, K, being what they already know, the second column, W, being what they want to know, the third column, completed after the reading activity, being what they have learned, and the fourth column, the plus column, becoming the basis of what they write about.

Other components of written language include working memory, executive planning, and attention. Working memory deficits might be helped by using graphic organizers, story maps, and writing wheels, all of which serve as memory aids and help the child store information long enough to use it in writing tasks (Feifer & De Fina, 2002). Executive planning deficits can be remediated with the use of a variety of cognitively based writing techniques such as COPS and POWER (Feifer & De Fina, 2002). Attention problems may be rehabilitated by breaking down tasks into smaller steps or by using cognitive-behavioral approaches such as self-talk and memory aids.

D'Amato and Rothlisberg's (1996) S.O.S. educational intervention model, developed to serve students with traumatic brain injuries, can easily be adapted for use with children with written language disorders. This ecologically based, contextually specific model advocates intervention in all areas of the learner's life. *Structure* relates to the physical organization of the environment and consistency in adult behaviors and classroom and home procedures, Organization refers to planning for learning tasks, organization of learning tasks, and using learning activities that are relevant to everyday life. Strategies refer to a variety of planning and self-monitoring techniques that take into account learning styles, student strengths and needs, and the use of peer assistance (D'Amato & Rothlisberg, 1996; Reynolds & French, 2003).

## EVALUATION OF INTERVENTION MODELS AND STRATEGIES

The evaluation of interventions is necessary not only to assess effectiveness with particular children, but also to facilitate the development of effective intervention models that can be applied to other children with similar problems. Unfortunately, a number of methodologic problems complicate outcome evaluations. For example, a comparison of the production and use of written language, pre- and post-treatment, would appear straightforward. This approach, however, is complicated by difficulties associated with finding measures that are independent of the therapies being used. Similarly, the issue of spontaneous recovery that typically occurs in the period immediately following injury makes such evaluations even more difficult. Evaluations of interventions must assess treatment integrity and acceptability with regard to the child, professionals, and families; however, it is difficult to standardize interventions across these domains. Evaluations of interventions for neuropsychological impairments are particularly difficult because there is so little consistency between the way any two children, even those with similar patterns of strengths and weaknesses, respond to treatment. In addition, there has been continuing concern about the ethical implications of testing rehabilitation models that withhold treatments known to be effective. While the use of both quantitative and qualitative outcome, or evidence-based, evaluation is preferred (Eslinger & Oliveri, 2002), particularly as interventions expand into nonmedical settings, the legitimacy of qualitative approaches continues to be questioned. Because of these and numerous other confounding factors, school psychologists and school neuropsychologists have not developed effective ways to evaluate interventions for children with impairments.

Notwithstanding these complications, a number of studies have examined, at least in a preliminary fashion, the effectiveness of writing interventions. Hillis and Caramazza (as cited in Rapscak & Beeson, 2000) compared several single-subject treatments and concluded that (1) patients with the same presumed locus of impairment benefited from different treatment approaches, (2) different treatment approaches could be equally appropriate for the same impairment, and (3) a particular treatment strategy could affect several different levels of processing impairment. Further, the patient's response to treatment could yield additional data that resulted in the diagnostic process continuing throughout rehabilitation (Rapcsak & Beeson, 2000).

In another study that demonstrated multiple benefits from an intervention, researchers showed that treatment of semantic deficits by means of teaching distinctions among semantically related items resulted in improved written naming, as well as generalization to oral naming and repetition tasks. Other studies aimed at strengthening the lexical and nonlexical spelling routes have documented improvements in writing (Rapcsak & Beeson, 2000). Yet other studies have evaluated the use of a writing prosthesis for the paralyzed right hand in children who have agraphia associated with aphasia (e.g., Lorch, 1995). Children exhibited superior linguistic content in written composition produced with the aided hemiparetic right hand when compared to composition with the nonparalyzed left hand. Armstrong and Macdonald (2000) reported on the use of a splint that allowed a young patient to use his dominant hand to write directly on a computer screen and to receive computer-generated auditory feedback about his writing performance. Results showed improvements in both the quality and quantity of written productions. De Partz (1995) reported on successful efforts to teach an adult patient with a graphemic buffer deficit to break down long written words into shorter segments that he could then dictate to himself and write down; it is very likely that such a strategy could be taught effectively to learners.

Gersten and Baker (2001) completed a meta-analysis of 13 group studies that examined writing interventions with elementary school-age students and reported a moderate effect size (.81) across treatments. They noted that both good writers and writers with deficits benefited when classroom teachers used innovative rather than traditional teaching techniques. Improvements were noted in the quality of writing across all genres and across all methods of evaluation, in student understanding of the writing process, and in students' perceptions of themselves as writers. The impact on student perceptions was similar to findings reported by Baker and Hubbard (2002) in a related study.

Wong, Butler, Ficzere, and Kuperis (1997) and others have demonstrated the usefulness of guided interactive dialogue between peers to help them plan the writing of essays and then in helping them revise their first drafts. Although there appeared to be no significant differences between the impact of teacher and peer feedback, what did seem to matter was that feedback systems were both elaborate and explicit (Baker & Hubbard, 2002). Mortley, Enderby, and Petheram (2001) reported the success of an intervention that used a computer to improve functional writing in a patient with surface dysgraphia. These innovative researchers used a compensatory strategy based on residual oral spelling skills, a computer to provide intensive practice, and a dictionary. Harris and Graham (1996) taught students to use self-directed prompts during writing tasks and found improvements in both the quantity and quality of written products. Students were better able to set writing goals, monitor progress, assess and record results, self-reinforce, and use self-talk to focus or refocus behavior. Results were similar to those found by Marlowe (2000), who recommended using self-talk with children who had disorders of executive function that also affected written language. She believed that such strategies could help with verbal mediation of complex tasks and self-regulation of behavior.

Researchers are beginning to plan and implement intervention studies that examine working memory and executive functions as they influence written productions. For instance, Hooper and his colleagues (2002) used Denckla's model with its four key domains—initiating behavior, sustaining behavior, inhibiting/stopping behavior, and set shifting—to examine the role of executive functions in written language among 55 elementary schoolchildren with and without writing deficits. They found that children with writing problems performed worse in each of these domains than did children without writing problems. If writing is, at least in part, a problem-solving process, executive functions that control planning and organizing written productions clearly contribute in important ways.

## CONCLUSION

School neuropsychology has made major strides in recent years, particularly in the assessment of deficits, including their localization and severity. While substantial progress has occurred in assessment, less progress has been made in treatment, especially evidence-based treatment of agraphias. To a large degree, the lack of progress reflects the multidimensional nature of writing, especially in children and adolescents who have widely divergent premorbid writing skills. Similarly, progress in the area has been limited by methodologic problems that impede still nascent research in the area. Clearly, there is considerable room for empirical research aimed at evaluating the successful elements of treatment proposed by the many models that currently inform the field. Aside from these issues, school psychologists and school neuropsychologists face other issues related to agraphia. Because motivation plays such a critical role in treatment, satisfaction with treatment plays an important role in treatment success (Bauer, 2002). Client satisfaction is taking on new importance as a fee-for-benefit model gradually supplants the more traditional fee-for-service model (Bauer, 2002). In the case of recovering learners, or very young learners, of course, the issue of client satisfaction is somewhat compromised by their neurocognitive status and their inability to provide accurate reports of satisfaction and progress (Bauer, 2002). A continuing need in the field of neuropsychological assessment and rehabilitation deals with the issue of developing culturally sensitive instruments for use with diverse populations (Hebben & Milberg, 2002). This need is likely to increase, given rapid growth in minority populations in the United States. Bauer has argued that neuropsychologists must understand the values, attitudes, and worldviews that have an impact on how members of culturally diverse groups report and use information about their own disabilities or those of their children. Bauer also has discussed three additional issues of concern: (1) The impact of variables such as age and educational level on neuropsychological test scores must be identified; (2) more effective means of evaluating executive and problem-solving skills are needed; and (3) the impact of motivation and social-behavioral issues on test performance must be better understood.

Advances in computer technology and neuroimaging have resulted in neuropsychologists becoming increasingly competent to read and interpret rehabilitation-related results. Computer-assisted neuropsychological assessment has resulted in tests being administered, scored, and interpreted by computer. The advantages of such assessment include standardized administration, well-controlled stimulus presentation, and relatively objective interpretation of test results. However, the very objectivity of such assessments has resulted in the loss of a rich source of clinical history that can be useful in understanding a child's unique issues. School psychologists and neuropsychologists are being challenged to come up with ways to use computer technology as an adjunct to, and not a substitute for, standardized evaluations.

Other challenges facing school psychologists and school neuropsychologists include examining the various typologies of writing disorders and making a determination about those that explain the writing process most effectively. Continued examination of assessment methods is important, as is developing an understanding of comorbid disorders that have an impact on written language. Bauer (2002) has recommended a close look at the biological basis of written language disorders with a view to developing more effective interventions for home and school. Finally, researchers (e.g., Ricker, 1998) have raised questions regarding the affordability of rehabilitation and schools' responsibility to pay for therapeutic care (which is prohibitively expensive), particularly in the case of low-income children and their families.

The disciplines of clinical and school neuropsychology have come a long way since their inception, when the understanding of brain-behavior relationships and their application to classrooms were viewed as controversial at best and unnecessary at worst (Reynolds & Fletcher-Janzen, 1997; Stringer, Cooley, & Christensen, 2002). Today, school neuropsychology is finding application in broad academic and behavioral domains, including that of written language. School psychologists and neuropsychologists are increasingly valued for their ability to integrate the principles of neurology, psychiatry, and psychometry to bear upon referral issues and to provide information that can help school personnel with the effective management of not only acquired, but also developmental written language disorders. This chapter is testimony to the progress that has been made, yet it is equally clear that many important questions remain unanswered and that there is considerable potential for additional research in both qualitative and quantitative areas.

## REFERENCES

Ardila, A. (2001). Acquired language disorders. In M. O. Ponton & J. Leon-Carrion (Eds.), *Neuropsycbology and the Hispanic patient: A clinical handbook* (pp. 87–103). Mahwah, NJ: Erlbaum.

Armstrong, L., & Macdonald, A. (2000). Aiding chronic written language expression difficulties: A case study. *Aphasiology, 14*(1), 93–108.

Bain, A. M., Bailet, L. L., & Moats, L. (2001). *Written language disorders: Theory into practice* (2nd ed.). Austin, TX: ProEd.

Baker, S., Gersten, R., & Graham, S. (2003). Teaching expressive writing to students with learning disabilities: Research-based applications. *Journal of Learning Disabilities, 36*(2), 109–124.

Baker, S., & Hubbard, D. (2002). Best practices in the assessment of written expression. In A. Thomas & J. Grimes (Eds.), *Best practices in school psychology IV* (Vol. 1, pp. 867–883). Bethesda, MD: National Association of School Psychologists.

Baron, I. S. (2004). *Neuropsychological evaluation of the child.* Oxford, England: Oxford University Press.

Bauer, R. M. (2002). To infinity and beyond: Clinical neuropsychology in the 21st century. In A. Y. Stringer, E. L. Cooley, & A. Christenson (Eds.), *Pathways to prominence in neuropsychology* (pp. 267–295). New York: Psychology Press.

Beeson, P. M., & Rapcsak, S. Z. (1998). The aphasias. In P. J. Snyder & P. D. Nussbaum (Eds.), *Clinical neuropsychology: A pocket handbook for assessment* (pp. 403–425). Washington, DC: American Psychological Association.

Benson, D. F., & Ardila, A. (1996). *Aphasia: A clinical perspective.* Oxford, England: Oxford University Press.

Berninger, V. W. (1994). Future directions for research on writing disabilities: Integrating endogenous and exogenous variables. In G. R. Lyon (Ed.), *Frames of reference for the assessment of learning disabilities: New view on measurement issues* (pp. 419–440). Baltimore: Brookes.

Berninger, V. W., Abbott, R. D., Abbott, S. P., Graham, S., & Richards, T. (2002). Writing and reading: Connections between language by hand and language by eye. *Journal of Learning Disabilities, 35*(1), 39–57.

Carr, E., & Ogle, D. (1987). K-W-L plus: A strategy for comprehension and summarization. *Journal of Reading, 30*(7), 627–631.

Crawford, L., Helwig, R., & Tindal, G. (2004). Writing performance assessment: How important is extended time? *Journal of Learning Disabilities, 37*(2), 132–143.

D'Amato, R. C., & Rothlisberg, B. A. (1996). How education should respond to students with traumatic brain injury. *Journal of Learning Disabilities, 9*(6), 670–684.

De Partz, M. (1995). Deficit of the graphemic buffer: Effects of a written lexical segmentation strategy. In R. S. Berndt & C. C. Mitchum (Eds.), *Cognitive neuropsychological approaches to the treatment of language disorders: A special issue of neuropsychological rehabilitation* (pp. 129–147). Hillsdale, NJ: Erlbaum.

Ellis, A. W. (1982). Spelling and writing (and reading and speaking). In A. W. Ellis (Ed.), *Normality and pathology in cognitive functions.* London: Academic Press.

Ellis, A. W. (1988). Normal writing processes and peripheral acquired dysgraphias. *Language and Cognitive Processes, 3,* 99–127.

Englert, C. S. (1990). Unraveling the mysteries of writing through strategy instruction. In T. E. Scruggs & B. Y. L. Wong (Eds.), *Intervention research in learning disabilities* (pp. 186–223). New York: Springer-Verlag.

Englert, C. S., & Raphael, T. E. (1988). Constructing well-formed prose: Process, structure, and metacognitive knowledge. *Exceptional Children, 65*(6), 513–520.

Eslinger, P. J., & Oliveri, M. V. (2002). Approaching interventions clinically and scientifically. In P. J. Eslinger (Ed.), *Neuropsychological interventions: Clinical research and practice* (pp. 3–15). New York: Guilford Press.

Farmer, J. E., & Brazeal, T. J. (1998). Parent perceptions about the process and outcomes of child neuropsychological assessment. *Applied Neuropsychology, 5,* 194–201.

Feifer, S. G. (2004, April). *The neuropsychology of written language disorders: Diagnosis and intervention.* Workshop presented at the 38th Annual Convention of the National Association of School Psychologists, Dallas, TX.

Feifer, S., G., & De Fina, P. A. (2002). *The neuropsychology of written language disorders: Diagnosis and intervention.* Middletown, MD: School Neuropsych Press, LLC.

Fryburg, E. L. (1997). *Reading and learning disability: A neuropsychological approach to evaluation and instruction.* Springfield, IL: Charles C. Thomas.

Gaillard, W. D., Xu, B., & Balsamo, L. (2002). Neuroimaging and disorders of communication. In P. J. Accardo, B. T. Rogers, & A. J. Capute (Eds.), *Disorders of language development* (pp. 124–148).Timonium, MD: York Press.

Gersten, R., & Baker, S. (2001). Teaching expressive writing to students with learning disabilities: A meta-analysis. *Elementary School Journal, 101,* 251–272.

Gould, B. W. (2001). Curricular strategies for written expression. In A. M. Bain, L. L. Bailet, & L. C. Moats (Eds.), *Written language disorders: Theory into practice* (2nd ed., pp. 185–220). Austin, TX: ProEd.

Gregg, N. (1995). *Written expression disorders.* Dordrecht, The Netherlands: Kluwer Academic.

Hartlage, L. C., Asken, M. J., & Hornsby, J. L. (Eds.). (1987). *Essentials of neuropsychological assessment.* New York: Springer.

Harris, K. R., & Graham, S. (1996). *Making the writing process work: Strategies for composition and self-regulation.* Cambridge, MA: Brookline Books.

Havey, J. M. (2002). Best practices in working with students with traumatic brain injury. In A. Thomas & J. Grimes (Eds.), *Best practices in school psychology IV* (Vol. 2, pp. 1433–1445). Bethesda, MD: National Association of School Psychologists.

Hebben, N., & Milberg, W. (2002). *Essentials of neuropsychological assessment.* New York: Wiley.

Hinckley, J. L. (2002). Models of language rehabilitation. In P. J. Eslinger (Ed.), *Neuropsychological interventions: Clinical research and practice* (pp. 182–221). New York: Guilford Press.

Hooper, S. R. (2002). The language of written language: An introduction to the special issue. *Journal of Learning Disabilities, 35*(1), 2–7.

Hooper, S. R., Swartz, C. W., Wakely, M. B., De Kruif, R. E. L., & Montgomery, J. W. (2002). Executive functions in elementary school children with and without problems in written expression. *Journal of Learning Disabilities, 35*(1), 57–69.

Lezak, M. D. (1995). *Neuropsychological assessment* (3rd ed.). Oxford, England: Oxford University Press.

Lorch, M. P. (1995). Disorders of writing and spelling. In H. S. Kirshner (Ed.), *Handbook of neurological speech and language disorders* (pp. 295–324). New York: Marcel Dekker.

Lord-Maes, J., & Obrzut, J. E. (1996). Neuropsychological consequences of traumatic brain injury in children and adolescents. *Journal of Learning Disabilities, 29*(6), 609–618.

Margolin, D. I. (1984). The neuropsychology of writing and spelling: Semantic, phonological, motor and perceptual processes. *Quarterly Journal of Experimental Psychology, 36A,* 459–489.

Margolin, D. I., & Goodman-Schulman, R. (1992). Oral and written spelling impairments. In D. I. Margolin (Ed.), *Cognitive neuropsychology in clinical practice* (pp. 263–297). New York: Oxford University Press.

Marlowe, W. B. (2000). An intervention for children with disorders of executive functions. *Developmental Neuropsychology, 18*(3), 445–454.

Mather, D. S. (2003). Dyslexia and dysgraphia: More than written language difficulties in common. *Journal of Learning Disabilities, 36*(4), 307–318.

Mortley, J., Enderby, P., & Petheram, B. (2001). Using a computer to improve functional writing in a patient with surface dysgraphia. *Aphasiology, 15*(5), 443–461.

Murdoch, B. E. (Ed.). (1990). *Acquired neurological speech/language disorders in childhood.* London: Taylor & Francis.

Naglieri, J. A. (2002). Best practices in interventions for school psychologists: A cognitive approach to problem solving. In A. Thomas & J. Grimes (Eds.), *Best practices in school psychology IV* (Vol. 2, pp. 1373–1392). Bethesda, MD: National Association of School Psychologists.

Ogle, J. W. (1867). Aphasia and agraphia in St. George's Hospital. *Report of the Medical Research Counsel of St. George's Hospital (London), 2,* 83–122.

Owens, R. E., Jr. (1999). *Language disorders: A functional approach to assessment and intervention* (3rd ed.). Needham Heights, MA; Allyn & Bacon.

Ponton, M. O., & Monguio, I. (2001). Rehabilitation of brain injury among Hispanic patients. In M. O. Ponton & J. Leon-Carrion (Eds.), *Neuropsycbology and the Hispanic patient: A clinical handbook* (pp. 307–319). Mahwah, NJ: Erlbaum.

Rapp, B., & Beeson, P. M. (2003). Dysgraphia: Cognitive processes, remediation, & neural substrates. *Aphasiology, 17*(6), 531–534.

Power, J. P. (2002). Preparing school psychologists as interventionists and preventionists. In M. A. Shinn, H. M. Walker, & G. Stoner (Eds.), *Interventions for academic and behavior problems II: Preventive and remedial approaches* (pp. 1047–1118). Bethesda, MD: NASP Publications.

Rapscak, S. Z. (1997). Disorders of writing. In L. J. G. Rothi & K. M. Heilman (Eds.), *Apraxia: The neuropsychology of action* (pp. 149–172). Hove, England: Psychology Press.

Rapcsak, S. Z., & Beeson, P. M. (2000). Agraphia. In S. E. Nadeau, L. J. G. Rothi, & B. Crosson (Eds.), *Aphasia and language: Theory to practice* (pp. 184–220). New York: Guilford Press.

Reynolds, C. R. (1986). Transactional models of intellectual development, yes. Deficit models of process remediation, no. *School Psychology Review, 15,* 256–260.

Reynolds, C. R., & French, C. L. (2003). The neuropsychological basis of intelligence revised—Some false starts and a clinical model. In A. M. Horton, Jr. & L. C. Hartledge (Eds.), *Handbook of forensic neuropsychology* (pp. 35–92). New York: Springer.

Reynolds, C. R., & Fletcher-Janzen, E. (Eds.). (1997). *Handbook of clinical child neuropsychology* (2nd ed.). New York: Plenum Press.

Ricker, J. H. (1998). Traumatic brain injury rehabilitation: Is it worth the cost? *Applied Neuropsychology, 5,* 184–193.

Robertson, J. (2000). Increasing access to modern foreign languages to pupils with special educational needs: A neuropsychological perspective. *Support for Learning, 15*(2), 62–66.

Roeltgen, D. P., & Blaskey, P. (1992). Processes, breakdowns, and remediation in developmental disorders of reading and spelling. In D. I. Margolin (Ed.), *Cognitive neuropsychology in clinical practice* (pp. 263–297). New York: Oxford University Press.

Rourke, B. P., Bakker, D. J., Fisk, J. L., & Strang, J. D. (1983). *Child neuropsychology: An introduction to theory, research, and clinical practice.* New York: Guilford Press.

Sattler, J. M., & D'Amato, R. C. (2002). Brain injuries: Theory and rehabilitation programs. In J. M. Sattler (Ed.), *Assessment of children: Behavioral and clinical applications.* San Diego, CA: Jerome M. Sattler.

Snyder, P. J., & Nussbaum, P. D. (Eds.). (1998). *Clinical neuropsychology: A pocket handbook for assessment.* Washington, DC: American Psychological Association.

Stringer, A. Y., Cooley, E. L., & Christensen, A. (2002). *Pathways to prominence in neuropsychology: Reflections of twentieth-century pioneers.* New York: Psychology Press.

Teeter, P. A., & Semrud-Clikeman, M. (1997). *Child neuropsychology: Assessment and interventions for neurodevelopmental disorders.* Boston: Allyn & Bacon.

Telzrow, C. F. (1991). The school psychologist's perspective on testing students with traumatic brain injury. *Journal of Head Trauma Rehabilitation, 6,* 23–34.

Turkstra, L. S. (2000). Should the shirt be tucked in or left out? The communication context of adolescence. *Aphasiology, 14*(4), 349–365.

Uzzell, B. (1998). Neuropsychological rehabilitation models. In J. Leon-Carrion (Ed.), *Neuropsychological rehabilitation: Fundamentals, innovations, and directions* (pp. 41–46). Delray Beach, FL: St. Lucie Press.

Weekes, B. (1996). Surface dyslexia and surface dysgraphia. *Cognitive Neuropsychology, 13*(2), 277–315.

Whitten, J. C., D'Amato, R. C., & Chittooran, M. M. (1992). A neuropsychological approach to intervention. In R. C. D'Amato, & B. A. Rothlisberg (Eds.), *Psychological perspectives on intervention: A case study approach to prescriptions for change* (pp. 112–136). White Plains, NY: Longman.

Wong, B. Y. L., Butler, D. L., Ficzere, S. A., & Kuperis, S. (1997). Teaching adolescents with learning disabilities and low achievers to plan, write, and revise compare-contrast essays. *Learning Disabilities Research and Practice, 12,* 2–15.

Ylvisaker, M. (1998). *Traumatic brain injury rehabilitation: Children and adolescents* (2nd ed.). Newton, MA: Butterworth-Heinemann.

Ylvisaker, M., Szekeres, S. F., & Haarbauer-Krupa, J. (1998). Cognitive rehabilitation, organization, memory, and language. In M. Ylvisaker (Ed.), *Traumatic brain injury rehabilitation: Children and adolescents* (2nd ed., pp. 181–220). Newton, MA: Butterworth-Heinemann.

# CHAPTER 36

# Understanding Psychopharmacology with Learners

THOMAS M. DUNN and PAUL D. RETZLAFF

THIS CHAPTER is intended to help inform clinicians working in school settings about psychopharmacology. Our intention is to create a practical guide to help school neuropsychologists and school psychologists, as well as others actively involved in the treatment of schoolchildren. We begin by discussing several issues regarding psychotropic medication for children, including rising prevalence rates, psychiatric evaluations, and drug outcome studies. We also address five major classes of medications, their indications and side effects, and other information useful to the school psychologist. We finish with a list of specific recommendations for the safe use of medications with children.

## TRENDS

The use of psychotropic medication has soared in the United States since the late 1980s. For example, the use of antidepressants in adults tripled during the 1990s (Foote & Etheredge, 2000). It is estimated that this trend is even more prevalent in children than in adults (Olfson et al., 1998). Similar trends have been found in preschoolers as well (Zito et al., 2000). The release of the selective serotonin reuptake inhibitors (SSRIs), such as Prozac and Zoloft, provided drugs that were safer and better tolerated than previous antidepressants. With more and more adults using such medications and reporting good efficacy without dangerous side effects, these medications started to be prescribed more and more for children (Popper, 2002), typically by primary care physicians (Zito et al., 2002).

It is very difficult to get firm base rates on the number of schoolchildren taking psychotropic medications. Studies designed to measure such numbers often run into significant logistical and methodological issues (Gadow, 1997). Base rates are also wildly variable depending on population, geography, age group, and so on (Popper, 2002). Despite this, the U.S. Food and Drug Administration (FDA) has speculated that more than 11 million prescriptions for antidepressants were written for children in 2002 (Goode, 2004). Also taking into consideration the growing number of stimulants and antipsychotics being prescribed, there could be an astonishing number of schoolchildren taking psychotropics (Olfson, Marcus, Weissman, & Jensen, 2002).

Although use of psychotropic medication is quickly on the rise among schoolchildren, often there is no FDA approval for pediatric use of these medicines. This is not unique to psychiatry, as nearly 75% of the drugs approved for adult use do not have FDA approval for use in children (Nahata, 1999). The FDA allows drug companies to extrapolate their efficacy and safety data from adults to children. This allows physicians to utilize off-label prescribing practices, or to use medications to treat conditions or groups without specific FDA approval for those particular uses. Blumer (1999) found that roughly 70% of the medications listed in the *Physicians' Desk Reference* did not contain pediatric dosing information, nor does the book list specific safety information for use in children. It may be difficult to find standard dosing information, side effect profiles, and other drug information as these apply to learners. As a result, teachers and parents have trouble finding information about psychotropic medicine, have too little information, or misinformation.

Despite not being able to find specific drug information on children, being knowledgeable about psychotropic medications in general is important for psychologists. With increasing numbers of learners taking such medications, the school psychologist or school neuropsychologist is likely to be seen as the best resource for teachers, parents, and students to explain the effects of these medications. Further, teachers and psychologists may be among the first to recognize whether medications are working or notice undesirable effects of the medicine. Because patients who are prescribed psychotropics often have weeks or months between doctor visits, it is likely that parents and teachers will be the first to observe drug efficacy and side effects. Informed observations about both the desirable and undesirable side effects of psychotropic medication can help provide feedback to the prescribing physician to make changes in the drug regimen to provide the maximum benefit to the child.

## DECIDING WHICH CHILDREN TO MEDICATE

The decision whether to medicate a child is a complicated one. Certainly, unilateral decisions based on a teacher's or school administrator's recommendation is inappropriate; in some states, such recommendations are spurring legislation specifically targeted at making such actions illegal. However, the behavior of the learner in school is a significant variable in the decision to medicate. A thorough psychological and, if indicated, neuropsychological evaluation is necessary to determine whether a child's behavior truly meets diagnostic criteria. Part of any thorough evaluation is a physical check-up by a physician who can look for organic causes for atypical behavior. In an ideal world, a child psychiatrist would be consulted for the appropriateness of psychotropic medication. However, these specialists often are located only in urban centers or are otherwise difficult to access. The vast majority of learners will likely have medication prescribed by a primary care physician, physician's assistant, or nurse practitioner.

Carlson (2002) writes that beginning pharmacological treatment of a child is a complicated task that is undertaken only after extensive evaluation of the child and with input from parents and teachers to help accurately make a diagnosis. She also advocates blood work (including CBC and liver function tests), pregnancy tests when appropriate, thyroid levels, and an electrocardiogram. With these tests complete, an appropriate medication is prescribed based on efficacy studies, which medicine is best tolerated, and what medication may have worked in the past for the child or for another family member with a similar presentation (Carlson, 2002; Diamond, 2002). Follow-up visits to ascertain whether the medication is effective and to ensure that it is well tolerated are also a requirement, although often overlooked.

When the decision to medicate a child is reached, it is important to keep in mind that psychotropics are unlike antibiotics or other short courses of medicines. Often, the correct dosage of the medication is determined only after assessing the child's symptoms and behavior and adjusting the dosage accordingly. Side effects of the medication are also taken into consideration and may lead to an adjustment of the dosage. It may take several visits to the physician to find a dose that eases symptoms but does not cause intolerable side effects. The therapeutic effect of the medicine may not be apparent until several weeks after it is started. This is due to structural changes in neurons secondary to changes of neurotransmitter levels in the synaptic gap brought about by the medication. Such changes are also responsible for some unpleasant side effects that may occur if psychotropics are stopped suddenly. Although all changes in medication regimens should be at the direction of the prescribing physician, it is advised that dosage be tapered off when discontinuing pychotropic use.

There are other considerations when medicating a child. There continues to be a stigma about mental health issues in schools and elsewhere. A child may resist taking medication at school. To lessen this resistance, there are various options. In some cases, for example, the child takes the medication at home and not at a nurse's office. Many of the drugs for treating Attention-Deficit/Hyperactivity Disorder (ADHD) now have an extended release preparation and no longer need to be dosed in the middle of the day. Some drugs may be delivered transdermally. This allows the child to benefit from receiving intermittent doses of the drug without having to ingest it in the middle of the day.

No matter what the drug, its dose, or the route of administration, it is important that the mental health professionals included in the treatment plan remember that they still have a role to play once the medication has been started. They must continue to monitor the child's symptoms and behavior to note whether there is improvement. Equally important is to note whether side effects of the medication are becoming an issue. For example, some medications are sedating, so a once-disruptive learner may sleep though class. This new problem could be caused by the medicine, and a change in dose could ease such side effects. Occasionally, more serious side effects result. Antidepressants, for example, can induce a manic episode, and it is important to monitor whether a child recently placed on such a medication might be showing signs of mania. Follow-up psychological assessment is important to determine whether the medication is effective.

## MECHANISM OF ACTION

To appreciate psychotropic medication, it is important to have a basic understanding of how these medicines exert their influences, although in some cases we simply do not have a full and complete understanding of how the medication is working. The vast majority of psychotropics exert their influence at the synaptic gap between neurons. This is known as the *site of action*. The specific mechanism by which medications exert their influence is known as the *mechanism of action*. This mechanism is different for each class of medication, but most are thought to mediate the action of neurotransmitter substance (the chemical messenger allowing neurons to signal each other). Psychotropics typically are either agonists that are thought to cause an increase in the overall level of neurotransmitter substance (or create a situation where existing neurotransmitter levels are enhanced, such as by enhancing receptor affinity). Antagonists, by comparison, are medicines that decrease the level of neurotransmitter substance, or prevent the neurotransmitter substance from binding with a receptor site.

## CLASSES OF MEDICATIONS

There are more than a dozen common neurotransmitters (and more being discovered and described regularly); those that are primarily involved in psychopharmacology are dopamine, norepinephrine, serotonin, and GABA. Many psychotropics are described by their effects on a particular neurotransmitter. Psychotropic drugs can be grouped into six major categories: antipsychotics, antidepressants, mood stabilizers, antianxiety medicines, stimulants, and a miscellaneous category. The miscellaneous category contains medications that are not readily classified and often not considered psychotropics because they typically have qualities that make them useful in treating more than just mental illness. It should also be noted that many of these medications have been found to be useful across categories. For example, antidepressants have been shown to be effective when treating anxiety. Most of these medication classes have similar mechanisms of action. The specific mechanism of action is discussed for each class of drugs.

### Antipsychotics

The field of psychopharmacology and biological psychiatry as we know it today can trace its roots to a single drug: the antipsychotic Thorazine (generic name chlorpromazine). This medicine was first manufactured in France in the mid-twentieth century. It was used as a sedative for surgery patients before its calming properties were noted to be useful for ameliorating some of the more severe signs and symptoms of psychosis, particularly in Schizophrenia. In 1954, the FDA granted approval for the use of the drug, which had initially been introduced by SmithKline as an antiemetic (antinausea medication). Thorazine began to be used in the treatment of Schizophrenia and within a few years was being widely used in the United States. Soon, other drug companies started to conduct research and development into similar medicines. Prior to the release of Thorazine, there was no widespread use of medication for mental illness.

Thorazine and other traditional or typical antipsychotics, such as Mellaril, Prolixin, Moban, and Haldol, all exert their effects by blocking a specific dopamine receptor in the brain known as the $D_2$ receptor (see Table 36.1). Although this typically results in an impressive reduction of some psychotic symptoms, there have been major concerns about this particular class of drugs. Because widespread dopamine receptors in the brain are being blocked with such medicines, systems that are highly dopamanergic in nature are also affected. Most notably affected is the extrapyramidal motor system, with structures such as the substantia nigra and the basal ganglia (caudate, putamen, globus pallidus). The pyramidal motor system is involved in voluntary movement, and the extrapyramidal motor system is indirectly involved with motor behavior by coordinating muscular activity. If the extrapyramidal motor system is not functioning, a variety of extrapyramidal symptoms can result, such as bradykinesia, rigidity, dyskinesia, tremor, and dystonia. These symptoms often result when the traditional antipsychotic medications are used at high doses and/or for long periods of time. This condition can resemble Parkinson's disease, with repetitive movements, difficulty walking (hence the phrase "Thorazine shuffle"), and other motor deficits. These side effects can be permanent. Using these medicines at lower doses and also prescribing drugs useful in Parkinson's disease, such as Cogentin, eases many of these side effects.

The second major concern about the use of the typical antipsychotics is their ability to address both the positive and negative symptoms of Schizophrenia. Generally, these medicines are known to relieve only the positive symptoms of the disease, such as delusions, hallucinations, and bizarre behavior. Many of the negative symptoms are left intact, such as social isolation, poor grooming, and inappropriate affect. Despite the inefficacy of these drugs for the negative symptoms for Schizophrenia and the side effects, for almost 40 years there were no other medicines that were as effective in the treatment of psychosis and Schizophrenia.

In the early 1990s, a new antipsychotic called Clozaril became available in the United States after a stormy introduction in Europe. The drug was revolutionary. Not only was it effective in reducing both the positive and negative symptoms of Schizophrenia, but it did not have the side effect profile of the earlier antipsychotics. However, it had a significant drawback: It was associated with a condition known as agranulocytosis, a shortage of white blood cells. This resulted in several deaths when the drug was first released in Europe. Despite this, it was far more effective than other drugs available and it was approved for use in the United States. Other drugs that work with a similar mechanism of action, such as Abilify, Geodon, Risperdal, Seroquel, and Zyprexa, were released in the 1990s and later. They have been collectively labeled the *atypical antipsychotics* (see Table 36.1) because they work differently from the traditional $D_2$ antagonist antipsychotics and are more effective without the same undesired side effects. They are in wider use than the traditional antipsychotics. The older medicines are still available and may be used in low doses if a patient does not respond to the atypical antipychotics.

The mechanism of action for the atypical antipsychotics is more complicated than simply blocking a single dopamine receptor. Instead, these medications jointly block select dopamine and serotonin receptors. This interferes with a complex interaction between serotonin- and dopamine-producing neurons, with the net effect of inhibiting the dopamine system that is widely thought to be controlling the signs and symptoms of Schizophrenia (Green, 2001). Most patients tolerate these medications; however, a common complaint regarding this class of medications is weight gain, often because of changes in appetite (Nasrallah, 2003).

**Table 36.1**
Common Antipsychotics

| Drug Name | | | FDA-Approved for Use in Children? | Common Side Effects | | |
| Trade Name | Generic Name | Other Common Uses | | Arousal | Metabolism | Cardiovascular |
| --- | --- | --- | --- | --- | --- | --- |
| Abilify | aripipazole | | No | | | |
| Clozaril | clozapine | | 16 and older | Sedation | Weight gain, dry mouth, agranulocytosis | Orthostatic hypotension |
| Geodon | ziprasidone | Acute agitation | No | Agitation and insomnia | | Linked to heart dysrhythmias |
| Haldol | haloperidol | Agitation | 3 and older | Sedation | Tardive dyskinesia | |
| Mellaril | thioridazine | | 2 and older | Sedation | Tardive dyskinesia | Linked to heart dysrhythmias |
| Moban | molindone | | 12 and older | Sedation | Tardive dyskinesia | |
| Prolixin | fluphenazine | Agitation | 12 and older | Sedation | | |
| Risperdal | risperidone | Acute agitation | 16 and older | | Weight gain, prolactin elevation (may cause amenorrhea and breast enlargement) | |
| Seroquel | quetiapine | Mood liability in Borderline Personality | No | | Weight gain, may induce cataracts | Orthrostatic hypotension |
| Thorazine | chlorpromazine | | 6 months and older | Sedation | Dry mouth, tardive dyskinesia | |
| Zyprexa/Zydis | olanzapine | Bipolar Disorder | No | Sedation | Weight gain | |

These medications are also found to be beneficial in conditions other than Schizophrenia, such as Bipolar Disorder, Pervasive Developmental Disorder, and other conditions that tend to be associated with agitation, behavioral outbursts, and impulsive behavior (Kowatch, Sethuraman, Hume, Kromelis, & Weinberg, 2003). This is why it is not uncommon to see atypical antipsychotics prescribed for learners with no history of Schizophrenia or psychosis, especially when the child is known to have limited behavioral controls. However, these are off-label uses without clear empirical research in such choices.

### Antidepressants

There are several classes of antidepressants, each of which has a slightly different mechanism of action. The older classes of antidepressants are described first and briefly. The newer and better-known antidepressants are discussed in greater detail because they are widely prescribed and have benefits that are not limited just to depression.

Medicines designed to ease the symptoms of depression have been in use since the 1950s. One of the earliest antidepressants, Tofranil, was discovered after testing a variety of antihistamines for mood-elevating effects (Pletscher, 1991). This drug became the prototypical tricyclic antidepressant (TCA), named after its three-ring chemical structure (see Table 36.2). These are generally known to be effective for depression in children (Green, 2001), but the TCAs such as Anafranil and Elavil have the potential to cause cardiac irritability and are quite toxic if taken in sufficient quantities. They also have side effects that can be unpleasant, including dry mouth, blurred vision, and constipation. TCAs have to be distributed judiciously to suicidal patients, as an overdose can be fatal. For these reasons, and with the advent of newer medicines with far fewer side effects, TCAs are not often prescribed. It should be noted that Tofranil may be effective in a variety of conditions in addition to depression. Green (2001) reviews these, including conduct disorder with depression, enuresis, ADHD, separation anxiety, and panic disorder. Again, we see the secondary uses as central to the practice of the school neuropsychologist.

An early alternative to the TCAs was medications inhibiting the enzyme that metabolizes monoamine neurotransmitters (including norepinephrine, serotonin, and dopamine). Examples of this kind of medicine are the drugs Nardil and Parnate. When the enzyme monoamine oxidase (MAO) is inhibited, it is thought to increase the overall level of monoamines in the synapse and easing the symptoms of depression. These medications, called MAO inhibitors, have also been known to be effective in the treatment of depression (Ryan et al., 1988). Despite their efficacy, particularly in depression resistant to TCA treatment (Diamond, 2002), they tend to deactivate the enzyme tyramine, which may cause undesirable effects. Most notable is the inability to metabolize tyramine that is ingested in a variety of foods, such as chocolate and aged food such as cheese, wine, and yogurt. A buildup of tyramine in the bloodstream can lead to a dangerous elevation of blood pressure known as a hypertensive crisis. Patients taking this medication need to keep a careful watch on their diet to be certain that they are not ingesting foods that could lead to this condition. Unfortunately, this can be difficult for children, who might not understand that some foods can be dangerous. MAO inhibitors are also known to have dangerous drug interactions

**Table 36.2**
Common Tricyclic (TCA) and MAO Inhibitor Antidepressants

| Drug Name | | Mechanism of Action | FDA-Approved for Use in Children? | Other Common Uses | Common Side Effects | | |
| --- | --- | --- | --- | --- | --- | --- | --- |
| Trade Name | Generic Name | | | | Arousal | Metabolism | Cardiovascular |
| Anafranil | clomipramine | TCA | 10 and older for OCD | OCD, Bulimia, Panic Disorder | | Bad breath, belching | May be associated with dysarthmias |
| Elavil | amitriptyline | TCA | 12 and older | Chronic pain | Sedation | Dry mouth | |
| Nardil | phenelzine | MAO inhibitor | 17 and older | | | Can be dangerous when eaten with certain foods | |
| Parnate | tranylcypromine | MAO inhibitor | 17 and older | | | Can be dangerous when eaten with certain foods | |
| Tofranil | imipramine | TCA | 6–11 for enuresis, 12 and older for depression | OCD, Bulima, ADHD | | Dry mouth | |

with other medicines, particularly some cold medications. Undesired drug interactions and potential hypertensive crisis make MAO inhibitors difficult medicines to take, particularly for children, who may be unable to monitor themselves. Therefore, these medications are also prescribed less frequently, and, like TCAs, if a patient is taking them, it is often because he or she has failed a trial on newer classes of antidepressants.

Among the advantages of the newer classes of medications is the lack of a potentially fatal overdose and no longer needing to closely monitor the intake of certain foods. For many patients, the psychopharmacological treatment of their depression is balanced against the side effects of such medications. The landscape of antidepressants (and arguably, psychopharmacology in general) changed dramatically with Eli Lilly's release of Prozac (fluoxetine). This was the first drug belonging to a class of antidepressants known as the selective serotonin reuptake inhibitors (SSRIs). Prozac (and other drugs in this class, such as Celexa, Lexapro, Luvox, Paxil, and Zoloft) is a serotonin agonist, exerting its effects by preventing the reuptake (or recycling) of serotonin into the neuron and out of the synaptic gap (see Table 36.3). The net result is an agonist effect on serotonin; therefore, more of the neurotransmitter is available. It takes several weeks for the elevation of serotonin to be utilized as the neurons need to add receptor sites for the serotonin to exert its effects. Once the medicine begins to work, the SSRIs are known to be effective antidepressants without many undesirable side effects. With the availability of an antidepressant that can be tolerated by a wide range of people, the number of users of these medicines tripled in the 1990s (Foote & Etheredge, 2000).

Other SSRIs followed, including, most notably, Zoloft and Paxil (see Table 36.3). These drugs would soon be touted for their amelioration of depressive symptoms with relatively few side effects. Further, the side effects that do exist often subside after several weeks of use. A notable exception to this is a common complaint from adult users that they find their libido is decreased and that they have difficulty achieving orgasm. This presents a much more substantial issue to adult users than to children and adolescents. Largely because they are well tolerated, the SSRIs have been widely used in children and adolescents suffering a wide variety of mental health issues beyond depression. This class of drugs is used in the treatment of eating disorders, posttraumatic stress disorder, panic disorder, obsessive-compulsive disorder, and other anxiety disorders (Cheer & Figgitt, 2002; Donnelly, 2003; Rosenblum & Forman, 2003; Sheehan, 2002; Thomsen, 2000).

Since the advent of the SSRIs, drug companies have started to introduce medicines that selectively act on neurotransmitters other than serotonin. So-called second-generation reuptake inhibitors (SGRIs) tend to agonize dopamine and norepinephrine. This results in the reduction of symptoms related to depression and anxiety, as is the case with the SSRIs. Table 36.4 on page 814 lists these medications (Remeron, Serzone, Desyrel, Effexor, Cymbalta) and their mechanisms of action. It is notable that Wellbutrin, another drug in this class, has been demonstrated to be effective in the treatment of ADHD (Spencer & Biederman, 2002).

Despite evidence that antidepressants may be useful in treating children, it should be noted that of all the medications available, only Prozac has FDA approval for use as an antidepressant in children and adolescents. It is also important to emphasize that in late 2003, the FDA released a pubic health advisory to health care

**Table 36.3**

Selective Serotonin Reuptake Inhibitor Antidepressants

| Drug Name | | Other Common Uses | FDA-Approved for Use in Children? | Common Side Effects | | |
| --- | --- | --- | --- | --- | --- | --- |
| Trade Name | Generic Name | | | Arousal | Metabolism | Cardiovascular |
| Celexa | citalopram | | No | Insomnia | Dry mouth, upset stomach, nausea, sexual dysfunction | |
| Lexapro* | escitalopram | | No | Insomnia | Dry mouth, upset stomach, nausea, sexual dysfunction | |
| Luvox | fluvoxamine | OCD | 8 and older for OCD | Sedation | Dry mouth, sexual dysfunction | |
| Paxil | paroxetine | OCD, situational anxiety | FDA has rescinded approval for use in children | | Dry mouth, constipation, sexual dysfunction | |
| Prozac/ Prozac Weekly | fluoxetine | OCD, anxiety | 7 and older for depression and OCD | | Agitation | Dry mouth, sexual dysfunction |
| Zoloft | sertraline | OCD, anxiety | 8 and older for OCD | | GI upset, dry mouth, sexual dysfunction | |

*Lexapro is a single isomer of Celexa.

**Table 36.4**

Common Second-Generation Reuptake Inhibitors

| Drug Name | | | | Common Side Effects | | | |
|---|---|---|---|---|---|---|---|
| Trade Name | Generic Name | Site of Action | FDA-Approved for Use in Children? | Other Common Uses | Arousal | Metabolism | Cardiovascular |
| Cymbalta | duloxetine | Serotonin and norepineph-rine | No | | | Nausea, dry mouth, consti-pation | |
| Desyrel | trazodone | Serotonin and norepineph-rine | No | Excellent sleep aid | Very sedating | Dry mouth | May cause priapism |
| Effexor | venlafaxine | Serotonin and norepineph-rine | No | Generalized anxiety | | Nausea | |
| Serzone | nefazadone | Serotonin and norepineph-rine | No | May reduce fibromyalgia symptoms | May be sedating | Dizziness, nausea | |
| Remeron | mirtazapine | Serotonin and norepineph-rine | No | | Sedation | Increased ap-petite, weight gain | |
| Wellbutrin/ Zyban | bupropion | Dopamine and norepi-nephrine | No | Smoking cessa-tion, ADHD | Restlessness Sleep dysfunction | | |

professionals about pediatric patients being at increased risk for suicide attempts and suicidal ideation when taking antidepressants. After a preliminary review of antidepressants, the FDA reported that eight—Celexa, Prozac, Luvox, Remeron, Serzone, Paxil, Zoloft, and Effexor—may be associated with increased suicidality and urged caution when prescribing these medications to children and adolescents. It should be noted that all patients when first prescribed antidepressants may be at higher risk for suicide than patients not taking such medicines. Suicidal ideation is a common symptom of depression and is often seen in patients who are not medicated. However, patients who are being treated with medicines may be more likely to experience an increase in energy levels while still feeling depressed. This may give them the energy to act on suicidal impulses that were earlier dampened by low levels of energy. It is important that all patients being treated for depression with medication be closely monitored for risk of suicide.

During 2004, concerns that learners seem to be in particular danger of increased suicidal ideation when taking antidepressants escalated and was widely reported in the media. One reasonable explanation for increased suicidal ideation is children and adolescents have increased impulsiveness. The FDA acknowledged this possibility in 2003 and urged physicians to warn their patients. British authorities have been more aggressive. The FDA's equivalent in the United Kingdom, the British Medicines and Healthcare Products Regulatory Agency, declared an outright ban on pediatric prescribing for most of these medicines in December 2003, excepting only Prozac. Their reasoning for this has been the equivocal results in the efficacy of such medications in pediatric patients and the possibility that they may be harmful to some children. It should be noted that any connection between suicidality and the SSRIs or SGRIs is still not yet well understood and establishing a definitive cause-and-effect relationship is fraught with methodological issues.

Despite these issues, in late 2004 the FDA issued a "black box warning" for most antidepressant medications following an examination of relevant studies by independent researchers. Such warnings are typically used when a potential danger has been noted with a drug and stops short of withdrawing approval for a drug. Often medicines that are required to carry a black box warning are pulled from the market (Lasser et al., 2002). The black box warns of increased risk of suicidality in children and adolescents and urges that prescribing these medications be balanced with clinical need. It advises watching children closely after they are started on antidepressants and advises warning all care givers.

With the concerns about suicidality and children, coupled with continuing concerns that these medications may not be as effective in children as in adults (Sommers-Flanagan & Sommers-Flanagan, 1996), some caution should be exercised before starting a child or adolescent on an antidepressant. Sommers-Flanagan and Sommers-Flanagan cogently argue that the following conditions should be met before a referral is made for psychopharmacological intervention in schoolchildren:

- Depressed mood persists without clear environmental influences, such as death of a parent, family discord, or recent move.
- The symptoms associated with the depression are both severe and are physiological in nature, such as sleep disturbance, appetite changes, somatic complaints, and changes in weight.

- The depression is resistant to a course of psychotherapy (10 to 15 sessions).
- The patient and his or her family understand the risks and benefits to medication.

Finally, it should be restated that all patients, but particularly children and adolescents, should be closely monitored for suicidal ideation when beginning a course of antidepressants.

## Antianxiety Medication

Medicine used for its calming properties can trace its roots back to the early 1900s, when barbiturates were first manufactured in Germany. This class of medication, including drugs such as pentobarbital (Nembutal), was the first to be used in clinical practice as a sedative and sleeping medication. These medications were widely prescribed well into the twentieth century, when risks associated with them began to come to light. Medicines in this class can be quite addictive, and prolonged use can lead to dependence. They were widely used as drugs of abuse in the 1960s and 1970s. Finally, barbiturates can be lethal when taken in large quantities or in combination with alcohol.

With their propensity for abuse and dependence, coupled with their lethality in certain situations, barbiturates have fallen out of favor for the treatment of mental illness. This drug class continues to have some applications in anesthesia, but since the advent of a newer class of antianxiety medicine, barbiturates are rarely used. Therefore, our discussion of antianxiety medications focuses on the benzodiazapines.

The first benzodiazapine, Librium, was first marketed in the United States in the 1960s as an alternative to barbiturates for anxiety and insomnia. It was found to have excellent anxiety-reducing properties, it could be used to induce sleep, and it was not nearly as dangerous as barbiturates if overdosed. The benzodiazapines depress the respiratory drive and can also be dangerous if taken with alcohol or other central nervous system depressants (such as narcotics). All of the benzodiazapines are GABA agonists. GABA is believed to be the neurotransmitter responsible for inhibiting neural firing, and increased levels are associated with sedation and relief from anxiety. The benzodiazapines (see Table 36.5) that are in wide use today (Ativan, Dalmane, Halcion, Librium, Klonopin, Valium, Xanax) are generally broken down into categories that describe how long it takes to metabolize the medicine—their half-life. Those drugs with the shortest half-lives are effective in the management of insomnia, allowing the patient to take the medication (even late at night) and have most of the drug clear the system by morning. This prevents the patient from feeling "drugged" in the morning, as may occur with medicines that have a longer half-life. The longer half-life benzodiazapines are used in managing of anxiety disorders, as these patients typically need a dose that persists for the entire day.

There are a variety of treatments for anxiety, and effective psychotherapy (particularly a cognitive-behavioral approach) has been found to be beneficial with children and adolescents (Kendall, 1994). Psychotherapy is often the first treatment modality used with anxious children. Although the benzodiazapines are known to be effective, they are also sedating, and learning may be difficult if a child is taking these medications. Further, long-term use of benzodiazapines is

**Table 36.5**
Common Antianxiety Medications

| Drug Name | | FDA-Approved for Use in Children? | Half-Life | Common Side Effects | | |
|---|---|---|---|---|---|---|
| Trade Name | Generic Name | | | Arousal | Metabolism | Cardiovascular |
| Ativan | lorazepam | No | 10–20 hours | Highly sedating | | |
| Librium | chlordiazepoxide | No | 5–30 hours | Highly sedating | | |
| Klonopin | clonazepam | No | 18–50 hours | Highly sedating | | |
| Valium | diazepam | No | 20–80 hours | Highly sedating | | |
| Xanax | alprazolam | No | 12 hours | Highly sedating | | |

*Note:* Both the SSRIs and SGRIs are widely used as effective anxiety medications. Most benzodiazapines are addicting and prolonged use can lead to dependences. These medicines often are prescribed only for less than 2 weeks to prevent dependence.

not indicated. Use for more than about 14 days can result in dependence and then withdrawal if the medicine is not tapered. The most efficient use of the benzodiazapines in the treatment of children and adolescents is short-term use following a significant psychological stressor (death of parent, etc.) while other means of support are being marshaled, such as establishing a therapeutic relationship and increasing social support.

As mentioned, there is increasing evidence to suggest that the SSRIs and SGRIs may also be effective in treating anxiety, particularly obsessive-compulsive disorder and social anxiety. These medications are an alternative to the benzodiazapines for schoolchildren who do not respond to psychotherapy. In addition to the SSRIs and SGRIs, there are several other drugs that may be effective for anxiety. The use of beta blockers is beginning to show promise in situational anxiety and will be discussed later. BuSpar (a nonbenzodiazapine) has been shown to be as effective as Valium when treating anxiety. This is noteworthy, because BuSpar is not addicting, nor is there an overdose issue. It should be noted that patients who have previously taken Valium tend to respond differently to BuSpar than do patients who have never taken the drug. People who have previously taken Valium find BuSpar to be less effective. Diamond (2002) speculates that this is because some patients who have experienced the powerful calming effects of Valium do not regard other drugs as effective.

## Mood Stabilizers

The mood stabilizers are a class of medications indicated for patients suffering from Bipolar Affective Disorder. These medications are known to help limit the number and severity of manic episodes. For decades, the medication of choice has been lithium, first used in the 1950s. The mechanism of action for lithium is complex and not well understood (Agranoff & Fisher, 2001). The drug is used in the management of Bipolar Disorder in children and adolescents and is often paired with an antidepressant (Biederman, Mick, Spencer, Wilens, & Faraone, 2000). Lithium is also known to be a difficult drug for patients because of its side effects (excessive thirst, GI irritability, weight gain, etc.). Lithium can also have unfavorable interactions with other drugs. Given these side effects, patients often will not adhere to the prescription, either skipping doses or not taking it at all. Fortunately, in the past decade, antiepileptic medications have been found to be effective in the treatment of Bipolar Disorder (Keck, Nelson, & McElroy, 2003); these include Depakote, Lamictal, Neurontin, Tegretol, and Topamax (see Table 36.6).

The mechanism of action of the antiepilepsy drugs is not well understood (Harwood & Agam, 2003). They have been found to be effective in stabilizing mood in children and adolescents without some of the toxic effects resulting from higher doses of lithium (Wagner et al., 2002). These drugs are also safe enough to be used with lithium as adjunctive drug therapy. The side effects are slight, primarily involving sedation, but some children experience hair loss, weight gain, and tremors. These medicines are also sometimes prescribed as an adjunct to help treat a variety of conditions where a disruption of mood is prominent, including cyclothymia, psychosis, Schizophrenia, personality disorders, and aggressive outbursts (Green, 2001; Steiner, Saxena, & Chang, 2003).

**Table 36.6**
Common Mood Stabilizing Drugs (for Use in Bipolar Disorder)

| Drug Name | | Other Common Uses | FDA-Approved for Use in Children? | Common Side Effects | | |
| --- | --- | --- | --- | --- | --- | --- |
| Trade Name | Generic Name | | | Arousal | Metabolism | Cardiovascular |
| Depakote/ Depakene | divalproex/ valproic acid | Aggressive behavior, Schizophrenia | No | Tremor | Weight gain, upset stomach, hair loss | |
| Lamictal | lamotrigine | Aggressive behavior, Schizophrenia | 2 and older for seizures | | Rash, nausea | |
| Eskalith/ Lithobid | lithium | | 12 and older | Fatigue, fine tremor | Increased thirst, nausea, vomiting, diarrhea | May be associated with dysarthmias |
| Neurontin | gabapentin | Aggressive behavior, Schizophrenia, pain control | 12 and older for seizures | Fatigue, dizziness | | |
| Symbyax | olanzapine and fluoxetine | | No | Sedation, weakness | Weight gain, increased appetite | |
| Tegretol | carbamazepine | Aggressive behavior, Schizophrenia | 6 and older for seizures | Sedation | | |
| Topamax | topiramate | Aggressive behavior, Schizophrenia | 2 and older for seizures | May cause word-finding difficulty | Associated with glaucoma | |

*Notes:* Most mood stabilizing drugs are dosed based on weight and blood serum level, so doses are highly variable. All of these drugs, except lithium, are antiepilepsy drugs. Other drugs typically associated with epilepsy are also being used as second-line medicines for Bipolar Disorder.

The newest addition to medicines used to treat Bipolar Disorder is *Symbyax*. The FDA approved this drug for the treatment of Bipolar Disorder in adults in late 2003. While Symbyax is a new preparation, it combines two older medicines, the antidepressant Prozac and antipsychotic Zyprexa.

## Medication Used in the Treatment of Attention-Deficit/Hyperactivity Disorder

Since the mid-1930s, amphetamines, or stimulants, have been used to treat ADHD in children, as well as used as diet drugs and by the military to stave off fatigue (Chiarello & Cole, 1987; Rafalovich, 2000). The use of stimulants is controversial and under intense discussion (see Haber, 2000; Hinshaw, Klein, & Abikoff, 2002; Spencer, Biederman, Wilens, & Faraone, 2002). Considering these controversies is impossible in the scope of this chapter, except to reiterate that before any medication is recommended, the learner should receive a thorough psychological evaluation and be given an accurate diagnosis. Similarly, it is also evident from the literature that medication is most effective when used in combination with psychotherapy and other psychosocial interventions (Spencer et al., 2002).

The number of prescriptions for stimulants has grown from fewer than 2 million in 1991 to over 10 million in 2001, and an estimated 6% of all schoolchildren are using such medicines (Volkow & Swanson, 2003). The drugs typically used to treat ADHD are listed in Table 36.7; however, many other medications may be used in the treatment of this disorder (e.g., SSRIs, atypical antipsychotics, mood stabilizers).

The therapeutic mechanism of action of the stimulants is complex and, again like most psychotropics, not well understood. It is most likely related to these medicines' effect as dopamine agonists and their ability to increase dopamine availability in the striatum, leading to increased attention and concentration as well as decreased impulsivity (Volkow & Swanson, 2003). Often, stimulants have beneficial effects on attention and concentration with decreasing hyperactivity in the majority of ADHD children. Indeed, many people with no problems with attention and concentration would notice an increase in their ability to focus if they took a low dose of amphetamines. Often, the major concern about children taking these drugs is the side effects. Some are slight and generally not concerning, such as feeling jittery, needing less sleep, weight loss, and increased heart rate and blood pressure. However, amphetamines are addictive and their use is often abused, and a patient may develop withdrawal symptoms if the stimulants are stopped suddenly. Most of the stimulants are on Schedule II of the Controlled Substances Act. This schedule includes drugs that are known to have a high potential for abuse with severe psychic or physical dependence.

Although the stimulants have medicinal value and are also used for other conditions (such as narcolepsy, fatigue secondary to medical conditions, and intractable depression), the focus of drug development for ADHD has been drugs that are not stimulants. Given the role of norepinephrine in higher cortical functions related to attention, alertness, vigilance, and executive function, it is likely that noradrenergic activity is involved (Biederman & Spencer, 1999). Drugs that agonize norepinephrine may be beneficial in the treatment of ADHD. Wellbutrin, for example, has been shown to sometimes be beneficial (Spencer & Biederman, 2002) and has a mechanism of action similar to Strattera. Like Wellbutrin, Strattera

**Table 36.7**

Drugs Commonly Prescribed for Attention-Deficit/Hyperactivity Disorder

| Drug Name | | Drug Class | Indication for Use | FDA-Approved for Use in Children? | Common Side Effects | | |
|---|---|---|---|---|---|---|---|
| Trade Name | Generic Name | | | | Arousal | Metabolism | Cardiovascular |
| Adderall | amphetamine/ dextroamphetamine | Amphetamine | ADHD | 3 and older | Agitation | Weight loss, addicting | |
| Cylert | pemoline | Amphetamine | ADHD | 3 and older | Agitation | Weight loss, addicting, hepatic failure | |
| Dexedrine/ Dextrostat | dexadrine | Amphetamine | ADHD | 3 and older | | Weight loss, addicting | |
| Focalin | dexmethylphenidate | Amphetamine | ADHD | 6 and older | | Weight loss, addicting | |
| Provigil | modafinil | Stimulant (not schedule II) | Excessive sleepiness | No | Agitation, insomnia | Weight loss | |
| Ritalin/ Concerta | Methylphenidate | Amphetamine | ADHD | 6 and older | Agitation | Weight loss, addicting | Increased heart rate |
| Strattera | atomoxetine | Norepineph-rine reuptake inhibitor | ADHD | 6 and older | | Upset stomach | |

*Note:* The PDA recommends that Cylert not be used as a frontline drug for ADHD due to possible liver failure danger.

is a norepinephrine reuptake inhibitor. It is FDA-approved for use in children and adolescents to treat ADHD. It is not a controlled substance because it does not have many of the concerns that accompany the stimulants. It is still too new to judge whether this drug will become a front-line ADHD medicine or an adjunct. If it is shown to be as effective as the stimulants, then it will likely revolutionize the treatment of ADHD (Kratochvil, Vaughan, Harrington, & Burke, 2003).

### MISCELLANEOUS DRUGS

There are a number of medications commonly prescribed for mental health reasons that are not often thought of as psychotropics. There are also medications that are psychotropics that cannot be classified easily elsewhere or are not in widespread use. These medications are listed in Table 36.8.

A number of medications listed in Table 36.8 are FDA-approved for use in children, although they belong to an older class of medication. Orap, for example, is approved for children age 12 and older for the treatment of Tourette syndrome. Desyrel is known to be less effective than the other antidepressants, but it has a secondary benefit of being heavily sedating. This allows the option of prescribing a medicine for sleep that does not belong to the benzodiazapines. Finally, there are two types of medicines that are known to help with anxiety disorders by their effect of blocking adrenaline receptors. Both Catapres and Inderal are hypertension medicines. Catapres has been known to be effective in the treatment of Posttraumatic Stress Disorder and ADHD. Inderal has the benefit of keeping the sympathetic nervous system in check. Without a sympathetic response, the "fight or flight" response to stress and anxiety cannot mobilize. This keeps patients who suffer from situational anxiety (such as public speaking or fear of flying) from experiencing the dry mouth, sweaty palms, racing heart, and tremors that often accompany exposure to an anxiety-provoking situation. It can be taken when needed and generally is well tolerated.

## STATE-DEPENDENT LEARNING

State-dependent learning refers to an increased ability to remember material when it is recalled in the same state as it was learned. For example, state-dependent learning has been demonstrated in college students ingesting caffeine (Kelemen & Creeley, 2003) and in divers learning word lists both underwater and on a small boat (Emmerson, 1986). This effect has also been found for states created by mood and anxiety (Lang, Craske, Brown, & Ghaneian, 2001). This presents an interesting dilemma when considering whether children may also experience this effect when trying to learn information while medicated. The effects of psychotropics on learning in children is not well understood. Although examples of state-dependent learning are prevalent for both people and animals, there are few published studies explicitly examining this effect in children taking psychotropics. Becker-Mattes, Mattes, Abikoff, and Brandt (1985) conducted a thorough review of the literature regarding methylphenidate (Ritalin) and found no evidence of state-dependent learning. Although well documented in the literature, state-dependent learning does not appear to be a pervasive problem with children and adolescents taking psychotropic medications. Further study is necessary to fully understand this phenomenon.

**Table 36.8**
Miscellaneous Drugs

| Drug Name | | | | | Common Side Effects | | |
| Trade Name | Generic Name | Drug Class | Indication for Use | FDA-Approved for Use in Children? | Arousal | Metabolism | Cardiovascular |
| --- | --- | --- | --- | --- | --- | --- | --- |
| BuSpar | buspirone | Unique: non-benzodiazapine anxiety medicine | Generalized anxiety | No | | | |
| Catapres | clonidine | Alpha blocker: antihypertensive | PTSD, ADHD | No | Fatigue | Dry mouth | Orthostatic hypotension |
| Desyrel | trazodone | Antidepressant | Insomnia | No | | Dry mouth | |
| Inderal | propranolol | Beta blocker: antihypertensive | Situational anxiety | No | | | Orthostatic hypotension |
| Orap | pimozide | Dopamine antagonist | Psychosis, Tourette's syndrome | 12 and older for Tourette's | | Extrapyramidal symptoms | |

## CONCLUSION

Psychiatric medications are of particular concern when used on children. Some see medications as a "silver bullet" fixing all problems with the swallowing of a pill. This is rarely the case. Medications should probably never be the first course of treatment. For many children, however, medications will improve school performance, psychological condition, and quality of life. Extending Sommers-Flanagan and Sommers-Flanagan's (1996) guidelines, a number of steps should be taken prior to medication prescription and after:

- A thorough evaluation by a school neuropsychologist should be performed.
- The psychopathology should persist without clear environmental influences, such as family discord or a recent move.
- The symptoms should be both severe and physiological in nature, such as sleep disturbance, appetite change, and somatic complaints. Further, the symptoms should be without volitional control.
- The psychopathology is resistant to a course of psychotherapy or a classroom modification plan.
- The patient and family should understand the risks and benefits to medication.
- The most qualified provider available should be consulted, preferably a child psychiatrist for anything except ADHD, which pediatricians are well qualified to handle.
- The psychopathology should be behaviorally monitored before and after the prescription of medication.
- Any and all side effects, particularly those associated with learning (such as sedation) should be documented and reported to the medication provider.
- Follow-up visits should be frequent and fixed.
- There should be no changes to the medication regimen (e.g., dose, time of day taken, stopping the medication) unless specifically directed by the prescribing physician.
- Treatment planning should include the goal of discontinuing the medication as soon as possible.

One thing is certain with respect to psychotropics and children. This will be a major societal debate for many years to come.

## REFERENCES

Agranoff, B. W., & Fisher, S. K. (2001). Inositol, lithium, and the brain. *Psychopharmacology Bulletin, 35,* 5–18.

Becker-Mattes, A., Mattes, J. A., Abikoff, H., & Brandt, L. (1985). State-dependent learning in hyperactive children receiving methylphenidate. *American Journal of Psychiatry, 142,* 455–459.

Biederman, J., Mick, E., Spencer, T. J., Wilens, T. E., & Faraone, S. V. (2000). Therapeutic dilemmas in the pharmacotherapy of bipolar depression in the young. *Journal of Child and Adolescent Psychopharmacology, 10,* 185–192.

Biederman, J., & Spencer, T. J. (1999). Attention-deficit/hyperactivity disorder (ADHD) as a noradrenergic disorder. *Biological Psychiatry, 46,* 1234–1242.

Blumer, J. L. (1999). Off-label uses of drugs in children. *Pediatrics, 104,* 598–602.

Carlson, G. A. (2002). Clinical aspects of child and adolescent psychopharmacology. In S. Kutcher (Ed.), *Practical child and adolescent psychopharmacology* (pp. 70–90). New York: Cambridge University Press.

Cheer, S. M., & Figgitt, D. P. (2002). Spotlight on fluvoxamine in anxiety disorders in children and adolescents. *CNS Drugs, 16,* 139–144.

Chiarello, R. J., & Cole, J. O. (1987). The use of psychostimulants in general psychiatry: A reconsideration. *Archives of General Psychiatry, 44,* 286–295.

Diamond, R. J. (2002). *Instant psychopharmacology* (2nd ed.). New York: Norton.

Donnelly, C. L. (2003). Pharmacologic treatment approaches for child and adolescents with posttraumatic stress disorder. *Child and Adolescent Psychiatric Clinics of North America, 12,* 251–269.

Emmerson, P. G. (1986). Effects of environmental context on recognition memory in an unusual environment. *Perceptual and Motor Skills, 63,* 1047–1050.

Foote, S. M., & Etheredge, L. (2000). Increasing use of new prescription drugs: A case study. *Health Affairs, 19,* 165–170.

Gadow, K. D. (1997). An overview of three decades of research in pediatric psychcopharamcoepidemiology. *Journal of Child and Adolescent Psychopharmacology, 7,* 219–236.

Goode, E. (2004, February 3). Stronger warning urged on antidepressants for teenagers. *New York Times,* p. A1.

Green, W. H. (2001). *Child and adolescent clinical psychopharmacology* (3rd ed.). Philadelphia: Lippincott.

Haber, J. S. (2000). *ADHD: The great misdiagnosis.* Dallas: Taylor Publishing.

Harwood, A. J., & Agam, G. (2003). Search for a common mechanism of mood stabilizers. *Biochemical Pharmacology, 66,* 179–189.

Hinshaw, S. P., Klein, R. G., & Abikoff, H. B. (2002). Childhood attention-deficit hyperactivity disorder: Nonpharmacological treatments and their combination for medication. In P. E. Nathan (Ed.), *A guide to treatments that work* (2nd ed., pp. 3–23). London: Oxford University Press.

Keck, P. R., Jr., Nelson, E. B., & McElroy, S. L. (2003). Advances in the pharmacologic treatment of bipolar depression. *Biological Psychiatry, 53,* 671–679.

Kelemen, W. L., & Creeley, C. E. (2003). State-dependent memory effects using caffeine and placebo do not extend to metamemory. *Journal of General Psychology, 130,* 70–86.

Kendall, P. C. (1994). Treating anxiety disorders in children: Results of a randomized clinical trial. *Journal of Consulting and Clinical Psychology, 62,* 100–110.

Kowatch, R. A., Sethuraman, G., Hume, J. H., Kromelis, M., & Weinberg, W. A. (2003). Combination pharmacotherapy in children and adolescents with bipolar disorder. *Biological Psychiatry, 53,* 978–984.

Kratochvil, C. J., Vaughan, B. S., Harrington, M. J., & Burke, W. J. (2003). Atomoxetine: A selective noradrenaline reuptake inhibitor for the treatment of attention deficit/ hyperactivity disorder. *Expert Opinion on Pharmacotherapy, 4,* 1165–1174.

Lang, A. J., Craske, M. G., Brown, M., & Ghaneian, A. (2001). Fear-related state dependent memory. *Cognition and Emotion, 15,* 695–703.

Lasser, K. E., Allen, P. D., Woolhandler, S. J., Himmelstein, D. U., Wolfe, S. M., & Bor, D. H. (2002). Timing of new black box warnings and withdrawals for prescription medication. *Journal of the American Medical Association, 287,* 2215–2220.

Nahata, M. C. (1999). Inadequate pharmacotherapeutic data for drugs used in children: What can be done? *Pediatric Drugs, 1,* 245–249.

Nasrallah H. (2003). A review of the effect of atypical antipsychotics on weight. *Psychoneuroendocrinology, 28*(Suppl. 1), 83–96.

Olfson, M., Marcus, S. C., Pincus, H. A., Zito, J. M., Thompson, J. W., & Zarin, D. A. (1998). Antidepressant prescribing practices of outpatient psychiatrists. *Archives of General Psychiatry, 55,* 310–316.

Olfson, M., Marcus, S. C., Weissman, M. M., & Jensen, P. S. (2002). National trends in the use of psychotropic medications by children. *Journal of the American Academy of Child and Adolescent Psychiatry, 41,* 514–521.

Pletscher, A. (1991). The discovery of antidepressants: A winding path. *Experientia, 47,* 4–8.

Popper, C. W. (2002). Child and adolescent psychopharmacology at the turn of the millennium. In S. Kutcher (Ed.), *Practical child and adolescent psychopharmacology* (pp. 13–37). New York: Cambridge University Press.

Rafalovich, A. (2000). The conceptual history of attention deficit hyperactivity disorder: Idiocy, imbecility, encephalitis, and the child deviant, 1877–1929. *Deviant Behavior, 22,* 93–115.

Rosenblum, J., & Forman, S. F. (2003). Management of anorexia nervosa with exercise, and selective serotonergic reuptake inhibitors. *Current Opinion in Pediatrics, 15,* 346–347.

Ryan, N. D., Puig-Antich, J., Rabinovich, H., Fried, J., Ambrosini, P., Meyer, V., et al. (1988). MAOIs in adolescent major depression unresponsive to tricyclic antidepressants. *Journal of American Academy of Child and Adolescent Psychiatry, 27,* 755–758.

Sheehan, D. V. (2002). The management of panic disorder. *Journal of Clinical Psychiatry, 63*(Suppl.), 17–21.

Spencer, T. J., & Biederman, J. (2002). Non-stimulant treatment for attention deficit/hyperactivity disorder. *Journal of Attention Disorders, 6*(Suppl.), S109–S119.

Spencer, T. J., Biederman, J., Wilens, T. E., & Faraone, S. V. (2002). Novel treatments for attention deficit/hyperactivity disorder in children. *Journal of Clinical Psychiatry, 63*(Suppl.), 16–22.

Sommers-Flanagan, J., & Sommers-Flanagan, R. (1996). Efficacy of antidepressant medication with depressed youth: What psychologists should know. *Professional Psychology: Research and Practice, 27,* 145–153.

Steiner, H., Saxena, K., & Chang, K. (2003). Psychopharmacologic strategies for the treatment of aggression in juveniles. *CNS Spectrums, 8,* 298–308.

Thomsen, P. H. (2000). Obsessive-compulsive disorder: Pharmacological treatment. *European Child and Adolescent Psychiatry, 9*(Suppl.), 176–184.

Volkow, N. D., & Swanson, J. M. (2003). Variables that affect the clinical use and abuse of methylphenidate in the treatment of ADHD. *American Journal of Psychiatry, 160,* 1909–1918.

Wagner, K. D., Weller, E. B., Carlson, G. A., Sachs, G., Biederman, J., Frazier, J. A., et al. (2002). An open-label trial of divalproex in children and adolescents with bipolar disorder. *Journal of the American Academy of Child and Adolescent Psychiatry, 41,* 1224–1230.

Zito, J. M., Safer, D. J., dosReis, S., Gardner, J. F., Boles, M., & Lynch, F. (2000). Trends in the prescribing of psychotropic medications to preschoolers. *Journal of the American Medical Association, 283,* 1025–1030.

Zito, J. M., Safer, D. J., dosReis, S., Gardner, J. F., Soeken, K., Boyles, M., et al. (2002). Rising prevalence of antidepressants among U.S. youths. *Pediatrics, 109,* 721–727.

# CHAPTER 37

# Integrating Evidence-Based Neuropsychological Services into School Settings: Issues and Challenges for the Future

MATTHEW C. TRAUGHBER and RIK CARL D'AMATO

THE CHAPTERS THAT comprise this volume collectively illustrate the considerable utility of a neuropsychological paradigm for inclusive school-based psychological service delivery. The basis for widespread neuropsychological practice in schools, however, requires further scrutiny; in fact, some have argued against neuropsychological practice in this setting (e.g., Reschly & Gresham, 1989). With this in mind, this final chapter considers the potential role and contribution of neuropsychology against the backdrop of several noteworthy changes (impending and prospective) occurring in the field of school psychology (e.g., a growing emphasis on evidence-based interventions). The chapter serves several purposes: to reiterate the contemporary philosophy underlying neuropsychological practice in schools, its intended applications, and acknowledged limitations; to clarify the place of neuropsychological assessment in an evolving school-based psychological services model; to acquaint readers with the emerging standards by which neuropsychological methods will be judged and to weigh the current state of empirical evidence underlying school neuropsychological practice; and to propose several key objectives that school neuropsychology must meet to ensure its relevance to education. It seems evident that the fate of neuropsychology practice in schools will, in large part, hinge on the extent to which the role of neuropsychologists is clearly defined, the unique benefits of their services are recognized, and the evidence supporting their practices continues to be established.

## THE EMERGENCE OF NEUROPSYCHOLOGY IN THE SCHOOLS

That neuropsychological principles could improve education by broadening our understanding of learning disorders was suggested by Orton as early as the 1920s

(Orton, 1937). Some 40 years later, Gaddes (1968) presented one of the first formalized approaches to addressing learning disabilities rooted in neuropsychological principles (Horton, 1997). The term "school neuropsychology" subsequently permeated the literature via a 1981 special issue of *School Psychology Review* devoted to advancing the relevance of neuropsychology to education (Hynd, 1981) and several other articles and chapters promoting school neuropsychology appearing around this time (Hynd & Hartlage, 1983; Hynd & Obrzut, 1981). The expanding science of neuropsychology was promoted as a promising foundation from which to understand and treat children with learning problems and brain-based disorders (Reynolds, 1981, 1986).

Indebted to these preliminary efforts, a maturing vision of the role of school neuropsychology in education has materialized, more clearly defining both the nature of the field and its applicability to school-based practice (e.g., D'Amato, 1990; D'Amato, Rothlisberg, & Leu Work, 1999; Gaddes & Edgell, 1994; Teeter & Semrud-Clikeman, 1997; Whitten, D'Amato, & Chittooran, 1992, 1997). This perspective can be characterized as an approach to understanding child functioning and neurodevelopment that emphasizes the reciprocal relationship between behavior and the brain. Practice from a neuropsychological perspective implies awareness of, and assigns considerable substance to, the potential neurobehavioral origins of each learner's academic and mental health problems; although neuropsychological practice requires specialized training (see Hynd & Reynolds, this volume), one need not be credentialed as a neuropsychologist or use neuropsychological tests to identify with this approach (Telzrow, 1985). Neuropsychologists attend to the many factors that impact behavior, and their neurobiological focus is balanced by an acknowledgment of the developmental, ecological, and psychosocial origins of childhood problems (D'Amato et al., 1999).

It should be reemphasized that neuropsychological assessment for intervention is not intended to usurp the role of equally important psychological theories and approaches (Gaddes & Edgell, 1994; Hynd & Hartlage, 1983; Teeter & Semrud-Clikeman, 1997). Instead, a neuropsychological perspective can be viewed as one compatible and essential piece of a comprehensive and integrated approach to meeting learners' needs, alongside a diversity of paradigms that include cognitive, developmental, family systems, and behavioral psychology, among others (see Teeter & Semrud-Clikeman, 1997, for an illustration of an integrated neurodevelopmental framework).

## NEEDS, OPPORTUNITIES, AND ADVANCES IN SCHOOL PSYCHOLOGY

Calls for reform from within and outside the field of school psychology have intensified, emphasizing the need for more intervention-focused and ecologically oriented forms of practice (Harrison et al., 2003; Sheridan & Gutkin, 2000). The Conference on the Future of School Psychology in 2002 represented a major step toward initiating such reforms and establishing school psychology goals for the twenty-first century (Sheridan & D'Amato, 2003/2004). Participants in this historic conference generated action plans for achieving positive outcomes for children, families, and schools (Dawson et al., 2003; Ehrhardt-Padgett, Hatzichristou, Kitson, & Meyers, 2003; Harrison et al., 2003; Sheridan & D'Amato, 2003/2004).

The resulting agenda for change outlined a number of key school psychological practice elements that warrant greater attention and focus: increased prevention and intervention services, corresponding with expanded roles in schools; the impact of diversity on school psychological services; the value of home-school partnerships; addressing the shortage of school psychologists; the possibility of comprehensive educational and mental health services through schools; the need for action research and qualitative inquiry; and the importance of collaboration across professions in education and all of psychology. Two additional themes also emerged from the conference that are particularly relevant for neuropsychological practice in schools: reduced emphasis on traditional individual assessment and a commitment to promoting evidence-based practice. Based on these themes, it seems reasonable to assume that the expansion of (and demand for) neuropsychological practice in the educational setting will be largely determined by the extent to which the following two objectives are accomplished:

1. The position of neuropsychology along the continuum of educational and psychological service delivery in schools is established. Displacement of the traditional "test and place" model of school psychological service delivery has been proposed for some time, and at this juncture a de-emphasis and reduction in the use of standardized ability testing appears a near certainty for most learners. The future reauthorization of the Individuals with Disabilities Education Act is likely to adopt changes whereby identifying and serving students with certain disabilities will no longer mandate cognitive testing. At the same time, many have called for comprehensive school-based health and mental health services to better promote the psychosocial and academic development of *all* children, youth, and families (Nastasi, 2000; Tharinger, 1995) with problem solving and prevention serving as primary goals (Conoley & Gutkin, 1995; Sheridan & Gutkin, 2000). What implications do these changes in service delivery hold for school neuropsychologists?
2. School neuropsychology continues to strengthen its scientific basis. Given the recent prioritization of evidence-based practice in both education and psychology, it is imperative that the validity of neuropsychological assessment and the efficacy of neuropsychology-driven instructional and intervention strategies undergo critical examination. Neuropsychologists are faced with the challenge of proving that their practices both improve learner outcomes and are congruent with the ecology of schools.

## Establishing the Role of the School Neuropsychologist

The predominant psychometric assessment practices (e.g., the use of an IQ-achievement discrepancy criterion) employed in schools have fallen from favor for many educators due to a number of inherent limitations (Dombrowski, Kamphaus, & Reynolds, 2004; Fuchs, Mock, Morgan, & Young, 2003). A problem-solving approach to assessment and intervention of academic and behavioral problems has been proposed as a more acceptable alternative (Reschly & Ysseldyke, 2002). School-based problem solving incorporates the three basic elements of (1) identifying and defining the problem, (2) generating and implementing solutions, and (3) evaluating the chosen solution (Deno, 2002).

Continual monitoring of progress is a fundamental element of problem solving; when initial solutions prove ineffective, they are modified or new ones developed. Consistent with the problem-solving philosophy, a *responsiveness to intervention* (RTI) framework is one approach that has been advocated to address the identification and intervention of learning problems (Vaughn & Fuchs, 2003) and is briefly described here. Under the RTI framework, curriculum-based measurement (CBM) is used to identify learners in need of additional instruction in a basic skill area such as reading fluency or mathematics. Such learners receive evidence-based supports beyond that offered in the general education curriculum, and their progress is continually monitored using CBM. The learning disability designation and special education services eligibility is given to learners who fail to improve despite such rehabilitation efforts.

Although promising, the research into school-wide implementation of RTI models remains largely exploratory, and problematic aspects of the RTI model have been noted (Fuchs et al., 2003; Vaughn & Fuchs, 2003). For instance, Dombrowski et al. (2004) cautioned that RTI models do not allow for uniformity of diagnosis and limit communication regarding phenomenological characteristics of a particular child's learning problem across practitioners and schools. These authors, in addition to the use of assessment and progress monitoring using CBM, also espoused requiring dual evidence of substandard norm-referenced achievement test performance in their model of learning disability identification in order to lend uniformity to the categorization across schools and states. Regardless of the exact shape the identification and rehabilitation of learning problems ultimately takes, however, school psychology will increasingly rely on strategies rooted in the principles of problem solving.

The multistage neuropsychological model proposed by Teeter and Semrud-Clikeman (1997) demonstrated how neuropsychology can contribute to service delivery for children who present with severe learning challenges; their model incorporates many previously discussed assumptions of problem solving. In Teeter and Semrud-Clikeman's model, learners who present with conditions that have obvious neurocognitive bases, such as suspected traumatic brain injury (TBI), may warrant immediate neuropsychological evaluation upon referral. School psychologists have been and will be faced with increasing numbers of such referrals. Advances in emergency medicine and transportation, along with improved neonatal care, have been shown to result in growing numbers of learners entering school affected by neurodevelopmental impairment and who therefore require specialized services or interventions (Gaddes, 1981; Haak & Livingston, 1997). And the true number of children who suffer a TBI is believed to exceed those identified with and receiving services for TBI, suggesting that this group of learners is actually underserved (Carney, du Coudray et al., 1999; Walker, Boling, & Cobb, 1999). Identification, intervention, and progress monitoring for learner problems that are *not* believed to be neurologically based, however, would typically prompt the use of behaviorally based interventions or instructional modifications initially facilitated by the school psychologist or school neuropsychologist. If a learner fails to improve despite these strategies, or lingering questions remain regarding the nature of the problem, standardized cognitive assessment represents the next step under this model. Subsequent to this stage, psychologists and educators should be able to identify effective interventions for most learners, and prior to this juncture, neuropsychological assessment would generally be unnecessary given what we now know. In fact, most learners who display problems in learning and behavior display no obvious neurological impairment (Gaddes, 1981; Lyon, Fletcher, & Barnes, 2003). A comprehensive neuropsychological evaluation does become appropriate, however, when school-related problems are not only resistant to remediation but also continue to defy standard analysis; in other words, at an advanced stage of "problem solving." When uncertainty regarding the nature of and solutions to individuals' problems persists, a neuropsychological evaluation can generate unique hypotheses and help resolve the question of how best to intervene (D'Amato et al., 1999).

In addition to changes in the approach to identifying and intervening in school-based problems, an expanded role in school-based service delivery is also likely to characterize the future of school psychology. The potential contribution of school psychology practitioners extends well beyond the prescribed, traditional gatekeeper role (Nastasi, 2000). It has been proposed that the school-based practitioner increasingly act as a key participant in and coordinator of the comprehensive health and mental health care of learners (Bucy, Meyers, & Swerdlik, 2002; DeMers, 1995; Sheridan & Gutkin, 2000). Schools have been suggested as logical *hubs* of service delivery for children based on aspects of accessibility and cost-effectiveness, and sentiment is growing for a move to full-service schools where learners are offered a wider array of health services (both universal and targeted) provided by an array of school- or community-based professionals (Carlson, Paavola, & Talley, 1995; Reschly & Ysseldyke, 2002). It is estimated that, even at present, schools provide 70% to 80% of the mental health services children receive (Ringeisen, Henderson, & Hoagwood, 2003), and schools represent the most common setting for the delivery of health promotion programming as well (Rothlisberg, D'Amato, & Palencia, 2003).

Nastasi (2000) has addressed the requisite skills and competencies for comprehensive health care delivery by school psychologists in the twenty-first century. A psychologist as health care provider recognizes the need for integrated service delivery and is attuned to the educational, health, mental health, and social service needs of learners across agencies and professional disciplines. The psychologist crafts and coordinates services reflective of the multitude of ecological variables that influence the well-being and achievement of children and their families. This professional provides or coordinates a continuum of services, ranging from prevention to treatment, addressing a broad spectrum of health-related issues, including chronic medical, neurodevelopmental, neurological, and other health-related conditions. Effectual cooperation with other professionals is essential to ensure that the services children and families receive are both integrated and comprehensive. The knowledge and skills of school neuropsychologists are ideally suited to such a role in a wide-ranging system of service delivery, given their expertise in service provision and professional collaboration with regard to the educational, psychosocial, and medical needs of children affected by the type of severe neurodevelopmental impairments that have increasingly fallen under the purview of schools. If and when schools undertake the responsibility of meeting the needs of all children, including those with severe problems, the services of professionals trained in school neuropsychology will likely assume greater import and relevance.

## SCHOOL NEUROPSYCHOLOGY AS EVIDENCE-BASED PRACTICE

It will progressively be the case that school neuropsychologists, if they are to be perceived as integral professionals in the school setting, must demonstrate both the validity of their assessment practices and the empirical justification underlying the interventions they choose.

*Validity Issues in School Neuropsychological Assessment* Despite significant improvements in imaging technology, now the primary tool for diagnosing neurological impairment, neuropsychological assessment maintains its unique role in identifying the functional consequences of impairment and formulating interventions (Long, 1998). Those trained in neuropsychology who practice in schools will be infrequently consulted regarding diagnostic questions; instead, their assistance will be sought for questions regarding integration of the learner back into the school setting or development of appropriate instructional strategies. However, the psychometric adequacy of neuropsychological instrumentation has been the subject of concern both from within (e.g., Reynolds, 1997; Sbordone, 1998) and outside (e.g., Reschly & Gresham, 1989) the field for some time. With regard to long-standing neuropsychological tests currently in use, observed limitations include insufficient normative data, a narrow understanding of the performance of nonimpaired individuals, and less than ideal evidence of reliability and validity. Referring to adults, Sbordone has written, "The neuropsychologist . . . who tries to search for empirically demonstrated relationships between neuropsychological test scores and specific vocationally related behaviors, often finds that such empirical evidence is 'embarrassingly limited'" (p. 15). The same should be said for children's academic and school behavior: There is currently little empirical basis for predicting the association between neuropsychological test performance and school outcomes (Long, 1998). In their current state, it is unclear whether neuropsychological findings incrementally improve the choice of intervention or outcomes for common learning disabilities, although evidence pertaining to this question may be produced in the future (Kalat & Wurm, 1999).

Although the clinical expertise of neuropsychologists can be quite valuable, unfortunately some neuropsychologists in the past have relied on subjective criteria rather than objective data when interpreting and drawing conclusions from test results (Franzen & Wilhelm, 1998; Reynolds, 1997). Such questionable practices are not necessarily unique to neuropsychologists, however; the educational enterprise in general has a poor history of selecting and using empirically substantiated measures.

Although new neuropsychological instrumentation is promising, much work remains to confirm the psychometric adequacy of instruments such as the NEPSY and the Dean-Woodcock Neuropsychological Battery (Davis & D'Amato, this volume; Sattler & D'Amato, 2002). Indeed, neuropsychologists working in schools must be cautious when generating decisions and recommendations, as inferences formed on the basis of neuropsychological instruments may lack empirical support (Long, 1998). A thorough discussion of the psychometric limitations of neuropsychological tests for children is available elsewhere (Reynolds, 1997). Nonetheless, it deserves mention that an ambitious objective for school neuropsychologists is to develop a body of support for their practices through empirical evaluation and applied research.

In school neuropsychology, considerable attention should be directed to understanding and generating *ecological* validity, generally defined as the functional and predictive relationship between the learner's test performance and that learner's behavior both at school and in other real-world settings (Sbordone, 1998). How confidently can school psychologists generalize the results of evaluations conducted under controlled conditions, chosen to elicit optimum performance, to the markedly different circumstances of the common school classroom? Few instruments used to assess neuropsychological integrity in children have been evaluated for the strength of their ecological validity (Franzen & Wilhelm, 1998). This manner of support can be difficult to obtain given the many environmental factors in addition to neuropsychological substrates that merge to influence school performance (Hartlage & Templer, 1998). Then again, school neuropsychologists can take advantage of their status as practitioners internal to the school system by evaluating the extent to which the observed behavior of the child in this natural environment (including academic performance and teacher, peer, and family interactions) is consistent with findings and conclusions gleaned from the neuropsychological assessment. For interested parties, other authors have outlined procedures for evaluating the ecological validity of neuropsychological tests (Franzen & Wilhelm, 1998).

School neuropsychologists also have the opportunity and duty to evaluate the treatment validity and social validity of their assessment practices. Do the findings from neuropsychological assessments lead to interventions effective above and beyond that which would occur in the absence of such assessment? Are the products of neuropsychological assessments not only germane to learners' school functioning but also perceived as relevant by others in the educational environment? These are questions all practitioners in schools must consider.

*Evidence-Based Interventions and School Neuropsychology*   The expansion and refinement of evidence-based education, mental health, and medicine has become a national priority (Chambless & Ollendick, 2001; Ringeisen et al., 2003). A growing emphasis on evidence-based practice has also occurred in applied psychology, motivated largely by such realities of practice as less than desirable child/patient outcomes, the persisting research-to-practice gap, and increased external demands for accountability. Consequently, a series of ambitious ventures by various organizations to identify and advance treatment and intervention approaches supported by credible research (evidence-based interventions [EBIs]) have been undertaken. Panels, task forces, and committees devoted to identifying and promoting EBIs have proliferated over the past decade. Following in the footsteps of the task force of the Clinical Psychology Division (12) of the American Psychological Association (APA), which commenced development of a system for rating the empirical support for psychotherapeutic treatments in the mid-1990s, more than 10 groups representing psychology and education are or have been involved in efforts to evaluate and disseminate intervention research pertinent to their respective fields, including APA Divisions 53 (Society of Clinical Child and Adolescent Psychology) and 16 (School Psychology), the National Reading Panel, and the U.S. Department of Education (Kratochwill & Shernoff, 2003). In addition, a number of texts and journal special issues commissioned or inspired by these groups and devoted to the dissemination and preservation of effective psychotherapeutic treatments for children and adolescents have been published (e.g., Gutkin, 2002; Kazdin & Weisz, 2003; Nathan & Gorman, 2002; Roth & Fonagy, 1996).

*APA Division 16 Task Force Criteria for Evidence-Based Interventions*　The Task Force on Evidence-Based Interventions in School Psychology (2003) recently produced, under the sponsorship of Division 16 and the Society for the Study of School Psychology and endorsed by the National Association of School Psychologists, a Procedural and Coding Manual containing a comprehensive and rigorous set of criteria for evaluating school-based interventions (Kratochwill & Stoiber, 2002). These criteria currently serve as the standard in evidence-based practice in school psychology. For a comprehensive review of the work of the Task Force and development of the coding manual, the reader is referred to the special issue of School Psychology Quarterly devoted to the topic (Gutkin, 2002), earlier published reports of the Task Force's progress (e.g., Kratochwill & Stoiber, 2000a, 2000b; Stoiber & Kratochwill, 2000), and the Procedural and Coding Manual itself. Readers are encouraged to familiarize themselves with the manual, which can be retrieved online (http://www.sp-ebi.org), and the established criteria for rating studies. It is possible that features of the manual highlighted here may be changed in future editions.

The stated purpose of the Task Force was to "identify, review, and code studies of psychological and educational interventions for behavioral, emotional, and academic problems and disorders for school-aged children and their families" (Task Force on Evidence-Based Interventions in School Psychology, 2003, p. 9). The manual provides detailed criteria and instructions for coding intervention outcome studies. Separate submanuals exist for studies of group-based and single-participant experimental designs (supplementary coding options also exist for quasi-experimental designs). These criteria, reproduced from the manual, are displayed in Tables 37.1 and 37.2.

The manual employs a dimensional rating system; many methodological characteristics of interventions are rated from 0 to 3 in accordance with the level of support, in essence placing responsibility on the consumer to judge whether or not the evidence warrants use of that intervention (Levin, O'Donnell, & Kratochwill, 2003). Studies or interventions nominated for review are classified under one of five content domains: (1) school- and community-based intervention programs for social and behavioral problems; (2) academic intervention programs; (3) family and parent intervention programs; (4) schoolwide and classroom-based programs; and (5) comprehensive and coordinated school health services. School neuropsychologists will be interested in interventions in each area; however, given the learner populations on whom school neuropsychologists often focus (e.g., learners with severe impairments), the content domain of comprehensive and coordinated school health services may emerge as especially relevant and the domain under which many neuropsychological interventions could be placed. Also of note is that the Task Force recommends the use of treatment manuals or other procedural guidelines to aid in evaluation efforts and the consistent implementation of EBIs in schools.

Several concerns regarding the evaluation of an intervention's evidence have been raised. One source of debate has been the merit of efficacy versus effectiveness studies (Fonagy, Target, Cottrell, Phillips, & Kurtz, 2002; Kratochwill &

**Table 37.1**

EBI Task Force Coding Criteria and Coding Options for Group-Based Studies

I. General Characteristics

  A. General Design Characteristics

    Random-assignment designs (if random assignment design, select one of the following)

- Completely randomized design
- Randomized block design (between-subjects variation)
- Randomized block design (within-subjects variation)
  - Randomized hierarchical design

    Nonrandom-assignment designs

- Nonrandomized design
- Nonrandomized block design (between-subjects variation)
- Nonrandomized block design (within-subjects variation)
- Nonrandomized hierarchical designs
- Optional coding of quasi-experimental designs

    Overall confidence of judgment on how participants were assigned

- Very low, □ Low, □ Moderate, □ High, □ Very high, □ N/A,
- Unknown/unable to code

  B. Statistical Treatment

    Appropriate unit of analysis: □ Yes □ No

    Family-wise error rate controlled: □ Yes □ No

    Sufficiently large $N$: □ Yes □ No

      Statistical Test: _____

- level: _____

      ES: _____

      $N$ required: _____

    Total size of sample (start of the study): _____

      Intervention group sample size: _____

      Control group sample size: _____

  C. Type of Program (select one)

- Universal prevention program
- Selective prevention program
- Targeted prevention program
- Intervention/Treatment
- Unknown

  D. Stage of Program (select one)

- Model/demonstration programs
- Early stage programs
- Established/institutionalized programs
- Unknown

  E. Concurrent or Historical Intervention Exposure

- Current exposure
- Prior exposure
- Unknown

II. Key Features for Coding Studies and Rating Level of Evidence/Support

  (3 = Strong evidence, 2 = Promising evidence, 1 = Weak evidence, 0 = No evidence)

*(continued)*

**Table 37.1** *Continued*

A. Measurement

Use of outcome measures that produce reliable scores for the majority of primary outcomes (select one of the following)

☐ Yes, ☐ No, ☐ Unknown/unable to code

Multi-method (select one of the following)

☐ Yes, ☐ No, ☐ N/A, ☐ Unknown/unable to code

Multi-source (select one of the following)

☐ Yes, ☐ No, ☐ N/A, ☐ Unknown/unable to code

Validity of measures reported

☐ Yes, validated with specific target group

☐ In part, validated for general population only

☐ No

☐ Unknown/unable to code

**Rating for Measurement** (select 0, 1, 2, or 3): ☐ **3** ☐ **2** ☐ **1** ☐ **0**

B. Comparison Group (select one of the following)

Type of comparison group

☐ Typical intervention

☐ Typical intervention (other) specify: _____

☐ Attention placebo

☐ Intervention elements placebo

☐ Alternative intervention

☐ Pharmacotherapy

☐ No intervention

☐ Wait list/delayed intervention

☐ Minimal contact

☐ Unable to identify type of comparison group

**Rating for Comparison Group** (select 0, 1, 2, or 3): ☐ **3** ☐ **2** ☐ **1** ☐ **0**

Overall confidence rating on judgment of type of comparison group

☐ Very low, ☐ Low, ☐ Moderate, ☐ High, ☐ Very high, ☐ Unknown/unable to code

Counterbalancing of change agents

☐ By change agent

☐ Statistical

☐ Other

Group equivalence established (select one of the following)

☐ Random assignment

☐ Post hoc matched set

☐ Statistical matching

☐ Post hoc test for group equivalence

Equivalent mortality

☐ Low attrition (less than 20% for post)

☐ Low attrition (less than 30% for follow-up)

☐ Intent to intervene analysis carried out (findings: _____)

C. Primary/Secondary Outcomes Are Statistically Significant

Evidence of appropriate statistical analysis for primary outcomes

☐ Appropriate unit of analysis (rate from previous code)

☐ Family-wise/experimenter-wise error rate controlled when applicable (rate from previous code)

☐ Sufficiently large N (rate from previous code)

☐ Sufficiently large N (rate from previous code)

**Table 37.1** *Continued*

Percentage of primary outcomes that are statistically significant (select one of the following)

☐ Significant primary outcomes for at least 75% of the total primary outcome measures for each key construct

☐ Significant primary outcomes for between 50% and 74% of the total primary outcome measures for each key construct

☐ Significant primary outcomes for between 25% and 49% of the total primary outcome measures for any key construct

**Rating for Primary Outcomes Statistically Significant** (select 0, 1, 2, or 3):
☐ **3** ☐ **2** ☐ **1** ☐ **0**

Evidence of appropriate statistical analysis for secondary outcomes

☐ Appropriate unit of analysis

☐ Family-wise/experimenter-wise error rate controlled when applicable (rate from previous code)

☐ Sufficiently large *N* (rate from previous code)

Percentage of secondary outcomes that are statistically significant (select one of the following)

☐ Significant primary outcomes for at least 75% of the total secondary outcome measures for each key construct

☐ Significant primary outcomes for between 50% and 74% of the total secondary outcome measures for each key construct

☐ Significant primary outcomes for between 25% and 49% of the total secondary outcome measures for any key construct

**Rating for Secondary Outcomes Statistically Significant** (select 0, 1, 2, or 3):
☐ **3** ☐ **2** ☐ **1** ☐ **0**

Overall summary of questions investigated

Main effect analyses conducted: ☐ Yes ☐ No

Moderator effect analyses conducted: ☐ Yes ☐ No

Specify results: _____

Mediator analyses conducted: ☐ Yes ☐ No

Specify results: _____

D. Educational/Clinical Significance

Categorical diagnosis data

Pretest: Diagnostic information regarding inclusion into the study presented

☐ Yes, ☐ No, ☐ Unknown

Posttest: Positive change in diagnostic criteria from pre- to posttest

☐ Yes, ☐ No, ☐ Unknown

Follow-up: Positive change in diagnostic criteria from posttest to follow-up

☐ Yes, ☐ No, ☐ Unknown

Outcomes assessed via continuous variables

Posttest: Positive change in percentage of participants showing clinical improvement from pre- to posttest

☐ Yes, ☐ No, ☐ Unknown

Follow-up: Positive change in percentage of participants showing clinical improvement from posttest to follow-up

☐ Yes, ☐ No, ☐ Unknown

*(continued)*

**Table 37.1**   *Continued*

Subjective evaluation

Pretest: Importance of behavior change is evaluated

   □ Yes, □ No, □ Unknown

Posttest: Importance of behavior change from pre- to posttest is evaluated positively by individuals in direct contact with the participant

   □ Yes, □ No, □ Unknown

Follow-up: Importance of behavior change from posttest to follow-up is evaluated positively by individuals in direct contact with the participant

   □ Yes, □ No, □ Unknown

Social comparison

Pretest: Participant's behavior is compared to normative data

   □ Yes, □ No, □ Unknown

Posttest: Participant's behavior has improved from pre- to posttest when compared to normative data

   □ Yes, □ No, □ Unknown

Follow-up: Participant's behavior has improved from posttest to follow-up when compared to normative data

   □ Yes, □ No, □ Unknown

**Rating for Educational/Clinical Significance** (select 0, 1, 2, or 3): □ **3** □ **2** □ **1** □ **0**

E.  Identifiable Components

Evidence for primary outcomes (rate from previous code): □ **3** □ **2** □ **1** □ **0**

Design allows for analysis of identifiable components (select one): □ Yes □ No

Total number of components: _____

Number of components linked to primary outcomes: _____

Clear documentation of essential components (select one): □ Yes □ No

Procedures for adapting the intervention are described in detail (select one): □ Yes □ No

Contextual features of the intervention are documented (select one): □ Yes □ No

**Rating for Identifiable Components** (select 0, 1, 2, or 3): □ **3** □ **2** □ **1** □ **0**

F.  Implementation Fidelity

Evidence of acceptable adherence

   □ Ongoing supervision/consultation

   □ Coding intervention sessions/lessons or procedures

   □ Audio/video tape implementation

   □ Entire intervention

   □ Part of intervention

Manualization (select all that apply)

   □ Written material involving a detailed account of the exact procedures and the sequence in which they are to be used

   □ Formal training session that includes a detailed account of the exact procedures and the sequence in which they are to be used

   □ Written material involving an overview of broad principles and a description of the intervention phases

   □ Formal or informal training session involving an overview of broad principles and a description of the intervention phases

Adaptation procedures are specified (select one): □ Yes □ No □ Unknown

**Table 37.1** *Continued*

**Rating for Implementation Fidelity** (select 0, 1, 2, or 3): ☐ **3** ☐ **2** ☐ **1** ☐ **0**

    G. Replication
        ☐ Same intervention
        ☐ Same target problem
        ☐ Independent evaluation

**Rating for Replication** (select 0, 1, 2, or 3): ☐ **3** ☐ **2** ☐ **1** ☐ **0**

    H. Site of Implementation
        School (if school is the site, select one of the following options)
            ☐ Public, ☐ Private, ☐ Charter, ☐ University affiliated, ☐ Alternative, ☐ Not specified/unknown
        Nonschool site (if it is a nonschool site, select one of the following options)
            ☐ Home, ☐ University clinic, ☐ Summer program, ☐ Outpatient hospital, ☐ Partial inpatient/day intervention program, ☐ Inpatient hospital, ☐ Private practice, ☐ Mental health center, ☐ Residential treatment facility, ☐ Other (specify), ☐ Unknown/insufficient information provided

**Rating for Site Implementation** (select 0, 1, 2, or 3): ☐ **3** ☐ **2** ☐ **1** ☐ **0**

    I. Follow-up Assessment
        ☐ Timing of follow-up assessment: specify _____
        ☐ Number of participants included in the follow-up assessment: specify _____
        ☐ Consistency of assessment method used: specify _____

**Rating for Follow-up Assessment** (select 0, 1, 2, or 3): ☐ **3** ☐ **2** ☐ **1** ☐ **0**

III. Other Descriptive or Supplemental Criteria to Consider
    A. External Validity Indicators
        Sampling procedures described in detail: ☐ Yes ☐ No
            Specify rationale for selection: _____
            Specify rationale for sample size: _____
            Inclusion/exclusion criteria specified: ☐ Yes ☐ No
            Inclusion/exclusion criteria similar to school practice: ☐ Yes ☐ No
            Specified criteria-related concern: ☐ Yes ☐ No
        Participant characteristics specified for treatment and control group
        Details are provided regarding variables that:
            Have differential relevance for intended outcomes: ☐ Yes ☐ No specify: _____
            Have relevance to inclusion criteria: ☐ Yes ☐ No specify: _____
        Receptivity/acceptance by target participant population (treatment group)
        Generalization of effects
            Generalization over time
                Evidence is provided regarding the sustainability of outcomes after intervention is terminated: ☐ Yes ☐ No specify: _____
                Procedures for maintaining outcomes are specified: ☐ Yes ☐ No specify: ___
            Generalization across settings
                Evidence is provided regarding the extent to which outcomes are manifested in contexts that are different from the intervention context: ☐ Yes ☐ No specify: _____
                Documentation of efforts to ensure application of intervention to other settings: ☐ Yes ☐ No specify: _____
            Generalization across persons
                Evidence is provided regarding the degree to which outcomes are manifested with participants who are different from the original group of participants for which the intervention was evaluated: ☐ Yes ☐ No specify: _____

*(continued)*

**Table 37.1** *Continued*

B. Length of Intervention
  □ Unknown/insufficient information provided
  □ Information provided (if information is provided, specify one of the following)
    weeks _____ , months _____ , years _____ , other _____

C. Intensity/dosage of Intervention
  □ Unknown/insufficient information provided
  □ Information provided (if information is provided, specify both of the following)
    length of intervention session _____ , frequency of intervention session _____

D. Dosage Response
  □ Unknown/insufficient information provided
  □ Information provided
    Describe positive outcomes associated with higher dosage: _____

E. Program Implementer (select all that apply)
  □ Research staff, □ School specialty staff, □ Teachers, □ Educational assistants, □ Parents, □ College students, □ Peers, □ Other, □ Unknown/insufficient information provided

F. Characteristics of the Intervener
  □ Highly similar to target participants on key variables (e.g., race, gender, SES)
  □ Somewhat similar to target participants on key variables
  □ Different from target participants on key variables

G. Intervention Style or Orientation (select all that apply)
  □ Behavioral, □ Cognitive-behavioral, □ Experiential, □ Humanistic/interpersonal, □ Psychodynamic/insight-oriented, □ Other (specify), □ Unknown/insufficient information provided

H. Cost Analysis Data
  □ Unknown/insufficient information provided
  □ Information provided
    Estimated cost of implementation: _____

I. Training and Support Resources (select all that apply)
  □ Simple orientation given to change agents
  □ Training workshops conducted
    # of workshops provided _____
    Average length of training _____
    Who conducted training (select all that apply)
    □ Project director, □ Graduate/project assistants, □ Other (specify),
      □ Unknown
  □ Ongoing technical support
  □ Program materials obtained
  □ Special facilities
  □ Other (specify)

J. Feasibility
  Level of difficulty in training intervention agents (select one of the following)
    □ High, □ Moderate, □ Low, □ Unknown
  Cost to train intervention agents (specify if known): _____
  Rating of cost to train intervention agents (select one of the following)
    □ High, □ Moderate, □ Low, □ Unknown

*Source:* From *Procedural and Coding Manual* by Task Force on Evidence-Based Interventions in School Psychology, June 2, 2003. Retrieved from http://www.sp-embi.org/_workingfiles /EBImanual1.pdf. Adapted with permission from the *Procedural and Coding Manual* of the Task Force on Evidence-Based Interventions in School Psychology.

I.  General Characteristics

    A.  General Design Characteristics

        Type of single-participant design

- ☐ Within-series design
  - ☐ Simple phase change
  - ☐ Complex phase change
- ☐ Between-series design
  - ☐ Comparing two interventions
  - ☐ Comparing interventions with no interventions
- ☐ Combined-series design
  - ☐ Multiple baseline across participants
  - ☐ Multiple baseline across behaviors
  - ☐ Multiple baseline across settings
  - ☐ Multiple probe design
- ☐ Mixed design
  - ☐ Combined single-participant and group design
  - ☐ Combined single-participant design
    - ☐ Within-series design
    - ☐ Simple phase change
    - ☐ Complex phase change
  - ☐ Between-series design
    - ☐ Comparing two interventions
    - ☐ Comparing interventions with no interventions
  - ☐ Combined-series design
    - ☐ Multiple baseline across participants
    - ☐ Multiple baseline across behaviors
    - ☐ Multiple baseline across settings
    - ☐ Multiple probe design
- ☐ Other (specify)

    B.  Other Design Characteristics (when randomization is used)

        Unit of assignment to conditions

- ☐ Individual, ☐ Classroom, ☐ School, ☐ Other (specify), ☐ N/A (randomization not used)

        Type of assignment to conditions/groups (select one of the following)

- ☐ Random after matching, stratification, blocking
- ☐ Random, simple (includes systematic sampling)
- ☐ Nonrandom, post hoc matching
- ☐ Nonrandom, other
- ☐ Other (specify)
- ☐ Unknown/insufficient information provided
- ☐ N/A (randomization not used)

        Overall confidence of judgment on how participants were assigned to conditions/groups (select one of the following)

- ☐ Very low, ☐ Low, ☐ Moderate, ☐ High, ☐ Very high, ☐ N/A, ☐ Unknown/unable to code

*(continued)*

**Table 37.2** *Continued*

Equivalence of conditions/groups tested at pretest (select one of the following)
    ☐ Yes, ☐ No, ☐ Unknown/insufficient information provided, ☐ N/A (randomization not used)

Total sample size (start of study): _____
Intervention sample size _____ ☐ N/A (randomization not used)
Control sample size _____ ☐ N/A (randomization not used)

  C. Type of Program (select one)
    ☐ Universal prevention program
    ☐ Selective prevention program
    ☐ Targeted prevention program
    ☐ Intervention/treatment
    ☐ Unknown

  D. Stage of the Program (select one)
    ☐ Model/demonstration programs
    ☐ Early stage programs
    ☐ Established/institutionalized programs
    ☐ Unknown

  E. Concurrent or Historical Intervention Exposure (select one)
    ☐ Current exposure, ☐ Prior exposure, ☐ Unknown

II. Key Features for Coding Studies and Rating Level of Evidence
  (3 = Strong evidence, 2 = Promising evidence, 1 = Weak evidence, 0 = No evidence)

  A. Measurement: Issues of Reliability and Validity
    Use of outcome measures that produce reliable scores (select one of the following)
      ☐ Yes, ☐ No, ☐ Unknown/unable to code
    Multi-method (select one of the following)
      ☐ Yes, ☐ No, ☐ N/A, ☐ Unknown/unable to code
    Multi-source
      ☐ Yes, ☐ No, ☐ N/A, ☐ Unknown/unable to code
    Validity of measures reported
      ☐ Yes, ☐ No, ☐ Unknown/unable to code

**Rating for Measurement** (select 0, 1, 2, or 3): ☐ **3** ☐ **2** ☐ **1** ☐ **0**

  B. Quality of Baseline
    Participant 1 (would replicate this section for each participant)
      Length: At least 3 data points during baseline (select one of the following)
        ☐ Yes, ☐ No, ☐ Unknown/insufficient information provided
      Stability: Variability in scores does not eliminate the detection of treatment effects (select one of the following)
        ☐ Yes, ☐ No, ☐ Unknown/insufficient information provided
      Overlap: Extreme scores during baseline do not overlap with most scores during intervention phase (select one of the following)
        ☐ Yes, ☐ No, ☐ Unknown/insufficient information provided
      Level: Behavior is serious enough during baseline to warrant an intervention (select one of the following)
        ☐ Yes, ☐ No, ☐ Unknown/insufficient information provided
      Trend: Behavior is not systematically increasing or decreasing in the desired direction of intervention effects during baseline
        ☐ Yes, ☐ No, ☐ Unknown/insufficient information provide

**Table 37.2** *Continued*

**Rating of Quality of Baseline for Participant 1** (select 0, 1, 2, or 3): □ **3** □ **2** □ **1** □ **0**

**Average Rating of Quality of Baseline across Participants**

**Overall Rating of Quality of Baseline** (select 0, 1, 2, or 3): □ **3** □ **2** □ **1** □ **0**

    C. Measures Support Primary and Secondary Outcomes (*manual includes a table to complete this section for multiple outcomes and for null/negative findings*)

        Visual analysis (*tables completed for each primary and secondary outcome for each participant*)

            Change in level (select one of the following)

                □ Large, □ Moderate-to-large, □ Moderate, □ No change, □ Unknown/ insufficient information provided

            No-to-minimal score overlap (select one of the following)

                □ Yes, □ No, □ Unknown/insufficient information provided

            Change in trend (select one of the following)

                □ Yes, □ No, □ N/A (no trend present), □ Unknown/insufficient information provided

            Adequate length (select one of the following)

                □ Yes, □ No, □ Unknown/insufficient information provided

            Stable data (select one of the following)

                □ Yes, □ No, □ Unknown/insufficient information provided

**Rating of Visual Analysis for Participant 1** (select 0, 1, 2, or 3): □ **3** □ **2** □ **1** □ **0**

    Reporting effect sizes (*tables completed for each primary and secondary outcome*)

    Measures support primary outcomes

        Average rating for measures supports primary outcomes across participants using score from visual analysis

**Overall Rating for Measures Support Primary Outcomes** (select 0, 1, 2, or 3): □ **3** □ **2** □ **1** □ **0**

    Measures support secondary outcomes

        Average rating for measures support secondary outcomes across participants using score from visual analysis

**Overall Rating for Measures Support Secondary Outcomes** (select 0, 1, 2, or 3): □ **3** □ **2** □ **1** □ **0**

    D. Educational/Clinical Significance

    Categorical diagnosis data

        Baseline phase: Diagnostic information regarding inclusion into the study presented

            □ Yes, □ No, □ Unknown

        Intervention phase: Positive change in diagnostic criteria from baseline to intervention

            □ Yes, □ No, □ Unknown

        Follow-up phase: Positive change in diagnostic criteria from intervention to follow-up

            □ Yes, □ No, □ Unknown

    Outcomes assessed via continuous variables

        Intervention phase: Positive change in percentage of participants showing clinical improvement from baseline to intervention

            □ Yes, □ No, □ Unknown

        Follow-up: Positive change in number of participants showing clinical improvement from intervention to follow-up

            □ Yes, □ No, □ Unknown

*(continued)*

**Table 37.2** *Continued*

Subjective evaluation

    Baseline phase: Importance of behavior change is evaluated

        □ Yes, □ No, □ Unknown

    Intervention phase: Importance of behavior change from baseline to intervention is evaluated positively by individuals in direct contact with the participant

        □ Yes, □ No, □ Unknown

    Follow- up: Importance of behavior change from intervention to follow-up is evaluated positively by individuals in direct contact with the participant

        □ Yes, □ No, □ Unknown

  Social comparison

    Baseline phase: Participant's behavior is compared to normative data

        □ Yes, □ No, □ Unknown

    Intervention phase: Participant's behavior has improved from baseline to intervention when compared to normative data

        □ Yes, □ No, □ Unknown

    Follow-up: Participant's behavior has improved from intervention to follow-up when compared to normative data

        □ Yes, □ No, □ Unknown

**Rating for Educational/Clinical Significance** (select 0, 1, 2, or 3): □ **3** □ **2** □ **1** □ **0**

  E. Identifiable Components (*identical to corresponding section in Table 37.1*)

**Rating for Identifiable Components** (select 0, 1, 2, or 3): □ **3** □ **2** □ **1** □ **0**

  F. Implementation Fidelity

    Participant 1 (*would rate for each participant*)

      Evidence of acceptable adherence (*identical to corresponding section in Table 37.1*)

      Manualization (select all that apply) (*identical to corresponding section in Table 37.1*)

      Adaptation procedures are specified (select one): □ Yes □ No □ Unknown

**Rating for Implementation Fidelity for Participant 1** (select 0, 1, 2, or 3): □ **3** □ **2** □ **1** □ **0**

**Average Fidelity Rating across Participants:**

**Overall Rating for Fidelity** (select 0, 1, 2, or 3): □ **3** □ **2** □ **1** □ **0**

  G. Replication

    Same intervention

      □ Yes, □ No, □ Unknown

    Same target problem

      □ Yes, □ No, □ Unknown

    Independent evaluation

      □ Yes, □ No, □ Unknown

**Rating for Replication** (select 0, 1, 2, or 3): □ **3** □ **2** □ **1** □ **0**

  H. Site of Implementation (*identical to corresponding section in Table 37.1*)

**Rating for Site Implementation** (select 0, 1, 2, or 3): □ **3** □ **2** □ **1** □ **0**

  I. Follow-up Assessment (*identical to corresponding section in Table 37.1*)

**Rating for Follow-up Up Assessment** (select 0, 1, 2, or 3): □ **3** □ **2** □ **1** □ **0**

III. Other Descriptive or Supplemental Criteria to Consider

  A. External Validity Indicators (*identical to corresponding section in Table 37.1*)

*Source:* From *Procedural and Coding Manual* by Task Force on Evidence-Based Interventions in School Psychology, June 2, 2003. Retrieved from http://www.sp-ebi.org/_working files /EBImanual1.pdf.Adapted with permission from the Procedural and Coding Manual of the Task Force on Evidence-Based Interventions in School Psychology.

Stoiber, 2002; Lonigan, Elbert, & Johnson, 1998). An efficacy study entails examination of an intervention's effect on specific outcome variables under tightly controlled, laboratory conditions using precise research methodology, including randomization, control groups, and well-defined inclusion criteria (Lonigan et al., 1998). Alternatively, effectiveness research denotes intervention studies carried out in naturalistic settings under authentic practice conditions (Fonagy et al., 2002). There are advantages and disadvantages inherent in each of these methods of inquiry. Efficacy research allows for greater understanding of the causal mechanisms contributing to intervention outcomes (Stoiber & Reinemann, 2001). However, the conditions of efficacy research may only minimally resemble those of the actual settings in which the intervention would ultimately be implemented. The heterogeneity of intervention targets and agents, the fidelity with which the intervention is applied, and many other setting-specific factors can all moderate the effect of interventions. Such "noise" factors go unexamined by studies that employ restricted samples while isolating the effect of the intervention variables of interest, and it cannot be assumed that treatments supported by efficacy studies will fit neatly into the ecology of real-world situations or engender a similar degree of change with diverse intervention agents and recipients (Chambless & Ollendick, 2001; Chorpita, 2003). Because such contextual variables often dictate the degree to which interventions succeed, the external validity of interventions tested under controlled conditions and then applied to real-world settings has been questioned (Ringeisen et al., 2003). The findings of applied effectiveness research, conversely, possess greater ecological validity and generalizability. Yet inferences drawn from findings of effectiveness studies are limited by inevitable threats to internal validity present in these designs (Levin et al., 2003; Stoiber & Reinemann, 2001).

To address the issue of efficacy versus effectiveness, researchers have endorsed a framework for the identification of EBIs that merges the two approaches and considers contextual variables. Controlled trials will always remain a necessity in establishing support for a particular intervention or approach (Levin et al., 2003). However, Kratochwill and Shernoff (2003) have argued that the *evidence-based* designation should be granted only to interventions that have demonstrated significant effects under the conditions of implementation and evaluation in practice, citing the four-tiered framework advanced by Chorpita (2003) as a means of establishing the generalizability of intervention effects that account for influential contextual variables. Under this framework, the initial efficacy study is just one factor in the ultimate determination of an intervention's applicability. Initial field-based studies would examine the degree to which effects are maintained in the real-world setting, along with potential confounds that arise and the feasibility of implementation (transportability studies). Subsequently, the effect of the intervention in practice, at various stages of removal from the original researcher and intervention agents, would be assessed (dissemination and system evaluations studies). Under this framework, efficacy is a necessary, but not sufficient, condition for establishing an intervention's evidence base (Chorpita, 2003; Lonigan et al., 1998), and smaller-scale practitioner-conducted research can play an important role in providing additional support, beyond controlled trials, for an intervention.

It has also been argued that efforts to identify efficacious treatments pay insufficient attention to the role of psychological theory in intervention development, evaluation, and application (Hughes, 2000). The argument underscores the importance of understanding the causal mechanisms that bring about change when addressed through intervention. According to Hughes, the most scientifically sound interventions will possess not only treatment efficacy but a strong underlying theoretical conceptualization as well:

> Without the knowledge of the mechanisms responsible for treatment benefits, the psychologist cannot make intelligent decisions regarding how to tailor the intervention in practice settings that differ from research psychotherapy settings and with clients who also differ from clients involved in efficacy studies. (p. 304)

This argument is germane to the practice of neuropsychology in the schools, as many neuropsychological inferences have been based largely on *theorized* links between the brain and behavior, and neuropsychologists may ascribe greater consequence to brain-behavior considerations in intervention development than those practicing from alternative (and sometimes theoretically based) paradigms. In fact, Kratochwill and Stoiber (2002) hypothesized the emergence of theoretical schisms within the field of school psychology as one possible trajectory of the EBI movement. Such a scenario might occur if interventions aligned with certain theoretical approaches are consistently found to possess greater empirical evidence than those associated with other orientations. From an integrative service delivery perspective, school neuropsychologists should certainly hope to avoid such a schism from what could be perceived as complementary bases of practice. As discussed, contemporary neuropsychological principles are compatible with those that distinguish other psychological traditions. Discounting neurobiological explanations would serve to limit the intervention options available to address the problems learners encounter. Yet the potential for conflict underscores the necessity that school-based neuropsychologists demonstrate both the efficacy and effectiveness of their practices; this might be the case even more for neuropsychologists given lingering skepticism over the application of neuropsychological theory and practice to education (Gaddes & Edgell, 1994).

What evidence exists for the effectiveness of school neuropsychological interventions? To answer this question, it may help to clarify what qualifies as a neuropsychological intervention, because the understanding of this concept is often unclear (Eslinger & Oliveri, 2002). Some neuropsychological interventions were developed specifically to accommodate or rehabilitate individuals' neuropsychological functioning (e.g., individualized learning strategies). These are typically categorized as either compensatory, remedial, or a combination of these two approaches (D'Amato et al., 1999; Rothlisberg et al., 2003). Other interventions, though rooted in what we know about the brain, learning, or behavior, do not explicitly target neuropsychological functions per se. A range of evidence-based approaches to the remediation of reading disorders (e.g., phonological awareness instruction), for example, is available to educators (Joseph, this volume; Lyon et al., 2003; Shaywitz, 2003). Such methods are generally neither unique to neuropsychology nor differentially selected on the basis of neuropsychological strengths and deficits, even though in most cases, they have been informed by neurocognitive research. In this respect, many interventions referred to as neuropsychological, whether directed toward children with neurodevelopmental disorders, TBI, or more common learning disabilities, borrow from or adopt the methods of other psychological paradigms. The effective school neuropsychologist will typically recommend interventions or strategies that draw from several psychological traditions, often simultaneously (D'Amato & Rothlisberg, 1992, 1997).

The current evidence supporting school-based neuropsychological interventions is modest but growing. The chapters of this volume provide a wealth of intervention and programming suggestions designed to address difficult learner problems that school psychological practitioners will face, some possessing a stronger research base than others. In general, however, the question of empirical support is difficult to answer given the range of neuropsychological disorders and the diversity of treatment approaches available. Intervention in lower-incidence child problems, such as TBI, tends to be more closely associated with neuropsychology. Yet intervention research in this area has not been shown to be especially persuasive.

The field of neuropsychology has, to an extent, responded in kind to the evidence-based movement with internal appeals for a more scientific and empirical approach (e.g., Eslinger & Oliveri, 2002) and evaluation of the evidence underlying particular areas of practice. For instance, several syntheses of the support for cognitive rehabilitation in adult patients with acquired brain injury have been published (e.g., Carney, Chestnut, et al., 1999; Chestnut et al., 1999; Cicerone et al., 2000). Few systematic studies of neuropsychological practices with children have been conducted, however, and studies of neuropsychology practice in schools are rare (Gaddes & Edgell, 1994). The vast majority of child-based intervention recommendations, though based on clinical experience and anecdotal evidence of success, have lacked rigorous empirical validation (D'Amato et al., 1999).

Carney, du Coudray, et al. (1999) synthesized a variety of child-focused intervention research in the area of learners with TBI. These authors reviewed the support for five separate aspects of programs designed to meet the treatment needs of children with acquired brain injury, including the efficacy of special education programs for children with TBI and family support interventions. Based on their review, they concluded that interventions relied more on clinical experience than any empirical data. The authors characterized the studies reviewed as suffering from methodological flaws and generally of experimental designs incapable of providing convincing evidence of intervention effectiveness. They found no randomized controlled trials and few comparative studies in the body of selected research described as primarily exploratory. The authors expressed the need not only for controlled studies but also for longitudinal studies comparing the course of children with and without TBI, and they criticized the common practice of pooling children with diverse impairments into study samples. Evaluations of clinic-based programs displayed variable results and typically lacked the rigor necessary for generalization. Notably few studies were found on school-based special education programs delivered by personnel trained in providing services to students with TBI. This is obviously an understudied area; school neuropsychologists can take the initiative both to contribute to the development of high-quality programs in this area (e.g., Clark & Hostetter, 1995) and to evaluate program outcomes. Carney, du Coudray, et al. (1999) also found no randomized controlled trials comparing families who received supports with those who received no supports. This represents another area of needed research given the impact family variables have on outcomes for both learners and their family members (Prentiss, 1997). Moreover, schools sometimes fail to offer the family-centered services that are required for learners with severe disabilities.

Such findings signal the necessity of documenting the effectiveness of school neuropsychological interventions while improving on the methodological limitations of past research. Independent replication of research into promising interventions and programs will also be essential. Of note is that the Division 16 Task Force Procedural and Coding Manual rating criteria favor interventions tested in schools over those studied in nonschool settings. It is thus imperative that school neuropsychologists evaluate interventions and their effectiveness in the school context. In addition, neuropsychologists practicing in schools must deliver, recommend, and advocate for intervention approaches that possess the strongest evidence base. Preserving the commitment to evidence-based practice may be difficult in cases where the preferred approach or interventions strategy is unsupported.

## FUTURE DIRECTIONS

Based on its utility for learners who display neurodevelopmental impairment or who struggle with learning or behavioral problems that defy standard analysis and solutions, the neuropsychological approach is certainly relevant to school-based practice. It also appears that it could become increasingly more important in the future for schools or districts to employ professionals who possess neuropsychological expertise (even as schools incorporate problem-solving models; D'Amato, Hammons, Terminie, & Dean, 1992). As our understanding of the relationship between the brain, learning, behavior, and school performance becomes more sophisticated, the psychologist versed in brain functioning will be increasingly valuable to schools striving to comprehensively meet both the educational and mental health needs of their students.

The place of neuropsychology in schools is not assured, however. Much of the future of neuropsychological practice in schools will depend on the empirical endeavors of neuropsychologists. The following are several potential objectives that, if met, will enhance the viability of neuropsychology in the schools; many of these can be traced back to expressed goals, discussed throughout this volume, for the fields of school neuropsychology and school psychology:

- Neuropsychological principles should be applied to an increasingly broader range of school-based problems. This may include using specialized knowledge of the brain to design prevention programs or encourage the facilitation of environments associated with optimal neuropsychological outcomes, while advocating against policies or conditions detrimental to neurological functioning (e.g., high-TBI-risk behaviors, environmental toxins, malnutrition).
- A proactive approach to practice should be stressed. For example, based on knowledge of the developmental course of brain injury, school neuropsychologists can help staff and parents prepare and develop plans to address behavioral and academic obstacles expected in learners with neurodevelopmental impairment before they emerge. School psychologists might also strive to play a greater role in prevention and intervention services directed toward *young* children (e.g., prereading groups formed from neuropsychological screening, behavior/social skills groups for individuals with nonverbal learning disabilities).
- Effective collaboration with families, school colleagues, and community resources is essential. The nature of this requirement is more extensive in schools

than in clinic-based neuropsychological services, which may involve less patient/family contact following a neuropsychological evaluation. The accessibility of school neuropsychologists must be much greater. Given the impact of family variables on children with severe problems and the likely unfamiliarity of many school staff with intervention approaches for such children and their diverse service needs, comprehensive services will be difficult to achieve (Prentiss, 1997). The formation of meaningful relationships is a must for neuropsychologists in the schools, not only to improve child outcomes but also to demystify practices that may be esoteric to many non-neuropsychologists. One aspect of effectively working with a range of stakeholders will involve the transfer of pertinent neuropsychological knowledge to parents or fellow staff through consultation. School neuropsychologists must consciously offer people-friendly services and avoid acquiring the reputation of being an isolated professional in the school. In addition, cooperation with medical personnel and professionals external to the school will help ensure the most advantageous outcomes for learners and should be promoted.

• Psychologists should function as scientist-practitioners in the true sense of the term. In the face of continued failure to uncover aptitude-treatment interactions (Reschly & Ysseldyke, 2002), it is imperative that practitioners not only choose interventions backed by research but also systematically *evaluate* the outcomes of their services, focusing as much on program evaluation as on assessment, and rely less on subjective evidence of success. Although clinic-based neuropsychologists may offer recommendations for school personnel based on evaluation findings, school-based practitioners, with daily access to learners and classrooms, are in a position to monitor progress toward goals and accordingly adjust the components or intensity of interventions. Greater attention must be paid to selecting targets of intervention, to identifying key outcome indicators for learners, and to objectively judging attainment of those benchmarks. And because interventions are customarily carried out by professionals other than the psychologist, the assessment of treatment fidelity and acceptability among intervention agents is also valuable, as these variables can be consequential learner outcomes. Trainers of school neuropsychologists can promote a scientific approach to intervention by providing instruction in evaluation methodology and emphasizing the essential role of applying such methods to practice.

• To be seen as legitimate school practice, empirical study of neuropsychological methods must begin to occur *in* the schools on a larger scale. Although all practitioners cannot be expected to carry out field-based research, some can take the initiative to make what may be one of the largest contributions toward establishing the transportability of neuropsychological research findings from the laboratory into real-life settings. Such efforts will help answer the question. Is this intervention or program effective in the school setting? given the unique contextual variables of that school. School neuropsychologists should generate, disseminate, and advocate for those interventions that have garnered both laboratory and field-based support. In addition, responsibility for confirming the ecological validity of school-based neuropsychological assessment and intervention for infants, children, and adolescents lies largely with those who have access to the school. If neuropsychological interventions are to be successful with individuals, with groups of children and youth, and schoolwide, they must fit the natural ecology of each given school (Sheridan & Gutkin, 2000). For better or for worse, school neuropsychologists have a duty to be forthright about the limitations of neuropsychological assessment and intervention practices while striving to overcome them.

Additional issues relative to the practice of neuropsychology in schools bear consideration. The current and predicted future shortage of school psychologists and school psychology faculty has been a subject of considerable concern (McIntosh, 2004). The fact that few programs offer training in neuropsychology (D'Amato, Dean, & Holloway, 1987; Leavell & Lewandowski, 1988) compounds the difficulties related to provision of neuropsychological services in schools. Unanticipated legislative enactments or economic changes that might affect school psychological service delivery will likewise impact school neuropsychology (Curtis, Hunley, & Grier, 2004; Davis, McIntosh, Phelps, & Kehle, 2004). External forces could shape the demand for school neuropsychologists, along with the availability of neuropsychological specialization among school psychologists-in-training. Questions regarding the feasibility and cost-effectiveness of internal neuropsychological services also need to be addressed (Pelletier, Hiemenz, & Shapiro, 2004). Although it has been speculated here and elsewhere how neuropsychology can be incorporated into school-based psychological service delivery, it is uncertain how neuropsychological practice will look in schools given recent changes in the law, society, and the world.

**Evaluating School Neuropsychological Research: An Illustrative Example**

For the purpose of illustrating the standards by which intervention research will be judged in the future, an evaluation of a recently published study according to Procedural and Coding Manual criteria[1] for group-based designs is presented. Our goal here is notto critique the study chosen, but to demonstrate for researchers and practitioners the characteristics of intervention research that EBI reviewers will rate and that should be taken into consideration when choosing interventions.

Jepsen and VonThaden (2002) investigated the effects of a cognitive education program on cognitive, academic, and adaptive outcomes for adolescent students attending an alternative school due to neurological and developmental disabilities or Autism. This particular study serves as a useful exemplar because (1) the intervention described is based on neuropsychological principles and theory, (2) the population studied resembles the type of learner that school neuropsychologists may frequently focus on, and (3) the intervention was conducted in a school setting and targeted outcomes tied to scholastic functioning.

The intervention investigated by Jepsen and VonThaden (2002) incorporated cognitive education into special education classrooms of "adolescents with chronic, long-standing impairments whose limited academic progress and maladaptive behaviors prohibited them from participating in less restrictive public school programs" (p. 201). Materials from the Reitan Evaluation of Hemispheric Abilities and

---

[1] Note that the *Procedural and Coding Manual* indicates that designated members of the Task Force committees will evaluate intervention research and assign ratings. Specific "decision-making procedures" regarding this process are contained in the manual. The evaluation of research presented here has not been sanctioned by the Task Force, and it may be the case that Task Force-designated reviewers would arrive at conclusions with regard to the study's support that vary from our own. In addition, the authors of the study evaluated were not contacted to provide any information or data not reported in the article describing the study, and not all *Coding Manual* criteria are commented on.

Brain Improvement Training (REHABIT) curriculum were used as part of a mediated teaching approach emphasizing development of metacognitive skills. Forty-six participants were matched according to demographic attributes and diagnostic category (multiple handicaps, neurologically impaired, genetic disability, Pervasive Developmental Disorder) and randomly assigned to either treatment classrooms or to control classrooms. The intervention group received 1 hour per week of cognitive education for 9 months; the control group received typical academic programming. Change was assessed through pre-post testing using a cognitive measure (the Cognitive Assessment System [CAS]), an achievement measure (the Woodcock-Johnson Revised), and an adaptive measure (the Adaptive Behavior Scale). Significant between-group and within-individual effects were observed on each of the outcome measures at posttest.

The study (as presented in the article) would likely receive ratings of strong evidence or promising evidence on several Task Force criteria for group-based design (see Table 37.1). Strengths include the design (a random block design incorporating a "typical contact" comparison group was employed and clearly described), the statistically significant primary and secondary outcomes, the use of outcome measures demonstrating adequate reliability, and a test for moderator effects (by disability category). The extensive intervention agent training built into the program, along with the ongoing consultation to intervention agents provided, also represent favorable components. Although the sample was smaller than ideal, it could be perceived as acceptable given the relatively rare treatment population. In addition, the site of the intervention was a school rather than a clinical or other nonschool setting.

Although the data connected to primary and secondary outcomes appear promising, it is at the same time clear that, when considered against Task Force criteria, additional evidence and a more comprehensive report of the findings would lend greater support to these conclusions. Unmet EBI criteria subsequently described could prevent this intervention from receiving a favorable rating; although some of these criteria have only infrequently been met historically by researchers (especially the "supplementary" criteria), increasingly rigorous standards for intervention research necessitate their consideration. For example, higher ratings are given to studies that provide data displaying evidence of clinically/educationally significant change. No such data were provided for the current study (although the authors did report personal anecdotal observations of positive change in the way participants learned and approached academic tasks). Although pre-post gains on CAS scores were statistically significant, they remained very low (e.g., mean treatment group increase from 55.0 to 58.9). It is not clear how relevant these changes were to the stakeholders in that setting, or whether any classroom performance changes experienced were significant in the eyes of teachers. Task Force ratings also consider the magnitude of the intervention effects (beyond mere statistical significance). However, effect sizes for the gains in measures of cognition, achievement, and adaptive behavior were not reported in the paper.

The rating criteria underscore a preference for treatments that have standardized implementation procedures, or manualization. It is unclear whether the cognitive education intervention was manualized, however, potentially preventing consistent implementation or precise replication in future studies. According to the manual, another relevant criterion is the extent to which intervention components are explicitly described. In this study, the intervention was described in general terms. Several additional limitations were also present. The researchers failed to address a potential change agent effect or counterbalance change agents as part of the design. Generalizability was compromised because only minimal information was provided about the demographic characteristics of the participants and the school/community/geographic location where the intervention occurred. The sampling procedures, including the inclusion/exclusion criteria, were unclear (e.g., How/Why were these 46 learners chosen?). No information was provided regarding characteristics of the change agents, and few contextual features were reported that would allow for adaptation to other settings. In addition, no evaluation of separate/multiple components was attempted (although the authors did list this as a limitation in the research). The creators of the Procedural and Coding Manual emphasized the importance of evaluating intervention fidelity/adherence. Although regular consultation to change agents that occurred might have met this standard in part, it appears that no test for implementation fidelity was incorporated into the design. Evidence of consumer satisfaction or acceptance might also have strengthened the rationale for adopting this intervention elsewhere. These comments demonstrate only a cross-section of the complete criteria for evaluating studies.

It should be noted that the feasibility of incorporating all or most of the safeguards covered in the EBI manual will vary, and in fact may be extremely difficult or costly, based on the nature of the topic under study and setting constraints. In the defense of the authors whose study was reviewed here, several of the areas of limited evidence noted may have been the result of unavailable or unreported data due to journal page limitations or other unknown reasons. Obviously, these researchers were not privy to a copy of the manual, and as such it may be inappropriate or unfair to hold them up to standards that in reality are especially difficult to attain. Despite the idealistic nature of the Task Force standards, intervention researchers will benefit from becoming familiar with the criteria. The advantage of such a manual is that the criteria by which research will be judged are stated explicitly. The incorporation of the majority of research components covered in the manual into designs will ensure rigorous methodology and ultimately allow for greater confidence in the effectiveness of interventions under study, as well as in their adaptability and generalizability.

## CONCLUSION

The prescriptions for a flourishing specialty of school neuropsychology offered in this chapter are ambitious; there is much work to be done before widespread, evidence-based neuropsychological practice in schools becomes a reality. In fact, many areas of psychology are struggling to achieve evidence-based status. The relative treatment validity even of functional behavioral assessment, a widely accepted methodology, appears unconfirmed in light of recent research (Gresham et al., 2004). In any case, it is important to imagine the direction school neuropsychology could take and what must occur for its role to solidify. Undoubtedly, the information value of brain research to education will continue to grow for both neuropsychologically impaired and normal students (Byrnes & Fox, 1998). Future school neuropsychologists can help ensure that such advances extend to school practice and ultimately result in promising outcomes for children, families, and schools.

# REFERENCES

Bucy, J. E., Meyers, A. B., & Swerdlik, M. E. (2002). Best practices in working in full-service schools. In A. Thomas & J. Grimes (Eds.), *Best practices in school psychology IV* (pp. 281–291). Bethesda, MD: National Association of School Psychologists.

Byrnes, J. P., & Fox, N. A. (1998). The educational relevance of research in cognitive neuroscience. *Educational Psychology Research, 10*(3), 297–342.

Carlson, C. I., Paavola, J., & Talley, R. (1995). Historical, current, and future models of schools as health care delivery settings. *School Psychology Quarterly, 10*(3), 184–202.

Carney, N., Chestnut, R. M., Maynard, H., Mann, N. C., Patterson, P., & Helfland, M. (1999). Effect of cognitive rehabilitation on outcomes for persons with traumatic brain injury. *Journal of Head Trauma Rehabilitation, 14*(3), 277–307.

Carney, N., du Coudray, H., Davis-O'Reilly, C., Zimmer-Gembeck, M., Mann, N. C. & Helfand, M. (1999). *Rehabilitation for traumatic brain injury in children and adolescents* (Evidence report no. 2, supplement, Contract 290-97-0018 to Oregon Health Sciences University). Rockville, MD: Agency for Health Care Policy and Research.

Chambless, D. L., & Ollendick, T. H. (2001). Empirically supported psychological interventions: Controversies and evidence. *Annual Review of Psychology, 52*, 685–716.

Chestnut, R. M., Carney, N., Maynard, H., Mann, N. C., Patterson, P., & Helfland, M. (1999). Summary report: Evidence of the effectiveness of rehabilitation for persons with traumatic brain injury. *Journal of Head Trauma Rehabilitation, 14*(2), 176–188.

Chorpita, B. F. (2003). The frontier of evidence-based practice. In A. E. Kazdin & J. R. Weisz (Eds.), *Evidence-based psychotherapies for children and adolescents* (pp. 42–59). New York: Guilford Press.

Cicerone, K. D., Dahlberg, C., Kalmar, K., Langenbahn, D. M., Malec, J. F., Bergquist, T. F., et al. (2000). Evidence-based cognitive rehabilitation: Recommendations for clinical practice. *Archives of Physical Medicine Rehabilitation, 81*, 1596–1615.

Clark, E., & Hostetter, C. (1995). *Traumatic brain injury: Training manual for school personnel.* Longmont, CO: Sopris West.

Conoley, J. C., & Gutkin, T. B. (1995). Why didn't: Why doesn't: School psychology realize its promise? *Journal of School Psychology, 33*(3), 209–217.

Curtis, M. J., Hunley, S. A., & Grier, E. C. (2004). The status of school psychology: Implications of a major personnel shortage. *Psychology in the Schools, 41*(4), 431–442.

D'Amato, R. C. (1990). A neuropsychological approach to school psychology. *School Psychology Quarterly, 5*(2), 141–160.

D'Amato, R. C., Dean, R. S., & Holloway, A. F. (1987). A decade of employment trends in neuropsychology. *Professional Psychology: Research and Practice, 18*, 653–655.

D'Amato, R. C., Hammons, P. F., Terminie, T. J., & Dean, R. S. (1992). Neuropsychological training in American Psychological Association-Accredited and nonaccredited school psychology programs. *Journal of School Psychology, 30*, 175–183.

D'Amato, R. C., & Rothlisberg, B. A. (Eds.). (1997). *Psychological perspectives on intervention: A case study approach to prescriptions for change.* Prospect Heights, IL: Waveland Press.

D'Amato, R. C., Rothlisberg, B. A., & Leu Work, P. H. (1999). Neuropsychological assessment for intervention. In T. B. Gutkin & C. R. Reynolds (Eds.), *Handbook of school psychology* (3rd ed., pp. 452–475). New York: Wiley.

Davis, A. S., McIntosh, D. E., Phelps, L., & Kehle, T. J. (2004). Addressing the shortage of school psychologists: A summative overview. *Psychology in the Schools, 41*(4), 489–495.

Dawson, M., Cummings, J. A., Harrison, P. L., Short, R. J., Gorin, S., & Palomares, R. (2003). The 2002 multisite conference on the future of school psychology: Next steps. *School Psychology Quarterly, 18*(4), 497–509.

DeMers, S. T. (Ed.). (1995). School psychology and health care [Special issue]. *School Psychology Quarterly, 10*(3).

Deno, S. L. (2002). Problem solving as "best practice." In A. Thomas & J. Grimes (Eds.), *Best practices in school psychology IV* (pp. 37–55). Bethesda, MD: National Association of School Psychologists.

Dombrowski, S. C., Kamphaus, R. W., & Reynolds, C. R. (2004). After the demise of the discrepancy: Proposed learning disabilities diagnostic criteria. *Professional Psychology: Research and Practice, 35*(4), 364–372.

Ehrhardt-Padgett, G. N., Hatzichristou, C., Kitson, J., & Meyers, J. (2003). Awakening to a new dawn: Perspectives of the future of school psychology. *School Psychology Quarterly, 18*(4), 483–496.

Eslinger, P. J., & Oliveri, M. V. (2002). Approaching interventions clinically and scientifically. In P. J. Eslinger (Ed.), *Neuropsychological interventions: Clinical research and practice* (pp. 3–15). New York: Guilford Press.

Fonagy, P., Target, M., Cottrell, D., Phillips, J., & Kurtz, Z. (2002). *What works for whom? A critical review of treatments for children and adolescents.* New York: Guilford Press.

Franzen, M. D., & Wilhelm, K. L. (1998). Conceptual foundations of ecological validity in neuropsychological assessment. In R. J. Sbordone & C. J. Long (Eds.), *Ecological validity of neuropsychological testing* (pp. 91–112). Delray Beach, FL: St. Lucie Press.

Fuchs, D., Mock, D., Morgan, P. L., & Young, C. L. (2003). Responsiveness-to-intervention: Definitions, evidence, and implications for the learning disabilities construct. *Learning Disabilities Research and Practice, 18*(3), 157–171.

Gaddes, W. H. (1968). A neuropsychological approach to learning disorders. *Journal of Learning Disabilities, 1,* 523–534.

Gaddes, W. H. (1981). Neuropsychology, fact or mythology, educational help or hindrance? *School Psychology Review, 10*(3), 322–330.

Gaddes, W. H., & Edgell, D. (1994). *Learning disabilities and brain function: A neuropsychological approach* (3rd ed.). New York: Springer.

Gresham, F. M., McIntyre, L. L., Olson-Tinker, H., Dolstra, L., McLaughlin, V., & Van, M. (2004). Relevance of functional behavioral assessment research for school-based interventions and positive behavioral support. *Research in Developmental Disabilities, 25,* 19–37.

Gutkin, T. B. (2002). Evidence-based interventions in school psychology: The state of the art and directions for the future [Special issue]. *School Psychology Quarterly, 17*(4).

Haak, R. A., & Livingston, R. B. (1997). Treating traumatic brain injury in the school: Mandates and methods. In C. R. Reynolds & E. Fletcher-Janzen (Eds.), *Handbook of clinical child neuropsychology* (2nd ed., pp. 482–505). New York: Plenum Press.

Harrison, P. L., Cummings, J. A., Dawson, M., Short, R. J., Gorin, S., & Palomares, R. (2003). Responding to the needs of children, families, and schools: The 2002 multisite conference on the future of school psychology. *School Psychology Quarterly, 18*(4), 358–388.

Hartlage, L. C., & Templer, D. I. (1998). Ecological issues and child neuropsychological assessment. In R. J. Sbordone & C. J. Long (Eds.), *Ecological validity of neuropsychological testing* (pp. 301–313). Delray Beach, FL: St. Lucie Press.

Horton, A. M., Jr. (1997). Human neuropsychology: Current status. In A. M. Horton, Jr., D. Wedding, & J. Webster (Eds.), *The neuropsychology handbook* (2nd ed., pp. 3–29). New York: Springer.

Hughes, J. N. (2000). The essential role of theory in the science of treating children: Beyond empirically supported treatments. *Journal of School Psychology, 38*(4), 301–330.

Hynd, G. W. (Ed.). (1981). Neuropsychology in the schools [Special issue]. *School Psychology Review, 10*(3).

Hynd, G. W., & Hartlage, L. C. (1983). Brain-behavior relationships in children: Neuropsychological assessment in the schools. In G. W. Hynd (Ed.), *The school psychologist: An introduction* (pp. 231–267). Syracuse, NY: Syracuse University Press.

Hynd, G. W., & Obrzut, J. E. (1981). School neuropsychology. *Journal of School Psychology, 19*(1), 45–50.

Jepsen, R. H., & VonThaden, K. (2002). The effect of cognitive education on the performance of students with neurological developmental disabilities. *NeuroRehabilitation, 17,* 201–209.

Kalat, J. W., & Wurm, T. (1999). Implications of recent research in biological psychology for school psychology. In T. B. Gutkin & C. R. Reynolds (Eds.), *Handbook of school psychology* (3rd ed., pp. 271–290). New York: Wiley.

Kazdin, A. E., & Weisz, J. R. (2003). *Evidence-based psychotherapies for children and adolescents.* New York: Guilford Press.

Kratochwill, T. R., & Shernoff, E. S. (2003). Evidence-based practice: Promoting evidence-based interventions in school psychology. *School Psychology Quarterly, 18*(4), 389–408.

Kratochwill, T. R., & Stoiber, K. C. (2000a). Diversifying theory and science: Expanding boundaries of empirically supported interventions in schools. *Journal of School Psychology, 38,* 349–358.

Kratochwill, T. R., & Stoiber, K. C. (2000b). Empirically supported interventions in school psychology: Conceptual and practical issues: Part II. *School Psychology Quarterly, 15,* 233–253.

Kratochwill, T. R., & Stoiber, K. C. (2002). Evidence-based interventions in school psychology: Conceptual foundations of the procedural and coding manual of Division 16 and the Society for the Study of School Psychology Task Force. *School Psychology Quarterly, 17*(4), 34–389.

Leavell, C., & Lewandowski, L. (1988). Neuropsychology in the schools: A survey report. *School Psychology Review, 17*(1), 147–155.

Levin, J. R., O'Donnell, A. M., & Kratochwill, T. R. (2003). Educational/psychological intervention research. In W. M. Reynolds & G. E. Miller (Eds.), *Handbook of psychology: Vol. 7. Educational psychology* (pp. 557–581). Hoboken, NJ: Wiley.

Lonigan, C. J., Elbert, J. C., & Johnson, S. B. (1998). Empirically supported psychosocial interventions for children: An overview. *Journal of Clinical Child Psychology, 27*(2), 138–145.

Long, C. J. (1998). Neuropsychological tests: A look at our past and the impact that ecological issues may have on our future. In R. J. Sbordone & C. J. Long (Eds.), *Ecological validity of neuropsychological testing* (pp. 1–14). Delray Beach, FL: St. Lucie Press.

Lyon, G. R., Fletcher, J. M., & Barnes, M. C. (2003). Learning disabilities. In E. J. Mash & R. A. Barkley (Eds.), *Child psychopathology* (2nd ed., pp. 520–586). New York: Guilford Press.

McIntosh, D. E. (Ed.). (2004). Addressing the shortage of school psychologists [Special issue]. *Psychology in the Schools, 41*(4).

Nastasi, B. K. (2000). School psychologists as health-care providers in the 21st century: Conceptual framework, professional identity, and professional practice. *School Psychology Review, 29*(4), 540–554.

Nathan, P. E., & Gorman, J. M. (Eds.). (2002). *A guide to treatments that work* (2nd ed.). New York: Oxford University Press.

Orton, S. T. (1937). *Reading, writing, and speech problems in children.* New York: Norton.

Pelletier, S. L., Hiemenz, J. R., & Shapiro, M. B. (2004). The application of neuropsychology in the schools should not be called school neuropsychology: A rejoinder to Crespi and Cooke. *School Psychologist, 58*(1), 17–24.

Prentiss, D. (1997). *Pediatric brain injury and families: The parental experience.* Unpublished doctoral dissertation, University of Northern Colorado.

Reschly, D. J., & Gresham, F. M. (1989). Current neuropsychological diagnosis of learning problems: A leap of faith. In C. R. Reynolds & E. Fletcher-Janzen (Eds.), *Handbook of clinical child neuropsychology* (pp. 503–519). New York: Plenum Press.

Reschly, D. J., & Ysseldyke, J. E. (2002). Paradigm shift: The past is not the future. In A. Thomas & J. Grimes (Eds.), *Best practices in school psychology IV* (pp. 3–20). Bethesda, MD: National Association of School Psychologists.

Reynolds, C. R. (1981). Neuropsychological assessment and the habilitation of learning: Considerations in the search for the aptitude x treatment interaction. *School Psychology Review, 10*(3), 343–349.

Reynolds, C. R. (1986). Transactional models of intellectual development, yes: Deficit models of process remediation, no. *School Psychology Review, 15,* 256–260.

Reynolds, C. R. (1997). Measurement and statistical problems in neuropsychological assessment of children. In C. R. Reynolds & E. Fletcher-Janzen (Eds.), *Handbook of clinical child neuropsychology* (2nd ed., pp. 180–203). New York: Plenum Press.

Ringeisen, H., Henderson, K., & Hoagwood, K. (2003). Context matters: Schools and the "research to practice gap" in children's mental health. *School Psychology Review, 32*(2), 153–168.

Roth, A. D., & Fonagy, P. (1996). What works for whom? *A critical review of psychotherapy research.* New York: Guilford Press.

Rothlisberg, B. A., D'Amato, R. C., & Palencia, B. N. (2003). Assessment of children for intervention planning following traumatic brain injury. In C. R. Reynolds & R. W. Kamphaus (Eds.), *Handbook of psychological and educational assessment of children: Intelligence, aptitude, and achievement* (2nd ed., pp. 685–706). New York: Guilford Press.

Sattler, J. M., & D'Amato, R. C. (2002). Brain injuries: Formal batteries and informal measures. In J. M. Sattler (Ed.), *Assessment of children: Behavioral and clinical applications* (4th ed., pp. 440–469). San Diego, CA: Jerome M. Sattler.

Sbordone, R. J. (1998). Ecological validity: Some critical issues for the neuropsychologist. In R. J. Sbordone & C. J. Long (Eds.), *Ecological validity of neuropsychological testing* (pp. 15–42). Delray Beach, FL: St. Lucie Press.

Shaywitz, S. (2003). *Overcoming dyslexia: A new and complete science-based program for reading problems at any level.* New York: Alfred A. Knopf.

Sheridan, S. M., & D'Amato, R. C. (2003/2004). Proceedings of the multisite conference on the future of school psychology. Published in *School Psychology Quarterly, 18*(4), 347–454 and *School Psychology Review, 33*(1), 1–126.

Sheridan, S. M., & Gutkin, T. B. (2000). The ecology of school psychology: Examining and changing our paradigm for the 21st century. *School Psychology Review, 29*(4), 485–502.

Stoiber, K. C., & Kratochwill, T. K. (2000). Empirically supported interventions in schools: Rationale and methodological issues: Part I. *School Psychology Quarterly, 15,* 75–115.

Stoiber, K. C., & Reinemann, D. H. S. (2001). All interventions are not created equal: The case against an anything goes approach to psychotherapy. *School Psychology Quarterly, 16*(2), 229–238.

Task Force on Evidence-Based Interventions in School Psychology. (2003, June 2). *Procedural and coding manual.* Retrieved January 20, 2004, from http://www.sp-ebi.org /_working files/EBImanual1.pdf.

Teeter, P. A., & Semrud-Clikeman, M. (1997). *Child neuropsychology: Assessment and interventions for neurodevelopmental disorders.* Boston: Allen & Bacon.

Telzrow, C. F. (1985). The science and speculation of rehabilitation in developmental neuropsychological disorders. In L. C. Hartlage & C. F. Telzrow (Eds.), *The neuropsychology of individual differences: A developmental perspective* (pp. 271–307). New York: Plenum Press.

Tharinger, D. (1995). Roles for psychologists in emerging models of school-related health and mental health services. *School Psychology Quarterly, 10*(3), 203–316.

Vaughn, S., & Fuchs, L. S. (2003). Redefining learning disabilities as inadequate response to instruction: The promise and potential problems. *Learning Disabilities Research and Practice, 18*(3), 137–146.

Walker, N. W., Boling, M. S., & Cobb, H. (1999). The pediatric neuropsychologist: Training of school psychologists in neuropsychology and brain injury: Results of a national survey of training programs. *Child Neuropsychology, 5*(2), 137–142.

Whitten, J. C., D'Amato, R. C., & Chittooran, M. M. (1992). A neuropsychological approach to intervention. In R. C. D'Amato & B. A. Rothlisberg (Eds.), *Psychological perspectives on intervention: A case study approach to prescriptions for change* (pp. 112–136). Prospect Heights, IL: Waveland Press.

Whitten, J. C., D'Amato, R. C., & Chittooran, M. M. (1997). A neuropsychological approach to intervention. In R. C. D'Amato & B. A. Rothlisberg (Eds.), *Psychological perspectives on intervention: A case study approach to prescriptions for change* (pbk. ed., pp. 112136). Prospect Heights, IL: Waveland Press.

# Appendix A: Sample Neuropsychological Questionnaire

MICHAEL J. TINCUP, RIK CARL D'AMATO,
JONATHAN E. TITLEY, and RAYMOND S. DEAN

UNIVERSITY *of*
## NORTHERN COLORADO

## Neuropsychological Questionnaire

**Neuropsychology Laboratory**
Psychological Services Clinic
College of Education and Behavioral Sciences

Michael J. Tincup, Rik Carl D'Amato, Jonathan E. Titley, and Raymond S. Dean

### *Child Version*

---

**Instructions**

This form is to be completed via an interview with a school neuropsychologist or individually and then reviewed. One copy is provided to the parent(s)/guardian and another copy is used by the neuropsychologist during the interview. Both are collected at the end of the interview. All information is confidential and will only be used by appropriate school or clinic personnel. In some instances, you may have difficulty remembering specific information. If this is the case, please write in "CR" for cannot remember. The information that you provide will aid in the evaluation of your child, so please attempt to fully complete the questionnaire. When completed, kindly return the form to the appropriate office.

---

## DEMOGRAPHICS & HOME ENVIRONMENT

**Child's Name:** _____ **Sex:** _____
                     Last          First          Middle

**Home Address:** _____
                  Street                City & State           Zip Code

**Date of Birth:** _____ **Age:** _____ **Home Telephone:** _____

**Child's School:** _____ **Grade:** _____ **Date Tested:** _____

**Race:** _____ **Primary Language Spoken at Home** _____

**Please place a check on the appropriate line that describes your child:**

|  | Adults with whom child is living | Nonresident adults involved with child |
|---|---|---|
| Natural Mother | _____ | _____ |
| Natural Father | _____ | _____ |
| Stepmother | _____ | _____ |
| Stepfather | _____ | _____ |
| Adoptive Mother | _____ | _____ |
| Adoptive Father | _____ | _____ |
| Grandparents | _____ | _____ |
| Other | _____ | _____ |

**With regard to the adults who live with the child and/or nonresidential adults associated with the child, please provide the following information:**

**Individuals Living with the Child:**

Father's or Stepfather's Name: _____ Age: _____

Occupation: _____ Educational Level: _____

Employer: _____ Office Telephone: _____

Mother's or Stepmother's Name: _____ Age: _____

Occupation: _____ Educational Level: _____

Employer: _____ Office Telephone: _____

**Individuals Not Living with the Child:**

Nonresident's Name: _____ Age: _____

Occupation: _____ Educational Level: _____

Extent of involvement with child: _____

_____

_____

_____

Nonresident's Name: _____ Age: _____

Occupation: _____ Educational Level: _____

Extent of involvement with child: _____

_____

_____

_____

**Please list all of the children in the family beginning with the eldest and working down to the youngest. Briefly describe any difficulties associated with each child (e.g. medical, social, academic, or behavioral). Place a check mark next to the name of the child currently being assessed.**

| Name of Child | Sex | Age | Relationship | Difficulties |
|---|---|---|---|---|
| _____ | ____ | ____ | _____ | _____ |
| _____ | ____ | ____ | _____ | _____ |
| _____ | ____ | ____ | _____ | _____ |
| _____ | ____ | ____ | _____ | _____ |
| _____ | ____ | ____ | _____ | _____ |

## REASON FOR REFERRAL

**Describe below the difficulties or reasons for which your child is being assessed. Please include a brief history.**

_____

_____

_____

_____

_____

_____

_____

_____

_____

Referred by: _____

## PREGNANCY, BIRTH, AND DEVELOPMENT

**Please answer the following questions in relation to the child currently being assessed.**

### Pregnancy

1. Did the mother have any accidents or infections during pregnancy? [ YES  NO ] If yes, please explain:

_____

_____

_____

2. Was medication taken during pregnancy? [ YES  NO ] If yes, please list and explain:

_____

_____

3. Did the mother smoke during pregnancy? [ YES  NO ] If yes, indicate average number of cigarettes per day: _____

4. Did the mother consume alcohol during pregnancy? [ YES  NO ] If yes, indicate how often (for example, 1 drink a day, week, month, etc.): _____

_____ .

**Birth and Postnatal**

1. Was he/she a full term baby? [ YES  NO ] If no, how many weeks premature or postmature (overdue) was he/she? Premature: _____weeks  Postmature: _____weeks.

2. Type of delivery (please check one):     Caesarean _____          Normal _____

3. Any unusual characteristics of delivery (for example, breech or induced)? [ YES  NO ] If yes, please specify: _____

_____

_____

4. What was his/her birthweight? _____ lbs. _____ oz(s).

5. Was there mention of anoxia (interruption of baby's breathing at birth)? [ YES  NO ]

6. Was there any evidence to suggest the possibility of injury to him/her before or during birth? [ YES  NO ] If yes, please describe: _____

_____

_____

7. Was there an incubation period? [ YES  NO ] If yes, how long: _____

8. Was there any delay in establishing a successful feeding formula? [ YES  NO ] If yes, how long was the delay and what were the results: _____

_____

_____

9. Was there significant weight loss? [ YES  NO ]

10. Excessive crying? [ YES  NO ]

11. Was the baby normally happy _____ ; upset _____ ; nervous _____ ; other _____

**<u>Development</u>**

**Please rate your child on the following skills (place check on line):**

| | Good | Average | Poor |
|---|---|---|---|
| Walking | ____ | ____ | ____ |
| Running | ____ | ____ | ____ |
| Jumping | ____ | ____ | ____ |
| Skipping | ____ | ____ | ____ |
| Throwing | ____ | ____ | ____ |
| Catching | ____ | ____ | ____ |
| Buttoning | ____ | ____ | ____ |
| Tying Shoelaces | ____ | ____ | ____ |
| Cutting w/ Scissors | ____ | ____ | ____ |
| Athletic Ability | ____ | ____ | ____ |

**If you can recall the age at which your child reached the following developmental milestones, please fill in the column under age. If you cannot recall, check one of the items at the right (early, average, or late).**

| | Age (months) | Early | Average | Late |
|---|---|---|---|---|
| Smiled | _____ | ___ | ___ | ___ |
| Sat without support | _____ | ___ | ___ | ___ |
| Crawled | _____ | ___ | ___ | ___ |
| Stood without support | _____ | ___ | ___ | ___ |
| Walked without assistance | _____ | ___ | ___ | ___ |
| Spoke first words (no mama/dada) | _____ | ___ | ___ | ___ |
| Said phrases | _____ | ___ | ___ | ___ |
| Pronunciation clear to strangers | _____ | ___ | ___ | ___ |
| Spoke in sentences | _____ | ___ | ___ | ___ |
| Toilet trained | _____ | ___ | ___ | ___ |
| Rode a bike w/out training wheels | _____ | ___ | ___ | ___ |
| Buttoned clothing | _____ | ___ | ___ | ___ |
| Tied shoelaces | _____ | ___ | ___ | ___ |
| Named colors | _____ | ___ | ___ | ___ |
| Said alphabet in order | _____ | ___ | ___ | ___ |
| Learned to read | _____ | ___ | ___ | ___ |

## ACADEMICS

**For each year (current and last year), place a check on the line which best describes your child's academic performance in each area.**

### Current Year

|           | Poor | Weak | Average | Good | Excellent |
|-----------|------|------|---------|------|-----------|
| Reading   | ___  | ___  | ___     | ___  | ___       |
| Arithmetic| ___  | ___  | ___     | ___  | ___       |
| Spelling  | ___  | ___  | ___     | ___  | ___       |
| Writing   | ___  | ___  | ___     | ___  | ___       |

### Last Year

|           | Poor | Weak | Average | Good | Excellent |
|-----------|------|------|---------|------|-----------|
| Reading   | ___  | ___  | ___     | ___  | ___       |
| Arithmetic| ___  | ___  | ___     | ___  | ___       |
| Spelling  | ___  | ___  | ___     | ___  | ___       |
| Writing   | ___  | ___  | ___     | ___  | ___       |

**Please answer the following questions.**

Did your child attend pre-school? [ YES  NO ] If yes, how many years? _____

Age your child entered first grade: _____

Has your child repeated any grades? [ YES  NO ] If yes, which one(s): _____

**Please list the schools attended by your child:**

| Name and Location | Grades | Dates Attended |
|-------------------|--------|----------------|
| _____ | _____ | _____ |
| _____ | _____ | _____ |
| _____ | _____ | _____ |
| _____ | _____ | _____ |
| _____ | _____ | _____ |
| _____ | _____ | _____ |
| _____ | _____ | _____ |

## ACCOMPLISHMENTS AND INTERESTS

What are your child's main hobbies and interests? _____

_____

_____

What are your child's areas of greatest accomplishment? _____

_____

_____

What does your child enjoy doing most? _____

_____

_____

What does your child dislike doing most? _____

_____

_____

## SOCIAL HISTORY

Describe your child's relationship with his/her father/stepfather, and what forms of discipline are most often used? _____

_____

Describe your child's relationship with his/her mother/stepmother, and what forms of discipline are most often used? _____

_____

Describe your child's relationship with his or her brothers and sisters: _____

_____

_____

Has your child been in contact with any unusual or odd family, friends, neighborhood, or community influences? [ YES  NO ] If yes, please describe: _____

_____

_____

_____

Describe your child's relationships with peers and close friends: _____

_____

_____

Describe the neighborhood in which your child lives (safety, opportunities for play or recreation, facilities, etc.): _____

_____

_____

**MEDICAL  HISTORY** **(Completed by Parent or Guardian)**

Child's present height, weight and general appearance: _____

_____

**Please indicate which of the following diseases your child has had:**

| Disease | Please circle one | If yes, please give child's age, approximate amount of time out of school, and describe any reaction to the illness. |
|---|---|---|
| Measles | [ YES  NO ] | |
| Whooping Cough | [ YES  NO ] | |
| Mumps | [ YES  NO ] | |
| Chicken Pox | [ YES  NO ] | |
| Pneumonia | [ YES  NO ] | |
| Diphtheria | [ YES  NO ] | |
| Scarlet Fever | [ YES  NO ] | |
| Rheumatic Fever | [ YES  NO ] | |
| Polio | [ YES  NO ] | |
| Influenza | [ YES  NO ] | |

Has your child had any other diseases? [ YES  NO ] If yes, please describe: _____

_____

_____

_____

**If your child's medical history includes any of the following, please note the age when the incident or illness occurred and any other pertinent information.**

Any operations? [ YES  NO ] If yes, please explain: _____

_____

_____

_____

Any hospitalization(s) for illness(es) other than operations? [ YES  NO ] If yes, please explain:

_____

_____

_____

Any head injuries? [ YES  NO ] If yes, please indicate whether or not your child lost consciousness and describe: _____

_____

_____

_____

Has your child displayed any of the following: persistent headaches; dizziness; insomnia; change in weight; or altered states of consciousness (for example, changes in taste or smell, or hallucinations)? [ YES  NO ] If yes, please explain: _____

_____

_____

Has your child ever had an extremely high fever? [ YES  NO ] If yes, please give age and describe:

_____

_____

Any convulsions? [ YES  NO ] If yes, please explain: _____

_____

_____

Any allergies? [ YES  NO ] If yes, please explain: _____

_____

Any eye or ear problems? [ YES  NO ] If yes, please explain: _____

_____

Any persistent or present medical problems experienced by your child? [ YES  NO ] If yes, please explain duration and extent of problem(s): _____

_____

_____

Are any medication(s) currently being taken by your child? [ YES  NO ] If yes, please list and explain:

_____

_____

Has your child ever been administered oxygen? [ YES  NO ] If yes, please explain: _____

_____

_____

Any history of abuse? [ YES  NO ] If yes, please explain severity and duration: _____

_____

_____

Any drug use (narcotics, barbiturates, psychedelics)? [ YES  NO ] If yes, please list and explain:

_____

_____

Were there any orthopedic problems which affected the child's crawling, walking or other kind of movement? [ YES  NO ] If yes, what type of disorder (Foot, arm, leg, other): _____

_____

Any contact with chemicals at school, work, or home? (pesticides, heavy metals, gases)? [ YES  NO ] If yes, please explain: _____

_____

Any family history of neurological or psychiatric illness? [ YES  NO ] If yes, please list and explain:

_____

_____

Any history of seizures in the family? [ YES  NO ]

Child's subjective complaints (current problems in child's own words): _____

_____

_____

**MEDICAL HISTORY** (Completed by School Neuropsychologist NOT Parent)

Provisional diagnosis: _____

Treatments: _____

EEG: _____

Skull X-ray: _____

CT/MRI scan: _____

**CURRENT FUNCTIONING** (Completed by Parent or Guardian)

**Please indicate which of the following difficulties your child has experienced and explain for each area the outcome of his or her problem:**

**Motor Functioning**

A.  Evidence of paralysis, muscle weakness or lack of coordination?  (Parent may give examples, such as difficulty in driving, fatigue, loss of bowel or bladder control, or right-left disorientation) [ YES  NO ]

_____

B.  Presence of tremors in the limbs? [ YES  NO ] _____

_____

C.  Difficulties with gait or posture (for example, stiffness, restricted range of movement)? [ YES  NO ]

_____

D.  Evidence of psychomotor retardation or hyperactivity? [ YES  NO ] _____

_____

**Auditory Functioning**

A.  Any hearing loss? [ YES  NO ] _____

B.  Disturbed by high pitched sounds/ringing in the head? [ YES  NO] _____

_____

C.  Difficulties perceiving simple pitch relationships (for example, tone deaf) or inability to reproduce basic rhythms (for example, cannot tap out time)? [ YES  NO ] _____

_____

## Tactile Functioning

A.  Any complaints of loss of sensation (for example, numbness, pins and needles; sense of touch not as discriminating; less sensitive to pain or change in temperatures)? [ YES  NO ] _____

## Visuo-Spatial Functioning

A.  Any visual problems (for example, double vision)? [ YES  NO ] _____

B.  Any difficulties in spatial orientation (for example, gets lost easily)? [ YES  NO ] _____

C.  Any experiences of distortions of body image (for example, change in size of the hands) or other visual hallucinations (for example, distortion of shape and distance of furniture)? [ YES  NO ] _____

## Language Ability

A.  Any problems in comprehending speech and responding to directions? [ YES  NO ] _____

B.  Any difficulties in verbal fluency (for example, inability to find the right word; garrulous speech; slurring of words)? [ YES  NO ] _____

## Memory Processes

A.  Has the child noticed a general deterioration in memory or only specific problems for certain materials (for example, able to recognize faces but cannot remember names)? [ YES  NO ] _____

B.  Adequacy of short-term memory (for example, ability to retain a new telephone number while phoning)? _____

C.  Adequacy of recent memory (for example, can remember day to day events; able to learn new information)? _____

D. Adequacy of remote memory (for example, can remember historical facts and recollect childhood incidents)? _____

_____

**Higher Neurocognitive Processes**

A. Any deterioration in general intelligence functioning in your child? [ YES  NO ] _____

_____

_____

B. Does you child have more difficulty coping at school? [ YES  NO ] _____

_____

_____

C. Is there any loss of efficiency of planning, organizing, and problem-solving? [ YES  NO ] _____

_____

_____

**Personality Organization**

A. Have you, relatives, or friends noticed any personality change/deterioration in your child? [ YES  NO ]

_____

  i. thinking disorder: _____

  ii. mood disorder (bizarre; agitated): _____

  iii. behavior (bizarre; agitated): _____

B. Self-concept (how does the child feel about themselves and their problems)? _____

_____

C. Any changes in sexual behavior (is you child sexually active or extremely interested in sex)?
   [ YES  NO ] _____

_____

D. How does the child function in unstructured situations (for example, what do they do in their free time? Has there been any loss of initiative?) _____

_____

## Behavior

**Please check any of the following behaviors or tendencies that are typical of your child:**

| | | |
|---|---|---|
| ___ Overeats | ___ Impulsive reactions | ___ Loss of control |
| ___ Suicide attempts | ___ Withdrawal | ___ Nervous habits |
| ___ Difficulty concentrating | ___ Vomiting | ___ Difficulty sleeping |
| ___ Takes too many risks | ___ Lazy | ___ Eating problems |
| ___ Aggressive behavior | ___ Crying excessively | ___ Outbursts of anger |
| ___ Drinks alcohol | ___ Fitful sleep | ___ Nausea |

## SUPPLEMENTARY INFORMATION (Completed by Parent or Guardian)

**Please list the names, positions, and addresses of any other professionals consulted, why they were consulted, as well as the dates of the consultation(s):**

1. Name:_____  Date: _____

Address: _____

Position: _____  Reason: _____

2. Name:_____  Date: _____

Address: _____

Position: _____  Reason: _____

Has your child been tested previously? [ YES  NO ] If yes, please provide date(s) and test(s) used:

Date: _____  Test(s) administered: _____

Date: _____  Test(s) administered: _____

Date: _____  Test(s) administered: _____

Signature: _____  Date: _____

Print Name: _____

Relationship to Child: _____

Revised November 2004

# Appendix B: Sample Report of Psychological Examination

JANIECE POMPA

**SALT LAKE CITY SCHOOL DISTRICT**
**Department of Special Education**
**REPORT OF PSYCHOLOGICAL EXAMINATION**

**Name:** Suzy Kuger    **Date of Birth:** 10-28-95    **C.A.** 9-3    **Grade:** 4

**Date of Exam:** 11-1-2003    **School:** Poe Elementary

**Examiner:** Janiece Pompa, Ph.D., Licensed Psychologist

---

## REASON FOR REFERRAL

Suzy Kuger is a 9-year-old right-handed Caucasian female who was referred for psychological evaluation in order to generate treatment recommendations regarding her reading disability. At the time of the evaluation, Suzy was prescribed the following medications per day: 20 mg Adderall for attention-deficit hyperactivity disorder (ADHD), and 40 mg Zoloft for depression.

Early History: The history was given by Sandra Kuger, Suzy's mother. She stated that the pregnancy and Suzy's birth were normal. Mrs. Kuger stated that Suzy was "a good baby" who slept well. She achieved developmental milestones within normal limits, and displayed a normal activity level as an infant and a young child. She was described as "sweet-natured" but "willful."

School History: Mrs. Kuger reported that in preschool, Suzy's teachers had some difficulty managing her because of attention and behavior problems. She had difficulty staying in the group circle, and was distractible. In kindergarten, the teacher felt she should be tested for ADHD, as Suzy was so interested in what the other children were doing that the teacher could not get Suzy to focus on what she should be doing.

At Poe Elementary, Suzy had been placed in a resource classroom by first grade due to problems learning reading, and distractibility. Mrs. Kuger stated that Suzy's self-esteem "started spiraling down" and she started acting out. In second grade, the teacher "managed to drag her through," although she was still in resource and was falling further behind. At that time, Mrs. Kuger realized that Suzy was having difficulty with reading. Although she had good phonetic skills, she had to sound out words every time she encountered them. In third grade, Mrs. Kuger enrolled Suzy in a private reading course. However, she only completed half of it because she was having such a difficult time remembering letters on a page and working on short-term memory drills. That year Suzy started fights, punched another child in the face, destroyed property, and stole from the teacher. Mrs. Kuger stated that they were in the principal's office "three times a week."

873

In March, 2004, Suzy was transferred to a self-contained classroom at Longfellow Elementary, She currently is "doing okay," although she still struggles with reading, When someone tells her to do something, she sometimes becomes defiant and has been in the time-out booth five times so far this year. Mrs. Kuger stated that for the first three weeks of the year Suzy was a model student and came home with almost perfect scores.

In October her best friend moved away, and her behavioral problems increased. She subsequently dropped a level in the behavioral system used in the classroom and has been going downhill academically and behaviorally ever since.

Psychological Symptoms: Mrs. Kuger stated that at home, Suzy can quickly escalate into an episode of rage, where she begins pounding, kicking, and punching, and Mr. Kuger will try to hold her down in order to calm her. Mr. Kuger stated that now that Suzy is having less stress at school her behavior at home has improved, although she still "freaks out" when she does not get her way. When Suzy turned on the TV and her father turned it off, she became very angry and started throwing things at her father. She has run away several times and her parents have had to call the police. The Kugers have been attending a parenting class for parents of children with oppositional defiant disorder, which Mrs. Kuger feels has been very helpful in enabling them to control Suzy's outbursts.

Mrs. Kuger stated that Suzy has "endless energy" but is not hyperactive. She is prescribed half a tablet of trazodone at night to sleep, as she has a hard time settling down at bedtime. However, she can watch a movie, play on the computer for hours, and can sit still if she is interested in an activity. Suzy has never attempted suicide, but occasionally engages in suicidal talk. When very frustrated, she has stated that she should kill herself and everyone would be better off.

On the positive side, Mrs. Kuger stated that Suzy has many friends. She is also very attached to her parents, and still likes to hold her mother's hand when she falls asleep. She and her younger sister care about each other and play together, and Suzy is very protective of her.

Medical History: Mrs. Kuger stated that Suzy was very healthy, and has suffered no chronic illnesses, head injuries, or neurologic illness.

Family Situation: Suzy lives at home with her parents and 7-year-old sister.

TESTS ADMINISTERED
Wechsler Intelligence Scale for Children-IV (WISC-IV)
California Verbal Learning Test-Children's Version (CVLT-C)
Rey Complex Figure Test
Delis-Kaplan Executive Function System (D-KEFS)
Trail Making Test Parts A and B
Woodcock-Johnson III Tests of Achievement (selected subtests)
Behavior Assessment for Children (completed by Mr. and Mrs. Kuger and Suzy's teacher, Bea Haive)
Conners' Parent Rating Scale-Revised: Long Version (completed by Sandy and Jerry Kuger)
Conners' Teacher Rating Scale: Long (completed by Suzy's teacher)
Review of records
Clinical interview

BEHAVIORAL OBSERVATIONS: Suzy presented as a cheerful, active child who was appropriately dressed in a pink sweatshirt and jeans. After entering the office, she actively explored the room, playing with each of the examiner's toys. She played loudly with several toys, and at times would talk over her mother on unrelated topics.

During testing, Suzy was initially very focused and on-task during structured activities. She talked out loud to guide herself through visual-perceptual tasks, such as assembling blocks to match a model. Although she was initially very cooperative, after working for approximately an hour during the first session, Suzy became progressively more restless. She pulled her jacket over her head, protested that she could not do the tasks, and would balk when harder tasks were introduced. She frequently asked to go to the bathroom, or would play with various toys while working. She was not responsive to tangible rewards such as candy. As a result, subsequent testing sessions were limited to one hour.

Due to Suzy's resistance to many of the assessment tasks, it is felt that the results of the evaluation may be a slight underestimate of her actual cognitive ability. However, it is felt that the current results are an accurate reflection of her performance in an extended testing situation, giving an example of how she might perform across the school day.

TEST RESULTS

General Intellectual Ability: The WISC-IV was administered as a measure of Suzy's verbal and nonverbal intellectual abilities. Her scores were as follows (mean = 100, SD = 15):

| | Scaled Score | %ile rank | | Scaled Score | %ile rank |
|---|---|---|---|---|---|
| **Verbal Comprehension Index** | **104** | **61** | **Working Memory Index** | **65** | **1** |
| Similarities | 13 | 84 | Digit Span | 7 | 16 |
| Vocabulary | 14 | 91 | Letter-Number Seq. | 1 | 0.1 |
| Comprehension | 6 | 9 | | | |
| **Perceptual Reasoning Index** | **110** | **75** | **Processing Speed Index** | **109** | **73** |
| Block Design | 11 | 63 | Coding | 10 | 50 |
| Picture Concepts | 12 | 75 | Symbol Search | 13 | 84 |
| Matrix Reasoning | 12 | 75 | **FULL SCALE IQ** | **99** | **47** |

Suzy's Perceptual Reasoning Index fell within the high average range, suggesting that her ability to process nonverbal information and nonverbal reasoning ability fall within the high end of the average range. Her Processing Speed and Verbal Comprehension Indexes fell within the average range, suggesting average performance on measures of mentally processing and quickly writing down simple information; processing verbal information; and verbal reasoning. Suzy's Working Memory score fell within the extremely low range, suggesting very poor ability to keep information in short-term memory while performing operations on that information. Suzy's score on the Working Memory Index was significantly lower than her scores on the other three indexes, suggesting that working memory is a significant weakness for her when compared to her other cognitive abilities.

Suzy demonstrated a high amount of variability between her subtest scores. Her scores on subtests measuring knowledge of vocabulary words and verbal concept formation were above average, and were relative strengths for her when compared to her other scores. Her score on a measure of visual-motor speed in visually scanning and marking symbols as same or different was also above average. Suzy's scores on tests measuring working memory in remembering numbers forwards and backwards and ordering sequences of numbers and letters presented auditorally was below average, and constituted relative weaknesses for her. It should be noted that Suzy's raw score on the Letter Number Sequencing task was 0, as she seemed to have difficulty understanding task instructions, became very fidgety, and was unwilling to make a meaningful effort, though the task was explained to her several times. Suzy's score on a measure of verbal reasoning in explaining the reasons for various social norms and rules was below average, which also constituted a relative weakness for her. Her score on this test was lowered by responses characteristic of behavior-disordered children, such as stating that if she found a wallet, she would keep the money inside of it rather than returning it to its owner. All other subtest scores fell within the average range.

Verbal Memory: On the CVLT, which required her to learn a list of 15 words repeated 5 times, Suzy learned 47 total words, which was average for her age (T = 53). She learned 5 words after the first presentation, which fell within the average range (Z = -.05), and suggests average initial attention span for auditory verbal information. She had learned 12 words by the last presentation, which also fell within the average range (Z = 0.5). Her learning slope was average (Z = 0.5), and suggested adequate verbal learning with repetition when compared to peers.

After presentation of a second list, Suzy learned 10 words, which was far above average (Z = 2.5), and suggested no significant proactive interference. Suzy's recall of the first list after a short and longer delay without and with cues fell within the average range (Z = 0.5 – 1.0). Her use of effective verbal learning strategies (clustering by category) was above average. She demonstrated increased recall of words from the end of the list (Z = 1.5) and fewer than average words from the beginning (Z = –1.5) and the middle of the list (Z = – 0.5), suggesting that she may have been somewhat passive in learning the verbal material.

Suzy displayed 11 perseverations (repetitions of words that she had already said) and 6 intrusions (saying words that were not on the list), both of which fell within the average range (Z = 0.5 and Z = 0.0, respectively), and suggests adequate ability to self-monitor and keep track of her responses and source memory ability. When presented with a list of target and distractor words, Suzy recognized all 15 correct words with no false positives, suggesting excellent ability to encode, store and recognize verbal information.

Suzy obtained a copy score of 24.5 on the Rey Complex Figure, suggesting that her visual-motor skills are below average (6-10th percentile). Her scores of 14.5 after a 3-minute delay (T = 43, 24th percentile) and 13 after a 30-minute delay (T = 40, 16th percentile) were both slightly below average. However, her recognition score of 20 (T = 48, 42nd percentile) suggests average visual memory in recognizing parts of the figure. Her recognition was somewhat better than her immediate and delayed recall, but not significantly so.

Executive Functioning: On Trails A, which required her to draw lines between numbers on a page in order, Suzy's speed (22 seconds) was average (Anderson, Lajoie and Bell, 1995), suggesting adequate visual-motor speed. On Trails B, which required her to draw lines between alternating numbers and letters on a page in order, Suzy's speed (80 seconds) was almost 2 standard deviations slower than the mean, suggesting poor mental tracking and speed of cognitive processing. She made no errors on Trails A, but made 3 definite errors on Trails B and at least 3 false starts to an incorrect stimulus. She tended to try to connect the letters in order, rather than alternating numbers and letters according to the directions. Suzy's very poor working memory may have accounted for her extreme difficulty in completing this task.

On the D-KEFS, Suzy obtained average scores on measures of verbal fluency (letter and category) as well as category switching. Her category fluency (SS = 15) was relatively better than her letter fluency (SS = 9). This may be because letter fluency requires more organization and effort in searching and retrieving items from memory. Suzy's ability to quickly retrieve words from alternating categories (category switching) was above average (SS = 13), suggesting adequate ability to verbally switch back and forth between two response categories.

Suzy's performance on the D-KEFS color-word interference test suggested low average ability to retrieve color names from memory (SS = 8). Her speed of word reading (SS = 7) was slightly below average, consistent with her diagnosed reading disability. Her ability to name the colors of ink in which a dissonant name of a color was printed (SS = 8), and her score on the inhibition-switching condition (SS = 10) both fell within the average range, suggesting adequate ability in inhibiting the name of a color from interfering with identification of the color in which that word was printed, as well as adequate ability to switch to naming the word instead of the color in which the word was printed under certain conditions.

On the D-KEFS tower test, Suzy's total achievement subtest score of 9 suggests adequate ability to plan moves in order to construct a tower according to a model, using specific rules. She did commit a significant number of rule violations during this task (12), and it is not known whether she had difficulty inhibiting her behavior, or was deliberately choosing to violate the rules in order to accomplish the task more quickly.

Achievement Testing: To evaluate Suzy's level of achievement across a variety of academic subjects, she was administered the Woodcock-Johnson Tests of Achievement-Third Edition (WJ-III). On this test, Suzy achieved an Academic Skills score of 82, which corresponds to the 12th percentile for students her age. This score indicates that when averaged across the areas of reading, writing, and mathematics, Suzy's skills fall within the low average range, lower than the level expected based on her IQ scores, age and grade placement.

Suzy's WJ-III subtest and cluster scores are given below:

| Subtest | Scaled Score | Percentile | Age Equivalent |
|---|---|---|---|
| Letter/Word Identification | 82 | 11 | 7-8 |
| Reading Fluency | 82 | 11 | 7-8 |
| Story Recall | 118 | 88 | >21 |
| Understanding Directions | 100 | 50 | 9-3 |
| Calculation | 91 | 28 | 8-4 |
| Math Fluency | 91 | 27 | 8-6 |
| Spelling | 77 | 6 | 7-6 |
| Writing Fluency | 97 | 43 | 9-0 |
| Passage Comprehension | 81 | 11 | 7-3 |
| Applied Problems | 93 | 31 | 8-4 |
| Writing Samples | 82 | 11 | 7-3 |
| Word Attack | 92 | 29 | 7-11 |

| Cluster Score | Scaled Score | Percentile | Age Equivalent |
|---|---|---|---|
| Broad Reading | 78 | 7 | 7-6 |
| Basic Reading Skills | 86 | 17 | 7-9 |
| Broad Math | 92 | 30 | 8-4 |
| Math Calculation Skills | 91 | 28 | 8-5 |
| Broad Written Language | 81 | 10 | 7-9 |
| Written Expression | 89 | 22 | 8-2 |
| Oral Language | 107 | 67 | 10-6 |
| Academic Skills | 82 | 12 | 7-8 |
| Academic Fluency | 87 | 19 | 8-1 |
| Academic Applications | 86 | 17 | 7-7 |

**Reading:** Suzy's Broad Reading score falls within the low range, lower than would be predicted given her IQ scores and her Oral Language score, and below average for her age and grade placement. Her Basic Reading score was somewhat higher, falling within the low average range. This cluster includes a measure of phonetic skill, and her average score on this subtest raised her cluster score. Suzy performed within the low average range on tasks that required her to identify a set of increasingly difficult words (Letter/Word Identification); rapidly read simple sentences and answer yes-no questions about what was read (Reading Fluency); and read complex sentences and paragraphs and understand what was read (Passage Comprehension). Based on these scores, Suzy appears to have a disability in reading, characterized by difficulties in visual perception of symbols and working memory. It should be also noted that she continues to reverse the letters "b" and "d" both in writing and reading.

**Mathematics:** Suzy's broad mathematics skills and math calculation skills both fall within the average range, within the level expected based on her age, grade placement and IQ scores. Suzy performed within the average range on the Calculation subtest, where she was required to solve a variety of age-appropriate mathematics problems that were already structured for her on the page. She also performed within the average range on the Math Fluency and Applied Problems subtest, suggesting adequate ability to solve simple addition, subtraction, multiplication, and division problems, as well as word problems that were read to her and practical mathematics problems pictured on a page. There was no indication of a mathematics disability.

**Oral Language:** Suzy's Oral Language score falls within the average range, at the level expected based on her age, grade, placement and IQ scores. This suggests that Suzy's reading disability is not the result of an overall disability in oral language development. On Story Recall, Suzy was required to listen to a set of short stories and then to recall these stories as accurately as possible, and her score on this subtest fell within the high average range, suggesting excellent verbal memory. This score is consistent with her scores on the CVLT as well. Her ability to understand and carry out directions presented auditorally fell within the average range, suggesting adequate auditory processing skills. There was no indication of a receptive or expressive language problem.

**Writing:** Suzy's Broad Written Language score and her Written Expression score both fell within the low average range, somewhat lower than would be expected given her IQ score, but within average limits based on her age and grade placement. She performed within the low range on a spelling task, and within the low average range on a task where there was no time limit and she was required to write words or sentences which met prespecified grammatical or spelling criteria or fit within a certain context (Writing Samples). She performed within the average range on a task requiring her to rapidly write simple sentences using three specified words (Writing Fluency). Suzy's difficulties in writing are likely a function of her delayed reading development.

Attention and Behavior: On the CPRS-R (Long), Mr. and Mrs. Kuger's responses resulted in severely atypical elevations on the following scales: Oppositional, Cognitive Problems/Inattention, Conners' ADHD Index, Conners' Global Index: Restless-Impulsive, Conners' Global Index: Emotional Lability, Conners' Global Index: Total, and DSM-IV: Total Scales, indicating that they see Suzy as having severe problems in all of these areas. They both also rated her as mildly atypical on the Psychosomatic scale. Mrs. Kuger's ratings also indicated that she rated Suzy as severely atypical on the DSM-IV: Inattentive scale, moderately atypical on the Hyperactivity scale, and mildly atypical on the DSM-IV: Hyperactive-Impulsive scale. Mr. Kuger also rated Suzy as severely atypical on the Social Problems and DSM-IV: Hyperactive-Impulsive scales. He rated Suzy as moderately atypical on the DSM-IV: Inattentive scale.

On the CTRS-R (Long), Ms. Haive's responses resulted in severely atypical ratings on the following scales: Oppositional, Conners' ADHD Index, Conners' Global Index: Emotional Lability, Conners' Global Index: Total, DSM-IV: Hyperactive-Impulsive, and DSM-IV: Total scales. She rated Suzy as moderately atypical on the Cognitive Problems/Inattention, Hyperactivity, Conners' Global Index: Restless-Impulsive, and DSM-IV: Inattentive scales. Both the parents and the teacher rated Suzy with a sufficient number of symptoms on the Inattentive scale to suggest a possible DSM-IV diagnosis. None of them rated her as having a significant number of Hyperactive-Impulsive symptoms severe enough to warrant that diagnosis.

Mr. and Mrs. Kuger and Ms. Haive also completed the BASC to provide information regarding their perceptions of Suzy's current psychological and behavioral status. All responses on caution indexes were within the acceptable range with the exception of Mr. Kuger's response on the F scale, which fell within the extreme caution range. This suggests that Mr. Kuger rated Suzy's behavior extremely negatively, more so than the other respondents. However, it is felt that his ratings were valid and interpretable.

Both parents' responses resulted in clinically significant elevations on the following scales: Aggression, Conduct Disorder, Externalizing Problems Composite, and Attention scales, indicating that they both see Suzy as having significant problems in these areas. Mr. Kuger also rated Suzy as having clinically significant problems on the following scales: Hyperactivity, Depression, Internalizing Problems Composite, Atypicality, and the Overall Behavioral Symptoms Index. He rated Suzy within the "at-risk" range on the Anxiety and Withdrawal scales, suggesting potential problems that should continue to be monitored. Mrs. Kuger rated Suzy as displaying problems within the at-risk range on the Hyperactivity scale, Depression scale, and Overall Behavioral Symptoms Index.

Ms. Haive's responses resulted in clinically significant elevations on the following scales: Hyperactivity, Aggression, Conduct Disorder, Externalizing Problems Composite, and Overall Behavioral Symptoms Index. She rated Suzy as falling within the at-risk range on the following scales: Depression, Attention, Learning Problems, School Problems Composite, and Atypicality.

On the Adaptive scales, Mr. and Mrs. Kuger both rated Suzy within the at-risk range on the Social Skills and Leadership scales. Mr. Kuger rated Suzy as having clinically significant problems in Adaptability and on the Adaptive Scales Composite. Mrs. Kuger rated Suzy as falling within the at-risk range on Adaptability, and on the Overall Adaptive Scales Composite. Ms. Haive's ratings on the Adaptability scales indicated that she saw Suzy as falling within the average range on the Social Skills and Leadership scales. She rated her as at-risk on the Study Skills scale and Adaptive Scale Composite, and in the clinically significant range in Adaptability.

**SUMMARY AND RECOMMENDATIONS:** Results of the current evaluation indicate that Suzy's perceptual reasoning falls within the high average range, while her verbal comprehension and visual-motor speed fall within the average range. These abilities constitute relative strengths for her. Suzy's verbal memory as well as certain aspects of executive function such as verbal fluency, ability to switch cognitive set, and ability to solve visual problems fall within the average to high average range and are also strengths for Suzy.

However, Suzy demonstrates marked weaknesses in working memory and weaker visual than verbal memory. Her adequate phonetic skills and difficulty acquiring sight words, as well as her tendency to reverse letters, suggests difficulties in visual processing of and visual memory for symbols. These problems will make it very difficult for Suzy to acquire the adequate sight-word vocabulary she needs in order to be a fluent reader.

Academic testing indicates that Suzy demonstrates marked weakness in reading, writing and spelling skills, while her math skills, oral language, verbal memory, and auditory processing are adequate. Her overall academic skills, speed of performing simple academic tasks, and ability to apply basic cognitive skills to academic tasks all fall within the low average range.

Results of behavioral inventories completed by Suzy's parents and teacher indicate that Suzy displays marked oppositional behavior, inattention, restlessness and impulsivity, and emotional lability. She does demonstrate some hyperactivity at times, but her primary problem appears to be in the area of inattention. Suzy's primary difficulties appear to be externalizing, as she obtained high ratings in the areas of aggression and conduct disorder. Although she displays possible symptoms of depression, these symptoms appear to come and go depending on environmental circumstances, and do not appear to constitute a clinical depression. Suzy also received relatively low ratings on measures of adaptability, social skills, and leadership ability.

Due to her ADHD and cognitive difficulties, especially her very poor working memory, it is likely that Suzy has become very frustrated with academic tasks, leading to oppositional, defiant, and aggressive behavior. Her placement in a self-contained classroom with the classification of emotionally disturbed appears to be appropriate, and her educational needs seem to have been met adequately by this placement.

The following are recommended:

1. Academic intervention should focus on helping Suzy continue to develop her phonetic skills, but she also needs to develop an adequate sight-word vocabulary. Because rote memory is the only way to learn sight words, flash cards are recommended to help Suzy learn and remember words. This may be done by first introducing the word, using it in a sentence, writing it on a card, and asking Suzy to pronounce it. She can then write the word on a card and write the word in a sentence in order to help her memorize the word. Printing the words on colored index cards may also facilitate her memory for them. It may be most helpful to begin with the 150 most common words found in printed English according to the *Word Frequency Book.* Suzy may begin by reading simple books within her instructional level, then progress to books that are slightly more difficult than her reading level. Frequent reading aloud with feedback and correction will be critical in helping Suzy develop her oral fluency skills.

2. It may be helpful to monitor the efficacy of Suzy's reading instruction by applying curriculum-based measurement to see whether Suzy is achieving adequate growth in reading throughout the school year. Curriculum-based measurement is presently being performed with all resource students in the Salt Lake District. If Suzy has not yet been assessed, it may be helpful to call the Special Programs Department of Salt Lake School District and request that a school psychologist or a resource teacher perform a brief reading assessment now and several weeks or months later in order to assess Suzy's rate of growth.

3. In order for Suzy to participate more fully in class and discussion periods, strategies such as previewing material, reviewing the content of an assignment, and talking through the assignment prior to class, will be helpful in enabling Suzy to participate meaningfully in discussion.

4. It is recommended that Suzy receive reading tutoring over the summer or read aloud regularly with a parent, in order to prevent academic regression.

5. It is highly recommended that Suzy's parents and teacher obtain Sally Shaywitz's book *Overcoming Dyslexia,* which provides a comprehensive review of the research on brain functioning, as well as intervention, and practical suggestions for remediation, and potential classroom accommodations.

6. It is recommended that teachers try to accommodate Suzy's poor working memory by repeating material over and over again, having her repeat it back to ensure

understanding, and checking periodically to make sure that Suzy knows what she is supposed to do. Suzy also needs to be taught and encouraged to ask for help when she does not understand material, in order to advocate for herself in the classroom.

7. It is recommended that Suzy be referred back to her physician to determine whether she is receiving the optimum amount of medication, as she continues to display significant problems with attention in the classroom.

8. The following may also be helpful:

## ATTENTION SUGGESTIONS

### External Aids
< In classes and lectures, Suzy should sit front and center. If necessary, she may want to have a friend nudge or prompt her to pay attention
< Set a timer or alarm watch as a reminder to pay attention
< Place a symbol or picture card in an obvious place in the work area as a reminder to maintain attention
< Organize the work environment and eliminate distractions
< Use written cue cards with questions to focus self (for example, "What should I be thinking about now?")
< Suzy's teacher may want to utilize a beep tape with incentives in the classroom to maximize Suzy's attention
< Use a Pocket PC with keyboard to take notes in class, or ask a good student to take notes. If another student is taking notes, Suzy should jot down keywords in order to be actively involved in the learning process.
< Suzy may wish to tape record lectures for review later.
< Suzy's parents may want to ask teachers for lesson plans in advance and review them with Suzy, in order to help her organize her thoughts and follow classroom instruction with greater comprehension.
< Suzy is likely to perform better if exams are untimed, and taken over a period of time in short intervals.

### Internal Strategies
< Suzy's parents may want to time her to see how long he can pay attention, then set progressively longer goals, rewarding her when goals are achieved
< Focus self through use of self-talk (for example, "What should I be doing now?" "What do I need to do next?") while working on a task
< Talk to self out loud or silently ("I am putting my keys on the table") to help remember where things are or what one is doing
< To focus on conversations, repeat back what has been said, paraphrasing the material (for example, repeating the time, date and place of a planned activity)
< When reading or studying, taking rest periods and short breaks within and between tasks
< When trying to focus on a task, eliminate distractions as much as possible
< Focus on doing one task correctly, rather than doing several things at once
< Focus on the consequences of not paying attention and remembering the information at a future time ("I need to focus and remember this, or my teacher will be mad at me")

*Website*
< www.ADDvisor is an excellent website for people of all ages who have ADHD.

*Support Groups*
< CHADD (537-7878) provides information and support groups for ADHD children and adults

*References for Adults*
< P. Quinn (ed.) ADD and the college student. Washington, D.C.: Magination Press, 1994.
< M. Gordon and S. Keiser (eds.), Accommodations in higher education under the Americans with Disabilities Act (ADA). New York: Guilford Press, 1998.
< Hallowell, E. and Ratey, J. Driven to distraction. New York: Pantheon, 1994.
< Hallowell, E. and Ratey, J. Answers to distraction. New York: Pantheon, 1994.
< Hartmann, T. ADD success stories. Grass Valley, California: Underwood Books, 1995.
< Nadeau, K. Adventures in fast forward: Life, love and work for the ADD adult.
< Murphy, K. and Levert, S. Out of the fog: Treatment options and coping strategies for adult attention deficit disorder.

*References for Parents*
< Attention deficit disorders intervention manual [school suggestions] and/or Parent's guide to attention deficit disorder. Hawthorne Educational Services, P.O. Box 7570, Columbia, MO 65205. 1-800-542-1673
< Cohen, M. The attention zone: A parent's guide to attention deficit/hyperactivity disorder. 1997
< Goldstein, S. A parent's guide: Attention-deficit hyperactivity disorder in children. 1991
< Hallowell, E. and Ratey, J. Driven to distraction. New York: Pantheon, 1994.
< Hallowell, E. and Ratey, J. Answers to distraction. New York: Pantheon, 1994.
< Hartmann, T. ADD success stories. Grass Valley, California: Underwood Books, 1995.
< Ingersoll, B. Daredevils and daydreamers: New perspectives on attention-deficit/ hyperactivity disorder. 1997
< McEwan, E. Attention deficit disorder: helpful, practical information. Colorado Springs, Colorado: Waterbrook Press, 1995.
< Phelan, T. All about attention deficit disorder. 1996

*References for Kids*
< Gordon, M. My brother's a world-class pain: A sibling's guide to ADHD-hyperactivity. 1992
< Janover, C. Zipper: The kid with ADHD.
< Quinn, P. Putting on the brakes: Young people's guide to understanding attention deficit hyperactivity disorder. 1992
< Quinn, T. Grandma's pet wildebeest ate my homework.

---

Janiece L. Pompa, Ph.D.
Psychologist

---

Names have been changed to protect the identity of those tested.

# Appendix C: Sample Neuropsychological Evaluation

LEESA V. HUANG, CHERISE D. LEREW, and RIK CARL D'AMATO

UNIVERSITY *of*
## NORTHERN COLORADO

College of Education and Behavioral Sciences
Division of Professional Psychology
Neuropsychology Laboratory

**\* CONFIDENTIAL REPORT \* CONFIDENTIAE REPORT
FOR AUTHORIZED PERSONNEL ONLY**

### Neuropsychological Evaluation

| | | | |
|---|---|---|---|
| **Name:** | Jane Husman | **Date of Birth** | 00/10/94 |
| **Address:** | 1919 63rd Avenue<br>Greeley, CO | **Chronological Age:** | 7 year, 6 month |
| **Telephone:** | (777) 633–3333 | **Grade:** | 2nd |
| **Parent(s):** | Marcia Garcia (Mother)<br>Lilia Husman (Grandmother) | **School:** | Garfield Elementary |
| **Date of Evaluation:** 02/00/00 | | **Handedness:** | Right |

## REASON FOR REFERRAL

Jane was referred to the UNC Neuropsychology Laboratory by Ms. Judy Winter, School Psychologist at Garfield Elementary, and Ms. Marcia Garcia, Jane's mother. After completing an educational evaluation in September 0000, Ms. Winter believes that Jane's profile has some indicators of neuropsychological difficulties. Ms. Garcia reported concerns regarding the inconsistency of Jane's performance on standardized tests, which indicate that she is functioning in the average range as compared to her same aged peers, while her classroom performance is significantly below average as noted by her general education teachers. In addition, Ms. Garcia stated that recently Jane has become increasingly aware of her academic difficulties and struggles daily with all aspects of her school life.

## EVALUATION PROCEDURES

> Clinical Interview (Ms. Garcia, Ms. Husman, and Jane)
> Review of Educational Records
> The Das-Naglieri: Cognitive Assessment System (CAS)
> The McCarthy Scales of Children's Abilities (Motor Scales)
> The Test of Memory and Learning (TOMAL)
> The NEPSY—A Developmental Neuropsychological Assessment (NEPSY)
> The Revised Children's Manifest Anxiety Scale (RCMAS)
> The Parent Stress Inventory (PSI)
> The Sentence Completion Test (SCT)
> The House-Tree-Person Drawings (HTP)
> The Wishes and Fears Personality Inventory

## BACKGROUND INFORMATION

Jane is a 7 years, 6 months old female who recently relocated with her family to Colorado in July 0000 from New Mexico. Currently, she resides with her mother and her grandmother. She also lives with her cousins, Cindy and Brian, who are both in secondary school. At the time of the evaluation, Jane reported infrequent contact with her biological father.

According to Ms. Garcia, she had a difficult pregnancy, especially during the first five months. She reported regular doctor visits and taking prenatal vitamins. She denied the intake of substances or drugs at any time during the pregnancy. Labor was reported to be difficult and Ms. Garcia stated that she received an excessive amount of pain medication while in the hospital. Ms. Garcia indicated that Jane obtained all developmental milestones within age appropriate ranges, with the notable exception of language.

Jane's medical history revealed that at the age of 6 months, she contracted croop and was hospitalized for a few of days. Ms. Garcia stated that Jane has frequent nasal stuffiness and has had several ear infections. Jane's family reported a history of depression. Ms. Garcia related that Jane's hearing is within the average range. Jane's vision was determined to be far-sighted by the school, but within the average range.

Jane's language delays are clearly evident and pervasive in all settings. Ms. Husman indicated that Jane tends to speak softly or whisper in nearly all situations and is embarrassed about her speech. Ms. Garcia indicated that it is difficult to understand Jane due to grammatical errors and poor articulation, so she "translates" what Jane is saying to other people, especially for those outside of the immediate family. Ms. Garcia stated that sometimes even she has a hard time understanding what Jane is trying to convey, but tries to be positive and patient with her. Jane frequently gets frustrated with people if they have trouble understanding or misunderstand her. According to her family, Jane also struggles to understand oral directions on a daily basis and requires repetition and rephrasing to ensure comprehension.

Ms. Garcia has concerns regarding Jane's gross motor skills. Ms. Garcia and Ms. Husman reported that Jane has an awkward gait and is accident-prone. When walking down stairs, Jane uses the same foot to descend each stair, instead of alternating her feet. Ms. Husman indicated that Jane is able to walk down the stairs alternating feet, however, she must be reminded and the activity must be modeled at the same time. Jane's mother and grandmother both relayed that Jane is unable to skip and seems to lack the necessary motor coordination skills needed to learn skipping.

Jane is currently in the second grade at Garfield Elementary School. Despite two school changes this academic year, Jane's educational history appears to be somewhat stable. Her family believed that moving to a smaller school setting would be beneficial to Jane because she would receive increased teacher support and provide a less overwhelming social situation. According to educational records provided by Ms. Garcia, Jane had good attendance the first quarter with no absences and poor attendance in the second quarter with 13 absences. Ms. Garcia explained that illnesses were a major factor in these absences.

At school, Jane's mother reported that Jane demonstrated an extremely low frustration tolerance. She is unable to perform in the regular education classroom setting at a level indicated by the standardized testing results. According to those results, Jane excels in the areas of reading and writing. Spelling also is an area of strength. Math seems to be an area of relative weakness, which causes excessive frustration and anxiety. Ms. Garcia is concerned that Jane's awareness of her difficulties is negatively impacting motivation and her ability to succeed in the classroom.

Jane is presently receiving special education services under the funding category of Speech/Language Disability. She was receiving resource room level support at the beginning of the year, however, the Individualized Education Plan (IEP) team decided that Jane met the goals written in the IEP and was functioning at or above the level of the students in the resource placement. Therefore, her placement was changed to a regular education setting with individual or small group Speech/Language pull-out services. Since then, her frustration with school has increased significantly and her family has observed Jane making negative comments about herself such as "I'm stupid" or "I'm not good enough."

Ms. Garcia and Ms. Husman both described Jane as a shy, quiet, and sensitive child. Both Jane's mother and grandmother reported that she misreads social cues given by her peers and is prone to crying when her peers ignore or tease her. Ms. Garcia stated that at school, Jane has few or no friends and that within the home environment; she has limited contact with peers her age. Ms. Husman reported that Jane tends to prefer adult company and her social circle consists of those extended family members who again, tend to be older. While on the playground at school, Ms. Garcia reported that Jane tends to be an observer instead of a participant and she rarely initiates interactions with peers. Ms. Husman observed that Jane tends to choose friends that exhibit bullying or aggressive behavior and Ms. Husman believes that it is a coping mechanism to keep Jane from being a target. At least once a week, Ms. Husman will have lunch with Jane because no one will sit with her during lunch. Ms. Husman states that Jane enjoys these lunch arrangements and requests her grandmother be present more often.

## BEHAVIORAL OBSERVATIONS

This evaluation was completed in a single session lasting approximately six to seven hours. In the morning, Jane appeared to be tired, yet friendly. She separated from her family with some coaxing, particularly from her mother. Jane seemed to be anxious in the assessment setting and was attentive to the environment. Initially, Jane was shy and withdrawn with the examiner and used head nods or hand motions to communicate, though she was cooperative and complied with the examiner's numerous requests. Jane became increasingly verbal throughout the course of the session and began initiating conversation.

During the assessment, Jane needed an excessive amount of reinforcement and reassurance from the examiner in order to complete some of the items. She appeared to be anxious when given timed tasks, yet did fairly well. Jane did well when completing tasks that were easy for her; however, she lacked persistence when presented with challenging activities. She appeared to use a trial-and-error method as her main problem-solving strategy. Her performance declined when she began noticing she was making errors and as her frustration level rose. She appeared to fatigue easily, so frequent breaks were provided. On school like tasks, alternating frustrating tasks with less challenging activities were necessary to maintain Jane's motivation and interest. Jane's attention span began to wane quickly after several subtests. In order to sustain attention, verbal reminders and consumable reinforcers were provided for Jane to remain on tasks.

During informal interactions, she seemed hesitant and spoke little. Jane's break time activities were silent for the most part with the same underlying themes while playing with toy figurines. When the examiner attempted to join her, she maintained parallel play and interaction was limited. She had difficulty transitioning back from the break to the assessment and it usually took her several minutes before she was putting forth complete effort. She denied thoughts of hurting herself or others. The following assessment appears to be a valid and reliable assessment of Jane's neuropsychological functioning.

## EVALUATION RESULTS AND INTERPRETATION

### Review of Prior Evaluation Results

Ms. Garcia brought copies of a prior individual psychological assessment conducted on 00/24/00 by Ms. Winter, Colorado Licensed School Psychologist; Compuscore Summary and Report Dated 00/07/00; an IEP dated 10/01/00; and speech-language assessment results for review.

The Wechsler Intelligence Scale for Children–Third Edition (WISC-III) profile indicated significant scatter among her verbal and nonverbal subtests as shown below:

| VERBAL TESTS | SCALED SCORE | PERFORMANCE TEST | SCALED SCORE |
|---|---|---|---|
| Information | 7 | Picture Completion | 9 |
| Similarities | 10 | Coding | 13 |
| Arithmetic | 1 | Picture Arrangement | 4 |
| Vocabulary | 5 | Block Design | 6 |
| Comprehension | 1 | Object Assembly | 9 |
| (Digit Span) | 5 | (Symbol Search) | 6 |
| | | (Mazes) | 7 |
| **Verbal IQ** | **71** | **Performance IQ** | **89** |
| **Full Scale IQ** | **77** | | |
| **Verbal Comprehension** | **77** | **Perceptual Organization** | **83** |
| **Processing Speed** | **99** | **Freedom From Distractibility** | **61** |

Her verbal subtests indicate that her abilities are within the Borderline range. She demonstrated below average vocabulary, though she appears to have adequate conceptual understanding as she was able to determine relationships between two words. She was able to answer questions regarding factual knowledge within the low average range. Jane appears to have significant weaknesses in mental arithmetic and social judgment. She also appears to struggle with repeating a series of numbers. Her overall nonverbal performance was found to be within the Low Average range and determined by Ms. Winter to be the most valid indicator of Jane's cognitive abilities. Jane was able to differentiate essential from nonessential details in order to determine a missing part of a picture. She had a relative strength in digit coding, which requires the child to learn symbols related to numbers under a specific time constraint. Tasks that involved sequencing pictures to determine cause and effect were difficult for her. Although she was able to put together puzzles that entail part-to-whole skills, on an activity that required arranging blocks according to an abstract visual stimulus, Jane performed in the Low Average range.

The Beery Buktenica Developmental Test of Visual-Motor Integration–2nd Edition (VMI) was administered to assess fine motor skills. According to the results, Jane is functioning within the Average range, though she struggled to copy complex abstract visual designs due to angling and distortion errors.

The Woodcock-Johnson III Tests of Achievement (WJ-III) was administered to Jane in September 2001. Average scores range from 90 to 110. The results indicated average scores in the broad areas of reading (Standard Score = 107), writing (Standard Score = 106), and math (Standard Score = 91). Reading and writing are areas of relative strengths, while math scores are commensurate with her nonverbal ability. She appeared to have particular difficulties on tasks that involved math story problems.

The Behavior Assessment System for Children (BASC) both Parent and Teacher Response Scales (PRS and TRS, respectively) were administered. Although both profiles indicated an overall Behavioral Symptom Index T-score within the Average range (BASC PRS = 52; BASC TRS = 52), several scales within the at-risk range were noted. Jane's teacher and parent both indicated concerns with Withdrawal, Attention Difficulties, and Social Skills. Jane's teacher also indicated concerns with behavior that would be considered odd or immature at an at-risk level, while Ms. Garcia indicated concerns regarding Adaptability within the clinically significant range.

According to results of the speech language evaluation, Jane displayed deficits in receptive (Peabody Picture Vocabulary Test-Third Edition, Form B; Standard Score = 69; Mean = 100; Average Range = 85–115) and expressive language, auditory processing, and auditory perception. Her severity rating is moderate disability, which indicates that language skills are below the average range and have an effect on her ability to participate in educational settings. Errors are noticeable and interfere with communication.

The Das-Naglieri: Cognitive Assessment System (CAS)

The CAS is an assessment tool that measures the child's overall cognitive abilities. This test is broken down into four sections. The first section, planning, is a measure for problem-solving skills, ability to develop plans, and impulse control. The next section is attention, which measures one's ability to selectively attend to some stimuli and ignore others. The last two sections, successive and simultaneous, measure the child's processing abilities. The scores on all of the sections are combined to give an overall index of the child's cognitive abilities. Normal scores on each subtest range from 8 to 12. Jane's results on the CAS are depicted in the table as follows:

| CAS Subtest | Scaled Scores |
|---|---|
| Matching Numbers | 8 |
| Planned Codes | 11 |
| Planned Connections | 7 |
| Nonverbal Matrices | 9 |
| Verbal-Spatial Relations | 1 |
| Figure Memory | 12 |
| Expressive Attention | 12 |
| Number Detection | 4 |
| Receptive Attention | 8 |
| Word Series | 3 |
| Sentence Repetition | 5 |
| Speech Rate/Sentence Questions | 6 |

| PASS Scale | Standard Score (Mean = 100; SD=15) | Classification | Confidence Interval 95% |
|---|---|---|---|
| Planning | 92 | Average | 84–102 |
| Attention | 88 | Low Average | 80–99 |
| Simultaneous | 83 | Low Average | 76–92 |
| Successive | 67 | **Significantly Below Average** | 62–77 |
| Full Scale | 76 | Below Average | 71–83 |

Jane earned a CAS Full Scale Score of 92, which falls within the Average classification. Her scores on the separate subtests that comprise the Full Scale were scattered and inconsistent. Due to the variability of subtest and scale scores, the CAS Full Scale score may not be an accurate representation of her overall cognitive abilities.

Jane earned a score of 92 on the Planning Scale, which is in the Average range. This score reflects her ability to make decisions about how to complete tasks, self-monitoring levels, and problem-solving skills. The Matching Numbers subtest required the ability to scan a row of numbers to find and underline two of the same numbers—Jane performed in the lower end of the average range. Planned Codes requires the child to replicate symbols that go with letters, requires skills such as visual-motor dexterity and speed of mental operation. This was a relative strength for Jane as her performance fell in the Average range. The Planned Connections subtest measures planning, motor speed, visual scanning, and visual-motor integration. It also measures immediate recognition of the symbolic significance of numbers and the ability to scan continuously, visual acuity, attention, and concentration. Jane's score on this subtest was in the Low Average range.

Jane earned a score of 88 on the Attention Scale, which is in the Low Average range. This score reflects her ability to focus her cognitive activity to attend to some stimuli and avoid being distracted by other stimuli in the tests. Expressive Attention requires that the child focus on and name a particular feature of a picture, while ignoring a conflicting aspect of the picture. Jane performed in the higher end of the Average range on this subtest. The number Detection subtest required Jane to scan a row of numbers and underline specific numbers. She performed in the Well Below Average range and demonstrated difficulty remembering which numbers to underline and which numbers to ignore. She continued to work slowly to ensure accuracy. The Receptive Attention subtest entails visual scanning, attention, and concentration in order to match pictures. Jane performed within the Average range.

Jane earned a score of 83 on the Simultaneous Processing Scale, which is in the Low Average range. This score reflects her ability to determine a relationship between parts of a task and work with information in groups. The Nonverbal Matrices subtest requires the child to display the skills of perceptual organization and classification abilities by figuring out which part of a matrix is missing. Jane performed in the Average range on this subtest. Verbal-Spatial Relations is a task that entails the ability to identify position or location within a picture according to verbal directions. Jane did poorly on this subtest indicating that she struggles immensely with positional concepts, which may be related to language difficulties she experiences. Jane performed in the upper end of the Average range on a task that required her to look briefly at an abstract design and identify the design within a complex visual pattern (Figure Memory).

Jane earned a score of 67 on the Successive Processing scale, which is in the Well Below Average range. This score reflects her ability to comprehend and perceive stimuli in sequence and the execution of movements in order. The Word Series subtest requires that a child repeat a series of words in the particular order it was administered. Jane performed in the Well Below Average range on this task. The Sentence Repetition is a task that involves the repetition of sentences with nonsensical content. Jane also scored in the Well Below Average range. On the Speech Rate subtest, Jane was asked to repeat a short list consisting of several common words ten times as fast as she can. Her scores reflect Below Average performance. Overall, this suggests that Jane's performance may be impacted by the previously documented language, auditory processing, and auditory perception difficulties.

The Test of Memory and Learning (TOMAL)

Jane was administered the TOMAL to assess memory skills. The TOMAL is broken down into two sections, verbal and nonverbal. The scores on all of the sections are combined to give an overall index of the child's memory abilities. Normal scores on each subtest range from 8 to 12. Jane's results on the TOMAL are depicted in the table as follows:

| Verbal Subtests | Scaled Scores | Nonverbal Subtests | | Scaled Scores |
|---|---|---|---|---|
| Memory for Stories | 6 | Facial Memory | | 5 |
| Word Selective Reminding | 10 | Visual Selective Reminding | | 6 |
| Object Recall | 8 | Abstract Visual Memory | | 12 |
| Digits Forward | 3 | Visual Sequential Memory | | 12 |
| Paired Recall | 9 | Memory for Location | | 11 |
| **Composite Indexes** | **Memory Index (Average Range = 90 – 110)** | **Percentiles** | **Classification** | |
| Verbal Memory Index (VMI) | 81 | 10 | Low Average | |
| Nonverbal Memory Index (NMI) | 94 | 35 | Average | |
| Composite Memory Index (CMI) | 87 | 19 | Low Average | |
| Delayed Recall Index (DRI) | 77 | 6 | Low | |

Overall, Jane's Composite Memory Index (CMI) was found to be in the Low Average range, with her Nonverbal Memory Index (NMI) being better developed in the Average range than her Verbal Memory Index (VMI). Jane's Delayed Recall Index (DRI) was found to be in the Low range, suggesting that her immediate memory skills are stronger and that over time, Jane's memory decreases with regard to quantity (e.g., number of items she can remember) and the quality (e.g., sequence).

Jane's VMI score was found to be in the Low Average range. Memory for Stories involved the reading of a story to Jane. She was then required to remember and repeat the stories told to her. She performed in the Low Average range on this task. She was unable to recall names and struggled with details and sequence of the story, especially after a time delay. The Word Selective Reminding subtest is a task in which the child is asked to learn a word list with reminders and prompts for each trial. Jane was able to successfully learn an eight-item word list within the Average range; however, after a specified amount of time, she was only able to recall five items. Object Recall is a subtest that requires a child to recall a list that is provided visually. Jane performed in the lower end of the Average range. The Digits Forward subtest had Jane repeat numbers that the examiner read. This task requires memory and attention span; Jane performed in the Well Below Average range on this task, which is commensurate with previous testing results. Paired Recall is the last verbal memory subtest administered. This subtest is a verbal paired-association learning task with verbal reminders. Jane performed in the Average range.

Jane's NMI was found to be in the Average Range. The Facial Memory subtest required Jane to recognize and remember human faces. She performed in the Well Below Average range, however, after a short time delay, Jane was able to identify faces within the Average range. The Visual Selective Reminding subtest is a task which involves remembering the location of a series of dots on a page that has been divided into six partitions. Her performance was in the Low Average range, yet again, after a short time delay, she was able to recall the locations within the Average range. The Abstract Visual Memory task required Jane to remember and recognize meaningless geometric shapes. She performed in the higher end of the Average range on this task. Jane completed the Visual Sequential Memory subtest within the higher end of the Average range. This subtest entailed the recall of sequences and geometric figures. The Memory for Location task requires spatial memory and recall of location of dots in a grid.

The McCarthy Scales of Children's Abilities (Motor Scales)

Jane was administered the Motor Scales (tests 9 to 13) of The McCarthy Scales of Children's Abilities given gross motor concerns raised by Ms. Garcia and Ms. Husman. This rather outdated measure was used as a gross and qualitative estimate of the abilities. A wide variety of the tasks are game-like and are non-threatening so the child is able to proceed easily through a number of activities assessing gross motor skills. Several trials are given in order to allow the child to practice and be successful after demonstration and verbal guidance from the examiner. It should be noted that on nearly all gross motor trials, Jane needed at least two trials and approximately half of the time, still did not receive full credit. Her overall Motor Score was found to be within the Below Average range even with special assistance and additional practice.

Leg Coordination assessed the maturity of motor coordination in the lower extremities. Walking backwards, walking on tiptoe, walking a straight line, standing on one foot, and skipping allow opportunities to observe the broad stance and balance of a child. Jane received partial credit on all items, except the last item, where she received no credit. She is able to walk at least five steps backwards; however, she waved her arms excessively in order to maintain balance. After two trials, Jane was able to walk three steps on tiptoe. While walking on a straight line, Jane exhibited fairly good balance for approximately nine feet and only stepped off the line twice. She was able to maintain her balance while standing on one foot for approximately six seconds with her right foot and seven seconds with her left foot. At this time, Jane is unable to skip.

Arm Coordination assessed the maturity of motor coordination in the upper extremities using three activities: ball bouncing, catching a beanbag, and aiming a beanbag at a target. Each of the activities allowed two or more trials in order to obtain the "Best Score." Jane was able to bounce a ball eight times in a row without a miss on the second trial. With both hands, she was able to catch the beanbag two of three tries. With just her right hand (dominant hand), Jane was able to catch the beanbag only one of three times. She was unable to catch the beanbag with her left hand after three trials. When aiming the beanbag at a target with her right hand, Jane was able to hit the target board each time, though it missed the hole. When using her left hand, Jane was only able to hit the target board once out of three tries and missing the hole.

Imitative Action is a subtest consisting of four simple motor tasks to observe general motor skills and an opportunity to note eye preference through a tube. Jane was able to imitate all four motor tasks requested by the examiner. She was assessed as right handed and demonstrated a right eye preference. Draw-A-Design and Draw-A-Child involves the copying of abstract shapes and designs and drawing a child of the same sex. Both subtests involve fine motor and perceptual skills. She appeared to have approximately average performance in this area, though she displays minor distortions in copying abstract designs.

The NEPSY—A Developmental Neuropsychological Assessment

The NEPSY is a measure of neuropsychological functioning. It provides performance information for attention, language, sensorimotor, and visuospatial processes. Average performance on the core domains falls between 85 and 115. Jane's scores are presented below.

| | Scaled Scores | Confidence Interval | Classification |
|---|---|---|---|
| **Attention/Executive Function** | 88 | 80-100 | **Borderline** |
| Tower | 6 | | |
| Auditory Attention | 6 | | |
| Visual Attention | 13 | | |
| **Language** | 77 | 71-89 | **Below Expected** |
| Phonological Processing | 6 | | |
| Speed Naming | 8 | | |
| Comp. Of Instructions | 5 | | |
| **Sensorimotor** | 100 | 90-110 | **At Expected** |
| Fingertip Tapping | 10 | | |
| Imitating Hand Positions | 12 | | |
| Visuomotor Precision | 8 | | |
| **Visuospatial** | 101 | 91-111 | **At Expected** |
| Design Copying | 15 | | |
| Arrows | 5 | | |

Jane's overall neuropsychological performance on the NEPSY ranged from below expected level to expected level. Her domain scores were inconsistent when compared to each other. There was a significant difference between her language score and both the sensorimotor score and visuospatial performance. This suggests a significant weakness in language abilities when compared to her performance on the other scales.

The Attention/Executive Functions Domain assesses a broad range of abilities, such as visual and auditory attention and the ability to plan. Jane's responses on this measure fell within the borderline range, as compared to same age peers. Her scores indicate a strength in her ability to attend to visual stimuli and locate target pictures quickly. However, her performance suggests that she has a weakness in her ability to plan, monitor, self-regulate, and problem-solve compared to peers her same age. She also displayed a weakness in her capacity to attend to simple auditory stimuli. This suggests that she may have difficulty with attention.

The Language Domain assesses the components of speech, language, reading, spelling and writing. Jane's performance on this measure falls within the below expected range for children her age. Jane was in the expected range on a measure that required her to access and produce familiar words in alternating patterns rapidly. Her performance suggests that she has difficulty with the ability to process and respond to verbal instructions and identify words from segments. She may be having problems processing and comprehending verbal messages that are complex. These results are consistent with the results obtained from the school evaluation and the parent report. Jane also displayed a weakness on a task that required her to identify a picture from orally presented word segments. Her problems could suggest a phonological processing problem that could eventually affect reading and spelling. Poor attention could also influence these findings.

The Sensorimotor Functions domain assesses the components of sensorimotor functions such as the ability to produce rapid, accurate, and coordinated finger and hand movements. Jane's responses reflect an expected level of functioning on tasks that require finger dexterity, processing tactile information, and imitating hand positions.

Jane's performance on the Visuospatial Processing domain falls in the expected range compared to other peers her same age. This domain measures visuospatial skills with coordinated motor activity and the ability to accurately perceive direction, orientation, and the angle of lines. She displayed a significant strength on the ability to integrate visual stimuli with motor coordination. However her scores suggest a significant weakness on the ability to judge direction and estimate distance. This could indicate a tendency to misjudge the location of objects in space, or could be due to poor planning. There was a significant discrepancy between these two scales that occurs in less than 1% of the peers her age.

The Revised Children's Manifest Anxiety Scale (RCMAS)

The RCMAS is designed to aid in the understanding of a child's level of anxiety as well as the nature of her anxiety. This measure yields scores in four dimensions of anxiety, which include total anxiety, physiological anxiety, worry/oversensitivity, and social concerns/concentration. A lie scale is also included to help determine the child's degree of honesty when answering the questions. High scores suggest a presence of anxious thoughts or behaviors. On the total Anxiety scale, average scores range from 40 to 60. On the other scales, the average scores range from 7 to 13.

| Scales | Standard Scores | Percentiles | Ranges |
|---|---|---|---|
| **Total Anxiety** | **41** | **18** | **Average** |
| Physiological Anxiety | 5 | 5 | Low |
| Worry/Oversensitivity | 9 | 46 | Average |
| Social Concerns/Concentration | 8 | 28 | Average |

According to the Standard Scores obtained on the RCMAS, Jane reported average levels of anxiety in all areas. However, the responses corresponding to the Lie Scale indicate that she answered in a socially desirable manner in an attempt to present herself favorably. The results reported may not be an indicator of Jane's true feelings of anxiety. Rather it may be an underestimate of her overall anxiety level.

The Parent Stress Inventory (PSI)

The PSI is a measure that examines various factors that contribute to stress. Scores are calculated for the Child Domain, which is child related stress issues, and for the Parent Domain, which includes parent related stress issues. An overall composite is found for the child and parent domains combined. Scores between the 20th and 80th percentile are considered normal. Scores above the 80th percentile are of concern.

Jane's characteristics appear to be a major factor contributing to the overall stress in the parent-child relationship. Ms. Garcia's and Ms. Husman's responses on the overall Child Domain were ranked in the 99th and 97th percentiles, respectively. The response pattern indicated that the family experiences Jane as placing many demands and Jane demonstrates difficulty adapting to environmental changes. Both mother and grandmother reported that Jane frequently exhibits symptoms of depressed mood.

The individual and overall scores for the Parent Domain for Ms. Garcia fell outside of the normal range. This suggests that Ms. Garcia considers personal stressors as being significant, in addition to considering life in general to be a major stressor for her (92nd percentile). The individual and overall scores for the Parent Domain for Ms. Husman fell in the normal range. This suggests that Ms. Husman does not consider personal stressors as being significant. However, she does consider life in general to be stressful for her. This score was above the 99th percentile.

Projective Tests and Measures

The *Sentence Completion Test* presented a series of sentence stems designed to explore feelings, thoughts, behaviors, and perceptions about self and world. Jane's responses indicated awareness and perceptions regarding poor peer relationships. Depressed affect was a common theme throughout her answers, especially when discussing the academic setting. Family appears to be a source of strength for her.

The *House-Tree-Person Drawing* Test (HTP) required Jane to draw a picture of a house, a tree, and a person. The HTP is utilized to reflect the child's perception of herself, home life, and their relationship with the family. Jane appears to view herself as lonely and having difficulties with interpersonal relationships with peers. Immaturity and some depressive tendencies were evident. This could be related to her confidence about relationships and social situations. Again, family relations appear to be important to Jane and her drawings indicate her home environment as positive and loving.

The *Wishes and Fears Inventory* is a self-report instrument that allows an individual to express her feelings and thoughts. Jane displayed great difficulty on this measure and was not able to complete this test given significant expressive language difficulties.

## EVALUATION SUMMARY

Jane's evaluation was completed to address concerns regarding possible neuropsychological difficulties that may be interfering with her academic performance and success. She is a 7-year-old second grade student whose overall intellectual abilities were found to be within the Borderline range. However, significant discrepancies and scatter exist in her cognitive profile, which may indicate that the obtained overall score may not be the best indicator of her cognitive skills. The scores obtained on a memory assessment indicated that Jane's nonverbal memory is better developed than her verbal memory, especially after a short time delay. Her delayed verbal memory skills are poorly developed. According to the NEPSY, she displayed average abilities in attention/executive functioning, sensorimotor, and visuospatial. The language areas (including understanding and expressing oral/auditory language) appear to be a significant weakness for her. She may be experiencing both moderate levels of anxiety and depression due to difficulties she encounters in the school setting both academically and socially. Familial relations continue to be an area of strength for her.

## DIAGNOSTIC IMPRESSIONS

Primary Handicapping Condition: Speech/Language Disability
   (Including 315.31 Mixed Receptive-Expressive Language Disorder)

Secondary Handicapping Condition: Seriously Identifiable Emotional Disturbance
   Rule Out 299.80  Pervasive Development Disorder
   Rule Out 300.4    Dysthymic Disorder

Rule Out Learning Disability

## EVALUATION RECOMMENDATIONS

1. Jane displays significant primary and secondary handicapping conditions that hinder her school progress. Ms. Garcia should contact the school and share the information included in this report so that a positive collaboration between home and school can be established. In addition, Ms. Garcia may wish to request that school personnel consider the possibility of eligibility for additional special education services.

2. Since it is close to the end of the school year, the issue of retention may surface in the school setting. It is the opinion of the evaluators that Jane should be promoted to the next grade, with appropriate academic support in the aforementioned areas, so that she will continue to be successful.

3. At this time, Jane is consistently able to follow one-step directions. Two-step directions can be introduced. Jane will need to orally repeat directions and may need several verbal

reminders given by an adult. At school, Jane's teacher(s) may consider combining visual and auditory reminder cues for multiple step directions to assist Jane in following directions.

4. Jane tends to wait for others to ask her if she needs assistance. For example, she needs to continue her self-advocacy and assertive skills by asking for assistance and clarification questions. Her teacher and parents could work with her in this area.

5. Jane needs to work on completing all academic tasks with increasing independence. At this time, she needs to complete as much of her assignment as she can before she may ask for help from a peer or a teacher. A plan should be developed that would explain in detail how she should work and attempt to solve her assignments for two to five minutes before asking for help from others. A certain number of items may then need to be completed prior to seeking assistance again.

6. Jane demonstrated a low frustration level and is unable to complete assignments. Adults need to working on helping her develop effective coping and problem-solving skills. At school, Jane's teacher could modify the number of items for completion and gradually work up to the full amount. At home, Ms. Garcia could set a specific time limit, such as five minutes, for completing a specific amount of homework before allowing a break. This time could be increased slowly. She should also have a discussion with her teacher and parents regarding appropriate ways to cope and express her frustration. Again, a clear plan could be developed so when she becomes extremely frustrated she as well as the adults in her life will know what steps to follow.

7. Jane and her family have stressed how poorly her peers treat her and how sad it is for her not to have any friends at school. It is recommended that Jane, her parents, and school personnel seriously discuss what could be changed in her current school placement to better meet her social needs. It is recommended that the individuals involved with Jane work together to design a social component for Jane at school so she will not feel so isolated. A friendship group could be developed in her classroom, the class could study friendship, and inappropriate peer relations, or she could be provide with a mentor/friend from her classroom.

8. Jane appears to have difficulties verbally interacting with peers. She should receive individualized role-playing based psychological services that emphasize conversational skills with same age peers. A social skills group by the school counselor or school psychologist would be helpful for her to work on particular skills in addition to helping her meet other children. But she will need training before participating in such a group. Her speech therapist could also work with Jane in this area.

9. When having lunch with family members, Jane may want to invite a peer to join them from her classroom so that she gains practice in social skills. Her teacher could be consulted initially to develop a list of children who may be willing to eat with her and serve as a friend.

10. For math problems, Jane appears to benefit from the use of manipulatives to perform calculations. As her confidence increases, she may wish to use a number line instead of physical manipulatives. At this time, it is not recommended that calculator skills be introduced. But they may need to be considered in future years.

11. Jane needs additional time to respond verbally. If possible, ask her to think about a specific question that the teacher will ask in class. This would assist in boosting her self-esteem and may positively reward the behavior of participation in class.

12. Ms. Garcia appears to be concerned about Jane's gross motor difficulties because she fears for Jane's safety. The examiner recommends a complete physical therapy evaluation be conducted due to the below average scores she obtained during the evaluation.

13. Her family (as well as school personnel) should continue to make positive comments about her on a frequent basis in order to improve her self-esteem. These comments should be related to something she has done (e.g., showing compassion or assertiveness), instead of a physical trait (e.g., beauty and clothes). Continue to highlight Jane's successes and remind her that she is capable of completing tasks.

14. Since she prefers older peers and adults, caution must be taken to avoid treating her like a "very young child." Jane should be able to speak for herself, especially if she is in a comfortable situation. Encourage her to speak a little louder and allow her time to express herself. Family members and educational personnel should praise her for her attempts to speak with others as well as her successes.

15. Continue to monitor vision (e.g., farsightedness) and its impact on her fine and gross motor skills. She should be evaluated on a regular basis in this area and parents and teachers should observe her vision and motor related skills regularly.

16. Due to language difficulties, it may be anticipated that she will have difficulties with applied mathematics problems. It will be important to identify math operational words to help her understand which operation to use (e.g., together, how many LEFT, in all, etc.)

17. In regard to testing accommodations and modifications, Jane will need to be placed in a very small group or individualized setting. Allow her time to read the directions and provide an opportunity for her to ask questions throughout the test. She may need a quiet setting with little stimulation when taking tests.

18. Judging and estimating objects in space appears to be an area of weakness for Jane. This may be why she appears so accident prone. Direct instruction and additional practice may be needed in this area. Practice in the fine and gross motor areas will allow her to develop these skills both at home and in school. Activities may include drawing, art, running, throwing, and more physical education related activities.

19. Jane appears to benefit from repeated practice in order to be successful. Allow Jane additional time within her schedule for practice of her skills. All home and school routines and schedules should be clear, followed regularly, and reinforced.

20. Jane needs to work on broadening her repertoire of strategies and problem-solving skills. Work to teach Jane "how" to approach problem solving and skill development. She will need extra help with organization and knowledge development. It is as important to teach Jane how to complete an assignment as it is to teach her the subject content. Thus, *content* and *method* should both be the focus of her educational achievement. Encourage creative approaches to help her solve tasks.

21. Jane needs to continue working on adaptive skills such as remembering her address, phone number, and birth date in the event that she needs to contact her home. She also should study how to respond in emergency situations.

_____
Leesa V. Huang, Ph.D.
Nationally Certified School Psychologist Number 12345

_____
Cherise Lerew, Ph.D.
Licensed Colorado School Psychologist Number 23456

_____
Rik Carl D'Amato, Ph.D.
Professor and Director, Neuropsychology Laboratory
Nationally Certified School Psychologist Number 22334

_____
Names have been changed to protect the identity of those tested.

# Appendix D: Sample Neuropsychological Evaluation

KIMBERLY A. ROOT, DAVID HULAC, and RIK CARL D'AMATO

UNIVERSITY *of*
## NORTHERN COLORADO

COLLEGE OF EDUCATION AND BEHAVIORAL SCIENCES
DIVISION OF PROFESSIONAL PSYCHOLOGY
NEUROPSYCHOLOGY LABORATORY

| | | | |
|---|---|---|---|
| **Name:** | Sonja Theresa Lopez | **Evaluation Dates:** | 00-00-0000 |
| **Grade:** | 4th | **Teacher:** | Mrs. James |
| **Handedness:** | Left | **Date of Birth** | January 12, 0000 |
| **School:** | Jackson Elementary | **Chronological Age:** | 10 years, 10 months |

## Reason for Referral

Sonja Lopez was referred by her mother, Mrs. Maria Lopez, to the University of Northern Colorado (UNC) Neuropsychological Laboratory due to concerns about a traumatic brain injury Sonja experienced some years ago. Mrs. Lopez wanted to learn about specific interventions and teaching strategies that would help her daughter improve her ability to learn in the classroom.

## Evaluation Procedures

> Clinical Interview (with Mrs. Lopez and Sonja)
> Review of School Cognitive and Achievement Testin g
> > Wechsler Intelligence Scales for Children-III
> > Woodcock-Johnson Achievement Test
> Review of Medical Records
> Cognitive Assessment System (CAS)
> NEPSY: A Developmental Neuropsychological Assessment
> Wechsler Individual Achievement Test, 2nd edition (WIAT II)
> The Behavioral Assessment Scale for Children (BASC)
> > Parent Report Form (with Mrs. Lopez)
> > Teacher Report Forms (with Mrs. James and Mrs. Smith)
> > Self-Report Form (with Sonja)
> The Vineland Adaptive Behavior Scales (with Mrs. Lopez)
> The Draw-a-Picture and Tell-a-Story Test

## Clinical History and Background Information

Sonja lives at home with her biological mother and father on a ranch in rural Northeastern Colorado. Her family raises and trains horses. This activity is one in which Sonja is a regular participant. Her 18-year-old brother Andre does not currently live at home full time, but visits regularly since he is attending Colorado State University, a local college, majoring in veterinary science.

901

Sonja's family's history revealed no significant cognitive, academic, or medical difficulties. Sonja's mother and father are both graduates of Colorado State University. Mrs. Lopez graduated with a degree in psychology and Mr. Lopez with a degree in ranch management. Her mother stays at home so she can help run the family business and care for Sonja. Sonja's father is a full time trainer who runs their family business from the ranch. Mr. Lopez was described as a quick learner who did well in school. Mrs. Lopez described herself as finding school more difficult, but she was able to succeed and graduated on schedule.

Sonja's medical history before the age of three years was reportedly unremarkable. Her mother indicated that Sonja weighed nine pounds at birth. There was no report of any drug, alcohol, or tobacco use during Mrs. Lopez's pregnancy and there were reportedly no complications at birth. Mrs. Lopez believes that Sonja experienced no significant illnesses or injuries until she was three-years-old. At that time, Sonja snuck out of the house to go look at the family's horses. When her mother finally found her, Sonja was in a horse stable, unconscious with blood that had been matted at the back of her head.

She was taken to the hospital where it was determined that she had been kicked in the chin by a horse. The force of the blow struck the right side of her chin causing a "perfect break" along her jaw. While in the hospital, Sonja underwent a CAT scan and an MRI to determine if there had been any "significant" brain damage. The results of both tests revealed no structural brain problems. A neurological report dated 00-00-0000 indicated that she should have a "full recovery" after some minor rehabilitation. However, Mrs. Lopez indicated that Sonja "acted different" after the accident and she believes it has changed Sonja significantly. Mrs. Lopez reported that Sonja's previous physical examination took place recently at which point all medical tests including both hearing and vision revealed no significant deficits.

Sonja is a 10-year-old 4th grader who is attending Jackson Elementary in rural Colorado. She described school as a fun place for her to be and indicated that she enjoys her teacher and her school friends. Science is Sonja's favorite subject while math is the subject with which she indicated having the most difficulty. Sonja's mother reported that her daughter initially showed problems with her academics at the end of first grade. At that point, school personnel suggested that Sonja be retained for another year to help her "mature." Although she was retained, Sonja continued to demonstrate problems with reading. Mrs. Lopez explained that Sonja also has difficulty with spelling as well as mild difficulty with mathematics and written expression. For her to be successful in writing and math, it is necessary for problems or stories to be read to her. These concerns continue in her current classroom.

In January, as a result of these academic concerns, and after a variety of interventions, Sonja was placed in a special education resource room with a Traumatic Brain Injury (TBI) classification. She receives a few hours of small group help each day from the teacher in the Learning Disabilities class. However, Mrs. Lopez describes her daughter's progress in school as having reached a plateau, and hopes for advice on effective strategies and interventions to help address her daughter's academic difficulties.

Sonja's self care and life skills were reported to be good. In school, Sonja typically finishes her assignments on time. Her mother describes Sonja as self-driven, responsible, and business-like. Sonja takes care of some of the animals at the ranch and is responsible for the care of two horses. Mrs. Lopez believes that Sonja has excellent interpersonal skills. She is responsible for presenting her horses at horse shows and has regular contact with many adults. Mrs. Lopez explained that many people were impressed with her daughter's ability to interact in ways that made her appear to be much older than her 10-years. Sonja herself says that she enjoys her interactions with her peers, her parents, and her teachers.

## Behavioral Observations

Sonja was assessed over two consecutive days. She worked for 5 hours each day in 2 _ hour segments. Sonja was initially shy when she first met the examiners. However, she soon relaxed and was a full and cooperative participant in all of the assessments. On both occasions, Sonja was casually but neatly dressed and appeared to be well groomed. Her eye contact and socialization skills seemed appropriate for a 10-year-old girl. Sonja appeared to work hard on all of the tasks that were required of her, although she looked bored when having to complete reading comprehension and writing tasks. Sonja denied the intention of hurting herself or others. She showed no indications of hearing or vision problems or impulsive behaviors. Sonja's performance on the current assessment appears to represent a valid and reliable sample of her neuropsychological abilities.

## Evaluation Results

### *Wechsler Intelligence Scales for Children-III* (WISC-III)

Sonja completed the WISC III in preparation for her Individualized Education Plan in a report dated 00-00-0000. The following results were reported by Dr. David Smith, a Licensed School Psychologist who worked with Sonja at Jackson Elementary School. Jackson is part of the Colorado Regional Inter-District Special Education Cooperative (C-RISE-C). The WISC-III provided information on both verbal and nonverbal problem solving abilities. Average scores on the verbal and performance subtests lie between 8 and 12, while the average composite standard score falls between 85 and 115. Sonja's scores are listed below:

| Verbal Scale | | Performance Scale | |
|---|---|---|---|
| Subtests | Scaled Scores | Subtests | Scaled Scores |
| Information | 6 | Picture Completion | 3 |
| Similarities | 6 | Coding | 7 |
| Arithmetic | 5 | Picture Arrangement | 9 (s) |
| Vocabulary | 7 | Block Design | 4 |
| Comprehension | 6 | Object Assembly | 3 |
| Digit Span | 6 | Symbol Search | |

| | Standard Scores | Score Ranges | Percentile Ranks | Classification |
|---|---|---|---|---|
| Verbal IQ | 78 | 73-85 | 7 | Borderline |
| Performance IQ | 71 | 66-82 | 3 | Borderline |
| Full Scale IQ | 72 | 67-79 | 3 | Borderline |
| Verbal Comprehension | 80 | 74-88 | 9 | Low Average |
| Perceptual Organization | 70 | 65-81 | 2 | Borderline |
| Freedom from Distractibility | 75 | 69-87 | 5 | Borderline |

Sonja's performance on tests measuring problem solving abilities fell within the Borderline range and was better than 3% of same-age individuals in the general population. Her ability to solve problems using language and her nonverbal problem solving skills also fall within the Borderline range. Children with similar cognitive profiles have difficulty acquiring new information and solving novel problems. Sonja's verbal problem solving abilities were evenly developed. Sonja's nonverbal problem solving abilities are also evenly developed with one exception. Her performance on activities that required a nonverbal knowledge of human events or social intelligence fell within the Average range. Sonja's relative strength in this area suggested that she is able to visually recognize and comprehend a situation and is able to organize components into a logical sequence.

The following instruments and procedures were administered at the UNC Neuropsychology Laboratory with the exception of the Woodcock-Johnson Achievement Test.

### Cognitive Assessment Scale (CAS)

The CAS measures both cognitive and neuropsychological processes. The assessment can provide evidence about Sonja's planning and attending skills as well as her ability to process information as a whole or in a specific order. Average scores on the composite areas fall between 85 and 115. On the individual subtests, the average scores fall between 7 and 13. Sonja achieved the following scores:

| Planning Subtests | | Attention Subtests | |
|---|---|---|---|
| Matching Numbers | 7 | Expressive Attention | 7 |
| Planned Codes | 10 | Number Detection | 8 |
| Planned Connections | 6 | Receptive Attention | 7 |
| | | | |
| Simultaneous Subtests | | Successive Subtests | |
| Nonverbal Matrices | 7 | Word Series | 10 |
| Verbal-Spatial Relations | 11 | Sentence Repetition | 8 |
| Figure Memory | 8 | Sentence Questions | 9 |

| | Scaled Score | Percentile Rank | 95% Confidence Interval | Classification |
|---|---|---|---|---|
| Planning Composite | 85 | 16 | 78-96 | Low Average |
| Attention Composite | 84 | 14 | 77-95 | Low Average |
| Simultaneous Composite | 92 | 30 | 85-100 | Average |
| Sequential Composite | 94 | 34 | 87-102 | Average |
| Full Scale Composite | 84 | 14 | 79-90 | Low Average |

On the CAS, Sonja's performance fell within the Low Average range. There was no significant difference between any of Sonja's scores. However, her ability to process information holistically as well as her ability to work sequentially and to follow specific patterns fell within the Average range. On tasks that required her to focus on necessary information while ignoring extraneous information, Sonja's performance fell within the Low Average range and was better than 14% of other children her age. Finally, her ability to set goals, make strategies, and to monitor the effectiveness of those strategies fell within the Low Average range.

Children who perform well on the successive subtests are able to work with information that is presented sequentially. Tasks that require sequential processing include if-then directions as well as instructions and mathematical algorithms. It would appear that Sonja is able to keep several pieces of information in her head and perform tasks in the correct order.

Children who perform well on the simultaneous composite are able to look at an entire situation and make sense of all of the information in its entirety. Looking at pictures or maps or performing tasks that do not require sequential demands are all simultaneous tasks. Sonja performed her best when she was asked to point to a picture that best fit a description given orally. She had more trouble when she was required to understand a nonverbal concept and complete a pattern that was given pictorially. Her ability to reproduce drawings by memory fell within the Average range. Sonja's performance on the planning subtests suggested that she has difficulty finding useful strategies for solving problems. When given a new task, it is necessary for an individual to set a goal, evaluate the best means for achieving such a goal, implementing those means, and evaluate their progress toward goal achievement. Finally, Sonja's attention skills fell within the Low Average range. Attention is measured by seeing how well an individual focuses on relevant information and ignores irrelevant information. This measure provided new information that was not available from the Wechsler scale.

### NEPSY

The NEPSY is a measure of neuropsychological functioning. The NEPSY provides performance information on attention, language, sensorimotor, visualspatial, and memory processes as well as executive functioning capabilities. Average performance on the subtests falls between 8 and 13 and average performance on the core domains falls between 85 and 115. Sonja achieved the following scores:

| | Scaled Scores | | Scaled Scores |
|---|---|---|---|
| **Attention Subtests** | | **Visualspatial Subtests** | |
| Tower | 3 (w) | Design Copying | 15 (s) |
| Auditory Attention | 9 | Arrows | 9 |
| Visual Attention | 13 (s) | | |
| **Language Subtests** | | **Memory Subtests** | |
| Phonological Processing | 4 (w) | Memory for Faces | 9 |
| Speeded Naming | 10 (s) | Memory for Names | 6 (w) |
| Comprehension of Instructions | 7 | Narrative Memory | 9 |
| **Sensorimotor Subtests** | | | |
| Finger Tapping | 8 | | |
| Imitating Hand Positions | 9 | | |
| Visuomotor Precision | 9 | | |

| | Standard Scores | Percentile Rank | Classification |
|---|---|---|---|
| Attention Domain | 88 | 21 | Borderline |
| Language Domain | 80 | 9 | Below Expected Level |
| Sensorimotor Domain | 89 | 23 | Borderline |
| Visuospatial Domain | 112 | 79 | Above Expected Level |
| Memory Domain | 86 | 18 | Borderline |

Sonja's overall neuropsychological functioning performance on the NEPSY falls within the Below Expected Level to Above Expected Level range based on her age. Such wide variability is typical of children with a history of TBI. Sonja displayed particular strengths on the domains measuring her visuospatial skills. Sonja's score on the Visuospatial Domain was a 112, which is Above Expected for her age level. Therefore, Sonja performed better than 79% of children her age on the visuospatial tasks. This reflects her well developed ability to synthesize visual information, understand the relationship between objects in space and adopt a variety of perspectives and rotate objects mentally.

Sonja performed in the Borderline range on the Attention, Memory and Sensorimotor Domains. Sonja's standard score on the Attention domain was an 88, which places her in the 21st percentile. Performance in this area reflected Sonja's ability to focus her attention, sustain her attention for a required period of time, and shift her attention as tasks change. Sonja had particular difficulty with a task that required her to place rings on pegs in a certain order and in a certain amount of moves. It appeared that Sonja could put them in the right order, but had difficulty understanding and remembering the rules as to the number of moves she was allowed. This particular task measures executive functioning, which is an individual's ability to set goals, plan for ways of achieving goals, and evaluate one's own progress toward a particular goal. However, Sonja's ability to merely sustain visual and auditory attention was Average.

Sonja's score on the Memory domain was an 86, which places her in the 18th percentile. This reflected her difficulty in remembering objects immediately and after a delay in time. Specifically, Sonja had difficulty with a task that required her to remember names of individuals. She did better on memory tasks that required her to remember information from a story and remember faces. Sonja's performance on the Sensorimotor domain was an 89, which is at the 23rd percentile. This score reflects Sonja's difficulties in performing a variety of requested tasks with her hands, such as tapping her fingers in a specified manner. Sonja's language processing abilities fell within the below expected range of performance. Sonja struggled with processing and understanding verbally presented information. She displayed her lowest performance on a task measuring her phonological processing skills. This measure also provided new information that was not previously available.

### *Woodcock-Johnson Achievement Test–3rd Edition* (WJA-III)

Sonja completed the Woodcock-Johnson Achievement Test–3rd Edition in preparation for an eligibility decision and development of a possible Individualized Educational Plan (IEP). This measure was administered by Ms. Carlson, a certified special education teacher at Jackson Elementary and information is provide in a report dated 00-00-000. The WJA-III is a measure of academic functioning, that measures an individual's reading, writing and mathematics abilities. Each of the three different areas is broken into three parts: academic skills, academic fluency, and skill application. The reading tests measure the examinee's ability to read single words, the ability to understand paragraphs, and the ability to determine the truth of simple sentences under time pressure. The written expression tests included a spelling test, writing to prompts, and the ability to write simple, complete sentences using picture and word cues. The mathematics tests measured math calculation, math application, and the ability to do simple addition, subtraction and multiplication problems quickly. The average standard score on each of the subtests of the WJA-III is 100, and the average range is between 85 and 115. Sonja's scores are listed below:

| Subtests/Clusters | Standard Scores | Percentile Ranks | Classifications |
|---|---|---|---|
| **Oral Language (Extended)** | 98 | 43 | Average |
| Oral Expression | 98 | 44 | Average |
| Listening Comprehension | 98 | 46 | Average |
| Story Recall | 108 | 71 | Average |
| Understanding Directions | 88 | 21 | Low Average |
| Oral Comprehension | 108 | 71 | Average |
| | | | |
| **Broad Reading** | 63 | 1 | Very Low |
| Basic Reading Skills | 78 | 7 | Low |
| Reading Comprehension | 57 | 0.2 | Very Low |
| Letter –Word Identification | 70 | 2 | Low |
| Reading Fluency | 63 | 1 | Very Low |
| Passage Comprehension | 71 | 3 | Low |
| Spelling of Sounds | 91 | 28 | Average |
| Word Attack | 89 | 23 | Low Average |
| | | | |
| **Broad Written Language** | 68 | 2 | Very Low |
| Basic Writing Skills | 64 | 1 | Very Low |
| Written Expression | 74 | 4 | Low |
| Spelling | 68 | 2 | Very Low |
| Writing Fluency | 66 | 1 | Very Low |
| Writing Samples | 92 | 31 | Average |
| Punctuation and Capitals | 94 | 34 | Average |
| | | | |
| **Broad Math** | 85 | 16 | Low Average |
| Math Calculation | 85 | 16 | Low Average |
| Applied Problems | 89 | 22 | Low Average |
| Math Fluency | 66 | 1 | Very Low |
| Quantitative Concepts | 64 | 1 | Very Low |

Sonja's overall performance on the WJA-IIII was better than only one percent of children her own age. Sonja demonstrated an overall strength in the area of oral expression. Her ability to remember information that has been spoken to her and her ability to follow directions fell within the Average range. Her ability to answer questions about a paragraph that were read to her also fell within the Average range. On tasks that required Sonja to see and define pictures, her performance fell within the Average range suggesting that her verbal knowledge base appears appropriately developed.

Sonja's performance on reading tasks fell in the Very Low range and was better than only one percent of students her own age. Sonja's reading profile was somewhat atypical. As is usually the case, children who learn how to read first develop their phonemic awareness skills or their ability to associate each letter or cluster of letters with a sound. On tasks that measured phonemic awareness, Sonja's performance fell within the Low Average range, but was much higher than her overall reading score. After solidifying their phonemic awareness skills, students then learn how to decode words. When asked to recognize nonsense words, Sonja's performance again fell within the Low Average range, but was much higher than her other reading abilities. After learning decoding skills, students begin to develop their vocabulary along with their sight word vocabulary. Once the vocabulary and sight word base are built, a student is able to develop their reading comprehension skills by linking what they read with the rest of their knowledge base. Sonja's knowledge of words and word meanings fell within the Low range suggesting that her vocabulary has not been sufficiently developed. Further, her ability to understand a sentence or paragraph well enough to insert a missing word fell within the Very Low range and is better than only 2 out of 1000 people Sonja's age. Even though Sonja's overall knowledge of words fell within the Average range, it appears that Sonja's reading difficulties involve linking a written word to a concept that she understands. Sonja's reading difficulties appear to be compounded when she is required to link several words that she does not recognize into a sentence.

Sonja's overall writing ability fell within the Very Low range. Sonja's ability to spell words and write simple sentences fell within the Very Low range. However, the content of her writing and the thoughts behind her writing appeared to be appropriate for a student her age. It is the mechanics of writing that seemed to cause Sonja the most difficulty. While she apparently understands the rules of punctuation and capitalization, she appears not to fully understand sentence structure and correct word usage. As a result, her ability to express her well-developed thoughts in writing becomes obscured by the structure of her sentences.

Mathematically, Sonja's performance fell within the Low Average range. It would appear that math is a relative strength for Sonja with her calculation skills and her ability to apply her mathematical knowledge being equally developed. However, her ability to do simple mathematical calculations under time pressure fell within the Very Low range. While Sonja seemed to have a good sense of the tasks necessary to succeed mathematically, she took a long time to complete these tasks, and may often make computational errors.

### *Wechsler Individual Achievement Test–2nd Edition* (**WIAT–II**)

Sonja completed two selected subtests from the WIAT-II. The passage comprehension subtest required her to read paragraphs and answer questions about those paragraphs as well as to read certain passages aloud. The Written Expression subtest required her to write a paragraph and to combine two sentences into a compound sentence. Both tasks are more authentic assessments of reading comprehension and written expression abilities since they required Sonja to use all of the strategies and skills that she knows to be successful on the assessments. The average standard score on each of the subtests of the WIAT-II is 100, and the average range is between 85 and 115. Sonja achieved the following scores:

| Subtests | Standard Score | Percentile | Classification |
|---|---|---|---|
| Reading Comprehension | 65 | < 1 | Extremely Low |
| Written Expression | 72 | 2 | Borderline |

On the reading comprehension activities, Sonja's performance fell within the Extremely Low range. Sonja's reading speed was very slow given that she required several minutes to read each short paragraph and attempted to scan the passage to find the answer. When required to read out loud, Sonja was unable to read the sentences with fluency. She made many self-corrections while reading, and when she came to an unfamiliar word she could not use contextual clues or phonetic decoding skills to determine the meaning of the word. Sonja could not recognize words such as could, reasons, or floppy.

On tasks measuring written expression, Sonja's abilities fell in the Borderline range of functioning. Her paragraph had many spelling errors, but only one punctuation error. When required to spell the same words on more than one occasion, she actually produced two different spellings which suggested that Sonja makes guesses at the correct spelling of words and does not use consistent spelling strategies when attempting to spell words correctly. It appeared that Sonja was unable to spell any words that were more than one syllable in length. It was also apparent that Sonja did not know how to construct sentences that were longer than a simple noun-verb sentence. In her paragraph, Sonja's letters were all correctly formed with no reversals. She was also able to copy words correctly and accurately.

### The Behavior Assessment Scale for Children (BASC)

The BASC is a behavior rating scale completed by Sonja's parents, teachers, and herself. It investigates Sonja's behaviors in her home, school, and peer environments. Information is collected to determine appropriate and/or inappropriate behaviors in an effort to develop appropriate interventions. The average range for each score, as well as the composite score, lies between 40 and 60 points. In most areas, scores that fall between 60 and 70 suggest the child is at-risk for developing a problem in a particular area. Scores that fall above 70 suggest that the respondent's perception of the child's behavior suggests clinically significant problems within a particular area. On the adaptive scales, scores that fall between 30 and 40 are considered to be at-risk while scores that fall below 30 are considered to be clinically significant. Scores that fall in the low or average range are not considered to be areas of concern.

### BASC–Parent Rating Form

Sonja's mother, Mrs. Lopez completed the parent survey form achieving the following scores:

| Parent Report Form | Scaled Scores (Mother) | Percentile (Mother) | Range (Mother) |
|---|---|---|---|
| Externalizing problems | 30 | 1 | Low |
| Hyperactivity | 30 | 1 | Low |
| Aggression | 32 | 2 | Low |
| Conduct Problems | 37 | 4 | Low |
| Internalizing Problems | 34 | 3 | Low |
| Anxiety | 40 | 15 | Average |
| Depression | 34 | 1 | Low |
| Somatization | 39 | 9 | Low |
| Atypicality | 38 | 3 | Low |
| Withdrawal | 44 | 31 | Average |
| Attention problems | 47 | 44 | Average |
| Behavioral Symptoms | 31 | 1 | Low |
| Adaptive Skills | 48 | 42 | Average |
| Adaptability | 61 | 86 | Average |
| Social skills | 47 | 38 | Average |
| **Leadership** | **37** | **11** | **At-Risk** |

Sonja's mother's responses are consistent with those of children who show few emotional and behavioral difficulties. She viewed Sonja as being relatively free from anxiety, depression, and other attention problems. Her responses also suggested that Sonja was not overly aggressive or hyperactive, and she demonstrated no conduct problems. Sonja's abilities to engage in appropriate social discourse and to adapt to changing environments appear to be average. Mrs. Lopez's responses did indicate that Sonja's leadership skills fall in the At-Risk range. Sonja's mother highlighted two critical items saying that she sometimes wets her bed and sometimes sleeps with her parents.

### BASC—Teacher Rating Form

Sonja's classroom teacher, Mrs. James, and her teacher's aide also completed a BASC. The results of Mrs. James' responses are reported first:

| Teacher Report Form | Scaled Scores (Teacher) | Percentile (Teacher) | Range (Teacher) |
|---|---|---|---|
| **Externalizing problems** | **66** | **91** | **At-Risk** |
| **Hyperactivity** | **68** | **94** | **At-Risk** |
| **Aggression** | **66** | **91** | **At-Risk** |
| Conduct Problems | 59 | 87 | Average |
| **Internalizing Problems** | **61** | **63** | **At-Risk** |
| Anxiety | 45 | 37 | Average |
| Depression | 43 | 26 | Average |
| **Somatization** | **64** | **90** | **At-Risk** |
| Attention Problems | 57 | 75 | Average |
| **Learning Problems** | **74** | **98** | **Clinically Significant** |
| **Atypicality** | **64** | **92** | **At-Risk** |

| | | | |
|---|---|---|---|
| **Withdrawal** | **61** | **87** | **At-Risk** |
| **School Problems** | **66** | **91** | **At-Risk** |
| Behavioral Symptoms | 59 | 82 | Average |
| Adaptive Skills | 50 | 50 | Average |
| Adaptability | 41 | 20 | Average |
| Social skills | 60 | 83 | High |
| Leadership | 50 | 50 | Average |
| Study Skill | 49 | 44 | Average |

When interpreting the teacher's BASC, it is important to note that Mrs. James may have been excessively negative in responding to some of the questions. With that in mind, it will be important to use caution when interpreting Sonja's scores. The classroom teacher's responses suggested that Sonja demonstrates learning problems that are Clinically Significant. Sonja also displayed behaviors that are associated with hyperactivity and aggression that are in the at-risk range. Sonja's teacher sees her as being at-risk for having school problems, being withdrawn, and displaying atypical behaviors. Her responses do not indicate significant levels of conduct problems, anxiety, depression or attention problems. It appears that Sonja's adaptive skills such as her ability to adapt to new situations, to interact with other people, and to be a leader when needed are all appropriately developed for a student her age.

Mrs. James' responses suggested that Sonja has significant learning problems that make school difficult for her. It is possible that when confronted with the many assignments that Sonja finds difficult, she begins to display behaviors that help her avoid difficult work. These may include hyperactive behaviors such as talking too loudly, acting silly, calling out in class, aggressive behaviors such as arguing, when she does not get her way, displaying tantrums or refusing to do an assignment. It is also possible that Sonja's learning problems cause a great deal of frustration for her teacher and possibly disrupt other students in the classroom. However, the teacher's responses also indicated that Sonja tries hard and takes her time when completing assignments. She indicated that Sonja has a good sense of humor, good problem solving skills, and seems to be creative.

### BASC—Teacher's Aide Report

The teacher's aide, Mrs. Smith, also completed the BASC, and her results are reported below:

| Teacher Report Form | Scaled Scores (Aide) | Percentile (Aide) | Range (Aide) |
|---|---|---|---|
| Externalizing problems | 53 | 71 | Average |
| Hyperactivity | 48 | 51 | Average |
| Aggression | 50 | 64 | Average |
| Conduct Problems | 59 | 87 | Average |
| Internalizing Problems | 52 | 69 | Average |
| Anxiety | 49 | 53 | Average |
| Depression | 48 | 55 | Average |
| Somatization | 59 | 84 | Average |
| Attention Problems | 46 | 42 | Average |
| Learning Problems | **61** | **85** | **At-Risk** |
| Atypicality | 55 | 83 | Average |

| | | | |
|---|---|---|---|
| Withdrawal | 42 | 20 | Average |
| School Problems | 54 | 68 | Average |
| Behavioral Symptoms | 49 | 57 | Average |
| Adaptive Skills | 51 | 54 | Average |
| Adaptability | 59 | 79 | Average |
| Social skills | 54 | 67 | Average |
| Leadership | 48 | 44 | Average |
| Study Skill | 43 | 27 | Average |

Mrs. Smith, the teacher's aide who is working with Sonja's classroom also sees Sonja as having learning difficulties. However, her responses do not demonstrate the same level of concern as do the classroom teacher's responses. The only area of concern highlighted by Mrs. Smith was in the area of learning problems which fell in the at-risk range. Otherwise, the teacher's aide does not see behaviors that are unusually aggressive or hyperactive. She identified Sonja as having appropriate social skills, leadership skills, and a good ability to adapt to new situations.

### BASC – Sonja's Self-Report

Sonja herself also completed a BASC survey with the help of a reader. Her scores are listed below:

| **Clinical Scales** | T Score | Percentile | Classification |
|---|---|---|---|
| Attitude To School | 42 | 28 | Average |
| Attitude To Teachers | 49 | 56 | Average |
| Atypicality | 37 | 6 | Low |
| Locus of Control | 41 | 23 | Average |
| Social Stress | 35 | 4 | Low |
| Anxiety | 42 | 28 | Average |
| Depression | 41 | 13 | Average |
| Sense of Inadequacy | 40 | 12 | Average |
| | | | |
| **Adaptive Scales** | | | |
| Relations With Parents | 51 | 38 | Average |
| Interpersonal Relations | 58 | 80 | Average |
| Self-Esteem | 57 | 73 | Average |
| Self-Reliance | 47 | 31 | Average |
| **Composites** | | | |
| School Maladjustment | 45 | 38 | Average |
| Clinical Maladjustment | 37 | 9 | Low |
| Personal Adjustment | 54 | 56 | Average |
| Emotional Symptoms Index | 38 | 7 | Low |

Sonja's responses are consistent with those of students who are confident and self-assured in their outlook toward the world. In the areas of self-esteem, self-reliance, and relationships with school, her parents, and her friends, her responses were all typical for a young lady of her age. Sonja has a high opinion of her teacher and believes that she is able to be successful at school and at home.

### *Vineland Adaptive Behavior Scales* (Vineland)

The Vineland provides information concerning significant strengths and weaknesses which affect Sonja's daily functioning. An interview was completed with Mrs. Lopez. Sonja's adaptive functioning ranged from moderately low to moderately high. Within the communication domain, Mrs. Lopez rated Sonja's ability to express herself verbally as adequate. Similarly, her ability to understand what is being said to her was rated as adequate. Sonja's written language was more difficult for her and was ranked in the moderately low range. Her mother perceived Sonja's daily living skills as being moderately high. She described Sonja as being able to take care of herself, being able to complete domestic tasks, and being able to function within the community. Sonja's social skills were rated in the adequate range. In the Socialization Domain, Mrs. Lopez viewed Sonja's coping skills as being more developed than her leisure skills or her ability to relate to and interact with peers. Specifically, she perceived Sonja's coping skills to be in the moderately high range. Her interpersonal skills and her leisure skills were rated in the adequate range.

### *The Draw-a-Picture and Tell-a-Story Test* (DAP-TAS)

The DAP-TAS test required Sonja to draw a picture, while she and the examiner made up a story together. This test is thought to measure the student's perceptions of herself as well as her social and emotional adjustment. Sonja took a long time to draw her picture and was very careful to get details exact, often erasing and re-drawing portions of her picture. This was similar to information provided by both her mother and her teacher. Her story was concrete and literal and related to individuals who enjoyed riding horses. Her story centered around enjoying taking care of animals, being outdoors, and worrying that her animals were not receiving proper care. She spoke of some typical family conflict and the effect it could have on a child's life. In general, the story seemed to reflect her life, her likes, and her strengths and difficulties.

## Evaluation Summary

Sonja's neuropsychological evaluation was completed in an attempt to address some of the concerns her mother has noted concerning Sonja's academic difficulties. Mrs. Lopez's main academic concerns related to Sonja's reading comprehension and writing. Mrs. Lopez is concerned that she may have neuropsychological problems related to a traumatic brain injury sustained at age three after being kicked in the jaw by a horse. Sonja's cognitive scores suggested that she has borderline to low average cognitive abilities. She has consistent verbal and nonverbal cognitive abilities. Sonja's simultaneous and sequential processing abilities are well developed and are considered to be average for an individual her age. Her planning and attention abilities are in the low average range. Sonja's academic strengths are in oral expression and mathematics.

Sonja displayed a broad range of neuropsychological skills and abilities. Such variability is expected in a child who has experienced a traumatic brain injury. This reflects her well developed visuospatial abilities including her ability to synthesize visual information, understand the relationship between objects in space and adopt a variety of perspectives and rotate objects mentally. Her ability to process information holistically appears to be Average for a student her age. Her memory, ability to sustain attention, and ability to develop an effective plan all fell within the Low Average range. Sonja displayed mild to moderate needs in the areas of maintaining attention, using language, sensorimotor activities, and short and long term memory. So too, phonological processing (including individual sounds within works) and processing verbally presented rules were difficulties for Sonja.

Academically, Sonja struggles with reading and written expression. It appears that Sonja has had extensive phonemic awareness training in her past and is able to do exercises that measure the relationship between individual sounds and individual letters. However, she is unable to apply those phonemic awareness skills to regular English words. Moreover, she has great difficulty with her reading comprehension skills which relate to her ability to not only recognize words but to connect those words to the rest of her knowledge base. When writing, Sonja is able to form her letters correctly, use punctuation and capitalization appropriately, and express her thoughts in a relatively clear manner. However, she has difficulty with sentence structure, noun-verb agreement, and spelling.

Various measures and reports indicated that Sonja displays few behavioral or adaptive functioning difficulties. Although her classroom teacher reported a number of concerns from her view, Sonja does not appear to display symptoms of depression or anxiety. The major concern highlighted in school was her significant learning problems. When taking care of herself, Sonja reportedly seems able to complete domestic tasks and advocate for herself in the community. She appeared to have good coping and interpersonal skills. Sonja gave the impression of a confident, self-assured, happy child, typical of her age. In fact, her experiences with horse shows and helping on the family ranch seem to have enabled her to develop strong interpersonal skills.

Children who have traumatic brain injuries have a difficult time learning new material and overcoming their weaknesses. Sonja may frustrate her teachers and parents by appearing to learn a skill one minute, and then forgetting how to do that skill soon afterward. Punishments and privileges may have little effect on Sonja because she may have difficulty attaching the consequence to the intended behavior. Thus, when working with Sonja, it is best to establish an environment that will allow for her to do well. Modifications will be needed to help her find success.

As previously detailed, Sonja displays numerous strengths which have and can continue to be used to compensate for her neuropsychological needs. These strengths should continue to be developed and should be used to help her succeed now and for years to come. Her strengths and abilities include excellent interpersonal skills with both peers and adults and good adaptive skills that enable her to care for herself and advocate for herself. Sonja is also able to understand and use oral language well and she has the skills necessary to be successful in many hands-on activities. Such activities could also utilize her strong visual skills.

## Diagnostic Impressions

**Primary Handicapping Condition:**      Traumatic Brain Injury
**Secondary Handicapping Condition:**    Learning Disability

Traumatic Brain Injury by History
315.00 Reading Disorder
315.2 Disorder of Written Language

## Evaluation Recommendations

Based on the results of this evaluation, the following recommendations are offered to Mr. and Mrs. Lopez and the Jackson Child Study Team to help Sonja achieve and maintain optimal functioning.

1. Mr. and Mrs. Lopez should make an appointment with the school psychologist and principal at Sonja's school to discuss the findings of this evaluation and to share some of the difficulties that Sonja faces. A copy of this report should also be provided to the school. These specialists should then schedule a meeting for Mr. and Mrs. Lopez and Sonja's teachers to discuss this evaluation and how recommended suggestions could be implemented.

2. Sonja's placement in special education should be continued. It is important that she be provided with some one-to-one instruction and be offered help with activities that she is struggling with in the regular education classroom. The special education and regular education teachers should communicate daily concerning Sonja's needs and progress.

3. Sonja has difficulty acquiring new information and solving novel problems. Thus, it is better to plan ahead in an effort to help Sonja succeed. Her teachers and parents should consider the following:
   - Exercises should be converted into factual, visual presentations that can be studied and memorized.
   - Multiple opportunities should be provided for review and practice in all environments (home, school, community). Increased opportunities for review and practice can be provided through team teaching, informing parents of current and upcoming school topics, reducing the number of topics to master in each class, carrying one theme over several content areas, reviewing new topics daily to reinforce new learning, providing model problems to follow, shortening tests, allowing extra time, and explaining connections between new and previously learned material.
   - Visual reminders of learning goals can be kept in the classroom and at home as learning helpers.
   - Learning strategies should be explicitly taught to Sonja.
   - Concepts can be taught through multisensory instruction (written, oral, pictorial, tactile).

4. Sonja's oral language is a strength for her. It is recommended that she be allowed to complete work orally to utilize this strength. Some suggestions include:
   - Labeling everyday objects with their names to increase familiarity with written words. This is important for Sonja because she has difficulty linking written words to the concepts she already knows.

- Having her complete assignments orally, instead of through writing.
- Obtaining audio recordings of books she is reading in classes so that she can listen to a story as she reads along in the book.

5. Phonological processing remains an area of relative difficulty for Sonja. It is recommended that she receive explicit instruction in phonics, with a focused emphasis on development of sound/symbol relationships. Reading readiness can be fostered and developed with an emphasis on sound/letter pairs, rhyming games, and activities that encourage recognition of words with the same beginning, ending, or middle sounds.

6. Reading comprehension skills can be developed by teaching strategies that good readers use, such as:
   - Previewing the text and self-questioning during the preview,
   - Teaching new vocabulary before a new passage or unit. This is particularly important for Sonja, who does not seem to have a solid vocabulary.
   - Teaching color-coded highlighting strategies (yellow for main idea, green for relevant details).
   - Patterned word lists and techniques that increase memorization of common words may be helpful

7. Written language knowledge and skills are another area of need for Sonja. It is recommended that:
   - She be encouraged to practice her written language by writing down telephone messages, copying short announcements, etc., both at home and at school.
   - Written language requirements should be decreased by allowing her to dictate short answers or use fill-in-the-blank, true-false, and/or matching formats for test questions.
   - When taking standardized or other tests, she may require the use of a scribe. The scribe should write down Sonja's responses as Sonja dictates them.
   - Tests should be read aloud and Sonja be allowed to respond orally
   - Alternatives should be offered for written assignments. For example, she could make a diorama, theatrical presentation, model or illustration. This would build on her skill strengths.
   - New skills can be developed by providing keyboarding and word-processing instruction and teaching prewriting and organizational structures, such as outlines, story mapping, webs, or other graphic organizers.

8. Sonja has a difficult time focusing on relevant material and ignoring extraneous material. To help her learn, individual and environmental modifications may be needed. It is recommended that:
   - Directions be shortened, focusing on the essential or most important parts. Directions may also need to be repeated.
   - It may be necessary to slow down and repeat main points, avoiding elaboration on ancillary details
   - Sonja should be allowed extra time to process information and finish her work
   - Distractions should be reduced by allowing Sonja to work in a study carrel or another quiet area of the classroom. Some learners find that headphones or other ear plugs also help block out classroom noise.

9. Mathematics is an area of relative strength for Sonja's although she may have difficulty under time constraints, which could leading to errors. It is recommended that Sonja be allowed extra time to complete problems and assignments correctly.

10. The symptoms of brain injuries are confusing and difficult for other people to understand. Sonja needs to learn about the nature of her particular brain injury including her neuropsychological strengths and weaknesses. By learning about her strengths and weaknesses, she can better advocate for her needs and educate her teachers and peers when she begins middle and high school. Her peers may also be more helpful when they understand why Sonja has difficulties in learning.

11. It will be important for the school staff and Sonja's parents to recognize that there will be significant variability in Sonja's performance. It is to be expected that Sonja will do some things well and some things poorly. Further, it will not be unusual for Sonja to appear to have mastered a skill at one moment, and then to have forgotten that skill in the next moment. Sonja should not be punished or admonished for such behaviors as it is common amongst children with TBI.

12. In two to three years, a reevaluation of Sonja's neuropsychological capabilities should be undertaken to determine her level of progress and if modifications are needed in her program. Since individuals like Sonja change learning styles often, focused mini-evaluations should be held a few times a year or more.

13. If Sonya's parents or teachers would like additional information, a number of books are available that discuss learning and reading strategies. One popular book recently released to the general public offers new and innovative teaching strategies. It is called Overcoming dyslexia: A new and complete science-based program for reading problems at any level, by Dr. Sally Shaywitz. The book, published by Knoph in 2003, is available at most bookstores and online.

Thank you for this referral. It was a pleasure to have the opportunity to work with Sonja.

_____
Kimberly Root, BA
School Psychologist-in-Training

_____
David Hulac, MA
School Psychologist-in-Training

_____
Rik Carl D'Amato, Ph.D.
Professor and Director
Neuropsychology Laboratory
Nationally Certified School Psychologist

_____

Names have been changed to protect the identity of those tested.

# Appendix E: Sample Neuropsychological IEP

## KENDRA J. BJORAKER

University of Minnesota Medical School
Pediatric Neuropsychology Clinic

### Individualized Educational Program 2004-2005

**Name:** Michael Smith
**Age:** 12 years 9 months
**Grade:** 6th grade

### Present Level of Functioning, Achievement, and Performance

**What does this student do well within the following areas, and what concerns are there for the student?**

Based on the findings of his most recent independent evaluation through the University of Minnesota, Pediatric Neuropsychology Clinic, and previous private and educational evaluations, Michael Smith was identified as having the following diagnoses: dyslexia, dysgraphia, language disorder, written language disorder, Major Depression, Psychotic Disorder Not Otherwise Specified, and Oppositional Defiant Disorder. All these diagnoses culminate in impairments that affect his capacity to function in the classroom. He shows deficits that compromise his alertness, focus, effort and accuracy; his capacity to manage and organize materials and complete classroom assignments within routine timelines. Further, his language processing deficits clearly affect his ability to follow directions or initiate and complete tasks. Michael's emotional and behavioral dysfunctions should be taken into consideration in regard to the impact this will have on his day-to-day academic achievement, his ability to learn, and his overall motivation and cooperation. Michael's emotional/behavioral issues impact his academic/communication needs, requiring an embedded approach that addresses his behaviors, emotional needs in concert with academic and communication needs.

**Educational:**

**How does this student perform within the curriculum and on age appropriate tasks?**

*Strengths*: Michael demonstrates a relative strength in his applied math abilities.

*Concerns*: Michael demonstrates below average reading skills, mildly impaired overall language and language processing skills, and well below average written language skills.

**Social/Emotional/Adaptive Behavior:**

**How does the student manage feelings and interact with others? How well does the student adapt to different environments?**

*Strengths*: One-on-one relationships with an adult are positive. He is very athletic and participates in organized sports involving teams. Michael is amiable when not under debilitating stress, presents as polite, helpful, loyal to his friends, and generous. He performs best in a multi-sensory learning situation when the tasks are very structured and understood.

*Concerns*: Michael has a marked deficit in behavioral and emotional regulation which was corroborated by results of numerous behavior rating scales across settings, formal testing, and interviews. Michael is experiencing severe psychological adjustment problems. He is sensitive to criticism, and reacts with anger and hostility, and because of real or perceived issues in his environment, he trusts few people and is constantly on guard to prevent others from doing him harm or injustice. When Michael feels threatened, he blames others for his problems and reacts with either aggression or has a "total power shut down." Michael endorsed a number of extreme and bizarre thoughts suggesting the presence of psychosis in times of inescapable stress and threatening situations. The aforementioned issues can be expected to have a pervasive impact on Michael's development of academic abilities, his social skills, and his interpersonal relationships. Inter-related are his impaired self-regulatory (attention, concentration, and planning) functions which allow for efficient, appropriate, goal-directed application of intelligence in a complex, changing environment.

Although Michael demonstrated a mild impairment in a highly structured setting, it is evident that he does have some capacity to execute behavior in a flexible and well-planned manner as demonstrated by this evaluation. However, in settings where structure is limited, he is capable of exhibiting very dramatic, and at times, dangerous levels of behavioral and emotional dysregulation. Michael craves attention, and often uses negative behavior to get the attention. The difficulties he is currently experiencing are likely to be a combination of genetic predisposition as well as how he has responded to his environment over the years. Michael endorsed depression, and with this, suicidal ideation. Depression refers to a state of sadness characterized by emotional despair and physical lethargy; both characteristics described of Michael by his mother, grandmother, and himself. Pessimism, depression, and hopelessness pervade his life, and to manage his emotions Michael withdraws, and becomes self-deprecating, often needing a great deal of reassurance and affirmation. Additionally, Michael endorsed and demonstrates feelings and thoughts of anxiety. Taken together, Michael's deficits may be reflected in numerous ways, including slowing of processing time, distractibility, and a limited range of awareness, fatigue, safety risks, inappropriate behavior (sexual, aggression), depression, and reduced productivity of material presumed to be known all of which are exacerbated by his reported significant language disorder and his reading disability intensifying each of the above mentioned deficits.

**Physical/Motor:**

**How are the student's vision, hearing, coordination, and general health?**

*Strengths*: No reported problems with hearing or general health; however, Michael does wear glasses. Motor skills were acquired within normal age level expectations. Michael is very athletic in that he plays soccer, swims, works out at the gym, and rock climbs.

*Concerns*: Fine motor speed and coordination was in the low average range using his right dominant hand, and in the mildly impaired range with his left nondominant hand. He was in the mildly impaired range using both hands together, suggestive of problems with fine motor coordination and speed. Additionally, Michael was below average in his ability to coordinate more complex visual-motor movements resulting in difficulties with spatial location appreciation in addition to coordinating more complex visual-motor movements.

**Communicative:**

**How does the student listen, speak, understand language, and express him or herself?**

*Strengths*: Michael expresses himself well when talking to others about subjects that are of high interest. He has average ability when using the information found within the linguistic context of the sentence to determine the meaning of an unknown word. Michael's performance was within the average range on a task requiring interpretation of semantic relationships in sentences, for example, to identify location or direction (spatial relations), include time relationships (temporal relations), and include serial order (sequential relations).

*Concerns*: Michael's overall language score was in the mildly impaired range. In receptive language, he scored in the mildly impaired range on a task requiring him to interpret, recall, and execute oral commands of increasing length and complexity that contain concepts requiring logical operations. He scored in the moderately impaired range on a task requiring him to perceive relationships in the meaning of words that are categorized by part-whole. Impairment indicates that Michael does not associate related words automatically or efficiently. Adequate ability to perceive relationships in the meaning of words and form word associations is essential for classroom listening and reading comprehension. Deficits in recognizing and using word associations influence his ability to make predictions, create meaning, make inferences, and use analogical reasoning for problem solving.

In expressive language, Michael's performance was in the mildly impaired range on tasks requiring the formulation of simple, compound, and complex sentences and difficulty with the ability to assemble syntactic structures into grammatically acceptable and semantically meaningful sentences. Comparatively, he was within the mildly impaired range on a task requiring the recalling and the reproduction of sentence surface structure as a function of syntactic complexity. Impairments in these areas indicate that Michael has difficulties in the generative language aspects related to planning and producing sentences for conversation, classroom discourse, academic interactions, and written language (i.e., taking notes, remembering the teacher's instructions, and copying from the chalkboard). Deficits in these areas indicates that he is experiencing difficulty in formulating descriptions, questions, responses, or conversation, as well as affecting his speaking ability in that there is a lack of variation in sentence structures used to express intents. Michael has difficulties expressing himself verbally or in written language.

Michael was in the severely impaired range in his ability to use pragmatic rules of language by having him judge the appropriateness of language used in specific environmental situations, or actually use language appropriate to given environmental conditions. Pragmatic competency in language production is assessed by asking the examinee to express a specific communicative intent; to recognize appropriate topics for conversation; to select relevant information of directions or request; to initiate conversation or turn-taking; to adjust the communication level to situational factors such as age or relationship; to use language for expressing gratitude, sorrow, and other feelings; and to judge the pragmatic appropriateness of the language behaviors of others who are engaged in the above activities.

**Cognitive:**
**How does the student think, problem solve, and learn within the environment?**

*Strengths*: Testing completed while at the Sunshine Program, and Garfield Public Schools using the *Wechsler Intelligence Scale for Children-Third Edition* (WISC-III), yielded a Verbal IQ score of 91, a Performance IQ score of 120, and a Full Scale IQ score of 105. In comparison to age-related peers, Michael's overall intellectual functioning is in the average range of intellectual functioning with nonverbal reasoning ability significantly more developed (superior range) than his verbal reasoning ability (average range). In regard to memory, testing revealed superior ability in his storage and retrieval of new information given in list form and high average ability with visually presented information; however, on a task requiring him to encode and recall lengthy orally presented passages he performed in the mildly impaired range.

*Concerns:* Michael's emotional and behavioral dysfunctions should be taken into consideration in regard to the impact this will have on his day-to-day academic achievement, his ability to learn, and his overall motivation and cooperation. Michael's emotional/behavioral issues impact his academic, cognitive, and communication needs, requiring an embedded approach that addresses his behaviors and emotional needs in concert with academic and communication needs.

### Statement of Educational Needs

**By integrating the assessment and functioning levels, address the needs of the whole child. Identify priority areas that directly relate to the student's own instructional and environmental needs.**

Needs:

- The ability to speak and be understood and the ability to comprehend what others are saying to him.
- A variety of opportunities to continue vocabulary development.
- An individualized curriculum in reading, writing mechanic/written language, and overall language.
- Instruction in independent work and study skills.
- Minimal transitions and changes in his day (space, staff, students, etc.). Visual aids such as a graphic hourly schedule (consider day-at-a-glance or PDA), warnings when a transition is about to take place, extra time to make transitions.
- Instruction in social skills and problems solving skills.
- A program which provides time for Michael to learn strategies to address his mental health needs so he can succeed academically.
- A proactive positive behavior plan.
- An environment which provides adequate structure and high expectations for individual behavior and cooperative learning in a nonpunitive proactive positive behavior plan developed through a functional behavioral assessment.
- An environment which supports him in meeting those expectations.

- A highly directed individualized plan to monitor Michael's suicidal ideations or expressions either verbally or through drawings with appropriate communication with both in-school and out patient mental health professionals and parents.
- Friendship support outside of school (extracurricular activities).
- Practical organizational format capitalizing on his visual strengths.
- Visual representation of directions (represented by utilizing the chalkboard, demonstrations, and visual cues).
- Opportunity for conversation.
- Practice formulating and asking questions about desires and needs, both academic and behavioral/emotional.
- Practice looking for cue words in environment.
- Assessment of interests.
- Functional behavioral analysis.
- Central Auditory Processing assessment.
- Behavioral support plan.
- A small group setting for instruction with opportunities for one to one instruction.
- Development of word processing/keyboarding skills to augment his written language deficits.
- A phonologically based reading program.
- Transportation behavior monitoring program.

### Interventions, Adaptations, Accommodations, and Modifications

**Emotional/Behavioral:**

- Regularly assess, monitor, and act accordingly for suicide ideation as per crisis intervention plan set forth by the school system.
- Low student to teacher ratio 3:1.
- Limit situations which result in inappropriate behavior (having to wait, task length and difficulty, peer involvement).
- Provide signals to alert Michael to quit inappropriate behaviors as defined in goals. These can be a hand signal or an agreed upon single word, or a look.
- Provide clear and concise classroom expectations and consequences.
- Speak with Michael privately about what he is doing wrong and what he should be doing instead.
- Avoid the use of confrontational techniques.
- Designate a "cooling off" location within the classroom.

- Assign activities that require some movement.
- Use praise generously.
- Avoid power struggles.
- Ignore attention-getting behavior.
- Avoid criticizing Michael.
- Communicate frequently with Michael's parents.
- Monitor levels of tolerance and be mindful of signs of frustration.

**Receptive/Expressive Language/Auditory Processing Disorders:**
- A full language based program, with a visual, hands on approach.
- Because Michael has receptive and expressive language disabilities he will do better with short, highly structured tasks, interspersed with quiet periods. Repetition of clearly defined oral instructions is required.
- Training in auditory discrimination is important so that Michael can learn to distinguish between differences in speech sounds and phonemes. For instance, activities could incorporate word-pairs which differ in their initial or final consonants (e.g., bat/pat, sad/sap) or in their medial vowels (e.g., bet/bat, bell/ball).
- Enhance Michael's auditory attention through games or exercises which require him to listen to specific questions and to execute the instruction included in that question.
- Monitor social communication in all settings and teach appropriate responses directly.
- Pre-teach new information and new vocabulary.
- Provide highly structured directions and information one-step at a time.
- Provide rephrased information using smaller linguistic units.
- Provide comprehension check by asking for demonstration or paraphrase rather than repetition of information.

**Reading:**
- Research on dyslexic children suggests that the single most important part of treatment is for the child to receive individualized tutoring in a phonics-based approach to reading to remediate a deficiency in phonological coding. Useful programs typically incorporate synthetic phonic approaches, which teach sound-letter relations and blending as well as phoneme awareness skills. Other important treatment elements include: training of rhymes, segmenting (phonemes and how they are made); letter/sound correspondence (taught explicitly); substitution, blending, rhyming; decodable text and spelling.

- Provide a program such as Orton-Gillingham (or variations thereof such as Slingerland, Project Read, Lindamood-Bell, among others) involve structured, sequential, multi-sensory teaching of written language that meet these recommendations.
- Repeated reading of the same text will help improve Michael's fluency. Listening to books on tape and repeatedly reading along will also help fluency. Michael will benefit from additional rehearsal, repetition, and review of verbal material to be learned.
- Direct, individualized instruction in written expression, spelling and reading (with a phonics-based approach) by reading specialist with the goal of explicitly teaching phonological decoding and word recognition.
- Recommendations from the National Teacher Education Task Force of the International Dyslexia Association suggest that interventions be multi-sensory and include the following content:
    content and structure of the English language
    phonology and phonological awareness
    sound/symbol relationships (in both directions)
    types and patterns of syllables
    syntax (grammar, sentence variation, mechanics of language)
    semantics (meaning of language)
- Allow extended time on tests and have tests read to him. Also, consultation from the school psychologist regarding ways of helping Michael develop coping strategies for test-taking, might also be helpful.
- Testing by recognition (e.g., multiple choice) as opposed to recall (e.g., fill-in-the-blank) to compensate for retrieval difficulties.

**Dysgraphia/Written Language:**
- Concentrate on handwriting fluency as a separate activity. Help Michael to set his own standards and evaluate the quality of his written work by comparison to his own best. The quality of Michael's handwriting will not necessarily indicate lack of motivation.
- Give separate grades for content of written work and mechanics (spelling, capitalization, punctuation). The quality of the ideas should be emphasized over the quantity of the written output.
- Minimize or eliminate rote-writing tasks such as copying passages or problems from the chalkboard or textbook.

- In math Michael may find it easier to organize his work if he uses graph paper, or if he turns regular paper sideways to keep the columns lined up.
- Adjust written assignments in terms of length and/or time allowed for completion.
- Michael should use a word processor with spell-check availability.
- Provide Michael with a proofreader to correct spelling and/or mechanical errors on his classroom and homework assignments.
- Michael will have significant difficulty with efficient/accurate note-taking during lectures or class discussions. He should be supplied with a copy of teacher's note.
- Allow Michael to begin projects or assignments early.
- Michael should be provided with a 'writing binder'. This 3-ring binder could include:

  A model of cursive or print letters on the inside cover (this is easier to refer to than one on the wall or blackboard).

  A laminated template of the required format for written work. Make a cut-out where the name, date, and assignment would go and model it next to the cutout. Three-hole punch it and put it into the binder on top of his writing paper. Then he can set up his paper and copy the heading information in the holes, then flip the template out of the way to finish the assignment.
- Reduce the copying elements of Michael's assignments and tests. For example, if he is expected to 'answer in complete sentences that reflect the question,' have him do this for three questions that you select, then answer the rest in phrases or words (or drawings). If he is expected to copy definitions, allow him to shorten them or give him the definitions and have him highlight the important phrases and words or write an example or drawing of the word instead of copying the definition.

**Academic:**
- Michael will receive instruction in a small group (3-4 students) setting with opportunities for one to one instruction in all academic areas.
- Additional time for completion of tests in a setting where Michael has less distractions and fewer students present. The tests are to be read to him. The time should be limited to the time he can remain engaged and scored based on the problems completed.
- Michael should be provided with advanced notice for all assignments or projects to allow for additional time to complete them.
- He should be allotted no more than an hour of "on task" homework. Anything not completed should not be graded. On task is monitored by his parents or caregiver.

- Limit distractions such as having in a closed as opposed to an open classroom, an opportunity to use a study carrel, etc.
- Provide materials for doing tasks in each class (pencils, paper, calculator, notebooks).
- Provide an additional set of textbooks for home use.
- Provide strategies to organize Michael's day with a Personal Digital Assistant.
- All academic work should be presented at his reading level.
- Monitor the amount of time Michael is spending on homework, and making alterations in required workload if necessary especially if parents are meeting with resistance and his behavioral and emotional functioning deteriorates in the face to the perceived workload burden.
- Modifying requirements to permit verbal responses on tests of knowledge.

### Related Services

**Emotional/Behavioral:**
- Individual therapy with a cognitive-behavioral focus three times per week.
- Group therapy one time per week.
- Provide Michael with an educational assistant.
- Special transportation will be provided because his needs require attendance at a school that is outside of his home school's boundaries.

**Receptive/Expressive Language/Auditory Processing Disorders:**
- Michael needs speech and language therapy four times per week, 30-minute sessions.
- Michael needs indirect speech and language services within the classroom setting.

**Dysgraphia/Written Language:**
- Occupational therapy two times per week.

| | |
|---|---|
| **Special Education Teacher** | **School Psychologist** |
| **Regular Education Teacher** | **School Counselor** |
| **Parent** | **Principal or Designee** |
| **Parent** | **Student** |

Names have been changed to protect the identity of those tested.

# Appendix F: Neuropsychology Organizations and Web Sites

RIK CARL D'AMATO and ELIZABETH A. McGRAIN

At the time this text was printed, these web sites were operating and offered useful information. Since there are literally hundreds of thousands of sites available, we are providing only an extremely small sample of what can be found online. We did not select sites in any special order or ranking and do not necessarily recommend these sites over others. Space limited the number of sites we could offer. We recommend that information obtained from any web site be considered vigilantly and suggest that certified or licensed school psychologists or school neuropsychologists be consulted before providing any type of diagnosis, intervention, or services to children, youth, teachers, or families. Some information offered via the web is erroneous while other information serves as a wonderful resource. Again, we recommend caution when using web sites as resources.

## PROFESSIONAL ORGANIZATIONS

American Psychological Association (APA) Division of Clinical Neuropsychology (Number 40)
http://www.div40.org

American Psychological Association (APA) Division of School Psychology (Number 16)
http://www.indiana.edu/~div16

American Psychological Society (APS)
http://www.psychologicalscience.org

Autism Society of America (ASA)
http://www.autism-society.org/site/PageServer

Brain Injury Association of America (BIAA)
http://www.biausa.org/Pages/splash.html

Children and Adults with Attention-Deficit/Hyperactivity Disorder (CHADD)
http://www.chadd.org/WEBPAGE.CFM?CAT_ID=5&SUBCAT_ID=23&SEC_ID=9

Coalition of Clinical Practitioners in Neuropsychology (CCPN)
http://www.neuropsych.com/CCPN.htm

Council for Exceptional Children (CEC)
http://www.cec.sped.org

Council for Learning Disabilities (CLD)
http://www.cldinternational.org/c/@YKQiPH9ZRboEc/Pages/home.html

International Neuropsychological Association (INS)
http://www.the-ins.org

International School Psychology Association (ISPA)
http://www.ispaweb.org/en

National Academy of Neuropsychology (NAN)
http://www.nanonline.org

National Association of School Psychologists (NASP)
http://www.nasponline.org

National Organization for Rare Disorders, Inc. (NORD)
http://www.rarediseases.org

## HELPFUL WEB SITES

Atlases of the Brain
http://medlib.med.utah.edu/kw/brain_atlas/index.html

Dictionary of Psychology
http://www.explore-dictionary.com/psychology/N/Neuropsychology.html

Internet Special Education Resources (ISER)
http://www.iser.com/index.shtml

Intervention Central
http://www.interventioncentral.org

Medical Dictionary at MedicineNet.com
http://www.medterms.com/script/main/hp.asp

National Center for Learning Disabilities
http://www.ncld.org

National Center on Low-Incidence Disabilities
http://nclid.unco.edu/newnclid/index.php

National Institute on Drug Abuse
http://www.nida.nih.gov

National Institutes of Health (NIH)
http://www.nih.gov

Neuroimaging Tutorials
http://www.neuropsychologycentral.com/interface/content/links/links
_interface_frameset.html

Neuropsychology Central
http://www.neuropsychologycentral.com

Neuropsychology Resources
http://www.psychwatch.com/neuropsy_page.htm

NIMH Autism Spectrum Disorders
http://www.nimh.nih.gov/publicat/autism.cfm

School Psychology Resources on Line
http://www.schoolpsychology.net

Special Education Resources on the Internet (SERI)
http://seriweb.com

Special Services Hotlist
http://wneo.org/hotlists/specialserv.htm

The American Board of Professional Neuropsychology
http://abpn.net/index.php

The American Board of Professional Psychology
http://www.abpp.org

The Educator's Reference Desk
http://www.eduref.org

The Human Brain: A Learning Tool
http://www.marymt.edu/~psychol/brain.html

The Laboratory of Brain and Cognition
http://lbc.nimh.nih.gov

The Scientific Review of Mental Health Practice
http://www.srmhp.org/online-articles.html

The Whole Brain Atlas
http://www.med.harvard.edu/AANLIB/home.html

Trauma Academy with Dr. Bruce Perry
http://www.childtrauma.org

Virtual Hospital: Dissections of the Real Brain
http://www.vh.org/adult/provider/anatomy/BrainAnatomy/BrainAnatomy.html

# Index

## A

Abnormalities, developmental, 584
Academic achievement, 94, 214, 215, 217, 237, 249, 276, 303, 334, 338, 339, 341, 353, 376, 390, 404, 453, 502, 577, 590, 624, 644, 647, 648, 651, 667, 692, 761, 765, 767, 785
Academic assessment, 230
Accountability, 176, 538, 540, 833
Accreditation, 8, 16
Acculturation, 637, 643, 645
Achievement. *See* Academic achievement
Acquired immunodeficiency disease (AIDS):
  complications to neural development and, 77
  related to neurodevelopment, 77
Adaptive behavior, 64, 78, 230, 311, 467, 475, 553, 577, 671, 778, 851
Adolescents, 15, 17, 25, 28, 30, 77, 123, 183, 192, 230, 239, 243, 389–390, 394–395, 417, 425–426, 433–435, 460–462, 469, 470, 473, 477, 480, 511, 516, 565–568, 577, 585, 608, 641–643, 650, 671, 684, 687, 777–778, 789, 798, 812, 815–816, 818, 822, 834, 849–850
  neurological development, 23–24

African American, 30, 69, 444, 489, 511, 522, 562, 585, 587, 637–638, 643, 646–647, 651
Aggression. *See* Violence
Agraphia, 781–784, 787, 793–794, 797–798
Agyria, 73
Alcohol, 11, 19–20, 30, 64, 66, 68–69, 71, 77, 101, 158, 185, 194, 213, 221, 275, 447, 561–569, 575–579, 591, 589–590, 596–598, 609–610, 639, 816
Alzheimer's disease, 58, 79, 280, 295, 616–617, 710
American Board of Professional Neuropsychology, 10
American Board of Professional Psychology, 10
American Psychological Association (APA), 8–9, 12, 16, 226, 354, 513, 536, 538, 639, 833–834
Americans with Disabilities Act, 365, 371, 415
Amygdaloid, 58, 563
Anafranil, 810–811
Anemia, 185, 221, 452, 514
Anencephaly, 45, 62, 64, 71, 153
  neural tube abnormalities and, 69
Angelman syndrome, related to neurodevelopment, 79–80
Anomia, 101, 374
Antianxiety medication, 807, 816–817

# M